In this book, Dr Donald Charrett and Philip Loots generously share their knowledge and insights gleaned by decades of interdisciplinary experience on projects around the world. Not only does the book provide a detailed map of the principles which are common across the globe, it also alerts readers to the hidden shoals of differences upon which projects might otherwise founder. For those setting sail on the waters of infrastructure procurement law, this book is an essential navigation tool.

Dr Matthew Bell, Senior Lecturer and Co-Director of Studies for Construction Law,
Melbourne Law School, The University of Melbourne

If one were to read this book from cover to cover, one would emerge with a deep and fulsome understanding not just of the legal issues critical to infrastructure project conception and delivery, but also a more profound understanding of the similarities and differences between common and civil law approaches.

Simon Bellas, Partner Jones Day Singapore

The authors have provided an excellent compendium of the legal principles which govern the delicate relationships between parties from different jurisdictions and legal systems in the modern environment of international infrastructural development. The book covers all of the complex challenges which face those advising clients involved in international infrastructural development, from the confluence between common law and civil law systems to the unique obstacles which arise in cross-border construction disputes. This is an essential addition to a construction lawyer's library.

Adriaan Hoeben, Senior Counsel, Construction and Engineering –
Eversheds Sutherland Dubai

This is a comprehensive and insightful guide to the myriad of issues that can arise on infrastructure construction projects and is a very valuable resource, not just for lawyers, but for consultants, owners, and contractors. What makes this text unique is its in-depth analysis of the practice of construction law internationally, but in a way that is accessible to a wide audience.

Sharon Vogel, Partner Singleton Urquhart Reynolds
Vogel LLP, Toronto Canada

CONTRACTS FOR INFRASTRUCTURE PROJECTS

Contracts for Infrastructure Projects: An International Guide to Application provides a guide to the law relating to construction contracts for infrastructure projects; it is intended for the use of engineers and other professionals who are involved in the negotiation and administration of construction contracts, to enable them to understand the risks involved, and how to minimise them. The principles of construction law outlined in this book apply to small construction contracts as well as very large contracts for which the contract sum may be in the billions of dollars.

The focus of the book is on construction contracts entered into by commercial organisations operating in a business environment. Contract law generally assumes that such parties are of equal bargaining power and puts relatively few fetters on their ability to agree on the terms of their bargain. However, where legislation impacts on the execution of construction projects or the operation of construction contracts it may be of major importance in protecting the rights of weaker parties or third parties.

It is assumed that the users of this book will be familiar with the general concepts of tendering and contracting for engineering and construction projects but may not have any formal knowledge of the law. To the extent possible, the emphasis is on general principles of contract law that are widely accepted in many jurisdictions. Examples are drawn from case law in a number of common law jurisdictions, as well as from civil codes.

PRACTICAL LEGAL GUIDES FOR CONSTRUCTION AND TECHNOLOGY PROJECTS

Series Editor

Donald Charrett

The books in this series provide lawyers and construction professionals with the relevant knowledge, resources and practical guidance to understand the contemporary construction industry and the law necessary to achieve successful outcomes for construction projects. The topics covered include front-end issues such as project procurement, the production, negotiation and administration of contracts, and the avoidance of disputes, as well as backend issues such as taking part in, managing or resolving disputes. The series aims to keep abreast of the technologies that have increasing impact in changing traditional ways of working, contracting and resolving disputes.

FIDIC CONTRACTS IN ASIA PACIFIC

A Practical Guide to Application

Donald Charrett

CONTRACTS FOR CONSTRUCTION AND ENGINEERING PROJECTS

Second Edition

Donald Charrett

CONTRACTS FOR INFRASTRUCTURE PROJECTS

An International Guide to Application

Philip Loots and Donald Charrett

For more information, please visit: www.routledge.com/Practical-Legal-Guides-for-Construction-and-Technology-Projects/book-series/PLGCTP

CONTRACTS FOR INFRASTRUCTURE PROJECTS

AN INTERNATIONAL GUIDE TO APPLICATION

PHILIP LOOTS AND DONALD CHARRETT

informa law
from Routledge

First published 2022
by Informa Law from Routledge
4 Park Square, Milton Park, Abingdon, Oxon OX14 4RN

and by Informa Law from Routledge
605 Third Avenue, New York, NY 10158

Informa Law from Routledge is an imprint of the Taylor & Francis Group, an informa business

British Library Cataloguing-in-Publication Data
A catalogue record for this book is available from the British Library

Library of Congress Cataloging-in-Publication Data
Names: Loots, Philip C., author. | Charrett, D. E. (Donald Eric), author.
Title: Contracts for infrastructure projects : an international guide / Philip Loots, Donald Charrett.
Description: Abingdon, Oxon ; New York, NY : Routledge, 2022. |
Series: Practical legal guides for construction and technology projects | Includes bibliographical references and index.
Identifiers: LCCN 2021050609 | ISBN 9781032074290 (hardback) | ISBN 9781032074269 (paperback) | ISBN 9781003206873 (ebook)
Subjects: LCSH: Construction contracts. | Infrastructure (Economics—Law and legislation.
Classification: LCC K891.B8 L66 2022 | DDC 343.07/8624—dc23/eng/20220208
LC record available at https://lccn.loc.gov/2021050609

ISBN: 978-1-032-07429-0 (hbk)
ISBN: 978-1-032-07426-9 (pbk)
ISBN: 978-1-003-20687-3 (ebk)

DOI: 10.4324/9781003206873

Typeset in Times New Roman
by Apex CoVantage, LLC

This book is dedicated with grateful thanks to our wives, Diana Loots and Jeyami Charrett, whose understanding and forbearance of our time-consuming writing has made this book possible.

CONTENTS

ILLUSTRATIONS

TABLES

AUTHOR BIOGRAPHIES

PROFILES

Philip Loots has practised exclusively as a construction lawyer for more than 40 years and is a recognised authority on construction law. He has worked in the Middle East, Africa, Australia, Asia and elsewhere internationally. In addition to writing numerous articles in this field, he has authored and co-authored a number of books including *Practical Guide to Engineering and Construction Contracts; Construction Law and Related Issues*; *Engineering and Construction Law* and *The Application of Contracts in Developing Oil and Gas Projects.* He is a past editor of *Construction Law International*, the magazine of the International Construction Projects Committee of the International Bar Association. Philip provided input to various FIDIC contact drafting committees and was a FIDIC Mediator and Arbitrator.He holds the position of Adjunct Professor at the Centre for Mining, Energy and Natural Resources, Faculty of Law, University of Western Australia. He practises as a Solicitor in Western Australia and is admitted as an Attorney and Notary Public in the Republic of South Africa. Philip is a Mediator, an International Arbitrator and a Statutory Adjudicator in Western Australia and the Northern Territories, Australia. He is a Fellow of the Chartered Institute of Arbitrators. Philip has had extensive experience as board member and General Counsel for leading international contractors and is engaged in and overseeing the drafting and negotiating all forms of construction contracts and advice on all aspects of construction law including claims and disputes. More recently he has had considerable mega-project experience. Work has included contracts for marine structures, dredging, pipelines and underground work. He served as counsel in the negotiations and legal team for the operator Chevron on the USD$54Bn Gorgon LNG project for five years, and for four years as in-house counsel for the EPC contractor Bechtel on the $37Bn Wheatstone LNG project. Philip has a B Comm LLB and attended the PMD at Harvard Business School, and subsequently the Executive Negotiation Program at Harvard. Philip serves on the Law Council of Australia /Law Society of Australia Construction and Infrastructure Committee. Most recently he participated in the successful defence of a claim of approximately US$2billion in International Arbitration brought against a major Oil and Gas Company.

Donald Charrett is a barrister, arbitrator, mediator, expert and dispute board member practising in technology, engineering and construction disputes. Prior to joining the Victorian Bar, he worked as a solicitor at a large Australian law firm. His construction law briefs have included arbitration, litigation, mediation, expert determination, facilitation of experts' conferences, and membership of dispute boards. He is a member of the FIDIC President's List of Adjudicators and a Fellow of the Chartered Institute of Arbitrators. He was named as Best Construction Law Practitioner, Australia 2016 by *Business Worldwide Magazine*. In 2019, 2020 and 2021WhosWho Legal included him on their list of Thought Leaders – Construction, saying "Donald is an excellent and knowledgeable lawyer". Prior to becoming a lawyer, he worked as an engineer for over thirty years, including twelve years as a director of a consulting engineering firm. Dr Charrett's engineering experience includes computer applications, structural design, managing engineering projects, acting as an expert witness and management roles in contract negotiation and administration, insurance, international joint ventures and corporate restructuring. From 2012 to 2014 he was non-executive chairman of consulting engineering company AMOG. Dr Charrett has published widely on legal and engineering subjects, and presented conference papers, workshops and training courses in Australia and internationally. He is a Senior Fellow at the University of Melbourne, teaching a Master of Construction Law subject on international construction law. His legal publications include articles on expert evidence, FIDIC contracts, dispute boards, dispute avoidance and resolution, contract risk, forensic engineering, contractual lessons from past projects, design and construct contracts, *quantum meruit*, solidary liability, construction insurance, professional indemnity insurance and reinsurance. He is the author of *Contracts for Construction and Engineering Projects,* joint author of *The Application of Contracts in Developing Oil and Gas Projects* and the editor of *FIDIC Contracts in Asia Pacific, The International Application of FIDIC Contracts*, and *Global Challenges Shared Solutions*.

ACKNOWLEDGEMENTS

We would like to thank our many colleagues who have contributed to this book, and to those who have encouraged our writing endeavours. In particular we are indebted to the Honourable Wayne Martin AC QC for writing the Foreword; Ian Thorpe and Peter Byford of e3Advisory for reviewing and commenting on Chapter 15 and for David Hudson's facilitation of the same; George Matta and Jonathan Shahady of Tracey Brunstrom & Hammond for assistance with Chapters 14 and 15 and for preparing their diagrams; Shamala Devi, Sundaram Jaishankar, Phillip Greenham, and David Charrett for their insights on Chapter 29; and Dr Matthew Bell of the University of Melbourne, Simon Bellas of Jones Day Singapore, and Adriaan Hoeben of Eversheds Sutherland Dubai for their endorsements.

Publication of this book would not have been possible without the professional expertise and hard work of Routledge staff. We thank Terry Clague, Guy Loft, and Amelia Bashford of Routledge, who have been unfailingly encouraging and helpful in publishing this book. The copyediting team have done an excellent job on the difficult task of editing the lengthy manuscript and ensuring consistency of style and presentation, for which we are most grateful. However, any shortcomings in the book are our sole responsibility.

Perth and Melbourne
September 2021

FOREWORD

Wayne Martin AC QC

Construction has been a vital part of human endeavour since the earliest days of civilisation. The creation of basic shelter providing protection from predators and the elements was essential for the survival of our forebears, who were nomadic hunter-gatherers. As agriculture and permanent settlements evolved, the complexity and sophistication of our building and infrastructure needs evolved with them.

Monumental buildings became the hallmark and legacy of the first great civilisations – the pyramids in Egypt, the Acropolis in Athens, the Pantheon and the Colosseum in Rome – taking just some examples from the region around the Mediterranean. During the Middle Ages communities around the world devoted generations of labour and a large part of their limited resources to the creation of magnificent structures exalting the glory of their deity – massive Christian cathedrals in Europe, monumental religious altars in South America, and extraordinary pagodas and temples throughout Asia.

Industrialisation took construction requirements beyond the spheres of residential, religious, and community needs into many different and complex areas, requiring increasingly sophisticated plant, equipment, and infrastructure. The ingenuity and innovation of humankind responded to the challenges of a mechanised and technological world with exponential increases in the capacity and efficiency of our building, engineering, and construction industries. Those industries became the fundamental drivers of developed economies – providing jobs and transport and satisfying basic human needs for water, housing, warmth (through electricity), health (through hospitals), and education (through schools and universities) and enabling the extraction of the minerals and resources and the manufacture of the materials needed to create these facilities.

A transparent and effective legal regime for the certain allocation of risk, responsibility, and reward amongst the principals, contractors, subcontractors, and end users involved in construction projects is an essential component of an efficient construction industry. Where all of those participants are within one jurisdiction, the applicable legal regime will be that of the jurisdiction.

However, the overwhelming trend of globalisation, which has dominated recent decades, has captured almost all areas of trade and commerce, including construction. Top-tier contractors operating internationally have become a ubiquitous feature of most developed and many developing economies. Multinational firms providing the full range of professional services needed to support the construction industry have become a dominant feature of the professional landscape. Many, if not most, major construction projects now involve participants beyond the country in which the project is located.

This book responds to the need created by the globalisation of the construction industry. Lawyers advising participants in that industry can no longer rely upon domestic texts which deal only with the laws of a particular jurisdiction. In this seminal work they will find a truly cosmopolitan compilation of the sources of law which govern the rights and obligations of participants in transnational construction projects.

The authors comprehensively develop the thesis earlier propounded by others[1] to the effect that it can now be said that there is a coherent body of international law applicable to construction which can be regarded as a division of the *lex mercatoria*[2] and described as *lex constructionis*. The development of suites of internationally recognised construction agreements by organisations like FIDIC and NEC and the resolution of disputes by reference to a body of law developed through international arbitration form significant planks in this thesis. Perhaps the best evidence of the authors' hypothesis is the book itself, which reveals a coherent body of law applicable to construction projects which transcends national boundaries.

Readers should not however think from these remarks that this book has an academic or theoretical focus. To the contrary, it is an essentially practical and contemporary work which covers all the topics which are likely to engage the attention of lawyers and advisers, whether they are involved in the 'front end' of contract negotiation and documentation or the 'back end' of disputes. A glance at the index will reveal the breadth of the topics addressed, from general principles of contract law in common law and civil law and UNIDROIT systems to the suites of international agreements in common use and the various types of construction contracts, followed by a detailed international analysis, chapter by chapter, of every issue which might possibly arise in connection with a construction project, from entry into the contract through to completion or earlier termination and the resolution of disputes. The appendices provide mines of essential information covering the matters which should be considered when drafting a construction contract, risk factors applicable to particular types of works, the preparation of claims, global claims, and a bibliography of international resources.

I have no doubt that this important work will fill a gap in the resources available to those providing legal advice to the international construction industry, and I commend the authors on the diligence, commitment, and scholarship which has been applied to bring this comprehensive treatise to fruition.

The Honourable Wayne Martin AC QC

September 2021

The Honourable Wayne Martin AC QC was Chief Justice of Western Australia between 2006 and his retirement from the bench in July 2018. As Chief Justice he created and managed the Arbitration List of the Supreme Court of Western Australia and published many decisions in that field. Prior to his appointment, he practised at the Western Australian Bar in the field of commercial litigation, mainly involving disputes in the mining, energy,

1 For example Charles Molineux, 'Moving towards a Lex Mercatoria – a Lex Constructionis' (1977) 14(1) *Journal of International Arbitration* 55.

2 International Merchant Law.

resources, construction, and financial sectors. He is a qualified and experienced mediator and as a member of 39 Essex Chambers (London, Singapore, and Kuala Lumpur) and Francis Burt Chambers (Perth) is taking appointments as an international arbitrator and mediator. In 2012, he was appointed as a Companion in the General Division of the Order of Australia for his eminent service to the judiciary and the state's legal system. He serves as a part-time judge of the Courts of the Dubai International Financial Centre at first instance and on appeal.

LIST OF CASES

LEGISLATION

CHAPTER 1

Introduction

CONTENTS

1.1 Objectives of this book

This book is intended to be a practical guide to the law relating to construction contracts as applied to infrastructure projects. It is intended for engineers, lawyers, contract administrators, owners, contractors, and other professionals who are involved in the negotiation and administration of construction contracts, to enable them to understand the risks involved, and how to minimise them. The principles of construction law outlined in this book apply to small construction contracts as well as very large contracts for which the contract sum may be in the billions of dollars.

The focus of this book is on construction contracts entered into by commercial organisations operating in a business environment. The law generally assumes that such parties are of equal bargaining power, and, depending on the jurisdiction, puts relatively few fetters on their ability to agree on the terms of their bargain. Construction contracts are typically very detailed in defining the allocation of risks and the scope of each party's obligations and rights. In a real sense the terms of the contract constitute the private law governing the parties' conduct. The widespread international use of standard form contracts and international arbitration to resolve construction disputes, and a *lex mercatoria*, establish widely followed norms of international construction law that are articulated in this book.

The book does not attempt to address the particular features of construction contracts related to building works on domestic housing for individual consumers. It should be noted

DOI: 10.4324/9781003206873-1

that many jurisdictions have specific legislation that regulates domestic building contracts intended to provide consumer protection for individuals who may not be familiar with construction, and who may have limited bargaining power to negotiate appropriate contract terms with the building and professional contractors who execute the building work. Consequently, there is considerably more statutory intervention into freedom of contract in domestic building contracts than in other types of construction contracts.

It is assumed that the users of this book will be familiar with the general concepts of tendering and contracting, but not necessarily have a formal knowledge of the law relevant to infrastructure projects.

Construction law encompasses a number of legal doctrines in addition to the law of contract, such as equity, tort law, and the requirements of statutes. As the emphasis in this book is on construction contracts, these other legal doctrines are not covered in any detail, except to the extent that they affect contractual relationships. To the extent possible, the emphasis is on general principles of contract law that are widely accepted in many jurisdictions.

1.2 *Lex constructionis*

The book has the ambitious aim of endeavouring to cover, in a general way, the practice of construction law as it is applied internationally. Such a construction contract may be 'domestic' where the contracting parties and the construction are carried out in one country. Alternatively, it may be 'international' where the contracting parties are from different countries, or the subject matter of the contract is executed in more than one country. Both domestic and international construction contracts are subject to the relevant laws relating to the entry into, execution, and termination of construction contracts, and to the laws relevant to the execution of the construction works in the country where they are executed.

Countries generally have statute laws that may govern aspects of contracts in general, or construction contracts in particular. An example of the former is a law which provides relief to a party which has entered into an unfair contract, for example *Unfair Contract Terms Act 1977* (UK) and *Consumer Rights Act (2015)* (UK). An example of the latter is the statutory entitlement to progress payments and the process of adjudication for their rapid recovery during the execution of a construction contract in ***Security of Payment*** **legislation**, for example *Building and Construction Industry Security of Payment Act 2004* (Singapore).

One fundamental aspect of a construction contract is that it involves construction of a physical facility that is attached to or forms part of the land that is located at a specific place on the earth's surface, in a particular country. Construction projects typically require considerable human resources and have the potential to significantly impact the environment. Because of their responsibility for their citizen's well-being, countries generally have statute laws that constrain the ways in which construction projects may be executed. An example of laws regulating the employment of labour are *Labour Law (2018 Amendment)* (China) and *Labour Contract Law (2012 Amendment)* (China). An example of laws to protect the environment are *General Law of the Environment (Law No 28611)* (Peru) and *Law of the National System of Environmental Assessment (Law No 29325)* (Peru).

Not only do statute laws regulating contracts and/or construction contracts and the execution of construction projects vary from country to country, but there may well be a number of different jurisdictions within one country, each with their own statutes to regulate particular aspects. For example, Australia has six States and two Territories, each of which has its own jurisdiction over construction work carried out within its own geographical area. Thus, there are eight different *Security of Payment Acts*, with significant differences in detail.

The plethora of different legislation relevant to construction contracts and construction projects across the many jurisdictions around the world makes it impractical to try and cover the details of statute law in a book such as this. This has been briefly covered for a number of jurisdictions around the world in books recently published on the international application of FIDIC contracts.[1] For each of the jurisdictions considered, these books tabulate relevant legislation if the governing law of the contract is in the jurisdiction and if the construction work is carried out in the jurisdiction. The length of each of those tables emphasises the extent to which construction law is subject to statutory constraints, both in the execution of the construction work, and in the operation of a construction contract.

Accordingly, the main focus of this book is on ***lex constructionis*** – the law relating to construction projects which is widely accepted internationally in legal jurisdictions subject to the rule of law and which recognise the parties' freedom of contract, irrespective of the specific impact of statute law. The principles of freedom of contract and ***pacta sunt servanda***[2] form the basis of construction law around the world and ensure that there is a thriving international construction industry. Construction contracts can be executed in the knowledge that, notwithstanding local law differences, there are appropriate methods of dispute resolution, broad agreement on what constitutes a just outcome in most situations, and international norms that ensure remedies can be realised. Knowledge and analysis of the differences may well stimulate desirable improvements in local law and further convergence in approaches between jurisdictions.

There are a number of difficulties with writing a text on construction contract law as it applies internationally, including the following:

- The differences between 'families' of law such as civil law and common law.
- The differences in legal terminology between different jurisdictions.
- In a particular common law jurisdiction, the common law in relation to a specific issue may be overruled by statute law.
- The relevant law in one country (or jurisdiction) may differ from that in another country/jurisdiction, whether a common law or civil law jurisdiction.

The authors have endeavoured to give some examples of relevant statute law applicable to contracts in general and construction contracts in particular to illustrate the similarities and differences in the practice of construction law in different countries. However, it should be noted that in view of the wide ambit of construction contract law, the large number of jurisdictions and the speed with which legislation can be promulgated or amended, it is

1 Donald Charrett (ed), *The International Application of FIDIC Contracts A Practical Guide* (Informa Law from Routledge, 2020); Donald Charrett (ed), *FIDIC Contracts in Asia Pacific A Practical Guide to Application* (Informa Law from Routledge, 2022).

2 A Latin phrase that means that agreements are to be kept.

not possible for any assessment of statute law to be correct and comprehensive, even at a single point in time. Readers should therefore consult construction law texts specific to their relevant country/jurisdiction to determine details of the statute and other law that applies to their situation. A (non-exhaustive) bibliography of texts for construction law, FIDIC contracts, and for certain countries is provided in the References section.

1.3 Contract law and construction contract law

Construction contract law is a subset of general contract law, and it is generally consistent with the principles that apply to contract law in general. As noted earlier, jurisdictions may have specific statute laws that define specific requirements for construction contracts, for example the entry into a construction contract or constraints on the method of resolution of construction disputes. However, many aspects of construction contract law are not dependent on the subject matter of the contract (ie construction) and are accordingly not distinguished from general contract law. For example, the principles which underlie the formation of a construction contract are generally not dependent on the nature or special features of a construction contract, and accordingly there is typically no specific contract construction law related to contract formation. For example, the 'battle of the forms' in the formation of a construction contract is no different in principle or substance to the battle which may occur in many other types of commercial contract where the contract conditions offered by one party are responded to by a counter-offer on different terms by the other party. However, the 'battle of the forms' is frequently exhibited in its most acute form as a result of the complexity of the documents which comprise a major construction contract, the often protracted 'arm-wrestling' during the pre-contractual negotiations which results in a complex series of communications, and the frequent desire of the Employer[3] for the Contractor to commence work on the Site before all of the contractual issues are 'ironed out.'

In order to keep this book within manageable limits, the authors have focused on those aspects of construction contracts which are peculiar to contracts of that nature and have provided only a limited coverage of general contract law. Contract law is covered extensively in other publications, often in considerable detail on specific issues in the legal literature.

1.4 Common law and civil law

Whilst 'the law' in any **legal jurisdiction**[4] is unique, there are two main law 'families' used throughout the world that are relevant to construction law: the common law system and the civil law system. A number of Islamic countries apply Shari'a law, derived from the Koran, and Jaeger and Hök have articulated how the principles of this Islamic law may apply to construction contracts.[5] Gibb has detailed the background to Shari'a law that provides an insight into its foundations and its application in Islamic countries.[6] This book however is

3 The definitions of capitalised terms are in the Glossary and are defined in the text where they are in bold.
4 A legal jurisdiction refers to a geographic area that is subject to a unique set of laws.
5 Axel-Volkmar Jaeger & Götz-Sebastian Hök, *FIDIC – A Guide for Practitioners* (Springer, 2010) 49–53.
6 H A R Gibb, 'The Shari'a,' www.answering-islam.org/Books/Gibb/sharia.htm (accessed 15 January 2021).

confined to a brief consideration of the differences between the common law and civil law, to the extent that it is significant in relation to construction contracts.

The **common law** legal system originated in England in the Middle Ages, and England introduced it into most of the colonies that constituted the British Empire around the world. Notwithstanding the ultimate independence of all those former colonies, the common law (in its local version) has been retained in those countries. Countries which still have a(n essentially) common law system include England and Wales, Ireland, Northern Ireland, the United States, Singapore, Malaysia, Brunei, Pakistan, India, Sri Lanka, Ghana, Cameroon, Canada, New Zealand, Fiji, Papua New Guinea, Hong Kong, and Australia. Some countries have a mixed common law and civil law system, including Nicaragua, Israel, South Africa, Scotland in the UK, Greece, the Philippines, the Seychelles, Quebec in Canada, Louisiana in the USA, and Puerto Rico.

The essential feature of the common law is that the law is stated by judges in their reasoning in giving judgement in the disputes brought before them. It is 'common' to all of the courts within a given legal jurisdiction, so that the legal result of a particular controversy does not depend on which judge or court hears the case. A common law court is required to follow the principles in previous decisions in the same legal jurisdiction, unless they are inconsistent with a higher court's decision or determined to be wrong in law. This doctrine is known as ***stare decisis***. The reasoning in the **case law** published in **Law Reports** that results from the judgements of judges is, collectively, the written statement of the common law. It may vary from one legal jurisdiction to another, and it may change and evolve over time. Nevertheless, many legal principles of the common law have been established and have remained essentially unchanged for hundreds of years, and still represent good law today. As will be noted from several cases referred to in this book, some of the common law principles that may still apply to a modern construction contract were articulated in England over 150 years ago.[7]

By contrast to the common law, in a **civil law** system, the governing legislature enacts detailed legislation that endeavours to codify the law in a given area. Pejovic describes civil law in the following terms:

> Civil law has its origin in Roman law, as codified in the Corpus Iuris Civilis of Justinian. Under this influence, in the ensuing period the civil law has been developed in Continental Europe and in many other parts of the world. The main feature of civil law is that it is contained in civil codes, which are described as a 'systematic, authoritative, and guiding statute of broad coverage, breathing the spirit of reform and marking a new start in the legal life of an entire nation.' Most civil codes were adopted in the nineteenth and twentieth centuries: French Code Civil, 1804, Austrian Bürgerliches Gesetzbuch, 1811, German Bürgerliches Gesetzbuch, 1896, Japanese Minpo, 1896, Swiss Zivilgesetzbuch, 1907, Italian Codice Civile, 1942. Between these codes there are some important differences, and they are often grouped in the Romanic and the Germanic families. Even though the civil codes of different countries are not homogenous, there are certain features of all civil codes which bind them together and 'sets them apart from those who practice under different systems.'

7 For a number of construction law cases from the nineteenth century that are still referred to, see Alfred A Hudson, *The Law of Building, Engineering, and Ship Building Contracts and of the Duties and Liabilities of Engineers, Architects, Surveyors, and Valuers Vol II* (Sweet & Maxwell, 4th edn 1914, abridged and reprinted 2001).

> Civil law is largely classified and structured and contains a great number of general rules and principles, often lacking details. One of the basic characteristics of the civil law is that the courts main task is to apply and interpret the law contained in a code, or a statute to case facts. The assumption is that the code regulates all cases that could occur in practice, and when certain cases are not regulated by the code, the courts should apply some of the general principles used to fill the gaps.[8]

Codification of the law is a comprehensive statement of all the principles that determine the legal outcome resulting from a given set of factual circumstances. In practical terms, complete codification of a given area of the law into a **contract code** is not possible, as it can only take into account foreseeable situations. Furthermore, any given codification may have gaps consciously left by the drafters, and these gaps leave scope for the application of judge-made law in the form of individual judgements.

Under the civil law in a given legal jurisdiction, there may be more than one code that applies to contracts of a given type. For example, in China there is a code applying to contracts in general, *PRC Contract Law* [428 Articles], and a specific code applying additional provisions to construction contracts: *PRC Construction Law* [85 Articles (1998 law)]. There are also *Regulations on the Quality Management of Construction Projects*.

Civil law jurisdictions may distinguish between contracts of a 'standard' type which are governed by particular statutory rules (so called **nominate contracts**) and one-off or **bespoke contracts** (in civil law terminology, **innominate contracts**). Construction contracts are one important class of nominate contracts, in which the relevant law defines the default rules which will automatically apply, except to the extent that the parties expressly or implicitly deviate from them (within the limits of what is permitted by the law). Thus, under civil law, there is a comprehensive codified framework in which every construction contract is embedded, which will apply unless the parties make specific alternative provisions in their contract.

There are significant differences in approach to drafting a contract under a common law or a civil law system. Jaeger and Hök have identified the differences as follows:

> Due to the fact that there is only a limited amount of statute law, common law practitioners will often attempt to create their own independent little contract world. The approach is to include statutes and case law in the terms of the contract if deemed useful or to circumvent it with great skill if considered a nuisance. Important terms will be defined and strictly used within the contract. Civil law practitioners on the other hand embed the contract into a grid of legal rules which consist of entire legal codifications. They will limit themselves to adjust the legal framework if possible. As a consequence contracts governed by civil law will be shorter than those governed by common law. Civil law practitioners will rely on implied terms and other provisions of the relevant codes[9] [citations omitted].

8 Pejovic, Caslav, 'Civil Law and Common Law: Two Different Paths Leading to the Same Goal' (2001) *VUWLawRw* 42; (2001) 32(3) *Victoria University of Wellington Law Review* 817, www.victoria.ac.nz/__data/assets/pdf_file/0008/830780/Pejovic.pdf (accessed 15 July 2018).

9 Axel-Volkmar Jaeger & Götz-Sebastian Hök, *FIDIC – A Guide for Practitioners* (Springer, 2010) 131.

1.4.1 Convergence of common law and civil law

However, the procedural differences between the common law and civil law have become much less in recent years. Increasingly, more of the law in common law countries is explicitly stated in legislation. This can take the form of a statute that codifies the common law or, alternatively, a statute that modifies an aspect of the common law inconsistent with modern society's expectations (as perceived by legislators). Statutes may also form new 'social legislation' that mandates desirable community outcomes not achieved by the common law. Examples of such laws that impact construction projects include legislation for health and safety and environmental protection. *Statutory Adjudication* laws are a recent example of 'social legislation' aimed at promoting prompt payment and redressing contractual imbalances of power.

The courts in civil law countries are relying to a much greater extent than previously on the precedential value of court judgements on a similar issue, because the answer to a legal issue may not be found in the codes. Whilst previous civil law court judgements may not have the authority that *stare decisis* has in the common law, well-reasoned judgements of other courts can be persuasive in cases where the legal issues are the same and the facts similar. For example, in the Swiss First Civil Law Court case *A.________ SA v. B.________ SA, 4A_124/2014*[10] the court referred to previous decisions in support of its findings on the jurisdiction of an arbitral tribunal and its ability to review the factual findings of an arbitral tribunal. Further, in some jurisdictions the decisions of the court of last resort are binding for lower courts, for example in Argentina.[11] In a book on FIDIC contracts, the authors list a significant number of cases from the French and German civil law jurisdictions, as well as cases from various common law jurisdictions.[12]

It is probably true that today there are no pure common law or civil law systems anywhere in the world. Landskron looked at this issue in some detail and concluded that in spite of the differences between the respective sources of law, the approaches of judges in common law and civil law systems to statutory interpretation were not essentially different, and there were no intrinsic differences between the two systems that justified their classification into different 'legal families.' Thus: 'Although each legal family represents similarity of the historical development, this does not mean anymore similarity of individual jurisdictions.'[13] Nevertheless, considering the broad characteristics of the common law and civil law systems is a useful way of considering their features in a comparative law sense. There are, for example, still different approaches to interpretation (or construction) of contract terms between the common law and civil law.

10 A case in which the court considered whether a DAB decision was a precondition to referring a dispute to arbitration under the 1999 FIDIC Red Book.

11 Cerámica San Lorenzo; Supreme Court of the Republic of Argentina; 307:1094; July 4, 1985; SAIJ.

12 Axel-Volkmar Jaeger & Götz-Sebastian Hök, *FIDIC – A Guide for Practitioners* (Springer, 2010) xix–xxx.

13 Rolf Landskron, *Common Law and Civil-Law Legal Families: A Misleading Categorisation* (LLM (Rsrch), Bond University, 2008) 144, http://epublications.bond.edu.au/theses/landskron/ (accessed 20 July 2010).

Another 'convergence' between the common law and civil law is that, despite the differences of form, procedure, and terminology, in many factual situations, the two systems will arrive at essentially the same substantive result. There is frequently broad agreement on what constitutes a just and equitable outcome in a given situation, despite the different potential routes to achieve it. The ability of international arbitral tribunals comprised of members from different countries and legal systems to agree on an award is testament to widely held concepts of justice. For example:

- Under the common law, a clause stipulating a consequence for breach of a term of the contract will be an unenforceable **penalty** if the consequence is out of all proportion to the legitimate interests of the innocent party in performance of the primary obligation.[14] As with many common law principles, the penalty doctrine is long-standing,[15] and has recently been redefined and refined in Australia,[16] England,[17] and New Zealand.[18]
- Although penalties are generally acceptable under civil law (ie the pre-agreed amount of damages for breach of contract or non-performance can be higher than the actual damages that could reasonably be expected), s343B of the *German Civil Code* authorises the courts to reduce an unreasonably high penalty amount. If penalty clauses for late performance exceed 0.2–0.3% of the contract price per day, or if there is no cap to the amount (5% is considered reasonable), the penalty clause will usually be declared void.[19]

This book cites many cases from various common law jurisdictions as authority for propositions of law, mainly because they are readily available in English and familiar to the authors. In many cases those propositions will also apply in civil law jurisdictions, notwithstanding different legal terminology.

Further, the influence of international arbitration in bridging the systems of common law and civil law should not be underestimated. In an international arbitration, one of the parties may be from a common law system whilst the other may be from a civil law jurisdiction. Different parts of the contract may be performed in the different jurisdictions. A number of different legal jurisdictions may be involved in different aspects of execution of the project. In a dispute determined by international arbitration, the Arbitrators may not only be from different countries but also from different legal systems (common law and civil law). Inevitably in such cases, common ground in relation to legal principles must be sought between the potentially conflicting requirements. This issue is discussed further in ¶4.6.

14 . The rule against penalties is a rule of contract law based on public policy. It is a question of construction of the parties' contract judged by reference to the circumstances at the time of contracting; the public policy is that the courts will not enforce a stipulation for punishment for breach of contract. *Cavendish Square Holdings v Makdessi* [2015] 3 WLR 1373, [243] per Lord Hodge.

15 *Dunlop Pneumatic Tyre Co Ltd v New Garage & Motor Co Ltd* [1915] AC 79.

16 *Andrews v ANZ Banking Group Ltd* (2012) 247 CLR 205; *Paciocco v Australia and New Zealand Banking Group Ltd* [2016] HCA 28.

17 *Cavendish Square Holdings v Makdessi* [2015] 3 WLR 1373.

18 *127 Hobson Street Limited v Honey Bees Preschool Limited* [2020] NZSC 53.

19 Axel-Volkmar Jaeger & Götz-Sebastian Hök, *FIDIC – A Guide for Practitioners* (Springer, 2010) 43.

1.5 Differences between legal concepts in the common law and civil law systems

The difficulties that can arise because of the differences between the legal concepts in the civil law and common law systems have been discussed by Jaeger and Hök in the context of FIDIC standard form construction contracts:

> The idea for this book was born out of the belief that the increasing dissemination of FIDIC forms of contract throughout the Civil Law world requires a different approach to the subject matter than that which is found under the Common Law. An English native speaker will naturally not encounter many difficulties when reading the FIDIC forms, although of course the wording used will sometimes be subject to interpretation. Again an English native speaker will usually be familiar with the underlying legal principles, which mostly derive from Common Law, despite the fact that some Civil Law-inspired features have been incorporated in the FIDIC books. Thus there is a clear need to explain Common Law concepts and legal terms in the context of Civil Law. This may often prove to be difficult as the very nature of Civil Law language is in many respects different from Common Law language. Both systems have terms which are often difficult to translate literally because of the fact that the terms reflect legal concepts which are unknown in the other legal world.
>
> Although many difficulties in understanding the wording may be overcome if the terms and concepts are carefully explained, the English wording may sometimes be in direct contradiction to Civil Law concepts and practice. Whether the FIDIC wording will then prevail depends on the strength of the *pacta sunt servanda* principle. Civil Law systems usually determine and categorise the very nature of a contract. If the contract falls within the limits of a nominated contract, the relevant default rules (*lois supplétives, dispositives Recht*) and additionally the relevant mandatory rules will apply. Whether the FIDIC based contract will be recognized as an agreement *sui generis* [belonging to a species all of its own; unique] or at least as a valid agreement although being in contradiction to the law must be ascertained on a case by case basis.[20]

A detailed examination of the differences between civil law and common law as it applies to contracts in general is outside the scope of this book. Nevertheless, it is worth highlighting the existence of some general civil law concepts that are either alien to the common law, or the civil law deals with them differently to the common law (and even the civil law terminology may have no counterpart in the common law):

- Pre-contractual duties;
- Duties to negotiate in good faith;
- The formal requirements for entering into a contract;
- The essential elements which determine the validity of a contract;
- Construction of contract terms;
- Filling of gaps in the terms of the contract, for example FIDIC contracts are referred to in Estonia to fill gaps in the law;
- Good faith and fair dealing in the execution of a contract;
- Enforceable obligations in respect of third parties to a contract;
- Penalty clauses;
- Cap on liability;
- Judicial powers to adapt contracts to changed circumstances;

20 Axel-Volkmar Jaeger & Götz-Sebastian Hök, *FIDIC – A Guide for Practitioners* (Springer, 2010) vii.

- Remedies for non-performance or breach of contract, for example specific performance (a court order compelling a party to fulfil its obligations to another party under a contract);
- ***Culpa in contrahendo*** (culpable conduct during contract negotiations);
- Unjust enrichment (a benefit received for which the recipient is obliged to make restitution to the party at whose expense it was unjustly obtained);
- ***Negotiorum gestio*** (enables one who intervenes without authority in another's affairs for the latter's benefit to claim reimbursement and indemnity);
- Changed circumstances (hardship clause);
- Disputes relating to non-contractual claims may be non-arbitrable (eg Pakistan and fraud);
- 'Set-off,' 'abatement,' or similar rights;
- Limitation periods for bringing an action for breach of contract (eg three years in India);
- Proof of loss;
- Extinguishing liability will not apply in some jurisdictions which do not allow contractual waiver of liability in cases of gross negligence or fraud;
- Torts (eg business libel/defamation in Canada and a number of civil law jurisdictions);
- The registration and effects of non-registration of local agents; and
- Companies.

It must be stressed that, although there may be substantial commonality between the manner in which these concepts are dealt with in different civil law jurisdictions, ultimately the law on any issue is that articulated in the appropriate code in the specific jurisdiction, perhaps as construed by judges. Just as the common law on a specific issue may be different in Canada from that in New Zealand, so the law on specific performance may differ significantly between Germany and France.

1.6 Common law

In adjudicating a dispute between two contracting parties in court, a common law judge will decide the outcome based on the body of applicable law relevant to the particular circumstances of the dispute. The applicable law may include law enacted by the Government in legislation or regulations (**statute law**), that which is found in the judgements of previous court cases (the common law), as well as that separate body of law known as **equity** which was developed in the UK Court of Chancery to supplement, correct, and mitigate the strict rules of common law. Judgements of superior courts in the common law jurisdictions are published in a wide range of Law Reports, and these form the primary source and authority for the common law. Judges are also required to determine the meaning of statutory provisions where this is in issue in a dispute, and statutes must therefore be interpreted and applied in accordance with any such judge-made 'clarification.' The significance and importance of reported judgements of relevant cases in determining the application of common and statute law therefore cannot be overemphasised.

Determining the applicable common law to a particular dispute in a given jurisdiction may not be an easy matter, because of the potentially wide source of judgements, and the differences between different jurisdictions or even between judges within the same jurisdiction. In principle, the judgements in other common law jurisdictions may be consistent with the common law in a particular legal jurisdiction and relied upon by the judges in that jurisdiction if the factual circumstances are sufficiently similar. However, any judgement from a different legal jurisdiction (and that includes a different State or Province in the same country) must be carefully reviewed for any relevant differences in the applicable statutory framework, or whether it has been overruled by a relevant court in the applicable jurisdiction. Australia (unlike the USA) has a unified common law, and the High Court is its final arbiter. The High Court has stated that intermediate appellate courts and trial judges in Australia should not depart from decisions on common law or on the interpretation of Commonwealth legislation or uniform national legislation in intermediate appellate courts in another jurisdiction unless they are convinced that the interpretation is plainly wrong.[21] Notwithstanding the High Court's admonitions on comity between Australian courts, in the absence of High Court authority on a particular issue, it is not unknown for courts in different States to disagree on the content of Australian common law.[22] In the absence of binding authority in Australia, a judgement from a superior court in England, Singapore, or another common law country may be very persuasive authority as to the applicable common law, however it is not binding. In this book, judgements from a range of common law countries are quoted as authority for various principles of construction law; however, these may not necessarily apply in all common law jurisdictions.

As an illustration of the different ways in which the common law of negligence has developed in different jurisdictions, Australia and the United Kingdom have different tests in respect of the duty of care that a person owes to another to avoid that person suffering economic loss. The three-stage test for imposing a duty of care on a person to avoid economic loss to another enunciated by the House of Lords[23] has been specifically rejected by five justices of the Australian High Court.[24] More recently the Australian High Court differed from the UK Supreme Court in respect of the scope of the doctrine of penalties. The Australian High Court held that equitable relief against penalties had not been subsumed into the common law rule and that the rule against penalties was not limited to cases arising out of breach of contract.[25] The UK Supreme Court held that the rule against penalties was confined to cases arising out of contractual breach.[26]

Notwithstanding the common law principles applicable to construction contracts in general in a particular legal jurisdiction, the doctrine of freedom of contract means that contracting parties may decide that those principles should not apply to their particular contract. In the event that the contractual terms evince the parties' clear intention to 'cover the field' in respect of a certain aspect, the common law is ousted to that extent.[27]

---

21 *Farah Constructions Pty Ltd v See-Day Pty Ltd* [2007] HCA 22.

22 For example, see the discussion on the admissibility of the surrounding 'matrix of facts' in ¶2.13.4.

23 *Caparo Industries Plc v Dickman* [1990] 2 AC 605 at 617–618 per Lord Bridge of Harwich.

24 *Sullivan v Moody* [2001] HCA 59; 207 CLR 562; 75 ALJR 1570.

25 *Andrews v ANZ Banking Group Ltd* [2012] 247 CLR 205.

26 *Cavendish Square Holdings v Makdessi* [2015] 3 WLR 1373.

27 For example, in *Tan Hung Nguyen v Luxury Design Homes* [2005] 21 BCL 46 at 58, Einstein J decided that a particular contractual clause was intended by the parties to exclude common law rights to relief for repudiatory conduct.

Conversely, unless the parties have intended to exclude common law rights, those rights will complement the contractual rights specifically provided for in terms. It is a well-established common law principle that clear words are needed to rebut the presumption that a contracting party does not intend to abandon any remedies for breach of contract arising by operation of law.[28] Contract terms may state that common law rights or rights 'otherwise at law' are specifically preserved in addition to the rights conferred by the contract. In every case, whatever words are used, whether common law rights are preserved or excluded is a question of the meaning of the terms of the contract.

An example of a case in which the question was whether the parties had excluded the operation of the common law is the case of *J-Corp v Mladenis*.[29] The question before the judge in this case was whether specified liquidated damages of $NIL for delay was intended to exclude a claim for common law damages. The judge at first instance, and the Court of Appeal, construed the terms of the contract to be that the parties did not express in clear and unambiguous terms an intention to exclude the common law right to damages for breach of the builder's obligation to complete the Works on time. As with other cases on construction of contract terms, this case turned on its own facts, and does not stand for any wider proposition in respect of the meaning of the words NIL for the specified amount of liquidated damages in a contract. Whether or not such a phrase is intended to exclude the common law right to damages for breach of contract for delay will depend on the construction of the specific terms of the relevant contract.

In *Adapt Constructions Pty Ltd v Whittaker and Luff*[30] Burns J also came to the conclusion that common law damages for delay were available where the contract provided for a rate of liquidated damages of $Zero. This was because there were no clear words in the contract evidencing an intention that the Employer would have no remedy for breach of the contract by failure to complete the Works within the prescribed time.

The common law itself may, however, be subject to the omnipotent power of a written *Constitution* which provides an overarching statute of universal application in the given legal jurisdiction. The following statement was made by the Chief Justice of the Australian High Court in relation to the situation in Australia, but is of much wider application:

> In one respect, the existence of a written Constitution as the basic law of a federal democratic society has a specific implication for the substantive content of the rule of law. The source of law-making authority is the Constitution, and the law, including the common law as developed by the courts, must conform to the Constitution. The Federal Parliament and the High Court both owe their existence to the Constitution. However law is made in Australia, it must be consistent with the Constitution. And so must any substantive principle said to flow from the rule of law itself.[31]

Further: 'Whether the common law is a separate source of judicial power, must in any event take account of the power of Parliament (acting within the *Constitution*) to alter the common law.'[32] That is a statement of general application in any common law jurisdiction:

28 *Gilbert-Ash (Northern) Ltd v Modern Engineering (Bristol) Ltd* [1974] AC 689; *Concut Pty Ltd v Worrell* [2000] HCA 64; [2000] 75 ALJR 312.

29 [2009] WASCA 157.

30 [2015] ACTSC 188.

31 Gleeson CJ, 'Courts and the Rule of Law' (2001) Speech in the Rule of Law Series at Melbourne University (7 November 2001), www.hcourt.gov.au/speeches/cj/cj_ruleoflaw.htm#_edn6 (accessed 5 August 2010).

32 Ibid.

subject only to the relevant *Constitution*, the legislature has unlimited legislative power to cover all areas of law comprehensively with its statutes, to the exclusion of the common law. In England, with no written *Constitution*, the conventional view is that the legislature does have unlimited power.[33] However, certain members of the House of Lords (now the Supreme Court) have expressed the view that there could be limits to this power:

> In exceptional circumstances involving an attempt to abolish judicial review or the ordinary role of the courts, the Appellate Committee of the House of Lords or a new Supreme Court may have to consider whether this is [a] constitutional fundamental which not even a sovereign Parliament acting at the behest of a complaisant House of Commons cannot abolish.[34]

The process the court uses to determine (construe) what a document (such as a contract or a statute) means is referred to as **construction** of the words used. The process of construction of the terms of a contract is discussed further in ¶2.13.

Although, in principle, the common law is specific to a particular jurisdiction (eg there is one common law in Australia which may be different to the common law in England in respect of a particular legal issue), there are considerable commonalities across jurisdictions, particularly in the field of construction law. Thus, it is common for judgements in one common law jurisdiction to cite with approval a judgement from another jurisdiction, for example a Canadian judgement may cite an Australian High Court case as support for the principles of the common law applicable in Canada. Although judgements from a wide range of international jurisdictions are increasingly cited in judgements in common law countries, this is hardly a new phenomenon. For example, in the seminal negligence (and most widely cited English) House of Lords case of *Donoghue v Stevenson*, Lord Atkin in 1932 referred to a US case in the New York Court of Appeals as support for the principle of manufacturer's liability even in the absence of a contractual relationship. One could reasonably anticipate that, with our shrinking (or flat[35]) world in which there are increasingly more sophisticated tools for cross jurisdictional legal research (eg LawCite in AUSTLII), such citation and common jurisprudence will become even more common in the future.

It is hardly surprising that there is significant commonality between the common law in different jurisdictions, when one remembers that the common law grew from its single root in England. Applicable English common law was taken at a given point in time to most of the colonies established by England around the world and incorporated by the enactment of reception statutes (with the exception of the USA). The received common law was subsequently gradually changed by judgements in local courts and, increasingly, by local statute. An interesting example of a significant departure from the English common law was the *Indian Contract Act 1872*, which applies in India, Pakistan, Sudan, and Malaysia – 'a straightforward and easily readable codification of the Common Law of Contracts with some enlightened improvements.'[36]

---

33 Tom Bingham, *The Rule of Law* (Penguin, 2010) 160–170.

34 *R(Jackson) v Attorney General* [2005] UKHL 56 [102] per Lord Steyn.

35 Thomas L Friedman, *The World Is Flat a Brief History of the Twenty-First Century* (Farrar, Straus and Giroux, 2005).

36 Robert Knutson (ed), *FIDIC An Analysis of International Construction Contracts* (Kluwer Law International, 2005) xvii.

The strength of the common law is that, over time, it has produced a large volume of case law in which judges have applied the law to a range of different situations. This leads to predictability, as contracting parties can be reasonably sure of the law that applies before they enter into a contract. Such predictability is very appealing to commercial parties, who frequently choose the law of a common law jurisdiction with a well-developed body of common law to achieve that result: 'As a practical matter, no civil law legislature can ever address the full spectrum of factual possibilities in the breadth, depth and detail of the case law of the common law courts of even a smaller jurisdiction.'[37]

1.7 Case law

The primary references for the common law are the written judgements made by judges in the common law courts. The judgement of a judge 'at first instance' (ie the first judge to hear a case) will be a part of the common law, provided it is not overturned by the judgement of a 'higher' court, that is a court with the jurisdiction to determine whether the judgement of the lower court was incorrect. The judgements of the highest court in a given jurisdiction thus determine, in their judgements, the current state of the common law in that jurisdiction. Thus, the higher a court in a given jurisdiction, the more definitive is its statement of the prevailing common law.

The hierarchy of the common law courts in England is:

- Supreme Court (President, Vice President, and Justices). In October 2009 the Supreme Court took over the functions of the Appellate Committee of the House of Lords, whose justices were known as the Law Lords: Lord Chancellor, Lords of Appeal in Ordinary, and peers who had exalted judicial experience;
- High Court: Court of Appeal (Master of the Rolls and Lord Justices of Appeal);
- High Court: Queen's Bench;
- County Court; and
- Magistrates Court.

Thus, a judgement of the Supreme Court (and in judgements before October 2009, the House of Lords) may overturn a judgement made by the Court of Appeal, which previously may have overturned a judgement made by the Queen's Bench Division of the High Court. It is therefore necessary in considering the statement of the common law in a judgement to establish which court it was made in, and if a lower court, whether or not that judgement has been overturned by a higher court. Judgements made in the Supreme Court/House of Lords are clearly the most definitive statement of the common law of England available.

Because of its nature and its long history, statements of the common law on a particular issue may derive from judgements made in the eighteenth century, or even earlier. Whilst the majority of such judgements are reasonably available in law libraries to lawyers residing in major cities in the common law world, they may be unavailable to others. This is particularly so if the judgement is very old or made by a judge in a non-mainstream court. Recent (say within the last ten years or so) judgements in many jurisdictions are now readily available to the general public over the internet. Accordingly, in this book, we have

37 Encyclopedia Britannica.

attempted to refer to such 'online' cases to the extent possible, to encourage readers to refer to the source cases for the legal propositions advanced. Whilst such recent cases may not be the most definitive statement of the common law, they have the considerable advantage of availability. Furthermore, frequently the judges in modern cases canvass the relevant common law, and summarise the salient points from the relevant judgements, often quoting extracts from older judgements.

Another useful source of case law is a 'casebook' in which an editor has extracted the significant parts of the seminal judgements on a particular topic to provide a concise summary of the common law. One such early casebook on construction law is still such a useful reference that it was reprinted 87 years after its original publication date: ***Hudson's Fourth Edition Volume of Cases***.[38] A more modern such casebook is *Powell-Smith & Furmston's Building Contract Casebook*.[39] Such casebooks generally not only provide the relevant judgements (or appropriate extracts from them) of some of the most important cases but also commentary or headnotes that highlight the significance of the judge's reasoning.

1.8 Mandatory and non-mandatory laws

Both common law and civil law systems endeavour to give effect to binding voluntary agreements entered into by legal persons, subject to the overarching effect of the applicable law and public policy. It is a 'paramount policy of the law that people should keep faith and fulfil their promises.'[40] A **legal person** is an entity on which the legal system confers rights and obligations and includes natural persons and artificial bodies such as corporations or companies.

The term 'contract' encompasses more obligations than those arising from mere agreement, summed up by the following definition from the US *Uniform Commercial Code*:

> '**Contract**,' as distinguished from 'agreement,' means the total legal obligation that results from the parties' agreement as determined by [the Uniform Commercial Code] as supplemented by any other applicable laws.[41]

The total legal obligation includes not only the specific agreement made by the parties but also the more complete set of rules comprised by the governing law or the proper law of the contract (see ¶2.6). In a common law jurisdiction, the proper law of the contract will include both statute law as well as the relevant common law.

The various provisions of the relevant statutes of the proper law of the contract may be either **mandatory law** or alternatively may be **non-mandatory law** and only apply to the extent that the parties have not agreed otherwise. Mandatory law is based on public policy

38 This book is a 2001 reprint of Alfred A Hudson, *The Law of Building, Engineering, and Ship Building Contracts and of the Duties and Liabilities of Engineers, Architects, Surveyors and Valuers with Reports of Cases and Precedents Vol II* (Sweet & Maxwell, 4th edn 1914).

39 Michael Furmston, *Powell-Smith and Furmston's Building Contract Casebook* (Blackwell Publishing, 4th edn 2006).

40 *Aquagenics Pty Ltd v Break O'Day Council* [2010] TASFC 3, [16] per Evans J.

41 §1.201(b)(12) of the *Uniform Commercial Code* (USA).

and as it cannot be excluded by the parties, it is a significant constraint on the principle of freedom of contract. This applies in both common law and civil law jurisdictions, however the dividing line between mandatory and non-mandatory law varies from one legal jurisdiction to another.

Determining whether a provision of a particular law is mandatory or non-mandatory can only be determined by construction of the law itself, although some recent statutes in for example France explicitly state when their rules are mandatory. Even the 'rules' of construction of a document may depend on whether it is a civil law or common law jurisdiction, or more accurately on the 'rules' of the particular jurisdiction. Thus, for example, the extent to which extraneous material (ie material not included in the words of the document itself) can be taken into account in construction of a document is different in England to France. This difference between English and French law is illustrated by the following extract from a UK House of Lords judgement:

> As Professor Catherine Valcke explains in an illuminating article ('On Comparing French and English Contract Law: Insights from Social Contract Theory') (16 January 2009), French law regards the intentions of the parties as a pure question of subjective fact, their volonté psychologique, uninfluenced by any rules of law. It follows that any evidence of what they said or did, whether to each other or to third parties, may be relevant to establishing what their intentions actually were. There is in French law a sharp distinction between the ascertainment of their intentions and the application of legal rules which may, in the interests of fairness to other parties or otherwise, limit the extent to which those intentions are given effect. English law, on the other hand, mixes up the ascertainment of intention with the rules of law by depersonalising the contracting parties and asking, not what their intentions actually were, but what a reasonable outside observer would have taken them to be.[42]

In practice there are two types of mandatory rules of law. The first, **domestic mandatory rules of law** of a given legal jurisdiction, apply to all contracts for which the proper law of the contract is the law of the jurisdiction. The second, **international mandatory rules of law**, have to be applied, even if the proper law of the contract is that of another jurisdiction. Whilst the **forum** (the place where the issue is being decided) will generally apply its own international mandatory rules, it is also possible for international mandatory rules of another jurisdiction to be applied.[43] For example, a construction contract in relation to a project built in France could have, for example, German law as the proper law of the contract, but the statutory liability of a contractor of ten years for latent structural defects under French law (***garantie décennale***) is a mandatory international rule of law and cannot be derogated from.

Examples of mandatory laws include the following:

- The limitation period for bringing an action in court for breach of contract (the **law of the forum** or ***lex fori***).
- Liability for latent defects in many civil law countries – *garantie décennale* in France and other countries such as Belgium, Luxemburg, Algeria (art. 554 *Civil*

42 *Chartbrook Limited v Persimmon Homes Limited* [2009] UKHL 38, per Lord Hoffman.

43 Thalia Kruger, 'Feasibility Study on the Choice of Law in International Contracts – Overview and Analysis of Existing Instruments' (2007) *Hague Conference on Private International Law* 10, 11, www.hcch.net/upload/wop/genaff_pd22b2007e.pdf (accessed 24 September 2010).

Code), Angola, Cameroun (art. 1792 *Civil Code*, French jurisdiction), Chile (art. 2003–3 *Codigo Civil*), Egypt, Malta, Morocco, Portugal, Romania (art. 1483 *Civil Code*), Spain, Tunisia, United Arab Emirates (art. 880 *Civil Code*).[44]

- The Australian *Consumer Law* (a schedule to the *Competition and Consumer Act 2010* (Cth)), which provides remedies for loss 'by' misleading or deceptive conduct that can bypass contractual agreements between the contracting parties.
- 'Consumer' legislation that specifies mandatory provisions to address the imbalance in bargaining power between individual persons and large corporations, for example in the *Domestic Building Contracts Act 1995* (Vic).

An example of a mandatory law with a long reach is the *Bribery Act 2010* (UK). This *Act* applies not only to the UK and UK companies, but the UK courts have jurisdiction if an offence is committed by a legal person with a close connection to the UK, or by a corporation which does business in the UK, regardless of where the alleged offence was carried out.

Where a provision of a statute is non-mandatory, it may not be obvious that the agreement of the parties in a contract has replaced that particular provision. As an example, the provisions of the *Civil Liability Act 2002* (Tas) which provide for proportionate liability of 'concurrent wrongdoers' in a claim for economic loss or damage to property in an action for damages arising from a failure to take reasonable care, are non-mandatory. Section 3A(3) of that *Act* provides that:

> This Act, other than Part 7, does not prevent the parties to a contract from making express provision for their rights, obligations and liabilities under the contract in relation to any matter to which this Act applies and does not limit or otherwise affect the operation of such an express provision.

In a case in which a Contractor wished to take advantage of the provisions of the *Act*, the judge found that the provisions of the contract, taken as a whole, contracted out of the proportionate liability provisions. This was so, even though the contract did not explicitly refer to the issue of proportionate liability. It was sufficient that there was an express provision to the contrary in their contract. Evans J said:

> I am satisfied that it is appropriate to consider those provisions of the contract from which, or by resort to which, it may be determined that the parties made provision for their rights, obligations and liabilities under the contract in relation to any matter to which the *Civil Liability Act* applies.[45]

Thus, even though the parties may be unaware of the implications, or even existence of a relevant non-mandatory law, its provisions will apply unless the parties make different provisions in their contract. In civil law jurisdictions a statute is generally intended to be a complete codification of the law on a specific issue, and civil law statutes are therefore usually more comprehensive and detailed than in common law jurisdictions. Although many of the provisions of the statutes relevant to construction law may be non-mandatory,

44 Axel-Volkmar Jaeger & Götz-Sebastian Hök, *FIDIC – A Guide for Practitioners* (Springer, 2010) 314.
45 *Aquagenics Pty Ltd v Break O'Day Council* [2010] TASFC 3.

they provide a default set of rules that will apply in the absence of agreement to alternative provisions by the parties (referred to as **suppletive** or **default rules**). In France and Germany for instance, there are so-called nominate contracts for which the statutes provide comprehensive sets of default rules which typical parties to typical contracts would opt for, based on the presumed intention of the parties. In accordance with the principle of freedom of contract, the parties can opt to derogate from those rules and provide for their own choice of rules in their contract. However, if they do not do so by way of an express or implied term in the contract, the default rules will still apply, whether or not the parties are aware of them: 'Thus, for example, a German based FIDIC contract will include Section 631 et seq. *German Civil Code*, whereas a French construction contract will include art 1792 et seq. *French Civil Code*.'[46]

Although common law jurisdictions generally do not have such comprehensive or codified legislation in respect of construction contracts, there is nevertheless the vast field of common law that will apply to a contract, unless the contract makes provisions to the contrary. Because of the substantial number of judgements which potentially make up the common law applicable to construction contracts, made over some hundreds of years and in a number of different jurisdictions, it is not always straightforward to determine what the common law is on a particular issue. A well-drafted contract will therefore typically not rely only on the provisions of the common law but will make explicit provision for the specific agreement made by the parties.

1.9 Topics covered by this book

Chapter 2 considers general contract law in the context of both common law and civil law, including hardship provisions and good faith. The various types of laws potentially impacting international contracts are identified. The governing law of the contract is discussed in the context of freedom of contract, and the complications that can arise if the parties fail to choose the governing law. The *UNIDROIT Principles of International Commercial Contracts* are introduced as a modern statement of the *lex mercatoria* (the Law Merchant), and their application to international contracts is discussed. The availability of contract codes in civil law and certain common law jurisdictions to determine the relevant contract law is noted. The requirements for formation of contracts under common law, civil law, and the *UNIDROIT Principles* and the various remedies for failure to perform contractual obligations are documented. Contract terms can be explicit or implicit; understanding the meaning of the words in a contract is determined by the process of construction which follows well-established rules which differ somewhat between jurisdictions and are not always straightforward to apply. The chapter concludes with a discussion of the prevention principle, sometimes expressed as preventing a party from taking advantage of his/her own wrong in enforcing a contract.

Chapter 3 covers the specific features of construction contracts. It discusses various types of construction contracts and their allocation of risks between Employer and Contractor. The features of some collaborative contracts are defined: early contractor

46 Axel-Volkmar Jaeger & Götz-Sebastian Hök, *FIDIC – A Guide for Practitioners* (Springer, 2010) 128.

involvement (ECI), incentivised target cost, alliance contracts and Public-Private Partnerships. The laws applicable to construction contracts are outlined, with reference to the governing law of the contract, the laws of the Site, and applicable legislation for the seat of the dispute determination. A case study is presented on the impact of COVID-19 on the execution of construction projects and the operation of construction contracts. Implied terms in construction contracts are outlined. Standard forms of contract and their advantages are distinguished from bespoke contracts. Standard form contracts from a number of different organisations are outlined, with FIDIC contracts and NEC contracts discussed in more detail. Guidance is provided on the contract as a contract management tool and drafting of construction contracts. The chapter concludes with a list of references on construction law, FIDIC contracts, NEC contracts, and case law.

Each jurisdiction has laws that impact on contracts for construction work: for the governing law of the contract, for the site of the construction work, or for the seat of dispute resolution. Chapter 4 explores the question of whether there are universally accepted principles of construction law, a *lex constructionis*. Three issues are discussed that can promote greater uniformity in the international practice of construction law: the use of FIDIC contracts, international commercial arbitration, and the modern statements of the *lex mercatoria*. A list of 20 principles of *lex constructionis* is proposed.

The succeeding chapters are devoted to individual topics of importance to construction contracts, each of which should be appropriately addressed in some form in any comprehensive and well written construction contract. Readers may note that these chapter headings are consistent with those in the contracts published by the International Federation of Consulting Engineers (**FIDIC** – *Fédération Internationale des Ingénieurs-Conseils*). These contracts are used extensively around the world for a large range of different types of work. In the authors' opinion, these are well-written and structured construction contracts which have appropriately addressed risk allocation between the contracting parties in an even-handed and transparent fashion, and the chapter headings of those contracts comprise of an appropriate framework for the consideration of construction contracts in general. FIDIC contracts are discussed in ¶3.10.1.

The final chapter addresses the impact of information and communications technology (ICT) on construction contracts: in the operation of construction contracts, in the execution of construction projects, and in the resolution of disputes. In the authors' view, improving the notorious low productivity in the construction industry will require the implementation of appropriate ICT, either in the form of enhancement applications or disruptive applications. Chapter 29 provides examples of enhancement applications and disruptive applications that can contribute to achieving better value in the construction of infrastructure that is essential for affordable, sustainable, healthy, peaceful, and happy lifestyles for as many people as possible in the modern world.

A glossary of terms commonly encountered in relation to construction contracts is included at the end of this book to assist readers who may not be familiar with some of the legal and industry terms used. It should be emphasised that some of these terms may have defined meanings in a particular contract, and these may be different to those given here. Consistent with general principle, the text of the relevant contract must always be consulted first to determine what it is that the parties have agreed, and this applies equally to the meaning of words that may otherwise be in common usage.

If this book assists in the understanding of the differences and commonalities between construction law as practiced around the world and the more efficient execution of such construction projects, including the avoidance or efficient resolution of their seemingly inevitable disputes, then the authors' efforts will have been worthwhile.

CHAPTER 2

Contract law

CONTENTS

DOI: 10.4324/9781003206873-2

2.1 Introduction

This chapter discusses contract law in the context of different legal systems around the world and considers some of the common issues and differences in contract law in general. The specific aspects of construction law as a species of contract law are considered in more detail in Chapter 3.

The world is a big place – as at 2021 there were 193 member states in the United Nations, each of which presumably has the sovereignty to enact laws that could impact on the practice of contract and construction law, at least within its borders. As discussed in Chapter 1, the legal systems of those member states comprise a number of broadly defined 'families' of law – common law, civil law, Shari'a law, and socialist law, to name the most widely recognised. Each of these families has certain characteristics which distinguish it from the other members of the family. Even within the broad common law family, there are identifiable differences in the law between jurisdictions. However, as discussed in ¶1.4.1, some of these differences may be more apparent than real.

2.2 Contracts

A **contract** is a legally binding agreement voluntarily entered into between two or more parties that is enforceable in a court of law according to its terms. In modern societies, where there is a division of labour and an emphasis on individual autonomy, it is the law of contract which enables the exchange of goods and services to take place in an orderly and predictable way. The fact that the law will enforce contracts provides predictability, which is of great importance to trade and industry, as it enables businesses to plan for the future and to allocate risks. It is no exaggeration to say that the law of contract forms the basis of a stable and peaceful society governed by the rule of law.

Enforceable contracts are also fundamentally important for international trade, as they provide the parties with the reassurance that they can plan their commercial affairs on the assumption that their agreement will be honoured. The modern globalised world could not function without contracts that are mutually recognised and enforceable across jurisdictions. Notwithstanding the sometimes-virulent minority opposition to globalisation, it is widely recognised that promotion and enhancement of international trade is fundamental to improving the living standards of the world's poor. Ricky Gordon posits: 'Although there are inevitable problems that occur from globalisation processes, especially between developing and developed nations, it has been found that over time these processes do enhance labour standards as a fundamental faculty of human rights.'[1]

International construction is a significant element of world trade, and it is often directly associated with major improvements in infrastructure that improve the health and living standards of the people in less developed countries. Construction has many international dimensions. The Contractors and suppliers for large construction projects in many parts of the world are frequently from another country, particularly where international finance or aid is involved. It is vital to obtaining competitive prices for such projects that the contracting parties can have confidence that their contractual expectations will be fulfilled.

The concepts which form the basis of the modern law of contract are not of recent origin. The Romans had very refined laws governing the performance of contracts, and many of those principles form the foundation of modern contract law, not only in civil law jurisdictions but also for common law. So pervasive is the influence of Roman law that it is still referred to in modern judgements; for example under Scottish law, old Roman law is still used in order to determine the obligations of the parties of a contract and even in tort. Thus, a Scottish court has said:

> If a person is employed under a contract *locatio operis faciendi*, 'for services' rather than 'of service,' the law does not hold the employer vicariously liable for wrongs committed by the contractor in the course of the employment. Such a person is an independent contractor, and is personally liable only, not being subject to detailed direction or control from the employer in the manner of performing the work. His contract is not to serve, but to bring about a required result in his own way, and if, in so doing, he injures a third party, he alone is responsible.[2]

Unless the contracting parties agree at all times on what the Contract means, and the consequences of breach or non-fulfilment of the terms of the Contract, such a 'binding' agreement would be illusory unless there is a mechanism for resolving disputes which will be accepted by, or could be enforced on, all parties. Under the rule of law, the courts have ultimate authority in respect of interpretation and enforcement of the Contract terms or deciding on the consequences of breach of the Contract.

As discussed in more detail in ¶4.3, contract law around the world is founded on two fundamental doctrines, operating within a legal system complying with the rule of law. The first of these, freedom of contract, sets the 'ground rules' which govern the parties' rights to enter into the Contract of their choice. The second, the principle of *pacta sunt servanda*, governs the performance of a contract after it has been entered into.

2.2.1 The contact terms prevail over the common law

The supremacy of the specific contract terms over any common law provisions that might otherwise apply has been summed up as follows:

1 Ricky Gordon, 'Do Globalisation Processes Enhance or Undermine Labour Standards as a Fundamental Faculty of Human Rights?' (2020) *Edith Cowan University* 8.

2 *Stewart & Anor v Malik* [2008] ScotSC 12 (29 April 2008), cited in Axel-Volkmar Jaeger & Götz-Sebastian Hök, *FIDIC – A Guide for Practitioners* (Springer, 2010) 3.

> A basic principle of the common law of contract, to which there are no exceptions that are relevant in the instant case, is that parties to a contract are free to determine for themselves what primary obligations they will accept. They may state these in express words in the contract itself and, where they do, the statement is determinative; but in practice a commercial contract never states all the primary obligations of the parties in full; many are left to be incorporated by implication of law from the legal nature of the contract into which the parties are entering. But if the parties wish to reject or modify primary obligations which would otherwise be so incorporated, they are fully at liberty to do so by express words.[3]

One important consequence of freedom of contract in the common law world is that the parties will be held to the specific bargain they have made, irrespective of whether it is fair, reasonable, or consistent with common practice or 'normal' contracts of that type. The starting point for any question in relation to a contract is therefore: 'What does the Contract require?' If the relevant provisions of the Contract are clear and unambiguous and are not in conflict with statute law or public policy, then, at least in the common law world, those provisions will generally prevail over any common practice or what might be considered fair and reasonable or what has happened in the past in respect of other contracts in similar circumstances. No matter how sympathetic a common law judge might be to the plight of a Contractor who entered into a loss-making contract, the terms of the Contract alone, subject to any mandatory law (see more on this later in the chapter), will determine the outcome in any legal proceedings.

Case study: Contractor held to onerous bargain

This principle was well illustrated in *Bottoms v York Corporation*,[4] where an inexperienced Contractor entered into a contract to construct a sewer, without being provided with any geotechnical information or making any investigations. In the event, the material encountered in the excavations required an extremely expensive form of construction that the Contractor had not allowed for. The Employer refused to change the Contract conditions as it was entitled to do, and the Contractor refused to complete the Contract Works. In a court case in which the Contractor sought damages for breach of contract and for an alleged wrongful seizure of the plaintiff's equipment, the judge made comments that would be equally relevant in similar circumstances today:

> I do not see any way of relieving the plaintiff from this contract into which he entered, and my judgment, therefore, must be in favour of the Corporation. At the same time, I think he has been hardly used, and I express my regret that the Corporation did not do what they were entitled to do, that is, refuse the lowest tender. I do not think that he and they were on level or on equal terms in coming to this bargain, and I think greater precaution should have been taken to inform him of the inevitable liability, of the inevitable loss, ruin, which was before him if he entered into the contract upon these terms.

---

3 *Photo Production v Securicor Ltd.* [1980] AC 827 per Lord Diplock.
4 (1892) Alfred A Hudson, *Hudson's Fourth Edition Table of Cases* (Sweet & Maxwell, 4th edn 1914) 208.

2.2.2 The contract terms and civil law

As discussed in ¶1.4, contract law is codified in civil law jurisdictions. Whether inconsistent contract terms prevail over the provisions of the relevant *Civil Code* depends on whether the provisions of the statute are mandatory or non-mandatory. For example, the provisions in respect of a nominate contract constitute default rules that the contract can deviate from explicitly or implicitly. However, any contract terms inconsistent with mandatory *Civil Code* provisions will not be enforceable.

2.3 Hardship provisions

2.3.1 Frustration

It is evident from the discussion in ¶2.2.1 that there is no general common law provision to relieve parties from hardships that arise from unforeseen circumstances not contemplated by the Contract. That is, any provisions dealing with hardship must be provided by the terms of the Contract itself. It is only in situations where performance of the Contract becomes impossible through circumstances not contemplated by the Contract that the common law provides the remedy of **frustration**. Frustration is 'the termination of a contract by operation of law on the emergence of fundamentally different situation,'[5] and:

> Frustration occurs whenever the law recognizes that without default of either party a contractual obligation has become incapable of being performed because the circumstances in which performance is called for would render it a thing radically different from that which was undertaken by the contract. *Non haec in fodera veni*. It was not this that I promised to do. . . . There must be as well such a change in the significance of the obligation that the thing undertaken would, if performed, be a different thing from that contracted for.[6]

2.3.2 Force majeure

Force majeure has different meanings in common law and civil law systems. Under the common law, *force majeure* is an exceptional event or circumstance which cannot be resisted or controlled and which satisfies the criteria stated in the Contract. Accordingly, it is not a term of art with a defined meaning in common law jurisdictions; any *force majeure* provisions that provide for unforeseen circumstances must be defined in the Contract.

In civil law systems, *force majeure* is defined in the relevant *Civil Code* and operates independently of party agreement, which means that it will protect an obligee even if the Contract does not contain a *force majeure* clause. Good faith is the bedrock principle in *Civil Codes* on which various 'hardship' provisions are founded. However, as illustrated in the following examples, there is no uniformity as to what events will constitute *force majeure*, and these differ significantly between jurisdictions.

Force majeure is considered in more detail in Chapter 25.

5 *Davis Contractors Ltd v Fareham Urban District Council* [1956] A.C. 696, 720 per Lord Reid; cited with approval in *Codelfa Construction Proprietary Limited v State Rail Authority of New South Wales* (1982) 149 C.L.R. 337, 357.

6 *Davis Contractors Ltd v Fareham Urban District Council* [1956] A.C. 696, 729 per Lord Radcliffe; cited with approval in *Codelfa Construction Proprietary Limited v State Rail Authority of New South Wales* (1982) 149 C.L.R. 337, 357.

2.3.2.1 UAE

Article 273 of the *UAE Civil Code* is barely distinguishable from common law frustration, as it depends on impossibility of performance, and has the consequence that the Contract is brought to an end:

> (1) In contracts binding on both parties, if *force majeure* supervenes which makes the performance of the contract impossible, the corresponding obligation shall cease, and the contract shall be automatically cancelled.
>
> (2) In the case of partial impossibility, that part of the contract which is impossible shall be extinguished, and the same shall apply to temporary impossibility in continuing contracts, and in those two cases it shall be permissible for the obligor to cancel the contract provided that the obligee is so aware.

2.3.2.2 France

The consequences of *force majeure* are different in other civil law jurisdictions. For example, in France a Contractor may be entitled to be indemnified above a certain threshold as a consequence of *sujétions imprévues* – technical difficulties of an unforeseeable nature and of sufficient magnitude to fundamentally affect the Contractor's performance. The threshold may be determined from the case law in a particular circumstance. Whilst the solution will take into consideration the intention of the parties and their agreed risk allocation, the administrative courts are free to decide a right of indemnification of the Contractor for *sujétions imprévues* notwithstanding any contract clause to the contrary.[7]

2.3.2.3 Philippines

Article 1174 of the Philippines *Civil Code* provides:

> Except in cases expressly specified by the law, or when it is otherwise declared by stipulation, or when the nature of the obligation requires the assumption of risk, no person shall be responsible for those events which could not be foreseen or which, though foreseen, were inevitable.

Arguably, this Article could apply as a defence to breach of contract as a consequence of failure to perform contractual obligations arising from the impact of COVID-19, for example failure to complete the Works by the contractually specified date for completion.

2.3.2.4 *UNIDROIT Principles*

The *UNIDROIT Principles* include similar provisions using the terminology of 'hardship.' Article 6.2.3 defines 'hardship' as follows:

> There is hardship where the occurrence of events fundamentally alters the equilibrium of the contract either because the cost of a party's performance has increased or because the value of the performance a party receives has diminished, and
>
> (a) the events occur or become known to the disadvantaged party after the conclusion of the contract;

---

7 Mark Frilet, 'France' in Robert Knutson (ed), *FIDIC An Analysis of International Construction Contracts* (Kluwer Law International, 2005) 79, 83.

(b) the events could not reasonably have been taken into account by the disadvantaged party at the time of the conclusion of the contract;
(c) the events are beyond the control of the disadvantaged party; and
(d) the risk of the events was not assumed by the disadvantaged party.

The effects of hardship can be ameliorated by a court (or an arbitral tribunal) as provided for in Article 6.2.3 of the *UNIDROIT Principles*:

(1) In case of hardship the disadvantaged party is entitled to request renegotiations. The request shall be made without undue delay and shall indicate the grounds on which it is based.
(2) The request for renegotiation does not in itself entitle the disadvantaged party to withhold performance.
(3) Upon failure to reach agreement within a reasonable time either party may resort to the court.
(4) If the court finds hardship it may, if reasonable,

   (a) terminate the contract at a date and on terms to be fixed, or
   (b) adapt the contract with a view to restoring its equilibrium.

2.3.3 Other remedies

In France ***imprévision*** provides that the Contractor has the right to indemnification when there is a major change in economic factors existing at the time of contracting and which destroys the contractual equilibrium:

> The *imprévision* theory is based on the *rebus sic stantibus* principle, which is the venerable principle limiting the 'sanctity of contract' theory (*pacta sunt servanda*). The Contractor has the right to indemnification when there is a major change in economic factors existing at the time of contracting and which destroys the contractual equilibrium (*bouleversement de l'économie du contrat*). It is not the magnitude of the event by itself which is sufficient to trigger the right of indemnification but its major impact on the Contractor's obligations.[8]

2.4 Good faith

Good faith is a general obligation which forms part of every contract in civil law systems,[9] and some common law jurisdictions.[10] However, it does not apply as a matter of law in many common law jurisdictions such as England and Australia. Where good faith does not apply as a matter of law, parties can include an obligation to act in good faith as an express contract term, and breach of that obligation will entitle the innocent party to damages. The duty of good faith extends to:

---

8 Ibid.

9 For example *Civil Code* (Germany) s242; *Civil Code* (France) Article 1134; *Indonesian Civil Code* Article 1338(3); *Civil Code* (Japan) Article 1(2); *Civil Code* (Peru) Article 1362.

10 For example USA: *Uniform Commercial Code* s1–203 and *Restatement of Contracts (Second)* s1–203; Canada: *Bhasin v Hrynew* 2014 SCC71; [2014] 3 SCR 494.

> an obligation to act honestly and with a fidelity to the bargain; an obligation not to act dishonestly and not to act to undermine the bargain entered or the substance of the contractual benefit bargained for; and an obligation to act reasonably and with fair dealing having regard to the interests of the parties (which will, inevitably, at times conflict) and to the provisions, aims and purposes of the contract, objectively ascertained.[11]

The NEC contracts import a good faith obligation in the following terms:

> The Parties, the *Project Manager* and the *Supervisor* shall act in a spirit of mutual trust and cooperation.[12]

2.4.1 Case study: Contractual obligation of good faith

In a contract for mining operations, the parties agreed to act in good faith in all matters relating to carrying out of the Works, derivation of rates, and interpretation of the Contract. The Contractor agreed to carry out contract mining operations at rates based on cost estimates but inflated its cost estimates to obtain additional payment. At trial, the judge found that in a contract requiring disclosure of confidential operating costs, a contractual obligation of good faith required the Contractor to formulate those costs honestly,[13] and this was upheld on appeal.[14] The judge awarded substantial damages for breach of the good faith obligation, and this was upheld by the High Court.[15] The judge at first instance found that an express contractual obligation to act in good faith required the parties to act honestly, and with goodwill and cooperation where the contract did not define rights and obligations or provide any mechanisms for the resolution of disputes. He also held that the contractual obligation of good faith did not prevent a party pursuing its legitimate commercial interests by exercising express contractual rights, and the pursuit of those interests did not require consideration of the other party's interests. Unless it is clearly not intended, the meaning of good faith would seem to be the same whether the obligation is implied or express.

Good faith does not involve one party putting the interests of the other contracting party ahead of its own interests, and may not be onerous:

> A duty to act in good faith, where it exists, is a modest requirement. It does no more than reflect the expectation that a contracting party will act honestly towards the other party and will not conduct itself in a way which is calculated to frustrate the purpose of the contract or which would be regarded as commercially unacceptable by reasonable and honest people. This is a lesser duty than the positive obligation to use all reasonable endeavours to achieve a specified result which the contract in this case imposed.[16]

---

11 *Paciocco v ANZ Banking Group* (2015) 321 ALR 584, [288] per Allsop CJ.
12 NEC4 Engineering and Construction Contract clause 10.2.
13 *Thiess Contractors Pty Ltd v Placer (Granny Smith) Pty Ltd* [1999] WASC 1046 (2000) 16 BCL 130.
14 Ibid. 255.
15 *Placer (Granny Smith) Pty Ltd v Thiess Contractors Pty Ltd* [2003] HCA 10; (2003) 19 BCL 431.
16 *Astor Management AG v Atalya Mining PLC* [2017] EWHC 425 [98].

Sir Rupert Jackson,[17] Kennedy-Grant,[18] and Mosey[19] have discussed the role of good faith in construction contracts, and Bailey compared good faith in civil law and common law systems.[20] Brown and Conrad state that good faith is the third principle of contract law in France and discussed its meaning and reach in the following terms:[21]

> Before the 2016 contract reform, the scope of good faith was limited to the performance of the contract, however courts had recognized the need to act in good faith during negotiations. As a result, the 2016 reform has extended the principle of good faith to pre-contractual negotiations and formation stages. Hence, the new rule is that 'Contracts must be negotiated, formed and performed in good faith,' this provision being 'a matter of public policy.'[22]
>
> Despite the fact that the notion of good faith was neither defined in the *1804 Civil Code* nor its new version, many court decisions have helped understand what this principle implies for parties to a contract. However, it is generally admitted that good faith will imply that the parties must behave 'loyally' with each other (*devoir de loyauté*). A good example of the application of this principle is a case arising out of a situation in which an Employer had realised that the surface of the building to be covered by the Contractor was half what it was supposed to be. Here, the Supreme Court upheld the Employer's claim for a refund, despite the fact that the contract was concluded on a lump sum basis. The court ordered the Contractor to pay the difference, because the Contractor, whilst it could not ignore that the actual surface was much smaller than the one anticipated in the contract, failed to inform the Employer of the same, and this behavior was found to amount to a lack of good faith.[23]

In the authors' view, good faith is an element of *lex constructionis* – see ¶4.8.1.1.

2.5 Applicable laws impacting international contracts

The legal issues that can arise from the execution of the Works under an international construction contract are many and varied. Whilst there is generally a single law or set of laws (ie the law of a specific legal jurisdiction) that governs the legal consequences of the rights and obligations the parties have assumed under their contract (the proper law of the contract), there are other laws that apply to the execution of the Works and other interactions between the parties, or between the parties and other stakeholders, for example employees, property owners, and government departments. The most common types of law that may be associated with the entry into, execution of, and issues and disputes arising from an international contract are as follows:

---

17 Sir Rupert Jackson, 'Does Good Faith Have any Role in Construction Contracts?' (2018) *Paper presented to the Society of Construction Law in London on 6 March 2018*. https://www.scl.org.uk/papers/does-good-faith-have-any-role-construction-contracts (accessed 8 December 2021).

18 Tómas Kennedy-Grant QC, 'Good Faith, Unconscionability, Unreasonableness – What on Earth Do They Have to Do with Construction Law' in Donald Charrett (ed), *Global Challenges Shared Solutions* (Society of Construction Law Australia, 2013) 48–62.

19 David Mosey, 'Good Faith in English Construction Law – What Does it Mean, and Does It Matter?' (2015) 4 *International Construction Law Journal* 392.

20 Julian Bailey, 'Comparing Good Faith in Civil and Common Law Systems' (2018) *Society of Construction Law*. https://www.scl-na.org/library/papers/comparing-good-faith-civil-and-common-law-systems (accessed 8 December 2021).

21 David Brown & Michael Conrad, 'France' in Donald Charrett (ed), *The International Application of FIDIC Contracts* (Informa Law from Routledge, 2020) 167.

22 *Civil Code* (France), Article 1104.

23 Civ.3ème, 2 March 2005, n°03–18080.

(1) The law of the place where a contract is made (***lex loci contractus***) – this may be relevant to determining whether the contract was validly made.
(2) The law of the habitual residence of a person (***lex domicilii***) – this may be relevant to determining whether a party has the legal capacity to enter into a contract.
(3) The proper law of the contract (***lex contractus***).
(4) The law(s) governing non-contractual obligations, for example torts (such as site accidents), unjust enrichment – generally the law of the place where the wrong was committed (***lex loci delicti commissi***).
(5) The laws applicable to the execution of the Works at the Site, for example health and safety issues, quality issues, employment law, building permits, customs – generally the laws of the place where the Site is situated (***lex loci rei sitae***).
(6) The law relating to ***in rem* claims** (the disposition of property) (***lex rei situs***).
(7) The procedural law that applies to any court proceedings, including the coercive power of the court in support of arbitration proceedings (law of the forum or ***lex fori***).
(8) The substantive law that gives an arbitral tribunal jurisdiction to determine a dispute instead of the courts (***lex arbitri***) – the law of the 'seat' of arbitration (***lex loci arbitri***).
(9) The law applying to a corporation which does business in a country (eg the *Bribery Act 2010* (UK)).

The essence of an international construction contract is that more than one country is involved in the entry into, the execution and termination of the Contract, and the resolution of disputes arising from the Contract. By way of example, the contracting parties may be from different countries, each of which is different to a third country where the Site is located. The Contract may have been concluded in a fourth country, and the parties may agree to arbitration being conducted in a fifth country (the seat of arbitration) under the arbitration law of a sixth country. The successful party in the arbitration may take legal proceedings in the courts of a seventh country to enforce the arbitration award, because that is where the unsuccessful party has significant assets.

2.6 Governing law of the contract

The **governing law of the contract** (also known as the **proper law of the contract**) is the law that governs the parties' contractual relations. It provides the legal rules for determining issues in connection with its formation, validity, interpretation, and the rights and obligations of the contracting parties. As discussed in ¶4.3.3, the overarching principles of freedom of contract and *pacta sunt servanda* generally result in the contracting parties having the freedom to determine the proper law of the contract, subject to any applicable mandatory law. The parties can make an explicit choice of the proper law of the contract by means of a **choice of law** clause in their Contract. Where they do so, this is generally unproblematic, providing it is not in conflict with the mandatory law of the forum. The parties' explicit choice of law will usually be applied by a court in the event that a dispute is referred to it.

The principle of party autonomy to determine the governing law of a contract is widely upheld, and many international agreements on choice of law do not constrain the choice of a legal system to one that has a link to the Contract. For example, neither *Rome I*[24] nor the *Inter-American Convention on the Law Applicable to International Contracts*[25] require such a link.

However, where the parties have made no such explicit choice (perhaps because they cannot agree on the appropriate law as each prefers the laws of its own legal jurisdiction) and there is more than one legal jurisdiction whose laws may govern the Contract, there is a **conflict of laws.** In such a case the judge or arbitral tribunal adjudicating a dispute must determine the proper law of the contract by the appropriate **conflict of laws rules**. The application of such conflict of laws rules in any dispute situation may involve a complicated interaction between the facts of the case and the **procedural law**[26] and **substantive law**[27] of different legal jurisdictions, where there is no unanimity of conflict of laws rules. The topic of conflict of laws is well outside the parameters of this book, however there are many texts available on the subject.

An Australian court considered the following factors were relevant where the parties had not made an explicit choice of the proper law:

> An important feature of the proper law of an international contract is that, subject to questions of public policy and bona fides, the parties are free to choose what the proper law will be: *Vita Food Products Inc v. Unus Shipping Co Ltd* [1939] AC 277. If, on construing the contract, the court is unable to conclude that the parties intended that contract to be governed by reference to a particular system of law, the court identifies a proper law by ascertaining the system of law with which the transaction has its closest and most real connection: *Bonython v Commonwealth of Australia* [1951] AC 201; *Akai Pty Ltd v. People's Insurance Co Limited* [1996] HCA 39; (1996) 188 CLR 418 at 440–1. But whether the proper law is ascertained from the intention of the parties, or under the *Bonython* test, makes no difference to those aspects of the contract – which might, on some accounts of the law, extend to its formation, validity, interpretation, and the rights and obligations of the parties under it – that are decided in accordance with the proper law of the contract. Other systems of law besides that of the forum and the proper law can sometimes come to bear upon the contract – as when its performance is illegal under the law of the place where it is to be performed. However it can be seen that one of the purposes of recognising a proper law of contract is to allow the parties to have freedom of choice about the system of law that will govern their relations, to the extent that other systems of law do not impose themselves upon the formation, performance or enforcement of the contract. That purpose is also advanced by applying the substantive/procedural distinction articulated in *John Pfeiffer v. Rogerson* (2000) 203 CLR 503 to litigation concerning international contracts.[28]

In some cases where the parties have not included a choice of law clause in the Contract, the arbitral tribunal has determined that, as the subject matter of the Contract does not have sufficiently close connections with any particular legal jurisdiction, the proper law

24 *Regulation (EC) No 593/2008* of the European Parliament and of the Council of 17 June 2008 on the law applicable to contractual obligations. Corrigenda dated 4 July 2008 and 14 August 2009.

25 www.oas.org/juridico/english/treaties/b-56.html (accessed 30 June 2020).

26 Procedural law regulates the formal requirements of the way a dispute about substantive law issues is to be conducted in court or another judicial tribunal.

27 The law applying to the substance of a legal relationship, for example a contract, in contrast to the procedural law.

28 *Garsec v His Majesty the Sultan of Brunei* [2008] NSWCA 211 [128] per Campbell JA.

of the contract is the international *lex mercatoria*.[29] It is worth noting that the use of such a transnational or non-state body of law is specifically provided for in *Rome I*, which provides in the Preamble: 'This Regulation does not preclude parties from incorporating by reference into their contract a non-State body of law or an international convention.' The *lex mercatoria* is considered in more detail in ¶4.7, and the *UNIDROIT Principles of International Commercial Contracts* as a contemporary modern statement of the *lex mercatoria* in ¶2.7.

It is evident from the list of potentially applicable laws in ¶2.5 that not all of the choice of relevant law is subject to party autonomy. Only items (3) and (8) can be selected by the parties in their Contract. A disputing party may have some choice in relation to (7) by choice of an appropriate forum in which to start legal proceedings – so-called forum shopping. However, the remaining laws will be subject to determination in accordance with mandatory law or conflict of laws rules. Where this is disputed, the court of the forum that is required to determine the issue will apply the applicable conflict of laws rules (or as they are sometimes referred to, the rules of **private international law**) that apply in that jurisdiction to determine what is the applicable law for the issue(s). One of the many possible problems in applying conflict of laws rules is the issue of ***renvoi***, which occurs when a forum court is directed by its choice of laws rules to the law of another country whose rules in turn direct the matter back to the forum court.

2.7 The *UNIDROIT Principles of International Commercial Contracts*

In the authors' view, the *UNIDROIT Principles of International Commercial Contracts* (***UP***) represent a contemporary statement of the modern content of the *lex mercatoria* that has practical application to international commercial contracts, and specifically to international construction contracts.

The *UP* have been referred to in a significant number of publicly reported international arbitrations, in which the question of the choice of law has frequently been a live issue. As at January 2018, the Unilex website listed a total of 194 international arbitration awards which have referred to the *UP* and noted that the real number is undoubtedly considerably more because arbitration awards are generally confidential to the parties and therefore many awards are not publicly accessible. The details of the publicly available arbitration awards that have referred to the *UP* (without any identification of the parties) are accessible by keywords, in abstract, and in a number of cases, the full text of the judgement/award is available.[30]

The number and variety of the arbitration awards which have referred to the *UP* provide a range of situations in which arbitral tribunals have found the *UP* relevant to the law applying to the contract in dispute. One of the significant applications in arbitration has been to apply the *UP* as the governing law of the contract where the parties have not made an express choice, or to supplement or reinforce national law. This is discussed in more detail in the following section.

29 For example Arbitral Award 9875 ICC (1999), www.unilex.info/case.cfm?pid=2&do=case&id=675&step=Abstract (accessed 22 January 2021).

30 www.unilex.info/dynasite.cfm?dssid=2377&dsmid=13620&x=1 (accessed 6 March 2020).

As a set of principles, the *UP* are complementary to and supportive of the specific Contract which applies to a given situation, in a similar way that the common law, civil law, or statute law applies to regulate the entry into, and execution (performance) and termination of, the Contract in the given legal system. In addition, the *UP* incorporate the rules to be followed in construing the Contract, as well as the *UP* themselves. However, because the *UP* are transnational, they do not and cannot have the legal force of a national legal system, which is based on government power. Any force that the *UP* have can only be derived from the parties themselves. Furthermore, any such power the parties themselves have invested in the *UP* will be illusory, unless that power is supported by one or more relevant legal systems, for example the legal system of a country in which enforcement of an arbitration award is sought.

The *UP* have received endorsement by UNCITRAL in the following terms:

> Congratulating UNIDROIT on having made a further contribution to the facilitation of international trade by preparing general rules for international commercial contracts, . . .
>
> Commends the use of the 2010 edition of the UNIDROIT Principles of International Commercial Contracts, as appropriate, for their intended purposes.[31]

2.8 Application of the *UP* to international contracts[32]

In contracts where the parties have expressly referred to the *UP*, then in accordance with the principle of freedom of contract, they will generally apply to the extent and in the manner that the parties have provided for in their Contract. This statement is subject to the constraints on freedom of contract discussed in ¶4.3.4 and ¶4.3.5, that is subject to any applicable statute law and no conflict with public policy. Thus, as one possibility, the parties may explicitly nominate the *UP* as the system of law to govern their Contract, to the exclusion of any national law that would otherwise apply based on the application of the well-established principles of conflict of laws. Any dispute arising under such a contract could, in principle, be resolved by the award of a properly constituted arbitral tribunal sitting anywhere in the world. If, as UNIDROIT suggests, the *UP* are sufficiently developed as a *lex mercatoria*, an arbitral tribunal would not need to refer to any national law to determine the meaning of the Contract, and the law of the contract (the *lex contractus*) would be the *UP*.

Interface with national law does, however, occur where:

- A dispute is litigated in court.
- Support of the courts is required in the conduct of an arbitration.
- An arbitration award is appealed.
- An arbitration award needs to be enforced.

31 Report of the United Nations Commission on International Trade Law on the work of its 45th session, 25 June–6 July 2012, 33, https://documents-dds-ny.un.org/doc/UNDOC/GEN/V12/551/54/PDF/V1255154.pdf?OpenElement (accessed 6 March 2020).

32 This topic is discussed in more detail in Donald Charrett, *Contracts for Construction and Engineering Projects* (Informa Law from, 2nd edn 2021) Chapter 36.

These applications of the relevant national law may involve issues relating to the entry into, execution, or termination of the Contract, the subject of the dispute. In any such case, or where a party referred a contractual dispute to litigation in the courts instead of arbitration, the court in the relevant jurisdiction may be required to enquire into the legal basis for the Contract and the arbitration and/or the arbitration award, and the extent to which the *UP* are compatible with the local law.

Thus, if contracting parties explicitly nominated the *UP* as the law governing their Contract, a court would generally be expected to uphold the parties' bargain, unless the choice of the *UP* as the governing law or specific aspects of the *UP* were in breach of a relevant statute or public policy. For example, although *Rome I* allows the incorporation of a non-state body of law into a contract, a European court would limit the parties' choice of governing law to a national system of law, and in the absence of the parties' choice would apply the conflict of laws rules in *Rome I* to determine the applicable law.[33] The extent of application of the chosen *UP* in these circumstances would depend on the relevant national law.

As another example, Article 869 of the *Colombian Commercial Code* states that Contracts that are performed in Colombia will be governed by Colombian law; it would be expected that even if the *UP* were chosen by the parties, a Colombian court would limit their application to issues not addressed by Colombian law, and then only to the extent that the *UP* were not inconsistent with Colombian law. There are other countries where the courts may not recognise non-state rules of law as the governing law of the contract.[34]

Even where the parties have not explicitly nominated the *UP* as the applicable law of the contract, a number of judges and arbitral tribunals have found them to be a valuable source of international law. For example:

> The UNIDROIT Principles of International Commercial Contracts are a reliable Fonti [*sic*] of international commercial law in international arbitration for they 'contain in essence a restatement of those "principes directeurs" that have enjoyed universal acceptance and, moreover, are at the heart of those most fundamental notions which have consistently been applied in arbitral practice.'[35]

However, this is not universally accepted:

> the UNIDROIT Principles could certainly be used for reference by the parties involved for the voluntary regulation of their contractual relationship, in addition to helping the arbitrator in confirming the existence of particular trade usages, but they cannot constitute a normative body in themselves that can be considered as an applicable supranational law to replace a national law, at least as long as the arbitrator is required to identify the applicable law by choosing the rule of conflict that he considers most appropriate, in accordance with the provisions laid down by the international conventions and as provided for in the rules of arbitration within the scope of which he operates.[36]

33 Guido Carducci, 'The Impact of the EU "Rome I" Regulation on International Litigation and Arbitration, A-National Law, Mandatory and Overriding Rules' (2011) 22(2) *ICC International Court of Arbitration Bulletin* 31, 36.

34 For example Australia: see Donald Charrett, 'Australia' in Willem Calkoen (ed), *Perspectives in Practice of the UNIDROIT Principles 2016* (IBA, 2019) 12.

35 ICC 9797 www.unilex.info/case.cfm?pid=2&do=case&id=668&step=FullText (accessed 31 July 2021).

36 ICC 9419 www.unilex.info/case.cfm?pid=2&do=case&id=664&step=FullText (accessed 31 July 2021).

It is clear from the cases that the *UP* are not totally consistent with the law in all jurisdictions. They incorporate some civil law concepts that are inconsistent with English common law, particularly in relation to the admissibility of evidence of pre-contract negotiations in determining the intentions of the parties.

2.9 Contract codes

2.9.1 Civil law jurisdictions

It is apparent from the foregoing discussion on the application of the common law, as revealed by a myriad of court judgements, that determining the law of contract as applied in any given common law jurisdiction in a particular situation may not be a trivial exercise. The situation is somewhat different in civil law jurisdictions, such as most European countries, China, and so on, where the law of contract is contained in a contract code. Thus, to determine the law of contract in for example Germany, one has recourse to a single readily available document, the German *Civil Code*, which sets out all the applicable rules, rather than a large, ill-defined and ever-expanding set of judicial precedents enshrined in case law. As noted later in the chapter, some common law jurisdictions also have contract codes, for example India and the USA.

It should be noted however that the extent of codification of the law of contract in civil law countries varies considerably. 'Codification' can be carried out at a very detailed level, with many hundreds of rules necessary to cover the myriad different permutations and combinations of circumstances that could arise in the wide variety of possible contractual situations. Conversely, 'codification' may be undertaken at a high level of abstraction, in which the code states general principles only. In the latter case, the importance of court decisions that construe or interpret the terms of the code, and apply them to specific fact situations, may assume greater importance than where the code is very detailed.

2.9.2 Common law jurisdictions

2.9.2.1 India

Some common-law jurisdictions have codified contract law into a comprehensive series of written rules that provide a 'one-stop shop' for determining the applicable law. An interesting example of a significant departure from the English common law of contract was the *Indian Contract Act 1872*, which contains 238 clauses and applies in India, Pakistan, Sudan, and Malaysia – 'a straightforward and easily readable codification of the Common Law of Contracts with some enlightened improvements.'[37]

2.9.2.2 USA

The *US Restatement (Second) of Law of Contracts* prepared by the American Law Institute is a codification of US contract law, and although it does not have statutory authority in any jurisdiction, it is continually resorted to by judges as having great persuasive authority as

37 Robert Knutson (ed), *FIDIC An Analysis of International Construction Contracts* (Kluwer Law International, 2005) xvii.

an explanation of what the law is. Also in the USA, the ***Uniform Commercial Code*** (***UCC***) is a product of the American Law Institute and the National Conference of Commissioners on Uniform State Laws: 'The *UCC* is a comprehensive modernization of various statutes relating to commercial transactions including sales, leases, negotiable instruments, bank deposits and collections, funds transfers, letters of credit, bulk sales, documents of title, investment securities, and secured transactions.'[38] It has been enacted (sometimes with modifications to suit local conditions or presentation style) in all of the 50 US states, as well as in the District of Columbia, the Commonwealth of Puerto Rico, Guam, and the U.S. Virgin Islands. The *UCC* contains some 400 clauses to provide a code of contract law for many common types of contract; these nominated contract types do not include construction or building contracts.

2.9.2.3 Australia

Wright and Ellinghaus wrote a 27-clause *Australian Contract Code* (***ACC***) to provide a concise statement of the existing common law rules that affect contractual transactions.[39] This is intended to be a plain English statement of contract law at a high level of abstraction that can be easily read and understood by non-lawyers. It has no legislative authority, but, in the words of the authors:

> The *ACC* could provide the basis for Australian participation in this movement [harmonisation of contract law], particularly with our Asian trading partners. The *ACC* is compatible with codes of contract law adopted or being adopted by other countries in our region, for example China.[40]

In empirical research involving the *ACC*, *UP*, and case law, Ellinghaus and Wright found that:

- Overall, decisions applying detailed rules were no more predictable than decisions applying broad principles, however, decisions applying broad principles were significantly more predictable in easier cases.
- Broad principles were more likely to lead to just outcomes.
- Broad principles were more accessible than detailed rules.
- Broad principles were significantly more efficient.[41]

Whilst the *ACC* has not received any statutory support, and in the period since it was written the number of contract cases in the Law Reports has continued to burgeon, the authors consider that it is a very useful concise summary of the current law of contract in Australia. Its brevity (only 27 clauses) is a result of its high level of generality. The use

38 www.ali.org/index.cfm?fuseaction=publications.ppage&node_id=86 (accessed 6 March 2020).

39 M P Ellinghaus & E W Wright, 'An Australian Contract Code' (1992) Law Reform Commission of Victoria Discussion Paper No 27, 1. The *ACC* was reproduced by kind permission of the authors in: Philip Loots & Donald Charrett, *Practical Guide to Engineering and Construction Contracts* (CCH, 2009) 359–361.

40 E Wright & M Ellinghaus, 'Submission to Standing Committee on Legal and Constitutional Affairs on Harmonisation of Legal Systems' (2005), www.aph.gov.au/house/committee/laca/harmonisation/subs/sub013.pdf (accessed 26 March 2011).

41 M P Ellinghaus & E W Wright, 'The Common Law of Contracts: Are Broad Principles Better than Detailed Ones? An Empirical Investigation' (2005) 11(2) *Texas Wesleyan Law Review* 28, University of Melbourne Legal Studies Research Paper No 122, http://ssrn.com/abstract=771204 (accessed 6 March 2020).

of plain English without any legal definitions makes it easy for non-lawyers to use. In the *ACC* authors' words:

> The potential advantages of codifying contract law are obvious. Having authoritative statements of the rules in one document makes it easy for any person who wishes to consult the law to find it. Codifying the law also creates an opportunity to simplify it. This makes it more accessible both to lawyers and to non lawyers. These two features of codes promote greater awareness of the law, and encourage its use.[42]

A notable feature of the *ACC* is the central role played by the concept of 'unconscionability' as an organising principle which can subsume many existing contractual doctrines. This approach is consistent with a number of High Court cases which have referred to the concept of conscience in respect of contractual or 'equitable' obligations. The *ACC* authors' use of 'unconscionable' as meaning 'offending against conscience' was chosen in preference to rival concepts such as 'justice,' 'reasonableness,' 'fairness,' and 'good faith,'[43] all of which can be found in the case law.

The significance of the *ACC* and empirical research into its efficacy is directly relevant to the international theme of this book:

> Our research may also have transnational implications. We are now living in a global environment in which there is a growing, and probably irresistible, movement towards the international harmonisation of contract law. This objective is unlikely to be achieved except through agreement on statements of broad principles in canonical form. If the common law is to remain a world force in this new order, then it may itself have to be restated in such a form.[44]

2.9.3 UNIDROIT Principles

Extending that idea beyond the common law world, the authors consider that the use of the *UP* as the governing law of a contract in which disputes are determined by international arbitration is the most appropriate way of achieving a truly international contract code, divorced from the specific laws of any country. The *UP* represent a consensus of the best international rules for the entry into and execution and termination of a commercial contract, and are supported by substantial scholarship and practical application by judges and arbitral tribunals. This is discussed further in ¶4.7.1.

2.10 Formation of contracts

2.10.1 Common law

Classical contract law defines what is a contract by reference to the formal elements which ensure that the contract is legally enforceable, that is enforceable through the courts. The formal elements of a contract under English law are:

---

42 M P Ellinghaus & E W Wright, 'An Australian Contract Code' (1992) Law Reform Commission of Victoria Discussion Paper No 27, 4.

43 Ibid. 8.

44 Ibid. 29.

- An agreement (made up of offer and acceptance),
- Supported by 'consideration,'[45]
- Made between legal persons who intend to be legally bound by the agreement,
- Containing terms which are clear and certain.

An agreement is formed when one person accepts an offer made to her/him by another person. **Consideration** consists of the exchange of something of value between the parties to the contract (although a court will not enquire as to its real value – $1 may suffice). The transacting parties must be legal persons capable of assuming legal obligations. They intend to be legally bound if they intend their agreement to be enforceable through the legal system in the event that it is not properly performed. The essential terms of the agreement must be articulated clearly by the parties. If all of these formal elements of a contract are established, the obligations in the contract become legal obligations. Conversely, if any of the formal elements are not established, a legally enforceable contract has not been formed, for example there may be no contract if an essential term has been omitted, left to be agreed on later, or expressed in ambiguous language. Subject to statutory and common law exceptions, the parties to a contract are the only ones with **privity of contract** which enables them to enforce its terms.

2.10.2 Civil law

The requirements for validity of a contract in civil law jurisdictions are expressed in various ways. The following are the general requirements for the validity and effectiveness of binding contracts according to Brazilian law:

(1) The contracting parties shall have full capacity and authority to contract,
(2) The object of the contract shall be lawful, possible, determined or determinable, and
(3) The formalities required by law, if any, must be observed.[46]

Subsection 2 Offer and Acceptance in the *Law of Contract, the General Regime of Obligations, and Proof of Obligations* in the *French Civil Code*[47] contains the general provisions relating to the formation of a contract. Article 1113 provides that:

> A contract is formed by the meeting of an offer and an acceptance by which the parties demonstrate their will to be bound.
> This may stem from a person's declaration or unequivocal conduct.

Section 2 Validity of the Contract in the *Law of Contract, the General Regime of Obligations, and Proof of Obligations* in the *French Civil Code*[48] contains the general provisions relating to the validity of a contract. Article 1128 provides:

45 However, consideration is not required if a contract is executed as a deed, also known as a **specialty**.
46 Thiago Fernandes Moreira & Caio Gabra, 'Brazil' in Donald Charrett (ed), *The International Application of FIDIC Contracts A Practical Guide* (Informa Law from Routledge, 2020) 80.
47 www.textes.justice.gouv.fr/art_pix/THE-LAW-OF-CONTRACT-2-5-16.pdf (accessed 6 March 2020).
48 Ibid.

The following are necessary for the validity of a contract:

1. the consent of the parties;
2. their capacity to contract;
3. content which is lawful and certain.

The essential conditions required for a valid contract in Romania are regulated by the *Civil Code* as the framework law[49] in the domain of contracts and are:

- The legal capacity to contract,
- The mutual consent of the parties,
- A determined and legitimate object, and
- A lawful and moral cause.[50]

2.10.3 UNIDROIT Principles

The *UP* contain the following provisions in respect of the formation of a contract:

> Art. 2.1.1 A contract may be concluded either by the acceptance of an offer or by conduct of the parties that is sufficient to show agreement.
>
> Art 2.1.2 A proposal for concluding a contract constitutes an offer if it is sufficiently definite and indicates the intention of the offeror to be bound in case of acceptance.

2.10.4 Summary

Whilst these various provisions highlight subtle differences in the requirements for the formation of a contract, the following appear to be common features:

- The legal capacity to contract,
- The mutual consent of the parties to be bound by a legal relationship, and
- Content which is lawful and certain.

2.11 Rights and remedies for failure to perform contractual obligations

Contract law provides a range of rights and remedies which the parties to a contract may access to resolve disputes concerning the performance of their contractual obligations. A failure to perform a contractual obligation is known as a **breach of contract**. Depending on the circumstances of the parties' contracting and of the breach of contract, the available legal and equitable remedies in a jurisdiction may include:

- Damages,
- An order for specific performance of the contract,
- An injunction to prevent continuation of a breach of contract,

---

49 Framework laws are laws that are more specific than constitutional provisions. They lay down general obligations and principles but leave to governing authorities the task of enacting the further legislation and other specific measures.

50 Cremona Cotovelea, 'Romania' in Donald Charrett (ed), *The International Application of FIDIC Contracts a Practical Guide* (Informa Law from Routledge, 2020) 318.

- Rectification of incorrectly expressed terms in the contract,
- A declaration as to the legal status of the contract, or
- An order that the contract is at an end.

Contract law is the primary but not the only law which imposes obligations on parties to a transaction associated with a contract. A transaction may have elements which give rise to legal liability, independently of whether or not a contract exists and has been breached. Other forms of legal liability may arise from statements or conduct by the parties:

- In the course of negotiating their contract, but before any contract arises,
- In the course of unsuccessful negotiations for a contract,
- During the performance of a contract.

For example, in Australia a transaction may involve statements or conduct by one of the parties which can later be characterised as:

- Misleading or deceptive conduct in contravention of the *Australian Consumer Law* (**ACL**),
- Unconscionable conduct,
- Negligence or deceit under the law of torts,
- The unjust enrichment of one party, resulting in a liability to make restitution where there is no subsisting contract (*quantum meruit*),
- Involving a fiduciary relationship and generating liability for breach of fiduciary obligation, or
- Generating other equitable and property law rights independent of the existence of a contract.

Thus, the same transaction may be used to argue for alternative remedies in other areas of law such as tort and/or restitution or for statutory remedies. In addition, a contracting party may owe a duty to a third (non-contracting) party as a consequence of conduct engaged in the execution of a contract. For example, in a contract for supply of materials for the construction of a supermarket, the Northern Territory Court of Appeal held that the supplier owed a duty of care to supply the materials in a timely fashion to avoid economic loss to a non-contracting party.[51]

The specific contractual and non-contractual remedies available in any given situation will depend on the applicable law, for example the governing law of the contract, the law of the forum, the *lex loci delecti commisi*, the *lex loci rei sitae*, and so on as relevant. These laws will inevitably be specific to the jurisdiction, notwithstanding broad agreement as to basic principles of law and justice.

2.12 Explicit contract terms

As noted earlier, one of the formal elements of contract formation is the existence of clear terms. Contract terms can and usually do take two forms: explicit and implicit (also referred to as express and implied terms). Explicit terms are those that the parties have

51 *Metal Roofing and Cladding Pty Ltd v Eire Pty Ltd* (1999) 9 NTLR 82; (2000) 16 BCL 466.

expressly articulated. For construction contracts, the explicit terms are usually but not necessarily in writing, and may be very voluminous, incorporating not only General Conditions of Contract and Special Conditions of Contract but also functional and technical specifications, drawings, and (possibly) bills of quantities. It is up to the parties in negotiating a contract to decide the extent to which they consider it appropriate and necessary to cater specifically in explicit terms for the circumstances they foresee may arise during the operation of the Contract.

It is normal practice for construction contracts to be in writing, which has the obvious benefit of articulating in a permanent form the terms that the parties have agreed. In common law jurisdictions a wholly written contract enlivens the **parol evidence rule**, which generally means that oral (parol) evidence is not admissible to add to, vary, or contradict the written terms.[52] If there is any dispute between the contracting parties as to what the words in the contract mean, it is the task of the court (or an arbitral tribunal) to determine what the words mean, that is to 'construe' the contract.

2.13 Construing the terms of a contract

The aim of this process is to determine what the parties' intentions were at the time they entered into the Contract. The process of construction of contract terms in common law jurisdictions is based on principles laid down by the courts over a long period of time. In civil law jurisdictions the principles of construction of contract terms are in the *Civil Codes*.

2.13.1 Common law – Australia

The complexity of contract construction is highlighted by the lengthy textbooks that detail the process.[53] In *Mount Bruce Mining Pty Limited v Wright Prospecting Pty Ltd*[54] the High Court articulated the following general principles in construing the terms of a contract in Australia:

> 46. The rights and liabilities of parties under a provision of a contract are determined objectively,[55] by reference to its text, context (the entire text of the contract as well as any contract, document or statutory provision referred to in the text of the contract) and purpose.[56]
> 47. In determining the meaning of the terms of a commercial contract, it is necessary to ask what a reasonable businessperson would have understood those terms to mean.[57] That enquiry will require consideration of the language used by the parties in the contract,

52 *Bacchus Marsh Concentrated Milk Co Ltd (in liq) v Joseph Nathan & Co Ltd* (1919) 26 CLR 410; *F W Nielsen (Canberra) Pty Ltd v P.D.C. Constructions (A.C.T.) Pty Ltd* (1987) 3 BCL 387, 390.

53 For example The Hon Justice Kim Lewison, *The Interpretation of Contracts* (Sweet & Maxwell, 6th edn 2019); Sir Kim Lewison & David Hughes, *The Interpretation of Contracts in Australia* (Thomson-Reuters Sydney, 2012) (Australia).

54 [2015] HCA 37 per French CJ, Nettle & Gordon JJ.

55 *Electricity Generation Corporation v Woodside Energy Ltd* (2014) 251 CLR 640, 656 [35]; [2014] HCA 7.

56 *Codelfa Construction Pty Ltd v State Rail Authority of New South Wales* [1982] 149 CLR 337, 350 (citing *Reardon Smith Line Ltd v Yngvar Hansen-Tangen* [1976] 1 WLR 989, 995–996; [1976] 3 All ER 570, 574), 352; [1982] HCA 24. See also Sir Anthony Mason, 'Opening Address' (2009) 25 *Journal of Contract Law* 1, 3.

57 *Electricity Generation Corporation v Woodside Energy Ltd* [2014] 251 CLR 640, 656–657 [35].

the circumstances addressed by the contract and the commercial purpose or objects to be secured by the contract.[58]

48. Ordinarily, this process of construction is possible by reference to the contract alone. Indeed, if an expression in a contract is unambiguous or susceptible of only one meaning, evidence of surrounding circumstances (events, circumstances and things external to the contract) cannot be adduced to contradict its plain meaning.[59]

49. However, sometimes, recourse to events, circumstances and things external to the contract is necessary. It may be necessary in identifying the commercial purpose or objects of the contract where that task is facilitated by an understanding 'of the genesis of the transaction, the background, the context [and] the market in which the parties are operating.'[60] It may be necessary in determining the proper construction where there is a constructional choice. . . .

50. Each of the events, circumstances and things external to the contract to which recourse may be had is objective. What may be referred to are events, circumstances and things external to the contract which are known to the parties or which assist in identifying the purpose or object of the transaction, which may include its history, background and context and the market in which the parties were operating. What is inadmissible is evidence of the parties' statements and actions reflecting their actual intentions and expectations.[61]

Contractual 'intention' has been defined by the Australian High Court as follows:

> Although the word 'intention' is used in this context, it is used in the same sense as it is used in other contractual contexts. It describes what it is that would objectively be conveyed by what was said or done, having regard to the circumstances in which those statements and actions happened.[62] It is not a search for the uncommunicated subjective motives or intentions of the parties.[63]

2.13.2 Common law – England

In the UK a court can have regard to all the background circumstances reasonably available to the parties in construing the terms of a contract.[64] This has resulted in UK courts adopting a broad view of the commercial purpose of contracts, and using a 'business common sense' approach to determining what the parties' objective intentions were 'to avoid frustrating

58 Ibid.

59 *Codelfa Construction Pty Ltd v State Rail Authority of New South Wales* [1982] 149 CLR 337, 352. See also Sir Anthony Mason, 'Opening Address' (2009) 25 *Journal of Contract Law* 1, 3.

60 *Electricity Generation Corporation v Woodside Energy Ltd* [2014] 251 CLR 640, 657 [35], citing *Codelfa Construction Pty Ltd v State Rail Authority of New South Wales* [1982] 149 CLR 337, 350, in turn citing *Reardon Smith Line Ltd v Yngvar Hansen-Tangen* [1976] 1 WLR 989, 995–996; [1976] 3 All ER 570, 574.

61 *Codelfa Construction Pty Ltd v State Rail Authority of New South Wales* [1982] 149 CLR 337, 352; *Reardon Smith Line Ltd v Yngvar Hansen-Tangen* [1976] 1 WLR 989, 995–996; [1976] 3 All ER 570, 574.

62 *Codelfa Construction Pty Ltd v State Rail Authority of NSW* [1982] 149 CLR 337, 348–353 per Mason J; *Royal Botanic Gardens and Domain Trust v South Sydney City Council* (2002) 76 ALJR 436; 186 ALR 289.

63 *Ermogenous v Greek Orthodox Community of SA Inc* [2002] 209 CLR 95, 105–106 [25] per Gaudron, McHugh, Hayne and Callinan JJ.

64 *Reardon Smith Line Ltd v Yngvar Hansen-Tangen* [1976] 1 WLR 989, 995–997.

the reasonable expectations of businessmen.'[65] In *Investors Compensation Scheme v West Bromwich Building Society*,[66] Lord Hoffman noted that the 'old intellectual baggage of "legal" interpretation has been discarded' in favour of judges interpreting documents according to the common sense principles by which any serious utterance would be interpreted in ordinary life. He summarised the modern principles of construction as follows:

(1) Interpretation is the ascertainment of the meaning which the document would convey to a reasonable person having all the background knowledge which would reasonably have been available to the parties in the situation in which they were at the time of the contract.

(2) The background was famously referred to by Lord Wilberforce as the 'matrix of fact,' but this phrase is, if anything, an understated description of what the background may include. Subject to the requirement that it should have been reasonably available to the parties and to the exception to be mentioned next, it includes absolutely anything which would have affected the way in which the language of the document would have been understood by a reasonable man.

(3) The law excludes from the admissible background the previous negotiations of the parties and their declarations of subjective intent. They are admissible only in an action for rectification. The law makes this distinction for reasons of practical policy and, in this respect only, legal interpretation differs from the way we would interpret utterances in ordinary life. . . .

(4) The meaning which a document (or any other utterance) would convey to a reasonable man is not the same thing as the meaning of its words. The meaning of words is a matter of dictionaries and grammars; the meaning of the document is what the parties using those words against the relevant background would reasonably have been understood to mean. The background may not merely enable the reasonable man to choose between the possible meanings of words which are ambiguous but even (as occasionally happens in ordinary life) to conclude that the parties must, for whatever reason, have used the wrong words or syntax (see *Mannai Investments Co. Ltd. v. Eagle Star Life Assurance Co. Ltd.* [1997] 2 WLR 945).

(5) The 'rule' that words should be given their 'natural and ordinary meaning' reflects the common sense proposition that we do not easily accept that people have made linguistic mistakes, particularly in formal documents. On the other hand, if one would nevertheless conclude from the background that something must have gone wrong with the language, the law does not require judges to attribute to the parties an intention which they plainly could not have had. Lord Diplock made this point more vigorously when he said in *The Antaios Compania Neviera S.A. v. Salen Rederierna A.B.* 1985 1 A.C. 191, 201:

> if detailed semantic and syntactical analysis of words in a commercial contract is going to lead to a conclusion that flouts business commonsense, it must be made to yield to business commonsense.

These principles have been confirmed in a number of UK Supreme Court cases.[67]

---

65 *Homburg Houtimport v ASgrostin Private* [2004] 1 AC 715, paras 10–12 per Lord Bing.

66 [1997] UKHL 28; [1998] 1 All ER 98; [1998] 1 WLR 896.

67 For example *Chartbrook Limited v Persimmon Homes Limited* [2009] UKHL 38; *Rainy Sky SA v Kookmin Bank* [2011] UKSC50; [2011] 1 WLR 2900; *Arnold v Britton* [2015] UKSC 36; *Wood v Capita Insurance Services* [2017] UKSC 24.

2.13.3 Canons of construction

In addition to these general principles, in appropriate circumstances common law courts apply a number of canons of construction if the language used is not clear and unambiguous and the parties have not expressed a contrary intention. These canons are not rules of law but guides to the interpretation of the English language.

Sir Kim Lewison and David Hughes list the following canons of construction:

(1) In order to arrive at the true interpretation of the document, a clause must not be considered in isolation, but must be considered in the context of the whole document.[68]

(2) In construing a contract all parts of it must be given effect where possible, and no part of it should be treated as inoperative or surplus.[69]

(3) Where a contract is a standard form of contract to which the parties have added special conditions, then unless the contract provides otherwise greater weight must be given to the special conditions, and in case of conflict between the general conditions and the special conditions, the latter will prevail. However, in interpreting a standard form there is less room for the influence of the special background applicable to any particular transaction.[70]

(4) Where a contract contains general provisions and specific provisions, the specific provisions will be given greater weight than the general provisions where the facts to which the contract is to be applied fall within the scope of the specific provisions.[71]

(5) Where the contract expressly mentions some things, it is often to be inferred that other things of the same category which are not expressly mentioned were deliberately omitted. Similar principles apply to the express inclusion of obligations dealing with a particular area of application.[72] This canon is referred to by its Latin name: ***expressio unius est exclusio alterius***.

(6) An express term in a contract excludes the possibility of implying any term dealing with the same subject matter as the express term.[73]

(7) Where there is doubt about the meaning of a contract, the words will be construed against the person who put them forward. This canon is referred to by its Latin name: ***contra proferentem***.[74]

(8) A contract will be construed so far as possible in such a manner as not to permit one party to it to take advantage of their own wrong.[75]

(9) Where the words of a contract are capable of two meanings, one of which is lawful and the other unlawful, the former construction should be preferred.[76]

---

68 Ibid. 283.
69 Ibid. 291.
70 Ibid. 293.
71 Ibid. 297.
72 Ibid. 298.
73 Ibid. 302.
74 Ibid. 304.
75 Ibid. 316.
76 Ibid. 320.

(10) The expression of a term which the law implies as a necessary part of the contract has no greater effect than the implied term would have had.[77]

(11) If it is found that things described by particular words have some common characteristic which constitutes them a genus, the general words which follow them ought to be limited to things of that genus. This canon is referred to by its Latin name: ***ejusdem generis***.[78]

(12) A word of ambiguous meaning may take its character from the surrounding words if they have a common characteristic. This canon is referred to by its Latin name: ***noscitur a sociis***.[79]

(13) In an appropriate case where a plural subject is followed by a plural predicate the plurals may be distributively construed, thereby breaking down the plurals into its component singulars.[80]

(14) Where two constructions of an instrument are equally plausible, upon one of which the instrument is valid, and upon the other of which it is invalid, the court should lean towards that construction which validates the instrument.[81]

(15) The reasonableness of the result of any particular construction is a relevant consideration in choosing between rival constructions. However, the court has no power to remake or amend a contract for the purpose of avoiding a result which is considered to be inconvenient or unjust.[82]

(16) Where a construction would produce an unfair result, the court will often require clear words to support the construction in question.[83]

(17) There is a presumption of interpretation that a contract does not require performance of the impossible, but this may be rebutted by clear words.[84]

The application of these canons of construction by courts is not necessarily straightforward or consistent, evidenced by the 64 pages devoted to the case law applying these canons in the Lewison and Hughes text quoted. Dixon J cautioned:

> [H]owever much help and guidance may be obtained from the principles and rules of construction, their controlling force in determining the conclusion is likely to be confined to cases where the real meaning is undiscoverable or where the court of construction, sceptical of the foresight of the draftsman or of his appreciation of the situation presented, is better content to supply the meaning by a legal presumption than subjectively.[85]

2.13.4 Complexities in construing contract terms

In common law jurisdictions a contract will typically be construed by objective consideration of its text, context, and purpose, with due regard to the commercial context. In the interpretation of a particular word or clause, some leeway is given by the basic

77 Ibid. 323.
78 Ibid. 325.
79 Ibid. 332.
80 Ibid. 334.
81 Ibid. 335.
82 Ibid. 338.
83 Ibid. 342.
84 Ibid. 343.
85 *Cody v JH Nelson Pty Ltd* [1947] 74 CLR 629, 647.

rule that a contract is to be interpreted as a whole, so that the literal meaning of a word or sentence may be controlled by the rest of the contract. The evidence of surrounding circumstances or 'matrix of facts' is generally admissible to assist in the interpretation of a contract to understand the background of the transaction, or if the language is ambiguous or susceptible of more than one meaning. However, evidence of the 'matrix of facts' is not admissible to contradict the language of the contract where it has a plain meaning.[86]

The extent to which the surrounding 'matrix of facts' will be considered varies between jurisdictions. For example, in Australia, the NSW Court of Appeal considers that ambiguity is a conclusion to be reached after consideration of evidence of surrounding circumstances, rather than a precondition to the admissibility of evidence of surrounding circumstances.[87] Conversely in Western Australia, the Court of Appeal considers that the true rule is that surrounding circumstances cannot be relied on to determine whether an ambiguity exists if it is not apparent from a consideration of the text of the document as a whole.[88]

The tools for the construction of contracts are generally well known within a common law jurisdiction, but their application to a particular set of facts can vary between judges. This was brought into sharp focus in the case of *MT Højgaard a/s v E.ON Climate and Renewables UK Robin Rigg East Ltd* where three learned judges of the Court of Appeal, construing the same documents, considering the same case law, and applying the same tools of construction, came to the opposite conclusion to the five judges of the Supreme Court and the judge at first instance.[89] This highlights the difficulties faced by parties considering entering into a construction contract comprising an intersecting web of legal and 'technical' documents – even skilled and experienced practitioners may come to differing conclusions as to how the documents would be construed by the fictitious 'reasonable' person in possession of the relevant background information.

2.13.5 Civil law

The *Law of Contract, the General Regime of Obligations, and Proof of Obligations* in the *French Civil Code*[90] contains the following provisions in Chapter III Contractual Interpretation:

> *Art. 1188.* – A contract is to be interpreted according to the common intention of the parties rather than stopping at the literal meaning of its terms.
>
> Where this intention cannot be discerned, a contract is to be interpreted in the sense which a reasonable person placed in the same situation would give to it.
>
> *Art. 1189.* – All the terms of a contract are to be interpreted in relation to each other, giving to each the meaning which respects the consistency of the contract as a whole.
>
> Where, according to the common intention of the parties, several contracts contribute to one and the same operation, they are to be interpreted by reference to this operation.

86 *Codelfa Construction Pty Ltd v State Rail Authority of NSW* [1982] 149 CLR337, 352; [1982] HCA 24 per Mason J.

87 *Cherry v Steele-Park* [2017] NSWCA 295.

88 *Hancock Prospecting Pty Ltd v Wright Prospecting Pty Ltd* [2012] WASCA 216, [76].

89 Donald Charrett, *The Application of Contracts in Construction and Engineering Projects* (Informa Law from Routledge, 2nd edn 2022) Chapter 8.

90 www.textes.justice.gouv.fr/art_pix/THE-LAW-OF-CONTRACT-2-5-16.pdf (accessed 6 March 2020).

> *Art. 1190.* – In case of ambiguity, a bespoke contract is interpreted against the creditor and in favour of the debtor, and a standard-form contract is interpreted against the person who put it forward.
> *Art. 1191.* – Where a contract term is capable of bearing two meanings, the one which gives it some effect is to be preferred to the one which makes it produce no effect.
> *Art. 1192.* – Clear and unambiguous terms are not subject to interpretation as doing so risks their distortion.

With the exception of Article 1188, these rules of construction are very similar to the common law rules referred to previously. In contrast to the common law approach of determining the parties' intentions objectively, the civil law approach in Article 1188 gives primacy to the parties' subjective intentions; only if these cannot be discerned is an objective approach taken.

2.13.6 UNIDROIT Principles

Article 4.1 of the *UP* takes a similar approach to the *French Civil Code*:

> (1) A contract shall be interpreted according to the common intention of the parties.
> (2) If such an intention cannot be established, the contract shall be interpreted according to the meaning that reasonable persons of the same kind as the parties would give to it in the same circumstances.

Chapter 4 of the *UP* contains eight Articles on the interpretation of the terms of contracts. Article 4.4 [Reference to contract or statements as a whole], Article 4.5 [All terms to be given effect], Article 4.6 [*Contra proferentem* rule] and Article 4.7 [Linguistic discrepancies] are probably consistent with most common law rules of contract construction. However, Articles 4.1 [Intention of the parties], Article 4.2 [Interpretation of statements and other conduct], Article 4.3 [Relevant circumstances], and Article 4.8 [Supplying an omitted term] allow for a greater amount of factual material to assist in interpreting the meaning of a contract, particularly in allowing for evidence of pre-contractual negotiations, earlier drafts of the contract, and each party's subjective intent than is generally applicable to many common law rules.

In *Chartbrook Limited v Persimmon Homes Limited*,[91] Lord Hoffmann confirmed the traditional exclusionary rule of the inadmissibility of evidence of pre-contractual negotiations. Referring to *UP* Article 4.3, he noted that this reflects the French philosophy of contractual interpretation, which is altogether different from that of English law:

> English law, on the other hand, mixes up the ascertainment of intention with the rules of law by depersonalising the contracting parties and asking, not what their intentions actually were, but what a reasonable outside observer would have taken them to be. One cannot in my opinion simply transpose rules based on one philosophy of contractual interpretation to another, or assume that the practical effect of admitting such evidence under the English system of civil procedure will be the same as that under a Continental system.[92]

---

91 [2009] UKHL 38.
92 Ibid. [39].

However, this issue is not without controversy, as several common law judges have argued in favour of a flexible application of the exclusionary rule whenever a cautious use of the pre-contract material would enable the court to arrive at a meaning of the contract that accorded with the ascertainable intention of the parties. In *Proforce Recruit Limited v The Rugby Group Limited*,[93] LJ Arden suggested that consideration should be given to the possibility of admitting evidence of pre-contractual negotiations in interpretation questions on a wider basis than the law presently permits. In her view, 'it may be appropriate to consider a number of international instruments applying to contracts,' such as the UNIDROIT Principles which 'give primacy to the common intention of the parties and on questions of interpretation requires regard to be had to all the circumstances, including the pre-contractual negotiations of the parties (Article 4.3).'

2.14 Implied contract terms

Irrespective of the thoroughness with which the parties have articulated their bargain explicitly in formal contract documents, it is almost inevitable that certain relevant issues or circumstances will not be addressed. In civil law systems the *Civil Codes* generally provide the tools for judges or arbitral tribunals to 'fill in the gaps' in the contract as expressed by the parties.

2.14.1 Types of implied terms

In common law, it is the role of the implied terms in a contract to 'fill in the gaps' in the explicit terms that the parties have articulated. Implied terms can be:

- Implied by law as an incident of contracts in general, or contracts of a particular class (such as construction contracts).
- Implied *ad hoc* – the term that the parties would have put into the contract had they turned their mind to it for the specific circumstances of the particular contract. It is the parties' actual or presumed objective intention, determined from the nature and context of the transaction.
- Implied by statute. For example, provisions of the Scheme for Construction Contracts may be implied terms of contract by virtue of s114 of the *Housing Grants Construction and Regeneration Act 1996* (UK).
- Implied by trade or custom and usage in a particular trade or industry.
- Implied by the parties' conduct where they have acted as if the term existed.

It is important to note that implied terms cannot be inconsistent with the explicit terms of the contract, which define the agreement that the parties actually made. Thus, a court will not imply a term by law or *ad hoc* if that term is inconsistent with the explicit terms of the agreement that the parties have made. For example, courts have implied a term in construction contracts that the Employer must ensure that the contract administrator acts independently, honestly, and fairly, and take the rights and interests of both Employer and

93 [2006] EWCA Civ 69.

Contractor into account when acting as a certifier.[94] However, such an implied term can be displaced by a specific contractual term that the contract administrator is to act as the agent of the Employer in all matters. Provided such a term does not breach public policy and is not contrary to any statute, it will be enforced by a court, no matter how unfair its operation may appear to be.

The courts of Singapore view the process of contractual interpretation as being distinct from the question of whether a term should be implied into a contract based on the mutual intentions of the parties.[95]

It is possible to exclude implied terms by a specific provision that only the express terms set out in the contract will bind the parties, thereby excluding any further implied terms. Although this approach is used in the USA, it is not common in Australia, perhaps because both parties may see the advantage of implication of terms to deal with the unexpected in a manner consistent with legal precedent.

2.14.2 Criteria for ad hoc *implied terms*

The following is a commonly accepted expression of the criteria that must be satisfied before a term will be implied *ad hoc* in a particular contract:

(1) It must be reasonable and equitable.
(2) It must be necessary to give business efficacy to the contract, so that no term will be implied if the contract is effective without it.
(3) It must be so obvious that 'it goes without saying.'
(4) It must be capable of clear expression.
(5) It must not contradict any express term of the contract.[96]

These principles were recently considered by Lord Neuberger to represent a clear, consistent and principled approach. Although 'it could be dangerous to reformulate the principles' laid down by Lord Simon, Lord Neuberger noted the following:

(1) Implication of a term is 'not critically dependent on proof of an actual intention of the parties' when negotiating the contract. The question is what notional reasonable people in the position of the parties at the time they were contracting would have agreed.
(2) A term should not be implied into a detailed commercial contract merely because it appears fair or merely because one considers that the parties would have agreed to it if it had been suggested to them – these are necessary but not sufficient grounds for including a term.
(3) It is questionable whether the requirement of reasonableness and equitableness will usually, or ever, add anything.
(4) The second and third requirements, business necessity and obviousness, can be alternatives in the sense that only one of them needs to be satisfied, although it is probably rare where only one is satisfied.

---

94 *Perini Corporation v Commonwealth of Australia* [1969] 2 NSWR 530, 542–545.

95 *Foo Jong Peng v Phua Kiah Mai* [2012] SGCA 55, [29]–[43]; *Sembcorp Marine Ltd v PPL Holdings Pte Ltd* [2013] SGCA 43, [24].

96 *BP Refinery (Westernport) Pty Ltd v Shire of Hastings* [1978] 52 ALJR 20, 26 per Lord Simon.

(5) If obviousness is approached by reference to the 'officious bystander' it is vital to formulate the question to be posed to him or her with the utmost care.
(6) Necessity for business efficacy involves a value judgment. A more helpful way of putting this requirement is that a term can only be implied if without it the contract would lack commercial or practical coherence.[97]

Whether a contract 'works' has a bearing on the question of whether a term is needed to give it business efficacy.[98]

2.14.3 Terms implied by law

As an example, the following terms are implied by law in Australia as an incident of all contracts, to the extent that they are not displaced by the explicit contract terms:

- Neither party shall do anything to prevent or delay the other from performing the contract (sometimes referred to as the prevention principle).[99]
- Each party agrees to do all that is necessary to be done on his/her part to enable the contract to be performed (**implied term of cooperation**).[100]

The implied term of cooperation has been expressed as follows:

> Where in a written contract it appears that both parties have agreed that something should be done which cannot effectively be done unless both concur in doing it, the construction of a contract is that each agrees to do all that is necessary to be done on his part for the carrying out of that thing though there may be no express words that effect.[101]

However: 'The law can enforce co-operation only in a limited degree – to the extent that it is necessary to make the contract workable.'[102]

2.15 Prevention principle

The **prevention principle** is sometimes expressed as preventing a party from taking advantage of his/her own wrong in enforcing a contract. The following illustrate the application of this principle:

- 'The essence of the prevention principle is that a party cannot insist on the performance of a contractual obligation by the other party if it itself is the cause of the other party's non-performance.'[103]

---

97 *Marks and Spencer plc v BNP Paribas Securities Services Trust Company (Jersey)* Ltd [2015] UKSC 72, [21].

98 *Renard Constructions (ME) Pty Ltd v Minister for Public Works* [1992] 26 NSWLR 234, 258 per Priestley JA.

99 *Barque Quilpé Ltd v Brown* [1904] 2 KB 264, 274 per Vaughan Williams LJ.

100 *McKay v Dick* [1881] 6 AC 251, 263 per Lord Blackburn; *Butt v M'Donald* (1896) 7 QLJ 68, 70–71 per Griffiths CJ; *Secured Income Real Estate (Aust) Ltd v St Martin's Investments Pty Ltd* [1979] 144 CLR 596, 607 per Mason J.

101 *Mackay v Dick* [1881] 6 AC 251, 263.

102 *Mona Oil Equipment & Supply Co Ltd v Rhodesia Railways Ltd* [1949] 2 All ER 1014, 1018 per Devlin J.

103 *Spiers Earthworks Pty Ltd v Landtec Projects Corp Pty Ltd (No 2)* [2012] 287 ALR 360; [2012] 28 BCL 282; [2012] WASCA 53, [47] per McLure P.

- The operation of the prevention principle can be modified or excluded by contract.[104]
- '[It is] a positive rule of law of contract that conduct of either promisor or promisee which can be said to amount to himself "of his own motion" bringing about the impossibility of performance is in itself a breach.'[105]
- 'It is a principle very well established at common law that no person can take advantage of the non fulfilment of a condition the performance of which has been hindered by himself.'[106]
- 'If the owner by the ordering of extra work or by the doing or omitting to do any act he ought to have done or omitted has delayed the contractor in beginning the work or necessarily increased the time finishing the work he thereby disentitles himself to claim the penalties for non-completion provided by the contract.'[107]

2.16 Entire agreement

An **entire agreement** clause is to the effect that the written terms of the contract constitutes the entire agreement and understanding between the parties, and that any representations made during negotiations prior to entry into the contract have no contractual effect.

Such provisions may go further and state that the express terms are exhaustive of the rights, obligations, and liabilities of each of the parties to the other. An example of such an entire agreement term is in the UK standard form contract MF/1 General Conditions of Contract published by the Association of Consulting Engineers:

> The Purchaser and the Contractor intend that their respective rights, obligations and liabilities as provided for in the Conditions shall be exhaustive of the rights, obligations and liabilities of each of them to the other arising out of, under or in connection with the Contract or the Works, whether such rights obligations and liabilities arise in respect of or in consequence of a breach of contract or statutory duty or a tortious or negligent act or omission which gives rise to a remedy at common law. Accordingly, except as expressly provided for in the Conditions, neither party shall be obligated or liable to the other in respect of any damages or losses suffered by the other which arise out of, under or in connection with the Contract or the Works, whether by reason or in consequence of any breach of contract or of statutory duty or tortious or negligent act or omission.

Properly worded, such an entire agreement clause would preclude claims for common law damages for breach of contract and confine a plaintiff to those remedies exclusively defined in the contract. In *Strachan & Henshaw Ltd v Stein Industrie (UK) Ltd*,[108] the UK Court of Appeal upheld the above entire agreement contract provision, even though that meant that it reduced important contractual obligations to unenforceable declarations of intent and made assumed contractual rights worthless. In contrast, in *Mostcash Plc v Fluor Ltd*, the UK Court of Appeal considered that the only realistic and commercial meaning

104 *Probuild Constructions (Aust) Pty Ltd v DDI Group Pty Ltd* [2017] NSWCA 151, [117] per McColl JA, Macfarlan JA and Beazley ACJ agreeing.
105 *Southern Foundries (1926) Ltd v Shirlaw* [1940] AC 701, 717 per Lord Atkin.
106 *Roberts v Bury Improvement Commissioners* [1870] LR 5 CP 310, 326 per Blackburn J.
107 *Ottowa Northern and Western Railway Co v Dominion Bridge Co* [1905] 36 SCR 347, 359 per Davies J.
108 (1997) 87 BLR 52, CA; [1997] 63 Con LR 160; (1998) 14 Const LJ 370.

of the words in the entire agreement/exclusive remedy provisions was that they were not intended to exclude a claim for damages.[109]

If the wording of an entire agreement is clear and wide enough, it can expressly exclude or negate all implied terms, claims in tort generally, and claims for tortious misrepresentation. Further, because such provisions are intended and often expressed to be intended to survive termination of the contract, the question of whether common law rights are preserved or excluded will depend on the express provisions of the termination clause.[110]

An entire agreement clause will not, however, be effective in precluding claims under statutes that cannot be contracted out of. For example, claims for misleading or deceptive conduct in contravention of the *Australian Consumer Law* in respect of pre-contract negotiations. The statutory rights conferred by the *ACL* cannot be contracted out of, and accordingly damages[111] or other remedies[112] are available to a party who has suffered loss or damage by another party's misleading or deceptive conduct prior to entry into, or during execution of, the contract.

The advantage of properly drawn entire agreement/exclusive remedy clauses is that they provide some certainty: the contract terms constitute an exclusive code of the rights and obligations of the parties in the one document, and users of the contract do not require knowledge of or reference to the common law. At the stage of negotiating contract terms, the parties want certainty and to avoid disputes. However, if there is subsequently a dispute, both parties will want the widest possible range of remedies, either within or outside the contract. Accordingly, a party entering into a contract should give very careful consideration to an entire agreement clause before agreeing to it.[113]

109 [2002] EWCA Civ 975; [2002] BLR 411; [2002] 83 Con LR 1.

110 Roberta Downey, 'The Contract is King . . . and Queen – the Use of Entire Agreement Clauses in Construction Contracts' (2003) Society of Construction Law (Paper based on the highly commended entry in the Hudson Prize Competition 2002, May 2003) 7–9 www.scl.org.uk/papers/contract-king-and-queen-use-entire-agreement-clauses-construction-contracts (accessed 31 July 2021).

111 *Australian Consumer Law* (Cth) s 236.

112 Ibid. ss 237–241, 248.

113 Roberta Downey, 'The Contract is King . . . and Queen – the Use of Entire Agreement Clauses in Construction Contracts' (2003) Society of Construction Law (Paper based on the highly commended entry in the Hudson Prize Competition 2002, May 2003) 14 www.scl.org.uk/papers/contract-king-and-queen-use-entire-agreement-clauses-construction-contracts (accessed 31 July 2021).

CHAPTER 3

Construction contracts

CONTENTS

DOI: 10.4324/9781003206873-3

3.1 Types of contracts

3.1.1 Construction contracts

Construction contracts can be defined in various ways. The following definition is used for the purposes of this book:

> any contract where one person [this includes a corporation] agrees for valuable consideration to carry out construction works, which may include building or engineering works, for another.[1]

In general terms, the parties to a construction contract are the **Employer** (also referred to as the Client,[2] Principal,[3] or the Owner) for whom the work is done, and the **Contractor** who carries out the work. Moreover, a **subcontract** in which a **subcontractor** undertakes construction work for a principal contractor is a species of construction contract and is frequently 'back-to-back' with the **head contract** between the Employer and the **Head Contractor**. Thus, the Contractor under the head contract functions as the Employer in a subcontract, and the subcontractor functions as the Contractor. In this book, the construction contract being referred to is referred to as the **Contract**.

The scope of a construction contract may be comprehensively defined by legislation to be narrower or broader than the earlier definition. Where relevant legislation relates to construction contracts the legislation must be consulted for the precise definition.

The Singapore statutory definition of construction contracts in the *Building and Construction Industry Security of Payment Act 2004* (Sing) is similar to the scope of the

1 Stephen Furst & The Hon Sir Vivian Ramsey, *Keating on Construction Contracts* (Sweet & Maxwell, 8th edn 2006) 1.
2 NEC4 Engineering and Construction Contract.
3 Australian Standards.

UK definition.[4] As there will inevitably be some differences between statutory definitions, the relevant legislation always should be referenced to determine the statutory scope of a construction contract in any jurisdiction.[5]

3.1.2 Building contracts

A particular species of construction contract is a **building contract** for the construction of a 'building.' Such contracts may be distinguished from contracts for the construction of infrastructure or industrial facilities such as an offshore oil and gas platform or a mineral processing facility. In a particular context there may be a need to determine whether a construction contract is also a building contract because of specific legislative requirements – see ¶3.1.2.3 later for an example.

The following examples illustrate different definitions in different jurisdictions.

3.1.2.1 Example 1: Definition of building work in the Peoples Republic of China

Construction Law Article 2:

> This Law shall be adhered to in engaging in building operations and in the exercise of supervision and administration over building operations within the territory of the People's Republic of China.

The building operations referred to in this Law mean construction of all types of housing and the construction of their ancillary facilities as well as their matching installation operations of wiring, piping, and equipment.

3.1.2.2 Example 2: Definition of building in Malaysia

Street, Drainage and Building Act 1974 (Malaysia)
The definition of 'building' in s3:

> includes any house, hut, shed, or roofed enclosure, whether used for the purpose of a human habitation or otherwise, and also any wall, fence, platform, staging, gate, post, pillar, paling, frame, hoarding, slip, dock, wharf, pier, jetty, landing-stage or bridge, or any structure support or foundation connected to the foregoing.

4 Sections 104 & 105 of the *Housing Grants, Construction and Regeneration Act 1996* (UK).

5 For example, s5 of the *Building and Construction Industry Improvement Act 2005* (Cth) has a definition of 'building work' that is similar in some respects to the definition of 'construction work' in the *Security of Payment* legislation but does not include work related to single-dwelling houses.

3.1.2.3 Example 3: Definition of building in Victoria

Section 3 of the *Building Act 1993* (Vic) defines 'building' as including structure, temporary building, temporary structure, and any part of a building or structure. The limits of this definition have been determined by the courts. For example, an advertising hoarding attached to a brick wall was found to be a building pursuant to s3 of the *Building Act 1993* (Vic),[6] whereas a railway overpass was held not to be a 'building.'[7]

The significance of this definition is that limitation periods for bringing an action in court depends on whether it is a building action or not. Section 134 of the *Building Act 1993* (Vic) limits the time at which a building action can be commenced in court to ten years from the date of issue of the certificate of occupancy, where building action means an action (including a counterclaim) for damages for loss or damage arising out of or concerning defective building work, which includes the design, inspection, and issuing of a permit in respect of building work.[8]

There are similar provisions in other Australian jurisdictions limiting the time to ten years during which a building action can be commenced.[9] Such limitations on the time for bringing an action do not apply to a construction contract unless it is also a building contract according to the relevant statutory definition. Thus, where a railway overpass was held not to be a 'building,' the normal six-year period from the accrual of the cause of action applied,[10] rather than the ten-year limitation period for a building action.

3.1.3 Other contracts

Although a contract for design only may satisfy the statutory definition of construction contract or building contract in the relevant legislation, such contracts do not involve 'construction' as such, and for the purposes of this book are not considered to be construction contracts. Accordingly, only passing reference is made to contracts which involve design only.[11] Conversely, although a design and construct contract includes design, it also involves construction and therefore falls within the definition adopted earlier.

Building contracts for **domestic building work** in connection with the construction of a home form a discrete type of building contract with particular characteristics, many of which are derived from the statutory requirements of legislation intended to protect the interests of consumer homeowners. The particular features for **domestic building contracts** are outside the scope of this book, which does not attempt to address the unique characteristics of such contracts.[12]

6 Finding into death without inquest by Victorian Coroner, COR 2013 1338, 7. www.coronerscourt.vic.gov.au/resources/151c4daa-ecf1-4693-9c08-a6bb98801f68/alexanderdavidjones_133813.pdf (accessed 17 June 2018).

7 *Australian Rail Track Corporation Ltd v Leighton Contractors Pty Ltd* [2003] VSC 189.

8 Section 129.

9 *Environmental Planning and Assessment Act 1979* (NSW) s109ZK; *Development Act 1993* (SA) s73; *Building Act 1996* (NT) s159; *Construction Practitioners Registration Act 1998* (ACT) s27.

10 As determined from the applicable *Limitation of Actions Act*, for example s5 of the *Limitation of Actions Act 1958* (Vic).

11 Various aspects of design contracts are discussed in Donald Charrett, *Contracts for Construction and Engineering Projects* (Informa Law from Routledge, 2nd edn 2022).

12 Domestic building contracts are covered in Philip Britton, Matthew Bell et al., *Residential Construction Law* (Bloomsbury Academic, 2021).

3.2 Delivery of construction projects

The legal mechanism for delivery of a construction project is a construction contract between Employer and Contractor. As a species of commercial contract that addresses the particular features of construction projects enumerated in ¶4.2 later, international construction contracts have a number of features that give them some unique characteristics. Those unique characteristics arise by operation of statute or common law or because of specific terms that are incorporated in most construction contracts, or because of the nature of construction work.

Construction contracts may also be combined with contracts for the operation of the constructed facilities, in contractual manifestations such as **PPP** (Public-Private Partnership), **BOOT** (Build, Own, Operate, Transfer), **BOO** (Build, Own, Operate), **BOT** (Build, Operate, Transfer), and **BOTT** (Build, Operate, Train, Transfer). In each of these types of contracts there are various project-specific provisions in respect of the operations phase (which may be very long term, perhaps over 30 years) which are outside the scope of this book. Nevertheless, the principles discussed in respect of construction contracts are relevant to the construction phase of PPP- and BOOT-type contracts.

3.3 Contract documents

There are no rules which govern the type or content of the documents which make up a construction contract (**contract documents**). Ultimately it is a matter for the contracting parties to decide which documents are to have contractual force. As noted in ¶4.2 later, because of the legal and technical complexity of many construction contracts, particularly contracts for large projects, the required design, scope, time, cost, and quality requirements of the work and the finished project are defined by extensive technical documentation. Many of these complex and lengthy technical documents are typically incorporated into the Contract so that their requirements are enforceable contractual obligations.

Thus, the contract documents for a construction contract typically contain both 'legal' and 'technical' documents. 'Legal' documents usually include the form of agreement and **conditions of contract** – the contract documents which specify the parties' overall obligations under the Contract and the allocation and consequences of risks. The conditions of contract may consist of **General Conditions** (the conditions of contract in a standard form contract which are of a general nature and are not specific to the project, the parties, the Site, or the specific scope of work) and **Special Conditions** (the conditions of contract in a standard form contract which are specific to the project, the parties, the Site, or the specific scope of work, and supplement or replace provisions in the General Conditions). 'Technical' documents may include Employer's requirements, specifications,[13] drawings, bills of quantities,[14] and schedules.

As noted in ¶2.13.3 earlier, one of the common law canons of construction of the terms of a contract is that all parts of it (ie both 'legal' and 'technical' documents) must be given effect to if possible, and no part should be interpreted as inoperative or surplus. Similar provisions apply in civil law jurisdictions, for example see ¶2.13.5.

13 A specification is a document which describes technical requirements for the Works to be constructed.

14 A bill of quantities (**BoQ**) is a schedule briefly describing each different type of constructional element and listing the quantity of each required for a complete construction project.

Table 3.1 Order of precedence of contract documents in FIDIC rainbow suite

	2017 Red Book	2017 Yellow Book	2017 Silver Book
(a)	the Contract Agreement	the Contract Agreement	the Contract Agreement
(b)	the Letter of Acceptance	the Letter of Acceptance	the Particular Conditions Part A – Contract Data
(c)	the Letter of Tender	the Letter of Tender	the Particular Conditions Part B – Special Provisions
(d)	the Particular Conditions Part A – Contract Data	the Particular Conditions Part A – Contract Data	the General Conditions
(e)	the Particular Conditions Part B – Special Provisions	the Particular Conditions Part B – Special Provisions	the Employer's Requirements
(f)	the General Conditions	the General Conditions	the Schedules
(g)	the Specification	the Employer's Requirements	the Tender
(h)	the drawings	the Schedules	the JV Undertaking (if the Contractor is a JV)
(i)	the Schedules	the Contractor's Proposal	any other documents forming part of the Contract
(j)	the JV Undertaking (if the Contractor is a JV)	the JV Undertaking (if the Contractor is a JV)	
(k)	any other documents forming part of the Contract	any other documents forming part of the Contract	

Where the Contract states that the contract documents are mutually explanatory, all the Contract documents are accepted with equal status and the normal legal rules of interpretation will apply. A document specially prepared for the Contract by the parties, such as a specification or bills of quantities, should be given special weight in any case of ambiguity or inconsistency, as against a printed standard document prepared by others, such as the General Conditions themselves.

Because a contract is not contained in one single document but in a number of documents, it is recommended to establish an order of priority of the documents in order to avoid having to resort to litigation to resolve disputes as to the interpretation of the Contract. More than one document may seek to regulate the same matters, or changes may have occurred during the contract negotiations which may lead to discrepancies between documents. It is therefore important to know which documents will take priority when interpreting a contract. If no order of priority is specified in the Contract, the general rule of interpretation in most countries is that the specific takes precedence over the general.

The possibility of inconsistencies between different contract documents indicates the need to state the order of precedence of contract documents in the event of inconsistency between them. For example, sub-clause 1.5 of the 2017 FIDIC Red Book, Yellow Book and Silver Book provide for the order of precedence shown in Table 3.1.

It can be seen from Table 3.1, as is typical for construction contracts, the 'technical' documents such as the Employer's requirements, Schedules, Specification and drawings are lower in the order of precedence than the 'legal' documents – the Contract Agreement, the Particular Conditions, and the General Conditions.

On the face of it, it would normally be expected that the allocation of a specific risk in the conditions of contract would take precedence over provisions in the 'technical' documents. Nevertheless, in *Clancy Docwra Ltd v E.ON Energy Solutions Ltd*[15] the court held that the scope of works had been modified by a document appended to the Contract which clarified the subcontractor's tender in relation to adverse ground conditions. This modification of the allocation of the risk for ground conditions was regardless of an express term of the conditions of contract which allocated ground risk to the subcontractor. In construing all the contract documents, Mrs Justice Jefford held that the tender clarifications were a particularisation of the subcontractor's obligations under the scope of works, and therefore the allocation of risk in the conditions of contract did not include the risk for works that were excluded by the tender clarifications incorporated in the Contract.

This case is a salutary reminder of the importance of parties to a construction contract ensuring that all contractual documents, including 'technical' documents, are consistent with the 'legal' conditions of contract. It is also a reminder that the meaning of a contract from construing all of the contract documents as a whole may give a different answer to that provided by the 'legal' documents alone. The case study in ¶6.12.1 highlights the difficulty of construing 'contractual documents of multiple authorship, which contain much loose wording' and 'the somewhat diffuse documents which constituted, or were incorporated into, the "design and build" contract in this case.'

Appendix A contains a number of checklists of issues that an Employer's agent should consider when drafting a construction contract to achieve the best result. Most, if not all of these issues will be covered in standard form General Conditions or Contract Data to be completed for the particular project.

3.4 Types of construction contract

It is clear from the range of issues relevant to construction contracts outlined earlier and the variety of ways that contracting parties can decide on the scope and division of work and risk allocation that there are a number of different types of construction contract. The following broad classification of types of construction contracts will be adopted for the purposes of this book, although it must be emphasised that because of the uniqueness of each construction project and the parties' freedom of contract, there are no 'bright line' distinctions between different types of contracts, and a particular contract may be a combination of more than one of the following types:

- **EPC/turnkey contract**, in which the Contractor takes total responsibility for the engineering, procurement and construction (**EPC**), and provides a fully equipped facility ready for operation (at the 'turn of the key').[16] The Contractor assumes the design risks.

15 [2018] EWHC 3124 (TCC).

16 In spite of the similarities of the acronyms EPC and EPCM, they are at opposite ends of the risk allocation spectrum. See Philip Loots & Nick Henchie, 'Worlds Apart: EPC and EPCM Contracts: Risk Issues and Allocation' (2007) *International Construction Law Review* 252.

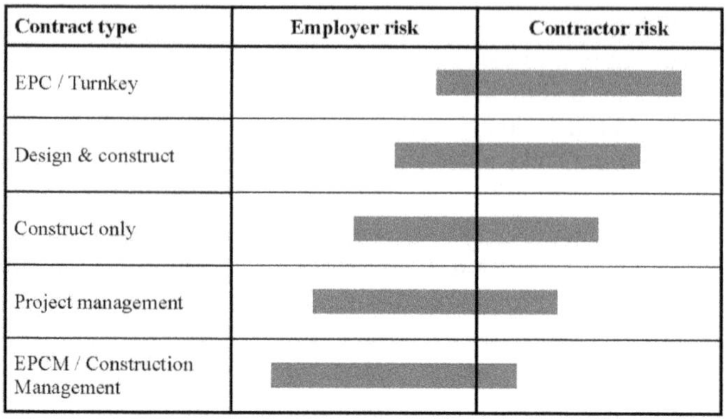

Figure 3.1 Allocation of risks between Employer and Contractor in different types of contract

- **Design and construct contract**, in which the Contractor prepares the design to satisfy the Employer's requirements, and then constructs that design. The Contractor assumes the design risks.
- **Construct only contract**, the 'traditional' form of construction contract between an Employer and Contractor in which the Contractor constructs the design prepared for the Employer by the Employer's engineer/architect (who has a separate design contract with the Employer). In the USA construct only contracts are referred to as design-bid-build (**DBB**). The Employer assumes the design risks.
- **Project management contract**, in which the Employer engages a **Project Manager** to act as its agent with control over the whole project, which may or may not be divided into discrete parts. The Employer assumes the design risks.
- **Construction management contract**, also called an **engineer, procure and construction management contract (EPCM)**, in which the Employer engages a **Construction Manager** to act as the Employer's agent to program, coordinate, and manage the design and construction activities which are divided into packages which are separately undertaken by trade contractors contracted directly to the Employer. The Employer assumes the design risks.

Within each type of contract there may also be variations because of different methods of payment, or different risk allocation. For example, EPC contracts may be lump sum or cost reimbursable, and this is a significant aspect of the risk allocation between the contracting parties. In the USA, construction management contracts typically require the Construction Manager (usually a licensed general contractor) to guarantee the cost of the project (referred to as construction management at risk). Although the boundaries between these different types of construction contracts are not fixed, each type can generally be distinguished from the others by the location of risk allocation on the spectrum of Employer/Contractor risks. This is illustrated diagrammatically in Figure 3.1.[17]

17 After Colin Carter, in Scotland, A Report by the Rt Hon Lord Fraser of Carmyllie QC, *The Holyrood Inquiry*, SP Paper No 205 (2004) 80.

The common feature of all these types of construction contracts is that the Employer and the Contractor each have separate rights and obligations arising from the defined scope, with the result that each separately accepts liability for some of the inherent risks in a construction project. Separately, either the Employer or the Contractor accepts each of the risks that make up the totality of the project risks. This allocation of risks results in what are often referred to as adversarial contracts, as the materialisation of a risk can have substantial time and/or cost consequences for one party which it seeks to avoid by adversarial means.

3.5 Collaborative contracts

3.5.1 Features

In contrast to adversarial contracts, collaborative contracts involve parties working together cooperatively and sharing risks:

> Collaborative contracting is where parties work together to achieve common outcomes. Collaborative contracts are underpinned by parties working together in good faith, focusing on fixing problems and not blame, managing risk equitably and jointly where appropriate, promoting transparency, and avoiding disputes.[18]

There are larger costs at the early stages of a project for collaborative contracting as it requires an investment in Employer leadership resources, and the tender process is more expensive than for adversarial contracts. However, long-term savings may be achieved by a lower construction cost, fewer time and cost overruns, and reduced disputation. They are likely to be more suited to large-scale, complex, and high-risk projects.

Collaborative contracts have a number of unique characteristics which set them apart from the adversarial construction contracts discussed earlier. The tender process will need to be appropriately structured to attract bids and enable suitable contract documentation to be developed. Selection of the Contractor on price alone is inappropriate, as non-cost criteria such as competence, track record on collaboration, and key project personnel are very important factors for success.[19] Collaborative contracting will not be successful unless there is trust between the parties, and this needs strong leadership to promptly identify and resolve issues as they arise. Formal processes such as written agreements to collaborate, start-up workshops, and ongoing senior management meetings are desirable to maintain collaborative working. Dispute Boards as discussed in ¶28.1.2 are a proven method of assisting the parties to avoid disputes.

Collaborative approaches have obvious benefits in dealing with unknown unknowns such as COVID-19 where the parties have established mechanisms to manage risks on a best for project basis.

18 Australian Government Department of Defence Capability Acquisition and Sustainment Group, 'Collaborative Contracting Better Practice Guide Version 1.0' (28 September 2017) 4, https://www1.defence.gov.au/sites/default/files/2020-06/collaborative_contracting_better_practice_guide.pdf (accessed 31 March 2021).

19 Philip Loots & Dr Donald Charrett, 'Reconsidering Procurement Criteria and Procedures for Major Infrastructure Projects: Why the use of "Price" as the Determining Factor in Construction Procurement Decisions is Wrong' (2017) *International Construction Law Review* 69.

3.5.2 Early contractor involvement contract

In an early contractor involvement contract (**ECI contract**) the Employer engages the Contractor during the planning and design development phase to obtain the benefit of the Contractor's construction expertise before the design is finalised. The Contractor works collaboratively on pricing with the Employer and the Employer's designers to determine a fixed price or guaranteed maximum price for the construction phase. This collaboration ensures that buildability issues are addressed at an early stage in the design before it is finalised. The ECI contract is initially let on the basis of a target construction price which is subsequently converted to a lump sum or guaranteed maximum price at the end of the design development phase.

An ECI contract has a number of advantages for the Employer. It retains flexibility to develop and refine its requirements, particularly valuable when the scope is uncertain or evolving. The Employer gains the benefit of the Contractor's skill and expertise to embed innovation and buildability into the design, whilst having visibility and some control of project costs. An ECI contract is appropriate when there is a tight time for Completion, and when the Employer wants to avoid adversarial tensions. The disadvantages include the administrative burden and once appointed there is no genuine competition for the ECI Contractor.

3.5.3 Incentivised target cost contract

This type of contract is the culmination of a collaborative process during the planning and design development phase of a project. A small number of shortlisted contractors work collaboratively with the Employer to define the project in sufficient detail to determine a target price. The successful respondent is then engaged under an incentivised target cost contract.

In an incentivised target cost contract, the Contractor is rewarded or penalised based on its performance measured against a target cost. The Contractor is responsible to achieve the target dates for Completion, subject to normal provisions for EOTs. It is paid its actual reimbursable costs plus allowances for corporate overhead and profit, plus risk/reward amounts. The incentive structure may include painshare/gainshare or early completion bonus. The Contractor is liable for its breaches of contract, which may have liability caps and exclusions of indirect and consequential losses.

Such contracts are highly interactive and promote innovation. The risk management process gives the parties early warnings. It requires strong contract management skills. Whilst it is collaborative on cost risk, the Contractor is responsible for the time and quality risks. Incentivised target cost contracts have been used for a number of NSW infrastructure projects: freeway upgrades, and a number of projects for Sydney Metro City & Southwest.

3.5.4 Alliance contract

In an **alliance contract** the risks and rewards are intended to be shared in a non-adversarial relationship between the parties. Alliance contracts have been widely used by governments in Australia, and in 2015 the Australian Government published 'National

Alliance Contracting Guidelines – Guide to Alliance Contracting.'[20] That Guide provides the following summary of the essential characteristics of an alliance contract with a Government Owner[21] (Employer):

> Alliance contracting is delivering major capital assets, where a public sector agency (the Owner) works collaboratively with private sector parties (Non-Owner Participants or **NOPs**). All participants are required to work together in good faith, acting with integrity and making best-for-project decisions. Working as an integrated, collaborative team, they make unanimous decisions on all key project delivery issues. The alliance structure capitalises on the relationships between the participants, removes organisational barriers and encourages effective integration with the owner.
>
> **Risk sharing v risk allocation**
>
> The most significant difference between traditional contracting methods and alliance contracting is that in alliancing, all project risk management and outcomes are collectively shared by the participants. In more traditional methods of risk allocation, specific risks are allocated to participants who are individually responsible for best managing the risk and bearing the risk outcome. This concept of collective risk sharing provides the foundation for the characteristics that underpin alliance contracting including collaboration, making best-for project decisions and innovation. If substantial and significant risk is allocated to individual participants, then it may not be an alliance and those characteristics may not be necessarily required or appropriate.
>
> Alliance agreements are premised on joint management of risk and opportunity for project delivery. All participants jointly manage that risk within the terms of an 'alliance agreement,' and share the outcomes of the project (however, the financial outcomes are not always shared equally between the Owner and the NOPs).

The term integrated project delivery (**IPD**) is used in the USA for a contractual mechanism that aligns the interests of all contracting parties. The following definition of IPD indicates that it is closely allied to alliance contracting:

> Integrated project delivery (IPD) is a relatively new procurement process that is gaining popularity as the use of BIM expands and the AEC facility management (AEC/FM) industry learns how to use this technology to support integrated teams. There are multiple approaches to IPD as the industry experiments with this approach. The American Institute of Architects (AIA), the Association of General Contractors (AGC), and other organizations have published sample contract forms for a family of IPD versions (AIA, 2017). In all cases, integrated projects are distinguished by effective collaboration among the owner, the prime (and possibly sub-) designers, and the prime (and possibly key sub-) contractor(s). This collaboration takes place from early design and continues through project handover. The key concept is that this project team works together using the best collaborative tools at their disposal to ensure that the project will meet owner requirements at significantly reduced time and cost.[22]

An alliance contract requires a commitment from the contracting parties to a 'no blame' culture in relation to errors, mistakes, defects, poor performance, and disputes. Each party

---

20 © Commonwealth of Australia 2015, www.infrastructure.gov.au/infrastructure/ngpd/files/National_Guide_to_Alliance_Contracting.pdf (accessed 17 March 2021).

21 Defined as the entity which will own the asset to be delivered by the alliance and generally has responsibility for the procurement of the alliance.

22 Rafael Sacks, Chuck Eastman, Ghang Lee, & Paul Teicholz, *BIM Handbook: A Guide to Building Information Modeling for Owners, Designers, Engineers, Contractors, and Facility Managers* (John Wiley & Sons, 3rd edn 2018) 7.

agrees not to bring a legal claim against other parties, typically with narrow exceptions, for example wilful default, repudiation of the alliance agreement, or failure to pay money due under the alliance agreement. Remuneration is typically based on payment at agreed rates, with a painshare/gainshare fund available for distribution (or not) based on overall project performance with respect to an agreed target.

Alliance contracts have been successfully used for projects procured by private sector and government Employers in Australia[23] and elsewhere. For example, Heathrow Terminal 5 was successfully delivered by an agreement that had the hallmarks of an alliance contract identified earlier.[24] Alliance contracts are particularly suitable where the Contractor is not in a position to manage or price risks because there are complex interfaces or operational constraints, where there are technical challenges requiring innovation, or there is scoping uncertainty or time constraints. Notwithstanding their advantages, alliance contracts are not appropriate for every project:

> Under alliance contracting, risks are shared between government and the private party. Alliances may work well in some circumstances but recent practice has been increasingly wary of the model due to uncertainty about the overall cost of construction and potential to put off rather than deal with risk issues early (chapter 12). Alliances may nevertheless still have their place. In particular, they may offer value in specific circumstances where projects must proceed out of necessity, but where substantial risk cannot be clearly allocated to one party. For example, because risks are difficult to identify and quantify or there is disagreement over the price. These examples should be rare in an effectively-planned infrastructure environment.[25]

The adoption of new technologies in construction projects may require collaborative contracting to achieve the potential advantages. For example, the full benefits of building information modelling (BIM) are difficult to achieve when there is a multiplicity of contracts involving Employer, designers, Contractor, subcontractors and suppliers. This is discussed further in ¶29.5.1.

3.5.5 Public-Private Partnerships

One definition of a Public-Private Partnership (PPP) is as follows:

> A long-term contract between a private party and a government entity, for providing a public asset or service, in which the private party bears significant risk and management responsibility, and remuneration is linked to performance.[26]

There is a wide range of PPPs which vary in the extent of involvement and risk taken by the private party. The World Bank notes the spectrum of PPP arrangements in Table 3.2.[27]

---

23 The first reported alliance contract in Australia was the Wandoo oil and gas platform in Western Australia in 1994.

24 Philip Loots & Donald Charrett, *Practical Guide to Engineering and Construction Contracts* (CCH, 2009) 354–358.

25 Australian Government, *Productivity Commission Inquiry Report Public Infrastructure* (No. 71, 27 May 2014) 122, www.pc.gov.au/inquiries/completed/infrastructure/report (accessed 17 May 2021).

26 https://ppp.worldbank.org/public-private-partnership/overview/what-are-public-private-partnerships (accessed19 May 2021).

27 https://ppp.worldbank.org/public-private-partnership/agreements (accessed 19 May 2021).

Table 3.2 Spectrum of public and private ownership in PPP arrangements

		Extent of private sector participation
Public owns and operates assets	Utility restructuring Corporatisation Decentralisation	Low
	Civil works Service contracts	
Public-Private Partnerships	Management and operating contracts	
	Leases *Affermage* contracts[28]	
	Concessions BOT projects DBO contracts	
	Joint Venture / Partial divestiture of public assets	
Private sector owns and operates assets	Full divestiture	High

Many PPP arrangements separate the concession contract between the government and the private entity delivering a public service (often referred to a special purpose vehicle (**SPV**)) from the contract to construct the facility (usually a design and construct contract) and the contract to manage the facility (the facilities management contract). Such PPP arrangements are far from new. In 1887 the Quebec Bridge and Railway Company was incorporated to build and operate a railway bridge across the St Lawrence River, pursuant to various *Acts* passed by the Government of Quebec. The bridge only became financially viable when the Government of Quebec granted a subsidy and guaranteed the bonds of the Quebec Bridge and Railway Company (the SPV). The SPV subsequently let a design and construct contract to the Phoenix Bridge Company.[29]

The World Bank publishes guidance on PPP contractual provisions[30] and standardised PPP contracts and contract clauses.[31]

28 An ***affermage* contract** is public-private sector arrangements under which the private operator is responsible for operating and maintaining the utility but not for financing the investment. http://regulationbodyofknowledge.org/glossary/a/affermage/ (accessed 19 May 2021).

29 Donald Charrett, *The Application of Contracts in Construction and Engineering Projects* (Informa Law from Routledge, 2nd edn 2022) 272.

30 https://ppp.worldbank.org/public-private-partnership/library/guidance-ppp-contractual-provisions-2019 (accessed 19 May 2021).

31 https://ppp.worldbank.org/public-private-partnership/standardized-ppp-contracts-and-contract-clause (accessed 19 May 2021).

3.6 Laws applicable to construction contracts

3.6.1 The impact of applicable laws

As used here, 'laws' means all national, state, or provincial legislation, statutes, *Acts*, decrees, rules, ordinances, orders, treaties, international law and other laws, and regulations and by-laws of any legally constituted public authority that apply to or are in connection with a construction contract.

The applicable laws can impact the operation of a construction contract in various ways:

- The provisions of mandatory law will override any contractual provisions.
- A construction contract must be executed in accordance with the applicable laws irrespective of the contract wording.
- Non-mandatory law may provide default options if they are not covered or explicitly derogated from by the specific terms of the Contract.

As discussed in ¶2.5 earlier, it is apparent that there are potentially a substantial number of laws that impact on the entry into, operation of, and termination of a contract; the design and execution of the Works; and the resolution of any disputes that arise from or are in connection with the Contract. Subject to the desirability of the Conditions of Contract comprising an accurate contract management manual, it is not the place of contract documents to constitute a complete definition of the parties' legal rights and obligations, or a project management manual (nor would it be feasible). Accordingly, the Conditions of Contract, even in a well-written and comprehensive contract, can never identify all of the applicable laws that may define the parties' rights and obligations in all circumstances.

Construction of any significant infrastructure or facility in the modern world is a complex undertaking in which the interests of many stakeholders must be considered, and a myriad of legal obligations complied with. Those involved at the 'coalface' of a construction project administering the Contract as Engineer, Employer, or Contractor need to be generally aware of their legal obligations under the applicable laws, so that they can make the appropriate enquiries as to their specific obligations in particular circumstances. Complex or unusual situations will undoubtedly require input from competent construction lawyers experienced in the relevant jurisdiction. Over 2000 years ago, Vitruvius advised the architect (constructor) of the need for constructors to be aware of relevant construction law:

> [A]s for principles of law, [an Architect] should know those which are necessary in the case of buildings having party walls, with regard to water dripping from the eaves, and also the laws about drains, windows, and water supply. And other things of this sort should be known to architects, so that, before they begin upon buildings, they may be careful not to leave disputed points for the householders to settle after the works are finished, and so that in drawing up contracts the interests of both employer and contractor may be wisely safe-guarded. For if a contract is skillfully drawn, each may obtain a release from the other without disadvantage.[32]

32 Marcus Vitruvius Pollo (translated by Morris Hicky Morgan), *Vitruvius: The Ten Books on Architecture* (Dover Publications, 1960) 11.

3.6.2 Types of relevant laws

Whilst it may be possible for the parties to a contract to select the governing law of the contract, they have no choice over the jurisdiction of the Site where the construction takes place, and any relevant statute law in that jurisdiction applicable to the Site or the Works will apply, irrespective of the governing law of the contract. The laws applicable to a construction contract can be considered under the following headings:

- The governing law of the contract,
- Laws applicable to the execution of a construction project at the Site in a country,
- Laws applicable to the resolution of disputes.

The governing law of the contract provides the laws for *inter alia*: entry into a contract, termination of a contract, and contractual liability. Laws applicable to the resolution of disputes include, *inter alia*: **limitation periods** for commencing legal proceedings, statutory requirements for construction disputes, court rules, and arbitration laws.

The laws applicable to the execution of a construction project will generally be those of the country where the Site or the Works are located. These include, *inter alia*: occupational health and safety; protection of the environment; heritage; labour laws; planning and building permits; registration and licencing of professionals, contractors, subcontractors, and trades; design and moral rights; copyright; the product produced from the Works; first nation people's rights; execution and standard of building work; property rights; liability for defective work; and nuisance.

In addition to the examples of general differences between civil law and common law systems identified in Chapter 1, there are a number of construction law specific issues where there may be differences in principle or arising from specific legislation between jurisdictions.[33] The following sections identify a range of issues that may be subject to legislation in a particular jurisdiction. They distinguish between the governing law of the contract, laws applicable to the execution of a construction project, and laws applicable to the resolution of disputes, since each of these may relate to different jurisdictions.

The following sections contain examples of applicable laws from various jurisdictions that illustrate the extent of legislation that construction practitioners need to be aware of.[34]

3.6.3 Applicable laws if the governing law is that of the jurisdiction

3.6.3.1 Entry into a construction contract

Issue	**Example**
Contracts generally	*Contract Law 1999* (China) *General Provisions of the Civil Law 2017* (China)
Construction contracts	*Civil Code* (France) Articles 1787 to 1799–1, and Article 1831–1 *Construction and Housing Code (Title II 'Promotion immobilière')* (France) *Code of Public Procurement* (France)

33 Statutory incursions into freedom of contract are discussed in more detail in ¶4.3.4.

34 These examples are taken from Donald Charrett (ed), *The International Application of FIDIC Contracts A Practical Guide* (Informa Law from Routledge, 2020). For each of the 18 jurisdictions in that book, the applicable laws are tabulated for the issues covered in 3.6.3, 3.6.4, and 3.6.5.

3.6.3.2 Termination of a construction contract

Issue	Example
Frustration/fundamental change of circumstances	*Interpretation II of the Supreme People's Court of Several Issues Concerning the Application of The Contract Law* (China)
Bankruptcy, insolvency, liquidation	*Enterprise Bankruptcy Law* (China)
Guarantees under forms of Security	*Civil Code* (France) Articles 2284*ff* *The Law of 16 July 1971* (France) on the regulation of retention guarantees applicable to private construction contracts

3.6.3.3 Dispute resolution

Issue	Example
Limitation periods	*General Provisions of the Civil Law 2017* (China)
Liability	*Contract Law 1999* (China) *Construction Law (2019 Amendment)* (China)
Adjudication	*Housing Grants, Construction and Regeneration Act 1996* (UK)
Arbitration	*Arbitration Law of the People's Republic of China (2017 Amendment)* (China)

3.6.4 Applicable laws if the Site is in the jurisdiction

3.6.4.1 Operation of a construction contract[35]

Issue	Example
Registration and administration of professionals – Engineers, Architects, Quantity Surveyors, Certifiers, Building Surveyors, Surveyors	*Construction Law (2019 Amendment)* (China) *Administrative Provisions on the Qualifications of Project Supervising Enterprises (2016 Amendment)* (China) *Administrative Provisions on Certified Jian Li (2016 Amendment)* (China) *Provisions on the Administration of Certified Constructors (2016 Amendment)* (China)
Registration/licencing of Contractors and subcontractors	*Administration of Qualifications of Enterprises in the Construction Industry (2018 Amendment)* (China)
Subcontracting	*Measures for the Administration on the Construction by Subcontract of House-building and Municipal Infrastructure Projects (2014 Amendment)* (China)
Use of liens/Assignment of debts	*Contract Law 1999* (China)
Retention money	*Measures for the Management of Construction Project Quality Deposits* (China)
Labour	*Labor Law (2018 Amendment)* (China) *Labor Contract Law (2012 Amendment)* (China)

35 Table 3.7 in ¶3.13 identifies which of these types of law apply in 18 jurisdictions.

Issue	Example
Design/Moral rights	*Regulation on the Administration of Survey and Design of Construction Projects (2017 Amendment)* (China)
Copyright	*Copyright Law (2010 Amendment)* (China) *Regulation for the Implementation of the Copyright Law (2013 Amendment)* (China)
Patent	*Patent Law (2008 Amendment)* (China) *Detailed Rules for the Implementation of the Patent Law (2010 Amendment)* (China) *Regulations on Construction Technology (2014 Amendment)* (China)
The product being produced from the Works	*Law of Integral Management of Solid Waste* (Legislative Decree N° 1278) (Peru)
First nation people's land rights	*Law of Native Communities and Agrarian Development of the Jungle* (Law Decree N° 22175) (Peru)
Work affecting adjacent property to the Site	*General Provisions of the Civil Law 2017* (China)
Heritage	*Cultural Relics Protection Law (2017 Amendment)* (China)
Environment	*Law of the People's Republic of China on Prevention and Control of Pollution from Environmental Noise (2018 Amendment)* (China) *Law of the People's Republic of China on Environmental Impact Assessment (2018 Amendment)* (China)
Planning	*Urban and Rural Planning Law (2015 Amendment)* (China)
Local procurement	*Public Finances (Management) Act 1995* (PNG)
Building and construction permits, execution of construction work	*Measures for the Administration of Construction Permits for Construction Projects (2018 Amendment)* (China)
Standard of construction work	*Regulations on the Quality Management of Construction Projects* (China)
Health and safety	*Regulations on the Safety Management of Construction Projects* (China)
Calibration of testing apparatus, equipment, and instruments	*National Building Regulation* (Peru)
Ownership of Plant and Materials	*Property Law* (China)
Employer's sale of Contractor's Equipment, surplus material, wreckage, and Temporary Works	*Civil Code* (France) Articles 1582*ff*
Insurance	*Social Insurance Law of the People's Republic of China (2018 Amendment)* (China)
Statutory rights that coexist with contractual rights	*Contract Law 1999* (China) *Construction Law (2019 Amendment)* (China)
Liability for defective work	*Construction Law (2019 Amendment)* (China) *Regulations on the Quality Management of Construction Projects* (China)
Liability for nuisance	*Civil Code* (France) Articles 1240*ff*

3.6.4.2 Termination of a construction contract[36]

Issue	Example
Bankruptcy, insolvency, liquidation	*Enterprise Bankruptcy Law* (China)
Decennial liability and liability generally for the total or partial collapse of structures	*Civil Code* (France) Articles 1792*ff* *Civil Code* (France) Articles 1240*ff*

3.6.5 Dispute resolution

Dispute before a local board / Adjudication	*Public Procurement Act* (Supreme Decree N° 082–2019-EF) and its *Regulation* (Supreme Decree N° 344–2018-EF) (Peru) *Public-Private Partnership Law* (Legislative Decree N° 1362) and its *Regulation* (Peru)
Limitation periods	*General Provisions of the Civil Law 2017* (China)

3.6.6 Applicable legislation if the 'seat' of the dispute determination is the jurisdiction[37]

Dispute resolution	*Code of Civil Procedure* (France)
Limitation periods	*General Provisions of the Civil Law 2017* (China)
Adjudication	*Construction Industry Payment and Adjudication Act 2012* (Malaysia)
Arbitration	*Arbitration Law of the People's Republic of China (2017 Amendment)* (China)

3.6.7 Freedom of contract

However, outside of specific statutory requirements, the parties' freedom to contract on their own terms will generally be recognised by courts, irrespective of conceptual and terminological differences:

> Conceptual incompatibilities between common-law-inspired FIDIC concepts and German law undeniably exist. However, German law should be taken as sufficiently flexible to tolerate different solutions as long as the legal outcome in terms of remedies, etc. is not totally different and does not additionally cause unacceptable disadvantage to the other Party. Since FIDIC contracts have been said to provide fairly balanced solutions, it is hardly arguable that German law requires the amendment of FIDIC wording in the event of merely formal differences between FIDIC wording or concepts on the one hand and German law on the other hand. For instance, it would be difficult to argue that German law requires the use of an Employer's agent and cannot tolerate a more independent role like that of the FIDIC Engineer.[38]

36 1 Table 3.8 in ¶3.13 identifies which of these types of law apply in 18 jurisdictions.

37 Table 3.9 in ¶3.13 identifies which of these types of law apply in 18 jurisdictions.

38 Götz-Sebastian Hök & Henry Stieglmeier, 'Chapter 10 Germany, 193' in Donald Charrett (ed), *The International Application of FIDIC Contracts A Practical Guide* (Informa Law from Routledge, 2020).

3.7 Case study: Statutory intervention arising from the impact of COVID-19

The worldwide advent of COVID-19 in 2020 resulted in an unprecedented range of legislation, firstly to deal with the health impacts, and secondly to deal with the economic impacts. That legislation significantly constrained freedom of contract in many situations, not least of which those laws and regulations that impacted construction projects and construction contracts. The legislative interventions that are relevant to construction were measures that constrained:

- The execution of construction projects,
- The operation of construction contracts, and
- Resolution of disputes arising out of COVID-19.

In some jurisdictions the impacts were a result of legislation specifically addressing the construction industry, and others were part of more general government actions to control the spread of COVID-19 or to provide economic support. The following are some of the COVID-19 specific measures introduced in various jurisdictions.

3.7.1 Execution of construction projects

Restrictions on travel – countries and regions closed their borders to non-residents, for example Australia closed its borders to non-residents and banned most international travel by residents; most Australian states closed their borders to residents of other states for months.

Shut down of construction sites – some countries shut down construction sites after the onset of infection, for example Singapore issued an advisory that all building works as defined in the *Building Control Act* were required to cease with effect from 7 April 2020 to 4 May 2020; Malaysia only permitted 'essential services' to operate in the period from 18 March to 31 March. The Philippines only permitted construction of essential facilities (health care facilities and isolation quarantine facilities) and priority projects under the Build Build Build Infrastructure Program to continue during the period of enhanced community quarantine from 16 March 2020. Small-scale construction activities intended for private and personal use were permitted during the subsequent period of modified enhanced community quarantine.

Constraints on working on construction sites – for example following a more severe second wave of infections in Victoria in July 2020, the operation of construction projects was restricted as follows:

- Large-scale construction comprising any project of more than three stories was limited to a maximum of 25% of normal employees on-site compared to normal operations, a high risk COVID-19 safe plan was required, and workers could only work at one site in a discrete shift.
- Small-scale construction comprising any building project of three stories or less was limited to a maximum of five workers (including supervisors), a universal COVID-19 safe plan was required, and workers could only work at one site in a discrete shift.
- State and civil construction projects were exempt from reduction targets but were required to implement a high risk COVID-19 safe plan.

Increased hours of working – for example New South Wales permitted construction sites to operate on weekends and public holidays irrespective of what consents might otherwise allow.

Physical distancing was the primary method of protection mandated in many countries, requiring all persons outside their homes to be separated by a distance of 1.0, 1.5, 1.8, or 2 metres.

Additional OHS precautions – many jurisdictions required additional health precautions to be implemented, for example wearing of face masks outside the home. Singapore issued an advisory on supporting mental well-being of workers under COVID-19 work arrangements; the Philippines required temperature checks prior to entering workplaces.[39]

Stringent cleaning protocols were required including frequent handwashing and sanitizing, by regularly and frequently disinfecting contact surfaces in an endeavour to prevent infection, and deep cleaning of premises where infection had occurred.

Enhanced documentation of employees – for example Singapore required mandatory daily declarations and updating by employers of work permits in the construction sector on stay-home notices; Victoria mandated enhanced record keeping to ensure that persons who had been in close contact with an infected person could be identified, advised, and tested.

Isolation of infected personnel – personnel diagnosed with COVID-19 were required to isolate from others, typically for a period of 14 days.

Quarantine – many countries required incoming travellers to be quarantined for 14 days. Some countries required particular areas of high risk to be quarantined from outside contact, for example Singapore issued an advisory requiring foreign employees in the construction sector to be quarantined in their accommodation from 20 April to 4 May.

Labour laws – some constraints on the employment of labour were temporarily put in abeyance, for example in Singapore employers were permitted to introduce flexible work schedules to use unused working hours to offset overtime hours; the Philippines permitted (1) reduction of workhours and/or workdays per week; (2) rotation of workers or alternately provided work within the week; and (3) forced leave, where the employees were required to go on leave for several days a week or weeks utilising any leave credits.[40]

Labour payments – some countries introduced new requirements to protect the incomes of infected persons, for example in Indonesia the salary of a documented infected worker was required to be paid in full for up to 14 days, a worker categorised as a suspect COVID-19 infection and quarantined/isolated was required to be paid in full during the quarantine/ isolation period, and a worker unable to work due to COVID-19 illness was required to be paid wages in accordance with applicable laws. Singapore required employers to notify the Ministry of Manpower of any cost-saving measures affecting employee's salaries.

3.7.2 Operation of construction contracts

3.7.2.1 Philippines

The Philippines Department of Labor and Employment issued Labor Advisory No 18 of 2020 applying to all employers, including contractors and subcontractors in the private sector that specified:

> The employer shall shoulder the cost of COVID-19 prevention and control measures such as but not limited to the following: testing, disinfection facilities, hand sanitisers, personal

39 Philippines Department of Public Works and Highways (DPWH) Department Order No. 39, series of 2020, dated 19 May 2020.

40 DOLE Labor Advisory No. 18, series of 2020, dated 16 May 2020.

protective equipment (PPEs, ie face mask), proper orientation and training of workers including IEC materials on COVID-19 prevention and control.[41]

3.7.2.2 Singapore[42]

Singapore acted early to provide relief for the impacts of the pandemic in the *COVID-19 (Temporary Measures) Act 2020* (Sin) (*the Act*), passed on 7 April 2020. Part 2 of the *Act* contains a number of measures for temporary relief for inability to perform an obligation in a scheduled contract after 1 February 2020 caused by a COVID-19 event.

The *Act* provides for a prescribed period of six months. A construction contract is a scheduled contract. The *Act* provides that where a party (A) to a scheduled contract is unable to perform a contractual obligation caused to a material extent by a COVID-19 event and has served a notification for relief with the other party or parties to the contract (B), then despite any law or anything in the contract, B may not take a number of actions for the specified period. The prohibited actions included commencing or continuing court or arbitral proceedings, enforcement of security, making an application for bankruptcy, or winding up or termination of a contract. Any applicable *force majeure* clause in the Contract and the *Frustrated Contracts Act* (Singapore) will prevail over the provisions of the *Act*.

Section 6 of the *Act* provides for additional relief for inability to perform an obligation in a construction or supply contract as a consequence of a COVID-19 event:

- Subject to specified conditions, the term of a performance bond is to be extended to a date seven days after the end of the prescribed period.
- B may not make a call on the performance bond for the specified period.
- For the purposes of calculating liquidated damages payable under the Contract after 1 February 2020 and before the expiry of the prescribed period, any period for which the inability exists is to be disregarded in determining the period of delay.
- The inability to perform an obligation in the Contract to a material extent caused by a COVID-19 event is a defence to a claim for a breach of contract for the period after 1 February 2020 and before the expiry of the prescribed period.

The *Act* also provides for an assessor to determine whether the non-performance of a party was in fact due to a COVID-19 event, and 'seek to achieve an outcome that is just and equitable in the circumstances of the case.' The assessor's determination may require a party to the contract to do anything or pay any sum of money to discharge any obligations under the Contract and require a party to a contract to pay reasonable costs incurred by another party in the performance of the Contract. With leave of the court, judgement may be entered in the terms of the assessor's determination.[43]

The measures in the *Act* are only temporary and will only freeze legal rights and obligations in place while it is in force, allowing proceedings to be commenced, if necessary, after the prescribed period.

41 Guidelines on the Cost of COVID-19 Prevention and Control Measures, 18 May 2020, www.dole.gov.ph/news/labor-advisory-no-18-series-of-2020-guidelines-on-the-cost-of-covid-19-prevention-and-control-measures/ (accessed 6 August 2020).

42 The *COVID-19 (Temporary Measures) Act 2020* (Sin) is discussed in more detail in chapter 12 of Donald Charrett, *Contracts for Construction and Engineering Projects* (Informa Law from Routledge, 2nd edn 2021).

43 Ibid. Part 2 Division 4.

3.8 Implied terms in construction contracts

A number of terms are implied by law as an incident of construction contracts, to the extent that they are not displaced by the explicit contract terms. Bailey identified a number of terms implied by the common law specific to construction contracts, including the following:[44]

- The materials used will be of good and proper quality.
- The work performed by the Contractor in a design and construct contract will be reasonably fit for the purpose which is agreed or known by the Contractor when it entered the Contract.[45]
- The materials supplied and the workmanship in a construct-only contract will be fit for their purpose, to the extent they are within the Contractor's control.
- The Contractor will perform its work properly, including completing the work it has undertaken, and in a good and workmanlike manner.
- The Contractor will use due skill and care in performing its contractual obligations.

These implied terms are discussed in more detail under the relevant chapters later.

As noted in ¶2.14, in addition to terms implied by the courts *ad hoc* in order to give construction contracts business efficacy, certain statutes also imply certain contract terms. The provisions of each such statute must be construed to determine whether such implied terms are mandatory or can be contracted out of by the parties. This issue is considered further later in the chapter.

In some cases, the courts will imply a term into a contract because it was obviously intended by the parties' conduct. In *Trollope and Colls Ltd v Atomic Power Construction Ltd*,[46] the subcontractors were asked by the Head Contractor to commence work before all the terms of the subcontract work had been agreed after the submission of tender. The court held that a term was to be implied in the subcontract that the Variation clause in that contract applied retrospectively to the valuation of changes made before the contract was finalised. In *Dong v Monkiro Pty Ltd*, Hall J quoted the *Trollope* decision and stated:

> [t]he law has adopted a practical approach to the operation of commercial contracts having regard to earlier dealings between contracting parties. The law does not assume that acceptance of an offer cannot have retrospective effect so as to make the contract apply to things done earlier in anticipation of the contract.[47]

The courts will take notice of any reasonable custom that can be proved satisfactorily, even if it gives an unusual meaning to the words used. For example, in *Patman & Fotheringham Ltd v Pilditch*,[48] the custom that figured dimensions are to be preferred to scaled dimensions was referred to.

Implied terms are not confined to common law systems. The *UNIDROIT Principles of International Commercial Contracts* (discussed in ¶2.7 and ¶4.7.1) provide in Article 5.1.1

44 Julian Bailey, *Construction Law Volume I* (Informa Law, 1st edn 2011) 163–189.
45 *Independent Broadcasting Authority v EMI Electronics* (1980) 14 BLR 1, 48 per Lord Scarman.
46 [1963] 1 WLR 333, [1962] 3 All ER 1035 (QB).
47 [2005] NSWSC 749, [63].
48 (1904) Alfred A Hudson, *Hudson's Fourth Edition Table of Cases* (Sweet & Maxwell, 4th edn 1914) 372.

that 'The contractual obligations of the parties may be express or implied.' Article 5.1.2 provides the possible sources of implied obligations that may go further than under the common law:

> Implied obligations stem from
> (a) the nature and purpose of the contract;
> (b) practices established between the parties and usages;
> (c) good faith and fair dealing;
> (d) reasonableness.

3.9 Standard contract forms and 'bespoke' contracts

3.9.1 Forms of construction contract

Written construction contracts take one of the following general forms:

- Standard form contract,
- Standard form contract with modifications, and
- Bespoke contract, specifically written for a particular construction contract.

Every construction contract is unique in a number of ways, at least because of the identity of the contracting parties and location of the construction site and the nature and timing of the Works to be carried out at that Site. Conversely, there is a large measure of standardisation in the provisions of contracts of a particular type, because of the desire of contracting parties not to 'reinvent the wheel,' and to obtain the economic benefits of a predictable contractual environment which reduces the transaction costs of negotiating and entering into a contract. This standardisation of contractual terms has led to the evolution of a number of standard form contracts, prepared by a range of organisations. As used here, a **standard form contract** refers to General Conditions of contract prepared by an organisation independent of the contracting parties, in a standard form intended to be used by many parties for a number and range of construction contracts of a particular type.

Standard form contracts have a long history in the common law world. Bailey notes that there were a number of standard forms that were in use in England by the end of the nineteenth century prepared by the War Department, the Builder's Association and the Institute of British Architects, and the London County Council.[49] In 1888 the American Institute of Architects and the National Association of Builders co-sponsored the 'Uniform Contract,' the first national standard form contract in the USA.[50]

The project, party, Site- and construction-specific 'legal' requirements are frequently recorded in what are termed the Special Conditions (or **Particular Conditions**) of a standard form contract, usually prepared by lawyers. Special Conditions may also be required to replace or supplement General Conditions that are inconsistent with mandatory law, where it is desirable to draw attention to relevant applicable laws that must be complied with, or where the Employer wishes to change some provisions (often the risk allocation) in the

49 Julian Bailey, *Construction Law* (Informa Law, 1st edn 2011) 116.

50 Justin Sweet, 'The Historical Emergence of Construction Law' (2007) 34(1) *William Mitchell Law Review* 6.

General Conditions. Clearly, the Special Conditions for a construction contract must be prepared specifically for the particular requirements of the individual circumstances of that contract, as the technical documents (specifications, drawings etc) must also be.

3.9.2 Standard form contracts

The General Conditions of a standard form contract define the legal obligations of each party to the contract in respect of the issues arising that are known from the long history of construction contracts to be of general and widespread application. Typically, a standard form contract is the result of a collaborative effort of a number of people with a range of perspectives on how such contracts have operated in the past, and how they should operate in the future. Most such standard form contracts are the result of an evolutionary process, in which successive editions take account of previous operational experience and the difficulties of interpretation or implementation that have been identified by courts in the published case law, or by changes in relevant legislation.

The form of contract (or suite of contracts) published by any organisation will reflect a particular view on how the various types of risk are to be allocated between the contracting parties for any particular type of construction contract. Within the generally accepted risk allocation for a particular type of contract, many standard form contracts aim to allocate risk to the contracting party best able to manage it (known as the **Abrahamson Principles**[51]), whereas other standard form contracts implicitly or explicitly endeavour to put one of the contracting parties in an advantageous position with respect to allocation of certain risks. Accordingly, it is important to understand the provenance of a standard form contract that is proposed to be used.

3.9.2.1 The need for different standard forms

Part of the evolution of standard form contracts over the last 20 or 30 years has been the recognition that different types of construction contracts have distinctly different requirements, and that standard form contracts should be prepared accordingly. The range of procurement options now in use for major projects demands a greater variety of contractual provisions than are provided by a single standard form contract. Whereas in the past a single form contract was advocated for construction work, project experience has demonstrated the pitfalls of using a standard form contract in circumstances for which it was not designed.

For example, construction of Parliament House in Canberra was procured in the 1980s by construction management of 320 trade subcontracts in a **fast track** design and construction process.[52] The Employer entered into the major trade contracts using a Construction Manager as both agent and superintendent. The trade contracts used a largely unamended version of the NPWC3 Edition 3 contract, a standard form government contract designed for use in traditional lump sum construction contracts. Parliament House Construction Authority recognised that this standard form contract was not ideally suited to the project,

---

51 Max W Abrahamson, 'Risk Management' (1983) *International Construction Law Review* 241, 244.

52 For a discussion of the procurement of the Australian Parliament House, see Donald Charrett, *The Application of Contracts in Construction and Engineering Projects* (Informa Law from Routledge, 2nd edn 2022) 188–193.

since it was not designed for construction management or fast track delivery of design and construction; however, at that time there was no suitable alternative.[53] In its report on the management experience of Project Parliament, the Australian Parliament House Authority highlighted the inappropriateness of such *ad hoc* adaptation, and suggested that the need to develop a suitable form of contract conditions for construction management was one of the most important lessons from the project.[54]

Standard form contracts specific to each type of construction contract are now available, so that it is generally unnecessary for users to make modifications to the General Conditions to use, for example, a standard form contract designed for construction only for a project procured by construction management.

3.9.2.2 Advantages of standard form contracts

There are many advantages of using a standard form contract (particularly one that aims to be even-handed as between the contracting parties), including more certainty in the meaning of contract terms and reduced contracting costs. The meaning of the words used in specific clauses of standard form contracts have been considered judicially in published case law, and such a judge's determination of the meaning of the words used would normally provide a persuasive precedent for other judges to follow in respect of the same wording. Such judicial pronouncements do not however constitute legal authority, since every contract must be construed as a whole, and the terms of a standard contract must therefore be construed in relation to their use in the particular circumstances:

> The decision on a particular contract cannot amount to a principle of law. It follows that a court should always be open to persuasion that a decision, even of a higher court, on the construction of the same standard form was erroneous. The same applies *a fortiori* to arbitration.[55]

The case for a standard and more efficient approach to contracting in the oil and gas industry for the UK continental shelf has been well articulated as follows:

> Invitations to Tender issued by UKCS [UK continental shelf] operators in the past typically contained individual specific contract terms and conditions. More often than not these terms would differ from the form previously seen by contractors thus necessitating a fresh review on each and every occasion. A variety of contracts, legal and project/operational personnel will typically be involved in this process. The contract form issued by the operator would normally be drafted in the operator's favour, anticipating, and receiving, lengthy qualifications by tenderers. Tenderers in turn would demand more concessions than they would expect the operator to agree to as 'negotiation' was expected. Often lengthy discussion followed, involving many individuals, before an agreed position was reached.
>
> The above process, on an industry wide basis, taking into account the number of operators, contractors and suppliers involved in the whole range of exploration, development and production activities covered, has a very significant resource and cost impact.
>
> What does this process achieve? For many who have worked with this arrangement over many years the belief is that that it achieved very little. Risk is not managed or allocated where it can

53 Parliament House Construction Authority, Commonwealth, *Project Parliament: The Management Experience* (Commonwealth of Australia, 1990) 115.

54 Ibid. 32.

55 John Uff, 'The Interplay of Contract Terms and Common Law' (Paper given at a meeting of the Society of Construction Law, 5 November 1991) 2.

> most appropriately be borne, rather it is pushed from one party to another depending on prevailing market conditions. Additional insurance costs can result and contract costs may be increased due to uncertainties and/or contingencies being added. Ultimately, however, the contracts that are signed by different operators and contractors often end up being remarkably alike.[56]

It is noteworthy that the large UK oil and gas industry promotes the economic advantages arising from a standard approach to contracting, whereas the Australian oil and gas and other resource industries still seem to be wedded to the approach of bespoke contracts (generally written on behalf of the owner/operator Employer) with conditions of contract peculiar to each owner/operator and each project. It is suggested that the use of bespoke contracts ultimately achieves very little other than adding unnecessary costs and uncertainty to the contracting process. Any apparent advantage that may appear to be achieved by the use of contracts that alter the traditional 'balance' between Employer and Contractor by transferring risk to the Contractor is likely to be illusory, because of higher costs either on the current or future contracts. A rational Contractor will increase its tender price if it understands that a particular form of contract requires it to accept risks that it cannot properly manage. Any lack of Contractor understanding of such risks leads to underpricing its tender. This may appear to give an advantage to the Employer but is likely to result in increased disputation under the contract and higher costs on future contracts, arising from the collective understanding of the performance of contracts within the construction industry.[57]

3.9.3 Standard contract forms with modifications

One of the potential drawbacks to the use of standard form contracts is that, because of the variety of interest groups involved in their production, the ultimate form of the General Conditions as published may represent a compromise between conflicting interests which may not be totally acceptable to anyone.[58] The inevitable result is modifications to the standard terms which must be negotiated between the contracting parties prior to entry into the Contract. The ambit of such modifications will generally depend on the extent to which the contracting parties are not prepared to accept the allocation of risk provided for in the standard terms.

To the extent that each such proposed modification of a standard form contract requires careful assessment of the potential cost and risk by each contracting party, there may be little difference from the process involved in negotiating a bespoke contract. However, provided the cumulative effect of such nonstandard terms is not such as to change the entire character of the standard form of contract, the departures from the norm can be readily identified and assessed.

---

56 Standard Contract for the U.K. Offshore Oil and Gas Industry General Conditions of Contract for Construction Part 2 Guidance Notes, Edition 2 October 2003, published by LOGIC (Leading Oil and Gas Industry Competitiveness) 1.

57 Philip Loots, 'Construction of Major Infrastructure Projects in the Energy Sector: Controlling Spiralling Development Costs' (2013) *AMPLA Yearbook* 173.

58 Whilst standard form contracts are widely used in Australia, a 2014 survey revealed that 84% of standard forms were amended. The incidence of modification of Australian standard forms ranged from 88% for AS4000 to 98% for AS4300: Professor John Sharkey, Matthew Bell et al, 'Standard Forms of Contract in the Australian Construction Industry' (June 2014) *The University of Melbourne* 35. A subsequent attempt to update AS2124–1992 and AS4000–1997 resulted in a draft for public comment DR AS11000:2015 that did not achieve a consensus, and accordingly has not been issued.

The clearest way of incorporating such departures from a standard form is to include the amendments in the Special Conditions or by means of 'red lining' the original text to ensure that all additions and deletions are clearly and unambiguously identified. Deviation from the General Conditions in this way allows the parties to identify such changes readily and is preferable to the rewriting of the General Conditions incorporating the desired modifications. If standard form General Conditions have been rewritten, much time may later be wasted by all parties associated with the project in attempting to locate and identify amendments which have been made, omissions often being the most difficult of these. Only once this has been done can the significance of the amendments be established and quantified.

The importance of carefully assessing all amendments to the General Conditions of a standard form contract cannot be overemphasised.[59] The case law is replete with examples of such amendments where ill-considered amendments or deletions have resulted in a contract that failed to provide adequately for circumstances that were foreseen in the standard form General Conditions.

3.9.3.1 The consequences of inappropriate amendment of standard form contracts

The Japan International Cooperation Agency (**JICA**) has formulated sample bidding documents for use in connection with civil works contracts for which it provides loan funds. These sample documents incorporate the FIDIC MDB Harmonised Edition 2010 and the FIDIC Plant and Design Build Contract (1st edn 1999) (see ¶3.10.1 later) which JICA considers balance the risks fairly between the Employer and the Contractor. It strongly discourages modifications to these contract conditions such that this balanced risk allocation is upset, highlighting the following potential consequences of excessively high risks allocated to the Contractor:

(1) Higher bid price,
(2) Bid failure and disruption of project implementation,
(3) Non-participation in the bid of conscientious and capable contractors,
(4) Contract award to a bidder who fails or was not capable of estimating the risks properly,
(5) Poor construction quality and delay to the progress of the work due to lack of risk contingency,
(6) Undermining the relationship of mutual trust and respect between the Employer and the Contractor,
(7) Repetition of groundless claims from the Contractor,
(8) Frequent disputes between the Employer and the Contractor, and
(9) In an extreme case eventual termination of the contract.[60]

JICA notes that if the originally contemplated risk distribution in a standard form contract is altered to a large extent and the risks allocated to the Contractor become excessively

59 The extent of modifications to standard forms in Australia is such that the Special Conditions may be longer than the General Conditions that they modify: Professor John Sharkey, Matthew Bell et al, 'Standard Forms of Contract in the Australian Construction Industry' (June 2014) *The University of Melbourne* 35.

60 Japan International Cooperation Agency (JICA), 'Check List for One Sided Contracts' (2011) 1, www.jica.go.jp/english/our_work/types_of_assistance/oda_loans/oda_op_info/guide/c8h0vm0000aoeprl-att/guide02.pdf (accessed 21 May 2021).

high, 'These situations interfere with the smooth implementation of projects financed by Japanese ODA loans and, may not bring the Employer any good result.'[61]

Higher bid prices as a consequence of unbalanced contracts are also noted by ConsensusDocs in the USA: 'Studies show risk-shifting clauses easily increase prices by 20%; fair contracts avoid inflated contingencies.'[62]

3.9.4 Bespoke contracts

Bespoke contracts for large construction projects are very common in Australia; they are frequently drawn up by solicitors who are very experienced in construction law and usually acting for the Employer. Accordingly, it can be expected that bespoke construction contracts included in tender documents will be more 'Employer friendly,' and the risk allocation may be significantly different to the standard form construction contracts. A tenderer faced with a proposed bespoke contract should ensure that the terms are very carefully and thoroughly scrutinised by an experienced construction lawyer to determine the impact of the risk allocation and other contract terms, and to propose acceptable alternatives if necessary. Such a process is invariably expensive, as it requires high calibre legal resources to go through each clause and consider its likely operation in the light of the contract as a whole, existing case law, and the usual allocation of risks as between Contractor and Employer. Even if major issues such as price and timing of a tender are acceptable, the importance of and time and energy involved in negotiating a substantial number of significant changes to a proposed contract should not be underestimated.

It is trite that the actual terms of the contract that the parties enter into will govern their contractual relationship for the duration of the contract and in respect of its termination. Those terms can be very one-sided, unreasonable, and unfair, but if that is the bargain that the parties have made (and it is not contrary to public policy or statute), a court or an Arbitrator will enforce it strictly in accordance with its terms. A party signing up to a bespoke contract should be under no illusions as to the likely outcome of terms that favour the other party: it should be assumed that those terms will be administered and enforced to achieve the expressed contractual intention. Even in the context of partnering or alliancing contracts, it would be naive to assume that the formal contract will be 'tucked away in a drawer' and not used in the day-to-day administration of the contractual relationship.

The application of the following chapters to bespoke (and standard form) contracts should be read in the knowledge that the case law referred to may not be relevant in a particular case because of differences in contract wording, or because of specific provisions in the bespoke contract which change the 'normal' situation covered by the common law.

3.10 Standard form contracts

In response to the use of different methods of project procurement and changes to traditional risk allocation, the standard contract forms of the twenty-first century have evolved to a level of variety and complexity not seen in earlier versions. The range of standard form contracts has expanded

61 Ibid.

62 www.consensusdocs.org/wp-content/uploads/2019/05/10-Reasons-Why-Brochure.pdf (accessed 25 May 2021).

considerably to encompass most if not all of the commonly used methods of procurement. Standard forms have also been prepared to cater for the demands of more risk to be borne by the Contractor than is the case in traditional standard form contracts. Further, the inevitable demand for project-specific modifications to standard forms has led to the incorporation of more alternative options for specific clauses to cater for the wide range of user preferences, particularly in the area of risk allocation. The availability of computerised tools to prepare a number of the standard form contracts with optional or alternative clauses greatly simplifies the mechanical process of producing contract documents and thereby reduces the cost.[63]

Standard form construction contracts are produced by different organisations in many countries. *The International Compendium of Construction Contracts* discusses the standard form construction contracts most commonly used in 37 countries.[64] A table in that book identifies the 'construction law' issues that are covered by the standard form contracts in those 37 countries. Of the 15 issues identified there is no uniformity as to which of those issues are covered, for example the standard form contract in Austria covers only three of the issues, whereas 13 of the issues are covered by the standard form contract in Ecuador.

In addition to the contracts identified in *The International Compendium of Construction Contracts*, there are standard form contracts in other countries, and standard forms for government projects, for example the Government of NSW uses its own GC21 contract.[65] Various professional organisations publish standard forms of contract, for example:

- Engineering Advancement Association of Japan, ENAA Model Form International Contract for Power Plant Construction (2012);
- Institution of Engineering and Technology, Model Form of Contract MF/ 1 (Revision 6) for the design, supply, and installation of electrical, electronic, and mechanical plant (2014); and
- The Association of Consulting Architects (UK) publishes a suite of partnering contracts, a suite of alliance contracts and standard form contracts for buildings and subcontracts.[66]

The International Chamber of Commerce (**ICC**) is the institutional representative of more than 45 million companies in over 100 countries. It publishes a number of standard form contracts for cross-border agreements, intended to be fair and balanced for all parties by defining comprehensive sets of rights and obligations. These include the following construction contracts:

- ICC Model Turnkey Contract for Major Projects (2007),
- ICC Model Subcontract, and
- ICC Model Contract for the Turnkey Supply of an Industrial Plant.[67]

63 For example, the US ConsensusDocs contracts use Microsoft Word based technology to allow easy customisation of over 100 contract documents to suit individual project requirements. The collaboration technology allows control of who has access to review or edit documents and maintains a version control system. www.consensusdocs.org/contracts/# (accessed 25 May 2021).

64 Phillip Greenham & the Society of Construction Law Australia (eds), *The International Compendium of Construction Contracts* (De Gruyter, 2021).

65 https://buy.nsw.gov.au/resources/gc21 (accessed 25 May 2021).

66 https://acarchitects.co.uk/publications/ (accessed 25 May 2021).

67 https://iccwbo.org/content/uploads/sites/3/2016/11/ICC-Model-Contracts-Catalogue-1.pdf (accessed 27 May 2021).

ConsensusDocs is a suite of standard form construction contracts endorsed by 36 participating associations in the USA representing design professionals, owners, constructors, subcontractors, and sureties. The aim of these contracts is as follows:

> ConsensusDocs contracts and forms attempt to fairly and appropriately allocate risks to the Party in the position to manage and control the risk. The practices articulated in the documents are forward-thinking, and may not always represent the status quo, but rather a better path forward to achieve project results. The goal of the multi-disciplined drafters was to create documents that best place the Parties to a construction contract in a position to complete a project on time and on budget with the highest possibility of avoiding claims.[68]

ConsensusDocs publishes 'over 100 documents that incorporate fair risk allocation and best practices to represent the project's best interests.' The following categories illustrate the wide range of contracting models now available in standard form contracts:

- General contracting,
- Collaborative,
- Design-build,
- CM [Construction Management] At-Risk,
- Subcontracting,
- Program Management, and
- Public-Private Partnership.[69]

The Institution of Chemical Engineers publishes a suite of contracts for creating new process plants and working on existing structures. They are drafted by a team of legal and industry professionals to reflect best practice for project delivery in the process industries.[70] The international contracts have been prepared to reflect the particular needs of international contracting in various jurisdictions:

- Lump Sum, The International Red Book, first edition, 2007;
- Reimbursable, The International Green Book, first edition, 2007;
- Target Cost, The International Burgundy Book, first edition, 2007; and
- Subcontracts, The International Yellow Book, first edition, 2007.[71]

The following sections contain details of the two most important standard form contracts intended for international construction contracts.

3.10.1 FIDIC

The *Fédération Internationale des Ingénieurs-Conseils* (FIDIC) (known by its English name of the International Federation of Consulting Engineers) is an organisation representing independent consulting engineers. It publishes standard form Conditions of Contract that are used in many countries and are probably the most widely used for international

---

68 ConsensusDocs Guidebook (2020) 5, www.consensusdocs.org/wp-content/uploads/2020/05/All-Associations.Guidebook.November.2020Updates.pdf (accessed 27 May 2021).
69 www.consensusdocs.org/contracts/ (accessed 27 May 2021).
70 www.icheme.org/knowledge/forms-of-contract/ (accessed 28 May 2021).
71 www.icheme.org/knowledge/forms-of-contract/the-contracts/ (accessed 28 May 2021).

construction contracts in the world. Although they have a common law pedigree, they are intended to be used in any legal jurisdiction whether common law, civil law, or any other type of law. The first FIDIC contract was published in 1957, based on the fourth edition of the Institution of Civil Engineers (**ICE**) Conditions of Contract. The first edition of the ICE contract was published in 1945.

FIDIC standard form contracts are prepared by a Contracts Committee appointed by the FIDIC Board. The Contracts Committee comprises engineers and lawyers from both common law and civil law jurisdictions. Draft contracts are circulated for friendly review by engineers and lawyers from around the world – there were 43 friendly reviewers of the 2017 Silver Book from 24 countries. Some proposed updates have been printed as a Test Edition that was subsequently revised for the final edition based on feedback from users. The large number of individuals involved from many countries with extensive contract, construction, engineering, and legal skills highlights FIDIC's comprehensive process of drafting contracts that acknowledge the importance of the many stakeholders, and their endeavours to produce balanced contracts that represent best international practice.

FIDIC General Conditions are explicitly based on a fair and equitable risk/reward allocation between the Employer and Contractor in conformance with the Abrahamson Principles and are widely recognised as striking an appropriate balance between the reasonable expectations of the contracting parties.[72]

The FIDIC contracts clearly have a common law 'pedigree' but are intended to be (and are) used where the law of the contract is a civil law jurisdiction. They are rarely used in Australia, Canada, Singapore, the UK, France, and Germany, no doubt because of the widespread use of local standard form contracts which have evolved to meet the specific requirements and usages in those jurisdictions. Of the 38 countries in *The International Compendium of Construction Contracts*, FIDIC contracts are noted as used in 21 countries, including in Europe, Asia, the Middle East, Africa, and South America.

It is suggested that their use in many countries may be promoted by the need to attract the expertise of international contractors to construct modern, large scale infrastructure, as well as the influence of multilateral development banks (**MDBs**) which often provide financing. A number of MDBs use FIDIC General Conditions in their Standard Bidding Documents. MDBs that have embraced FIDIC General Conditions include the World Bank, Asian Development Bank, Black Sea Trade & Development Bank, European Bank for Reconstruction and Development, Caribbean Development Bank, and the Inter-American Development Bank. The extensive international input into the drafting of FIDIC General Conditions and its acceptance as an appropriate contract for international contracts is evidenced by the World Bank's implementation of the 2017 Red Book in its 2019 Standard Procurement Document.[73]

The standard forms of construction contract between Employer and Contractor, subcontracts between Contractor and subcontractor, and guides shown in Table 3.3 are available from FIDIC.[74]

72 FIDIC, *The FIDIC Golden Principles* (FIDIC, 1st edn 2019).

73 http://pubdocs.worldbank.org/en/865231562944956956/SPD-Request-for-Bids-WORKS-after-prequalification.docx (accessed 28 August 2020).

74 These FIDIC contracts were listed on the FIDIC website (www.fidic.org/bookshop) (accessed 25 May 2021).

Table 3.3 FIDIC Contracts available in 2021[75]

	Works Contract	**Subcontract**	**Guide**
Red Book	Conditions of Contract for Works of Civil Engineering Construction – Third Edition 1977		
	Fourth Edition 1987	Conditions of Subcontract for Work of Civil Engineering Construction – First Edition 1994	Red Book (1987 Red Book) Guide – First Edition 1989 EC Corbett, *FIDIC 4th – A Practical Legal Guide* (Sweet & Maxwell, 1991) Standard Letters and Notices
	First Edition 1999	Conditions of Subcontract for Construction – First Edition 2011	FIDIC Contracts (1999 editions) Guide – First Edition 2000 EIC [European International Contractor's] Contractors Guide to the FIDIC Construction Contract (1999 Red Book) 2001
	Second Edition 2017		
Yellow Book	Conditions of Contract for Electrical and Mechanical Works – Third Edition 1987;		Electrical and Mechanical Works (1987 Yellow Book) Guide – First Edition 1988
	Conditions of Contract for Plant and Design-Build – First Edition 1999	Conditions of Subcontract for Plant and Design (Yellow Book 1999) – First Edition 2019	FIDIC Contracts (1999 editions) Guide – First Edition 2000 EIC [European International Contractor's] Contractors Guide to the FIDIC Construction Contract (1999 Red Book) 2001
	Second Edition 2017		
Orange Book	Conditions of Contract for Design-Build and Turnkey – First Edition 1995		Design-Build and Turnkey (1995 Orange Book) Guide – First Edition 1996
Silver Book	Conditions of Contract for EPC/Turnkey Projects – First Edition 1999		FIDIC Contracts (1999 editions) Guide – First Edition 2000 EIC Contractors Guide to the FIDIC EPC/Turnkey Contract (1999 Silver Book) – Second Edition 2003
	Second Edition 2017		

75 Documents listed on the FIDIC bookshop website https://fidic.org/bookshop (accessed 25 May 2021).

	Works Contract	Subcontract	Guide
Pink Book	Conditions of Contract for Construction – Multilateral Development Bank Harmonised Edition for Building and Engineering Works Designed by the Employer – Version 1: 2005		
	Version 2: 2006		Guide to the March 2006 release of the MDB Harmonised Construction Contract
	Version 3: 2010		
Green Book	Short Form of Contract – First Edition 1999		
Gold Book	Conditions of Contract for Design, Build and Operate Projects – First Edition 2008		DBO (2008 Gold Book) Contract Guide – First Edition 2011
Blue-Green Book	Form of Contract for Dredging and Reclamation Works – First Edition 2006		
	Second Edition 2016		
Emerald Book	Conditions of Contract for Underground Works – First Edition 2019		

The major contracts, often referred to as the **rainbow suite** because of the distinctive colour of their covers, cover the major types of construction contract used internationally: construction of the design prepared by the Employer, design and construct, and EPC/turnkey. There are differences between the standard forms in the rainbow suite in who carries out the design (Employer or Contractor), who administers the contract (Engineer or Employer's Representative), the form of Dispute Board (standing or ad hoc, DAB or DAAB), and how the Contractor is paid (remeasurement of lump sum). These differences are summarised for the 1999 and 2017 rainbow suite in Table 3.4.[76]

One of the advantages of using a FIDIC standard form contract is the wealth of information available in books and articles that provide detailed guidance on the rainbow suite; a number of these are listed in the references.

3.10.2 New Engineering Contract

The New Engineering Contracts (**NEC**) are published by the Institution of Civil Engineers (ICE). The first edition of NEC was released in 1993 following a fundamental review of alternative contract strategies, and a belief that existing standard form contracts (including

76 An outline of the differences between the 1999 and 2017 rainbow suites is in: Donald Charrett, *Contracts for Engineering and Construction Projects* (Informa Law from Routledge, 2nd edn 2022) Chapter 11.

Table 3.4 Differences between 1999 and 2017 FIDIC standard forms of contract between Employer and Contractor

<table>
<tr><th>Red Book First Edition 1999</th><th>Red Book Second Edition 2017</th><th>Yellow Book First Edition 1999</th><th>Yellow Book Second Edition 2017</th><th>Silver Book First Edition 1999</th><th>Silver Book Second Edition 2017</th></tr>
<tr><td colspan="2">Design by Employer</td><td colspan="4">Design by Contractor</td></tr>
<tr><td colspan="4">Contract administered by Engineer</td><td colspan="2">Contract administered by Employer's Representative</td></tr>
<tr><td>Standing DAB</td><td>Standing DAAB</td><td>Ad hoc DAB</td><td>Standing DAAB</td><td>Ad hoc DAB</td><td>Standing DAAB</td></tr>
<tr><td colspan="2">Contractor paid on remeasurement basis</td><td colspan="4">Contractor paid on lump sum basis</td></tr>
</table>

the ICE Conditions of Contract) did not represent the best interests of the parties. NEC was drafted from the beginning without making use of any other contract. NEC employs a radically different approach to the ICE Conditions of Contract, the last (seventh) edition of which was published in 1999. The drafters' aims were that the new NEC contract would:

- Be more flexible in its scope than existing standard forms,
- Provide a greater stimulus to the good management of projects than existing standard forms, and
- Be expressed more simply and clearly than existing forms.[77]

The resulting suite of contracts, now in their fourth edition, aim to provide international all-purpose contracts. NEC contracts provides a combination of uniquely drafted provisions and a complex structure of options which provides the flexibility for virtually any form of project procurement. Because of the extent of user choice as to what is to be included in an NEC contract, it is more of a model form, rather than a standard form. Stimulus to good contract management is provided by an emphasis on communications, cooperation and programming, and the need for clear definition of various types of information at the outset. Clarity and simplicity are intended to be achieved by the use of non-legalistic language using short sentences and avoiding cross-references, and the omission of familiar phrases such as 'variations.'[78] The contract forms are supported by guidance notes and flowcharts, as well as a User's Group with over 400 members around the world. The NEC website includes a history of NEC contracts, how they work, and dictionaries of defined terms.[79] A significant innovation is the requirement for a risk register to be created, and a specified procedure to be followed to manage identified risks.

The NEC contracts have many protagonists who suggest that their use results in improvements in project management and job satisfaction. The ECC Guidance Notes articulate its collaborative approach as follows:

77 Brian Eggleston, *The New Engineering Contract: A Commentary* (Blackwell, 1996) 2.
78 Ibid. 3.
79 www.neccontract.com.

> The ECC [Engineering and Construction Contract] is therefore intended to provide a modern method for employers, designers, contractors and project managers to work collaboratively. It also enables them to achieve their own objectives more consistently than has been possible using more traditional forms of contract. Use of the ECC is intended to lead to a much reduced risk to the Employer of cost and time overruns and the poor performance of the completed projects. It should also lead to a much increased likelihood of achieving a profit for the Contractor and his subcontractors and suppliers.
>
> . . .
>
> Inevitably on any construction engineering project there will be uncertainty and risks involved in carrying out works. The ECC allocates the risks between the Parties clearly and simply. But it also helps to reduce the likelihood of those risks occurring and their subsequent impact, if they do occur, by the application of collaborative foresight and risk reduction procedures. In this way, it aims to improve the outcome of projects generally for parties whose interests might seem to be opposed.[80]

The current NEC comprehensive suite of contracts cover Works, facilities management, services, and supply, as shown in Table 3.5.

Table 3.5 NEC standard form contracts

		NEC3[81]	**NEC4**[82]
Works	**ECC**	Engineering and Construction Contract	Engineering and Construction Contract
	ECSC	Engineering and Construction Short Contract	
	ECSS	Engineering and Construction Short Subcontract	
	ECS	Engineering and Construction Subcontract	Engineering and Construction Subcontract
	ALC		Alliance Contract
	DBO		Design Build and Operate Contract
	FMC		Facilities Management Contract
Services	**PSC**	Professional Service Contract	Professional Service Contract
	PSSC	Professional Service Short Contract	
	TSC	Term Service Contract	Term Service Contract
	TSSC	Term Service Short Contract	
	AC	Adjudicator's Contract	
	DRSC		Dispute Resolution Service Contract
Supply	**FC**	Framework Contract	Framework Contract
	SC	Supply Contract	Supply Contract
	SSC	Supply Short Contract	

80 NEC3 Engineering and Construction Contract Guidance Notes (2013) 3.
81 www.neccontract.com/NEC3-Products/NEC3-Contracts (accessed 26 May 2021).
82 www.neccontract.com/NEC4-Products/NEC4-Contracts (accessed 26 May 2021).

Table 3.6 Allocation of financial risk in ECC Main Option clauses

A	Priced contract with activity schedule	↓ Increasing Employer risk	↑ Increasing Contractor risk
B	Priced contract with Bill of quantities		
C	Target contract with activity schedule		
D	Target contract with Bill of quantities		
E	Cost reimbursable contract		
F	Management contract		

The Engineering and Construction Contract (**ECC**) is structured to be used for all construction and engineering disciplines such as civil, electrical, mechanical, and building work, and whether the Contractor has full design responsibility, some design responsibility, or no design responsibility. It contains six Main Options for different types of payment, one of which must be selected. These are shown in Table 3.6, which illustrates the change in allocating financial risks between the Contractor and the Employer. There are three options for dispute resolution procedures in NEC4 (two in NEC3), one of which must be chosen. Other secondary options are included, which may be included if required.

NEC contracts have clearly been well received by many sectors of the construction and engineering industry in the UK and have been adopted for a number of substantial projects including the Channel Rail Link, Heathrow Terminal 5, Crossrail, and procurement of £9.3Bn of construction for the 2012 Olympics in London. In the early 1990s Sir Michael Latham's review of procurement *Constructing the Team* recommended that a lightly amended NEC contract should become a national standard for the public as well as the private sector.[83] The UK Government is now using NEC contracts instead of the previous government standard form contract GC Works.

NEC contracts have not been widely used outside the UK; the option of a Dispute Avoidance Board in a new Option W3 in the Engineering and Construction Contract in NEC4 appears to be aimed at making NEC4 a viable alternative to FIDIC contracts for international use. In an article critiquing the suitability of the NEC4 contract for international use, representatives of the European International Contractors (**EIC**) encapsulated its strengths and weaknesses as follows:

> The philosophies behind the NEC contract are those of collaboration and mutual trust and cooperation. The contract can be a success if both parties believe in these principles and dedicate the appropriate resources to manage the contract with these at their core. The parties must understand that they will have to provide sufficient, appropriate and skilled resources to ensure proper contract management. Typically, this means a greater investment in such resources than for other standard forms of contracts. The risk is that not only contractors, but also clients, do not always wish to allocate and dedicate the required level of investment in such resources and the parties depart from these philosophies.[84]

The authors of this article concluded that international contractors may have concerns that the cooperative approach and simple structure of the core clauses would not be adopted,

83 Nicholas Gould, 'NEC3: Construction Contract of the Future?' (Paper presented to the Society of Construction Law International conference, Singapore in February 2007, September 2007) 1.

84 Mathias Fabich, Nabeel Khokhar, Ian Cowling, & Stefan Ciufu-Hayward, 'The NEC4 Contract – Fit for Purpose for International Use?' (2018) *International Construction Law Review* 28, 42.

questioning whether the international market is fit for or ready to adopt the principles in NEC forms of contract.[85]

3.11 The contract as a contract management tool

The primary and most important function of the content of the documents comprising a construction contract is, as precisely as possible, to define the agreement that the parties have made. If there is a dispute between the parties as to what their agreement comprises, it is the contract documents that will be referred to by any third-party neutral person called upon to adjudicate the dispute. Such a third-party neutral will look for the objective meaning of the words that the parties have used in their contract documents (at least in the first instance). The contract documents need to define the scope of work to be carried out by the Contractor, the required quality of the Works, the time in which the Works must be completed, and the payments and timing of payments that will be made by the Employer for that work. Further, there are likely to be overarching constraints on the way the work is carried out (eg it must be carried out safely and in accordance with all relevant legislation), as well as the consequences for non-performance. In defining the rights and obligations of the contracting parties, the contract implicitly 'allocates' risks to the parties, that is it defines (or should define) which party must bear the contractual consequences of a risk event materialising.

It is apparent that the Contractor must comply with the requirements of the Contract to avoid the risk of a claim by an Employer for a breach of contract. It should be self-evident that the Contractor needs to be familiar with the provisions of the Contract, in order that it can fulfil its obligations in respect of time, cost, and quality during the execution of the Works. The Contractor will normally be familiar with the 'technical' documents comprising the Contract, that is drawings and specifications, as it refers to these as a matter of course in the execution of its work. However, some of the 'legal' documents comprising the Contract may not appear, at first sight, to be the type of documents that the Contractor would be familiar with in its day-to-day execution of its work. In particular the General Conditions of contract may appear to the Contractor to be confined to esoteric legal matters that will only become relevant in the event of a dispute. It is submitted that if the Contractor takes this view and consigns the General Conditions 'to the bottom drawer' during the execution of the Works, there will almost inevitably be disputes over whether the work was executed in accordance with the requirements of the Contract. The General Conditions will almost certainly define such important day-to-day issues as the procedures for submitting payment claims, the required notification of work additional to the original contract scope that should be classified as a Variation, requests for drawings or materials that the Employer is required to provide, and so on. It is therefore imperative that the Contractor's personnel responsible for management of the project are completely familiar with all of the requirements of the Contract, and strictly comply with them.

In view of this importance of the 'legal' parts of a contract in the day-to-day execution of the Works, it is submitted that a well-written construction contract will also provide a practical contract management tool that, if used properly, will materially assist the Contractor in carrying out its contractual obligations. The FIDIC and the NEC suites of contracts have paid particular attention to this aspect of their application; it is hardly surprising that these

85 Ibid.

contract suites are also intended to be used as contract and risk management manuals, given their provenance from the International Federation of Consulting Engineers and the Institution of Civil Engineers respectively.

3.12 Drafting construction contracts

The modern form of construction contracts, whether standard form or bespoke, has evolved over a period of more than 150 years, influenced by the decisions of English and other common law courts. A perusal of textbooks on construction law and cases in the nineteenth century reveals sophisticated contracts with clauses covering the ambit of most modern construction contracts. Then, as now, clauses in contracts were changed following court decisions that did not give effect to the contract writer's subjective intentions.

The following commentary prefacing a set of 289 'standard' clauses for construction contracts was published over 100 years ago but is still relevant advice on the drafting of modern construction contracts.

> In order to draft a complete set of conditions of contract, all the conditions should be consistent one with another, as well as with the conditions in the specification.
>
> Each covenant or condition to be performed by the parties to the contract should provide a remedy or power to arise in case of default. If this is not done, and the party injured is left to his rights and remedies at common law, and as these rights in a complicated set of conditions are often difficult of determination, it is far better that they should be clearly defined. . . .
>
> Having regard to the decisions of the Courts upon onerous covenants by contractors, is not safe to leave anything in doubt or obscurity if it is desired that the conditions should be capable of being enforced.
>
> In contracts containing so much detail, general words cannot always be relied upon. It is advisable, therefore, when using any such words, to add matters which such words are intended to include, with an express provision that such addition does not limit the general words.
>
> It must be borne in mind that, in settling the form of conditions of a building or engineering contract, regard must be had to the ordinary practice of the engineer or architect, who is to use and enforce them, because however well conditions may be drafted, unless they are used and applied as they should be, they may be the source of danger rather than of advantage. . . .
>
> Courts and juries are not inclined to assist employers in enforcing onerous conditions, and will not find, or construe contracts to mean, that the contractors have bound themselves hand and foot to onerous and ruinous conditions unless it is quite clear that they have done so.[86]

3.13 Applicable laws in various jurisdictions

Tables 3.7–3.9 show examples of applicable laws in a number of jurisdictions. Table 3.7 illustrates applicable laws that apply to the operation of a construction contract where the Site is in the jurisdiction; Table 3.8 illustrates applicable laws that apply to the termination of a construction contract where the Site is in the jurisdiction; Table 3.9 illustrates applicable laws that apply to dispute resolution where the Site is in the jurisdiction.

86 Alfred A Hudson, *Hudson's Fourth Edition Table of Cases* (Sweet & Maxwell, 4th edn 1914) 487.

Table 3.7 Applicable laws for the operation of a construction contract where the Site is in the jurisdiction[87]

	Australia	**Brazil**	**China**	**Czech Rep Republic**	**Fiji**	**France**	**Germany**	**Ghana**	**Hong Kong**	**Italy**	**Malaysia**	**PNG**	**Peru**	**Romania**	**South Africa**	**Sri Lanka**	**Switzerland**	**UAE**
Registration and administration of professionals[88]	√	√	√	√	√	√	√	√	√	√	√	√	√	√	√	√	√	√
Registration/ licencing of Contractors and subcontractors	√		√		√			√	√		√		√	√	√	√	√	√
Subcontractors			√	√		√			√	√	√		√	√				√
Use of liens/ assignment of debts	√	√	√	√	√	√	√	√	√	√	√			√			√	√
Labour	√	√	√	√	√	√	√	√	√	√	√	√	√	√	√	√	√	√
Design/moral rights	√	√	√	√	√	√		√		√	√			√	√	√	√	
Copyright	√	√	√	√	√	√	√	√	√	√	√	√	√	√	√	√	√	√
The product being produced from the Works	√	√			√		√	√	√	√	√		√	√		√		√
First nation people's land rights	√	√			√			√					√		√			
Planning	√		√	√	√	√	√	√	√	√	√	√	√		√	√	√	√

87 The specific legislation for each country is identified in Donald Charrett (ed), *The International Application of FIDIC Contracts A Practical Guide* (Informa Law from Routledge, 2020).

88 Professionals include engineers, architects, quantity surveyors, certifiers, building surveyors, surveyors.

	Australia	Brazil	China	Czech Rep Republic	Fiji	France	Germany	Ghana	Hong Kong	Italy	Malaysia	PNG	Peru	Romania	South Africa	Sri Lanka	Switzerland	UAE
Work affecting adjacent property to the Site	√	√	√	√	√	√	√	√	√	√	√		√				√	√
Heritage	√	√	√	√	√		√	√	√	√	√		√	√	√	√	√	
Environment	√	√	√	√	√	√	√	√	√	√	√	√	√	√	√	√	√	√
Public procurement	√	√		√						√	√	√						
Local procurement								√			√				√			
Building permits, construction work, Standard of work	√	√	√	√	√	√	√	√	√	√	√	√	√	√	√	√	√	√
Health and safety	√	√	√	√	√	√	√	√	√	√	√	√	√	√	√	√	√	√
Calibration of testing apparatus etc				√			√	√		√	√		√	√	√	√		
Ownership of plant and materials	√	√	√	√			√	√		√		√	√	√				
Employer's sale of Contractor's Equipment etc	√				√	√		√	√	√		√		√				√
Insurance	√	√	√	√	√	√	√	√	√	√	√	√	√	√	√	√		√
Statutory rights that coexist with contractual rights	√		√		√		√	√	√	√	√	√	√			√		
Liability for defective work	√	√	√	√	√	√	√	√	√	√	√	√	√	√	√			√
Liability for nuisance	√	√			√	√	√	√	√	√	√		√	√		√		√
Other issues	√		√	√	√				√		√			√		√		

Table 3.8 Applicable laws for termination of a construction contract where the Site is in the jurisdiction[89]

	Australia	Brazil	China	Czech Rep Republic	Fiji	France	Germany	Ghana	Hong Kong	Italy	Malaysia	PNG	Peru	Romania	South Africa	Sri Lanka	Switzerland	UAE
Bankruptcy, insolvency, liquidation	√	√	√	√	√	√		√	√	√	√	√	√	√	√	√		√
Decennial liability and liability for structural collapse		√				√				√			√	√	√			√
Other	√													√				

Table 3.9 Applicable laws for dispute resolution where the Site is in the jurisdiction[90]

	Australia	Brazil	China	Czech Rep Republic	Fiji	France	Germany	Ghana	Hong Kong	Italy	Malaysia	PNG	Peru	Romania	South Africa	Sri Lanka	Switzerland	UAE
Dispute before a local board / Adjudication	√						√	√		√	√		√	√	√	√		
Limitation periods	√	√	√	√	√	√	√	√	√	√	√	√	√	√	√	√	√	√

89 The specific legislation for each country is identified in Donald Charrett (ed), *The International Application of FIDIC Contracts A Practical Guide* (Informa Law from Routledge, 2020).
90 Ibid.

CHAPTER 4

Lex constructionis[1]

CONTENTS

1 This chapter is an edited and updated version of the paper: Dr Donald Charrett, '*Lex constructionis* – or My Country's Rules' first published in (2021) *International Construction Law Review* 61, published by Informa Law, London.

DOI: 10.4324/9781003206873-4

4.1 Introduction

Contract law in all countries is based on the twin principles of freedom of contract, and *pacta sunt servanda*. However, each jurisdiction has laws that impact on contracts for construction work. Local laws apply if the governing law of the contract is in the jurisdiction, if the Site of the construction work is in the jurisdiction, or if the seat of dispute resolution is in the jurisdiction. This chapter explores the question of whether there are universally accepted principles of construction law, a *lex constructionis*, or whether it is trumped in every jurisdiction by local laws that differ from international norms. Three issues are discussed that support the concept of *lex constructionis* in the international practice of construction law: the use of FIDIC contracts, international commercial arbitration, and the *lex mercatoria*.

The chapter concludes with a proposed list of 20 principles of *lex constructionis* that take into account the unique features of construction projects and construction contracts.

4.2 Construction contracts

Construction law is the law relating to construction projects: their design, construction, maintenance, and operation. The legal mechanism for delivery of a construction project is a construction contract between Employer and Contractor. It defines their rights and obligations and allocates the risks between them. As a species of commercial contract that addresses the issues of construction projects enumerated later, international construction contracts have a number of features that make them *sui generis*. As discussed later, the authors posit that, notwithstanding local laws, there are widely accepted principles of construction law that constitute a *lex constructionis*. That *lex* is a subset of *lex mercatoria* that takes account of the specific aspects of construction law that distinguishes it from commercial law in general.

There are a number of unique distinguishing features of construction law. These can be conveniently considered under a number of issues that are generally relevant to all construction projects. Under each of the following headings a number of distinguishing features are identified.

4.2.1 Scope

The subject matter of the contract relates to construction of a unique facility which will be affixed to the land at a specific location over a specific period of time. That fixing to the land results in the constructed facility becoming part of the real property of the landowner when attached.

The required design, scope, time, cost, and quality requirements of the Works and the finished project are defined by extensive and complex technical documentation. The Employer (generally) has the right to increase or decrease the originally agreed scope of work by the issue of **Variations**,[2] and the Contractor is obliged to carry out or omit the varied work. The execution of the construction work and/or the performance of the Contract may be supervised by a person who is not a party to the Contract.

4.2.2 Risk

There are many risks in a construction project – known knowns, known unknowns, and unknown unknowns. Ground conditions are never completely known, including geotechnical conditions, groundwater, contamination, or heritage items. Weather conditions can have a significant impact on construction activities and delay completion.

Freedom of contract may be constrained, for example *Statutory Adjudication* legislation that mandates payment obligations and makes some provisions illegal, such as pay when paid clauses. In addition, many aspects of the execution of a construction project are subject to government laws and regulations.

There are usually a series of independent and interrelated contracts between a number of different parties: for example Employer/consultant, Employer/Contractor, Contractor/subcontractor, Contractor/surety, Contractor/insurer.

Construction activities are potentially dangerous to personnel and may involve heavy machinery, working at heights, or working in confined spaces. Construction involves significant environmental impacts: noise, dust, smells, vibration, nuisance, water run-off, sediment, and erosion. Other impacts on external stakeholders may include adverse impacts on adjacent property.

Insurance of the Works is usually mandatory and is a significant risk transfer mechanism. Insolvency of parties to interrelated contracts may impact performance.

4.2.3 Time

The time for performance of a construction contract may extend over a number of years, including a period after completion of construction (and when the Employer is in possession of the Site) during which the Contractor is liable to rectify defects.

---

2 A Variation is an increase, decrease or change to the originally agreed scope of work, as directed by the Employer, which the Contractor has a contractual obligation to perform.

There are usually significant financial consequences arising from late contract completion – the Employer cannot generate revenue from the facility until it is operational, and the Contractor is typically subject to liquidated damages for late completion.

4.2.4 Cost

The contract sum and cash flow is typically substantial – 'There must be a "cash flow" in the building trade. It is the very lifeblood of the enterprise.'[3]

The Contractor is usually required to provide security for its performance.

4.2.5 Quality

A construction contract may involve the assumption of obligations that are very long term, for example maintenance or liability for defects arising many years after construction was completed. Construction work apparently completed in accordance with contractual requirements may contain latent defects which only manifest themselves many years after construction was completed.

4.2.6 Disputes

Disputes are common and frequently involve complex technical issues and large volumes of documents.

A number of these features impact third parties and are subject to various laws, such as environmental impact or work, health, and safety regulations. Other third-party impacts are subject to legal doctrines such as tort or the law of nuisance. However, the majority of the issues listed are matters between the contracting parties and are therefore regulated by the terms of their contract.

4.3 International contract law

International contract law is based on the two fundamental principles of freedom of contract and *pacta sunt servanda*. These principles are universal in jurisdictions subject to the rule of law, the necessary precondition for the exercise of the parties' autonomy and the enforcement of their rights and obligations.

4.3.1 Freedom of contract

Freedom of contract is the ability of legal persons (eg natural persons over 18 years of age and properly constituted companies) to enter into a binding agreement to do anything, provided it is not contrary to the law or public policy (and in some jurisdictions, morals). Freedom of contract and *pacta sunt servanda* are long-standing principles enshrined in the common law.[4] Courts have a natural bias to uphold freedom of contract and to take a narrow view of any statutory constraint,[5] even if one of the parties has accepted risks that it cannot manage or insure for.

---

3 *Modern Engineering (Bristol) Ltd v Gilbert Ash (Northern) Limited* (1973) 71 LGR 162, 167 per Lord Denning MR.
4 *Printing and Numeral Registering Co. v Sampson* (1875) L. R. 19 Eq. 462.
5 *Colin John Fitzgerald v F J Leonhardt Pty Ltd* (1997) 189 CLR 215 per Kirby J.

This freedom to contract about anything has a long history in the English common law. Well over 100 years ago Sir George Jessel MR stated that freedom of contract was the paramount public policy in English common law:

> if there is one thing which more than another public policy requires it is that men of full age and competent understanding shall have the utmost liberty of contracting, and that their contracts when entered into freely and voluntarily shall be held sacred and shall be enforced by Courts of justice.[6]

A more recent and succinct statement was given by Gillard J: 'Subject to public policy and statute law, parties to a contract can agree to do anything.'[7]

Freedom of contract is enshrined in legislation in both common law and civil law jurisdictions.

Malaysia is a common law country, but it has a detailed statute (derived from the *Contracts Act 1872* (India)) that effectively constitutes a default contract code. The *Contracts Act 1950* (Malaysia) enshrines freedom of contract in statute in the following terms:

> s1(2) Nothing herein contained shall affect any written law or any usage or custom of trade, or any incident of any contract, not inconsistent with this Act.
>
> s24 The consideration or object of an agreement is lawful, unless –
>
> (a) it is forbidden by a law;
> (b) it is of such a nature that, if permitted, it would defeat any law;
> (c) it is fraudulent;
> (d) it involves or implies injury to the person or property of another; or
> (e) the court regards it as immoral, or opposed to public policy.

In each of the preceding cases, the consideration or object of an agreement is said to be unlawful. Every agreement in which the object or consideration is unlawful is void.

However, the very freedom of contract provided in the *Contracts Act 1950* (Malaysia) gives the parties the freedom to derogate from its provisions. In *Ooi Boon Long v Citibank NA*[8] Lord Brightman held that s1(2) of the *Contracts Act 1950*,

> does not say that the contracting parties are unable by agreement to vary the legal consequences spelt out by the Act. Section 1 (2) has no effect on the freedom of contracting parties to decide upon what terms they desire to contract.

Therefore, if parties desire to oust the application of a certain provision of the *Contracts Act 1950* (Malaysia), their intention should be made clear expressly.

Freedom of contract is also a fundamental principle under civil law systems, for example

> In this jurisdiction [Philippines] contracts are enforced as they are read, and parties who are competent to contract may make such agreements within the limitations of the law and public policy as they desire, and the courts will enforce them according to their terms.[9]

---

6 *Printing and Numeral Registering Co. v Sampson* (1875) L. R. 19 Eq., 462, 465 per Sir George Jessel MR.

7 *Abigroup Contractors Pty Ltd v Transfield Pty Ltd & Obayashi Corporation* [1998] VSC 103 [86].

8 [1984] 1 M.L.J. 222 (Malaysian Privy Council).

9 *Lambert v Fox* 26 Phil 588 [Philippines], cited in Edgardo L Paras, *Civil Code of the Philippines Annotated Volume Four* (Rex Book Store, 14th edn 2000) 332.

In this case the principle is enshrined in statute – Art 1306 of the *Civil Code of the Philippines* states:

> The contracting parties may establish such stipulations, clauses, terms and conditions as they may deem convenient, provided they are not contrary to law, morals, good customs, public order or public policy.

Article 1102 of the Law of Contract, the General Regime of Obligations, and Proof of Obligations in the French *Civil Code* provides:

> Everyone is free to contract or not to contract, to choose the person with whom to contract, and to determine the content and form of the contract, within the limits imposed by legislation.[10]

As the common law and statutory definitions of the principle make clear, the parties' freedom of contract is not unlimited, as it is subject to any statutory constraints or prohibitions on conduct that is in conflict with public policy (or morals). Clearly both of these vary from jurisdiction to jurisdiction, with the result that both contract law and construction law are inevitably conditioned by the relevant jurisdiction.

The universal application of freedom of contract is reinforced by its statement in principles that may be regarded as private codifications or restatements of international contract law (modern statements of the *lex mercatoria*, discussed further in ¶4.7). Article 1.1 (Freedom of contract) of the *UNIDROIT Principles of International Commercial Contracts 2016*[11] provides for freedom of contract in the following terms: 'The parties are free to enter into a contract and to determine its content.' *Trans-Lex Principle* No. IV.1.1 – Freedom of contract states: 'The parties are free to enter into contracts and to determine their contents (principle of party autonomy).'[12]

4.3.2 Pacta sunt servanda

Once parties have exercised their freedom to enter into a contract, they have the legal rights and obligations they have agreed to. Those rights and obligations would be illusory if the parties did not fulfil their agreement. The principle of *pacta sunt servanda* is therefore the essential obverse of the principle of freedom of contract.

Article 1.3 (Binding character of contract) of the *UP* gives effect to the principal of *pacta sunt servanda* in the following terms:

> A contract validly entered into is binding upon the parties. It can only be modified or terminated in accordance with its terms or by agreement or as otherwise provided in these Principles.

The universality and importance of this principle for construction law has been aptly summed up as follows:

10 www.textes.justice.gouv.fr/art_pix/THE-LAW-OF-CONTRACT-2-5-16.pdf (accessed 6 March 2020).

11 www.unidroit.org/english/principles/contracts/principles2016/principles2016-e.pdf (accessed 15 January 2021).

12 www.trans-lex.org/principles/of-transnational-law-(lex-mercatoria) (accessed 15 January 2021).

> the principle of *pacta sunt servanda* . . . is universal to all legal systems. This means that the vast majority of construction disputes are fought and won or lost primarily over the wording of the contract (and alleged facts).[13]

The following quotation is perhaps the clearest pointer to the primacy of the contract and the fundamental importance of the words in the contract, vindicating the twin principles of freedom of contract and *pacta sunt servanda*:

> Finally, deep in the night, with no one else around, most lawyers in their heart of hearts will admit – the Contract usually decides the issues, despite what the law is.[14]

Of course, *pacta sunt servanda* would be illusory in the absence of a mechanism to enforce the rights and obligations the parties have agreed to. In a jurisdiction subject to the rule of law, the courts will give effect to *pacta sunt servanda* by holding the parties to their bargain. If necessary, the coercive powers of the state can be called in aid to enforce a court judgement. Thus, for example, if contracting parties have agreed that any disputes will be settled by arbitration, the courts will generally stay any court proceedings commenced in breach of their agreement to arbitrate.

4.3.3 Governing law of the contract

Freedom of contract generally enables contracting parties to choose the law that governs their contractual relations, known as the governing law of the contract or the proper law of the contract; to agree on the scope of their rights and obligations; to agree on the allocation of risks between themselves; and to agree to resolve their disputes by private and confidential arbitration by an arbitral tribunal of their choice in accordance with procedures they have chosen. The governing law of a contract provides the legal rules for determining issues in connection with its formation, validity, interpretation, and the rights and obligations of the parties. This is discussed further in ¶2.6.

4.3.4 Statutory incursions into freedom of contract

Statutory incursions into freedom of contract are ubiquitous and increasing in both common law and civil law jurisdictions. In the most general sense, every statute whose subject matter is relevant to the content of a contract potentially impacts on freedom of contract by prescribing certain required conduct in particular circumstances or proscribing certain conduct in other circumstances.

Further, all applicable laws impacting on any aspect of a construction project explicitly constrain the parties' freedom of contract, particularly in how the work can be carried out and how it impacts on third parties, for example laws relating to labour, health and safety, the environment, and so on. In many cases such statutory intervention is indirect where the subject matter of the legislation only peripherally impacts the performance of the obligations under the contract. The emphasis in this book is on providing examples of statutes that apply directly to

---

13 Robert Knutson (ed), *FIDIC An Analysis of International Construction Contracts* (Kluwer Law International, 2005) xvi.

14 Ibid. xix.

the subject matter of a contract under consideration, and to understand how relevant statutory provisions operate in conjunction with the terms of the specific contract in the particular circumstances. Thus, the statutory constraints on freedom of contract considered here are those which explicitly circumscribe the terms regulating the parties' own commercial agreement. Of necessity, the examples of statutory intervention on freedom of contract referred to in this book are considered in isolation of the terms of any specific contract.

The natural bias of courts to uphold freedom of contract and to take a narrow view of the construction of statutes which reduce that freedom is encapsulated in the following statement by His Honour Justice Kirby:

> Certainly, there are plenty of judicial dicta to suggest that courts will be slow to imply, where the applicable legislation is silent, a prohibition which interferes with the rights and remedies given to parties by the ordinary law of contract. This reluctance probably grows out of a recognition of the multitude of legislative provisions, important and unimportant, which may nowadays indirectly impinge upon the contractual relations of parties and, if enforced with full rigour, cause harsh and unwarranted deprivation of rights. In part, this reluctance may be no more than a species of the general rule of statutory construction that legislation will not be interpreted to deprive parties of basic rights at common law without a clear expression of the legislative will to do so[15] [citations omitted].

However, notwithstanding the universal acceptance and powerful reach of the principle of freedom of contract, legislatures around the world have seen the need for statutory intervention to ameliorate the potentially draconian results which can arise. The aim of such statutory intervention is typically to ensure that public policy principles are not subverted by private agreement.

The three categories of laws relevant to construction are (1) project-related laws – subject to the jurisdiction of the Site where the Works are carried out; (2) contract-related laws – subject to the jurisdiction of the governing law of the contract; and (3) dispute resolution laws – subject to the law of the 'seat' of the dispute resolution.

4.3.4.1 Project-related laws

All applicable laws impacting on any aspect of a construction project explicitly constrain the parties' freedom of contract, particularly in how the work can be carried out and how it impacts on third parties, for example laws relating to labour, health and safety, or the environment. Laws relating to activities, people, and property at the Site of a construction project will generally apply irrespective of the governing law of the contract.

The following are examples of project-related laws that constrain the parties' freedom of contract:

- Protective measures in favour of subcontractors, for example *Law on Subcontracting 1975* (France);
- Liability generally for the partial or total collapse of structures, for example *Civil Code* (France) Articles 1792–1792-6; *Civil Code* (UAE) Article 880;
- Deemed acceptance of Variations by the Employer, for example *Civil Code* (Brazil) Article 619;

15 *Colin John Fitzgerald v F J Leonhardt Pty Ltd* (1997) 189 CLR 215, 243.

- Interim payments, for example *Construction Contracts Act 2013* (Ireland) s3; and
- Rules relating to property in goods, for example *Property Law* (China), *Personal Property Securities Act 2017* (Fiji), *Personal Property Security Act 2011* (PNG).

Although much of the construction law in common law jurisdictions has traditionally been determined by the common law, there has been increasing statutory intervention to alleviate long-standing challenges inherent in the application of classical contract theory to construction. Perhaps the greatest of these challenges has been to ensure the prompt and reliable flow of payments through the contractual chain. As far back as the 1880s, US states enacted mechanic's lien statutes to protect unpaid subcontractors, labourers, and materialmen who had performed work on private property by granting them equitable interests in the improved real estate.[16] Following the Latham Report on procurement and contractual arrangements in the UK construction industry,[17] the UK enacted legislation that provided a statutory right to progress payments and for disputes to be determined provisionally by adjudication.[18] Similar legislation, restricted to adjudication of payment disputes, has been implemented in all Australian States and Territories,[19] and a number of other jurisdictions.[20]

The constraints on freedom of contract from such *Statutory Adjudication* legislation is quite profound as, depending on the jurisdiction, it may provide statutory regulation of the following issues in legislation that cannot be contracted out of:

- The Contractor may have a statutory entitlement to progress payments, and an automatic entitlement to payment if the payer does not respond to a payment claim.
- There may be no contractual defenses to court enforcement of an adjudicated amount as a judgement debt.
- 'Pay when paid' and 'pay if paid' clauses are void.
- An unpaid party may stop work irrespective of contractual terms.
- Parties have the right to submit a defined type of dispute to adjudication, and the legislation defines formal adjudication procedures. There are strict time limits for adjudication, and parties may not be able to choose the Adjudicator.
- In some jurisdictions project bank accounts are required to provide a trust over monies payable to subcontractors.

---

16 Philip L Bruner, 'The Historical Emergence of Construction Law' (2007) 34(1) *William Mitchell Law Review* 1, 6.

17 Sir Michael Latham, 'Constructing the Team' (July 1994) Final Report.

18 *Housing Grants, Construction and Regeneration Act 1996* (UK).

19 NSW: *Building and Construction Industry Security of Payment Act 1999*; Victoria: *Building and Construction Industry Security of Payment Act* 2002; Northern Territory: *Construction Contracts (Security of Payments) Act 2004*; West Australia: *Building and Construction Industry (Security of Payment) Act 2021*; Australian Capital Territory: *Construction Industry (Security of Payment Act) 2009*; South Australia: *Building and Construction Industry Security of Payment Act 2009*; Tasmania: *Building and Construction Industry Security of Payment Act 2009*; Queensland: *Building Industry Fairness (Security of Payment) Act 2017*.

20 New Zealand: *Construction Contracts Act 2002*; Singapore: *Building and Construction Industry Security of Payment Act 2004*; Isle of Man: *Construction Contracts Act 2004* (IoM); Malaysia: *Construction Industry Payment and Adjudication Act 2012*; Ireland: *Construction Contracts Act 2013*; Ontario: *Construction Act 1990*.

4.3.4.2 Contract-related laws

Examples of contract-related laws that constrain the parties' freedom of contract include the payment of penalties, for example *Civil Code* (Romania), *Conventional Penalties Act 1962* (South Africa); unfair contract conditions, for example *Standard Business Terms Act* (Germany), *Unfair Contract Terms Act* (UK); and bribery and corruption, for example *Bribery Act 2010* (UK).

Notwithstanding parties' agreement on the amount of liquidated damages payable in the event of specified breaches of contract, *Civil Code* provisions may allow subsequent adjustment, for example *Civil Code* (France) s1152 and *Civil Code BGB* (Germany) s343.

Many *Civil Codes* provide for relief from contractual stipulations if *force majeure* or hardship arising from a change in circumstances since the contract was executed prevent performance, such as the *Civil Code* (Philippines) s1174, *Civil Code* (Indonesia) s1245, *Civil Code* (Peru) ss1315 and 1440, and *Civil Code* (France) s1148.

4.3.4.3 Dispute resolution laws

The law applying to the conduct of dispute resolution will be that of the 'seat' of the forum where the dispute resolution takes place. If the dispute is litigated in court, the law of the forum of the court will apply. If the parties have chosen arbitration, then the arbitration law at the 'seat' of the arbitration will apply. In accordance with the principle of party autonomy, parties are free to choose the jurisdiction of an arbitral 'seat' that is different to the jurisdiction of the governing law of the contract, or the jurisdiction of the Site where the construction work is performed. In many instances that will be the case where the contracting parties choose a neutral forum for arbitration, so that neither party has any 'home ground' advantage.

As noted earlier, *Statutory Adjudication* legislation may apply to the provisional resolution of disputes in the jurisdiction where the construction is carried out. However, this does not negate the parties' right to final resolution of a dispute by international arbitration in a neutral forum. Any party choice of an alternative method of dispute resolution is of course subject to any mandatory applicable law. For example, as noted later, a Dispute Board determination may not be final and binding in some jurisdictions, notwithstanding contractual agreement that it is. Some jurisdictions such as some Australian States prohibit pre-agreed arbitration of 'consumer' disputes, such as those arising in domestic building contracts.

4.3.5 Public policy constraints on freedom of contract

Public policy is largely concerned with the potential for manifest unfairness or injustice in a given situation. Courts may disregard or refuse to give effect to contractual obligations which, whilst not directly contrary to any express or implied statutory prohibition, nevertheless contravene 'the policy of the law.'

The somewhat nebulous concept of public policy has a very powerful reach in civil law systems. In the European community, most of whose member states have civil law legal systems, parties have a similar freedom of contract to that applying under common law systems and are free to choose (within certain limits) the law which is to apply to their contract. The *Convention on the Law Applicable to Contractual Obligations* (***Rome I***)[21] provides in Article 3.1 that 'A contract shall be governed by the law chosen by the parties.' However, it also provides in Article 21 that:

> The application of a provision of the law of any country specified by this Regulation may be refused only if such application is manifestly incompatible with the public policy (*ordre public*) of the forum.

It is suggested that one public policy that is universally applicable is that parties to a contract may not exclude the jurisdiction of the courts. This could be inferred from the sovereign nature of governments to pass laws, and their exclusive right to compel persons within the jurisdiction to submit to those laws. Accordingly, a contract term having the effect of ousting the jurisdiction of the court will not be upheld by a court.[22]

The principle of freedom of contract that allows the parties to choose their own method of dispute resolution outside the court system is clearly the foundation principle for international arbitration. There is a tension here between the parties' freedom of contract and the public policy that it is impermissible to oust the jurisdiction of the courts. The widespread use and acceptance of international arbitration in such treaties as the ***New York Convention***[23] has generally settled this tension in favour of freedom of contract. In a recent case in England, the High Court confirmed that the standard *Scott v Avery* clause[24] found in several trade association standard contract forms has the effect of excluding the English courts' power to grant interim relief.[25] The apparent tension between the public policy principle of the courts' ultimate authority to decide legal rights and the parties' freedom of contract right to adopt alternative dispute resolution mechanisms is discussed further in Chapter 28.

Another example of the tension between the principle of freedom of contract and public policy is illustrated by the Canadian Supreme Court's approach to the application of exclusion clauses. In the case of *Tercon Contractors Ltd v British Columbia (Transportation and Highways)*[26] the judges agreed that, even if an exclusion clause is valid and applicable, the court may nevertheless decide to

> refuse to enforce the valid exclusion clause because of the existence of an overriding public policy, proof of which lies on the party seeking to avoid enforcement of the clause, that outweighs the very strong public interest in the enforcement of contracts.[27]

---

21 *Regulation (EC) No 593/2008* of the European Parliament and of the Council of 17 June 2008 on the law applicable to contractual obligations. Corrigenda dated 4 July 2008 and 14 August 2009.

22 See for example *Brooks v Burns Philp Trustee Co Ltd* [1969] HCA 4; *Baulderstone Hornibrook Engineering Pty Ltd v Kayah Holdings Pty Ltd* (1998) 14 BCL 277.

23 *United Nations 1958 New York Convention on the Recognition and Enforcement of Foreign Arbitral Awards.*

24 A clause that says that neither party in a dispute will bring an action in court until arbitration has been conducted.

25 *B v S* [2011] EWHC 691 (Comm).

26 [2010] SCC 4.

27 Ibid. [123].

Other examples of situations in which courts have refused to enforce a contractual agreement on the grounds that it is against public policy include the following:

- Imposing a penalty for breach of contract (*Andrews v Australia and New Zealand Banking Group Ltd* [2012] HCA 30);
- Unlawful conduct (*Gaffney v Ryan* [1995] 1 Qd R 19);
- Economic duress – the application of illegitimate pressure to achieve an agreement (*DSND Subsea Ltd v Petroleum Geo Services ASA* [2000] BLR 530);
- Conduct prejudicial to the administration of justice (*Trendtex Trading Corporation v Credit Suisse* [1982] AC 679);
- Conduct prejudicing the impartiality of public officials (*Wilkinson v Osborne* [1915] HCA 92);
- Conduct prejudicial to national or international security (*Foster v Driscoll* [1929] 1 KB 470); and
- Unreasonable restraint of trade (*Esso Petroleum Co Ltd v Harper's Garage (Stourport) Ltd* [1967] UKHL 1).

4.4 *Lex constructionis*

4.4.1 What is it?

As defined in ¶1.2, *lex constructionis* is the law relating to construction projects which is widely accepted internationally in jurisdictions subject to the rule of law and which recognise the parties' freedom of contract, irrespective of the specific impact of statute law. It is a subset of *lex mercatoria* (the law merchant), a long-standing legal concept that has regained prominence and importance in the modern globalised world.

The 'new' *lex mercatoria* dates from 1957.[28] Its significance is encapsulated in the introductory speech at the London colloquium on 'The New Sources of the Law of International Trade with Special Reference to East-West Trade' in 1962:

> The evolution of an autonomous law of international trade, founded on universally accepted standards of business conduct, would be one of the most important developments of legal science in our time. It would constitute a common platform for commercial lawyers from all countries, those of planned and free-market economy, those from civil law and common law, and those of fully developed and developing economy, which would enable them to cooperate in the perfection of the legal mechanism of international trade.[29]

In the authors' view, by replacing 'international trade' with 'international construction' this statement is the lodestar for *lex constructionis*.

There are three theories of the meaning of *lex constructionis* that can be derived from the broader category of *lex mercatoria*:

(1) A 'mass' of rules and principles for the law of construction, devoid of any internal consistency or systematic quality.

---

28 Klaus Peter Berger, *The Creeping Codification of the New Lex Mercatoria* (Wolters Kluwer, 2010) 1.

29 Professor Clive M Schmitthoff, cited in Klaus Peter Berger, *The Creeping Codification of the New Lex Mercatoria* (Wolters Kluwer, 2010) 4.

(2) The totality of usages that are refined according to the needs of construction.
(3) An independent, supranational legal system.[30]

The first of these theories, based on the universally recognised principle of party autonomy in contract law, is that *lex constructionis* supplements the well-known categories of applicable domestic law. The second theory is based on statutory or judicial acceptance of trade usages as a factual supplement to the applicable domestic law. Both of these theories limit the ultimate development and application of *lex constructionis* by the constraints of domestic law.

In the authors' view, the third theory is supported by a conjunction of modern developments that make such a supranational system possible. As discussed later, these developments comprise widely used and accepted international standard form construction contracts, the articulation of the new *lex mercatoria*, and the application of international arbitration to finally resolve disputes.

Consistent with the preceding definition, *lex constructionis* is comprised of the following four elements: the governing law of the contract, the contract between the parties, the law applying to the project at the Site, and the law applying to the final resolution of disputes.

4.4.2 Why is it important?

Construction is an important industry in every country of the world. It is important because it generally represents a significant component of gross national product;[31] it is important because it employs many people: in professional occupations, in skilled trades, and in less skilled jobs such as labouring.[32] But perhaps most important of all, it provides the infrastructure on which modern life depends: the facilities to mine and process natural resources; transport infrastructure; energy generation and distribution infrastructure; the provision of clean water and water treatment; and the built environment.

The construction industry is of particular importance in less developed countries. It is fundamental to the achievement of the United Nations' Sustainable Development Goals (**SDG**),[33] to improving health and life expectancy, and advancing standards of living to reduce the gap between the living standards of the developed and less-developed countries.

Construction is a very international industry. The scale of large construction projects, and the time required to construct them, provide attractive opportunities for experienced Contractors to operate internationally and transfer their skills and technology to other countries.

---

30 Klaus Peter Berger, *The Creeping Codification of the New Lex Mercatoria* (Wolters Kluwer, 2010) 61–62.

31 Construction is one of the largest sectors of the world economy, equivalent to 13% of GDP. Annual expenditure on construction related expenditure is of the order of USD 10 trillion: McKinsey Global Institute, 'Reinventing Construction: A Route to Higher Productivity' (February 2017) 1.

32 The construction industry employs approximately 7% of the global workforce. http://oecdinsights.org/2016/08/22/global-construction-sector-corporate-responsibility/ (accessed 22 April 2021).

33 The SDGs are the United Nations' framework for continuing development priorities such as poverty eradication, health, education, and food security and nutrition, a wide range of economic, social, and environmental objectives. United Nations, 'Resolution adopted by the General Assembly on 25 September 2015' 6, https://documents-dds-ny.un.org/doc/UNDOC/GEN/N15/291/89/PDF/N1529189.pdf?OpenElement (accessed 25 March 2021).

In the authors' view, *lex constructionis* is important in providing a legal framework within which the international construction industry can thrive and prosper by promoting best practice for successful projects in which the contracting parties' legitimate expectations can be realised. It can lead to better value for money by enabling less-expensive projects with fewer disputes and fewer insolvencies, and it can promote international trade and greater comity between nations.

The following examples provide some historical and other evidence of *lex constructionis*.

4.4.3 Examples of lex constructionis

4.4.3.1 Significant convergence between the common law and civil law

The significant convergence between common law and civil law is discussed in ¶1.4.1.

4.4.3.2 Liability for incorrect cost estimates

In 15 BC Vitruvius noted in his seminal architectural books that in Ephesus an architect was liable for construction cost overruns in excess of 25% above his estimate.[34]

Two thousand years later, an architect in Australia could similarly be legally liable for cost overruns in excess of his/her estimate. An architect who was retained to plan a residence to a price specified by the client and represented that the house could be built for that price in accordance with the plans he drew up, was found to have engaged in misleading or deceptive conduct in contravention of the *Trade Practices Act 1974* (Cth) (now *Australian Consumer Law*).[35]

4.4.3.3 Contractor's liability for defective work

The oldest known written legal code, the *Code of Hammurabi* (c 1750 BC), prescribed the financial consequences if a builder built a house that was defective:

> 232 If it ruin goods, he shall make compensation for all that has been ruined, and inasmuch as he did not construct properly this house which he built and it fell, he shall re-erect the house from his own means.
>
> 233 If a builder build a house for some one, even though he has not yet completed it; if then the walls seem toppling, the builder must make the walls solid from his own means.

Thus, in the event that the consequences of the defective work were confined to property damage, the builder was liable for reinstatement costs. That is still the situation today. For example, in the UK recently, the Contractor was liable for rectification costs arising from the structural failure of wind turbine towers that occurred within two years of installation. The failure occurred as a result of an unknown error in the specified design standard, in the absence of negligence.[36]

---

34 Marcus Vitruvius Pollo (translated by Morris Hicky Morgan), *Vitruvius: The Ten Books on Architecture* (Dover Publications, 1960) 281.

35 *Coleman v Gordon M Jenkins & Associates Pty Ltd* (1993) 9 BCL 292.

36 *MT Højgaard a/s v E.ON Climate and Renewables UK Robin Rigg East Ltd* [2017] UKSC 59.

The *Code of Hammurabi* provided that the builder could be put to death for a collapse that killed someone. In the twenty-first century strict OHS laws have been enacted to protect life; if defective work constructed negligently results in a death, a contractor is liable to severe penalties under industrial manslaughter laws.[37]

4.5 FIDIC Contracts

FIDIC (*Fédération Internationale des Ingénieurs-Conseils*) publishes standard form Conditions of Contract that are used in many countries and are the most widely used international construction contracts in the world. The following contracts are commonly referred to as the rainbow suite:

- Conditions of Contract for Construction – First Edition 1999, Second Edition 2017 (**Red Book**);
- Conditions of Contract for Plant and Design-Build – First Edition 1999, Second Edition 2017 (**Yellow Book**); and
- Conditions of Contract for EPC/Turnkey Projects – First Edition 1999, Second Edition 2017 (**Silver Book**).

As discussed in ¶3.10.1, FIDIC contracts are drafted by a Contracts Committee with international representation and are reviewed by friendly reviewers from many different countries and jurisdictions. They are based on a fair allocation of risks and rewards. Although they have a common law heritage, they are used in many countries, in both civil law and common law jurisdictions. Because of their genesis from the common law Institution of Civil Engineers' contract, they are more detailed than typical construction contracts in civil law jurisdictions, which rely on *Civil Codes* for many legal rights and obligations.

It is submitted that the detailed articulation of the contracting parties' rights and obligations in FIDIC contracts as the outcome of the drafting process by engineers and lawyers from many jurisdictions is a significant contribution to *lex constructionis*. The Contracts Committee has distilled common practices in international construction contracting into a form that is broadly consistent with domestic law in many countries and is therefore widely accepted.

The extensive international input into the drafting of FIDIC General Conditions and its acceptance as an appropriate contract for international contracts is evidenced by the World Bank's implementation of the 2017 Red Book in its 2019 Standard Procurement Document.[38] The Particular Conditions of Contract in the World Bank Standard Procurement Document does not change the balanced risk/reward allocation in the General Conditions, and mainly comprises 'social provisions' to provide protections for labour, local communities, and the environment that may not be adequately covered by legislation is less-developed countries.

37 For example, Queensland, the ACT and Victoria have industrial manslaughter laws that apply to negligent conduct causing death. Maximum penalties are up to 20 years' imprisonment and/or a fine of AU$ 320,000 (US$ 240,000) for senior officers and AU$ 10 million (US$ 7.6 million) for body corporates.

38 http://pubdocs.worldbank.org/en/865231562944956956/SPD-Request-for-Bids-WORKS-after-prequalification.docx (accessed 28 August 2020).

Each of the printed FIDIC rainbow suite standard forms comprise General Conditions, Guidance for the Preparation of Particular Conditions, and Forms. A FIDIC contract comprises the General Conditions as published by FIDIC, as amended by Particular Conditions to comply with the governing law of the contract, and the law of the Site where the Works are performed.

The extent to which the FIDIC contracts contribute to *lex constructionis* may be gauged from the extent to which Particular Conditions essential for conformity with local law are required. A recently published book on the application of FIDIC contracts contains chapters on 18 jurisdictions from around the world, each written by a locally experienced construction law practitioner.[39] The brief for these chapter authors included a requirement to identify what Special Provisions in the Particular Conditions were necessary for consistency with local laws in circumstances where FIDIC General Conditions are incompatible or inconsistent with the governing law of the contract, the law of the Site, or the laws of the seat of the dispute determination.

Tables 4.1 through 4.3 identify the issues in each of the preceding categories that the chapter authors identified as requiring Special Provisions in the Particular Conditions for conformity with local law. It should be noted that as a consequence of freedom of contract, the jurisdictions for the governing law of the contract and the law of the seat of arbitration could be different from the law of the Site for a specific construction project. The parties will of course have no choice as to the law of the Site, as this is automatically the law of the country where construction occurs.

Table 4.1 FIDIC General Conditions are incompatible or inconsistent with governing law of the contract

Jurisdiction	**Particular Conditions**
Brazil[40]	• Exclude indirect damages • Time for notification of claims to be consistent with statutory limitations
China[41]	• Subcontracting the whole Works or main structure not permitted
Czech Republic[42]	• Replace liquidated damages with contractual penalty • Replace financing charges with contractual penalty or statutory interest
France[43]	• Payment of subcontractors by the Employer • Termination of the construction contract by the Employer
Germany[44]	• Limitation of liability • Define 'indirect loss' • Performance security • Cessation of Employer's liability

(*Continued*)

39 Donald Charrett (ed), *The International Application of FIDIC Contracts A Practical Guide* (Informa Law from Routledge, 2020).

40 Thiago Fernandes Moreira & Caio Gabra, Chapter 5.

41 Sun Yiwen, Chapter 6.

42 Lukas Klee, Vojtech Hradecny & Anastazie Jegorova, Chapter 7.

43 David Brown & Michael Conrad, Chapter 9.

44 Götz-Sebastian Hök & Henry Stiegelmier, Chapter 10.

Table 4.1 (Continued)

Jurisdiction	Particular Conditions
Italy[45]	• Acknowledgement that the contract has been completed by expert parties fully aware of the content and the implications
Malaysia[46]	• Copyright
Peru[47]	• Implied terms • Time-bar clauses are illegal • Fitness for purpose – Yellow & Silver Books • Meaning and scope of liability for fitness for purpose • Liquidated or delay damages must be considered *penalidades* • Limitation period of liability • Defects Notification Period is a timeframe of responsibility • Contractual waiver of liability is illegal • Definition of parties' specific liabilities and scope of work
Romania[48]	• Fit for purpose obligation • Limitation period for liability • Bankruptcy, insolvency, liquidation • 'Unusual clauses' • Specific requirements for public procurement contracts
South Africa[49]	• Unfair or unreasonable Particular Conditions unenforceable • Builder's lien • Innocent or negligent representation • Election in case of breach of clauses 8.7 & 8.8 • Termination for Contractor's default
United Arab Emirates[50]	• Defects Notification Period • No exclusion of gross negligence • No contracting out of statutory prescription periods for bringing a claim • Exceptional circumstances • Termination

No Particular Conditions are necessary for the use of FIDIC contracts subject to the governing law of the common law jurisdictions of Australia,[51] Fiji,[52] Ghana,[53] Hong Kong,[54] Papua New Guinea,[55] Sri Lanka,[56] or the civil law jurisdiction of Switzerland.[57]

45 Nicola Davide Romano, Chapter 13.
46 Ben Bury & Julie-Ann Pemberton, Chapter 14.
47 Jaime Gray & Jonnathan Bravo, Chapter 16.
48 Cremona Cotovelea, Chapter 17.
49 Johan Beyers, Chapter 18.
50 Erin Miller Rankin & Samantha Lord Hill, Chapter 21.
51 Donald Charrett, Chapter 4.
52 Nicholas Barnes & Melvin Chand, Chapter 8.
53 Kwame Amankwah-Twum & Priscilla Tara Buckman, Chapter 11.
54 Ben Bury & Julie-Ann Pemberton, Chapter 12.
55 Joseph Barbaro, Andrew McCormack, Nick Thorne, Ryan Warokra & Kenneth Imako, Chapter 15.
56 Harsha Cabral, Malith Mendis & Chamaka Ambagahawita, Chapter 19.
57 Sam Moss, Tino Schneider & Jean-Rodolphe Fiechter, Chapter 20.

Table 4.2 FIDIC General Conditions are incompatible or inconsistent with the laws of the Site

Jurisdiction	Particular Conditions
Brazil	• Defect notice period
China	• Construction contract cannot materially change the bidding documents and proposals • Defects Notification period cannot be more than two years • Retention is limited to 5% • Commencement date of Defects Notification Period
Italy	• Provisions relating to bankruptcy, insolvency, and liquidation
Romania	• Design • Taking over the Works

Table 4.3 FIDIC General Conditions are incompatible or inconsistent with the laws of the seat of the arbitration or relevant laws on dispute determination

Jurisdiction	Particular Conditions
Brazil	• Engineer's decision not final and binding • Dispute Board decision not final and binding
Czech Republic	• Dispute Board decision not enforceable

No Particular Conditions are necessary for the use of FIDIC contracts where the Site is in Australia, Czech Republic, Fiji, France, Germany, Ghana, Hong Kong, Malaysia, Papua New Guinea, Peru, South Africa, Sri Lanka, Switzerland, or United Arab Emirates.

No Particular Conditions are necessary for the use of FIDIC contracts where the seat of the dispute determination is in Australia, China, Fiji, France, Germany, Ghana, Hong Kong, Italy, Malaysia, Papua New Guinea, Peru, Romania, South Africa, Sri Lanka, Switzerland, or United Arab Emirates.

Considering the range of jurisdictions covered, there are a relatively small number of changes that need to be made to FIDIC General Conditions for their international use. In the authors' view, Tables 4.1–4.3 highlight the extent to which FIDIC contracts approach an international norm, and support for *lex constructionis*.

4.6 International commercial arbitration

Freedom of contract allows parties to select arbitration to finally resolve disputes, rather than the courts. Arbitration is frequently preferred over litigation in court for construction disputes because of features such as confidentiality, and the exercise of party autonomy to tailor a suitable process and select a tribunal with appropriate legal and technical skills. For international disputes, international arbitration is also preferred as it avoids any perceived home country bias in domestic courts.

The importance for *lex constructionis* of the adoption of the *New York Convention* by over 160 countries cannot be overstated. The *New York Convention* ensures that international arbitration is accepted in the majority of countries as a binding method of dispute resolution, so that court proceedings can be stayed to permit arbitration, and arbitral awards can be enforced in most jurisdictions.

International arbitration is well suited to the resolution of international construction disputes. International arbitral tribunals typically comprise practitioners from different jurisdictions and legal systems, and there are many international arbitrators with expertise in handling complex construction disputes and their extensive technical documentation.

International arbitration is well supported by a number of international organisations. These organisations promote principles, rules, and procedures that are widely accepted as international norms, independent of legal systems. The following are a few examples of such organisations, and their publications that support international arbitration practice:

- The United Nations Commission on International Trade Law (**UNCITRAL**),[58]
- The International Bar Association (**IBA**) (80,000 members in 170 countries),[59]
- The Chartered Institute of Arbitrators (**CIArb**) (16,000 members in 149 countries),[60]
- The International Chamber of Commerce (**ICC**).[61]

There are also many institutions that publish arbitration rules and administer international arbitrations, such as the ICC Court of Arbitration, the London Court of International Arbitration (**LCIA**),[62] the Singapore International Arbitration Centre (**SIAC**),[63] and the Hong Kong International Arbitration Centre (**HKIAC**).[64] Notwithstanding the inevitable differences in rules and procedures, it is submitted that there is broad consensus on the principles of international arbitration that promote consistency of approach and just and equitable outcomes.

A considerable degree of international comity in arbitration law is evidenced by the 116 jurisdictions that have based their arbitration law on the *UNCITRAL Model Law on*

---

58 UNCITRAL publishes: Convention on the Recognition and Enforcement of Foreign Arbitral Awards 1958 – New York Convention (165 parties); UNCITRAL Model Law on International Commercial Arbitration 2006 (83 countries, 116 jurisdictions); UNCITRAL Arbitration Rules. https://uncitral.un.org/en/texts/arbitration (accessed 8 September 2020).

59 IBA publishes Rules on Taking of Evidence in International Arbitration; Guidelines on Party Representation in International Arbitration; Guidelines on Conflicts of Interest in International Arbitration; Guidelines for Drafting International Arbitration Clauses. www.ibanet.org/Publications/publications_IBA_guides_and_free_materials.aspx (accessed 8 September 2020).

60 CIArb publishes International Arbitration Practice Guidelines; ADR Procedures in Arbitration; Consumers and Parties with Significant Differences of Resources; Multi-Party Arbitrations; CIArb Code of Professional and Ethical Conduct. www.ciarb.org (accessed 8 September 2020).

61 ICC publishes ICC Rules of Arbitration; Procedure; Practice Notes; Checklists; ICC Terms of Reference; ICC procedural timetable. https://iccwbo.org/dispute-resolution-services/ (accessed 8 September 2020).

62 www.lcia.org (accessed 8 September 2020).

63 www.siac.org.sg (accessed 8 September 2020).

64 www.hkiac.org (accessed 8 September 2020).

International Commercial Arbitration (***Model Law***).[65] This uniformity of arbitral law coupled with respected international organisations that administer international arbitrations is a significant contributor to *lex constructionis*.

Arbitration is discussed in more detail in ¶28.11.

4.7 *Lex mercatoria*

The Law Merchant or ***lex mercatoria*** can be defined as an a-national system of best practice in international commercial law, which has evolved by international custom and usage, and which is free from legal technicalities. As noted earlier, *lex constructionis* is a subset of *lex mercatoria*, which applies to the broad class of international commercial contracts.

The *lex mercatoria* has a long history:

> *Lex mercatoria* (from the Latin for 'merchant law'), often referred to as 'the Law Merchant' in English, is the body of commercial law used by merchants throughout Europe during the medieval period. It evolved similar to English common law as a system of custom and best practice, which was enforced through a system of merchant courts along the main trade routes. It functioned as the international law of commerce. It emphasised contractual freedom and alienability of property, while shunning legal technicalities and deciding cases *ex aequo et bono*. A distinct feature was the reliance by merchants on a legal system developed and administered by them. States or local authorities seldom interfered and did not interfere a lot in internal domestic trade. Under *lex mercatoria* trade flourished and states took in large amounts of taxation.[66]

However, the concept of *lex mercatoria* is of limited practical value unless its content can be determined. Fortunately, there are at least two modern expressions of *lex mercatoria* that can be applied to international construction contracts: the *UNIDROIT Principles of International Commercial Contracts*[67] and the *TransLex Principles*.[68]

There are many references discussing *lex mercatoria*, but few discussing *lex constructionis*.[69]

---

65 https://uncitral.un.org/en/texts/arbitration/modellaw/commercial_arbitration/status (accessed 15 January 2021).

66 https://en.wikipedia.org/wiki/Lex_mercatoria (accessed 5 March 2020).

67 www.unidroit.org/contracts#UPICC (accessed 9 September 2020).

68 www.trans-lex.org/principles/of-transnational-law-(lex-mercatoria) (accessed 10 September 2020).

69 A Google search on 9 September 2020 yielded the following in English: Charles Molineaux, 'Moving Towards a Constrcution Lex Mercatoria – A Lex Constructionis' www.trans-lex.org/126700/_/a-lex-constructionis-14-j-int-l-arb-1997-no-1-at-55-et-seq/; Yuliya Pshenichnaya, 'Lex constructionis as the legal source of the international construction contract' www.hse.ru/en/edu/vkr/206782720; CEC Jansen, 'The Case for the European Lex Constructionis' https://research.vu.nl/en/publications/the-case-for-the-european-lex-constructionis; Novoselov Mikhail Alexandrovich, 'Application Lex Constructionis for the Regulation of International Construction Contracts in Russia' http://urvak.org/articles/bizne-vypusk-4-primenenie-lex-constructionis-v-ros/; Lukas Klee, *International Construction Law* (Wiley Blackwell, Hoboken NJ, 2nd edn, 2018) Chapter 5.

4.7.1 UNIDROIT Principles of Commercial Contracts[70]

4.7.1.1 What is UNIDROIT?

UNIDROIT is the International Institute for the Unification of Private Law, an independent intergovernmental organisation with its seat in Rome. It studies needs and methods for modernising, harmonising, and co-ordinating private, and in particular commercial, law as between states and groups of states. UNIDROIT's 63-member states are drawn from the five continents and represent a variety of different legal, economic, and political systems as well as different cultural backgrounds.[71]

4.7.1.2 What are the *UNIDROIT Principles*?

The *UNIDROIT Principles of International Commercial Contracts* (*UP*) are a set of a-national principles that apply to the formation, validity, interpretation, performance, and termination of commercial contracts.

They are considered to be a modern statement of a *lex mercatoria* for international contracts which are drafted by legal experts from many countries, common law, and civil law in which the rules are not derived from any particular national law. Accordingly, the *UP* embody contractual principles which are, or can be, recognised by the laws of any country, whether common law or civil law.

There have been four editions of the *UP*: 1994–120 articles, 2004–185 articles, 2010–211 articles, and 2016–211 articles. A helpful Table of Correspondence is available to cross reference the Articles in the four editions and identify new or changed clauses or comments.[72] The 2016 *UP* are available in the official languages of English, French, German, Italian, and Spanish as well as Chinese, Japanese, Korean, Portuguese, Romanian, and Turkish.[73] In addition to the text of the Principles, a version with comments in English and French is also available, in which the reasons for and application of each subclause is explained.[74] Many provisions are illustrated by examples of applicable contractual situations.

The dynamic nature of the *UP* in responding to contemporary developments is evident in the addition of new chapters on set-off, assignment of rights, and limitation periods in the 2004 edition, and the new chapter on plurality of obligors and obligees in the 2010 edition. The 2016 edition is not intended as a revision of the previous edition but was altered marginally to take better into account the special needs of long-term contracts.[75]

---

70 A more detailed discussion of the use of the *UNIDROIT Principles* in international construction contracts is in Donald Charrett, *Contracts for Construction and Engineering Projects* (Informa Law from Routledge, 2nd edn 2022) Chapter 36; Donald Charrett, 'The Use of the UNIDROIT Principles in International Construction Contracts' (2013) 1 *International Construction Law Review* 507.

71 www.unidroit.org (accessed 8 September 2020).

72 UNIDROIT, *UNIDROIT Principles of International Commercial Contracts* (UNIDROIT, 2016) xxxvii.

73 www.unidroit.org/instruments/commercial-contracts/unidroit-principles-2016 (accessed 6 March 2020).

74 UNIDROIT, *UNIDROIT Principles of International Commercial Contracts* (UNIDROIT, 2016), www.unidroit.org/unidroit-principles-2016/unidroit-principles-2016-overview/english-integral (accessed 24 August 2021).

75 UNIDROIT, *UNIDROIT Principles of International Commercial Contracts* (UNIDROIT, 2016) vii.

The *UP* and explanatory notes on each clause are available on the UNIDROIT website.[76] There is a considerable literature available on the *UP*, and their application to contractual issues in various national legal systems.[77] Also available are citations of court and arbitration cases in which the *UP* have been considered. These are available by jurisdiction, and by subject. They have also usefully been tabulated by sub-clause, so that it is easy to find the treatment a particular sub-clause has been given in different jurisdictions.[78] The IBA recently published a book – *Perspectives in Practice of the UNIDROIT Principles 2016*[79] – that contains country perspectives on the application of the *UP* in 28 countries, and summaries of court and arbitration cases from many countries illustrating how the various provisions of the *UP* have been applied in a variety of situations.

4.7.1.3 How are the *UNIDROIT Principles* applied?

The possible applications of the *UP* are aptly summed up in the Preamble:

> These Principles set forth general rules for international commercial contracts.
>
> They shall be applied when the parties have agreed that their contract be governed by them.
>
> They may be applied when the parties have agreed that their contract be governed by general principles of law, the *lex mercatoria* or the like.
>
> They may be applied when the parties have not chosen any law to govern their contract.
>
> They may be used to interpret or supplement international uniform law instruments.
>
> They may be used to interpret or supplement domestic law.
>
> They may serve as a model for national and international legislators.

The *UP* have been applied in these various ways by many hundreds of arbitral tribunals and courts around the world.[80]

4.7.1.4 What are the benefits of using the *UNIDROIT Principles*?

The *UP* are a private codification of civil law, approved by an intergovernmental institution. Although neither treaty, nor compilation of usages, nor standard terms of contract, they are in fact a manifestation of transnational law:

> The UNIDROIT Principles of International Commercial Contracts are a reliable Fonti [sic] of international commercial law in international arbitration for they 'contain in essence a restatement of those "principes directeurs" that have enjoyed universal acceptance and,

---

76 www.unidroit.org/contracts#UPICC (accessed 24 August 2021).

77 www.unilex.info/dynasite.cfm?dssid=2377&dsmid=13623&x=1 (accessed 24 August 2021).

78 www.unilex.info/dynasite.cfm?dssid=2377&dsmid=14311 (accessed 24 August 2021).

79 www.ibanet.org/Publications/Perspectives-in-Practice-of-the-UNIDROIT-Principles-2016.aspx (accessed 6 March 2020).

80 www.unilex.info/instrument/principles (accessed 8 September 2020); IBA, *Perspectives in Practice of UNIDROIT Principles 2016* (IBA, 2019), www.ibanet.org/Publications/Perspectives-in-Practice-of-the-UNIDROIT-Principles-2016.aspx (accessed 9 October 2020).

> moreover, are at the heart of those most fundamental notions which have consistently been applied in arbitral practice.'[81]

The *UP* comprise rules 'broadly recognised throughout the world and the practice of international contracts.'[82] In the authors' view, the *UNIDROIT Principles of International Commercial Contracts* (*UP*) represent a contemporary statement of the modern content of the *lex mercatoria* that has practical application to international commercial contracts, and specifically to international construction contracts.

4.7.1.5 *UNIDROIT Principles* on hardship and *force majeure*

The *UP* include provisions that provide principles applicable to situations where contractual performance as originally anticipated is adversely affected by unforeseen circumstances. These provisions are particularly relevant to the contractual issues in construction projects arising from the COVID-19 pandemic in 2020.[83]

Whilst these provisions provide adjustment mechanisms to relieve a party from the consequences of events that impose excessively onerous financial burdens, they do so within the principles of freedom of contract and *pacta sunt servanda.* In circumstances where the performance of a contract becomes more onerous for a party because of hardship,[84] it is still required to perform its obligations.[85] However, it is entitled to request renegotiation of the contract; in the event that the parties fail to reach agreement within a reasonable time, either party may resort to the court.[86] The court has the power to terminate the contract or adapt the contract with a view to restoring its equilibrium.[87]

The *force majeure* provisions excuse performance in circumstances where

> the non-performance was due to an impediment beyond its control and that it could not reasonably be expected to have taken the impediment into account at the time of the conclusion of the contract or to have avoided or overcome it or its consequences.[88]

Non-performance is only excused for the reasonable period in which the impediment operated and is subject to notice within a reasonable time.[89]

A party that owes an obligation other than one to pay money is required to perform unless, *inter alia*, performance is impossible in law or fact, or performance or enforcement is unreasonably burdensome or expensive.[90]

---

81 ICC Award No 9797 www.unilex.info/principles/case/668 (accessed 8 September 2020).

82 ICC Award No 8264 www.unilex.info/principles/case/658 (accessed 9 September 2020).

83 For a discussion of the application of the *UNIDROIT Principles* on hardship and *force majeure* to address the contractual impacts of non-performance arising from the COVOID-19 pandemic, see: UNIDROIT Secretariat, 'The UNIDROIT Principles of International Commercial Contracts and the COVID-19 Health Crisis' www.unidroit.org/english/news/2020/200721-principles-covid19-note/note-e.pdf (accessed 7 September 2020).

84 Hardship is defined in Article 6.2.2 Definition of hardship.

85 Article 6.2.1 Contract to be observed.

86 Article 6.2.3 Effects of hardship.

87 Ibid.

88 Article 7.1.7 *Force majeure.*

89 Ibid.

90 Article 7.2.2 Performance of non-monetary obligation.

These articles have been introduced, either literally or with only few modifications, in a number of national codifications, including People's Republic of China (only *force majeure*), Russian Federation, France, Argentina, Estonia, Lithuania, and Brazil.[91]

4.7.1.6 Summary

The *UP* represent a set of overarching principles that are appropriate to regulate an international construction contract in a manner that is fair to all parties, straightforward to apply, predictable in outcome, independent of a particular national legal system, and generally consistent with the contract law and principles in any country (with some exceptions).

4.7.2 TransLex Principles

4.7.2.1 Content

The *TransLex Principles* are a recent manifestation of what Klaus Berger refers to as the 'creeping codification of the *lex mercatoria.*' These principles are based on compilation of a list that

> reproduces all those rules and principles of the new *lex mercatoria* as black-letter law which have been accepted in international arbitral and contract practice together with comprehensive comparative references. The list unifies the various sources that have fostered the evolution of a transnational commercial legal system into one single, open-ended set of rules and principles: reception of general principles of law, codification of international trade law by 'formulating agencies,' case law of international arbitral tribunals, the law-making forces of international model contract forms and general conditions of trade, and the analysis of comparative legal science.[92]

The recognition that the 'new' *lex mercatoria* is constantly evolving and needs to draw on all relevant sources for its legitimacy has resulted in a different approach to UNIDROIT. The *TransLex Principles* take into account comparative research and the comprehensive case law of international arbitral tribunals. '[T]he most significant contribution is not the list per se, but the technique that gave rise to and is meant to ensure its open-endedness and continuing evolution: the technique of creeping codification.'[93]

A basic difference between the *UNIDROIT Principles* and the *TransLex Principles* is that the latter is not limited to the field of international commercial contract law. The TransLex

> list follows the decision-making practice of international arbitration and therefore contains legal principles that are related to those fields of law which play a predominant role in international arbitral case law, such as international company law, conflict of laws, rules of evidence, the international law of expropriation and general arbitration law.[94]

91 UNIDROIT Secretariat, 'The UNIDROIT Principles of International Commercial Contracts and the COVID-19 Health Crisis' 4, www.unidroit.org/english/news/2020/200721-principles-covid19-note/note-e.pdf (accessed 7 September 2020).

92 Klaus Peter Berger, *The Creeping Codification of the New Lex Mercatoria* (Wolters Kluwer, 2010) 256.

93 L Yves Fortier, 'The New, New *Lex Mercatoria,* or Back to the Future' (2001) 17(2) *Arbitration International* 121, 127.

94 Klaus Peter Berger, *The Creeping Codification of the New Lex Mercatoria* (Wolters Kluwer, 2010) 258.

The *TransLex Principles* are maintained in an online database, easily accessible to practitioners in any jurisdiction. The website has four sections as follows (as at 11 September 2020):

- **Principles**, comprising 143 *TransLex Principles* in 14 chapters, 1408 full text comparative references, and 2193 contract clauses
- **Bibliography**, containing 1025 entries on transnational law
- **Materials**, comprising a collection of contemporary materials on transnational and arbitration law (86 documents)
- **Archive**, comprising 62 rare historical documents on arbitration and ADR (including England's oldest surviving arbitral award from AD118)

4.7.2.2 *TransLex Principles* on hardship and *force majeure*

The *TransLex Principles* contain provisions on hardship[95] and *force majeure*[96] applicable to situations where contractual performance as originally anticipated is adversely affected by unforeseen circumstances. These provisions are similar to the corresponding *UNIDROIT Principles*. In respect of hardship,[97] there is a good faith obligation to renegotiate the contract if there is a need to adapt it to changed circumstances;[98] failing party agreement a court can adapt the contract to the changed circumstances or terminate the contract.[99] Non-performance as a consequence of *force majeure* is excused for the period of the impediment, subject to reasonable notice. Any limitation period is suspended so as not to expire before one year after the relevant impediment has ceased to exist.[100]

As with the corresponding *UP* discussed earlier, these provisions are particularly relevant to the contractual issues in construction projects arising from the COVID-19 pandemic in 2020 by providing a mechanism for equitable changes to contractual obligations arising from circumstances outside the control of either party.

4.8 Proposed principles of *lex constructionis*

It was earlier suggested that *lex constructionis* can promote best practice for successful projects in which the contracting parties' legitimate expectations can be realised. In the authors' view, those legitimate expectations are typically along the following lines.

The Employer expects completion of the project on time, for the contract price and to the agreed standard of quality, and timely and adequate communication from the Contractor of any departures from the original scope of works, the materialisation of risks, and any claims.

The Contractor expects prompt payment of all amounts due under the Contract, and the freedom to carry out the construction in accordance with the Contract without hindrance

95 No. IV.6.7 – Duty to renegotiate; No. IV.6.8 – (Re-) Negotiation agreement / clause (*pactum de negotiando*); No. VIII.1 – Definition [hardship]; No. VIII.2 – Legal consequences [of hardship].

96 No. VI.3 – *Force majeure*.

97 No. VIII.1 – Definition [hardship].

98 No. IV.6.7 – Duty to renegotiate.

99 No. VIII.2 – Legal consequences [of hardship].

100 No. VI.3 – *Force majeure*.

by the Employer. Also, timely and adequate communication from the Employer of the materialisation of any risks, communication of instructions and assessment of claims.

It is submitted that the principles proposed in ¶4.8.1, if followed, would fulfil those expectations. The proposed principles have been formulated taking into account the unique features of construction projects and construction contracts discussed earlier, the Abrahamson Principles of balanced risk allocation,[101] the FIDIC General Conditions in the rainbow suite, the FIDIC Golden Principles,[102] and 'social obligations' owed to third parties. They are also influenced by Charles Molyneaux's paper on this topic in which he formulated a 'modest Mosaic ten' principles.[103]

One of the criticisms that could be directed to the proposed (or any) principles of *lex constructionis* is that they cannot cover all situations, nor can they necessarily be applied in their entirety in many situations. The following discussion of principles in the context of *lex mercatoria* is equally applicable to the proposed principles of *lex constructionis*:

> General principles do not necessarily have pre-set conditions for application. Instead they merely constitute 'rules of optimal application' which means that they may be complied with in varying degrees. The required degree of compliance depends not only on the actual but also on the legal options open to the target group. Application of general principles therefore requires a substantial process of weighing up contradictory principles and rules. General principles are therefore always subject to a continual discussion about the effectiveness and scope[104] [citations omitted].

4.8.1 Proposed principles

4.8.1.1 Overarching principles

(1) *Pacta sunt servanda.*

(2) ***Rebus sic stantibus*** – doctrines or rules relating to changed conditions.

(3) The parties must act in accordance with good faith and fair dealing in construction contracts.

4.8.1.2 Scope

(4) The contract defines, in writing, the original scope of work and the known conditions at the Site.

(5) The Employer has the right to instruct Variations consistent with the original scope of the Contract, and the Contractor has the obligation to carry out all such Variations.

(6) Construction works must be carried out so as to protect the health and safety of workers.

(7) Construction works must not adversely affect the environment or the interests of third parties.

101 Max W Abrahamson, 'Risk Management' (1983) *International Construction Law Review* 241, 244.

102 Donald Charrett (ed), *The International Application of FIDIC Contracts A Practical Guide* (Informa Law from Routledge, 2020) Chapter 2.

103 Charles Molineux, 'Moving towards a Lex Mercatoria – a Lex Constructionis' (1977) 14(1) *Journal of International Arbitration* 55.

104 Klaus Peter Berger, *The Creeping Codification of the New Lex Mercatoria* (Wolters Kluwer, 2010) 201.

(8) Subject to any contractual requirements, the Contractor selects the methods and timing of the Works.

4.8.1.3 Risk

(9) Each risk is allocated to the party best able to manage and control it and the consequences if it eventuates, or to the party who will derive any benefit or suffer the least consequences if the risk eventuates.
(10) A party is not allocated risks that it cannot insure for or has insufficient financial resources to bear.
(11) The Contractor is responsible for the Works whilst it is in possession of the Site.

4.8.1.4 Time

(12) The parties have a reasonable time to perform their obligations and exercise their rights.
(13) The Contractor provides the Employer with prompt and adequate notice of any unexpected conditions that affect its performance, the occurrence of any risk events, and any claims.
(14) The Employer provides the Contractor with prompt and adequate notice of the occurrence of any risk events that affect the Contractor, instructions, and responses to claims.
(15) The Contractor is liable to pay damages if it does not complete the Works by the contractually agreed date.

4.8.1.5 Cost

(16) The Employer has adequate financial resources to complete the Contract.
(17) The Contractor provides security for its performance.
(18) The Employer pays the Contractor its contractual entitlements promptly.

4.8.1.6 Quality

(19) The Contractor either rectifies defects in the Works or pays damages to reinstate the Works to the contractually specified quality.

4.8.1.7 Disputes

(20) Unresolved disputes are finally determined by arbitration.

4.8.2 Discussion

Space does not permit a detailed exposition of each of the preceding principles. Some would probably be accepted as implied terms that go without saying. Others may be more controversial.

The overarching principles are contained in statements of the *lex mercatoria*, such as the *UNIDROIT Principles*. In the authors' view they are important for successful execution of construction projects that frequently take place over a long time and involve changed circumstances. In particular, the requirements of honesty, fairness, and reasonableness inherent in the good faith principle will necessarily be relied upon to resolve amicably (where possible) many of the expected and unexpected issues that can arise during the execution of a construction contract.

The principles on scope acknowledge the complexity of construction projects, the possibility that the scope may need to change, and that the Works impact on third parties and the environment. Risks are inherent in any construction project, and their appropriate allocation is often critical to achieving a successful project.[105]

The principles on time reiterate the requirement of reasonableness and emphasise the importance of adequate and timely communication from Contractor to Employer and vice versa. Damages for late completion are appropriate to compensate the Employer for its inability to make commercial use of the constructed facility from the agreed date.

Certainty and promptness of payment are usually of great importance to the Contractor and may be critical to its solvency. The requirement for a Contractor to rectify or pay for defect rectification is merely a construction specific implementation of *pacta sunt servanda*.

The near universal implementation of the *New York Convention*, the norms of international arbitration, and the finality and enforcement of awards are the basis for arbitration to be the most appropriate method for resolving international construction disputes.

4.9 Conclusion

The impact of COVID-19 on construction projects reinforced some aspects of *lex constructionis*, specifically the legislated adjustments to working methods on construction sites to ensure worker safety. Conversely, the frequent lack of legal or contractual provisions suitable to make appropriate adjustments for unforeseen circumstances in situations such as COVID-19 indicates the need for wider application of the principles of *lex constructionis*.

The foundations of *lex constructionis* already exist: a *lex mercatoria*, international contracts that can be implemented in any jurisdiction and international arbitration of disputes in accordance with widely accepted laws and rules that results in final awards that can be enforced in most jurisdictions.

It is submitted that the 20 principles of *lex constructionis* proposed can encourage projects that provide better value for money, and promote international trade and greater comity between nations whilst fulfilling the parties' legitimate expectations. As with the *lex mercatoria*, the *lex constructionis* is 'not carved in stone but has always been, still is, and will always be subject to constant review, textual refinement and adaptation to new developments in international business practice.'[106]

The closest approach to a *lex constructionis*, that is as an independent, supranational legal system not subject to the vagaries of a particular jurisdiction, may be achieved by:

- Use of an internationally accepted standard form of contract such as FIDIC,

105 For a discussion of the consequences of inappropriately allocating risk, see JICA's 'Check List for One Sided Contracts' in ¶3.9.3.1. www.jica.go.jp/english/our_work/types_of_assistance/oda_loans/oda_op_info/guide/c8h0vm0000aoeprl-att/guide02.pdf (accessed 9 September 2020).

106 Klaus Peter Berger, *The Creeping Codification of the New Lex Mercatoria* (Wolters Kluwer, 2010) 277.

- *UNIDROIT Principles* (or *TransLex Principles*) as the governing law of the contract, and
- International arbitration as the final method of dispute resolution.

Such a contract exercises the parties' freedom of contract and is de-localised to the maximum extent achievable for a construction contract. It must always be accepted that the construction of a facility at a particular location in a specific jurisdiction will be subject to laws applicable to construction projects in that jurisdiction. However, it is submitted that there is considerable international agreement on many of the overarching principles underlying laws to protect the health and safety of workers, protection of the environment, and the rights of third parties impacted by construction, and these are probably the least controversial of the proposed principles of *lex constructionis*.

CHAPTER 5

Entry into a contract

CONTENTS

The commentary contained in this chapter generally applies to all types of construction contracts.

5.1 Tender appraisal, selecting a Contractor, and advising on a construction contract

Very often an engineer, architect, or quantity surveyor is called upon to prepare the necessary contract at the tender stage. This assumes that a choice of contracting strategy[1] and the basis of pricing[2] have already been decided upon by the Employer. That in itself requires a realistic and clear understanding of the capabilities and expectations of the Employer.[3] The nature of the contract is normally discussed with the Employer and very often one or other standard form contracts is agreed upon.[4] Whilst it would normally be safe to advise the Employer to contract on one of the standard forms commonly utilised in the industry, the professional should be careful not to suggest a document totally unsuitable for its use given the circumstances of a particular contract. For example, it would be negligent to prepare a tender utilising standard terms and conditions published for use in a contract where the design is prepared by an architect or engineer when the contract is intended to be a design and construct contract in which the Contractor prepares the design.

Appendix A contains details of 31 issues that should be considered when drafting a contract.

---

1 Philip Loots & Nick Henchie, 'Worlds Apart: EPC and EPCM Contracts: Risk Issues and Allocation' (2007) *International Construction Law Review* 252.

2 Philip Loots & Dr Donald Charrett, 'Reconsidering Procurement Criteria and Procedures for Major Infrastructure Projects' (2017) *International Construction Law Review* 69.

3 Donald Charrett, *Contracts for Construction and Engineering Projects* (Informa Law from Routledge, 2nd edn 2022) Chapter 7; Dr Donald Charrett, 'Design Life or Service Life: What is the difference?' (2017) *International Construction Law Review* 16.

4 See ¶3.10 for a discussion of standard form contracts.

DOI: 10.4324/9781003206873-5

If, however, the professional feels that it is outside his or her expertise to give proper advice on the form of contract, then he/she should either seek or advise the Employer to seek legal advice.

After tenders have been received and opened, the Employer's agent is invariably charged with considering the tenders. This consideration is vitally important, and the professional must exercise care in making his or her assessment. The professional should take into account matters such as the Tenderers' reputations, the performance of the Tenderers on other projects, the solvency of the Tenderers and their ability to perform the work with adequate resourcing, and consider carefully the prices or rates tendered. If necessary, meetings should be held with the Tenderers to ascertain the relevant information and adequate enquiries made to confirm its veracity.

Written bid-clarification logs with each Tenderer should be kept contemporaneously and signed off progressively by both parties. Construction contracts often bind the parties for a protracted period of time and involve considerable sums of money. It is therefore vital for the successful completion of the Works that a positive relationship between the parties is properly established from the outset.

The architect, engineer, or quantity surveyor should not be a slave to merely promoting the lowest tendered price.[5] There are matters which have to be taken into account in assessing the ability of a Tenderer to complete the Works satisfactorily within its tendered price; these include its projected workload and its reputation for spurious claims and litigation. Proper advice, therefore, entails a consideration of each and every element which ultimately contributes to the successful completion of the Contract.

5.2 Letters of intent

A **letter of intent** is a document issued prior to entry into a contract which signifies the Employer's intent to enter into a contract with a preferred Tenderer at a future time.[6] It is used where, notwithstanding the absence of agreement on all aspects of the legal arrangements, the Employer wishes to preserve the benefits of a contractor's tender. At a given point in time, the Employer may not wish or be able to make the full commitments entailed by a contract, but may nevertheless desire the Contractor not to withdraw its tender, and to commence to ready itself for, or even make a start on, the Works. A properly drawn letter of intent can provide an Employer with those benefits whilst at the same time providing time for subsequent negotiation to agree on all formal contract clauses. Such a letter will not normally constitute an acceptance of the tender, nor oblige the Employer to enter into a formal contract.[7] The general position is that properly drawn letters of intent are at most non-promissory statements of intention.[8] Letters of intent should, however, be treated with extreme caution.

There may also be significant benefits for a Contractor arising from the issue of a letter of intent. A letter of intent may amount to a promise by the Employer that if the Contractor undertakes some work it will receive payment even if no contract is entered into.[9] Provided the Contractor

5 Philip Loots & Dr Donald Charrett, 'Reconsidering Procurement Criteria and Procedures for Major Infrastructure Projects: Why the Use of "Price" as the Determining Factor in Construction Procurement Decisions is Wrong' (2017) *International Construction Law Review* 69.

6 As was the case in *British Steel Corp v Cleveland Bridge and Engineering Co Ltd* [1984] 1 All ER 504.

7 *Turriff Construction Ltd v Regalia Knitting Mills Ltd* (1971) 9 BLR 20.

8 *Australian European Finance Corp Ltd V Sheahan* (1993) 60 SASR 187.

9 *British Steel Corp v Cleveland Bridge and Engineering Co Ltd* [1984] 1 All ER 504.

is careful to comply with its terms, such a letter can provide a legally enforceable obligation on the Employer for it to pay for work done prior to, or even in the absence of, a subsequently concluded formal contract. For example, in *Cox Constructions Pty Ltd v Décor Ceilings Pty Ltd (No 2)*,[10] the Contractor issued a letter of intent to a subcontractor which made reference to a formal agreement to be signed 'in due course,' but the subcontractor was nevertheless instructed to commence work. In the event, the parties could not agree on the terms of the formal agreement, and the parties remained bound by the terms of the letter of intent for the work done.

Typically, a letter of intent is issued after agreement on the essential terms of a contract, with some provisions requiring further negotiations before they are agreed. The legal effect of a letter of intent will depend on normal legal principles, that is on construction of its terms to determine the intention of the parties. Depending on its terms and the surrounding matrix of facts, the nature of a letter of intent can be one of the following:

- A binding contract in which, pending execution of a formal contract for the whole of the project, the parties have assumed reciprocal obligations towards each other whose content is defined by the terms of the letter.[11]
- An 'if' contract whereby one party makes a standing offer to the other that if it carries out the defined performance of services, that other party will be remunerated for its performance. However, no obligation to perform is created and the reciprocal obligation to remunerate is limited by the express and implied terms of the offer in the letter of intent.[12]
- No contract has come into existence.[13]

A properly drafted a letter of intent will preclude a contract coming into existence until the parties have agreed on its terms, irrespective of whether the Contractor commences work in anticipation of a contract or not. In the case of *Abigroup Contractors Pty Ltd v ABB Service Pty Ltd (formerly ABB Engineering Construction Pty Ltd)*,[14] the subcontractor commenced work on site on the basis of a letter of intent and in anticipation of agreement on a contract with the Head Contractor. The parties never agreed on the terms of the contract, and the court held that no contract had come into existence. The subcontractor was therefore entitled to be paid for its work on the basis of a *quantum meruit*.[15]

In view of the potential consequences of a poorly drafted letter of intent inadvertently resulting in contractual obligations, the parties should be careful to ensure that their intentions regarding the enforceability or unenforceability of a letter of intent are made abundantly clear.

5.3 Preliminary agreements

Participants in the construction industry frequently enter into preliminary agreements which anticipate a further or subsequent agreement being entered into. Such preliminary

---

10 (2007) 23 BCL 347.

11 *AC Controls Ltd v British Broadcasting Corporation* (2002) 89 Con LR; [2002]; EWHC 3132; *Cox Constructions Pty Ltd v Décor Ceilings Pty Ltd (No 2)* (2007) 23 BCL 347.

12 Ibid.

13 *British Steel Corp v Cleveland Bridge and Engineering Co Ltd* [1984] 1 All ER 504; *Abigroup Contractors Pty Ltd v ABB Service Pty Ltd (formerly ABB Engineering Construction Pty Ltd)* [2004] NSWCA 181; (2005) 21 BCL 12.

14 [2003] NSWSC 665; (2005) 21 BCL 12.

15 Reasonable remuneration or 'as much as he has earned' (Latin). *Quantum meruit* is discussed in ¶21.12.

agreements are typically made where the Employer and Contractor require more certainty than would be provided by a letter of intent, but before they have finalised all the provisions of a formal agreement. As with a letter of intent, such an agreement should be carefully drafted to ensure that it incorporates the parties' intentions.

The leading case on the enforceability of preliminary agreements in Australia is *Masters v Cameron*,[16] a 1954 decision of the High Court. In *Masters v Cameron*, a vendor and purchaser signed an agreement for the sale of a farming property. The agreement stated that it was 'made subject to the preparation of a formal contract of sale which shall be acceptable to my solicitors on the above terms and conditions.' A deposit was paid. The purchasers however later declined to proceed with the sale. The High Court found that there was no contract unless and until a formal contract was signed.

In reaching its decision, the High Court formulated three categories in which to place preliminary or 'subject to contract' agreements. The three categories of preliminary contracts are as follows:

(1) Where the parties have reached finality in arranging all the terms of their bargain and intend to be immediately bound to the performance of those terms, but at the same time propose to have the terms restated in a form which will be fuller or more precise but not different in effect.
(2) Where the parties have completely agreed upon all the terms of their bargain and intend no departure from or addition to that which their agreed terms express or imply, but nevertheless have made performance of one or more of the terms conditional upon the execution of a formal document.
(3) Where the intention of the parties is not to make a concluded bargain at all, unless and until they execute a formal contract, that is the preliminary agreement is a mere 'agreement to agree.'[17]

There may also be a fourth class in which a preliminary agreement constitutes a binding contract. Such a case arises where, upon the proper construction of the preliminary agreement, it is apparent that the parties were content to be bound immediately and exclusively by the terms which they have agreed on, whilst expecting to make a further contract in substitution for the first contract, containing, by consent, additional terms.[18]

Into which category a preliminary agreement falls depends on the intention of the parties and is a question of construction of the words they have used. When drafting preliminary agreements, careful consideration should therefore be given to the intended effect of the preliminary agreement. As cautioned by McHugh J:

> However, the decisive issue is always the intention of the parties which must be objectively ascertained from the terms of the document when read in the light of the surrounding circumstances. If the terms of a document indicate that the parties intended to be bound immediately, effect must be given to that intention irrespective of the subject matter, magnitude or complexity of the transaction.[19]

16 (1954) 91 CLR 353.
17 Ibid. 360.
18 *GR Securities Pty Ltd v Baulkham Hills Private Hospital Pty Ltd* [1986] 40 NSWLR 631, 634 per McHugh JA.
19 Ibid.

The NSW Supreme Court in *Banque Brussels Lambert SA v Australian National Industries Ltd*[20] set out a number of factors to be considered when determining whether a letter of intent gives rise to contractual obligations. These factors may also be applied by analogy to preliminary agreements. The factors are:

(1) The ordinary rules of construction and interpretation relating to contracts apply.
(2) The overriding test is whether the parties intended that a binding contract would come into existence, as deduced from the document as a whole, seen against the background of the practices of the particular trade or industry and the surrounding circumstances.
(3) A presumption exists, in commercial transactions, that the parties intend for documents to be contractually binding and the onus of disproving this presumption rests with the party asserting that the document is not binding.

Set out next are a number of general drafting recommendations to assist the clarity of drafting of preliminary agreements and to protect each party's position:

- Don't use the ambiguous phrase 'subject to contract.' Instead, expressly state the extent to which a preliminary agreement is to be enforceable or unenforceable. For example, a preliminary agreement might state it is only enforceable to the extent that it authorises early works such as Site preparation.
- Expressly provide that either party may terminate the preliminary agreement in the event the parties are unable to agree on the subsequent formal documentation. This allows the parties to neatly end their relationship, however it will not be appropriate in all circumstances.
- Where a preliminary agreement authorises the early performance of Works by the Contractor, a form of contract (eg the form of contract issued with the invitation to tender along with agreed rates and prices) should be incorporated into the preliminary agreement so that the risk allocation and contractual mechanism for the early Works is prescribed. This avoids disputes (for example, as to the payment process, including the method used to value the work performed).
- Again, for early Works, where a capped amount is provided for, expressly state that the cap is the maximum amount which may be recovered by the Contractor prior to the formal documentation being signed and include an express waiver of any additional amounts.

5.4 The letter of acceptance

This describes the formal acceptance by the Employer of the Contractor's tender for the execution of the Contract Works. Communication of acceptance to the Contractor brings the Contract into existence. With the exception of postal delivery, the Contractor must actually receive the Employer's acceptance before it has been communicated. The common law rule in respect of postal acceptance is that it has been communicated when posted.

For clarity, the **letter of acceptance** should contain the following:

20 (1989) 21 NSWLR 502.

- A complete list of the contract documents including the tender documentation,
- Confirmation of all the adjustments made between Employer and Contractor in correcting errors or eliminating qualifications in the tender,
- The agreed contract price, and
- All amendments to the proposed conditions of contract agreed to prior to the award of the Contract.

5.5 Formal contract agreement

Many conditions of tender require the parties to enter into a formal contract agreement. Such formal contract agreements are frequently entered into long after the work has been commenced on Site, and on occasions one of the parties fails or refuses to enter into such an agreement. In such a situation, the prior dealings between the parties may amount to a preliminary agreement. However, as noted earlier, the terms of the parties' agreement short of the unexecuted formal agreement must be construed to determine which of the *Masters v Cameron* categories the preliminary agreement is in. It may be that the preliminary agreement defines the extent of the parties contractual obligations (as in *Cox Constructions Pty Ltd v Décor Ceilings Pty Ltd (No 2)*[21]), or it may be that no concluded agreement has been reached (as in *ABB Engineering Construction Pty Limited v Abigroup Contractors Pty Limited*[22]).

It is clear from the cases that the formal requirements for entry into a contract will not be satisfied whilst there is any disagreement on the formal terms. However, one party may accept the contractual terms proffered by the other, by conduct in commencing the work without protest.[23] In those circumstances it could be a breach of contract not to enter into a formal contract that was required by the terms accepted by conduct. However, this does not necessarily imply that a failure to enter a formal contract, having agreed to do so, would amount to breach of contract, as this would depend on the circumstances.

21 (2007) 23 BCL 347.
22 [2003] NSWSC 665; (2005) 21 BCL 12.
23 *Brambles Holdings Limited v Bathurst City Council* [2001] NSWCA 61; (2001) 53 NSWLR 153 at [71]–[81].

CHAPTER 6

General provisions

CONTENTS

6.1 Definitions

Reference should always be made to the definitions section of a contract as a first step when analysing conditions of contract. The definitions are a series of key words used throughout the contract documents and are often identified in a contract by initial capital letters or italics to distinguish them from the natural meaning of the same words. If the same terms or words are used in contract documents other than the General Conditions (such as the Special Conditions or a specification), in the absence of a specific definition, it would generally be inferred that the same defined meaning was intended. This is particularly the case if a word is capitalised as in the definitions section of the General Conditions.

Notwithstanding that various terms have a usually accepted meaning within the construction industry, the explicit contract definitions will always prevail over 'normal' usage. In this book, certain terms have been used for consistency, such as reference to the contracting parties as the Employer and the Contractor, and the person responsible for administering the Contract as the

DOI: 10.4324/9781003206873-6

Engineer. The meaning of these words and other 'terms of art' used in this book are defined in the Glossary. In the context of a particular contract (Contract), these terms should be replaced by the actual defined terms, with their meanings amended as required by the Contract.

6.2 Communications

Formal communications such as approvals, notices, and requests or determinations are usually required to be in writing, and the acceptable method of transmission may be defined in the Contract. 'Writing' may include electronic records, as in the 2017 FIDIC rainbow suite: '"written" or "in writing" means hand-written, type-written, printed or electronically made, and resulting in a permanent record.'[1]

If electronic communications are acceptable, the agreed system should be stated. The significance and importance of electronic communications are recognised in the US ConsensusDOCS, which includes 'ConsensusDocs 200.2 – Electronic Communications Protocol Addendum':

> The Electronic Communications Protocol Addendum is unique in the construction industry, comprehensively setting standards, processes and protocols that Parties will use to facilitate the accurate and secure transmittal of Electronic Communications among them during their Project. It is ideally intended to be completed no later than at the time the Owner and Contractor are preparing their Agreement, but may be entered into by amendment to an existing contract at any time. The 200.2 is a flexible document that can be used in any ConsensusDocs Agreement or in other contract Agreements.[2]

Example: Notices and communications

The 2017 FIDIC rainbow suite states that all Notices and other communications

(a) shall be:

  (i) a paper-original signed by the Contractor's Representative, the Engineer, or the authorised representative of the Employer (as the case may be); or

  (ii) an electronic original generated from any of the systems of electronic transmission stated in the Contract Data (if not stated, system(s) acceptable to the Engineer), where the electronic original is transmitted by the electronic address

or both, as stated in these Conditions; and . . .[3]

There may also be a contractual requirement that defined types of communications such as approvals, certificates, consents, and communications shall not be unreasonably withheld or delayed, for example 2017 FIDIC rainbow suite sub-clause 1.3. It is good practice to have default or deeming provisions to ensure that failure to issue a critical communication will not have adverse implications for the innocent party. For example, if the certificate of the Engineer is a condition of the liability of the Employer, the absence of the certificate will prevent the Contractor from recovering payment due to it, even if the Engineer's conduct is unreasonable.[4] The 2017 FIDIC

1 Sub-clause 1.2(d).

2 www.consensusdocs.org/wp-content/uploads/2019/02/200.2_Guidebook_08_12_13-1.pdf (accessed 5 January 2021).

3 Sub-clause 1.3(a).

4 *In re De Morgan, Snell & Co. and Rio De Janeiro Flour Milling Co.* (1891) Alfred A Hudson, *Hudson's Fourth Edition Table of Cases* (Sweet & Maxwell, 4th edn 1914) 185, 194.

rainbow suite contains many deeming provisions that ensure that the consequences of failure to act by a Party or the Engineer are defined. For example, if the Engineer does not issue a Notice to the Contractor that its programme does not comply with the Contract within the prescribed time, the Engineer shall be deemed to have given a Notice of No-objection.[5]

The importance of strict compliance with the formal and time requirements for communications, and the serious consequences of non-compliance (including time-bars discussed in ¶27.3.4), should not be underestimated.

6.3 Proper law of the contract

Contracts do not exist as mere pieces of paper in a vacuum – they formalise the obligations the parties have agreed to, according to some system of law. The proper law of the contract should be stated in the Contract to avoid any later dispute about it. As discussed in ¶2.6, the applicable or proper law of the contract is the law which the contract is subject to and which governs construction of its terms. The proper law of the contract is also referred to as the governing law of the contract, or the substantive law. These terms all refer to the particular system of law that governs the interpretation and validity of the contract, the rights and obligations of the parties, the mode of performance, and the consequences of breach of contract.[6]

Choice of law of the proper law of the contract often gives rise to particular difficulties in international contracts and there is no easy answer to the question as to whose law should apply. The Employer may seek to apply the law of its own country or the Site, and the Contractor may seek to apply another law with which it is familiar. If the parties state nothing, then the governing law will be determined according to the rules of law applied by the court of the country seized with any legal proceedings, or by an arbitral tribunal. This is not a situation that the parties should willingly allow to happen by lack of precision in the Contract, since decisions which involve the proper law of the contract may need to be taken at any time when it is being performed and, to say the least, certainty in this area is most desirable.

The parties can generally choose the proper law of the contract by an explicit provision in the Contract. For example, the 2017 FIDIC rainbow suite provides for the Parties to nominate the proper law of the contract in the Contract Data; if not stated, sub-clause 1.4 applies the law of the Country where the Site is located. The only qualifications on the parties' unfettered choice are that it must be (1) bona fide, (2) legal, and (3) not in conflict with public policy.

What this complexity highlights is that a carefully thought out and appropriate choice of law clause is essential in any international construction contract, since it is only then that the parties are likely to have a reasonable understanding of what the applicable law is, and thereby avoid the expense of a dispute about the conflict of laws rules that will determine the proper law of the contract.

If the parties, because they cannot agree that one of the laws of their respective countries should apply, elect to choose a third country's law as the applicable law, then they should take care to choose a law that they are familiar with, and are confident that it will uphold the bargain they have agreed. There are a number of issues to consider in choosing the governing law of the contract:

5 2017 FIDIC Yellow Book sub-clause 8.3.

6 *Compoagnie d'Armement Maritime SA v Compagnie Tunisienne de Navigation SA* [1971] A.C. 572, 603 per Lord Diplock.

- Are there any legal constraints on selecting the governing law in the country of the Site or the domiciles of the contracting parties?[7]
- Is the proposed law reasonably well developed and well known?
- Is legal advice on the proposed law readily available?
- Is the proposed law familiar to the contracting parties and Arbitrators?
- Is the chosen law predictable?
- Are there any potential inconsistencies with the laws of the country of the Site?
- Is the choice of law contrary to public policy or statute law in the forum where any action may be taken to enforce the terms of the Contract?
- The preferences of the contracting parties.
- Availability of reference materials (eg books, legislation, case law) in the language for communication in the Contract.

The modern tendency is to adopt an objective approach to the determination of the proper law of a contract where the parties did not themselves effect a choice – that is to determine 'the system of law by reference to which the contract was made or that with which the transaction has its closest and most real connection.'[8] The legal system with which the transaction has its closest and most real connection would, in most cases, be the one which the courts would presume to have objectively been intended by the parties. In determining that objective intention, courts would have regard to a number of matters, including the places of residence or business of the parties, the place of contracting, the place of performance, and the nature and subject matter of the contract.[9]

A choice of law clause in a contract may also refer to the (non-exclusive) jurisdiction of a particular court to resolve any disputes between the parties. The law relating to the exercise of jurisdiction by a court is referred to as the law of the forum, and it may be different to the proper law of the contract. Similarly, an arbitration agreement in a contract may refer to the law governing the existence and proceedings of the arbitral tribunal, sometimes referred to as the *lex arbitri* (or the law of the seat of arbitration), and this may also be different to the proper law of the contract.[10]

Normally, if the parties have not agreed upon any specific law to govern the procedure and administration of any arbitration, then the law in force in the place (or 'seat') where the arbitration takes place (law of the forum) will be that which is applicable. This may be to the disadvantage of the parties as the procedural law of the place of arbitration may not provide adequate procedures such as security for costs, laws relating to the discovery of documents, and for interim awards. Clearly, the choice of *lex arbitri* should be based on informed knowledge so as to ensure that there are no surprises.

6.4 Ambiguities or discrepancies in contract documents

Normally, any ambiguities or discrepancies in the contract documents affecting the work to be undertaken by the Contractor are to be explained and adjusted by the Engineer's instructions.

7 For example, Article 869 of the *Colombian Commercial Code* states that contracts that are performed in Colombia will be governed by Colombian Law.

8 *Bonython v Commonwealth* [1950] HCA 37; (1950) 81 CLR 486, 499. *Rome I* art 21 contains a similar provision: 'The contract should be governed by the law of the country with which it is most closely connected.'

9 *Akai Pty Ltd v People's Insurance Co Ltd* [1996] HCA 39; (1996) 188 CLR 418; (1996) 141 ALR 374; (1996) 71 ALJR 156.

10 *Enka Insaat v e Sanayoi AS v OOO Insurance Company Chubb* [2020] UKSC 38.

The Engineer normally has no contractual authority to resolve disputed matters of the legal construction of the Contract documents.[11] Similarly, the Engineer normally has no authority to order additional payments or deductions on the basis that the Contractor should be excused or penalised for misconstruing the Contract in a sense different from its true construction.

Where a genuine mistake or conflict or ambiguity exists which cannot be resolved or reconciled by the order of precedence defined in the Contract (if any) or the ordinary rules of construction – for example dimensional or other discrepancies occurring between the bills, specification, or drawings (including working drawings), or within any one of these documents – then the Engineer normally has the last word in order that s/he may maintain control over the physical work. In that event s/he normally only has power to award the Contractor compensation for changes which constitute a Variation to the Works under the Contract.

Where the Engineer has to explain the Contract in the event of an ambiguity or discrepancy, s/he is obliged to follow the legal rules of interpretation. In addition to the rules of construction discussed in Chapter 2, the following rules developed by common law courts (subject to any contrary intention expressed in the Contract) may assist in determining the meaning of a Contract which is not clear:

- Obvious clerical errors will be read as corrected.
- The words take precedence where there is a discrepancy between numbers given both in written form and in figures.
- Where part of a contract is in a standard printed form, any alterations or additions written in for the particular contract will outweigh any inconsistent standard clauses.
- Corrections and erasures are presumed to have been made before signature of the Contract, and therefore to be valid. Alterations proved to have been made after execution of the Contract are not valid unless agreed to by both parties.
- There is also a presumption that a change of words implies a change of meaning, and that the same word or phrase is intended to have the same meaning throughout a contract.
- If it is not possible to reconcile the various documents making up a construction contract, they may be interpreted in the way least favourable to the drafter of the document because s/he had control over the drafting of the Contract (*contra proferentem*).[12]

It should be noted that the *contra proferentem* rule may have no application in respect of standard forms of contract. The matter of construction of standard forms was commented upon in *Tersons Ltd v Stevenage Development Corp*,[13] where Pearson LJ pointed out that the ICE general conditions are not a

> partisan document . . . but a general form . . . prepared and revised jointly by several representative bodies' and 'it would naturally be incorporated in a contract of this kind and should have the same meaning whether the one party or the other happens to have made the first mention of it in the negotiations.

11 However, see *Bottoms v York Corporation* (1892) Alfred A Hudson, *Hudson's Fourth Edition Table of Cases* (Sweet & Maxwell, 4th edn 1914) 208, in which the contract provided

> that in case any dispute, question or difference arises as to the value of any particular work not clearly stated in the bill or schedules, or with regard to any other matter or thing connected with the contract, such dispute, question or difference shall be decided by the engineer, whose decision and award shall be final and binding upon all parties.

12 See also *UNIDROIT Principles of International Commercial Contracts 2016* Article 4.6.

13 [1965] 1 QB 37, [1963] 3 All ER 863 (QB).

Where work is not included in all the Contract documents – for example where work is shown on one of the Contract drawings and not on another – a Contractor will sometimes argue that this is a discrepancy and that it is entitled to claim a Variation. Since the natural presumption is that work shown on any one of the Contract documents is to be done, the Contractor will only be able to recover additional costs where the drawings are genuinely misleading, and it did not and had no reason to anticipate the additional work. Under such circumstances the Contractor may also be entitled to an extension of time (EOT) for Completion. Such an issue must be resolved by the true construction of the Contract documents.

Because of the practical difficulty of ensuring that every single item required for completion of construction of the project is shown on the drawings or otherwise defined in the specification, it is common to have a contract 'catch-all' clause which clearly makes the Contractor liable to provide everything necessary for the scope of work defined in the Contract.

Example: Contractor's general obligations

> The Works shall include any work which is necessary to satisfy the Employer's Requirements, Contractor's Proposal and Schedules, or is implied by the Contract, and all works which (although not mentioned in the Contract) are necessary for stability or for the completion, or safe and proper operation, of the Works.[14]

Such is the extensive and complicated nature of major construction contracts that discrepancies or errors can easily occur in the documentation and, having regard to the exigencies of tendering, it is not unreasonable that the Employer, whose agents have prepared the Contract documents in detail over perhaps a long period of time, should be the one to bear the loss if an undetected mistake occurs, rather than a Contractor who is required to price the work at comparatively short notice. However, whether the Employer accepts the risk of such mistakes in the Contract documents will depend upon the terms of the relevant contract.

Example: Contractor responsible for errors in Employer's Requirements

> The Employer shall not be responsible for any error, inaccuracy or omission of any kind in the Employer's Requirements as originally included in the Contract and shall not be deemed to have given any representation of accuracy or completeness of any data or information, except as stated in this Sub-Clause below. Any data or information received by the Contractor, from the Employer or otherwise, shall not relieve the Contractor from the Contractor's responsibility for the execution of the Works.[15]

The 'final' decision of the Engineer or Employer's Representative in resolving difficulties in interpretation of the Contract is, of course, generally open to review by an Arbitrator or the courts.

14 2017 FIDIC Yellow Book sub-clause 4.1.
15 2017 FIDIC Silver Book sub-clause 5.1.

An issue may arise where there is an inconsistency as to the order of precedence of the drawings and the specifications, where the Contract in question does not specify how to resolve such ambiguities. A number of cases[16] suggest that in the absence of an express provision in the Contract stating what is the order of precedence in the Contract documents, the specifications come before the drawings. This also accords with industry practice.[17]

6.5 Rectification of contract terms

Where the parties agree orally on the terms to be set down in a written contract, but a mistake is made and the writing does not set out their agreement accurately, the courts will correct the Contract provided the prior agreement and the mistake are proved clearly. This process is referred to as **rectification**.

In *Monaghan County Council v Vaughan*,[18] A contracted with B to remove rubble. In the written contract that was eventually signed there was a term for a payment, but the clause was ambiguous as to whether the payment was to be made by or to A. It was proved that the parties had, in fact, agreed that the terms of the Contract should be that A would make the payment and the written contract was rectified to make this clear.

Where the date for Completion was omitted it was held that there could be no contract rectification.[19]

The cases in which the courts will grant rectification are limited by the necessity of proving prior agreement by the parties on the particular point. Most of the disputes concerning interpretation are on points which were never thought about by the parties or the drafter when the Contract was being drawn up, and accordingly are not subject to rectification.

6.6 Erection information

The Contractor may be required to provide, within the time stated in the programme or in the Contract, certain vital information required by the Contract. This commonly includes information required by the Employer's designers, such as drawings and details necessary for the design of suitable foundations or other temporary works and means of support, details of access required, and details of any necessary connections to the plant – for example holding down bolts, power, and services.

The timing of the provision of this information may be vital to the time for Completion of the Works as a whole, and Employers may therefore be well advised to make some provision in the Contract for a reduction in the contract price (liquidated damages) should the specified information not be provided by the Contractor within the time specified in the Contract for reasons within the Contractor's control.

---

16 For example *Jorey v Thiange* (1894) 11 CU 154.

17 For example, the 1999 and 2017 FIDIC Red Books state that the Specification take precedence over the Drawings in the order of precedence of the contract documents.

18 [1948] IR 306.

19 *Kemp v Rose* [1858] 114 RR 429.

6.7 Drawings

In general, the drawings and specifications are the quantitative and qualitative descriptions of the Works. The Contractor is obliged to construct the Works, which, by definition, normally include the work shown on the drawings.

Contract conditions frequently prohibit the Contractor from using for construction any drawings issued for the purposes of tendering or for procurement uses and require that only drawings marked 'issued for construction' may be used for construction. Once so issued, such drawings constitute an order or instruction to the Contractor to carry out the work contained therein. This may be of significance where such drawings result in substantial increases or decreases of constructed quantities over those shown in bills of quantities or in the tender.

It is important to note that the Contractor should take instructions and directions only from the Engineer (or Employer's Representative if there is no Engineer) or, subject to the limitations contained in the Contract, from the Engineer's Representative (or persons delegated by the Employer's Representative). The Contractor is also usually obliged to comply with the Engineer's instructions on any matter, whether mentioned in the Contract or not, provided such instructions fall within the limits of the Engineer's authority. This is discussed further in Chapter 8.

6.8 Errors in drawings

A fault in the drawings or specification may necessitate additional work on the Contractor's part. If, prior to the conclusion of the Works, the Contractor discovers that the drawings are defective, it must usually execute the extra work. Whether or not it is entitled to extra remuneration or a time extension generally depends on who is responsible for provision of the defective drawings or specification.

Construction only contracts should provide that the Employer is responsible for drawings and information provided to the Contractor by it or the Engineer, and for the details of any special work that may have been specified to the Contractor. If the drawings, information, or details are incorrect, the Engineer can usually require the Contractor to correct the drawings or make any necessary alterations to the work at the Employer's expense, in which case the Contractor should be entitled to recover not only the costs incurred but also an allowance for profit. The Contractor would then usually also be entitled to an extension of time for Completion if it could show that delay on the critical path had been caused by the need for it to correct erroneous Employer's drawings, information, or details.

On the other hand, if a standard method of measurement[20] is adopted and any measurable item of work is omitted from the bill of quantities, it may be an implied term that the Contractor will be entitled to payment for the execution of the omitted work on the basis of prices quoted for the same or similar items in the bill, or at a reasonable valuation.

Construction contracts normally provide that the Contractor is responsible for any errors or omissions in the Contractor's drawings and is required, at its own cost, to carry out any alterations or remedial work caused thereby. This would include modification of the drawings and of any information based thereon.

It must be remembered that where the Contractor carries out the design of the Works, it is solely responsible for the design. It cannot transfer responsibility for design to the Engineer on the grounds that the Engineer has 'approved' the drawings. If the Engineer fails to detect an error

20 A standardised and defined procedure for preparing bills of quantities.

in the drawings which, as a competent professional engineer it ought to, this is a matter between the Employer and the Engineer, governed by the terms of the Engineer's engagement. Whilst the Contractor may complain that the error in question was not identified, the Contractor ought not to have committed the error in the first place. The Contractor may, however, have a valid claim for extra remuneration and/or time where the error or omission in the Contractor's drawings resulted from errors or omissions in the Employer's drawings or other written information supplied by the Employer or the Engineer to the Contractor. This would not however apply in a design and construct contract where the Contractor had warranted its liability for the design notwithstanding any pre-contract design work carried out by the Employer.

The extent of the Contractor's responsibility under the Contract in relation to errors or omissions in the Contractor's drawings and information will extend to the correction of the drawings and carrying out any of the remedial work to the plant or Works necessary in consequence thereof. It may also extend to the cost of correcting work done by a third party in reliance upon the Contractor's drawings or information that has proved to be in error. However, the terms of the Contract will govern the Contractor's responsibility.

6.9 Employers use of Contractor's drawings and documents

Construction contracts should provide a perpetual limited licence to the Employer to use the Contractor's drawings and documents for those purposes necessary for completing, operating, maintaining, adjusting, modifying, and repairing the Works, subject to payment of the contract price. The Contract may require the Contractor to supply electronic copies of drawings produced by Computer Aided Design (**CAD**) as the most appropriate medium. The requirements for such electronic drawings should be specified in detail to ensure that they contain all the original design information and metadata so that they are usable by the Employer for subsequent modifications or repair with the appropriate software.

Assignment of copyright in the drawings and documents is not required for protection of the Employer's rights in respect of the construction, operation, modification, or maintenance of the facilities. Accordingly, copyright should be retained by their author to ensure that they are legally entitled to use the intellectual property they created in the drawings and documents in subsequent projects. The Employer should not be entitled to use the drawings, for example, to build a similar plant. Nor should it be entitled to use the drawings for the manufacture of spare parts, other than for purposes of repairing the Works. This position is recognised in the US ConsensusDocs.

The Contractor is not usually required in construction contracts to disclose to the Engineer or the Employer confidential manufacturing drawings, design knowledge, or manufacturing practices, processes, or operations. Such matters are the essence of the Contractor's competitive advantage and there can be little justification for requiring their disclosure save in the most exceptional circumstances. It is, however, normal practice to require the Contractor to provide civil and structural engineering calculations, as these may be required in the future for modifications or to check the design capacity against new or different requirements. Such calculations may be required by the Contract to include electronic copies of the data used for computer analysis.

6.10 Supply of services

Where the Contractor supplies services, it will be an implied term of the Contract that the supplier will carry out its services with reasonable skill and care.[21]

---

21 *Seadrill Management Services Ltd v OAO Gazprom* [2010] EWCA Civ 691, [27]–[28].

6.11 Duty to exercise reasonable skill and care

A party who has undertaken to perform work pursuant to a contract carries an implied obligation to perform work using reasonable skill and care. This is a term which is implied at common law.[22] Where a contracting party is a professional person, who holds himself or herself out as possessing a particular skill, it is the implied contractual duty of that person, when employed to do work which requires the application of that skill, that he or she will exercise reasonable skill and care in the art he or she professes.[23] Dillon LJ in *Hawkins v Chrysler (UK) Ltd*[24] held that

> The general position . . . is that a professional man who is called in to advise is bound, and impliedly undertakes, to use reasonable skill and care in advising, but is not responsible for providing a perfect result or a perfect building.[25]

6.12 Obligation to achieve a particular result

In *Hall v Burke*,[26] Lord Esher said:

> There were two well-known kinds of contract – first, a customer might ask a manufacturer to make a machine according to a given plan, or according to a plan supplied by the customer; in that case the manufacturer would only have to make the machine according to the plan, and in a workmanlike manner. Secondly, a customer might ask the manufacturer to make a machine for a particular purpose, not supplying any plan, but leaving it to him to make it for that purpose; in that case, unless the contrary was expressly stated in the contract, the manufacturer would have to make a machine fit for that purpose. There might be a third kind of contract, where both parties said that they would jointly endeavour to make a machine that would do its business, when there would be no warranty that it would affect its purpose.

An obligation to achieve a particular result is breached when the result is not achieved.[27] This is not the same as an obligation to use reasonable care. In regard to the obligation of a professional person:

> The law does not usually imply a warranty that he will achieve the desired result, but only a term that he will use reasonable care and skill. The surgeon does not warrant that he will cure the patient. Nor does the solicitor warrant that he will win the case. But when a dentist agrees to make a set of false teeth for a patient, there is an implied warranty that they will fit his gums: see *Samuel v Davis* [1943] K.B. 526.[28]

---

22 *Greaves & Co (Contractors) Ltd v Baynham Meikle & Partners* [1975] 1095, 1099 per Lord Denning MR; *Astley v Austrust Ltd* (1999) 197 CLR 1, 21 [46]–[48].

23 *Barclays Bank plc v Fairclough* (1994) 68 BLR 1; *Platform Funding Ltd v Bank of Scotland plc* (2008) 120 Con LR 201, [15], per Moore-Bick LJ.

24 (1986) 38 BLR 36.

25 (1986) 38 BLR 36, 53. See also *Orlit Pty Ltd v JF&P Consulting Engineering Pty Ltd* (1992) 11 BCL 260, 267, per Moynihan J.

26 (1886) 3 T.L.R. 165.

27 *Greaves & Co (Contractors) Ltd v Baynham Meikle & Partners* [1975] 1 WLR 1095, 1099, per Lord Denning MR; also Geoffrey Lane LJ, 1103; *Holland Hannen & Cubbits (Northern) Ltd v WHTSO* (1985) 35 BLR 1, 30, per Dillon LJ; *Platform Funding Ltd v Bank of Scotland plc* (2008) 120 Con LR 201 (CA).

28 *Greaves & Co (Contractors) Ltd v Baynham Meikle & Partners* [1975] 1095, 1100 per Lord Denning MR.

There are cases where a person has applied reasonable skill and care, according to the prevailing standards of their profession yet has been unable to produce a particular result. If a person is subject to an express contractual obligation to achieve a particular result, they will be liable for failing to achieve that result even if they have otherwise acted with reasonable skill and care.[29]

6.12.1 Case study: Contractual obligation to achieve a particular result

In the case of *Mt Højgaard A/S v E.ON Climate and Renewables UK Robin Rigg East Limited*[30] the Contractor was required to design and construct an offshore wind farm in which the foundations were to have a service life of 20 years. The litigation in this case arose from the failure of the grouted connections between piled foundations and the towers supporting the wind turbines. The grouted connections were designed to accepted international Standards and verified by an independent certifying authority. There was no negligence in the design of the grouted connections. However, there was a serious (and unknown at the time) error in the contractually specified Standard for the design of the grouted connections that resulted in their failure in service within two years.

In the Supreme Court Lord Neuberger referred to English case law going back over 100 years as support for the primacy of a contractual requirement to construct a work capable of carrying out a specified duty; such a duty may entail that more is required than compliance with the specification.[31] Accordingly, the Contractor was liable for the cost of rectifying the failed grouted connections, notwithstanding that it complied with the specified Standard, and exercised due skill and care in preparing the design. Accordingly, there is a heavy onus on a designer where a fitness for purpose obligation is imposed by a contract. In such a case, following international standards or the current state-of-the-art will not avail a designer where a standard or the current state-of-the-art is inadequate.[32]

The *Højgaard* case is significant because the issues were addressed by learned judges in three courts: it was initially decided in the Technology and Construction Court, reversed in the Court of Appeal, and the first instance judge's decision was reinstated by the Supreme Court. Ultimately, as is frequently the case, the outcome depended on construction of the documents comprising the Contract. What is of particular interest in this case is that the three learned judges of the Court of Appeal, construing the same documents, considering the same case law and applying the same tools of construction, came to the opposite conclusion to the five judges of the Supreme Court and the judge at first instance. This highlights the difficulties faced by parties considering entering into a construction contract comprising an intersecting web of legal and 'technical' documents – even skilled and experienced practitioners may come to differing conclusions as to how the documents would be construed by the fictitious 'reasonable' person in possession of the relevant background information.[33]

29 *Costain Ltd v Charles Haswell and Partners Ltd* [2009] EWHC B25 (TCC), [52]–[59], per DHCJ Fernyhough QC.

30 [2017] UKSC 59.

31 *MT Højgaard a/s v E.ON Climate and Renewables Robin Rigg East Ltd* [2017] UKSC 59, [38]–[43].

32 For a case in which a designer was found liable for not following the provisions of an unpublished draft Standard, see Donald Charrett, *Contracts for Construction and Engineering Projects* (Informa Law from Routledge, 2nd edn 2022) Chapter 10.

33 For a detailed discussion of the three judgements in this case, see Donald Charrett, *Contracts for Construction and Engineering Projects* (Informa Law from Routledge, 2nd edn 2022) Chapter 8.

6.13 Duty to act honestly

It is an implied term of a contract that a party is to act honestly in the performance of its obligations and the assertion of its rights under that contract.[34] A fraudulent payment claim is one where the maker of the claim knows that it is not entitled to the amount claimed.[35] Because it is impermissible for a Contractor to make a fraudulent payment claim, such payment claim will have no contractual effect, and may attract criminal sanctions. A fraudulent payment claim may be distinguished from a payment claim which is for an amount that is in excess of the payee's true entitlement, yet in respect of which the payee genuinely believes it is entitled to payment of the amount claimed.

6.14 Duty to provide accurate design information

It will usually be an implied term that the information supplied is accurate where a Contract imposes an obligation upon one party to provide design information to another so as to enable that other to perform its works.[36]

6.15 Compliance with statutes, regulations, and laws

The Employer may not rely on the Contractor's non-compliance with regulations as a breach of contract if it insisted that the work be carried out in conflict with them. But if work not specifically mentioned in a construction contract is necessary to comply with building regulations or other laws, such work will generally have to be executed by the Contractor at no additional charge as part of the Works. This applies even where the Contract does not specifically require that the work must be done in accordance with the regulations, and even though the Contractor may be put to greater expense in completing the work in this manner.

A contract which contravenes a statute, by-law, or statutory regulation is illegal. This means that it is tainted in the eyes of the civil courts – the parties do not necessarily commit a crime, but the courts will, as a general rule, refuse to enforce such a contract.

This applies even where the party wishing to enforce the Contract did not realise when s/he made it that it was illegal, on the general principle that ignorance of the law is no excuse. But where only the use to be made of a facility is contrary to by-laws or involves planning consent, the Contractor may enforce the Contract if it did not know of the intended infringement or genuinely believed that the Employer would get the necessary consent.[37]

If the Contractor notifies the Engineer before carrying out work that, as designed, it will involve infringements, it seems that the Contractor would normally be entitled to a Variation order and adjustment of the contract price. The Contractor is not bound to do the original work, which is legally impossible, and has no authority to alter the work so as to avoid an infringement without a Variation Order. There will, however, be many cases in

---

34 *Jones v Dalcon Construction Pty Ltd* [2006] WASCA 874, [26], per Pullin JA (dissenting).

35 *Duchess of Marlborough v Vanbrugh* 9 Mod 23, 25–26 [88].

36 *London Borough of Merton v Leach* (1985) 32 BLR 51, 81–83, per Vinelott J; *Scottish Power plc v Kvaerner Construction (Regions) Ltd* 1999 SLT 721.

37 *Townsends Builders Ltd v Cinema News* [1959] 1 WLR 119, [1959] 1 All ER 7 (CA); *Best v Glanville* [1960] 1 WLR 1198.

which the specification is sufficiently general to allow a choice to the Contractor, and in these cases it must, without extra payment, choose to do the work so as to comply with the regulations.

There is in any event, usually a general contractual obligation on the Contractor to comply with any law or statutory regulation applicable to the Works and to give all notices and pay all fees that may be required, for example sub-clause 1.13 of the 2017 FIDIC Yellow Book.

Apart from its specific contractual obligations, there is an overarching legal obligation on the Contractor to comply with all laws relating to the design and manufacture or construction of the Works, both in the country of manufacture and where the Works are to be erected. The Contractor must also comply with all laws relating to the erection and operation of the Works in that country during the construction stage, and whilst the Contractor is responsible for its operation.

6.16 Duty to act reasonably in exercising rights

There is no general rule of law in England that a party to a contract is only entitled to exercise his or her rights in a reasonable way.[38] However, the law will now, in certain circumstances, impute to the parties the unstated intention that certain rights should be exercised reasonably. An obligation or a condition of a right to exercise contractual rights reasonably may be imposed by implication of law, or by implication from the facts surrounding a transaction. The implication of a requirement of reasonableness may be made in a construction contract just as it may in any other form of commercial contract.[39] For example, an Employer's contractual right to approve any proposed bondsman proffered by the Contractor may be subject to the implied condition that the Employer's right of refusal is not to be exercised unreasonably.[40]

6.17 Site

The **Site** is constituted by the places made available by the Employer for execution of the Works, but the Contractor may also have to carry out work at locations other than the Site. Engineering projects are frequently constructed over wide areas, perhaps already occupied by the Employer or other persons, and the location on which the 'site' works are carried out may only form a small part. These other areas may also have no readily recognisable limitations or boundaries. Pipe-laying work, for instance, may take place under public roads, or may traverse gardens, fields, or open country, or occur within an existing complex of engineering works or under the sea. Accessibility in all such contracts is of vital practical importance, as is possession of some, but not necessarily all, of the land occupied by the Employer for the purposes of temporary works. In addition, working space outside the

38 *Blackpool & Fylde Aero Club Ltd v Blackpool Borough Council* [1990] 1 WLR 1195, 1202, per Bingham LJ.

39 *Onesteel Manufacturing Pty Ltd v United KG Pty Ltd* [2006] SASC 119, [33], per Debelle J (22 BCL 449, 24 Const LJ 431.

40 *Arbiter Investments Ltd v Wiltshier (London) Ltd* (1987) 14 Con LR 16.

immediate width or area of the Works or of the Employer's land may be essential – for example on one or both sides of the trench in a pipe-laying contract.

Contract documents are frequently silent about this, yet a precise definition of the Site is obviously essential for the operation of clauses dealing with damage to land or crops not being on the Site, and with possession of the Site, storage facilities, and laydown areas. It is therefore essential for the specification or bills (or drawings) to describe exactly the area over which the Contractor is entitled to have freedom of operation for the purposes of the Contract, and also any special rights of access across adjoining land or restrictions on the use of the Employer's land. The Contractor may have the risk of timely access to any locations on which it has to carry out Works that do not form part of the Site.

6.18 'Buildability'

'Buildability' refers to the capacity of a design to be implemented physically in a manner that is safe, sound, and otherwise in accordance with the terms of the relevant construction contract. The question may arise as to which party accepts the risk that the relevant design will be impossible to implement in a manner that is safe, sound, and otherwise in accordance with the terms of the Contract. The issue usually arises in the context of the original design for the Works requiring some modification to produce a satisfactory physical end-product, and the parties disagreeing over the financial consequences, as between themselves, of the modification being made. A contract may, for example, expressly excuse the Contractor from performing the Works it has promised to do to the extent that the Works are 'physically impossible.'[41]

Where the design has been supplied by an Employer to a Contractor and the design has been prepared by a consultant to the Employer, there is no warranty on the part of the Employer implied by law that the design is capable of being implemented to meet the requirements of the Contract. This will certainly be the case where the Contractor could reasonably, after reviewing the design itself, have discovered the impossibility of building the design.[42] However, it may be the duty of the designer towards the Employer to ensure that the design which the Contractor is given is, in the circumstances of the particular project, 'buildable.'[43] There are no absolute principles of law involved, and the allocation of risk between the parties essentially depends upon the arrangements they make.[44] A Contract may provide in terms that the Employer takes responsibility for the risk of there being an error in a design which it has prepared or commissioned and provided to the Contractor.

6.19 Proportionate liability

The following section, relating to liability arising from a breach of contractual provisions, might be seen as more appropriate in Chapter 27 Dispute Avoidance and Resolution.

41 *Turriff Ltd v The Welsh National Water Development Authority* (1979, unreported, Sir William Stabb QC).

42 *Thorn v The Mayor and Commonalty of London* (1876) LR 1 HL 120.

43 *Equitable Debenture Assets Corporation Limited v William Moss Group Limited* (1984) 2 Con LR 1, 21–22, per Judge Newey QC; *Department of National Heritage v Steensen Varming Mulcahy* (1998) 60 Con LR 33 and 85 [124]–86 [126], per Judge Bowsher QC.

44 *Codelfa Construction Pty Ltd v State Rail Authority of New Wales* (1982) CLR 337, 355, per Mason J.

However, as discussed herein, the operation of proportionate liability legislation may be avoided by appropriate provisions in the Contract. Accordingly, it is appropriate to consider the ambit of proportionate liability under general provisions in this chapter.

In situations where a person has suffered loss caused by the actions of more than one person, the traditional position has been that a plaintiff can choose to take action against one or more of the wrongdoers and execute judgement for the entire amount of the damages against any one of the defendants found to be jointly and severally liable. This principle of joint and several liability can result in a person being legally liable for 100% of the damages, even though that person's causal contribution to the damage was very minor. One of the consequences of joint and several liability is that the legal burden of paying damages for defective building work may be suffered disproportionately by those parties with insurance (because these were the parties the plaintiff elected to sue).

All Australian jurisdictions have enacted proportionate liability legislation which encompasses claims for damages for economic loss or damage to property arising from a failure to take reasonable care, and for breaches of the *Trade Practices Act* and *Fair Trading Acts*.[45] Proportionate liability does not apply to claims involving fraud or personal injury, nor does it affect the operation of contributory negligence, agency, or vicarious liability. A defendant to proceedings in relation to a building or construction dispute may plead the defence of proportionate liability in order to minimise the amount of damages it may be liable for. In order to successfully invoke the defence of proportionate liability, it is likely that the following elements must be present and proved:

(1) There is a claim for damages for economic loss or damage to property caused by either:
  (a) a failure to take reasonable care – whether in tort, contract, under statute, or otherwise; or
  (b) misleading or deceptive conduct.

(2) There is a 'concurrent wrongdoer' – that is a person who is one of two or more persons whose acts or omissions caused (independently of each other or jointly) the loss or damage suffered by the plaintiff.

The application of proportionate liability legislation in complex construction disputes can introduce substantial additional complexity in the proceedings and make an out-of-court settlement much more difficult to achieve. Because of this complexity, and the significant differences between legislation in different jurisdictions, a plaintiff should be aware of the relevant proportionate liability legislation that applies in the particular jurisdiction which governs the dispute. An Employer should consider whether it is appropriate and permissible to include in the Contract a provision to contract out of the application of the proportionate liability legislation.[46] Further, although the issue has not been decided by a superior court,

45 *Wrongs Act 1958* (Vic) Part IVAA Proportionate liability; *Civil Liability Act 2002* (NSW) Part 4 Proportionate liability; *Civil Liability Act 2003* (Qld) Chapter 2 Part 2 Proportionate liability; *Law Reform (Contributory Negligence And Apportionment of Liability) Act 2001* (SA) Part 3 Apportionable liability; *Civil Liability Act 2002* (WA) Part 1F Proportionate liability; *Civil Liability Act 2002* (Tas) Part 9A Proportionate liability; *Civil Law (Wrongs) Act 2002* (ACT) Chapter 7A; *Proportionate Liability Act 2005* (NT).

46 The relevant legislation in NSW, Western Australia, and Tasmania expressly permits parties to exclude, modify, or restrict the operation of proportionate liability. The Queensland legislation specifically prohibits contracting out of its provisions. There is no express provision, either way, as to contracting out of the proportionate

there are good arguments that in all States and Territories the relevant proportional liability legislation does not apply to arbitrations conducted under the applicable *Commercial Arbitration Act*.[47]

In South Africa the *Apportionment of Damages Act*, 34 of 1956 *inter alia* provides for the apportionment of loss arising from the wrongful negligent action of defendants amongst them, in proportion to their respective degrees of fault. It should be noted, however, that these provisions do not apply to contractual liability for damages.[48]

Article 290 of the *UAE Civil Code* permits a Court (or arbitral tribunal) to reduce the level of damages, or not to order damages at all, if it finds that the person suffering harm participated by his/her own act in bringing about or aggravating the harm.[49] Where a number of parties are responsible for the breach, each of them shall be responsible in their proportionate share and the Court (or arbitral tribunal) may make an order against them in equal shares or by way of joint or several liability.[50] Accordingly, notwithstanding that the Contract may identify certain Contractor risk and Employer risk events, to the extent that the Court (or arbitral tribunal) finds that both parties were responsible for bringing about the harm that occurred, it may decide to apportion liability as it sees fit.[51]

It should be noted that joint and several liability is the norm in most jurisdictions; proportionate liability only applies in a few jurisdictions apart from Australia

---

liability legislation in the Australian Capital Territory, the Northern Territory, South Australia, or Victoria, nor in respect of the Commonwealth provisions contained in the *Australian Consumer Law*.

47 David Levin, 'Proportionate Liability in Arbitrations in Australia?' (2009) 25 *Building and Construction Law* 298. See also *Aquagenics Pty Ltd v Break O'Day Council (No 2)* [2009] TASSC 89.

48 Johan Beyers, 'South Africa' in Donald Charrett (ed), *The International Application of FIDIC Contracts: A Practical Guide* (Informa Law from Routledge, 2020) 334, 352.

49 *UAE Civil Code*, Article 290.

50 Ibid. Article 291.

51 Erin Miller Rankin & Samantha Lord Hill, 'The United Arab Emirates' in Donald Charrett (ed), *The International Application of FIDIC Contracts A Practical Guide* (Informa Law from Routledge, 2020) 386, 404.

CHAPTER 7

The Employer

CONTENTS

7.1 Obligations of the Employer

A fundamental and overriding generalised implied principle is that neither party shall do anything to hinder the other from performing the Contract. This is known as the 'prevention principle.' This principle is sometimes expressed by saying that a party cannot take advantage of its own wrong in enforcing a contract.[1]

1 *Roberts v Bury Commissioners* (1870) L.R. 5 C.P. 310, 326 per Blackburn J; 329 per Kelly C.B.

DOI: 10.4324/9781003206873-7

An equally important generalised and implied principle is a positive obligation to do anything which may be necessary to enable the other to perform its obligations.[2]

> Where in a written contract it appears that both parties have agreed that something should be done which cannot effectively be done unless both concur in doing it, the construction of the contract is that each agrees to do all that is necessary to be done on his part for the carrying out of that thing though there may be no express words to that effect.[3]

For an example of this in the context of a duty to provide necessary information to the Contractor during construction, see *London Borough of Merton v Leach*.[4]

As the contract party for whom the construction work is done, the Employer must either be the owner of the land on which construction is to take place or must have a legal right from the owner to permit things to be fixed to the land. Certain obligations of the Employer in relation to matters which are within the Employer's or owner's (and therefore the Employer's) control, or where assistance from the Employer may be required, may be crucial in enabling the Contractor to complete on time. Any failure by the Employer to comply with such requirements could lead to delay in the Completion of the Works on Site and hence to claims from the Contractor.

However, notwithstanding that such matters appear to be within the Employer's control, the Contractor may assume the risk of such matters through specific provisions of the Contract, either through express obligations or by giving warranties in relation to such matters. It is therefore important that the terms of the Contract are clear as to which party accepts a particular risk – it should not be assumed that the 'normal' allocation of risk necessarily applies, particularly in the case of bespoke contracts. Accordingly, the parties must always review the Contract to establish which party accepts a particular risk under that contract, rather than assuming that some 'usual practice' applies.

7.2 Obligations which are not the subject of express provisions

Among the obligations and responsibilities of the Employer which may not be the subject of express provisions are:

(1) Nomination and appointment
  (a) The Employer may be required to nominate and appoint a certifier or his/her substitute.
  (b) The Employer may be required to nominate subcontractors or suppliers ready to contract in suitable terms with the Head Contractor.
  (c) Where a certifier is to act in accordance with his/her own independent opinion or decision, not to obstruct, interfere with, or improperly influence them in doing so.

2 *London Borough of Merton v Leach* (1985) 32 B.L.R 51, 73–82 per Vinelott J.
3 Per Lord Blackburn in *Mackay v Dick* (1881) 6 A.C. 251, 263.
4 *London Borough of Merton v Leach* (1985) 32 B.L.R 51, 73–82 per Vinelott J.

(2) The Site

The Employer must:

(a) Not misrepresent the physical state of the Site,
(b) Give an adequate degree of undisturbed possession of the Site,
(c) Secure undisturbed possession of the Site as against other contractors or persons employed by the Employer, and
(d) Give the Contractor good title to quiet possession of the Site as against third persons.

(3) Information

The Employer:

(a) Must give all necessary information required by the Contractor in good time, and
(b) Meet special obligations with regard to timing and content of instructions and Variations.

(4) Works

(a) The Employer must permit the Contractor to carry out the whole of the Works.

If a consultant is employed by the Employer, the consultant will discharge a number of these responsibilities as agent of the Employer, but some of these matters lie solely within the control of the Employer.[5]

7.3 The Employer's financial arrangements

Clearly, one of the Contractor's prime objectives during execution of a Contract is to be paid promptly for the work it has done in accordance with the provisions of the Contract. Prior to entry into the Contract, a prudent Contractor will always investigate the ability of the contracting Employer to fulfil its payment obligations, and this requires an understanding of the way in which the project will be financed, and the relationship between the contracting parties and the financiers. There are a variety of contractual ways in which a Contractor can minimise its risk in respect of payment, and some of these are discussed later in the chapter. However, in the final analysis, if a Contractor is not prepared to accept the inherent risks, the most appropriate risk reduction strategy is not to enter into the Contract.

The following issues are factors that, if applicable, may have a significant bearing on the Employer's contractual payment obligations:

(1) The corporate structure of the Employer: a stock-exchange listed 'blue-chip' company or is it a $2 'shell' company?
(2) Is the Employer a joint venture in which each constituent company only has several (and not joint and several) liability?

5 Atkin Chambers, *Hudson's Building and Engineering Contracts* (Sweet & Maxwell, 12th edn 2010), [3–138] (***Hudson's***).

(3) Is the project funded from the Employer's (or its parent company's) balance sheet, or is it externally financed?
(4) Is the Employer the owner of the property on which the construction is to be carried out? If not, the Contractor does not have the 'security' of the land to fall back on if the Employer breaches its payment obligations under the Contract.
(5) Is there litigation involving material amounts of money to which the Employer is a party?

The outcome of enquiries on these factors may lead the Contractor to identify specific risks in connection with the ongoing ability of the Employer to fund the project and pay progress payments as they fall due. Funding constraints may also influence an Employer's attitude to authorising Variations. In such situations the Contractor should seek to have appropriate mechanisms incorporated into the Contract to reduce these risks of non-payment. There are a variety of contractual mechanisms which can be adopted, including the following:

(1) On request by the Contractor, the Employer must provide reasonable evidence that financial arrangements are in place which will enable it to make payments as required under the Contract, for example sub-clause 2.4 [Employer's Financial Arrangements] in the 1999 and 2017 FIDIC rainbow suites.
(2) A parent company guarantee of performance by its subsidiary.
(3) A tripartite arrangement between the Employer, Contractor, and financier, providing appropriate security for payment of the Contractor.
(4) The ability to be paid for off-site materials.
(5) Constraints on assignment of the Contract by the Employer, for example sub-clause 1.7 [Assignment] in the 1999 and 2017 FIDIC rainbow suites.

Each of these contractual mechanisms requires careful drafting, not only in the construction contract itself but also the terms of any collateral contracts. Some of these issues have been discussed by Mead.[6]

7.3.1 Example: FIDIC provisions on Employer's financial arrangements

Sub-clause 2.4 of the 2017 FIDIC rainbow suite requires that the Employer's arrangements for financing its obligations under the Contract to be detailed in the Contract Data. The Employer is required to immediately notify the Contractor if it intends to make any material change to these arrangements affecting its ability to pay the outstanding part of the Contract Price. Where the Contractor receives an instruction to execute a Variation valued at greater than 10%

6 Patrick Mead, 'Current Trends in Risk Allocation in Construction Projects and Their Implications for Industry Stakeholders' (2006) 22 *Building and Construction Law* 407, 416–417.

of the Contract Price, does not receive timely payment, or becomes aware of a material change in the Employer's financial arrangements, it may request the Employer to provide reasonable evidence of its ability to make payments. The Employer is required to provide the requested evidence of financial arrangements that have been made to enable it to pay the outstanding part of the Contract Price within 28 days.

7.4 Import permits and licenses

Usually it is the Employer's obligation under the Contract to obtain any permits or licenses necessary for commencing performance before the commencement date of the Contract. It is also usually the Employer's obligation under the Contract to obtain any remaining import permits or licenses in time to enable the plant to be delivered to Site without any delay being experienced on importation into the country where the Site is located. Failure to do so could result in delay and in claims by the Contractor for additional time and payment.

The Contractor generally has an obligation to give the Employer whatever information it may need to permit the Employer to obtain any necessary import permits or licenses. The Contract should require the Contractor to provide this information in good time and, where possible, the latest date for provision of the information to the Employer should be required to be specified in the tender submission (such as in the tender programme).

The normal practice in relation to customs and import duties is that these are borne by the Employer, whether the primary obligation under the relevant law to pay such duties and taxes is imposed on the Employer or the Contractor. If the law of the country where the Site is located requires the Employer to pay these duties, it should be required under the Contract to pay them. If the Contractor is required either by the law of the country concerned or by the Contract itself to pay such duties and taxes, the Contract should require the Employer to reimburse the amount to be paid.

In addition, the Contract should impose a positive obligation upon the Employer to assist the Contractor in obtaining clearance through customs of plant and Contractor's equipment, and in obtaining any necessary government consent to the re-exportation of Contractor's equipment when it is removed from the Site, for example sub-clause 2.2 [Permits, Licences and Approvals] in the 1999 FIDIC rainbow suite and sub-clause 2.2 [Assistance] in the 2017 FIDIC rainbow suite.

7.5 Consents to access land required for construction

The fact that any necessary consents for the construction of the Works may have been obtained from relevant authorities may not be sufficient to ensure that the Works can, in fact, proceed. Permits to work may be required where the Works are being provided to the Employer as part of some larger project being undertaken by the Employer for a third party.

A **wayleave easement** is permission to make or use a way across private land and includes permission to erect structures such as overhead transmission lines to bring adequate and reliable power to the Site. If the Employer is responsible for obtaining particular consents, wayleaves, and approvals under the Contract, the Contractor should have identified in its tender, and should have stated in the programme the time by which the Employer is required to obtain those consents, wayleaves, and approvals. If the Employer fails to do so in time, the Contractor may be delayed in Completion and may claim additional payments and possibly an extension of time from the Employer.

7.6 Appointment of a construction professional as contract administrator

Where the Contract provides for the Works to be administered or supervised by the Employer's consultant, some of the services performed are performed simply as servant or agent of the Employer, such as, for example the supply of drawings and information or the issue of Variation Orders. Other functions may involve the exercise of a discretion. In *London Borough of Merton v Leach*, Vinelott J described the architect's discretionary powers in the following terms:

> The contract also confers on the architect discretionary powers which he must exercise with due regard to the interests of the contractor and the building owner. The building owner does not undertake that the architect will exercise his discretionary powers reasonably; he undertakes that although the architect may be engaged or employed by him he will leave him free to exercise his discretions fairly and without improper interference by him.[7]

Examples of the Employer's consultant's discretionary powers are in the evaluation of Contractors' claims both as to time and money, and the deduction of liquidated damages for delay. The legal status of these certification functions has been variously described as 'somewhere between those of a servant and those of an arbitrator,'[8] and 'independent, impartial, fair and honest.'[9] Given the importance of the certifier's role to the Contractor, construction contracts usually identify the certifier in the original contract documentation and cover eventualities such as death, retirement withdrawal, or disqualification.

The Employer is under an implied duty to appoint a certifier, or a successor, within a reasonable time. Refusal to do so may be a breach going to the root of the contract and justify termination if the Contract requires the exercise of certifying functions of this kind.[10] An Employer cannot appoint itself to replace a certifier.[11]

---

7 [1985] 32 B.L.R. 51, 78.
8 *Perini Corporation v Commonwealth of Australia* (1969) 12 B.L.R. 82, 98 per MacFarlan J.
9 *Scheldebouw BV v St James Homes (Grosvenor Dock) Ltd* [2006] B.L.R. 113, [34] per Jackson J.
10 Atkin Chambers, *Hudson's Building and Engineering Contracts* (Sweet & Maxwell, 12th edn 2010) 3–165.
11 *Scheldebouw BV v St James Homes (Grosvenor Dock) Ltd* [2006] B.L.R. 113, [34] per Jackson J, [45].

7.7 Examination of the Site

An Employer, in the absence of an actionable misrepresentation or deliberate concealment, or of some express warranty, owes no implied duty to a Contractor, whether of disclosure or otherwise, in either contract or tort in regard to the pre-existing state of the Site. A similar position has been taken in the US, when rejecting any implied duty of disclosure.

The word 'site' normally includes reasonable working space and access on land of the Employer joining the immediate footprint of a structure:

> Subject to express exclusions, the 'site for the work' must, in the case of a completely new structure, comprise not only the ground actually to be occupied by the completed structure but so much area around it as is within the control of the owner and is reasonably necessary for carrying out the work efficiently and in accordance with generally accepted construction practice.[12]

7.8 Nomination of specialist subcontractors and suppliers

The Employer may wish to optimise its supply chain and the holding of spare parts for ongoing maintenance by standardising its sources of supply and the intellectual property licenses which it holds. It achieves this by nominating suppliers and products for use in the construction of its project. In practice, the Employer or its consultant obtains quotations from subcontractors against full contract documentation already prepared by the consultant, so that a subsequent instruction to the Contractor to place an order will usually not merely involve the consultant's naming of a desired subcontractor but also directions to the Contractor of the exact terms of the subcontract against which the subcontractor has quoted.

The nominated subcontract 'package' should therefore comply with all reasonable requirements of the Contractor to enable it to fulfil its main contract obligations and be capable of rapid acceptance by the Contractor. It is advisable to ensure that the subcontractor acknowledges the order to satisfy the principles of offer and acceptance and consideration leading to a legally binding subcontract. It goes without saying that the Employer and its consultant must fulfil their obligations in this regard in sufficient time to enable the Contractor to fulfil its obligations and carry out its work economically and timeously. It is implied that the Employer or the consultant will nominate a supplier or subcontractor willing to enter into a subcontract in a form consistent with the obligations of the head contract.[13]

In *Leslie v Metropolitan Asylums District Managers*,[14] Romer J. stated that: 'The [contractors] clearly could not be compelled to enter into a [sub-] contract which did not adequately protect them.' The Contractor, by placing an order with a subcontractor without protest, particularly where there is an express right to object, will usually be held to have waived any breach of this term, or be estopped from alleging it: 'if the terms of those

12 *R v Walter Cabot Construction* (1964) 44 D.L.R. (3d) 82, 93 per Mahoney J., Fed Ct. of Canada, quoted and approved on appeal by Urie J. in the Federal Court of Appeal (1977) 69 T.L.R. (3d) 542.

13 Atkin Chambers, *Hudson's Building and Engineering Contracts* (Sweet & Maxwell, 12th edn 2010) 3–163.

14 (1901) 1 L.G.R. 862, 868.

[sub-] contracts prove insufficient to properly protect the [Contractor], that is their fault or misfortune and they cannot hold [the Employer] liable in any way.'[15]

Should a nominated subcontractor fail, there is a duty on the Employer to renominate a new nominated subcontractor in their place within a reasonable time.[16] Should the Contract make no provision for the additional loss and expense,[17] the Contractor could object to the nomination of the second subcontractor on that ground, and if it did so, neither side would be in breach, resulting in an impasse, which could presumably only be resolved either by agreement or by the Employer exercising power to omit the remaining subcontract work.[18]

7.9 Drawings and instructions

The 'traditional' method of procurement is one whereby a consultant is engaged by an Employer to design and supervise the project, and in which the Contractor is required to construct the Works to the consultant's designs and specifications and (perhaps) under their supervision. Usually the consultant only produces design drawings and specifications in sufficient detail to allow Tenderers to price the Works. The final required detail remains to be specified by way of later post-contract instructions contained in 'working drawings' or specification details, which are not intended to amount to Variations or changes which will entitle the Contractor to any adjustment of the contract price. Such instructions should be distinguished from post-contract instructions and Variations which are required if the Employer or designer wishes to make any change to the originally contemplated work.

If there are parts of the Works on which a final decision has not yet been reached at the time of contracting, or nominated subcontractors are to be used, these can be accommodated by the use of contingent or provisional sum items in the bills of quantities or specification.

In more complex projects such as pipelines, or road or railway contracts, possession of the Site may be given progressively in stages, as the required construction drawings for each stage of the Works are made available to the Contractor. The late provision of such required design information is a fertile area for Contractor claims: 'In such cases, it may only be a question of semantics as to whether to describe claims for delay so caused as being based on late information rather than on late possession.'[19]

If the Employer's consultant fails to issue drawings or other necessary information or approvals within a reasonable time, they will, as the Employer's agent, commit a breach of contract for which the Employer will be liable in damages to the Contractor.

An Employer does not warrant the certifier's competence in performing certification or discretionary functions during the supervisory stage of the contract,[20] nor does the

---

15 Ibid.

16 *North West Metropolitan Regional Hospital Board v T.A. Bickerton & Son Ltd* [1970] 1 W.L.R. 607, 613 per Lord Reid.

17 *Bilton v Greater London Council* [1982] 1 W.L.R. 794.

18 See *Fairclough Building Ltd v Rhuddlan Borough Council* (1985) 30 B.L.R. 34.

19 Atkin Chambers, *Hudson's Building and Engineering Contracts* (Sweet & Maxwell, 12th edn 2010) 3–159.

20 *Pacific Associates v Baxter* [1990] 1 Q.B. 993; [1989] 3 W.L.R. 1150.

Employer give a warranty to the Contractor as to the adequacy of the design by the consultant. There is, however, a fairly widespread lack of understanding of the duty which the Employer owes the Contractor not to interfere with the certifier where the certifier is required by the Contract to act fairly as between the parties and exercise his/her own judgement. This has been termed as a 'negative duty,' but it has also been held that the Employer owes the Contractor an affirmative duty to use its best endeavours to see to it that the certifier does carry out the required functions properly, for example where, to the Employer's knowledge, the certifier is failing to perform its function at all, or is going outside the proper terms of reference by taking into account extraneous considerations not warranted by the terms of the Contract.[21]

7.10 Shop drawings

A 'construct only' contract may envisage a series of information exchanges, which may take the form of initial design drawings to be supplied by the Employer's consultant structural engineer, followed by preparation of detailed shop drawings or fabrication or installation drawings by the Contractor or their subcontractor. **Shop drawings** are drawings of all the dimensional, material, and fabrication details required for manufacture of components such as structural steel or joinery in a workshop They are usually required to be submitted for review by the Employer's consultant, and also, in certain cases, by a second 'lead' consultant for co-ordination purposes. The consultant's review within a stated period of time is required prior to the Contractor being allowed to proceed with manufacture or fabrication and the subsequent work of installation. This procedure is common in contracts involving fabrication of structural steel.

There will often be two stages of Employer obligations, namely the initial preparation and issue of design drawings to the Contractor, either in the contract documents themselves or subsequently, and the later review of the Contractor's fabrication or installation drawings when received. The level of detail to be provided in the initial drawings should be clearly stated and the interface between design drawings and shop drawings clearly defined. While it will not be realistic for Contractors to assert a duty to supply all required information at the outset of a construction contract, a realistic degree of 'lead time' to enable the Contractor to place orders and organise and properly pre-plan their work may usually be legitimately required.

The Employer should ensure that any review of the Contractor's shop drawings by the Employer's consultants is carried out within the time allowed in the Contract and does not release the Contractor from any of its contractual obligations to construct the Works in accordance with the Contract. Any such clause should not imply any 'approval' by the Employer's consultant but provide an opportunity to require correction before manufacture if a shop drawing does not comply with the requirements of the Contract. If the consultant does not require any changes to a shop drawing, it is more appropriate to issue a notice of no-objection rather than 'approval.'

21 *Perini Corporation v Commonwealth of Australia* (1969) 12 B.L.R. 82.

7.10.1 Example: GC21 clause on review of Contractor's documents

1. Unless the Contract provides otherwise, the Contractor must submit *Contractor's Documents* to the Principal at least 21 days before the date the Contractor proposes to use them for procurement, manufacture, fabrication or construction. *Contractor's Documents* must be submitted progressively with sufficient detail to demonstrate what is proposed. The number of copies must be as stated in Contract Information item 28.
2. The Principal need not respond to the Contractor about the *Contractor's Documents*.
3. If the Principal objects to the *Contractor's Documents*, the Contractor must take the objections into account and discuss them with the Principal. The Contractor must correct any Fault, error or omission in the *Contractor's Documents*.
4. Nothing the Principal does or omits to do in connection with the *Contractor's Documents* makes the Principal responsible for the *Contractor's Documents*, or prevents the Principal from relying on or enforcing any right under the Contract or otherwise.[22]

7.11 Novel and risky designs and Employer's interference in design

The Employer may encourage the designer to adopt a novel design in order to save costs.

Case study: No negligence in failure of novel design

In *Turner v Garland & Christopher*[23] it was held that a failure by a designer to succeed with a new method of which he had professed no expertise was not negligence. In that matter a designer was employed to prepare plans and superintend the erection of model lodging houses for an Employer. The Employer instructed the designer to use a new patent concrete roofing which was cheaper than lead or slate. The concrete roofing failed and had to be removed and replaced. The Employer brought an action for negligence against the designer. The judge

> charged the jury that, though failure in an ordinary building was evidence of want of competent skill, but if out of ordinary course an architect is employed in some novel thing in which he has not experience, failure is consistent with skill.[24]

The decision has been criticised on the basis that the case was decided well over 100 years ago and conditions in the construction industry and the law have changed out of all recognition since then. It is suggested that it is probable that the result of that case would be different if it were to be heard today.[25]

22 NSW Government GC21 (Edition 2) General Conditions of Contract Clause 40.
23 (1853) Alfred A Hudson, *Hudson's Fourth Edition Table of Cases* (Sweet & Maxwell, 4th edn 1914) 1.
24 Ibid.
25 Sarah Lupton, *Cornes and Lupton's Design Liability in the Construction Industry* (John Wiley & Sons, 5th edn 2013) 151.

Case study: High degree of care required in novel design

A more recent case is that of *Independent Broadcasting Authority v EMI Electronics Limited and BICC Construction Limited*,[26] which involved a design and construct contract for a 381 metre high television mast. The mast collapsed three years after completion in conditions of fog, severe ice, and snow. The cause of the failure was wind excited oscillation assisted by some degree of asymmetric icing on the stay wires. The design and construct contractors asserted in their defence that the design of the mast was 'both at and beyond the frontier of professional knowledge at that time.' Viscount Dilhorne rejected this assertion and Lord Edmund-Davies had the following to say:

> What is embraced by the duty to exercise reasonable care must always depend on the circumstances of each case. They may call for particular precautions (*Readhead v Midland Railway Company* (1869) L.R. 4 QB, 379 at 393). The graver the foreseeable consequence of failure to take care, the greater the necessity for special circumspection (*Paris v Stepney Borough Council* [1951] AC 367), and 'Those who engage in operations inherently dangerous must take precautions which are not required of persons engaged in the ordinary routine of daily life' (*Glasgow Corporation v Muir* [1943] AC 448 per Lord Macmillan at 456). The project may be alluring. But the risks of injury to those engaged in it, or to others, or to both, may be so manifest and substantial and their elimination may be so difficult to ensure with reasonable certainty that the only proper course is to abandon the project altogether. Learned counsel for BICC appeared to regard such a defeatist outcome as unthinkable. Yet circumstances can, and have at times arisen, in which it is plain common-sense that the decision is foolhardy. The law requires even pioneers to be prudent.[27]

The view taken by the court was therefore that in the circumstances of a novel design the designer was required to exercise a very high degree of care to discharge its duty of reasonable skill and care.

In *Randaree & Others NNO v W H Dixon & Associates* Kotze JA articulated the designer's duty to warn the Employer of risks in relation to novel designs:

> The architect or engineer is under a special duty to take the best advice available upon the use of such new techniques, and to advise his Employer of any potential risks; and where the selection of the technique is the architects, the onus of justifying this action will be correspondingly heavier, since nearly all building and civil engineering techniques are empirical in origin and have evolved gradually by experience and trial and error, and non-traditional methods are notoriously susceptible to unexpected difficulties and failure.
>
> . . .
>
> The said rule presumably applies *a fortiori* where tried and normal standards are deviated from.[28]

26 (1980) 14 B.L.R. 9.
27 Ibid. 28.
28 1983 (2) SA 1 (A).

Increases in cost of construction very often leads the Employer to instruct its agent to reduce the quality of the Works by both omission and Variations. If this occurs it is the duty of the designer to advise the Employer of the likely outcome of its instructions, which may be sufficient to discharge the designer from liability. If, however, the Employer's instructions would lead to a defective design or a contravention of the law, the designer will not be discharged from his/her tortious and professional liability. S/he may have no alternative but to resign if the Employer will not agree to an adequate and legal design.

7.12 Contractor's access to, and possession of, the Site

7.12.1 Possession of the Site

In general, the Employer is required to grant the Contractor access to the Site on a specified date, or if not specified, within a reasonable time. If no date for handing over the Site is specified, there is an implied term that the Site will be handed over to the Contractor within a reasonable time of signing the contract.[29] A sufficient degree of uninterrupted and exclusive possession must be provided to permit the Contractor to carry out its work unimpeded and in the manner of its choice, so as to complete the contract by the Date for Completion required by the Contract documents. As Vaughan Williams LJ famously put it:

> If in the contract one finds the time limited within which the builder is to do the work, that means, not only that he is to do it within that time, but it means also that he is to have that time within which to do it.[30]

The Employer should be aware that in linear projects such as pipelines, roads, and railways access to the entire Site may be required to enable the Contractor to carry out the Works efficiently and in the manner costed in its tender. Any interruption to the planned sequence of such works caused by lack of access to a part of the Site can result in expensive delays or demobilisation/remobilisation costs.

Clearly, in contracts for the provision of electrical and mechanical Works or involving 'modular' construction where, in general, a substantial portion of the work will be carried out otherwise than on the Site, the whole of the Site does not necessarily need to be made available to the Contractor from the commencement date of the Contract. In such contracts, the latest date and successive dates by which the Contractor requires access to the Site should be stated, for example in the Contract programme. Where the Work is divided into separable portions, specific dates for access to each separable portion should be identified in the Contract. If no date is specified it should be clear from the Contract programme how much time the Contractor requires for its work

29 *Roberts v Bury Commissioners* (1870) L.R. 5 C.P. 310, 320 and 325; *Freeman v Hensler* (1900) 64 J.P. 260 per Collins L.J.

30 *Wells v Army & Navy Co-operative Society* (1902) Alfred A Hudson, *Hudson's Fourth Edition Table of Cases* (Sweet & Maxwell, 4th edn 1914) 393; see also *Arterial Drainage Co. v Rathangan Drainage Board* (1880) 6 L.R. Ir.513; *Carr v Berriman Pty Ltd* (1953) 27 A.L.J.R. 273; *Penvidic v International Nickel of Canada* [1976] 1 S.C.R. 267.

on the Site, and, in such circumstances, the general requirement is that the Employer should grant access within a reasonable time. The difficulty with this position is that the Engineer's or the court's assessment of an objectively reasonable time may not coincide with the Contractor's requirements determined (in hindsight) by its actual performance on the Site.

Because the Contractor is generally expressly responsible for the safety of the Works during construction, necessitating a high degree of effective control over the Site, if it is intended that the Site should remain occupied partly or wholly by the Employer, its servants, agents, or other contractors, express provision for this should be made in the Contract. On the face of it, the Contractor is entitled to possession of the whole of the Site until Completion or practical completion, and the Employer is not, in the absence of an express right, entitled to take possession of parts of the Work before completion of the whole.

7.12.2 Access to the Site

The granting of access generally implies not only the handing over of the Site to the Contractor but also the provision of the means of access for all plant and Contractor's equipment to the Site. This obligation on the Employer (if contained in the Contract) should be no problem where road or railway access is already available. Where, however, the Works are to be constructed on a 'green field' site and the Employer is to provide the means of access and adequate 'lay-down' areas, these must be available on time. Further, the extent of the Employer's obligations should be stated in the specification to the Contract, including any special requirements relating to access such as dimensions and the load-bearing capacity. If access is to be by rail or sea, limitations on the size or weight of loads should also be specified in the Contract.

The Contractor should be aware that 'sufficient' access for preliminary survey work provided under the Contract will not only be short of full possession, but it may not provide access in a timely fashion to all parts of the Site to carry out the survey work in an efficient and sequential manner. As with other areas of the Contract, explicit definition of the meaning of 'sufficient access' should enable the Contractor to properly price the risks implicit in being provided less than full possession of the Site from the first date that on-site work is planned.

Note that the definition of 'Site' in the Contract may be confined to land that the Employer owns or has a lease over; the Site may not cover all areas of land on which the Contractor has to carry out construction work to fulfil its contractual obligations. For example, the Site may not include public roads and bridges on which the Contractor has to carry out modification work necessary to provide access for heavy plant and equipment. In such a case, the Employer may have no contractual obligation to provide access to the Contractor in a reasonable time or even at all, and the Contractor would accordingly assume the associated risks.

7.12.3 Restrictions on access to the Site

The NEC Contract anticipates that the entire Site will not be made available to the Contractor for the duration of the contract, because it expressly provides for access dates to parts of the Site to be set out in the Contract Data. In other contracts, as stated earlier, this should be clarified. Where the word 'possession' of the Site is used, this may mean a temporary and revocable right of occupation flowing from and only to the extent reasonably required for the work to be undertaken by the Contractor.

It can be expected that during construction the Contractor may experience temporary restrictions on small parts of the work as a result of site instructions and Variations. The possession obligation has been described as an initial duty to afford possession and control of the Site as a whole, but once this has been given, any subsequent deprivation will be in a different category. The consequences of such deprivation will depend on the degree of undisturbed possession or access to be afforded, which will vary with the nature of the project; the Contractor's entitlement will depend on the precise terms of the Contract or a more generalised implied term against unreasonable interference with the Contractor's freedom of working. Thus, an instruction to cease work on a particular structure due to design changes has been held not to be a breach of the primary obligation to provide possession (but will most likely give rise to relief under other terms of the contract, such as 'Variations').[31]

Should strikes either by the Contractor's or subcontractor's employees prevent access or possession of the Site, the risk is usually subject to the express provisions of the Contract.

7.12.3.1 Case study: Access to the Site

In *L.R.E. Engineering v Otto Simon Carves*,[32] subcontractors' work on a steelworks was interrupted when 90% complete by a violent and unlawful strike and picketing at the entry points to the Site by the Employer's striking employees. The subcontract provided that:

> access and possession of the site shall be afforded to the [sub-] contractor by the [head] contractor in proper time for the execution of the work. The [sub-] contractor shall have access by means only of those roadways and railway sidings of [the Employer] as shall be made available.

The court held, upholding the Arbitrator, that there had been no breach of contract. The Contractor had 'afforded access,' since it had made available the physical means of access as promised, and the opportunity of making use of it. It was the activities of a third party which had prevented the subcontractor from taking advantage of the opportunity.

31 *Imprefed (Pty) Ltd v National Transport Commission* [1993] S.A. 94 A.D.
32 (1981) 24 B.L.R. 27.

7.12.3.2 Case study: Restrictions on working hours on the Site

In *Codelfa Construction Ltd v State Rail Authority of New South Wales*[33] the Contractor was advised by the government Employer that it could construct a tunnel through suburban Sydney on a 24 hour/day 7 day/week basis. Third parties adjacent to the Site obtained an injunction that prevented three shifts and Sunday working. The Contractor sued the Employer for the additional loss and expense it incurred on the basis of an asserted implied term that the Employer would extend the time for Completion and indemnify the Contractor against the losses caused by the restrictions on its access to the Site. The High Court of Australia overturned the NSW Court of Appeal and found that there was no such implied term. In the circumstances, the High Court found that the contract had been frustrated.[34]

7.12.4 Access to the Site by other contractors

Where the Contract contemplates that the Employer will itself, or together with other contractors, do work or supply materials in connection with the Work, they will almost invariably be liable for damage suffered by the Contractor as a result of their failure to do the Work or supply materials at the proper time, or by obstructing the Contractor by any extended presence on Site. Usually when the Employer contracts directly with another contractor or supplier, the Employer will be responsible to the Contractor for the other contractor's or suppliers' due performance of its obligations.

7.12.4.1 Case study: Employer's obligation for other contractors

In a contract for the construction of a new railway line the Employer engaged another contractor to provide a junction to the Employer's existing line.[35] The other contractor failed to do its work in time to enable the Contractor to obtain access to its own Works in constructing the new length of line. The result was that the Contractor had to make more expensive arrangements for access. The Supreme Court of Canada held that the Employer was in breach of contract and must pay damages.[36]

Sometimes circumstances are such that, particularly in the case of subcontracts, the work will inevitably be subject to interruption or dislocation by other subcontractors or the Contractor. The type of work being undertaken might also be an important factor.

33 (1982) 149 C.L.R. 337.

34 Atkin Chambers, *Hudson's Building and Engineering Contracts* (Sweet & Maxwell, 12th edn 2010) 3–155, states that this decision has been widely regarded as controversial, however it could be justified on the basis that the injunctions were obtained under the general law which, in theory, should have been well known to the Contractor.

35 *Penvidic v Walter Cabott Construction* (1964) 44 D.L.R. (3d) 82, 93, per Mahoney J., Fed. Ct. of Canada, quoted and approved on appeal by Urie J. in the Federal Court of Appeal (1977) 69 T.L.R. (3d) 542.

36 See also *Neodox Limited v Swinton and Pendlebury Borough Council* 5 B.L.R. 34, and *Swanson v Government of Manitoba* (1963) 40 D.L.R. (2d), Canada, affirmed (1964) 44 D.L.R. (2d) 632.

7.12.4.2 Case study: Disruption of subcontractor's work

In *Smith & Montgomery v Johnson Bros*,[37] the work involved tunnelling for a sewer, in which continuity of work is exceptionally important for technical reasons. The tunnelling subcontractor undertook the 'execution of the work . . . according to the dimensions and specifications as set forth in the contract between the [Head Contractor and the Employer].' In the Contract specification, the Employer reserved the right to stop the excavation and require the Contractor to complete the sewer and backfilling up to such point as the Engineer might direct, before proceeding further with the excavation, and the Contractor was not thereby entitled to demand any allowance or compensation. The Engineer exercised this power, with the result that the Contractor ordered the subcontractor to temporarily stop work. The subcontractor claimed damages. The Contractor contended that the head contract specification was incorporated into the subcontract, but even if it was not, there was no express term obliging the Contractor to permit the subcontractor to do the work continuously. The court held that the specification was not incorporated for the purpose of the clause in question, and in the absence of an express term, there was an implied term that the Contractor should permit the subcontractor to proceed in a reasonable manner without any undue or unreasonable delay or suspension of their operations, and the Contractor was accordingly liable for damages.

7.13 The Engineer's access to the Site

To give effect to the many powers of the Engineer, a right of access to the locations where Works are being carried out would normally be implied. Many contracts go further however and provide unfettered access to all such locations for the Engineer and persons authorised by it. Any person can be authorised by the Engineer under such a clause so that, for instance, it could authorise access for visitors or others not directly concerned with the supervision of the Contract. Insofar as some of the places relevant to the Works may not be in the occupation or control of the Contractor (eg subcontractor's or manufacturer's premises such as fabrication yards), the Contract should require the Contractor to enable access to such facilities. Without a contractual right for access to all relevant locations, the Employer and its agents may not be able to make the inspections required to confirm that progress and quality are in accordance with the requirements of the Contract.

7.14 Preliminary works on the Site

Any building, structure, foundation, or means of access on the Site to be provided by the Employer must generally be in a condition suitable for the reception, movement, installation, and maintenance of the Works within the time or times indicated in the programme. However, it is not unusual to find provisions to the effect that the Contractor warrants that it has considered or inspected such a building, structure, foundation, or means of access on the Site (as known prior to entering into the Contract), and effectively that it releases the Employer from any claims for costs or delay arising out of those matters.

37 (1954) 1 D.L.R. (2d) 392, Canada.

If the Contract provides that the Employer is responsible for particular structures, foundations, and so on, or of any alterations to existing structures, the Contractor will, by submitting its programme, have provided the Engineer and the Employer with the time at which it requires those structures, foundations, and so on, or of any alterations to existing structures. Unless these are ready on time, delays will occur, and the Employer could find itself faced with claims for additional payment and extension of time in consequence. The time by which any necessary civil engineering work must have been completed for the commencement of electrical and mechanical work must be stated in the programme, and the Employer and Engineer will have to ensure that these are ready on time.

7.15 Temporary works and methods of working

It is particularly important in the Employer's interest that the Contract should not specify the particular method of working to be adopted, since if it does and that method becomes impracticable, the Contractor may be in a position to recover additional payment for the changed method of construction necessary to achieve Completion.

In relation to working methods or temporary works which have not been expressly prescribed by the Contract, and which may or may not affect the final permanent works, the Employer and its employees and consultants generally have no contractual power to intervene or give instructions, and, if they do so, may expose the Employer to claims for wrongful interference. In the absence of any express stipulation, an Employer has no right to dictate the order in which the Works will be carried out or to alter it. If the Contractor is prevented from carrying out the Works in the order of its choice, the Contractor may for that reason be entitled to damages for wrongful interference; many Variation clauses only allow changes in the permanent works described in the Contract, and do not confer power in regard to temporary works or methods of working where these have been left to the Contractor and will not affect the final permanent works.[38]

7.16 Variations ordered by the Employer

The nature and extent of the Employer's powers to issue Variations to the Works is usually set out in the Contract. Variations should not change the 'character' of the work being undertaken, or, put differently, should not be outside the 'scope of the contract.'[39] They should be ordered before Completion, because by then, the Contractor's equipment and personnel may have been re-allocated or partially or completely demobilised. Once a Variation has been ordered, the same considerations for the Employer's supply of any necessary further drawings or information within a reasonable time are precisely the same as in the case of the original construction work.[40]

The power to order Variations almost invariably includes the power to omit work, however this typically will not permit such omitted work to be carried out by the Employer or other contractors. For example, sub-clause 13.1 of the 2017 FIDIC

38 Atkin Chambers, *Hudson's Building and Engineering Contracts* (Sweet & Maxwell, 12th edn 2010) 3–158.
39 Or, as put by the US Court of Claims, be a 'cardinal change.'
40 *A MacAlpine Ltd v Transvaal Provincial Administration* [1974] 3 S.A.L.R. 506.

rainbow suite provides that 'Other than as stated under Sub-Clause 11.4 [Failure to Remedy Defects], a Variation shall not comprise the omission of any work which is to be carried out by the Employer or by others unless otherwise agreed by the Parties.'

Contracts sometimes contain unrealistic provisions requiring the time and cost impact of Variations ordered to be agreed prior to their being carried out by the Contractor. Circumstances may arise in which the number, nature, and extent of Variations which have to be issued not only call for additional administrative resources to be committed by the Contractor to deal with the situation, but it may become impossible for the Contractor to comply with the notice requirements at all. The physical execution of the additional work with existing resources may also not be possible, creating a dilemma as to whether to proceed with the work, accelerate the work and run the risk of being refused additional time and money, or be penalised. The cumulative effect of a 'blizzard' of Variations may result in delay and disruption which exceeds the sum of the parts. It may be implied that extras and alterations will be ordered at a reasonable stage (and in a reasonable manner) in relation to the Works as a whole so as to permit its economic and orderly execution without disruption or additional costs to the Contractor. Variations are fertile ground for disputes when they result in delays and extra cost.[41]

Variations are considered in more detail in Chapter 20.

7.17 The Contractor must be allowed to carry out the whole of the Works

Unless there is an express power to omit work in the Contract, the Employer must allow the Contractor to carry out the whole of the Works, and if the Employer prevents the Contractor from doing so, the Employer will be in breach of contract and liable for damages.[42]

Even if a term could be implied so as to allow the Employer to vary the Works, it does not follow that it is necessary to imply a term under which a fixed price is to be varied with any Variation. In *SWI Ltd v P&I Data Services Ltd*,[43] a term relating to a reduction in a fixed price could not be implied.

Where a Variation clause in the Contract entitles the Employer to omit work, it is implicit in most contracts that the Employer must genuinely require the work not to be done at all. In the absence of an express term of the Contract authorising the Employer to have omitted work carried out by others, it is impermissible for the Employer to exercise its power to omit work with a view to having the work carried out by someone else.[44] The rationale behind this is that a power to make omissions should not be construed as to allow an Employer to avoid the fundamental bargain struck with the Contractor.[45]

41 *Group Five Building Ltd v Minister of Public Works* [1993] 2 S.A. 593 per Corbett C J.

42 *Tancred Arrol & Co v The Steel Company of Scotland* (1890) 15 App. Cas 125, (a case involving the supply of steel for the construction of the Forth Bridge).

43 [2007] B.L.R. 430.

44 *Gallagher v Hirsch* N.Y. 45 App Div 467 (1899) New York; N.Y. Supp. 607; *Carr v JA Berriman* [1953] HCA 31; (1953) 89 CLR 327; *Commissioner for Main Roads v Reed & Stuart Pty Ltd* [1974] HCA 53; (1974) 131 CLR 378.

45 *Abbey Developments Ltd v PP Brickwork Ltd* (2003) C.I.L.L. (H.H. Judge Lloyd QC, as considered and applied by Jackson J. in *Trustees of the Stratfield Saye Estate v AHL Construction Ltd* [2004] EWHC 3286 (TCC)).

Provisional sum[46] work has been treated as definitive and not contingent, so that its omission under a power to vary the Works, if intended to have the work done by another contractor, has been held to be outside that power to vary and in breach of contract, entitling the Contractor to damages.[47]

7.18 Administration of the Contract

The adage 'time equals money' is particularly significant in the construction industry. The costs of labour, plant, and material can escalate at an alarming rate and it is only through proper administration of the Contract that these costs are properly managed and controlled.

The failure to install adequate project controls and procedures at the outset, to issue instructions on time, to provide necessary information when required, or to limit the amount of Variations and extra work orders can cause substantial critical delays to the Contractor's programme. Very often this leads to the Contractor submitting substantial claims for extensions of time, loss of productivity, additional preliminary and general expenses, and the like. The Engineer, as agent of the Employer, should be diligent to administer the Contract so as to avoid these delays and minimise such claims.[48]

46 See ¶19.2 for a definition of provisional sum.

47 *AMEC Building Ltd v Cadmus Investment Co Ltd* (1996) 13 Const L.J. 50, 65–66.

48 *Croudacre Limited v London Borough of Lambeth* [1984] 1 Con LR 12; *Fairclough Building Limited v Ruddlan* BC [1983] 3 Con LR 30; *Perini v Commonwealth of Australia* (1969) 12 BLR 82.

CHAPTER 8

The Engineer

CONTENTS

DOI: 10.4324/9781003206873-8

8.1 Engineer's duties and authority

8.1.1 Introduction

Many construction contracts refer to the role and responsibilities of the Engineer (or Project Manager, Architect or Superintendent). Where an Engineer/Project Manager/Architect/Superintendent is specified in the Contract, it is usually defined as the person, firm, or company which is to act as such for the purposes of the Contract. It should be noted that the role of the 'Engineer' in the NEC ECC is undertaken by two entities: the Project Manager and the Supervisor. The term 'Engineer' is used in this book for the entity (or entities) that administers the Contract and fulfils the role(s) defined in the Contract. For grammatical consistency the Engineer is assumed to be a firm or company.

The construction contract itself defines the duties and authority that the Engineer assumes in respect of the Contract, although the Engineer is not a party to that contract. The Engineer is usually engaged under a separate contract with the Employer (**Engineer's contract**), and therefore has no contractual relationship with the Contractor. The Engineer may be an employee of the Employer, in which case the Engineer's contract is a contract of employment. Clearly, the Engineer's duties and authority under the Engineer's contract should be consistent with the Engineer's duties and authority under the construction contract if conflicts in the execution of those duties are to be avoided.

The Engineer fulfils an important and difficult role in respect of a construction contract; the role is particularly difficult if an employee of the Employer is appointed. Under the Engineer's contract, it has duties to advance the Employer's interests, and act as the Employer's agent in issuing instructions to the Contractor. It is paid by the Employer. However, the Engineer also has a duty in respect of achievement of the contractual aim of the Employer and Contractor, in pursuit of which the Engineer is usually required to hold the balance between the competing commercial imperatives of the parties to the Contract. In that decision-making or certification role, the Engineer is required to consider the interests of both Employer and Contractor and act independently, fairly, and probably reasonably.

Tenderers are entitled to know the identity of the proposed Engineer at the tender stage. The Tenderer's knowledge of the reputation and integrity of the Engineer may be a factor in determining the price and terms on which the Tenderer will tender for the work. The Contractor usually relies heavily upon the reputation, ability, and professional integrity of the Engineer in carrying out its delegated duties such that not only will project documentation be delivered in a timely fashion, but the Contractor will receive its due time and cost entitlements under the Contract. For this reason, and subject to the precise terms of the Contract, the Employer may sometimes be unable to change the identity of, or replace, the Engineer without the Contractor's consent. For example, in the FIDIC 2017 Red Book and Yellow Book, 'The Employer shall not replace the Engineer with a person (whether a legal entity or a natural person) against whom the Contractor raises reasonable objection by a Notice under this Sub-Clause.'[1] There is no such constraint in the NEC ECC where 'The

1 Sub-clause 3.6.

Client may replace the Project Manager or the Supervisor after notifying the Contractor of the name of the replacement.'[2]

Full particulars of any restrictions placed by the Employer on the Engineer in respect of any of the duties normally assigned to it should be included in the Contract, or otherwise disclosed to the Contractor, in order that the Contractor is properly informed of such restrictions. The Contractor should carefully review the manner in which its Variations, EOT claims, and delay cost claims will be assessed by the Engineer. Importantly, the contractual mechanisms should give comfort to the Contractor that its claims will be assessed by the Engineer fairly and honestly. It may be prudent for the Contractor to ensure it is provided with a copy of the Engineer's contract to provide reassurance that the scope of the Engineer's engagement by the Employer is consistent with the Contract.

The Engineer itself has no ostensible or implied authority to vary the Contract. Nor does it have authority to vary the Works themselves in any way merely by reason of its position as Engineer. Such authority as it has must be found in the express terms of the Contract itself, for example the power to order a Variation.

8.1.2 The functions and obligations of the Engineer[3]

In 'traditional,' construction only contracts in which a consulting engineer provides full services, the Employer contracts with the engineer to prepare the designs and contract documentation, call and evaluate tenders and make recommendations on the appropriate Contractor, supervise the construction work, and administer the Contract on behalf of the Employer.[4] After the Employer and Contractor have signed the Contract, the engineer becomes the Engineer under the Contract. The Engineer generally has two differing but co-existing roles under the Contract, which have been described as the 'agency function' and the 'decision-making function.'[5] In undertaking its agency function, the Engineer acts on the instructions of the Employer, whereas in undertaking its decision-making function, the Engineer has to make decisions that balance the sometimes conflicting interests of the Employer and the Contractor.

There are a number of roles fulfilled by an engineer in connection with a major construction project. The role of a particular engineer prior to and after the Contract has been entered into may include one or more of the following:

(1) Promoting the functional and technical aspects of the project to potential project sponsors/financiers/regulatory authorities.

---

2 Clause 14.4.

3 This topic is discussed in more detail in Donald Charrett, *Contracts for Construction and Engineering Projects* (Informa Law from Routledge, 2nd edn 2021) Chapter 2.

4 For a standard form contract for the engagement of an engineer, see the FIDIC, *Clients/Consultants Model Services Agreement* (FIDIC, 5th edn 2017) (**White Book**).

5 *Scheldebouw BV v St. James Homes (Grosvenor Dock) Ltd* [2006] EWHC 89, [21].

(2) Advising the Employer at the concept stage of a project on possible options for project delivery, including suitable design and construction concepts, cost estimates and project procurement options (including appropriate forms of contract).
(3) Calling tenders on behalf of the Employer.
(4) Assessment of Tenderer's proposals and advising the Employer on the most appropriate company to be contracted to execute the Works.
(5) Preparation of preliminary designs to refine concepts and enable more realistic cost estimates to be determined.
(6) Preparation of design documentation in sufficient detail to enable Tenderers to determine appropriate construction methods and prepare accurate tenders for the construction costs.
(7) Project managing the project on behalf of the Employer, including monitoring progress, and reporting on the Contractor's achievement of contractual time, cost and quality obligations.
(8) Preparation of 'for construction' drawings and documentation.
(9) Technical review and inspection of the Contractor's work, including assessment as to whether the Contractor's fabrication and erection methods will have any adverse impact on the suitability of the as constructed design to fulfil its purpose in accordance with the design assumptions.
(10) Administering the construction contract on behalf of the Employer, including an assessment of the Contractor's compliance with the contractual requirements, and taking proactive steps to foresee and manage risks so that the Contractor achieves the requirements of the Contract.
(11) Issuing instructions to the Contractor on behalf of the Employer, particularly with respect to Variations.
(12) Assessing the Contractor's claims for time and money and certifying the Contractor's progress to enable the Employer to make progress payments as required by the construction contract.
(13) Conducting tests and inspections and certifying that the contractually specified quality is achieved.
(14) Adjudication of contractual disputes between the Contractor and Employer.

In this book, the term '**engineer**' is used for the person/entity providing one or more 'engineering' (including project management) services in relation to one or more aspects of a construction project, such obligations being defined under the engineer's contract with the Employer. The term '**Engineer**' is used for the person(s)/entity who fulfils the contract administration role of the Engineer (referred to in some contracts as the Project Manager, Architect, or Superintendent) under a construction contract.

The various roles of the engineer/Engineer at the different stages of a project are shown in Table 8.1. The table shows the role of Adjudicator as being potentially filled by the Engineer, as still occurs under some contracts, for example NPWC3 in Australia. However, as discussed in ¶8.1.11, this is not consistent with the current view that the Engineer should not be adjudicating on disputes that may arise from its own decisions.

Table 8.1 The roles of the engineer/Engineer

	Role of engineer under its contract with the Employer		Role of the Engineer under the construction contract		
	Project Manager	**Designer**	**Contract Administrator**		**Adjudicator**
			Agency function	**Decision-making function**	
Pre-construction	1. Promoting the functional and technical aspects of the project to potential project sponsors/ financiers/regulatory authorities. 2. Advising the Employer at the concept stage of a project on possible options for project delivery, including suitable design and construction concepts, cost estimates, and project procurement options (including appropriate forms of contract). 3. Calling tenders on behalf of the Employer. 4. Assessment of Contractors' proposals and advising the Employer on the most appropriate Contractor to be contracted to execute the Works.	5. Preparation of preliminary designs to refine concepts and enable more realistic cost estimates to be determined. 6. Preparation of design documentation in sufficient detail to enable Contractors to determine appropriate construction methods and prepare accurate tenders for the construction costs.			

	Role of engineer under its contract with the Employer		Role of the Engineer under the construction contract		
	Project Manager	**Designer**	**Contract Administrator**		**Adjudicator**
			Agency function	**Decision-making function**	
Construction	7. Project managing the project on behalf of the Employer, including monitoring progress, reporting on the Contractor's achievement of contractual time, cost, and quality obligations.	8. Preparation of 'for construction' drawings and documentation. 9. Technical review and inspection of the Contractor's work, including assessment as to whether the Contractor's fabrication and erection methods will have any adverse impact on the suitability of the as constructed design to fulfil its purpose in accordance with the design intent.	10. Administering the construction contract on behalf of the Employer, including an assessment of the Contractor's compliance with the contractual requirements, and taking proactive steps to foresee and manage risks so that the Contractor achieves the requirements of the Contract. 11. Issuing instructions to the Contractor on behalf of the Employer, particularly with respect to Variations.	12. Assessing the Contractor's claims for time and money and certifying the Contractor's progress to enable the Employer to make progress payments as required by the Contract.[6] 13. Conducting tests and inspections and certifying that the contractually specified quality is achieved.[7]	14. Adjudication of contractual disputes between the Contractor and Employer.

6 Under the NEC ECC, this role is undertaken by the *Project Manager*.
7 Under the NEC ECC, this role is undertaken by the *Supervisor*.

The contractual responsibilities of the Engineer may be different in forms of contract other than conventional construction only contracts. For example, in a design and construct contract, the Engineer will not prepare 'for construction' drawings, as this is the responsibility of the Contractor.

The Engineer, in its contract with the Employer, is the Employer's agent, at least in respect of its agency functions where the Engineer is upholding the Employer's interests. Whether the Engineer is also acting as the Employer's agent in respect of its decision-making functions depends on the specific terms of the Contract.

Traditionally, in discharging the decision-making functions under a construction contract, the Engineer was not acting as agent of the Employer but was impartial as between the Employer and Contractor. Indeed, the role was previously seen by the courts as 'quasi-judicial,' thereby rendering the Engineer immune from suit by either the Employer or Contractor for wrongful certification made negligently, but honestly and in good faith.[8] That immunity no longer holds, and the modern position is that the Engineer, as an independent professional, may be liable to the Employer under contract and in tort for damages arising from negligent certification.[9] However, in the absence of clear words in the Contract to the contrary, the Engineer is still required to discharge its decision-making functions fairly, impartially, and honestly (and arguably, reasonably[10]), even if directly employed by the Employer. This position was summed up by McFarlan J in the case of *Perini Corporation v Commonwealth of Australia*[11] as follows:

> [T]he cases make plain that throughout the period of performance of all these duties, the senior officer [Engineer] remains an employee of the government or semi-government body [Employer], but that in addition and while he continues as such an employee he becomes vested with duties which oblige him to act fairly and justly and with skill to both parties to the contract.[12]

Thus, whilst the Engineer cannot be regarded as independent of the Employer, the Engineer remains obliged to act in respect of its decision-making functions in a manner which is independent, impartial, fair, and honest. It is the Engineer's obligation to form opinions objectively and not simply adopt the subjective views of the Employer. It is ultimately a matter of arriving at the right decision in the circumstances, as opposed to a decision which defaults to advancing the interest of the Employer.[13]

Judges have used a variety of other words to express the obligations of the Engineer, including: 'independence and impartiality,'[14] 'act in a fair and unbiased manner,' and 'reach such decisions fairly, holding the balance between his client and the contractor';[15] 'he must

---

8 *In the matter of an Arbitration between de Morgan, Snell & Co, and the Rio De Janeiro Flour Mills and Granaries Ltd* (1891) per Mathew J: Alfred A Hudson, *Hudson's Fourth Edition Table of Cases* (Sweet & Maxwell, 4th edn 1914) 185, 195.

9 *Sutcliffe v Thackrah* [1974] AC 727. See also *Pullen v Gutteridge Haskins & Davey Pty Ltd* [1993] 1 VR 27 for concurrent liability of an engineer in tort as well as in contract.

10 Scott Lambert, 'The Superintendent and AS 4902 – General Conditions for Design and Construct' (2001) 17 *Building and Construction Law* 251, 253.

11 [1969] 2 NSWLR 530.

12 Ibid. 536.

13 See *Costain Limited and Ors. v Bechtel Limited & Ors* [2005] EWHC 1018 (TCC) and *Sutcliffe v Thackrah* [1974] AC 727, 737 per Lord Reid, 740–741 per Lord Morris.

14 *Dixon v South Australian Railways Commissioner* [1923] HCA 45; (1923) 34 CLR 71 per Isaacs J.

15 *Sutcliffe v Thackrah* (1974) AC 727, 737 per Lord Reid.

be fair and he must be honest' and 'impartially and fairly';[16] 'honestly and impartially';[17] 'fairly, impartially and in accordance with the powers given to him by the conditions'[18] and 'to hold the balance fairly as between employer and contractor.'[19] Acting 'honestly and fairly' has been held to mean 'when that individual is not dishonest, is just and impartial and conducts him or herself in a reasonable manner.'[20]

The requirement of impartiality in its decision-making functions would require very plain words in the Contract to negate it. For example, even in the case of an Engineer's contract that specifically provided that the Engineer was the agent of the Employer in 'all matters relating to the design and construction of the project,' the court found that in exercising its certifying functions under the construction contract, the Engineer was required to act honestly and impartially and was not acting as the Employer's agent in the strict legal sense.[21] The court also found, controversially,[22] that the Superintendent's power to extend time was capable of being exercised in the interests both of the Employer and the Contractor (even after the Contract had come to an end), and the Superintendent was obliged to act honestly and impartially in deciding whether to exercise this power.[23]

Mr Justice Jackson (as he then was) summed up the position of the decision maker (in this case the construction manager) as follows:

> (1) The precise role and duties of the decision-maker will be determined by the terms of the contract under which he is required to act.
> (2) Generally the decision-maker is not, and cannot be regarded as, independent of the employer.
> (3) When performing his decision-making function, the decision-maker is required to act in a manner which has variously been described as independent, impartial, fair and honest. These concepts are overlapping but not synonymous. They connote that the decision-maker must use his professional skills and his best endeavours to reach the right decision, as opposed to a decision which favours the interests of the employer.[24]

8.1.3 Example: Engineer's duties and authority under FIDIC contracts

The Engineer's duties and authority are defined as follows in the FIDIC 2017 Red Book and 2017 Yellow Book:

> Except as otherwise stated in these Conditions, whenever carrying out duties or exercising authority, specified in or implied by the Contract, the Engineer shall act as a skilled professional and shall be deemed to act for the Employer.

16 *Sutcliffe v Thackrah* (1974) AC 727, 740, 741 per Lord Morris.
17 *Peninsula Balmain Pty. Limited v Abigroup Contractors Pty. Limited* [2002] NSWCA 211; (2002) 18 BCL 322.
18 *Cantrell v Wright and Fuller Ltd* [2003] EWHC 1545 (TCC); (2003) 91 Con LR 97.
19 *Scheldebouw BV v St James Homes (Grosvenor Dock Ltd)* [2006] EWHC 89, [24] per Jackson J.
20 *Kane Constructions Pty Ltd v Sopov* [2005] VSC 237; (2006) 22 BCL 92, [617].
21 *Peninsula Balmain Pty Ltd v Abigroup Contractors Pty Ltd* (2002) 18 BCL 322, 338 per Hodgson JA.
22 Adrian Baron, 'The Superintendent's Discretion to Extend Time: A Long Story Must Be Told to Satisfy "the Earnest Inquirer"' (2007) 23 *Building and Construction Law* 410.
23 Ibid. 343.
24 *Scheldebouw BV v St James Homes (Grosvenor Dock Ltd)* [2006] EWHC 89, [34] per Jackson J.

> The Engineer shall have no authority to amend the Contract or, except as otherwise stated in these Conditions, to relieve either Party of any duty, obligation or responsibility under or in connection with the Contract.
>
> The Engineer may exercise the authority attributable to the Engineer as specified in or necessarily to be implied from the Contract. If the Engineer is required to obtain the consent of the Employer before exercising a specified authority, the requirements shall be as stated in the Particular Conditions.
>
> There shall be no requirement for the Engineer to obtain the Employer's consent before the Engineer exercises his/her authority under Sub-Clause 3.7 [Agreement or Determination]. The Employer shall not impose further constraints on the Engineer's authority.[25]

However sub-clause 3.6 Agreement or Determination provides:

> When carrying out his/her duties under this Sub-Clause, the Engineer shall act neutrally between the Parties and shall not be deemed to act for the Employer.

8.1.4 Obligations of Employer's agent

Not all construction contracts involve the appointment of an Engineer, for example the FIDIC Silver Book provides for an Employer's Representative, rather than an Engineer. Such an Employer's Representative acts as the agent of the Employer for all purposes, and the Contract will not usually require him/her to take any account of the interests of the Contractor in arriving at any determination of the Contractor's liability in respect of time, cost, or quality issues under the Contract. The Australian standard form PC-1 1998 explicitly refers to the Contract Administrator who 'will give Directions and carry out all its other functions under the Contract as the agent of the Owner (and not as an independent certifier, assessor or valuer).'[26]

The distinction between the obligations of the Employer's agent and that of the 'traditional' Engineer in respect of the decision-making functions may be more apparent than real. Arguably, the Employer's Representative/contract administrator may only be required to act honestly, not necessarily fairly or reasonably. However, in the cases that have considered the role of the Employer's agent, the courts have used very similar words to those that have been applied to the obligations of the Engineer. In a contract in which there was no Engineer, the court found that the power of the Employer to value Variations 'in its sole discretion' was to be exercised 'honestly, bona fide, and reasonably.'[27] In the *Peninsula Balmain Pty Ltd v Abigroup Contractors Pty Ltd* case referred to earlier, Hodgson JA found that the Project Manager, acting as agent of the Employer, was still required to exercise its certifying functions honestly and impartially. And in a case where the Employer's Representative took the place of the Engineer in the ICE Conditions of Contract, the court nevertheless found that the Employer was bound to act honestly, fairly,

25 Sub-clause 3.2.
26 Section 3.1.
27 *WMC Resources Ltd v Leighton Contractors Pty Ltd* [1999] WASCA 10; (2000) 16 BCL 53, 62 per Ipp J.

and reasonably in arriving at its judgement, even where no such obligation was expressed in the contract.[28]

8.1.5 Contractual obligations of the Employer and Contractor with respect to the Engineer

The Employer has implicit (and sometimes explicit[29]) contractual obligations to ensure that the Engineer fulfils its duties in accordance with the requirements of the Contract, and not to interfere with the impartiality of the Engineer in the exercise of its certifying functions. McFarlan J in *Perini* found implied terms of the Contract that the Employer had a positive obligation to ensure that the Superintendent acts honestly and impartially in carrying out its certification functions,[30] and a negative obligation not to do anything that would prevent it from a proper discharge of its contractual mandate.[31]

The Employer's positive obligation requires it to use reasonable endeavours to ensure that the Engineer carries out its duties in accordance with the requirements of the Contract.[32] Those duties include both making certifications and making those certifications within the time provided for. Many construction contracts provide a dispute resolution mechanism to resolve any dispute concerning an Engineer's direction, and this provides an avenue for either the Employer or the Contractor to have a wrong direction (including a certification) corrected.[33] In any event, the Employer would be unable to benefit from instructing the Engineer not to comply with its obligations of independence and impartiality, as the Employer cannot rely on the absence of the Engineer's certification to avoid payment to the Contractor.[34]

In addition to seeking to have an Engineer's incorrect direction or certification corrected, if the Engineer does not act in conformity with the Contract requirements (eg within the time required under the Contract or honestly and impartially), the Contractor may be able to seek damages for breach of contract, and possibly in tort[35] from the Employer as provided for by the dispute resolution clauses of the Contract.

If the Employer has entered into an agreement with the Engineer restricting the Engineer's authority to valuing the Contractor's Works to a specified money limit, the Employer has a duty to communicate that restriction to the Contractor before the Contract is entered into.[36] If an Engineer is required to act independently or impartially, for example, in certifying the value of work performed by the Contractor, it will be unlawful for the Employer to attempt to interfere with the independence of or to influence the Engineer to act in its favour.[37]

---

28 *Balfour Beatty Civil Engineering Ltd v Docklands Light Railway Ltd* (1996) 78 BLR 42.

29 For example AS2125–1992 clause 23, AS4000–1997 clause 20.

30 *Perini Corporation v Commonwealth of Australia* [1969] 2 NSWLR 530, 545.

31 Ibid. 543.

32 *Multiplex Constructions Pty Ltd v SOR Pty Ltd* (2001) 17 BCL 174, 178.

33 For example under sub-clause 3.7.5 of the 2017 FIDIC Yellow Book, if either Party is dissatisfied with an Engineer's determination, it may issue a Notice of Dissatisfaction within 28 days, and then proceed to obtain the DAAB's decision under sub-clause 21.4.

34 *Hickman & Co v Roberts* [1913] AC 229.

35 *Multiplex Constructions Pty Ltd v SOR Pty Ltd* (2001) 17 BCL 174, 178.

36 *Imperial Chemical Industries Ltd v Merit Merrell Technology Ltd* [2017] EWHC 1763 (TCC), [37] per Fraser J; *Imperial Chemical Industries Ltd v Merit Merrell Technology Ltd* [2018] EWHC 1577 (TCC), [17], per Fraser J.

37 *Minster Trust Ltd v Traps Tractors Ltd* [1954] 1 WLR 963, 975 per Devlin J; *Perini Corp v Commonwealth* (1969) 12 BLR 82, 106–108 (2 NSWR 53) per Macfarlan J (NSW Sup Ct); *Balderstone Hornibrook Pty Ltd v*

8.1.6 Fraud, collusion, and undue influence

As detailed earlier, whilst the Engineer is not independent, it is required to place itself in a position of 'independence' and act honestly when undertaking its decision-making functions under the Contract, namely, certification, assessment, and valuation roles. For example, in issuing a final payment certificate, the Engineer's function is to determine fairly, independently, and honestly what is finally due and owing by the Employer to the Contractor.[38] Thus, where the Engineer issued a certificate fraudulently, the certificate was of no force and effect.[39] Similarly, where an incorrect certificate was induced by the fraudulent representation of the Contractor to the Engineer, the certificate was not binding.[40]

Case law references to circumstances which have been held to interfere with the Engineer's independence were summarised by Warren CJ:

> First of all, with respect to the role of the superintendent, interference leading to [lack of] impartiality can arise in a series of circumstances. These include when the superintendent allows judgment to be influenced; when the superintendent is in a position whereby the certificate is deprived of value; when the superintendent acts in the interests of one of the parties and by their direction; when the position is misconceived and the superintendent acts as mediator; when there is not sufficient firmness in order to decide questions based on his or her own opinion; where judgement and conduct are controlled by the principal; and where the superintendent considers the assent of the principal to be necessary, has ceased to be a free agent and does not give full disclosure of every communication between the superintendent and the principal. Finally, the superintendent may lose independence without actually intending to do so or even without knowledge they have done so[41] [citations omitted].

However, where an Engineer independently and honestly but negligently issues a certificate, the Employer must nevertheless pay that amount. As noted later, such negligence would entitle the Employer to institute an action in contract and tort against the Engineer.[42]

8.1.7 The Engineer's obligations to the Employer

The Engineer's obligations to the Employer are primarily governed by the contract between the Engineer and the Employer. It is usually an implied (if not explicit) term of that contract that the Engineer has a duty to exercise reasonable care and skill in the performance of its duties (the 'duty of care'). Since the Engineer's duties include both the agency and the decision-making functions, the obligation to exercise reasonable care and skill applies to both. If it fails to carry out any of its functions with due skill and care, and the Employer thereby suffers damage, the Engineer may be liable to the Employer in both contract and

Qantas Airways Ltd [2003] FCA 174, [90]-[93] per Finkelstein J; *D&C Property Pte Ltd v Four Seas Construction Co Pte Ltd* [1997] SGHC 216, [37]-[53] per Tan Lee Meng J.

38 *Hoffman v Meyer* (1956) (2) SA 752, 758.

39 *Wilson v Holt* (1886) 4 HCG 220; *Maw v Mackenzie* (1953) (2) SA (A); *Saperstein v Harris* (1909) TH 170.

40 *Capstick and Co Ltd v Keen* (1933) NPD 556.

41 *Kane Constructions Pty Ltd v Sopov* [2005] VSC 237; (2006) 22 BCL 92, [623].

42 *Hoffman v Meyer* (1956) (2) SA 752, 757–8; *Laidlaw v The Hastings Pier Company* (1874) Alfred A Hudson, *Hudson's Fourth Edition Table of Cases* (Sweet & Maxwell, 4th edn 1914) 13; *Clemente v Clarke* (1880) Alfred A Hudson, *Hudson's Fourth Edition Table of Cases* (Sweet & Maxwell, 4th edn 1914) 541.

tort. The extent of any such liability will depend substantially on the terms of the Engineer's contract with the Employer.

Consequently, if an Engineer negligently certifies incomplete or defective work in its decision-making function, and as a result of this the Employer overpays the Contractor, or becomes obliged to do so, the Employer may recover the damages caused by the Engineer's breach of contract. For example, in a case where the builder erected houses in an unskilled or unworkmanlike manner with inferior materials, the Architect who had negligently certified payment was found to be liable to the Employer.[43] The same applies *a fortiori*, if the Engineer's incorrect certification is the result of fraud.

In the absence of any contractual modification, the duty of care owed by a professional is that stated by Windeyer J in reference to an architect's design work:

> An architect undertaking any work in the way of his profession accepts the ordinary liabilities of any man who follows a skilled calling. He is bound to exercise due care, skill and diligence. He is not required to have an extraordinary degree of skill or the highest professional attainments. But he must bring to the task he undertakes the competence and skill that is usual among architects practising their profession. And he must use due care. If he fails in these matters and the person who employed him thereby suffers damage, he is liable to that person. This liability can be said to arise either from a breach of his contract or in tort.[44]

In Australia (in contrast to England), it is the task of the Court to determine the standard of the duty of care which the law expects of ordinary skilled persons exercising or professing the skill of an Engineer administering a building contract.[45] A court will have regard to the evidence of contemporaneous practices accepted as proper by a responsible body of professional opinion as to the general level of skill and diligence possessed and exercised by the members of the branch of the profession to which the Engineer belongs. However, currently accepted professional practice is not necessarily decisive.[46]

In deciding the requisite degree of skill and care, a court will also have regard to a precaution usually observed by a reasonable and prudent person.[47] If specialised knowledge is required, the Engineer should therefore make use of the services of an appropriate expert. Where a project is based on new techniques of construction, an engineer would be well advised to heed the following rule formulated in Hudson's 11th edition:

> the architect or Engineer is . . . under a special duty to take the best advice available upon the use of such new techniques, and to advise his employer of any potential risks, and where the selection of the technique is the architect's, the onus of justifying his action will be correspondingly heavier, since nearly all building and civil engineering techniques have been arrived at by empirical means, materials have evolved gradually by experience and trial and error, and untried, non-traditional or high technology methods and materials are notoriously susceptible to unexpected difficulties and failure.[48]

---

43 *Armstrong v Jones* (1869) Alfred A Hudson, *Hudson's Fourth Edition Table of Cases* (Sweet & Maxwell, 4th edn 1914) 6.

44 *Voli v Inglewood Shire Council* (1962–1963) 110 CLR 74, 84.

45 *John Holland Construction & Engineering Pty Ltd v Majorca Projects Pty Ltd and Bruce Henderson Pty Ltd* (1997) 13 BCL 235, 248 per Byrne J.

46 *Rogers v Whittaker* (1992) 175 CLR 479 per Mason CJ, Brennan, Dawson, Toohey & McHugh JJ.

47 *Paris v Stepney Borough Council* 1951 AC 367, 382.

48 I N Duncan-Wallace, *Hudson's Building and Engineering Contracts* (Sweet & Maxwell, 11th edn, 1995) 293–294.

Under the doctrine of freedom of contract, the Employer and Engineer are free to agree to any terms that do not conflict with any legislation or public policy. Accordingly, a court will (perhaps reluctantly) uphold terms limiting or even excluding liability, provided they are sufficiently clear. Properly drawn up, such terms can limit liability in tort as well as under the contract: the 'tort duty . . . must yield to the parties superior right to arrange their rights and duties in a different way.'[49]

Further, properly drawn up disclaimers can preclude reliance that would otherwise result in a relationship of the type necessary for a duty of care to be owed, or for liability for misrepresentation under the *Hedley Byrne* principle (see ¶8.1.8).

8.1.8 The Engineer's obligations to the Contractor

Since there is no contractual relationship between the Engineer and the Contractor, it has been widely believed that the Engineer under a construction contract cannot under any circumstances be liable to a Contractor who has suffered purely financial loss by making a contract on the faith of misleading information, or on advice given to it negligently by the Engineer – for example in a front end engineering design (**FEED**), or a bill of quantities, or drawings, and so on. There are, however, several possible bases of liability based on negligent acts or omissions resulting in pure economic loss, the tort of misrepresentation (under the *Hedley Byrne* principle), or in Australia under the *Australian Consumer Law* as a result of misleading or deceptive conduct.

Damages arising from negligent acts or omissions resulting in purely economic loss have been recognised in Australia since the case of *Caltex Oil (Australia) Pty. Limited v The Dredge 'Willemstad,'*[50] and the principles have been discussed in a number of cases since.[51] In these situations of pure economic loss, reasonable foreseeability of harm is by itself insufficient to found a relevant duty of care, and liability has only been found in cases where sufficiently special circumstances have existed to found the requisite degree of 'proximity.' The High Court have laid down a variety of matters as 'salient features' in respect of negligence that may result in a person's liability for another person's pure economic loss, and these include: assumption of responsibility, and reliance by and vulnerability of the person suffering the loss. Some of these factors may be present in the Engineer's relationship with the Contractor.

The seminal House of Lord's case of *Hedley Byrne & Co Ltd v Heller & Partners*[52] established that a person who, by failure to take reasonable care, made a misleading statement to another, could be liable for the foreseeable economic loss suffered as a result of the second person's reliance on the misrepresentation. Whilst the ambit of this tort of misrepresentation is constrained by the requirement that the statement must be made in circumstances where it is known that it will be relied on as the basis of action, it

49 *BG Checo International Ltd v British Columbia Hydro and Power Authority* [1993] ISCR 12, cited in Patrick Mead, 'Liability of the Superintendent for Wrongfully Certifying' (1999) 15 *Building and Construction Law* 81, 84.

50 (1976–1977) 136 CLR 529.

51 For example *Perre v Apand Pty Ltd* (1999) 164 ALR 606; *Bryan v Maloney* [1995] HCA 17; (1995) 182 CLR 609; (1997) 13 BCL 104; *Woolcock v CDG Pty Ltd* [2004] HCA 16; (2004) 78 ALJR 628; (2004) 20 BCL 176.

52 (1964) AC 465.

nevertheless considerably widened the circumstances in which a person can be held liable to another where there is no contractual relationship between them. In Australia, the *Hedley Byrne* principle is now regarded as a subset of that species of negligence that results in pure economic loss, a field of the common law in which there are significant differences between Australia and England.

There have been several attempts by Contractors, both in England and Australia, to seek damages for the pure economic loss said to have been caused by an Engineer's negligent certification.[53] Whilst to date none of these have been successful, the comments made by the judges have left open the possibility that such claims could be successful in the future. In a case in which the judge refused to strike out a Contractor's claim against the Engineer as not disclosing a cause of action, Cole J said:

> Assuming such reliance [by the Contractor on the Engineer's certification] is established that may, but not necessarily will, give rise to the necessary proximity to sustain a duty of care. Whether it does or not may depend upon the particular circumstances detailed in the pleadings coupled with a consideration of any concepts of policy which may be apposite.[54]

Notwithstanding the fact that the Contractor's senior personnel are generally skilled engineers and, in a position to evaluate statements made by the Engineer, the Engineer may therefore be liable to the Contractor for damages if it makes any negligent oral or written statement about the conditions for the work, and so on, in a situation which implies that the Contractor may rely on them. This would apply even if the statements were not made in the Contract. For example, the Engineer could be liable if it advised the Contractor of its conclusions about the conditions of the Site, without giving the Contractor the detailed results of those investigations so that it could draw its own conclusions, or if the Engineer mislead the Contractor as to the difficulty of the Works by negligent design criteria for the permanent works set out in the tender document.[55]

Patrick Mead reviewed the issues involved in whether an Engineer could be liable for wrongfully certifying pursuant to the *Trade Practices Act* (now *Australian Consumer Law*).[56] In the absence of case law authority determinative of this issue, Mead noted a number of obstacles which make such a claim difficult. These include: whether the Engineer's certifying role is conduct 'in trade or commerce'; whether it could be misleading or deceptive conduct to perform a contractual obligation in the precise terms in which it agreed that obligation would be performed; whether the issue of the certificate in reality has the potential to mislead or deceive; and whether the Contractor's loss can be characterised as 'by' the Engineer's misleading or deceptive conduct. Notwithstanding these obstacles, Mead concludes that

53 *Pacific Associates Inc v Baxter* [1990] 1 QB 993; *P. & E. Phontos Pty Ltd v McConnel Smith & Johnson Pty Ltd* (1993) 9 BCL 259; *R W Miller & Co Pty Ltd v Krupp (Australia) Pty Ltd* (1995) 11 BCL 74, 147; *John Holland Construction & Engineering Pty Ltd v Majorca Projects Pty Ltd* (1996) 13 BCL 235.

54 *P. & E. Phontos Pty Ltd v McConnel Smith & Johnson Pty Ltd* (1993) 9 BCL 259, 264.

55 MW Abrahamson, *Engineering Law and the I.C.E. Contracts* (F & N Spon, 4th edn 1995) 459.

56 Patrick Mead, 'Liability of the Superintendent for Wrongfully Certifying' (1999) 15 *Building and Construction Law* 81, 101–104.

> the superintendent would be ill-advised to assume that it will be immune from such action, particularly in circumstances where one or other of the parties to the building contract goes into liquidation owing moneys to the other. In particular, it is likely that there will be an increase in the number of claims brought against the superintendent pursuant to the TPA [*Trade Practices Act*], given that the conduct sought to be impugned will be judged at the time it occurs, rather than by reference to the antecedent contractual structure, which might otherwise preclude recovery on a tortious basis.[57]

8.1.9 Ambiguities and discrepancies

Usually the Contract will make provision for the Engineer's power to order extra payment to a Contractor in the event of an ambiguity or discrepancy, where that ambiguity or discrepancy arises in documents prepared by or on behalf of the Employer and causes additional cost that a reasonably skilled Contractor could not have reasonably foreseen.

Where the Engineer issues an instruction to resolve an ambiguity or discrepancy, it would require clear words in the Contract to preclude the Contractor from its entitlement to additional payment and an EOT (if appropriate) for the resulting Variation.

8.1.10 Engineer's instructions

The Engineer should take care in ordering extra work and, prudently, should seek express authority before doing so. Very often the contract between the Engineer and the Employer in fact requires such confirmation. Certain contracts between the Employer and the Engineer prohibit the granting of extensions of time or the payment of money arising out of claims without the prior approval of the Employer. While such provisions may be called for in the interests of good governance and the avoidance of corruption, they may also have the opposite effect. The Employer should at the outset draw such limitations on the powers of the Engineer to the attention of the Contractor, who is not normally party to the agreement between the Engineer and the Employer or aware of its contents and such limitations.

For example, the standard form contract for civil engineering government work in Hong Kong makes it clear that the Engineer is subject to the directions of the Employer:

> (a) The Engineer shall carry out the duties and may exercise the powers specified in or necessarily to be implied from the Contract.
>
> (b) Before carrying out any such duty or exercising any such power, the Engineer may be required under the terms of his appointment by the Employer to obtain confirmation that the Employer has no objection to the Engineer's proposed course of action and, in the event of an objection, to act in accordance with the Employer's direction. If the Engineer is subject to any such requirements, particulars thereof shall be set out in the Appendix to the Form of Tender.[58]

---

57 Ibid. 104.

58 General Conditions of Contract for Civil Engineering Works 1999 (Government of Hong Kong SAR), Clause 2.1. See also similar provisions in the General Conditions of Contract for Mechanical & Engineering Works 1999, General Conditions of Contract for Building Works 1999 and the General Conditions of Contract for Design and Build Contracts 1999 in respect of the Engineer/Architect/Survey/Supervising Officer.

In acceding to the Contractor's request for extra payment or extensions of time, which are very often contemplated by standard form contracts, the Engineer must exercise due care in assessing the Contractor's entitlement under the relevant Contract. Its position can be precarious as, on the one hand, a failure to accede to a request for an extension of time within a reasonable period might lead to the Employer being held in breach of contract (and time becoming 'at large'), while on the other hand an over-generous extension of time could deprive the Employer of its entitlement to liquidated damages.

8.1.11 Adjudication of disputes

In addition to its decision-making role in certifying the Contractor's entitlements to time and money under the Contract, under some older forms of contract the Engineer was also required to act as Adjudicator and decide disputes between the Employer and the Contractor, for example FIDIC Conditions of Contract for Works of Civil Engineering Construction (4th edn 1987) sub-clause 67.1. In a specific situation, whether or not the Engineer acts as certifier or Adjudicator depends on the wording of the relevant clause pursuant to which it acts, as well as the nature of the dispute.[59]

In making a determination on such a dispute the Engineer does not act as Arbitrator nor observe the technicalities of arbitration, but is nevertheless required to act honestly, impartially, fairly, and independently. Provided the Engineer acts honestly, it will probably not be liable to the Employer. In contracts which specify that the Employer is bound by the decision of its designated Engineer without recourse to arbitration or to court, this, of course, can have serious consequences.

In circumstances where the Engineer has a contractual role as Adjudicator, it is very often placed in the position of being a 'judge in its own cause,' as the disputes often concern allegations relating to the Engineer's own conduct in administering the Contract. This is not consonant with modern conceptions of procedural fairness. It is unrealistic to expect that the Engineer could bring an impartial mind to determining whether one of its previous decisions was correct, particularly in circumstances where a decision could be adverse to the Engineer's own commercial interests.

Current widely used international construction contracts avoid this perceived conflict of interest by assigning the role of the Adjudicator to an independent entity, for example the DAB or DAAB in the FIDIC rainbow suite, and the Adjudicator in the NEC ECC.

8.2 Delegation by the Engineer

8.2.1 Engineer's authority to delegate

It is normal for the Engineer to delegate certain powers to the **Engineer's Representative**, provided this is authorised by the terms of the Contract. This should be done in writing with a copy to the Contractor and to the Employer. The Engineer may, in writing, alter or withdraw any such delegation in the future. It is important to note that the Engineer

59 See *Sutcliffe v Thackrah* [1974] A.C. 727; [1974] 1 All E.R. 859; [1974] 1 Lloyds Rep. 318; (1974) 118 S.J.148 HL.

cannot, simply by way of delegation, relinquish its decision-making responsibilities under the Contract. That is, it is the Engineer who has to ultimately and objectively arrive at the right decision.

Unless an adequate written delegation takes place, the Contractor is not bound to obey any of the instructions of the Engineer's Representative or to pay any attention to him/her or their views (unless, of course, they are instructions of the Engineer transmitted by the Resident Engineer, such as working drawings issued under the name of the Engineer). In cases of difficulty where an Engineer refuses to delegate and the Resident Engineer and Engineer are not acting consistently with each other, ignoring the Engineer's Representative is the Contractor's only effective remedy in order to bring about a more satisfactory state of affairs.

8.2.2 Engineer's Representative

The Engineer's Representative is typically appointed to watch and continually supervise the construction of the Works and to test and examine any materials to be used and workmanship to be employed. S/he is usually merely the inspector and assistant of the Engineer and has only negative powers, namely to condemn bad work or material. In an engineering contract the status of the Engineer's Representative is equivalent to that of the clerk of works in a building contract. S/he is entitled to be present on any part of the Works at any time and to make tests of, and inspect, all work in progress.

Where the Engineer is a firm of Consulting Engineers in private practice a Resident Engineer or Engineer's Representative from the Consulting Engineer's own permanent staff is sometimes employed for the particular project and paid by the Employer. The details of the Resident Engineer's employment contract may be important in determining whether the Engineer is vicariously liable to the Employer for the negligence of the Engineer's Representative.

8.2.3 Instructions of the Engineer's Representative

The Contractor need not, and indeed dare not, obey any instruction of an Engineer's Representative unless there has been an appropriate delegation in writing by the Engineer itself.

The Contractor should treat instructions issued by the Engineer's Representative on behalf of the Engineer (eg correspondence issued and signed on behalf of the Engineer) with caution. Unless accompanied by a written delegation, steps ought to be taken immediately to ensure such instructions were issued with the full knowledge and sanction of the Engineer. Where there is a written delegation of powers, and the Contractor disagrees with the Engineer's Representative, notwithstanding that the Employer will be fully bound by a Representative's decision within the terms of the delegation, it is advisable for the Contractor to insist upon a decision from the Engineer, who must confirm, or vary, the decision of the Engineer's Representative and cannot decline to do so. Similarly, the Contractor should apply to the Engineer for confirmation of any instruction or decision of the Representative whenever there may be any doubt as to his/her authority in relation to such instruction or decision. See, for example sub-clause 3.4 of the 2017 FIDIC Yellow Book which enables the Contractor to query any instruction or Notice given by an Engineer's delegated assistant, and deems the Engineer to have confirmed such an instruction if it does not respond within seven days.

In *Attorney General v Briggs*,[60] under the terms of a contract, the plans were subject to the approval in writing of the Employer's principal engineer. The Contractor carried out work on the basis of plans approved by the Engineer's Representative. The court held that the approval of the Engineer's Representative did not bind the Employer. Similarly, the Contractor has no right to payment for performing extra work without a prior instruction from the Engineer.

8.3 Instructions of the Engineer

8.3.1 Implied authority to give instructions

An Engineer's authority to bind the Employer is derived from the agreement between the parties, the construction contract, and usage. When an engineer is employed to perform an act in the course of her/his profession, s/he has implied authority to do whatever is normally and reasonably incidental to the performance of such act. For example, in *R H Morris Ltd v Barlow*[61] it was held that an architect who had been authorised to conclude a construction contract on behalf of the Employer has implied authority to stipulate the usual terms and conditions.

Where the Engineer's authority is not expressly limited, it has implied authority from the Employer to do all that is reasonably necessary to enable it to fulfil its agency and decision-making functions under the Contract. Accordingly, it is not necessary for the Contractor to specifically enquire as to the actual scope of authority in the Engineer's contract before acting on instructions. However, as outlined earlier it is often prudent to do so to ensure that there are no impediments to the Engineer carrying out its decision-making functions fairly and impartially.

The Contractor must proceed with the Works in accordance with the decisions and instructions given by the Engineer. The Contractor may dispute any such decisions and instructions (eg by seeking an instruction for a Variation from the Employer or an EOT from the Engineer), but must still proceed with the work. If oral instructions are given by the Engineer to the Contractor, the Contractor is normally entitled to require the Engineer to confirm these in writing. If the Contractor does request such confirmation, it is not normally required to proceed in accordance with the instructions until such written confirmation has been given.

Similarly, if any oral decision given by the Engineer is likely to involve the Contractor in extra cost or delay, it would be sensible and advisable for the Contractor to require such decision to be confirmed in writing.

8.3.2 'As soon as is practicable'

If the Engineer instructs that work is to be carried out 'as soon as practicable,' this does not mean whenever the Contractor deems fit, nor is it necessarily a reasonable time.

60 (1855) 1 Jur (NS) 1084.
61 (1953) (1) PH A1 (c).

In *Hydraulic Engineering Co v McHaffie*,[62] A contracted in July to make machinery for delivery at the end of August, and B contracted with it to make a part of the machinery 'as soon as possible.' B knew that A's delivery date was August but did not complete its part of the machine until the end of September, and A refused to accept it. The delay by B was due to it not having a foreman competent to make necessary parts at the time of the agreement. The court held that B was liable: 'as soon as possible' meant that, although it was not bound to leave aside all other work, it was to do the work in the shortest time reasonably possible given the resources which A was entitled to expect B to have. It is suggested that 'practicable' in this context has the same meaning as 'possible.'

8.3.3 Engineer's instructions on Contractor's methods of working

The extent of the Engineer's power to give instructions controlling the method of working necessary for the proper execution of the work is set out in the Contract. The degree of interest in and control over the Contractor's method of working (if any) will vary from contract to contract. The Engineer usually has wide powers to give directions, demand information, and control work. However, without some express wording or implication in the Contract, the Engineer will not normally (subject to its power to suspend work on safety grounds) have the power to do more than stipulate the form of the permanent work as the final result which it requires. In the absence of such express provision, the choice of method of working and the effective control of the Site is the Contractor's alone.[63] The consequence of this is that in the event of a structural failure in the permanent works as a result of the Engineer's design of the Works, the cost of repair of any damage which results and cost of reinstatement of the Works themselves would be borne by the Employer, who would normally seek to recover that from the Engineer.

The Engineer's powers specified in the Contract sometimes include control over the Contractor's method of working and temporary works. There are significant risks for the Employer in agreeing to give the Engineer this power, which should make clear that any such instruction does not relieve the Contractor of responsibility for safe working and for completion of the Works in accordance with the Contract. Where the Contract enables the Engineer to issue instructions as to the method of working to be adopted, the exercise of this power might amount to a Variation if the Engineer's method of working is not prescribed in the Contract. If this were not so the Engineer might require a cheaper process (where alternative processes are differentially priced in the Contract) and the Contractor might object on grounds of safety or stability of the Works and call for a more expensive process to be adopted. The risk and responsibility for safety of the temporary works would then be assumed by the Engineer.

The Engineer may also require a safer but more expensive process of construction. For instance, the technical documents not uncommonly confer express power on the Engineer to decide whether particular methods should be used in different parts of the Works (eg the amount of temporary support in a tunnel excavation). Whether the Engineer's decision in

62 (1878) 4 QBD 670; 27 WR 221.

63 See *Clayton v Woodman and Sons (Builders) Ltd* [1962] 2 All ER 33 (CA).

such matters would entitle the Contractor to extra payment would depend on the terms of the Contract. However, contractually unauthorised interference in the Contractor's methods of working will almost invariably constitute a Variation.

There is no doubt that particular requirements of the Engineer as to methods of working can amount to a Variation if not contemplated by the Contract – even where the Engineer refuses to issue a Variation order.[64] Should circumstances give rise to substantial and necessary modifications (of a kind not anticipated by the Contract), the Engineer and/or Employer should, as a matter of practicality, invite the Contractor to scope the extent of modification work required, and, save for exceptional circumstances, instruct the existing Contractor to perform such works by issuing an instruction to vary the Works. To do otherwise (eg instruct a third party to perform the Variation) could constitute an act of prevention on the part of the Employer as it could lead to a contractual impasse and not allow the Contract to flow as intended.[65]

Where an arbitration clause gives the Arbitrator express power to open up, revise, and review the Engineer's decisions, the Arbitrator could substitute his/her own exercise of, for instance, the Engineer's powers in terms of the conditions, and would be able to award additional payment. It is important to note that decisions of the Engineer not made in accordance with the requirements of the Contract may not be capable of being 'opened up, reviewed, and substituted' by the Arbitrator in the event of a dispute. For example, where the Engineer has issued notices in breach of contract or where late certification has occurred. In these circumstances, the Engineer's decisions are 'irreversible,' and the Contractor is entitled to seek relief by way of the alternative of either a declaration or damages.[66]

8.4 Replacement of the Engineer

The Employer may terminate the named Engineer's powers to act for and bind it under the Contract and may appoint a substitute. Such dismissal of the Engineer will bring an end to its powers. It may, however, also be a breach of the Engineer's contract, for which it would be entitled to damages from the Employer. In the absence of a clause in the Contract entitling it to do so, the Employer generally cannot unilaterally appoint a new Engineer to exercise the functions entrusted by the Contract to the first Engineer without the consent of the Contractor.[67]

In the case of a change of Engineer, it is the Employer's Engineer at the time of the certificate who must certify and not the Engineer who supervised the work, and so on, to which it relates.[68] The new Engineer cannot generally repudiate its predecessor's decisions, but it usually has power to correct or modify interim certificates.

---

64 See, for instance, the Arbitrator's finding in the House of Lords case, *Brodie v Cardiff Corporation* (1919) AC 337, 347.

65 See *North West Regional Hospital Board v T A Bickerton Ltd* [1970] 1 All ER 1039 and *Holland Hannen & Cubbitts (Northern) Ltd v Welsh Health Technical Services Organisation* (1981) 18 BLR 80.

66 See *United Australia Ltd v Barclays Bank Ltd* [1941] AC 1, 29–30 per Atkin LJ; *Ciavarella v Balmer* (1983) 153 CLR 438, 449 per Gibbs CJ, Mason, Wilson, Deane and Dawson JJ.

67 Philip Loots, *Construction Law and Related Issues* (Juta & Co, 1st edn 1995) 350.

68 *Kellett v Mayor of Stockport* (1906) 70 JP 154.

8.5 Determinations by the Engineer

8.5.1 Scope of determinations

A decision of the Engineer in the exercise of its decision-making function is referred to as a **determination**. Many construction contracts provide that either party may dispute an Engineer's determination under the dispute resolution provisions of the Contract. For example, the 2017 FIDIC Yellow Book provides that if either Party is dissatisfied with a determination of the Engineer, it can give a 'Notice of Dissatisfaction with the Engineer's Determination' within 28 days and then submit a Dispute to the DAAB.[69] In resolving such a dispute, a Dispute Board or Arbitrator generally has the power to open up and revise the decision of the Engineer, for example Rule 5(k) of the DAAB Procedural Rules and sub-clause 21.6 of the 2017 FIDIC Yellow Book. Whilst it is possible for the parties to make the Engineer's determination binding and unreviewable by an Arbitrator or the Court, it would require very clear words to do so. In the absence of such very clear words, the Court will also generally have the power to open up and revise the decisions of the Engineer.[70]

However, the parties to a contract can always agree that a particular determination made by the Engineer or even one of the contract parties is binding and unreviewable, and there are cases in the Law Reports where there were contractual provisions to that effect.[71] For example, in a contract which provided for the Employer to undertake a valuation 'in its sole discretion,' an Arbitrator or a court did not have the power to open up, review, or revise a certification made by the Employer, provided it was made honestly, bona fide, and reasonably and in accordance with the contract.[72]

8.5.2 The Engineer's determination with respect to time

The Engineer has a duty, when administering the Contract, to determine such extensions of time as are claimed. It is usually the Engineer and not the Employer who must determine and grant any such extension. The Engineer, as set out earlier, is obliged to reach a decision independently, impartially, fairly, and honestly. This normally involves the Engineer having regard to both the interests of the Employer as well as the Contractor in arriving at its decision whether to grant the Contractor an EOT.[73] The Engineer is then required to convey this decision to the Contractor within a reasonable time after extra or additional work or other special circumstances have arisen. This will enable the Contractor to comply with the programming requirements of the Contract, and it forms one of the most important decision-making functions of the Engineer.

It is important for the Engineer to appreciate that where the Contractor meets unexpected difficulties, such as industrial delay, it may be entitled to an EOT for completing the relevant separable portion/milestone, although it has agreed to take the risk of such difficulties so

69 Sub-clause 3.7.

70 *Beaufort Development (NI) Ltd v Gilbert Ash NI Ltd* (1998) 59 Con LR 66 per Lord Hoffmann.

71 For example *In re De Morgan, Snell & Co. and Rio De Janeiro Flour Milling Co.* (1891) Alfred A Hudson, *Hudson's Fourth Edition Table of Cases* (Sweet & Maxwell, 4th edn 1914) 185.

72 *WMC Resources Ltd v Leighton Contractors Pty Ltd* [1999] WASCA 10; (2000) 16 BCL 53, 69 per Ipp J.

73 See *Peninsula Balmain Pty Ltd v Abigroup Contractor Pty Ltd* [2002] NSWCA 211; (2002) 18 BCL 322, 343.

far as payment is concerned – even where the Contract is a pure lump sum form. It is also important to note that the Contractor is often only entitled to an EOT to the extent that it has strictly complied with the relevant notice provisions of the Contract and where it has taken steps to mitigate the effect of the delay event. Although *Peninsula Balmain Pty Ltd v Abigroup Contractors Pty Ltd*[74] suggests that an Engineer's power to extend time may be capable of being exercised to overcome the effects of a time bar in some contracts, a Contractor would be well advised to strictly comply with all contractual notification provisions with respect to EOTs. Many contracts have strict time-bars that preclude claims that are not submitted within the specified time and do not authorise the Engineer to extend time in such circumstances.

8.5.3 Engineer's change of mind

The Engineer normally has no power to alter the Contract requirements by giving a binding approval of work which infringes the requirements of the Contract, nor are its powers normally affected merely because of its previous approval. The Contractor therefore remains exposed to having to redo bad work under the defects clause, whether or not the Engineer has approved it.

If the Engineer reverses its approval, the Contractor has a remedy in arbitration or litigation if it believes that the final disapproval is wrong. The Employer may allow the work to remain without prejudice to a claim for damages, rather than risk liability for the cost of having the work redone if it loses in arbitration. Where the defect is not serious and the cost of rectification is disproportionately high, the Arbitrator may not award the full cost of having the defect made good, but only the reduction in value of the Works because of the defect.

This position may perhaps be unfair to the Contractor, particularly if the Employer replaces an incompetent Engineer and the new Engineer goes back on its predecessor's approvals. However, the Contractor normally has an independent duty to ensure that its work is up to the required contractual standard, and it should not be entitled to rely on the Engineer to ensure that the requirements of the Contract are fulfilled.

If the description of materials in the specification is followed by 'or other approved' or words to that effect, or the only requirement is that particular work is to be done to the Engineer's approval, the specification requirements are fulfilled when materials or work are approved by the Engineer. In this situation the Engineer has no power to disapprove of materials or work of its own motion at a later stage.[75]

Apart from the final payment certificate, no prior approval, test, payment, or certificate will normally avail the Contractor if work is subsequently found to be defective. The Engineer usually has the power, if agreed to by the Employer and Contractor in the Contract, to allow nominal defects to remain and to certify a reasonable deduction from the contract price. However, the Engineer's own express prior approval of work during the course of construction may preclude it from subsequently ordering its removal and re-execution at the Contractor's expense on the basis of estoppel or waiver, provided it did not exceed its authority in originally approving the Works.

---

74 Ibid. 343.

75 MW Abrahamson, *Engineering Law and the I.C.E. Contracts* (F & N Spon, 4th edn 1995) 149.

8.5.4 Approval of workmanship and plant

The manner of execution or standard of workmanship can be set out in the Contract in different ways. Normally, for the reasons given earlier, detailed instructions as to the manner of execution will not be given but will be found indirectly in references to technical standards in the specification. They may also be found indirectly in the form of tolerances that are required to be met or in specific test results to be achieved. Where no specific standards have been included in the Contract, the work must be done in a proper and workmanlike manner. In addition, the work must be in accordance with recognised good practice. This expression implies that the manner of execution must be such as is commonly known and acceptable to experienced contractors.

If the Contractor intends to carry out work in a novel or experimental way it should give details at the tender stage or submit its proposal to the Engineer during performance of the Contract so as to enable the Engineer to form a view and, if appropriate, to instruct the Contractor not to use it.

Certain contracts require examination and testing of plant at the place of manufacture, and inspection of certain work before it is covered up, for example foundations. Provision should be made accordingly in the contract documents for this inspection to be carried out by the Engineer or its Representative. On receipt of the Contractor's notice that plant or other work is available for inspection, the Engineer may either notify the Contractor that checks are unnecessary or carry out the appropriate examination, measurement, or testing, without unreasonable delay. If the Engineer takes no action the Contractor will be entitled to use or cover up the work in question after the expiry of a reasonable time. The Contractor would, however, be well advised not to cover up any such work without serving notice on the Engineer of the date when it intends to do so.

The Engineer is normally entitled to give an instruction to the Contractor to expose any part of the Works at any time before Taking-Over, to check whether the work is in conformance with the requirements of the Contract. Instructions of this nature from the Engineer may disturb the regular progress of the Works and may entitle the Contractor to an EOT and costs if the work is found to be satisfactory.

It may be desirable to permit the Engineer to use an independent inspector. Either the Engineer's right to appoint an independent inspector must be provided for in the Contract, or the Engineer must obtain the Contractor's consent. If the Engineer has power to appoint an independent inspector, it will be sensible to include in the Contract a list of those inspectors from whom the Engineer may make a choice. The Engineer's right to choose an independent inspector normally creates no problem, however the Contractor has good reason not to agree to the Engineer having an unfettered right to appoint inspectors from outside its own organisation, for such an inspector might, for example, turn out to be one of the Contractor's competitors.

The Engineer is normally entitled to inspect, examine, test, and check on the Contractor's or subcontractor's premises where the manufacture of plant takes place. If plant is being manufactured on a subcontractor's premises, the Contractor should be required under the Contract to include in its subcontract permission for the Engineer to perform its inspection activities at the subcontractor's premises. It will be necessary to obtain such permission from all subcontractors engaged in manufacture of any part of the plant, including the right of independent inspection. It is usually necessary for the Contractor to secure 'back to back' agreements with its subcontractors in this area of the Contract. The Contractor and its subcontractors would normally be entitled to limit the required access for inspection solely to the areas of their works where manufacture of plant for the Contract is taking place, and to normal working hours.

If the Engineer has not attended the tests after having received adequate prior notification, but should have done so, it will usually be obliged to accept the validity of the test readings contained in the results. The Contractor should ensure that the Contract does not give the Employer any right to insist on retesting if its Engineer has not availed itself of the opportunity to witness the tests when they were first done.

The obligation to provide facilities for testing is frequently part of the Contractor's obligations, which it must allow for in the Contract price. The Engineer is normally required to certify that the tests have been passed. The Engineer can either issue a certificate to the Contractor to that effect or endorse a test certificate issued by the Contractor.

The Engineer's right to reject plant is usually dependent on certain conditions. The plant must either be defective or otherwise not in accordance with the Contract for the Engineer to take this action. This is a question of fact. The Engineer need not have inspected, examined, or tested the plant in order to reject it. It can do so on the basis of the results not conforming to the requirements of the Contract. The presence of the Engineer at the tests in order to take such action is not usually obligatory. The Engineer's decision is based on its opinion, which decision may normally be disputed under the dispute resolution provisions of the Contract. If the decision is wrong, the Contractor may be entitled to compensation for all costs incurred as a consequence of the incorrect rejection. The Engineer's right to reject plant should be restricted to cases where the defects, or non-compliance with the Contract, are of some importance. It should not be entitled to reject any plant containing minor defects which do not affect the commercial operation of such plant.

In the event of rejection, the Engineer should be obliged to notify the Contractor immediately of its decision. The notice should state the Engineer's objections with reasons. The extent of detail given by the Engineer in relation to its objections will depend upon the circumstances. The Engineer should say why it considers the plant defective or otherwise not in accordance with the Contract, so that the Contractor has a basis for determining whether or not to dispute the Engineer's decision.

The Engineer may normally require rejected plant to be retested even if the reason for rejection is unrelated to a failure to pass tests provided for in the Contract. If it so requires, the tests must be repeated under the same terms and conditions. Besides bearing the costs which it has incurred because of the repetition of such tests, the Contractor may also have to bear any additional costs incurred by the Employer, including the costs of the Engineer.

A decision by the Engineer to reject any plant or construction may be contentious because of the substantial costs involved. Nevertheless, if the Contract gives the Engineer the power to reject plant with defects, the Contractor is required to comply with the Engineer's instructions and correct the alleged defects. Delay and disturbance may result and, if the Engineer is ultimately found to have rejected the plant improperly, the Contractor would normally be entitled to an EOT and additional costs.

8.5.5 Delivery of plant and equipment to Site

The Contractor is normally required to have the Engineer's written permission to deliver any plant or Contractor's equipment to the Site. This is to facilitate co-ordination and planning of resources, procedures, and facilities on the Site. Appropriate lay-down, storage, fabrication, and workshop areas must be designated. The Contractor is responsible for the reception of plant and Contractor's equipment at Site including responsibility for offloading. Permission from the Engineer to deliver to Site does not release the Contractor from its obligations. Obligations in respect of ownership, care, custody, control, and risk of Contractor's equipment, plant, and materials on Site must be clearly defined in the Contract.

8.5.6 Approval by the Engineer

Where the Contract provides for an unconditional final payment certificate, if the Engineer issues a final payment certificate whilst being aware of the existence of certain defects, the certificate will protect the Contractor even in respect of other defects where no dishonesty on the part of the Engineer existed. In such cases, once the Works have validly been approved by the Employer or the Engineer as provided for in the Contract, the Contractor is entitled to payment and is not liable for defects which existed when approval was expressed, even though they manifested themselves only at a later stage. However, many construction contracts provide that, notwithstanding the issue of a final payment certificate, the Contractor must remedy defects appearing within a certain time.

A contract may also provide that, within a stipulated time after acceptance of the Works, the Employer must advise the Contractor of all defects or omissions and that thereafter the Contractor's liability shall be restricted to such complaints. The exception will be for latent defects in the Contractor's work which were not capable of being identified when the certificate was issued.

A construction contract may provide that a dispute about the expression of approval by the Engineer, or its refusal to do so, may be referred to arbitration. If the arbitration provisions are invoked, the Arbitrator's award will take the place of the Engineer's decision or its failure to decide. If the Engineer is dismissed by the Employer after it has expressed its approval with the Works or has given a certificate, the dismissal has no effect on the validity of such prior acts.

Where the Contract requires a statement that the Works have been completed to the Engineer's satisfaction, a certificate will not be valid as a final payment certificate unless it actually states that the Works have been completed and maintained to its satisfaction. It has, for instance been held that a certificate that the Works were completed to the supervisor's satisfaction was provided where the supervisor certified for a 'final instalment'[76] and for the release of the second half of the retention money,[77] but not where an architect wrote 'Balance due as per conditions' in the margin of the Contractor's account.[78]

---

76 *Lowther v Swan & Co* [1915] TFD 494 (SA).

77 *Machin v Sume* (1892) 18 VLR 472; *Borough of Stratford v J H Ashman Ltd* [1960] NZLR 503.

78 *Goodman v Layborn* (1881) Roscoe's *Digest of Building Cases* 4 ed 162 (CA).

Once any claim by the Contractor is approved by the Engineer, the Contractor may claim immediate payment; the Employer is not entitled to withhold it until other claims by the Contractor have been settled.

The Engineer's final payment certificate may be made conclusive, at least on some points, by excluding the right to arbitration. Such conclusive final payment certificate by the Engineer is a two-edged sword for the Employer. If the final payment certificate is made conclusive on payment, the Contractor cannot recover any payment unless it is included in a certificate. However, the Employer cannot go behind a certificate and claim to pay less than the amount certified, even if it includes, for instance, the value of extras which were not ordered properly. This is subject to the exception that the certificate may be reopened or dispensed with if the Engineer was disqualified when it was made or if it delegated its powers. The certificate may also be dispensed with if the Employer prevents the Engineer from issuing it. Where the Employer has power to appoint a substitute Engineer, failure to appoint a substitute for an Engineer who dies or arbitrarily refuses to exercise its powers would probably be a breach of an implied term by the Employer, so as to give the Contractor a right to payment without a certificate.

8.5.7 Work to be to the satisfaction of the Engineer or Employer

The extent of the Contractor's obligation to complete, and the effect of having to carry out the Contract to the satisfaction of the Engineer, are issues which must be clearly formulated in the Contract.

Although now unusual, a construction contract may require the Contractor to perform the Works to the satisfaction of the Engineer. In such a case, the Engineer must act reasonably in deciding whether the Contractor's works are adequate.[79] The courts will construe such a clause as meaning that the Contractor must comply with its completion obligations to the objective satisfaction of a reasonable person, unless there is clear language in the Contract showing that work is to be carried out to the subjective and personal satisfaction of the Engineer or Employer. An Engineer or Employer administering the Contract should therefore apply the standard of objective reasonableness in certifying the Contractor's work, unless the Contract clearly allows for the Engineer's subjective satisfaction. The Engineer's approval may be either express or implied, and whether payment will constitute approval will depend on the facts of each case.

If, by providing for the subjective approval of the Engineer, the terms of the Contract are such as in effect to make the Engineer judge in its own cause, these provisions will receive a restrictive interpretation by the courts. In such cases, common law principles require that when weighing its approval, the Engineer must act honestly. Whilst a court will not 'open up, revise or review' an Engineer's decision if made honestly in accordance with the Contract, it may be set aside if made dishonestly, and such a dishonest decision would not preclude payment to the Contractor.

Where the language of the clauses in the Contract do not expressly or by necessary implication make the Engineer the sole arbiter of the end product whose approval is the overriding and decisive factor, the issue of a final payment certificate by it would not prevent

---

79 *Ripley v United States* (1912) 233 U.S. 695, 701–702.

a court or an Arbitrator enquiring as to whether the Contract had been properly performed. In a contract of this type, the Contractor's obligation is essentially to perform the Contract in accordance with the specification, and the Engineer's certificate is not decisive.

Where the work must be completed to the satisfaction of the Engineer, the Contract may also require that the work be completed in accordance with the plans and specifications, and that it furthermore be approved by the Engineer. However, where the undertaking of the Contractor is in the form in which the supply of good materials and the performance of good workmanship is subordinated to the satisfaction of the Employer and that of the Engineer, if the Employer and the Engineer are satisfied, the undertaking of the Contractor is taken to be fulfilled.

Certain English cases have regarded the Engineer's approval as an additional safeguard and the requirements of the Contract are therefore not overridden by its or any other third party's approval, thereby leaving the Employer free to dispute the quality of work despite a certificate or approval.[80] These cases highlight the importance of sufficiently explicit wording in the Contract to make clear whether the Engineer's approval is the only or overriding requirement as to the sufficiency of the work, or whether it is merely an added protection for the Employer.

8.5.8 The Engineer exceeding its authority

Where the Engineer exceeds its authority under the Contract, its certificate will not be valid and binding on the Employer. For example, where the terms of a Contract provide that a final payment certificate shall not be granted for three months after the completion of the Contract, a certificate by the Engineer issued before such period has elapsed would not be binding. Where an Engineer had authority to issue progress certificates as to the value of work actually completed, certificates issued on plan measurement were held to be outside its powers.[81]

Where a detailed account is attached to a certificate and it is evident that the Engineer had exceeded its authority by including certain items, the certificate, being divisible, is nevertheless binding in respect of the remaining items. Even where the Engineer has exceeded its authority, if the circumstances are such that the Employer has ratified its conduct or is estopped from denying authority, the certificate may be binding.[82]

80 see I N Duncan-Wallace, *Hudson's Building and Engineering Contracts* (Sweet & Maxwell, 11th edn 1995) 754–756, and in particular *Newton Abbott Development Co Ltd v Stockman Brothers* (1931) 47 TLR 616; *Billyack v Leyland Construction Co* [1968] 1 All ER 783 (KB).

81 *Rudland & Son v Gwelo Municipality* (1933) SR 119.

82 *Dunbar & Co v Escombe Avenue Nursing Home* (1921) WLD 45, 48.

CHAPTER 9

The Contractor

CONTENTS

DOI: 10.4324/9781003206873-9

9.1 Contractor's general obligations

A construction contract is a contract for work and materials.

The work, materials, and plant which the Contractor[1] is or may be required to carry out and complete or provide under the Contract is commonly referred to as the **Works**. The Works generally includes Variations, rectification of defects, temporary works, and equipment.

9.1.1 Contractor's role – construct only contracts

In most common law countries, the 'traditional' practice for Employers wishing to engage in a building or engineering contract was that they would appoint an architect or engineer to advise on the Works and also upon the preparation of the Contract under which they are to be constructed, to act as the Employer's agent and administer the Contract on behalf of the Employer. In such a 'construct only' contract, the architect or engineer would design[2] the project and supervise or inspect the work of the Contractor; approve work, temporary works, and methods of working[3] and independently and fairly certify interim and final payments, Completion of the Works, delay for the purposes of liquidated damages, if appropriate; and then issue a final certificate to bring the project to its conclusion. Where

1 Generally so described in most construction contracts; although also described as 'Main Contractor' in the UK, and 'Prime Contractor' in the US. In the authors' view, it is regrettable that *Hudson's Building and Engineering Contracts* (Sweet & Maxwell, 12th edn 2010) has adopted the term 'Construction Professionals' in place of 'Architects, Engineers and Surveyors,' suggesting that Contractors are not 'Construction Professionals.' Just one major Design-Build Contractor, Bechtel (with a turnover of US$21.8 billion in 2019) and operating in 160 countries on seven continents, employs over 50,000 employees of which a substantial number are 'construction professionals.'

2 Design encompasses all plans, drawings, sketches, instructions, and descriptions that determine the way the Works (or parts of it) are to be constructed. Design includes the writing or selection of specifications as well as the production of plans and drawings and any element of choice on the part of the designer, such as requirements as to materials or working methods.

3 Particular attention should be given to whether 'approval' of temporary works and methods of working attracts legal liability for the adequacy of the same, because many structures are unstable during various stages of construction and the Contractor is often relied upon for its expertise. The litany of avoidable failures of partially constructed structures due to shortcomings in the design or execution of temporary works and errors in methods of working is endless.

the Employer has retained professional designers to produce the Employer's design and specifications for the project, the professional designer will generally have obligations in contract and in tort in respect of the design produced while retained by the Employer. The Employer and its advisers will need to have determined in advance what the design life and the service life of the object to be constructed is to be.[4]

If plans and specifications are provided to the Contractor to work to, the Contractor will normally have to do no more than carry out the work according to the plans and specifications in a workmanlike manner and using proper materials, subject only, in cases of very obvious prospective unsuitability, to a duty of the Contractor to warn the Employer or its designer.

When express undertakings are given by the Contractor as to design or suitability, they will usually prevail, notwithstanding compliance in all other respects with the contract requirements. If the Contractor expressly undertakes to carry out work which will perform a certain duty or function and in conformity with the plans and specifications, and it turns out that the Works constructed in accordance with the plans and specifications will not perform that duty or function, the express obligation to construct the work capable of carrying out the duty in question overrides the obligation to comply with the plans and specifications, and the Contractor will be liable for the failure of the work notwithstanding that it is carried out in accordance with the plans and specifications. The Contractor will not be entitled to extra payment for amending the work so that it will perform the stipulated duty.[5] See the case study in ¶6.12.1 for an example of a Contractor's liability for defective work notwithstanding that it had complied with the contractually specified design requirements.

Hudson's Building and Engineering Contracts notes an increasing tendency in the UK and elsewhere for Employers to use a construction management professional (typically known as a Project Manager) other than an architect or engineer. Such a Project Manager will act as either the Employer's agent or act independently in obtaining the design and construction – an architect or engineer as appropriate, a single Head Contractor, or a Management Contractor, or trade Contractors to carry out specified elements of the construction. This change in paradigm from the 'traditional' practice focuses more on procuring functions rather than a direct professional relationship with architects or engineers. Accordingly, the Project Manager is the conduit through which the Employer receives the design and construction elements of the project.[6]

This new paradigm is implemented in the NEC contracts, which divide the traditional functions of the Engineer between the Project Manager and the Supervisor. The Project Manager administers the contract on behalf of the Employer so that its object is achieved,[7] gives instructions to the Contractor,[8] and certifies payments. The Supervisor carries out tests, monitors the Contractor's testing, and may carry out testing itself to ensure that the contractually specified quality is achieved.[9]

---

4 Donald Charrett, *The Application of Contracts in Construction and Engineering Projects* (Informa Law from Routledge, 2nd edn 2022) 87–90.

5 *Steel Co. of Canada v Willand Management Ltd.* [1966] S.C.R. 746.

6 Atkin Chambers, *Hudson's Building and Engineering Contracts* (Sweet & Maxwell, 12th edn 2010) 2–201 (*Hudson's*).

7 For example NEC3 Engineering and Construction Contract section 42 Searching for and notifying Defects.

8 For example NEC3 Engineering and Construction Contract section 15 Adding to the Working Areas; section 17 Ambiguities and inconsistencies; section 19 Prevention.

9 NEC3 Engineering and Construction Contract section 40 Tests and inspections.

9.1.2 Contractor's role – design and construct contracts

Where the Employer undertakes any significant preliminary design which forms the basis of the contract, the Contractor is often required to complete the design. The question of responsibility for defects in the Employer's design often depends upon when the Contractor is to undertake a review of that design and the extent of the review required. Some contracts require the Contractor to conduct a review and to notify the Employer of any discrepancy or defect without responsibility in the early stages of the contract, such as the FIDIC Gold Book.[10] Others, such as the 2017 FIDIC Silver Book[11] and ENAA[12] place responsibility on the Contractor to review the Employer's design prior to contract, thereby placing a frequently impossible task within the time allowed and a costly burden on all tenderers. The FIDIC Silver Book approach effectively provides the Employer with a review by all tendering contractors, who must identify problems or defects in the design and provide their solution before the Contract Price is agreed with the successful tenderer (the Contractor). However, it is a costly, time-consuming, and fruitless activity for the unsuccessful tenderers, the cost of which must be recovered elsewhere. Enlightened Employers contribute a fixed sum towards the costs of all pre-qualified Tenderers who submit a tender on this basis.

In design and construct[13] and EPC contracts, the Contractor is completely responsible for the design. An EPC contract is a species of design and construct contract in which the Employer deals directly with the Contractor on a 'turnkey' basis, and the Contractor assumes full responsibility for the project from inception to completion. In such a contract, the Contractor carries more risks than in a 'conventional' design and construct contract. This is illustrated by the difference in risk allocation between the 2017 FIDIC Yellow Book (design and construct) and the 2017 FIDIC Silver Book (EPC). The following Employer's risks in the 2017 Yellow Book sub-clauses are Contractor's risks in the 2017 Silver Book:

4.7 Errors in setting out.

4.12 Unforeseeable physical conditions.

8.5(c) Exceptionally adverse climatic conditions.

8.5(d) Unforeseeable shortages and the availability of personnel or Goods caused by epidemic or government actions.

---

10 Sub-clause 5.1 General Design Obligations:

Within the period stated in the Contract Data, calculated from the Commencement Date, the Contractor shall give Notice to the Employer's Representative of any error, fault or other defect found in the Employer's Requirements or these items of reference (including design criteria and calculations, if any).

11 Sub-clause 5.1 General Design Obligations:

The Contractor shall be deemed to have scrutinised, prior to the Base Date [28 days prior to the submission of tender], the Employer's Requirements (including design criteria and calculations, if any).

12 ENAA Model Form of International Contract for Power Plant Construction (2012) GC 9.2:

The Contractor confirms that it has entered into the contract on the basis of reasonable examination of:
(a) the data relating to the Works (including any data as to boring tests) provided by the Owner;

13 Also referred to as design and build contracts.

The single point of responsibility in the use of a design and construct or EPC contract avoids the complexities of management and litigation where issues arise such as questions of whether defects are attributable to defective design, defective materials, or defective workmanship. Other advantages claimed for design and build contracts by *Hudson's* include:

(1) Cost savings arising from a more efficient design process once the Contractor is in control of the design.
(2) The potential for increased value born of the Contractor's likely greater understanding of the relationship between labour and material costs and the cost relationships between components of the design.
(3) Time savings as a result of the potential to overlap the production of the design with the commencement of the construction when both are within the control of the Contractor by contrast with the time required to complete the design before tendering by Contractors in a traditional design-bid-build situation.
(4) Reduced administration costs for the Employer when the administration of the building contract itself is not required.
(5) In lump sum or guaranteed maximum price design and build contracts the advantage to the Employer of early price certainty.[14]

The extent to which these potential advantages to an Employer are achieved in practice will depend on the conditions of contract, the scope and competence of the Contractor's design, and the amount of Employer's involvement in the design.

The Employer having made known its requirements for a design and construct contract, it is the Contractor which employs its own professional advisers or its internal professionals to produce the complete or final design of the project. Most Contractors employ either directly or indirectly professional designers who are members of the relevant professional bodies and would be expected to conform to the rules and standards of those professional bodies. It is submitted that the convenience and benefits derived from single point responsibility for design and construction is usually the deciding factor in selecting a design and construct contract. A reduced time for delivery of the completed facility may also be a compelling reason to select a design and construct contract over a 'traditional' contract.

Remuneration for a design and construct contract may be based either on a lump sum or cost plus fixed fee or some other variant, depending upon the resources and experience of both the Employer and the Contractor. A danger which presents itself to the Employer in this type of contract is that if the Employer is not sufficiently experienced or lacks confidence in its choice of Contractor and employs its own architects or engineers to protect its own interests, mixed messages, claims of interference and disruption, and split responsibility are likely to be the result.

The Contractor's basic obligations under the Contract for the design, manufacture, delivery, erection, and testing of the plant and Works all within the time for Completion should be clearly set out in the contract documents.

14 Atkin Chambers, *Hudson's Building and Engineering Contracts* (Sweet & Maxwell, 12th edn 2010) 3–107.

9.1.3 Inspection of Site and pre-contractual site information

9.1.3.1 Site information

The Contractor is usually obliged to inspect and examine the Site prior to entry into the Contract, and to obtain all necessary information so far as these activities are practicable. The Employer will usually provide available factual information on foundation conditions, but often with an express disclaimer of any responsibility for its accuracy. In subsequently considering issues such as latent conditions, the time allowed for tendering, the information provided by the Employer, and the nature of the Site would no doubt be considered in determining what would be practicable in the circumstances. The consequence of a disclaimer of warranty or representation by the Employer in relation to the physical conditions or suitability of the Site would be that the Contractor would not be entitled to resile from the Contract on the grounds of an innocent misrepresentation. However, the Employer may be subject to a specific duty of disclosure where it is in possession of information adversely affecting the interests of the Contractor at the time of tender.

In *Royston Urban District Council v Royston Builders Ltd*[15] it was held that if the Contractor can show that in the Contract documents, or before or at the time when the Contract was made, the Employer gave any definite information about Site conditions, and so on, whether orally or in writing, in a form or in circumstances which implied particularly that the information might be relied on by the Contractor, then the Employer may be liable if the information is not correct. The information may be binding either on the grounds that it is a term of the Contract, a warranty that the information is correct, or that the Employer and Contractor have entered into a collateral contract about the information quite separate from the contract.[16] Many contracts have an express clause to negate any such implication, for example: 'The Employer shall have no responsibility for the accuracy, sufficiency or completeness of such data and/or items of reference, except as stated in Sub-Clause 5.1 [General Design Obligations].'[17]

There is a further obligation on the Employer if there has been any positive warranty or representation given or made to the Contractor in relation to the Site. In this respect, the Employer may be liable for an inaccurate statement of fact made with the intention of inducing the Contractor to enter into the contract, or it may be liable in tort in this regard. In Australia and other jurisdictions that prohibit misleading or deceptive conduct,[18] the Employer's failure to provide all the information it promised (even if inadvertent) or the provision of incorrect information may also enable the Contractor to make a claim of misleading or deceptive conduct in breach of legislation.

---

15 (1961) 177 EG 589.

16 See also *Morrison-Knudsen International v The Commonwealth* [1972] 46 ALJR 265.

17 2017 FIDIC Silver Book sub-clause 2.5.

18 For example *Competition and Consumer Act 2010* (Cth); *Fijian Competition and Consumer Act 2010; Consumer Protection Act 1999* (Malaysia).

Case study: Misleading or deceptive conduct

The alternative remedies available for the statutory cause of action arising from misleading or deceptive conduct are well illustrated by the case of *Abigroup Contractors Pty Limited v Sydney Catchment Authority (No. 3)*.[19] In this case, at the tender stage the Employer represented that it had no plans of an outlet pipe in the vicinity of a dam spillway to be built, and in reliance on this the Contractor entered into a fixed lump sum contract and took the risk of the actual rock level. In fact, the Employer did have a plan of the outlet pipe, and had this been revealed, the Contractor would have made a much greater allowance for rock excavation in its tender. In an action for damages under the *Trade Practices Act 1974* (Cth) (the predecessor to the *Competition and Consumer Act 2010* (Cth)), the NSW Court of Appeal held that the incorrect representation that there was no plan of the outlet pipe was misleading and deceptive conduct and awarded the Contractor damages for the discrete loss it incurred in undertaking additional rock excavation caused 'by' the misleading and deceptive conduct. Because the Contractor accepted the risk of the actual rock level in its tender, it had no contractual basis to recover the cost of the unforeseen additional rock excavation. This case illustrates the power of the *Competition and Consumer Act 2010* to create new grounds for a remedy unavailable under contract law.

Notwithstanding the remedies that might be available to a Contractor to recover costs resulting from the provision of misleading information by the Employer at the tender stage, both parties have a very real interest in ensuring that comprehensive and accurate information is made available to Tenderers. The following statement by McDougall J is, it is suggested, widely applicable:

> Both [the Employer] and prospective tenderers had an interest in ensuring, or assuming, that the information was as accurate as possible. For [the Employer], the interest was to produce a tender which accurately priced the likely works and did not contain a massive margin for latent conditions, the risk of which tenderers were required to assume. For tenderers, the interest was the converse.[20]

Unexpected difficulties which could have been foreseen are generally a matter for the Contractor to surmount at its own expense in order to discharge its express obligation to complete the described work.

9.1.3.2 Disclaimers

Any disclaimer of accuracy of quantities in the preamble to bills of quantities given by the Employer should be read in the context of whether the Contract is a lump sum contract, schedule of rates contract, or schedule of quantities contract. While the Contractor is generally obliged to satisfy itself of the quantities, it is generally not the Contractor's responsibility to recalculate the quantities in a schedule of quantities contract, whereas in a lump sum or schedule of rates contract the Contractor may have to recalculate the

19 [2006] NSWCA 282.
20 *Abigroup Contractors Pty Ltd v Sydney Catchment Authority* [2005] NSWSC 662.

quantities either from the drawings or by independent means for the sake of its own protection. A detailed analysis of the function, nature, and effect of bills of quantities was discussed by Wallace.[21]

A contractual disclaimer of responsibility for representations will not exclude liability for fraud. In *Pearson & Son Ltd v Dublin Corporation*,[22] the Engineer had shown a wall on the Contract drawings in a position which it knew was not correct. The court held that the clause in the Contract, to the effect that the Contractor would satisfy itself as to the dimensions, levels, and nature of all existing works and that the Employer did not hold itself responsible for the accuracy of information given, was no defence to liability to the Contractor for fraud. Exclusion clauses also cannot be applied to defeat claims for misleading and deceptive conduct in breach of legislation.[23]

9.1.3.3 Collateral contracts, warranties, and representations

A **collateral contract** by which the Contractor agrees to enter into a contract on the Employer's oral or written promise that certain information is correct need not be made in so many words but may be implied from the parties' statements and behaviour. Such an agreement may be enforced even though it is not referred to in the Contract documents. However, the courts will not enforce a collateral agreement where it would be inconsistent with the head contract: 'A collateral contract, which may be either antecedent or contemporaneous, being supplementary only to the head contract, cannot impinge on it, or alter its provisions or the rights created by it.'[24] The courts take a strict view of collateral warranties, and require that the contractual words must 'speak for themselves.'[25] Extrinsic evidence will not normally be admissible to prove the content of the collateral contract, particularly where it would contradict or vary the written terms of the Contract. It is important to note that not every representation can be used to create a contractual relationship.

Whether or not a statement is intended to be binding as a warranty depends on the intention of the parties. Their intention is, however, judged objectively – if the form or circumstances of the statement are such that a reasonable person would believe that the Employer intended to warrant the information, the Employer is bound, even though in its own mind it did not intend to do so. A statement about the nature of subsoil made casually or in passing, even in the Contract documents, might not amount to a warranty, particularly if it were practicable for the Contractor to find out the actual conditions; but a definite and clear statement made to influence the Contractor in pricing would do so.[26]

21 I.N. Duncan Wallace, 'The Use of Bills of Quantities in Civil Engineering and Building Contracts' (1975) 6(3) *Journal of Maritime Law and Commerce* 409.

22 [1907] AC 351.

23 See *Henjo Investments Pty. Ltd. v Collins Marrickville Pty. Ltd.* (1988) A.T.P.R. 40–850; *Clark Equipment Australia Ltd. v Covcat* (1987) 71 A.L.R. 367 *Keen Mar Corporation Pty. Ltd. v Labrador Park Shopping Centre Pty. Ltd.* (1989) A.T.P.R. (Digest) 46–048, 53,146; *Benlist Pty. Ltd. v Olivetti Australia Pty. Ltd.* (1990) A.T.P.R. 41–043; and *John G. Glass Real Estate Pty. Ltd. v Karawi Constructions Pty. Ltd.* (1993) A.T.P.R. 41–249.

24 *Hoyt's Pty Ltd v Spencer* [1919] HCA 64; (1919) 27 CLR 133, 147 per Isaacs J.

25 Stephen Furst & the Hon Sir Vivian Ramsey, *Keating on Construction Contracts* (Sweet & Maxwell Limited, 8th edn 2006) 3–102, 3–117.

26 See *Bentley (Dick) Productions Ltd v Smith (Harold) (Motors) Ltd* [1965] 1 WLR 623; [1965] 2 All ER 65 and *Bank of Ireland v Smith* (1968) 102 ILTR 69, 75.

Hospital Products Ltd v United States Surgical Corporation[27] provides an outline of the general principles on representations made in the course of contractual negotiations and notes that the intention of the parties has to be ascertained in an objective manner and could only be deduced 'from the totality of the evidence.' In other words, the statement relied upon must be promissory and not merely representational for it to constitute a collateral warranty.[28]

A misrepresentation is fraudulent if the representation is made knowing that it is not true; reckless if it is made without knowing that it is untrue but 'with a reckless indifference whether . . . it is true or false'[29] or with 'a reckless disregard of the interest of the other contracting party.'[30]

If the Contractor enters into a loss-making contract in reliance on a statement made by the Employer which does not become contractually binding, the Contractor will nevertheless have remedies at common law if the statement was made negligently, fraudulently, or recklessly. Further, the Contractor may have a remedy under legislation if it suffered a loss as a result of misleading or deceptive conduct constituted by a misrepresentation.

If there is a warranty or collateral contract between the parties that, for instance, Site conditions are as stated, then the Contractor has all the remedies for breach of contract if they are not so, even if the Employer had reasonable grounds for believing that the statement of the conditions was correct.

It is necessary to determine the exact scope of a representation. For example, the wide scope of a statement that 'the soil is sand' is clear, but to state merely that bore-holes were made by the X company and that the following are the results supplied by the company, is a representation that bore-holes were in fact made by the particular company and that the results given to the Contractor are the results furnished by the company – not that the results are an accurate representation of the soil in the bore-holes, or that they are representative of the soil in the area in general.

In *Boyd & Forest v Glasgow & SW Railway Co*,[31] Lord Atkinson suggested (but expressed no conclusion on the point) that there might be a warranty that, for instance, a journal of bores supplied was prepared with 'reasonable skill, care and accuracy,' or that skilful people were appointed to do the boring, or that the documents submitted to the Contractors should reasonably answer the description of a journal of bores. In *M.G.I.C.A. (1992) Ltd. v Kenny & Good Pty. Ltd*,[32] a valuation report was found to contain implied representations not only that the opinions expressed were held, but also that they were based on reasonable grounds, were the product of due care and skill, and were safe to be relied upon. Thus, a statement that 'in the Engineer's opinion the soil is silt' may not only be a representation that the opinion is held, but it might also be a representation that the Engineer has reasonable grounds for holding the opinion, the opinion is the product of the exercise of due care and skill in geotechnical engineering and can be relied on by the Contractor.

---

27 [1984] HCA 64 [20]; (1984) 156 CLR 41, 61 per Gibbs CJ.
28 Ibid.
29 *Pearson & Son Ltd v Dublin Corporation* [1907] AC 351, 353, per Lord Loreburn LC.
30 *Boyd & Forest v Glasgow & SW Railway Co* (1912) SC (HL) 93, 104.
31 (1912) SC (HL) 93, 96.
32 (1996) 140 A.L.R. 313, 356–357 per Lindgren J.

9.1.3.4 Representations by the Engineer

Although the Employer may bind itself, the Engineer generally has no apparent authority under the Contract to bind the Employer by any extraneous assurance, for example as to the feasibility of the design, the accuracy of the quantities, or the conditions of the Site. Where the Engineer is a full-time employee of the Employer, as distinct from a consulting engineer who is acting as agent for the Employer, the Engineer may however have wider authority. The Employer will therefore not usually be bound if the Engineer gives an assurance without special authority, but the Engineer may be liable to the Contractor for breach of warranty of authority.[33]

The Employer may be liable for a misrepresentation by the Engineer if the Engineer had special authority to make the representation to give such information to Tenderers. The Employer can also be held vicariously liable for the Engineer's conduct both under the law of agency and pursuant to legislation, for example prohibiting misleading or deceptive conduct. The intention of certain legislation is to widen the common law principles relating to agency.[34]

9.1.4 Work to be in accordance with the Contract

The Contractor may be entitled to refuse to carry out work specified in the Contract if it is legally impossible to execute, without being liable to pay damages for breach of contract. This does not mean that the Contractor is entitled to damages for loss of profit if the Employer abandons the Works because they are impossible to complete. In the case of a construct only contract where the Contractor has no responsibility for design, if the Contractor does the work described in the Contract it is usually entitled to payment, even though the work does not achieve the result intended by the Employer, for example if it carries out welding to a defined procedure but the specified material and weld are such that the weld is liable to break. However, even if the Contractor is not responsible for the preparation of the design of the Works, it is not excused from responsibility for defects in the Works, where it ought to have been clear to the Contractor that the design was materially deficient.[35]

The Contractor will be liable for breach of contract if it does not construct what it has contracted for, even if that is impossible. In a case where a shipbuilder had contracted to supply a ship to carry 1800 tons dead weight and in accordance with a model approved by the purchaser, the shipbuilder maintained it was impossible to build a ship according to the model that would carry the specified weight. Lord Rutherford Clark held that this was no defence: 'The fact remains that the defenders undertook a contract which they could not fulfil and they are consequently liable in damages for the breach.'[36]

Where the Works, whether in whole or in part, are or become prohibited by law (eg under environmental or licensing regulations), or infringe private or other persons' legal rights which can be protected by injunction or otherwise, the Works may become legally impossible to perform. Such an illegal contract is void and unenforceable.

33 I N Duncan-Wallace, *Hudson's Building and Engineering Contracts* (Sweet & Maxwell Limited, 11th edn 1995) 281–283.

34 See *T.P.C. v Sun Alliance Australia Ltd.* (1994) A.T.P.R. 41–286.

35 *Steel Co of Canada Ltd v Willand Management Ltd* [1066] 1 WLR 1317, 1333, per Lord Denning MR.

36 *A.M. Gillespie & Company v John Howden & Company* (1885) 22 SLR 527, 528.

9.1.5 Difficult or more expensive performance

If performance becomes more difficult or expensive than contemplated by the Contractor, but remains possible, the Contractor will not be relieved of its duty to complete for the contract price, unless it can establish circumstances which warrant a Variation of the scope of the Works or constitute adverse physical conditions for which contractual relief is provided. Difficulty of performance is not equal to impossibility of performance.

The basic principle is that, in the absence of an express representation, an Employer who uses a professional adviser does not warrant that completion according to its adviser's plans or design is practicable, and that, even in the absence of express provisions for protection of the Works, the risk in regard to the execution of and safety of the Works remains with the Contractor until the Works have been re-occupied by the Employer.

A Contractor who expressly or impliedly undertakes to complete a project according to the contract drawings and design, thereby impliedly warrants its ability to do so, and if it cannot do so, will be liable in damages. As a result, any additional work which is required to achieve completion must be carried out by the Contractor at its own expense if it is to discharge its liability under the Contract. Such work will not qualify for additional payment as a Variation even if the Contractor has been formally instructed to do the work in question.[37]

Case study: Difficulty in driving piles

In a Canadian contract for the supply and driving of interlocking steel piles, the specification provided that although soundings and borings had been carefully taken, the Contractor was to take its own sounding levels and borings before tender; the Contractor was deemed to satisfy itself as to the accuracy of the information contained in the plans and specifications. The soil was described as 'sand, gravel, few stones, loose clay, stiff and sticky clay, tough clay.' The Contract expressly stated that no claim would be entertained for unforeseen difficulties in carrying out the work and the Contractor was to visit the Site and make its own estimates of difficulty arising out of the execution of the work.

The Contractor described pile-driving as unusually severe. It alleged that the soil was in fact a material called 'hard pan' with many large boulders embedded in it, necessitating unforeseen work including the use of explosives, which the Contractor alleged was entirely outside the Contract, and claimed compensation on a *quantum meruit* basis. In the Exchequer Court of Canada, the Contractor succeeded, subject to a deduction of one-third for delays attributable to the Contractor.

On Appeal, the Supreme Court of Canada held that the Contractor had undertaken to drive piles in soil which they had agreed to investigate, and which the Employer did not guarantee. The obligation of the Contractor was not to drive piles in a specified soil, but in a specified place. The risk was on the Contractor and must be borne by the Contractor if it misjudged the Works to be performed and miscalculated the cost. Taschereau J stated that expenses incurred for unforeseen difficulties must be considered as being included in the

37 *Thorn v the Mayor and Commanlty of Londomn* [1876] 1 App. Cas. 120, 135. This case dealt with the demolition of the old London Bridge and its replacement using wrought iron caissons, instead of traditional cofferdams, resulting in considerable extra expense to the Contractor due to the inability of the caissons to withstand the tide pressures.

amount of the tender, and the Contractor had the legal obligation to execute the Contract for the price agreed upon; in the same way it would have been its indisputable right to benefit if the soil had been more favourable and easier than foreseen.[38]

The same applies to the reinstatement or repair if the Works have been damaged by some external cause. The Contractor's obligation to complete must be clearly distinguished from the Contractor's responsibility for suitability of the work or the adequacy of its design once it has been completed.

9.1.6 Physical impossibility – frustration

If, at the time of entering into the Contract, it is impossible for the Contractor to carry out the work by any means, then subject to the terms of the Contract, it will not be liable for breach of contract. However, if the Contractor has warranted that the work is possible or has positively and absolutely contracted to do the work, it will be liable in damages for failure to perform.[39] The Contractor can be protected from the consequences of contracting to carry out impossible or illegal work by an appropriate clause in the Contract.

Example: Contractor not liable for impossible or illegal work

Clause 13(1) of the ICE Conditions of Contract (Seventh edition) provides:

> Save insofar as it is legally or physically impossible the Contractor shall construct and complete the Works in strict accordance with the Contract to the satisfaction of the Engineer.

There is a difference between work which is impossible to execute and work which is more difficult or requires more equipment or temporary works than the Contractor anticipated. Should the Contractor do altered work to avoid a physical impossibility, it may be entitled to extra payment for it, depending on the terms of the Contract.

Where a supervening cause renders the performance of the Contract impossible after the parties enter into it, then upon such a cause occurring, the Contract is said to be frustrated and both the Employer and the Contractor are excused from further performance. A succinct definition of frustration of a contract is: 'The termination of the contract by operation of law on the emergence of a fundamentally different situation.'[40]

Frustration of a contract occurs:

> whenever the law recognises that without default of either party a contractual obligation has become incapable of being performed because the circumstances in which performance is called for would

38 *R v Paradis and Furley Inc* [1942] S.C.R. 10.
39 Stephen Furst & the Hon Sir Vivian Ramsey, *Keating on Construction Contracts* (Sweet & Maxwell, 8th edn 2006) 6–030, 186.
40 *Davis Contractors Limited v Fareham Urban District Council* [1956] AC 696, 723 per Lord Reid.

> render it a thing radically different from that which was undertaken by the contract. . . . It was not this that I promised to do. . . . There must be as well such a change in the significance of the obligation that the thing undertaken would, if performed be a different thing from that contracted for.[41]

When a contract is frustrated, it comes to an end with respect to any future obligations of the parties, but accrued rights and obligations remain intact.[42] As the Contract does not remain binding, the Contractor is therefore not entitled to be paid. But it has been held that, where performance is impossible and the Contract is frustrated, the Employer is not entitled to derive monetary advantage from the unfinished work of the Contractor, and it must pay the Contractor for such benefit as it has obtained (assuming the benefit was not destroyed by the supervening event).[43] It has also been held that, in an entire contract where the Contractor is to be paid at 'intervals' and the contract works are damaged or destroyed, the Employer is not entitled to recover the amount already paid.[44]

The common law position is that a Contractor is entitled to a *quantum meruit* as a consequence of the frustration of a contract, although courts are slow to find that a contract has been frustrated. A number of common law jurisdictions have passed legislation dealing with the consequences of frustrated contracts which ameliorate the common law rules, and effectively provide for a statutory *quantum meruit*.[45]

Frustrated contracts are in fact quite rare, because circumstances that make contracts impossible to perform are very unusual. Typically, the work can be varied so that it can be carried out, albeit with cost and time consequences.

Case studies: Frustration

In *Metropolitan Water Board v Dick Kerr & Co*,[46] the Contractor was to build a reservoir under an ICE contract of July 1914. War broke out in August 1914, and in February 1916 all work was stopped by order of the government which commandeered the Contractor's plant and materials. Lord Dunedin said that these events:

> made the contract, if resumed, a work under different conditions from those of the work when interrupted . . . the contract being a measure and value contract, the whole range of prices might be different, It would in my judgment amount, if resumed, to a new contract.

In *Wong Lai Ying & others v Chinachem Investment Co Ltd*, a landslip carried a 13-storey block of flats onto a partially completed building, completely obliterating

41 *Davis Contractors Limited v Fareham Urban District Council* [1956] AC 696, 729 per Lord Radcliffe. The High Court accepted that *Davis Contractors* states the common law on frustration in Australia in *Codelfa Construction Pty Ltd v State Rail Authority of New South Wales* (1982) 149 CLR 337.

42 *Baltic Shipping Co v Dillon* (1993) 176 CLR 344; (1993) 111 ALR 289; (1993) 67 ALJR 228, 297.

43 *Cutter v Powell* (1795) 101 ER 573.

44 *Anglo-Egyptian Navigation* Co *v Rennie* (1875) LR 10 CP 271.

45 *Frustrated Contracts Act 1978* (NSW); *Frustrated Contracts Act 1988* (SA); *Australian Consumer Law and Fair Trading Act 2012* (Vic) Part 3.2; *Contracts Act 1950* (Malaysia) s57(2); *Law Amendment and Reform (Consolidation) Ordinance* (Cap 23) (HK) ss16(2), 16(3).

46 [1916–17] All ER 122, 1918 AC 119, 34 TLR 113.

the Site. As a consequence, the building permit expired. These events were held by the Privy Council to have frustrated the contract.[47]

In *Codelfa Construction Pty Ltd v State Rail Authority of New South Wales*, the contract was found to be frustrated when an injunction was granted preventing the Contractor from working seven days a week, because 'the performance of the contract in the events which have occurred is radically different from performance of the contract in the circumstances which it, construed in the light of surrounding circumstances, contemplated.'[48]

In *Davis Contractors Ltd v Fareham Urban District Council*,[49] the Contractor, working under a fixed-price contract, claimed that the contract had been frustrated because of unexpected inflation and failure to secure skilled labour, and because the work had cost vastly more than they contemplated and had taken much longer. Their claim was rejected because the primary obligation was capable of being performed.

See ¶2.3 for a discussion of hardship provisions that may apply in difficult circumstances that fall short of impossibility to perform.

9.1.7 Contractor's obligations as to quality of work and materials

The Contractor's specific obligations in respect of quality of work and materials may depend on the terms of the Contract. A term is generally implied that a Contractor will perform its work properly, including completing the work it has undertaken to perform[50] and will do so in a good and workmanlike manner.[51] In other words, the Contractor has an implied duty to carry out its work with due skill and care, meaning the skill and care of an ordinarily competent contractor in the circumstances of the actual Contractor.[52]

A Contractor impliedly undertakes to use materials of good quality, and where materials are expressly specified, this means that they must be good of their expressed kind and free from defects. When goods are not described or only described in general terms, there will be reliance on the Contractor that both the workmanship and materials will be reasonably fit for the purpose for which they are required, unless the circumstances of the Contract are such as to exclude any such obligation.[53]

The obligation to supply good materials in the absence of express description includes the obligation to choose materials suitable for the purpose for which they are intended. Similarly, workmanship will include the use of suitable materials and practises such that the work and materials are suitable for their required purpose once the Work is completed.

47 [1984] CLY 381; 13 BLR 81 (PC).

48 (1982) 149 CLR 337, 363.

49 [1956] 2 All ER 145, AC 696, 54 HLR 289 HL.

50 *Perry v Sharon Development co Ltd* [1937] 4 All ER 390, 396, per MacKinnon LJ (CA).

51 *Emcor Drake & Scull Ltd v Sir Robert McAlpine Ltd* [2004] EWCA Civ 1733, [14], per Clarke LJ.

52 *Young & Marten Ltd v McManus Childs Ltd* [1969] 1 AC 454, 465, per Lord Reid.

53 *Myers v Brent Cross Garage* [1934] 1 K.B. 46, 55, per du Parq J; *Young & Marten Ltd v McManus Childs Ltd* [1969] 1 CA.C. 454.

The obligation to use materials of satisfactory quality is absolute and independent of fault.[54] For any such term to be implied, the Employer must be relying, to the actual or presumed knowledge of the Contractor, upon the Contractor's skill and judgement and not upon their own or that of their agent. This reliance need not be exclusive, provided it is substantial.[55] As with all implied terms, any of these terms may be displaced by explicit terms in the Contract.

If, due to physical or environmental limitations the Contractor is unable to perform its work in a good and workmanlike manner, and it is obvious that the requested work cannot be performed satisfactorily, it is the duty of the Contractor to draw this to the attention of the Employer and ask the Employer what it wishes to do. In other words, where a Contractor knows or ought to know that the Works that it is asked to perform will be defective, or otherwise unsatisfactory for their known purpose, the Contractor should not proceed with the Works unless it has drawn the particular deficiency to the attention of the Employer or its agent and sought instructions on how to proceed. The fact that a structure is 'built down to a price' does not excuse the presence of defects in the structure.[56] When considering the adequacy of a Contractor's workmanship, regard is to be had to the whole of the Works which the Contractor has undertaken to perform.[57]

9.1.8 Fitness for purpose

If the Employer informs the Contractor, whether by express words or other conduct that the Employer requires the goods for a particular purpose, it will be an implied term of the Contract of supply that the goods will be reasonably fit for that purpose.[58] Whether the particular purpose for which the goods were intended to be used was understood by the Contractor is a question of fact. Sometimes the purpose of the purchase will be so obvious that only one purpose could be in the mutual contemplation of the parties.[59]

Example: Fitness for Purpose

The *United Nations Convention on Contracts for the International Sale of Goods* (***CISG***) provides that goods

> are fit for any particular purpose expressly or impliedly made known to the seller at the time of the conclusion of the contract, except where the circumstances show that the buyer did not rely, or that it was unreasonable for him to rely, on the seller's skill and judgement;[60]

54 *Hancock v Brazier (Anerley) Ltd* (1966) 1 W.L.R. 1317, per Diplock L.J.; *Young & Marten v McManus Childs Ltd* [1969] 1 A.C. 454.

55 See *Cammell Laird Ltd v Manganese, Bronze & Brass Co. Ltd.* [1934] A.C. 402 and *Att. Gen of Canada v Laminated Structures* (1961) 28 D.L.R. (2d) 92.

56 *Brown v Gilbert-Scott* (1992) 35 Con LR 120, 124–125 per Recorder Coles QC.

57 *Barclays Bank plc v Fairclough Building Ltd* (1994) 68 BLR 1, 13, per Beldam LJ.

58 *Slater v Finning Ltd* [1997] AC 473, 486, per Lord Steyn. See also *J Murphy & Sons Ltd v Johnson Precast Ltd* [2008] EWHC 3024 (TCC), [114]-[127].

59 *Henry Kendall & Sons v William Lillico & Sons Ltd* [1969] 2 AC 31at 93, per Lord Morris.

60 Article 35(b).

The *CISG* has entered into force in 96 countries and applies to contracts of sale of goods between parties whose places of business are in different States when (1) when the States are Contracting States; or (2) when the rules of private international law lead to the application of the law of a Contracting State,[61] unless the parties have excluded the application of the *CISG*.[62]

In *Corben v Hayes*,[63] it was stated that unlike a warranty of good workmanship, a warranty that the work will answer the purpose for which it is intended is not implied in every contract of work. The essential element for the implication of such a term is that the Employer should be relying, to the knowledge of the Contractor, upon the Contractor. Similarly, in *Karl Meuller Construction Ltd v Commissioner for N W Territory*,[64] it was stated that a Contractor may be said to be responsible for design defects to the extent that it must build what the contract calls for, or be liable in damages, even if it is difficult or impossible to do so.

But the Contractor does not thereby warrant that an incompetent or unsuitable design will work, unless it has done so expressly. If a Contractor has guaranteed that the work will perform a certain function, it is responsible for the performance of that function, notwithstanding that the design provided by the Employer is incapable of performing that function. For example, in a roofing contract where the Employer specified the brand of adhesive that failed, the Contractor was nevertheless liable for the repair costs because it had provided a five-year guarantee that all the work specified would remain weathertight. Richie J held:

> The agreement to furnish a written guarantee 'that all work above specified will remain weathertight' for five years in my view constitutes at the very least an express undertaking 'to carry out work which will perform a certain . . . function in conformity with plans and specifications' and in accordance with the principles stated in the paragraph last above cited, I think that it follows that when a works so constructed does not perform the function which the contractor agreed that it would perform, the contractor is liable for the failure of the work and is not entitled to extra payment for repairing it 'so that it will perform the stipulated duty.'[65]

It is clear then, that for any such term to be implied in a building or engineering contract, the Employer must be relying upon the Contractor's skill and knowledge and not upon their own or those of the agent, to the actual or presumed knowledge of the Contractor.

Under the common law, the Contractor's obligations in a design and construct contract probably include the requirement that the completed design must be fit for purpose unless the Contract contains explicit provisions to the contrary.[66] Many standard form contracts define an explicit fit for purpose obligation on Completion.

---

61 Article 1.

62 Article 6.

63 Unreported, April 27, 1964, 4 Court of New South Wales, cited by Sugerman J.A. in *McKone v Johnson* [1966] 2 N.S.W.R. 471.

64 (1991), 73 D.L.R.4th 234, 244 (NWT CA).

65 *The Steel Company of Canada Limited v Willand Management Limited* [1966] S.C.R. 746, 754. See also *Greater Vancouver Water District v North American Pipe & Steel Ltd* (2021) BCCA 337 in which a pipe supplier was liable for defects in coatings applied according to the Employer's specifications but were not free from defects as warranted by the Contractor.

66 For example *Independent Broadcasting Authority v EMI Electronics Ltd* (1980) 14 BLR 9, 47 per Lord Scarman; *Greaves & Co (Contractors) Ltd v Baynham Meikle & Partners* [1975] 1095, 1098 per Lord Denning MR.

Example: Contractor's fit for purpose obligation

The 2017 FIDIC Silver Book states:

> The Contractor shall execute the Works in accordance with the Contract. When completed, the Works (or Section or major item of Plant, if any) shall be fit for the purpose(s) for which they are intended, as defined and described in the Employer's Requirements or, where no purpose(s) are so defined and described, fit for their ordinary purpose(s).

As noted in ¶9.1.2, sub-clause 5.1 deems the Contractor to have scrutinised the Employer's Requirements (including design criteria) prior to the Base Date, and the Employer has no responsibility for errors in the Employer's Requirements.

9.1.9 Contractor's obligations as to quality of design

While every case will depend upon its own facts, generally speaking, if plans and specifications are provided to a Contractor to work to, and particularly if the Employer uses its own designer for this purpose, the Contractor will not normally have to do more than carry out the work according to the plans and specifications in a workmanlike manner and using proper materials. This applies even if the Contractor may be well aware of the purpose for which the work is required. The Employer will normally be unable to complain about the unsuitability of the final result if it is due solely to exact compliance with that design. However, in situations in which it is very obvious that the outcome will be unsuitable, the Contractor has a duty to warn the Employer or its designer. This is discussed further in ¶9.1.10.

Usually, if the Contractor designs or selects materials for the Works, either because the Contractor provides the whole design itself or because part of the design is left to the Contractor's choice, there will be an implied term that the work and materials will be suitable for the purpose in the absence of express terms to a different effect. Care should be taken in the choice of modern forms of design and build contracts because they vary significantly in the nature and extent to which express terms limit or impose design obligations as regards care and skill and fitness for purpose.

Certain design and build contracts make express provision for the standard to which the Contractor must design, but in many cases where standard forms of contract make some provision for the Contractor to design elements of the Works, this is done without expressly stating that the Contractor's design must be fit for purpose. The NEC3 Engineering and Construction contract states: 'The *Contractor* designs the parts which the Works Information states he is to design.'[67] The standard to be applied to the Contractor's design is not expressly stated, but it is clearly envisaged that the Contractor must produce a suitable design unless the parties agree to limit the responsibility of the Contractor to the exercise of reasonable skill and care by the adoption of Options clause X15.[68]

67 Clause 21.1.
68 See also the Guidance notes on Option X15.

The Employer may wish to impose its requirements for the ultimate design by way of producing some level of design undertaken by professional designers on its behalf prior to the Contract.[69] The question which this procurement methodology gives rise to is: to what extent is a Contractor, who has expressly contracted to produce a design that is to be fit for purpose, responsible for the failure of the project to perform as required, when significant portions of the design is provided by the Employer as part of its specifications or requirements in advance of the Contract? Is the responsibility of the Contractor limited to the exercise of due care and skill in producing the design, or to provide a product which is fit for purpose?

As noted in ¶9.1.8, sub-clause 4.1 of the 2017 FIDIC Silver Book provides that when completed, the Works shall be fit for the purposes for which the Works are intended as defined in the Contract and does not distinguish between aspects of the Works previously designed by the Employer, making the Contractor responsible for the suitability of the whole of the Works regardless of the source of the design. This is consistent with *Hudson's* submission that 'Arguably the simplest contractual method by which to achieve price certainty in a design and build project where the Employer has produced elements of the design is in making the Contractor responsible for the entirety of the design.'[70]

This single point design responsibility is based on the ability of the Contractor to complete the Works fit for purpose having been given a relatively short period for tendering and incurred significant costs in checking the Employer's data and design. There are inherent risks in this approach, and risk-pricing on the part of the Contractor and choosing the lowest lump sum price will not necessarily achieve the desired outcome.[71]

9.1.10 Contractor's duty to warn of defective design

Although it might reasonably be expected that the Employer carries the design risk if the design has been prepared on its behalf and the Contractor is engaged only to construct that design, there may be circumstances in which the Contractor has a duty to warn the Employer of design defects. Trew discussed several such cases and identified that a duty to warn could arise from the obligation to act with the skill and care of a reasonably competent Contractor, or from the Employer's reliance on the experience, judgement, and skill of the Contractor.[72]

Whether a duty to warn is breached will depend upon the circumstances. A Contractor is not expected to examine and approve the details of an engineer's work or design; only relatively obvious errors judged in the light of the knowledge to be expected from a Contractor of the type employed will give rise to a duty to warn.[73]

---

69 The American Institute of Architects (AIA) form of design build contract provides for procurement in 2 stages: part 1 is the initial design by an architect and part 2 is the detailed design. The Contractor takes responsibility for the design in both parts.

70 Atkin Chambers, *Hudson's Building and Engineering Contracts* (Sweet & Maxwell, 12th edn 2010) 3–127.

71 See Philip Loots & Dr Donald Charrett, 'Reconsidering Procurement Criteria and Procedures for Major Infrastructure Projects' (2017) 1 *International Construction Law Review* 69.

72 Stephen Trew, 'Contractors Duty to Warn: The Extent to Which the Contractor is Now Liable for Design Defects' (2001) 17 *Building and Construction Law* 386. See also: Owen Hayford, 'Watch Out! The Duty to Warn on Construction Projects' (2008) 24 *Building and Construction Law* 163.

73 *Steel Co of Canada Ltd v Willand Management Ltd* [1066] 1 WLR 1317, 1333, per Lord Denning MR.

In certain situations in which the Contractor has a duty to warn of a design deficiency of which a reasonably competent Contractor should be aware, the duty to warn will be satisfied by warning the Employer's consultant. In other situations, the Contractor may be required to warn the Employer directly, depending on the seriousness of the potential defect and the consultant's response to the warning.

Case study: Failure to warn the Employer

In *Plant Construction plc v Clive Adams and Associates*,[74] a subcontractor was required to comply with the Employer's Engineer's instructions in regard to temporary works. The subcontractor considered that an 'Acrow' prop system of support for an existing floor above the proposed works which had been instructed by the Employer's Engineer was dangerously inadequate. The subcontractor had protested of the danger of the proposals to the Head Contractor's structural engineer and in the presence of the Head Contractor's engineering representative. The subcontractor eventually yielded to the Contractor's structural engineer's advice to comply with the Employer's instructions.

The English Court of Appeal held the subcontractor liable for failing to warn the Head Contractor. It appears that this decision turned on the subcontractor's actual knowledge that the design of the temporary works was inherently dangerous and inadequate. The Court of Appeal expressly reserved the position in respect of where imputed rather than actual knowledge was alleged, and also where a design defect was only economic, and not dangerous.

When using the work of other contractors, see *Chevalier v Tompkins*.[75]

9.1.11 Contractor's obligation to complete

9.1.11.1 Scope of the obligation

Construction contracts usually include an express undertaking by the Contractor to complete the work. When considering whether ancillary work or work necessary to achieve completion of the described work constitutes a Variation or entitles the Contractor to additional payment, the words 'so far as the necessity for providing the same is reasonably to be inferred,' or similar words, must be borne in mind. It is essential to consider first the nature of a construction contract in order to appreciate the extent of the parties' obligations.

In all contracts of work and labour, the Contractor is obliged to construct and complete any work, whether described or not, ancillary to or necessary to achieve completion of the work described in the Contract. This work may be of two kinds – work which on the true construction of the Contract will inevitably be required to complete the described work ('indispensably necessary work' as it is sometimes called) and work which may contingently be required to complete, for example to overcome difficulties which may be encountered during construction.

74 [2000] B.L.R. 137.
75 (1915) 48 Québec L.R. (S.C.) 53, 56.

Without express provision, difficulties in the latter category will usually be part of the Contractor's obligation to complete – subject to the law of impossibility. Under the lump sum form of contract, the cost of both categories of work is included in the contract price. In the schedule of quantities or schedule of rates forms of admeasured contracts, the Contractor will be entitled to additional payment in respect of indispensably necessary work only where there has been a failure of the bills to conform in detail with incorporated standard methods of measurement.[76] Where the Contractor has been required to price a specified method of construction on a bill of quantities or drawings, as opposed to the work necessary to achieve an end-result, any contingently necessary work will generally entitle the Contractor to additional payment.

When disputes arise, or more attractive opportunities present themselves, the Contractor cannot voluntarily abandon work, and demand payment for work done to date. This is an implied obligation and most likely also an express obligation contained in the Contract. The Contractor who, in breach of contract, has failed to complete the work in accordance with the Contract will be unable to sue for the price, or even part of it, for work done, in the absence of express provision for interim payment (subject to the doctrine of substantial performance, and statutory provision for interim payments).

The Contractor's obligation to complete the Work on time free from patent defects, is, in the absence of a provision to the contrary, usually satisfied by allowing the Employer to take possession, and may be expressed in the Contract as 'substantial' or 'practical completion.' See ¶16.1 for a discussion of substantial completion.

9.1.11.2 Additional work necessary for completion

The effect of the Contractor's obligation to complete is that, in the absence of express qualification, the Contractor binds itself to do any additional work which may be necessary to bring it to the point of Completion, including any work necessitated by defects in the design. That is not to say that the Contractor necessarily warrants the suitability of the design of the work for its ultimate purpose after Completion, nor must it necessarily carry out additional work at its own expense. In order to determine upon whom the burden of any additional cost falls, the type of contract needs to be considered and the specific terms of the Contract must be construed. The same applies to the question of whether the Contractor is entitled to an extension of time. A consistent policy as to the physical obligation to complete in the face of major engineering difficulties and the financial responsibility for indispensably necessary work in the event of such event should be stated in the Contract.

The ideal for the Contractor under a 'construct only' contract is that if a part of the Employer's design is impracticable from the point of view of Completion, the Contractor is excused from further performance. Considerable assistance in clarifying the parties' rights and obligations under the Contract (if not the ultimately prevailing provisions) may be found in the technical contractual documents, and those responsible for drafting bills of quantities or specifications should endeavour to deal with these questions expressly on the basis that the conditions of contract by themselves may not give adequate guidance in a field where major disputes are most likely to occur.

---

76 See *Bryant and Son v Birmingham Hospital Saturday Fund* [1938] 1 All E.R. 503, and *A E Farr Ltd v The Admiralty* [1953] 2 All ER 512 (QB).

In a design and construct contract, the Contractor explicitly assumes the time and cost risks involved in modifying an impractical design and/or method of working so that the Works can be completed.

9.1.11.3 Methods of working

In electrical, mechanical, and civil contracts, **plant** generally means machinery and apparatus to be provided under the Contract for incorporation into the **permanent works**. **Equipment** or Contractor's equipment generally means all appliances and machinery required for the execution of the Works by the Contractor which do not form part of the permanent works and are ultimately removed from the Site. In some contracts the term plant is used to describe the Contractor's equipment, for example AS 2124–1992 uses the term 'Constructional Plant' to refer to appliances and things used in the execution of the work under the Contract but not forming part of the Works. Some case law uses the term 'plant' for what is referred to herein as equipment.[77] Clearly, very different considerations apply to plant and Contractor's equipment. Care must be exercised to avoid confusion between plant and equipment.

Temporary works in construction contracts may either be Works that are removed at the end of the Contract (eg a specially constructed temporary access road) or Works required during construction that are retained as part of a permanent structure (eg a flooded cofferdam). Temporary works in either category may sometimes be priced in the bills of quantities as part of the Works as a whole and sometimes not. It is not unusual to provide separate amounts for temporary works in the bills of quantities which qualify for purposes of interim payment.

In construction contracts the design of temporary works is usually left entirely to the Contractor and is regarded as being outside the Engineer's mandate. Where the Contractor carries out these functions, the Employer should ensure that the Contract requires that the Contractor carries Contractor's all-risks insurance and insurance for design liability in respect of the temporary works.

As noted in ¶7.15, it is usually in the Employer's interest to avoid prescribing exactly the method of working to be adopted by the Contractor, and to make plain that the Contractor's prices are inclusive of any method of working found to be necessary in order to produce the finished Works. Where methods of working or temporary works are described in the Contract, it is common practice for the Employer to disclaim responsibility for such description by stating that no warranty is given as to their efficacy and that the Contractor is free to adopt other methods subject to the Engineer's approval.

Where the Employer is concerned with quality assurance, it may be advisable to give the Engineer the necessary authority under the Contract to vary the design of temporary works for safety or other reasons. The Employer should however be aware that the exercise of any such right may relieve the Contractor of liability for the temporary works. Recently it has become the practice of Employers who wish to have close control over quality assurance and timeous completion by the Contractor to specify both the methods of working and temporary works, thereby carrying full responsibility for such decisions.

77 For example *P & E Phontos Pty Ltd v New South Wales Land and Housing Corp* (1987) 7 Aust Const LR 54; 4 BCL 45.

However, in the case of Employer design, while the Contractor is obliged to complete the Works, the Contractor does not owe any duty in regard to its subsequent performance, safety, durability, or suitability after Completion, provided the work has been carried out using proper standards of materials and workmanship in exact accordance with the Employer's design.

9.1.11.4 Unforeseen difficulties

No defence is available to the Contractor for matters which pre-exist the date of the Contract in the event of damage to the Works or Site difficulties. Should supervening causes or events occur during construction, these will also be at the Contractor's risk unless they have the effect of permanently preventing Completion of the project. Damage which can be repaired such as fire, flood or civil commotion must be repaired at the expense of the Contractor, and without an extension of time unless otherwise provided for in the Contract.

The Contract must address (and should limit) the Contractor's express and implied continuing obligation to carry out and complete the Works in accordance with the Contract in relation to hidden defects.

9.2 Security

9.2.1 Performance security

In the absence of specific agreement, neither the Contractor nor the Employer is obliged to provide any form of security for the due fulfilment of their obligations. It is, however, customary to require the Contractor to furnish a **performance security**. If a Contract makes provision for the furnishing of security it is generally to be regarded as a fundamental term of the Contract, and continued failure to provide the security is a fundamental breach of contract entitling the Employer to resile from the Contract. Performance securities include performance bonds provided by a bank or insurance company, retention funds and performance guarantees by a **surety** (a person who makes itself responsible for the performance of the Contractor's obligations). Where the Contractor is a non-listed limited company, the directors may be asked to guarantee its performance of the Contract personally, although this would defeat the protection afforded to them by the use of a limited liability company.

There is no reason why an Employer should not be asked by the Contractor to provide a guarantee of payment (including Variations). This requirement is a frequent and serious omission from conditions of contract, although many modern standard form contracts make provision for it. See ¶7.3 for a discussion of the Employer's financial arrangements and ¶7.3.1 for an example of a relevant FIDIC provision.

The Employer should keep the performance security in force until the Contractor has executed, completed, and remedied defects in the Works in accordance with the Contract. Employers should note specifically that they usually cannot make claims under the performance security once the final payment certificate has been issued after the end of the defects liability period, and they are generally obliged to return the security within a specified number of days after the issue of that certificate. The Employer's recourse to the performance security will be governed by the terms of the Contract.

Once the Contractor has completed its obligations in relation to the Works it should be entitled under the Contract to the return of the performance security issued on its behalf, in order that it may arrange for its formal cancellation. By the time the Contractor is entitled to receive the final payment certificate it is usually abundantly clear to the Employer whether it has any grounds for claiming under the performance security or not. As such, contracts generally provide for the return of security at this time.

It is customary in most countries for security to be furnished by the Contractor in an amount of 10% of the tender sum. Since a definite tender sum is set out in the tender, and the requirement is that security be furnished by the successful Tenderer in an amount of 10% of such tender sum, once such a bond has been furnished and accepted by the Employer, the Contractor's obligation is generally fulfilled. If there are large increases in the Works, the Employer may consider obtaining a further bond as security for the increased scope at its own cost and with the express consent of the Contractor (unless the Contract provides otherwise).

The form of security must be examined by the Employer and any doubtful points referred for legal advice if necessary. On-demand performance bonds are to be preferred over sureties by reason of their being independent rather than accessory obligations. Approval or disapproval of security given must be carefully considered since the sanction, if unsatisfactory security is put up, is for the Employer to treat the Contract as repudiated and seek damages for breach of contract.

9.2.2 Discharge of a surety's obligations

Where the Contractor fails to fulfil its obligations, its surety may, with the consent of the Employer, assume the Contractor's obligations and complete the Works. This may apply even though the Contractor's estate may have been sequestrated.

It is sufficient to state here that prejudicial conduct on the part of the Employer may discharge the surety from its obligations, subject to the express terms of the Contract. For example, a quantity surveyor appointed by the Employer to issue certificates to enable interim payments to be made to the Contractor, may issue these certificates recklessly in disregard of the relevant contractual provisions. This may result in overpayments being made to the Contractor which would prejudice both the Employer and the surety as surety. It may, based on the circumstances of the particular case, be found that there is an implied undertaking by the Employer to the surety that interim payments will be made in accordance with the terms of the Contract; as soon as the prejudicial conduct occurs, the surety is automatically and fully discharged whatever the ultimate amount of the prejudice might turn out to be.

The distinction between the cases where the surety is wholly discharged owing to the creditor's dealing with a security given by the principal debtor, and the cases where owing to such dealing it is only discharged proportionately, according to the actual loss proved to have been sustained, is dealt with in the latter part of the judgement of Blackburn J in *Pollak & another v Everette*,[78] and is summarised by Cotton LJ in *Carter v White*.[79]

---

78 (1876) 1 QBD 669.
79 (1888) 25 Ch D 666, 670.

Case study: Discharge of surety

In *Nathanson & another v Dennil*,[80] the defendant stood surety for the performance of a building Contractor under a Contract in terms of which the building Employers were entitled to hold certain retention moneys until the completion of the Contract. The building Employers agreed to relax their rights to retain these moneys and paid the builder prematurely in full what was due to him. It was held that the building Employers, by agreeing to forgo their right to the retention moneys, had made a material alteration in the original agreement which discharged the surety from its obligation.

9.2.3 Forms of security

In view of the legal uncertainties surrounding the enforceability of sureties' obligations, which are due in part to their nature being that of accessory obligations, it is suggested that the purpose of furnishing security would be better served if unconditional performance bonds payable on demand (also known as demand guarantees) were used for this purpose. These are independent obligations entered into between the guarantor (typically a bank or insurance company) and the Employer and are therefore more distant from the effect of conduct under the Contract. Where the form of the performance bond is expressly set out in the tender there can be no issue over its subsequent approval by the Employer.

Deeds of suretyship, acknowledgements of debt, and other instruments of indebtedness often contain clauses providing for the amount of the indebtedness to be proved by way of a certificate given by an official of the creditor. Such certificates are stipulated to be either conclusive proof of the amount of the indebtedness or prima facie proof of the amount of the indebtedness. In the latter case the production of the certificates places the onus on the debtor to establish that the certificate is incorrect. In the absence of a stipulation relating to certificates, the onus would be on the creditor to prove the amount of the indebtedness.

9.3 Subcontractors

9.3.1 Subcontracts

In the traditional system of contracting in the construction industry the whole of the work is initially let to the Head Contractor. There is no general obligation[81] for the Contractor to personally carry out the Works it has undertaken to perform. However, certain contracts may contain an express prohibition against subcontracting the whole or any part of the Works,[82] or subcontracting the whole of the Works may be prohibited by statute.[83] Thus,

80 (1904) TH 289.
81 Under English, Australian, Hong Kong, or Singapore law.
82 *Linden Gardens Trust Ltd v Lenesta Sludge Disposals Ltd* [1994] 1 AC 85, 103, per Lord Browne-Wilkinson; *Poh Lian Construction Pte Ltd (in liq) v Lauw Wisaggeni* [2019] SGHC 114, [90] – [99], per Kannan Ramesh J.
83 For example in China. See Sun Yiwen, 'China', 155 in Donald Charrett (ed), *FIDIC Contracts in Asia Pacific A Practical Guide to Application* (Informa Law from Routledge, 2022).

subject to the provisions of the Contract, the Contractor usually has the right to subcontract parts of the physical construction of the Works to subcontractors. The Contract may not require the written approval of the Employer or its agent to subcontract if the work is of a 'rough and indiscriminate kind,' where it is immaterial who does it.[84]

However, the Contractor does not have the right to subcontract where the Contract is let by reason of some special skill or quality of the Contractor.[85] In *British Waggon Co v Lea*, it was held that:

> [W]here a person contracts with another to do work or perform services and it can be inferred that the person had been selected with reference to his individual skill, competency or other personal qualifications, it can be inferred that the contract is at an end if that person refuses to perform the contract notwithstanding that the person who tendered to take the place of the contracting party may be equally well qualified to do the service.[86]

Engineering subcontractors tend often to be specialists who carry out limited parts of the Works, such as piling. In complex projects, it is not uncommon for the majority of the Works on a substantial contract to be carried out by a large number of trade subcontractors. Performance by a subcontractor constitutes vicarious performance on behalf of the Contractor, who remains fully responsible for the work, save where the Head Contract provides otherwise. It follows that a contract for specialist site-investigation work is likely to be one which may not be sublet without consent of the Employer.

If provided for in the Contract, the Employer has the right to nominate subcontractors (**nominated subcontractors**). Details of nominated subcontractors and the particular problems that can arise when a subcontractor is nominated are discussed in Chapter 10.

Subcontracting does not result in an assignment of liability: The Contractor remains liable to the Employer for the due performance of the Works in accordance with the requirements of the Contract.[87] That is, the Contractor is liable to the Employer for any defective work done by or delay caused by a subcontractor, irrespective of the subcontractor's liability to the Contractor, or who nominated the subcontractor. Contractors can best protect themselves from subcontractor's failures by entering into subcontracts which are 'back-to-back' with the head contract.[88]

Before agreement on, or recommendation of (depending on the terms of the Contract), a subcontractor, the Employer or its agent should properly enquire into the subcontractor's suitability for its part of the Works. This promotes proper workmanship from the start and mitigates against the pitfalls of both litigation against the subcontractor and interference

84 *British Waggon Co v Lea* (1880) 5 QBD 149.

85 *Knight v Burgess* (1864) 33 LJ Ch 727, 730, per Stuart V-C; *Southway Group Ltd v Wolff* (1991) 57 BLR 33; *Advanced National Services Pty Ltd v Daintree Contractors Pty Ltd* [2019] NSWCA 270, [56]–[63] per Gleeson JA.

86 (1880) 5 QBD 149.

87 *Adelaide to City Corporation v Jennings Industries Ltd* (1985) 156 CLR 274, 289, per Brennan J; *Wong Mee-wan v Kwan Kin Travel Services Ltd* [1995] 2 HKLR 542, 545, per Lord Slynn (PC); *Rail Corporation NSW v Fluor Australia Pty Ltd* [2009] NSWCA344, [84], per MacFarlan JA; *NP Integrated Technology Ltd v Entwistle* [2017] EWHC B21 (TCC), [57] per HHJ Russen QC.

88 Although there will differences in the timing of payments, remembering that 'pay-if-paid' and 'pay-when-paid' provisions are widely outlawed by statute. See Table 28.2.

with co-ordination of the Works. Exercising legal remedies against the Head Contractor is not as satisfactory to the Employer as having the work done properly in the first place.

Subcontracts are found in most construction work, since very few Contractors have the resources to carry out the whole of a project themselves. Furthermore, the Contractor does not incur obligations towards the subcontractor's workers which it would incur if it employed those workers directly.[89]

9.3.2 Contractor's liability to subcontractor

The Contractor is, subject to the terms of the subcontract, liable to a subcontractor for breach of the subcontract if the Contractor's default prevents it from earning the subcontract price (eg by causing the head contract to be cancelled). Similarly, a subcontractor is, subject to the terms of the subcontract, liable to the Contractor if the subcontractor's breach of its subcontract results in the Contractor's liability to the Employer or causes other loss to the Contractor.

9.3.3 'Back-to-back' subcontracts

The parties can make any contractual provisions they like regarding subcontracting. The allocation of risk as between the Contractor and the subcontractor for the work to be performed by a subcontractor is a matter for agreement between the Contractor and the subcontractor in the subcontract. In general, a contract can confer rights and duties only upon those who are parties to it. The rights or duties of a subcontractor are therefore in no way affected by the terms of the head contract, unless these are expressly incorporated into the subcontract.

The terms of the head contract must be carefully considered when preparing subcontracts, to ensure that they are consistent and truly 'back-to-back' where necessary. In a 'back-to-back' subcontract the subcontractor automatically becomes liable for any act or omission which causes breach of the head contract. The general incorporation of the terms and conditions of the head contract by reference will usually not suffice, as this may create problems of interpretation and may not achieve the effect intended. The wholesale incorporation by reference without adaptation or amendment of the terms of the head contract into a subcontract may create significant ambiguity and confusion as to what the applicable terms of the subcontract are.[90]

Where a subcontract provides that the terms of the head contract are incorporated 'back-to-back,' it will not usually be intended that literally all the terms of the head contract including the contract price are incorporated into the subcontract.[91] Unless there is an express term in a subcontract incorporating the terms of the head contract, those terms are not incorporated in the subcontract.

---

89 *Leighton Contractors Pty Ltd v Fox* [2009] HCA 35, [21].

90 See Julian Bailey, *Construction Law Vol 3* (Informa Law, 2nd edn 2016) 1521. See *Alsthom Ltd v Yokogawa Australia Pty Ltd (No 7)* [2012] SASC 49, [89] – [92], per Bielby J; *Mainteck Services Pty Ltd v Stein Heurty* [2014] NSWCA 184.

91 See *Spandeck Engineering (S) Pte Ltd v China Construction (South Pacific) Development Co Pte Ltd* [2005] SGCA 59, [16].

Case study: Back-to-back subcontract

The risks in an incomplete back-to-back subcontract were illustrated in *Chandler Bros Ltd v Boswell*.[92] Some of the terms of the head contract were included in a subcontract, but a particular term by which the Employer's Engineer had the power to order the Contractor to remove a subcontractor was not included in the subcontract. The subcontract also set out that the subcontractor agreed to carry out the work in accordance with the terms of the head contract. The court held that the Engineer's power in the head contract was not incorporated into the subcontract. The Head Contractor therefore breached the subcontract if it obeyed an order to dismiss the subcontractor; if it did not, however, it breached the head contract.[93]

A more useful device, adopted by some standard forms of subcontract, is to require the subcontractor to perform so that the Contractor is not caused to be in breach of the head contract. This device is likely to be effective as regards the standard or quality of work. But as regards time, it is much more difficult to devise obligations which will ensure that the subcontractor performs to a programme which satisfies the needs of the head contract. Any programme fixed in advance is vulnerable to the need to make adjustments before or even during the performance of the subcontract work. A device which is likely to be effective is to require the subcontractor to start only as and when instructed to do so, but it may be difficult to secure the subcontractor's agreement. A subcontractor may be expressly required to work in accordance with the Head Contractor's programme of Works as adjusted from time to time under the head contract, without being entitled to additional compensation for any prolongation of the head contract program due to Variations being made under the head contract.[94]

9.3.4 Control of subcontractor's work

In the absence of appropriate terms in the subcontract, the Head Contractor has the right only to prescribe to the subcontractor what final results its work is to produce; it has no right to prescribe how the subcontractor is to do the work, or to order it to submit to the detailed organisation of the project. The Engineer should therefore ensure that a proper subcontract is executed between the Contractor and subcontractor so that, in relation to subcontracted work, the Engineer will be able to effectively exercise its powers of control under the head contract, through the Head Contractor. If this is not done, a subcontractor is entitled to refuse to obey the Engineer's instructions. Whilst the Employer is protected

92 [1936] 3 All ER 179 (CA).
93 See also *Mills v McWilliams* (1914) 33 NZLR 718.
94 *Martin Grant & Co Ltd v Sir Lindsay Parkinson & Co Ltd* [1984] 53 BLR 31.

in theory by the right to terminate the Contract, the practical result of termination may be that the Employer and subcontractor will be competing to extract damages from the Contractor, in addition to the inevitable delay and disruption resulting from a new contractor taking over the work.

It is important to note that *Security of Payment* legislation in Australia and other jurisdictions outlaws contractual provisions for 'pay when paid' or 'pay if paid' schemes.[95] That is, a subcontract cannot include a valid provision that makes the Contractor's payment to the subcontractor conditional on the Contractor receiving payment from the Employer. The provisions prohibiting 'pay when paid' schemes apply both to construction work and related goods and services supplied or undertaken to be supplied under a construction contract. One of the avowed aims of such legislation is to ensure that the parties to construction contracts have a statutory right to the progress payments that are the 'lifeblood' of the industry: 'There must be a "cash flow" in the building trade. It is the very lifeblood of the enterprise.'[96]

9.4 Setting out

The Contractor should be obliged to set out the work to points, lines, and levels of reference given to it by the Engineer. Notwithstanding that the Engineer may have checked any setting out done by the Contractor, the responsibility for the correct setting out of the work should remain with the Contractor. If, during the work, any error appears in the setting out, the Contractor is normally obliged to rectify the error at its own expense, unless the error results from incorrect information supplied by the Employer or the Engineer or by default of another contractor. In that event, the cost (together with profit) of correcting the error should be paid by the Employer. The responsibility and liability for this issue will of course depend on the terms of the relevant Contract.

It is usually the Employer's responsibility to provide the Contractor with the basic reference points. The Engineer is generally required to furnish the necessary levels and reference points (usually on its drawings) to enable the Contractor to achieve the 'true and proper' setting out required.

95 *Housing Grants, Construction and Regeneration Act 1996* (UK) s113; *Building and Construction Industry Security of Payment Act 1999* (NSW) s12; *Building and Construction Industry Security of Payment Act 2002* (Vic) s13; *Building and Construction Industry (Security of Payment) Act 2021* (WA) s14; *Construction Contracts (Security of Payments) Act 2004* (NT) s12; *Construction Industry (Security of Payment Act) 2009* (ACT) s14; *Building and Construction Industry Security of Payment Act 2009* (SA) s12; *Building and Construction Industry Security of Payment Act 2009* (Tas) s16; *Building Industry Fairness (Security of Payment) Act 2017* (Qld) s74; *Construction Contracts Act 2002* (New Zealand) s13; *Construction Contracts Act 2004* (Isle of Man) s10; *Building and Construction Industry Security of Payment Act 2004* (Singapore) s9; *Construction Industry Payment and Adjudication Act 2012* (Malaysia) s35; *Construction Contracts Act 2013* (Ireland); *Construction Act 1990* (Ont) ss6.5(4), 6.6(4).

96 *Modern Engineering (Bristol) Ltd v Gilbert Ash (Northern) Limited* (1973) 71 LGR 162, 167 per Lord Denning MR.

Example: Setting out

Sub-clause 4.7 of the 1999 FIDIC Yellow Book provides for the following responsibilities and liabilities:

> The Contractor shall set out the Works in relation to original points, lines and levels of reference specified in the Contract or notified by the Engineer. The Contractor shall be responsible for the correct positioning of all parts of the Works, and shall rectify any error in the positions, levels, dimensions or alignment of the Works.
>
> The Employer shall be responsible for any errors in these specified or notified items of reference, but the Contractor shall use reasonable efforts to verify their accuracy before they are used.
>
> If the Contractor suffers delay and/or incurs Cost from executing work which was necessitated by an error in these items of reference, and an experienced contractor could not reasonably have discovered such error and avoided this delay and/or Cost, the Contractor shall give notice to the Engineer and shall be entitled subject to Sub-Clause 20.1 [*Contractor's Claims*] to:
>
> (a) an extension of time for any such delay, if completion is or will be delayed, under Sub-Clause 8.4 [Extension of Time for Completion], and
> (b) payment of any such Cost plus reasonable profit, which shall be included in the Contract Price.

The power to order rectification of errors under the Contract should not be limited to inaccurate setting out but should include dimensional inaccuracies of any kind at any stage of the Works. This power generally derives from the Engineer's or Employer's power to order the re-execution of defective work.

Some of the most difficult problems in interpreting certain of the standard contract forms may be illustrated by reference to the Contractor's liability if an error in setting out is found only during the defects liability period after practical completion. The question then arises as to whether the Contractor is liable to make good the error as part of its responsibility for rectification of defects. If it is not liable under the Contract in that way, the Employer may have a common law remedy in damages. It is also unlikely that the Engineer may vary the Works in the defects liability period by altering the position of the Works although they are situated in accordance with its instructions.

9.5 Site data

The Contractor should be responsible under the Contract for its own interpretation of the data made available to it. This would include whatever information may have been provided to the Contractor with the tender documents in relation to the Site, its physical characteristics, the climate, and so on. The application of this information is relevant to both the design and the construction of the Works. For example, if a design and construct Contractor were to conclude (incorrectly) from the details of the weather conditions provided by the Employer that there was no necessity for taking any special measures to protect particular items of plant from corrosion and the plant was designed accordingly, it will be for the Contractor to correct its design at no cost to the Employer; if the Contractor had made proper enquiries from local records as to the severity of the corrosive atmosphere, it would have concluded that special precautions were necessary in the design of the plant.

Notwithstanding that it is the Contractor's responsibility to properly interpret the Site data which is provided to it, it is in the interests of both Employer and Contractor that the Contractor be provided with all available relevant information in the possession of the Employer. The possible consequences of not providing all information available to the Employer are discussed in the case study in ¶9.1.3.1.

9.6 Sufficiency of the accepted contract amount

The Contract should state clearly that the Contractor has fixed the contract price in the light not only of all the information made available to it by the Employer, but also in the light of its own enquiries as to the possibility of carrying out the Works. In general, it should be required to have satisfied itself as to the general circumstances at the Site, provided that access has been made available to it, and as to the general labour and logistical situation at the Site.

The Contractor is generally responsible for any misunderstanding it may have in relation to the Works, or incorrect information, however it has obtained it, unless it has been obtained in writing from the Engineer. Formal inspection of the Site by prospective Tenderers with the Engineer in attendance can reduce the risk of misunderstandings and subsequent claims by the Contractor against the Employer. A detailed record should be kept of what was viewed, what questions were raised, and what answers were given.

9.7 Unforeseeable physical conditions

9.7.1 Contractor's entitlements

In the absence of specific contractual provisions, the Contractor is not entitled to additional payment or an EOT if it encounters unexpected adverse conditions or artificial obstructions (**latent conditions**) at the Site that make construction more time-consuming and expensive than anticipated. This is so, even if the physical conditions could not reasonably have been foreseen by a contractor skilled in carrying out work of the relevant type. Physical conditions include natural physical conditions, physical obstructions (man-made), pollutants, and heritage items.

Where the Contract does provide for additional time or payment for unforeseeable latent conditions, there are invariably requirements for the Contractor to submit a notice. It is essential to serve the notices set out in the Contract, which are usually and rightly an essential precondition of payment. On the other hand, it is not always easy for a Contractor to comply with the requirements as to the contents of the necessary notice. The courts are likely to require a meticulous compliance with such notice requirements. Accordingly, it is in the Contractor's interest to read very carefully and comply with the requirements of the Contract immediately when unforeseeable physical conditions or obstructions are encountered which are thought to justify a claim.

Example: Requirements for a Contractor's Notice of unforeseeable physical conditions

Sub-clause 4.12.1 of the 2017 FIDIC Yellow Book specifies the following requirements for the Contractor's Notice:

> After discovery of such physical conditions, the Contractor shall give a Notice to the Engineer, which shall:
>
> (a) be given as soon as practicable and in good time to give the Engineer opportunity to inspect and investigate the physical conditions promptly and before they are disturbed;
> (b) describe the physical conditions, so that they can be inspected and/ or investigated promptly by the Engineer;
> (c) set out the reasons why the Contractor considers the physical conditions to be Unforeseeable; and
> (d) describe the manner in which the physical conditions will have an adverse effect on the progress and/or increase the Cost of the execution of the Works.

'Unforeseeable' is defined as 'not reasonably foreseeable by an experienced contractor by the Base Date.'[97]

The contractual relief for adverse physical conditions should be carefully defined and should not be read by the Contractor, or the Engineer, as giving them *carte blanche* to claim or award extra time and payment if the Contractor has failed to assess a risk correctly.

9.7.2 Types of obstructions and conditions

Where there are artificial obstructions by underground public services, the presence of which prevent the Contractor from getting effective possession of the Site, the Contractor may, depending on the terms of the Contract, initiate a claim against the Employer not only due to adverse physical conditions (latent conditions) but also due to the Employer's failure to give access to the Site. That may be useful for the Contractor if notices required to be given under the Contract in respect of adverse physical conditions have been overlooked, but possession was actually prevented. The subject matter of a successful claim will in practice usually be some physical condition of the ground below the surface.

Where the consequences of 'weather conditions or conditions due to weather conditions' are excluded from relief granted to the Contractor under the adverse physical conditions clause, difficulties of interpretation can arise from these words. While floods or landslides would seem to come within the description, the common experience of an unusually high water table leading to unexpectedly wet ground is more difficult to assess.

97 Sub-clause 1.1.87.

The words 'artificial obstructions' (or similar) are aimed primarily at unexpected wreckage, underground culverts, municipal services, foundations, and the like. Uncharted wreckage, culverts, sewers, or services are a commonplace occurrence in offshore installations and in excavations in streets or highways. The bills of quantities or specifications in pipe-laying or sewerage contracts may require all such obstructions to be located, diverted, or supported at the Contractor's expense whenever they cross the line of the trench or excavation or interfere with construction operations. In general, it is submitted that, in cases of doubt, the bill or specification, being specifically prepared by the parties for the Contract in question, may be more specific than the General Conditions of contract in defining what unforeseeable physical conditions are. Where the Contractor is entitled to payment for unforeseeable physical conditions, the Contractor has a remedy for these types of unforeseen difficulties only and not, for example, for 'normal' unforeseen difficulties in procuring the necessary Contractor's Equipment, labour, or materials.

9.7.3 Not reasonably foreseeable

Where the Contract stipulates that in order for the Contractor to be entitled to relief, the adverse physical conditions and artificial obstructions must be of such a nature that they could not have been reasonably foreseen by an experienced contractor (eg as in the FIDIC Red and Yellow Books), it should be borne in mind that these words probably give rise to the most frequent disputes of fact which come before engineering arbitrators. The word 'reasonably' introduces an element of degree. Apart from this, the application of the words to a given set of circumstances can be extraordinarily difficult. Engineering arbitrators tend to construe the expression as meaning reasonably foreseen by a contractor experienced in the type of work being carried out.

Case studies: Unforeseeable physical conditions

In *CJ Pearce & Co Ltd v Hereford Corporation*,[98] the Contractors knew before tender that a sewer at least 100 years old had to be crossed in the course of laying a new sewer and that they could expect to meet the sewer anywhere under an embankment supporting a main road. The old sewer fractured when the Contractors disturbed the surrounding soil. The court held that the condition could have been 'reasonably foreseen,' so the Contractors were not entitled to extra payment on the basis of an adverse physical condition and artificial obstruction clause for renewing the old sewer, backfilling the excavation, and so on.

Conversely, in *Bryant & Son Ltd v Birmingham Hospital Saturday Fund*,[99] it was held that it was not reasonable to expect Contractors who had seen two trial holes, to search a site overgrown with grass and find three more holes of which they were not aware, but which did show evidence of rock.

98 (1968) 66 LGR 647.
99 (1938) 1 All ER 503 (KB).

In pricing, an experienced and reputable Contractor will know that there are risks ranging from the totally unforeseeable, through the improbable, to the probable. Where there is no contract clause providing relief from adverse physical conditions and artificial obstructions which could not have been reasonably foreseen,[100] it will price the risks higher than in the case of a tender for which such a clause operates.[101] For totally unforeseeable risks a Contractor may add a percentage based on its experience of the particular class of work, but in doing so may prejudice its chances of securing the Contract when tendering against the reckless or inexperienced.

9.7.4 Giving notice

Where notice of adverse conditions in writing is required, such notice is a condition precedent to a claim,[102] and the Engineer or an Arbitrator has no discretion in the matter. It not infrequently happens, however, that a situation requiring notice is met with, and considerable expense may be incurred before the cause has been diagnosed, for example if steel sheet piling cannot be driven further, it may be due to a defect in the piles or to an artificial obstruction or to unexpected rock or very hard ground. Even where a condition has been diagnosed, the equipment or work necessary to deal with it effectively (eg the size of pile and hammer, or the choice of sumps or well-pointing) may not be decided upon for some time and after much trial and error. Nevertheless, the notice required by the terms of the Contract often requires both diagnosis and cure to be stated, and a forecast of delay or interference, and this has to be provided within a short time after the Contractor becomes aware of the unforeseen physical conditions. Very few notices comply strictly with such requirements in practice. Where compliance is difficult, the original notice should be supplemented at the earliest possible time with the necessary further information. To make the position clear beyond doubt, notices should refer specifically to the clause in terms of which they are made, with a reservation of the right or a statement of intent to claim under that clause. Such a notice should also identify the area of work involved. New notices should be given if conditions are encountered later on in some different area of the Works.

Example: Reasonable requirements for notifying unforeseeable physical conditions

The 2017 FIDIC Red and Yellow Books define notice requirements on encountering unforeseeable physical conditions that can reasonably be complied with – see the preceding case study. Following receipt of such a Notice, the Engineer is required to inspect and investigate the physical conditions within seven days (sub-clause 4.12.2), and subsequently issue appropriate instructions (sub-clause 4.12.3). If the Contractor complies with the contractual requirements, it is entitled to an EOT and/or payment of additional Cost (sub-clause 4.12.4), subject to compliance with sub-clause 20.2 [Claims for Payment and/or EOT]. Sub-clause 20.2.1 requires a Notice describing the event or circumstances giving rise to the Claim within 28 days, and sub-clause 20.2.4 requires a fully detailed Claim within 84 days after the Contractor became aware of the unforeseeable physical conditions (subject to a longer period agreed by the Engineer).

---

100 For example 2017 FIDIC Silver Book sub-clause 4.12 [Unforeseeable Difficulties].

101 For example 2017 Yellow Book sub-clause 4.12 [Unforeseeable Physical Conditions].

102 See *Monmouth C v Costello & Kemple* (1964) 63 LGR 131 and *Blackford & Sons (Caine) Ltd v Christchurch Borough* [1962] 1 Lloyd's Rep 349.

9.8 Repudiation and defective performance

The Contractor's wrongful and total abandonment of the Works before Completion is clearly a repudiatory breach of contract, entitling the Employer to accept the repudiation and terminate the Contract. The question arises as to whether defective performance of the Works may constitute repudiation in some circumstances.

In the case of a lump sum contract, if the Contractor substantially completes the Works, even though there are defects, that will be regarded as due performance. Generally, defective workmanship will not be regarded as a default and certainly not as a repudiatory breach, especially where the Contract provides a remedy for Works which do not comply with the Contract.

During the execution of the Works and before the contractually specified date for Completion, there may be defects that the Contractor has not yet rectified. Such temporary disconformities are not regarded as a breach of contract if they are rectified before Completion. In *Kaye (P & M) Ltd v Hosier and Dickinson Ltd*,[103] Lord Diplock said in connection with the JCT 63 contract:

> Upon a legalistic analysis it might be argued that the temporary disconformity of any part of the works with the requirements of the contract, even though remedied before the end of the agreed construction period, constituted a breach of contract for which nominal damages could be recoverable. I do not think that makes business sense. Provided that the contractor puts it right timeously I do not think that the parties intended that any temporary disconformity should of itself amount to a breach of contract by the contractor.

In some circumstances grossly defective workmanship will amount to a repudiatory breach. However, so far as standard forms are concerned, they usually contemplate defects and provide a procedure for the correction or removal of defective materials and workmanship, so that it must be rare when defective workmanship can amount to a repudiatory breach such as to entitle the Contractor to treat a subcontract as repudiated.

Case study: Contractor's repudiation

In *Sutcliffe v Chippendale & Edmondson*, the court concluded that the Contractor had repudiated the contract as a result of a combination of circumstances, including defective work:

> I take the view that the whole combination of circumstances that then existed . . . did justify the plaintiff in ordering the contractors off the site. I think that their manifest inability to comply with the completion date requirements, the nature and number of complaints from subcontractors and [their] own admission that in May and June the quality of work was deteriorating and the number of defects was multiplying, many of which [they] had tried unsuccessfully to have put right, all point to the truth of the plaintiffs expressed view that the contractors had neither the ability, competence nor the will by this time to complete the work in the manner required by the contract.[104]

103 [1972] 1 All ER 121, 11972] 1 WLR 146.
104 (1981) 18 BLR 149.

9.9 Avoidance of interference

Where the Contractor is engaged on a multidiscipline site where its work forms only a part of some larger project of the Employer, it will be particularly important to ensure that there is no conflict between the work being done by the several contractors on the Site such as might obstruct or disturb the regular progress of the Works being constructed by the Contractor. The Contractor may, depending on the terms of the Contract, be entitled to an extension of time and additional payment if another contractor employed directly by the Employer causes it delay, for example sub-clause 4.6 of the FIDIC rainbow suite. If, for instance, materials supplied by that other contractor are defective, the Engineer may have to give a Variation order and an extension of time for any extra work and delay suffered by the Contractor. It will therefore be important at the tender stage to identify the times during which access by other contractors will be required in order that, if these dates are crucial, appropriate provision is made in the programme.

The Employer should be entitled to retain control over those who are to be permitted to enter the Site. This control should be operated through the Engineer. However, this may be inconsistent with the Contractor's statutory obligations in regard to the Site. For example, in Australia, the Contract may appoint the Contractor as the 'principal contractor' on the Site; the principal contractor has specific statutory duties in respect of, *inter alia*, site induction, security of the Site, and management of health and safety.[105]

9.10 Contractor's equipment

The Contractor is generally obliged under construction contracts to provide all the equipment it needs for the purposes of the Works. Some such equipment, for example diving service vessels or craneage, may well already be available on Site, and if the Contractor is to be permitted to use it for the purposes of the Works, this must be specified. Because the Contractor's equipment is usually deemed to be on Site exclusively for the purposes of the Works, the Contractor is usually not permitted to remove it until either it is no longer required, or the Engineer permits it to do so. This applies whether the Contractor's equipment concerned belongs to the Contractor or has been hired.

9.11 Employer's equipment and free-issue material

All equipment to be made available by the Employer to the Contractor should be identified by reference to a schedule attached to and forming part of the Contract. The place and duration of the use of equipment should also be specified. More recently on some remote sites each item of mobile equipment is fitted with a satellite tracking device which logs its daily activities. (The tracking of activities of individual workers through personal tracking devices, by consent, has also helped the daily analysis of where bottlenecks and delays are being incurred, eg drawing free-issue materials from the Employer's stores.)

105 For example *Work Health and Safety Regulation 2017* (NSW) Parts 6.3–6.5.

The Contractor is usually permitted under construction contracts to request the Employer to make available for the execution of the Works any Employer's equipment which may be available on the Site. Provided the relevant equipment is listed in the Contract as equipment that the Employer will make available to the Contractor, the Employer must make it available if the Contractor so requests, but generally the Contractor must pay for its use. The Employer is generally required at all times to be responsible for the safe working of its equipment whilst it is being operated for the Contractor, unless the Contract provides otherwise. This does not generally, however, release the Contractor from any liability if, in giving instructions for the operation of the equipment, it requires it to be operated in an unsafe manner. The risks and allocation of responsibility for the safe execution of tandem lifts warrants particular attention.

If the Contractor is required to make any of its equipment available at the Employer's request to others, or provides services to others engaged on the Site, it should be entitled to be paid for such services. The same considerations of safety apply.

9.12 Assignment

9.12.1 What is it?

Assignment is the means by which a party may legally transfer to another the whole or part of its rights or obligations under a contract. Subject to the terms of the Contract, a party is permitted to assign to another person its benefit under a contract, including any debt due to it under the Contract.[106] When the Contractor assigns part of its obligation to perform the work, the effect is similar to a subcontract save that the assignee is in direct contract with the Employer, and the Contractor no longer has liability for that work. An assignment is a transfer, recognised by the law, of a right of one person to another. Most rights are capable of assignment. This may be achieved in a number of ways. Assignments are sometimes brought about by operation of law.

An assignment, in common with other legal transactions, is distinct from a contract to make an assignment. An assignment does not generally require consideration. But a contract to assign, in order to be enforceable, must comply with the same requirements as any other contract, including the need for consideration. An assignment of a right arising under a contract is a further exception to the doctrine of privity in that rights or burdens are conferred upon persons who are not party to the Contract.

9.12.2 Assignments not permitted

Construction contracts and subcontracts often contain terms restricting or prohibiting assignments. Such terms have the effect of making any purported assignment invalid as against the other party to the Contract. However, the right to prevent an assignment may be lost by waiver. Thus, if the Contractor assigns his right to receive payment, the Employer will waive its right to object if payment is made to the assignee.

106 *Southway Group Limited v Wolff* (1991) 57 BLR 33, 43, per Parker LJ, 52 per Bingham LJ.

Example: 2017 FIDIC rainbow suite sub-clause 1.7

> Neither Party shall assign the whole or any part of the Contract or any benefit or interest in or under the Contract. However, either Party:
>
> (a) may assign the whole or any part of the Contract with the prior agreement of the other Party, at the sole discretion of such other Party; and
> (b) may, as security in favour of a bank or financial institution, assign the Party's right to any moneys due, or to become due, under the Contract without the prior agreement of the other Party.

9.12.3 Effects of assignment

Upon a valid assignment, the assignor loses its rights in the things assigned. The assignee acquires the right to sue in its own name. However, if the assignment is equitable, the assignor may need to be made a party to the action. The right acquired is subject to any rights of the other party against the assignor, including the right of set-off. Thus, if a Contractor assigns money payable under a certificate, the Employer may set off against the assignee any claim for defects or delay. The Employer cannot counterclaim, but the set-off may reduce or extinguish the debt.

9.12.4 Assignment of benefit of subcontract

The Employer may wish to make provision in the Contract for the possibility of assigning subcontractors' subcontracts with the Contractor to a substitute contractor, or to itself. In the event that the Contractor becomes insolvent, is unable to complete the Contract, or repudiates it before completion, the Employer will be faced with appointing a substitute contractor. In those circumstances, the delay and disruption to the project will be minimised if the existing subcontracts can be assigned to the substitute contractor. Where a subcontractor's obligations extend beyond the end of the defects liability period, it may be appropriate for the subcontract to be assigned to the Employer itself.

The Contract can make provision for either of these scenarios by defining the circumstances in which the Contractor is obliged to assign the benefit of subcontracts. However, for this provision to be effective, a 'back-to-back' provision must be included in each of the subcontracts, so that the subcontractors are obliged to agree to assignment of the subcontracts in the specified circumstances. One way in which this is sometimes done is to require that each subcontractor execute a Deed Poll in which it commits to signing a specified form of Deed of Novation with a substitute contractor on receipt of written instructions from the Employer.

9.12.5 Assignment of warranties

This topic has acquired currency through the creation of contractual warranties intended to replace claims previously available in tort. The assignees are those subsequently acquiring an interest in construction works. Thus, parties involved in carrying out a construction project, particularly the designers and other professionals, may be asked to give forms of warranty with the intention that these may be assigned to subsequent owners of the project. In accordance with the principles discussed earlier, the benefit of such a warranty is generally assignable without need of express provision or consent.

However, an assignment can do no more than to transfer rights available to the assignor; it is not capable of creating new rights in favour of an assignee. Thus, while the Employer can in theory assign the right to have a structure adequately designed, it is unclear what right would be transferred to sue for damages in the event of breach. A further difficulty would arise where a structure is sold to a number of different purchasers. The assignment to each of the right to have the structure properly designed creates a number of problems as to what enforceable right (if any) has been transferred to each purchaser. These problems are capable of resolution, in principle, by the terms of the document to be assigned, particularly if created by deed (so as to avoid problems of consideration). Thus, the nature and extent of rights to be transferred may be defined, as well as the damage that may be claimed in the event of a breach. A solution which avoids these problems is to draft the document in the form of a **novation**, whereby the assignee third party may take over the full contractual rights of the developer/Employer, as though named as an original party to the transaction.

The effect of a contract expressly made with the intention that the benefit be assigned to another party was considered by the Court of Appeal in *Darlington Borough Council v Wiltshier Northern Ltd.*[107] This concerned the familiar method of financing local authority development works by use of a bank (Morgan Grenfell) as the primary employer. The Court of Appeal held the council entitled to recover the damages, following *Linden Gardens*[108] case.

107 [1995] 1 WLR 68, 79.
108 *Linden Gardens Trust Ltd v Lenesta Sludge Disposals Ltd* [1994] 1 AC 85.

CHAPTER 10

Subcontracting

CONTENTS

DOI: 10.4324/9781003206873-10

10.1 Rights and obligations

The advantage of subcontracting to the Employer is that while the Works may actually be performed by various specialists, the Head Contractor alone remains responsible for the whole operation and, perhaps most importantly, for the co-ordination of its own work and that of subcontractors. Sums included in the head contract and designated as **prime cost items** usually represent work intended to be subcontracted. The Employer must pay the actual cost of prime cost items. Prime cost work often represents an important part of a project which has not been designed in any detail, and which is to be subcontracted to a nominated specialist who will furnish the design. By contrast, a **provisional sum** usually represents work of uncertain scope which may be subcontracted. Prime cost sums and provisional sums are discussed in ¶20.4.

A common feature of head contracts is for the Employer to retain the right to make direct payments to a nominated subcontractor. These provisions recognise that payments due to a nominated subcontractor are generally fixed by the Engineer, so that the Contractor acts merely as a channel for payment. However, neither nomination nor direct payment to subcontractors gives a subcontractor the right to sue the Employer and no privity of contract is created. The only exception to this principle is where the Employer obtains a collateral warranty from the subcontractor.

10.2 The subcontractor's liability to the Employer

10.2.1 Contractual liability

Since a subcontract is made between the Contractor and the subcontractor only, the Employer has no contractual rights against, or duties to, a subcontractor, unless it makes a separate contractual arrangement. The effect of the normal position is that in the event that the Contractor becomes insolvent or goes into liquidation, the Employer cannot extract payment of any damages directly from a subcontractor (including a nominated subcontractor) resulting from its delay or defective work. The damages must be paid by the subcontractor to the liquidator of the Contractor, and the Employer can then (apart from its contractual rights over the plant and Contractor's equipment, etc) only receive a dividend as an ordinary creditor of the Contractor for the loss it has suffered.[1]

This Employer can obtain contractual rights against a subcontractor by means of a direct contract between the Employer and the subcontractor which is back-to-back with the head contract. The Contract can require that a subcontractor must execute a collateral contract in which it guarantees performance of the subcontract and give warranties concerning its design and workmanship to the Employer. The Employer can ensure that such a provision is given effect to in each of the subcontracts entered into by the Contractor as a condition of its approval of the subcontractors. Such a

1 MW Abrahamson, *Engineering Law and the ICE Contracts* (E & FN Spon London, 4th edn 1979) 139.

collateral contract ensures that the Employer has direct recourse against the nominated subcontractor. This may be useful in circumstances where the Employer wishes to pursue the subcontractor for breach of its subcontract directly or does not have recourse against the Head Contractor for the subcontractor's defective work or material (for example, because the Contractor is insolvent).

Whilst such a collateral contract will not help the Employer if the subcontractor becomes insolvent, it may, apart from other advantages, prevent a liquidation of convenience intended to escape the consequences of an unprofitable subcontract using the *Bickerton* decision.[2] Given the uncertainties, it may be important in many circumstances for the Engineer to ensure that such a collateral contract is made to protect its client, or that an indemnity be given by a subcontractor directly to the Employer.[3]

10.2.2 Subcontractor's liability in negligence

A subcontractor will ordinarily owe a duty of care to an Employer in respect of harm or injury to persons, or damage to other property, including the Employer's property, that may be caused by the subcontractor's failure to exercise reasonable skill and care.

In the case of *Independent Broadcasting Authority v EMI Electronics and BICC Construction Ltd*,[4] it was not disputed that, even when there is no contractual relationship between an Employer and a subcontractor who it has nominated, the subcontractor owes a duty of care in tort to the Employer, and will be liable to the Employer for the consequences of negligence, whatever form that negligence takes. In that particular case, it was held to be negligent design by the nominated subcontractor which resulted in a 1250-foot high television mast collapsing. This case is discussed in more detail in ¶7.11, noting that a high degree of care is required in a novel design.

Whether an Employer can sue a domestic subcontractor for negligent workmanship is not clear, but it is submitted that there is, indeed, a duty of care to the Employer owed by the subcontractor.

10.3 Employer's liability to subcontractor

Construction contracts generally do not give the Employer the right to make direct payment to subcontractors other than any nominated subcontractor. The Engineer can only certify payment to the Contractor by the Employer, at the same time indicating in that certificate what proportion of the sums so certified should be paid over to the subcontractors. The Engineer cannot validly issue a certificate to the Contractor for payment to a subcontractor as it is not the agent of the Contractor and can only validly certify payments to be made by the Employer. Generally, therefore, the Employer pays the Head Contractor, from whom

2 *North West Metropolitan Regional Hospital Board v T A Bickerton & Sons Ltd* [1970] 1 All ER 1039.

3 Stephen Furst & the Hon Sir Vivian Ramsey, *Keating on Construction Contracts* (Sweet & Maxwell, 8th edn 2006) [12–050–12–051].

4 (1980) 14 BLR 1.

the subcontractor recovers its share of payment or damages. Clearly, the subcontractor may lose if the Contractor becomes insolvent after it has received payment from the Employer but before it pays the subcontractor.

However, some contracts contain a provision that enables the Employer to make an election either to pay the subcontractor directly or to pay to the Contractor in order for payment to be made to the subcontractor. Once a certificate on one basis has been issued, a certificate cannot validly be issued for a lesser amount thereafter. After the Engineer has issued to the Contractor a Final Payment Certificate for payment in full for all its work, the Engineer has exhausted its mandate (*functus officio*) and is precluded from issuing an amended certificate dealing with payment to the subcontractor. Should a second (invalid) certificate be issued, the validity of the first certificate is not destroyed.

A subcontract creates no privity of contract between the subcontractor and the Employer, and accordingly a subcontractor cannot sue the Employer directly for payment or extra expenses or damages in contract. The subcontractor can sue only the Head Contractor for the price of the subcontracted work. Even though the Employer is enriched (receives a benefit), a subcontractor has no right to recover money from the Employer in restitution for unjust enrichment by the subcontractor performing its work on the Employer's land.[5] A right of action may, however, exist on the basis of unjust enrichment in certain circumstances.

In exceptional cases it may be implied that an Employer has entered into a direct contract with a subcontractor for the work or materials. However, even if the subcontractor was nominated by the Employer and the subcontract negotiated by its Engineer would not be sufficient to create a direct contract and preclude the Contractor's liability; the Engineer is taken to be acting as the Contractor's agent in any negotiations on subcontract terms.

If, however, the Employer, or the Engineer acting clearly for the Employer and with the Employer's authority, negotiates with or gives an instruction directly to the subcontractor, this may create a direct contract. This would negate the whole object of the subcontracting system from the Employer's point of view; the rules set out earlier would not apply and the Employer would be bound to ensure that the subcontractor is paid. In *Wallis v Robinson*,[6] the Engineer, in the presence of the Employer, asked a subcontractor to carry out work by a process which was more expensive than the process specified and told the subcontractor that it would be paid extra. The court held that a contract was created between the Employer and the subcontractor under which the subcontractor could recover the extra payment directly from the Employer.[7]

---

5 *Lumbers v W Cook Builders Pty Ltd (in liq)* (2008) CLR 635; [2008] BLR 581; *Yew Sang Hong Ltd v Hong Kong Housing Authority* [2008] BLR 563 (HKCA); *United Electrical Co Ltd v Wing Hong Contractors Ltd* [2011] HKCFI 638, [40]–[45], per Sakhrani J; *Lonsdale Investments Pty Ltd v OM (Manganese) Ltd(No3)* [2012] WASC 185, [1129]–[1133], per Corboy J; *Skilled Group Ltd v CSR Viridian Pty Ltd* [2012] VSC 290, [23]–[39], per Vickery J.

6 (1862) 130 RR 841.

7 MW Abrahamson, *Engineering Law and the ICE Contracts* (E & FN Spon London, 4th edn 1979) 255.

An Employer that directs a subcontractor to carry out additional work may also become liable to the subcontractor on the basis of a *quantum meruit* arising from the Employer's unjust enrichment from the benefit received. A claim for a *quantum meruit* may be available to a person where there is no subsisting contract governing that person's right to compensation for work carried out at the direction of another. *Quantum meruit* is discussed further in ¶21.12.

The principles applicable to unjust enrichment were applied in *ABB Power Generation Ltd v Chapple & Ors*,[8] where a scaffolding subcontractor (Chapple) to one of ABB's contractors was successful in claiming a *quantum meruit* from ABB for the reasonable cost of extra work that was not recoverable under Chapple's subcontract. There was no contractual relationship between ABB and Chapple. ABB was held to be enriched by obtaining the benefit of certain scaffolding modification work it ordered to suit its agreement with other contractors on site. The unjust element arose from the circumstances that Chapple was given to understand by ABB that the extra costs would be met. This case emphasises that, in giving effect to the principles of restitution for a benefit unjustly received, courts are prepared to look beyond the contractual relationships that had previously been regarded as defining the limits of a party's obligations.

10.4 Subcontractor's other remedies

A subcontractor may, depending on the terms of its subcontract, be entitled to stop work for due cause, but in the absence of appropriate contractual or statutory protection this has substantial risks. The threat to stop work may constitute repudiation of the subcontract entitling the Contractor to resile from the subcontract and claim damages from the subcontractor. Actual stoppage may constitute the Contractor's repudiation of the Contract, entitling the Employer to withhold certificates. This could precipitate the Contractor's insolvency, in which the subcontractor may lose the payments which the Contractor has already received in respect of the subcontractor's work.[9]

The subcontractor's position is however protected in many jurisdictions if it stops work in circumstances where it has not been paid and it complies with the provisions of the relevant *Security of Payment* legislation.

10.5 Nominated subcontractors

10.5.1 Nomination

Subcontractors who are chosen by the Contractor are often referred to as domestic subcontractors. Nominated subcontractors are those subcontractors of the Contractor nominated by the Employer.

It may be considered desirable for the Employer or the Engineer to control the choice of specialist subcontractor to ensure that standardisation of equipment or desired quality or performance is achieved. The Employer's aim is to have control over the most appropriate subcontractor to deliver a defined part of the work (possibly including negotiation of price

8 [2001] WASCA 412.

9 M W Abrahamson, *Engineering Law and the ICE Contracts* (E & FN Spon London, 4th edn 1979) 255.

and subcontract terms), whilst holding the Contractor liable for any lack of performance by the subcontractor under the terms of the head contract. Not surprisingly, nomination of subcontractors by the Employer can give rise to some difficult issues, because of the inherent tension between the Employer's desire for control whilst maintaining the Contractor's sole liability for time, cost, and quality of the Works. Although standard form contracts still make provision for nominated subcontractors, the practice is not as common as it used to be, and there are good reasons, as discussed later, for an Employer to use alternative approaches.

In *North West Metropolitan Regional Hospital Board v T A Bickerton & Sons Ltd*,[10] the court described the process of nomination which has developed in the construction industry in England:

> The scheme for nominated subcontractors is an ingenious method of achieving two objects which at first sight might seem incompatible.
>
> The employers want to choose who is to do the prime cost work and to settle the terms on which it is to be done, and at the same time to avoid the hazards and difficulties which might arise if they entered into a contract with the person they have chosen to do the work.
>
> The scheme creates a chain of responsibility. Subject to a very limited right to object, the principal contractor is bound to enter into a contract with the employer's nominee, but it has no concern with the terms of that contract, for those terms are settled by the employers and their nominee.

Nominated subcontractors may be named in the Contract, or they may be subsequently nominated under a power given to the Engineer in the Contract. If nominated subcontractors are named in the tender documents, the Contractor has a reasonable opportunity before entering into the Contract to object to those nominated, or to prepare its tender price based on an assessment of the risks associated with subcontracting with them. There are, of course, many practical reasons why nominations may not be made until after the head contract is executed.

The usual procedure for letting a nominated subcontract is for the Engineer to obtain competitive quotations for the work in question direct from prospective subcontractors, and then, under powers contained in the head contract, to instruct the Contractor to place an order with the chosen tenderer. The terms of the subcontract will largely be settled before the nomination, usually by incorporating a standard form, but both the Contractor and subcontractor may seek to amend or alter the terms. The head contract usually gives the Contractor some protection by giving it a right of reasonable refusal to engage a nominated subcontractor.[11]

The allocation of risk as between the Employer and the Head Contractor for work performed by a nominated subcontractor is a matter for agreement between the Employer and the Head Contractor.[12] Contracts typically require the Head Contractor to be responsible to the Employer for the nominated subcontractor's works, even though the Head Contractor

10 [1970] 1 All ER 1039 (HL); 68 LGR447 (HL).

11 For example, 2017 FIDIC Red Book sub-clause 5.2.2. Compare *Naylor Group Inc v Ellis-Don Construction Ltd* [2001] 2 SCR 943, [49].

12 *Sinclair v Woods of Winchester (No2)* [2006] EWHC 3003 (TCC), [30]–[33], per HHJ Coulson QC.

neither selected nor exercised control over those works.[13] The Head Contractor may even be prohibited, expressly or impliedly, from carrying out the works of the nominated subcontractor even if the nominated subcontract is terminated.[14] A Head Contractor may not however be legally compelled to enter into a subcontract.[15]

10.5.2 Problems of nomination

In general, construction Contracts which provide for nominated subcontracts will entitle the Contractor to an extension of time and to suspension for any delay in nomination by the Employer (or the Engineer as the case may be) if the Contractor gives the necessary notice. The problems of delay in nominating the replacement subcontractor are illustrated in *North West Metropolitan Regional Hospital Board v TA Bickerton and Sons Ltd*,[16] discussed further in ¶10.5.5.

In the case of work provided for by a provisional sum to be executed by a nominated subcontractor who defaults in its obligations, the Contractor may attempt to have a second subcontractor nominated by the Engineer and claim any additional payment made to the second subcontractor. The Contractor may also argue that, if it is instructed by the Engineer that it must complete a subcontractor's work itself or by its own subcontractor after default, it is entitled to have the work valued as a Variation. The Contractor may also claim an increase on contract rates for the difficulties in taking over partly completed work. The main practical objection to allowing the Head Contractor to recover in these situations is that the Employer then has no redress for the loss it has suffered because of the subcontractor's default, and the guilty subcontractor escapes the consequences. If, moreover, the Head Contractor recovers the full cost of the work from the Employer, it has no substantial claim against the subcontractor since it has not suffered any loss. The Employer usually cannot recover the extra payments it makes to the Head Contractor directly from the subcontractor, since it has no contract with the nominated subcontractor.

A similar problem occurs in relation to the Head Contractor's liability for defective work by nominated subcontractors.

If an Employer considers it necessary to nominate a subcontractor, both Employer and Engineer need to be scrupulous in respecting the contractual relationship between Contractor and subcontractor, and in fulfilling all the Employer's contractual obligations in respect of the nominated subcontractor. In many cases, it is preferable for the Contract to leave the choice of subcontractors up to the Contractor, whilst retaining the Employer's reasonable power of veto over subcontractors and suppliers.

---

13 *John Lang Construction Ltd v County and District Properties Ltd* (1982) 2 Con LR 1, 32–33, per Webster J; *Equitable Debenture Assets Corporation Ltd v William Moss Group Ltd* (1984) 2 Con LR 1, 32–33, per Judge Newey QC; *Gema Metal Ceilings (Far East) Pte Ltd v Iwatani Techno Construction (M) Sdn Bhd* [2000] SGHC 37, [66], per Chan Seng Onn JC.

14 *TA Bickerton & Son Ltd v North West Metropolitan Regional Hospital Board* [1970] 1 WLR 607, 609, per Lord Reid, 624 per Viscount Dilhorne; cf *Adelaide City Corporation v Jennings Industries* (1985) 156 CLR 274, 280–281, per Wilson J.

15 *Leslie v Metropolitan Asylums District Managers* (1901) 2 Arch Law Rep 36, 42, per Romer LJ, 68 JP 86 (CA).

16 [1970] 1 All ER 1039 (HL); 68 LGR 447 (HL).

10.5.3 *Minimising the problems of nomination*

As discussed in ¶10.2, the Employer can enter into a collateral contract with a subcontractor in which the subcontractor has a direct contractual obligation to the Employer that it will comply with its obligations under the subcontract with the Contractor. In these circumstances, the Employer has a contractual right to seek recourse directly from the subcontractor for breach of its subcontract. The reasons for the Employer entering into such a collateral contract are even more compelling in the case of nominated subcontractors.

10.5.4 *Objection to nomination*

The Contractor is generally given a right to make reasonable objection to a nominated subcontractor, particularly if the nominated subcontractor refuses to enter into a subcontract which provides that in respect of the subcontract works, the nominated subcontractor will indemnify the Head Contractor against the Head Contractor's liabilities under the head contract.

For example, the 2017 FIDIC Yellow Book sub-clause 4.5.1 [Objection to Nomination] provides as follows:

> The Contractor shall not be under any obligation to employ a nominated Subcontractor whom the Engineer instructs and against whom the Contractor raises reasonable objection by giving a Notice to the Engineer, with detailed supporting particulars, no later than 14 days after receiving the Engineer's instruction. An objection shall be deemed reasonable if it arises from (among other things) any of the following matters, unless the Employer agrees to indemnify the Contractor against and from the consequences of the matter:
>
> (a) there are reasons to believe that the Subcontractor does not have sufficient competence, resources or financial strength;
> (b) the subcontract does not specify that the nominated Subcontractor shall indemnify the Contractor against and from any negligence or misuse of Goods by the nominated Subcontractor, the nominated Subcontractor's agents and employees; or
> (c) the subcontract does not specify that, for the subcontracted work (including design, if any), the nominated Subcontractor shall:
>
> (i) undertake to the Contractor such obligations and liabilities as will enable the Contractor to discharge the Contractor's corresponding obligations and liabilities under the Contract; and
> (ii) indemnify the Contractor against and from all obligations and liabilities arising under or in connection with the Contract and from the consequences of any failure by the Subcontractor to perform these obligations or to fulfil these liabilities.

The Head Contractor may have no right to object to a nominated supplier, despite the terms of the quotation negotiated by the Employer, which may incorporate special conditions exempting the supplier from liability to the Head Contractor for the materials. In such cases, the Head Contractor will probably not be liable for defective materials supplied by the nominated supplier.

What does not appear to have been decided in any construction case is whether there is any liability in tort on an Engineer for the negligent nomination of a subcontractor. The position is complicated by the contractual terms entitling a contractor, in limited circumstances and for a limited time, to reject a nomination. But it is conceivable that an Engineer may be liable in negligence in the nomination of an obviously incapable subcontractor.

10.5.5 The duty to renominate

In the event that a nominated subcontractor goes into liquidation, the question arises as to whether the Employer has a duty to nominate a new subcontractor. As with most such questions, the answer depends on the words of the contract and how those words are properly construed.[17]

In *North West Metropolitan Regional Hospital Board v TA Bickerton and Sons Ltd*,[18] the Contractor agreed to build some hospital buildings under the contract form published by the Royal Institute of British Architects (**RIBA**). The Architect refused to make a further nomination when a subcontractor nominated under a prime cost sum went into liquidation. The court held that the RIBA contract did not give the Contractor the right or the duty to do any of the prime cost work itself. Accordingly, the Head Contractor was entitled to extra payment for completing the subcontract work in the absence of a second nomination. The consequences of the Architect's misguided logic in refusing to nominate a second subcontractor was that, under such circumstances, the Employer was obliged to reimburse the Head Contractor for any losses that resulted and grant extensions of time for any delay the Head Contractor may have suffered.

By contrast, in *Reilly (RM) Ltd v Belfast Corporation*[19] it was held that, if a nominated subcontractor went into liquidation, there was no duty on the Employer to make a second nomination. Lord MacDermott CJ, quoting clause 1(1) of JCT 63, said:

> The work covered by ordinary subcontracts made by the Head Contractor would not reduce the latter's field of performance, and I can find nothing in the head contract to suggest that subcontracts with a nominated subcontractor were to stand in any different position.
>
> If my view on this is right, a construction which would place an obligation on the employers to renominate seems to be founded on little more than wishful thinking.

Lord Reid distinguished this case from the *Bickerton* case in the following terms: 'I would agree that, if the principal contractor had any duty under the main contract to do prime cost work itself, it would follow that the employer would not be bound to make a second nomination.'[20]

In the absence of a specific provision in the Contract on the obligations arising from withdrawal of a nominated subcontractor, the outcome will depend on whether or not there is an implied term that the Employer has a duty to renominate if the original nominated subcontractor withdraws. If there is no such implied term, the Contractor can only recover

---

17 '[T]he provisions of the RIBA form of contract are so confused and obscure that no conclusion can be reached without a long and complicated chain of reasoning.' *North West Metropolitan Regional Hospital Board v TA Bickerton and Sons Ltd* [1970] 1 All ER 1039, 1045 per Lord Reid.

18 [1970] 1 All ER 1039 (HL); 68 LGR 447 (HL).

19 [1970] NI 68.

20 *North West Metropolitan Regional Hospital Board v TA Bickerton and Sons Ltd* [1970] 1 All ER 1039, 1043 per Lord Reid.

damages from the original subcontractor of the difference between the original and the later subcontractor's price. However, if there is such an implied term, the Employer has a duty to nominate a new subcontractor within a reasonable time and is liable to the Contractor for any additional costs arising.

10.5.6 Payments to nominated subcontractors

Construction contracts which provide for nominated subcontractors generally provide for the Employer to elect to pay all nominated subcontractors directly (ie 'supply only' subcontractors as well as subcontractors for work). The Employer's power to make direct payment to nominated subcontractors effectively enables the Employer to secure payment of the earlier accounts by the Contractor, or pay them itself, when the time for the next certificate arises. The Engineer deducts the amount of the direct payment in and from any later certificates to the Contractor.

A clause in the head contract giving the Employer the right to pay nominated subcontractors directly provides important security to nominated subcontractors, since the payment may be made even after the bankruptcy or liquidation of the Head Contractor. If there is no direct payment clause, in the event of the Contractor's insolvency, the Employer must pay any money due for a subcontractor's work to the liquidator of the Head Contractor. The subcontractor's only right then is to prove for a dividend in the liquidation as an ordinary creditor.

Every payment under the Contract made by the Employer must first be made to the Contractor, or in the event of its insolvency, its liquidator. As such, in paying the subcontractor directly, the Employer must rely on its right to recoup those direct payments from money becoming payable to the Contractor in later certificates. However, it may be that the plant, retention, and payments due to the Contractor may not be sufficient to recoup the Employer's expenses and damages in completing the Works. In the event of the Contractor's insolvency, the Employer may be required to pay to the liquidator amounts due to the Contractor that include sums paid directly to nominated subcontractors. In such circumstances the Employer may be unable to recover the amount of the direct payments.

If any immediate risk to Completion arises whereby the Employer must take all or part of the Works out of the Contractor's hands, the Employer may not be inclined to add to those expenses by making payments directly to subcontractors for work for which the Contractor has already been paid. That said, subcontractors who have not been paid will most likely require payment of arrears as an inducement to complete their work.

A contract will generally provide that the Employer may not pay a subcontractor directly if the Head Contractor states in writing to the Engineer and subcontractor that it had reasonable cause for failing to pass over the payments included in previous certificates (whether, in fact, it had reasonable cause or not). If this is the case under the Contract, it gives the Contractor the power to prevent direct payment. However, unless the Engineer is fully informed, it may be inappropriate to allow it to prejudge disputes between the Contractor and a subcontractor in order to decide whether the Contractor had reasonable grounds for not paying, such as delay or damage by the subcontractor to the Contractor's work, or special credit terms agreed between the Head Contractor and subcontractor.

A construction contract may provide that (for the reason of business efficacy) the Contractor is bound to inform the Engineer of the facts which are its reasons for withholding payment and also, if only a partial withholding is justified, of the amount which it feels justified in not paying to the subcontractor. In such circumstances, the Contract will generally provide the Engineer with the power to decide whether the facts reasonably justify withholding the payment.

Where a contract provides for direct payment to nominated subcontractors, the Employer will usually be provided with a personal discretion; it is not bound to pay directly on the Engineer's certificate. Even if it were provided that the Employer shall pay directly, a subcontractor would not be entitled to enforce direct payment since it is not a party to the Contract (although it may be regarded as a stipulation for the benefit of a third party).

10.5.7 Design approved before nomination

If, before the Contractor tenders, the Employer has commissioned another person to prepare the design of the structure, the Contractor may not be liable for design defects of a nominated subcontractor where the head contract is a construct only contract with no obligation for design.

In the Irish case of *Norta Wallpapers Ltd v John Sisk, & Sons Ltd (Dublin)*,[21] specialists in 'system built' superstructures were commissioned to design and erect a superstructure, including the roof and roof lights. Later they were nominated as subcontractors under the standard contract to the Contractor and completed the work. Within six months, there were major leaks which an Arbitrator held to be due 85% to defective design, 12% to use of inferior materials, and 3% to bad workmanship. The Contractor was held liable for the last two items but not the defective design by the subcontractors.

The *Norta* case can be contrasted with the House of Lords decision in *Independent Broadcasting Authority v EMI & BICC*[22] where the Head Contractor had contractual responsibility for the project, including the design and performance of the mast. Accordingly, it was held liable for the negligent design of the nominated subcontractor who had prepared the design before the head contract was entered into.

10.5.8 Delay on the part of a nominated subcontractor or supplier

If a nominated subcontractor causes delay without repudiating its subcontract, the Contractor generally remains liable and may pass on the Employer's claim to the subcontractor in default. However, some forms of contract provide expressly for an extension of time on the grounds of delay by a nominated subcontractor. This effectively deprives the Employer of a remedy, save under any direct warranty.

The House of Lords ruled that a clause in a head contract, which gave a Head Contractor a financial remedy for delay and disruption arising from causes 'beyond the contractor's control,' entitled the Contractor to compensation for losses flowing from a nominated subcontractor's supply of defective goods, where the Head Contractor had no influence over the quality of goods supplied.[23]

21 (1977) 14 BLR 49 [Ir Sup Ct].
22 (1980) 14 BLR 1.
23 *Scott Lithgow Ltd v Secretary of State for Defence* (1989) 45 BLR 1.

Where the nominated subcontractor repudiates, it appears to follow from the *Bickerton* case that the Employer will be responsible for any unreasonable delay in providing a replacement subcontractor. However, the outcome in any particular case will depend on the construction of the specific words of the Contract.

In *Percy Bilton Ltd v Greater London Council*,[24] the Contractor accepted the nominated subcontractor's repudiation after it went into liquidation. Some time elapsed before another nominated subcontractor entered into a subcontract. The Employer levied liquidated damages for delay in completion. The Contractor argued that as soon as the original nominated subcontractor had 'withdrawn' there would have to be an immediate renomination of a subcontractor to avoid a breach of contract by the Employer. The House of Lords held that the delay resulting from the was not the responsibility of the Employer. Lord Fraser held:

> Withdrawal of a nominated subcontractor is not caused by the fault of the employer, nor is it covered by any of the express provisions of clause 23. . . accordingly, withdrawal falls under the general rule and the Head Contractor takes the risk of any delay directly caused thereby.

Where a nominated subcontractor has achieved apparent completion and defects are thereafter discovered in the work, the question arises whether this can constitute delay on the part of nominated subcontractors.

These facts occurred in the case of *J Jarvis & Sons Ltd v Westminster Corporation*,[25] where defects were discovered in bored piles after the subcontractor had withdrawn from the site. The necessary remedial work resulted in substantial delays to the head contract. Lord Dilhorne held:

> A practical completion certificate can be issued when owing to latent defects the works do not fulfil the contract requirements and . . . under the contract works can be completed despite the presence of such defects. Completion under the contract is not postponed until defects which became apparent only after the work had been finished had been remedied. . . . I conclude that the [subcontractor] had completed the subcontract works to the reasonable satisfaction of the Architects and the [Head Contractor] and so were not guilty of delay.

Accordingly, as in the *Percy Bilton* case, the subsequent delay was not covered by the extension of time clause, and the Head Contractor remained responsible for the delay.

Unless otherwise provided for in the Contract, failure of a nominated subcontractor to complete by its contract date, or other delays caused to the Contractor by default of a nominated subcontractor, do not authorise the Engineer to extend the Contractor's time for Completion.

10.5.9 Liability for defects

One of the problems relating to subcontracts is that of determining the obligations of the Head Contractor in respect of materials and work of nominated subcontractors, and thus determining the rights of the Employer in the event of default by a nominated subcontractor.

---

24 [1982] 2 All ER 623 (HL); (1981) BLR 1; (1982) 20 BLR 1.
25 [1970] 1 WLR 637.

There is generally no problem in regard to the express description of the work. This will become incorporated in the head contract by virtue of the nomination. The problem arises when the subcontractor's work, while complying with the express terms of the head contract and subcontract, is not of good quality or not fit for its purpose.

Generally, the Head Contractor will be responsible both for the quality and for the fitness of materials used, unless there are circumstances which are such as to negative the existence of either term. Where there is a nominated supplier, the materials will have been specifically chosen by the Architect or Engineer, so that the Head Contractor will not be responsible for their fitness or suitability.

In *Young & Marten v McManus Childs*,[26] the House of Lords held that the choice of tiles made by only one manufacturer excluded the warranty of fitness but was not sufficient to exclude the implication of a warranty of quality in the head contract, so that the Head Contractor was liable for latent defects in the tiles. Lord Pearce expressed his view thus:

> It is frequent for builders to fit baths, sanitary equipment, central heating and the like, encouraging their clients to choose from the wholesales' display rooms the bath or sanitary fittings which they prefer. It would, I think, surprise the average householder if it were suggested that simply by exercising a choice he had lost all right of recourse in respect of quality of the fittings against the builder who normally has a better knowledge of these matters.
>
> Of course, if a builder warned him against a particular fitting or manufacturer and he persisted in his choice, he would obviously be doing so at his own risk. And a builder can always make it clear that he is not prepared to take responsibility for a particular kind of fitting or material.

In the case of *Gloucestershire Country Council v Richardson*,[27] the Head Contractor discovered, during the course of construction works, defects in pre-cast concrete columns provided by a nominated supplier. The form of contract (RIBA form, 1939 edition) did not permit the Contractor to object to the terms of the nominated supply contract, which was subject to a limitation of liability. It was held that the Head Contractor was not liable for the quality (or the fitness) of the components and was not therefore in breach of contract. Lord Wilberforce held:

> The design, materials, specification, quality and price were fixed between the employer and the sub-supplier without any reference to the contractor: and so far from being expected to secure conditions or warranties from the sub-supplier, he had imposed upon him special conditions which severely restricted the extent of his remedy. Moreover, as reference to the head contract shows, he had no right to object to the nominated supplier. . . . In these circumstances, so far from there being a good reason to imply in contract . . . a condition or warranty binding the contractor in respect of latently defective goods, the indications drawn from the conduct of the contracting parties are strongly against any such thing.

10.5.10 Repudiation by nominated subcontractor

A further problem arises if a nominated subcontractor repudiates. Is the Contractor itself obliged to complete the work at its own expense, so far as this exceeds the agreed subcontract price, or must the Employer pay the additional cost of finding an alternative

26 [1968] 2 All ER 1169 (HL).
27 [1968] 2 All ER 1181 (HL), [1969] 1 AC 480.

subcontractor? As discussed in ¶10.5.5, in *North Western Metropolitan Regional Hospital Board v T A Bickerton and Sons*,[28] it was held that under the 1963 JCT the Architect was obliged to renominate, so that the Employer must bear the loss. The decision was based on the fact that the Contract contemplated that prime cost work could be carried out only by a nominated subcontractor. The decision may therefore apply to other forms of head contract. However, where a contract contains express provisions dealing with parties' rights upon the default of a nominated subcontractor, there may be little application for the *Bickerton* principle.

A combination of the preceding problems occurs if a nominated subcontractor repudiates leaving defects in partly completed work. If the facts are similar to the *Young & Marten* case, the Head Contractor would be liable for the quality of the subcontractor's work. However, in *Fairclough v Rhuddlan BC*,[29] the Head Contractor was *prima facie* liable for the work of the subcontractor but was held not to be under any responsibility for defects discovered after the subcontractor had repudiated. The decision relied on the principle established in the *Bickerton* case, that the Head Contractor had neither the right nor the duty to carry out work within a prime cost sum.

Unless the Contract provides otherwise, there is no implied obligation on an Employer to make a second nomination should the first nominee subcontractor repudiate its subcontract after becoming contractually bound to the Head Contractor. Similarly, unless the Contract imposes liability on the Employer to compensate the Contractor, the Employer, in the absence of express provision, is under no duty to intervene in, advise, or direct the Head Contractor in regard to terminating the contract of the defaulting nominated subcontractor.[30]

10.6 Subcontractor's compliance with instructions

In some contracts a subcontractor is expressly required to comply with the Engineer's instructions. The subcontractor may not only undertake to carry out and complete the subcontract works in accordance with the subcontract documents, but it may also agree to conform with such directions as the Contractor may give to achieve co-ordination of progress and, impliedly, with all Engineer's instructions which are authorised by the head contract and which relate to the subcontract work. However, unless expressly provided for in the subcontract, the Engineer is not empowered to issue instructions direct to the subcontractor and there is no obligation on the subcontractor to obey them if they are issued.

There may be special provisions in the subcontract as to what procedure is to be followed if the subcontractor fails to comply with the Engineer's instruction properly issued through the Contractor or the Contractor's own directions. The primary question is whether Contractors' claims for delay or disruption can be offset against sums certified as due to a subcontractor. In *Dawnays v F G Minter & Trollope and Colls Ltd*[31] the Court of Appeal

28 [1970] 1 All ER 1039 (HL); 68 LGR 447 (HL).
29 [1983] 3 Con LR 30.
30 *James Longley v Reigate Borough Council* (1982) 22 BLR 31 (CA).
31 [1971] 2 All ER 1389, 2 Lloyd's Reg 192 (1970) 1 BLR 16.

held that there could be no deductions from certified sums apart from those specifically authorised by the Contract.[32]

For that reason, Contractors' own forms, such as that in *Gilbert-Ash (Northern) Ltd v Modern Engineering (Bristol) Ltd*,[33] nearly always include an express right of deduction from certified sums.

10.7 Repudiation

If a subcontractor removes itself and its staff completely from the Site,[34] that will readily be held to be a repudiation by conduct. However, complete suspension of all work does not amount to evidence of an intention to repudiate the contract if there is a reason for it.

In *F Treliving & Co Ltd v Simplex Time Recorder Co (UK) Ltd*,[35] a subcontractor threatened to suspend work, and did so substantially because its claim for disruption (which had been agreed and promised) was not met. Judge Stabb took the view that the use of the words 'suspend the works,' far from being a repudiation of the contract, was a positive affirmation of it: 'Suspend eliminates the essential quality for repudiation by refusal to go on and introduces a temporary quality into the stop.'

Similarly, in *Hill (JM) & Sons Ltd v London Borough of Camden*,[36] a Contractor was held to be entitled to suspend the Works because it was not being paid certified sums and its claims for loss and/or expense were being ignored by the Architect. The Employer purported to determine the subcontractor's employment under clause 27 of JCT 1963, but the Employer served the notices, not the Architect. They were held to be invalid, as was the determination. Moreover, the Contractor was held to have reasonable grounds for suspending the work.

Such breaches of Contract, as they are not repudiatory breaches, do not entitle the innocent party to refuse to perform its own obligations.

10.8 Refusal to indemnify the Contractor

Where a subcontractor or supplier of goods refuses to enter into a subcontract in which it will indemnify the Contractor, the Head Contractor will be well advised to avoid using such subcontractor or supplier.

As stated earlier, there is no privity of contract between the Employer and the subcontractor. The contractual relationship is between Employer and the Head Contractor, with the result that the Head Contractor is liable to the Employer for defects in a subcontractor's work and materials. This applies even where the Head Contractor waives its rights by entering into a

32 The case was subjected to some criticism in *Gilbert-Ash (Northern) Ltd v Modern Engineering Bristol Ltd* ([1974] AC 689 (HL)) by the Lords of Appeal in Ordinary. The principle of *Dawnay's* case was, however, reaffirmed by the Court of Appeal shortly afterwards in *Kilby and Gayford Ltd v Selincourt Ltd* [1973] 229 Estates Gazette 1343 (1976) 3 BLR 104 (CA), and accepted by the House of Lords in *Mottram Consultants Ltd v Bernard Sunley & Sons Ltd* [1975] 2 Lloyd's Rep 197 (1976) 2 BLR 31 (1975) 118 SJ 808.

33 [1974] AC 689 (HL).

34 For example, *Marshall v Mackintosh* (1898) 78 LT 750, 46 WR 580, 14 TLR 458.

35 (1981, unreported).

36 (1981) 18 BLR 31.

subcontract negotiated by the Employer's agent which deprives it of its rights against the subcontractor; see *Young & Marten Ltd v McManus Childs Ltd.*[37]

In order to overcome the difficulties raised by a subcontractor's refusal to indemnify the Contractor and the absence of privity of contract between Employer and subcontractor, particularly in the case of a nominated subcontractor, a direct contract between the subcontractor and the Employer should be considered. A condition of the nomination by the Employer of a specialist as a subcontractor to the Head Contractor would be that the specialist would guarantee performance of the subcontract directly to the Employer and in parallel with its obligation to the Head Contractor.

In addition to performance, where the Head Contractor initially carries no design liability towards the Employer and the Employer later wishes to nominate a specialist to carry out a design, supply and install subcontract, the most convenient way of protecting the Employer in the event of the Head Contractor's refusal to accept design liability would be for the nominated subcontractor to provide a guarantee in respect of such design directly in favour of the Employer.

10.9 Collateral contracts of warranty

There can be a collateral contract of warranty between a nominated subcontractor and an Employer. Even if there is no contractual relationship between an Employer and a nominated subcontractor or supplier, there may be an unwritten collateral contract of warranty, the terms of which are, in essence: 'If you nominate me or specify my goods, I warrant to you that they will be fit for the purpose I have held them out to be.'

However, a collateral contract of warranty must be proved by evidence that it was so intended. In *Heilbut Symons & Co v Buckleton*,[38] Lord Moulton said that collateral contracts 'must be proved strictly. Not only the terms of such contracts but the existence of an *animus contrahendi* on the part of all the parties to them must be clearly shown.'

In *Shanklin Pier Ltd v Detel Products Ltd*,[39] a pier company was induced to specify the use of a certain paint because of statements made by the manufacturers that it would be proof against sea damage. When it failed, the Employer succeeded in an action against the manufacturers on the grounds of a collateral contract of warranty.

10.10 Payment to subcontractors

10.10.1 Direct payment by the Employer

Usually, payment is made by the Employer to the Head Contractor, who in turn will pay the various subcontractors for the work that they have carried out. Direct payment is not normally made by the Employer to subcontractors.

The issue arises as to what happens when the Head Contractor refuses or is unable to make payment to its subcontractors. The terms of the head contract may permit (but not require) the Employer to make direct payment to subcontractors if the Head Contractor does

37 [1968] 2 All ER 1169 (HL).
38 (1913) AC 30.
39 [1951] 2 All ER 471, [1951] 2 KB 854, [1951] 2 Lloyd's Rep 187.

not make payment of the amounts due and payable to subcontractors. The subcontractor will not have an enforceable right to payment against the Employer unless there is a distinct agreement between the Employer and subcontractor which requires the Employer to make payment to such subcontractor. This is because there is no privity of contract between the Employer and the subcontractor.[40]

Terms of the head contract entitling the Employer to make direct payment to a subcontractor usually involve nominated subcontractors (discussed in ¶10.5.6), because the Employer will wish to ensure that cash flow to nominated subcontractors on its project is maintained and work on its project is able to continue even if the Head Contractor is unable or unwilling to continue with the Works. Care has to be taken to avoid the Employer becoming liable to pay twice for the same work and terms of this nature generally provide that if the Employer does make a direct payment to a subcontractor this will have the effect of discharging the Employer's indebtedness to the Head Contractor in the amount of the direct payment or will create a debt owed by the Head Contractor to the Employer.[41]

If an Employer makes payment to a subcontractor of an amount owed by the Head Contractor to the subcontractor, the Employer will have a right of restitution to reimbursement from the Head Contractor where the Head Contractor uses the payment made by the Employer to discharge the debt owed by the Head Contractor to the subcontractor.[42] Unless there is an agreement between the Employer and the Head Contractor that the Employer making direct payment to the subcontractor will discharge the Employer from any obligation to pay the same amount to the Head Contractor, the Employer will not be discharged from its debt to the Head Contractor.[43]

10.10.2 Mechanisms for Employer payments in the event of the Contractor's insolvency

Difficulties may arise if such contractual provisions are held to be unenforceable against the liquidator or trustee in bankruptcy of the Head Contractor. The amount payable to the Head Contractor, if paid to the subcontractor, may be regarded as a chose in action forming part of the Head Contractor's bankrupt estate at the time of winding up or bankruptcy. The basis of this objection is that the direct payment provision gives the subcontractor an unfair preference as regards the other unsecured creditors of the Head Contractor.[44]

The following are circumstances in which a means of direct payment may be applied without objection under insolvency laws because the ***pari passu*** principle of insolvency law is not violated.

40 *A Vigers Sons & Co Ltd v Swindell* [1939] 3 All ER 590, 593–594, per Asquith J; *Yew Sang Hong Ltd v Hong Kong Housing Authority* [2008] BLR 563 [HKCA]; *Sanctuary Systems Ltd v Orient International Holdings Hong Kong Co Ltd* [2014] HKCFI 243, [72] – [73] per Au-Yeng J; *Eltraco International Pte Ltd v Sennet Electrical Engineering Pte Ltd (in liq)* [2003] SGHC 40, [30], per MPH Rubin J (appeal dismissed) 4 SLR(R) 384; *Management 3 Group Pty Ltd (in liq) v Lenny's Commercial Kitchens Pty Ltd* [2011] FCAFC 162, [61].

41 *New Civilbuild Pte Ltd v Guobena Sdn Bhd* [2000] 1 SLR(R) 368, [57] – [58], per Lai Siu Chiu JC. For an example of a contract provision, see 2017 FIDIC Red Book sub-clauses 5.2.4 and 14.6.1.

42 *Re Cleadon Trust Ltd* [1939] Ch D 286; *Plaza West Pty Ltd v Simon's Earthworks (NSW) Pty Ltd* [2008] NSWSC 753, [71], per Hammerschlag J (affirmed [2008] NSWCA 279.

43 *Hoo Cheong Building Construction Co Ltd v Jade Union Investment Ltd* [2004] HKCFI 21, [46], per Barma J.

44 The Singapore *Security of Payment* legislation permits an Employer to make direct payment to the claimant for an adjudicated amount that is unpaid by the respondent.

An express trust may be used. This involves the creation of an express trust over money paid by an Employer to a Head Contractor, in favour of the subcontractors of the Head Contractor. It is dependent upon the establishment of the necessary intention to create a trust, certainty as to the subject matter of the trust, and certainty as to the identities of the beneficiaries of the trust.[45] However, the certification of amounts attributable to subcontractors' work, and preconditions requiring the Head Contractor to have made payment in respect of previous certificates, does not give rise to a trust in favour of the subcontractor over monies payable or paid by the Employer to the Head Contractor.[46]

If, before a Head Contractor's insolvency, there is a direct payment agreement in place between the Employer, the Head Contractor, and the subcontractor that permits or obliges the Employer to make direct payment to the subcontractor, such an agreement will not fall foul of insolvency rules against direct payment. This is because, by making direct payment, the Employer is discharging a primary liability to the subcontractor.[47]

Where the right of the Head Contractor to payment from the Employer is conditional, and the condition entitling the Head Contractor payment has been satisfied, the Head Contractor is entitled to payment upon satisfaction of the condition, for example, the provision by it of evidence of it having paid its subcontractor for work performed. If the Contract provides that the Head Contractor does not have an entitlement to payment in respect of sums attributable to the work performed by its subcontractors if it does not provide such evidence, it does not have an entitlement to payment in respect of such sums if the evidence is not provided. The Employer may then make payment to the unpaid subcontractors and discharge of the unpaid amounts with the result that the Head Contractor is not entitled to payment of such amounts from the Employer.[48] In these circumstances, the *pari passu* principle of insolvency law is not violated because the money that is paid directly to the subcontractor is not money in respect of which the Head Contractor may claim a proprietary right.[49]

If an Employer enters into a direct contract with the subcontractor that should the subcontractor perform the relevant work, the Employer will pay directly for that work, the subcontractor will be entitled to bring an action in contract against the Employer for payment once the work is performed, but the subcontractor will not be entitled to claim on a *quantum meruit*.[50]

---

45 *Salvo v New Tel* [2004] NSWSC 675, per McDougall J; *Glen Eight Pty Ltd v Home Building Pty Ltd* [2005] NSWSC 309, [12], per Young CJ in Eq.

46 *Veitchi & Co v Crowley Russell & Co* 1972 SC 225, 229–230, per Lord Hunter.

47 *Sydenhams (Timber Engineering) Ltd v CHG Holdings Ltd* [2007] EWHC 1129 (TCC), [87]–[89], per HHJ Coulson QC; *Brian Fabrications Ltd v Merchant City Developments Ltd* [2003] BLR 512.

48 *Re Trout and Finch Ltd* [1954] 1 All ER 127; *Re Cooper, ex parte Smith* (1965) 10 FLR 369; *Re CG Monkhouse Properties* [1968] SR (NSW) 429; *Veitchi & Co v Crowley Russell & Co* 1972 SC 225; cf *British Eagle International Airlines Ltd v Compagnie Nationale Air France* [1975] 1 WLR 758.

49 *Glow Heating Ltd v Eastern Health Board* (1988) 6 ILT 237; 8 Const LJ 56 [High Ct of Ireland]; *Golden Sand Marble Factory Ltd v Easy Success Enterprises Ltd* [1999] 2 HKC 356; Soo, 'Invoking Security in Hong Kong Construction Contracts' (2001) *ICLR* 113; Bateson and Barton, 'Subcontractor Insolvency – Issues for Head Contractors in Hong Kong' (2002) *ICLR* 540; Soo, 'Protecting Against Insolvency of Contractors in Hong Kong' (2003) 19 *Const LJ* 406, 411.

50 *Sweeting v Asplin* (1840) 7 M&W 165 [151ER 723]; *Tang Ng v Fung Kung Ha* [1962] HKLR 101; *Yee Sang Metal Supplies Co v Defag Construction Co* [1969] HKCFI 12 (affirmed [1971] UKPC 28).

10.10.3 'Pay when paid' provisions

Many Head Contractors seek to limit their own obligations to pay for work performed/materials supplied (and thus their own side of the contractual bargain) by introducing 'pay if paid,' and 'pay when paid' provisions into their subcontracts. Such provisions severely distort the contractual bargain, to the detriment of the subcontractor. They are inequitable, unfair, and legally questionable.

Where such provisions apply, the subcontractor is strictly obliged to perform its side of the bargain, but the Head Contractor's corresponding obligation is greatly reduced, being only obliged to make payment when, or if, it receives payment from the Employer. The Head Contractor is seeking a one-sided contract, under which the subcontractor must perform, but the Head Contractor will only pay when it receives payment from the Employer, or if the Employer pays at all. The subcontractor is in contract only with the Head Contractor and should be able to expect to receive payment in return for work performed. The Head Contractor's own financial arrangements and, indeed, its own contractual links with other parties (including the Employer) are irrelevant to the subcontract and should have no bearing on its obligations to its subcontractors.

In the authors' view, a Head Contractor should not subcontract unless able and willing to pay its subcontractors directly in return for work and materials supplied, in accordance with reasonable payment terms. If the Head Contractor is unable to meet its side of the bargain and accept the obligations, it should not subcontract nor expect the subcontractor to carry out work. One of the principal objections to the use of such provisions from the subcontractor's point of view is that it will leave the subcontractor unsure as to the amount and timing of payment, with no practical way of monitoring and, if necessary, enforcing the entitlement to receive payment.

As discussed in ¶9.3.4, many common law jurisdictions have now prohibited such practices by legislating against their use.[51]

The preceding said, if a subcontract provides that its payment terms are 'back-to-back' with those of the corresponding head contract, this may be sufficient to render the subcontract payment mechanism a pay-when paid-clause[52] (and unenforceable in those jurisdictions with *Security of Payment* legislation).

---

51 *Housing Grants, Construction and Regeneration Act 1996* (UK) s113; *Building and Construction Industry Security of Payment Act 1999* (NSW) s12; *Building and Construction Industry Security of Payment Act 2002* (Vic) s13; *Building and Construction Industry (Security of Payment) Act 2021* (WA) s14; *Construction Contracts (Security of Payments) Act 2004* (NT) s12; *Construction Industry (Security of Payment Act) 2009* (ACT) s14; *Building and Construction Industry Security of Payment Act 2009* (SA) s12; *Building and Construction Industry Security of Payment Act 2009* (Tas) s16; *Building Industry Fairness (Security of Payment) Act 2017* (Qld) s74; *Construction Contracts Act 2002* (New Zealand) s13; *Construction Contracts Act 2004* (Isle of Man) s10; *Building and Construction Industry Security of Payment Act 2004* (Singapore) s9; *Construction Industry Payment and Adjudication Act 2012* (Malaysia) s35; *Construction Contracts Act 2013* (Ireland); *Construction Act 1990* (Ont) ss6.5(4), 6.6(4).

52 *Massford (HK) Ltd v Wah Seng General Contractors* [2005] HKCA 425; *Tim Lee Construction Engineering Co Ltd v Kwong Wah* [2012] HKCFI 557, [27]–[44]; [2013] HKCA 146. Compare *Wo Hing Engineering Ltd v Pekko Engineers Ltd* [1998] HKCFI 425, [41]–[49]; *Brighton Engineering Ltd v Cheerise Asia Ltd* [2011] HKCFI 567, [52], per DHCJ Cheng SC.

10.11 Set-off

Set-off, involving the offsetting of one debt against another, is well established in common law. In building and civil engineering subcontracts the use of set-off by the Head Contractor against interim payments due to a subcontractor can often be a major cause of conflict and concern, involving, as it does, interference by the Head Contractor in the subcontractor's vital cash flow.

If a Head Contractor considers that there is, or might be, a claim against a subcontractor, it may wish to use the commercial leverage given to it by its control over the flow of money down the 'payment chain' to the subcontractor. Accordingly, it will set-off its claim against the next interim payment due to the subcontractor.

Some non-standard set-off provisions give the Head Contractor a wide and arbitrary power and put the subcontractor's cash flow at potential risk. This is particularly acute where the Head Contractor's right of set-off is not tied to any objective test, such as for example, the subcontractor's actual liability, but is instead tied to the subjective 'opinion' or 'bona fide estimate' of the Head Contractor. In this situation the Head Contractor is given a contractual right to act subjectively as judge in its own cause.

This ability to interfere in the subcontractor's cash flow is potentially open to great abuse. Some claims which Head Contractors seek to offset are genuine and sustainable, but others are at the very least questionable and some are patently spurious. The prospects of further work with the contractor, the relative inequality in financial strength, and the substantial time and cost to seek redress in court are often factors which weigh heavily on subcontractors in such situations.

Interim payments are of vital importance to the subcontractor as the basis of the cash flow (and perhaps its very solvency) upon which its continuing work on Site relies. Lord Denning, in particular, recognised its importance, saying in *Modern Engineering (Bristol) Ltd v Gilbert Ash (Northern) Limited*: 'There must be a cash-flow in the building trade. It is the very lifeblood of the enterprise.'[53]

Governments in a number of common law jurisdictions have recognised the fundamental importance of ensuring cash flow down the contractual chain by implementing *Security of Payment* legislation. As outlined in ¶4.3.4.1, such legislation provides a statutory right to progress payments and for disputes to be determined quickly, economically, and provisionally by adjudication. Where such legislation is in force, it cannot be contracted out of, and provides statutory rights (additional to any contractual rights) that a subcontractor can invoke to counteract any inappropriate withholding or set-offs by the Head Contractor.

In jurisdictions that do not have *Security of Payment* legislation, the parties to a subcontract can acknowledge the importance of cash flow to both parties by the inclusion of adjudication provisions in the subcontract whereby the subcontractor may refer any questionable set-off claim to a neutral adjudicator for a rapid interim ruling.

It is notable that the set-off provisions used by a significant number of Head Contractors still include a clause of the type which was roundly condemned in *Gilbert-Ash (Northern) Limited v Modern Engineering (Bristol) Limited* (supra). The clause in that instance provided that

53 (1973) 3 WLR 121; (1973) 71 LGR 162.

> [i]f the subcontractor fails to comply with any of the conditions of this subcontract, the contractor reserves the right to suspend or withhold payment of any monies due or becoming due to the subcontractor.

In other words, in the event of even a minor breach by the subcontractor, causing little or no financial loss, the Head Contractor would be entitled to withhold any money due, thereby extracting a penalty out of all proportion to the breach. The court confirmed unequivocally that such penalty clauses cannot be supported by the courts and are unenforceable. However, such clauses still regularly appear in subcontract conditions in certain quarters giving the Head Contractor a potent short-term cash flow weapon and an undue degree of arbitrary control over the subcontractor's cash flow.

10.12 Contractual abuses

Some of the many other contractual abuses to which subcontractors and suppliers are subjected include:

(1) Significant delays in receiving information about the project and serious shortcomings in the project information when it is provided. In particular, specialists are commonly invited to tender on the basis of grossly inadequate information and may often be threatened by dire consequences – including omission from future tender lists – if they wisely decline to commit themselves to give a price until full information about the project and their obligations has been made available.

(2) Arbitrary control by the Head Contractor of the time period for Completion, and of the time programme in general. In particular, some Head Contractors seek to enter into subcontracts on the basis that the time for Completion will be 'as directed by the Head Contractor,' and some seek to take arbitrary powers to 'accelerate' the subcontract work with such acceleration powers commonly tied so the Head Contractor's partial and subjective 'opinion' regarding the progress to date.

(3) Deduction of the cash discount from payments which are made late.

(4) Unrealistic and impractical – and often uninsurable – obligations on the specialist to 'protect' its work for an extended period, long after satisfactory completion of its other obligations and after leaving the Site. Such obligations are a common feature of many management contracts, together with other common features such as the obligation for the specialist to 'co-ordinate' with other specialist firms on Site.

(5) The Head Contractor's unilateral right of termination without compensation.

(6) Starving the subcontractor's cash flow with a view to forcing the subcontractor into inequitable compromises – 'wiping the slate clean' – meaning the release of payments which are properly due to the subcontractor in exchange for a waiver by the subcontractor of all claims against the Head Contractor.[54]

54 *Security of Payment* legislation is intended to avert this type of contractual abuse by Head Contractors.

A further example of common abuse is one in which the Engineer includes sums due to a nominated subcontractor. Payment of these is made to the Contractor. It considers, however, that it has been caused loss and expense by the subcontractor, so it withholds payment. The subcontractor then proceeds to sue for an order for payment. The Contractor then raises two defences: one by way of counterclaim:

- Firstly, it asserts that it has a claim against the subcontractor for a sum in excess of the certified sum.
- Secondly, it claims that there is a dispute of fact between the Contractor and the subcontractor and that by the terms of their contract this dispute must be referred to arbitration.

The Contractor may then apply to court for a stay of the proceedings. In the meantime, the subcontractor, deprived of cash flow, must get on with the subcontract, and the Contractor will remain in possession of the monies. By the terms of the contract such arbitration can often not be commenced until after Completion. This situation occurs frequently and occasions much litigation.

CHAPTER 11

Design

CONTENTS

DOI: 10.4324/9781003206873-11

11.1 General design obligations

11.1.1 What does 'design' cover?

The design of a constructed facility involves all the large and small decisions required to determine its form, how its elements work individually and in combination to fulfil their functional requirements, what materials will be used in construction, how these are connected, how the facility is to be constructed, and how it should be maintained and operated. It is the design that determines not only the form and nature of the construction but also the economic characteristics of the constructed facility, such as its durability, the ongoing operating and maintenance costs, and ultimately its commercial life.

Design should be interpreted widely to cover all plans, drawings, sketches, instructions, and descriptions that determine the way the Works (or parts of it) are to be constructed. Design includes the writing or selection of specifications as well as the production of plans and drawings and any element of choice on the part of the designer, such as requirements as to materials or working methods.[1] The 'design' may concern a small part of the Works – for example the size and form of a bracket – or the whole concept (such as, say, the process line of a process plant). Design involves choice in the work processes as well as materials:

> In a construction context, the essential element of the function of design is choice, that is, the selection of the appropriate work processes and materials to meet the indicated or presumed requirements of the owner. The due discharge of the design obligation, therefore, will depend upon and be measured by the suitability of the work and materials for their required purpose once completed and in place.[2]

The word 'design' may be contrasted with the output of the designed Works – in other words the capacity or performance of the Works. A requirement that the Works must be able to produce a certain number of articles or volume of product per hour is not its design per se, it is a functional specification of the Employer's performance requirements. However, a requirement that must be met to make a specific process work is a matter of design, for example the minimum temperature to avoid brittle fracture in a pipeline.

The designs must either be specified (in performance terms if they are to be executed by the Contractor) or be provided by the Employer or the Engineer (if the Contractor's contractual obligations are limited to construction only). A design that is provided may be developed by the Employer's engineer and presented to the Contractor in a highly developed form. The complete documentation of a design usually includes drawings in addition to written documentation such as a specification and/or operating and maintenance manuals.

---

1 I N Duncan-Wallace, *Hudson's Building and Engineering Contracts* (Sweet & Maxwell, 11th edn 1995) 293.
2 Ibid. 517.

Ordinarily, certain parts of an installation (such as, for example transformers) may not have been designed in detail by the designer of the overall facility. The question then arises as to whether the Contractor is responsible for the design of such portions of the installation. The answer to that question must be found in the contract documents and it is only if those documents provide for such design, either expressly or as a matter of reasonable inference, that the Contractor will be responsible for it. The extent of the Contractor's 'design' of such an item of plant in a design and construct contract may be confined to the detailed specification accompanying the procurement documents. Although the manufacturer carries out the detailed design of the plant, the Contractor is liable to the Employer if it is not fit for the purpose for which it was installed. In such a case, the Contractor may have recourse against the plant manufacturer, if the plant does not fulfil the requirements of the specification or contains inherent design defects. However, the Contractor's specification of functional and performance requirements may be the 'design' that is deficient, in which case the Contractor would have no recourse against the manufacturer.

11.1.2 Design and the implementation of design

One of the reasons why construction disputes frequently involve a number of parties is because the design and the implementation of design are usually performed by different legal entities, even in design and construct contracts. When a defect becomes apparent it is frequently not clear whether the defect arises from a defect in design, or a defect in construction, that is the implementation of the design. This is often significant in terms of insurance coverage, as CAR policies typically exclude occurrences arising from design defects.

Case study: The scope of design

A crane driver was injured when the jib of a crane fell on him. The jib fell because a luffing rope came away from its anchorage point and because the anchorage system of the crane did not comply with the *Inspection of Machinery Regulations*. The Contractor responsible for the design, supply, commissioning, and maintenance of the crane was insured under a products liability policy which had an exception clause that the insurer was not liable for claims in respect of bodily injury caused by or arising out of any defective design of structural steel products. In an appeal by the insurer against the finding that it was liable to indemnify the Contractor, Ryan J considered that 'design' in the sense of the policy was not confined to matters in the plans submitted to the government department to enable the chief inspector to specify the safe working load of the crane:

> The design of the product and the construction of the product itself are distinct matters. The design is an idea or conception; it is, as his Honour stated, quoting from the Oxford English Dictionary 'a plan or a scheme conceived in the mind of something to be done, the preliminary conception of an idea that is to be carried

> into effect by action.' When a decision was made on the site to fit a particular method of anchorage that involved two things: a decision on the design of the method of anchorage, and the execution of that decision by fitting that anchorage. If the design decision was not defective but its execution was it could not be said that the injury arose out of the defective design of the product. On the other hand if the design itself was defective and the injury arose from that defect the insurer could rely upon the clause to exempt itself from liability.[3]

The cause of the accident was determined from the evidence to be that the luffing rope of the crane was not anchored in accordance with the standard. The method of anchorage was a site decision after the crane had been rigged on site. Ryan J held that the cause of the accident was attributable to a defect in design, not to some defect in the execution of a design. That is, the site decision on the method of anchorage was an aspect of the design. Accordingly, the insurer was not liable because of the exception for design in the products liability policy.[4]

Distinguishing between design and the implementation of design is particularly acute in the design of tunnels using the observational method. In essence the observational method requires the design of different support types for the different types of material expected from the geotechnical investigation undertaken prior to construction. It is subject to confirmation based on the actual ground conditions encountered during tunnel excavation. Which support type is installed at any given location within the tunnel is based on the assessment of actual ground conditions encountered by a suitably qualified geologist or geotechnical engineer. Thus, the support design is not based on providing a single universal design for the worst-case condition, but rather relies on in situ geotechnical observations and mapping to vary the support locally to address variations in conditions observed in the field and the use of a range of support types designed for these variations in conditions.

Case studies: Tunnel failure a result of design or implementation of design?

In assigning liability for a tunnel failure, the question arises as to whether the selection of previously designed types of support based on the observation of geotechnical conditions encountered in the tunnel excavation is an aspect of the design or an implementation of the design. This question has been answered differently in two cases arising from tunnel failures.

In *Thiess Pty Ltd and John Holland Pty Ltd v Parsons Brinkerhoff Australia Pty Ltd*,[5] McDougall J held that the site activities of the geotechnical engineer were design obligations:

3 *Vosten v The Commonwealth* [1989] 1 Qd R 693, 708.
4 Ibid. 709.
5 [2016] NSWSC 173.

533 However, I do agree that the relevant obligations of PSM [the geotechnical site engineer] were design obligations. That seems to me to follow inevitably from the observational approach to design. The design was not something fixed immutably at the commencement of the project. It was something to be assessed and, if necessary, modified, as the project progressed. PSM's obligations under its Consultancy Agreement, as I have identified them earlier, gave it a role in that ongoing process of design.

534 First, PSM was required to assess the suitability of the support system specified in the light of conditions actually encountered. And second, PSM was required to specify the support system to be adopted, in the light of ground conditions actually encountered. Of necessity, part at least of those obligations had to be performed on site.

535 In Vosten [*Vosten v The Commonwealth* [1989] 1 Qd R 693], Ryan J (who gave the judgment of the Full Court) considered whether the specification of the method of anchorage of the luffing rope of a crane constituted 'design.' The evidence was that the decision, how to anchor the luffing rope, was one made on site once the crane had been rigged. His Honour held that the selection of a particular method of anchorage was 'a decision on the design of the method of anchorage.'

536 In my view, that analysis applies in the present case. An obligation to decide whether a specified support design is appropriate, and should continue to be used, is an integral part of the design of the support to be used. Indeed, that is so a fortiori bearing in mind the observational approach to design. And likewise, the specification of a support system to be used is an integral element of the design of that support system.[6]

In *SSE Generation Ltd v Hochtief Solutions AG*,[7] a tunnel that had been designed by the observational method suffered a substantial failure during the two-year defects liability period. The judge at first instance found the cause of the collapse to have been insufficient shotcrete and rock bolts being provided where there were poor rock conditions, even though the geologist whose rock classifications determined which type of support to use exercised reasonable skill and care. The majority in the appeal held that the geologist's designation of tunnel support was part of the implementation of the design, but was not part of the design, and was therefore not a Defect in the Works due to the Contractor's design.[8] That finding meant that the contractual provision limiting the Contractor's liability for its design to reasonable skill and care was not engaged, and the Contractor was liable for the rectification costs.

11.1.3 Contractual responsibility for design

Where the Contract documents provide for the 'design, supply, and installation' of an item, the design will be part of the work which the Contractor has expressly undertaken to perform or to have performed through a subcontractor, and for which the Contractor will be liable towards the Employer. Where, however, the Contract documents refer only

6 *Thiess Pty Ltd and John Holland Pty Ltd v Parsons Brinkerhoff Australia Pty Ltd* [2016] NSWSC 173.

7 [2018] CSIH 26 CA162/12.

8 *SSE Generation Ltd v Hochtief Solutions AG* [2018] CSIH 26 CA162/12 [349], [350] per Lord Menzies; [362], [375] per Lord Glennie.

to 'supply and installation,' an obligation to design can only arise by implication. The fact that the item concerned is one which, from its nature, obviously requires to be designed will not itself be sufficient to justify an inference that the Contractor is to be responsible for the design. On the contrary – the omission of any reference to design is *prima facie* inconsistent with the design forming part of the work which the Contractor has undertaken to do, and the proper inference will ordinarily be that such design was to be the subject of an Engineer's instruction issued in terms of the Contract. There may, of course, be cases where (notwithstanding the omission from the Contract documents of any express reference to design) the inference that the Contractor is to be responsible for the design of a specialist item may be properly drawn from the terms of the Contract. Such cases will, however, be exceptional.

Where the design is done by a subcontractor, whether nominated or otherwise (see Chapter 10 for commentary regarding nominated subcontractors), the Contractor will similarly be responsible to the Employer if the subcontractor's design work is not fit for purpose. Where a nominated subcontract is concluded, there is ordinarily no privity of contract between the Employer and the nominated subcontractor; the subcontractor makes its contract with the Head Contractor as principal, and the Employer has no recourse against the subcontractor.[9] The Employer's recourse is against the Contractor, who in turn has recourse under its subcontract against the defaulting subcontractor.

The relationship between the various parties concerned in the execution of a project is governed by the express or implied terms of the contracts which each party has with one or more of the others. In determining which party has contractual responsibility for design, the first enquiry is therefore to ascertain the parties between whom the relevant contractual relations exist, and then to look at the terms of the specific contracts and construe them. The issue of design in respect of construction contracts cannot be dealt with in the abstract but must be considered by reference to the particular contracts which are entered into between the Employer and the Head Contractor, and between the Head Contractor and its subcontractors.

The emphasis in construing the terms of the Contract must be put on the form in which the design is given to the Contractor. This usually presents no problem where the designs are provided as part of the invitation to tender or are described there and provided in complete form later, including drawings. When however, the designs are specified without drawings, the problems of interpretation may be more difficult. The Engineer or the Employer may, for instance, just specify a design by giving a fairly sketchy description of what they want in correspondence or at meetings (which may or may not be confirmed by the minutes) or just orally. Both parties are well advised to have any such vague specification clarified. At the very least the Contractor should confirm in writing as soon as possible any specification or design it thinks that it has received. The Employer and the Engineer should likewise strive to avoid any doubts as to whether any design has been specified by them or not. None of the parties will benefit from a situation where part of the liability for defects in design is not definitely allocated between them.

9 See *Hampton v Glamorgan County Council* [1917] AC 13 (HL) and *Frederick W Nielsen (Canberra) Pty Ltd v PDC Constructions (ACT) Pty Ltd* (1987) 71 ACTR 1 (1987) 3 BCL 387 which followed *Hampton* on this point.

Thus, where all the Contractor has to do is to execute and complete the Works shown on the drawings and described in the bills of quantities and specification supplied by the Employer, the Contractor is usually not liable for design unless the Contract specifically refers to a design requirement from the Contractor. This principle has been summarised as follows:

> If a skilled person promises to do a job, that is, to produce a particular thing, whether a house or a motor car or a piece of machinery, and he makes no provision, as a matter of bargain, as to the precise structure or article which he will create, then it may well be that the buyer of the structure or article relies on the judgment and skill of the other party to produce that which he says he will produce. That, however, is only another way of formulating the existence in such circumstances of an implied warranty. On the other hand, if two parties elected to make a bargain which specifies in precise detail what one of them will do, then, in the absence of some other express provision, it would appear to me to follow that the bargain is that which they have made; and so long as the party doing the work does that which he has contracted to do, that is the extent of his obligation.[10]

11.1.4 Breach of design obligation

In the case where nothing is stated either in the head contract or in the specialist subcontract documentation about any design function which may have to be undertaken by the subcontractor, the engineer engaged by the Employer cannot usually divest itself of its design responsibility.[11] If an engineer undertakes to design a structure for reward, it undertakes that the various parts of the project will be properly designed with the necessary skill and care required for those parts of the work, whether the skill demanded is a strictly engineering skill or not. To this extent it guarantees the professional competence of those to whom it chooses to delegate its function. There is no difficulty in this approach in the case of the Employer's own engineering consultants, against whom it will have contractual recourse in the event of a design failure. However, the Employer's engineer will not have any such recourse in the case of design carried out by a subcontractor to the Contractor. In the engineer's own as well as the Employer's interest, the Contractor should therefore obtain express guarantees of the suitability of the work and its design from a subcontractor in favour of the Employer and of itself.

The measure of damage for breach of the design obligation will obviously differ widely according to the nature of the breach; it may be nominal if the error can be rectified simply at an early stage; it may be for loss of value or loss of commercial profitability in the case of a non-fundamental suitability breach and will usually be the cost of repair or replacement in the case of a fundamental breach.

It is generally the case that the Contractor has a duty to notify the Employer or the Engineer of designs provided which it considers defective or otherwise inadequate. This may be an explicit duty under the Contract or may arise under the common law. The 2017 FIDIC Red Book provides that each Party shall advise the other and the Engineer of any known or probable future events which may have adverse effects; these include design defects that adversely affect the performance of the Works when completed.[12] Similarly the

---

10 *Lynch v Thorne* [1956] 1 All ER 744 (CA) 744, 748 per Lord Evershed MR.

11 *Moresk v Hicks* [1966] 2 Lloyd's Rep 338.

12 Sub-clause 8.4.

NEC4 ECC requires the *Contractor* and the *Project Manager* to give an early warning of any matter that could impair the performance of the *works* in use, which clearly includes design defects.[13] This complex area of the law was discussed by Hayford.[14]

If a designer does not have the necessary expertise, it is proper for it to inform the client accordingly and either itself engage, or to advise the Employer to engage, a person with the required expertise.[15] In *Young v Tomlinson*,[16] architects were held negligent in the design of a wall which was defective 'owing to the architect having moved a little out of their specialised field' and in not having sought the advice of structural engineers for the design.

11.1.5 Site investigation

The Site must be examined by the designer before the design is prepared. Whilst not limiting the extent of such inspection, the designer would firstly look for all things that are readily apparent on the Site which might affect its design and, secondly, ascertain the nature and load-bearing capacity of the foundation material. In this latter regard it usual to engage a specialised geotechnical engineer to perform the tests and to prepare a report.

Case study: Geotechnical investigations are normally required

In *Eames London Estates v North Herts District Council*,[17] a designer agreed with the local authority's building inspector that three-quarters of a ton per square foot bearing capacity was the load that the local authority wanted for this particular Site. The whole of the Site of the structure was on made-up ground and on part of the Site there had been an old railway embankment which was well consolidated. The designer did not obtain bore-holes or advise that bore-holes should be taken or that specialist engineer's advice be obtained. Although the Site was filled, the ordinance survey map showed that a railway crossed only part of the Site. Evidence was given at the trial that a proper investigation would have indicated that simple shallow foundations would be bound to lead to serious uneven and continuing settlement. It was held that the designer could not shed his responsibility by ascertaining what the local authority would accept. Specifying three quarters of a ton per square foot indicated that he appreciated the inferior nature of the ground and he was therefore put on enquiry that further investigation or specialist design was required. The designer was held to be negligent:

> I consider it normal practice for an architect (or engineer/designer) to draw his client's attention to the need for ground conditions to be investigated; also for the client to be advised of the possible need to carry out a detailed site investigation if the architect (or engineer/designer) was uncertain in any way of the type and bearing capacity of the ground.

13 Sub-clause 15.1.

14 Hayford, Owen, 'Watch out! The Duty to Warn on Construction Projects' (2008) 24 *Building and Construction Law* 163.

15 See *Equitable Debenture Assets Corporation Limited v Moss (William) Group Limited* (1984) 2 Con. L.R. 1; (1984) 1 Const. L.J.131 QBD (OR); *Moresk Cleaners Limited v Hicks* [1966] 2 Lloyd's Rep 338.

16 [1979] 2 NZLR 441.

17 [1980] 259 EG 491.

Similarly, a designer who accepts the results of borings taken by someone engaged by its employer will not necessarily escape liability if its design is inadequate based upon those borings. In *Moneypenny v Hartland*,[18] an engineer was held negligent in failing to examine the nature of the soil in which to place foundations for a bridge. As a result, he had grossly underestimated the cost of construction. In *Columbus v Clowes*,[19] an architect was held negligent in failing to measure and survey a site himself. In consequence he had drawn plans and specifications on the basis of dimensions smaller than the actual dimensions of the Site. In both cases the error had resulted from relying on inaccurate information supplied by a third person, but the court held that it was the duty of the engineer or architect to ascertain the information for himself.

The architect or engineer must be alive to problems which might arise during the construction phase. Notwithstanding having taken care to obtain sufficient information about subsoil conditions for the purpose of the initial design, the designer will be liable if it fails to confirm those conditions during its supervision of the work. Extensive tests might even be required at this stage and allowance is very often made in the bills of quantities for the professional to instruct the Contractor to obtain such tests. Indeed, on contracts where soil conditions and compaction are significant elements, such as major roadworks, a soils laboratory is often established on site.

A designer is not only restricted to considerations which pertain to the specific Site in question but must look beyond the Site to the neighbouring land in circumstances where a careful and competent designer would have observed defects in adjoining land or where it would not have built until there had been a further site investigation or an expert's report of the condition of the subsoil. Issues such as the effect on the water-table, lateral support afforded to the adjoining land, and the right to install rock-anchors should also be considered. The effect of vegetation and extremely dry or wet weather on soil movement also needs to be taken into account in preparing foundation designs that will preclude unacceptable settlement or heaving of structures. For example, in *Balcomb & another v Wards Construction (Medway) Limited*, it was said:

> I find the conclusion inescapable that in 1971 a competent engineer encountering London clay as in this case would have made enquiries whether there had been trees on the site and finding that there had been would have caused moisture content and plastic limit tests to be carried out. Had that course been taken it is not disputed and there can be no doubt that [the designer] would have advised that the proposed foundations were inadequate.[20]

The exercise of reasonable care may require the designer to make reasonable enquiries concerning the rights of neighbours, for example whether there are any restrictions on the use to which the Site may be put. In the event of the designer not undertaking such an investigation it would be prudent to warn the client that it has not done so, as all of the preceding may give rise to claims for which the Employer may be liable to the Contractor under the Contract.

18 [1826] 1 C&P 352.
19 [1903] 1 KB 244.
20 [1981] 25D 765.

The designer should ensure that it informs its client of the consequences of the design it has prepared, and if necessary, ensure that the Employer makes fully informed decisions where there are possible tradeoffs between implementation cost and risk. Whilst there are inevitable risks in adopting novel designs, failure is not necessarily evidence of negligent design. In a case brought by an Employer against his architect who had specified a novel patented roof design (which cost only a quarter of the cost of a conventional roof), the judge noted:

> But if out of ordinary course, and you employ him about a novel thing, about which he has had little experience, if it has not had the test of experience, failure may be consistent with skill. The history of all great improvements shows failure of those who embark in them; this may account for the defect of roof.[21]

However, if the designer proposes a design alternative to reduce the cost, it should advise the Employer of possible risks. In one case, consulting engineers designed a swimming pool with slab foundations on silt notorious for its settlement, on the basis that it was cheaper than piled foundations. The Employer was not consulted on the choice of foundation design, nor advised of the possibility of differential settlement in the slab foundations constructed. After the slab foundations failed the consulting engineer was found liable in negligence. The court noted the designer's obligation to advise the Employer of alternative designs in the following terms:

> If the only foolproof method of dealing with the possibility of settlement of the kind that has happened was piling the whole centre, and if that course was or might be feasible, we consider that the respondent [designer] ought reasonably to have put that course before the appellant [Employer] for its consideration coupled (if appropriate) with an investigation into feasibility.
>
> . . .
>
> If it was not possible to pile the whole centre and the only foolproof method of dealing with the problem was to move to another site, again the respondent ought reasonably to have put that course before the appellant for its consideration.[22]

11.1.6 Liability for choice of materials and fitness for purpose

Designers are under the same duty in selecting materials as they generally are in relation to design, and they will incur liability to their client if they select materials without reasonable skill and care. They should make their own enquiries as to the suitability of materials or products and should not rely on manufacturers' literature or recommendations. If they do not do so, they risk being in breach of duty.

A designer who selects materials and specifies them so that the Contractor has no choice as to what materials to buy will remove the Employer's cause of action against the Contractor in respect of the implied warranty of fitness for purpose. The Employer can still rely on the implied warranty as to quality, at least in cases where the defect complained of

21 *Turner v Garland and Christopher* (1853) Alfred A Hudson, *Hudson's Fourth Edition Table of Cases* (Sweet & Maxwell, 4th edn 1914) 1, 2.

22 *Pullen v Gutteridge Haskins & Davey Pty Ltd* [1991] 1 VR 27, 52, 53 per Brooking, Tadgell and Hayne JJ.

is one of quality rather than fitness for purpose. The problem cannot be avoided by adding a qualification 'or other approved' material as that has been interpreted as simply affording the designer a latitude of choice.[23]

In *Sealand of the Pacific v Robert C McHaffie Limited*,[24] naval architects were retained by Sealand to make some alterations in an underwater aquarium. A supplier of concrete products recommended a certain product to Sealand and, subsequently, to McHaffie. The use of the product for the purpose recommended was unusual and, in the event, proved unsuitable. In the action by Sealand against the supplier of the product, against McHaffie, and against an employee of McHaffie, the supplier was held liable, but the actions against McHaffie and the employee were dismissed. On appeal it was held that the cross-appeal of Sealand against the dismissal of its action against McHaffie should be allowed. McHaffie owed Sealand a contractual duty to make further enquiries and not simply to rely on the supplier's recommendations. Such further enquiries would have revealed the unsuitability of the product for its proposed use.

The Employer should be aware that the obligation relating to materials is sometimes diminished contractually, for example, that the architect 'shall not be responsible for any material component, system, or workmanship, or failure to perform in accordance with the claims of the manufacturers, suppliers, contractors or subcontractors.'

11.1.7 Providing a misleading estimate to the Employer

Reasonable care and skill must be exercised in making an estimate of the construction cost. In *Moneypenny v Hartland*[25] the engineer was held responsible for a mistake made in its estimate. A similar conclusion was reached in *Savage v Board of School Trustees*.[26]

Where there is a limit placed on the construction budget by the Employer and the tenders do not come within the estimate because of negligence, a designer might well lose its fees – see *Nicolaides v Skordiss*.[27] The designer should consider whether the budget limit is likely to be exceeded and, if so, warn its Employer before tenders are called.

In Australia, the expression of a designer's estimate of construction cost would usually convey the opinion that it is honestly held on rational grounds involving an application of relevant expertise. If those elements were not in fact present, the designer could be liable for misleading or deceptive conduct in breach of the *Australian Consumer Law*.[28] See ¶4.4.3.2 for a case in which an architect engaged in misleading and deceptive conduct in preparing a cost estimate.

---

23 *Leedsford Limited v Bradford Corporation* (March 1960, unreported); *Young & Marten Ltd v McManus Childs Ltd* [1968] 2 All E.R. 1169 (HL).

24 (1974) 51 DLR (3rd) at 702.

25 [1826] 1 C&P 352.

26 [1951] 3 DLR 39.

27 (1973) (2) SA 370 (N).

28 For example *Bateman v Slatyer* (1987) 71 ALR 553, 559; *MGCIA (1992) Ltd v Kenny & Good Pty Ltd* (1996) 70 FCR 236.

11.2 Fitness for purpose

11.2.1 Design contract

In the absence of an express warranty in respect of fitness for purpose in a contract between a designer (engineer or architect) and the Employer, the designer must exercise the degree of skill, care, and diligence of an ordinary competent person practising that profession. The common law does not require that the designer warrant that the design will be fit for its intended purpose, only that s/he will exercise due skill and care.[29]

As an example of the distinction between the exercise of due skill, care, and diligence and a fit for purpose design, in the case of *Manufacturers Mutual Insurance Limited v The Queensland Government Railways*,[30] a railway bridge collapsed in an unprecedented flood because the piers had insufficient strength to withstand the forces they were subjected to. The High Court held that, although the design was not negligent, it was 'faulty' as the existing engineering knowledge was inadequate, and accordingly the insurance exclusion for faulty design operated to deny indemnity for the loss. This is apparently a case in which the design was executed with professional skill in accordance with accepted engineering practice, yet the Employer suffered loss because the design was not fit for its purpose. Other examples in which the design was not fit for purpose notwithstanding that it was prepared with reasonable skill and care are discussed in ¶6.12.1 (*MT Højgaard a/s v E.ON Climate and Renewables UK Robin Rigg East Ltd*[31]) and ¶11.1.2 (*SSE Generation Ltd v Hochtief Solutions AG*[32]).

11.2.2 Contractor's design

The situation is different however in respect of any design for which the Contractor is responsible. In that case, the common law position is that the Contractor warrants that the design will be fit for its intended purpose. The exercise of due skill and care alone may be insufficient in such a case, as a design that fails in some way will not be fit for purpose notwithstanding that the designer may have exercised due skill and care.

The principle of the Contractor's liability for fitness for purpose of any design it is responsible for has been expressed as follows:

> Unlike a warranty of good workmanship, a warranty that the work will answer the purpose for which it is intended is not implied in every contract for work. The essential element for implication of such a term is that the Employer should be relying, to the knowledge of the contractor, upon the latter's skill and judgment and not upon his own or those of his agents.[33]

A design and construct contract is characterised by an express provision that the Contractor is responsible for the overall design. On the other hand, a 'traditional' construct only construction contract usually has no express provisions relating to design. The extent

29 *Voli v Inglewood Shire Council* (1962–1963) 110 CLR 74, 84.
30 (1968) 118 CLR 314.
31 [2017] UKSC 59.
32 [2018] CSIH 26 CA162/12.
33 *Corben v Hayes* (Unreported, Full Court of NSW, 27 April 1964), cited in *McKone v Johnson* [1966] 2 NSWLR 471.

to which the Contractor or a subcontractor is responsible for the overall design in the absence of an express provision therefore depends upon whether such an undertaking is implied in the construction contract.

11.2.2.1 FIDIC contracts

The Contractor prepares the design under the 2017 FIDIC Yellow Book which has an explicit fitness for purpose obligation:

> When completed, the Works (or Section or Part or major item of Plant, if any) shall be fit for the purpose(s) for which they are intended, as defined and described in the Employer's Requirements (or, where no purpose(s) are so defined and described, fit for their ordinary purpose(s)).[34]

The 2017 FIDIC Red Book may specify that the Contractor shall design any part of the Permanent Works, in which case:

> the Contractor shall be responsible for this part and it shall, when the Works are completed, be fit for such purpose(s) for which the part is intended as are specified in the Contract (or, where no purpose(s) are so defined and described, fit for their ordinary purpose(s)).[35]

11.2.2.2 NEC4 ECC contract

A different approach to design by the Contractor is taken by NEC4 ECC, which states that it 'should be used for the appointment of a contractor for engineering and construction work, including any level of design responsibility.' It can therefore be used for a traditional construct only contract in which the Employer is responsible for the design, a design and construct contract in which the Contractor is responsible for the design, or any combination of Employer design/Contractor design in between. The Contractor's design obligations are provided in clause 21.1: 'The Contractor designs the parts of the works which the Scope states the Contractor is to design.' Design of Equipment is provided for in clause 23.1: 'The Contractor submits particulars of the design of an item of Equipment to the Project Manager for acceptance if the Project Manager instructs the Contractor to.' Optional clause X15 The Contractor's design provides in X15.1 that it is 'not liable for a Defect which arose from its design unless it failed to carry out that design using the skill and care normally used by professionals designing works similar to the *works*.'

If optional clause X15 is included in an NEC4 ECC contract, the Contractor will not have an obligation to provide a design that is reasonably fit for the purpose made known to the Contractor, as the lesser standard of due skill and care will apply. If optional clause X15 is not included, the Contractor's fit for purpose obligations will depend on the specific wording of the Scope (information which specifies and describes the *works* or states any constraints on how the *Contractor* Provides the Works[36]) and the applicable law. The Scope should therefore define the extent of the Contractor's design obligations and state

34 Sub-clause 4.1.
35 Sub-clause 4.1(e).
36 NEC4 ECC clause 11.2 (16).

the purpose of the design work. It should be carefully worded to ensure that other parts of the Scope are not inconsistent with a fitness for purpose obligation if that is required.

11.2.3 Supply of materials

In a construction contract, in addition to plant, the Contractor will be required to supply materials to be incorporated in the permanent works. As regards the Contractor's responsibility for materials installed, as a general rule:

> a person contracting to do work and supply materials warrants that the materials which he uses will be of good quality and reasonably fit for the purpose for which he is using them unless the circumstances of the contract are such as to exclude any such warranty.[37]

The warranty of fitness for purpose will usually be excluded and the Contractor will not be responsible where the Contractor is required to supply articles of a particular brand:

> A man goes to a repairer and says 'Repair my car; get the parts from the maker of the car and fit them.' In such a case it is made plain that the person ordering the repairs is not relying on any warranty except that the parts used will be parts ordered and obtained from the maker. On the other hand, if he says: 'Do this work, fit any necessary parts,' then he is in no way limiting the person doing the repair work, and the person doing the repair work is, in my view, liable if there is any defect in the material supplied, even if it was one which reasonable care could not have discovered.[38]

If the make of an item is specified either in the Contract documents or by an Engineer's instruction, the Contractor will usually not be responsible for its design, safety, or adequate functioning if it should turn out that the item is unsuitable. However, even where the Engineer or Employer has selected an item, the Contractor will be liable in the event that it is not fit for purpose if it has provided a warranty that the items to be used will be free of defects – see ¶9.1.8 earlier. Where the Contractor itself selects the item, it will be responsible for the item's fitness for purpose.

11.3 Design life and service life

11.3.1 Design of constructed facilities

Those responsible for the design of constructed facilities are constrained by, *inter alia*, the laws of physics; the known, available, and usable mathematics; and the known 'state of the art' of the relevant technology. Notwithstanding the continual advances in technology and the state of the art, the design of facilities will continue to create new frontiers and reveal hitherto unknown gaps in our knowledge. In this book **state of the art** refers to the art and science that would be applied by competent and experienced practitioners involved in the

37 *Myers (G H) & Co v Brent Cross Service Co* [1934] 1 KB 46, 51 per Du Parcq J, approved in *Helicopter Sales (Aust) Pty Ltd v Rotor-Work Pty Ltd* (1974) 4 ALR 77, 82.

38 *Myers (G H) & Co v Brent Cross Service Co* [1934] 1 KB 46, 51 per du Parcq J.

relevant practice of engineering at that time, not necessarily the science of engineering as known to academics researching at the cutting edge of known technology.

Notwithstanding the availability of cheap and extremely powerful computing facilities, and the evolution of new technologies such as artificial intelligence, in the writers' view, the design of facilities will (at least for the foreseeable future) rely on the skill and professionalism (including both art and science) of engineers and other professional practitioners.[39] We can reasonably expect and require that those professionals be trained, skilled, experienced, and up to date with the state of the art as defined earlier. Does that mean that they can 'guarantee' a specific outcome in respect of the facilities they design? Specifically, can a designer, using up-to-date and state of the art knowledge, guarantee that a facility will have a specific service life in every situation?

All constructed facilities (buildings, infrastructure, structures, and equipment for the extraction of natural resources or for the processing of natural resources into manufactured products etc) are designed on the basis of certain assumptions, to perform specific functions over a service life (which may be implicit). The required functions, required service life, and assumptions made for the design of a facility will be referred to as the **design parameters**. A facility as a whole, and its individual components, must be designed individually and collectively so as to comply with the design parameters.

Whilst certain design parameters may be precisely known or are able to be calculated, many parameters can only be estimated on the basis of mathematical calculations, statistical measurement, experiment, or engineering experience. For example, the required functionality may be capable of precise definition (eg a power station required to generate 500MW of power at a 90% availability for a service life of 30 years), whereas other parameters fundamental to the design may have to be determined by experiment, for example the practically achievable thermal efficiency of the coal fuelling the power station. Important design parameters arising from the forces of nature, such as wind loading, earthquake loading, or the maximum anticipated flood level, are generally determined on the basis of professional consensus based on experience at the relevant location and statistical analysis of the available records.

11.3.2 Service life

As defined here, the **service life** of a constructed facility is the time that it is in functional operation. The service life can only ultimately be determined in retrospect, that is at the end of the functional life of the facility. From the prospective view of a contract for the construction of a facility, the Employer will have a service life in mind that it requires (and expects) the facility to achieve. The **required service life** is the service life specified by the Employer, for example the Technical Requirements for the Robin Rigg wind farms in the Solway Firth between England and Scotland required that 'All parts of the Works, except wear parts and consumables shall be designed for a minimum service life 20 years.'[40]

39 The 1828 Royal Charter Institution of Civil Engineers defined civil engineering as the 'art of directing the great sources of power in nature for the use and convenience of man.'

40 *MT Hojgaard A/S v E.ON Climate and Renewables UK Robin Rigg* [2015] EWCA Civ 407, [35].

The service life of a facility is of fundamental importance to the long-term owner of that facility since it is required to deliver an economic return over its service life. Further, the facility may have to be replaced when it is no longer functional. Long-term facility owners are usually interested in long service lives, subject always to the economics of procurement and available funding. A rational decision on the optimum required service life for a long-term owner would be determined on the basis of the minimum net present value:

> Fenwick and Rotolone (2003) explored the economics of service life for civil infrastructure from a long term asset owner's perspective. They adopted the AASHTO (2006) definition of service life as the period of time that the structure is expected to be in operation, and considered a simple example of a culvert, exploring service lives between 30 and 300 years. For almost all cases over a range of feasible interest rates, a service life of 300 years before replacement proved to be the most economical outcome on a net present value basis.[41]

The determination of the net present value of a facility includes consideration of the operational costs:

> In targeting a service life performance for a structure, the asset owner needs to be aware not only of the initial cost of creating the structure, but its service life and the long term cost of maintaining and repairing it over that service life, and finally its replacement cost.[42]

The required service life is one of the objectives of the design process, and will usually coincide with the design life:

> A service life performance must be formulated into specific design criteria to provide the designer with objectives for the design which are then encapsulated in specification requirements that must be met by the builder during the construction. The codes usually define a design life that implies a particular service life regarded by society as acceptable. For example, AS5100 (2004) [Australian Standard for Bridge Design] adopts a design life of 100 years. BS5400.1 (1988) [British Standard code of practice for the design and construction of steel, concrete and composite bridges – General Statement] assumes a design life of 120 years and AASHTO [American Association of State Highway and Transportation Officials] (2006) is based on a design life of 75 years. It is usual to simply apply these codes and standards that imply a particular assumption of service life performance. These are based on current materials and technologies and perhaps inhibit achieving very long service lives through the use of new materials or combinations of materials and new technologies.[43]

The required service life is ultimately the choice (explicit or implicit) of the sponsor (or funder) of a project. A required service life in excess of the norm is implicit in an explicit specification of design life in the relevant contract. For example, the second Gateway Bridge over the Brisbane River in Brisbane, Australia, was required to have a design life of 300 years, a world first and far in excess of the typical 50- to 100-year design life of infrastructure in Australia.

---

41 John Connal & Marita Berndt, 'Sustainable Bridges – 300 Year Design Life for Second Gateway Bridge' www.outokumpu.com/SiteCollectionDocuments/Research-paper-Susstainable%20Bridges.pdf (accessed 13 August 2015).

42 Ibid.

43 Ibid.

11.3.3 Design life

A facility is designed, implicitly or explicitly, to perform for its intended purpose with expected maintenance but without major repair being necessary for a certain period of time, defined here as **design life**. Design life is thus the expected service life that results from the design process. For example, in the context of structural design, Australian Standard AS1170.0:2002[44] defines design working life as:

> Duration of the period during which a structural element, when designed, is assumed to perform for its intended purpose with expected maintenance but without major structural repair being necessary.
>
> NOTE: In the context of this Standard, the design working life is a 'reference period' usually stated in years. It is a concept that can be used to select the probability of exceedance of different actions [sets of concentrated or distributed forces acting on a structure (direct action) or deformation imposed on a structure or constrained within (indirect action)].

A design and construct contract may specify a design life for specific components, for example the headrace tunnel for the Glendoe hydroelectric scheme in Scotland was required to have a design life of 75 years.[45] The following example in a design specification for sewerage lagoons defines the requirement for both design life and service life:

> All equipment shall be designed and constructed to have a working life of at least 15 years, working 24 hours a day, 365 days per year. Valves and pipework shall be designed and constructed of materials that shall have a design life of 30 years. Structures such as concrete and steel shall be designed and constructed of materials that have a design life of 50 years and be maintenance free for 50 years.[46]

The requirement that structures shall be designed and constructed of materials to have a design life of 50 years and be maintenance free for 50 years arguably includes a specification of both design life of 50 years (explicit) and a required service life of 50 years (implicit in 'maintenance free for 50 years').

As indicated earlier, the design life is an outcome of the design process using current state of the art design techniques, taking into account a range of relevant factors such as site information, prevailing environmental conditions, durability, operational parameters, and material behaviour. Design standards are typically based on a design life of 50 years for normal structures, for example Australian Standard Structural design actions AS1170.0:2002.[47]

Design standards are based on the current state of the art of design, and, as noted earlier, the design life is an expectation of the service life that will be achieved by a properly designed facility constructed in accordance with the design. Properly designed in accordance with a design standard means applying the design standard methodology to the correct data. By its nature, the design life can only be a prediction of the service life, not a guarantee. As Lord Justice Jackson noted in respect of a provision in a design standard

44 Structural design actions Part 0: General Principles.
45 *SSE Generation Ltd v Hochtief Solutions AG* [2018] CSIH 26 CA162/12 [368].
46 *CH2M Hill v New South Wales* [2012] NSWSC 963 (2014) 30 BCL 35, [99].
47 F3.

(J101): 'The authors of J101 regarded paragraph F301 as appropriate for a structure with design life of 20 years. No-one suggests that that provision would achieve a structure with a guaranteed life of 20 years.'[48]

There can be many reasons why the service life may ultimately prove to be less than the design life, for example a structure may be subjected to loads for which it was not designed, necessary maintenance may not have been performed, the facility may not have been operated correctly, the operating conditions may have been different to those on which the design was based, or the state of the art of the design may have been inadequate. The distinction between design life and service life was succinctly articulated by Lord Justice Jackson: 'If a structure has a design life of 20 years, that does not mean that inevitably it will function for 20 years, although it probably will.'[49]

11.3.4 Warranties

Where a contract specifies a design life and/or a service life, the question arises as to whether these are subject to a contractual warranty. The answer will depend on the proper construction of the terms of the contract. In view of the technical complexity of the documents in many construction contracts, this is often not a straightforward task, and one in which highly experienced judges may differ.

A contractual warranty for the service life of a facility is a warranty that the facility will be fit for purpose for the period of the warranty. It is submitted that a warranty for the design life of a facility is confined to a warranty that the facility has been designed in accordance with the current state of the art of design using the correct design parameters. Whilst it is anticipated that the service life will at least be equal to the design life, for the reasons discussed earlier, that may not be achieved. Based on these meanings of warranties, the fact that a service life warranty is breached does not automatically mean that a corresponding design life warranty is breached. As the preceding examples show, a design can be prepared with due skill and care according to the prevailing state of the art for a specified design life, yet the required service life is not achieved.

The fit for purpose warranty in the FIDIC contracts referred to in ¶11.2.2.1 earlier is effectively a service life warranty. The warranty in option X15 of NEC4 ECC referred to in ¶11.2.2.2 earlier is effectively a design life warranty.

11.3.5 Case study[50]

The case of *MT Højgaard a/s v E.ON Climate and Renewables Robin Rigg East Ltd* brought the issue of service life and design life into sharp focus. The grouted connections in offshore wind turbine towers failed within two years of installation, and within the defects liability period. The towers clearly failed to achieve the

48 *MT Hojgaard A/S v E.ON Climate and Renewables UK Robin Rigg* [2015] EWCA Civ 407, [93].
49 Ibid. [91].
50 This case is discussed in detail in Donald Charrett, *Contracts for Construction and Engineering Projects* (Informa Law from Routledge, 2nd edn 2022) Chapter 8.

20-year service life required by the Contract. The towers were designed according to the prevailing state of the art with due care and skill in accordance with a design standard containing a major error.

In the Court of Appeal Lord Justice Jackson accepted that, notwithstanding the failure to achieve a service life of 20 years because of the design standard error, the towers had a design life of 20 years. Accordingly, he recognised a contractual difference between service life and design life.[51]

In the Supreme Court, Lord Neuberger, in obiter accepted that there was a strong argument that the meaning of 'The design of the foundations shall ensure a lifetime of 20 years in every aspect without planned replacement' 'did not guarantee that the foundations would last 20 years without replacement, but that they had been designed to last 20 years without replacement.'[52] That is, he suggested that a design life warranty is not necessarily a warranty of the service life.

11.4 Design for which the Contractor is responsible

11.4.1 Employer's requirements

In any contract in which the Contractor is responsible for the overall design, the Contract documents must spell out in detail the **Employer's requirements** for the facility. These include the performance requirements, as well as other data and information provided by the Employer, a statement of intended purpose of the facility and criteria for testing and performance of the completed Works. The Contract may also contain more detailed and prescriptive information on specific design requirements.

It is apparent that the more precisely the Employer specifies its requirements, the less the opportunity for the Contractor to 'cut corners' by providing lower quality equipment and construction. The Employer has a long-term focus on performance, operation, and durability; the Contractor has a short-term focus on minimising its expenditure on construction and for the rectification of defects during the defects liability period. The Employer must therefore specify the basis of design in sufficient detail such that its long-term operating costs are not inappropriately increased by design choices made by the Contractor to minimise the capital cost.

It is common in design and construct contracts for the Contractor to accept liability for the accuracy and correctness of the Employer's requirements, subject to certain defined exceptions for which the Employer remains liable. For example, the 2017 FIDIC Silver Book provides:

> The Employer shall not be responsible for any error, inaccuracy or omission of any kind in the Employer's Requirements as originally included in the Contract and shall not be deemed to have given any representation of accuracy or completeness of any data or information, except as stated in this Sub-Clause below. Any data or information received by the Contractor, from the Employer or otherwise, shall not relieve the Contractor from the Contractor's responsibility for the execution of the Works.

51 *MT Højgaard a/s v E.ON Climate and Renewables UK Robin Rigg East Ltd* [2015] EWCA Civ 407, [91].
52 *MT Højgaard a/s v E.ON Climate and Renewables Robin Rigg East Ltd* [2017] UKSC 59, [30].

However, the Employer shall be responsible for the correctness of the following portions of the Employer's Requirements and of the following data and information provided by (or on behalf of) the Employer:

(a) portions, data and information which are stated in the Contract as being immutable or the responsibility of the Employer,
(b) definitions of intended purposes of the Works or any parts thereof,
(c) criteria for the testing and performance of the completed Works, and
(d) portions, data and information which cannot be verified by the Contractor, except as otherwise stated in the Contract.[53]

The Contractor should be alert at the tender stage to ensure that it does not accept liability for Employer-provided data and information which it cannot verify unless it clearly understands and prices the risks. This is particularly the case where front-end engineering and design has been done by others. In particular, the Employer is the one who should understand the intended purpose and should take contractual responsibility for its adequate definition.

Particular attention should be placed on the criteria for testing and performance of the completed Works, since this may ultimately be the determinant of whether the requirements of the Contract have been satisfied or not. Considerable detail is needed to avoid ambiguity and potential dispute: the specifications need to cover what is to be tested and when, who is to carry out the tests, the specific procedures to be adopted, the criteria to be used in assessing performance, and the consequences of the tests not satisfying all of the criteria. Liquidated damages for failure to achieve levels of mechanical performance or volumes of production are to be distinguished from liquidated damages for late Completion and may run concurrently. Tests on Completion are discussed more fully in Chapter 16.

11.4.2 Review/approval by the Employer

If the Contractor is responsible for design, its designer is free to adopt any design that fulfils the requirements of the Contract, subject to any contractual requirements in respect of the Employer's role in the design such as 'review' or 'approval.' It is apparent that design decisions are fundamental to the safety, functionality and durability of any facility throughout its life, and these are all issues which the Employer has an interest in as the ultimate owner and/or operator of the facility. Further, design changes required to correct errors or to achieve improved performance are very much more costly to implement after construction has been commenced.

Thus, the Employer has a very real interest in ensuring that the design has been properly carried out, and it is for this reason that it frequently has a contractual role in reviewing or approving the Contractor's design before construction commences. The purpose of the review or approval is to enable the Engineer to satisfy itself, on behalf of the Employer, as to the general suitability of the design for its intended purpose and its compliance with the requirements of the Contract. For example, the 2017 FIDIC Yellow Book has detailed provisions for the Engineer to review all Contractors Documents nominated for review and issue a Notice of No-objection before these documents can be used for construction.

53 Sub-clause 5.1.

The Employer/Engineer may strongly express a preference for certain materials or methods of construction, but the Contractor nevertheless remains responsible for the adequacy of the design, and its conformance to the requirements of the Contract. Where the Employer's/Engineer's 'suggestions' are likely to lead to an unsatisfactory result, it is the Contractor's designer's duty to warn of the consequences. A Contractor would be most unwise to implement any Employer's 'suggestions' that it disagreed with, without a written direction. Similarly, an Employer should avoid giving the Contractor any directions as regards design for which the Contractor is responsible, in order to preserve the liability for design assigned in the Contract. If the Employer has strong preferences for certain plant or materials it should include them as part of the Employer's Requirements so that the Contractor has a contractual obligation to supply them, subject to appropriate warranties.

Where the Contractor is responsible for the design of the Works it should submit its drawings to the Engineer in accordance with the details given in the programme or elsewhere in the Contract. The Contractor should also provide the Engineer with general arrangement and detailed drawings to the extent specified in the Contract as the work proceeds, or as the Engineer may require. The Engineer may have an unfettered right under the Contract to request the Contractor to provide drawings and information, although the Contractor does not usually have to submit confidential or manufacturing drawings (shop drawings) for approval. The exact extent to which the Employer can have an input into design by review/approval of the drawings is ultimately a question of construction of the terms of the Contract.

If the Engineer fails to signify its rejection or approval of such drawings within the specified time, the drawings are normally deemed to be approved. The Engineer should be required to sign or otherwise identify 'reviewed' or 'approved' drawings so that there can be no argument later as to what has been reviewed/approved. Once Contractor's drawings have been reviewed/approved or deemed to have been reviewed/approved by the Engineer, construction contracts usually provide that they may not be departed from either by the Contractor or by the Engineer. Thus, the Contractor will need to resubmit drawings for the review/approval process if at any later stage it finds errors or wishes to make changes.

A construction contract should expressly provide that the Engineer's review or approval of the Contractor's drawings does not imply approval that the design satisfies the requirements of the Contract and does not relieve the Contractor of its responsibility for its design. There is a tension between the Employer's legitimate desire to have an influence on the Contractor's design (manifested contractually by review or approval), and the Contractor's sole responsibility for the design. Notwithstanding a disclaimer that the Employer's approval does not relieve the Contractor from any obligation or responsibility, it may not be fully effective to avoid all liability for an 'approved' submission. The Employer's interests in ensuring the design satisfies the requirements of the Contract can generally be achieved by review followed by issue of a No-objection Notice. 'Approval' should generally be avoided.

Irrespective of the Employer's contractual rights to review/approve, if an error in the Contractor's design is discovered at any stage prior to Completion, the Employer should, as part of its duty to mitigate damage, give the Contractor an opportunity to correct it.[54]

54 *Columbus Co v Clowes* [1903] 1 KB 244, 247.

11.4.3 Design responsibility for permanent and temporary works

In construction work, many designs are not stable or self-supporting until the last part of the construction or work is in place, hence the need for temporary works. In situ concrete is one of the best examples: form work must be constructed to withstand the hydrostatic pressures of the wet concrete, and the formwork must be temporarily supported by a structure capable of safely supporting the entire dead load of the wet concrete until it has hardened and can carry load itself. The Contractor is usually fully responsible for the design of such temporary works, irrespective of who carried out the design of the permanent works.

In a construct only contract, the engineer's design responsibility to the Employer may not be confined to the suitability of the facility to fulfil its function in its final constructed condition. Where an excepted risk (generally those risks that the Contractor expressly does not accept liability for under the Contract) includes a cause due to the engineer's design of the Works, these words could mean either a defect of (1) the design of the permanent works which would affect their safety or stability after completion, or (2) the design of the temporary works or method of working to be adopted which was prescribed or provided by the Engineer or the Contract documents. It is also suggested that the Contractor would not be liable if a design defect of the permanent works designed by others incidentally had the effect of causing damage during construction where temporary support or other special measures would not reasonably be required for an adequate design.

In a situation where damage is apprehended but has not yet occurred, the Engineer is normally enabled under the Contract to suspend the Works if the suspension is necessary for the safety of the Works or any part thereof. Subject to the provisions of the Contract, such a power would normally extend to any risk of damage to the Works, irrespective of which party had contractual responsibility for design of the relevant part.

11.4.4 Revision of the design during construction

The duty of design is a continuing duty which extends until the structure is complete or finally fit for its purpose: see *Brickfield Properties v Newton*,[55] *London Borough of Merton v Lowe*,[56] *University Court of the University of Glasgow v William Whitfield*.[57]

11.5 Contractor's warranties

Design and construct contracts typically include express warranties by the Contractor that its design and documents, the execution and completed Works will comply with the laws of the country and the documents forming the Contract. The Contractor may also be required to give other warranties in respect of issues such as the exercise of due skill care and diligence in the execution and completion of the work, the engagement of the design consultants nominated in the tender, the checking and acceptance as suitable of any preliminary design carried out by the Employer and included in the Contract, and that the design will be fit for its intended purpose.

55 [1971] 1 WLR 862.
56 (1981) 18 BLR 133.
57 (1989) LJ Cons 5, 73.

In the absence of such express contractual provisions, the substance of some of these warranties may be implied terms in any event. Their inclusion in the Contract as express warranties ensures that the Employer has a remedy in damages if any of these terms are breached. However, the wording of the Contract provisions may mean that the 'warranties' are in fact essential conditions of the Contract, breach of which would entitle the Employer to terminate the Contract in addition to seeking damages. A contractual term in which the Contractor acknowledges that the Employer has relied on the warranties as an essential precondition to entering into the Contract may well have this effect.

It should be noted that Variations amend the scope of the Works, but do not vary the Contract. Accordingly, a Contractor's warranty that it will execute the Works in accordance with the documents forming the Contract will generally include the Contract documents as modified by Variations.

11.6 Technical standards and regulations

The technical standards and regulations that the design must comply with may change over the time that the Works are being carried out, particularly in large projects which are executed over a number of years. It is generally essential for the Employer that, at Taking-Over, the completed facility satisfies the technical standards and regulations, as well as the laws in force prevailing at that time. The cost of implementing changes to ensure conformance with this requirement to an already constructed design may be considerable.

The Contractor should ensure that any changes to the design or construction required to comply with revised technical standards, regulations, or laws constitute a Variation, thereby entitling it to an EOT and additional remuneration. In the absence of such a contractual provision, a prudent Contractor will ensure that it has had an adequate allowance in its price for the cost of this risk.

The FIDIC 2017 Yellow Book provides that the Contractor's documents, the execution of the Works and the completed Works shall comply with the Country's technical standards, and applicable Laws and other standards specified in the Employer's requirements in force when the Works are taken over by the Employer.[58] However, if the Contractor suffers delay and/or incurs an increase in Cost as a result of any change in Laws, the Contractor is entitled to an EOT and/or payment of such Cost.[59] If technical standards change after the Base Date, the Engineer may issue a Variation if it considers that compliance is required and involves changes to the execution of the Works.[60]

11.7 Cold commissioning, hot commissioning, training, and Taking-Over

Commissioning and training are peculiar to mechanical plant and are usually inextricably linked. **Commissioning** means bringing something newly produced into working condition. Where the Contractor has a contractual obligation to provide plant as part of

58 Sub-clause 5.4.
59 Sub-clause 13.6.
60 Sub-clause 5.4.

the Works, it almost invariably has a contractual obligation to at least carry out cold commissioning for that plant. **Cold commissioning** means that the plant has been tested, checked, and run to demonstrate that it is ready to be placed into operation, and consists of dry commissioning and wet commissioning. **Dry commissioning** means the plant has been manufactured, trial-fit, passed quality control testing, disassembled, and packed ready for transport without solvents or process fluids yet introduced. **Wet commissioning** means operation of plant for the first time for the purposes of trialing or testing its performance, and the discharge of waste as in pipelines, transformers, pumps, and the like. **Hot commissioning** is a phase of commissioning when the plant and systems are energised, and when the actual performance of the individual plant components is demonstrated and confirmed against their specified performance, involving the introduction of feedstock and process fluids.

Taking-Over is the point at which the Employer takes responsibility for the functioning and operation of the facility. The party with contractual responsibility for hot commissioning depends on the point at which Taking-Over takes place. If this is immediately after cold commissioning, the Employer has the responsibility for hot commissioning all of the items of plant so that it functions properly in accordance with the specifications.

There are clearly risks for the Contractor if the Employer (rather than the Contractor) carries out hot commissioning. In the event that the entire facility fails to achieve the specified functional output, it may be difficult for the Contractor to ascertain whether the output shortfall was the result of a defect, or operator unfamiliarity or incompetence with the operational requirements of the specific plant. The time and expense of subsequently determining the reason for and resolution of any failure to achieve the contractually specified output could be considerable. It is therefore normally in the Contractor's interest to have contractual responsibility for hot commissioning, including carrying out any required performance tests. If this cannot be achieved, the Contractor would be wise to ensure that it at least has the contractual right to audit the hot commissioning, and to attend the performance tests.

The Contract may require the Contractor to provide training in the use of the plant for the Employer's personnel prior to Taking-Over. Any such requirements should be carefully specified, so that both parties clearly understand the number of personnel to be trained, the extent to which and when training is required, and the required outcome of that training. If the training is required to achieve a specified level of competence, then it and the qualities and abilities of the Employer's personnel should be clearly defined in the Contract. The opportunities for on-the-job training during commissioning will depend to a significant extent on whether the Contractor has responsibility for hot commissioning or not. Whilst there may be opportunities for some on-the-job training during cold commissioning, this would usually need to be substantially supplemented by formal training if the Contractor does not have responsibility for hot commissioning.

The specified requirements for the required training should also cover whether the Contractor is required to pay trainees or provide transport or accommodation during the training, and whether the training can be carried out at the Site. Any delay caused by the Employer providing its personnel for training after the scheduled date would normally entitle the Contractor to an EOT and delay costs if it extended the date for Taking-Over.

11.8 As built documents

The Contractor is normally required to provide the Employer with a set of 'as built' documents showing the exact as built locations, sizes and details of the work as executed. Where this is a contractual requirement, it is normally a precondition to Taking-Over. The Employer's need for these drawings for the subsequent operation, maintenance and modification of the constructed facility is obvious, and it would have little leverage to obtain these after the Contractor has left the Site. In view of their importance, the form and extent of these documents may be specified in the Contract, or they may have to be submitted to the Engineer for approval.

The Contractor should not underestimate the resources needed to satisfy the contractual requirements for preparation and submission of as built documents. In order to avoid delay of Completion, the documents should be prepared progressively during the execution of the work and submitted to the Engineer with sufficient time to allow for its review and/or approval.

11.9 Operation and maintenance manuals

The Employer clearly needs to have operation and maintenance manuals of all plant provided as part of the Works in sufficient detail so that it can operate, maintain, dismantle, reassemble, adjust, and repair it during its life. The Contract should therefore provide that the Works are not complete for the purposes of Taking-Over until the Contractor has supplied appropriately detailed operation and maintenance manuals to the Employer. As with as built documents, these must usually be provided prior to Completion. The Employer may also require provisional copies of these documents prior to carrying out any Tests on Completion, to ensure that its personnel have sufficient training and familiarity with the equipment to conduct or supervise the tests. Such provisional operation and maintenance manuals may need to be updated with the results of the Tests on Completion to produce the final manuals.

It is prudent for the Employer to ensure that the Contract clearly specifies the requirements for the form of the operation and maintenance manuals, particularly if it has specific requirements for electronic documents. As most of these documents may be sourced from the Contractor's plant supply subcontractors, it is appropriate for any specific contractual requirements for operation and maintenance manuals to be included in the plant subcontracts let by the Contractor.

In a large project with many items of plant, the resources required for producing a coherent and properly indexed set of operation and maintenance manuals may be substantial, and the task needs to be properly planned as part of the project schedule to ensure that it does not cause delay to Completion. The Contractor may be 'encouraged' to provide the specified operation and maintenance manuals in time by a contractual provision that failure to do so by the time for Completion will result in a reduction in the contract price.

CHAPTER 12

Staff and labour

CONTENTS

It is important to note that the following information is project specific and will be heavily regulated by the local legislation and workplace and industrial agreements where the relevant Works are to be performed.

12.1 Engagement of staff and labour

Construction contracts normally provide that the Contractor is solely responsible for paying the wages of and all expenses in connection with all staff and labour employed on the project. Any provision by the Employer of its personnel must be specifically provided for. Any such clause should clearly specify the obligations of both parties in the event that there is a shortcoming in the performance of any personnel provided by the Employer.

The responsibility of paying local income tax relating to those employed, and detailed provisions relating to housing, feeding, and transport of the Contractor's personnel should be specified in the Contract.

12.2 Rates of wages

The purpose of clauses which require the payment of minimum rates of wages, 'fair wages' clauses as they are usually called, is to give the Employer some assurance that strikes by the Contractor's workmen will be kept to a minimum. There is usually no specific sanction in the Contract for enforcement of this requirement other than the general right to terminate the Contract for 'persistent and flagrant' neglect of any obligation, which itself does little more than restate the common-law situation in which an Employer would be entitled to treat the Contract as repudiated.

DOI: 10.4324/9781003206873-12

The Contract may provide that the Contractor is entitled to an extension of time as the result of a strike. Such entitlement may only arise if the strike does not involve the Contractor's personnel, for example the FIDIC Yellow Book provides that the Contractor is entitled to an EOT for an Exceptional Event arising from a 'strike or lockout not solely involving the Contractor's Personnel and other employees of the Contractor and Subcontractors.'[1]

Even if the Contract provides for an EOT resulting from a strike by the Contractor's personnel, the Contractor is typically only entitled to an EOT for industrial delay to the extent that it took all reasonable steps to preclude or mitigate the effect of the industrial delay. It is important for the Contractor to identify at the earliest possible stage of the Contract (preferably pre-execution) the degree to which, from a practical sense, the Contractor is required to 'mitigate.' For example, is the Contractor expected to exhaust all its legal options, or rather utilise its dispute resolution procedures as a priority? Often a well-documented and ongoing process involving input by the Employer/Engineer would assist the Contractor in identifying what is expected in order for it to be entitled to an EOT for industrial delay.

It should be noted that the Head Contractor does not assume responsibility for industrial relations of its subcontractors unless the terms of the Contract specifically stipulate otherwise. If, however the Contractor is charged with the responsibility of the management of all industrial relations as a result of the head contract, it would then be prudent for the Head Contractor to share its industrial risk with its subcontractors by appropriate terms in the subcontracts.

12.3 Persons in the service of the Employer

Some contracts have a provision that the Contractor may not recruit or attempt to recruit personnel employed by the Employer (and vice versa), for example 2017 FIDIC Yellow Book sub-clause 6.2. The wording of any such clause should be carefully reviewed to ensure that the contractual obligations on the Contractor do not constitute an unreasonable restriction on the right of employees to change employment. A clause which unreasonably interfered with an individual's freedom of employment could be struck out by a court as a breach of public policy.

12.4 Labour laws

The Employer has a legitimate interest in ensuring that the Contractor complies with all relevant labour laws, as well as the prevailing industrial conditions such as agreements negotiated with the relevant unions. Not only is the Employer interested in minimising the likely incidence of strikes, but under some circumstances it could be liable under statute in respect of unpaid workers' wages. Accordingly, as a condition precedent to payment of a progress claim, the Contract may give the Employer the right to require the Contractor to submit a statutory declaration that all its employees and its subcontractor's employees have been paid all moneys due and payable to them.

The Employer is also concerned that the Contractor's employees comply with all applicable legislation, particularly health and safety legislation which usually place legal obligations to provide safe and healthy premises on the owner of the premises in addition to the Contractor carrying out the Works. A breach by the Contractor of this requirement would normally render it liable to indemnify the Employer for any damage suffered as a consequence.

1 2017 FIDIC Yellow Book sub-clause 18.1(d).

12.5 Working hours

The normal working hours and days should be specified, and during these hours, the Contractor is entitled to carry out work on Site without interruption. The Engineer usually has power, after consulting the Employer and Contractor, to direct that work should be done outside these times and, provided the need for this has not arisen through default of the Contractor, the Contractor is usually entitled to recover the extra cost involved, together with profit. Similarly, where the Engineer orders the Contractor to expedite progress in order to compensate for delays for which the Contractor does not carry the risk, the Contractor would be entitled to claim the resulting cost of working additional hours. It is only where the Contractor requests such permission to make up for delays for which it is responsible that it is not entitled to any payment for doing so.

In the absence of any contractual provisions to the contrary, the Contractor is at liberty to make use of its possession of the Site as it wishes, subject to any statutory requirements. The Contract often requires that no work is to be done outside normal working hours or on locally recognised days of rest unless provision for such night, Sunday, and holiday work is included in the Contract, or unless some emergency arises, or the Engineer gives its consent. The Contractor should not assume that, if it is necessary to work outside normal working hours in order for it to achieve Completion within the time for Completion the Engineer will necessarily be in a position to give its consent, particularly where any restrictions on working hours are imposed so as not to inconvenience persons living in the locality or to enable other work on site to be carried out. It is however, in the Contractor's interest that the Contract provides that such consent will not be unreasonably withheld, as an unreasonable refusal to grant permission may found a claim for an EOT. Where approval for such work outside normal working hours is given, the Contractor may be liable for the additional costs of supervision by the Engineer or Employer's personnel.

The Contract must give the Engineer a general right to call for accelerated progress to make up lost time for it to have the power to do so. In the absence of such a contractual right, the Engineer has no power to order acceleration, even in the event that the Contractor is expected to finish after the contractual Date for Completion and thereby incur liquidated damages.

Whilst workers are entitled to refuse to work overtime, their contract of employment would not usually permit them to unreasonably withhold their agreement to do so. To minimise the risk of delays and costs, it must be made clear to employees/unions in advance (via project agreements/letters of offer) what operational requirements the project will demand, setting out also the appropriate overtime loading in order to ensure that any subsequent requests to work overtime are reasonable. Not offering adequate compensation for working overtime will increase the risk of industrial strike action and/or have an effect on the Contractor's ability to claim an extension of time, which could further compromise project schedules.

Ultimately, the power of an Employer, Contractor, or subcontractor to expedite progress is still subject to local industrial relations laws. To determine whether additional hours are reasonable, factors to be taken into account include:

(1) Any risk to the employee's health and safety that might arise if the employee worked the additional hours,
(2) The employee's personal circumstances (including family responsibilities),
(3) The operational requirements of the workplace or enterprise,

(4) Any notice given by the employer of the requirement or request that the employee work the additional hours,
(5) Any notice given by the employee of the employee's intention to refuse to work the additional hours,
(6) Whether any of the additional hours are on a public holiday, and
(7) The employee's hours of work over the four weeks ending immediately before the employee is required or requested to work the additional hours.

Payment of higher rates (or at least the anticipation of it) is likely to be a key factor in deciding whether additional hours are reasonable or not. It is therefore important to expressly identify the type of overtime anticipated (eg Sundays or simply Mondays to Saturdays) in agreements with the relevant employees/unions as part of operational requirements. This would also include setting out the expected categories of premium rates of pay.

12.6 Contractor's personnel

The Engineer typically has the power to require the Contractor to remove any person 'employed' on the Site. In this context, the term 'employ' is to be read in the wide sense of 'make use of,' and accordingly persons 'employed' are not confined to employees.[2] The Engineer should therefore have the power to order removal from the Works of a partner in a contracting firm, or of a subcontractor, although neither is an employee of the Contractor. Where persons employed on the Works are included in the definition of the Engineer's power of removal, but they are employed away from the Site, the Engineer may nevertheless order such persons to be removed 'from the Works.'

It is important for the Contractor to ensure that its employees meet any criteria which are stipulated for employment on the project, for example are capable of communicating satisfactorily in the agreed language of the Contract.[3]

If the Engineer, without justification, orders an employee to be removed, the Contractor's remedy will generally be to claim damages. Damages are not an effective remedy, since it may be difficult to prove tangible loss beyond the salary or wages of a substitute (and that only if the Contractor cannot make full use elsewhere of the services of the employee dismissed), however valuable the employee may be to the Contractor's organisation. The person dismissed may have a right of action against the Engineer for defamation, since the order implies that he/she has misconducted himself/herself or has been incompetent or negligent.

2 For the meaning of 'employ,' see *Carter v Great West Lumber Co* [1919] 3 WWR 901, applied in *Re Merchant Nurseries Pty Ltd; Corporate Affairs Commission v Rowley* (1985) 10 ACLR 143. In *Carter*, it was said that a doctor or solicitor, though in one sense *employed* by their client cannot be considered an employee. Similarly, the receivers in *Re Merchant Nurseries* were not disqualified as receivers of Merchant Nurseries Pty Ltd on the basis that, although their accounting firm (who they were partners of) had been employed by Merchant Nurseries in the past, they were never employees.

3 The common law will give effect to contracts expressed in a language other than English. If contracting parties enter into a contract in a certain language, and have the contract translated into a second language, the first language version of the Contract will constitute the true version of the Contract unless otherwise provided for: see *Affluent Construction Co Ltd v Yu Cheung Yin* [2018] HKCFI 1452, [64]–[73], per DHCJ To.

12.7 Records of Contractor's personnel and equipment

It is important for the Contractor to maintain accurate and detailed records of the day-to-day manning and plant and equipment on the Site. Maintenance of these records is usually a contractual requirement and is required to assist the Engineer in assessing the Contractor's claims for payment, and in particular, claims for additional payment.

The Contract may require the Contractor to give the Employer access to its statutory returns. The purpose of having access to these returns is that it gives the Employer the right to demand a pre-contract specific representation from the Contractor. If the Employer found out after the Contract was executed that the representation was untrue, then (even though the Contractor subsequently complied with its other contractual obligations in all respects) the Employer might be entitled to rescind the Contract for innocent or fraudulent misrepresentation – possibly because a Contractor with a past record of non-compliance would be more likely to, for example, attract trade union interference, or engage in unsafe work practices or non-compliance with equal opportunity obligations.

The degree of interest in, and control over, the Contractor's labour force and working methods permitted to the Engineer must be clearly defined in the Contract. The Engineer would not be entitled to this type of information without a specific contractual right.

Careful consideration should be given before the secondment of personnel from one company to another, and the merging of teams from the Employer and the Contractor, as this may create split responsibility and confuse accountability. Any secondment of personnel from the Employer to the Contractor (or vice versa) should be pursuant to a separate agreement that specifies responsibilities in a way that maintains the Contractor's obligations under the Contract.

12.8 Key personnel

The Employer may consider the experience and expertise of certain Contractor's personnel one of the important factors in achieving a successful project. If the employment of such key personnel on the project in defined roles is required, it must be included in the Contract; otherwise, the Contractor has the right to employ such personnel as it sees fit (at least until there is cause for complaint by the Engineer or Employer). Such provisions may take the form of pre-approved personnel named in the Contract or require the Engineer's approval of persons proposed for the defined key roles. As with other approvals by the Engineer, a time should be stated within which any rejection must be notified to the Contractor.

The UK decision *Fitzroy Robinson Limited v Mentmore Towers Limited; Fitzroy Robinson Limited v (1) Good Start Limited (2) Anglo Swiss Holdings Limited*[4] deals with the issue of a party's duty to disclose circumstances affecting the validity of a pre-contractual statement regarding key personnel. In that case the judge found that a consultant's representations on the appointment of a particular person as the team leader was one of the main reasons for the consultant's engagement. The key individual resigned before the consultant was engaged, but the Employer was not advised. The judge held this to be a fraudulent misrepresentation

4 (2009) EWHC 1552 (TCC).

and awarded damages for consultant's fees arising from the disruption and duplication of work.

Apart from the particular duty to disclose the resignation of proposed key personnel from a firm to a prospective client, the finding in this case sounds a general warning to Contractors and consultants that they are under a duty to disclose to their prospective clients any circumstances that render untrue pre-contractual statements regarding key personnel.

It follows that parties preparing pre-bid statements, documentation, and bid agreements should bear this decision in mind when making such representations and should be mindful of whether accompanying qualifications may be required before executing project agreements. As an added caution it is necessary to engage in open and frank disclosure of any alteration of circumstances during the course of projects that would render pre-contractual statements untrue to avoid any potential legal liability for such nondisclosure.

CHAPTER 13

Plant, materials, and workmanship

CONTENTS

13.1 Manner of execution

Certain items of temporary works and construction equipment may be designed to be more conveniently left in situ, for example certain items of piling, formwork, or the remnants of tunnel boring machines. Where this is intended by the Contractor, the Contract must make provision for it. For example, provision must be made for the amount to be retained in respect of disestablishment and clearing the Site, disposal of scrap and hazardous materials, transport costs of re-export of equipment, and duties or penalties on equipment which has been imported for temporary use.

If the design has been supplied by the Employer to the Contractor, and the design has been prepared by a consultant to the Employer, there is no warranty on the part of the Employer implied by the common law that the design is capable of being carried out so as to meet the requirements of the Contract.[1] Under Singapore Law, building regulations require developers and others to ensure that building works are designed and carried out such that they meet a minimum 'buildable design score.'[2] Builders are required to ensure that construction of building works will meet a 'minimum constructability score'[3] so as to ensure that buildings that are designed are in fact 'buildable.' **Buildability** means the ability

1 *Thorn v The Mayor and Commonalty of London* (1876) 1 App Cas 120.
2 *Building Control (Buildability) Regulations 2011* (S199/2011) (Sing) Regulation 4.
3 Ibid. Regulation 5.

DOI: 10.4324/9781003206873-13

of a design to be implemented physically in a manner that is safe, sound, and otherwise in accordance with the terms of the relevant construction contract; it may embrace both the physical possibility of implementing a design, and the practical ability to do so.[4] A contract may however expressly excuse the Contractor from performing the Works it has promised to do if those works are 'physically impossible.'[5]

13.1.1 Implied warranties

Construction contracts usually expressly require that the materials used by a Contractor are to be new and of suitable quality.[6] A Contractor who undertakes to do work and supply materials impliedly warrants that the materials will be of good and proper quality, unless the circumstances of the case show that the parties intended otherwise. The law will imply obligations that, in so far as the documents are silent, the materials and workmanship shall be of reasonable (or merchantable) quality and suitable for their intended purpose. Although goods may be of good quality, they may be unsuitable for a particular purpose.

The Contractor who assumes responsibility for design under a construction contract assumes implied responsibility that the result of its work will be reasonably fit for the purpose for which it is agreed or known to be required provided that the Contractor is aware of the particular purpose at the time of entering into the Contract[7] and there are no contractual terms or circumstances existing at the time the Contract was entered into which negative the implication of the warranty.[8] A fitness for purpose warranty will be implied where a Contractor has expressly assumed responsibility for designing and constructing a structure, meaning that the obligation of the Contractor will be a warranty of performance,[9] and will be more than that of exercising reasonable skill and care.[10] An obligation to use reasonable skill and care is not the same as an obligation to achieve a particular result; for example 'The surgeon does not warrant that he will cure the patient. Nor does the solicitor warrant that he will win the case.'[11] If a person has undertaken an express obligation to achieve a particular result, they will be liable for failing to achieve that result even if they have otherwise acted with reasonable skill and care.[12] If the Employer or its agent does not specify a particular matter of design, and the selection of the materials is left to the Contractor, the design must be suitable for the purposes for which the element is to be used.[13]

4 *Pickard Finlason Partnership Ltd v Lock* [2014] EWHC 25 (TCC), [198], per HHJ Stephen Davies.

5 *Turriff Ltd v The Welsh National Water Development Authority* (1979, OR, Sir William Stabb QC), reported in J Uff & Furst (eds), *Construction Law Yearbook 1994* (Chancery Law Publishing, 1994) 126–130.

6 The 2017 FIDIC Red Book does not expressly require the Contractor to ensure that the materials it uses are of a satisfactory quality, however, clause 7 of the contract contains a detailed procedure for the inspection and testing of materials used by the Contractor, with the Engineer being empowered to reject unsatisfactory materials. The JCT Standard Building Contract 2016 edition clause 2.3.3 requires the materials to be to the Architect/Contract Administrator's reasonable satisfaction.

7 *Fluor Ltd v Shanghai Zenhua Heavy Industry Co Ltd* [2016] EWHC 2062 (TCC), [531], per Edwards-Stuart J.

8 *Independent Broadcasting Authority v EMI Electronics* (1980) 14 BLR, 44–45, per Lord Fraser, 47, per Lord Scarman; *Reed v Perditis* [2005] SASC 136, [27], per Besanko J; *Jurong Town Corp v Sembcorp Engineers & Constructors Pte Ltd* [2009] SGHC 93, [7], per Chan Seng Onn J; *Millenia Pte Ltd v Dragages Singapore Pte Ltd* [2018] SGHC 193, [409], per Quentin Loh J.

9 *Fugro Spatial Solutions Pty Ltd v Cifuentes* [2011] WASCA 102, [144], per McLure P.

10 *Hawkins v Chrysler (UK) Limited* (1986) 38 BLR 36, 55, Neill LJ.

11 *Greaves & Co (Contractors) Ltd v Baynham Meikle & Partners* [1975] WLR 1095, 1099, per Lord Denning MR; see also *Healthcare at Home Ltd v Common Services Agency* [2014] UKSC 49, [1]–[3], per Lord Reed.

12 *Costain Ltd v Charles Haswell & Partners Ltd* [2009] EWHC B25 (TCC), [52]–[59], per DHCJ Fernyhough QC.

13 *Cleightonhills v Bembridge Marine Ltd* [2012] EWHC 3449 (TCC), [47], per Akenhead J.

If a Contractor has not assumed responsibility for design and has simply agreed to supply materials and build a structure according to a given design, the implied warranty as to fitness for purpose only relates to the materials supplied and the Contractor's workmanship to the extent that they are within the Contractor's control; the Contract is not a warranty in respect of the fitness for purpose of the design.[14]

These implied warranties arise under the common law and are analogous to the implied warranties that arise under sale of goods legislation.[15] Under English and Singaporean sale of goods legislation, contracts for the sale of goods are subject to an implied term that they will be of 'satisfactory quality,' meaning the standard that a reasonable person would regard as satisfactory, taking account of any description of the goods, the price, if relevant, and all other relevant matters.[16] Whether one or both of the two separate warranties for materials (reasonable quality and fit for their intended purpose) will be implied by law in relation to materials depends on the facts of each case.

In *Young and Marten Ltd v McManus Childs Ltd*,[17] roofing Contractors subcontracted the supply and laying of replacement tiles after a representative of the developer suggested the type of replacement tiles to lay. After 12 months, the tiles began to disintegrate. The facts excluded a warranty for fitness of purpose because the developers chose the tiles. However, the Contractors were still liable for breach of the warranty of merchantable (reasonable) quality.

By contrast *in Gloucestershire County Council v Richardson*,[18] the House of Lord's held that there was no implied warranty by the Contractor that concrete columns supplied were of merchantable quality and fit for their intended purpose. In this case, the Contractor was directed by the Employer's architect to enter an agreement with a nominated supplier, and the Contract did not expressly allow the Contractor to reasonably object to this. Furthermore, the quotation that the Contractor was directed to accept contained conditions limiting the nominated supplier's liability for defects.

In *Helicopter Sales (Aust) Pty Ltd v Rotor-Work Pty Ltd*,[19] the Australian High Court held that on the facts of the case neither warranty was implied in relation to the materials supplied by a helicopter repair company. The relevant circumstances that led the Court to this conclusion were that the contract was predominantly a service contract, and renewing parts was merely incidental. The service company was obliged to comply, and did comply, with Department of Civil Aviation requirements and the manufacturer's manual, the service company was only allowed to use replacement parts supplied by the manufacturer's authorised distributor, the service company had to obtain a duly certified release note for replacement parts, and the Employer knew the service company was not equipped to carry out scientific tests to ensure the absence of latent defects in the parts supplied to it.

A Contractor's general insurance policy for its business operations may not cover the Contractor against any liability it may have for breach of a fitness for purpose obligation;

14 *NP Integrated Technology Ltd v Entwistle* [2017] EWHC B21 (TCC), [38](1)], per HHJ Stephen Davies.

15 For example in England: *Sale of Goods Act* 1979 (UK); *Supply of Goods and Services Act* 1982 (UK); Australia: *Sale of Goods Act 1896* (Qld); *Sale of Goods Act 1895* (WA); *Sale of Goods Act 1895* (SA); *Sale of Goods Act 1896* (TAS); *Sale of Goods Act 1972* (NT); *Goods Act 1958* (Vic) s 19(a) and (b)), and Part 3–2, Division 1 of the *Australian Consumer Law* (being Schedule 2 to the *Competition and Consumer Act 2010* (Cth); Hong Kong: *Sale of Goods Ordinance (Cap 26)* (HK); Singapore: *Sale of Goods Act (Cap 393, 1999 revised edition)* (Sing).

16 *Sale of Goods Act 1979* (UK) s14(2A); *Consumer Rights Act 2015* (UK) s9(2); *Sale of Goods Act* (Cap 393, 1999 revised edition) (Sing) s14(2A); *Supply of Goods Act* (Cap 394, 1999 revised edition) (Sing) s4(2A).

17 [1969] 1 AC 454.

18 [1969] 1 AC 480.

19 (1974) 132 CLR 1.

a Contractor may only undertake to exercise reasonable skill and care in performing its obligations, and not warrant fitness for purpose of what it designs and builds.[20]

A fitness for purpose warranty will be implied in plant or equipment hire agreements meaning that the supplier of plant or equipment will be taken to warrant that the plant or equipment supplied is reasonably safe and suitable for its usual purpose.[21] If the plant or equipment is hired together with an operator, it may be an implied term of the Contract that the operator will be properly skilled, qualified, and trained.[22] That said, the question of the 'fitness' of goods or services for a particular purpose may be considered having regard to the 'suitability' of those goods or services for the known or intended purpose.[23] A manufacturer of construction products subject to European law will usually be required to ensure that its products comply with the *European Construction Products Regulations*.

13.1.2 Exclusion of the warranty for merchantable quality

From the cases considered, a Contractor's warranty for merchantable quality materials will not be implied if the Employer directs the Contractor to purchase certain materials and accepts specific conditions limiting liability for defects as in *Gloucestershire County Council*, and/or if factual circumstances make a warranty for reasonable quality practically impossible as in *Helicopter Sales*.

13.1.3 Exclusion of the warranty for materials to be fit for purpose

A Contractor's warranty for materials to be fit for purpose is more easily excluded than the warranty of merchantable quality. This is because if a Contractor is directed to obtain certain materials from a nominated subcontractor, the Employer takes the risk that the materials will not be fit for purpose. Therefore, this term will only be implied if an Employer relies on the Contractor's skill and experience. For example, in *Martin v McNamara*,[24] the Employer relied on the Contractor's recommendation of substitute roof tiles after it was found that there would be delay in the provision of the originally specified roof tile. The Contractor was liable because it was made clear that the Employer was relying on the Contractor's skill and experience in relation to substituting the specified tiles.

13.1.4 Warranty of skill, care, and competence

The law may also imply a warranty that a Contractor will construct a building with the skill, care, and competence of an ordinary contractor and in accordance with good building practice. The obligation is usually regarded as being of such importance that it is set out in an express contractual term.[25] If services, as opposed to goods are provided

---

20 *SSE Generation Ltd v Hochtief Solutions AG* [2016] Scots CSOH 177, [159]–[164], per Lord Woolman (appeal allowed on unrelated grounds [2018] CSIH 26).

21 *Nea Pty Ltd v Magenta Mining Pty Ltd* [2005] WASC 106, [235]–[238], per EM Heenan J.

22 *Kay Lim Construction & Trading Pte Ltd v Soon Douglas (Pte) Ltd* [2012] SGHC 186.

23 *Maersk Oil UK Ltd v Dresser Rand (UK) Ltd* [2007] EWHC 752 (TCC), [68]–[69], per HHJ Wilcox.

24 *Martin v McNamara* [1951] SR Q 225, 232.

25 For example SIA Building Contract (1st edn 2016) (Sing) clause 11(1)(a); JCWC Standard Form of Building Contract (2006 edn) (HK) clause 2.1(1)(i); JCT Standard Building Contract (2016 edn) (UK) clause 2.1;

pursuant to a contract as part of the business, it will be implied that the supplier will carry out its services with reasonable skill and care.[26] Although the Contractor might not be responsible for the preparation of the design of the Works, the Contractor is not excused from responsibility for defects in the Works where it ought to have been clear to the Contractor that the design was materially deficient.[27] If circumstances arise in which a Contractor is unable perform its work in a good and workmanlike manner, and it is obvious to the Contractor that the work cannot be performed satisfactorily, it is the duty of the Contractor to draw this matter to the attention of the Employer, and seek directions as to what it wishes to do. In Singapore, Hong Kong, most jurisdictions of Australia and many other jurisdictions, but not in the UK, builders are required to be licensed in order to legally to perform building work and may be disciplined or even deregistered if they fail to carry out their work in a competent manner.

In *Brian Geaney Pty Ltd v Close Constructions Pty Ltd*,[28] the plaintiff Geaney wanted to construct a building on land he had acquired. He consulted with an architect (who drew the initial building design based on a stud frame) and a structural engineer (who designed the foundations) and contracted with Close Constructions Pty Ltd to (re)design and construct the building. Geaney discussed ways to lower the contract price with Close by using blocks as a substitute for the stud frame construction, and this change was adopted by Close. The completed building had two major defects: inappropriate foundations for the heavier load of the block walls, and lack of control joints in the block work, which contributed to extensive cracking of the walls. It was held that Close's contract was in substance a design and construct contract, as Close had itself modified the original designs prepared by the architect. As the defects were design defects, Close (builder and designer) breached an implied condition in that it did not construct the building with the skill, care, and competence of an ordinary builder undertaking a design and construct contract, or in accordance with good building practice.

This case illustrates that even if an Employer wants to change the design to cut costs, it does not obviate the Contractor's liability for foreseeable consequences that arise from a new design prepared by it. Furthermore, if the Employer relies on the Contractor's expert advice, the Contractor may find its liability can increase from one of construction only to the more onerous obligations in a design and construct contract.

13.1.5 Express warranties

Despite the law's ability to imply warranties of suitability, it may nevertheless be desirable in the Employer's interest that the Contract should contain express provisions in respect of the requirements for work and materials. In view of the operation of the *Competition and Consumer*

AS 4000–1997 (Aus) clause 29.1; 2017 FIDIC Red Book sub-clause 7.1(b).

26 *Supply of Goods and Services Act 1982* (UK) s13; *Consumer Rights Act 2015* (UK) s49(1); *Australian Consumer Law* s60, *Supply of Services (Implied Terms) Ordinance (Cap 457)* (HK) s5. *Seadrill Management Services Ltd v OAO Gazprom* [2010] EWCA Civ 691, [27]–[28], per Moore-Bick LJ; *Iliffe v Feltham Construction Ltd* [2014] EWHC 2125 (TCC), [100] and [112], per Stuart-Smith (appeal allowed on unrelated grounds: [2015] EWCA Civ 715).

27 *Steel Co of Canada Ltd v Willand Management Ltd* [1996] SCR 746, 753–754; *Brunswick Construction Ltd v Nowlan* (1974) 21 BLR 27 and 34–35, per Ritchie J [SCC].

28 [2003] Aust Torts Reports 81–719; [2003] QSC 393.

Act (2010) in Australia and its prohibition on misleading and deceptive conduct, it is undesirable for such warranties to be couched in terms of the 'best' quality or the 'highest' standards of workmanship, as such terms may promote disputes. Suitable contractual provisions should require that, unless otherwise expressly described in the Contract documents, all materials should be new, non-hazardous and suitable for their purpose, and all work should be carried out in a proper workmanlike and careful manner, in accordance with recognised good practice.

Contractual warranties on workmanship in bespoke contracts sometimes go further than this and require that it also be fit for its purpose. Such an express contractual warranty may be problematic for a Contractor in a design and construct contract, as the fit for purpose requirement would apply to design work as well as site construction work and would usually not be covered under the designer's Professional Indemnity insurance. This issue is covered in more detail elsewhere.[29]

13.1.6 Employer's materials

Unless the Contract provides otherwise, the ordinary position is that the Contractor is not entitled to use existing materials in or on the Site which in law belongs to the Employer.

Although the Employer is often tempted to make use of its buying power to purchase materials for the use of the Contractor at a discount, there are risks if it does so. The Contractor would be entitled to an extension of time and possibly to suspension of the Works or damages if there is any failure or delay by the Employer or its supplier in making materials available. Further, if the Employer supplied materials are faulty the Contractor will be entitled to a Variation order for any extra work this causes.[30]

13.2 Inspection

If the Engineer delays unreasonably in inspecting or notifying the Contractor that an examination of the work is unnecessary, the Contractor should not cover the work, but would normally be entitled to an extension of time for Completion and to compensation where it has suffered a loss as a result of such delay.

It is usually made plain in the Contract that, with the possible exception of the Final Payment Certificate, no approval or passing of work, or payment, or certificate, can bind the Employer or Engineer if the work is later found to be defective. A previous approved covering-up does not protect the Contractor if a subsequent re-opening discloses defective work. This is because although the issue of an interim payment certificate is based upon the Engineer's valuation of the work performed (and which in principle includes an allowance for defective work), the absence of an allowance for defects does not constitute acceptance of defective work.[31] A further rationale for allowing revision to certified progress if defects are discovered later, is that a progress payment is merely an interim payment on account (eg expressly provided in AS 2124–1992 cl 42.6 and NPWC 3 cl 42.5 standard form contracts).

29 Donald Charrett, *Contracts for Construction and Engineering Projects* (Informa Law from Routledge, 2nd edn 2022) Chapter 23.

30 *Macintosh v Midland Counties Railway* (1845) 14 M & W 548; *W H Gaze & Sons Ltd v Corporation of Port Talbot* (1929) 93 JP 89.

31 See *Construction Services Civil Pty Ltd v J & N Allen Enterprises Pty Ltd* (1985) 5 Aust Const LR (Pt 2) 14; 1 BCL 363, SC(SA); *Re Sanders Constructions Pty Ltd and Eric Newham (Wallerawang) Pty Ltd* [1969] Qd R 29; *Ownit Homes Pty Ltd v Batchelor* [1983] 2 Qd R 124, 134 per Thomas J.

Where defects are approved by the Engineer (eg the misalignment of a structure which the Employer does not wish to demolish), it is advisable for the Contractor to confirm an Engineer's approval of such work which is not up to specification as a Variation. This is because damages in a construction contract represent the amount of both demolition and reconstruction of a defective structure.[32]

It must be borne in mind that in offshore work, the cost of rectification of defective work may be considerably less than the cost of searching for and locating defects, and mobilising suitable vessels and personnel to reach the Works in order to carry out the rectification, for example charter of a diving service vessel or a more expensive spread together with diving services and certification personnel.

13.3 Testing

The Contractor is normally obliged to pay for testing in any event for:

(1) Tests shown clearly as intended by the Contract documents to be carried out by the Contractor, other than such tests as may be ordered at will in any part of the work, and
(2) Tests intended of the finished Works, or any part of them, and made to determine the ability of the finished Works to fulfil their intended function (as opposed to tests of their materials or workmanship to determine their compliance with the Contract), provided that the tests in question are described with sufficient particularity in the Contract for the Contractor to be able to make a proper allowance for them when pricing (**Performance Tests**).

Usually, mention of tests in any bills of quantities will mean that they are the subject of a provisional sum, in which case the Contractor will be paid for carrying them out.

Any test ordered which does not fall within the preceding definition is usually paid for by the Employer or Contractor depending upon the outcome of the test. Tests which confirm that the work conforms with the Contract should be paid for by the Employer, whereas tests which reveal defective work should be paid for by the Contractor, in addition to the costs of rectification of the defective work.

The power of the Engineer to require defective work to be re-executed during the course of construction is important and would normally imply that it has power to order tests which may reveal defects. Other powers comparable to the power to order tests which are usually incorporated into the General Conditions of Contract are the power to order the opening or uncovering of work, and the power to order a search for defects.

If goods are supplied that fail to comply with the statutory warranty of quality under the sale of goods legislation, under Singaporean law generally in consumer transactions but in commercial transactions only where the breach of warranty is more than slight, and under Australian, English, and Hong Kong law generally, it is open to the purchaser to reject those goods if they fail to meet the applicable contractual or statutory requirements. If goods are accepted by the purchaser, the right of rejection is lost. The Employer will nevertheless have a right to claim either damages for breach of warranty or an abatement of the purchase price.[33]

---

32 *Bellgrove v Eldridge* (1954) 90 CLR 613.

33 *Sale of Goods Act 1979* (UK) s11(4) and 53(1); *Sale of Goods Act 1923* (NSW) s54(1); *Sale of Goods Ordinance (Cap 26)* (HK) ss13(3) and 55; *Sale of Goods Act (Cap 393, 1999 revised edition)* (Sing) s53(1); *Trac Time Control Ltd v Moss Plastic Parts Ltd* [2004] EWHC 3298 (TCC), [177] -[178] per HHJ Grenfell.

13.4 Ownership of plant and materials

In considering the question of ownership of materials and plant at any stage supplied either by the Employer or Contractor, the answer lies in the law of property. Materials and plant supplied by the Employer remain its property for the duration of the Contract. Materials and plant supplied by the Contractor under the Contract and fixed in place become the property of the owner of the Site by virtue of becoming a 'fixture' of the land, if property does not pass earlier by virtue of the Contract. It has been held that ownership of unfixed plant and materials passes to the Employer when included in a certificate for payment on the basis that this was the inference to be drawn from the Contract.[34]

In *Partington Advertising Co v Willing and Co*,[35] the court pointed out that a Contractor's equipment is treated differently from its material, since an individual item of equipment is not fixed to the Site with the intention of it remaining there permanently. The court held that ownership would pass in respect of a gantry crane installed as part of the permanent works, but which was used by the Contractor to install other mechanical equipment. In the terminology adopted here, this was an item of plant which was used during construction as Contractor's equipment.

The Contract should provide that the plant becomes the Employer's property either when plant is delivered to Site (in which case the Contractor should be entitled to payment for it), or when the Contractor has been paid the value of the plant. Similarly, in the event of suspension or delay attributable to the Employer, the Contractor should be entitled to be paid for plant which it has been prevented from delivering to Site or milestones frustrated by reason of a suspension order or delay. The Contractor (or a subcontractor) should be aware of the consequences of property in goods that have not been paid for passing to the owner of the Site by virtue of becoming fixtures, particularly if the owner of the real property is a different entity to the contracting entity. For example, in *Belgrave Nominees Pty. Ltd. v Barlin-Scott Airconditioning (Aust.) Pty. Ltd*,[36] the air-conditioning equipment installed by a subcontractor in a building became a fixture and part of the owner's real property. Notwithstanding that the Contractor who had engaged the subcontractor went into liquidation before the plant was paid for, the subcontractor had no right to remove the equipment, and the owner was granted an injunction requiring it to be reinstated.

Where there may have been substantial progress payments to the Contractor for plant in the course of manufacture prior to delivery to Site, there may be inadequate protection for the Employer. In such circumstances it may be appropriate to consider the inclusion of contractual provisions making the Contractor's entitlement to progress payments conditional upon the Contractor providing the Engineer with reasonable evidence of the value of the work done, the Contractor's right to transfer title to the Employer, and that it has suitably and sufficiently marked the plant in question as the Employer's property, as the Engineer may reasonably have required. Employers should, however, be aware that in some countries such provision would not be effective to vest ownership of the plant in the Employer, and detailed advice on the laws governing transfer of title in a country where the plant is being manufactured may need to be obtained.

---

34 *The Banbury and Cheltenham Direct Railway Company v Daniel* (1885) 54 LJCH 256.
35 [1896] 8 QB 913.
36 [1984] VR 947.

A clause which vests ownership of plant and materials in the Employer before they become fixed to the Works provides security to the Employer for money advanced to the Contractor. It also enables the Employer to ensure that, where the Contractor defaults in its obligations, the Employer can have the Works completed by another contractor with materials and plant already on the Site and to which the original Contractor has no claim.

Where advance payments, as opposed to progress payments, are included, Employers will normally protect their interests in the payments made by requiring the Contractor to provide an on-demand advance payment guarantee.

13.4.1 Effect of termination of the Contract

As a general rule, where an Employer terminates the Contract due to Contractor insolvency or breach, the Employer is not entitled to use the Contractor's materials, plant and equipment on the Site unless specifically permitted by the Contract.[37] It may be reasonably foreseeable that the deliberate and wrongful seizure of plant, equipment or materials would have the effect of driving the Contractor out of business with the consequence that the Contractor was unable to mitigate its loss; in such event the Contractor will be entitled to recover damages for conversion of its plant and equipment at prices prevailing at the date of judgement.[38] The situation is however different in respect of plant and materials if ownership has already been vested in the Employer. To provide additional protection for the Employer, the Contract may also stipulate that if the Employer takes over the work because of the Contractor's breach or insolvency, the Employer can take and use all plant, material and equipment owned by the Contractor on Site (see for example AS 2124–1992 cl 44.5). Such a clause permits another contractor to use everything (including equipment) owned by the defaulting Contractor that is necessary for Completion of the Works. However, where the Contractor's equipment is hired, such a clause will not affect the rights of the owner of the equipment.

Where the Employer becomes insolvent, its creditors enjoy a right to attach materials and plant owned by the Employer, but not the Contractor's plant, materials and equipment. The situation is different on the Contractor's insolvency. In *Kerr v Dundee Gas Light Co*,[39] a Contractor became bankrupt, leaving a crane and various materials on site. The Contractor's trustee in bankruptcy demanded delivery, which was refused, and the Employer used both equipment and materials to complete the Works and maintained their refusal to deliver after Completion. The court held that the Employer was entitled to use materials and the Contractor's equipment for Completion, subject to payment for the materials and the use of the crane, but must deliver up the crane upon Completion. This case is useful in distinguishing between Contractor's equipment and plant and materials.[40]

37 *P & E Phontos Pty Ltd v New South Wales Land and Housing Corp* (1987) 7 Aust Const LR 54; 4 BCL 45.

38 *Egan v State Transport Authority* (1982) 31 SASR 481. Note: In this instance, the date of judgement was 16 years after the plant and equipment had been wrongfully seized.

39 (1861) 23 D (Ct of Sess) 343.

40 See also *In re Winter, Ex parte Bolland* (1878) 8 Ch D 225.

CHAPTER 14

Commencement, delays, and suspension[1]

CONTENTS

1 The authors are indebted to George Matta and Jonathan Shahady of Tracey Brunstrom & Hammond for the diagrams used in this chapter.

DOI: 10.4324/9781003206873-14

14.1 Commencement of Works

14.1.1 Contractual obligations

The date of commencement of the Works is usually specified in the Contract and is the date from which the contractual date for Completion of the Works (**Date for Completion**) is computed, albeit usually implicitly. However, the Contractor's delay in commencement typically does not have the contractual consequences that lateness in Completion does.

It is desirable that the Contract should state a time limit within which the Engineer is to give the order to commence the Works, and the time period within which the Contractor is then to commence. The Contract may provide that the Contractor must commence the Works upon being given a 'notice to proceed' or similar notice.[2] A notice to proceed is frequently used because it gives the Employer flexibility as to when the Site is handed over, as opposed to a predetermined date in the Contract. It is also useful when there are a number of subcontractors working on a project who will require access to different portions of the Site at different times. In this way, the Contractor can coordinate the commencement date for each subcontractor to suit the circumstances at the time and avoid claims for damages from subcontractors should commencement dates be specified in individual subcontracts which the Contractor is unable to meet due to circumstances beyond its control.[3] In the absence of specified times, reasonable time periods would be implied from the date of acceptance of the tender.

It may be that the Contractor's Works must be integrated with works performed by other contractors, in which case it will be implicit that the Contractor must commence the Works within a reasonable time so as to coordinate with the works of the other contractors on the Site.[4] The Contract may provide that the Contractor is bound to perform the Works in accordance with the construction programme, failing which the Employer may give the Contractor notice to commence within a reasonable time. If the Contractor fails to commence within a reasonable time, the Employer may become entitled to terminate the Contract.[5] Certain contracts provide that the Contractor must commence the Works upon

2 For example 2017 FIDIC Red Book sub-clause 8.1.

3 *Scottish Power plc v Kvaerner Construction (Regions) Ltd* 1999 SLT 721.

4 See *Fairfield-Mabey Ltd v Shell UK Ltd* [1989] CILL 514, 516, per HHJ Bowsher QC; *Aries Powerplant Ltd v ECE Systems Limited* (1995) 45 Con LR 111, 123, per HHJ Lloyd QC.

5 *Bedfordshire CC v Fitzpatrick Contractors Ltd* (1998) 62 Con LR 64, 73, per Dyson J.

being given possession of the Site.[6] If the order to commence the Works is not given timeously, the Employer would ordinarily be liable to pay damages for breach of contract for any unreasonable delay. However, the Engineer can avoid damages for breach by giving an order to commence on time and granting an extension of time for Completion and costs to cover any delay in giving possession of the Site.

If the Contractor does not commence the Works due to causes sanctioned by the Engineer or wholly beyond the Contractor's control, the failure by the Contractor to proceed without delay would not be a breach of any contractual term requiring execution of the Works 'with due expedition and without delay' (the due diligence clause). However, unless the Contractor claims an extension of time, the time lost may eventually involve it in liquidated damages for delay in Completion. A Contractor may regard delays such as this on the critical path at the outset of a project as less important than delays towards the end of the project, reflecting its wish to avoid confrontation at an early stage in the project arising from default by the Employer. Such an approach is short-sighted; it is virtually impossible for the Contractor to fully assess its risks of subsequent delays arising from its own culpable actions later in the project and therefore its ultimate need for extensions of time to avoid liquidated damages. It would be sensible for a Contractor to make all legitimate claims for extensions of time in accordance with the requirements of the Contract to ensure that these are available at a later stage if necessary.

14.1.2 Possession of the Site

Depending on the specific terms of the Contract, the Employer's initial obligation is usually to give possession of the Site, or sufficient access, to the Contractor on the commencement date. Failure to give possession of the Site to the Contractor as provided for in the Contract amounts to a breach of the Employer's obligations, which may entitle the Contractor to claim damages and an extension of time for the breach. Reference should be made to ¶7.12.2 for a caution on the difficulties that a Contractor may face in relation to 'sufficient' access.

In the absence of an appropriate termination clause, mere delay by the Employer in fulfilling its obligations generally would not entitle the Contractor to terminate the Contract, unless time is of the essence in the Contract. Generally, time is only of the essence in a contract if there is a term to this effect, or it has been made so by a notice issued pursuant to one of the clauses in the Contract.

Once it has obtained possession of the Site, the Contractor is then generally entitled to remain in possession of the Site until Completion of the Works, unless the Contract has been lawfully terminated. However, there may be circumstances where the Contractor is required to give possession back to the Employer at some stage during the Contract period (for example, where the Contract requires the Employer to perform some works on the project prior to the Contractor completing its Works). It may also apply where there is provision for staged practical completion and handover of the Works.

6 See JCT Standard Building Contract (2016 edition) clause 2.4; JCWC Standard Form of Building Contract (2006 edition) clause 23.3; SIA Building Contract (1st edn 2016) clause 10(1).

In the absence of a specific contractual term to the contrary, the Contractor is entitled to possession of the Site to the exclusion of other contractors during performance of the Works. For this reason, a contract may provide that the Contractor must permit other contractors on Site to execute other works on behalf of the Employer. The Contractor should carefully assess the potential costs and risks of disruption that could arise from such joint possession prior to entering into the Contract. Legislation may impose work health and safety obligations on the Contractor for any contractors on the Site if the Contractor is the principal contractor for the Site.[7]

Possession of the Site by the Contractor is, in many cases, required only in sequence or stages, and 'the Site' may be an indeterminate area which it is difficult to define precisely. The definition of the Site provided in the conditions of contract is not usually, by itself, satisfactory, and whenever possible the other contract documents (if any) should define it and the available means of access to it as precisely as possible. Provision should also be made in the contract documents for areas needed by the Contractor for storage of materials or for reasonable access to the Site, notwithstanding that work may not actually be intended to take place in such areas either at all or for the time being.

14.2 Date for completion

14.2.1 Obligation to complete

Under the laws of England, Australia, Hong Kong, and Singapore, it is not necessary to demonstrate the 'fault' of the Contractor in completing late in order to claim damages. If the Contractor has promised to complete the Works by an agreed date, if the Contractor fails to complete by that date, the Contractor is in breach of contract unless it can justify its late performance.[8] Under German law: 'Fault is a prerequisite for delay as well as for non-performance or faulty performance. This means that without intent or negligence, there is no delay in a legal sense and damages cannot be claimed.'[9]

The Date for Completion must be specified by the Employer at the tender stage of a project, unless the Employer is asking Tenderers to compete on time for Completion. It may be expressed as a date (eg 1 March 2020) or a period of time (eg 107 days from the commencement date). The Date for Completion will change during the course of the Contract if the Contractor is granted any extension of time. Where the time for Completion is expressed as a number of days, the Date for Completion is calculated by adding that number of days to the planned commencement date, plus any extensions of time to which the Contractor is entitled under the Contract. If the Contractor fails to complete by the Date for Completion and any extension thereto, the Employer will be entitled to payment of damages or a reduction in price (depending on the relevant terms of the Contract). However,

---

7 For example under the *Environmental Planning and Assessment Act 1979* (NSW) s1.4 defines the 'principal contractor for building work means the person responsible for the overall coordination and control of the carrying out of the building work.'

8 *Westminster Corporation v J Jarvis & Sons Ltd* [1970] 1 WLR 637, 649, per Lord Wilberforce.

9 L Nicklish, 'Remedies of the Employer for Delay in Completion Under the Contract and at Law: Liquidated and Un-Liquidated Damages: Termination' in Lloyd (ed), *The Liability of Contractors* (Centre for Commercial Law Studies, Queen Mary College Longman Group, 1986) 96–97.

should the Employer cause the delay, it is not entitled to damages if the Contractor fails to complete within the stipulated time.

If no time for Completion of the Works is stipulated in the Contract, the legal inference will be that the Contractor is obliged to complete the Works within a reasonable time.[10] In *Astea (UK) Limited v Time Group Limited* HHJ Seymour QC summarised some of the matters that would be considered in determining what is a 'reasonable time':

> That broad consideration was likely to include taking into account any estimate given by the performing party of how long it would take him to perform; whether that estimate has been exceeded and, if so, in what circumstances; whether the party for whose benefit the relevant obligation was to be performed needed to participate in the performance, actively, in the sense of collaborating in what was needed to be done, or passively, in the sense of being in a position to receive performance, or not at all; whether it was necessary for third parties to collaborate with the performing party in order to enable it to perform; and what exactly was the cause, or where the causes of the delay to performance. The list is not intended to be exhaustive.[11]

A period of delay to the Works caused by risk for which the Contractor is contractually responsible is not to be included in the calculation of a reasonable time for Completion.[12]

The express obligation to complete by the Date for Completion has very important legal consequences. Its absolute nature means that the Contractor is effectively at risk with regard to the Works until Completion, subject to any express stipulation in the Contract to the contrary. Where the Contract fixes a Date for Completion, the Contractor is obliged to complete by that date. Obstacles to completion of the Work on time, such as inclement weather or adverse site conditions whether foreseeable or unforeseeable, will not excuse late performance unless there is an express contractual provision which relieves the Contractor from its obligations to perform timeously.[13] Where the time for the Contractor to complete its contractual obligations is vitally important (ie the Contract specifies that 'time is of the essence') and the Contractor fails to adhere to the time limit, the Employer may treat the Contract as terminated.

The actual date on which the Contractor achieves Completion is the **Date of Completion**. Where the Contract contains a mechanism for extending the time within which the Contractor is to complete the Works, and the time is extended, the Contractor's obligation is to complete the Works by the extended Date for Completion.[14] A Contractor is normally entitled to complete the Works before the Date for Completion, but cannot be required to complete the Works earlier unless there is an express contractual power entitling the Employer or its agent to order acceleration for the Contractor to achieve early Completion.[15]

If the Contractor fails to complete the Works timeously without excuse, the Employer is usually entitled to recover the damages it has sustained or stipulate a reduction in the contract price (depending on the terms of the Contract). Under the common law, the Employer would

---

10 *Mir Bros Trading company Pty Ltd v Cavasinni Constructions Pty Ltd* [2016] NSWSC 1873, [43], per Fagan J.

11 [2003] EWHC 725 (TCC), [144]; cited with approval in *Peregrine Systems Ltd v Steria Ltd* [2005] EWCA Civ 329, [15]; *Urban I (Blonk Street) Ltd v Ayres* [2013] EWCA Civ 816, [49], per Sir Terence Etherton C.

12 *Elvanite Full Circle Ltd v AMEC Earth & Environmental (UK) Limited* [2013] EWHC 1191 (TCC), [72], per Coulson J.

13 *Murray v Leisureplay plc* [2005] EWCA Civ 963, [29], per Arden LJ.

14 *Percy Bilton Ltd v Greater London Council* [1982] 1 WLR 794, 801, per Lord Fraser.

15 *Rennavi SpA v New Century Shipbuilding Co Ltd* [2007] EWCA Civ 58, [19], per Moore-Bick LJ.

be entitled to all the damages it suffered which were reasonably foreseeable at the time the Contract was entered into, however this position is frequently altered by specific contractual provisions. Damages may be subject to agreed limitations, as commercial realities usually dictate that at the time of negotiating the Contract, the Employer should accept a limit on the Contractor's liability for prolonged delay. For example, the parties may have agreed to exclude or cap the monetary value of certain types of damages to a percentage of the Contract price, such as loss of profit or 'consequential' losses (which should be explicitly defined). Alternatively, the parties may have agreed to cap damages by nominating an agreed pre-estimate of loss and damages in the form of **liquidated damages** for each day that the Date of Completion exceeds the Date for Completion. The terms of the Contract must be carefully construed to establish whether such liquidated damages are the Employer's sole remedy for late delivery of the Works, or whether common law (unliquidated) damages are also available.[16]

14.2.2 'Time of the essence'

The Contract may stipulate conditions which make 'time of the essence,'[17] but in arriving at a decision as to whether those conditions have been fulfilled, a court will consider the Contract as a whole.[18] In general, a specific stipulation as to time will rarely make time of the essence in a contract which provides for payment of liquidated damages for failing to complete by the Date for Completion.[19] The position is different in the US, where it has been held that if a contract fixes a time for Completion, completion by that date is of the essence, and the fact that liquidated damages may be recoverable in the event of late completion does not militate against this conclusion.[20]

Where the time for the performance in a contract has been stipulated and one party is in delay by reason of its failure to perform it within that time, but 'time is not of the essence of the contract,' the other party can make timely performance a fundamental term by requiring performance within a reasonable time. The non-defaulting party can do this by giving notice that, if the obligation is not complied with by a certain date (allowing a reasonable time), it will regard the Contract as at an end.[21] Where time is not of the essence of the Contract but one of the contracting parties elects to make it so by giving such a notice, it should ensure that the notice is clear and unequivocal, so that the other contracting party is aware of the consequences of a failure on its part to perform timeously.[22]

16 For example, the liquidated damages provision in the JCT80 standard form contract was found to be an exclusive agreement as the damages payable by the Contractor for late completion in *Temloc Ltd v Errill Properties Ltd* (1987) 12 Con LR 109 (Court of Appeal).

17 *Peak Construction (Liverpool) Ltd v McKinney Foundations Ltd* (1970) 1 BLR 111, 120, per Salmon LJ (CA); *Munkenbeck & Marshall v The Kensington Hotel Ltd* (2000) 78 Con LR 171, 178 [25], per HHJ Bowsher QC; *Cavy Offshore Ltd v Emerald Field Contracting Ltd* (1991) 55 BLR 1, 8 to, per Judge Thayne Forbes QC; CCA *Technologies Pte Ltd v Newcon Builders Pte Ltd* [2017] SGCA 53, [45]; *Versa-Tile Pty Ltd v 101 Construction Pty Ltd* [2017] VSC 73, [80], per Ginanne J.

18 *Lamprell v Guardians of the Poor of the Billericay Union* (1849) 3 Exch 283, 309.

19 *Lamprell v Guardians of the Poor of the Billericay Union* (1849) 3 Exch 283, 308 per Rolfe B; *Global Time Investments Ltd v Super Keen Investments Ltd* [2000] HKCFA 104, per Lord Hoffman NPJ.

20 *Empire Energy Management Systems, Inc v Roche* CASFC No 03–1277, 24 March 2004.

21 *Laurinda Pty Ltd v Capalaba Park Shopping Centre Pty Ltd* (1989) 166 CLR 623.

22 *Rickards (Charles) v Oppenheim* [1950] 1 All ER 420 (CA); *Laurinda Pty Ltd v Capalaba Park Shopping Centre Pty Ltd* (1989) 166 CLR 623.

14.2.3 Liquidated damages

The Employer may claim liquidated damages for delay in Completion where, pursuant to the Contract, work has been taken out of the Contractor's hands and the Date for Completion is overrun. In this situation where the Contract is still operative, the Employer may recover from the Contractor not only the liquidated damages for the delay before taking over but also liquidated damages to cover the full period from the Date for Completion fixed by the Contract to the Date of Completion. The Contractor will be entitled to an extension of time only for unnecessary delay in getting a new Contractor to take over the work or unnecessary delay caused by the substitute Contractor.[23]

Where the Contract has been validly terminated for unreasonable delay, the position is different and the principles relating to breach of the entire Contract will apply. In these circumstances, the Employer is only entitled to recover liquidated damages for delay before termination of the Contract, plus its proven damages for delay after termination. In *British Glanzstoff Manufacturing Co Ltd v General Accident, Fire and Life Assurance Co Ltd*,[24] it was held that liquidated damages could not be claimed for the period after termination of the Contract when the whole Works were in another Contractor's hands.

Under the common law, the Employer will not be entitled to recover the liquidated damages nominated in the Contract if those liquidated damages were not a genuine covenanted pre-estimate of the damage that the Employer would suffer as a result of late completion of the Works,[25] that is if the liquidated damages amount to a penalty. (It should be noted however that the judges in some old cases referred to liquidated damages themselves as a penalty, eg *Wells v Army & Navy Cooperative Society*.) The common law penalty doctrine is long-standing,[26] and has recently been redefined and refined in Australia,[27] England,[28] and New Zealand.[29] There are differences between jurisdictions in the circumstances where the doctrine is applicable.

Contractual provisions for liquidated damages for late Completion have benefits for both the Employer and the Contractor. In the event of late Completion, the Employer will not have to undertake the time-consuming and expensive exercise of proving its actual losses. The Contractor knows before entering into the Contract the financial consequences for every day of late Completion; this avoids any uncertainty on what the damages will be and enables the Contractor to plan its work accordingly.

It is therefore in the Employer's (and usually the Contractor's also) interests not only for the liquidated damages rate specified in the Contract to be a genuine pre-estimate, but

23 *Geiger v Western Maryland Ry* (1874) Md 43 USA; cf *British Glanzstoff Manufacturing Co Ltd v General Accident Fire & Life Assurance Co Ltd* [1912] SC 591; [1913] AC 143.

24 [1912] SC 591; [1913] AC 143.

25 *Dunlop Pneumatic Tyre Company Limited v New Garage and Motor Company Limited* [1915] AC 79.

26 *Dunlop Pneumatic Tyre Co Ltd v New Garage & Motor Co Ltd* [1915] AC 79.

27 *Andrews v ANZ Banking Group Ltd* (2012) 247 CLR 205; *Paciocco v Australia and New Zealand Banking Group Ltd* [2016] HCA 28. In *Paciocco,* Kiefel J said that the question is 'whether a provision for the payment of a sum of money on default is out of all proportion to the interests of the party which it is the purpose of the provision to protect. This interest may be of a business or financial nature' [29].

28 *Cavendish Square Holdings v Makdessi* [2015] 3 WLR 1373. Lord Neuberger and Lord Sumption said that the true test is whether the provision is a secondary obligation which imposes a detriment on the party in breach 'out of all proportion to any legitimate interest of the innocent party in the enforcement of the primary obligation.'

29 *127 Hobson Street Limited v Honey Bees Preschool Limited* [2020] NZSC 53.

that there are contemporaneous records which document the rational basis on which it was determined. It is no bar to the validity of liquidated damages that the amount subsequently proves to be different (either higher or lower even to the extent of zero) to the actual damages suffered, provided it was a reasonable estimate of the foreseeable losses at the time the Contract was entered into.[30] Records of the basis of calculation of liquidated damages prepared at tender time would normally be very persuasive evidence to a court that the amount was a genuine pre-estimate of damages, and therefore not a penalty.

It should be noted that Employers must still prove their loss even where there is a liquidated damages clause for delay in some jurisdictions, for example Malaysia and Pakistan.[31] A court may reduce the specified liquidated damages in some jurisdictions, for example Japan, Korea, and the Philippines.[32] In some jurisdictions a court may increase the specified liquidated damages if a party can prove a higher loss, for example UAE.[33]

If the Contract does not contain a liquidated damages provision, or the liquidated damages provisions are unenforceable, the Employer will have to prove the damage it suffered through the late Completion of the Works in accordance with the usual rules for the recovery of damages.

14.2.4 Completion requirements in the specification

Where staged Completion of portions of the Works are required and this is set out in the Contract, it must clearly state which portions of the Works are to be completed by when, and further, the liquidated damages attached to late Completion of each portion. The Contractor must ensure that its tender and other cross-references to Completion are consistent with this requirement.

14.3 Programme

14.3.1 General requirements

The provision by the Contractor of a **programme** that includes a schedule of activities, their start times and durations is vital to the successful completion of the Contract. Nevertheless, it is not uncommon for the Contractor's programme to be inadequate or out of date, and this may be a factor in the rejection of claims for an extension of time and subsequent disputes:

> Central to most disputes remains the lack of any rigour in the management of the construction program. Amazing as it is, many contractors do not program the works in detail (perhaps preferring not to have an accurate record) and many clients do not specify a definitive program regime. Contracts typically assign responsibility for programming but fail to provide a means of dealing with the problem of non-compliance. This alone leaves these contracts unmanageable and the resolution of disputes as a 'global claim' farce. Within the melee that surrounds most projects, client organisations appear to prefer the cover that arbitration and other legal processes

30 *Clydebank Engineering & Shipbuilding Vo v Castaneda* [1905] AC 6 (House of Lords).

31 Donald Charrett (ed), *FIDIC Contracts in Asia Pacific: A Practical Guide to Application* (Informa Law from Routledge, 2021), 364 and 433.

32 Ibid, 314, 330 and 483.

33 Donald Charrett (ed), *The International Application of FIDIC Contracts* (Informa Law from Routledge, 2020), 404.

> give them whilst contractors, faced with extended cash-flow problems, play the expanded claims value game as a means of maximising their belated returns. The consequence is that disputes have grown in size and the time taken to deal with them has lengthened.[34]

It is for the Engineer and the Employer to decide in what form they require the programme – for example critical path network, linked bar chart, or PERT – in such detail as the Engineer may require. The actual form in which the programme is to be submitted by the Contractor should be identified by the Employer in the Contract documents, either by way of a sample or by reference to commonly understood types of programme, to avoid subsequent debate as to its adequacy. For example, a milestone programme may be provided by the Employer setting out the parameters within which the Contractor must carry out its work. It is not unknown for a Contractor to contrive disagreement on the programme from inception, thereby obstructing its true intent and value.

The programme is important for both Contractor and Employer, particularly from the Employer's point of view in relation to the obligations it is required to fulfil under the Contract, which may include provision of Employer's drawings, access to the Site, completion of any necessary civil engineering work, obtaining import licences, and so on. The programme prepared by the Contractor should therefore include both the Employer's and the Contractor's obligations, notwithstanding that it is generally the Contractor's sole responsibility to maintain this document. An accurate, properly prepared and maintained programme could also be crucial in determining the disrupting effect of any delays which may occur during the course of the Contract and whether the Contractor is entitled to an extension of time under the relevant extension of time provisions. A properly maintained programme is one in which the 'as built' progress is recorded for each activity, separate from the planned progress.

If a Contractor promises to work to a programme, the Contractor is bound to do so and will be in breach of the Contract if it fails to follow the programme.[35]

The programme should be sufficiently detailed to enable arrangements to be made by the Employer for access to, or possession of, the various parts of the Site in good time. In engineering contracts, possession is made available in stages more often than in building contracts. Advance notice is also often required to enable the Engineer to exercise any powers conferred upon it by the contract documents, to control and select the method of working, or to approve stages of construction, or to suspend the work on the grounds of safety. The Engineer should be fully informed at all times of the Contractor's intentions, and this can be particularly important if major technical difficulties are encountered. If the Contractor fails to follow the contract programme, the Engineer or the Employer may be empowered to order the Contractor to take such measures as are necessary so as to 'get back on track.'[36]

34 John Messenger, 'An Overview of Changes in the Construction Industry Since the Eighties' in Charles O'Neill (ed), *Human Dynamics in Construction Risk Management* (Contract Dynamics Sdn Bhd 2014) 54, 57.

35 See 2017 FIDIC Red Book sub-clause 8.3; AS 4000–1997 clause 32; *Fairfield-Mabey Ltd v Shell UK Ltd* [1989] CILL 514, 517, per HHJ Bowsher QC; *Council of the City of Plymouth v DR Jones (Yeovil) Ltd* [2005] EWHC 2356 (TCC), [34], per HHJ Coulson QC. See also Maclean, 'The programme under NEC3: the unacceptable truth' (2013) 29 *Construction Law Journal* 205.

36 See for example 2017 FIDIC Red Book sub-clause 8.7.

The Contract should be drafted so that the Engineer has the power to order the Contractor to revise the programme if the progress of the Works either falls behind or leads the programme. The Contract should be drafted in this way because it is far better that the parties should always be working to a programme which reflects the actual progress of the Works, rather than the desired progress. Construction contracts which provide the Engineer with this power generally also provide that if the Engineer requires a revised programme, the Contractor is entitled to be paid the cost of the revisions to the programme if the modifications arise for reasons for which the Contractor is not responsible.

Insofar as Completion dates are concerned, a construction programme is, in essence, a statement of the intended order of working rather than a statement of dates having contractual force. The Contractor is normally required under the Contract to submit, at the request of the Engineer, the order and the proposed method of working. Full information as to the Contractor's 'arrangements' – that is its methods and intentions – may also be required under the Contract at any subsequent time on the Engineer's request. It is suggested that this information should be incorporated as part of the Contract, as it will document not only the progress of the Contractor, but also the performance by the Engineer and the Employer of their obligations.

The practical implications if the Contractor fails to comply with its programme obligations under the Contract or recording its as built progress will be far reaching, as it will be deprived of valuable evidence upon which to have its claims for extension of time or costs of acceleration evaluated. Further, the Engineer may not be able to adequately judge the Contractor's applications for extension of time.

The Employer can achieve an effective sanction on the Contractor if it is stipulated that a programme must be provided by the Contractor at the tender stage. Alternatively, the Contract could require the programme to be provided before the Contractor is permitted to enter the Site, or that interim payments could be withheld by the Employer until the Contractor had complied with such an Engineer's request.

Since, in nearly all cases, it will be impossible for an Employer to show that the clause containing the Contractor's programme obligations is a fundamental term of the Contract or that it has suffered damage if its Engineer's requests are not complied with, neither an action for breach of contract nor the withholding of moneys otherwise due are in practice likely to be available to the Employer to enforce the Contractor to comply with its programme obligations. An important characteristic of engineering contracts, as compared to building contracts, is the much higher degree of interest in, and control over, the Contractor's methods of working by the Employer. The modern tendency is for the Employer, through the Engineer, to become more intimately involved with the monitoring of the Contractor's progress – on the basis that the legal remedies afforded the Employer in case of a breach are inadequate when compared with the benefits derived by the Employer in ensuring timely and satisfactory compliance by the Contractor.

If the Contract requires the Employer to provide information to the Contractor by a particular date, the programme may be used by the Contractor to justify a complaint that the late provision of that information has delayed the Works, thereby entitling it to an extension of time.

From the Employer's point of view the programme enables the Engineer to monitor the progress of the work, and thus to advise the Employer at an early stage whether the Contract will be completed timeously, or whether the Contractor should be ordered (if there is such a power under the Contract) to speed up the progress of the Works (acceleration). Where timely completion is of major importance and the Contract has discrete **milestone** dates for separable portions of the Works, a contractual provision enabling the imposition of liquidated damages for failure to achieve milestone dates in addition to liquidated damages for late Completion is recommended. For example, Annexure A of AS2124–1992 provides for liquidated damages to be specified for each separable portion.

14.3.2 Programme contingency

A prudent Contractor planning the Works will normally make a contingency allowance for possible delays arising from the materialisation of Contractor's risks (eg inclement weather), as it will not be entitled to an extension of time for such delays. Such a contingency can be hidden in the time estimates for each activity by adding an allowance to the time estimated to actually complete the activity. Alternatively, it can be shown as a period of time after the completion of the activities required for Completion until the Date for Completion; this period is sometimes inappropriately referred to as Contractor's 'float.'

Float is a term used in the critical path method of programming for the amount of free time available before an activity must start so that it does not extend the overall time for Completion. Activities on the critical path have zero float. The **critical path method (CPM)** of programming is a mathematical method of scheduling a set of project activities to determine the shortest overall time for Completion (the **critical path**). The time remaining from the planned completion of all the Contractor's activities required for Completion until the Date for Completion under the Contract is more appropriately termed **Contractor's contingency**.

Programmes which are agreed or approved by the Engineer, and which show Completion considerably in advance of the Date for Completion (ie which show Contractor's contingency in the programme) may, depending on the terms of the Contract, still be used by the Contractor to justify an extension of time claim (and associated delay costs) for issues such as the late supply of information by the Employer or the Employer's failure to give access to the Site. For example, sub-clause 8.5 of the 2017 FIDIC Red Book provides for an extension of time for a qualifying cause of delay 'if and to the extent that completion for the purposes of Sub-Clause 10.1 [Taking Over the Works and Sections] is or will be delayed.' Under such a contractual provision, the fact that the Contractor intends to complete the Works before the Date for Completion would not affect its ability to successfully raise a claim for an extension of time.

However, a contractual term which confines an extension of time for a qualifying cause of delay to one which will delay the Contractor in achieving Completion by the relevant Date for Completion would not give the Contractor the benefit of its programme contingency. In the authors' experience, such a contractual provision in which the Employer's delays can be deducted from the Contractor's contingency is not conducive to the preparation or maintenance of a realistic programme by the Contractor.[37] In this situation there is no incentive for the Contractor to include any contingency in its programme to allow for

37 This is often referred to as the Employer 'owning the float,' although for the reasons given earlier this is misleading terminology.

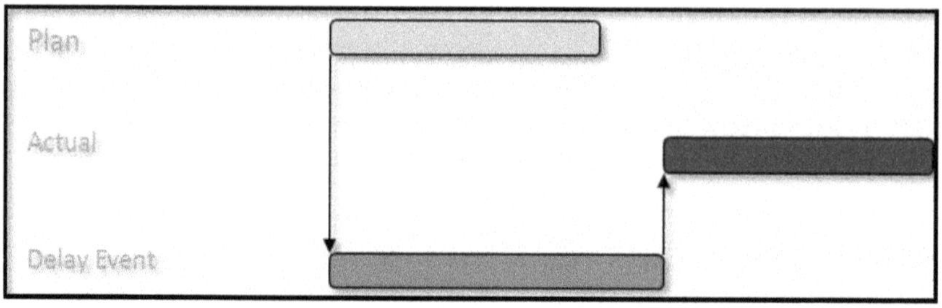

Figure 14.1 Pictorial representation of delay

the inevitable risks and vicissitudes of construction for which it will not be entitled to an extension of time. These risks to the Date of Completion are likely to be implicit in the Contractor's planning of its work, notwithstanding the programme it submits to the Engineer, which may have been prepared to show multiple critical paths all projecting Completion on the Date for Completion. Such a one-sided contractual provision is likely to lead to considerably more time disputes, since any delay to any critical path on the programme will, at least in theory, extend Completion beyond the contractual Date for Completion. This type of contractual provision may also result in the Contractor having two programmes: the contract programme which is provided to the Engineer and the Employer showing a multitude of critical activities, and the 'real' programme that has realistic estimates of activity durations and a Contractor's contingency which the Contractor actually uses to plan the Works.

14.4 Delay

A **delay** is any event which extends the duration of one aspect (or multiple aspects) of a project. Delay occurs where something happens later than expected or programmed, or where the work is not carried out in a timely manner.

Bramble and Callahan define delay as 'the time during which some part of a construction has been extended beyond what was originally planned due to circumstance impacting on the project.'[38] The **SCL Protocol**[39] defines a delay event as 'an event or cause of delay, which may be either a Employer Risk Event or a Contractor Risk Event.'[40] A delay event is illustrated in Figure 14.1.

It is important to note that the cause of the delay (delay event), actual delay, and the effect of the delay can be time distant apart, as shown in Figure 14.2.

In the case of a fixed commencement and completion date contract, both Employer and Contractor have their rights and obligations stipulated in the Contract. The Contractor becomes liable if it fails to achieve the Date for Completion due to its own fault and the

38 Barry B. Bramble & Michael T Callahan, *Construction Delay Claims* (Aspen Publishers, 6th edn 2017).
39 The Society of Construction Law Delay and Disruption Protocol (2nd edn, February 2017).
40 Ibid. 63.

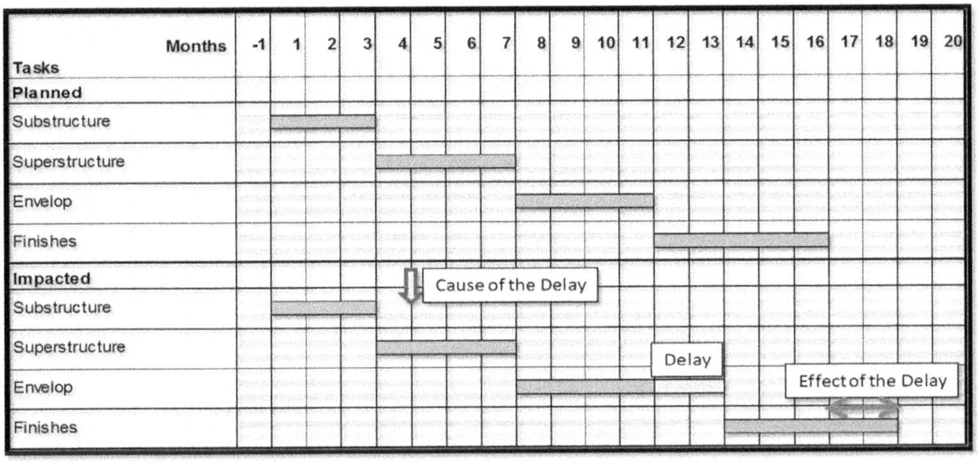

Figure 14.2 Delay event and effect of the delay

Employer is liable if it prevents the Contractor from achieving the Date for Completion. From a Contractor's perspective, any project which suffers delay and disruption may have serious consequences due to the possible imposition and enforcement of liquidated damages by the Employer and increased preliminaries and time-related costs.

Delay can be categorised as either critical delay or non-critical delay

The SCL Protocol defines **critical delay** as 'a delay to progress of any activity on the critical path [which] will, without acceleration or re-sequencing, cause the overall project duration to be extended.'[41]

A **non-critical delay** is a delay to an activity not on the critical path of the construction programme and therefore does not affect the project Completion date.

Delays may also be categorised as excusable, non-excusable, compensable, and non-compensable.[42] An **excusable delay** is a delay caused by the Employer or the Employer's agents or due to a neutral event beyond the control of the Contractor. The Contractor is usually entitled an EOT if it is an excusable delay. The SCL Protocol defines an Employer delay as 'any delay caused by an Employer Risk Event.' The SCL Protocol also defines an Employer Risk Event in respect of which the Contractor is entitled to compensation as a compensable event.[43] **Non-excusable delays** are those which are attributable to the Contractor or the Contractor's agents and therefore do not entitle the Contractor to an EOT or compensation.

Where a party is entitled to additional payment as a result of a delay event, it is referred to as a **compensable delay**. Where a delay event cannot be classified as compensable, it will be considered a **non-compensable delay** by default. Similarly, a delay event will

41 Ibid. 62.
42 P J Keane & A F Caletka, *Delay Analysis in Construction Contracts* (Wiley Blackwell, 2nd edn 2015) 6.
43 SCL Protocol, 61.

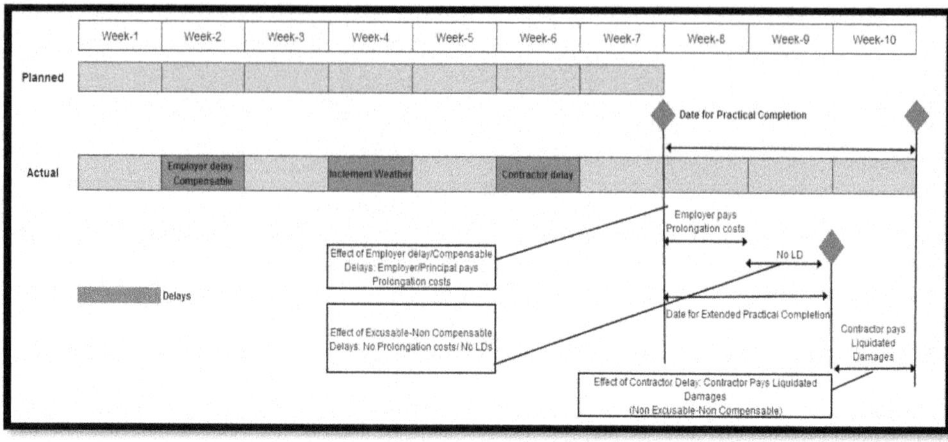

Figure 14.3 Effect of various delays on liquidated damages/costs

be considered as non-excusable if it cannot be proved as excusable. Excusable non-compensable delays are generally beyond the control of both the parties. Figure 14.3 highlights the effect of various delays on liquidated damages/costs.

In order to demonstrate that a delay is compensable as well as excusable, it must be shown that it impacts the Completion date and it must be proved as a critical delay to Completion of the Works (or section of the Works). Entitlement to additional time and delay costs depends on which party has caused the delay. The Contractor can claim additional time as well as extra costs and expenses incurred, if the Employer caused the critical delay events extending the Date for Completion. Similarly, the Employer can impose liquidated damages on the Contractor if the delay to the Date for Completion is caused by the Contractor.

14.5 Concurrent delay

14.5.1 What is concurrent delay?

Few construction law topics have generated as much confusion, debate, and controversy as the issue of concurrent delay.

> This arises from the conceptual difficulty of applying the principles of legal causation to complex delays in construction projects, and the commercial consequences arising from contractors' applications for extension of time to contract completion dates, relief from liquidated damages for delay, and compensation for delay costs.[44]

Much of that conceptual difficulty arises from the lack of a universally accepted definition of concurrent delay and the limitations of the cases that have considered concurrent delay.

44 Gordon Smith, 'What is the Malmaison Approach?' (2015) 1, www.gordonsmithlegal.com.au/resources/What%20is%20the%20Malmaison%20Approach%20-%20(19022015).pdf (accessed 17 August 2021).

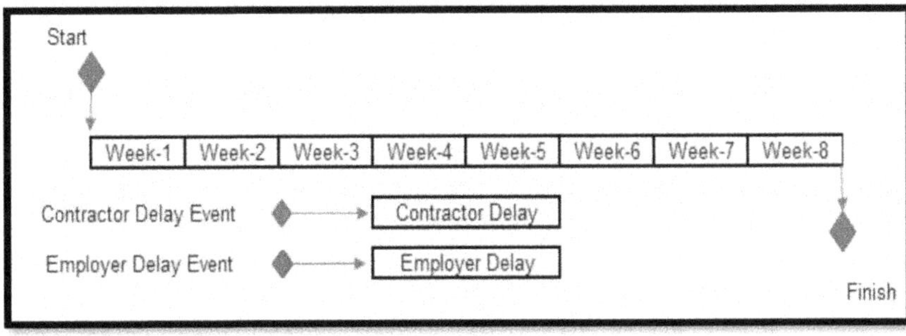

Figure 14.4 Pictorial representation of true concurrency

Marrin defined 'concurrent delay' as 'a period of project overrun which is caused by two or more effective causes of delay which are of approximately equal causative potency.'[45] This definition was accepted by the Court of Appeal in *North Midland Building Ltd v Cyden Homes Ltd.*[46] HH Judge Richard Seymour explains 'concurrent delay' as: 'when two things happen, either of which, had it happened on its own, would have caused delay, and one is a relevant event, while the other is not.'[47]

The SCL Protocol distinguishes between the common usage of 'concurrent delay' as 'the situation where two or more delay events arise at different times, but the effects of them are felt at the same time'[48] from 'true concurrent delay':

> True concurrent delay is the occurrence of two or more delay events at the same time, one an Employer Risk Event, the other a Contractor Risk Event, and the effects of which are felt at the same time. For concurrent delay to exist, each of the Employer Risk Event and the Contractor Risk Event must be an effective cause of Delay to Completion (i.e. the delays must both affect the critical path).[49]

The SCL Protocol considers true concurrent delay to be a rare occurrence. True concurrency is shown pictorially in Figure 14.4.

The Scottish case of *City Inn Ltd v Shepherd Construction*[50] highlighted that the term 'concurrent delay' may refer to a number of different situations. The term can apply in the broad sense where two delaying events have a causative effect on Completion even where they do not overlap in time. Alternatively, the term can apply in the narrow sense where two delaying events are contemporaneous or co-extensive and may or may not share a starting point and an end point in time.[51]

---

45 John Marrin QC, 'Concurrent Delay' (2002) 18 *Construction Law Journal* 436, 437.

46 [2018] EWCA Civ 1744 per Coulson LJ. See also *Adyard Abu Dhabi v SD Marine Services* [2011] EWHC 848 (Comm) per Hamblen J.

47 *Royal Brompton Hospital NHS Trust v Frederick Alexander Hammond (No.6)* (2000) 76 Con. L.R. 131, [31].

48 Ibid. [10.4].

49 SCL Protocol, [10.3].

50 [2010] CSIH 68.

51 *City Inn Ltd v Shepherd Construction* [2010] CSIH 68, [49] per Lord Osborne.

The SCL definition of true concurrency and the Marrin definition appear to apply to the narrow sense. Stephenson used the terms 'contemporaneously concurrent' (where events occur at exactly the same time) and 'non-contemporaneously concurrent' (where the events occur at different times but cooperate together to cause a single delay) for the terms in the narrow sense and broad sense respectively.[52]

Much of the uncertainty around concurrent delay in the literature and the cases arises because it is not always clear whether the term refers to 'true' concurrent delay in the narrow sense (as in the SCL definition), or concurrent delay in the broad sense.

In *Royal Brompton Hospital NHS Trust v Hammond*,[53] Judge Seymour clearly distinguished between the concurrent effects of sequential delays and true concurrency in the following terms:

> However, it is, I think, necessary to be clear what one means by events operating concurrently. It does not mean, in my judgement, a situation in which, work already being delayed, let it be supposed, because the contractor has had difficulty in obtaining sufficient labour, an event occurs which is a relevant event [ie an event which if on the critical path would give rise to an extension of time] and which, had the contractor not been delayed, would have caused him to be delayed, but which, in fact, by reason of the existing delay, made no difference. In such a situation although there is a relevant event, 'the completion of the Works is [not] likely to be delayed thereby beyond the Completion Date.'
>
> The relevant event simply has no effect upon the completion date. This situation obviously needs to be distinguished from a situation in which, as it were, the works are proceeding in a regular fashion and on programme, when two things happen, either of which, had it happened on its own, would have caused delay, and one is a relevant event, while the other is not. In such circumstances there is a real concurrency of causes of the delay.[54]

The following definitions are used in this book:

Concurrent delay is delay caused by more than one event when the causes are within the control or risk shared by both parties, that is concurrent delay in the broad sense.

True concurrent delay is the occurrence of two or more delay events at the same time, one an Employer risk event, the other a Contractor risk event, and the effects of which are felt at the same time, that is the SCL Protocol definition.

14.5.2 Cases on concurrent delay

In a review of English cases dealing with the Contractor's entitlement to an EOT where there is concurrent delay, Victoria Peckett identified three lines of cases:[55]

(1) The Contractor will be entitled to an EOT if the Contractor risk event and the Employer risk event are of approximately equal potency.[56]

---

52 Andrew Stephenson, 'Concurrency, Causation, Commonsense & Compensation (Part 1)' (2010) *International Construction Law Review* 166, 177.

53 (2001) 76 Con LR 148.

54 Ibid. 173–174.

55 Victoria Peckett, 'England' in CMS Guide to Concurrent Delay (July 2020), www.cms-lawnow.com/publications/2020/08/international-cms-guide-to-concurrent-delay-2020?cc_lang=en (accessed 17 August 2021).

56 *Henry Boot Construction (UK) Limited v Malmaison Hotel (Manchester) Ltd* (1999) 70 Con LR 32 per Dyson J; *Steria Ltd v Sigma Wireless Communications Ltd* [2008] BLR 79; [2007] EWHC 3454 (TCC) per Judge

(2) The 'first in time' event determines the cause of the delay, and the second in time is not an effective cause because the Contractor is already in delay.[57]
(3) The Contractor is entitled to an EOT where an Employer's risk event would have provided an entitlement to an EOT in the absence of the Contractor's risk event.[58]

In *City Inn Ltd v Shepherd Construction*,[59] the Inner House of the Scottish Court of Session took a different approach to the English cases. From his review of the authorities, Lord Osborne formulated a number of propositions:

(1) A relevant event must be shown to be a cause of delay to Completion.
(2) The causative effect of a relevant event is to be resolved by the application of principles of common sense.
(3) Causation can be determined by any acceptable factual evidence, not necessarily confined to a critical path analysis.
(4) If a dominant cause of delay can be identified, effect will be given to that without taking into account any causes that are not material.
(5) Where two causes are operative and neither is a dominant cause (concurrent causes) the delay may be apportioned between the causes. The apportionment should be carried out in a fair and reasonable way, taking into account the background to the decision making.[60]

It should be noted that later English cases have specifically stated that the apportionment approach is not in accordance with English law.[61] However, there was no critical path determined in *City Inn* and in the Outer House of the Court of Session Lord Drummond Young stated that the case was 'one of true concurrent causes.'[62] Whilst apportionment is likely to be inappropriate in the majority of cases where there is evidence of the impact of the various delaying events on the critical path, apportionment may be the only practical and fair approach where disentangling the precise impacts of different delay events is not possible. For this reason, Stephenson submits that:

> *City Inn* was an unusual case which required an unusual approach. It should not be regarded as inconsistent with the *Brompton Hospital* case; the two cases reflect the two approaches which may be taken, depending on the expert evidence available. However, in the vast majority of cases in large projects the expert evidence is likely to allow a *Brompton Hospital* analysis, which is more sophisticated and accurate and therefore should be adopted.[63]

Davies; *Walter Lilly & Company Ltd v DMV Developments Ltd* [2012] EWHC 1773 per Akenhead J.

57 *Balfour Beatty Ltd v Chestermount Properties Ltd* [1993] 62 BLR 1 per Colman J; *Royal Brompton Hospital NHS Trust v Hammond* (2001) 76 Con LR 148, [2000] EWHC Technology 39 per HHJ Seymour QC; *Great Eastern Hotel Company Ltd v John Laing Construction Ltd* [2005] EWCH 181 per HHJ David Wilcox; *Adyard Abu Dhabi v SD Marine Services* [2011] EWHC 848 per Hamblen J; *Saga Cruises BDF Ltd v Fincantieri SPA* [2016] EWHC 1875 per Sara Cockerill DHCJ.

58 *De Beers UK Limited v Atos Origin IT Services UK Limited* [2010] EWHC 3276 per Edwards-Stuart J.

59 [2010] CSIH 68.

60 Ibid. [42].

61 For example *Walter Lilly & Company Ltd v DMV Developments Ltd* [2012] EWHC 1773, [370] per Akenhead J.

62 *City Inn Ltd v Shepherd Construction* [2007] CSOH 190, [157].

63 Andrew Stephenson, 'Concurrency, Causation, Commonsense & Compensation (Part 1)' (2010) *International Construction Law Review* 166, 176.

The majority of the English cases and *City Inn* are based on the JCT contract, which requires the contract administrator to give an extension of time estimated to be fair and reasonable in the circumstances.

14.5.3 The SCL Protocol

In a 2015 paper Smith reviewed the case law on concurrent delay from the perspective of whether the cases supported the 'SCL view' enshrined in the 2002 SCL Protocol (the Contractor is entitled to an extension of time if there is a relevant event) or the 'critical path view' (which allows an extension of time only if there is a delay to Completion).[64]

Core principle 9 in the 2002 SCL Protocol in respect of the Contractor's entitlement to extension of time where there is concurrent delay states: 'Where Contractor delay to Completion occurs or has effect concurrently with Employer delay to Completion, the Contractor's concurrent delay should not reduce any EOT due.' In the 2017 second edition of the SCL Protocol, the SCL's original approach to concurrent delay was amended to reflect recent case law. It recommended that where the Employer delay will not result in the Works being completed later than would otherwise have been the case because they were already going to be delayed by a greater period because of the Contractor delay to Completion, the only effective cause of the delay to Completion is the Contractor risk event. This was said to be the consistent position taken in recent lower-level English court decisions. It is also consistent with Smith's conclusion that the *Malmaison* approach is confined to the rare situation of true concurrent delay. He noted that Contractors frequently rely on the (2002) SCL view, whereas Employers frequently rely on the critical path view.[65] Contractors are now on notice that the (2002) SCL view is not supported by case law, nor by the preference expressed in the 2017 SCL Protocol.

The SCL Protocol has no inherent status. It is intended to provide useful guidance on some of the common delay and disruption issues that arise in construction projects but is not intended to be a contract document.[66] Although it has been referred to in a limited number of cases,[67] its approach to concurrent delay has not been endorsed. Nevertheless, it contains a useful statement of a reasonable approach to concurrent delay:

> In considering whether concurrent delay exists, the Protocol recommends a common sense approach to delay analysis. In particular, the Protocol recognises that delay analysis is rarely precise down to the day (or even a few days). The application of common sense requires that the margin for imprecision should be taken into account in reaching a conclusion of concurrency.[68]

---

64 Gordon Smith, 'What is the Malmaison Approach?' (2015) 2, www.gordonsmithlegal.com.au/resources/What%20is%20the%20Malmaison%20Approach%20-%20(19022015).pdf (accessed 17 August 2021).

65 Gordon Smith,(2015) 2, www.gordonsmithlegal.com.au/resources/What%20is%20the%20Malmaison%20Approach%20-%20(19022015).pdf (accessed 17 August 2021).

66 SCL Protocol 1.

67 www.scl.org.uk/sites/default/files/documents/SCL%20Delay%20and%20Disruption%20Protocol%20-%20judicial%20references%20%5BUpdated%20August%20 . . . . pdf (accessed 19 August 2021).

68 SCL Protocol, [B10.11].

14.5.4 Analysis of concurrent delay

The cases make clear that any enquiry on concurrent delay must start with the words of the Contract. In many cases, the proper construction of the terms of the Contract may provide a clear answer to issues of concurrent delay. For example, the 1999 FIDIC Yellow Book provides that:

> The Contractor shall be entitled subject to Sub-Clause 20.1 [Contractor's Claims] to extension of the Time for Completion if and to the extent that the completion for the purposes of Sub-Clause 10.1 [Taking Over of the Works and Sections] is or will be delayed by any of the following causes:
> (a) . . .
> (e) . . . [69]

It is submitted that this entitlement to an EOT is not conditioned in any way by other delaying events for which the Contractor is responsible. If completion is delayed by any of the enumerated causes (a)–(e), the Contractor is entitled to an EOT irrespective of whether there is a concurrent delay caused by a Contractor risk event.[70] Accordingly, the situation under the 1999 Yellow Book is similar to that under the standard form JCT contract where Akenhead J noted: 'There is nothing in the wording of Clause 25 which expressly suggests that there is any sort of proviso to the effect that an extension should be reduced if the causation criterion is established. . . . The test is primarily a causation one.'[71]

Conversely AS 4300 provides that

> Where more than one event causes concurrent delays and the cause of at least one of those events, but not all of them, is not a cause of delay listed in Clause 35.5 (a) or (b) [entitling the Contractor to an extension of time], then to the extent that the delays are concurrent, the Contractor shall not be entitled to an extension of time for Practical Completion.[72]

This clearly allocates the risk of concurrent delay to the Contractor, as was done in the case of *North Midland Building Ltd v Cyden Homes Ltd* where the relevant JCT clause was amended to similar effect.[73]

In 2010 Stephenson reviewed the cases on concurrent delay and concluded that the *Malmaison* approach was not supported by more general cases relating to the causation of concurrent losses. He noted that the traditional 'but for' test of causation does not

---

69 Sub-clause 8.4 Extension of Time for Completion.

70 It is unfortunate that the 2017 FIDIC Yellow Book has departed from this clarity by adding the following:

> If a delay caused by a matter which is the Employer's responsibility is concurrent with a delay caused by a matter which is the Contractor's responsibility, the Contractor's entitlement to EOT shall be assessed in accordance with the rules and procedures stated in the Special Provisions (if not stated, as appropriate taking due regard of all relevant circumstances).

The Notes on the Preparation of Special Provisions refers to the SCL Protocol as one example of 'rules and procedures' but notes that different rules/procedures may apply different legal jurisdictions. In the authors' view this addition was a retrograde step that is only likely to increase the potential for disputes.

71 *Walter Lilly & Company Ltd v DMV Developments Ltd* [2012] EWHC 1773, [370] per Akenhead J.

72 General Conditions of Contract for Design and Construct AS 4300–1995, clause 35.5 Extension of time for Practical Completion.

73 [2018] EWCA Civ 1744, [39] per Coulson LJ.

work for concurrent delay, as it results in a conclusion that neither delaying event caused delay to Completion (because absent (only) one of the delaying events, the delay would still have occurred).[74] He suggested the proper approach to causation where the 'but for' test of causation does not apply in respect of concurrent delays is to apply common sense to the relevant facts having close regard to the purpose of the inquiry. The purpose of such an enquiry into causation is critical to determine which of many antecedent events will be considered to be the legal cause of the delay. The question is: having regard to the purpose of the enquiry, as a matter of common sense, should the delay entitle the Contractor to further remuneration and an extension of time?[75]

Stephenson suggested the following use of the common sense test of causation:

(1) If the delays are contemporaneously concurrent, consider the purpose for which the extension of time or compensation is being granted. That may be a single purpose such as to relieve the Contractor of liability for liquidated damages and to preserve the Employer's right to liquidated damages by ensuring that the prevention principle does not apply. Stephenson submits that where one of the purposes is to relieve the Contractor from liquidated damages, the Contractor is entitled to an EOT if one of the causes of delay is an excusable event.

(2) If the delays are not contemporaneously concurrent, the application of common sense principles will entitle the Contractor to an EOT if one of the causes of the delay is an excusable event, irrespective of whether another event was also part of the causal chain.[76]

The common sense test of causation has been endorsed by a number of cases in Australia[77] and England,[78] and common sense is explicitly referred to in a number of the concurrent delay cases[79] and the SCL Protocol. It is generally applicable to analysing liability for true concurrent delays, or for concurrent delays in the broader sense. The starting point must always be the proper construction of the terms of the Contract relating to delay and extensions of time. A properly prepared critical path programme that reflects the actual (or projected) sequence of events will usually provide the facts to which common sense principles of causation can be applied.

It is suggested by the authors that business common sense, reasonable outcomes and a common commercial purpose should guide the quest for a generally accepted international practice in resolving issues of concurrency.

74 Andrew Stephenson, 'Concurrency, Causation, Commonsense & Compensation (Part 1)' (2010) *International Construction Law Review* 166, 192.

75 Ibid. 190.

76 Ibid.

77 *March v M H Stramare Pty Ltd* (1991) 171 CLR 506; *Henville v Walker* (2001) 206 CLR 459; *I & L Securities Pty Ltd v HTW Valuers (Brisbane) Pty Ltd* (2002) 210 CLR 109;

78 *Galoo Ltd (in liq.) v Bright Grahame Murray (a firm)* [1995] 1 All ER 16.

79 *Great Eastern Hotel Company Ltd v John Laing Construction Ltd* [2005] EWCH 181 per HHJ David Wilcox; *City Inn Ltd v Shepherd Construction Ltd* [2010] ScotCS CSIH 68 per Lord Osborne; *Adyard Abu Dhabi v SD Marine Services* [2011] EWHC 848 per Hamblen J; *Walter Lilly & Company Ltd v DMV Developments Ltd* [2012] EWHC 1773 per Akenhead J.

14.6 Prolongation, disruption, and acceleration

When delay occurs, conflict often arises, hence the need to understand the difference between delay, prolongation, disruption, and acceleration.

- Prolongation – this is a time related concept.
- Disruption – an efficiency related concept.
- Acceleration – a resource allocation concept.

These three concepts relate to three different project aspects which are separate yet interrelated. They can all have significant impact on the costs borne by the Contractor and the Employer.

14.6.1 Prolongation

Prolongation is the extent to which a delay impacts Completion. The consequence of prolongation is a lengthened project duration, and this happens when a delay occurs on the critical path. A pictorial representation of prolongation is given in Figure 14.5.

A delay does not always extend the project Completion, that is it does not always result in prolongation. Figure 14.6 depicts a non-critical delay not resulting in prolongation.

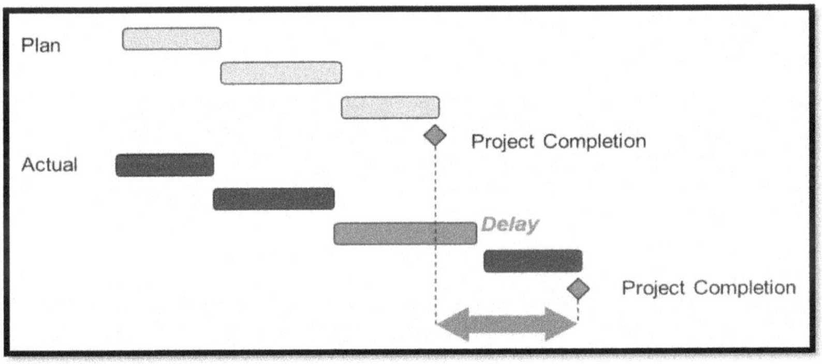

Figure 14.5 Pictorial representation for prolongation

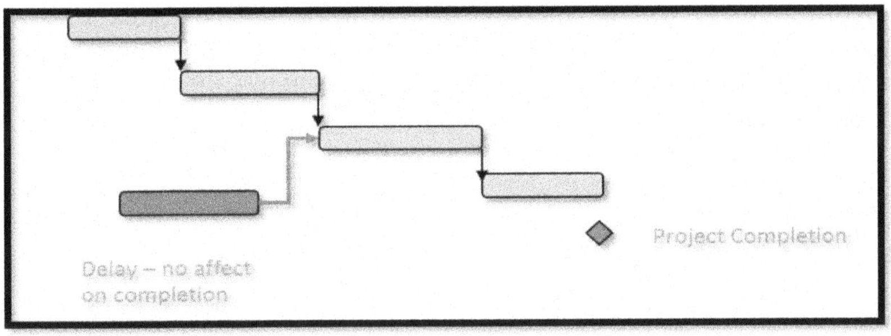

Figure 14.6 Pictorial representation of delay event not resulting in prolongation

14.6.2 Disruption

The SCL Protocol defines **disruption** as 'disturbance, hindrance or interruption to a Contractor's normal working methods, resulting in lower productivity or efficiency in the execution of particular work activities.'[80] Disruption does not necessarily result in a delay to progress or a delay to Completion, but almost inevitably results in increased costs.

The SCL Protocol lists the following productivity-based methods of analysis of disruption:[81]

(1) Project-specific studies:
   (a) Measured mile analysis,
   (b) Earned value analysis,
   (c) Programme analysis,
   (d) Work or trade sampling,
   (e) System dynamics modelling;
(2) Project-comparison studies;
(3) Industry studies.

The SCL Protocol also lists two cost-based methods of analysis of disruption, which it states provide the least robust support for a disruption claim and are inappropriate to use when productivity-based methods can reasonably be deployed:[82]

(1) Estimated v incurred labour,
(2) Estimated v used cost.

The Association for the Advancement of Cost Engineering (**AACE**) has listed, in order of preference, numerous methods[83] to calculate the loss of productivity (ie disruption). The first two methods, being 'Project specific studies,' are:

- Measured mile study,
- Earned value analysis.

The 'measured mile' calculation is perfectly applied where it compares identical activities in impacted and non-impacted sections of the project. The 'measured mile study' compares 'identical activities in impacted and non-impacted sections of the project in order to ascertain the loss of productivity resulting from the impact of a known set of events.'[84]

The 'earned value analysis' is based on the Contractor's estimate of the direct labour hours to be spent in each activity. Physical units of work completed multiplied by budget unit rates can be used to determine earned hours. The earned hours are then compared to the actual hours expended for the period of the impact and the difference between the two may be used to calculate the productivity loss experienced.[85]

80 SCL Protocol, Part A [5].
81 Ibid. 46–48.
82 Ibid. 49.
83 AACE, 'Estimating Lost Labor Productivity in Construction Claims' (2004) International Recommended Practice No. 25R-03, 8 and 9.
84 Ibid. 11.
85 Ibid. 12.

14.6.3 Acceleration

Acceleration is the application of additional resources to achieve a goal. Figure 14.7 is an example of acceleration where resources are added to reduce the duration of an activity.

Generally, when a project is disrupted or delayed, the Contractor accelerates to achieve the original planned duration. It is often a contractual obligation of the Contractor to mitigate any delays, even without instruction from the Employer. Disputes arise when the Contractor accelerates without the Employer's instruction or attempts to mitigate and ends up accelerating, thereby incurring further costs. Disputes may also arise because the cost of the acceleration may outweigh the benefit (or perceived benefit) gained.

Provision may be made in the Contract to entitle the Employer to require Completion of the Works or part thereof earlier than the initial Date for Completion stated in the Contract. In the absence of a specific contractual provision the Employer is unable to order acceleration of the Contractor's work, and accordingly a broadly worded acceleration clause is usually desired by Employers. For example, the JCT Design and Build Contract 2016 (DB 2016) provides an 'Employer friendly' version of an acceleration clause in Supplemental Provision 4. This clause enables the Employer to invite an 'Acceleration Quotation' if it wishes to investigate the possibility of achieving practical completion before the Completion Date for the Works. The Contractor is required to either provide an Acceleration Quotation or explain why it would be impractical to achieve practical completion earlier than the Completion Date. An Acceleration Quotation identifies the time that can be saved, the amount of adjustment to the Contract Sum, and any other conditions. If the Employer wishes to accept the Acceleration Quotation, it must issue a Confirmed Acceptance within the stipulated time.

A 'Contractor-friendly' version of DB 2016 would exclude Supplemental Provision 4 in the Contract Particulars.

For the Contractor to be able to take full advantage of an accelerated programme, the Contract must make it clear that the Employer, in agreeing to such an accelerated programme, is assuming the obligation to fulfil its obligations (which may, for example, include to give access and instructions as soon as practicable) in accordance with the timeframe set out in that accelerated programme.

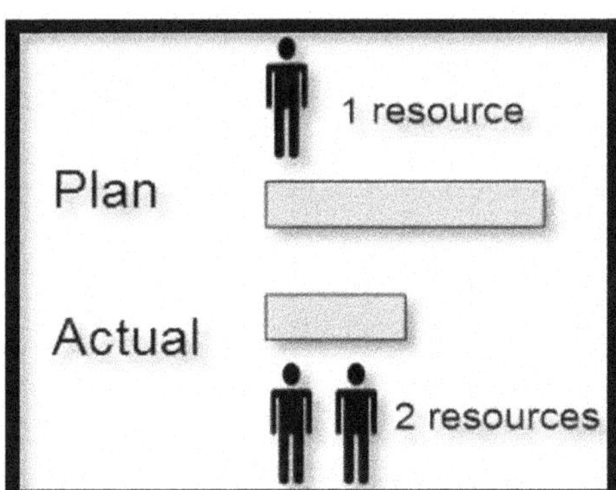

Figure 14.7 Acceleration

Regardless of whether the Employer is bound to complete its obligations in accordance with the approved accelerated programme, the danger to the Employer in the approval of such an accelerated programme exists in the difficulties that may arise, or delays that may result, from nominated subcontractors or suppliers whose quoted delivery or completion dates were arranged with the Date for Completion in view prior to the approval of the accelerated programme (which is presumably the Date for Completion set out in the Contract). The approval of such a programme may involve a changed series of Employer obligations in regard to information and access but does not necessarily result in a contractual obligation upon the Contractor to complete the Works by such earlier date. This depends upon whether the period between the accelerated Date for Completion (as shown in the accelerated programme) and the Date for Completion is shown as contingency on the Contractor's programme, or whether the earlier date is shown as a revised contractual Date for Completion of the whole of the Works. There is no logical reason why there cannot be a legal obligation upon the Employer and the Engineer to work to an accelerated programme while the Contractor duly becomes liable for breach and liquidated damages if it fails to complete by some considerably later date. The terms of the Contract will determine whether this is in fact the case.

A programme which is sufficiently detailed may constitute notice and may suffice as a demand in order to place the Employer or the Engineer in delay or breach, quite apart from the explicit requirements of the Contract. However, without strong evidence to indicate that the Employer is working to the revised dates as if contractually bound to do so, it is probable that the Contract Date for Completion (and other activities) remain as they were originally nominated until validly altered under the Contract.[86]

14.7 Extension of time for Completion (EOT)

14.7.1 Extension of time fundamentals

An **extension of time** (**EOT**) is a formal extension of the contractually specified Date for Completion approved by the Engineer or other person nominated in the Contract.

Time is an important issue in construction contracts[87] with delay claims cited as being perhaps the most common form of dispute in construction contracts.[88] Generally, standard form contracts and modern-day construction contracts provide a mechanism for extending the contractual time for Completion. From a Contractor's perspective, an EOT claim can be the most convenient method of recovering costs due to delayed Completion. EOT is also beneficial to the Employer as it establishes a new Completion date and prevents the time for Completion from becoming 'at large.'

The following questions should be asked when considering whether an event should entitle the Contractor to an extension of time:

(1) Has an event occurred which is the risk or responsibility of the Employer under the Contract (**Employer risk event**)?

86 See J B Dorter & J A Sharkey, *Building and Construction Contracts in Australia* (Thomson Reuters looseleaf) 9.70.

87 J Murdoch & W Hughes, *Construction Contracts Law and Management* (Taylor & Francis, 4th edn 2008) 189.

88 N J Carnell, *Causation and Delay in Construction Disputes* (Blackwell Publishing Ltd, 2nd edn 2005) viii.

(2) Did/will the event delay the progress of the Works?
(3) Did/will the delay to progress cause delay to the Works such that Completion will be delayed?

Questions (2) and (3) are questions of causation. The question of what causal connection is required is a question of law. As Lord Hoffman has said:

> Before answering questions about causation, it is therefore necessary to identify the scope of the relevant rule [which imposes liability/responsibility]. This is not a question of common sense fact; it is a question of law.[89]

and

> One decides, as a matter of law, what causal connection the law requires and one then decides, as a question of fact, whether the claimant has satisfied the requirements of the law. There is, in my opinion, nothing more to be said.[90]

These comments were made in the context of the test for causation of loss in breach of contract cases; the same logic applies to determining whether a Contractor is entitled to an extension of time under the Contract. The question becomes what causal connection is required under the Contract. This is a question of law, not fact.

14.7.2 Standard form contract requirements for EOT

The majority of standard form contracts (such as FIDIC, JCT, Australian Standard forms etc) have strict procedural requirements for EOT claims. While every standard form of contract specifies its own procedure to be followed, some process such as notification of a claim within a prescribed time are common amongst most standard form contracts.

Despite being of significant importance in claiming EOTs, many Contractors fail to follow the notice provisions required by the Contract.

> Contractors either do not want to create an adversarial working environment or do not sufficiently understand their obligations under the notice provisions. Most often, however, Contractors simply have insufficient time during a busy job to follow the specific notice procedures in the contract properly each time a change is encountered.[91]

The under-resourcing of competent contract administration staff can also be a factor.

A notice of delay (**NOD**) may not be a claim and may be considered as no more than a notice for information and intention to make a claim. When a NOD is given within the prescribed time it may provide the opportunity for the Employer to take some action to reduce or even eliminate the cause of the delaying event.

---

89 *Environment Agency v Empress Car Co* [1999] 2 AC 22 (HL).

90 Lord Hoffman, Causation (2005) LQR, Vol 121, page 592, 603.

91 Stephen B Shapiro, Charles F Mitchell & Michael J Cohen, *Notice Provisions in Construction Contracts* (Federal Publication Inc, 2nd Series, 1993) 3–93 Construction Briefings 1.

Failure to provide a notice for an EOT claim within the prescribed time frame may result in the loss of an entitlement to an EOT.[92] Common law courts are willing to uphold clearly drafted time bar clauses and to exclude the application of the prevention principle when prescriptive contractual procedures are not followed properly.[93] Against that, certain contracts contain such stringent and demanding notice requirements that they may be impossible to comply with in practice.

14.7.3 Contractor's entitlement to an EOT

The Contract commonly contains an express power for the Engineer to extend the time for Completion. Generally, an extension of time may be granted either for a delay caused by the Employer, or a delay not caused by the Employer, for example *force majeure*. However, unless the Contract expressly provides, the Engineer has no jurisdiction to extend the time where the Employer has by its own act prevented Completion within the time provided for in the Contract. The exercise of the power to extend time defined in the Contract may not go outside the terms of such power.

The conditions of contract will usually set out the conditions, including notice provisions, under which the Contractor is entitled to an extension of time for Completion. It is important to note that not all delay events give rise to an EOT. A careful examination of the governing contract condition is required to determine which causes of delay are claimable.

The procedures to be followed by the Contractor, the Engineer, and the Employer will also usually be set out in detail. Whether the Contractor can claim for extensions based on any causes other than those listed in the Contract should be made clear. For example, the Contract may provide that the Contractor is entitled to an extension of time for 'exceptionally adverse weather conditions.' What constitutes 'exceptionally adverse weather conditions' depends on the local climate and the time of the year. If the work operations are weather-sensitive, it may be wise to define 'exceptionally adverse' conditions more precisely in the Contract – for example wind above a certain strength, precipitation above a certain measure per 24 hours, and so on.

If the Contractor gives the necessary notice, it may not only be entitled to an extension of time for doing work, but possibly also to expenses where the delay was caused by matters that were the responsibility of the Engineer or the Employer, for example where it was misled by an ambiguity in the specifications and so on, or where materials were incorrectly rejected. The Contractor's entitlement in these circumstances will depend on the specific terms of the Contract.

With the increasing involvement of Employers in electrical and mechanical contracts (in providing design, drawings, engineering, materials, and equipment), the failure of the Employer to fulfil any of its obligations under the Contract may become a major cause for extension of time. Whether this is the case depends on the terms of the Contract. Contractors should be aware of the possibility of delays caused in these circumstances

92 *Australian Development Corporation Pty Limited v White Constructions (ACT) Pty Ltd & Ors* (1996) 12 BCL 317; *Multiplex Constructions Pty Ltd v The State of Queensland* unreported, Supreme Court of Queensland, 31 January 1997.

93 *CMA Assets Pty Ltd v John Holland Pty Ltd [No 6]* [2015] WASC 217.

and should be particularly careful in documenting such delays and complying with the notification provisions in the Contract for claiming an extension of time.

The Contractor may be delayed by other contractors when their performance is necessary for further performance by the Contractor. This may entitle the Contractor to an extension of time under the Contract. Any **suspension** of all or part of the Works, other than caused by the Contractor's default, is usually a cause for a claim for extension of time. In each case, the Contractor's entitlement to an extension of time depends on the specific terms of the Contract.

Industrial disputes may cause disputes between the parties to the Contract, particularly if the party with the ability to control or influence industrial relations does not bear the financial consequences of industrial disputes. For example, an industrial dispute limited to the employees of the Contractor may be capable of easy resolution by the Contractor and arguably, should not be a basis for an extension of time. Delays caused by industrial disputes may be frequent and inevitably cause delay to the Contractor, but the specific terms of the Contract determine whether such a dispute is a qualifying cause of delay for an extension of time. At one end of the spectrum, the Contract may provide that the Contractor is entitled to an extension of time in respect of all industrial disputes without an exception for disputes that are limited to the Contractor's employees. At the other end of the spectrum, an industrial dispute may only entitle the Contractor to an extension of time if it is confined in particular, limited circumstances to workers other than the Contractor's employees.

It should be easy to recognise the delaying effect of an industrial dispute whether occurring in the Employer's country, the Contractor's country, or any other country (eg through which the plant is transported). If, at the time the Contract is negotiated, the Employer refuses to accept any industrial disputes (even those outside the control of the Contractor) as a basis for extensions of time, this can only lead to higher prices to cover the risks involved, which would in the end be to the disadvantage of the Employer. It may also lead to subsequent disputation if the Contractor used spurious or tenuous grounds for claiming an extension of time.

14.7.4 Administration of EOT claims

The Contract should be drafted so that the Contractor is not allowed to wait until near the Date for Completion to present claims for extensions notified long ago if it could have presented them earlier. It is, however, often difficult for the Contractor to assess the consequences of an initial delay. A delay caused early in the work may be easy to overcome, while a delay in the later stages may have grave consequences. The Contractor is often required to notify the number of days extension claimed either with its claim or 'as soon as possible' or 'as soon as practicable' thereafter. As these expressions are flexible, it may be wise for the Contractor and Engineer to agree to let resolution of the number of days claimed wait until the situation can be better assessed (or better still, provide expressly for such later resolution in the Contract documents). However, such later resolution should not be so late as to prejudice the Contractor.

Subject to the express terms of the Contract, the Engineer must usually adjudicate an application for an extension of time at the time of the delay or within a reasonable time after the cause of delay has ended, even if that is after the Date for Completion originally fixed by the Contract. Further, the terms of the Contract will usually provide that the Engineer may not delay in notifying the Contractor of the length of the extension (if any) which it is prepared to certify and may not wait until after Completion of the Works, except where, for example, the duration is based on an average rate of progress.

The specific provisions of the time extension clause and the causes of delay will determine whether the Engineer may exercise the power to extend either prospectively and/or retrospectively.[94] For example, the NEC ECC contract requires an EOT to be given prospectively, whereas FIDIC contracts provide for EOTs to be given prospectively or retrospectively. The 1999 FIDIC Yellow Book provides:

> The Contractor shall be entitled subject to Sub-Clause 20.1 [Contractor's Claims] to an extension of the Time for Completion if and to the extent that completion for the purposes of Sub-Clause 10.1 [Taking Over the Works and Sections] is or will be delayed by any of the following causes: . . . [95]

In the case of *Obrascon Huarte Lain SA v Her Majesty's Attorney General for Gibraltar*[96] Akenhead J noted that this clause applied either prospectively or retrospectively:

> This suggests that the extension of time can be claimed either when it is clear that there will be delay (a prospective delay) or when the delay has been at least started to be incurred (a retrospective delay).[97]

However, it may be appropriate for the Engineer to defer a decision on extension of time where this is permitted by the Contract. For example, the Engineer may confirm that the Contractor has a basis for an extension, but that it is too early to quantify the number of days of the extension. Whether or not the Engineer is able to do so will depend on the terms of the Contract. A possible advantage of allowing the Engineer to defer a decision on an extension of time is that, depending on the circumstances and the time at which they occur, the Contractor may be able to mitigate some of the consequences of the delaying event, and the ultimate delay may in fact be less than that originally projected. However, whilst the Contractor may be motivated in this way by having to wait for the final decision, it often becomes insecure if it is not in a position to plan the execution of its work so as to avoid the imposition of liquidated damages, or to decide whether acceleration measures should be applied. Thus, even if the Engineer is able to defer a decision on an extension of time under the Contract, it should not defer such a decision unless it is clearly appropriate to wait, and in particular should not wait until after Completion to make an assessment just because it is convenient. In contracts where the time for Completion is long, it may be appropriate to give the Engineer power to award interim extensions of time, pending final assessment of the consequences of delaying events.

94 *Miller v London County Council* (1934) 151 LT 425.
95 Sub-clause 8.5.
96 [2014] EWHC 1028 (TCC).
97 [312].

If the Engineer does not administer the Contract in a timely manner and with due care as it is required do,[98] it may be precluded from allowing for liquidated damages in future payment certificates to the Contractor. Even if the Engineer's unreasonable delay in administering the Contract is caused by the Engineer acting independently from the Employer and not as agent of the Employer, the Employer may nevertheless be disentitled to damages, depending on the wording of the Contract.[99] Where due to supervening circumstances it has become impossible to perform the Contract within the stipulated time, the Contractor may not be liable for damages for late Completion if that is the true construction of the Contract. For example, this usually applies where the Contractor is prevented by *force majeure* (some superior power or force which cannot be resisted or controlled) or possibly because of ***casus fortuitous*** (a happening so exceptional or extraordinary as not to be foreseeable). It should be noted in this connection that mere difficulty of performance does not constitute impossibility. *Force majeure* is discussed in more detail in Chapter 25.

On receipt of a claim for an extension of time, the Engineer is usually required under the Contract to consult with both the Employer and the Contractor on the extension of time, if any, that is justified by the claim. After consultation, the Engineer should be required by the Contract to grant the Contractor such extension of time for Completion 'as may be justified'; in other words such extension as a fair and objective evaluation of the circumstances necessitates. However, the extension of time clause in the Contract will dictate the extension of time that the Engineer should grant. Both Employer and Contractor must be notified of the Engineer's decision.

Where a subcontractor is delayed for any of the reasons for which the Contractor would be entitled to an extension of time under the Contract, the head contract should provide that the Contractor is entitled to an extension if such delay prevents the Contractor itself from meeting the Date for Completion under the head contract. The Contractor should however take care that its subcontractors do not have a wider right of extension of time under their subcontracts than it itself has under the head contract, since this could expose the Contractor to liquidated damages in circumstances where it was unable to recover them from its subcontractors.

The converse of this situation is where a subcontractor causes a non-excusable delay under the subcontract, but which is an excusable delay under the head contract. If the Contractor is, as it must be, given an extension of time under the Contract to cover this delay, it is not liable to the Employer for liquidated damages for the period of the delay. It has therefore only suffered what may be a relatively minor loss because of the subcontractor's default, and this loss is all it can recover from the subcontractor (unless the subcontract has an applicable liquidated damages clause). The Employer cannot sue the subcontractor directly for the loss it has suffered, and it is therefore the Employer who is disadvantaged because of the subcontractor's delay.

The consequences of delay by the Contractor under the Contract may be a reduction of the contract price or liquidated damages for each day's delay and, after having reached a maximum value set out in the Contract, the Employer's right to terminate. It may be

98 For example, see J B Dorter & J A Sharkey, '*Building and Construction Contracts in Australia*' (Thomson Reuters loose-leaf) 7.500.

99 *Peters, Flamman & Co v Kokstad Municipality* (1919) AD 427.

difficult in practice to decide whether the delay of a part of the Works affects the whole Works, only that part of the Works or a larger part of the Works. It is suggested that the main criterion ought to be whether the rest of the Works can, in fact, be put to their intended use.

14.7.5 Extensions of time after the Works have been completed

The question may arise whether, after the Works have been completed, the Engineer can extend the time for Completion. In *Amalgamated Building Contractors Ltd v Waltham Holy Cross Urban District Council*,[100] the court held that under the then standard form JCT contract, the Architect could exercise its power to issue an extension of time at any time, including four months after the work had been completed. In *Fernbrook Trading Co Ltd v Taggart*,[101] the court considered the reasonableness of the Engineer exercising its discretion to extend time after the Date for Completion and held that in the circumstances, that is where the Contract did not expressly provide that the power to extend must be exercised prior to the Date for Completion, such extensions were validly given.

14.7.6 Delays due to the Employer's default – the prevention principle

The prevention principle (or doctrine of prevention) applies where an act by the Employer prevents the Contractor from undertaking its obligations and rights under the Contract (such as completing the Works by the Date for Completion). The principle was summarised by Gillard J:

> Where performance of a condition has been rendered impossible by the act of the grantee himself, the grantor is exonerated from performance of it. . . . This principle is applicable not to building contracts only but to all contracts.[102]

Put differently, where a contract stipulates the time for Completion of the Works by the Contractor, and the Employer causes delay to the Contractor's work so as to prevent the Contractor from completing the Works by the stipulated date, the Contractor will be excused from completing the Work by the stipulated date if there is no applicable extension of time mechanism available to the Contractor, or the Contract does not otherwise make provision for the time for performance in those circumstances. In these circumstances the time by which the Contractor is required to complete the Works will be 'at large'[103] and the

---

100 [1952] 2 All ER 452 (CA).

101 (1979) 1 NZLR 556, 558.

102 *Kilpatrick Green Pty Ltd v Leading Synthetics Pty Ltd* BC9802331, 32, citing *Dodd v Churton* (1897) 1 QB 562.

103 *Peak Construction (Liverpool) Ltd v McKinney Foundations Ltd* (1970) 1 BLR 111 (Court of Appeal). See Cowan & Bellhouse, 'Common Law "Time at Large" Arguments in a Civil Law Context' (2007) 23 *Construction Law Journal* 592; O'Connor & Landqau, 'Time at Large in Canada' (2011) *Journal of the Canadian College of Construction Lawyers* 71; *Holme v Guppy* (1838) 3 M&W 387 (150 ER 1195); *Davy Offshore Ltd v Emerald Field Contracting Ltd* (1991) 55 BLR 1, 87 per Judge Thayne Forbes QC; *Multiplex Constructions (UK) Limited v Honeywell Control Systems Limited (No.2)* [2007] BLR 195, 205 [48] per Jackson J; *Artlane Design Consultants Ltd v Chan Wen Mee May* [2009] HKCFI 570, [31] per Burrell J; *Chua Tian Chu v Chin Bay Ching* [2011] SGHC

Employer no longer has the right to liquidated damages. A court will not fix a new Date for Completion allowing for the Employer's delay, and the Contractor's obligation then becomes to complete the Works within a reasonable time.[104]

In determining what is a reasonable time, all relevant circumstances must be taken into account.[105] Diplock J outlined relevant factors to be considered as follows:

> In determining what is a reasonable time as respects any particular details and instructions, factors which must obviously be borne in mind are such matters as the order in which the engineer has determined the work shall be carried out. . ., whether requests for particular details or instructions have been made by the contractors, whether the instructions relate to a variation of the contract which the engineer is entitled to make from time to time during execution of the contract, or whether they relate to part of the original works, and also the time, including any extension of time, within which the contractors are contractually bound to complete the works.
>
> In mentioning these matters, I want to make it perfectly clear that they are not intended to be exhaustive, or anything like it. What is a reasonable time is a question of fact having regard to all the circumstances of the case.[106]

In *Wells v Army & Navy Co-op Society*,[107] the extension of time clause was held not to cover delay caused by the Employer's failure to give timely possession of the Site and delays in issuing drawings and instructions. Thus, notwithstanding that the Employer had the contractual authority to adjudicate on and make binding decisions in respect of extensions of time, the Employer was unable to recover liquidated damages because time was set at large because the extension of time clause was inadequate. By contrast, the point that liquidated damages could not be claimed as a result of delay caused by the Employer was not pressed in *Demolition & Construction Co Ltd v Kent River Board*,[108] because the contract provided for liquidated damages for delay caused by 'any cause whatsoever,' which are 'about as wide as any words can be.'[109] The contrast between these cases highlights the importance of construction of the terms of the Contract in determining whether the Employer's own actions disentitle it from claiming liquidated damages for late Completion.

126, [58]-[64] per Andrew Ang J; *Fongsoon Engineering ins) Pte Ltd v Kensteel Engineering Pte Ltd* [2011] SGHC 82, [24] per Belinda Ang Saw Saw Ean J; *Carillion Construction Ltd v Emcor Engineering Services Ltd* [2017] EWCA Civ 65, [54] per Jackson LJ; *Probuild Constructions (Aust) Pty Ltd v DDI Group Pty Ltd* [2017] NSWCA 151, [116] per McColl JA; *Hsin Chong Construction (Asia) Ltd v Henble Ltd* [2006] HKCFI 965, [21] per Reyes J; *Bluewater Energy Services BV v Mercon Steel Structures BV* [2014] EWHC 2132 (TCC), [516]-[518] per Ramsey J.

104 *Spiers Earthworks Pty Ltd v Landtec Projects Co Pty Ltd (No.2)* [2012] WASCA 53, [49] per McLure P; *Chua Tian Chu v Chin Bay Ching* [2011] SGHC 126, [104] per Andrew Ang J; *North Midland Building Ltd v Cyden Homes Ltd* [2017] EWHC 2414 (TCC), [11] per Fraser J; *North Midland Building Ltd v Cyden Homes Ltd* [2018] EWCA Civ 1744, [28] per Coulson LJ; *Shawston Engineering Ltd v DPG International Ltd* [2006] BLR 1, 5[11], 6[20], and 7[32], per May LJ; *Alsthom Ltd v Yokogawa Australia Pty Ltd (No 7)* [2012] SASC 49, [576], per Bleby J; *Lim Hoe Heng v Poh Choon Kia* [2012] SGCA 58, [52]-[55].

105 *Shinedean Ltd v Alldown Demolition (London) Ltd* [2006] 1 WLR 2696, 2701 [19] per May LJ, 2703 [27] per Sir Anthony Clarke MR; *Fong Chun Wing v Yee Yip Enterprises Ltd* [1988] HKCFI 87, [67]-[71] per Liu J.

106 *Neodox Ltd v Borough of Swinton & Pendelbury* (1958) 5 BLR 34 per Diplock J.

107 *Wells v Army & Navy Cooperative Society* (1903) Alfred A Hudson, *Hudson's Fourth Edition Table of Cases* (Sweet & Maxwell, 4th edn 1914), 346.

108 1963 2 Lloyd's Rep 6.

109 *Hydraulic Engineering Co v McHaffie* (1878) 4 QBD 671.

The rationale for the prevention principle is that the Employer cannot be permitted to take advantage of its own wrong.[110] The prevention principle was applied to construction contracts by Brooking J as follows:

> On occasion acts of prevention have been described as inconsistent with a claim to insist on completion within the stipulated time. . . [111]
>
> A wide variety of expressions have been used to describe the act of prevention which will excuse performance. At times words are employed which suggest that any act or omission preventing performance will suffice: . . . an act; . . . prevention; . . . 'acts or omissions' . . . acts, whether authorised by or breaches of the contract, . . . wrongful acts. . . 'fault' and 'fault or breach of contract' . . . 'act or default' . . . it may be quite legitimate conduct. . . [112]
>
> [But] what little authority there is supports the view which I would adopt as a matter of principle, namely that the ordering of variations after the due date which must substantially delay completion will, unless the contract provides otherwise, and in the absence of an applicable extension of time clause, disable the proprietor from recovering or retaining liquidated damages which might otherwise have accrued after the giving of the order, the employer's right in respect of amounts that have already accrued by way of liquidated damages not being affected.[113]
>
> Even in cases where the Employer cannot be said to have prevented the Contractor from completing by the relevant date because the Contractor would not have been able to complete by the due date in any event, prevention excuses performance of a promise to pay liquidated damages.[114] The cases for more than 100 years support this proposition.[115]

In *Multiplex Constructions (UK) Limited v Honeywell Control Systems Limited*[116] Jackson J reviewed the authorities on delays due to the Employer's default and derived the following three propositions:

(1) Actions by the employer which are perfectly legitimate under a construction contract may still be characterised as prevention, if those actions cause the delay beyond the contractual completion date.
(2) Acts of prevention by an employer do not set **time at large**, if the contract provides for an extension of time in respect of those events.
(3) Insofar as the extension of time clause is ambiguous, it should be construed in favour of the contractor.[117]

---

110 See also *Cheall v Association of Professional Executive Clerical and Computer Staff* (1983) 2 AC 180, 188–189.

111 *S.M.K. Cabinets v Hili Modern Electrics Pty Ltd* [1984] VR 391, 397 per Brooking J.

112 Ibid. 395–396.

113 Ibid. 398.

114 Ibid.

115 *Holme v Guppy* (1838) 3 M&W 387; 150 ER 1195; *Russell v Sa Da Bandeira (Viscount)* (1862) 13 CB NS 149, 206; 143 ER 59; *Parle v Leistikow* (1883) 4 LR (NSW) 84; *Dodd v Churton* [1897] 1 QB 562; *Baskett v Bendigo Gold Dredging Co, Ltd* (1902) 21 NZLR 166; *Wells v Army and Navy Cooperative Society* (1902) 86 LT 764 Alfred A Hudson, *Hudson's Fourth Edition Table of Cases* (Sweet & Maxwell, 4th edn 1914) 346; *Bunning Bros v Manea* (1911) 13 WALR 148; *Miller v London County Council* (1934) 151 LT 425, 426–7; *Perini v Greater Vancouver Sewerage and Drainage* District (1966) 57 DLR (2d) 307; *Peak Construction (Liverpool) Ltd v McKinney Foundations Ltd* (1970) 1 BLR 111; *Fernbrook Trading Co Ltd v Taggart* [1979] 1 NZLR 556.

116 [2007] EWHC 447 (TCC).

117 [56].

Where a breach of contract on the part of the Employer or a Variation by the Employer prevents the Contractor from completing the Works by the stipulated Date for Completion, the Contractor will usually be entitled to claim an extension of time for Completion of the Works. If an extension of time is not granted to the Contractor in circumstances where it ought to be granted, some contracts provide that time will not become 'at large,' but the Contractor's remedy for the failure to grant an extension of time will be an award of damages.[118]

Even if the Contractor is itself responsible for the Works being delayed by a certain period, concurrently with the delay for which the Employer is responsible, time may be 'at large.'[119] It does not follow that because time is 'at large' that the contract price is inapplicable and open to review where the Contract makes provision for the adjustment of the contract price in the event of the Contractor being delayed.[120]

Where time has been set 'at large' and liquidated damages no longer apply, the Employer would be able to claim general damages for delay once the Contractor has been placed in breach, that is a reasonable time has elapsed and the Contractor has failed to complete after having received a demand fixing a further date for performance which is reasonable in the circumstances.

The power given to the Engineer in the Contract to grant an extension of time (even in the absence of a request by the Contractor) and fix a new Date for Completion from which liquidated damages will run, is therefore for the Employer's benefit. Such a contractual provision, properly worded, enables the Engineer to grant an extension of time for delay caused by the Employer, even if the Contractor has not requested it. If, however, the Employer's delay amounts to a fundamental breach of the Contract, on ordinary contractual principles the Contractor would be entitled to bring the whole Contract to an end and claim full damages as a result.

14.7.7 Late certification of EOT

The Date for Completion is not extended until time extensions have been determined and certified by the Engineer, or by an arbitral tribunal or a court. The effect is that, although extensions of time applications may have been made by the Contractor seeking to extend the Date for Completion, the Employer may deduct liquidated damages if the Works are not completed by the Date for Completion prescribed in the Contract. Where it is subsequently shown that the extension sought was not timeously dealt with, or was wrongfully refused, the Contractor may have an action against the Engineer in tort to recover its damages. See the section on the Engineer's obligations to the Contractor in ¶8.1.8.

The Employer may sue for and recover liquidated damages from the Contractor, as well as deducting them from moneys due to the Contractor under the Contract. The liquidated damages are only for failure to complete on time, and not for any other breach of contract. The Contractor may not abandon the Works upon deduction of the liquidated

118 See *Spiers Earthworks Pty Ltd v Landtec Projects Co Pty Ltd (No.2)* [2012] WASCA 53, [15]-[63], per McLure P (considering clause 35.5 of AS 2124–1986 form of contract). See also *Severfield UK Ltd v Duro Felguera UK Ltd (No.2)* [2017] EWHC 3066 (TCC), [54]-[55] per Coulson J.

119 *Holme v Guppy* (1838) 3 M&W 387 (150 ER 1195).

120 *McAlpine Humberoak Ltd v McDermott International Inc (No.1)* (1992) 58 BLR 1, 22 per Lloyd LJ.

damages but must use the machinery provided in the Contract for the resolution of disputes. From a practical point of view however, the delay in such event might drive it into insolvency.

14.7.8 Delay by other contractors

In the absence of an express contractual provision to the contrary, the Contractor on a new project is entitled to undisturbed possession of the Site, to enable it to undertake the Works.[121] The specific contractual provisions will determine whether the Employer, by employing others on the Site, is in breach of an express or implied term that it should afford the Contractor undisturbed possession of the Site to carry out the Works without interruption by other contractors. If affording facilities for other contractors beyond what is reasonable involves the Contractor in any delay, the Contractor would normally be entitled to an extension of time or a suspension order, and a Variation order for any extra work.

It seems clear that requiring the Contractor to provide facilities to other contractors or organisations contracted to the Employer which could cause serious disruption to the Contractor's own method of working or organisation is not 'reasonable' unless the Employer's rights to carry out such activities or works is specifically provided for in the Contract or has previously been agreed to by the Contractor. It is suggested that should the Contractor grant permission to the Employer after the award of the Contract, it is entitled to make its permission conditional on payment of its reasonable costs as well as any appropriate extension of time. However, the Contractor's entitlement for payment will ultimately be a matter to be negotiated between the Employer and the Contractor if it is not dealt with in the Contract documents.

14.7.9 Delays in drawings and information

Where the design is not the responsibility of the Contractor, a common practice is for a contract to be let with relatively generalised drawings which are considered sufficient to enable a Contractor to price the bills, and to rely on detailed 'working drawings' or drawings issued 'for construction' or other information being supplied after work has started. Subject to the express terms of the Contract, it is implied that the Engineer must supply drawings and instructions in an opportune and timeous manner.[122] In *Wells v Army and Navy Co-op Society*, the court held that the Contractor is entitled to drawings, and so on, in time to pre-plan the work – '[Contractors] must within reasonable limits be allowed to decide for themselves at what time they are to be supplied with details.'[123]

It is suggested that it is necessary to imply such a duty on the Engineer to supply this information timeously in order to give the Contract business efficacy. However, it may be necessary for the Contractor to give adequate prior notice in writing that this information is required. The submission of a method statement and programme by the Contractor will be highly relevant in determining the time for the Engineer to exercise this duty and, if

121 *Penvidic v International Nickel* [1976] 1 S.C.R. 267, 276.

122 *Alfred McAlpine & Son (Pty) Ltd v Transvaal Provincial Administration* (1974) (3) SA 506 A.

123 (1903) Alfred A Hudson, *Hudson's Fourth Edition Table of Cases* (Sweet & Maxwell, 4th edn 1914) 346, 352 per Wright J.

sufficiently detailed, the method statement and programme may specify dates by which information is required and thus constitute due written notice.

The Contract usually requires notice to be given (although not necessarily in writing) before the Employer becomes liable for delay in giving other instructions unless they are obviously needed. For a common law remedy of damages for breach of contract where the time for performance is not fixed, a demand for performance must be made in which the due date for performance is laid down. The time allowed for performance must be reasonable in the circumstances. A distinction must be made between remedies which are provided by the Contract, and remedies which flow from the legal consequences of breach of contract. In the absence of an express exclusion of common law remedies, these will be available in addition to those agreed upon in the Contract, unless clearly inconsistent or contradictory.

Where the Contract requires that the Contractor shall give 'reasonable notice in writing' of its need for information from the Engineer, special attention should be accorded these words for various reasons: they qualify the time for the Engineer to exercise its duty to supply information, and they indicate that notice by the Contractor requiring the drawings by a fixed time is a necessity before the Contractor is entitled to rely upon its contractual remedies arising out of late information.

14.8 Damages for delay

In circumstances where liquidated damages are not available, if either party fails to fulfil its obligations timeously, the other may, subject to the terms of the Contract, be entitled to recover damages caused by the delay. Such damages may comprise loss of profit, or expenditure incurred in securing alternative facilities, provided that such damages were reasonably foreseeable when the Contract was concluded. For example, delay in the completion of a factory will not entitle the Employer to recover rental which it might have earned by letting the factory, unless the Contractor knew, or should have known at the time of entry into the Contract, that the Employer intended to enter into a lease after Completion.

If the Contractor sues the Employer for payment of the contract price, and it appears that the Contractor completed the work after the due date, the Contractor is not required to prove that the Employer did not suffer damage on account of the late performance.[124]

In the absence of a cancellation clause or special circumstances in which time is 'of the essence,' delay in completing the work timeously does not entitle the Employer to terminate the Contract. As discussed in ¶14.2.2, in exceptional circumstances time may be 'of the essence' of the Contract and, if not, the Employer may make time 'of the essence' by giving a notice.

Where the work is completed and taken over in time, the Employer may thereafter be deprived of beneficial possession should the Contractor have to remedy defects which appear during the defects liability period. Should this occur, the Employer may claim damages, but not liquidated damages, in respect of the period during which the defects were remedied. The burden of proving an entitlement to damages, and the quantum of damages, rests on the party claiming such damages.

124 *Hendricks and Soeker v Atkins* (1903) 20 SC 310; 13 CTR 517.

14.9 Due diligence in the execution of the Works

'Diligence' means the industrious or efficient allocation of economic resources towards achieving the contractual end.[125] A construction contract usually makes provision for termination for lack of due diligence in execution of the Works by the Contractor. A contractual clause requiring 'regular and diligent' progress requires the Contractor to maintain the orderly progress of the Works.[126] The test is largely an objective one. Lack of due diligence in the progress of the Works would justify termination of the Contract at common law only if preceded by a notice which was ignored.

There is no general implied obligation on a Contractor to 'get on with the work' once the Contractor has commenced the Works.[127] The law is different in Hong Kong, in that an obligation to proceed with reasonable or due diligence will usually be implied.[128] Should the Contractor decide to 'go slow,' this will not ordinarily amount in itself to a breach of contract.[129] However, if the Contractor illegitimately threatens to suspend its operations for the purpose of obtaining an economic benefit from the Employer, an absence of diligence and progress may be found.[130] An obligation that the Contractor is to complete its work efficiently may be implied.[131]

If the Employer delays terminating the Contract for lack of due diligence beyond a reasonable time, it may be held to have waived the right to terminate in that case, subject to any 'no waiver' clause in the Contract. This is particularly so where the Contractor is allowed to alter its position adversely, for example by buying expensive plant for the Works in the belief that it will be allowed to complete the Contract.

14.10 Consequences of suspension

If the activities of the Employer, or the Engineer as its agent, upset the Contractor's programme where, for example, plant or materials to be supplied by the Employer are not available in time, the Engineer may have a duty to suspend performance of all or part of the Works so that the Contractor becomes entitled to costs and an extension of time. If a suspension is not provided for in the Contract and the Contractor treats the suspension as an omission on the part of the Employer then, provided the necessary notice is served by the Contractor as required by the Contract, it will usually be entitled to claim a Variation under the variation clause and an extension of time under the extension of time clause. However, it will not be entitled to damages if the omission is properly made under the relevant clause(s) in the Contract.

---

125 *West Faulkner Associates v London Borough of Newham* (1994) 71 BLR 1, 12–13, per Simon Brown LJ.

126 *Hounslow LBC v Twickenham Garden Developments Ltd* [1971] 1 Ch 233, 269, per Megarry J.

127 *Greater London Council v Cleveland Bridge & Engineering Co Ltd* (1986) 34 BLR 50, 77, per Parker LJ; *CAA Technologies Pte Ltd v Newcon Builders Pte Ltd* [2017] SGCA 53, [61]–[82].

128 *Fong Chun Wing v Yee Yip Enterprises Ltd* [1988] HKCFI 87, [59], per Liu J; *Chan Shun Kei v Hong Kong Construction (Hong Kong) Ltd* [2014] HKCFI 189, [63], per Burrell J.

129 *J M Hill & Sons Ltd v London Borough of Camden* (1980) 18 BLR 31, 47, per Ormond LJ; *Multiplex Constructions (UK) Ltd v Cleveland Bridge UK Ltd* [2006] EWHC 1341 (TCC), [537]-[547], per Jackson J (affirmed [2007] EWCA 443; Paul Keating, 'Employers Remedy for Delay: Termination' in E Lloyd (ed), *The Liability of Contractors* (Longman, 1986) 62–63.

130 *Carillion Construction Ltd v Felix (UK) Limited* [2001] BLR 1, 8 [36] per Dyson J.

131 *Franks & Collingwood v Gates* (1983) 1 Con LR 21, 25, per Judge Newey QC.

Construction contracts should be drafted to provide that the Engineer is entitled to instruct suspension of the performance of the Contract at any time before the Works are taken over by the Employer (see for example sub-clause 8.9 of the 2017 FIDIC rainbow suite). The order to suspend under the Contract might relate to suspension of the progress of the Works before plant is ready for delivery, or suspension of delivery of plant or Contractor's equipment which is ready for delivery to the Site, or suspension of the erection of plant that has been delivered to the Site.

An instruction to suspend generally means that the Contractor must stop the specified performance as soon as is practicable. From receipt of such instruction, the Contractor must generally protect and secure the Works or plant affected. The duty to protect and secure usually rests with the Contractor regardless of whether the Works or plant are located at the Contractor's premises, at the Site, or elsewhere. It is usually the Contractor's responsibility to determine what will be adequate means of protection, but in case of doubt, it is recommended that the Contractor seeks the opinion of the Engineer.

Contracts should be drafted so that the Contractor is entitled to be paid all additional costs reasonably incurred by it because of suspension, unless the suspension is directed as a consequence of the Contractor's fault. Where additional cost is to be incurred by the Contractor in protecting and securing the Works or plant affected, the Contractor would be wise to obtain written instructions from the Engineer on the actions to be taken. Further, contracts should be drafted so that the Contractor is entitled to be paid the additional costs incurred in following the Engineer's instructions or deemed instructions to suspend, including the costs of demobilisation of the work force, of paying stand-by rates on hired equipment and the like, together with the additional costs incurred in resumption of the work ordered by the Engineer, including costs such as remobilisation of the work force.

Contracts should also be drafted so that after the passage of a specified period of time, the Contractor is entitled to be paid the value of plant as at the date of suspension, notwithstanding its failure to achieve milestones. This should oblige the Employer to pay the unpaid amount of the value of such plant, even if the Contractor has not reached a 'milestone' for payment according to the agreed terms of payment.

Where prolonged suspension occurs, the Contract should provide that the Contractor, by notice to the Engineer, is entitled to request permission to proceed within a reasonable period. Further, if such permission is not granted within that time, the Contractor is entitled to treat the suspension as an omission of that section of the Works, or, if the suspension affects the whole of the Works, to terminate the Contract. In these circumstances, the responsibility of care and risk of loss of the Works should pass to the Employer. However, this would not occur if the Contractor elects not to exercise its rights – in other words, if it decides to wait for an eventual resumption of the Works. In this event the Contractor is usually entitled to require the Employer to take over the responsibility for protection, storage, security, and insurance of the suspended Works. After having made such a request, the risk of loss or damage to the suspended Works under the Contract should pass from the Contractor to the Employer, depending on the terms of the Contract.

The terms of the Contract should also cover the situation where work resumes after suspension, and transfer of responsibility for the care and risk of loss of the Works passes from the Employer back to the Contractor. Where permission to proceed with or resume the Works after suspension is given, the Contractor and the Engineer should examine the Works to establish whether any deterioration or defect in the suspended Works or plant has occurred during suspension. The Contract should provide that the Contractor is obliged to make good any deterioration. Further, if such making good involves cost to the Contractor which would not have occurred but for the suspension, the Contract should provide that the Contractor is entitled to have the cost, together with profit, added to the contract price, as well as an extension of time where appropriate.

14.11 Waiver and estoppel

The question arises as to whether the principle of waiver or estoppel applies

> if the Employer leads the Contractor to believe that it does not require the work to be finished by the Date for Completion, and because of this the Contractor does not give notice of claims for extensions of time or slows down the work.[132]

Waiver is an election by a party not to enforce a right it is entitled to under a contract. An **estoppel** is a term which means that a party in legal proceedings is precluded from asserting a position contrary to that which it has already established by its promise, representation, or conduct where another party has relied on that promise. Thus, whenever a party has by its promise, representation, or conduct induced another to make an assumption that something is or will be the case, that party may be estopped from going back on the representation that led to the other party acting on the assumption to its detriment.

The English courts have developed the doctrine of waiver which may help the Contractor in this type of situation. In *Rickards (Charles) Ltd v Oppenheim*,[133] the defendant ordered a body for a Rolls Royce chassis. The date of delivery was 20 March 1948. The body was not completed on that date, but the defendant continued to press for delivery. The court held that the defendant had lost its right to refuse to take the body because it was not completed on 20 March. He had waived the date for completion by continuing to press for delivery after that date, and the manufacturers had continued to do work on the car as a result of the representation by its conduct that the defendant would not rely on the original date, so that it would have been unjust to allow it to go back on that representation.

Waiver may apply to the situation where one party to the Contract continues to unintentionally conduct itself in a manner that leads to the other party reasonably believing that it is waiving its strict contractual rights. Where the doctrine of waiver applies, these 'waived' rights are not lost completely, but the other party must be given an opportunity to put itself back in the position in which it would have been had it not relied on the conduct indicating that rights had been waived, for example by extending the time for Completion. Failing to terminate the Contract for delay in Completion, or to deduct the liquidated damages as they become due may, by itself, waive the right to claim for delay or create an estoppel. A right of termination which has arisen may also

132 *Rickards (Charles) v Oppenheim* [1950] 1 KB 616; [1950] 1 All ER 420 (CA).
133 [1950] 1 KB 616, [1950] 1 All ER 420 (Court of Appeal).

be waived if the Employer, with knowledge of its rights to terminate, makes advances of money to the Contractor for the purposes of the Contract or in any other way treats the Contract as still subsisting.[134]

The Engineer's authority to act as the Employer's agent does not normally extend to waiving contractual rights on behalf of the Employer. This is often made clear by a specific clause in the Contract such as: 'the Engineer has no authority to relieve either Party of any duties, obligations or responsibilities under the Contract.'[135]

The common law provisions in respect of waiver must, of course, give way to any specific provisions of the Contract to the contrary. For example, clause 7.3 of the NSW Government GC21 (Edition 2) General Conditions of Contract provides that: 'The terms of the Contract cannot be amended or waived unless both parties agree in writing.'

134 See *Re Garrud, Ex parte Newitt* (1881) 16 ChD 522.
135 1999 FIDIC Red Book sub-clause 3.1.

CHAPTER 15

Planning and programming[1]

CONTENTS

1 The authors are indebted to George Matta and Jonathan Shahady of Tracey Brunstrom & Hammond for his assistance in developing Chapter 15 and for the diagrams used.

DOI: 10.4324/9781003206873-15

15.1 Programme fundamentals

Communication of the overall strategy to all parties undertaking a construction project is of vital importance if it is to be successfully and timeously completed. As noted in ¶14.3.1, the usual form of communication is by a **programme**: a schedule of the activities, their start times, and durations required for Completion of the Works. Preparation of a programme requires a skillset of time management including both planning and scheduling.

Planning is the structured identification and visualisation of activities, events, and resources required to deliver a project as well as the relationships between them.

Scheduling is the analytical sequencing of activities based on their relationships. Scheduling is the mathematical calculation of activity timing and float thereby determining a project's duration and the critical path to its completion.

Planning and scheduling are distinct yet inseparable aspects for successfully managing projects. In construction, the combination of these two skills is commonly called programming.[2]

Common programming techniques include the critical path method (**CPM**), arrow or precedence network diagrams, timescaled networking, time-chainage charting, line of balance, Gantt or bar charts, and simple schedules.

The most widely used chart in the execution of projects today is the Gantt chart or horizontal bar chart. This chart was developed by Henry Gantt around 1910–1915[3] and shows graphically when an activity is to be carried out. It is easy to understand and read.

The critical path method was developed in the late 1950s, the precursors of which were developed and put into practice by Du Pont in the period 1940–1943 and contributed to the success of the Manhattan project.[4] The project evaluation and review technique (**PERT**) was developed by the US Navy and Booz Allen Hamilton in the 1950s and was applied to delivery of the Polaris submarine project.[5] It is a critical path network analysis scheduling method which allows for randomness in estimated start times and activity durations. The output of a CPM or PERT analysis can be used to produce a Gantt chart.

The cost of time and the increasing complexity of projects today have made the use of scheduling techniques imperative for the control of projects. The CPM methods are best used when the control of the project is related to the control of the interface between project participants. It is inconceivable to launch a space rocket or develop an oil field or a mine today without resorting to these techniques for the time control of activities, as well as for control of resources and cost. Other methods of scheduling may be more appropriate for certain types of projects, for example it is suggested that for a freeway, especially long ones, a line of balance would be a better method.

---

2 In some countries including the USA, 'scheduling' is also used to mean programming.

3 https://en.wikipedia.org/wiki/Gantt_chart (accessed 20 August 2021).

4 https://en.wikipedia.org/wiki/Critical_path_method#cite_note-4 (accessed 20 August 2021).

5 Ibid.

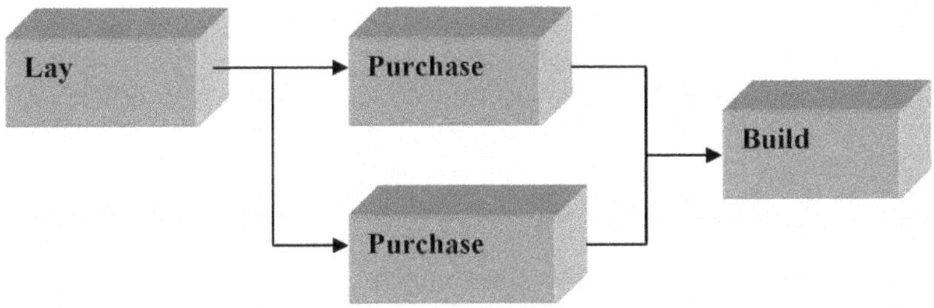

Figure 15.1 Nodes and activities in a network

With the advent of computerised programmes operating on relatively inexpensive computers, these powerful mathematical tools have been brought within the grasp of even small contractors.

Analysis of the activities in a network is the basis of all PERT or CPM programmes, and the computer has blurred the difference between 'node' (activity on node) and 'arrow' (activity on arrow) networks. Network analysis is founded on the concept that any project can be broken down into a number of discrete activities or tasks which must be accomplished to complete the project. A **network** is a representation of the logical sequence of activities and the relationship or the links between them. Prior to the common use of project scheduling software, the logical sequence was often represented by a network diagram with no scale or time. The use of project scheduling software means that network diagrams are generally no longer needed to model the activities in a project.

In a node network diagram, each activity is represented by a box called a node, and the relationships between the activities are represented by lines or arrows. A simple node network is illustrated in Figure 15.1.

The way that activities in a project are interrelated depends on the circumstances. In the construction of a building, for example, the foundations are laid before building the walls and putting on the roof. This is sometimes known as *hard logic*. **Network logic** is the term used to describe the relationships between activities. It describes the order in which things happen and specifies the **dependencies** – that is, which activities are dependent on other activities.

A **precedence network** is so called because it is based on the systematic listing of each of the activities' predecessors – the activities that must logically precede each activity. For example, the predecessor to building a wall is the laying of the foundation, as the building of the wall cannot start until the foundation is complete. By describing all the activities in a programme in this way a picture of the relationship between them is built up, which becomes the basis for a plan. Then, using appropriate computer software, all possible sequences of activities are examined to determine the shortest duration feasible outcome.

The activities used to build up the programme must be appropriate. One must consider the future uses of the plan, because before implementation, a plan is a map of the future. It needs to be reasonably general, and it needs to be broken down into meaningful component parts. The function of the programme before implementation, therefore, is to identify the essential elements of a project and to establish their relationships. Once a project is under way, the main function of the programme is to provide a benchmark against which the actual progress can be measured.

Activities must both divide the project into a linked pattern of essential tasks and provide appropriate information to the people who need it. The programme is the tool which satisfies both these needs.

The **duration** of an activity is the time it takes to complete the activity. At the planning stage, the duration of each activity is estimated. The computer software adds the activity durations together on the critical path it has calculated to establish the minimum overall time for the project. As the accuracy of the total time depends on the accuracy of the individual durations, it is important that they are estimated realistically.

A large part of the skill in programming lies in determining the appropriate level to which the project activities should be broken down as well as making realistic estimates of activity durations.

15.2 Contractual requirements for programmes

A construction contract will generally require a programme to be produced. The definitions and requirements for the programme will be specific to the Contract and may vary significantly from provisions in other contracts. It is important to understand the contractual requirements to ensure that the programme that is created complies with those requirements.

The programme needs to address the intended functions identified in the Contract. These may include regular reporting on progress, determination of EOTs, Variations, and Completion and risk allocation.

Other contract clauses that are commonly related to programmes include the following:

- Access,
- Date for Completion,
- Information and documentation reviews,
- Progress,
- Variations,
- Extension of Time.

Each of these clauses should be consulted to ensure that all relevant activities and durations are incorporated in the programme. For example, the Employer's review of design documents for the foundations will be a predecessor activity to constructing the foundations, and the contractually specified time for the Employer's review needs to be allowed for.

Contracts often require the programme to be revised and resubmitted whenever it ceases to reflect actual progress or is otherwise inconsistent with the Contractor's obligations, for example 2017 FIDIC Yellow Book sub-clause 8.3. The Contract may also have a monthly reporting requirement that requires comparisons of actual and planned progress, for example 2017 FIDIC Yellow Book sub-clause 4.20. Such contractual provisions implicitly require updating the programme on a regular basis to reflect actual progress. On a major project with hundreds or thousands of activities, significant resources need to be dedicated to this task.

15.3 The programme as a multipurpose tool

Preparing the programme enforces systematic thinking – defining the project effectively. The programme is a statement of policy. It defines the order in which things are to be done and the time available and should bring into focus what is required to happen in order to deliver a project.

The programme (being the output of planning and scheduling) can also be used to measure progress during the actual course of the project to record the true occurrence of events, delays, as well as any changes to the plan or project.

It is for the preceding reasons, that a programme has traditionally been considered a multipurpose tool that satisfies the following requirements, as shown in Figure 15.2:

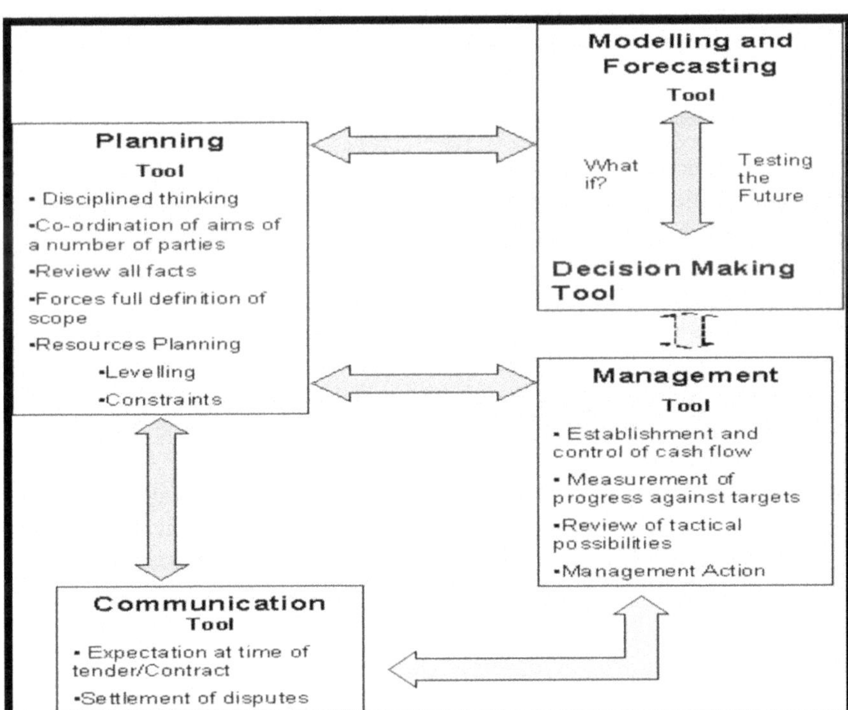

Figure 15.2 The programme as a multipurpose tool

- Planning tool;
- Management tool;
- Forecasting, modelling, and decision-making tool;
- Communication tool; and
- History-recording tool.

15.3.1 The programme as a planning tool

Once completed, the programme can be used to demonstrate 'the plan' to achieve the project milestones. The potential impact of planning decreases rapidly over time. Planning at the outset of any project, no matter whether it is at the commencement of the design phase or the construction phase, will have a far greater impact and provide a project with the best chance of successful delivery than if planning is ignored until problems arise.

The purpose of a programme as a planning tool includes the development of:

- A structure which encourages disciplined thinking;
- A medium for coordinating the aims and commitments of multiple parties;
- A review of all the facts and assumptions required to deliver the project;
- The full definition of the scope (content) of the project, including temporary and associated works; and
- Consideration of the resourcing of a project, including resourcing constraints and utilising float for resource levelling.

15.3.2 The programme as a management tool

The programme directs and focuses the attention of management personnel, allowing management of a project to be more efficient and effective. This is because the programme provides a benchmark against which progress can be monitored and evaluated. It is this evaluation that allows for the forecasting of potential impacts produced by actual events, and highlights changes, problem areas, and critical areas.

'What if' analysis can be applied to the programme to identify possible courses of action to overcome potential impacts and/or add value to the project. The programme also establishes control over the array of resources used within a project. This control over the utilisation of resources can be used to establish and manage the cash flow for a project throughout its entire duration.

Senior management requires an understanding of the 'big picture' and will usually require a 'rolled up' programme showing major activities and the critical path on no more than a few pages. The full programme with hundreds of discrete activities shown over many pages makes it hard to distinguish 'the trees from the woods.'

15.3.3 The programme as a modelling, forecasting, and decision-making tool

A programme is an abstract model of reality used to plan for the future. Therefore, it has all the problems of any model. Because its predictions are based on assumptions which can be subject to change as well as being abstract, it is likely that it will not include all the forces that will ultimately impact the project.

However, a model is an excellent tool for testing the possible outcomes by altering the assumptions, parameters, and so on. For example, how much time would be saved if:

- Early access to certain parts of the Work is allowed, and sequencing of fabrication and installation is optimised, or
- Certain parts are pre-assembled in modules for early installation prior to construction of other components.

'What if' exercises will allow the thinking through of such scenarios. This will help identify and mitigate future difficulties and problems in advance, and give a time estimate of the impact of such decisions.

Schedule risk (or range) analysis techniques can be used to model the effects of activity variables or delays on project dates. This analysis can also be utilised to determine delay contingencies for estimating more realistic project dates or changes in the timing of high-risk and low-risk activity paths.

15.3.4 The programme as a communication tool

The programme demonstrates the expectations of the parties at the time of tender or contract, representing an understanding of the scope, timing, and sequence of the Works. This allows for the Employer and Contractor to agree on dates by which project milestones are to be achieved. It is this advance communication that allows the planning of certain courses of action and interface points as well as the coordination to those at the workplace who carry out the plan.

The programme acts as a basis for measurement of the effect of time-related changes and issues such as delay, disruption, out of sequence work, acceleration, workplace availability, prolongation, and so on. This allows the Employer and the Contractor to use this information to communicate their ideas, theories, capabilities, and decisions.

15.3.5 The programme as a history-recording tool

The as-built programme is a record of the actual sequencing, timing, and duration of the project activities. This data can be analysed and used for different purposes, such as analysing project performance, as well as providing supporting evidence for making or assessing claims.

The as-built programme will identify the effectiveness of the Contractor's working methods and outline areas of underperformance. This information can then be used to make certain adjustments in order to improve the accuracy and effectiveness of the Contractor's working methods for future projects.

15.4 Forms of programmes

Programmes come in many forms. Often, they are such an everyday tool that they are not recognised as a programme. Some examples of types of programmes include the following:

- Schedule of dates,
- Simple bar chart/Gantt chart,
- Line of balance or time chainage,
- Network diagrams,

- Logic-linked Gantt chart,
- Flow charts,
- 4D modelling.

15.4.1 Schedule of dates

A schedule of dates is a simplistic programme form which states the main phases of a project as well as its start and finish dates, as shown in Table 15.1. It does not show relationships between each main phase or the activities within them. It can be used to simply identify when a main phase of the project does not align with the dates of the as-planned schedule of dates. This can indicate whether the project is either falling behind or is ahead of schedule.

15.4.2 Simple bar chart

A bar chart is a graphical representation of a list of activities in a project and their planned start and planned finish in the form of a bar, such that the length of the bar represents the duration of the activity.

'A bar chart is easily prepared and can be used to show estimated timing and duration of activities and to record actual progress.'[6] As demonstrated in Figure 15.3, this basic form is easy to comprehend and does not require complex software or skill to produce. It is basically a step up from the schedule of dates showing a visual representation of the main phases of a project.

Table 15.1 Example of schedule of dates

Task	**Start**	**Finish**
Prepare Design	01 Jan 09	30 June 09
Procure Material	30 March 09	01 August 09
Construction	01 May 09	30 November 09

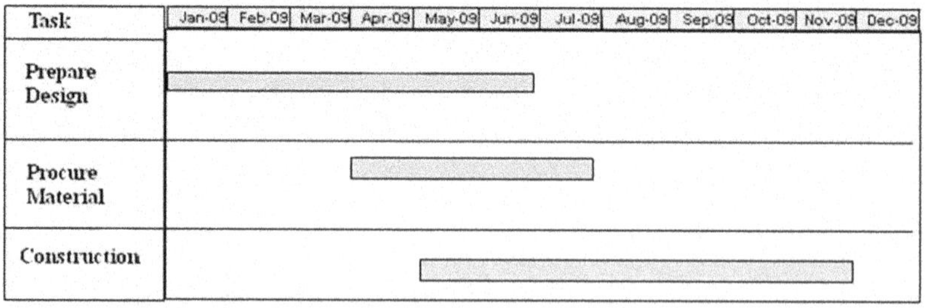

Figure 15.3 Simple bar chart

6 Roger Gibson, *Construction Delays: Extension of Times and Prolongation Claims* (Taylor & Francis, 1st edn 2008) 30.

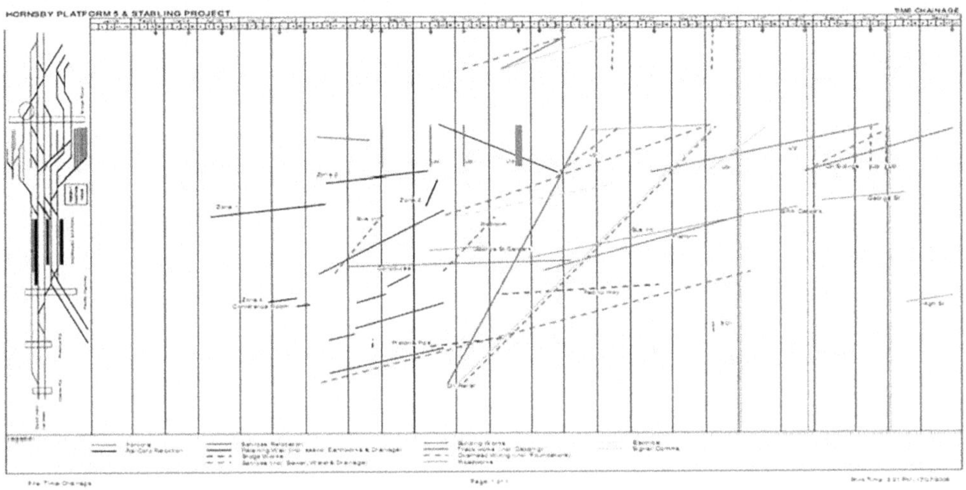

Figure 15.4 Time chainage diagram

The bar chart in Figure 15.3 is also a Gantt chart. A **Gantt chart**, at its simplest, is nothing more than activities represented by horizontal bars on a timescale, with the names of the activities in a column on the left.

15.4.3 Time chainage diagram

A time chainage diagram is a programme that is useful in linear construction (track, road, piping, tunnelling) with multiple work fronts. The **time chainage diagram** portrays the duration of activities through time as well as distance, portraying a geographical representation of project progress.[7] This is demonstrated in Figure 15.4. Time chainage diagrams are suitable for lineal projects as they display progress of distance and time whereas other programme forms show progress only in relation to time.

Figure 15.4 is a time chainage diagram, which is a particular form of visual representation of a programme. It is similar in form to the diagram that results from line of balance analysis. Line of balance is not the same as time chainage, although it often results in a visual presentation similar to a time chainage diagram.

Line of balance is a project/production analysis method designed to create a project in which each team or pool of resources works with minimal interruption. The resulting programme may have some activities starting later than they would in a programme prepared with CPM techniques. Because of the visual similarity of line of balance diagrams and time chainage diagrams and because line of balance analysis techniques will often be suitable to the linear types of projects that are readily represented on a

7 Ibid.

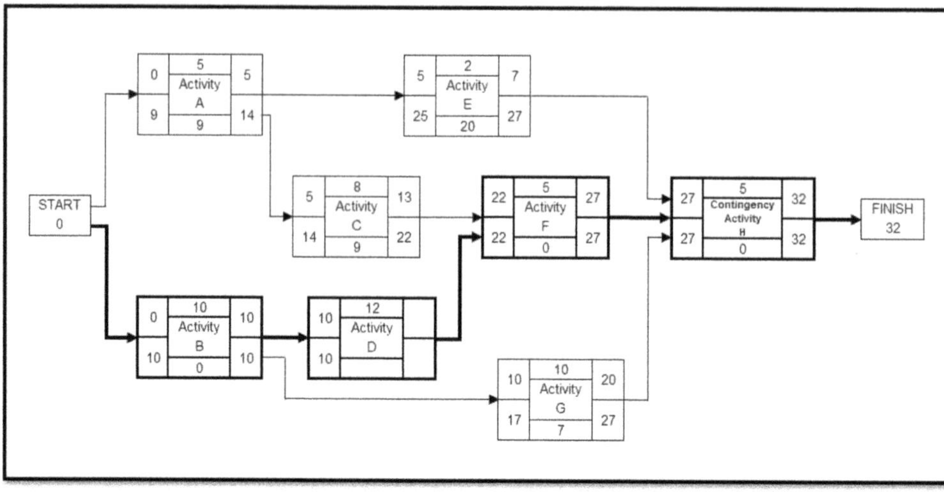

Figure 15.5 Network diagram portraying the critical path

time chainage diagram, it has become common place to equate line of balance and time chainage.

15.4.4 Network diagrams

Network diagrams are generally used for analysis purposes. A network diagram can be in conjunction with the critical path method. The CPM method uses a forward/backward pass to outline the relationship of each activity, which determines the critical path through a group of activities. An example of a network diagram analysed by CPM is shown in Figure 15.5 where the critical path is highlighted in bold.

It is very rare these days for construction programmers to prepare network diagrams like that in Figure 15.5. The network diagram, drawn by hand or by a draftsperson, used to be essential in order to do the forward pass and backward pass and thus work out the critical path and the float of all the non-critical activities. These days the project scheduling software does these calculations, making network diagrams unnecessary. Some project scheduling software will draw a network diagram of the programme, but it is usually much harder to understand than a logic-linked Gantt chart.

15.4.5 Linked bar chart/Gantt chart diagram

The most common programming format in the execution of projects is the linked bar chart, as shown in Figure 15.6. It is easy to understand and read. It contains more information than the simple bar chart. Not only does it show activity duration and start and finish dates, it outlines the relationship each activity has with one another. This is a fundamental tool needed to plan a project and the utilisation and supply of resources and develop the correct sequence of activities. The critical activities are depicted by solid bars.

ID	Activity Description	Dur	Early Start	Early Finish	Float
10	Prepare Design	5	01MAY	05MAY	0
20	Procure Door & Frame	5	06MAY	10MAY	20
30	Procure Bricks	10	06MAY	15MAY	0
40	Procure Roof Trusses	15	06MAY	20MAY	3
50	Start on Site	0	06MAY		3
60	Prepare Site	2	06MAY	07MAY	3
70	Pour Ground Slab	5	08MAY	12MAY	3
80	Brickwork	8	16MAY	23MAY	0
90	Install Door	1	19MAY	19MAY	12
100	Install Roof Trusses	2	24MAY	25MAY	0
110	Install Roof Sheeting	1	26MAY	26MAY	0
120	Construct Driveway	5	27MAY	31MAY	0
130	Practical Completion	0		31MAY	0
140	Delay Contingency	9	01JUN	09JUN	0
150	Date for Practical Completion	0		09JUN*	0

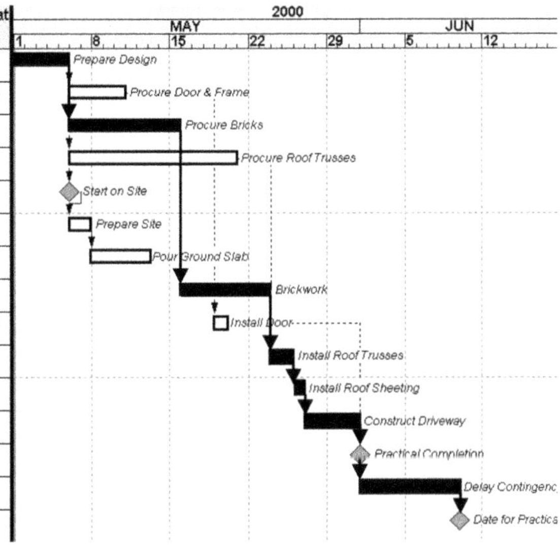

Figure 15.6 Linked bar chart/Gantt chart diagram

15.4.6 Flow chart

A flow chart shows the relationship between each major phase of a project and outlines the process of progression in each phase. An example of a flow chart demonstrating the phases in a typical design and construct project is shown in Figure 15.7. A flow chart does not show the details of activities, their relationships, or start and finish dates within each phase.

15.4.7 4D BIM

This form of programme takes the 3D design of a project and applies a time element to each component. For this to happen, each component of that project is given a duration and a start and finish date. It creates a 3D visualisation of the project being built over a period of time, referred to as 4D BIM (building information modelling). This visual representation of a project's construction sequence allows for a more in-depth analysis of the sequence of events. BIM is discussed in ¶29.5.1.

15.5 Preparing a programme

15.5.1 Purpose

The fundamental purpose of any programme is to convey the sequence of events, their relationship with each other, and their direction, to determine and demonstrate a considered estimate of the overall time required to achieve the project objectives.

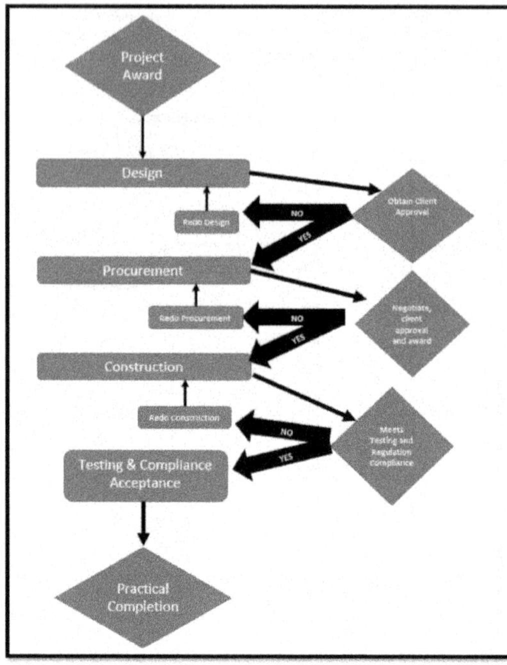

Figure 15.7 Flow chart for a typical design and construct project

15.5.2 Programming tools

Generally modern-day programmes are created using proprietary project management software that assists the project manager in developing the plan, assigning resources to tasks, tracking progress, managing changes, and analysing workloads.

Some of the common programming software tools, include the following:

- Primavera (P6),
- Microsoft Project,
- ASTA Power Project,
- Tilos (Time chainage), and
- Microsoft Excel.

15.5.3 Typical programme components

Every project is different, however in general terms a typical construction programme will generally be broken down into the following phases:

- Feasibility,
- Planning and approvals,
- Design,

- Procurement,
- Construction, and
- Commissioning.

The activities should be organised in a structured format which is generally aligns with the work breakdown structure (**WBS**) of the project.

The programme should specify the working calendar for each individual activity or resource. This for example may include a 5-day, 6-day, or 24-hour calendar and non-working days.

The programme should clearly identify the total float of each activity and the critical path to completion.

The programme may include a target (or nett) completion, a Contractor's contingency period, and a gross completion date, which may or may not equate to the Contract Date for Completion.

15.5.4 Steps in developing a programme

Before creating a programme, it is important to understand what the programme is intended to deliver. The following documents will help in creating the programme:

- The Contract (including Special Conditions and amendments to General Conditions),
- Drawings (architectural, structural, mechanical etc),
- Specifications,
- Cost plan, bill of quantities (BOQ), schedule of rates,
- Cash flow,
- Scope details, and
- Other relevant documents.

The following nine steps outline the typical process for developing a programme:

Step 1 – Create a work breakdown structure (WBS)

As described in Figure 15.8, the WBS subdivides the project work into smaller, more manageable pieces of work.

The highest-level components of a WBS are typically contract, design, procurement, construction, and commissioning. When considering a WBS it is important to recognise how the project will be constructed, procured, resourced, and/or managed.

Step 2 – Determine the calendars

A programme may have a single calendar for the entire project or multiple calendars for separable portions, different activities, and resources in the project.

Step 3 – Determine activities to reflect project chronology

According to the WBS and construction methodology, a sequence of activities can be developed. Activities and sub-activities will be created within the sub-groups defined by the WBS. The relationships between the activities recorded as dependency logic links should be added to identify the predecessor and successor activities for each activity.

Step 4 – Quantify the work for each activity

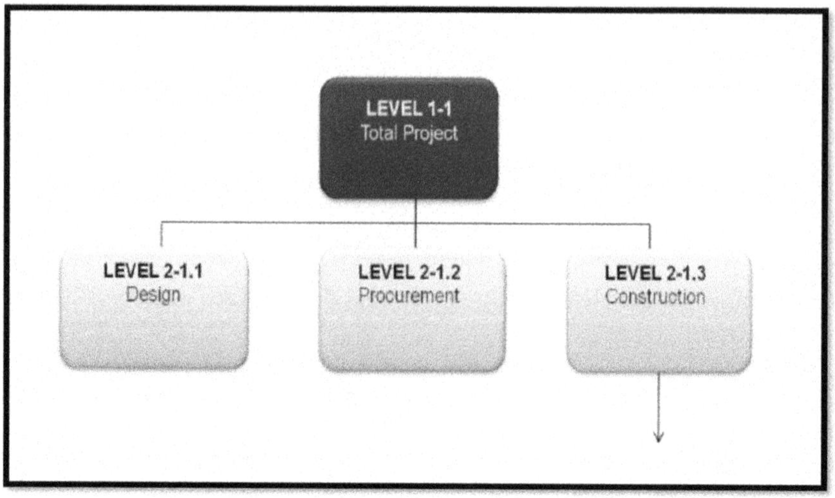

Figure 15.8 Work breakdown structure

Drawings, the bill of quantities, and advice from the Employer or subcontractors can be used to determine the quantity of work that is needed to complete certain aspects of a project.

Direct labour hours may be calculated using estimated quantities from material take-offs and estimating labour norms or in-house data. Calculated norm hours are for ideal working conditions not encountered in reality and are only used as a starting point. The norm hours are then multiplied by a theoretical site-specific productivity factor to arrive at the total on-site labour hour estimate. These site hours are then subsequently used to arrive at the total construction cost. The total site hours are used for labour manpower planning and resource allocation.

Step 5 – Determine the activity work days

The production rate for a variety of construction activities can be estimated based on historical data, industry guides, and project experience. The production rate can also be determined using the direct hours determined in Step 4 divided by the working hours per day divided by the normal crew size required for the activity.

Subject to the nature of the project environment, these production rates can be applied, as amended, to the quantity of measured work determined in Step 4 to calculate the expected total working time to complete the selected activity.

Step 6 – Estimate the activity duration

Following on from Step 5, the programmer can estimate appropriate activity durations according to the quantity of work required and intended resources.

The duration of the activity will account for the working calendar that has been assigned to the activity.

Step 7 – Resource levelling[8]

8 Resource levelling is defined as: 'A technique in which the start and finish dates are adjusted based on resource limitation with the goal of balancing demand for resources with the available supply' (Project Management Institute, *A Guide to the Project Management Body of Knowledge* (PMI, 7th edn 2021).

It is important to ensure the resources allocated to a particular set of activities are realistic and efficient. This can be ensured by consulting clients, contractors, and sub-contractors to clarify crew sizes and production rates for the specific project.

Step 8 – Constraints and assumptions

Where constraints are specified by the Contract, Employer, or other stakeholders, they must be incorporated into the programme.

These constraints may restrict start or finish dates for the entire project or an individual activity.

For example, if Site access is restricted to start no earlier than a particular date, the programme is required to have a 'no earlier than' start constraint on a 'Site access' activity.

Step 9 – Planning records

When constructing a programme it is important to make records of the calculations and planning process undertaken, such as:

- Logic behind estimates,
- Assumptions made, and
- Information and data received.

A programme register (the basis of schedule) should be generated for all versions of the programme issued.

15.6 Types of programmes

Programmes are prepared for different purposes, including the following:

- Development programme,
- Contract programme,
- Target construction programme, and
- Commissioning programme.

These are described in more detail next.

15.6.1 Development programme

A development programme is produced by the Employer very early in the project. It covers the overall timeline from project inception to operation.

A development programme is usually produced before design starts, based on little information, and requires considerable effort to identify project assumptions and risks. High level programmes are used as a basis for initial cost estimates and project feasibility.

This will be the first project timeline presented to senior decision makers and can create unrealistic expectations if assumptions, current conditions, and projections on which the programme is based are not clearly spelt out. If these programmes are underestimated, then it will be very hard to justify later increases to time and budget estimates. They can easily become the basis for drawn out future disputes.

15.6.2 Contract programme

The Contract programme (often referred to as the baseline programme) is usually prepared following award of a construction contract.[9] It communicates the Contractor's intended methodology, commitments between the parties, handover, and Completion dates which align with the requirements of the Contract.

The Contract programme is a yardstick for measurement of progress (ie status reporting) and forms the basis for extension of time claims, assessment of Variations, and evidence in disputes.

The programme should contain delay contingency allowances for all the delay risks assumed by the Contractor under the Contract. It should be stated at the outset that these contingency allowances belong to the Contractor if that is what is intended. See ¶14.3.2 for a discussion of Contractor's contingency.

In the authors' view, it is imperative to retain a copy of every programme in native format issued during the course of a project. These should clearly identify the date they are updated to reflect as-built status (which will usually be different to the date on which they were prepared or issued). As noted in ¶15.5.4, a programme register should be maintained for all versions of the programme issued, recording date of issue, update date, and to whom it was issued. Retaining a native copy of every programme issued can save substantial expenditure at a later date in justifying claims or resolving disputes.

15.6.3 Target construction programme

A target construction programme should reflect the Contract programme methodology but is generally set to a 'tighter' timeline than the Contract programme, with an aim to deliver a project as early as possible.

The purpose of the target construction programme is for the Contractor to drive subcontractors and consultants and it usually contains little or no delay contingency.

The purpose of this programme should be clarified at the time because it may be used against the Contractor later in litigation to show that the Contract programme which has been communicated to the Employer is misleading or deceptive.

15.6.4 Commissioning programme

The commissioning programme generally refers to the cold commissioning and hot commissioning of the Works. Cold commissioning involves bringing all the services, plant, and systems for the building or infrastructure Works online, following the completion of construction, so that the Works are 'functioning' and fit for operation.

Hot commissioning is the process of organising and starting up the activities which will occur once the project is complete. This is especially important in projects where the ongoing operations are complex – for instance processing plants, road tunnels, airports,

9 Philip Loots & Dr Donald Charrett, 'Reconsidering Procurement Criteria and Procedures for Major Infrastructure Projects: Why the Use of "Price" as the Determining Factor in Construction Procurement Decisions is Wrong' (2017) *International Construction Law Review* 69.

hospitals, and hotels. Off-site components of hot commissioning may commence many months before the physical project is complete (eg procuring equipment, hiring of staff to work in a new facility) and, in later stages, will have many interface points with the physical project (eg processing of materials, access for staff orientation and training, material stocking etc).

Commissioning is discussed in more detail in ¶11.7.

15.7 Updating the programme

Very few construction projects are built precisely on schedule. It is almost inevitable that problems will occur which throw the Contractor off schedule. For this reason the Contractor must update the project schedule frequently and at regular intervals (and as noted earlier may have a contractual obligation to do so). The Contractor faces severe consequences if it fails to update the programme. A common problem which is encountered is a dispute with subcontractors whose work was planned on the basis of the progress schedule and who have incurred increased costs as a result of the Head Contractor's abandonment of that schedule.[10]

For the Head Contractor the regular and frequent updating of the project programme is essential to maintain the accuracy of this vital management tool and to ensure that the schedule does not become the basis for a claim alleging delay and failure to schedule the work.

10 *E.C. Ernst Inc. v Manhattan Construction Company of Texas* 387 F. Supp. 1001 (1974).

CHAPTER 16

Tests on and after completion

CONTENTS

16.1 Completion

16.1.1 What constitutes completion?

Contracts often use the word 'completion' indiscriminately to mean either 'practical completion,' the later completion of all outstanding work, or the completion later still of the work of rectifying defects. It is necessary in every case to consider the usage of the word in the Contract carefully so as to decide which of these meanings is intended. For examples of clauses where these distinctions arise, see clauses dealing with care of the Works, clearance of the Site, damages for delay, and payment of retention money. The word is perhaps most frequently used in the sense of completion as at certification of practical completion except for any outstanding work still remaining to be done at that date.

Completion may mean performance of the entirety of the Contractor's Works being completion of the Contractor's physical deliverables. In *Wood Hall Ltd v the Pipeline Authority*,[1] it was held that although the Contractor was late in the performance of its work, and therefore in breach of contract, as the Contractor had nevertheless physically completed the work it promised to perform; there was 'completion' of the Works, notwithstanding that the Contractor may have fallen into breach of contract.

1 (1979) 141 CLR 443, 453 per Gibbs J.

DOI: 10.4324/9781003206873-16

The concept of 'completion' under the Contract will amount to a reference to completion of all the Contractor's Works in accordance with the Contract, and not just completion to the point that the Works in question are functional.[2] This will apply unless a contract makes specific reference to 'substantial completion' or 'practical completion.' When the Works are physically complete or certified as complete save for minor omissions or defects, or the Works are otherwise reasonably capable of their intended use,[3] the Works are commonly regarded as having reached **substantial completion.**[4] **Practical completion** and 'taking-over' may be regarded as having the same meaning. Practical completion and substantial completion usually mean that the Works are to be regarded as having reached a stage of physical or functional completion or have been certified as complete save for minor omissions or defects,[5] and the Works are otherwise reasonably capable of their intended use.[6]

Where the Works involves items of plant, Tests on Completion are usually required before the Employer takes possession of the Works and the Site, for example 2017 FIDIC Red Book sub-clause 10.1(a). Physical completion of the particular Works will not constitute 'completion' where testing and commissioning of plant is a pre-requisite. It is standard practice to also require 'as built' documents,[7] operations and maintenance manuals (**O&M manuals**), and similar documents to be satisfactorily completed and delivered to the Employer or its representative before 'completion.'[8]

'Completion' may refer to **sections** or portions of the Works (known as separable portions) so as to allow the Employer to take possession of sections or portions progressively. A Contractor may only be required to complete sections of the Works by specific dates if the Contract specifies that this is to be done.[9]

Where process plants are being constructed, commissioning and testing of each section individually may be required before 'completion' of each such section is achieved, and ultimately the whole of the Works will be required to be tested as one in order to achieve 'completion' of the whole of the Works. **Mechanical Completion** in projects which involve process plant usually means that the components of the plant have been physically completed, ready to be commissioned and may be achieved before or after tests to demonstrate that the plant is capable of being used as intended, depending upon how the Contract is worded.[10]

---

2 See *Hall v Van Der Heiden (No.2)* [2010] EWHC 586 (TCC), [44] per Coulson J; *Cordon Investments Pty Ltd v Lesdor Properties Pty Ltd* [2010] NSWSC 1073, [95]-[104] per McDougall J; *Ho Kwai Chun v Wong King Man* [2014] HKCFI 888, [25] per DHCJ Burrell; *Leighton Contractors (Singapore) Pte Ltd v J-Power SystemsCorp* [2009] SGHC 7, [11], per Choo Han Teck J.

3 See *Mariner International Hotels Ltd v Atlas Ltd* [2007] HKCFA 5, [27] per Bokhary J; *Lucas Stuart Pty Ltd v Hemmes Hermitage Pty Ltd* [2010] NSWCA 283, [31] per Macfarlan JA; *Walter Lilly and Company Limited v Mackay* [2012] EWHC 1773 (TCC), [372] per Akenhead J; *Willow Corp SARL v MTD Contractors Ltd* [2019] EWHC 1591 (TCC), [41] per Pepperall J.

4 The term 'Substantial Completion' is used in the JCWC Standard Form of Building Contract (2006 edn) (Hong Kong).

5 See *Mears Ltd v Costplan Services (South East) Ltd* [2019] EWCA Civ 502, [74(f)] per Coulson LJ.

6 *Walter Lilly & Co Ltd v Mackay* [2012] EWHC 1773 (TCC), [372] per Akenhead J; *Tennyson Estate Ltd v Boxwood Design Ltd* [2014] HKCFI 447, [20]-[21] per DHCJ S Wong SC; *Willow Corp SARL v MTD Contractors Ltd* [2019] EWHC 1591 (TCC), [41] per Pepperall J.

7 See 2017 FIDIC Red Book sub-clause 4.1; *LQS Construction Pte Ltd v Mencast Marine Pte Ltd* [2017] SGHC 148, [50]-[51] per Hoo Sheau Peng JC; *Alsthom Power Ltd v Somi Impianti SRL* [2011] EWHC 3941 (TCC), [14] per Akenhead J; cf: *Might Foundate Development Ltd v CCECC (HK) Ltd* [2001] HKCFI 715, [21] per Burrell J.

8 See 2017 FIDIC Red Book sub-clause 10.1; *Alsthom Power Ltd v Somi Impianti SRL* [2011] EWHC 3941 (TCC), [14] per Akenhead J; *LQS Construction Pte Ltd v Mencast Marine Pte Ltd* [2017] SGHC 148, [50]-[51] per Hoo Sheau Peng JC.

9 *Council of the City of Plymouth v DR Jones (Yeovil) Ltd* [2005] EWHC 2356 (TCC), [34] per HHJ Coulson QC; *University of Warwick v Balfour Beatty Group Limited* [2018] EWHC 3230 (TCC).

10 See AR Marshall, 'Process Plant: The ENAA Model Form Contract (2010 edition) – Comments and Comparisons' (2011) *International Construction Law Review* 138, 143–144.

The terminology **Completion** is used in this book to denote practical completion in the sense defined in the Contract.

16.1.2 Court interpretations of completion

In England, the Court of Appeal has taken a very literal interpretation of contractual terms when determining issues of completion.[11] By contrast, the Australian courts have recognised that the parties may agree that substantial completion is sufficient for completion, and that it may be unfair to penalise a party for falling short of a criterion contained in a contract when the overall performance required by the Contract has been achieved. The proposition comes down to the likely intent of the parties, defined by a reasonable commercial bystander. In *Luna Park (NSW) Ltd v Tramways Advertising Pty Ltd*,[12] an advertising contract required the contractors to display advertisements for 'at least eight hours per day.' The High Court interpreted this as requiring display for 'substantially' eight hours. Thus, the doctrine of substantial completion has been held to apply where a clause is not regarded as being broken by occasional small deficiencies. The case of *Luna Park* has been applied and followed in a number of instances.[13]

Obviously both the nature and extent of the uncompleted work or defects are relevant, and to say that substantial completion allows for minor deficiencies that can be readily remedied and which do not impair the Works as a whole is probably an accurate summary of what is a question of fact in each case.[14]

16.1.3 Implied warranty of completion

There is no implied warranty by the Employer that the Works can be completed or successfully carried out.[15] It is the duty of the Contractor to satisfy itself, prior to execution of the Contract, that the Works can be carried out in accordance with the plans, and that the Tests on Completion will be able to be passed.

16.2 Tests on Completion

Many contracts have a requirement for the Contractor to carry out **Tests on Completion**. The passing of such tests leads to the acceptance and **Taking-Over** of the Works by the Employer and regaining possession of the Site. The Engineer formally notifies that Completion has been achieved by issue of the **Taking-Over Certificate**. This is discussed further in Chapter 17.

Wherever possible, full details of the Tests on Completion should be agreed at the tender stage and described in detail in the Contract (normally in the specification) so that there can be no argument as to which tests the plant will be required to pass before the Works are taken over by the Employer.[16] The Contractor should plan ahead to ensure that adequate

11 See *Arcos Ltd v E A Ronaasen & Son 1368* [1933] AC 470.

12 (1938) 61 CLR 286.

13 See for example *Cell Tech Communications Pty Ltd v Nokia Mobile Phones (UK) Ltd* (1995) 58 FCR 365 and *Whipp v Cochrane* [2001] NSWSC 454.

14 See *Jacobs & Younger Inc v Kent* 230 NY 239, 129 NE 889.

15 *Robertson v Maurice Nichols (Pty) Ltd* (1938) NPD 34; *Neodox Ltd v Swinton and Pendlebury* (1958) 5 BLR 34.

16 See the 2017 FIDIC Yellow Book sub-clause 9.1, in which the Employer's Requirements describe the tests which the Contractor must carry out before being entitled to a Taking-Over Certificate.

power and consumables are available for the tests, and provide for what may be intricate coordination, especially if the Works are to be tested and taken over in sections. Special consideration must be given to the effect of other parts of the Works being incomplete. The Engineer's or Employer's approval must not be unreasonably, or dishonestly, or capriciously withheld.[17] What is reasonable is a question of fact. Sometimes, particularly where the Works involve the supply of computer software, perhaps for control systems, the tests cannot be agreed in detail at the tender stage. Where this is the case, the results to be achieved by the tests may be agreed at tender while details of the tests can be agreed later and incorporated into the Contract by way of amendment.

It is advisable for the Employer to arrange for its permanent operating and maintenance personnel to witness the operational tests and/or trial operation, which may coincide with the training of the Employer's personnel. In the case of a process plant, the supply of feedstock for trial operation and the disposal of any product (which usually becomes the property of the Employer) must be provided for.

If the Works are to be completed in sections and taken over in **stages,** each stage must be defined, and its precise geographical location must be defined. It may be convenient to formulate a table setting out the time for Completion, the amount of retention money to be released, and the amount of the delay damages applicable to each section and to the whole project.

When the Contractor believes that the Works have reached Completion, it should agree with the Engineer on a specific time for carrying out the specified tests. The possibility of lack of action by the Engineer regarding the Tests on Completion should be provided for in the Contract. This lack of action can take two forms that may prevent the Contractor from fulfilling the contractual conditions for Taking-Over:

- The Engineer fails to appoint a time for the tests after having received notice from the Contractor.
- The Engineer is absent at the time and place it has appointed.

In both instances, the Contractor should be entitled to proceed with the tests in the Engineer's absence. In the first instance it would be necessary for the Contractor to notify the Engineer of the date and place of the tests.

When the tests proceed in the absence of the Engineer, the tests should be deemed to have been made in the presence of the Engineer. The Engineer should not be able to later excuse itself for not having discovered a fault in the Works because it was not present at the tests. The results of the tests conducted in the Engineer's absence should then be accepted as accurate. The Engineer (or the Employer) cannot afterwards dispute the results of such tests on the grounds that the specific measurement was not adequate or accurate. It is, however, necessary that the Contractor performs all such tests that the parties have agreed upon in the Contract, and provide comprehensive documentation of the calibration of testing equipment, test measurements, and so on.

There is no reason why, when the Tests on Completion are agreed, the parties should not also agree and specify the services and facilities to be provided by the Employer and the Contractor for the tests. If the Employer is in default in providing such facilities, the Contractor may be entitled to compensation for costs incurred in providing the facilities itself and to an extension of time.

17 *Cammell Laird & Co v The Manganese Bronze and Brass Co* [1934] A.C. 402 (HL).

If approval is subject to the completion of certain tests which the Employer fails to carry out through its own fault, the Employer cannot withhold its approval because the Work has not satisfied other tests not agreed upon in the Contract.[18]

16.3 Delayed tests

Provision should be made in the Contract for the situation whereby the agreed Tests on Completion are unduly delayed by the Contractor. Notification from the Engineer to carry out the Tests on Completion should require the Contractor to make the tests within a stipulated time. If the Contractor then fails to make the tests required within the stipulated time, the Engineer may proceed with the tests itself. Any tests made by the Engineer would normally be at the risk and cost of the Contractor and the cost of the tests would be deducted from the contract price. The tests so made should be deemed to have been made in the Contractor's presence.

16.4 Failure to pass Tests on Completion

The consequences of the Works or any section thereof failing to pass the Tests on Completion must be provided for. When such failure occurs, either the Engineer or the Contractor should be entitled to require such tests to be repeated on the same terms and conditions. The Contractor should bear the cost of the repeated tests, the cost being deducted from the contract price.

The Tests on Completion are the formal means of establishing that the Works have been satisfactorily completed in accordance with the Contract and may be accepted by the Employer. It may therefore be that the Engineer and the Contractor disagree in their interpretation of the test results. If this is the case, it is suggested that the Contractor and the Engineer should be required to submit statements of their views to each other. The statements, accompanied by all relevant evidence, should be submitted within a specified period after such disagreement arises. In subsequent expert determination or arbitration, these statements may be important evidence in deciding whether the specific tests have been satisfactorily completed, and whether a repeated test was called for.

If failure of Tests on Completion occurs, the Contract may give the Engineer the choice between three options, a choice that it can only exercise after having duly consulted both the Employer and the Contractor:

- The first option is to order one further repetition of the tests. In other words, the Contractor would be obliged to make one more set of tests (but not more) at its own cost if so ordered by the Engineer.
- The second option is the right of the Employer to reject the Works (or section) with the right to terminate the whole of the Works or section or any part in respect of which it will be deprived substantially of the whole of the contractual benefit.
- The third option is to take over the Works notwithstanding that they have not passed the Tests on Completion. If the Employer elects to proceed on this basis, the Engineer must then issue a Taking-Over Certificate for the Works (or section). In this event, the contract price should be reduced. As the reduction

18 *Mackay v Dick* (1881) 6 App. Cas 251 (HL).

in value of the Works will vary according to why the tests were not passed, provision should be made for the Contractor and the Employer to agree in each specific circumstance, or to let the matter be decided by arbitration or expert determination. The minimum acceptable performance criteria should be clearly defined in the Contract.

The third option is often selected in cases where the performance falls only marginally short of that required by the Contract. In some contracts there may be provisions specifying pre-agreed damages for not passing certain levels of performance in the Tests on Completion. The calculation of performance damages will be based on the extent of the failure, and the method of calculation should be clearly stated in the Schedule of Performance Guarantees.

The Engineer is usually obliged to issue a Taking-Over Certificate to the Contractor and the Employer as soon as the Works or any section thereof have passed the Tests on Completion. The Engineer should do this without any application from the Contractor, although it would be good practice for the Contractor to make a formal request in writing to the Engineer.

16.5 Tests after Taking-Over

There may be tests to be carried out after Taking-Over (**Tests after Completion**), to verify that the Works comply with the Employer's performance requirements. FIDIC[19] emphasises the importance of specifying, in the Schedule of Performance Guarantees, the performance criteria which the facility will be required to achieve.[20] Usually Tests after Completion are carried out by the Employer and the Employer's operating personnel, with guidance from the Contractor's staff. If the Employer wishes the Contractor to carry out the Tests after Completion the Employer may be required to provide all electricity, water, fuel, consumables, materials, and so on for the tests and make personnel and plant available.[21]

Tests after Completion may comprise performance tests and availability tests. Performance tests are carried out shortly after Taking-Over, to measure the performance of the Works or section against the performance criteria specified in the Contract. Availability tests are carried out during the initial period of the defects liability period, to measure the availability of the Works or section during that period. In the case of EPC/Turnkey projects, it is usually necessary to demonstrate that the guaranteed performance is achieved under normal operating conditions.[22] Some jurisdictions may require mandatory testing of the Works after Taking-Over and before operation.

---

19 2017 FIDIC Yellow Book sub-clause 12.1.

20 The instructions to Tenderers should include information on the base physical input conditions (such as raw water quality for a water treatment plant) the Contractor can rely on to design and construct the facility to achieve such performance criteria (2017 FIDIC Yellow Book Notes on the Preparation of Special Provisions, Clause 12.1).

21 Consideration should be given to the provisions of sub-clause 12.1 in 2017 FIDIC Silver Book.

22 See 2017 FIDIC Silver Book sub-clause 12.1.

CHAPTER 17

Employer's Taking-Over

CONTENTS

17.1 Practical completion

17.1.1 Achievement of practical completion

Whether practical completion (Completion) has been achieved is primarily a question of fact[1] and judgement[2] which is to be determined having regard to what the Contractor undertook to supply, the definition of Completion in the Contract, and whether what the Contractor has provided is substantially in accordance with what the Contract required so as to constitute Completion. If the Works, or elements of the Works, are potentially unsafe, Completion will not have been achieved.[3] On the other hand, where a structure is physically complete but is not functioning entirely as it should, Completion may nevertheless have occurred.[4] For cases dealing with the meaning of 'substantial completion,' see *Dakin v Lee*.[5]

1 *Luen Tat Co v Valley View Co-operative Building Society Ltd* [1968] HKCFI 9, [12] per Huggins J; *Clyde Contractors Pty Ltd v Northern Beaches Developments Pty Ltd* [2001] QCA 314, [16] (18 BCL 144); *Laurence Constructions Pty Ltd v Nolks* [2010] NTSC 37, [43] per Southwood J.

2 See *Fairfield City Council v Abergeldie Contractors Pty Ltd* [2017] NSWSC 166, [33] per Ball J; *Laing O'Rourke Construction Ltd v Healthcare Support (Newcastle) Ltd* [2014] EWHC 2595 (TCC), [35]–[47] per Edwards-Stuart J.

3 See *Ser Kim Koi v GTMS Construction Pte Ltd* [2016] SGCA 7, [51]–[55], per Quentin Loh J.

4 *Bovis Lend Lease Ltd v Saillard Fuller & Partners* (2001) 77 Con LR 134; cf: *Mears Ltd v Costplan Services (South East) Ltd* [2019] EWCA Civ 502, [70] per Coulson LJ.

5 (1916) 1 KB 566.

DOI: 10.4324/9781003206873-17

The question of whether Completion has been achieved may be primarily a question of fact,[6] or it may be regarded as a mixed question of fact and law.[7] Patent defects in the Works (including defects of an aesthetic nature[8] which are more than trifling) will result in the Works not achieving Completion.[9] Where the Works appear to have been completed but contain latent defects which will ultimately prevent them from being used, the Contractor may still be regarded as having achieved Completion in spite of the presence of such latent defects (which by definition are unknown at the time).[10]

If the achievement of Completion is subject to the Engineer forming the opinion that the Works have reached a state of Completion, and unreasonably or in bad faith he or she fails to form that opinion and certify that the Works are practically complete, a court or tribunal is not prevented from concluding that Completion has been achieved, if objectively it has been achieved.[11]

Completion is usually certified by the Engineer's issue of a certificate of practical completion or a Taking-Over Certificate. Where the Engineer is obliged to issue a certificate of practical completion or a Taking-Over Certificate, this is usually a mandatory provision of the Contract. If the Contractor alleges Completion and if this is disputed by the Engineer, the Contractor's remedy is usually immediate arbitration.

17.1.2 The consequences of practical completion

The certification of Completion has a number of important effects. Completion usually represents the point at which possession of the Site is handed back to the Employer,[12] and the risk of damage to the Works will usually revert from the Contractor to the Employer. However, occupation of the Works by the Employer does not necessarily mean that the Works are practically complete if there are significant Works which remain incomplete or defective.[13]

Completion usually marks the end of the construction phase of the project and identifies the commencement of the defects liability period during which the Contractor's obligations are to complete outstanding work, and to repair and make good defects. The Employer or the Engineer may be precluded from instructing further Variations to the Works, depending upon the drafting of the Contract. The point in time at which the Employer's cause of action arises in respect of defective Works depends primarily upon the facts and the terms of the Contract in question.[14]

---

6 *Luen Tat Co v Valley View Cooperative Building Society Ltd* [1968] HKCFI 9, [12] per Huggins J; *Laurence Constructions Pty Ltd v Nolks* [2010] NTSC 37, [43] per Southwood J.

7 *Miller v Lida Build Pty Ltd* [2013] QCA 332, [15] per Gotterson JA.

8 *Mears Ltd v Costplan Services (South East) Ltd* [2019] EWCA Civ 502, [81] per Waksman J (appeal dismissed: [2019] EWCA Civ 502).

9 *Cordon Investments Pty Ltd v Lesdor Properties Pty Ltd* [2006] NSWSC 184, [61] per Bathurst CJ.

10 *Westminster Corporation v Jarvis & Sons Ltd* [1970] 1 WLR 637.

11 *Fairfield City Council v Abergeldie Contractors Pty Ltd* [2017] NSWSC 166, [33] per Ball J.

12 *Ascon Contracting Ltd v Alfred McAlpine Construction Isle of Man Ltd* (1999) 66 Con LR 119, 143 [80] per HHJ Hicks QC.

13 *Hall v Van Der Heiden (No 2)* [2010] EWHC 586 (TCC), [70] per Coulson LJ.

14 *Millenia Pte Ltd v Dragages Singapore Pte Ltd* [2018] SGHC 193, [470] per Quentin Loh J. Compare *Acme Metal Works Ltd v Shun Shing Construction & Engineering Co Ltd* [1990] 2 HKLR 474, 478–479 per

If retention money has been deducted from progress payments made to the Contractor, Completion usually entitles the Contractor to the payment of half of that retention money. A performance bond may be expressed so that it is reduced or becomes null and void upon the Engineer issuing a Taking-Over Certificate.

The risk of damage to or destruction of the Works usually passes from the Contractor to the Employer upon Completion, except for outstanding work and damage to the Works actually occasioned by the Contractor during the defects liability period. The Contractor or Employer's obligation to take out 'joint names' insurance against the risk of loss or damage to the Works may cease.[15] However, the Contractor's obligation to insure the Works is usually not completely extinguished.

It is important to distinguish between the Date of Completion, being the date on which the Works reached the physical state of being practically complete, and the Date for Completion, being the date required by the Contract for Completion.[16] Where the Date of Completion is later than the Contract Date for Completion, the Date of Completion marks the end of the period in respect of which the Contractor is liable to pay liquidated damages.

17.2 Taking-Over Certificate

The Contract may require the Engineer or the Employer to issue a Taking-Over Certificate upon the Works reaching the state of being practically complete.[17] This amounts to a positive obligation on the Engineer or Employer to monitor the state of the Works, and to issue a certificate when the Works are practically complete.[18]

Alternatively, the Contractor may be required to notify either the Engineer or the Employer when the Contractor believes the Works have achieved a state of Completion and apply for the issue of the Taking-Over Certificate.[19] It is important for the Contractor to be aware that this is a mandatory provision in certain contracts. If the Contractor fails to give due notification when it considers the Works to have achieved Completion under such a contract, Completion will not have been achieved, even if the Works are objectively in a state in which they have been practically completed.[20]

Where the Contractor is required to serve notice on the Engineer that the Works are complete, the Engineer must generally, within a stipulated time after the receipt of the Contractor's application, either issue a Taking-Over Certificate stating the date on which the Works were complete and ready for Taking-Over, or reject the application giving its reasons.

Nazareth J; *Agro Investment Overseas Ltd v Stewart Milne Group Limited* [2018] CSOH 120, [101] per Lord Clark.

15 *TFW Printers Ltd v Interserve Project Services Ltd* [2006] BLR 299 (CA).

16 *Re an arbitration between Taylor Woodrow International Ltd and the Minister of Health* (1978) 19 SASR 1, 26–27 per Bray CJ.

17 The FIDIC rainbow suite uses the term Taking-Over Certificate. The JCT Standard Building Contract (2016) clause 2.30 and the JCWC Standard Form of Building Contract (2006) clause 17.1 use the term Practical Completion Certificate.

18 See *Emson Eastern Ltd v EME Developments Ltd* (1991) 55 BLR 114, 122 per Judge Newey QC.

19 See for example AS 4000–1997, clause 34.6; SIA Building Contract (1st edn 2016) clause 22(2).

20 See *Vascroft (Contractors) Ltd v Seeboard plc* (1996) 78 BLR 132, 161–163, per Judge Humphrey Lloyd QC; *Embankment Place Hotels (Blackfriars) Ltd v Blackfriars Hotels Ltd* (2002) 85 Con LR 29, 43 [23]–44 [25] per Forbes J (affirmed [2003] EWCA Civ 588).

If the Engineer rejects the application, it should be careful to include details of any outstanding work required to be done, including repair, replacement, and making good of any defects required before the issue of the certificate. If the Engineer does not include this requirement, the defects and any outstanding work which the Engineer may not have drawn to the Contractor's attention will still generally be covered by the Contractor's obligation to remedy defects during the defects liability period.

The Contract may include a default mechanism for the eventuality that the Engineer or the Employer fails to respond to the Contractor's notification of Completion.[21] These typically provide that if the Engineer fails to respond to a Contractor's application for the Taking-Over Certificate within the stipulated time, the Engineer is deemed to have issued the certificate at the end of such period. An Employer may waive the requirements for Completion being achieved by taking over the Works notwithstanding that they are not practically complete.[22]

A Taking-Over Certificate may state that once identified works have been completed, Completion will have been achieved.[23] If the Works are incomplete, but only in minor respects[24] that do not prevent the Employer from using the Works for their intended purpose,[25] the Contractor is usually still entitled to a Taking-Over Certificate. Certain contracts may positively permit the Engineer or Employer to issue a Taking-Over Certificate although there are minor outstanding works (**punch-list items**), on condition that the Contractor completes those works within a particular time.[26] Under such circumstances, the Engineer or Employer will have a discretion to decide whether to certify that Completion has been achieved despite there being minor incomplete Works although that discretion must be exercised in a reasoned and not in an arbitrary way.[27]

Separate Taking-Over Certificates may be issued in respect of each section of the Works.

The Engineer or the Employer may issue a certificate at the end of the defects liability period recording the fact that the Contractor has remedied the defects which were required to be corrected during the defects liability period. This may be a condition precedent to the issue of a final payment certificate.[28]

There may be circumstances where the Engineer certifies the Works as complete, and the parties subsequently dispute whether the Works were in fact complete in the sense that they were fit for their intended purpose. An example is where the Works are taken over and certified prior

---

21 A contract may provide that Completion is deemed to have occurred on the date notified by the Contractor: see for example *GB Building Solutions Ltd v SFS Fire Services Ltd* [2017] EWHC 1289 (TCC) [64]–[65] per Stephen Davies J.

22 See *AMEC Foster Wheeler Group Limited v Morgan Sindall Professional Services Ltd* [2016] EWHC 902 (TCC) [35] per Edwards-Stuart J.

23 *Bovis Lend Lease Ltd v Saillard Fuller & Partners* (2001) 77 Con LR 134, 198 [185] per HHJ Thornton QC.

24 *Mears Ltd v Costplan Services (South East) Ltd* [2019] EWCA Civ 502, [74(f)] per Coulson J.

25 *Mariner International Hotels Ltd v Atlas Ltd* [2007] HKCFA 5, [27] per Bokhary PJ; *Lucas Stuart Pty Ltd v Hemmes Hermitage Pty Ltd* [2010] NSWCA 283, [31] per Macfarlan JA; *Walter Lilly & Co Ltd v Mackay* [2012] EWHC 1773 (TCC), [372] per Akenhead J; *Tennyson Estate Ltd v Boxwood Design Ltd* [2014] HKCFI 447, [20]–[21] per DHCJ S Wong SC; *Grocon Constructors (Qld) Pty Ltd v Juniper Developers No. 2 Pty Ltd* [2015] QCA 291, [59] per McKeekin J; *Willow Corp SARL v MTD Contractors Ltd* [2019] EWHC 1591 (TCC), [41] per Pepperall J.

26 SIA Form of contract: SIA Building Contract (1st edn 2016) clause 22(5); *Permasteelisa Pacific Holdings v Hyundai Engineering & Construction Co Ltd* [2005] 2 SLR(R) 270.

27 *Permasteelisa Pacific Holdings v Hyundai Engineering & Construction Co Ltd* [2005] 2 SLR(R) 270, 281 [18] per Judith Prakash J.

28 *Cantrell v Wright & Fuller Ltd* [2003] BLR 412, 441 [140]–442 [143] per HHJ Thornton QC.

to the requisite commissioning tests being undertaken because the Works required modification. In such a case, the Employer's entitlement to liquidated damages may be compromised.

The fact that the Engineer has issued a Taking-Over Certificate on Completion does not exempt the Contractor from liability under a defects liability clause requiring it to make good any defects that appear within a specified period from Completion of the Works.

17.3 Taking-Over the Works and sections

17.3.1 Taking-Over

Taking-Over, sometimes referred to as 'provisional acceptance,' occurs at the end of the construction stage of the Works or a section of the Works when, after passing the Tests on Completion, the Works are taken over by the Employer and the Contractor's obligations to remedy defects commence. Taking-Over is usually formalised by the issue of the Taking-Over Certificate, or the certificate of practical completion. Oral certification has been held to be sufficient where written certification is not specified.[29]

Since the Works are at the Contractor's risk until Taking-Over, the Employer is usually not entitled to use any part of the Works until a Taking-Over Certificate has been issued. Circumstances may arise where, before all the Tests on Completion have been passed, the Employer wishes to use part of the Works and does so in such circumstances that the Engineer is usually obliged to issue a Taking-Over Certificate for that part. When this happens, the Employer must give the Contractor the earliest possible opportunity of carrying out the Tests on Completion on the part of the Works taken over.

The occupation of a portion of the Works before Completion of the whole of the Works may constitute a significant change in risk affecting the Contractor's insurance policies. The Employer should therefore exercise extreme caution in taking over sections or parts of the Contractor's Works with the intention of having them completed by the Employer or a third party. This is especially so where the Contractor is willing, ready, and able to undertake such works itself.

Where the Employer does use part of the Works, the Contractor's defects liability obligation will generally commence on the date it was taken into use by the Employer, and the provisions relating to delay in Completion will not apply to that part of the Works being used.

Usually, three matters must be satisfied before Taking-Over can be affected:

(1) The Works must be completed in accordance with the Contract;
(2) The Works must have passed the Tests on Completion; and
(3) A Taking-Over Certificate must have been issued or deemed to have been issued.

17.3.2 Completion of the Works and defects

Where any portion of the Works is to be completed before the whole, such portion will usually qualify for a Taking-Over Certificate when complete for all practical purposes.

29 *Muyer v Gilmer* (1899) 18 NZLR 1291.

A dilemma may arise where the Works do not pass the Tests on Completion, but the Employer is obliged to take the Works over in order to mitigate losses and to satisfy sales orders made in the expectation of Completion. In these circumstances, the Employer may have good reason to resist the Works being at the Employer's risk.

The work outstanding should, as far as possible, be agreed at this stage, but the Contractor's contractual undertaking on Taking-Over should also include a general agreement to make good all existing defects. This will avoid any possible argument that it is not bound to make good defects which existed at the time of Completion but were not notified to the Contractor.

It is implied that the Engineer retains its powers in relation to subsequent acceptance of work that was incomplete at Completion. However, the Contract may not make it clear that the Engineer has powers to vary the work after Completion, since the Contractor's undertaking may be limited to finishing any outstanding work.

Outstanding non-essential work and reinstatement of ground or surfaces may be required to be done after Completion. For example, it is suggested that once an Employer can put a water purification works scheme into effective operation, Completion will have been achieved, notwithstanding that there may be a fair amount of non-essential work remaining to be done. Where there is likely to be any doubt about this, the Contract should deal with the matter expressly, particularly if Completion in stages is contemplated.

17.4 Final certificate

A **final certificate** is a statement by the Engineer or the Employer that the Contractor has completed all the Works in accordance with the Contract. A contract may provide that the final certificate provides conclusive evidence of the performance by the Contractor of its obligations. The terms of the Contract and the law governing the Contract will determine whether the final certificate absolves the Contractor from responsibility for latent defects which manifest themselves after the issue of the final certificate.

The correct application of the relevant Contract will determine when a final certificate must be issued, what it is required to state, the effect that it has between the parties and what form it is to be in. Under sub-clause 11.9 of the 2017 FIDIC Red Book, the Engineer is required to issue a Performance Certificate, which may be regarded as the equivalent of a final certificate, when the Contractor has completed all of its obligations under the Contract.

A final certificate will also usually contain a statement that the amount stated in it is the final amount which is due and payable by the Employer to the Contractor, or by the Contractor to the Employer.[30] Antecedent certificates, such as interim certificates, are overridden by a final certificate.[31]

30 See JCT Standard Building Contract (2016 edn) clause 4.26.2; *Penwith DC v VP Developments Ltd* [1999] EWHC Tech 231, [18] per HHJ Lloyd QC; *Tameside Metropolitan Borough Council v Barlow Securities Group Services Ltd* [2001] BLR 113, 121 [31] per Henry LJ.

31 *Mossop Group Pty Ltd v 1KW Adelaide Pty Ltd* [2018] SASC 186, [35] per Doyle J.

In *Cantrell v Wright & Fuller Ltd* it was held that:

> [A] final certificate often has a draconian effect on the rights of at least one of the parties to the contract. Thus, a final certificate contractual conditions and the final certificate itself must be strictly construed so as to ensure that the final certificate document conforms in all respects to the contractual requirements relating to both its form and to the circumstances when it may be issued.[32]

Preconditions for the issue of a final certificate may more generally include that:

- The Contractor has duly performed all of the Works that it was required to perform under the Contract;
- The Contractor has provided a unilateral release to the Employer from all further claims by the Contractor arising out of the Contract[33] (a bilateral release may be provided: see *Sabemo (SA) Pty Ltd v AIW Engineering Pty Ltd*[34]);
- The effect of the final certificate is to provide a conclusive statement of the Contractor's entitlement to payment for all matters arising out of the Contract; and[35]
- The Contractor has applied for the issue of a final certificate or made a 'final payment claim'[36] satisfying all the requirements of the Contract to show that the Works have reached the stage of finality, and the value of that work, and that the Contractor has otherwise performed its contractual obligations.[37]

Should the Employer wrongfully withhold the issue of a final certificate, equity will regard as done that which ought to be done,[38] or the Employer may, by its conduct, have waived its right to insist upon the issue of the final certificate.[39] It is not unusual for the Engineer or the Employer to attempt to agree the final value of the Works, and the remaining amount owing to the Contractor and other matters concerning the content of the final certificate with the Contractor.[40]

The final certificate usually represents the end of the Contractor's obligation to perform construction work, including the repair of defects, unless a defect correction certificate has been issued prior to the issue of the final certificate, in which case the Contractor's obligation will usually cease upon satisfaction of a defect correction certificate. The Contractor will usually be entitled to payment of any outstanding money, in particular retention money if a retention mechanism has been used, or alternatively to the return of another form of security such as a performance bond. If a final certificate is final and

32 [2003] BLR 412, 429 [81] per HHJ Thornton QC.

33 See the 2017 FIDIC Red Book sub-clause 14.12.

34 (1992) 9 BCL 280 [Sup Ct SA].

35 A final certificate is 'conclusive evidence of accord and satisfaction' between Employer and the Contractor so as to discharge the parties' respect of obligations subject to identify the exceptions in AS 4000–1997 clause 37.4.

36 See *Mackie Pty Ltd v Counahan* [2013] VSC 694, [65]–[69], per Vickery J.

37 See 2017 FIDIC Red Book sub-clause 14.11; SIA Building Contract (1st edn 2016) clause 31(9); JCT Standard Building Contract (2016) clause 4.25; AS 4000–1997 clause 37.4.

38 *Hightrade Construction Pty Ltd v Full Sea International Ltd* [2004] NSWSC 888, [18] per Campbell J.

39 Ibid. 17.

40 *Whittall Builders Co Ltd v Chester-le-Street DC* (1985) 11 Con LR 40, 54–55 per Mr Recorder Percival QC.

conclusive in its effect, the Contractor will usually be precluded from claiming an amount greater than that stated as due in the final certificate and the Employer will be discharged from paying any further or other amount.[41]

The final certificate may provide conclusive evidence of the adequacy of the work performed by the Contractor unless it is challenged within the period prescribed by the Contract. In such a case, the Employer is disentitled from seeking to exercise a right of set-off for countervailing claims on the basis of the adequacy of the work, for example the cost of rectifying defects which were not taken into account in the certificate, or delays to the Works which would otherwise have given rise to claims for liquidated damages. If that is the effect of the final certificate, it will 'put an end to disputes about the building operations.'[42]

That said, a final certificate may be only conclusive as to the Engineer's satisfaction that the Contractor has completed the Works, without constituting a final statement as to the adequacy of the work. This means that if latent defects become apparent after the issue of the final certificate, the Employer may be entitled to bring an action against the Contractor in respect of the defects.[43]

The Engineer will usually have no further power under the Contract to certify, being *functus officio* under the Contract.[44]

17.5 Interference with Tests on Completion

Where the Contractor is prevented from carrying out Tests on Completion through some cause for which the Engineer or the Employer or other contractors employed by the Employer are responsible, the Employer would normally be deemed to have taken over the Works on the date when the tests would otherwise have been completed, and the Engineer would be required to issue a Taking-Over Certificate accordingly. No Taking-Over Certificate should, however, be issued in such circumstances if the Works are not substantially complete in accordance with the Contract. Where the Works are taken over under these circumstances, the Contractor would not be absolved from carrying out the Tests on Completion and should be required to carry them out during the defects liability period. In these circumstances, the Contractor should be entitled to recover all additional costs reasonably incurred in making the Tests on Completion during such period.

---

41 See 2017 FIDIC Red Book sub-clause 14.4; AS 4000–1997 clause 37.4.

42 *James Png Construction Pte Ltd v Tu Chin Kwan Peter* [1991] 1 MLJ 499 (noted by Powell-Smith, [1992] *International Construction Law Review* 101); *Tarmac Construction Ltd v Esso Petroleum Co Ltd* (1996) 83 BLR 65, 106 per Judge Lloyd QC; *Hassell v Silent Vector Pty Ltd* [2002] WASC 250, [19]-[21] per Barker J.

43 See *Meredith Projects Pty Ltd v Fletcher Construction Pty Ltd* [2000] NSWSC 493, [25]–[26] per Rolfe J. Sub-clause 11.10 of the 2017 FIDIC Red Book makes each Party to the Contract liable for performance of any obligation which has not been fulfilled at the time of issuing a Performance Certificate. See also JCWC Standard Form of Building Contract (2006 edn) clause 32.9 under which the Contractor remains liable for latent defects that become apparent after the issue of a final certificate: SIA Building Contract (1st edn 2016) clause 27 (4) (b).

44 *Cantrell v Wright Fuller Ltd* [2003] BLR 412, 45 [99], per HHJ Thornton QC.

CHAPTER 18

Defects after Taking-Over

CONTENTS

18.1 Completion of outstanding work and remedying defects

18.1.1 Defects

The judicial interpretation of the term 'defective,' although derived in the context of insurance contracts, is that it 'simply denotes that the subject matter whether it be workmanship, design or material, is ineffective for the purposes for which it was intended.'[1] It is submitted that this definition is equally applicable to defective work in the context of construction contracts. In a general sense, a defect in a constructed facility is therefore a falling short in its ultimate functional requirements or fitness for purpose. Put more broadly, the word 'defect' may mean an element in the design and/or construction of work, or other delivery of goods or services, which in qualitative terms falls short of what should have

1 *Chalmers Leask Underwriting Agencies v Mayne Nickless Ltd* (1982) 2 ANZ Ins Cas, [0–463].

DOI: 10.4324/9781003206873-18

been supplied.[2] Whether or not a particular defect has contractual significance depends on the circumstances and the terms of the Contract. Some construction contracts use the term defect in a general sense (eg the 1999 FIDIC rainbow suite), whereas others may give it a particular contractual significance by using it as a defined term (eg NEC ECC) and the 2017 FIDIC rainbow suite. The terms of the Contract must be construed to determine which of these meanings is intended. Where the type of work for which the Contractor is contracted is aesthetic and does not add to the value of a property, the Employer is not disentitled from recovering substantial damages because what was supplied fell short of what ought to have been supplied, provided that what the Employer is claiming is compensation for a genuine loss.[3]

The principle was succinctly put by Oliver J:

> I know of no principle of damages which would dictate that a plaintiff who has stipulated for an article of a certain quality should be fobbed off with an inferior substitute merely because it is cheaper for a defendant who has broken his contract to supply it.[4]

For clarity, the term **defect** is used in this book to denote any defective work in the general sense. By contrast, the particular species of defect in which materials supplied or work carried out by the Contractor do not satisfy the requirements of the Contract will be referred to as a **Defect**.[5] Contracts frequently require that the Contractor is liable to rectify all defects 'discovered' before termination of the Contract. In such a contract the Contractor has an obligation not only to put its workmanship and materials in a condition which complies with the Contract before its completion, but also to rectify other defects for which it is not liable. The work involved in rectification of a defect which is not a Defect should be a Variation for which the Contractor is paid as provided for in the Contract.

As noted in ¶9.1.7, it is usually an implied (if not explicit) term in a construction contract that the Contractor must execute the work in a workmanlike manner, and that the materials used by it must be of a reasonable quality. In general, therefore, work which is not carried out in a workmanlike manner or materials which are not of reasonable quality constitute Defects. The Employer's cause of action will accrue at the point of taking possession, which will usually be the date of Completion.[6] Should the Employer, however, undertake to supply the materials, the Contractor will not be responsible for the unsuitability, or (possibly) the defective quality of materials selected by the Employer. If the Employer consults the Contractor before making a decision as to materials to be used and the materials later prove to be unsuitable for

2 See *Pearson Education Ltd v The Charter Partnership* [2005] EWHC 2021 (TCC), [122] per HHJ Thornton QC; *SAM Business Systems Limited v Hedley & Co* [2002] EWHC 2733 (TCC), [20] per HHJ Bowsher QC; *Schindler Lifts (Singapore) Pte Ltd v Paya Ubi Industrial Park Pte Ltd* [2004] SGHC 34, [83] per Judith Prakash J; *Longyuan-Arrk (Macao) Pte Ltd v Show and Tell Productions Pte Ltd* [2013] SGHC 160, [54] per Belinda Ang Saw Ean J; *Millennia Pte Ltd v Dragages Singapore Pte Ltd* [2018] SGHC 193,[226] per Quentin Loh J.

3 *NP Integrated Technology Pty Ltd v Entwistle* [2017] EWHC B21 (TCC), [116]-[119] per HHJ Stephen Davies; *Stone v Chappel* [2017] SASFC 72, [200]-[201] per Doyle J. *Tabcorp Holdings Ltd v Bowen Investments Pty Ltd* [2009] HCA 8, [20].

4 *Radford v De Froberville* [1977] 1 WLR 1262, 1284.

5 *Dymocks Books Arcade Pty Ltd v Capral Ltd* [2013] NSWSC 343, [93] per McDougall J; *Kone Elevator (HK) v Citybase Property Management Ltd* [2012] HKCFI 1022, [44]-[50] per Mr Recorder H Wong SC.

6 *Swansea Stadium Management Co Ltd v City & County of Swansea* [2018] EWHC 2192 (TCC), [57] per O'Farrell J; *Brewarrina Shire Council v Beckhaus Civil Pty Ltd* [2005] NSWCA 248, [69] per Ipp JA.

the contemplated purpose (ie defective), the Contractor generally would not be able to recover remuneration for its labour, unless it had safe-guarded itself by informing the Employer of the risks involved.[7]

Although unusual, a construction contract may specify that rectification of defects shall not be part of the Contractor's obligations. In such event the Contractor is responsible only for ensuring that its workmanship and the materials it supplies are of good quality and fit for purpose. The Employer would, however, be entitled to damages for breach of contract if Defects are discovered.

Damages are a conventional remedy at common law or under civil law for breach of contract or tort, giving rise to an obligation to pay damages by operation of law,[8] or because of a contractual stipulation. An award of damages for breach of contract is to compensate the Employer for its loss,[9] and to put the Employer in the position in which it would have been had the Contract been performed.[10]

'In a contract for the performance of building work, the plaintiff can recover the cost of rectifying defective or incomplete work because, by receipt of the money in substitution for performance, it is given the means of putting itself in the position it would have been in had the contract been performed.'[11] This measure of damages applies for actions founded in either contract or negligence. The cost of repairing the defects or bringing the Works to the standard required by the Contract must be reasonable.[12] Should the cost of rectifying a defect exceed the contract price for the performance of the original work, this does not, of itself, indicate any unreasonableness or disproportionality in undertaking remedial work.[13]

Where design forms part of the Works, damages for negligent design has been formulated as follows:

(1) The first stage is for a claimant in a claim against a construction professional for negligent design, to establish what would have happened if the construction professional had in fact exercised proper care and skill.

(2) If the claimant establishes that, if the construction professional had used proper care and skill, the claimant would have proceeded with the construction of the building in accordance with the proper design carried out by the construction professional then the measure of damages will be the cost of remedying the defect

---

7 *Miller v Cannon Hill Estates* [1931] 2 KB 113; *Myers (G H) & Co v Brent Cross Services* [1934] 1 KB 46; *Young & Marten v McManus Childs Ltd* [1968] 2 All ER 1191.

8 *Mann v Paterson Constructions Pty Ltd* [2019] HCA 32, [83] per Gageler J, [195] and [197] per Nettle, Gordon and Edelman JJ.

9 *Ruxley Electronics and Construction Ltd v Forsyth* [1996] AC 344, 360 per Lord Mustill.

10 See M Bell, 'After Tabcorp, for Whom Does the Bellgrove Toll? Cementing the Expectation Measure as the "Ruling Principle" for Calculation of Contract Damages' (2009) 32 *Melbourne University Law Review* 684; *Tabcorp Holdings Ltd v Bowen Investments Pty Ltd* (2009) 236 CLR 272, [15]; *FYD Investments Pty Ltd v Promptair Pty Ltd (No.2)* [2019] FCA 419, [236] and [242] per White J; *PND Civil Group Pty Ltd v Bastow Civil Constructions Pty Ltd* [2017] NSWCA 159, [59] per McDougall J.

11 *Westpoint Management Ltd v Chocolate Factory Apartments Ltd* [2007] NSWCA 253, [43] per Giles JA; *Kirkby v Coote* [2006] QCA 061, [47] per Keane JA, [93] per McMurdo J; *Lee v South* [2019] NZHC 646, [25] per Muir J.

12 In *Chocolate Factory Apartments Ltd v Westpoint Finance Pty Ltd* [2005] NSWSC 784, McDougall J held: 'It is hard to imagine a less meritorious claim for damages; or a more clear example of facts that justify a finding that the cost of rectification is not . . . reasonable.' Sub-specification skirting boards had been installed, a saving AUD$ 350; the Employer had no intention of removing and replacing them so as to ensure compliance with the Contract, yet it claimed AUD$112,815 from the Contractor as damages representing the cost of rectification.'

13 *Pravenkav Group Pty Ltd v Diploma Construction (WA) Pty Ltd (No.3)* [2014] WASCA 132, [77]; *Stone v Chappel* [2017] SASFC 72, [13] per Kourakis CJ.

but less a credit for any higher costs which would have been payable for a proper design in the first place.

(3) If, however, the claimant would have abandoned the project to construct the building if the construction professional had produced a properly prepared design, then the loss would be measured by reference to the wasted expenditure.[14]

The Employer is usually precluded from recovering damages from the Contractor in respect of defects arising during a defects liability period[15] unless the Employer has first given the Contractor the opportunity of undertaking the necessary rectification work (at the Contractor's expense) and the Contractor has failed to perform the required rectification. Giving the Contractor the opportunity of correcting a defect for which it is responsible is, in any event, a prudent step for the Employer to take in attempting to mitigate its loss.[16]

18.1.2 Defects liability period

Construction contracts generally stipulate a period after Completion and Taking-Over in which the Contractor has the obligation to rectify all Defects 'discovered.' This period is variously referred to as a 'defects correction period' (NEC ECC), a 'Defects Notification Period' (FIDIC rainbow suite), 'guarantee maintenance period,' 'maintenance period,' 'rectification period' (JCT forms of contract). This is also known as the **defects liability period**, which term is used in this book to define the period after Completion or Taking-Over during which the Contractor has a contractual obligation to rectify Defects. If parts of the Works are taken over separately, the defects liability period for such parts commences when they are taken over.

Whether the risk of damage or destruction to its work during the defects liability period remains with the Contractor (ie whether it must reconstruct the work if it is accidentally destroyed during that period) should be clearly stated in the Contract. In the absence of a clear statement that the Contractor remains liable, it would normally be implied that the Employer is subject to the risk of damage or destruction after Taking-Over.

A contractual mechanism will usually require either the Employer or the Engineer to notify the Contractor of Defects and require their repair so as to comply with the requirements of the Contract at the expense of the Contractor.[17] The Contractor's right of access to enter upon the land where the Works were performed so as to undertake any required corrections may be confirmed by an express contractual term.[18] In the absence of express contractual wording requiring the Contractor to correct Defects of which it has not been notified, the Contractor will not be under an obligation to correct such Defects.[19]

---

14 *Cooperative Group Limited v John Allen Associates Ltd* [2010] EWHC (TCC), [339] per Ramsey J.

15 *P&M Kaye Ltd v Hosier & Dickinson Ltd* [1972] 1 WLR 146, 166 per Lord Diplock; *Turner Corporation Ltd v Austotel Pty Ltd* (1994) 13 BCL 378, 394–396 per Cole J (NSW Sup Ct).

16 *Nouvelle Homes Pty Ltd v G&M Smargiassi* [2007] WASC 50, [16] per Blaxwll J; *Iggleden v Fairview New Homes (Shooters Hill) Ltd* [2007] EWHC 1573 (TCC), [77] per HHJ Coulson QC; *Pamax Ltd v Cross Max Interiors Ltd* [2008] HKCFI 266, [129] per DHCJ Gill; *Mul v Hutton Construction Ltd* [2014] EWHC 1797 (TCC).

17 *BHP Petroleum Ltd v British Steel plc* (2001) 74 Con LR 63 (CA).

18 See 2017 FIDIC Red Book sub-clause 11.7; NEC4 ECC clause 44.4.

19 *AMEC Foster Wheeler Group Limited v Morgan Sindall Professional Services Ltd* [2016] EWHC 902 (TCC), [41]-[47] per Edwards-Stuart J; *Yap Boon Keng Sonny v Pacific Prince International Pte Ltd* [2008] SGHC 161, [115] per Judith Prakesh J; *Thio Keny Thay v Sandy Island Pte Ltd* [2019] SGHC 175, [101]-[103] per Lee Seiu Kin J.

If the Defects discovered, or damage caused by such Defects during the defects liability period are successfully repaired or made good, this constitutes the whole of the Contractor's obligation. If a Contractor's express obligation is to correct Defects which 'appear' or 'occur' during the defects liability period, the obligation may include the correction of Defects which 're-appear' or 'recur.'[20] If the Defects are not successfully repaired, several remedies are open to the Employer, including termination of the Contract. The characteristic feature is, however, that the Contractor's liability for defects is limited to and dependent upon, it being able to repair the Defects.

If the Employer or the Engineer does not notify the Contractor about a Defect or damage, it will not be repaired. If the Employer or the Engineer does notify the Contractor, but later than can be considered reasonable, more difficult questions arise. If the late notice results in further defectiveness or damage that would not have occurred with an earlier notice, the Employer may have to bear the costs caused by the late notification.

As long as the Employer or the Engineer does notify the Contractor within the defects liability period, it is doubtful whether even a very late notification can be disregarded, and the Contractor deemed to be released from its obligations to repair the specific Defect or damage. A final inspection a few days before the end of the defects liability period may reveal Defects that will take a significant time to rectify, and the Contractor should then have a reasonable time to rectify those Defects.

There may be circumstances where it is necessary to imply the commencement date for the defects liability period. For example, if the Employer takes over a separable portion or any stage[21] of the Works, or omits a separable portion for whatever reason, and the defects liability period is expressed as commencing from a date referable to a stage which is no longer required, such an implied term would be necessary for the effective operation of the Contract. Without such an interpretation, there would be no certainty regarding the commencement of the defects liability period with its significant contractual consequences.

18.1.3 Maintenance and rectification of defects

The Contract may provide that, in addition to making good Defects, the Contractor is required to repair or maintain the Works for a specified period after the Date for Completion. This period, referred to as the **maintenance period** is normally for a year in engineering contracts. In this context, 'maintain' means to maintain in the same state as at the inception of the maintenance period. Such a 'maintenance' clause imposes on the Contractor a wider obligation than simply to make good Defects. The terms 'defects liability period' and 'maintenance period' are sometimes used interchangeably; however, the specific terms of the Contract should be referred to in order to determine the exact scope of the Contractor's obligations.

The maintenance obligation or the obligation to rectify Defects is in essence a valuable right to the Contractor to be permitted physically to return to the Site to maintain the Works and/or make good Defects. Subject to the terms of the Contract, an Employer may not

20 *ENS Ltd v Derwent Cogeneration Ltd* (1998) 62 Con LR 141, 150 per HHJ Havery QC.

21 A stage is a discrete part of the Works which must generally be completed before the next stage can be commenced, for example, design may constitute the first stage of a design and construct contract which must be completed and 'signed off' by the Employer before the Contractor is entitled to proceed with the construction stage. Completion of a stage may constitute the achievement of a milestone.

be able to rely on a maintenance or rectification of Defects clause to claim damages for Defects which were known to have existed before the inception of the maintenance period.

Because it is likely to cost more to have another contractor who is not familiar with the Works to do repairs, the Contractor is usually required to do all necessary repairs during a specified time after Completion. This will generally be over the teething period of the Works, even if the repairs, defects and so on, are not due to its fault. The Contractor usually bears the cost of repairs, rectification work, and of searching for the cause of defects only where such work is necessary as a result of its breach of contract.

18.1.4 Good and perfect condition

Where there is a fair wear and tear exception for the Employer's use this means that the Engineer cannot call for a brand-new finish at the end of the maintenance period – a matter of more importance, perhaps, in engineering contracts, where the maintenance period is sometimes substantially longer than in building contracts. The basic contractual obligation to complete is satisfied as soon as there is Completion as contemplated by the Contract, and only if, and to the extent that, work is not fully complete at that date will there be any obligation to do further work thereafter, other than in compliance with the terms of the defects liability or maintenance obligation.

Warranties of quality are often included in engineering and construction contracts, so as to provide certainty as to the nature and extent of the parties' respective rights and obligations. A warranty of quality or adequacy of the work may take effect from the time at which the work was completed, as distinct from the time at which the totality of the Works was completed.[22]

The Contractor must be available to do remedial work at any time during the defects liability period. Because the Contractor is usually liable only to make good Defects which are actually 'discovered' during the defects liability period, inspection on behalf of the Employer before the end of the period is important. Where the work is unsatisfactory due to design not carried out by the Contractor, the Contractor is not bound to do more by way of maintenance than to put the Works back to their original standard. In *Blome & Sinek v City of Regia*,[23] it was held that although granitoid pavements were not suitable for the climate, the Contractor's only duty in a maintenance period, where granitoid pavements had failed, was to do whatever was necessary to put them into first class condition.

18.2 Cost of remedying defects

The Contractor must bear the cost of remedying Defects because these have been caused by its breach of contract. However, it should not be liable for the cost of rectifying other defects which were the responsibility of others. Some contracts, for example, FIDIC require the Employer to notify the Contractor if it is not liable for the cost of rectifying defects, in which case the Variation procedure provided for in the Contract should be followed. Even if the Contractor considers that a defect is not a Defect for which it is liable, it is nevertheless usually required to carry out the necessary rectification work. In these circumstances it should make a claim for additional payment in accordance with the requirements of the Contract.

22 *Phillips Petroleum Co UK ltd v Snamprogetti Ltd* (2001) 79 Con LR 80 (CA).
23 (1919) 50 DLR 93 Can.

18.3 Extension of defects liability period

Extensions to the defects liability period when Defects appear or damage occurs must be provided for in the Contract.

The defects liability period for replacements and renewals carried out, and the extension of the defects liability period for the Works in the case of their being out of use when affected by a Defect or damage, should be set out in the Contract. When, in making good a Defect or damage the Contractor carries out a replacement or renewal, the replaced or renewed part should normally have its own defects liability period which runs from the time the repair or replacement is completed, subject perhaps to a maximum limit of time.[24]

It is also good practice to include in the Contract a requirement that the Contractor provide deeds of subcontractor warranties. The primary purpose of this is to provide the Employer with the benefit of enforceable contracts in which it can deal directly with the subcontractors to require them to undertake rectification, reinstatement, and replacement of any defective work under their subcontracts. However, a deed of subcontractor warranty can also provide the Employer with the benefit of an extended warranty period beyond the expiration of the defects liability period, during which the subcontractor would be required to rectify Defects in its work.

Defects or damage may result in the Works being unusable during the period of rectification. In practice there may be times when the whole of the Works will be out of commission during actual replacement or repair to only a part of the Works. The Contract should require that, under these circumstances, the defects liability period is extended accordingly.

18.4 Failure to remedy defects

The Contractor's failure to remedy a Defect or Defects notified may give the Employer a choice between three options. To be free to exercise such a choice, however, the Employer should first have fixed a final date for remedying the Defect(s) or damage by the Contractor. This should be done by written notice to the Contractor. The final time limit should give the Contractor a realistic opportunity to fulfill its obligations, due regard being given to the time already spent and the interests of the Employer.[25]

Before the Employer removes the obligation (and right) of the Contractor to undertake the rectification of Defects, the Employer must have regard to the general principle that, in the absence of a specific contractual provision to the contrary, the Contractor, 'as successful tenderer, should have the opportunity of performing the whole of the contract works.'[26] This is particularly so in the case of lump sum contracts which define the extent of the work in the specifications and drawings. The following cases illustrate this important principle, which applies as much to the Contractor's Defect rectification work during the defects liability period as to its work before Completion.[27]

24 See for example, 2017 FIDIC Red Book sub-clause 11.3.

25 Note the doctrine of prevention.

26 *BHP Petroleum Ltd v British Steel plc* (2001) 74 Con LR 63, 78–79 [70], per May LJ; *Nouvelle Homes Pty Ltd v G&M Smarglassi* [2007] WASC 50, [16], per Blaxwell J; *Pamax Ltd v Cross Max Interiors Ltd* [2008] HKCFI 266, [129], per DHCJ Gill; *Mul v Hutton Construction Ltd* [2014] EWHC 1797 (TCC), [25], per Akenhead J; *Owners – Strataplan 89041 v Gaylan Pty Ltd* [2019] NSWSC 619, [21] per Stevenson J.

27 *Trustees of the Stratfield Saye Estate v AHL Construction Ltd* [2004] EWHC 3286 (TCC), [35]-[36] per Jackson J; *Ipson Renovation Ltd v Inc Owners of Connie Towers* [2016] HKCFI 2117, [37], per Mimmie Chan J; *P&M Kaye Ltd v Hosier and Dickinson Ltd* [1972] 1 WLR, 166, per Lord Diplock.

Case studies: Contractor's right to carry out the Works

In *Commissioner for Main Roads v Reed & Stuart Pty Ltd*[28] an Employer's power to engage a third party to undertake contract work was discussed by the High Court of Australia. The lump sum contract in this instance included a term that 'if sufficient topsoil to meet the requirements of the works cannot be obtained within the right-of-way, the engineer may direct the contractor in writing to obtain topsoil from other locations.' The Engineer chose not to issue that direction and instead, engaged a third party at a cheaper rate. The High Court held that the Commissioner had breached the contract by engaging the third party.

In *Bethlehem Singapore Private Ltd v Barrier Reef Holdings Ltd*[29] it was held that:

> [S]eparating the act of deleting the works from the act of giving them to another will not avoid the application of the general principle [that] [t]he contract work cannot be taken away from the contractor to be given to someone else, and the same exercise cannot be performed by two stages making use of what is apparently authorised by a variations clause for the purpose. . . . The heart of the idea is that the contractor is entitled to do the work, the whole work including each small part of it, and it is just as much an infraction of the contractor's rights to be varied out of the performance of small but, it may be, profitable parts of the contract work as it would be to be varied out of the performance of large and fundamentally significant parts of the contract work.

It is also worth noting that in circumstances where the Employer engages a third party to undertake works during the currency of the Contract, this may offend contractual principles governing a party's obligation to mitigate its losses. This is particularly the case when the Contractor represents a cheaper option in undertaking the Works.[30] In *Pearce & High v Baxter*[31] the English Court of Appeal considered whether an Employer had a right to recover from the Contractor the money paid to a third party to rectify Defects, when the Employer failed to give the Contractor notice of such Defects. Although the English Court of Appeal awarded in the Employer's favour on the basis that only an explicit clause could override the Employer's entitlement to damages, the Employer was not permitted to recover more than the amount which it would have cost the Contractor itself to remedy the Defects. The Court's assessment 'is achieved as a matter of legal analysis by permitting the contractor to set off against the owner's damages the amount by which he, the contractor, has been disadvantaged by not being able or permitted to carry out the repairs himself, or more simply, by reference to the owner's duty to mitigate his loss.'[32]

If the Contractor fails to remedy the Defects after being given the opportunity, the first option available to the Employer is to carry out the work itself, or using others, at the Contractor's risk and cost. In *Turner Corporation Ltd (Receiver and Manager Appointed) v*

28 (1974) 131 CLR 378, 382.

29 (Unreported, NSW Supreme Court, Bryson J, 15 October 1987) 10.

30 See *Wenham v Ella* (1972) 127 CLR 454, 460–61, applied in *National Australia Bank v Nemur Varity Pty Ltd* (2002) 4 VR 252 and *Australian Capital Territory Gaming & Liquor Authority v Andonaros* (1991) 103 FLR 450.

31 (1999) BLR 101.

32 Ibid, 104.

Austotel Pty Ltd[33] it was held that for an Employer to have an entitlement to rectify defects it would need to be stated in the Contract. In *Turner*, the standard form contract JCC-A 1985 required a second notice to be issued to the Contractor to rectify before the Employer could undertake rectification works. This was not complied with. Cole J stated that 'the contract does provide a code which establishes the rights, obligations and liabilities of the parties, and the mechanisms by which completion of the Works is to be achieved. . . . The Proprietor has no general right to bring others onto the site to perform or complete portions of the Works.'[34]

The Employer should act in a reasonable manner and should not incur unnecessary or unreasonable costs. The costs properly incurred by the Employer in carrying out the rectification of Defects should be deducted from the contract price. The Contractor must therefore pay for the work, but it does not assume any responsibility for it. The Owner is able to recover the reasonable and necessary costs of rectification as set out *Bellgrove v Eldridge*[35] (discussed further in ¶18.11).

The second option is that the Employer may require a reasonable reduction in the contract price. Such reduction in the contract price must reflect the reduction of value of the Works for the Employer because of the defect or damage. The Contractor and the Engineer should normally try to agree on a reasonable reduction. If such agreement cannot be reached, the reduction will need to be fixed through the dispute resolution mechanisms provided for in the Contract.

The third option available to the Employer is termination of the Contract in respect of such parts of the Works as cannot be put to their intended use. The Employer can terminate the Contract for the whole of the Works when the Defect is such as will affect the use of the whole of the Works. This option is however limited when only specific parts of the Works are affected in this way. Clearly, this is a drastic option and cannot be exercised by reason of any defect or damage. The defect or damage must be such that the Employer has been deprived of substantially the whole of the benefit of the Works or a section thereof.

If it terminates the Contract, the Employer is entitled to recover all sums paid in respect of the Works or the affected section. It is also entitled to recover the cost of dismantling the Works or section and clearing the Site, and it is entitled to recover the cost of returning the plant to the Contractor or otherwise disposing of it in accordance with the Contractor's instructions. The Employer should therefore ask the Contractor for instructions relating to the disposal of the plant. If no instructions are forthcoming within a reasonable time, the Employer would be entitled to return the plant to the Contractor and recover its cost of doing so.

18.5 Removal of defective work

Replacing a defective part means removing it and installing another. If repairs and/or replacement of a defective part cannot be expeditiously carried out on the Site – that is, not without being clearly more cumbersome and time-consuming than repairs carried out elsewhere – the Contractor should be allowed to remove any such damaged or defective part from the Site. As the Employer has possession of the Site, any such removal requires the

33 (1994) 13 BCL 378.
34 Ibid, 394.
35 (1954) 90 CLR 613.

Employer's consent. It may be reasonable, as a condition of that consent, for the Contractor to provide additional security for the full replacement cost of the item removed from Site.

18.6 Further tests

Defects may have the effect of preventing the Works from achieving their specified performance. After rectification of such defects, it may be appropriate to repeat tests prescribed in the Contract and previously carried out. The cost of such tests would be borne by the Contractor if the defect was caused by its breach of contract, otherwise by the Employer.

18.7 Right of access

As the Contractor has an obligation to rectify Defects during the defects liability period when it is no longer in possession of the Site, it must be given reasonable access to the Works as necessary to carry out the required remediation, repairs, or maintenance. Reasonable access will take due account of the Employer's use of its facilities, security arrangements, and so on.

The Contractor impliedly must carry out the work without unduly interfering with the Employer's occupation of the Works. It is also implied that particular items must be done within a reasonable time from the Engineer's instructions.

The right of the Employer to require the Contractor to return to the Site and repair Defects will usually expire at the end of the defects liability period, even if there are existing Defects in the Works that were not apparent before or upon the expiry of that period.

18.7.1 Contractor to search

The Contract may explicitly give the Engineer the power to order the Contractor to search for the cause of a defect. Such a power appears to apply only in cases where a defect, imperfection, or fault is visible, but the precise cause is not known, and only when the cause has been ascertained will it be possible to decide whether the defect is one for which the Contractor is liable. This obligation can be extremely difficult, time-consuming, and costly.[36] The wider power to open up work during construction gives the Engineer power to order a search where no defect is visible; however, this would generally not apply during the defects liability period. After Completion the Contractor would be liable for the costs of searching only if materials or workmanship were not in accordance with the Contract or because of some other breach of contract.

Where the Contractor fails to identify the precise cause within a reasonable time, the Employer may be entitled to recover the reasonable costs of engaging a third party to investigate and report on the extent of defects for which the Contractor is responsible, including the cost of devising a remedial scheme.[37]

36 For example, in water-retaining structures.

37 *Peak Construction (Liverpool) Ltd v McKinney Foundations Ltd* (1970) 1 BLR 111, 121 per Salmon LJ (CA); *OBS (Nominees 1) v Lend Lease Construction (Europe) Limited* [2017] EWHC 25 (TCC), [174]-[175] per Stuart-Smith J.

18.8 Final payment certificate

The **final payment certificate** is a written confirmation to the Employer and the Contractor that the Engineer is satisfied that:

(a) The defects liability period for the Works (or the relevant part of it) has expired and
(b) The Contractor has fulfilled all its obligations under the Contract, including in respect of rectification of all known Defects in the Works (or the relevant part).

Issue of the final payment certificate usually triggers return of all retention monies and undertakings held as security for performance.

Contracts often have a defects rectification clause to the effect that the Contractor will be responsible for Defects appearing within a certain limited time after the Engineer issues the final payment certificate. The Contractor will then be bound to remedy Defects appearing within such time. The issue of a final certificate often extinguishes any future liability that a Contractor would otherwise have for defective design or workmanship.[38] A final payment certificate may actually be 'final' in the sense that the Contractor has no ongoing contractual liability in respect of latent defects subsequently coming to light. For example, in a contract in which Defects were discovered after the specified four years from the end of the defects liability period, the Contractor was not liable because the certificate for the final balance due was 'conclusive evidence of the works being duly completed.'[39] More commonly, a final payment certificate preserves the Employer's common-law rights in respect of damages for breach of contract for latent defects. In *National Coal Board v William Neill Ltd*,[40] the court found that the final certificate was conclusive that the Engineer himself was satisfied. However, in the absence of wording that the final certificate was conclusive, the Contractor was liable in respect of defects which became apparent only after the defects liability period had expired.

Where it is provided that a final payment certificate, save as regards all defects and insufficiencies in the Works or materials which a reasonable examination would not have disclosed, shall be conclusive evidence as to the sufficiency of the said Works and materials, and of their value, such a provision has been held to override a provision in an arbitration clause allowing an Arbitrator to review a certificate.[41] The phrase 'reasonable examination' in such a clause means 'reasonable examination from time to time during the progress of the work.'[42]

Where an Engineer has authority to approve work and it issues a certificate authorising final payment, such certificate is generally interpreted as a certificate of approval, even in the absence of a final payment certificate. This will not be the case, however, where approval is not a condition precedent to payment, and payment has been made with knowledge of

38 *Tarmac Construction Ltd v Esso Petroleum Co Ltd* (1996) 83 BLR 65, 106, per Judge Lloyd QC; *Haswell v Silent Vector Pty Ltd* [2002] WASC 250, [19]-[21], per Barker J.

39 *London School Board v Johnson* (1891) Alfred A Hudson, *Hudson's Fourth Edition Table of Cases* (Sweet & Maxwell, 4th edn 1914) 176.

40 [1985] 1 Q.B. 300.

41 *East Ham Borough Council v Bernard Sunley & Sons Ltd* [1965] 3 All ER 619 (HL).

42 Ibid.

Defects and bad workmanship. In such a case, the fact that the Employer has paid the Contractor would not debar the Employer from claiming in respect of defective work.

18.9 Unfulfilled obligations

The Contract may have a provision relating to the fulfilment of any unfulfilled obligations extant at the time of issue of the final payment certificate. Such a clause is desirable to confirm that, notwithstanding the formal certification that the Contractor has complied with its contractual obligations, the Contract continues on foot until all outstanding obligations have been complied with. In particular, the Employer may have outstanding obligations in respect of payment and return of securities, and the Contractor may have obligations in respect to removing equipment, surplus material, rubbish, and so on.

18.10 Clearance of Site

The Contractor may be given a limited period of time after issue of the final payment certificate to remove all its equipment, material, wreckage, rubbish, and temporary works from the Site. If it fails to do so within the specified time, the Employer should be empowered to take appropriate action at the cost of the Contractor.

18.11 Latent defects

A Defect which is a shortcoming, in the sense of a nonconformance with a contractual requirement, in design, work, or materials, which is unknown and imperceptible upon reasonable examination is referred to as a **latent defect**.[43] A latent defect has also been described as a defect which is not patent. Whether a defect is patent or latent is a factual matter. This may be significant for the purpose of determining when time starts to run under an applicable limitation statute. The fact that the defect was not detected at the time of handover or that the Work was approved by the Employer or its agent prior to or at the point of taking-over does not usually absolve the Contractor for its breach of obligation.[44] Unless the Contract provides to the contrary, there is generally no contractual requirement for the Contractor to rectify such a defect after the final certificate has been issued, as the Contract is at an end. Since latent defects constitute a breach of contract, the Contractor will, however, generally be liable for damages arising from such defects within the relevant limitation period for commencement of legal actions.[45] However, where the Engineer issues a final certificate that confirms the adequacy of the work performed by the Contractor on a final and conclusive basis, a right to bring an action may be excluded.[46]

43 *Sanfield Building Contractors Ltd v Kai Cheong* [2003] HKCFA 46, [26] per Bokhary PJ; *Pearson Education Ltd v The Charter Partnership* [2005] EWHC 2021 (TCC), [125] per HHJ Thornton QC (affirmed [2007] BLR 324).

44 *Saga Cruises BDF Ltd v Fincantieri SpA* [2016] EWHC 1875 (Comm), [163]-[172] per DHCJ Sara Cockerill QC.

45 *London Borough of Harrow v Engie Regeneration (Apollo) Ltd* [2018] EWHC 2575 (TCC).

46 *James Png Construction Pte Ltd v Tu Chin Kwan Peter* [1991] 1 MLJ 499 (noted by Powell-Smith, [1992] *International Construction Law Review* 101; *Tarmac Construction Ltd v Esso Petroleum Co Ltd* (1996) 83 BLR 65, 106 per Judge Lloyd QC; *Hassell v Silent Vector Pty Ltd* [2002] WASC 250, [19]-[21] per Barker J.

Although the limitation regimes applying in England, Hong Kong, Singapore, and Australia are similar, there are also significant differences between them which require careful attention. Time will start running for the purposes of an action in contract from the time that the breach of contract occurred, being the time the cause of action in contract accrued.[47] Limitation periods for commencement of actions in respect of breach of contract in Australia are generally six years from the date of the breach in respect of simple contracts[48] (three years in the Northern Territory[49]), and between 12 and 20 years for breach of contracts that have been executed as a deed.[50] The limitation period for actions based on misleading or deceptive conduct in breach of the *Australian Consumer Law* (being Schedule 2 of the *Competition and Consumer Act 2010* (Cth) is six years.[51] For the narrower class of 'building actions' (as defined in the relevant legislation), all Australian States and Territories except Queensland and Western Australia have a limitation period of ten years.[52]

Insofar as limitation periods for actions in contract, Australian law follows English law in that actions in contract commence running from the date of the relevant breach of contract, regardless of whether the claimant knew of the breach at the time it occurred, and regardless of whether any damage occurred at that time because of the breach.[53] English law differs from Australian law as to when a cause of action arises in negligence: under Australian law an action arises at the time when the defect first becomes known or manifest, which is not necessarily the time at which the damage first occurred.[54]

In Singapore, in contract, time starts running from the date of the breach of contract, and in negligence, time starts running from when damage first occurred, regardless of whether or not that damage was reasonably perceptible, meaning that the position in Singapore is essentially the same as that in England.[55]

In Hong Kong there is a six-year limitation period for the bringing of any action founded on breach of contract or in tort, including negligence.[56] The common law of Hong Kong

47 *Mostcash plc v Fluor Ltd* [2002] BLR 411, 428 [56] per Chadwick LJ.

48 *Limitation of Actions Act 1958* (Vic) s5(1)(a); *Limitation Act 1969* (NSW) s14(1)(a); *Limitation of Actions Act 1974* (Qld) s10(1)(a); *Limitation Act 1935* (WA) s38(1)(c); *Limitation Act 1985* (ACT) s11(1); *Limitation of Actions Act 1936* (SA) s35(a); *Limitation Act 1974* (Tas) s4(1)(a).

49 *Limitation Act* (NT) s12(1)(b).

50 12 years: *Limitation Act 1969* (NSW) s16; *Limitation of Actions Act 1974* (Qld) s10(3); *Limitation Act 1985* (ACT) s13; *Limitation Act* (NT) s14(1); *Limitation Act 1974* (Tas) s4(3); 15 years: *Limitation of Actions Act 1958* (Vic) s5(3); *Limitation of Actions Act 1936*(SA) s34; 20 years: *Limitation Act 1935* (WA) s38(1)(e).

51 *Australian Consumer Law* (Cth) s236(2).

52 *Building Act 1993* (Vic) s134; *Environment Planning and Assessment Act 1979* (NSW) s109 ZK; *Building Act 2004* (ACT) s142; *Development Act 1993* (SA) s73; *Building Act 1996* (NT) s160; *Building Act 2000* (Tas) s255.

53 *Building Insurers Guarantee Corporation v The Owners Strata Plan No. 57504* [2010] NSWCA 23, [46] per Handley AJA.

54 *Owners Corporation Strata Plan 61288 v Brookfield Multiplex Ltd* [2013] NSWCA 317, [17] per Basten JA (appeal allowed, on other grounds, [2014] HCA 36); *Melisavon Pty Ltd v Springfield Land Development Corp Pty Ltd* [2014] QCA 23, 38 per Margaret McMurdo P, [57]-[65] per Holmes JA; C J Rossiter & M Stone, 'Latent Defects in Buildings: When Does the Cause of Action Arise?' (1985) *Australian Law Journal* 606; Nicholas J Mullany, '"Concrete Cancer"- It's Limitation Implications' (1989) 5 *Building and Construction Law* 197; Nicholas J Mullany, 'Liability in Tort for "Concrete Cancer"' (1989) 5 *Building and Construction Law* 270; *Winnote Pty Ltd v Page* [2006] NSWCA 287, [40] per Mason P.

55 *Millennia Pte Ltd v Dragages Singapore Pte Ltd* [2018] SGHC 193, [479]-[480] per Quentin Loh J; see A Lavers, 'Defects in Construction: Recent Developments in the Law Relating to Limitation of Actions' (1987) 29 *Malay Law Review* 18.

56 *Limitation Ordinance Cap 347* (HK) section 4(1).

follows the English common law by holding that the cause of action in negligence accrues upon the occurrence of physical damage in a real and substantial sense, regardless of whether that damage is manifest.[57]

To the extent that the Contractor's liability for latent defects continues after the issue of the certificate, the Employer's common-law remedy will be ineffective after release of the securities if the Contractor is insolvent.

The normal situation is that damages for defective work are calculated on the cost of the necessary and reasonable work required to reinstate the facility to the condition it would have been in if the Contract had not been breached.[58] Only if it is not reasonable to carry out rectification work are damages based on the diminution of value.[59] In *Chocolate Factory Apartments v Westpoint Finance*, McDougall J stated that the *Bellgrove* High Court Case establishes four things:

(1) Damages for breach of the obligation to construct in accordance with the Contract and plans and specifications are measured by the cost of rectification, where it is necessary to undertake that rectification to produce conformity and where it is reasonable to adopt that course.
(2) In those circumstances, damages are not measured by comparing the value of the building which has been erected with the value it would have been if erected in accordance with the Contract.
(3) However, where rectification may be necessary to produce conformity, but it is not reasonable to do so, the true measure of loss is any diminution in value produced by the non-conformity with the Contract, plans, and specifications.
(4) It is a question of fact as to whether, in any particular case, rectification is both necessary (in the sense explained) and reasonable.[60]

One important consequence of the express obligation to rectify Defects is that time may begin to run against the Employer in respect of latent defects, for the purpose of limitation of actions laws, from the date of the completion of maintenance and not at some earlier stage when the defective work was carried out.[61]

57 *Bank of East Asia Ltd v Tsien Wui Marble Factory Ltd* (1999) 2 HKCFAR 349 (noted by R Glofcheski, 'The Law of Limitations as applied to Latent Building Defects' (2000) 16 *Construction Law Journal* 379; D Bateson & O Mak, 'Has the Dust Finally Settled on Latent Damage?' (2000) *International Construction Law Review* 675).

58 *Bellgrove v Eldridge* (1954) 90 CLR 613.

59 *Chocolate Factory Apartments v Westpoint Finance* [2005] NSWSC 784 per McDougall J.

60 Ibid.

61 See *Eskom v Stewarts & Lloyds of SA (Pty) Ltd* 1981 (3) SA 340 (A).

CHAPTER 19

Measurement and valuation

CONTENTS

19.1 Measurement

Issues relating to the contract price are discussed in detail in Chapter 21 for different types of contracts, categorised by reference to the different manner in which the contract price is calculated. Contract clauses on measurement and evaluation are required to evaluate the Contract price in any **measurement contract**,[1] that is, a contract in which payment to the Contractor for the Works is based on measurement of the actual amount of work done, for example, volume of excavation, tonnes of steel work erected, and so on, paid for at pre-agreed rates for the work.[2] Measurement contracts include bill of quantities contracts and schedule of rates contracts.

A **bill of quantities contract** incorporates a bill of quantities in the Contract. A **bill of quantities (BoQ)** is a schedule briefly describing each different type of constructional element and listing the quantity of each required for a complete construction project. A bill of quantities is prepared by a quantity surveyor, usually engaged by the Employer. A tenderer can prepare a tender from a BoQ by multiplying the unit rate for each different type of constructional element by its quantity and summing all the items. The bill of quantities is used to evaluate changes in the Works during the course of the Contract. This type of contract facilitates competitive tendering.

A **schedule of rates contract** incorporates a schedule of rates or schedule of prices in which the Contractor undertakes to do any or all of a number of described construction processes, involving the provision of construction equipment, work, and the supply of materials, at quoted prices per unit rather than being compounded against work items

1 Also known as a 're-measurable,' or 'measure and value' form of contract.

2 *Chan Chi Lam v Lam Woo & Co Ltd* [2017] HKCFI 421, [20]-[28] per Mimmie Chan J.

DOI: 10.4324/9781003206873-19

as in the bills of quantities. Such contracts are typically used where the work is not sufficiently preplanned or capable of estimation at the time of tender.

In a measurement contract it is not necessary for the Engineer or Employer to issue a Variation instruction in respect of the difference in quantities between the actual quantity of work performed and the estimate of quantities indicated in the bill of quantities or schedule of rates, save in respect of Work that is different from that in the Contractor's original scope of work.[3] In some places, calculation of the contract price based on measurement is considered to be a significantly more rational basis of determining the contract price from the Employer's point of view.[4] However, even in fixed lump sum contracts, the measurement and evaluation clauses may be important in valuing Variations using a schedule of rates or dayworks schedules.

19.2 Works to be measured

In measurement contracts, the ultimate quantities for which the Contractor will be paid are not those shown in the bill of quantities or schedule of rates but are the measured quantities of work actually carried out on the Completion of the Works.

It is of fundamental importance to appreciate that the sum named in the tender for a bill of quantities contract is not the ultimate contract price, as the tender sum is based upon the Works as quantified in the bill of (provisional) quantities provided in the tender documents. Errors due to mistakes in grossing-up the quantities at the rates in the bills in the tender sum will be rectified in calculating the final amount due to the Contractor, since the word 'measurement' in this context embraces recalculation. The description of an item in a bill of quantities defines the scope of work for which the scheduled rate applies. If there is no item describing the work required, a new rate may be appropriate. The same may apply in a schedule of rates contract.

The differences between quantities in bills of quantities and actuality are likely to be at their greatest in the valuation provisions applying to provisional quantity items. **Provisional quantity** items are employed in bills of quantities for work which is not reasonably predictable in quantity. For example, whereas the amount of excavation to accommodate an underground structure is predictable from the drawings, the excavation to reach firm ground that is adequate for supporting foundations or to remove pockets of unsuitable material is not, and these latter are often billed as provisional quantity items. Excavation may either be billed 'excavate in any material including rock' with the estimated overall quantities, or the general excavation item will be worded so as to exclude rock and a small provisional quantity extra-over will be inserted for that purpose. The use of the provisional quantity items merely emphasizes even more strongly, in the case of those items, that the billed quantities are not the actual and correct quantities of work to be carried out by the Contractor, and that possibly substantial differences between the billed and actual quantities are expected. Such substantial differences will, by themselves, usually be a Variation.

Provisional sums are amounts identified as such in the Contract against particular items of work, where the performance of the work is in the nature of a contingency,[5] and will only

3 *Chak Chiu Hung v Shiu Lock Hing* [1910] HKLR 242, 246 per Piggott CJ.

4 In Romania it is not permitted for public works contracts to be entered into on a lump sum basis: L Klee & C A Teodorescu, 'Romanian Experience with FIDIC Forms in Road and Bridge Construction' (2013) *International Construction Law Review* 432, 435–436.

5 *Multiplex Constructions (UK) Limited v Cleveland Bridge UK Ltd (No 6)* [2008] EWHC 2220 (TCC), [1017] per Jackson J (appeal allowed, on other grounds: [2010] EWCA Civ 139).

be performed should the Engineer instruct the Contractor to perform them. Only in that circumstance will the Contractor become entitled to payment for the work.[6] A provisional sum will usually be adjusted to reflect the cost or value of the actual work performed,[7] and this is usually done by way of measurement.

19.3 Method of measurement in a bill of quantities contract

In applying the bills of quantities to the Works it is necessary to take cognizance of the manner in which this can be done. It is obvious that detailed documents which are initially designed to describe the nature and extent of the work to be done and to affect an ultimate remeasurement of the whole Works will fail in their intention unless there is an agreement as to the exact technical manner of measuring the quantities of work. Thus, measurement of the cubic content of excavations could theoretically be based on:

- (i) Physical measurement of the excavated material, with or without an allowance for 'bulking', or
- (ii) Physical measurement of the void left by the excavation, or
- (iii) A theoretical calculation of the volume shown on the drawings of the structure to be accommodated by the excavation without any allowance for any necessary excavation for working space outside its area and depth, or
- (iv) A calculation as in (iii), but with physical measurement of, or an arbitrary price or allowance for, 'overbreak' outside the net volume of the structure.

A **standard method of measurement** is a standardised and defined procedure for preparing bills of quantities. If the Contract does not identify the method of measurement to be applied, difficulties may arise[8] and matters of custom and practice may be relevant to that determination. Standard methods of measurement are designed partly to achieve uniformity in the ways in which engineering or building work is to be subdivided into its component parts or items for the purposes of pricing in bills of quantities, and partly to indicate the principles or formulae to be applied when actually measuring or calculating the quantities of work done. By reason of the methods used in the various standard methods of measurement, the need for actual physical measurement of work is kept to a minimum, and, in the great majority of work, the quantities are arrived at by calculation from the Contract or later working drawings.

Undoubtedly the real purpose of such provisions in construction contracts is to incorporate by reference the various technical rules of measurement so that bills can be kept as short as possible, and so that there is no doubt as to what, for example, a cubic metre of ordinary excavation for a structure means[9] and how it is to be measured.

The Contractor may claim additional payment on the ground that there has been an 'omission of an item' from the bills where it can be shown that the provisions of the standard method have (often quite obviously) not been complied with in the bills. It may

6 *Amec Building Ltd v Cadmus Investments Co Ltd* (1996) 51 Con LR 105, 125–126 per Mr Recorder Kallipetis QC.

7 See JCT Standard Building Contract (2016 edn) clause 5.2.1; AS 4000–1997 clause 3; 2017 FIDIC Red Book sub-clause 13.4; JCWC Standard Form of Building Contract (2006 edn) clause 13.4; SIA Building (1st edn 2016) clause 28(5); *Midland Expressway Ltd v Carillion Construction Ltd* [2006] EWCA Civ 936, [31] Per May LJ.

8 *Lo Kwok Hung v Lee Shu Sum* [1986] HKCFI 303.

9 For example, to be measured 'net in situ,' by measurement in a 'banked stockpile,' or 'placed and compacted.'

be that such work is indispensably necessary to complete the described work; contingently necessary work may also not be mentioned in the bills. The ordinary rules of construction of the contract documents as a whole may indicate that the Contractor's price was inclusive of the allegedly extra work. Claims are advanced in other cases, based (when appropriate), on the allegation that the Contractor's price was for the cheaper of two alternatives, though there may be no overt indication of this in the bills' description of the item in question. Accordingly, it is essential that the items are described and divided on an agreed system so that the Contractor knows what it is pricing in each rate and price. The Engineer should therefore follow a standard method of measurement wherever possible.

In *Bryant and Sons Ltd v Birmingham Hospital Saturday Fund*,[10] the Contract was a measurement or quantities contract, with a clause incorporating a method of measurement which provided for separate items for excavating in soft material and in rock. The Architect knew that there was some rock on the Site but did not mention it in the plans or quantities. The court held that, for work in rock, the Contractor was entitled to reasonable extra payment above the general rate of excavating. In another case there was a clause in the Contract providing for the rectification of errors in description in the bill and an entitlement to extra payment, but the principle would appear to apply even without such a clause.[11]

Where the Contract requires that the bill shall be measured according to a standard method of measurement which provides for separate items to measure excavation in soft material and excavation in rock, even if the Engineer or Employer did not know, for instance, of the existence of rock, work in rock in a bill of quantities contract, or in Variations, cannot be priced under a rate for excavating in soft material. Such work must be priced as a Variation or, if excavation of the particular area was included in the original Contract, as an item included in the original Works, but to which no rate in the bill applies. In either case the Employer must pay a reasonable rate for the excavation in rock.

Where an item which is obviously necessary to complete the Works is omitted from the bill in error, it may be argued that the Contractor must supply the item without extra payment; in practice, extra payment is very often claimed and allowed.[12] If the item omitted is an item for which the standard method of measurement specifically requires a separate rate, then the standard method clause will prevail and the Contractor will be entitled to additional payment on measurement of the Works.

In a case where the bills stated that 'any additional excavation which may be required for working space, etc, will be paid for under separate items,' the only specific items for working space were in the portion of the bills relating to subsidiary parts of the Works. It was held by a majority of the House of Lords that the quoted words amounted to a promise to pay the Contractor extra for all working space required, whether or not described in a special item in the bills. In this decision Lord Pearson said:

> I think it is strictly correct to say that clause 57 does not impose on the building owner an obligation to draft his Bill of Quantities in conformity with the Standard Method of Measurement,

10 [1938] 1 All E.R. 503.

11 See *A E Farr v The Admiralty* [1953] 2 All ER 512 (QB); *Kelly and Hingle's Trustees v Union Government (Minister of Public Works)* (1928) TPD 272, 294 and 304.

12 *Patman and Fotheringham Ltd v Pilditch* (1904) Alfred A Hudson, *Hudson's Fourth Edition Table of Cases* (Sweet & Maxwell, 4th edn 1914) 368.

> but it would be natural and advisable for him to do so, as otherwise problems would arise in respect of the construction of the Bill of Quantities, and in respect of the application of the rates contained therein to the measurements taken in accordance with the procedure set forth in the Standard Method of Measurement.[13]

Where the method of measurement is not covered by the specification, or in the detailed description of an item of work in the bill of quantities, the above would not apply. The interpretation of general descriptions as to the extent to which they exclude the method is obviously capable of causing a great deal of difficulty. Where the amount of rock is known for example, it is bad practice to exclude the method by a general description and not to give separate items.

In a pure lump sum contract, the Contractor has no remedy in relation to the original contract work on the grounds that the bill was prepared wrongly, since the bill is part of the Contract only for pricing Variations.[14]

19.4 Valuation

A certificate of measurement need not usually be in any prescribed form and in each case, it is necessary to consider what kind of certificate is required by the Contract and whether terms of the statement or acts relied upon can constitute such a certificate. Unless so required by the Contract, the certificate need not be in writing. In *Elmes v Burgh Market Co* (1891),[15] a contract provided for payment 'on the surveyor certifying that the whole of the works are in a complete and satisfactory state.' The court held that an oral certificate was sufficient.

19.5 Errors in the preparation of bills of quantities

Care must be taken in preparing bills of quantities even if such bills are only provisional. The provisional quantities should not be so out of keeping that when the work comes to be performed, such quantities are grossly exceeded, leading to extensive claims by Contractors.

It is normally the function of a quantity surveyor engaged by the Employer to prepare bills of quantities, but architects and engineers often assume the responsibility. Under those circumstances, the same standards will apply to the architect and the engineer as to a quantity surveyor. Standard methods of measurement are in common use and any professional who prepares a bill of quantities is expected to be familiar with them.

Minor errors are likely to be insufficient to establish negligence, as was found in *London School Board v Northcroft*.[16] Conversely, the greater the errors, whether in number or consequence, the more difficult it will be to resist a finding of negligence.

---

13 *A E Farr v The Ministry of Transport* (1965) 5 BLR 97.

14 *Sharpe v San Paulo Co* (1873) LR 8 Ch App 597, 607 per James LJ (CA); *Soon Li Heng Civil Engineering Pte Ltd v Woon Contractors Pte Ltd* [2005] SGHC 34, [83]-[84] per Lai Siu Chiu J; *Danidale Pty Ltd v Abigroup Contractors Pty Ltd* [2007] VSC 391, [114]-[122] per Habersberger J; *FDC Constructions & Fitout Pty Ltd v Condensing Vaporisers Aust Pty Ltd* [2013] NSWSC 1073; *West Reg. Street (Property) Ltd v Central Demolition Ltd* [2018] CSOH 98.

15 Alfred A Hudson, *Hudson's Fourth Edition Table of Cases* (Sweet & Maxwell, 4th edn 1914) 170.

16 See Alfred A Hudson, *Hudson's Fourth Edition Table of Cases* (Sweet & Maxwell, 4th edn 1914) 147. See also *Tyrer v District Auditor of Monmouthshire* [1973] 230 EG 973.

19.6 Authority of Engineer to vary or fix rates

Although the quantities set out in the bill of quantities are usually stated to be estimated, the Engineer is often given the power in the Contract to vary a rate because more or less units of work or materials than shown in the bill are necessary to complete the work as originally described and the effect of the difference in quantity upon costs justifies such action. The Contract normally provides rights for review of rates and extension of time where this is justified. For example, the 2017 FIDIC Red Book provides that the Engineer can determine a new rate for an item of work if no specified rate or price is appropriate because the item of work is not of similar character, or the measured quantity is changed by more than 10% (subject to minimum percentage impacts on the Accepted Contract Amount and the Cost per unit quantity of the item).[17] In *J Crosby & Sons Ltd v Portland Urban District Council*,[18] Donaldson J held that the Engineer had the power to vary a rate where the bill rate referred to laying and so on of pipes in excavation to 5 ft only, but the Contractor laid the pipes at greater depths in order to comply with the original drawings.

Case study: New rates where actual quantities were substantially different from the quantities in the BoQ

The right of the Contractor to require, and the power of the Engineer to agree or fix, any adjusted rates as a result of differences in quantities on remeasurement was considered in the case of *Mitsui Construction Co Ltd v The Attorney General of Hong Kong.*[19] The Contractor, Mitsui, contracted to construct a tunnel 3,227 m in length. As the nature of the ground through which the tunnel was to pass could not be predicted accurately in advance, the Contract specified five different types of lining suitable for different ground conditions but did not specify where lining was to be required, or what type should be used. The Contract included bills of quantities priced by the Contractor for the estimated lengths of tunnel which were to be left unlined and to be lined with each of the different types of lining. In the event, there were substantial differences between the estimated lengths of each type of support in the bill of quantities and that actually constructed: the estimated length of tunnel to be unlined was 1,342 m, whereas the length left unlined was only 547 m; the estimated length of tunnel to be lined with the heaviest and most expensive type of lining was 275 m, whereas the length so lined was 2,448 m; the billed quantity of steel required for lining support was 40 tonnes, whereas the quantity required and used in the event was 2,943 tonnes. As a result of these differences, the work on the tunnel took much longer than it would have done if the quality and quantity of lining required had corresponded reasonably with the billed quantities. The Engineer exercised his power under the Contract to grant an extension of 784 days to 'compensate for the extra time required to cope with ground conditions executing the tunnel excavation and lining works.' The Contractor was paid for the

17 Sub-clause 12.3.
18 (1967) 5D.C BLR.
19 (1986) 33 BLR 1.

work executed and measured at the rates in the bills of quantities. However, it claimed that, given the events that had occurred, it was entitled to an adjustment of rates to be agreed with, or fixed by the Engineer. In the Privy Council their Lordships held that, on the construction of the Contract and the agreed facts, the differences between the measured quantities and the billed quantities were such as to give jurisdiction to the Engineer, if he was of the opinion that the nature and amount of the differences from the estimated items in the bills of quantities would render the billed rate for any item unreasonable or inapplicable, to agree with the Contractor or in the event of disagreement fix a suitable rate under the Contract.[20]

However, the fact that the quantity of work performed by the Contractor is greater or less than the quantity shown in its bill of quantities does not of itself and without more justify a re-rating.[21] Where the quantities on re-measurement differ radically from those indicated in the bill of quantities, the difference in quantities can be dealt with as a Variation. The make-up of the Contractor's tender may be relevant to any re-rating, and if so, will be admissible for that purpose in any court or arbitral proceedings concerning the issue of re-rating.[22]

If it is necessary for the Engineer to fix rates for a certain type of work because it has not been covered in the bills of quantities, it is necessary to determine whether, amongst other things, the Contractor's overheads are paid under other items in the bills. Where the Contract positively requires the Contractor to price all of its overhead expenditure in the form of a very comprehensive bill item for **Preliminaries**,[23] the Contractor will deviate from such a requirement at its own peril. In this situation, rates fixed by the Engineer will not contain an allowance for overheads, unless it can be shown that the type of work concerned directly increases overheads.

Claims which are based on the nature of an omission or addition, for example, the time when a particular item is ordered, or which affect part of the Site where work is to be carried out, rendering the contract prices unreasonable or inapplicable, merit careful consideration. Claims based upon the effect of differences in quantities may demand a disclosure of the composition of the Contractor's tender. Increases in quantities, for instance, usually do not necessarily justify a reduction in a rate or price and vice versa. Regard may be had to those cost elements the rate of which are fixed, and those that vary according to the volume of work. The Contractors tender make-up may be relevant to any re-rating and if so, it will be admissible for that purpose in any court or arbitral proceedings concerning the issue of re-rating.[24]

20 See Philip Loots, *Construction Law and Related Issues* (Juta & Co, 1995) 94.

21 See ICE Conditions of Contract (7th edn, 1999) clause 56(2); *Secretary for Justice v Sun Foo Kong (Civil) Ltd* [1997] HKCFI 331, [7]-[10] per Finlay J; *Tactful Construction & Engineering Ltd v Univic Engineering Ltd* [2019] HKCFI 1568, [19] per Mimmie Chan J.

22 *Maeda Corporation v HKSAR* [2014] BLR 22, 28 [35] – 29 [41] per Fok J.

23 Preliminaries are generally the first item in a bill of quantities in which the Contractor prices the provision of items applying to commencement of the Works, or the Works as a whole, for example, temporary offices, insurances, temporary lighting, hoardings, fencing, and so on. The item description will define whether it includes all of the Contractor's overheads or not.

24 *Maeda Corporation v HKSAR* [2014] BLR 22.

CHAPTER 20

Variations and adjustments

CONTENTS

20.1 Right to vary

20.1.1 Variations

Construction contracts are unusual amongst commercial contracts in that they generally have explicit provisions which enable the Employer to require the Contractor to carry out additional or different work to that originally required by the Contract, or to omit work from the agreed scope (Variation). Such varied work, (also referred to as an 'extra,' 'alteration,' 'addition,' or 'change'), is an omission, increase, decrease, or change to the originally agreed scope of work, as directed by the Engineer or the Employer.[1] Whether a Contractor has been instructed to perform a Variation depends upon what the Contractor was required to do, and what it is instructed to do. This requires an analysis of the Contractor's original scope of work.[2]

1 *Rotol Projects Pte Ltd v CCM Industrial Pte Ltd* [2014] SGHC 72, [10]-[11] per Quentin Loh J.
2 *Sopov v Kane Constructions Pty Ltd (No.2)* [2009] VSCA 141, [41]-[44] ([2009] BLR 468).

DOI: 10.4324/9781003206873-20

In order for work to qualify as a Variation, it is essential that the Contractor is required to do something different from that which it is otherwise required to do by the Contract.[3] Reasonableness may have a bearing on whether certain work required to be performed as part of the Contractor's original scope of work is a Variation.[4] A suspension, direction to change the method of working, resequencing of the Works, and an instruction to accelerate the Works is usually a Variation and a compensable matter. It is impermissible for the Employer to omit work for the purpose of giving it to another Contractor unless this is expressly permitted by the Contract.[5] Sub-clause 13.1(iv) of the 2017 FIDIC Red Book expressly permits the issuing of a Variation instruction which omits work, except where the work is to be carried out by others.[6] The power to vary may not be used to omit the entirety, or a substantial portion of a Contractor's Works.[7]

In the absence of a specific clause in the Contract giving the Employer or its agent the power to order extra or changed work as a Variation, the Engineer and the Employer have no power to do so, and the Contractor has the contractual right to refuse any request to carry out work which is different from the originally agreed scope of work. Refusal to give a Variation instruction may be regarded as wrongful if the Contractor performs the work in question which turns out to be outside the Contractor's scope of work.[8]

Conversely, if the Contractor alters the Works without contractual authority, the Contractor is not entitled to payment for the altered work. It will also have breached the Contract. Contract work has not been done and it is no defence in law that the Contractor has done equivalent or better work. The Contractor is bound to fulfil its contract and may not exercise its own choice in matters where it considers that it can improve on the plans and specifications. The Contractor will only be entitled to payment for additional work if it can show that the Employer consented to the alterations, and either knew, or should have known, that the alterations would increase the cost of the work.

Because the nature of construction contracts involves a significant risk of unforeseen events and circumstances, virtually all modern construction contracts give the Employer the power to order Variations.[9] Subject to the specific provisions of the Contract, the Contractor cannot refuse to carry out validly ordered Variations. Contracts generally do not contain any specific limitation on the power to order Variations, and often contain a clause that any Variation will not 'vitiate the contract.' However, there must be a limit to the extent of a Variation within the scope of the Contract, and this is discussed further in later sections.

---

3 *Martifer UK Ltd v Lend Lease Construction (EMEA) Ltd* [2016] CSOH 98, [20]-[25] per Lord Tyre; *CMA Assets Pty Ltd v John Holland Pty Ltd [No.6]* [2015] WASC 217, [251] per Allanson J.

4 *Petroleo Brasileiro SA (Petrobras) v Petromec Inc* [2013] EWCA Civ 150, [77]-[78] per Rix J.

5 *Commissioner for Main Roads v Reed & Stuart Pty Ltd* (1974) 131 CLR 378, 382; *Abbey Developments Ltd v PP Brickwork Ltd* [2003] EWHC 1987 (TCC), [45]-[47] per HHJ Lloyd QC.

6 See *Carr v JA Berriman Pty Ltd* (1953) 89 CLR 327, 348, per Fullagar J; *Sacon Constructions Pty Ltd v Kezarne Pty Ltd* [1997] NSWSC 474; *AGC Industries Pty Ltd v Karara Mining Ltd* [2019] WASC 140, [585]-[616], per Allanson J.

7 *Trustees of the Stratfield Saye Estate v AHL Construction Ltd* [2004] EWHC 3286 (TCC), [35]-[36], per Jackson J; *Ipson Renovation Ltd v Incorporated Owners of Connie Towers* [2016] HKCFI 2117, [37], per Mimmie Chan J.

8 *State Railway Authority (NSW) v Baulderstone and Hornibrook Pty Ltd* (1988) 5 BCL 117 [Sup Ct NSW, Cole J]; *Atlantic Civil Pty Ltd v Water Administration Ministerial Corporation* (1992) 39 NSWLR 468, 483–484, per Giles J.

9 Bingham LJ stated that: 'I do not, however, think that there is any class of contract in which the content of… fundamental terms is potentially as fluid as in the familiar forms of building and civil engineering contract. These contain terms which enable the contractor's work to be increased, decreased or varied, perhaps substantially, the period for performance to be extended, again substantially, and the contract price to be recalculated, upwards or downwards, in the light of events during the currency of the contract.': *Asheville Investments Ltd v Elmer Contractors Ltd* [1989] 1 QB 488, 507; See also *VK Holdings (HK) Ltd v Panasonic Eco Solutions (Hong Kong) Co Ltd* [2014] HKCFI 2358, [26], per Mimmie Chan J.

Few features of construction contracts of any kind cause more difficulty than Variations. Variations are blamed for cost overruns, delays, and disputes, although the root of the problem often lies deeper in bad organization and unseemly haste in starting work which has not been adequately scoped, designed, planned, and resourced.

Widespread malpractices in procurement systems and misunderstandings around contract pricing have led to Employers and the financiers being lulled into a false sense of security when entering into construction contracts.[10] As a result, many banks, Contractors, Employers, and engineers have had bad experiences with Variations and seek to protect themselves by appropriate wording of the Variations clause. It is therefore exceedingly difficult to achieve objective and balanced provisions for Variations that will be accepted as such by all concerned.

The need for Variations generally stems from the Employer. Variations are required either because the Employer did not take sufficient time to plan all details before inviting tenders, or because circumstances have changed and changes have to be made.[11] The natural starting point for regulating Variations therefore seems to be that the Employer, to a large extent, must bear the economic risk for cost overruns and delay caused by Variations. There are, however, nuances that must be taken into account. Variations of the Works are likely to cause disturbance and disruption to the Contractor's orderly and sequentially built-up work plan. Variations may cause delay. Inadequate preparation lays the Employer open to the often-contentious issue that many Contractors may try to use Variations as an excuse for their own poor planning and inefficiency, and as an excuse for a delay that would have occurred in any event.

The Employer should be aware, before the Contract is executed, that it will be expensive if it changes its mind and subsequently issues Variations. The Contractor is often in a position to hold out for its price before doing altered work because of the trouble and difficulty of bringing another contractor onto the Site, and the situation becomes even more problematic in the case of a turnkey contract in which the Contractor holds the intellectual property rights to the process, has obtained the statutory design approvals, and is the author and holder of the design details.

In consequence, drafting an acceptable set of Variation provisions is not easy. The provisions should not expose the Contractor to risks that should in all fairness be borne by the Employer. On the other hand, the provisions must give the Employer and the Engineer sufficient protection for their ability to direct a change in the Works.

20.1.2 Authority to order Variations

The Engineer, as agent of the Employer, usually has express authority under the Contract to order Variations at any time from signing of the Contract until the Works are taken over.[12] Usually construction contracts empower the Employer or the Engineer to direct the

10 Philip Loots & Dr Donald Charrett, 'Reconsidering Procurement Criteria and Procedures for Major Infrastructure Projects: Why the Use of "Price" as the Determining Factor in Construction Procurement Decisions is Wrong' (2017) *International Construction Law Review* 69; Faisal Manzoor Arain & Low Sui Pheng, 'PSSCOC and Variations, An Analysis of Consultant-Related Variations in School Building Projects' (2007) *International Construction Law Review* 366.

11 Philip Loots, 'Construction of Major Infrastructure Projects in the Energy Sector: Controlling Spiralling Development Costs' (2013) *AMPLA Yearbook* 173.

12 *Wilmot v Smith* (1828) 3 Carr and Payne 453; *Forman v The Lidesdale* 1900 AC 190; *Ashwell and Nesbit Ltd v Allen* (1912) in *Hudson's Fourth Edition Table of Cases* (Sweet & Maxwell, 4th edn 1914) 462.

Contractor to carry out variation work during the construction phase of the project, but not after practical completion has been achieved.[13]

Whilst the Engineer's power to order Variations is usually defined in the Contract, any limitations imposed by the Employer on the Engineer's powers contained in its terms and conditions of appointment should be disclosed to the Contractor, because the Contractor is not normally privy to the details of the contract between the Engineer and the Employer.

The Contract may require that the power to order Variations must be exercised only in a certain way; for example, that directions by the Engineer will be effective only when made in writing or, if verbal, when subsequently confirmed in writing. A Contractor should study the terms of the Contract and make certain in each case that the person who orders Variations has authority, and such authority is exercised in the manner specified.

An Engineer has no implied authority to order Variations or waive conditions in the Contract specifying how Variations may be ordered. Where the Contractor has executed extra work and the Contract is silent regarding Variations, the mere fact that it has carried out such extra work does not entitle the Contractor to claim additional remuneration. It follows that the Contractor may be liable for damages, the Employer may have a right of termination, and the Contractor may not be entitled to an extension of time for Completion because of the extra work.

Any entitlement to additional remuneration for extra work must therefore arise out of the terms of the Contract, or a new agreement, express or implied, or exceptionally on the principles of unjust enrichment. It is a question of fact whether such a fresh agreement has been concluded. In order to establish an implied agreement it is not sufficient to prove that the Employer consented to an alteration involving extra work; it must also be shown that it knew or should have known that the alterations would increase the cost of the work. An agreement relating to Variations may merely amend the original Contract, or it may constitute an independent new agreement. Where it constitutes an independent new agreement, if the Contractor finds it necessary to commence legal proceedings to obtain payment for Variations, it should probably sue on two separate causes of action, namely the original Contract and the new agreement.

If the Employer or the Engineer directs a Contractor to perform particular works which are not of the type or quantity which the Employer is empowered to direct under the terms of the Contract, or the procedure for issuing a Variation instruction under the Contract has not been followed, the Contractor may refuse to perform the work.[14] If the Contractor accedes to the direction given and performs the work, the Contractor is entitled to be paid for performing that work and will be taken to have waived its right to contest the legality of the instruction in question. In the absence of any distinct agreement for payment the Contractor will be entitled to a reasonable remuneration (*quantum meruit*).[15]

Under a typical Variations clause, the Engineer may order the Contractor to alter, amend, omit, add to, or otherwise vary any part of the Works. A Variation may entail not only an addition (which is by far the most usual variation of the Works in practice), but also an alteration to any parts of the Works which may change the substance of the Contractor's obligation to perform. For example, the Contractor's tender may have been based on a

13 See 2017 FIDIC Red Book sub-clause 13.1; AS 4000–1997 clause 36.1; Under the JCWC Standard Form of Building Contract (2006 edn) clause 4.1 Variations may be instructed, any time up to the issuing of a Final Certificate; Compare the JCT Standard Form of Prime Cost Contract (2016 edition) JCT PCC; *Treasure and Son Ltd v Dawes* [2008] BLR 24, 32 [36], per Akenhead J.

14 *Blue Circle Industries plc v Holland Dredging Co (UK) Ltd* (1987) 37 BLR 40.

15 *Kehr and Tucker Ltd v Astronomical Ltd* [2008] EWHC 2862 (TCC).

certain level of welding expertise to be utilized. The Contractor may be ordered to change to a very much higher level, perhaps not available amongst the Contractor's employees. The Engineer thus has the right at any time to change any aspect of performance of the work under the Contract, but not the terms and conditions of the Contract itself.

20.1.3 Extensions of time and Variations

If a contract contemplates the execution of Variations, it will depend on the construction of the Contract as to whether these have to be executed within the period provided for Completion of the Works.

The Contractor is normally entitled to an extension of time to complete the work if additional or extra work is authorized which increases the time required for Completion. However, what is the effect of a Contract which requires the Contractor to execute additional work within the time originally stipulated and subject to liquidated damages for late completion in circumstances where the terms of the Contract make the Employer judge in its own cause on questions of delay? In accordance with the principles used by courts to construe contracts, where the terms of the Contract are ambiguous, and one construction would lead to an unreasonable result, the court will be unwilling to adopt that construction. However, if there is no ambiguity in the Contract wording, then in accordance with the principle that parties will be held to the terms of their bargain, where a Contractor has undertaken to perform any additional work that may be ordered by the original Date for Completion, it will be required to do so, no matter how foolish that undertaking may have been.

The question of whether the ordering of Variations after the execution of a construction contract will affect the stipulated Date for Completion and the operation of the liquidated damages clause coupled with it cannot be answered without taking into account the relevant facts and circumstances. Even if the Contract contemplates Variations, the courts will as far as possible avoid a construction that the Works, so amended, must be completed within the stipulated time. Where the legal right to claim an extension of time has been established by the ordering of Variations, the Contractor still has to demonstrate the factual cause and effect of such Variations on the Date for Completion. If no detailed construction programme or method of delay analysis from which a critical path can be established has been agreed between the parties, the factual enquiry of whether extra and additional work has affected the Date for Completion may be highly speculative and time consuming.

In deciding whether the amount of extra or additional work fairly entitles the Contractor to an extension of time, the Engineer (or Arbitrator) may certainly allow for any omissions, but it is normally given no power to bring forward the Date for Completion when the time saved by omissions exceeds the time consumed by extras. Thus, even if there have been substantial omissions, only the original Date for Completion can be considered in deciding whether to terminate the Contract for lack of due diligence and in calculating liquidated damages for delay.

Construction contracts usually provide for the Engineer to grant a fair and reasonable extension of time to balance any delay caused by Variations.[16] If the Engineer orders a Variation which delays Completion by the Contractor and does not grant an extension of time, then time is set at large and the Date for Completion and liquidated damages no longer apply. The work as varied must then be completed within a reasonable time. This is

16 *Chaffer and Tassie v Richards* (1905) 26 NLR 207, 222.

the effect of the prevention principle discussed in ¶14.7.6, which provides that where an Employer prevents performance by its own act, it is not entitled to take advantage of its own wrong (in the absence of a special stipulation in the Contract). If the Contractor fails to complete the varied work within a reasonable time, the Employer may recover such damages as it can prove, but not the liquidated damages specified in the Contract.

Where the omissions and extras were ordered at about the same time and resulted in no inconvenience to the Contractor in switching labour from one portion of the work to another, only the net effect would be taken into account, but generally the time saved by omissions should not be set off against the additional time caused by Variations.[17] An analysis of the effects upon the critical path would provide a more precise approach. The contractual provisions may also be so worded that the Engineer, when considering whether or not to allow an extension of time as a result of the ordering of Variations, may deduct time saved as a result of omissions.

The virtually unfettered discretion apparently conferred upon the Engineer to grant an extension of time for Variations can also be exercised by an Arbitrator.

20.1.4 Form of the Variation Order

A Variation Order should be clearly identified as such. It should at least:

(a) Be in writing,
(b) Call itself a Variation Order, and
(c) Contain a description of the Variation or Variations required.

That said, an instruction to carry out a Variation must be issued in the manner and form set out in the Contract which permits its issue. The purpose of specifying the requirements which a written notice of Variation must comply with is to ensure that the Employer is not burdened with the cost of extra work that was not really ordered.[18] A written instruction may be in the form of the issue of a document described as a 'Variation Instruction,' the issue of a drawing, a Site Instruction or the minutes of the site meeting,[19] and it must be evident from the document that it was intended to operate as such an instruction.[20] If it is a contractual requirement that a 'Variation Instruction' must include certain information, a document issued to the Contractor that does not contain the required information will not constitute an instruction for the purposes of the Contract.[21] Put otherwise, unless a claimed 'variation' meets the contractual requirements for a Variation, it will not be a Variation for the purposes of the Contract.[22]

A distinction must be made between a Variation to the work undertaken under the Contract and a variation of the Contract. The Engineer generally has the power to order a Variation, but no power to require a variation of the Contract. As the Contract is

---

17 *Wilson v Holt* (1886) 4 HCG 220.

18 See *Brodie v Cardiff Corporation* [1919] AC 337 (HL(E)); *Tharsis and Copper Co v McElroy and Sons* (1878) LR 3 HL 1040, 1050, per Lord Blackburn (HL(Sc)); *Jaya Sarana Engineering Pte Ltd v GIB Automation Pte Ltd* [2007] SGHC 49, [50]-[53], per Sundaresh Menon JC; *Mann v Paterson Constructions Pty Ltd* [2019] HCA 32, [156]-[157], per Nettle, Gordon and Edelman JJ; *Timwin Construction Pty Ltd v Façade Innovations Pty Ltd* [NSWSC 548, [26], per McDougall J.

19 *Norwest Holst Construction Ltd v Co-Operative Wholesale Society Ltd* [1998] EWHC Technology 339, [292], per HHJ Thornton QC.

20 *Bluewater Energy Services BV v Mercon Steel Structures BV* [2014] EWHC 2132 (TCC), [66], per Ramsey J.

21 *West 3 Mechanical Contractors Ltd v Mizen Design Build Ltd* [2014] EWHC 4004 (TCC), [97]-[99], per Ramsey J.

22 See *Jones v Dalcon Construction Pty Ltd* [2006] WASCA 205, [21], per Wheeler J.

a consensual agreement between Employer and Contractor, only those parties may, by subsequent agreement, affect a variation of the Contract.[23]

20.1.5 Exceptions to Variation Orders made in writing

Where a dispute arises between the parties in relation to whether work constitutes extra work, an arbitration clause in an agreement may provide that an Arbitrator can award payment for Variations in the absence of a written order.[24] A court appointed referee can also make such a determination.[25]

A construction contract may provide that no extra work is to be done unless upon the written order of the Employer or its Engineer and that no claim for extra payment should be entertained unless supported by the written authority of the Employer. Notwithstanding such term, in some circumstances the Employer may not be able to deny liability for such work on the ground that it did not give written authority. In the case of *Liebe v Molloy*[26] the court found that a contract to pay for extra works should be implied if it can be inferred that the Employer:

(a) Had actual knowledge of the works as they were being carried out,
(b) Knew the works were 'outside the Contract,' and
(c) Knew that the Contractor expected to be paid for the works.

Otherwise, the work must have been requested, and the fact that the Contractor has performed 'out of scope' work is a necessary but insufficient condition to it being entitled to payment for that work.[27] It follows that where the Contractor performs extra work as a 'goodwill gesture,' it will not be entitled to payment.[28]

Where the Contract states that the Contractor is only entitled to additional payment if a written Variation instruction is given, there may be circumstances where the absence of a written Variation instruction will not prevent the Contractor from being entitled to payment. The Employer may have conducted itself so as to waive its right to rely upon the clause requiring a written Variation instruction to be given. If the Employer has lead the Contractor to believe that it will be remunerated for extra work and the Contractor has acted on that understanding, the Employer may be estopped from seeking to defend the Contractor's claim for additional payment on the basis of the particular contractual provision.[29] Also, the work may be so different from that contemplated by the Contract that it is not caught by the contractual provisions dealing with Variations, the contractual machinery for ordering and assessing Variations may have broken down by reason of the Engineer having abandoned or otherwise refused to fulfil its contractual valuation function,[30] or the contractual machinery for the ordering and valuation of the Variation may

23 *Firth v Thompson* [2001] NSWCA 131.
24 *Brodie v Cardiff Corp* [1919] AC 337.
25 *Atlantic Civil Pty Ltd v Water Administration Ministerial Corp* (1992) 39 NSWLR 468.
26 (1906) 4 CLR 347.
27 *Teras Offshore Pte Ltd v Teras Cargo Transport (America) LLC* [2017] SGHC(I) 04, [31], per Sir Henry Bernard Eder IJ.
28 *Dunn International Ltd v CDE* (1997) 57 Con LR 11 and 34–36, per Judge Lloyd QC.
29 *SHA Premier Constructions Pty Ltd v Lanskey Constructions Pty Ltd* [2019] QSC 81, [41]-[44], per Boddice J (appeal dismissed) [2019] QCA 177); *GPE Pte Ltd v Siemens Pte Ltd* [2018] SGHC 194, [15], per Chan Seng Onn J.
30 *Chun Wo Building Construction Ltd v Metta Resources Ltd* [2016] HKCFI 1357, [151]-[159], per Anthony Chan J.

simply have broken down.[31] The terms of the Contract may also have been varied and a new contract entered into to the effect that there is no need for a Variation instruction to be given in writing.[32]

20.1.6 Authorisation of Variations

It should be remembered that the Contractor has fundamental obligations under the Contract and may be already bound to do such indispensably or contingently necessary work as is required to bring the described work to Completion.

Where the Contractor seeks to recover payment for Variations, it must show that it has fulfilled any necessary condition precedent specified in the Contract, for example, the written instruction or order of the Employer or Engineer. The purpose of such a clause is to ensure that the Employer is properly informed of the effect of Variations and to provide a method for monitoring the cost and time effects on the project. It was held in *Jorey v Thiange*[33] that where the Architect's certificate that payment was due was a condition precedent to payment under the Contract, it was also a condition precedent to payment for Variations. The **Variation Order** may have to be sanctioned by the Engineer in writing, upon its official letterhead or printed form, expressly purporting to be an order as extra or additional work. In *Tharsis Sulphur and Copper Co v McElroy and Sons and others*,[34] mere reference in progress certificates did not constitute a written order, nor did sketches prepared in the architect's office and not signed by it.[35] The Employer may, however, be held to have waived its rights to insist on the provisions relating to written orders. An Engineer has no implied power to waive such a provision requiring a written order.[36]

The Contractor is not entitled to extra payment for a Variation which is not made by order of the Engineer but is merely allowed as a concession. In *Tharsis Sulphur and Copper Co v McElroy and Sons*,[37] the Contractor applied for permission to increase the width of girders because it could not make them as specified – at least not without incurring a great deal of expense. The court held that there was nothing to imply that the Engineer intended, when giving its oral consent, to agree to extra payment for the increase.

If the Engineer in such a case does give a written Variation Order without specifying that it is given at the request of the Contractor who is to carry out the change without extra payment, the Contractor in some cases may have a claim to payment. It may be difficult for the Employer to argue that the order was solely for the Contractor's benefit since the Employer may have avoided a delay for which the Contractor might have become entitled to an extension of time or otherwise have avoided a claim under the Contract. In *Simplex Concrete Piles Ltd v St Pancras Borough Council*,[38] the Contractor working under a design and construct contract found it impracticable to carry out the work as contracted. The

31 *Davy Offshore Ltd v Emerald Field Contracting Ltd* (1991) 55 BLR 1, 77–78, per Judge Thayne Forbes QC.

32 *Management Solutions and Professional Consultants Ltd v Bennett (Electrical) Services Ltd* [2006] EWHC 1720 (TCC), [11], per HHJ Thornton QC; *Built Interiors Pty Ltd v Three Dinosaurs Pty Ltd* [2003] NSWCA 290, [20] and [53]-[58], per Mason P.

33 (1894)11 CU 154.

34 (1878) 3 App Cas 1040 (HL), 1053.

35 *Myers v Sarl* (1860) 3 E and E 306.

36 *Sharpe v San Paulo Railway Co* (1873) LR 8 Ch App 597.

37 (1878) 3 App Cas 1040 (HL) 1053.

38 (1958) (unreported, see *Hudson's Building and Engineering Contracts* (Sweet & Maxwell, 9th edn 1965) 393).

Architect wrote 'we are prepared to accept your proposal that the piles . . . should be of the bored type in accordance with quotations submitted' (by the subcontractor). The court held that this letter was an Architect's instruction under the RIBA form and that the Contractor was entitled to be paid for the varied work in accordance with that quotation.

There is usually no express statement in a contract that Variations will be paid for on interim certificates, but since these form part of the permanent work executed, they would normally qualify for payment in that way in any event.[39]

All work done in accordance with the drawings and which forms part of the Contract is work done by the Engineer's order.[40] Such work may be additional work to the extent that the quantities of such work exceed the quantities which appear in the bill of quantities.[41]

20.1.7 Negative Variations – the omission of works

The Engineer should exercise caution when issuing a Variation to omit works under the Contract. In particular, if the work is still required to be done in order to achieve the final product, then, unless the Contract specifically enables the Engineer to do so, the Engineer should not take work out of the Contractor's scope and transfer it to the Employer or a third party. High Court case law in Australia favours the Contractor's right as successful Tenderer to undertake *all* works which are required under the scope of the Works for which it tendered.[42] The principles set out in these High Court cases in relation to a Variation clause which permits the omission of works have been aptly summarized as follows:

> [Such a clause] enables the Employer to omit work or part of the work under a contract but only where the work is not to be performed at all.
>
> The contract work cannot be taken away from the Contractor to be given to someone else, and the same exercise cannot be performed by two stages making use of what is apparently authorised by a variations clause for the purpose.
>
> Once it is established that a proprietor wishes to have work done, it is not a proper exercise of the power or an exercise within the ambit of the power to take any work out of the Contract as a step in the process of giving it to somebody else.[43]

Accordingly, the High Court has established the principle that it would be an unreasonable exercise of the Variation power, especially in a lump sum contract, for Contractor's work to be taken out of its hands for which it has tendered and successfully commercially bargained for. This principle is accepted elsewhere.[44] The above principle is of course subject to the express terms of the Contract which may override the common law principle and provide the Employer an unfettered right to omit work.

It would be an improper use of the power to vary if it is used to omit works (for which the Contractor would under the terms of the Contract be entitled to an extension of time),

---

39 See *Tersons v Stevenage Development Corporation* [1965] 1 QB 37.

40 See *Munro v Westville Town* [1903] 36 NSR 313; *Myers v Sarl* (1860) 3 E and E 306.

41 *Mitsui Construction Company Ltd v The Attorney General of Hong Kong* (1986) 33 BLR 1.

42 *Carr v J.A. Berriman Pty Ltd* (1953) 89 CLR 327; *Commissioner for Main Roads v Reed and Stuart Pty Ltd* (1974) 131 CLR.

43 *Bethlehem Singapore Private Ltd v Barrier Reef Holdings Ltd* (BC8701035) (unreported, NSW Sup Ct, 15 October 1987).

44 eg *Abbey Developments Ltd v PP Brickwork Ltd* [2003] EWHC 1987 (TCC), [45]-[47] per HHJ Lloyd QC.

with the intention of ensuring that the Contractor does not obtain that extension of time and is rendered liable to pay damages for delay.[45]

The Contractor should be aware that the Employer's power to omit work under the Variation clause in the head contract will not necessarily be the same as the Contractor's power to omit work under the Variations clause in its subcontracts. For example, in the case of *Chadmax Plastics Pty Ltd v Hansen and Yuncken (S.A.) Pty Ltd*,[46] the Architect issued a Variation that deleted 98% of a specified proprietary brand of wall finish and replaced it with a different finish. Whilst that Variation was valid under the head contract, the Contractor's deletion of 98% of the work of its subcontractor amounted to repudiation of the subcontract, for which the Contractor was liable in damages.

20.1.8 Variations exceeding a certain percentage

The Contract may provide for the contract price to be further increased or decreased if the net effect of all Variations results in a Variation greater than a specified percentage of the sum named in the tender. This is an arbitrary provision and may be inappropriate to the nature of this work being undertaken and the method of pricing the Contract.

There may be statutory constraints on the amount by which the total value of Variations can exceed the contract price. For example, EU public procurement law applies even after a contract has been entered into, and this law includes principles of equal treatment and transparency. These principles set boundaries to the extent of Variations that can be ordered without requiring a new contract award procedure.[47]

20.1.9 Payment for Variations

If additional work has been performed by the Contractor voluntarily, the Contractor generally will not be able to seek payment for this work.[48] If the Contractor chooses to put in extras without the knowledge or authority of the Employer, even if the latter is compelled to have the benefit of them because they cannot be removed (eg materials which cost more or are of a superior quality), the Employer is not obliged to pay additional remuneration.

In the absence of a specific agreement, a Contractor who has done authorised extra work which is not included in the contract price and for which there is no rate or price, is entitled to reasonable remuneration. This is illustrated by the case of *Parkinson (Sir Lindsay) and Co Ltd v Commissioners of Works*.[49] The contract was for the construction of a factory for £3,500,000. The conditions of contract included a wide Variation clause that gave the Employer or its Architect power at their absolute discretion: 'to modify the extent, character, sections quantities or dimensions of any works shown or described in the Contract or the levels or positions of any of the works or to order any portion

45 *Aoki Corporation v Hong Kong Institute of Education* [2004] HKCFI 34, [63], per Reyes J.
46 (1985) 1 BCL 52.
47 Lukas Klee, *International Construction Law* (Wiley Blackwell, 2nd edn 2018) 273–275.
48 *Tharsis Sulphur and Copper Co v M'Elroy and Sons* (1878) 3 App Cas 1040.
49 [1949] 2 KB 632, [1950] 1 All ER 208 (CA), discussed in *British Movietone News v London and District Cinemas* [1952] AC 166.

or portions of the works to be omitted . . . or to order additional work.' Further, there was a note in the bill of quantities that it was probable that further work to the value of approximately £500,000 would be ordered on a measured basis. As a result of delay by the Employer, the parties entered into a deed of Variation by which the Contractor agreed to adopt uneconomic working to complete by the original date. The deed specified that the Contract payments would be the actual cost to the Contractor plus a net remuneration of not less than £150,000 or more than £300,000. The deed confirmed all the other terms of the original contract. The Employer ordered extra works so that the total cost of the Works to the Contractor was £6,683,056. The Arbitrator found that the extra work was not different in character from that anticipated at the time of the deed of Variation, but that at the time the deed was made the Contractor contemplated that the actual cost of the finished work would not exceed £5,000,000, made up of the original contract work, plus the probable extras mentioned of £500,000 and £1,000,000 for uneconomic working. There was evidence that the Contractor's minimum and maximum remuneration was based on that estimated cost of the work. The court held that to have put the Contractor at the mercy of the Employer in making it liable to do whatever extra work the Employer required without any increase in their profits would have been absurd. On a true construction of the two contracts taken together, the power to order Variations did not entitle the Employer to require work materially in excess of £5,000,000, so that the Contractor was entitled to be paid a reasonable profit on work beyond that amount.

A contract that includes a bill of quantities, or a schedule of rates and prices for items of work, may provide that extra work is to be valued using the rates and prices indicated in the bill or the Contract, or that such rates and prices are to be used which in the opinion of the Engineer are appropriate or applicable to the work in question.[50] If the Contract does not include such details as to prices or rates, it may be permissible for the Engineer to scrutinise other potentially relevant material such as the build-up of the Contractor's tender. It may be left to the Engineer to assess a reasonable price for the Variation work if the Contract does not contain an applicable rate or price for the work in question.[51] The circumstances will dictate what a 'reasonable' rate is,[52] and a 'reasonable' rate may include time-related costs.[53]

Star Rate is a commonly used term for a reasonable rate for valuing a Variation derived from sources outside the Contract based on industry custom and practice. It is a rate which is 'derived from sources outside the terms of the contract but must be a rate which sits reasonably alongside existing contract rates and is one which, when applied to the varied work, will not throw the whole pricing structure of, or the financial return from, the contract out of balance.'[54]

Where the parties are faced with a binding Variation provision which contemplates the value of a Variation being agreed, the parties will be under a duty to cooperate with each

50 See AS 4000–1997 clause 36.4; JCT Standard Building Contract, 2016 edition, clause 5.6; *AJ Lucas Drilling Pty Ltd v McConnell Dowell Constructors (Aust) Pty Ltd* [2009] VSCA 310, [72].

51 See ICE Conditions (7th edn 1999) clause 52; 2017 FIDIC Red Book sub-clause 12.3; JCT Standard Building Contract (2016 edn) clause 5.10.

52 *Lucas Earthmovers Pty Ltd v Anglogold Ashanti Australia Ltd* [2019] FCA 1049, [266], per White J.

53 Ibid, 267–268.

54 *JDM Accord Ltd v Secretary of State* (2004) 93 Con LR 133, 197 [171], per HHJ Thornton QC; *Ruttle Plant Hire Ltd v Secretary of State for the Environment* [2007] EWHC 1773 (TCC), [9] and [19], per Jackson J.

other with a view to reaching agreement on the price of the Variation.[55] Where a contract provides for negotiations regarding the additional amount to be paid for as Variations, if negotiations fail, the Contractor is entitled to reasonable remuneration.[56]

In the case of additional work, if a contract provides for 'equitable adjustment' to the contract price in the event of Variations, the direct costs of performing the additional work[57] plus a profit margin will be taken into account.[58]

20.1.10 Work outside the Contract

If the Engineer acts purportedly in accordance with the Contract, and as a result radically changes the scope or character of the Works, for example, by varying the work or omitting specific items, an implied new contract may come into existence, replacing the original one, and the Contractor may claim a reasonable remuneration in terms of this new contract.[59] In practice this will occur infrequently since most Variation clauses are widely cast, and contracts are more often than not administered in their terms to completion of construction. This approach should be adopted with great caution.

The general statement of the Engineer's powers to order a Variation is usually along the lines of 'a variation of the form, quality or quantity of the works or any part thereof' and does not refer to a change in the character of the Works. The only reference to a change of character usually refers to a change in the character of any work included in the Contract, and not specifically of the Works as a whole. The Variation clause does not therefore usually authorize a transformation in the character of the whole Works.[60]

Abrahamson[61] draws a distinction between 'extra' and 'additional' work. The term 'extra work' has a specific meaning in construction contracts. Additional work may or may not be extra work.[62] To be regarded as 'extra work' the work must, in the first place, not be expressly or impliedly included in the Contract. 'Additional work' is usually work which

55 *Swallowfalls Ltd v Monaco Yachting and Technologies SAM* [2014] EWCA Civ 186, [32], per Long-more LJ; *Kennett Pty Ltd v Janssen* [2014] SASC 164, [169], per Blue J.

56 *Pavey and Matthews Pty Ltd v Paul* (1987) 162 CLR 221, 256; *Summers v Commonwealth* (1918) 25 CLR 144 (affirmed (1919) 26 CLR 180); *Update Construction Pty Ltd v Rozelle Child Care Centre* (1990) 20 NSWLR 251, 275, per Priestley JA; *Golden Singa Engineering (Singapore) Pte Ltd v Techfield Engineering Pte Ltd* [1993] SGHC 219; *Foundation Co of Canada Ltd v United Grain Growers Ltd* (1997) 34 BCLR (3d) 92, [128]-[133], per McEarchern CJ; *Trimis v Mina* [1999] NSWCA 140, [54], per Mason P [16 BCL 288]; *GEC Marconi Systems Pty Ltd v BHP Information Technology Pty Ltd* (2003) 128 FCR 1, [655]-[656], per Finn J; *Mowlem plc v Stena Line Ports Ltd* [2004] EWHC 2206 (TCC), [40], per HHJ Seymour QC; *McGlinn v Waltham Contractors Ltd (No.3)* [2007] EWHC 149 (TCC), [982], per HH J Coulson QC; *Cardno CCS Pty Ltd v Dwyer* [2007] QCA 263, [58], per Williams JA; *BMD Major Projects Pty Ltd v Victorian Urban Development Authority* [2007] VSC 409, [149], per Pagone J; *Equuscorp Pty Ltd v Haxton* [2012] HCA 7, [64]; *Benedetti v Sawiris* [2013] UKSC 50, [9], per Lord Clarke JSC; *Alwie Handoyo v Tjong Very Sumito* [2013] SGCA 44, [103]-[108]; *FDC Constructions and Fitout Pty Ltd v Condensing Vaporisers Aust. Ltd* [2013] NSWSC 1073, [66], per Slattery J; *Erith Holdings Ltd v Murphy* [2017] EWHC 1364 (TCC), [102], per O'Farrell J; *Mann v Paterson Constructions Pty Ltd* [2019] HCA 32, [14]-[19], per Kiefel CJ, Bell and Keane JJ;, [164], per Nettle, Gordon and Edelman JJ.

57 *Hong Kong Housing Authority v Leighton Contractors (Asia) Ltd* [2004] HKCFI 1217; *Maeda Corporation v HKSAR* [2014] BLR 22, 30 [47]-[49], per Fok JA.

58 *Weldon Plant Ltd v Commission for New Towns* [2001] 1 ALL ER (Comm) 264, 272–274, per HHJ Lloyd QC; *Chun Wo Building Construction Ltd v Metta Resources Ltd* [2016] HKCFI 1357, [257], per Anthony Chan J.

59 *Sir Lindsay Parkinson and Co Ltd v Commissioners of Works* [1949] 2 KB 632, [1950] 1 All ER 208 (CA).

60 *Alfred McAlpine and Son (Pty) Ltd v Transvaal Provincial Administration* (1974) 3 SALR 516.

61 MW Abrahamson, *Engineering Law and the ICE Contracts* (F & N Spon, 4th edn 1979) 115.

62 *De Martini v Elade Realty Corporation* 52 NYS 2d 487.

results from a change or alteration in plans concerning work which has to be done under the Contract, while 'extra work' relates to work which is not included within the Contract itself.[63] The distinction between additional work, extra work, and work which falls outside the Contract is relevant only where the Contract has explicit provisions for additional work and extra work. In the absence of such provisions, the Contractor is entitled to fair and reasonable remuneration for any additional work.[64]

Changes can fall outside the relevant Variation clause, such that the additional work is not within the contract. Abrahamson[65] cites the following examples:

- In a contract to do all carpentry, joinery, glazing, and tin work for certain houses, after the work was executed, the Employer added attics and ordered the Contractor to do the necessary additional carpentry work in windows and doors and added large stables suitable for an inn.[66]
- Where a contract gave the Employer the right to 'make any alterations that may hereafter be determined upon as necessary or desirable,' alterations in part of the route of a canal through deep ravines and hills resulted in at least 53 times the estimated quantity of cut stone and masonry.[67]
- Over 1,000 feet extra were added to the lower end of a sewer through soil of a different character and much more difficult to excavate. A change in location of the sewer from the centre of a street to the side seriously interfered with the working of ditching machines.[68]
- In a contract for supplying stone for ten buildings, the Employer was liable for loss of profits for reducing the number of buildings to five.[69]
- Where the Contract gave the Employer the power 'to exclude any item to increase or diminish the quantities to any extent,' the Employer was liable for reducing a tile drain from sixteen to seven-and a-half miles.[70]

The dividing line between omissions which are permissible under the Contract and a breach of the Contract may be fine and will ultimately turn on construction of the terms of the Contract. Thus, the necessary omission of a half a mile out of a contract for three and three-quarter miles of a canal and the elimination of other work totalling 41% of the contract work was held to be within a right to make deductions from the contract work; however, omitting 2½% of the work was held to be a breach of contract in which the Employer had the right 'to alter drawings in any way it may deem necessary for the public interest.'[71]

63 *Shields et al v City of New York* 84 App Div 502.

64 *Alfred McAlpine and Son (Pty) Ltd v Transvaal Provincial Administration* (1974) 3 SALR 516; *Reid v Batte* (1829) M & M 413; *Russell v Sa Da Bandeira (Viscount)* (1862) 13 CB (NS) 149; *Thorn v Mayor and Commonality of London* (1876) 1 App Cas 120; See also *Warner v Wright* (1908) EDC 14; *Compagnie Interafricaine de Travaux (Comiat) v South African Transport Services* (SATS) (1991) (4) SA 217 (A).

65 MW Abrahamson, *Engineering Law and the ICE Contract* (F & N Spon, 4th edn 1979) 115.

66 *Watson v O'Beirne* (1850) 7 Up Can QB 3451.

67 *Salt Lake City v Smith* 104 Fed 457.

68 *Boyd v South Winnipeg* (1917) 2 WWR 489 Can.

69 *McMaster v State of New York* 108 NY 542.

70 *Drainage District No 1 of Lincoln County v Rude* 21 F 2d 257.

71 *Kinser Construction Co v State of New York* 204 NY 381; *Whitfield Construction Co v City of New York* 244 NY 251.

Any possibility that Variations may be held to go outside the scope of the Contract should be avoided, since the Contractor is entitled to refuse to do them and is obviously in a position to hold out for its price because of the expense of bringing another contractor on to the Site. The Engineer and the Employer should be aware that the right to change the work after the Contract is made is not unlimited and should exercise caution in respect of issuing directions to change the Works in a radical or extensive way. If the Engineer is in any doubt as to whether extra work is outside the Contract, it should explain what is involved to the Employer, and preferably negotiate a supplementary agreement with the Contractor, fixing a revised programme and a price or rates for the new Works in advance.

The greatest danger is that Variations outside the Contract may be ordered by the Engineer unwittingly. If that happens and the work is done by the Contractor without fixing a price in advance, it will (since the work falls outside the Contract) normally be entitled to a reasonable remuneration without any reference to the Contract rates or prices, provided it can prove that the Engineer had authority to order the work. Such work may not merely be additional to the Contract Works but may involve such a complete transformation of the original contract plan that no original contract work can fairly be traced in the work carried out to be priced at the Contract rates. This is the *quantum meruit* 'holy grail' sought by Contractors, since it sets the original Contract aside and replaces it with reasonable remuneration for all work done, irrespective of whether a profit could have been made or not. Cases (successful and unsuccessful) that involved a claim for a *quantum meruit* for work outside the contract were discussed by Charrett.[72]

The Contractor may not, however, mislead the Employer. If it carries out work which it realizes does not fall within the right of Variations under the original Contract without claiming for payment outside the Contract when the work is ordered and accepts interim certificates under the original Contract including payment for the new work, it may be held to have impliedly agreed that the work will be done on the terms of the original Contract and at the original contract rates. In *Peter Kiewit Sons Company of Canada Ltd v Eakins*,[73] the court held that a Contractor who carried out extra work falling outside the Contract, knowing that it fell outside the Contract, must be taken to have agreed that the Contract rates will apply to the work. This case also held that the fact that the Contractor did the work under protest did not affect the position.[74]

A clear-cut restriction on Variations to a percentage of the original work is sometimes used in an attempt to avoid these problems, but this does not provide a satisfactory safeguard for the Employer against inadequate preparation of the Contract documents.

20.1.11 Differences in quantities

Even though a Contractor may have performed work additional to that which is expressly or impliedly included in the Contract, it does not follow that the Employer is necessarily liable to pay for such work. Whether or not work is expressly or impliedly included in the Contract depends in each case on the type of contract and its specific terms.

72 Dr Donald Charrett, 'Quantum meruit claims in construction law' (2002) 9 *Building Dispute Practitioners Society Newsletter* 6, 11–13.

73 [1962] 22 DLR (2d) 465 Can.

74 See also *Thorn v Mayor and Commonality of London* (1876) 1 App Cas 120, 127 and 128.

Except in a re-measurement contract, all differences between the billed and actual quantities usually fall to be valued under the Variation clause. Where extra or additional work is carried out, the first task of the Engineer is to decide whether or not a rate is 'applicable'; it is generally accepted in practice that the Engineer should have regard to the applicable standard method of measurement and the real content of the item, and not merely its description in the bill, that is, it should decide whether the various activities necessary for the execution of the varied work are the same as those necessary to execute the work covered by the original item. The problem of applicability or otherwise of rates is particularly important because the Contractor may have priced the work low in its tender, and when the work is varied, the Contractor may argue that in the circumstances the Contract rates do not apply and that in fixing 'reasonable prices' under this clause the Engineer must award a full rate for the new work.

The usual purpose of a power to vary rates is to deal with cases where the change in the amount, and so on, of a particular item affects the Contractor's economics in doing that item of work and its profitability. Where the 'rates set out in the Contract' are referred to, this means all the rates, including any preliminary items which may be affected by additional or extra work, and it is the Engineer's duty to apply a proper proportion of any particular item of preliminary work which is likely to be increased by the additional or extra work ordered. Special circumstances, such as the time when the Variation is ordered, may render those prices inapplicable and unreasonable.

It can be argued that, even when the Contract rates do not apply directly, the rates applicable for the extra or additional work are not intended to be reasonable prices in the abstract but are intended to be fixed with reference to all the circumstances, including the general level of the Contract rates and the original rates for any varied item. On this interpretation, if the Engineer varies work which is priced low, it may price the new work similarly. It is often argued that this is unreasonable because the Contractor might have had cheap supplies or some other special reasons for the original price which do not apply to the altered work. The solution appears to be that the Engineer must fix the price of the varied work by reference to all the actual circumstances, and only if the Contractor can prove special facts should it be allowed a full price. Where the Contractor has put a high rate on a particular item it should, in the same way, be entitled to an equivalent rate where the work is varied since it is generally entitled to allow for its profit in whichever rate it chooses.

At the same time the Engineer's obligation to fix 'reasonable prices' where contract rates are not applicable is paramount, and where a Variation involves a greatly increased or reduced quantity of work it is suggested that the Engineer is not entitled to apply particular rates too strictly by analogy but must have regard to the general level of the Contractor's rates and prices. It is also suggested that, where the overall work is greatly changed by Variations, the circumstances may indicate that the Engineer should depart even from that general level. In the last analysis, even a Contractor who deliberately under prices will normally do so on the basis of a particular volume and type of work which will bear some of its overheads or cost of idle plant without causing more than an estimated loss on direct costs.

The solution must be that the Engineer must consider all the circumstances including the Contract rates and prices where Contract rates are not directly applicable. This avoids large differences in rates hinging on whether there is a Contract rate directly applicable or not (which may be largely fortuitous). This appears to be most fair to both the Employer and the Contractor and is the solution to which Arbitrators generally incline. It is, however, not at all certain that a court would accept it, as a court may hold that prices are to be fixed in the abstract without regard to the original rates.

Rate-fixing is normally a give-and-take operation between Engineer and Contractor. Whilst lawyers may find the imprecision of the procedure difficult to accept, rigid legal rules would be difficult to formulate and would be arbitrary in application. The paper by C K Haswell,[75] and particularly the discussion,[76] are most informative on Variations in practice and the multitude of factors affecting the Contractor's distribution of costs and profits between the rates which make rigid rules inappropriate.

In measure and value contracts, where the bill of quantities represents an estimate of the work that the Contractor is to perform, the Contractor is entitled to be paid according to the quantity of work actually performed, which may differ from the quantity of work stated in the bill. It is important to appreciate that it is not necessary in such cases for a Variation order to be given to the Contractor in respect of the greater or lesser quantities.[77] If the Contractor fails to price an item in the bill, it is generally to be taken as covered by its other rates and prices.

20.2 Value engineering

Value engineering can be defined as '[A] systematic approach to delivering the required function at lowest cost without loss of quality, performance or reliability.'[78] Also known as value analysis.

Value engineering provisions may be included in a contract to encourage the Contractor to propose changes that will reduce costs. Such provisions typically define the share of value engineering cost savings between the Contractor and the Employer. Any such value engineering provisions in the Contract will need to be carefully structured to ensure that they will achieve the desired objective. Importantly, the Contractor will need to ensure that such provisions cannot be circumvented by the Employer using its powers to order Variations under the Contract. A prudent provision in the Contract would be that once the Contractor has proposed a 'cost saving initiative,' the Contract should provide an express mechanism that prevents the Engineer or Employer from initiating a Variation to capture all the benefit for itself. It may be that the concept of seeking cost savings for the Employer is inconsistent with a hard money lump sum contract, where the Contractor essentially bears the performance risk. Costs savings are perhaps best left to alliance and similar risk sharing arrangements.

Properly structured cost savings provisions in a design and construct contract should not dilute the normal contractual right of the Contractor to prepare the most cost-effective design it can produce by the exercise of its engineering skill, provided this is consistent with the requirements of the Contract.

75 CK Haswell, 'Rate Fixing in Civil Engineering Contracts' (1963/02) 24 *Proceedings ICE* 223.

76 1963/02 Vol 27 *Proceedings ICE* 192.

77 *J Cosby and Sons Ltd v Portland UDC* (1967) 5 BLR 121, 130, per Donaldson J; *Grinaker Construction (Transvaal) Pty Ltd v Transvaal Provincial Administration* (1981) 20 BLR 30 (Sth Afr Sup Ct); *Barter v Mayor of Melbourne* (1870) 1 AJR (Full Ct Sup Ct Vic); *JG King Pty Ltd v Patel* [2014] VSC 58, [84]-[111], per Kryou J.

78 David Blockley, *New Dictionary of Civil Engineering* (Penguin Books, 2005).

20.3 Variation procedure

Where the Employer is a large and cumbersome bureaucracy, government, or private organisation, the time taken to authorise a Variation Order may delay sensible progress of the Works. It is common practice for the Contractor to start work on a Variation on the basis of verbal or partially written information long before it has been formalised. Contractors should be aware that they do so at their own risk. Technically, the Contractor is in default if it starts work on a Variation before the Variation Order arrives. By acting this way, Contractors perpetuate the bad practice frequently adopted by Employers and Engineers in not adopting and following the contractual disciplines laid down in the Contract. Employers need to appreciate that delayed approval of a Variation may result in additional costs arising from the progress of the Works in accordance with the Contractor's programme.

The Contractor may receive a drawing or specification during the performance of the Contract which the Engineer considers to be further detail of the original scope of work, whereas the Contractor considers it to be a Variation. The only way the Contractor can handle this situation is by disputing the instruction as lying outside the agreed scope of work and requesting a Variation Order.

It may be desirable to establish a dialogue between the Contractor and the Engineer before the decision is taken on whether to issue a Variation Order. Normally the Engineer will want an estimate for the work in question and its effect on the programme. It is therefore desirable that as full information as possible be given to the Contractor. This is usually provided for in the Contract by giving the Engineer the power to make a **Variation Price Request**. The Contractor's submission in response to a Variation Price Request should contain a description of the work to be performed, and a price and programme for its execution. The Contractor should prepare any such submission carefully to ensure that it takes due account of the full impact of the varied Works, including not only the Variation itself, but its disruptive effect on the planning and progress of the other work and any impact on the Contractor's performance obligations. The Contractor's proposal should include a date by which the Variation Order has to be issued for the quoted price to be maintained. The Contractor's price should also include the costs of preparing the proposal.

In the event that the Engineer does not issue a Variation Order in response to the Contractor's proposal, the Contractor should be entitled to recover the costs it incurred in preparing the proposal. In the absence of such an entitlement, there is no constraint on the Employer requesting proposals for speculative variations. The 2017 FIDIC rainbow suite provides for payment of the Contractor's costs in preparing a proposal for a variation that is not proceeded with.[79]

Even omitting work often entails some work to be performed, for example, demobilization, removal of equipment, and so on. It is important that the description is detailed and accurate because this enables both parties to make better evaluations on the possible adjustments to the programme and the adjustment to the contract price. For the same reasons it is important to present clear proposals for the build-up of the programme for the execution of the Variation work; the Contractor's proposals for any necessary modifications to the programme or to any of the Contractor's obligations under the Contract must be appropriately justified. It does not follow automatically that an omission of work

79 Sub-clause 13.3.2.

will result in a reduced time for Completion or reduction in price: the opposite may be true. Each situation must be dealt with on its own merits.

The need for change in the programme will emanate from a Variation that authorises an extension of time; the change of the programme will follow the procedure for extension of the time for Completion.

The Contractor must also submit proposals for modifications to any Contractor's obligations other than complying with the programme. Changes in the Works may, for instance, affect the strength of the materials used or the capacity to withstand high or low temperatures and so on. This may change the basis for any performance guarantees or other guarantees given by the Contractor. The Contractor should have a certain freedom of choice on the presentation of its proposal. It might build up its proposal on the rates contained in the schedule of prices, if it deems them applicable, or by some kind of interpolation from the rates. It may also present merely a lump sum or special rates as its proposal for a negotiated adjustment of the contract price.

When it receives a Variation Order, the Contractor should be obliged to carry it out forthwith, regardless of whether agreement has been reached on the adjustment of the contract price or on an extension of the Date for Completion. If it intends to do so, the Contractor should give notice that it will be making a claim for the increased costs and an extension of time. It is common for a construction contract to include such a notice clause in any event.

20.4 Provisional sums and prime cost items

A **provisional sum** is a sum that the Contractor is directed by the Employer to include in its tender as part of the contract price to cover items of work, goods, or services that the Employer may or may not require, or for contingencies. The Contractor will only receive payment in respect of provisional sums expended following instructions by the Engineer. The payment normally comprises the actual amount expended plus a predetermined markup to cover overhead and profit. Provisional sums are not the same as the price of provisional quantities. Provisional quantities are items or components of work for which the requirements and quantities are not known at the time of tendering and for which the Contractor will be paid based on the actual amount of work carried out and the rates set out in the Contract.

Work which is definitely intended to be carried out by a nominated subcontractor (and which cannot therefore be regarded as provisional in character) should not be billed as a provisional sum but as a PC item.

The contract may define **prime cost items (PC items)**. A prime cost item is a specified item of known work, plant, or materials in a bill of quantities or the Contract which is assigned a dollar value by the Employer for tender pricing purposes (**prime cost sum**). That value may or may not cover the actual cost of the item; however, the final contract price includes the actual cost, plus any specified markup. The total prime cost in the Contract at the time it is executed is therefore likely to be different from the prime cost included in the contract price.

Trade discounts in respect of provisional sums or PC items may not be retained by the Contractor. In *Hippisley v Knee Brothers*,[80] auctioneers were to be paid a lump sum as commission and 'out of pocket expenses.' The court held that they were not entitled to

80 [1905] 1 KB 1.

retain trade discounts in respect of printing and advertising. Nor is the Contractor entitled to any discount for cash.[81]

In order to entitle the Contractor to obtain and keep a discount from a nominated subcontractor, the right to do so must be given to it both in relation to the Employer and in relation to the subcontractor. The subcontractor's principal concern is that it is paid within the number of days for the discount specified in the subcontract. Provided, therefore, that it is paid within that time, it must allow the discount whether or not it is paid before the head contractor receives payment from the Employer. As between the Employer and the Contractor, however, obviously the party who in fact finances the payment to the subcontractor should get the benefit of the discount.

Although in practice the industry is familiar with the use of the terminology of provisional sums and PC sums and the administration of the work which is the subject of them, it is perhaps not sufficiently realised how vague the usual contractual provisions regulating them are, and how many questions they leave unanswered. The obscurities may arise because:

(a) There is no definition of the terms, as such – reference must be made to a standard method of measurement, if there is one, which is applicable to the type of work being undertaken.
(b) There is generally no provision in the conditions of contract which clearly gives the Engineer power to nominate or select subcontractors or suppliers, or which relates this power specifically to either of these terms.
(c) No provision exists as to the time when the Contractor is supposed to make payments to suppliers or subcontractors, or as to the nature or extent of these payments.
(d) The provisions as to discounts relate to the amount paid to the subcontractor without any regard to the Contractor's right to set-off.

The financial and accounting position of work described in this way should be clearly regulated by the contractual terms. In practice, the Contract very often does not do so, nor does it make it clear that the Engineer is entitled to nominate subcontractors to carry out such work. Without such an express power, a nomination may be in breach of contract, since a power to omit work cannot be exercised so as to give the work to another contractor.

20.5 Daywork

Daywork means work which is usually performed on a piecemeal basis and which is not properly capable of being measured according to any method of measurement prescribed by the Contract. It is usually of a minor or incidental nature. Daywork schedules containing rates for labour and equipment are usually listed in the specification, bill of quantities, or schedule of rates which forms part of the Contract. The rates can be expected to be inflated[82] when compared to other rates in the Contract because of the piecemeal nature of the work typically performed as daywork.

Variation work paid according to a daywork schedule will only apply when the Engineer instructs its use. It is clearly in the Contractor's interest to maintain accurate and auditable documents such as signed and authorised labour timesheets, and records of equipment and

81 See *London School Board v Northcroft* (1889) Alfred A Hudson, *Hudson's Fourth Edition Table of Cases* (Sweet & Maxwell, 4th edn 1914 147.
82 *Roe Brickwork Ltd v Wates Construction Ltd* [2013] EWHC 3417 (TCC), [18] per Edwards-Stuart J.

materials used. The Contractor and the Engineer should agree before commencing the performance of dayworks how such records should be established. Too often, in practice, disagreement on the validity or appropriateness of the records occurs long after the work on the Variation has been finished.

Because of the difficulty of controlling daywork costs, the Contract usually contains a requirement for the Contractor to submit daily statements of labour, materials, and equipment used for the approval of the Engineer; this provides the opportunity to resolve any issues whilst the information is fresh and available. For example, the FIDIC rainbow suite requires daily submission of statements of daywork resources used for the Engineer to agree and sign.[83] Procurement of materials or equipment for dayworks not included in a daywork schedule may require quotations to be submitted for the approval of the Engineer.[84] Provision of the daily lists of labour employed and monthly statements of materials and equipment used is usually an important condition precedent to payment.

The Engineer may have complete discretion, subject to arbitration, to order dayworks for additional or substituted work, whether or not there are Contract rates which may apply, and to authorize payment upon a fair and reasonable value where the provision of details of labour, and so on, is impracticable.

A Contractor who has quoted a high rate may gain, and a Contractor who has quoted a low rate may lose by an order for work on a daywork basis, but the Contractor and Employer are aware of this by the daywork rates fixed in the daywork schedule in the Contract.

20.6 Contract price adjustments

Adjustment of the contract price to take account of changes in the cost of labour, materials, transport, and so on, and increases or decreases in cost resulting from changes in legislation of the country where the Site is located is normally provided for in the Contract.

Where the contract price is to be adjusted for changes in the cost of labour, materials, transport, or other costs, such adjustment may be calculated in accordance with an appropriate contract price adjustment formula which is stated in the Contract. Full details should be stated in the Contract, and the relevant indices to be used under the formula in calculating adjustments should be identified. It should be noted that if an adjustment formula is to be used, the Contractor should not be entitled to recover any increased cost which has resulted from its negligence or default. Thus, if the Contractor is in delay in consequence of matters for which it is responsible, it should not be entitled to claim any increase in cost occurring during that period of delay.

In the event that changes in cost result from alteration in the legislation of the country where the Site is located, or in its generally accepted interpretation, the Contract should provide for an adjustment in the price either upwards or downwards. It may be appropriate for the Contractor to take the risk of any changes in legislation, and so on, in its own country in which case the contract price would not be adjusted in consequence of any such changes.

The risk of fluctuations in currency exchange rates should be clearly allocated and provided for where items of plant and equipment are procured from foreign countries.

83 2017 FIDIC rainbow suite sub-clause 13.5; 1999 FIDIC rainbow suite sub-clause 13.6. The Employer signs the Contractor's daily daywork statement under the Silver Book, as there is no Engineer.

84 For example, 2017 FIDIC rainbow suite sub-clause 13.5. The Employer approves the quotation under the Silver Book, as there is no Engineer.

CHAPTER 21

Contract price and payment

CONTENTS

DOI: 10.4324/9781003206873-21

21.1 The contract price

21.1.1 Types of contract

The importance of timely and contractually correct payments to the Contractor has been expressed as follows:

> It is well recognised that progress payments are an integral and important part of construction contracts. They have been described as the 'lifeblood' of the contractor. If the contractor is deprived of the proper progress payments he may be placed in financial difficulties and incur substantial financing costs. However, it has also been pointed out that the position is not all one-way and that the employer too may be relying upon finance in order to perform the contract and that overpayment by the employer may equally cause him loss.[1]

The parties must have an appreciation of the various types of contract and the consequences that flow from the choice of how the **contract price** is arrived at. This forms part of the contracting strategy in which there are three essential requirements:

(i) Incentive – the primary aim is to provide an adequate incentive for efficient performance by the Contractor. This must be reflected by a corresponding incentive for the Employer to provide appropriate information and support timeously.
(ii) Flexibility – the primary aim is to provide the Employer with sufficient flexibility to introduce change which can be anticipated but not defined at the tender stage. An important requirement is that the Contract should provide for systematic and equitable evaluation of such changes.
(iii) Risk Sharing – the primary aim is to allocate all risks between the Employer and the Contractor. The fundamental principle that the particular risk should be allocated to the party best equipped to deal with it should be adhered to, if the best results are to be obtained. This must also take into account the management and control of the effects of such risks that materialise. The Contractor will include a risk contingency sum in its tender as protection against the risks it has been asked to bear.

1 *Secretary of State for Transport v Birse-Farr Joint Venture 1992* (1993) 62 BLR 36 per Hobhouse J.

It is apparent that, generally, Contractor's incentive and Employer's flexibility tend to be incompatible. For example, a lump sum contract imposes maximum incentive on the Contractor but also implies a very high level of constraint on the Employer against introducing change. The converse is true at the other extreme of a cost reimbursable plus percentage fee contract. Consideration of when to use each type of contract should concentrate on circumstances favouring their use rather than particular types of projects. It should not be assumed that the presence of one or more of the circumstances on a project will demand the use of a particular type of contract; other contract strategies may be suitable. For example, an early start to construction can be achieved by a reimbursable contract but also by management contracting, package deals, and two-stage tendering.

The distinction between the method of calculating the contract price in measurement contracts (bill of quantities and schedule of rates), in cost reimbursable contracts, and in target price contracts is of fundamental importance, as the Contractor's right to payment differs radically from the lump sum principle in these types of contracts. Care should be taken not to confuse a 'cost plus' contract with a 'reimbursable' contract, because reimbursement suggests an indemnity for expenditure incurred, whereas a 'cost plus' contract requires not only the reimbursement of a Contractor's cost but also payment of the profit margin on top.[2] The difference between 'cost' and 'profit' is well recognised.[3] It has been suggested that the 'cost plus' contract 'brings the Employer and Contractor together in a unity of interest, in sharp contrast to the adversarial relationship established in the traditional lump sum contract that so often leads to disputes.'[4]

It is necessary that the Engineer be in a position to appreciate the various types of contracts and the consequences that flow from the choice of contract, as well as the specific provisions of the Contract it is administering. For example, the Engineer ought to understand what is included or excluded in the contract price, the variable consequences regarding the Contractor's right to an extension of time or a change of rate arising from differences in quantities which occur on re-measurement, and when payment is to be made.

21.1.2 Contractor's entitlement to payment

If a Contractor's entitlement to payment is conditional upon it obtaining a payment certificate, and before that certificate is issued, the Contractor abandons the Works, the Contractor will not be entitled to payment for the Works it has performed.[5]

Substantial performance means something close to the achievement of practical completion.[6] If the Employer is able to take beneficial occupation of the completed Works and make use of them, the Contractor may be regarded as having substantially performed the Works,[7] and entitled to payment accordingly.

2 Julian Bailey, *Construction Law Vol II* (London Publishing Partnership, 3rd edn 2020) 6.10 footnote 30.

3 See *Petromec Inc v Petroleo Brasileiro SA Petrobras* [2005] EWCA Civ 891 at [91] – [95], per Longmore LJ.

4 Peter Cooper, *Building Relationships: The History of Bovis 1885–2000* (Cassell & Co, 2000) 48.

5 *Cleveland Bridge v UK Ltd v Multiplex Constructions (UK) Ltd* [2010] EWCA Civ 139, [88] – [90] per Sir Anthony May P.

6 *Big Island Contracting (HK) Ltd v Skink Ltd* (1990) 52 BLR 110, 114; *Mariner International Hotels Ltd v Atlas Ltd* [2007] HKCFA 5, [15] – [16] per Bokhary PJ.

7 *Cordon Investments Pty Ltd v Lesdor Properties Pty Ltd* [2010] NSWSC 1073, [169] per McDougall J (affirmed [2012] NSWCA 184).

Where a Contractor abandons the Works without justification under a lump sum contract which is an entire contract, the Contractor is not entitled to payment, even on a *quantum meruit* basis.[8] However, if the Employer has retained materials left by the Contractor on site, the Employer is required to pay for those materials.[9] Also, if the Employer has accepted the Works, and thereby received part or substantially all of what was promised, the Contractor is entitled to the contract price, less an abatement to reflect the shortcomings in the Contractor's work,[10] but is not entitled to be paid on a *quantum meruit*.

If the Employer has paid the Contractor more money than it is properly entitled to be paid, under the mistaken belief that a greater amount was owed to the Contractor than was in fact the case, the Contractor may be required to account to the Employer in restitution for the amount of the overpayment.[11] There must be a causative link between the mistake and payment.[12] However, recovery of any overpayment will usually be affected in practice by a contractual mechanism.[13] Any overpayment in one period is usually regulated by being the subject of an adjustment between the parties in a later payment period, or in the final accounting between the parties.

If an amount is paid as a result of an Adjudicator deciding that an amount is payable pursuant to a construction contract which is established in later proceedings (whether court or arbitration) to be an overpayment, it may be an implied term of the contract, or the contract may be interpreted to mean that the amount overpaid is recoverable.[14] If an overpayment is made in circumstances where the Employer knows or suspects it may be overpaying but the Employer expressly makes the payment on a 'without prejudice' basis, the Employer's reservation of rights will usually be sufficient to preserve its entitlement to reclaim any amount overpaid.[15]

Where there is no express agreement on the basis of a time charge, or rate per hour or per day, with any materials that are required being chargeable as well, but the party who performed the work in question regularly sent invoices calculated on a time charge basis,

---

8 *ISG Construction Ltd v Seevic College* [2014] EWHC 4007 (TCC), [7] per Edwards-Stuart; *Intake Instruments v Transnet Ltd* [2019] ZASCA 79, [44] – [48].

9 *Sumpter v Hedges* [1898] 1 QB 673; *Cleveland Bridge UK Ltd v Multiplex Constructions (UK) Limited* [2010] EWCA Civ 139.

10 *Ho Kwai Chun v Wong King Man* [2014] HKCFI 888, [83] – [91] per DHCJ Burrell; *Jaya Sarana Engineering Pte Ltd v GIB Automation Pte Ltd* [2007] SGHC 49, [38] – [39] per Sundaresh Menon JC; *Tung Ngar Air Condition & Steel Holdings Ltd v Hin Catering Group Ltd* [2017] HKCFI 1703, [133] – [134] per L Chan J.

11 *Dah Chong Hong (Engineering) Ltd v Henry Marble Co Ltd* [2007] HKCFI 200, [18] – [19] per Master Yu; *Mirimskaya v Evans* (2007) 114 Con LR 144, 163 [59] – 164 [64] per DHCJ Richard Fernyhough QC (TCC); *Leighton Contractors Pty Ltd v Public Transport Authority of Western Australia (No 6)* [2008] WASC 193, [335] – [343] per Le Miere J; *JDM Accord Ltd v Secretary of State* (2004) 93 Con LR 133, 182 [136] per HHJ Thornton QC.

12 *Leslie v Farrar Construction Ltd* [2015] EWHC 58 (TCC), [267(6)] per HHJ Stephen Davies (affirmed: [2016] EWCA Civ 1041).

13 *Imperial Chemical Industries Ltd v Merit Merrell Technology Ltd* [2017] EWHC 1763 (TCC), [194] per Fraser J; *Everwarm Ltd v BN Rendering Ltd* [2019] EWHC 3030 (TCC), [115] per DHCJ Nissen QC.

14 *Jim Ennis Construction Ltd v Premier Asphalt Ltd* [2009] EWHC 1906 (TCC), [22] – [25] per HHJ Stephen Davies; *Aspect Contracts (Asbestos) Ltd v Higgins Construction Plc* [2015] UKSC 38, [24] – [25]; *Jim Ennis Construction Ltd v Premier Asphalt Ltd* [2009] EWHC 1906 (TCC), [28] – [29] per HHJ Stephen Davies.

15 *HSM Offshore BV v Aker Offshore Partner Ltd* [2017] EWHC 2979 (TCC), [89] – [96] per Coulson J; *Birmingham City Council v Amey Birmingham Highways Ltd* [2018] EWHC 2875 (QB), [11] – [26] per Stuart-Smith J.

and they were not disputed, it may be inferred that the basis of charging was accepted by the person who requested the work.[16]

21.1.3 Set-off and abatement

Set-off is the deduction of an amount that is owing on a countervailing debt or claim, so as to reduce or extinguish the first liability. The law recognises various categories of set-off, these being grouped into five categories:

(1) Independent set-off,
(2) Transaction set-off,
(3) Contractual set-off,
(4) Current account set-off, and
(5) Insolvency set-off.[17]

Where the respective rights of the parties which are contended to have the effect of negating each other are 'substantially the same,' a right of set-off will exist.[18] If the respective rights of the parties are not 'substantially the same,' a countervailing claim will be incapable of being set-off.[19] Where the two claims arise under different contracts but relate to the same project, a claim under one contract may be closely related to a claim under another if the contract in question is financially interlinked.[20] If the contracts relate to completely different projects,[21] the only connection between them being the common identities of the contracting parties, a transaction set-off will not be permitted because the contracts will not be sufficiently connected.[22]

Judgement is given in the amount of the balance to the party to whom it is owed in cases where a transaction set-off arises.[23] A transaction set-off may be exercised in respect of an unliquidated amount if it is evident and reasonable to conclude that the actual amount of the set-off is likely to be greater than the amount claimed against the party seeking to exercise its right of set-off.[24] A contractual right of set-off has been said to only arise in respect of liquidated claims or debts, and not for unliquidated claims for damages, but there

16 *Clancy Consulting Ltd v Derwent Holdings Ltd* [2010] EWHC 762 (TCC).

17 See Julian Bailey, *Construction Law Vol II* (London Publishing Partnership, 3rd edn 2020) [6.404].

18 *Commissioner of Taxation v Linter Textiles Australia Ltd (in liq)* (2005) CLR 592, [41].

19 *Downsouth Constructions Pty Ltd v Jigsaw Corporate Childcare Australia Pty Ltd* [2007] NSWSC 597, [59] per McDougall J (25 BCL 276); *In re Paraguassu Steam Tramroad Co* (1872) LR 8 Ch App 254, 261 per Lord Selbourne LC.

20 *Hill Corcoran Constructions Pty Ltd v Navarro* [1992] QCA 017; *Popular Homes Ltd v Circuit Developments Ltd* [1979] 2 NZLR 642; *Lemina Pty Ltd v Phillips Construction Co Pty Ltd* (1987) 4 BCL 56 [Sup Ct NSW] per Bryson J; *Pollard Construction Co Ltd v Yung Yat Fan* [1999] HKCFI 632, [19] – [13] per Cheung J; *Geldof Metaalconstructie NV v Simon Carves Ltd* [2010] BLR 401, 413 [46] – [47] per Rix LJ; *Engineering Construction Pte Ltd v Sanchoon Builders Pte Ltd* [2010] SGHC 293, [20] per Quentin Loh J.

21 *Ellis Mechanical Services Ltd v Wates Construction Ltd* (1976) 2 BLR 57, [63] per Lord Denning MR; *Paul Y Construction Co-Ltd v A-G (HK)* [1992] HKCFI 265, [18] – [36] per Kaplan J.

22 *Success Mark Construction Engineering Ltd v Wang On Construction Engineering Ltd* [2000] HKFCI 1165, [11] per Burrell J; *Beck Interiors Ltd v Classic Decorative Finishing Ltd* [2012] EWHC 1956 (TCC), [13] – [15] per Coulson J.

23 *Stringfellow v Blyth* (2001) 83 Con LR 124,129 [24] per Sir Stuart Murray-Smith (CA).

24 *Concrete Equipment Australia (Trading) Pty Ltd v Bonfiglioli Transmission (Aust) Pty Ltd* [2010] NSWSC 393, [24] per Barr AJ; *Engineering Construction Pte Ltd v Sanchoon Builders Pte Ltd* [2010] SGHC 293, [28] per Quentin Loh J.

is authority from the English Court of Appeal that a right to set-off 'all amounts lawfully due' by one party to another includes unliquidated claims.[25] It is permissible for a set-off clause to be drafted so as to permit a party to set-off sums that it reasonably estimates to be due, even if those sums are not yet properly quantified or ascertained.[26]

Set-off against monies otherwise due may be limited or excluded by contract.[27] This limitation or exclusion by the contract will not apply unless the parties used clear words to indicate that it was their intention. There is generally a presumption allowing a set-off where such a right would otherwise exist, unless extinguished or limited by clear agreement.[28] In *Hermcrest plc v G Percy Trentham Ltd* it was held that a clause containing a clear agreement to exclude set-off operated to exclude the Contractor's right of transaction set-off, preventing it from seeking to set-off liquidated damages for delay against money otherwise owing to the subcontractor.[29] In a similar case, the Contractor was required to pay the amount owing to the subcontractor without deduction, but was entitled to pursue its claim against the subcontractor for liquidated damages by way of separate proceedings.[30]

Abatement is the exercise of a right which reduces or extinguishes a claim due to defective work having been performed. It is a common law right. It is not properly characterised as a set-off.[31] A contract may be ineffective to delimit a right of abatement if it only excludes or limits a right of set-off.[32] Where an Employer may also be entitled to reduce the amount that it pays on the basis of any countervailing claim it has for damages for delay, or other breaches of contract, such a deduction is properly characterised as being a set-off rather than an abatement.[33]

21.1.4 Contractor's rights for non-payment

Because a Contractor's obligation to perform work is usually independent of the Employer's obligation to pay for that work, a Contractor does not possess a general right at common law to suspend work if a progress payment is not made when it ought to be made.[34] The

25 *Geldof Metaalconstructie NV v Simon Carves Ltd* [2010] BLR 401.

26 *Watpac Constructions (NSW) Pty Ltd v Austin Corp Pty Ltd* [2010] NSWSC 168, [35] – [41] per McDougall J.

27 *Gilbert-Ash (Northern) Ltd v Modern Engineering (Bristol) Ltd* [1974] AC 689, 722–723 per Lord Salmon; *John Mowlem Construction plc v Secretary of State for Defence* (2001) 82 Con LR 140, 152 [30] – 153 [33] per Forbes J; *Jem Developments Pty Ltd v Hansen Yuncken Pty Ltd* [2006] NSWSC 1378, [28] – [30] per Austin J.

28 *Jia Min Building Construction Pte Ltd v Ann Lee Pte Ltd* [2004] 3 SLR 288, [43] per VK Rajah JC; *Jones v Dalcon Construction Pty Ltd* [2006] WASCA 205, [35] per McLure JA; *Jacobs UK Ltd v Skidmore Owings & Merrill LLP* [2008] EWHC 2847 (TCC), [54] per Coulson J; *Seadrill Management Services Ltd v OAO Gazprom* [2009] EWHC 1530 (Comm), [214] – [218] per Flaux J (appeal dismissed [2010] EWCA Civ 691); *Thomas Construction (Pty) Ltd v Grafton Furniture Manufacturers (Pty) Ltd* (1986) 3 Const LJ 216, 221 (Sth African Supreme Court, Natal Provincial Division) per Nienaber J; *Koh Lin Yee v Terrestrial Pte Ltd* [2015] SGCA 6, [15] – [16].

29 *Hermcrest plc v G Percy Trentham Ltd* (1991) 53 BLR 104.

30 *BWP (Architectural) Ltd v Beaver Building Systems Limited* (1988) 42 BLR 86, 96–97 per HHJ Esyr Lewis QC.

31 *Henriksens Rederi A/S v THZ Rolimex* [1974] 1 QB 233, 252 per Cairns LJ.

32 *Acsim (Southern) Ltd v Danish Contracting and Development Co Ltd* (1989) 47 BLR 55.

33 *Newfoundland Government v Newfoundland Railway Co* (1888) 13 App Cas 199, 212 (PC).

34 *Lim Poh yeoh v TS Ong Construction Pte Ltd* [2016] SGHC 17, [70] per Edmund Leow JC; *Goh Eng Lee Andy v Yeo Jin Kow* [2016] SGHC 110, [50] per Kannan Ramesh JC.

wrongful suspension of the Works by the Contractor may constitute repudiation of the Contract.[35] However, if there has been non-payment of a significant amount properly owing under the Contract, and the non-payment represents a breach of an essential term or serious breach of an innominate term of the Contract, the Contractor may elect to accept the repudiation and terminate the Contract, in this way bringing to an end the Contractor's obligation to perform the Works.[36]

If the Employer insists upon an incorrect interpretation of the Contract, for example, that liquidated damages are payable, when in fact there was no agreement as to the payment of liquidated damages, this may be characterised as repudiatory conduct on the part of the Employer.[37]

The Contractor is not entitled to reduce its labour force or other resources on the project ('go slow') where it has not been paid when it ought to have been paid, and the terms of the Contract require the Contractor to maintain reasonable progress.[38]

In principle, the common law allows the parties to a construction contract to agree upon whatever payment arrangements they want both in regard to the amount and the method of payment.[39] The parties may choose to use various bases for determining the remuneration of the Contractor, for example, the parties may agree that some parts of the contract price are to be paid on a 'lump sum' basis, while others are to be paid on a 'cost plus' basis.[40]

However, substantial inroads into this freedom of contract have been made in England, all Australian States and mainland Territories, New Zealand, Singapore, Malaysia, Isle of Man, Ireland, Ontario, and elsewhere by the enactment of *Statutory Adjudication* statutes aimed at mandating a right to periodic payment in regulated construction contracts and creating a fast track adjudication procedure for parties who believe that they have not been paid what is due to them. These statutes are not uniform, and care should be taken to ensure that the correct statute and case-law is applied, and to determine the commercial advisability of seeking such statutory protection.[41]

It should always be remembered that there may be avenues outside the Contract through which money may become due to the Contractor, for example, by way of damages, or statute.

---

35 *De Beers UK Ltd v Atos Origin IT Services UK Ltd* [2010] EWHC 3276 (TCC), [229] – [236] per Edwards-Stuart J.

36 *Wui Fu Development Co Ltd v Tak Yuen Construction Co Ltd* [1999] HKCFI 93; *CJ Elvin Building Services Ltd v Noble* [2003] EWHC 837 (TCC), [89] – [91] per Mr Recorder Akenhead QC.

37 *Len Lichtnauer Developments Pty Ltd v James Trowse Constructions Pty Ltd* [2005] QCA 214, [15] per McPherson JA (21 BCL 430). See D Jones, 'Construction Contractors: The Right to Stop Work' (Part 1) (1992) *International Construction Law Review* 310; D Jones, 'Construction Contractors: The Right to Stop Work (Part 2)' (1992) *International Construction Law Review* 433.

38 *Supamarl Ltd v Federated Homes Ltd* (1981) 9 Con LR 25, 28 per HHJ Hawser QC; *William Clark Partnership Ltd v Dock St PCT Ltd* [2015] EWHC 2923 (TCC), [2.51] per HHJ Stephen Davies; *Chun Wo Building Construction Ltd v Metta Resources Ltd* [2016] HKCFI 1357, [135] – [136] per Anthony Chan J.

39 In Romania public works contracts may not be entered into on a lump sum basis: L Klee & C A Teodorescu, 'Romanian Experience in FIDIC Forms in Road and Bridge Construction' (2013) *International Construction Law Review* 432, 435–436.

40 *Vassallo Constructions Pty Ltd v Andergrove Lakes Pty* Ltd [2014] FCA 862, [14] per Dowsett J.

41 See ¶28.9 for a more detailed discussion of statutory adjudication.

21.1.5 Lump sum contracts

Lump sum contracts provide for payment of a stipulated amount for the completion of specified Works (usually described by reference to an end result) to the satisfaction of the Employer by a certain date. Use of this type of contract implies that design is complete and final. In a lump sum contract, the Contractor is not entitled to the payment of any amount for the Works other than the amount contemplated by the Contract (unless it is a claim for breach of contract or other act by the Employer giving rise to a claim for damages or other relief).

Fixed price contracts are the most common form of lump sum contracts and provide for the payment of an agreed amount with provision for adjustment for Variations to the scope of work or scope of performance or any extra costs incurred as a result of delays but without adjustment for fluctuations in currencies or prices of equipment, labour, or materials. Commentary on contract Variations and adjustments necessitated by a change in the scope of the contract Works are discussed in Chapter 20. Areas of exposure to cost and time overrun in a lump sum contract should be clearly identified and understood.

In a pure lump sum contract the agreement for the Completion of the Works is for the construction of a whole body of work (for example, a road, a process plant, or an offshore platform) or for a package deal in which the Contractor is responsible for both detailed design and construction, for a lump sum price. It has been held by the courts that a lump sum price is an undertaking to accomplish a definite result for a fixed sum of money.[42] The price will not be altered unless there is some express contract provision such as a currency or price fluctuations clause, or unless the Contract Works have been varied or changed in some way on the order of the Employer or Engineer.[43] Subject to additional amounts that the Contractor is entitled to under the Contract (for example, as the result of Variations), the Contractor is only entitled to the lump sum set out in the Contract, regardless of how difficult or expensive it subsequently becomes to accomplish the result for the lump sum amount. On the other hand, if physical and other contingencies that the Contractor anticipated and priced for in its 'lump sum' do not materialise, the full amount of the lump sum price remains due to the Contractor.[44]

In *Sharpe v San Paulo Railway*[45] the Contractor entered into a pure lump sum contract to lay the San Paulo Railway from terminus A to terminus B. As a result of errors in the Engineer's plan, almost twice the quantities of excavation originally estimated were required to complete the line. The court held that the Contractor was entitled to no extra payment beyond the lump sum price in its tender. In such a contract no work indispensably necessary to achieve the result is an extra. The 'lump sum' is not to be reduced to take account of any overlap or double counting under any implied term.[46]

In *Williams v Fitzmaurice*,[47] the Contractor entered into a lump sum contract to build a house. Flooring was omitted from the specifications. The court held that the Contractor

42 *Thorn v the Mayor and Commonalty of London* (1876) 1 App Cas 120.
43 See *Commissioner for Main Roads v Reed and Stuart* (1975) 48 ALJR 641.
44 *Atkins Ltd v Secretary of State for Transport* [2013] BLR 193 at 207 [33] per Akenhead J.
45 (1873) LR 8 Ch App 597.
46 *Durian Pty Ltd v Penrith CC* (1991) 10 Const LJ 129 at 135–136, per Mahoney JA [NSWCA] (9 BCL 199).
47 (1858) 177 RR 1004.

was obliged to put in the flooring without extra payment as it was clearly indispensably necessary to complete the house.

In *Peters v Quebec Harbour Commissioners*[48] and in *Ibmac v Marshall Homes Ltd*,[49] the court held that, in a pure lump sum contract, the contract price will be altered only where the plans, and so on, are varied by the Employer who decides that a change is preferable, although not absolutely necessary, and not where the change is necessary to complete the project.

A Contractor who agrees to carry out work under a pure lump sum contract will be considered simply to have taken a voluntary commercial risk regarding the costs of that work and will be bound by the lump sum agreed in the Contract. If an item in a bill of quantities contract includes a lump sum against an item in the bill, the lump sum will be payable regardless of whether the actual quantity of work is greater or less than the indicative or approximate amount unless the Contract indicates otherwise.[50]

Where the ordinary features of a lump sum contract are altered by making the quantities in the bill of quantities part of the description of the work to be done, then the Contractor may be entitled not only to its lump sum for carrying out the quantities of work set out in the bill, but also to extra payment for any work carried out beyond that. However, since the courts have tended to lean towards the pure lump sum principle, this may be insufficient to incorporate the quantities into the Contract to create a measurement or schedule of quantities contract. Such incorporation may create a measurement contract, but this is not a conclusive test. In *Patman & Fotheringham Ltd v Pilditch*,[51] it was held with 'considerable doubt,' that such incorporation created a measurement contract. Accordingly, where quantities are incorporated as a description of the quantity of the work to be carried out for the contract price, it is advisable to state it explicitly in the definition of the contract price.

A lump sum contract may contain a **schedule of rates** or **schedule of prices**, a schedule in the Contract of the rates to be charged by the Contractor for specified labour, equipment, or material in the event that its use is directed by the Engineer. The Contract should make clear that any such document incorporated into a lump sum contract showing units of construction and prices (sometimes confusingly called a schedule of quantities) exists only for the purpose of valuing any Variations required during the execution of the Contract and has no legal effect beyond its use in the valuation of such Variations. It is sometimes used as a basis for interim payments. Such schedules may not even perform these functions but may simply be used as a guide issued to contractors at the tendering stage by the Employer's advisers so as to reduce the time and expense of the estimating process required to arrive at the lump sum. Such schedules do not form part of the Contract, and the Contract remains essentially a lump sum contract.

At common law, where a lump sum contract is an entire contract, the Contractor's entitlement to payment will not accrue until all of the Contractor's Works have been

48 (1891) 19 SCR 685 (Canada).

49 (Estates Gazette 20 April 1968) 208 EG 851.

50 *Hung Wan Construction Co Ltd v Hong Kong Kong Housing Authority* [2010] HKCFI 650, [19] per Saunders J.

51 Alfred A Hudson, *Hudson's Fourth Edition Table of Cases* (Sweet & Maxwell, 4th edn 1914) 368. See also *Ibmac v Marshall (Homes) Ltd* (1968) 208 EG 851.

completed.[52] Where a lump sum contract provides for payments in instalments, these may be based on the value of work it has performed, whether by measurement, completion of certain milestones, or other means.[53] Although the Contract is awarded on the basis of a single lump sum price, in all but the smallest of contracts it is likely that the payment of a proportion of this sum will be made to the Contractor on completion of each of a number of different stages of the Works.

Clearly an Employer (and the project financier) who obtains a lump sum tender fixes a contract price for work in order to know what its financial commitment is, and any relaxation of these rules would destroy the whole object of obtaining such a tender. The courts have held that in inviting a tender for a lump sum price there is no implied guarantee by the Employer that the plans, bills of quantities, or specifications supplied to Tenderers are accurate, or that the work can be carried out in accordance with them, for the quantities in the bills of quantities do not form part of the Contract nor do they form part of the description of the work to be done.

In *Thorn v the Mayor and Commonalty of London*,[54] foundations were to be put in with caissons according to plans to build Blackfriar's Bridge. The Contractors found this impossible. They eventually abandoned the attempt and completed the bridge in accordance with altered plans. The court held that while they were entitled to the contract payments for the original work actually completed and, under the particular form of contract, to extra payments for the work on the new plans, they were not entitled to damages for the added expense and delay in trying to do the original work.[55]

It is essential for the Contractor that the Works can be precisely estimated in advance, since, after carefully analysing the specification and the drawings, it must be able to ascertain all the various construction processes and the expenditure required. However, in putting forward plans, specifications, and a bill of quantities with the invitation to tender a lump sum price, the Employer is merely putting forward the estimate of an engineer as to how the required result may be achieved – it is not, without more, guaranteeing that the engineer is right. The Employer will, however, be liable if the plans, quantities, and so on, are fraudulent – that is, if it or the engineer puts them forward knowing they are incorrect, or does so recklessly, not caring whether they are correct or not; or if it represents or warrants that they are correct when they are not.

In Australia, the Employer will also be liable under the provisions of the *Australian Consumer Law* if its representations constitute misleading or deceptive conduct. In *Abigroup Contractors Pty Limited v Sydney Catchment Authority (No. 3)*[56] the Contractor entered into a fixed-price contract to construct the spillway for a dam, following a

52 *Sumpter v Hedges* [1898] 1 QB 673, 674 per AL Smith LJ; *Ruttle Plant Hire Ltd v Secretary of State for Environment Food & Rural Affairs* [2009] BLR 301, 310 [66] – 311[69] per Jacob LJ.

53 *Oceania Football Confederation Inc v Engineering Solutions & Systems Ltd* [2019] NZHC 1439, [170]; *Woo & Co Ltd* [2017] HKCFI 421, [20] – [28] per Mimmie Chan J.

54 (1876) 1 App Cas 120.

55 See also *McDonald v Workington Corporation* 1892 MR 230 (referred to in Alfred A Hudson, *Hudson's Fourth Edition Table of Cases* (Sweet & Maxwell, 4th edn 1914) 228), where the Contractor received no extra payment for unexpected work due to water in the soil; and *In re Baldisaro & MacGregor Ltd & the Queen in Right of Ontario* 48 DLR (3d) 517, where the Contractor obtained no relief for an unexpected high water level in the soil.

56 [2006] NSWCA 282. See Section 18 of the *Australian Consumer Law* (Schedule 2 of the *Competition and Consumer Act 2010* (Cth)).

tender process. The Employer did not disclose to the Contractor a drawing it had in its possession showing the rock level to be substantially lower than that indicated in its specifications. The Contractor claimed that the substantial additional excavation work it carried out and the consequent financial loss was caused by the Employer's misleading and deceptive conduct in not disclosing the relevant drawing at the tender stage. The Court of Appeal held that the Contractor was entitled to recover the substantial financial loss (in the range $4.5m- $7.5m) it had suffered from the misleading and deceptive conduct in breach of the *Trade Practices Act* (the previous legislation to the *Australian Consumer Law*), irrespective of whether or not it had made a loss on the contract overall.

If an Employer and Contractor enter into a construction contract without specifying the contract price, the Contractor will generally be entitled to reasonable remuneration in respect of the Completion of the Works, on the basis of an implied term.

With respect to the Contractor's performance obligations under a lump sum contract, it is worth noting that, in the absence of contract terms to the contrary, the Contractor tenders on the basis of a commercially bargained price by which it anticipates that it will be provided the opportunity to perform the entire Works in return for the contract price.[57]

21.1.6 Measurement contracts

Measurement or remeasurement contracts, also known as 'measure and value' contracts, involve any quantities reflected in the contract being provisional in nature; the final quantities of work performed by the Contractor are ascertained or 'measured,'[58] and the Contractor is paid at pre-agreed rates and prices for the work based on those measurements. The final cost of the Works may be greater than or less than the indicative contract price, depending upon the quantity of work actually performed.

Where it is impossible to know in advance what the Works will involve, the sum tendered by a contractor for a pure lump sum form of contract will allow for contingencies in the scope of work. The more ill-defined the scope of work, the higher those contingencies are likely to be. Marine construction and below ground work such as tunnelling and foundations may be particularly problematic if inadequate geotechnical investigation has been carried out. In such a case it may be in the Employer's own interest to use a **measurement contract** in which the Contractor is paid for the work it performs, based on measurement of the actual quantities of each different element of construction, applied to pre-agreed rates in the Contract. A measurement contract may use a (re-measured) bill of quantities which forms part of the Contract with a schedule of rates and prices, or where the precise volume of work to be undertaken by the Contractor is unknown, and the Contractor is unable to provide a fixed-price tender for the work,[59] a schedule of rates. The Employer then has the ability to direct the Contractor to perform work on a piecemeal basis as required from time to time.[60] The Employer should be aware that the total tendered figure in a schedule

57 Note *Carr v Berriman* Pty Ltd (1974) 131 CLR 378 where the Contractor, 'as successful tenderer, should have the opportunity of performing the works.' See ¶20.1.7 Negative Variations – the omission of Works on this point.

58 *Chan Chi Lam v Lam Woo & Co Ltd* [2017] HKCFI 421, [20] – [28] per Mimmie Chan J.

59 *Arcos Industries Pty Ltd v Electricity Commission of NSW* [1973] 2 NSWLR 186, 193 per Jacobs P; *In the matter of an application by Queensland Electricity Commission* (1991) 10 BCL 143 [Sup Ct Qld per Dowsett J.

60 *AAB Engineering & Inspection Services Pty Ltd v Brunel Energy Pty Ltd* [2004] WASC 124.

of quantities or schedule of rates contract is only an estimate. The Employer's attention should also be drawn to those circumstances where it may become liable for unanticipated extra payment, and where the date for Completion may be extended.

Alternatively, in a **cost reimbursable** contract (sometimes referred to as **cost plus**), the Contractor is reimbursed for the labour, materials, and equipment it uses on the Works, plus a margin for overheads and profit (if the relevant Contract definition provides for it). If such a measurement contract is used instead of a lump sum contract, the Employer will not pay for contingencies which do not materialize. In addition to having to provide invoices received from suppliers and subcontractors, the Contractor's records are often to be made available for inspection by the Employer on an 'open book' basis.[61] Costs which the Contractor seeks to recover must be reasonably and properly incurred.[62] Cost reimbursable contracts often require that the costs incurred by a Contractor as a result of its default, or of the default of its subcontractors or suppliers, are not recoverable costs.[63] Cost reimbursable contracts may also be qualified so as to limit the Contractor's total remuneration to a certain price, sometimes referred to as a 'guaranteed maximum price.'[64]

Despite the likelihood of lower overall contract prices in such situations, project financiers tend to prefer lump sum contracts, in the belief that they provide less risk of cost blowouts. Measurement contracts are not necessarily riskier, or even undesirable, when compared to lump sum contracts.[65]

21.1.7 Bill of quantities contracts

Bill of quantities contracts are now used predominantly in both the building and civil engineering industries and are normally used where the nature and extent of the work can be assessed fairly accurately, for example, road construction or bridge building. In these contracts the Employer's advisers have themselves analysed and assessed the drawings and specification, have broken down the entire project into its constituent trades and processes, and have then stated, directly by calculation from the drawings where possible or by estimation where not, approximate quantities for each construction process. When tendering, the Contractors are required to price the individual items in the bills of quantities, which are then grossed up to produce the total tender sum. The priced bill or schedule of quantities document usually fulfils a number of quite separate contractual functions, namely:

- (i) It forms part of the Contract.
- (ii) It indicates to Tenderers the nature and extent of the Works to be done with some precision.

61 *Secretary of State for Defence v Turner Estate Solutions Ltd* [2015] EWHC 1150 (TCC), [26] per Coulson J; *Grocon Constructors (Victoria) Pty Ltd v APN DF2 Project 2 Pty Ltd* [2015] VSCA 190.

62 *D&Z Constructions Pty Ltd v IHI Corporation* [2013] WASC 265, [70] – [73] per Martin CJ; *Prince Albert Pulp Co Ltd v Foundation Co of Canada Ltd* [1977] 1 SCR 200.

63 *Network Rail Infrastructure Ltd v ABC Electrification Ltd* [2019] EWHC 1769 (TCC).

64 See D W M Chan, A P C Chan, P T I Lam & J H L Chan, 'Exploring the Key Risks and Risk Mitigation Measures for Guaranteed Maximum Price and Target Cost Contracts in Construction' (2010) 26 *Construction Law Journal* 364; *AMEC Group Limited v Secretary of State for Defence* [2013] EWHC 110 (TCC).

65 *Bing Integrated Construction Pte Ltd v Eco Special Waste Management Pte Ltd* [2010] SGHC 310,[45] -[46] per Chan Seng Onn J.

(iii) It forms the basis for determining new rates where the existing rates are no longer applicable.
(iv) It is used as a basis for assessing interim payments.
(v) It is the exact measure of the work undertaken for the tender price, which is adjusted to become the contract price once the work is complete, and the actual quantities known.
(vi) It can, to a degree, indicate the composition of the tender to persons examining it on behalf of the Employer.
(vii) It provides a basis for comparing and adjudicating tenders.
(viii) The works programme, for execution of the Works, is compiled on the basis of the estimated quantities.
(ix) 'Extra' or 'additional' work is determined with reference to these quantities.[66]

If there are no Variations and the estimated quantities remain unchanged, the Contractor will be paid the tender sum. However, all quantities are remeasured during the course of the Contract, valued at the tendered rates or adjusted rates, and the amended tender sum accordingly then becomes the contract price.

The ultimate quantities can differ from the original contract quantities in two ways. Firstly, while the standard methods of measurement for measuring quantities may enable them to be calculated with precision from the drawings and specifications without any need for physical measurement on Site, the precise quantities of some work items cannot be the subject of exact calculation beforehand and will often need physical measurement. For example, the removal of soft or unsatisfactory material from excavations and the substitution of imported fill will depend upon ascertaining the suitability of the subsoil after excavation has taken place and on physical measurement or estimation of the quantities of unsuitable material ultimately replaced. Secondly, separate prices may be included for excavation in rock where found, which obviously cannot be determined precisely beforehand. This type of difference in quantities may occur in civil engineering contracts or in the engineering parts of building contracts, for example, excavation.

It is important to note that the actual quantity of work performed by the Contractor is likely to differ from the estimate of quantities indicated in the bill of quantities. A Variation instruction is not required in respect of those different quantities, with the exception of work that is different from that in the Contractor's original scope of work.[67]

Bills of quantities greatly reduce the cost of tendering and provide a more meticulous and accurate basis for comparing tenders and valuing Variations and interim payments.

21.1.8 Schedule of rates contracts

Where the Contractor is unable to provide a fixed price tender for the Work because the precise volume of work to be undertaken is unknown at the time of tendering, a schedule of rates contract may be used, in which the Contractor is paid a particular rate for certain

---

66 I N Duncan-Wallace, *Hudson's Building and Engineering Contracts* (Sweet & Maxwell, 10th edn 1979) 200.

67 *Chak Chiu Hung v Shiu Lock Hing* [1910] HKLR 242, 246 per Piggott CJ.

itemised activities, which allow the Contractor to be paid for the volume of work it performs.[68]

In a schedule of rates contract, the Contractor undertakes to do any or all of a number of described construction processes, involving the provision of construction equipment, work, and the supply of materials, at quoted prices per unit. A schedule of rates is used in repetitive work and is frequently used in contracts for the erection of process plants.

The rates in a schedule of rates contract may be adjusted over the course of a project in question, to reflect changes in cost,[69] or where a Variation order has been issued by the Engineer, or where the tender sum has been exceeded by a specified percentage. On the other hand, the Contract may stipulate that the rates are deemed to be inclusive of the cost of performing the items of work, even if unanticipated events occur rendering them more costly.[70] Where bills of quantities are used with this type of contract, they amount in substance to no more than a form of schedule of rates and often do not form part of the contract itself.

In such contracts there is, in principle, neither a stated total contract price nor any variation of the Contract Works as such, except where some construction process, method, or working condition different from that tendered for is ordered. The instructions given by the Engineer from time to time, or any drawings or specifications supplied by it, merely constitute the identification of the precise extent of the contract work and ultimately of the contract price.[71]

There are significant differences between a bill of quantities contract and a schedule of rates contract. In a bill of quantities contract the initial bill of quantities is prepared by a quantity surveyor based on measuring the quantities of all the individual discrete items of work identifiable from the drawings, usually prepared according to a standard method of measurement. When the Works are completed, the actual quantities installed are re-measured by a quantity surveyor, often from as-built drawings. In a schedule of rates contract, the Contract has rates for the itemised activities listed in the schedule of rates, perhaps without any estimate of the likely quantities. These activity rates are typically for an all-inclusive item of work which in a bill of quantities would encompass a number of individual quantities. For example, in a tunnel it may be known that five different types of material may be encountered, each requiring different types of support. A schedule of rates would itemise each of these support types for Tenderers to price at a rate per metre installed. The Contractor would ultimately be paid for the number of metres of each type of support installed in accordance with the schedule of rates, as documented in the construction records and readily verified. If a bill of quantities contract was used in this situation, there would be individual quantities in the bills of quantities for discrete activities, such as excavation in each type of rock, supply and placing of in-situ concrete,

68 See *Arcos Industries Pty Ltd v Electricity Commission of NSW* [1973] 2 NSWLR 186, 193 per Jacobs P; *ABB Engineering & Inspection Services Pty Ltd v Brunel Energy Pty Ltd* [2004] WASC 124.

69 *Simms Construction Ltd v GR Homes* Ltd [2012] NIQB 73.

70 See *Colas Ltd v Transport for London* [2018] EWHC 831 (TCC), [77]-[86] per O'Farrell J.

71 See *Arcos Industries v Electricity Supply Commission of New South Wales* (1973) 2 NSWLR 186; *Grinaker Construction (Tvl) Pty Ltd v Transvaal Provincial Administration* 1982 (1) SA 78 A; *Minister of Public Works v WJM Construction Co (Pty) Ltd* 1983 (3) SA 78 (A) in which a careful study of the contractual provisions found that the contract was a schedule of rates contract. See also *Coryell & others v DuBois Borough* 75 Atlantic Reporter 25.

fabrication and fixing of steel supports, and so on. The ultimate payment to the Contractor would require remeasurement of each of the quantities actually installed.

A widely held misconception is that a lump sum contract is preferable to a schedule of rates contract, because the former provides certainty as to price, whereas the latter does not. A lump sum contract is usually liable to adjustment for a number of reasons, including statutory intervention. The contract price in most lump sum contracts contains a significant contingency for increases in quantities estimated by the Contractor, whereas in a schedule of rates contract, the Contractor is paid for the actual quantities of work performed. In addition to this, the Contractor is likely to price for risks in a lump sum contract which may never eventuate.[72]

21.1.9 Cost reimbursable contracts

A cost reimbursable contract is used when the requirements of the Employer are vague or when it is desirable for the design to proceed concurrently with construction. Such contracts are also used when the Employer wishes to be directly involved in the management of the Contract, or to reduce the financial risk to the Contractor. An agreed fixed fee to cover overheads and profit is the most prudent form of remunerating the Contractor. However, it is not unknown for the Contractor to be reimbursed for all costs incurred during the fulfilment of the Contract, plus a fee defined as a percentage of the agreed actual cost to cover overheads and profit. The latter of course provides no incentive to the Contractor to limit the cost. Both parties may suffer from lack of motivation unless the Employer establishes effective controls, preferably by the operation of a joint planning and cost control team.

21.1.10 Target price contracts

An Employer may introduce additional incentives into a contract by offering the Contractor bonus payment for the achievement of some previously defined target in terms of time, cost, or performance. Time or performance targets may be set in any type of contract. Thus, a Contractor may earn a bonus for timely or early completion of the whole or some section of the Works in addition to the normal contractual payment related to work completed. The achievement of key intermediate completion dates is particularly important in projects which involve a number of different contractors in sequential installation and commissioning of process or manufacturing plant. A series of increasing bonuses tied to a sequence of key dates has been found to be a particularly successful form of incentive. Clearly, the target and bonus/penalty will be selected to encourage the Contractor to achieve the Employer's dominant objective. In some cases, the incentive will be related to a sliding scale of achievement, that is, if the Contractor misses the target by a small amount it will earn a portion of the bonus. In other situations, such as the fabrication of marine installations where the Employer may have to wait many months for installation should the

72 See Philip Loots & Dr Donald Charrett, 'Reconsidering Procurement Criteria and Procedures for Major Infrastructure Projects: Why the Use of "Price" as the Determining Factor in Construction Procurement Decisions is Wrong' (2017) *International Construction Law Review* 67; Philip Loots, 'Construction of Major Infrastructure Projects in the Energy Sector: Controlling Spiralling Development Costs' (2013) *AMPLA Yearbook* 173.

'weather window' be missed, where the processing of a crop is involved as in a sugar mill, or where tax incentives are involved, the bonus may be lost completely in the event of the target date not being achieved.

Cost targets may be introduced into cost reimbursable contracts to encourage efficient and economic working, something that is not always achieved in a simple cost plus contract. There are many types of incentive mechanism, the simplest being that which, in addition to the reimbursement of actual cost plus a percentage fee, the Contractor will be paid a share of any saving between the target and the actual cost, while the fee will be reduced should the actual cost exceed the target.

The administration of a target contract is more complex than in any other type of contract as the Employer or the Engineer is involved in the audit of actual cost and in the evaluation and/ or adjustment of the target. It is also desirable for the Employer or the Engineer to be involved in the planning of the Works and in the approval of the resources to be employed by the Contractor. One of the benefits frequently derived from this type of contract is the consequent focus, unity of purpose, and harmony generated between the parties. There are many examples of the successful use of such contracts for work involving exceptional risk or uncertainty, or where there is a particular benefit to the Employer to be gained by direct involvement in contract management, in the early appointment of the Contractor, and/or early completion of the project. It is important to note that, in any target contract the incentive must be sufficient to generate the desired motivation and that it is essential that the target figure tendered by the Contractor should be realistic and not depressed due to market forces. If the incentive is to be maintained, the target cost must be adjusted for inflation and for any substantial Variations or changes introduced by the Employer.

21.1.11 Mechanical and electrical plant contracts

Conditions of contract for electrical and mechanical work are usually based on a lump sum contract model and, in general, there is no necessity for quantities supplied to be measured. The terms of payment of the lump sum will generally be stated in the Contract. Whilst these are negotiable, it will be sensible at the tender stage for the Employer to specify its preferred terms. These may include an advance payment against an advance payment guarantee, progress payment during manufacture, payment on due delivery to Site or upon shipment, monthly payments as the work on Site proceeds, amounts due on taking over, retentions if any, and so on. Payments that are due on the achievement of such identified discrete points in the progress of the Works at which certain identified activities have been completed are commonly referred to as **milestone payments**.

Alternatively, Contractors may be informed that payments will be made from a line of credit made available to the Employer, in which case the terms of payment will depend upon the detailed provisions of the terms of the credit or other financing agreement and may involve valuation and certification at regular intervals by a third party acceptable to the lender.

In some circumstances, depending upon the nature of the plant and the work or installation, it may be appropriate that some part of the contract price should be established by the application of rates and/or prices specified in the Contract to measured quantities. Where such measurement is required, contractual provisions relating to the method of measurement to be applied should be included.

21.1.12 Provisional sums and prime cost items

Where the work is only to be performed should the Contractor be instructed to perform it, and is in the nature of a contingency,[73] provisional sums are used. Often provisional sums are used for work that is not sufficiently defined at the time of tender[74] to enable the Contractor to price it accurately, and the provisional sum will usually be adjusted to reflect the cost or value of the actual work performed.[75] Amounts are identified as such in a Contract against particular items of work, and only then will the Contractor become entitled to payment for the work.[76] Provisional sums may be valued by way of measurement or by way of a fixed price.

Prime cost items are used when there is an agreement to pay the Contractor's cost of performing the required works, plus a profit margin. The difference between a prime cost item and a provisional sum item is that generally under a prime cost item, the actual cost of materials is paid, whereas in a provisional sum item, the amount paid includes both the cost of materials and the cost of labour associated with performing work with those materials.[77] However, there is no settled meaning for prime cost, and it may include the actual cost of labour and materials. The precise wording of the Contract will determine the specific meaning of either term.

Provisional sums and prime cost items are discussed in more detail in ¶20.4.

21.1.13 Cost

The term 'cost' is often referred to in conditions of contract. It should be stated in the definitions section of the conditions of contract that, where any such reference is made, **cost** means only actual costs properly incurred plus allowable overhead charges, unless an entitlement to profit is expressly incorporated in the provision for the payment of 'costs.'

It was held in *Jameson Construction v Lacombe & NW Railway Co*,[78] that if a contractor is specifically to do work on a cost plus basis (or presumably to be paid 'expenses' or 'costs') the Contractor may recover only reasonable costs, but the burden is on the Employer to show that costs incurred were not reasonable.[79]

21.1.14 Contractor's overhead and profit

The Contractor may, depending on the terms of the Contract, be entitled to recover overhead and profit on top of extra costs that it may have incurred under certain of the General

73 *Multiplex Construction (UK) Ltd v Cleveland Bridge UK Ltd (No 6)* [2008] EWHC 2220 (TCC) at [1017], per Jackson J, appeal allowed on other grounds [2010] EWCA Civ 139.

74 *Plymouth & South-West Co-operative Society Ltd v Architecture, Structure and Management Ltd* [2006] EWHC 5 (TCC), [111] per HHJ Thornton QC; *Lloyds Bank plc v McBains Cooper Consulting Ltd* [2015] EWHC 2372 (TCC), [30 (note 2)] per Edwards-Stuart J.

75 *Midland Expressway Ltd v Carillion Construction Ltd* [2005] EWHC 2810 (TCC), [435] – [438] per May LJ.

76 *Amec Building Ltd v Cadmus Investments Co Ltd* (1996) 51 Con LR 105, 125–126 per Mr Recorder Kallipetis QC.

77 *Wabbits Pty Ltd v Godfrey* [2009] NSWSC 1299, [27] – [28] per Ward J.

78 (1926) 2 DLR 653.

79 See also *Title Guarantee and Trust Co v Pam* 155 NY Sup 333 and *Pattie Laboratories v Du Point Film Manufacturing* Co 3 FRD.

Conditions, for example, where it performs Variations under the Contract. The amount of the overhead and profit on-cost may be the subject of negotiations between Employer and Contractor, but in order that tenders from different Tenderers may be evaluated on an equal footing, it is desirable that the Employer insert an appropriate percentage at the tender stage. This also dispenses with the necessity of proof of overheads later on. The valuation of additional costs under the Contract may be defined as including overheads but excluding profit, and the percentage applicable should reflect this.

Overhead in this context usually refers to 'corporate' overhead or 'head office' overhead, that is, the expenses involved in maintaining a corporate head office with staff that manage the contractor's business, such as employing and paying staff and labour, submitting tenders for future work, invoicing for work done, and so on. As discussed in ¶19.6, site overheads are usually recovered under the Preliminaries item in a bill of quantities.

In the event of an extended suspension of the Works, recovery of corporate overhead not funded by work on Site can be problematic, as it is not amenable to a percentage on-cost.[80] An agreed daily rate in the Contract for delay to the Contractor's Works caused by the Employer will avoid the expense of subsequently proving both corporate and site overheads.

21.1.15 Terms of payment

Most construction contracts contain express provisions for interim payment. It is said that 'cash flow is the lifeblood of the construction industry.' Two of the most common forms of interim payment are payments of stipulated sums on completion of various defined stages of work (stage payments), or regular periodical payments based on interim valuation of work done to date (periodical valuation payments).

In civil engineering contracts, the work is usually measured monthly and paid for within a specified time of the Engineer's payment certificate. It will be sensible for the Employer to set out its proposed terms in its tender documents, for example, the amount of any down payment, the amount to be paid during the course of manufacture, the amount to be paid on shipment, monthly payment for work on Site, on commissioning, startup, and retention. A schedule annexed to the Contract is a suitable method of defining such agreed terms.

In process plant works there may be no Engineer to provide such a payment certificate, and payment may be made against the achievement of milestones. A Contractor should be aware that a delay affecting one or more milestones can have a devastating effect on its cash-flow because they have expended large amounts towards the achievement of those milestones but will not be eligible for payment until each milestone is achieved.

It is important to note that the provisions of the *Security of Payment* legislation in the relevant jurisdiction may override the common law, or even the provisions of the Contract itself in some circumstances. This legislation, enacted in a number of jurisdictions, ensures that any person who carries out construction work or who supplies related goods and services under a construction contract of a defined type has a statutory entitlement

80 Atkin Chambers, *Hudson's Building and Engineering Contracts* (Sweet & Maxwell, 12th edn 2010) 6–73.

to receive progress payments in relation to that work or those goods and services. The legislation establishes a procedure by which a party can claim a progress payment and seek rapid adjudication of any dispute that arises. Where the scope of construction work falls within the statutory definition, the timeframes and form of payment claims and certificates must comply with the provisions of the relevant *Act*. The statutory rights provided by the legislation cannot be contracted out of, and therefore apply despite contractual terms to the contrary. This is discussed further in ¶28.9.2.

21.1.16 Escalation of costs

If the contract price is not subject to adjustment for changes in the Contractor's costs, this should be stated in the Contract documents. If the contract price is subject to adjustment, then the relevant method of adjustment should be stated in a schedule annexed to the Contract and which forms part of the Contract.

Escalation (rise and fall, or fluctuation or 'up and down') clauses and formulae must be treated with caution as they can be arbitrary and do not always produce the desired effect. There is no legal requirement that a rise and fall clause actually reflects the impact of the change in costs to the Contractor.[81] The intention is that the Contractor be paid an increased sum should certain of the Contractor's costs increase from a fixed base date.[82] In the absence of a rise and fall provision, the Contractor takes the risk that rises in the costs of plant, labour, and materials will reduce the profitability of the project or even cause the Contractor to make a loss.[83]

Abnormal fluctuations in prices or cost do not normally have a frustrating effect upon a contract. However, in many civil law jurisdictions, should a Contractor's costs escalate substantially beyond what it could have allowed for in its tender, the Contractor may be entitled to seek an adjustment of the contract price.[84] Escalation in contract prices may even be written into statute,[85] or, on the other hand, may be, subject to limited exceptions, illegal.[86]

The intention of an escalation clause is to ensure that the Contractor is paid the current market rate for its work, which becomes especially important when Contractors undertake projects that may last for several years, during which significant and unpredictable fluctuations in the costs of inputs may occur.[87]

81 *Re Sanders Constructions Pty Ltd* [1969] Qd R 29, 37–39 per Hoare J.

82 *British Movietone News v London and District Cinemas Ltd* [1952] AC 166,185 per Viscount Simon.

83 *Aggressive Construction Co Ltd v Wai Kin Construction Ltd* [2018] HKCFI 744, [28] per Mimmie Chan J.

84 Mark Frilet, 'Management Contracting: A Civil Law Approach Based on the French Example' (1993) *International Construction Law Review* 337, 341–342; *UNIDROIT Principles of International Commercial Contracts* (2016) Articles 6.2.1–6.2.3.

85 A M Ismail, 'Globalisation and Contract Price in the International Public Works Agreements in the Egyptian State Procurement Law: New Trends' (2010) *International Construction Law Review* 92; Hamed, El Haggan & Yemia, 'Post Contract Change in Costs – A Study of Construction Contracts and the Egyptian Civil Law' (2012) 28 *Construction Law Journal* 187; E Garay, 'Quantifying Public Construction Claims in Argentina' (1989) *International Construction Law Review* 127.

86 eg in Finnish law: E Korhonen, 'Inflation and the Building Contract' (1984) *International Construction Law Review* 22.

87 *Leighton Contractors Pty Ltd v Public Transport Authority of Western Australia (No 6)* [2008] WASC 193, [71] per Le Miere J.

21.1.17 Entire contracts

The following discussion on common law principles needs to be read in the light of the various *Security of Payment Acts* in various jurisdictions, which may overcome the sometimes harsh application of the common law. This is discussed further in ¶28.9.2.

Contracts may be either 'divisible' or 'separable,' as opposed to 'entire,' depending upon the contracting parties' intention as determined from the terms of the contract itself.[88] If the performance by the Contractor of all or substantially all of its obligations is a condition precedent to its entitlement to payment, the contract is an **entire contract**, whereas if the parties contemplated that the financial consideration promised by the Employer was divisible, the contract is a **divisible contract** or **separable contract**.

It is important to note that even though the Contract may contemplate the Contractor being entitled to receive payment on an interim or progressive basis as the work proceeds,[89] such provisions are not inconsistent with it being an entire contract. Whether or not a contract is an entire contract depends on the construction of the Contract.[90]

Under an entire contract the Contractor may not be entitled to final payment, or return of any retention monies or performance securities, until all the Works have been completed free from defects or omissions.[91] In such a contract, interim payments are made as advances against the contract price.[92] A major consideration for a construction contract to be an entire contract, as opposed to a contract where the Contractor's entitlement to payment does not depend upon completion of all the Works, is that if the Contractor knows that it will only become entitled to payment of the contract price once it has completed all or substantially all of the Works in accordance with the Contract it will have an incentive to complete its Works in accordance with the Contract, rather than abandoning the Works if the project becomes unprofitable or performing work to a lesser standard than that required.[93]

The common law position is that where a Contractor fails to finish the entire work as provided for under an entire contract, it is not entitled to any payment. This was the situation in *Sumpter v Hedges*,[94] where the Contractor abandoned the Contract when it had virtually completed the contract building, and the Employer completed the work. It was held that the Contractor could recover nothing for the work it had done on the basis that the parties had entered into an entire contract. The Contractor was not entitled to any payment

---

88 *GEC Marconi Systems Pty Ltd v BHP Information Technology Pty Ltd* (2003) 128 FCR 1, [704] per Finn J; *Cordon Investments Pty Ltd v Lesdor Properties Pty Ltd* [2012] NSWCA 184, [94] – [95] per Bathurst CJ.

89 As Lord Morris said in *Gilbert-Ash (Northern) Ltd v Modern Engineering (Bristol) Ltd* [1974] AC 689, 699: 'It is manifest that it would not be reasonable or fair to expect a contractor to wait until the end of the period of erection of a large building before you received any money.'

90 *Purcell v Bacon* (1914) 19 CLR 249 per Griffith CJ.

91 *Hoenig v Isaacs* [1952] 2 All ER 176, 180 per Denning LJ (CA).

92 *Spandeck Engineering (S) Pte Ltd v China Construction (South Pacific) Development Co Pte Ltd* [2005] SGCA 59, [19].

93 Mc Pherson JA held in *Trade Indemnity Australia Ltd v Parkinson Air Conditioning Ltd* (1994) 11 BCL 39, 44 [QCA]: '[G]enerally speaking and apart from any agreed provision to the contrary, a contract for work and labour is regarded as entire, that is to say, the supplier has at law no right to payment in any amount until the whole of the work is completed. In practice the rigours of the common law rule are usually mitigated by providing for progress payments based either on completion of particular sections of the work or on the invoice value of material supplied and work done whether completed or not.' See also *Mann v Paterson Constructions Pty Ltd* [2019] HCA 32, [26] per Kiefel CJ, Bell and Keane JJ.

94 [1898] 1 QB 673. Considered by the Supreme Court of NSW in *Oliver v Lakeside Property Trust Pty Ltd* [2005] NSWSC 1040.

under the original contract because it had not completed the contract work. A new contract to pay for the work could not be implied merely because the Employer had completed the buildings, since it was not obliged to go to the expense of removing the buildings or to leave them on its land in a state in which they were a nuisance.

Note that under an entire contract, the Contractor may be able to recover costs for work performed even though the Contract has not been fully performed:

(a) If the failure to perform all of the Works is the Employer's fault[95]
(b) Where the incomplete work was accepted by the Employer[96]
(c) Where a new contract has been agreed to regarding the work[97]
(d) Where the principle of substantial performance is applicable. See *Hoenig v Isaacs*[98] in which it was held that even if it was a condition precedent to payment that the entire contract be completed, the Employer had waived the condition by taking the benefit of the work.

The doctrine of substantial completion is dealt with in ¶16.1.

21.2 Advance payment

Because the cost of financing a project is as much a valid cost to a project as steel and concrete, commercial circumstances can make it desirable for the Employer to make available advance payment or neutral funding to a Contractor, to provide immediate funds for, for example, mobilisation of staff and to procure long-lead and other items.[99]

The Employer will usually require the Contractor to provide some form of security for such an advance payment, typically in the form of a guarantee to be issued by an entity approved by the Employer. The required form of guarantee may be annexed to the conditions of contract, which might also permit another form as an alternative option for the Contractor. The Employer would normally be entitled to withhold its approval of another form which was less favourable to it than the form annexed to the Contract.

The entity which issues the performance security may insist on it having an expiry date around the time that it is expected to have been repaid. If the advance has not been repaid within say a month before the expiry date of the security, the Employer should request an extension to take account of possible delays or the provision of an acceptable substitute security. In the absence of such an extension, the Employer will probably have the right to call the guarantee and then proceed on the basis that the advance has been repaid.

If the Contractor fails to perform any work in respect of an advance or neutral funding payment, the Employer will be entitled to restitution of the amount paid because there will have been a total failure of consideration.[100]

95 *Phillips v Ellinson Bros Pty Ltd* (1941) 65 CLR 221, 233.
96 Ibid, 235.
97 Ibid, 234.
98 [1952] 2 All ER 176.
99 *Hall v Van Der Heiden (No2)* [2010] EWHC 586 (TCC), [12] per Coulson J.
100 *TTI Team Telecom International Ltd v Hutchison 3G UK Ltd* [2005] EWHC 762 TCC, [57] per HHJ Thornton QC; *Mirimskaya v Evans* (2007) 114 Cons LR 144, 163 [59] – 164 [64] per DHCJ Richard Fernyhough QC (TCC).

21.3 Application for interim payment certificate

The Contract usually provides for progress payments based on the value of work performed, although such a term cannot be implied as a matter of course, particularly if the contract is an entire contract.[101] **Progress payments** are no more than advances against the eventual contract price so as to provide the Contractor with a cash flow to fund the performance of the work. It has been said that progress payments or interim payments may be the 'life blood' of the Contractor.[102] Progress payments are ordinarily made after an **interim payment certificate** (which must comply with the contractual requirements) is issued by the Engineer as agent for the Employer.

Interim payment certificates provide a means for regulating incremental payments to the Contractor for work performed and inform the Employer as to the progress of the Works.[103] However, 'Interim claims and certifications are not intended to reflect down to the last dollar the amount of work actually done. It is a rough estimate, not an exact measurement.'[104]

Interim payment certificates do not purport to represent a permanently binding statement of the state or adequacy of the Works, or the Contractor's final entitlement to payment.[105] 'Interim certificates are valid and persuasive as evidence but are not conclusive.'[106] It is recognized by the courts that interim payment certificates are only approximate estimates and are not in any way conclusive. The mere inclusion by the Engineer of amounts claimed by the Contractor, or an omission by the Contractor to claim in respect of any matter or thing in any interim payment certificate cannot, therefore, without more, create a representation or an estoppel.

The right to receive payment in accordance with an interim payment certificate validly issued in accordance with the Contract will be upheld by a court.[107] The determination by a court regarding a Contractor's entitlement to payment in respect of a specific progress claim certified in an interim payment certificate will not prevent the Employer from reopening the issue of the Contractor's entitlement to payment in later proceedings on the accuracy of the payment certificate.[108] If the Engineer does not certify a progress claim

---

101 *CJ Elvin Building Services Ltd v Noble* [2003] EWHC 837 (TCC), [13] and [84] per Mr Recorder Akenhead QC; *Chun Lee Engineering Co Ltd v Aoki Corporation* [1991] HKCA 297, [26] per Clough JA.

102 *Melville Dundas Ltd v George Wimpey UK Ltd* [2007] 1 WLR 1136 per Lord Hoffman; *Dacy Building Services Ltd v IDM Properties LLP* [2018] EWHC 178 (TCC), [13], per Fraser J; *Compact Metal Industries Ltd v Enersave Power Builders Pte Ltd* [2008] SGHC 201, [52] per Andrew Ang J; *WY Steel Construction Pte Ltd v Osko Pte Ltd* [2013] SGCA 32, [18].

103 *Beaufort Developments (NI) Ltd v Gilbert-Ash NI Ltd* [1999] 1 AC 266, 275–276 per Lord Hoffman.

104 *SG Industrial Pte Ltd v Eros Electrical Engineering and Construction Pte Ltd* [1998] SGHC 299, [70] per Warren Khoo LHJ. See also *Henry Boot Construction Ltd v Alstom Combined Cycles Ltd* [2005] BLR 437, 451 [56] per Dyson LJ.

105 *Tharsis Sulphur and Copper Co v McElroy & Sons* (1878) LR 3 HL 1040, 1054 per Lord Blackburn (HL(Sc)); *PC Harrington Contractors Ltd v Multiplex Constructions (UK) Ltd* [2005] BLR 16, 22 [37] per Christopher Clarke J; *Kennett Pty Ltd v Janssen* [2014] SASC 164, [137] per Blue J; *Tactful Construction and Engineering (HK) Ltd v Univic Engineering Ltd* [2019] HKCFI 1568, [33] per Mimmie Chan J.

106 *AG Machin Design & Build Contractors Ltd v Long* (1992) 34 Con LR 121, 129 per Glidewell LJ (CA); *Wong Chuk Kin v Millennium Engineering Ltd* [2007] HKCFI 866, 866 [27] per DHCJ To; *SGL Carbon Fibres Ltd v RBG Ltd* [2012] CSOH 19, [24] per Lord Glennie; *Mansource Interior Pte Ltd v CSG Group Pte Ltd* [2017] SGHC 41, [56] – [60] per Vinodh Coomaraswamy J.

107 *Ivan Chin v HP Construction and Engineering Pte Ltd* [2015] SGCA 14, [21] per Menon CJ.

108 *Filipe v Inscope Solutions Pty Ltd* [2004] NSWCA 417, [5] per Hodgson JA.

within the stipulated period, the progress claim may be deemed to have been accepted, and the Contractor entitled to payment of the full amount claimed.[109]

In order for the Engineer to arrive at a correct evaluation of the work, the Contractor must supply information in support of its claim, especially if the nature and extent of the Work cannot be properly inspected.[110] The Contractor's application for an interim payment certificate must therefore be accompanied by such evidence of the value of the work done as the Engineer may reasonably require. As the Engineer will need to satisfy itself as to whether the amount applied for is fair and reasonable in all the circumstances, it should specify in advance what documentary and other evidence it will require to accompany the application in order that it may be certified. This may include copies of invoices, details of hours worked by the various grades of employees, and so on.

The specific wording of the Contract will determine whether an obligation to supply supporting information with a progress claim amounts to a condition which must be fulfilled before a payment certificate must be issued, or whether its non-fulfilment will entitle the withholding of payment.[111] A condition precedent to the obligation to issue a payment certificate may itself give rise to a dispute as to the adequacy of the information provided.[112]

Valuations which are made on an interim basis and on account may be adjusted in subsequent valuations. The Engineer may review and revise an interim payment certificate by issuing a further certificate to correct errors or misstatements in the earlier certificate. For this reason, if the information is not complete or precise, the adequacy of the information provided in support of an interim payment claim, whilst important, is not of such importance as to negate the obligation to issue a payment certificate and maintain the Contractor's cash flow.[113] It follows that where the Contract does not expressly or by implication make the provision of certain information a condition precedent to the making of a valid payment claim, a payment claim may still be valid even if it does not contain all of the supporting information required.[114]

A requirement that the Contractor provide evidence and information of the value of work to the satisfaction of the Engineer is different from a provision requiring the Contractor to provide such evidence and information as the Engineer may reasonably require, the latter being an objective standard absent in the former.[115] If a Contractor has,

---

109 *Algons Engineering Pty Ltd v Abigroup Contractors Pty Ltd* (1997) 14 BCL 215 [Sup Ct NSW]; *CJP Builders Ltd v William Verry Limited* [2008] BLR 545, 561 [91(a)] per Akenhead J; *Kyren Pty Ltd v Wunda Projects Australia Pty Ltd* [2012] SASCFC 23, [76].

110 *Brewarrina Shire Council v Beckhaus Civil Pty Ltd* (2003) 56 NSWLR 576, [16] per Ipp J A; *Sir Henry Boot Construction Ltd v Alstom Combined Cycles Ltd* [2005] BLR 437, 453–454 [66] per Dyson LJ; *Grocon Constructors (Victoria) Pty Ltd v APN DF2 Project 2 Pty Ltd* [2015] VSCA 190, [165] – [175].

111 *FPM Constructions Pty Ltd v Council of the City of Blue Mountains* [2005] NSWCA 314; *Karalis v Archonstruct Pty Ltd* [2008] SASC 368, [132] – [133] per Kourakis J.

112 *Brewarrina Shire Council v Beckhaus Civil Pty Ltd* (2003) 56 NSWLR 576, [72] per Young CJ in Eq. (dissenting).

113 Ibid, [79].

114 *London Underground Ltd v Pillar Broadway Ltd* (2003) 87 Con LR 205, 224 [48] – 226 [52] per HHJ Seymour QC; *Clarence Street Pty Ltd v Isis Projects Pty Ltd* (2005) 64 NSWLR 448, 460 [63] per Mason P; *Kersfield Developments (Bridge Road) Ltd v Bray & Slaughter Ltd* [2017] EWHC 15 (TCC), [33] – [37] per O'Farrell J.

115 *Onesteel Manufacturing Pty Ltd v United KG Pty Ltd* [2006] SASC 119, [68] per Debelle J (22 BCL 449, 24 Const LJ 431).

to the knowledge of the Employer, performed the work as a Variation, but has not kept sufficient records of the work performed, or of its value, it is not permissible to refuse to value the work or to give it a zero value in the absence of an express obligation to keep records.[116]

The validity of a payment claim may be challenged if the accuracy of a mandatory statutory declaration given by the person making a payment claim is brought into question.[117] A Contractor is not permitted to make a fraudulent payment claim. It is an implied term of a contract that a Contractor is to act honestly in making progress claims,[118] with the result that a fraudulent payment claim will have no contractual effect and a Contractor who makes a fraudulent payment claim may be subject to criminal sanctions.[119] Where the maker of the claim knows that it is not entitled to the amount claimed, the maker makes a fraudulent payment claim. The claim may represent that the work has been performed when the person making the claim knew that the work had not been performed,[120] or when the person making the claim knows that non-compliant goods were used.[121] Deliberately making a false representation to obtain payment is a crime, for example, *Fraud Act 2006* (UK) s2.

If the Contractor is applying for payment in respect of plant to be shipped, it must provide evidence of shipment, payment of freight and insurance, and any other documents required by the Engineer. As discussed in ¶13.4, the Contract may also have relevant provisions in relation to transfer of title for such plant before payment is due.

If the Contractor is, by its application, making a claim for additional payment, then it must provide the particulars necessary to enable the Engineer to assess the claim. The Engineer is entitled to satisfy itself that the payment is in fact due. For example, if the Contractor is entitled to reimbursement by the Employer of import duties paid for importation of the plant into the country where the Site is located, receipts for the payments made must be provided.

21.4 Interim payment certificates

21.4.1 Engineer's certification

Before issuing an interim payment certificate, the Engineer must satisfy itself that, *prima facie*, the Contractor is entitled to make the application in accordance with the Contract, and that the value of the work done has been correctly stated, that plant has been shipped, freight and insurance paid, and so on. The Engineer must apply the terms of the Contract to determine the amount for which the certificate should be issued, which may include items in respect of:

116 *Ruttle Plant Hire Ltd v Secretary of State for Environment Food and Rural Affairs* [2009] BLR 301, 307 [35] – [36] per Jacob LJ. Compare *Sabemo (SA) Pty Ltd v AIW Engineering Pty Ltd* (1992) 9 BCL 280 [Sup Ct SA].

117 *Metacorp Australia Pty Ltd v Andeco Construction Group Pty Ltd* (2010) 30 VR 141, [204] – [220] per Vickery J; *Robinson v St Kilda Road Pty Ltd* [2018] FCAFC 84.

118 *Jones v Dalcon Construction Pty Ltd* [2006] WASCA 205, [43] per Pullin JA (dissenting on the facts).

119 *Herniman v Smith* [1938] AC 305 (HL(E)); *R v Bassett* (1967) 51 Cr App R 28 (CA); *R v Silverman* (1988) 86 Cr App R 213 (CA); *Plaza West Pty Ltd v Simon's Earthworks (NSW) Pty Ltd* [2010] NSWSC 1426.

120 *O'Leary v R* [2013] EWCA Crim 1371.

121 *Tan Wai Kok v Hart Engineering (Pte) Ltd* [2005] SGHC 215, [111] per Lai Siu Chiu J.

- Measurement of the amount of work completed. If the Contract is prescriptive as to the application of a specific standard in measuring or valuing work, for example, the **CESMM**,[122] that standard must be applied.[123]
- Sums previously paid to the Contractor, and their subtraction from any valuation made in order to reach the sum due under a certificate.
- The interim certification of nominated subcontractors' or suppliers' accounts.
- Any special valuations of Variations.
- Possible claims by the Contractor under a very large number of clauses in the Contract which may not (unlike nominated subcontractors or varied work) strictly be regarded as the estimated contract value of the Works. In the evaluation of a Contractor's entitlement to compensation for items not specifically monetised in the Contract, the Contractor's tender rates may be used provided they are realistic and relevant.[124]
- Retentions and sums due to the Employer, say, for use of power on Site which the Engineer may certify as deductions from the amount claimed.
- Possible counterclaims by the Employer (insurance premiums on Contractor's default, uncovering of work, remedying defective work, liquidated damages, sale of plant and unused materials left on Site by the Contractor, and direct payment of subcontractors). Although it is normal to take into account countervailing claims and deductions as part of the calculation of what is due for work performed,[125] the Contract may require the Engineer to ignore such counterclaims when certifying. In this case the Employer should deduct the appropriate sums when making payment, usually with the exception of direct payment of subcontractors. For administrative reasons it is highly desirable for both the decisions and any necessary deductions to be recorded in the Engineer's certificates for payment, but this depends on whether it is permissible under the Contract.

Only the Engineer nominated in the Contract may issue an interim payment certificate.[126] The provisions of the Contract should be adhered to in respect of the person to whom a payment certificate is to be issued, that is, the Contractor or the Employer.

If the Engineer is given a discretion as to what is due on an interim basis, the exercise of that discretion will usually be subject to the implied condition that the Engineer must act honestly and reasonably in exercising the discretion. However, if the Contract is prescriptive as to the amount to be paid to the Contractor, questions of reasonableness do not usually arise.[127]

---

122 The Civil Engineering Standard Method of Measurement produced by the Institution of Civil Engineers.

123 *Obayashi-Gumi Ltd v Kian Hong Holdings Pte Ltd* [1987] SLR 94 [Sing CA]; *Demolition Services Ltd v Castle Vale Housing Action Trust* (1999) 79 Con LR 55.

124 *How Engineering Services Ltd v Linder Ceilings Floors Partitions plc* (1999) 64 Con LR 67, 73–74 [24] per Dyson J; *AJ Lucas Drilling Pty Ltd v McConnell Dowell Constructors (Aust) Pty Ltd* [2008] VSC 275, [14] Byrne J (affirmed [2009] VSCA 310).

125 *PC Harrington Contractors Ltd v Multiplex Constructions (UK) Ltd* [2008] 1 BLR 16, 22 [37] – [39] per Christopher Clarke J.

126 *General Iron and Hardware Co Ltd v Estate Molyneux and Oldham* (1911) 32 NLR 193.

127 *TSG Building Services plc v South Anglia Housing Ltd* [2013] EWHC 1151 (TCC), [38] per Akenhead J.

21.4.2 The efficacy of an interim payment certificate

The amount certified as payable pursuant to an interim payment certificate will not necessarily be representative of the final liability of the Employer to make payment to the Contractor, nor of the Contractor's right to payment for Work performed.[128] The final account at the end of the project will determine the parties' respective rights and obligations in respect of payment.

The Contract may make express provision as to whether the Employer is obliged to pay the amount specified in an interim payment certificate, or whether rights of abatement, set-off, or counterclaim (also known as 'contra charges,' or 'back charges') may be exercised by the Employer.[129] Under the common law, an Employer will be entitled to exercise a right of set-off or abatement against amounts stated to be owing in a certificate in the absence of any express provision to the contrary.

The Engineer has power to correct mistakes in an interim payment certificate, even in the absence of a specific term in the Contract.[130] However, greater certainty can be achieved if express provisions define the effect and procedure of correction. For example, questions may otherwise arise about whether a correcting certificate retrospectively amends a previous certificate, or a supplemental certificate is issued instead. Further, there are resulting uncertainties about the timing of payment obligations. The Contractor should recognise that a wide power of correction means that there is no certainty of the final result when a certificate is issued. It also makes time limits on the certifier's part pointless because the certifier can always correct a certified figure later on.

If time limits are too tight it may impact on the ability of a certifier to comply with professional standards, and this may cause unfairness. These concerns need to be borne in mind when a construction contract is drafted. An example of how this might be dealt with is in AS 2124–1992 (clauses 42.9 and 42.1) and JCC clause 10.08, where if a certifier fails to act within the time limit imposed, the Contractor is compensated through interest payments. An alternative is to deem the amount claimed to be approved. Ultimately, the appropriate solution in any given case will depend on what effect the parties want the certification to have.

It is a frequent source of complaint by Contractors that the Contract does not fix a time limit from receiving the Contractor's payment claim within which the Engineer is to issue a payment certificate. Where payments are to be made monthly, it is implied that there must be the minimum delay to enable such payments to be made monthly and the Contractor may, in such cases of delay, recover interest if the Contract provides for it.

Where a progress payment is made conditional on the interim payment certificate, the granting of the certificate is conclusive evidence of the amount certified to be due, and the Contractor is entitled to be paid that amount.[131] As such a certificate is issued for the

---

128 *Re Luen Cheong Tai Construction Co Ltd* [2008] HKCFI 466, [17] per Kwan J; *Wiggins Island Coal Export Terminal Pty Ltd v Monadelphous Engineering Pty Ltd* [2015] QSC 309, [42] per Jackson J; *BGC Construction Pty Ltd v Citygate Properties Pty Ltd* [2016] WASC 88, [94] – [98] per Tottle J; *AGC Industries Pty Ltd v Karara Mining services Ltd* [2019] WASC 140 at [720] per Allanson J.

129 *Mottram Consultants Ltd v Bernard Sunley & Sons Ltd* [1975] 2 Lloyd's Rep 197, 204 per Lord Cross; *Icon Co (NSW) Pty Ltd v Australia Avenue Developments Pty Ltd* [2018] NSWCA 339, [23] per Basten JA.

130 *Lawrence v Kern* [1910] 14 WLR 337 (Canada).

131 *P & M Kaye Ltd v Hosier & Dickinson Ltd* [1972] 1 All ER 121 (HL).

purpose of assessing interim payments only, it is not evidence of satisfaction with the Contractor's work or in any way binding or conclusive as to the quality of the work.

Such a certificate is regarded as the equivalent of cash and will found a claim in court for summary proceedings for debt so long as the Contract runs. It has been held that payment on a certificate is conditional upon the issue thereof.[132] It is important that the Contractor has possession of the original of each payment certificate since it will have to rely on the relevant document in legal proceedings should the Employer fail to make payment upon it.

21.4.3 The power to withhold certification

The Employer's right to withhold payment for defective work (including defective work by a subcontractor) is important if there is any danger that it may become necessary to take the Works or any part of it out of the Contractor's hands, since the payment withheld may be retained to meet the Employer's expenses in completing the Works. This right may have to be balanced against the possibility that withholding certificates may itself make it difficult for the Contractor to finance the Works and lead to its insolvency or liquidation, in which event the Employer may still be prejudiced.

The wording of the Contract should be such as to avoid the situation whereby a certificate in respect of any part of the Works, however large, may be withheld because of defective work, however small, contained in that part. If the Contractor is entitled to payment in accordance with the Contract, the Engineer is not normally entitled to withhold a certificate because of defects of a minor character which would not affect the use of the Works or because it disputes any part of the payment applied for. If the Engineer does dispute any part of the payment applied for, it should issue a payment certificate for the undisputed part. Further, the Contractor may have the benefit of the various *Security of Payment Acts* applicable in the relevant jurisdiction, whereby it can apply for rapid adjudication of a disputed payment claim in accordance with the legislative provisions.

Where a payment certificate sets out in detail how the amount is made up, the fact that some of the items shown should not have been included in the amount does not make the whole certificate bad. If the items incorrectly included are severable, they can be struck out and the certificate will be valid for the balance. Mere general instructions in a letter from the Engineer to the Contractor are not sufficient to constitute a valid certificate in regard to defects.[133] Matters of proof and procedure must not be ignored.

The Contractor is usually entitled under a construction contract to immediate arbitration on withholding of a certificate. Where a certificate of payment is issued to a Contractor, then withdrawn and replaced by a certificate reflecting a debit balance in favour of the Employer, such conduct is tantamount to withholding the certificate. The statutory provisions of the relevant *Security of Payment* legislation (if applicable) will usually provide the most time and cost-effective method for a Contractor (or subcontractor) to ensure that it receives progress payments.

132 *Scott v Sytner 9* SC 50; *Clark & Son v Jefferies* (1905) HC 238.
133 *Green v Page* (1905) TS 599.

21.5 Payment on interim payment certificates

21.5.1 Payment of certified amount

Where the Contract provides for a comprehensive scheme of certification of interim payments and adjustment of liabilities between the parties, with either party having the right to refer any dispute over the certification to arbitration or some other adversarial forum, the Contract may be construed as one under which the obligation of the Employer is to pay the amount certified; any issues concerning overpayment or underpayment can be resolved by further adversarial processes or by correction in a later certificate.[134]

However, if the Contract permits the Employer to withhold payment of an interim certificate on the grounds of exercising a counterclaim arising from a right of set-off or because it challenges the correctness of an interim certificate, the Employer may resist an application by the Contractor for summary judgement for the amount certified where the Employer, in good faith, and on reasonable evidential material, disputes the Contractor's entitlement to the amounts certified.[135]

A Contractor will normally be entitled to payment if the Employer should reasonably have been satisfied with the work: 'Where a contract requires that some task be performed to the "reasonable satisfaction" of one of the contracting parties, that standard is attained both if that party is in fact satisfied, and also if that party ought, as a reasonable person, be satisfied.'[136] What is or is not reasonable depends upon the facts and circumstances of each particular case.[137] Even where the Contract does not employ words such as 'to the reasonable satisfaction' the court will, wherever possible, imply a condition that the Employer should not unreasonably withhold its approval.[138]

Although the courts will tend to interpret clauses of this nature as restrictively as possible, a Contract is quite valid which makes approval by the Employer 'in its sole discretion' a condition precedent to payment, and, where the wording is clear and unambiguous, the court will give effect to such a condition.[139] Where the work is to be done to the taste of the Employer, a court would be extremely hesitant to say that its failure to approve had been unreasonable.[140] An Employer must at least act honestly, *bona fide,* and reasonably.[141] If the Employer is motivated by wilful caprice or dishonesty, the Contractor will be entitled to payment.[142]

Where dayworks are concerned, the Contractor charging on the basis of time spent in performing work, and the Contractor has submitted daily timesheets to the Employer as evidence of work performed and how long it took, if the Employer or the Engineer has countersigned those timesheets, such countersignature may constitute acknowledgement

---

134 *Sopov v Kane Constructions Ltd* [2007] VSCA 257, [78]- [100] per Whelan AJA; *Dial D Pty Ltd v Kingston Building (Australia) Pty Ltd* [2013] NSWCA 277, [34] – [35] per Ward JA.

135 *Jem Developments Pty Ltd v Hansen Yuncken Pty Ltd* [2006] NSWSC 1378.

136 *Adelaide Brighton Ltd v Ostabridge Pty Ltd* [2005] NSWSC 737 per Campbell J at [142], citing *Smith v Sadler* (1880) 6 VLR (L) 5, 6.

137 *Stadhard v Lee* (1863) 3 B and S 364, 373.

138 *Smith v Sadler* (1880) 6 VLR 5, 6; *Minster Trust Ltd v Traps Tractors Ltd & others* [1954] 3 All ER 136 (QB), 145.

139 *WMC Resources Ltd v Leighton Contractors Pty Ltd* [1999] WASCA 10; (2000) 16 BCL 53.

140 *Andrews v Belfield* (1857) 2 CB (NS) 779.

141 *WMC Resources Ltd v Leighton Contractors Pty Ltd* [1999] WASCA 10; (2000) 16 BCL 53.

142 *Andrews v Belfield* (1857) 2 CB (NS) 779; *Roberts v Bury Commissioners* (1870) LR 5 CP 310.

of the work performed and the Contractor's entitlement to payment.[143] Where a timesheet purports to incorporate contractual terms to which the parties have not otherwise agreed, the signing of the timesheet will not usually constitute an acceptance of those terms, but signature of a timesheet will ordinarily represent a record of work performed.[144] A countersignature does not, however, make the content of the timesheet conclusive.[145]

21.5.2 Is a payment certificate a condition precedent to payment?

Unless the Contract expressly provides that the issuing of a payment certificate is to be regarded as a condition precedent to payment, it will not be so regarded.[146]

The Contractor may recover payment without a payment certificate having been issued where the Engineer has colluded with the Employer and refused to certify, and where the Engineer has placed itself under the influence and control of the Employer. The Contractor is also entitled to payment without a certificate having been issued where the Engineer deliberately refuses to issue it,[147] or where it has misinterpreted its function and taken into account matters which the parties on a true construction of the Contract did not intend that it should.[148] These are specific examples of the following contractual principle:

> The applicable principles are that a party cannot insist on a condition if non-fulfilment of it is due to his own fault and that a party to a contract is absolved from performance where performance is prevented by the wrongful act of another contracting party.[149]

A Contractor is entitled to payment in the absence of a payment certificate where the terms of the Contract allow the Arbitrator to decide whether a certificate has been correctly withheld.[150] The same can be said for the determination of a statutory Adjudicator.

21.5.3 Employer's defences for non-payment

A question which is of cardinal interest to both Employers and Contractors is whether the Employer is entitled to resist a claim for payment of the sum shown in an interim

---

143 *Keller Ltd v Morrison Construction Ltd* [1998] EWCA Civ 19; *In the matter of Pan Interiors Ltd* [2005] EWHC 3241 (Ch), [41] – [42] per Warren J.

144 *Grogan v Robin Meredith Plant Hire* (1996) 53 Con LR 87 (CA); *Pak Lik Company v Sung Foo Kee Ltd* [1996] HKCA 654, [30] – [33] per Godfrey JA; *Waterfront Shipping Co Ltd v Trafigura AG* [2007] EWHC 2482 (Comm), [27] – [28] per Gloster J.

145 *JDM Accord Ltd v Secretary of State* (2004) 93 Con LR 133, 183 [142] – 184 [143] per HHJ Thornton QC; see *Ruttle Plant Hire Ltd v Secretary of State* (2004) 104 Con LR 110, 204 [332] – 205 [335] per HHJ Thornton QC; *Bluewater Energy Services BV v Mercon Steel Structures BV* [2014] EWHC 2132 TCC, [839] per Ramsey J.

146 *Dallman v King* (1837) 7 IJCP 6.

147 *In re Hohenzollern Actien-Gesellschaft fur Locomotivbahn and City of London Contract Corporation* (1886) 54 LT 596; (1886) Alfred A Hudson, *Hudson's Fourth Edition Table of Cases* (Sweet & Maxwell, 4th edn 1914) 100 [Note: this case was distinguished in *Briscoe & Co Ltd v Victorian Railways Commissioners* [1907] VLR 523; (1907) 13 ALR 308].

148 *Panamena Europea Navigacion (Companio Limitada) v Frederick Leyland and Co Ltd (F Russel and Co)* 1947 AC 428 (HL).

149 *Kendalls (NSW) Pty Ltd (in liq) v Sweeney* [2005] QSC 064, [64], citing *Panamena Europea Navigacion (Companio Limitada) v Frederick Leyland and Co Ltd (F Russel and Co)* 1947 AC 428 (HL).

150 *Brodie v Cardiff Corporation* 1919 AC 337 (HL); *Prestige v Brettell 1938* (55) TLR 59 (CA).

payment certificate by reason of the fact that defective work has been certified and the cost of remedying it will extinguish or reduce the amount of the claim on the certificate.

A defendant who is sued for payment for work done and materials supplied is entitled to raise, as a common law defence, that the work or materials were defective and, therefore, that it is not liable for the whole or part of the price. The contract in question would require very clear wording if the issue of an Engineer's certificate is intended to remove this right, as there is no particular reason why a payment certificate should put the Contractor in an especially favourable position.

In *Gilbert-Ash (Northern) Ltd v Modern Engineering (Bristol) Ltd*,[151] Viscount Dilhorn stated the principle as follows:

> It is of course true that the contract makes provision for payment as the work proceeds, but, it is to be observed, a fact to which I feel insufficient attention has been paid, that the contractor is only entitled to be paid on interim certificates for work properly executed. He is not entitled to be paid on interim certificates for work which is defective. The architect should only value work executed properly, that is to say, to his reasonable satisfaction: and no interim certificate is of itself conclusive evidence that the work was in accordance with the contract.[152]

The vital factor seems to be that any Employer who wishes to resist payment on a certificate must be in a position to quantify a counterclaim for the defective work. On the authority of *Gilbert-Ash* it should be possible to set up a counterclaim for defective work, even if unquantified, to resist summary proceedings by a Contractor for payment on an interim payment certificate. This is particularly so in the case where the Employer is in a position to show that a valid counterclaim exists which will exceed the value of the certificate but is not in a position to quantify such counterclaim within the short time period available for summary proceedings. In such circumstances, the Employer might suffer very serious prejudice by paying the certificate if, for example, the insolvency of the Contractor is imminent.

If the issue of a certificate is a condition precedent to an entitlement to payment, the Contractor is not entitled to payment unless and until a certificate has been issued. The Contractor is then only entitled to the sum stated in the certificate.[153] The absence of a certificate will provide a defence to an action for payment even if the Engineer in error but in good faith, formed the view that the Contractor was not entitled to the issue of a certificate.[154]

Misconduct on the part of the Employer in relation to the issue of a certificate will not give rise to a defence of absence of a certificate.[155]

Where the Contract contains an arbitration clause, in the event of there being a dispute over the amounts certified as owing in the payment certificate, the obtaining of an arbitrator's award is a condition precedent to the Contractor having an entitlement to

151 [1974] AC 689 (HL (E).
152 [1973] 3 All ER 195 (HL).
153 *Bennett (Construction) Ltd v CIMIC MBS Ltd* [2019] EWCA Civ 1515, [22] per Coulson LJ.
154 *Henry Boot Construction Ltd v Alstom Combined Cycles Ltd* [2005] BLR 437 [28] per Dyson LJ.
155 *Sharpe v San Paulo Railway Co* (1873) LR 8 Ch App 597, 612 per Mellish LJ (CA); *Butcher v Port* [1985] 1 NZLR 491.

payment.[156] If there is no dispute over the amounts certified in the payment certificate, court proceedings may be instituted by the Contractor to recover the amount stated to be owing.[157]

21.5.4 Non-payment of progress payments

The terms of the particular Contract govern the time by which payment owing is required to be made; under an entire contract, the Contractor is only entitled to payment from the completion of all of its work. In the absence of an express basis for determining when the Contractor is to be paid under a Contract, the Employer must pay the Contractor the sum due for the work performed within a reasonable time.[158]

The Employer's obligation to pay progress payments is enforceable. As set out in ¶28.9, *Security of Payment Acts* in a number of jurisdictions establish a statutory entitlement to recover progress payments, subject to compliance with the requirements of the legislation.

The possible consequences of not paying progress payments required in accordance with the Contract is illustrated by the case of *Fernbrook Trading Co Ltd v Taggart*.[159] The Employer breached the contract in failing to make progress payments for a total of 23 weeks, causing the Contractor to reduce labour on the Site because of financial difficulties. The court held that the Engineer had no jurisdiction to extend time on account of the Employer's breach of contract, which set the completion date at large with the effect that the Contractor was not liable to pay liquidated damages.

If payment is not made by the date or at the end of the period prescribed for payment, a breach of contract will occur.[160] Time is not usually 'of the essence' in the making of payment under a construction contract. It follows that the failure to make timeous payment will not ordinarily constitute breach of an essential term of the Contract so as to justify termination of the contract for non-payment.[161] However, a persistence in non-payment may amount to repudiatory conduct on the Employer's part, and in these circumstances the Contractor may elect to accept the repudiation and terminate the contract, in this way bringing to an end the Contractor's obligation to perform its Contract Works.

The Contractor does not possess a general right at common law to suspend work if a progress payment is not made when it ought to have been made.[162] In the absence of a contractual provision or repudiatory conduct by the Employer, a Contractor is not entitled to reduce its labour force or other resources on a project where it has not been paid when it

---

156 *Kirsch v H P Brady Pty Ltd* (1937) 58 CLR 36; *South Australian Railways Commissioners v Egan* (1973) 130 CLR 506; *J&H Manktelow Pty Ltd v Alloway Grazing Pty Ltd* [1975] 1 NSWLR 385.

157 *John Grant and Sons Ltd v The Trocadero Building and Investment Co Ltd* (1938) 60 CLR 1; *Codelfa Construction Pty Ltd v State Rail Authority of New South Wales* (1982) 149 CLR 337, 423 per Brennan J.

158 *Lam Geotechnics Ltd v Milichich* [2005] HKEC 1014, [55] per DH Muttrie; *Gomes v Moono Constructions Pty Ltd* [2012] NSWSC 909, [64] per Slattery J; *Bennett (Construction) Ltd v CIMIC MBS Ltd* [2019] EWCA Civ 1515, [42] per Coulson LJ.

159 (1979) 1 NZLR 556.

160 *Tombs v Wilson Connolly Ltd* (2004) 98 Con LR 44, 60–61 [50] per HHJ Coulson QC (TCC).

161 *Alan Auld Associates Ltd v Rick Pollard Associates* [2008] BLR 419, 423 [12] per Tuckey LJ; *Alliance Concrete Singapore Pte Ltd v Comfort Resources Pte Ltd* [2009] SGCA 34, [54] – [56]; *Dalkia Utilities Services plc v Celtech International Ltd* [2006] EWHC 63 (Comm), [130] per Christopher Clarke J.

162 *Mackel v Rafferty* [2014] NIQB 113, [18] –] 19] per Weatherup J; *William Clark Partnership Ltd v Dock St PCT Ltd* [2015] EWHC 2923 (TCC), [5.9] per HHJ Stephen Davies; *Triple Point Technology Inc v PTT Public Co Ltd* [2019] EWCA Civ 230, [63] – [66] per Sir Rupert Jackson.

ought to have been paid, and the contract terms require the Contract to maintain reasonable progress.[163] A wrongful suspension of the Works may constitute repudiation of the Contract by the Contractor,[164] because the obligation of a Contractor to perform work is usually independent of the Employer's obligation to pay for that work.[165]

Under certain contracts the Contractor is entitled to stop work after notice to the Engineer and the Employer in circumstances where either the Engineer failed to issue a payment certificate which had been properly applied for by the Contractor, or if the Employer failed to make any payment, or failed to comply with a Dispute Board or Adjudicator's ruling. For example, sub-clause 16.1 of the 2017 FIDIC Red Book provides that the Contractor can suspend work not less than 21 days after giving Notice that the Engineer has failed to issue an Interim Payment Certificate, the Employer has not complied with its payment obligations or complied with an Engineer's determination or a DAAB decision.

An application for payment by the Contractor is a proper application if it is made in accordance with the terms of the Contract, at the right time or at the right stage of construction and is accompanied by the evidence which the Engineer has required. Unjustified requests for further information are sometimes wrongfully used to obstruct or delay payment. If the Contractor has not justified its application for payment by the documents that accompany it, then the Engineer's failure to issue a payment certificate will be justified, and the Contractor will not be entitled to use the remedy of stopping the Works. If, however, the Contractor is entitled to use this remedy and does so, then it is entitled to be paid the cost occasioned by the stoppage and the subsequent resumption of work together with a profit allowance.

If the Employer wilfully, in the knowledge that the money is owing, refuses to make payment to the Contractor, and the Employer intends the non-payment to cause economic damage to the Contractor beyond economic damage caused by the non-payment itself, the Contractor may, under English law, be entitled to recover damages in tort for the loss or damage it suffers as a consequence of the Employer's refusal to pay; it may also constitute a repudiation of the Contract.[166] The tort of unlawful interference with economic relations is yet to be recognised in Australia.[167]

Note that where *Security of Payment* legislation applies and the legislative provisions have been complied with, the Contractor has statutory protection if it stops work because it has not been paid progress payments to which it is entitled. The Contractor may also seek a speedy adjudication by bringing a claim for non-payment under the relevant *Security of Payment* legislation, discussed further in ¶28.9.

163 *Supamarl Ltd v Federated Homes Ltd* (1981) 9 Con LR 25, 28 per HHJ Hawser QC; *William Clark Partnership Ltd v Dock St PCT Ltd* [2015] EWHC 2923 (TCC), [2.51] per HHJ Stephen Davies; compare *Chun Wo Building Construction Ltd v Metta Resources* [2016] HKCFI 1357, [135] – [136] per Anthony Chan J.

164 *De Beers UK Ltd v Atos Origin IT Services UK Ltd* [2010] EWHC 3276 (TCC), [229] – [236] per Edwards – Stuart J.

165 *Carillion Construction Ltd v Felix (UK) ltd* [2001] BLR 1, 8 [34] per Dyson, J; *DSND Subsea Ltd v Petroleum Geo-Services ASA* [2000] BLR 530, 546 [135] per Dyson J.

166 *Longwell Enterprises Ltd v McGowan* (1989) 37 CLR [BC Co Ct]; *Beacon Developments Corp v Schuler* (1997) 36 DLR (2d) 43 [BC SC]; *Creatiles Materials Co Ltd v To's Universe Construction Co Ltd* [2003] HKCA 359; *Chim Kee Machinery Co Ltd v SNE Engineering Co Ltd* [2013] HKCFI 836, [40] – [42].

167 *Sanders v Snell* (1998) 196 CLR 329.

Finally, the most drastic remedy of all may be provided for where the Contractor has made a proper application for payment and the Engineer has failed to issue a payment certificate. The Contractor may then be entitled to terminate the Contract.

21.5.5 'Pay when paid' clauses

Certain contracts contain 'pay-when-paid' provisions which entitle the party carrying out work to payment (typically a subcontractor) only when the payer (typically a Head Contractor) has been put in funds by a third party. In practice, this eliminates the need for the Head Contractor to finance the work of its subcontractors and passes on to the subcontractors the risk of non-payment due to insolvency of the Employer.[168]

If the Head Contractor has not been paid because of its own default, it will not be entitled to rely upon the 'pay-when-paid' clause.[169] 'Pay-when-paid' clauses, when permitted by statute to operate, will be interpreted according to their terms and upheld by the courts.[170] 'Pay-when-paid' clauses are void under New York law,[171] and under *Statutory Adjudication Acts*.[172]

While the correct application of a 'pay-when-paid' clause depends on its wording, a 'pay- when-paid' clause may be interpreted so as to entitle a Head Contractor to withhold progress payments from a subcontractor. However, such a clause does not entitle the Contractor to withhold a final payment for work completed, to a claim for compensation arising from a breach of contract[173] or for an extra-contractual claim.[174] If a subcontract provides that payment is to be 'back-to-back' with the head contract, that may indicate that payments are to be made on a 'pay-when-paid' basis.[175]

21.5.6 Interest on delayed payment

Construction contracts often provide that interest is due on a particular payment from one party to the other party from the time at which that particular payment should have been made. For example, sub-clause 14.8 of the 2017 FIDIC Red Book provides that the Contractor is entitled to financing charges, compounded monthly on the unpaid amount

168 *Teakwood Works Ltd v Shui On Construction Co Ltd* [1984] HKLR 235; *Brightside Mechanical & Electrical Services Group Ltd v Hyundai Engineering and Construction Co Ltd* (1988) 41 BLR 110 [Sing HC].

169 *Durabella Ltd v J Jarvis & Sons Ltd* (2001) 83 Con LR 145, 155 [19] per HHJ Lloyd QC.

170 *Schindler Lifts (Singapore) Pte Ltd v Paya Ubi Industrial Park Pte Ltd* [2004] SGHC 34, [33] per Judith Prakash J.

171 Thomas P Hanley, 'Enforcing New York Governing Law Clauses in Commercial Contracts' (2001) *International Construction Law Review* 681, 684.

172 See Table 28.2.

173 *Kim Hung Construction & Engineering Co Ltd v Standard Refrigeration & Engineering Co Ltd* [2016] HKCA 4, [7] – [16] per Kwan J.

174 *Iezzi Constructions Pty Ltd v Watkins Pacific (Qld) Pty Ltd* [1995] 2 Qd R 350; *Aesco Steel Inc v JA Jones Construction Co Ltd* (1988) 4 Const LJ 310 [US District Ct, ED Louisiana, 29 Nov 1985]; *Smith & Smith Glass Ltd v Winstone Architectural Cladding Systems Limited* [1992] 2 NZLR 473.

175 *Massford (HK) Ltd v Wah Seng General Contractors Ltd* [2005] HKCA 425; *Tin Lee Construction Engineering Co Ltd v Kwong Wah* [2012] HKCFI 557, [27] – [44] (appeal dismissed: [2013] HKCA 146); *Pfeiffer GmbH v Cheung Hay Kit* [2013] HKCFI 174, [26] per Zervos J. Compare *Wo Hing Engineering Ltd v Pekko Engineers Ltd* [1988] HKCFI 425, [41]-[49]; *Luen Fat Engineering & Construction Co v Hung Yip (HK) Engineering Co Ltd* [2015] HKCFI 182.

after 28 days from when the Employer receives the Interim Payment Certificate, or if the Engineer does not issue an Interim Payment Certificate, after 56 days from when the Engineer receives the Contractor's application for payment.

21.6 Retention money

21.6.1 Payment of retention money

It is common for a construction contract to provide that a portion of the amount certified in interim payment certificates be set aside or retained by the Employer until a later date when the Contract has been completed. These amounts withheld are referred to as **retention money** or the **retention fund**. This money is set aside as security for the due completion of the Works and to provide funds for the rectification of defects should the Contractor fail to do so. The percentage to be withheld, and the time for paying over to the Contractor of the retention money, depends upon the terms of the Contract. The Contractor is generally not entitled to payment of any of the retention money until it has achieved Completion.

Where the Contract has been lawfully terminated by the Contractor, it is entitled to all money retained up to the time of such termination. Where the Contractor is in breach and the Contract has been completed by someone else, and where the total amount paid out by the Employer is less than the contract price, the Contractor is usually entitled to claim the remaining balance out of the retention money.

Where a subcontractor has agreed to be bound by the same conditions in a subcontract as are binding on the Contractor in regard to the head contract, the Contractor is entitled to hold back a percentage of the payment due to the subcontractor, equivalent to the percentage withheld as retention money under the head contract. In any event, the Contractor's entitlement to retention from payments it makes to a subcontractor will be governed by the terms of the relevant subcontract.

A surety who has completed the Works where the Contractor is in breach is usually entitled to recover out of the retention money any loss incurred by it in completing the Works. Whether a surety may claim retention money in excess of the loss it has suffered depends upon the terms of the Contract. If an Employer pays over retention money before it is obliged to do so, its action may have the effect of releasing a surety for the Contractor.

The Contractor may, depending on the terms of the Contract, lose retention money if the Employer is sequestrated or goes into liquidation. Under certain forms of construction contract this is avoided by having retention money held by the Employer in trust for the Contractor. There are express statutory provisions in some of the *Security of Payment Acts* in Australia which state that retention money is to be held in trust for the Contractor,[176] or for subcontractors.[177]

Where the retention moneys are invested in the joint names of the Contractor and the Employer, such monies are not jointly owned by them. Rights in the fund accrue to one

176 *Building and Construction Industry (Security of Payment) Act 2021* (WA) s71; *Construction Contracts (Security of Payments) Act* (NT) s24.

177 *Building Industry Fairness (Security of Payment) Act 2017* (Qld) s9.

or other of the parties on the occurrence of predetermined events. Contrary to the normal procedure applicable to joint accounts, neither party has access to the retention money without the Engineer's certificate or until the date for payment has arrived.

The problem of insolvency of one of the parties arises where the retention money has been invested in an account in the joint names of the Employer and the Contractor. In such circumstances, the retention money invested in the joint names of the Employer and the Contractor is held in trust for the Employer as security for the due completion of the Works (unless the money is held in trust for the Contractor by virtue of *Security of Payment Act* provisions). If the Employer becomes insolvent or is placed in liquidation and the Contractor is allowed to complete the Works, the whole of the retention money will revert to it. If the executor (or liquidator) of the Employer should elect to terminate the Contract, it would have no greater rights than the Employer would have had, and the fund would revert to the Contractor. Where the Contractor completes the Works, or where it is prevented from doing so by the intervention of the Employer's insolvency or liquidation, the Contractor's right to be paid the whole of the retention money is not prejudiced in any way. In the event of the Contractor's insolvency or liquidation, the full amount of the retention money would accrue to its estate if the executor (or liquidator) should elect to complete the Works and in fact does so. If the executor (or liquidator) of the Contractor should elect to terminate the Contract, the Employer would be entitled to recoup out of the retention money any extra cost or expense arising out of the employment of another contractor to complete the Works. Any unexpended balance in the retention money would accrue to the Contractor's estate.

21.6.2 Time for payment of retention money

Usually, the first half of retention money is released on Completion. Practical completion of the whole Works can be certified notwithstanding that some work still remains to be done, but how and when any deduction should be made from payments otherwise due in respect of any outstanding work of this kind, or when and how the Contractor should be paid for it once it has done it, should be clarified in the Contract. See ¶17.1 for a discussion of practical completion and ¶16.1 for a discussion of the doctrine of substantial completion.

The second half of the retention money is usually to be released within a number of days after the expiry of the maintenance period or defects liability period (depending on the particular contract), minus only a deduction of such sum as may be necessary to cover the cost of remedying defects still existing at that time. Assuming there are defects remaining to be addressed at the expiry of the maintenance period or defects liability period, a maintenance certificate (or similar) will be issued when the necessary remedial work is finished. So, by implication, the money retained against this remedial work will usually have to be certified for or released at that time.

If the Employer has to sue the Contractor for further damages for failing to complete, it must give credit for any retention money which it holds. The Contractor will usually be entitled to the retention money where substantial completion is prevented by the Employer, for example, by interfering with the Contractor's possession of the Site.

21.7 Application for final payment certificate

21.7.1 Contractor's claim for final payment

The process by which a final account is reckoned usually involves the Contractor making a claim for its final payment under the Contract upon or after completion of all the Works, and the rectification of defects before the expiration of any defects liability period. If a contract makes the giving of notification of a claim, in a particular form and within a particular period, a condition to the entitlement to make the claim, it is for the party making the claim to demonstrate that the notification of the claim was given in accordance with the contract.[178]

The Contractor may require the Engineer to issue a **defects liability certificate** at the end of the defects liability period detailing that, in the opinion of the Engineer, there are no outstanding Defects, or alternatively listing the remaining known Defects. The Contractor is usually obliged to make an application for the final payment certificate within a certain number of days after the issue of the defects liability certificate, or, if there is more than one, the issue of the last defects liability certificate.

The Contractor should be in a position to have prepared a draft final account well before this time, and it will no doubt have discussed this with the Engineer. This is usually the last chance that the Contractor has to make claims for additional payment to deal with the pricing of any Variations that may not yet have been agreed. The final account should therefore be full and detailed in all particulars.

21.7.2 Discharge

It is common for contracts to require the Contractor to submit a written discharge to confirm that the total amount claimed in its application for the final payment certificate represents full and final settlement of all moneys due to the Contractor under or in connection with the Contract. Such a discharge would normally only become effective when the Contractor had received all outstanding payments due, and any retention and performance securities had been returned.

In the alternative to a written discharge, the Contract may provide that, after the due date for submitting its application for the final payment certificate, the Contractor releases the Employer from any claim under or in connection with the Contract. Such a clause places a heavy onus on the Contractor to submit all of its claims by the date provided for in the Contract.

21.8 Final payment certificate

21.8.1 Engineer's duties

After it has received the Contractor's application for a final payment certificate, the Engineer will assess the total value of work performed. This requires a meticulous final measurement of finished work (with no unfixed materials), of Variations, of PC and provisional sums, and measurements required by all the many other clauses affecting the contract price which

178 *Lucas Earthmovers Pty Ltd v Anglogold Ashanti Australia Ltd* [2019] FCA 1049, [497] per White J.

must be made before an accurate certificate can be given. When amounts previously paid to the Contractor are deducted from this gross figure, and allowable deductions, setoffs, and counterclaims are applied, the final account is determined. A final account is a calculation of the total value of work performed by a Contractor pursuant to the Contract and reflects the final amount due to the Contractor.[179]

The Engineer will be required to issue a final certificate for the amount owing on completion of the making good of defects. It may be inferred that it, or a contemporaneous certificate, should state the final sum due. The Contract should define when the final measurement and adjustment of the contract price (subject only to a retention of money for outstanding defects) should be completed, as well as the time for release of the performance bonds, and/or the parent company guarantee and the last instalment of the retention money.

Whilst the formalities of the Contract in respect of the final payment certificate should be observed by the Engineer, the courts may nevertheless accept other documents which clearly express an intention to accept the work as a final certificate.

Where the Engineer certifies in a final payment certificate that work has been carried out to its satisfaction, this concludes the Engineer's powers to correct or modify previous interim payment certificates, and it is therefore ***functus officio*** (ie has exhausted its mandate). Under such circumstances the Engineer has no power to correct or modify the final payment certificate of its own motion, but it appears that it (or an Arbitrator) may do so if either party raises a dispute under a contract clause which gives it the appropriate jurisdiction. Obvious clerical errors will be read as corrected.

If the Contractor fails to make its application for a final payment certificate, it is usually open to the Engineer to issue the final payment certificate on the basis of such particulars as it has for the amount that the Engineer deems correct. If the Contractor disagrees with this assessment, it may have only itself to blame. Unless it challenges the final payment certificate it will subsequently have to take the matter to arbitration or litigation. However, the exact position can be qualified depending on contract drafting. For example, in AS 2124–1992 clause 42.8, the final payment certificate is not triggered until the Superintendent receives the Contractor's final payment claim. This standard contract omits the provision which allows the Superintendent to initiate a certificate where the Contractor has not made a claim. By contrast, FIDIC and JCC contracts make provision for the Engineer to initiate a final payment certificate in the absence of a claim, provided certain conditions are met.

21.8.2 Breach of Engineer's certification duty

Errors or negligence on the part of the quantity surveyor or Engineer may mean that the final payment certificate is not entirely accurate in relation to either the valuation reflected in it, or the amount due to the Contractor. Such errors do not render a final payment certificate open to attack. All the more, they cannot preclude its enforcement as being contrary to public policy. Assuming a valid and enforceable underlying Contract, a final payment

179 *YJL London Ltd v Roswin Estates LLP* [2009] EWHC 3174 (TCC), [16] per Coulson J; *Longyuan-Arrk (Macao) Pte Ltd v Show and Tell Productions Pte Ltd* [2013] SGHC 160, [50] per Belinda Ang Saw Ean J; *Lau Fook Hoong Adam v GTH Engineering & Construction Pte Ltd* [2015] SGHC 141, [47] – [49] per Aedit Abdullah JC.

certificate is open to challenge only on very limited grounds such as fraud, collusion, or other serious misconduct. Where a challenge is successful on these grounds, the certificate will be void as it is contrary to public policy to enforce such certification.[180]

These grounds of challenge relate directly to the duties of certifiers. The certifier must make its determination fairly, impartially, and independently. See, for example, *Dixon v South Australian Railways Commissioner*,[181] where the High Court held that although there was no evidence on the facts to establish disqualifying conduct by the certifier, collusion (improper interference with the certifier's duties) would disqualify the certifier and hence void the certification. Further, if it could be shown that there was interference with a certifier's duties, it is not necessary to prove that the interfering party was a party to the misconduct – that is, that their actions were designed to interfere. In *Perini Corp v Commonwealth*,[182] it was held that the certifier (who was employed by the Employer) was entitled to consider information provided by others as well as its Employer's department policy but could not be controlled by the Employer and had to exercise its own discretion. There was also an implied term that the Employer not interfere with the certifier's ability to comply with its certification duties. Finally, in *Amann Aviation Pty Ltd v Commonwealth*,[183] Davies and Sheppard JJ applied *Perini* and *Dixon* in holding that the certifier in this case had a duty of fairness – to act without actual bias and not capriciously and only after giving due attention to the interests of both parties.

In practice, Engineers often delay issuing final payment certificates and issue supplementary certificates from time to time during the progress of what are frequently long, drawn-out negotiations with Contractors concerning final payment. The existence of a claim by the Contractor, however unjustified, could not possibly be, in law, a reason for an Engineer not certifying sums to which the Contractor is entitled, or for an Employer not paying such a sum. The process of detailed valuation or measurement may involve an element of give-and-take even when properly conducted and claims of a certain kind may raise questions embarrassing to the Engineer in its relationship with the Employer. For these reasons some Engineers treat the entire process of certification, and particularly final certification, as one of negotiation in which one item or concession can be balanced against another. Further, some Engineers regard themselves as inhibited from certifying unless agreement at each stage, and in particular final agreement, can be reached. This is a grossly wrong, if not unprofessional, approach. Contractors may have some protection against such behaviour under the various *Security of Payment* legislation, as this provides an avenue for rapid adjudication in circumstances of unpaid and disputed progress payments (which in some jurisdictions are specifically defined to include the final payment).

The hazards to Contractors in accepting 'equivalent payments' or the making of 'bucket settlements' embracing a plethora of contentious issues without motivation or itemisation and which may subsequently be disputed or come to light in a contract audit cannot be overemphasized; such practices frequently result in the Contractor's proper interests becoming progressively imperilled and may give rise to allegations of fraud or improper dealing.

180 *Redmond v Wynne* (1892) 13 LR (NSW) L39.
181 (1923) 34 CLR 71.
182 [1969] 2 NSWR 530.
183 (1990) 22 FCR 527.

21.8.3 Effect of the final payment certificate

The last chance that either party has of alleging a failure by the other party to fulfil its obligations under the Contract is prior to the issue of the final payment certificate. The importance of that certificate should therefore not be underestimated by the parties or by the Engineer.

The important question for the Contractor is whether the final payment certificate denotes approval of the Works which will be conclusive and binding on the Employer so as to prevent it subsequently raising such matters as defective performance and incorrect measurement in litigation or arbitration. It should be noted that if the final payment certificate is conclusive, it is conclusive as to these matters as well as to the work and materials being in accordance with the Contract. If it is binding, it will be binding as to varied work having been ordered by the Engineer also.

The precise effect of a final payment certificate depends on the specific contract clauses. It is commonly intended to be conclusive evidence of the value of the Works, that the work and materials are in accordance with the Contract, and that the Contractor has performed all its obligations under the Contract, for example, in standard contract NPWC3. The Engineer should therefore not issue the final payment certificate unless it is satisfied that it can professionally justify its conclusions that the Contractor is entitled to the final payment certificate. In these circumstances also, payment of the amounts certified in the final payment certificate by the Employer would be conclusive evidence that the Contractor has performed all its obligations under the Contract. Further, issuing of the final payment certificate means that the Contractor is also barred from making further claims against the Employer, for example, 2017 FIDIC rainbow suite.

If the final payment certificate does not satisfy all relevant contractual requirements, it may be held to be a special interim payment certificate and not the final payment certificate.[184] Some contracts provide that even the final payment certificate is not evidence of the value of work or that work has been satisfactorily carried out in accordance with the Contract or is an admission of the Employer's liability or approval of the Contractor's performance or compliance with the Contract. Further, a final payment certificate is not conclusive if there has been any fraud or dishonesty relating to any matter dealt with in the certificate or if arbitration or court proceedings under the Contract have been commenced.

In general, approval in a final payment certificate must be expressed in the manner and in the terms specified in the Contract. A certificate is not bad merely because it is based on measurement made by another person. Not every deviation from the requirements relating to the issue of a final payment certificate by an Engineer will render it invalid. As previously discussed, deviations may, however, cause the certificate to be construed in substance as a special interim payment certificate instead of a final payment certificate.

If an Engineer whose decision under the Contract is final and binding between the parties includes in its final payment certificate amounts due for extra work ordered orally, the Employer, in the absence of fraud or collusion, would be liable to pay the amount so certified, notwithstanding the fact that the Contract required extra work to be ordered in writing.[185]

---

184 *Shaw v Melbourne and Metropolitan Board of Works* (1898) 24 VLR 86.

185 *Laidlaw v Hastings Pier* Co (1874) Alfred A Hudson, *Hudson's Fourth Edition Table of Cases* (Sweet & Maxwell, 4th edn 1914) 13.

21.9 Currencies of payment

Where the Employer is able to offer payment in foreign currencies, such currencies should be identified in the tender documents and the Contract documents. Provision should be made in the Contract to fix the contract price so that there is to be no increase or decrease in the sums to be received by the Contractor because of fluctuations in the rates of exchange. This may be achieved either by specifying the contract price in defined proportions of more than one currency, or in one currency based on fixed rates of exchange for the other currencies. This would enable either party to offset the risk of fluctuating rates of exchange by buying or selling the foreign currency on forward markets and thus hedging their exposure.

In the interests of avoiding the cost of high-risk contingencies being built into the contract price, it may be appropriate to make provision in the Contract for the Employer to reimburse the Contractor for any loss arising from currency restrictions, or restrictions on the transfer of currency which are imposed by the government or other authorities in a country from which any payments are to be made.

21.10 Place of payment

The Contract may provide where payment is to take place. If not, payment must be made at the place where the work was done, at least if the Contract stipulated the place where the work has to be executed.[186] Payment into tax havens with no direct connection to the parties or the project and to other places of dubious repute are likely to attract the attention of the relevant authorities and create suspicion of a breach of the *Foreign Corrupt Practices Act 1977* (US), or the *Bribery Act 2010* (UK).

21.11 *Security of Payment* legislation

Security of Payment legislation has been promulgated in a number of jurisdictions, to 'ensure that any person who undertakes to carry out construction work or who undertakes to supply related goods and services under a construction contract is entitled to receive, and is able to recover, progress payments in relation to the carrying out of that work and the supplying of those goods and services.'[187] Because of the far-reaching nature of the provisions of such legislation for both Contractors and Employers, it is vital, when drafting and administering construction contracts to determine whether and how it applies in the particular contract circumstances. The objective is to improve the cash-flow of Contractors and subcontractors.

The *Acts* provide statutory rights that cannot be contracted out of, which are in addition to rights under the Contract (or replacing contractual rights if they conflict with mandatory provisions of the legislation). The *Acts* (with the exception of Malaysia) provide for 'regular and timely payments' by providing an entitlement to progress payments. They generally enable the contracting parties to agree on the mechanism for determining the valuation and timing of payments but provide default conditions in the absence of agreement. Some *Acts*

186 *Horne v Williams & Co* (1940) TPD 106.

187 *Building and Construction Industry Security of Payment Act 2002* (Vic), 3(1)].

provide a maximum time for payment after a payment claim is made, irrespective of party agreement.[188]

This important legislation is discussed in ¶28.9.3, which provides details of the statutory adjudication process to provide a provisionally binding resolution of a payment dispute. The reader is referred to comprehensive texts which are available, including those by Jacobs,[189] Davenport,[190] and Coulson.[191]

21.12 *Quantum meruit*

In circumstances where there is no applicable contract and a contractor is requested to perform work at the request of another person on a non-gratuitous basis, the contractor will normally be entitled under the common law to be paid reasonable remuneration (***quantum meruit***) for that work. *Quantum meruit* is a Latin phrase meaning 'what one has earned.' The legal basis under the common law is now accepted to be restitution for a benefit received by a person unjustly enriched at the expense of another person.[192]

The value of work performed on a *quantum meruit* is simply a fair commercial rate for that work.[193] If cost is used as the basis for determining a *quantum meruit*, the costs recoverable by the contractor will usually include direct costs and attributable off-site overheads and a profit margin as well as any applicable taxes.[194] The amount must be reasonable in all the circumstances and represent the market value of the goods and services provided.[195] If a contractor owns and operates an item of equipment that is fully depreciated, so that it has minimal operating costs, the market value for the use of that item of equipment may be considerably greater than its operating cost.[196]

The profit margin that may be applicable to the valuation of the Work performed on a *quantum meruit* basis is the margin applicable to the contractor who performed the work, not an average or expected margin of other participants in the construction industry.[197]

---

188 NSW: 15 days for payment to a Head Contractor, 20 days for a payment to a subcontractor: *Building and Construction Industry Security of Payment Act 1999* (NSW) s11; WA: 42 days: *Building and Construction Industry (Security of Payment) Act 2021* (WA) s20; NT: 30 working days: *Construction Contracts (Security of Payments) Act 2004* (NT) s13; Ontario: Owner to Contractor – 28 days, Contractor to subcontractor – 7 days after receiving payment: *Construction Act 1990* (Ont) ss6.4, 6.5.

189 Marcus S Jacobs QC, *Security of Payments in the Australian Building and Construction Industry* (Thomson Reuters (Professional) Australia Limited, 6th edn 2016).

190 Philip Davenport, *Adjudication in the Building Industry* (Federation Press, 3rd edn 2010).

191 HHJ Peter Coulson QC, *Construction Adjudication* (Oxford University Press, 2007).

192 *Pavey & Mathews Pty Ltd v Paul* (1987) 162 CLR 221.

193 *Mann v Paterson Constructions Pty Ltd* [2019] HCA 32, [203] per Nettle Gordon and Edelman JJ.

194 *ERDC Group Limited v Brunel University* [2006] BLR 255, 270 [45] per HHJ Lloyd QC; *Castle Trustee Ltd v Bombay Palace Restaurant Ltd* [2018] EWHC 1602 (TCC), [301] per Jefford J.

195 *Balfour Beatty Power Construction Australia Ltd v Kidston Goldmines Ltd* [1989] 2 Qd R 105, 135, per Dowsett J; *Len Lichtnauer Developments Pty Ltd v James Trowse Constructions Pty Ltd* [2005] QCA 214, [29] per McMurdo J (21 BCL 430); *BP Exploration Co (Libya) Ltd v Hunt (No 2)* [1979] 1 WLR 783, 840 per Robert Goff J; *Benedetti v Sawiris* [2013] UKSC 50, [15] – [17] per Lord Clarke JSC, [103] per Lord Reed JSC, [180] per Lord Neuberger PSC (noted by McInnes (2014) 130 LQR 8.

196 *Maeda Kensetu Kogya Kabushiki Kaisha v Bauer Hong Kong* [2019] HKCFI 916, [34] – [50] per Mimmie Chan J.

197 *ERDC Group Limited v Brunel University* [2006] BLR 255, 274 [119] per HHJ Lloyd QC.

A contractor's entitlement to payment for a *quantum meruit* accrues whether or not the contractor has demanded payment.[198]

It must be stressed that a contractor can only claim remuneration on a *quantum meruit* where there is no subsisting applicable contract for the work requested:

> Indeed, if there was a valid and enforceable agreement governing the claimant's right to compensation, there would be neither occasion nor legal justification for the law to superimpose or impute an obligation or promise to pay a reasonable remuneration. The quasi-contractual obligation to pay fair and just compensation for a benefit which has been accepted will only arise in a case where there is no applicable genuine agreement or where such an agreement is frustrated, avoided or unenforceable. In such a case, it is the very fact that there is no genuine agreement or that the genuine agreement is frustrated, avoided or unenforceable that provides the occasion for (and part of the circumstances giving rise to) the imposition by the law of obligations to make restitution.[199]

The mutually exclusive nature of contractual and restitutionary claims has been accepted in many other cases since *Pavey*.[200]

The following are examples of circumstances where a *quantum meruit* may be applied because there is no subsisting contractual relationship that governs the relevant relationship between the parties:

(1) No subsisting contract:
- Where there is no genuine agreement between the parties.[201]
- Where preparatory work done in expectation of a contract is made use of by an owner, and a contract is never concluded.[202]

(2) Existing agreement no longer applies because of frustration, avoidance, or unenforceability:
- Where the contract has been frustrated at common law or under a relevant statute.[203]
- Where work has been carried out under a void contract or under a contract unenforceable by statute.[204]

---

198 *Claymore Services Ltd v Nautilus Properties Ltd* [2007] BLR 452, 457–458 [39] per Jackson J.

199 *Pavey & Mathews Pty Ltd v Paul* (1987) 162 CLR 221, 256 per Deane J.

200 eg *Update Constructions Pty Ltd v Rozelle Child Care Centre Ltd* (1990) 20 NSWLR 251, 275 per Priestly JA; *Ansett Transport Industries (Operations) Pty Ltd v Alenia Aeritalia & Selenia SPA* (1991) 105 FLR 169, 174; *Gaymark Investments Pty Ltd v Walter Construction Group Ltd* (1999) 16 BCL 449; [1999] NTSC 143; *Trimis & Anor v Mina* [1999] NSWCA 140.

201 eg *Atlas Cabinets & Furniture Ltd v National Trust Co* (1990) 68 DLR (4th) 161; *ABB Power Generation Ltd v Chapple & Ors* [2001] WASCA 412.

202 eg *William Lacey (Hounslow) Ltd v Davis* [1957] 1 WLR 932; 2 All ER 712; *Sabemo Pty Ltd v North Sydney Municipal Council* [1977] 2 NSWLR 880.

203 Frustration under the common law is a high bar to overcome, and the following claims for a *quantum meruit* because the contract was frustrated failed because the court held the contract was not frustrated: *Davis Contractors Limited v Fareham Urban District Council* [1956] AC 696; *Peter Kiewit Sons' Company of Canada Limited v Eakins Construction Limited* (1960) 22 DLR (2d) 465. [1960] SCR 361; *Morrison-Knudsen Co Ltd v British Columbia Hydro & Power Authority* (1978) 85 DLR (3d) 186; (1991) 7 Const LJ 227.

204 eg *Gino D'Allesandro Constructions Pty Ltd v Powis* [1987] 2 Qd R 40; *Gray (Constructions) Pty Ltd v Hogan* [2000] NSWCA 26; *Lee Gleeson Pty Ltd v Sterling Estates Pty Ltd* (1991) 23 NSWLR 571; *Nunkuwarrin Yunti v AL Sealey Construction Pty Ltd* (1998) 72 SASR 21; (1998) 199 LSJS 76; *Great City Pty Ltd v Kemayan Management Services (Australia) Pty Ltd & Ors* [1999] WASC 70 (24 June 1999); *Pohlmann v Harrison* [1995] 2 Qd R 59.

(3) Existing agreement no longer applies because it has been repudiated.[205]

(4) Terms of existing agreement do not cover additional work:

- Where the Employer or her/his representatives do not issue an instruction for a Variation and wrongly but bona fide insist on the disputed work being carried out as part of the original contract obligations.[206]
- It is contended that work additional to an existing contract cannot reasonably be regarded as included in the scope of the contract.[207]

The concepts of restitution and unjust enrichment are also features of civil law systems that can apply in similar situations to those previously outlined. For example, under the *French Civil Code*, acts of performance under an annulled contract (deemed never to have existed) give rise to restitution,[208] as may be the case under a lapsed contract (the result if one of the necessary contractual elements disappears).[209] Restitution may be required for acts of performance after the termination of a contract.[210] Similar to the common law concept of paying for the value of unjust enrichment as a *quantum meruit*, the *French Civil Code* requires 'A person who benefits from an unjustified enrichment to the detriment of another person must indemnify the person who is thereby made the poorer to an amount equal to the lesser of the two values of the enrichment and the impoverishment.'[211] Unjustified enrichment is defined as: 'An enrichment is unjustified where it stems neither from the fulfilment of an obligation by the person impoverished nor from his intention to confer a gratuitous benefit.'[212]

21.13 Economic duress

On occasion, a Contractor or subcontractor which finds it is making a substantial loss on a contract will endeavour to put pressure on the Employer or Contractor to make payments that are additional to those due under the Contract. That pressure can take the form of a threat to repudiate the Contract, or not deliver the contracted for facilities by the contractually required date. In circumstances where late delivery of a facility may involve the Employer in breach of its own supply contracts, the real losses which would arise from delayed or non-delivery may be many times the potential liquidated damages or the recoverable damages for breach of contract. In this situation, an Employer may feel it has no real alternative but to agree to pay up, notwithstanding the lack of contractual liability.

An agreement to pay additional money in these circumstances may subsequently be voided under the doctrine of economic duress. The elements of economic duress are that

---

205 eg *De Bernady v Harding* (1853) 8 Ex 822; *Lodder v Slowey* [1904] AC 442; *Jennings Construction Ltd v Q H & M Birt Pty Ltd* (unreported, SC NSW, Cole J, 16 October 1988); *Renard Constructions (ME) Pty Ltd v Minister for Public Works* (1992) 26 NSWLR 234; (1992) 9 BCL 40; *Iezzi Constructions Pty Ltd v Watkins Pacific (Qld) Pty Ltd* [1995] 2 Qd R 350; *Sopov v Kane Constructions Pty Ltd* [2007] VSCA 257.

206 eg *Liebe v Molloy* (1906) 4 CLR 347; *Gigliotti Constructions Pty Ltd v Jalili* [1998] NSWSC 182.

207 eg *Sir Lindsay Parkinson & Co Ld v Commissioner of Works and Public Buildings* [1949] 2 KB 632.

208 Art 1178.

209 Art 1187.

210 Art 1229.

211 Art 1303.

212 Art 1303–1.

illegitimate economic pressure was applied to overcome free will so that there was no real consent to the agreement. Considerations relevant to application of this doctrine to construction contracts, and the hurdles to be overcome in demonstrating that economic pressure is 'illegitimate' are discussed by Loots & Charrett,[213] and in Keating,[214] including reference to two recent cases in the UK.[215]

213 Philip Loots & Dr Donald Charrett, 'Being Held to Ransom or "Wielding the Whip or the Rod": How Unscrupulous Dealing, Illegitimate Pressure and Tough Negotiating Tactics Can be Overcome by the Legal Remedy of Economic Duress' (2014) *International Construction Law Review* 211.

214 Stephen Furst & Vivian Ramsey, *Keating on Construction Contracts* (Thomson Sweet & Maxwell, 8th edn 2006) 199–201.

215 *DSND Subsea v Petroleum Geo-Services* [2000] B.L.R. 530; *Carillion Construction Ltd v Felix (UK) Ltd* [2001] B.L.R. 1.

CHAPTER 22

Termination by the Employer

CONTENTS

22.1 Default by the Contractor

What a Contractor has promised to do or not to do must be determined from the terms of the Contract. A breach of contract is a failure by a party to fulfil its contractual obligations. The Contractor is usually obliged to carry out and complete the Works described in the scope of works. It will be in breach of contract if it fails to complete the Works, even if it would have been unable to complete the Works exercising due skill and diligence.[1] Not all breaches of contract by either the Contractor or the Employer are sufficiently serious to entitle the other to terminate the contract. The primary

1 *Midland Bank Trust Co Ltd v Hett, Stubbs and Kemp* [1979] Ch 384, 434–435 per Oliver J.

DOI: 10.4324/9781003206873-22

consequence of a party committing a breach of contract is that it becomes liable to pay damages to the innocent party.[2]

It is only the breach of a fundamental term of the contract which entitles the innocent party to terminate. It will be recognized that termination of any construction contract is a drastic measure which, in practice, may be exceedingly difficult to execute. It is characteristic of many standard form contracts that resort to termination is expressly provided for only in the most serious circumstances.[3]

The Employer will often be better off by accepting a defective or delayed project, rather than by terminating the Contract and starting anew with another contractor which would involve loss of time and money that the Employer may have little chance of ever recovering. The position of the Contractor may therefore be better than appears from the Contract. Accordingly, it is of great importance to an Employer to contract with a Contractor upon whom it can rely, rather than relying on provisions for termination in the Contract.

It may on the other hand, be fairly easy to exercise the Employer's right to terminate the Contract and complete the Works when the plant has been delivered to the Site, provided that the remaining work is not of a highly specialized nature. It will be more difficult when the plant is still being manufactured at the Contractor's or at its subcontractor's premises, which may be in another country. Even if the Contractor is obliged to release the plant, the situation may prove to be complex.

Alternatively, the Employer may elect not to complete the Works. This may well be the least expensive solution where the Contract has proved a failure from the start, and little work has been carried out. In such cases, the value of the Works may be very small, if of any value at all, so that there may be no amount or a negative amount due to the Contractor. Equally, the work actually done may be of no useful value to the Employer.

22.2 Notice to correct

Construction contracts typically contain a provision enabling the Engineer to issue a notice to the Contractor, requiring it to make good any failure to carry out its contractual obligations under the Contract, and giving it a specified reasonable time to do so. Depending on the specific terms of the Contract, such a notice may or may not be a necessary precondition for termination by the Employer under the provisions of the Contract. That is, the Employer may have the power to terminate the Contract without notice on the happening of certain specified events.

22.2.1 Default notices or 'show cause' notices

A show cause notice requires the Contractor to correct specified breaches of contract and requires evidence that this has been done in a certain form and by a certain time.[4] A default notice is similar to a show cause notice but does not usually require the Contractor to provide

2 *Shaw v MFP Foundations and Pilings Ltd* [2010] EWHC 1839 (TCC), [40] per Edwards-Stuart J; *Out of the Box Pte Ltd v Wanin Industries Pte Ltd* [2013] SGCA 15, [10].

3 See *Tsakiroglou and Co Ltd v Noblee Thorl GmbH* [1960] 2 QB 180; and Asquith L.J. in *Sir Lindsay Parkinson and Co Ltd v Commissioner of Works* [1949] 2 KB 632.

4 2017 FIDIC Red Book sub-clause 15.1; JCWC Standard Form of Building Contract (2006 edn) clauses 35.1(1) and (2), AS 4000–1997, clauses 39.2 and 39.3; see *Dura (Australia) Constructions Pty Ltd v Hue Boutique Living Pty Ltd* [2012] VSC 99, [385]-[386], [391]-[392] and [403] per Dixon J.

evidence of it having corrected its defaults.[5] Examples of circumstances in which such notices are issued involve serious breaches of contract such as where the Contractor has suspended all its work or has failed to proceed regularly and diligently with its work, or where the Contractor is persistent in its disobedience of a notice or instruction issued by the Engineer. Failing to proceed regularly and diligently with the work does not require that the Contractor has reduced its work to the point that there was either no progress, or that progress was *de minimis*.[6]

The issuing of a default notice or show cause notice may be a contractual requirement and condition precedent to termination.[7] A contract may require as a precondition to the issue of a show cause notice or default notice that the Employer considers that damages may not be an adequate remedy for the Contractor's breaches of contract. A public authority may reasonably consider it to be in the public interest for the Works to be brought to completion as soon as practicable, so as to avoid detriment to the intended end users of the Works even though liquidated damages are payable by the Contractor for late completion.[8] The notice needs to do no more than to direct the Contractor's attention to what is amiss.[9] Under the FIDIC rainbow suite a default notice is required to state a 'specified reasonable time' within which the Contractor must make good its failure to perform its contractual obligations.[10]

In *Obrascon Huarte Lain SA v A-G (Gibraltar)*[11] the court held that:

> The specified time for compliance with Clause 15.1 notice must be reasonable in all the circumstances prevailing at the time of the notice. Thus, if 90% of the workforce had gone down with cholera at that time, the period given for compliance would need reasonably to take that into account, even if that problem was the Contractor's risk. It may well be relevant to take into account whether Clause 15.1 notice is coming out of the blue or if the subject matter has been raised before and the Contractor has chosen to ignore what it has been told. What is reasonable is fact sensitive.

22.3 Termination by the Employer

22.3.1 Contractual termination

Engineering and construction contracts usually make provision for circumstances in which the parties may terminate the Contract and provide for the consequences flowing from such termination. It is open to the parties to agree that breach of any obligation, whether or not such an obligation is an 'essential 'or 'innominate' term gives rise to a right to terminate.[12] In addition, construction contracts commonly contain a termination clause which entitles the Employer to

5 See JCT Standard Building Contract (2016 edn) clause 8.4.

6 See *Bayindir Insaat Turizm Ticaret Ve Sanayi A.S. v Islamic Republic of Pakistan* (ICSID Case No. ARB/03/29, Award of 27 August 2009), [255] (considering a FIDIC contract).

7 *Interserve Construction Ltd v Hitachi Zosen Inova AG* [2017] EWHC 2633 (TCC).

8 *Bath and North-East Somerset District Council v Mowlem plc* [2004] BLR 153, 161, per Mance LJ; *FPM Constructions Pty Ltd v Council of the City of Blue Mountains* [2005] NSWCA 340, [139], per Basten JA.

9 *Dura (Australia) Constructions Pty Ltd v Hue Boutique Living Pty Ltd* [2012] VSC 99, [397]-[398], per Dixon J (affirmed: [2013] VSCA 179).

10 Referred to as a Notice to Correct in sub-clause 15.1 of the 2017 FIDIC rainbow suite.

11 [2014] EWHC 1028 (TCC), [318(b)] per Akenhead J (appeal dismissed: [2015] EWCA Civ 712).

12 See *Obrascon Huarte Lain SA v A-G (Gibraltar)* [2014] EWHC 1028 (TCC), [318(a)] and [321] per Akenhead J; *Bunge Corporation v Tradax Export SA* [1981] 1 WLR 711, 715 per Lord Wilberforce; *Australian Development Corp Pty Ltd v White Constructions (ACT) Pty Ltd* (1996) 12 BCL 317, 359 per Giles CJ Comm D [Sup Ct NSW]; *Northrop Grumman Mission Systems Europe Limited v BAE Systems (Al Diriyah C4I) Ltd* [2014] 2014 EWHC 2955 (TCC), [67] per Ramsey J (appeal dismissed: [2015] EWCA Civ 844); see 2017 FIDIC

eject the Contractor from the Site, or otherwise to take the work substantially out of its hands. More recently, breaches of safety requirements, non-compliance with equal opportunity and environmental policies and legislation might be included in contracts as a cause for termination. Generally speaking, a contractual termination provision is regarded as being in addition to, and not in derogation of, the common-law rights arising from repudiation of a contract. Termination is an extreme remedy and should only be undertaken after seeking legal advice.

A wide variety of equivalent terminology is used in texts on contracts to describe the process in which a party brings a contract to an end by its own action before the contract has been fully performed by one or other or both parties. These terms include 'forfeiture,' 'determination,' 'termination', 'renunciation,' 'rescission,' and 'repudiation.' The term **termination** will be used in this book for the process in which a party brings a contract to an end by its own action before the contract has been fully performed by one or other or both parties.[13] Termination of a contract pursuant to a contractual power must be distinguished from what is sometimes referred to as determination of a contractor's employment by the Employer pursuant to contractual power, which contemplates that the Contractor will be discharged from performing further work but the underlying construction contract will continue to operate, with a monetary adjustment taking place between the parties in accordance with the contractual terms to take account of the effect on the Employer and on the Contractor as a result of the Contractor's employment being determined.[14]

Unless a party to a contract has express power to do so, it may not terminate an engineering or construction contract unilaterally before the contract has been fully performed.[15]

It may be very difficult to know whether a breach of contract by the Contractor is serious enough to entitle the Employer to bring the Contract to an end under the common law so as to avoid further harm by the Contractor, as opposed to allowing the Contractor to continue with the Works and merely claim damages. A termination clause in the Contract setting out the remedies and powers of the Employer is designed mainly to allow the Employer to take the work out of the Contractor's hands in certain clearly defined circumstances, where under the general law it may not be entitled to do this. Even if a clause of this kind and the Employer's common law rights overlap, it may be preferable to act under such a clause.

Despite the absence of any expression such as 'without prejudice to any other rights or remedies,' it is submitted that the rights conferred by an express termination clause would not be intended as a substitution for the innocent party's common-law rights in the absence of clear language to that effect. This is important because a large number of the matters on which such a clause is conditioned would also entitle the Employer to rescind the contract at common law.

The termination provisions usually set out the necessary prerequisites for a contractual right of termination by the Employer and may be described as a right 'to enter upon the Site and Works and expel the Contractor therefrom.' A termination clause of this kind is interpreted by the courts strictly against the Employer.

Red Book sub-clause 15 which requires that the breach in question be a 'material breach of the Contractor's obligations under the Contract.'

13 The position in the Middle East is considered in H Turner & M Scriven, 'Default and Termination Under Construction Contracts (With Certain Particular References to the Middle East)' (1995) *International Construction Law Review* 583.

14 *BMBF (No. 12) Ltd v Harland and Wolff Shipbuilding and Heavy Industries Ltd* [2001] EWCA Civ 862, [48] per Potter LJ; *Melville Dundas Ltd v George Wimpey UK Ltd* [2006] BLR 164, 174 [30].

15 *Nigel Witham Ltd v Smith* [2007] EWHC 3027 (TCC), [86], per HHJ Coulson QC.

22.3.2 Termination under common law

Contracts can be terminated in a number of circumstances at common law, including where the contract has been repudiated, or there has been an anticipatory breach or a breach of a serious term and the innocent party has elected to terminate the contract.[16] A further circumstance would be where the contract is terminated, prospectively or retrospectively due to frustration, illegality, death of a party, or pursuant to some other legal or equitable right; or where a right to terminate is conferred by statute and that right is exercised.

Repudiation is a common law termination procedure where one party is in breach of a fundamental term of a contract or has shown by her/his conduct an intention not to be bound by the contract terms, and the other (innocent) party elects to accept the repudiation, thereby bringing the contract to an end. A breach of contract constitutes a repudiatory breach where its effect is to deprive the innocent party of substantially the whole of the benefit which it was intended the innocent party would obtain from performance of the contract.[17]

A breach of an essential term or condition of a contract will permit the innocent party to elect to terminate the contract, regardless of the consequences of the breach.[18] In *Telford Homes (Creekside) Ltd v Ampurius Nu Homes Holdings Ltd*[19] the principal questions to be asked were framed as follows:

> The next thing to consider is the effect of the breach on the injured party. What financial loss has it caused? How much of the intended benefit under the contract has the injured party already received? Can the injured party be adequately compensated by an award of damages? Is the breach likely to be repeated? Will the guilty party resume compliance with his obligations? Has the breach fundamentally changed the value of future performance of the guilty parties outstanding obligations? The quantification of the financial consequences may provide a strong indication of the seriousness of the breach; if not purely financial but with the potential to cause physical harm or injury, a breach may justify the termination of the contract.[20]

The cumulative effect of breaches which do not justify termination of the contract individually may be sufficient to establish a basis for termination.[21] Put differently, a number of breaches of contract may, when taken together, manifest objectively 'a fundamental disregard of the contract' that constitutes a repudiation of it.[22] It is important to appreciate that a wrongful allegation of repudiation may itself amount to a repudiation, for example, if party A refuses to perform its contractual obligations because it believes that party B has repudiated the contract, and party A is wrong in that assertion, party A itself may have repudiated the contract, thereby entitling party B to terminate the contract.[23]

---

16 *Alliance Concrete Singapore Pte Ltd v Sato Kogyo (s) Pte Ltd* [2014] SGCA 35, [58]; *Phosagro Asia Pte Ltd v Piattchanine* [2016] SGCA 61, [51]-[52]; *Sports Connection Private Ltd v Deuter Sports GmbH* [2009] SGCA 22.

17 *Stocznia Gdynia SA v Gearbulk Holdings Ltd* [2009] BLR 196, 203 [14] per Moore-Bick LJ; *LED Linear (Asia) Pte Ltd v Krislite Pte Ltd* [2017] SGHC 150, [136]-[137] per Tan Lee Meng SJ.

18 *Fu Yuan Foodstuff Manufacturer Pte Ltd v Methodist Welfare Services* [2009] SGCA 23, [34].

19 [2013] EWCA Civ 577, [52] per Lewison LJ.

20 See *McNab NQ Pty Ltd v Walkrete Pty Ltd* [2013] QSC 128, [26] per de Jersey CJ.

21 *Anglo Group plc v Winther Browne and Co* (2000) 72 Con LR 118, 160 [227] per HHJ Tomlin CMG QC; *Rice v Great Yarmouth BC* (2001) 3 LGLR 41, 51 [37] per Hale LJ.

22 *Kyren Pty Ltd v Wunda Projects Australia Pty Ltd* [2012] SASCFC 23, [112].

23 *National Engineering Pty Ltd v Chilco Enterprises Pty Ltd* [1999] NSWSC 1105, [28] per Windeyer J; *Shyam Jewellers Ltd v Cheesman* [2001] EWCA Civ 1818, [63], per Potter LJ; *Able Contractors Ltd v Wui Loong*

A Contractor's conduct may constitute a repudiation of the contract, or a serious breach entitling the Employer to terminate, where the Contractor purports to terminate the Contract in circumstances where it is not entitled to do so;[24] where a Contractor abandons the Site with no intention of returning;[25] when the Contractor fails to comply with applicable construction plans in a very fundamental way;[26] or the Contractor becomes insolvent and stops the Works with little or no prospect of resuming.[27] Even if a small amount of work remains to be performed, a Contractor's conduct may be repudiatory.[28] If the Contractor refuses to go on with the Works unless a further payment is made to it, where the Contractor was not legitimately entitled to make that demand for payment,[29] such conduct will amount to a repudiation.[30]

The nature and gravity of the Contractor's delay may be important as to whether the Employer's entitlement is limited to recovering damages or giving an entitlement to terminate.[31] Where the Contractor is required to complete the Works by a particular date, but completion by that date is not stated to be 'of the essence' of the contract, should the Contractor not complete the Work by the required date, the Employer or its duly authorised agent may give the Contractor a notice requiring the Contractor to complete within a specified reasonable time, failing which the Employer may terminate the Contract.[32] The German and Swiss law apparently entitle the Employer to terminate the contract if the Contractor fails to complete the Works by the required date.[33] If a Contractor's progress is grossly or inexcusably poor, the Contractor's conduct may amount to repudiation or a breach of an essential or innominate term[34] of the contract, entitling the Employer to terminate the

---

Scaffolding Works Co Ltd [2012] HKCFI 914, [62] per Chu J.

24 *Carr v JA Berriman Pty Ltd* (1953) 89 CLR 327, 343 per Fullagar J; *Manx Electricity Authority v JP Morgan Chase Bank* [2003] EWCA Civ 1324, [36] per Rix LJ.

25 *Rubiera v Building and Handyman Group Limited* [2019] EWHC 1730 (TCC), [31]-[32] per DHCJ Veronique Buehrlen QC; *Basetech Services Pty Ltd v Leighton Contractors Pty Ltd* (No.6) [2016] FCA 1534, [642] per Besanko J.

26 *Trident Engineering Co Ltd v Mansion Holdings Ltd* [2000] HKCFI 1, [144], per DHCJ To (appeal dismissed [2001] HKCA 338).

27 *Chan Hong Seng Engrg and Const Pte Ltd v Vatten International Pte Ltd* [2002] SGHC 124, [44-[67], per Judith Prakash J; *Greenore Port Ltd v Technical and Guarantee Co Ltd* [2006] EWHC 3119 (TCC), [171]-[172] per Jackson J; *Wenn v Café San Paul Pty Ltd* [2008] QCA 18.

28 *San International Pte Ltd v Keppel Engineering Pte Ltd* [1998] 3 SLR(R) 447, 460 [29] per M Karthigesu.

29 See Philip Loots & Dr Donald Charrett, 'Being Held to Ransom or "Wielding the Whip or the Rod": How Unscrupulous Dealing, Illegitimate Pressure and Tough Negotiating Tactics can be Overcome by the Legal Remedy of Economic Duress' (2014) *International Construction Law Review* 211.

30 *Pickard Finlason Partnership Ltd v Lock* [2014] EWHC 25 (TCC), [274]-[278] per HHJ Stephen Davies; *Aggressive Construction Co Ltd v Wai Kin Construction Ltd* [2014] HKCFI 744, [81] per Mimmie Chan J; *Stepanoski v Aslan* (No.3) [2019] NSWSC 1445, [54]-[59] per Emmett AJA.

31 *Lawrence v Ciantar* [2019] NSWSC 464, [189]-[191] per Henry J; *Seadrill Management Services Ltd v OAO Gazprom* [2009] EWHC 1530 (Comm), [244] per Flaux J (appeal dismissed [2010] EWCA Civ 691); *Sabic UK Petrochemicals Ltd v Punj Lloyd Ltd* [2013] EWHC 2916 (TCC), [377]-[383] per Stuart-Smith J; *Engen Marine Engineering Pte Ltd* [2013] SGHC 148, [109]-[118] per Vinodh Coomaraswamy JC.

32 *Balog v Crestiani* (1975) 132 CLR 289, 296, per Gibbs J; *Discain Project Services Ltd v Opecprime Developments Ltd* [2001] EWHC Tech 450, [57], per HH J Seymour QC; *Lauro v The Marble House of Australia Pty Ltd* [2013] SASC 186, [134], per Blue J.

33 F Nicklisch, 'Remedies of the Employer for Delay in Completion under the Contract and, Law: Liquidated Damages and Unliquidated Damages: Termination' in Humphrey Lloyd (ed), *The Liability of Contractors* (Longman Group Ltd, 1986) 89–98; A Scherer & A Schneider, 'International Construction Contracts Under Swiss Law: An Introduction' (2007) 23 *Construction Law Journal* 559, 557–570; *DCT Projects Pty Ltd v Champion Homes Sales Pty Ltd* [2016] NSWCA 117, [44]-[52], per Gleeson JA.

34 An **innominate term** of a contract is between a condition and a warranty. Sometimes referred to as an intermediate term.

contract.[35] If the Contractor has performed work in a seriously defective manner,[36] and its attempts at remedial works are clearly inadequate, this may constitute repudiatory conduct.[37]

A party may show an intention to perform the contract in a manner that is substantially inconsistent with its obligations, and it is clear that the party will not perform the contract in any other way.[38] Whether a repudiation can be shown to have taken place is determined having regard to the nature of the contract, and all the objective circumstances of the case.[39] A Contractor which misinterprets its contractual obligations and attempts to perform its obligations in a manner which is inconsistent with its actual obligations does not necessarily exhibit repudiatory conduct.[40] If a party persists in adopting an untenable position even if that party believes it to be correct and which is materially opposed to its true obligations, that will usually constitute repudiatory conduct.[41] A party's breach of a fundamental contractual obligation, or conduct showing an intention no longer to be bound by its contractual obligations, are really different facets of the same thing. Repudiatory conduct gives the innocent party an election between continuing with the contract on foot and seeking damages for the breach or accepting the repudiation and terminating the contract.

On the other hand, in the case of a breach of an innominate term, the position would have to be determined contextually by looking at the nature of the term and the consequences that may flow or have flowed from the breach. If the consequences of the breach are not such as to deny the innocent party the benefit of the contract, the innocent party will not be entitled to terminate it. By way of example, in *A-G Botswana v Aussie Diamond Products Pty Ltd (No.2)*,[42] in a contract for the supply and commissioning of a drilling rig, the commissioning component of the sales price amounted to approximately 1% of the total price. Failures in the supplier fulfilling its commissioning obligations were held not to be sufficient to entitle the purchaser to terminate the contract for breach.

A major dilemma which may face an Employer confronted with a defaulting Contractor, particularly if the default occurs in the early stages of the work, is that the Employer cannot seek to recover damages for breach of contract until the work is complete – perhaps a number of years later. Yet the damage, in the shape of the cost of completion and perhaps even of the amount of delay likely to arise from the breach, may be more or less immediately ascertainable once a complete contract is let to a new Contractor.

Again, in certain rather special circumstances, an Employer may not wish to complete the Works at all, though it may have suffered severe financial loss of a different kind in an abortive

35 See *Wui Fu Development Co Ltd v Tak Yuen Construction Co Ltd* [1999] HKCFI 93, [25] per Findlay J.

36 See Paul Keating, 'The Control of Quality in Construction' All They Will Be the Way Is Running Presents Where' in J Uff & P Capper (eds), *Construction Contract Policy* (Kings College London, 1989) chapter 10, 142; *Mousa v Vukobratich Enterprises Pty Ltd* [2019] QSC 49, [196] per Henry J.

37 *Wyman- Gordon Ltd v Proclad International Ltd (No.3)* [2009] CSOH 98; *Osburn v Leggett* [1930] SASR 346; *Tennyson Estate Ltd v Boxwood Design Ltd* [2014] HKCFI 447, [22]-[23] per GHCJ S Wong SC.

38 *CFW Architects v Cowlin Construction Ltd* [2006] EWHC 6 (TCC), [113] per HHJ Thornton QC; *Pacific Brands Sport and Leisure Pty Ltd v Underworks Pty Ltd* [2006] FCAFC 40, [102]; *Koompahtoo Local Aboriginal Land Council v Sanpine Pty Ltd* (2007) 233 CLR 115, [44]; *Diploma Construction Pty Ltd v Marula Pty Ltd* [2009] WASCA 229, [88]-[97] per Newnes JA (26 BCL 172); *Biofuel Industries Pte Ltd v V8 Environmental Pte Ltd* [2018] SGCA 28, [20].

39 *Wesiak v D&R Constructions (Aust) Pty Ltd* [2016] NSWCA 353, [90] per McDougall J; *Seadrill Management Services Ltd v OAO Gazprom* [2009] EWHC 1530 (Comm), [239], per Flaux J (appeal dismissed [2010] EWCA Civ 691).

40 *Sweet and Maxwell Ltd v Universal Services Ltd* [1964] 2 QB 699, 734 per Pearson LJ; *GIB Automation Pte Ltd v Deluge Fire Protection (SEA) Pte Ltd* [2007] SGHC 48, [77] per Sundaresh Menon CJ.

41 *Austman Pty Ltd v Mount Gibson Mining Ltd* [2012] WASC 202, [546] per Kenneth Martin J; *Stepanoski v Aslan (No.3)* [2019] NSWSC 1445, [54] per Emmett AJA.

42 [2012] WASCA 73.

project. In each of these cases the Employer will wish to consider using its common-law remedy of termination. In many other situations the Employer may wish to keep its options open and use both remedies so that if its termination fails, for instance on common-law grounds, it can be supported on contractual grounds (or vice versa). However, where the Employer's rights under the contractual termination clause are mutually exclusive and inconsistent with common-law termination, it may be argued that the Employer must, in fact, make an election between exercising the common-law right of termination and the contractual right to terminate.

22.3.3 The effects of termination

If the Employer elects to accept a repudiation of the contract, or elects to terminate the Contract due to the Contractor's serious breach, the effect is not to terminate the Contract *ab initio*.[43] The parties' executory rights and obligations under the Contract come to an end, but secondary obligations come into existence, including an obligation to compensate the innocent party for the consequences of the termination of the contract.[44] Termination is accordingly prospective, not retrospective.[45] It is good drafting practice to specify which of the Contract's clauses are to survive termination,[46] such as dispute resolution provisions,[47] or a contractual right to recover overpayments.[48]

22.3.4 Contractual preconditions for termination

Termination clauses usually provide a list of identified defaults by the Contractor entitling the Employer to terminate the Contract. For example, the 2017 FIDIC Red Book provides for termination if the Contractor:

- Fails to comply with a Notice to Correct.[49]
- Fails to comply with a binding agreement or a final and binding determination of the Engineer,[50] or a decision of the Dispute Avoidance/Adjudication Board[51] and such failure constitutes a material breach of the Contractor's obligation under the Contract
- Abandons the Works or otherwise plainly demonstrates an intention not to continue performance of the Contractor's obligations under the Contract.[52]
- Without reasonable excuse fails to proceed with the Works in accordance with the provisions for commencement, delays, and suspension, or if there is a maximum amount of Delay Damages the Employer would be entitled to Delay Damages that exceeded this maximum amount.[53]

---

43 *Mi-Space (UK) Limited v Bridgewater Civil Engineering Ltd* [2015] EWHC 3360 (TCC), [118] per Edwards-Stuart J.

44 *Alfred McAlpine Construction Ltd v Panatown Ltd* [2001] 1 AC 518, 534 per Lord Clyde.

45 *Mann v Paterson Constructions Pty Ltd* [2019] HCA 32, [8]-[10] per Kiefel CJ, Bell and Keane JJ.

46 *Pipeline Services WA Pty Ltd Atco Gas Australia Pty Ltd* [2014] WASC 10, [7].

47 *Codelfa Construction Pty Ltd v State Railway Authority of New South Wales* (1982) 149 CLR 337, 365–366 per Mason J.

48 *Imperial Chemical Industries Ltd v Merit Merrell Technology Ltd* [2017] EWHC 1763 (TCC), [196] per Fraser J.

49 See 2017 FIDIC Red Book sub-clause 15.2.1 (a)(i).

50 2017 FIDIC Red Book sub-clause 15.2.1 (a)(ii).

51 2017 FIDIC Red Book sub-clause 15.2.1 (a)(iii).

52 2017 FIDIC Red Book sub-clause 15.2.1 (b).

53 2017 FIDIC Red Book sub-clause 15.2.1 (c).

- Without reasonable excuse fails to comply with a Notice of rejection given under defects and rejection provisions, or an Engineer's instruction regarding remedial work within 28 days after receiving it.[54]
- Fails to provide performance security.[55]
- Subcontracts the whole, or any part of, the Works in breach of the Contract or assigns the Contract without the required agreement under the terms of the contract governing assignment.[56]
- Becomes bankrupt or insolvent, goes into liquidation, administration, reorganisation, winding up or dissolution; becomes subject to the appointment of a liquidator, receiver, administrator, manager, or trustee; enters into a composition with the Contractor's creditors; or any act is done or any event occurs which is analogous to or has a similar effect to any of these acts or events under applicable laws.[57]
- Is found, based on reasonable evidence, to have engaged in corrupt, fraudulent, collusive, or coercive practice at any time in relation to the Works or the Contract.[58]

The Contractor may have the right to correct certain defaults within a specified time, whereas other defaults may justify immediate termination. In some cases the Employer has the alternative of taking part of the work out of the Contractor's hands. The Contract may require that, in the event of termination arising from the Contractor's default, the Employer is required to notify the Contractor with specific reference to the default.[59] The power of termination will be wrongfully exercised if the happening of one of the default events has not occurred.

The Engineer has power to withhold payment certificates for defective work, which may be prudent so as to have money in hand if termination becomes necessary. It is implied that the Engineer must give its notice within a reasonable time of the action of which it is complaining.

22.3.5 The Employer cannot 'reprobate and approbate'

Termination by the Employer will be wrongful if the Employer itself has been the cause of bringing about the event giving rise to the termination. The effect of a termination clause is to give the Employer the right to take possession of the Site and complete the Works, as well as to use the materials and plant and equipment on the Site. If the Employer ejects the Contractor, calls the bonds, completes the work, and uses the Contractor's materials, plant, or equipment, or holds retention money due to the Contractor, it must account to the Contractor, that is, it must show that the materials, plant, equipment, and money were expended reasonably.

Any attempt to terminate the Contract which is not in strict accordance with the termination clause and the common law may amount to a repudiation of the Contract by the Employer, and entitle the Contractor to accept such repudiation of the Contract and claim damages or a *quantum meruit*.[60] However, a wrongful termination under the contractual termination clause does not negate the validity of a termination under the common law where the Contractor's default in any event amounts to a repudiation.

---

54 2017 FIDIC Red Book sub-clause 15.2.1 (d).
55 2017 FIDIC Red Book sub-clause 15.2.1 (e).
56 2017 FIDIC Red Book sub-clause 15.2.1 (f).
57 2017 FIDIC Red Book sub-clause 15.2.1 (g).
58 2017 FIDIC Red Book sub-clause 15.2.1 (h).
59 *Marsden v Sambell* (1880) 43 CT 120; *Drew v Fosolyne* (1887) 18 WBD 590 (CA).
60 *Lodder v Slowey* (1904) AC 442; see also *Roberts v Bury Commissioners* (1870) LR 5 CP 310.

In *Wellington (Mayor, etc) v Roberts and McNaught*,[61] a termination clause entitled the Employer in certain circumstances to take the work out of the hands of the Contractor on notice and either carry it on under the direction of the city surveyor or re-let it to another contractor. An attempted termination was held to be invalid because the notice did not say that the Employer intended to take the latter course.

22.3.6 Termination may constitute a penalty

Where a termination clause is viewed as a 'penalty' a court will not uphold it. For example, in *Bysouth v Blackburn & Mitcham Shire (No 2)*[62] (*Bysouth*) the Employer purported to terminate a contract pursuant to a termination clause which provided that upon termination, the moneys previously paid to the Contractor should be deemed to be the full value of all work done and should satisfy all claims by the Contractor under the Contract. Further, the Employer argued that the deposit, all retention money and all materials, implements and plant on or about the Works should remain the absolute property of the Employer. The Full Court held that a provision which seeks to forfeit moneys already earned and the Contractor's property on the Works amounted to a penalty.

This was affirmed in *Egan v South Australian Railways Commissioner*[63] where the language of the termination clause was almost identical to the clause considered in *Bysouth*. The Full Court arrived at the same decision and held that the termination clause was a penalty.

In *Suburban Municipal Waterworks v Cochrane and Cherry*,[64] it was held that, where the Contract provided that the Engineer was to decide whether a default had occurred or not, such decision would be binding. Where the Contract contained no such provision and a dispute arose, this question would be decided by a court or arbitrator.

In *Roberts v Bury Commissioners*,[65] it was held that a clause in a contract empowering the Engineer to decide whether or not there had been a delay did not give it the power to decide whether the reason for such delay was attributable to the Contractor or the Employer.

22.3.7 Subcontracts

The Employer may seek to take over subcontracts after termination of the head contract. If, as is often the case, the Contractor's solvency is also in question, subcontractors will usually be pleased to carry on working for a solvent Employer. The Employer is to some extent in the hands of subcontractors in this situation. In the absence of a specific contractual provision, the Employer generally has no right to take over subcontracts on termination. But a subcontractor who refuses to make a reasonable contract with the Employer may not be entitled to recover damages from the Contractor for breach of the subcontract on the grounds that it failed to mitigate its losses. Further, the Employer may be able to exert some pressure through its right to pay or not to pay nominated subcontractors direct for work already done.

---

61 (1883) 2 NZLR (CA) 56.
62 [1928] VLR 562.
63 (1979) 24 SASR 5.
64 14 CTR 169.
65 (1870) LR 5 CP 310.

Subcontractors may urge that their accounts for work done prior to the termination should be met. In general they have no contractual authority to enforce these claims, but sometimes (eg if specially fabricated items from a nominated supplier are on very long delivery dates) there is a real sanction since recovery of their goods from the Site (which the Employer could usually not prevent if the goods were not fixed) or refusal to deliver goods fabricated and ready for delivery, could severely jeopardize Completion. The power to pay directly for such work with a right to deduct or recover from the Contractor is therefore a desirable contractual provision.

Without an applicable express power, the Employer who pays subcontractors directly in respect of sums owing by the Contractor will be unable to recover such sums, even on the Contractor's insolvency. To deal with this situation, it would be prudent for the Employer to insert a provision in the Contract requiring that the Contractor make provision in each subcontract for the subcontractor to novate the benefit of the subcontract to the Employer where required.

22.3.8 Termination due to insolvency

In the absence of a contractual provision to the contrary, the insolvency of one of the parties to a contract does not as a rule automatically terminate the contract, and the trustee for the insolvent party has the right to decide whether to abide by the contract or not. If the insolvent's trustee elects to hold the other contracting party to its obligations under the contract, it must tender complete performance of all the insolvent's obligations. If the trustee intends to abide by the contract, it should give notice to the other party, failing which the latter may treat it as being at an end. Where the trustee elects to abide by the contract, it steps into the shoes of the insolvent and is bound by all the terms of the contract. It will be bound by any terms relating to performance, liquidated damages for delay, submission of disputes to arbitration, and similar provisions.[66] However, where the trustee elects to resile from the contract, it cannot rely upon the contract unless an eligible claim was already in existence at the time it exercised such election.

A termination on any one of various insolvency grounds, while perfectly good against the Contractor itself, is probably void as against the trustee or liquidator as infringing a basic policy of the law of insolvency as the trustee may usually elect whether or not to perform in terms of the contract. A termination will be good against a trustee or liquidator, however, if exercised upon one of the other grounds such as a failure to maintain progress.

A subcontractor who is owed money by a Contractor who has become insolvent must claim against the insolvent estate in the same way as any other creditor. In many standard forms of contract there are clauses which authorise an Employer, in certain circumstances, to pay subcontractors directly and deduct the amounts of such payments from amounts due to the Contractor. Such a provision is annulled by the insolvency of the Contractor, as subcontractors may not be paid by the Employer in priority to the Contractor's trustee (but see *Wilkinson, Ex parte Fowler*[67]).

---

66 See *In re Keen and Keen, Ex parte Collins* [1902] 1 KB 5551.
67 [1905] 2 KB 713.

A contractual stipulation between the debtor and a creditor will usually not entitle the creditor to obtain a preference over other creditors otherwise than in accordance with the order of preference laid down by law. Accordingly, a clause which purports to vest property owned by the insolvent immediately prior to insolvency in someone other than the trustee would be contrary to the principles of the law governing insolvency and therefore void.[68] A clause purporting to give, after insolvency, to someone other than the trustee a power to control the use of property vested in the insolvent at the date of insolvency would also be invalid.[69]

These principles apply generally to construction contracts, but the exceptions may, in certain instances, be of importance in the case of such contracts.

If the other contracting party originally entered into the contract with the insolvent because of some special personal quality or skill which the latter possessed, it would seem that the contract would terminate on insolvency.[70] Contracts between Employer and architect or between Employer and consulting engineer would therefore normally terminate on the insolvency of the architect or consulting engineer.[71] Whether this rule would apply so as to terminate a contract between the Employer and Contractor on the insolvency of the Contractor, would depend on the circumstances of each case. Generally, however, where a Contractor is employed primarily because its tender is the lowest, the rule could have no application and the trustee could elect whether or not to continue with the Contract.

22.3.9 Liquidated damages for delay

An express provision in a contract providing for the payment of liquidated damages for delay has been held to apply only when the Contractor itself completes the Contract, and not when the Contract has been taken out of its hands and completed by someone else.[72] If liquidated damages have accrued before termination, an Employer could claim such liquidated damages from the Contractor.

22.4 Valuation at date of termination

The Employer is usually entitled to complete the Works itself or by any other contractor upon termination. If such completion results in extra costs being incurred, they are to be borne by the Contractor. Termination provisions are usually based upon the Employer retaining the finished part of the Works. The Contractor is therefore generally entitled to be paid for the work performed so far, less the costs incurred by the Employer. In the event of termination, some contracts permit the Employer to use any Contractor's equipment which is upon the Site, allowing the Contractor a fair price for such use.

The amount which the Contractor is entitled to be paid (or the amount it owes to the Employer) will usually be determined by valuation of the work completed in accordance

---

68 *In re Harrison, Ex parte Jay* (1880) 14 ChD 19 (CA); see also s 29 of the *Insolvency Act* 24 of 1936.
69 *In re Walker, Ex. parte Barter* (1884) 26 ChD 510 (CA), 519.
70 *Knight v Burgess* (1864) 33 LJ Ch 727.
71 cf *Stubbs v Holywell Ry* (1867) LR 2 Ex 311.
72 *British Glanzstoff Manufacturing Co Ltd v General Accident Fire and Life Assurance Co Ltd* 1913 AC 143 (HL).

with the provisions of the Contract, less any amounts owing by the Contractor for, for example, defective work, liquidated damages, advance payments, and so on.

22.5 Payment after termination

Whilst the valuation at the date of termination may ultimately amount to a significant sum payable to the Contractor, the exact amount of this sum is unlikely to be ascertained quickly. The Employer may not be in a position to determine the additional costs arising from another contractor completing the Works, including the correction of Defects, until the subsequent contract has been completed. Accordingly, there may be a substantial delay after termination before any money is paid to the Contractor, or its securities released.

22.6 Employer's entitlement to terminate for convenience

In the absence of an express provision in the Contract entitling the Employer to terminate the contract at will, it will not be permissible for the Employer to unilaterally terminate the Contract.[73] However, many construction contracts have a provision which entitles the Employer to terminate the Contract at any time for its own convenience. Such provisions, known as 'Termination for Convenience' clauses, are included in contracts where the Employer, for example, may wish to terminate a contract because of financial difficulties or lack of demand for the constructed facility, or the project has become economically unviable or statutory approvals have been withheld, making the project works impossible.[74] Termination for convenience clauses are also used in a subcontract so as to enable the Head Contractor to terminate the subcontract should the head contract itself be terminated.[75]

The Contractor would be well advised to scrutinise the provisions of such a clause carefully before it enters into the Contract, to ensure that the provisions in respect of notice and valuation on termination are fair and reasonable and will cover all its likely losses and damages attributable to the termination. The Contractor should also ensure that such a clause would not permit the Employer to terminate the Contract and carry out the work itself or give it to another contractor without adequate payment to the Contractor.[76] Termination for convenience clauses may permit termination of the Contract for any reason, provided the exercise of the termination power does not contravene any requirements of good faith and fair dealing.[77]

73 *Edwin Hill and Partners v Leakcliffe Properties Ltd* (1984) 29 BLR 43, [70]-[71] per Hutchison J. Note that the position is different under the law of the Netherlands, where an Employer is entitled to terminate a construction contract for convenience at any time: van Wassenaer, 'Update on the Netherlands – Reconstructing Construction' (2010) *International Construction Law Review* 114, 117–118.

74 See Misu, 'Termination or Employer's Convenience under the FIDIC Yellow Book 1999' (2013) 29 *Construction Law Journal* 138; 2017 FIDIC Red Book sub-clause 15.5; SIA Building Contract (1st edn 2016) clause 32(1); NEC4 Option X11.

75 *BAE Systems Australia Ltd v Cubic Defence New Zealand Limited* [2011] FCA 1434.

76 Clause 15.5 of the 1999 FIDIC Red Book expressly prohibited the Employer from terminating the Contract so as to give the work to another contractor; that prohibition has been removed from sub-clause 15.5 of the 2017 FIDIC Red Book. However, sub-clause 15.6 [Valuation after Termination for Employer's Convenience] entitles the Contractor to payment for 'the amount of any loss or profit or other losses and damages suffered by the Contractor as a result of the termination.'

77 See Albert Monichino, 'Termination for convenience: good faith and other possible restrictions' (2015) 31 *Building and Construction Law* 68; Tackaberry, 'Termination for Convenience' (April 2002, downloadable

22.7 Employer's financial remedies

The Employer is entitled to recover damages, usually being the difference between the cost of completing the outstanding work (which may be either the actual cost of completing the work, or an estimate of the likely cost of completing the work)[78] including the rectification of any defects,[79] less the amount of the contract price remaining unpaid.[80] The Employer's additional costs flowing from the termination will be attributed to the Contractor's repudiation or serious breach of contract, rather than the fact of termination by the Employer.[81] If the additional cost to complete is inflated due to the original Contractor having under-priced its tender, the fact of under-pricing will not impact the Employer's entitlement to damages.[82] The duty to mitigate its loss will not generally require the Employer to seek to allow the Contractor or a guarantor of the Contractor to complete the outstanding works.[83]

at www.scl. org.uk); Jennifer McVeigh & Kimie Tsukakoshi, 'Termination for Convenience: Not as Easy as it Sounds' (2013) 29 *Building and Construction Law* 122; *GEC Marconi Systems Pty Ltd v BHP Information Technology Pty Ltd* (2003) 128 FCR 1, [753], per Finn J; cf *Leighton Contractors Pty Ltd v Arogen* [2012] NSWSC 1370, [22], per McDougall J.

78 *Mousa v Vukobratich Enterprises Pty Ltd* [2019] QSC 49, [216] per Henry J.

79 *Barber v Oracle (NSW) Pty Ltd* [NSWSC 1370, [13] per Ball J.

80 *Hanison Construction Co Ltd v Diamond Term Ltd* [2012] HKCFI 311, [10] per Mr Recorder Chan SC; *Cordon Investments Pty Ltd v Lesdor Properties Pty Ltd* [2012] NSWCA 184, [202] per Bathurst CJ; *Sear v Kingfisher Builders (No.3)* [2013] EWHC 21 (TCC), [17] per Ramsey J; *Mousa v Vukobratich Enterprises Pty Ltd* [2019] QSC 49, [200]-[208] per Henry J.

81 *Castle Constructions Pty Ltd v Fekala Pty Ltd* [2006] NSWCA 133, [28] per Mason P; *LF Construction Pte Ltd v Yeo Pia Thian* [2007] SGHC 45, [30] per Belinda Ang Saw Ean J.

82 *Seaton Brick and Tile Co Ltd v Mitchell* (1900) 2 F 550; *Macmahon Mining Services Pty Ltd v Cobar Management Ltd* [2014] NSWSC 502, [34] per McDougall J.

83 *Greenore Port Ltd v Technical and Guarantee Co Ltd* [2006] EWHC 3119 (TCC), [36] and [184]-[189] per Jackson J.

CHAPTER 23

Suspension and termination by the Contractor

CONTENTS

23.1 Contractor's entitlement to suspend work

A breach of contract by the Employer, for example, failure to pay a progress payment to which the Contractor is entitled, does not automatically entitle the Contractor to suspend its work under the Contract. Absent a breach by the Employer of a fundamental obligation under the Contract justifying termination, the Contractor may be in breach of contract itself if it suspends work because of the Employer's breach of contract. A Contractor is, however, entitled to suspend work in the circumstances specifically provided for in the Contract or if it has statutory right to do so.

An example of a contractual clause referring to suspension can be found in standard form contract AS 2124–1992, clause 34.2. The NPWC3 standard form contract also provides for this situation in slightly more detail under its clause 34.3; a Contractor wishing to suspend the Works must provide written notification for this and explain reasons for the justification of the suspension. The 2017 FIDIC rainbow suite provides that the Contractor may suspend work not less than 21 days after giving a Notice identifying a specified failure of the Employer constituting a material breach of the Employer's obligations under the Contract.[1]

Each of the *Security of Payment Acts* in Australia defines circumstances in which a Contractor is permitted to suspend carrying out construction work or supplying related goods and services under a construction contract without breaching the contract. In NSW, Victoria, and Queensland, where the Employer fails to provide a payment schedule and pay the claimed amount or fails to pay all of the scheduled amount on or before the due date for the progress

1 Sub-clause 16.1.

DOI: 10.4324/9781003206873-23

payment, the Contractor is entitled to suspend work after giving notice of its intention to do so. The Contractor is not liable for any loss or expense incurred by the Employer as a result of its suspension. Further, the Employer is liable to pay any loss or expense incurred by the Contractor as a result of the removal of any part of the work or supply from the Contract.[2] In Western Australia and the Northern Territory, the Contractor has a similar right to suspend work if the Employer does not pay the amount of the Adjudicator's determination, without prejudice to any other contractual rights the Contractor may have.[3] As detailed in Table 28.2, the Contractor's right to suspend work for non-payment is also enshrined in the *Security of Payment* legislation in the UK, New Zealand, Singapore, Isle of Man, Malaysia, Ireland, and Ontario.

Where the Contract falls within the statutory definition of construction contract, these statutory rights to suspend work are a valuable addition to any rights the Contractor may have under the Contract. In any circumstances where a Contractor is entitled to suspend work, it must scrupulously follow the relevant provisions of the Contract or the applicable legislation in relation to notice and timing, to avoid itself breaching or possibly repudiating the Contract.

23.2 Termination by Contractor

23.2.1 Default of Employer

The profound consequences of default by the Employer are not always fully appreciated. As noted in Chapter 22, the Employer can terminate a contract under the common law for a sufficiently serious breach of contract by the Contractor, and this applies equally to termination by the Contractor for serious breaches by the Employer. In addition, construction contracts commonly contain a termination clause which entitles the Contractor to terminate the Contract in certain defined circumstances.

It may be very difficult for the Contractor to disengage from a contract, even if the Employer is in serious default of its obligations. The Contractor may have obligations towards vendors and subcontractors which will have to be paid whether or not the Contractor terminates, and these costs may not be able to be recovered from the Employer in the event of termination.

A Contractor also cannot be heard to say that a contract has become impossible and at the same time claim that the Contract should remain in existence so as to enable the Contractor to carry it on in a truncated form. This applies also where the Employer wrongfully prevents the Contractor from performing or in any way puts it out of the power of the Contractor to complete the Works. That is because of the doctrine of prevention, discussed in ¶2.15 and ¶14.7.6.

23.2.2 Repudiation by the Employer

Where an Employer demonstrates an inability or unwillingness to perform its obligations under the Contract,[4] or is in breach of an essential term of the Contract[5] (an act of repudiation),

2 *Building and Construction Industry Security of Payment Act 1999* (NSW) s27; *Building and Construction Industry Security of Payment Act 2002* (Vic) s29; *Building and Construction Industry Payments Act 2004* (Qld) s33.

3 *Building and Construction Industry (Security of Payment) Act 2021* (WA) s 62; *Construction Contracts (Security of Payments) Act 2004* (NT) s44.

4 *Matthews v Brodie* (unreported, Vic Supreme Court, 2 April 1980), 15 per McGarvie J.

5 *Tramways Advertising Pty Ltd v Luna Park (NSW) Ltd* (1938) SR (NSW) 632, 641–642 per Jordan CJ; *Associated Newspapers Ltd v Bancks* (1951) 83 CLR 322, 337; *DTR Nominees Pty Ltd v Mona Homes Pty Ltd*

this may give the Contractor the right to terminate the Contract under the common law. The act of repudiation may be either express or inferred from the Employer's conduct.

If the Employer terminates the Contract in circumstances where the Employer is not entitled to do so, it will be taken to have repudiated the Contract.[6] A contract may permit the Employer or the Engineer to suspend the Contractor's performance of the Works for a period of time,[7] but if the Employer engages a new contractor to perform the Work to the exclusion of the Contractor[8] or denies access to the Site in a manner which evidences an unwillingness to provide access to the Contractor at any time in the future,[9] this may constitute repudiatory conduct.

If the Employer uses its powers to order Variations so as to omit a sizeable amount of the Works for the purpose of giving it to another contractor, this will amount to a repudiation by the Employer;[10] if the Contractor requires timely instructions from the Employer or the Engineer in order to perform the Works and timely instructions are not given, this may also amount to repudiation by the Employer.[11] Failure to make a single progress payment may constitute repudiatory conduct, but not necessarily so;[12] however, repeated failure to pay money when it is due may constitute a repudiation[13] where the reason for non-payment is either a wrongful refusal to pay an amount which is properly owing[14] or substantial and seemingly financial incapacity.[15] If the Employer fails to pay the Contractor for work performed and there is evidence that the failure to pay is likely to continue, this may constitute repudiation.[16] The

(1978) 138 CLR 423, 430–431 and 435–436 per Stephen, Mason and Jacobs JJ.

6 *Eddy Lau Constructions Pty Ltd v Transdevelopment Enterprise Pty Ltd* [2004] NSWSC 273, [38] per Barrett J; *Britannia Pty Ltd v Parkline Constructions Pty Ltd* [2009] NSWSC 1302, [52]-[67] per White J (26 BCL 335); *Dura (Australia) Constructions Ltd v Hue Boutique Living Pty Ltd* [2012] VSC 99, [572] per Dixon J (affirmed: [2013] VSCA 179).

7 See 2017 FIDIC Red Book sub-clause 8.9.

8 *Trimis v Mina* [1999] NSWCA 140, [41] per Mason P (16 BCL 288); *Brani Readymixed Pte Ltd v Yee Hong Pte Ltd* [1995] 1 SLR 205.

9 *Carr v JA Berriman Pty Ltd* (1953) 89 CLR 327, 350 per Fullagar J; *Hayes v Stewart* [2002] EWCA Civ 513; *Vivergo Fuels Ltd v Redhall Engineering Solutions Ltd* [2013] EWHC 4030 (TCC), [519]-[520] per Ramsey J.

10 *Carr v JA Berriman Pty Ltd* (1953) 89 CLR 327, 350 per Fullagar J.

11 *Relative Mirait Services Pty Ltd v Midcoast Under Road Boring Pty Ltd* [2013] NSWSC 107, [50] per Latham J.

12 *Brani Readymixed Pte Ltd v Yee Hong Pte Ltd* [1995] 1 SLR 205, [19]; *Tombs and Wilson Connolly Ltd* (2004) 98 Con LR 44, 62 [54] per HHJ Coulson QC (TCC); *The Craftsmen Restoration and Renovations Pty Ltd v Boland* [2008] NSWSC 660, [61] per Howie J.

13 *Alan Auld Associates Ltd v Rick Pollard Associates* [2008] BLR 419; *Valilas v Januzai* [2014] EWCA Civ 436; *Stecon Sdh Bhd v Eco Tower Sdn Bhd* [2015] 4 MLRH 315, [26] per See Mee Chun J.

14 *Alan Auld Associates Ltd v Rick Pollard Associates* [2008] BLR 419, 425 [20] per Tuckey LJ; *Progen Engineering Pte Ltd v Chua Aik Kia* [2006] SGHC 159, [30]-[33] per Belinda Ang Saw Ean J; *Compact Metal Industries Ltd v Enersave Power Builders Pte Ltd* [2008] SGHC 201, [58] per Andrew Ang J; *Shyam Jewellers Ltd v Cheesman* [2001] EWCA Civ 1818, [57]-[58].

15 See *Progen Engineering Pte Ltd v Chua Aik Kia* [2006] SGHC 159, [30]-[33] per Belinda Ang Saw Ean J; *Compact Metal Industries Ltd v Enersave Power Builders Pte Ltd* [2008] SGHC 201, [58] per Andrew Ang J.

16 *Canterbury Pipe Lines Ltd v The Christchurch Drainage Board* (1979) 16 BLR 76, 115 per McMullin J (NZ CA); *CJ Elvin Building Services Ltd v Noble* [2003] EWHC 837 (TCC), [89]-[91] per Mr Recorder Akenhead QC; *Mirimskaya v Evans* (2007) 114 Con LR 144, 159 [48]-162 [56] per DHCJ Richard Fernyhough QC (TCC).

Contractor must specify the amount that is owed and the date on which the debt is payable.[17]

If the Employer or Engineer issues a payment certificate in an amount less than the amount claimed by the Contractor, but the amount certified is believed to be defensible[18] the Employer will not be taken to have repudiated the Contract.[19]

The *UNIDROIT Principles of International Commercial Contracts (2016)* Article 7.3.4 permits a contracting party who reasonably believes that the other party will not be able to meet its contractual obligations to demand adequate assurance of performance, and if such assurance is not forthcoming, to treat the other party as having repudiated the contract.

Where a Contractor seeks to accept repudiation of a contract because the Employer has delayed in giving possession of the Site or in giving drawings, plans, or instructions, in order to establish a breach of a material obligation by the Employer, the Contractor must allege and prove that such delay was wrongful in that it was unreasonable and material.[20] Mere lateness would not amount to repudiation, but to a breach entitling the Contractor to claim damages, provided the Employer or its Engineer had been placed in default.[21] Any such lateness on the Employer's part would also affect its right to claim damages for delay in Completion (see the discussion of the prevention principle in ¶14.7.6).

No reasons need to be given for a common law termination. Remarkably, if at the time of termination the Contractor gave an erroneous reason for terminating the Contract, it is entitled to justify the termination on other grounds even though they were not overtly relied upon at the time of termination (assuming that those other grounds would have justified termination).[22]

At common law, no formalities are required for an innocent party who wishes to accept a repudiation of a contract. All that is needed, in order for a repudiation to be accepted, is for the innocent party to act in such a way as to make it clear to the repudiating party, by objective conduct, that the innocent party treats the contract as being at an end.[23] It would, however, be prudent for the Contractor to advise its

---

17 *Shyam Jewellers Ltd v Cheesman* [2001] EWCA Civ 1818, [59].

18 *A L Stainless Industries Pte Ltd v Wei Sin Construction Pte Ltd* [2001] SGHC 243, [194] per Woo Bih Li JC; *Chua Tian Chu v Chin Bay Ching* [2011] SGHC 126, [24] per Andrew Ang J; *CAA Technologies Pte Ltd v H P Construction and Engineering Pte Ltd* [2015] SGHC 32, [56]-[60] per Tan Siong Thye J.

19 *Multiplex Constructions (UK) Limited v Cleveland Bridge UK Ltd* [2006] EWHC 1341 (TCC), [626]-[632] per Jackson J (affirmed [2007] EWCA 443; *Gibbs v Tomlinson* (1992) 35 Con LR 86, 111, per Mr Recorder Harvey QC.

20 *Stapelford Estates (Pty) Ltd and another v Wright* (1968) SA (1) (E), 4; *Kragga Kamma Estates cc and Another v Flanagan (720/93)* [1994] ZASCA 137; 1995 (2) SA 367 AD; [1995] 1 All SA 486 (A) (29 September 1994).

21 *Roberts v Bury Commissioners* (1870) LR 5 CP 310; *In re Trollope and Colls Ltd and Singer* (1913); Alfred A Hudson, *Hudson's Fourth Edition Table of Cases* (Sweet & Maxwell, 4th edn 1914) 649.

22 *Stocznia Gdynia SA v Gearbulk Holdings Ltd* [2009] BLR 196, 210 [44] per Moore-Bick LJ; *Alliance Concrete Singapore Pte Ltd v Comfort Resources Pte Ltd* [2009] SGCA 34, [63]-[64]; *Geldof Metaalconstructie NV v Simon Carves Ltd* [2010] BLR 401, 412–413 [45] per Rix LJ; *Imperial Chemical Industries Ltd v Merrit Merrell Technology Ltd* [2017] EWHC 1763 (TCC), [191] per Fraser J; *CAA Technologies Pte Ltd v Newcon Builders Pte Ltd* [2017] SGCA 53, [31]; *McIntyre v Quality Roofing Services Pty Ltd* [2019] SASFC 29, [41] per Tilmouth AJ; *Mousa v Vukobratich Enterprises Pty Ltd* [2019] QSC 49, [199] per Henry J; *Visual Building Construction Pty Ltd v Armistead (No.2)* [2019] NSWCA 280, [38] per Bell ACJ.

23 *Heyman v Darwins Ltd* [1942] AC 356, 361 per Viscount Simon LC; *Vitol SA v Norelf Ltd* [1996] AC 800, 810–811 per Lord Steyn; *BSkyB Ltd v HP Enterprise Services UK Ltd* [2010] EWHC 86 (TCC),

acceptance of repudiation to the Employer in writing, following legal advice on the appropriate wording.

23.2.3 Termination pursuant to a contractual right

The legal requirements for terminating pursuant to a contractual power may, however, be different from the requirements for terminating at common law. Certain construction contracts contain express provisions entitling the Contractor to terminate the Contract upon the Employer being in serious default, such as where the Employer has not paid an amount certified as owing by the due date for payment,[24] or under other circumstances such as where the Engineer has issued an instruction to the Contractor to suspend the Works, or where the Employer has become insolvent.[25]

If the Contract requires a period to elapse between the giving of a notice to correct a breach by the Employer and termination, then the Contract may not be terminated before the applicable period has expired.[26] If the Contract permits the Contractor to issue a termination notice following the issue of a default or 'show cause' notice, but the Contract does not specify the period following the issue of the default or 'show cause' notice, the right to terminate must be exercised within a reasonable time.[27] Because of the serious consequences which follow on a Contractor's termination, the courts usually insist that where a Contractor wishes to exercise a contractual right to terminate a contract, the Contractor must comply strictly with the Contract in exercising its right of termination.[28] Compliance of a termination notice with the terms of the Contract pursuant to which it was issued will be determined in a commercial or businesslike way, unless the terms of the Contract make it clear that the termination notice is to adopt a precise form or content. It does not necessarily follow that a party has waived its entitlement to terminate if it seeks performance of the other party's obligations after the right to terminate has crystallised.[29]

Generally, the effect of terminating the Contract pursuant to a contractual power will be similar to the effect of terminating at common law, meaning that the further performance of the Contract is ended but the parties' accrued rights and obligations persist.[30]

[1373] per Ramsey J; *ADS Aerospace Ltd v EMS Global Tracking Ltd* [2012] EWHC 2310 (TCC), [150] per Akenhead J.

24 See eg 2017 FIDIC Red Book sub-clause 16.2 (c).

25 See eg JCT Standard Building Contract (2016 edn) clause is 8.9 and 8.10; 2017 FIDIC Red Book sub-clause 16.2 (i)); JCWC Standard Form of Building Contract (2006 edn) clauses 36.1 and 36.2; SIA Building Contract (1st edn 2016) clause 33.

26 *Price v Carter* [2010] EWHC 1451 (TCC), [22]-[23] per Edwards-Stuart.

27 *Mvita Construction Co Ltd v Tanzanian Harbours Authority* (1988) 46 BLR 19, 31, per Nyalati CJ (CA Tanzania), considering the application of clause 63(1) of the 1969 FIDIC Conditions (noted by Streatfield-James [1990] *International Construction Law Review* 257).

28 *Obrascon Huarte Lain SA v A-G (Gibraltar)* [2014] EWHC 1028 (TCC), [318(d) – [321] per Akenhead J, considering sub-clause 15.1 of the 1999 FIDIC Yellow Book (appeal dismissed: [2015] EWCA Civ 712).

29 See *Pegler Ltd v Wang UK Ltd* [2000] BLR 218, 225 [35], per HHJ Bowsher QC; cf *Asia Engineering Ltd v Wing Hong Contractors Ltd* [1991] HKCFI 332, [29]-[39].

30 See eg JCT Standard Building Contract (2016 edn) clause 8, and AS 4000–1997 clause 39.10.

23.2.4 Termination due to frustration

When a contract is terminated by frustration, the whole contract is usually terminated.[31] Any accrued rights and obligations remain enforceable after the frustrating event, because the Contract is treated as having existed until the point when the frustrating event occurred.[32] As discussed in ¶2.3.1, frustration means the termination of the contract by operation of law or when the circumstances surrounding the performance of the contract change so fundamentally that the contract becomes incapable of being performed. It applies also where the performance called for in the changed circumstances is not what the parties promised.[33] There must have been a common assumption of fact, where after entering into the contract the fact changes, or a common assumption of a matter of law, where either the parties are mistaken in their assumption all along, or the law subsequently changes so as to render the assumption incorrect.[34] The changed circumstances must be permanent or indefinite in nature, as opposed to a change that is only of a temporary or transient nature,[35] and the change must take place after the contract was entered into.[36]

Although it has been commented that 'frustration' is not readily transportable into contracts governed by the laws of civil law systems,[37] this may be regarded as being controversial due to the developing modern *lex mercatoria* and long-established Roman Law principles.[38]

In contrast to the position where a contract is terminated after one party's repudiation, in which case the election of the innocent party is a critical matter,[39] the frustration of a contract occurs automatically. It may occur where a 'catastrophic event, caused by the act of neither party' has changed the nature of the work that the Contractor undertook in a fundamental way, although the occurrence of a catastrophic event is not a necessary condition for the frustration of a contract.

---

31 *Aurel Forras Pty Ltd v Graham Karp Developments Pty Ltd* [1975] VR 202; *Nelson v Kimberley Homes Pty Ltd* (1988) 4 BCL 289, 291 per Young J (Sup Ct NSW); *BP Exploration Company (Libya) Ltd v Hunt (No 2)* [1979] 1 WLR 783, 829 per Robert Goff J.

32 *Cantiare San Rocco SA v Clyde Shipbuilding and Engineering Co Ltd* [1924] AC 226 (HL(Sc)); *Codelfa Construction Pty Ltd v State Rail Authority of New South Wales* (1982) 149 CLR 337, 360 per Mason J; *Mann v Paterson Constructions Pty Ltd* [2019] HCA 32, [189] per Nettle, Gordon and Edelman JJ.

33 *Davis Contractors v Fareham Urban District Council* [1956] AC 696, 723 per Lord Reid, 728–729 per Lord Radcliffe; *Edwinton Commercial Corporation v Tsavliris Russ (Worldwide Salvage and Towage) Ltd (the 'Sea Angel')* [2007] EWCA Civ 547, [83]-[90] per Rix LJ; *Alliance Concrete Singapore Pte Ltd v Sato Kogoyo (S) Pte Ltd* [2014] SGCA 35, [33]-[37] and [47]; *Naylor Group Inc v Ellis-Don Construction Ltd* [2001] 2 SCR 943, [53].

34 *Codelfa Construction Pty Ltd v State Rail Authority of New South Wales* (1982) 149 CLR 337, 360 per Mason J.

35 *Metropolitan Water Board v Dick, Kerr and Co Ltd* [1918] AC 119, 128 per Lord Dunedin.

36 *Mc Alpine Humberoak Ltd v McDermott International (No.1)* (1992) 58 BLR 1, 18–19 per Lloyd LJ.

37 K Goedel, 'Recommendations for Review of the Conditions of Contract (International) for Works of Civil Engineering Construction – 3rd Edition March 1977' (1983) *International Construction Law Review* 50, 69.

38 See W W Buckland, 'Casus and Frustration in Roman and Common Law' (June 1933) 46(8) *Harvard Law Review* 1281–1300.

39 *Alliance Concrete Singapore Pte Ltd v Sato Kogyo (S) Pte Ltd* [2014] SGCA 35, [33]; *Heyman v Darwins* [1942] AC 356, 365 per Viscount Simon LC; *The 'Super Servant Two'* [1990] 1 Lloyd's Rep 1, 8 per Bingham LJ.

Under the laws of England, Australia, Hong Kong, and Singapore, if an event or state of affairs was known to the parties at the time the Contract was entered into, the fact that the Works which the Contractor has promised to perform are impossible affords no excuse to the Contractor. Usually there will have been a supervening event not arising from the default of either party to the Contract[40] of such a degree as to make performance of the Contract impossible, or nearly impossible.[41] An example would be where the Contract requires a party to use or supply a particular material, but without fault on the part of the Contractor, the material becomes unavailable. In *Alliance Concrete Singapore Pte Ltd v Sato Kogyo (S) Pte Ltd* it was held that a contract for the supply of ready mixed concrete in Singapore was frustrated when an unspecified source of sand for making the concrete, which was in Indonesia, became unavailable due to the Indonesian government banning the export of sand to Singapore. The court held that the position may be different where both parties contemplated a particular yet unspecified source of materials, where the source becomes unavailable.[42]

The impact of COVID-19 on the execution of construction projects has been substantial, requiring measures such as social distancing, reduction of workers permitted on a site, stringent cleaning protocols, isolation of infected workers, and other health measures. These measures have resulted in significant cost increases, and in some cases, suspension of construction works. However, the impacts have generally not reached the high threshold of making execution of the Works impossible, and accordingly are unlikely to have frustrated the Contract.

The possibility of high rates of inflation impacting the cost of plant, labour, and materials does not necessarily have the effect of frustrating the Contract,[43] but it has been held that an 'astronomical' increase in cost could lead to the Contract being frustrated.[44] It is for this reason that construction contracts sometimes include 'rise and fall' clauses.

A Contractor who has performed work pursuant to a frustrated contract is entitled to be remunerated for that work unless the Contract to perform the work is an entire contract, in which event the Contractor's work was incomplete.[45]

Legislation in Australia,[46] Hong Kong,[47] and Singapore[48] is similar in its operation to the *Law Reform (Frustrated Contracts) Act 1943* (UK), which applies where a contract has become impossible to perform or has otherwise been frustrated, thereby discharging parties from performing the contract. The legislation attempts to restore the parties to the position they would have been in but for the frustration, subject to the parties having changed their positions in performance of the contract to their detriment, the

40 *PT Arutmin Indonesia v PT Thiess Contractors Indonesia* [2013] QSC 332, [117] per Jackson J; *Tan Yong Hui v Aasperon Venture Pte Ltd* [2015] SGHC 169, [26] per Lai Siu Chiu SJ.

41 *Sir Lindsay Parkinson and Co Ltd v Commissioners of Works* [1949] 2 KB 632, 665 per Asquith LJ.

42 *Alliance Concrete Singapore Pte Ltd v Sato Kogyo (S) Pte Ltd* [2014] SGCA 35, [48]-[50]; Chen Han Toh, 'Correspondent Report – Singapore' (2015) *International Construction Law Review* 348, 53–57.

43 *Wates Ltd v Grater London Council* (1983) 25 BLR 1 (CA).

44 *Alliance Concrete Singapore Pte Ltd v Sato Kogyo (S) Pte Ltd* [2014] SGCA 35, [39].

45 *Appleby v Myers* (1867) LR 2 CP 651, 660–661; *Wai Lee Firm v Ku Chung Ming* [1911] HKLR 146.

46 *Frustrated Contracts Act 1978* (NSW); *Frustrated Contracts Act 1988* (SA); *Australian Consumer Law and Fair Trading Act 2012* (Vic).

47 *Law Amendment and Reform (Consolidation) Ordinance (Cap 23)* (HK) ss 16–18.

48 *Frustrated Contracts Act (Cap 115, 1985 revised edition)* (Sing).

objective being that neither party should be unjustly enriched at the other's expense.[49] The parties will not be put in the position they would have been in had the contract been performed.[50]

The parties may replace, modify, or supplement the principles of law laid down by the common law and statute by agreement.[51]

23.3 Payment on termination

23.3.1 Payment in accordance with the Contract

The Contractor's rights to payment on termination depend on whether the Contract was terminated under the common law or under the Contract:

> Where one party is entitled to determine the contract at common law, he will also be entitled to damages to compensate him for his loss. Where a party is terminating under an express provision of the contract, he will only be entitled to such further remedy as the contract gives him.[52]

If it is terminated under the Contract, the amount of payment due to the Contractor will be determined in accordance with the provisions of the Contract.

23.3.2 Payment under the common law

Under the common law, and in the absence of a contractual term to the contrary, if the Contractor elects to accept the Employer's repudiation of the contract, the Contractor then has a further election between the alternative remedies of damages for breach of contract, or a *quantum meruit* for the value of goods delivered or services provided.

If the Contractor elects damages for breach of contract, it is entitled to be placed in the position it would have been in had both parties fulfilled their obligations.[53] The Contractor will therefore be entitled to recover its loss of profit on the remaining work.[54] Put differently, an innocent Contractor will be entitled to recover as damages upon termination an amount equal to the contract price, less the value of any remaining works, less amounts already paid to the Contractor.[55]

---

49 *Law Reform (Frustrated Contracts) Act 1943* (UK) section 1(2).

50 *BP Exploration Company (Libya) Ltd v Hunt (No.2)* [1979] 1WLR 783, 799–800 per Robert Goff J; see Stewart Carter, 'Frustrated Contracts and Statutory Adjustment: The Case for a Reappraisal' (1992) *Contracts Law Journal* 66; J Mason, S Carter & L Tolhurst, *Mason and Carte's Restitution Law in Australia* (LexisNexis Butterworths, 2nd edn 2008) [1236]-[1268]; D Jones, 'Force Majeure in Australian Construction Law' (1995) *International Construction Law Review* 295.

51 See, for example, clause 40 of the AS 4000–1997 form of contract.

52 Michael Furmston, *Powell-Smith and Furmston's Building Contract Casebook* (Blackwell Publishing, 4th edn 2006) 440.

53 *Ranger v Great Western Railway Co* (1854) 5 HLC 72, 96–97 per Lord Cranworth LC.

54 *Shia Kian Eng v Nakano Singapore (Pte) Ltd* [2001] SGHC 68, [110] per Judith Prakash J; *Austman Pty Ltd v Mount Gibson Mining Ltd* [2012] WASC 202, [564] per Kenneth Martin J; *Kyren Pty Ltd v Wunda Projects Australia Pty Ltd* [2012] SASFC 23, [123]-[132]; *Redbourn Group Limited v Fairgate Development Ltd* [2018] EWHC 658 (TCC).

55 *Jebsen and Co Ltd v Watfield Technology Ltd* [2007] HKCFI 197, [94] per Mr Recorder Kwok SC.

A Contractor must adduce adequate evidence of the profit it would have made had it completed the Works.[56] In any event, if it is clear that a loss of profit has been suffered and provided the Contractor has not without justification failed to adduce evidence of the corresponding cost it would have incurred so as to produce a net profit figure,[57] the court will do its best to calculate the amount of that loss, and award damages in such amount.[58]

The Contractor will not be entitled to its loss of profit, or the full amount of its profit if it could have mitigated its damages but did not do so. If the Contractor accepts the Employer's repudiation of its obligations, and the Employer thereafter requests the Contractor to complete the Works, it may have to do so in order to mitigate its damages. The onus rests on the Employer to prove that the Contractor could have and did not mitigate its damages.

To the extent that the Contractor has purchased materials that were anticipated to be used but were not used in the performance of the Works the Contractor would be entitled to be paid the cost of purchasing those materials less the value of those materials in the Contractor's hands.[59]

If there are amounts which have been earned by the Contractor at the point of termination of the Contract but which have not been paid, they may be recovered as damages. Even if such amounts are not reflective of the cost to the Contractor of the work it has performed, or of the work remaining to be performed, a Contractor will be entitled to the payment of amounts due under the Contract.[60]

23.3.3 Quantum meruit

Where an innocent Contractor has performed work for a repudiating Employer, and the Contractor has elected to terminate the Contract, the Contractor is entitled under the common law of England, Singapore, and Hong Kong to recover a reasonable remuneration in restitution, that is, a *quantum meruit* for the work performed by it to the point of termination.[61]

In circumstances where the Contractor is in a loss-making situation on the Contract, such a *quantum meruit* is the equivalent of the holy grail, because it sets the Contract aside. The Contractor is then entitled to be paid a reasonable amount for the work done and materials and plant supplied, without reference to the remuneration agreed under the Contract. An Employer can protect itself from such uncapped liability by ensuring that the Contract has a provision which precludes a *quantum meruit* in the event that the Contract is repudiated.

---

56 *Paul Michael Pty Ltd v Urban Traders Pty Ltd* [2010] NSWSC 1246, [44] per White J; *Versa-Tile Pty Ltd v 101 Construction Pty Ltd* [2017] VSC 73, [35]-[38] per Ginnane J; *Caruso v Built It Pty Ltd (in liq) (No.2)* [2019] SASC 125, [99] per Parker J; *Tomlinson v Wilson* [2007] All ER (D), [44]-[46] per Judge Langan; *Sun Man Construction and Engineering Co Ltd v Smart Top Engineering Ltd* [2012] HKCFI 1373, [49]-[52] per DHCJ Lok.

57 See *Biofuel Industries Pte Ltd v V8 Environmental Pte Ltd* [2018] SGCA 28, [40]-[45].

58 *AJ Lucas Drilling Pty Ltd v McConnell Dowell Constructors (Aust) Pty Ltd* [2009] VSCA 310, [165].

59 *R J Grills Pty Ltd v Dellios* [1988] VR 136, 138–139 per Murray J.

60 *Drossos v Marvel Homes Pty Ltd* [2014] VSC 384, [48] per Kaye J.

61 *Lee Siong Kee v Beng Tiong Trading (1988) Pte Ltd* [2000] SGCA 57; BMI Tax Service Pte Ltd v Heng Keok Meng [2019] SGHC 09, [50]-[52] per Mavis Chionh JC; *EDRC Construction Ltd v HM Love and Co* (1994) 70 BLR 67, 88–91 (Court of Session); David Sawtell, 'Enrichment- Based Claims for a Quantum Meruit in Construction Disputes' (2019) *International Construction Law Review* 101.

Because a claim in *quantum meruit* represents an alternative to damages, the Contractor who elects to claim a *quantum meruit* is not entitled to recover an amount in respect of any loss of profit on the remainder of the Works;[62] and a Contractor claiming a *quantum meruit* must elect between claiming damages or a *quantum meruit* prior to the time of judgement being delivered.[63]

If following repudiation of the Contract, the Contractor elects to affirm the contract, it is not competent for the innocent party in subsequent proceedings to seek to recover a *quantum meruit*. Where the Contractor has performed all its obligations under the Contract, the Contractor's financial remedy is limited to recovery of the contract price.[64]

The option of a *quantum meruit* for all work done prior to repudiation by the Employer no longer applies in Australia in part owing to the 'unprecedented level of uncertainty and complexity' in evaluating a *quantum meruit* in such circumstances.[65] In *Mann v Paterson Constructions Pty Ltd*[66] the Australian High Court held that the Contractor was not entitled to a *quantum meruit* for all the work done prior to repudiation, as repudiation did not void the contract *ab initio*; the Contract governed the parties' accrued rights. It follows that the Contractor's financial remedy in Australia for that work lies in debt or in damages. It appears that under Australian common law a Contractor will not be entitled to recover a *quantum meruit* for an amount that would exceed the sum recoverable under the Contract for the work in question.[67]

It is worth noting that construction contracts approved by the World Bank accept that the Employer's liability is unlimited in the circumstances of termination because of the Employer's default. It is recognized that if the Contractor cannot limit its overall liability under the Contract, it would be unfair for the Employer to be able to do so.

---

62 cf *Thomas v Hammersmith BC* [1938] 3 All ER 201 (CA); *Edwin Hill and Partners v Leakcliffe Properties Ltd* (1984) 29 BLR 43.

63 *United Australia Ltd v Barclays Bank Ltd* [1941] AC 1, 29–30 per Lord Atkin; *Morrison-Knudsen Co Ltd v British Columbia Hydro and Power Authority* (1978) 7 Const LJ, 230–231 (85 DLR (3d) 186).

64 *Morrison-Knudsen Co Ltd v British Columbia Hydro and Power Authority* (1978) 7 Const LJ, 230–231 (85 DLR (3d) 186); *Taylor v Motability Finance Ltd* [2004] EWHC 2619 (Comm), [23] per Cooke J; *Lau Yeong Wood v Standard Oil Co of New York* [1908] HKLR 53, 57–58 per Piggott CJ; *Secretary of State for the Home Department v Raytheon Systems Ltd* [2014] EWHC 4375 (TCC), [53]-[56] per Akenhead J.

65 See *Sopov v Kane Constructions Pty Ltd (No.2)* [2009] VSCA 141, [24] in which the Victorian Court of Appeal held that 'where the claim is made on a *quantum meruit* the contract price does not impose a ceiling on the amount recoverable, though it may provide a guide to the reasonableness of the remuneration claimed.' This aspect was overruled together with much of the other Australian jurisprudence concerning the recovery of a *quantum meruit* post termination in *Mann v Paterson Constructions Pty Ltd* [2019] HCA 32 per Kiefel CJ, Bell and Keane JJ. Such a description of the exercise has been criticised as 'a little exaggerated, as courts and tribunals have for centuries grappled adequately with *quantum meruit* valuations, just as they have been able to engage with the inherent uncertainties associated with assessing damages for breach of contract' (Julian Bailey, *Construction Law II* (London Publishing Partnership, 3rd edn 2020) 833 footnote 428). See also *Mann v Paterson Constructions* (above), [87] per Gageler J, [180]-[186] per Nettle, Gordon and Edelman JJ.

66 [2019] HCA 32.

67 See *Mann v Paterson Constructions Pty Ltd* [2019] HCA 32, [201]-[217] per Nettle, Gordon and Edelman JJ. Their Honours did, however, acknowledge that there may be circumstances which warrant the awarding of a *quantum meruit* exceeding the contract price or the relevant part of it (at [215]-[216]). Gageler J held that the contract price, or relevant part of it would act as a limit, without exception (at [91]-[105]). Kiefel CJ, Bell and Keane JJ denied the existence of a *quantum meruit* remedy, all in the relevant circumstances.

CHAPTER 24

Care of the Works and indemnities

CONTENTS

24.1 Risks

The risks of loss or damage to property and of death and personal injury, and the legal responsibility for such eventualities between the Employer and the Contractor, should be allocated in a manner which reflects their respective ability to prevent such loss, damage, or injury from occurring. It is in the Employer's interests of obtaining the best tender prices that allocation of risks should also permit the Contractor to be able to assess its risks on a fair and reasonable basis, without having to allow in its tender price for contingencies that may never occur. Risks for which the Contract assigns the legal responsibilities and liability for the risks materialising to the Contractor are called **Contractor's risks** and those for which the Contract assigns the legal responsibilities and liability for the risks materialising to the Employer are called **Employer's risks**.

Risks of delay to Completion and control of costs in construction contracts include project planning and scheduling, legal, disputes, design, buildability, construction, financial, political, and insurance.

The insurance of the risks associated with the construction of thc Works must be distinguished from the legal responsibilities and liability of the parties assigned to them in the Contract. The apportionment of such responsibilities and liabilities between the

DOI: 10.4324/9781003206873-24

parties applies whether or not the associated risks are insured. In practice, many of the risks allocated to the Employer are risks for which insurance cannot be obtained, or which can only be insured with difficulty or at a very high premium.

Modern contracts typically enumerate the Employer's risks and the Contractor's risks and specify which party is responsible for each type of insurance required. Shortly after the FIDIC rainbow suite was released in 1999 Nael Bunni noted:

> The theory of Risk has developed in the past twenty years or so to such an extent that it is now common knowledge that for a contract to be performed in an effective manner, the inherent risks must be allocated to the contracting parties on some logical basis, which should be made known to them. Thus, it has been said that the main purpose of a contract is to identify the principles of allocating the risks facing the contracting parties.[1]

The NEC contracts require active risk management by, *inter alia*, requiring the Project Manager to maintain an up-to-date **Risk Register** and encouraging the Project Manager or the Contractor to give early warning of issues that could increase the total of the Prices, delay Completion or meeting a Key Date or impair the performance of the Works in use. The Risk Register is maintained by the Project Manager and identifies the risks listed in the Contract Data, early warning matters and records the decisions made in risk reduction meetings.[2]

Appendix B highlights the main risks relevant to construction of a number of types of infrastructure projects.

24.2 Indemnities

Construction contracts usually provide that the Contractor must indemnify the Employer in respect of risks assumed by the Contractor under the Contract and vice versa. An indemnity means a binding promise to keep another person financially harmless[3] against a loss.[4] Indemnities are commonly given by Contractors to Employers against loss and expense arising out of the carrying out of the Works, and may be against any claims made by third parties against the Employer;[5] claims that the Employer may have against the Contractor, such as where the Employer itself suffers a loss as a consequence of a breach of contract on the part of the Contractor.[6] The Employer commonly indemnifies the Contractor for claims that the Contractor may have against the Employer under the Contract.[7]

1 Nael Bunni, 'FIDIC's New Suite of Contracts – Clauses 17 to 19' http://www1.fidic.org/resources/contracts/bunni_0601.asp (accessed 12 January 2009).

2 NEC3 Engineering and Construction Contract clauses 16.1–16.4.

3 *Sunny Metal and Engineering Pte Ltd v Ng Khim Ming Eric* [2007] 3 SLR(R) 782, [35]-[39].

4 See *Matalan Discount Club (Cash and Carry) Ltd v Tokenspire Properties (North Western) Ltd* [2001] EWHC Tech 449, [89] per HHJ Seymour QC; *Caledonia North Sea Ltd v British Telecommunications plc* [2002] BLR 139, 158 [95] per Lord Hoffman; *Pacific Indemnity Underwriting Agency Pty Ltd v Maclaw No. 651 Pty Ltd* [2005] VSCA 165, [71] per Ormiston JA.

5 *Collins v Harland and Wolff* [1951] Lloyds Rep 458 (CA); *Davis v Commissioner of Main Roads* (1968) 117 CLR 529; *Browning v Bitupave Ltd* [2008] NSWSC 19.

6 The indemnity provides a remedy to the Employer which is distinct from the Employer's right to recover damages for breach of contract; see *Scottish and Southern Energy plc v Lerwick Engineering and Fabrications Ltd* [2008] CSOH 41.

7 See *Stent Foundations Ltd v MJ Gleeson Group plc* [2001] BLR 134, 136–137 per HHJ Bowsher QC; *Westerngeco Ltd v ATP Oil and Gas (UK) Limited* (2006) 115 Con LR 94.

A contract of insurance operates as an indemnity.[8] An action on an indemnity need not be founded on a breach of contract, and the rules limiting the recoverability of damages are not necessarily applicable.[9] An indemnity may apply if an effective cause of the loss was a matter for which the indemnitor took the risk, even though the loss in question was caused by more than one cause.[10] A contract of indemnity should not be confused with a contract of guarantee, which concerns an obligation which is secondary in nature and conditioned on breach of another's obligation. An indemnity represents an independent undertaking that is not necessarily conditioned upon a third party having committed a breach of an obligation.[11] A contract of guarantee must be in writing to be enforceable, whereas an indemnity does not.[12]

Such contractual indemnities not only make the risk allocation regime clear, but also may provide greater compensation than would be available for breach of contract alone. The relevant losses against which indemnities may be given include financial damage,[13] or loss of or damage to physical property,[14] harm or injury suffered by an employee of the Head Contractor as a consequence of the subcontractor's conduct,[15] or loss suffered as a consequence of the third party making a claim against the beneficiary of the indemnity.[16] Ascertaining the identity of the parties in whose favour the indemnity is given is not always a simple matter.[17]

Whilst it may be desirable for each party to have in place appropriate insurance that responds to losses arising from the enforcement of indemnities, such insurance may not be required under the Contract or available on commercially acceptable terms. Prior to entering into a contract, a prudent Contractor or Employer will carefully scrutinise the proposed contractual terms in respect of risk, indemnities, and insurance to ensure that they are, to the extent possible, consistent. Further, any uninsured risks must be both understood and acceptable within corporate guidelines if potentially large and perhaps unsustainable financial losses are to be avoided.

---

8 Once an indemnifier has paid money to a party indemnified in respect of the loss it has suffered due to the conduct of the third party, the indemnifier is entitled to exercise a right of subrogation meaning that it can exercise all of the indemnified party's rights and remedies against the third party: *Stewart v Atco Controls Pty Ltd* [2014] HCA 15, [50].

9 *The 'Eurus'* [1998] 1 Lloyd's 351 (CA); W Courtney, 'The Nature of Contractual Indemnities' (2011) 27 *Journal of Contract Law* 11–12, J W Carter & W Courtney, 'Indemnities Against Breach of Contract as Agreed Damages Clauses' (2012) *Journal of Business Law* 579; *Dinov v Allianz Australia in Insurance Ltd* [2017] NSWCA 270, [16] per Meagher JA.

10 *ENE Kos 1 Ltd v Petroleo Brasileiro SA (No 2)* [2012] 2 AC 164 and 189 [61] per Lord Clarke JSC; *Greenwich Millennium Village Ltd v Essex Services Group Plc* [2013] EWHC 3059 (TCC), [252]-[256] per Colson J (appeal dismissed: [2014] EWCA Civ 960).

11 *Associated British Ports v Ferryways NV* [2009] EWCA Civ 189, [1] per Maurice Kay LJ; *PT Jaya Sumpiles Indonesia v Kristle Trading Ltd* [2009] SGCA 20, [50]; *IWD No2 Pty Ltd v Level Orange Pty Ltd* [2012] NSWSC 1439, [67]-[68] per Stevenson J; *Erith Holdings Ltd v Murphy* [2017] EWHC 1364 (TCC), [88] per O'Farrell J.

12 *YJL Ltd v Jacobs One Ltd* [2017] EWHC 2625 (TCC); cf *Vossloh Aktiengesellenschaft v Alpha Trains (UK) Limited* (2010) 132 Con LR 32, 38 [21]-40 [25] per Sir William Blackburne.

13 *Rabilizirov v A2 Dominion London Ltd* [2019] EWHC 863 (QB).

14 *Anglian Water Services Ltd v Crawshaw Robbins and Co Ltd* [2001] BLR 173, 190 [91] per Burnton J.

15 *BI (Contracting) Pty Ltd v AW Baulderstone Holdings Pty Ltd* [2007] NSWCA 173.

16 See JCT Standard Building Contract (2016 edn) clauses 6.1 and 6.2 under which the Contractor provides an indemnity to the Employer for any expense or loss that the Employer suffers as a consequence of any injury or death to a person or harm to property that results from, among other things, the Contractor's default. The injury may be to a third person, and the damaged property may belong to a third party.

17 *South Seas Drilling Company v Esso Australia Ltd* (1988) 5 BCL 51 (Full Ct Sup Ct Vic).

24.3 Contractor's care of the Works

24.3.1 Accident or injury to workmen

There is an important distinction between the duty of care owed by an employer to an employee, and a person who is not an employee but carries on his/her own business, nevertheless carrying out work for the employer. The latter is commonly known as an 'independent contractor,' and the distinction between an employee and an independent contractor has been described as: 'The general discrimen between employees and independent contractors is the distinction between a contract of service and a contract for services.'[18] In the case of an employee, the employer owes, amongst other things, a duty of care to provide a safe system of work.[19] There are numerous factors that may be of relevance in determining whether an individual is an employee or an independent contractor but it is the substance of the total relationship which is of the greatest importance.[20] There is an increasing usage of engaging operatives from labour hire firms on the basis that such persons are not employees; the status of labour agency works was dealt with in *Smith v Carillion (JM) Ltd*.[21]

The Contract usually provides that the Contractor, or its subcontractors where appropriate, is liable for, and indemnifies the Employer against, any claims arising in connection with the death or injury of any of their respective employees, unless such death or injury is caused by acts or defaults of the Engineer, the Employer, or other contractors whom the Employer may have engaged to work on the Site. In such cases, the Employer should be required to indemnify the Contractor against all such claims arising. This is a fair apportionment of liability and both parties can arrange suitable insurance against these liabilities without difficulty.

Irrespective of the requirements of the Contract, the Contractor is bound to see that reasonable care is taken to supply its employees with, and to maintain, proper equipment and materials, and to see that its employees have a safe place of work and a safe system of work. The Contractor is also liable for any injury caused to an employee by the negligence of any other employee.

By contrast, an employer may have a lesser duty owed to an independent contractor.[22] Certain statutes benefit[23] 'employees' but not independent contractors in terms of the right to compensation from the employer for injuries sustained during employment, the right to be paid annual leave or sick leave, and to certain rights in the event of being unfairly dismissed. Different tax considerations apply where a worker is an employee compared to where a worker is self-employed, that is, an independent contractor.[24] Notwithstanding the differences in entitlements between employees and independent contractors, the Contractor is obliged to comply with applicable occupational health and safety legislation in respect of anyone working on the Site.

---

18 *Takacs v The Uniting Church* [2007] NSWSC 175, [43] per Rothman J (appeal allowed [2008] NSWCA 141, without affecting the validity of Rothman J's dicta); *Lee Ting Sang v Chung Chi-Keung* [1990] 2 AC 374, 382 (PC); *Tobiassen v Reilly* [2009] WASCA 26, [99].

19 *David Smith v Carillion (JM) Ltd* [2015] EWCA Civ 209.

20 See *Jennings v The Forestry Commission* [2008] EWCA Civ 581, [24] per Richards LJ.

21 [2015] EWCA Civ 209.

22 See *Miljus v CSR Limited (No 4)* [2012] NSWCA 96; *Leighton Contractors Pty Ltd. v Fox* [2009] HCA 35, [48]; *Pacific Steel Constructions Pty Ltd. V Barahona* [2009] NSWCA 406, [80]-[81]; *Luen Hing Fat Coating and Finishing Factory Ltd v Waan Chuen Ming* (2001) 14 HKCFAR 14.

23 eg *Personnel Contracting Pty Ltd. v CFMEU* [2004] WASCA 312: Construction workers engaged through an employment agency were independent contractors and incapable of being unfairly dismissed for the purposes of the *Industrial Relations Act 1979*.

24 *Hollis v Vubu Pty Ltd* (2001) CLR 21.

Many countries have enacted statutes and regulations to implement a system that pays benefits to injured workers. Employers are required by statute to take out workplace insurance for the benefit of employees. The position under English law[25] is that an injured worker will have an entitlement at common law to recover damages against his/her employer where the employer's negligence caused or contributed to the injury, and irrespective of negligence the employee may be entitled to payment of medical expenses and lost income. In Australia, statutory schemes for workers compensation operate in each State and Territory of Australia and at the Federal level[26] so as to ensure that workers who are injured during the course of their employment are entitled to receive compensation in respect of their injuries, regardless of whether the injury was caused by the negligence of the employer, the worker, or a third party; and to assist in the rehabilitation of injured workers.

In Hong Kong, the *Employees' Compensation Ordinance Cap 282* provides for the payment of compensation by employers to employees who are injured during the course of their work, irrespective of whether the injury was caused by the carelessness of the employer or the employee,[27] but does not include a person who is working in the capacity of an independent contractor.

Singapore provides a statutory entitlement to compensation to employees who are accidentally injured during the course of their employment, regardless of whether the injury arose from the carelessness of the employer, the employee, or another person under section 3(1) of the *Work Injury Compensation Act* (Sing).[28]

Contractual terms to the effect that the Contractor is liable for death or injury of its employees merely restate the common law and relevant statutory provisions. However, contractual indemnities ensure that the Employer will not suffer any loss in the event that an injured Contractor's employee chooses to seek compensation from a 'deep pocket' Employer.

Babcock v Brighton Corp[29] is a case which goes unusually far in holding the employer fully liable for the safety of its employees but may be taken as a warning of how careful a prudent employer will have to be to protect its workers in order to avoid liability. 'A,' an employee at an electrical substation, was injured while making a test because he removed a screen between the dead and live parts of the switchboard. 'A' had learnt to do this from a fellow employee and had then pointed out the dangers but had been told that if no risks were taken nothing would be done, and, in fact, the usual practice in the substation was to remove the screen. 'A' had later been appointed to do dangerous work, had been given a copy of the regulations, which forbade removal of the screen, and had been told to make himself familiar with them. The court held that A's employer was liable for his injuries in that it had not provided a safe

25 See Burnton J in *Employers' Liability Policy 'Trigger' Litigation* [2008] EWHC 2692 (QB), [33]-[36] (see also on appeal [2010] EWCA Civ 1096: *Employers Liability Policy 'Trigger' Litigation* [2012] UKSC 14, [10] per Lord Mance JSC).

26 *Workers Compensation Act 1987* (NSW) and *Workplace Injury Management and Workers Compensation Act 1998* (NSW); *Accident Compensation Act 1985* (Vic) and *Workplace Injury Rehabilitation and Compensation Act 2013* (Vic); *Workers Compensation and Rehabilitation Act 1981* (WA); *Workers Compensation and Rehabilitation Act 2003* (Qld); *Return to Work Act 2014* (SA); *Workers Rehabilitation and Compensation Act 1998* (Tas); *Workers Compensation Act 1951* (ACT); *Return to Work Act 1986* (NT); *Safety Rehabilitation and Compensation Act 1988* (Cth); see *John Holland Group Pty Ltd. v Robertson* [2010] FCAFC 88.

27 See *Lee Ting Sang v Chung Chi-Keung* [1990] 2 AC 374, 384 (PC); *Poon Chau Nam v Yim Siu Cheung* (2007) 10 HKCFAR 156, 170[27] per Ribiero PJ.

28 *Cap 354, 2009* revised edition.

29 [1949] 1 KB 339.

system of work simply by telling the employee to follow these regulations, and even if it had originally supplied a safe system it had allowed it to be ignored. 'A' was not himself guilty of contributory negligence because he had followed the example of his superiors.

24.3.2 Contractor's responsibility for the care of the Works

The Contractor is normally totally responsible for the care of the Works and all plant and materials on the site from the commencement date until the **risk transfer date**.[30] Even if the Contract does not expressly require the Contractor to take care of the Works, it may be implicit that the Contractor is to take the risk of damage being caused to the Works during construction. This means that the Contractor where necessary must construct temporary protective structures or take other precautionary measures. In certain civil law jurisdictions, the allocation of risk in respect of damage to the Works is determined by the prevailing *Civil Code* in the absence of express agreement between the parties.[31] The Contractor should also be required to be responsible for the care of any part of the Works upon which it is performing any outstanding work during the defects liability period until that work is completed. This reflects the philosophy that the Contractor should be responsible for matters which are within its control.

Should the Contractor have undertaken an obligation to maintain security at the Site where it is working or be under an obligation in tort to do so, it may engage a security firm to do so. A security firm will, however, usually only accept responsibility for providing security to a level promised in its contract, and to a standard usually requiring the exercise of reasonable skill and care. This means that a breach of contract together with causation of the loss that the claimant suffered must be shown before the security firm will be rendered liable to pay damages for any criminal acts having occurred due to a lapse in security.[32] Where individuals trespass or harass workers, injunctive relief may be available to restrain those persons from continuing their disruptive action.

If the damage to property on the Site is due to the negligence of a worker, responsibility for that damage is usually attributed to the worker's employer. This is known as 'vicarious liability.' Vicarious liability is imposed by the law for reasons of policy, being a redistribution of the incidences of loss from employees to employers, who are generally more able to bear a loss, even if the employer may not have been at fault personally.[33] The employer will accordingly be liable for the negligence of employees acting during the course of their work.

There is a distinction between an employee and an independent contractor where the actions of workers cause damage to the property of a third party, for example, plant or equipment of another contractor or injury to another contractor's workers. At common law an employer is not liable to a third party for damage caused by an independent contractor engaged by the employer. The reason for this is that the work that the independent contractor

30 See eg AS 4000–1997 clause 14.1; 2017 FIDIC Red Book sub-clauses 4.1 and 17.2.

31 See eg D Foigt, J Kirkiliene, S Kravale & M Mugu, 'Construction Law: An Overview of Recent Developments in the Baltics' (2008) *International Construction Law Review* 134, 143–145.

32 See *BGC Residential Pty Ltd v Fairwater Pty Ltd* [2012] WASCA 268, [41]-[55].

33 *Viasystems (Tyneside) Ltd v Thermal Transfer (Northern) Ltd* [2006] 2 QB 510, 528 [52] per May LJ, 529 [55] and 536–537[79] per Rix LJ; *Catholic Child Welfare Society v Institute of the Brothers of the Christian Schools* [2012] UKSC 56.

has agreed to undertake is not undertaken as a representative of the employer.[34] However, if the employer has directly authorised the doing of a tortious act by the independent contractor, or the circumstances are such that the employer owes a 'non-delegable' duty to a third party who is harmed or injured by the independent contractor's conduct, the employer will be liable for the conduct of an independent contractor.[35]

Often, an employee of a contractor on Site is seconded to another contractor, so is to be temporarily under the supervision of that other contractor. In such an event, acts of negligence resulting in physical damage to the Site may be attributable to both the employee's employer and the contractor to whom the employee was seconded.[36] The degree of control exercised over the conduct of a particular worker (meaning more than supervising the conduct of work) will be an important factor,[37] and before a worker's employment will be held to have been transferred for liability purposes, exceptional circumstances are required.[38]

24.3.3 Incidence of risk for damage to the Works

The Contract normally allocates the responsibility for damage to the Works until Completion between the Employer and Contractor, according to the nature of the risk or damage, and similarly makes special provision for the defects liability period. The risk of loss or damage occasioned by earthquake, flood,[39] hurricane, and the like lies with the Contractor until the Works have been completed, assuming the Contract provides for payment to be made on completion of the work.[40] The damage for which the Contractor is normally responsible is:

(a) 'Until Completion' – damage from any cause whatever, except:
    (i) the 'riot, war, invasion, etc' group of risks
    (ii) a cause due to the Engineer's design of the Works or
    (iii) any qualification justified by the 'legally and physically impossible' saving of the contractual conditions
(b) During the defects liability period, damage actually caused by the Contractor while working on the Site

In the event that loss or damage to the Works occurs through causes which fall within any of the Contractor's risks, the Contractor will have to make good the loss or damage

34 *R v Associated Octel Co Ltd* [1996] 1 WLR 1543, 1547 per Lord Hoffman; *Northern Sandblasting Pty Ltd. v Harris* (1997) 188 CLR 313, 366 per McHugh J.

35 *Fox v Leighton Contractors Pty Ltd* [2008] NSWCA 23, [47], per Basten JA (appeal allowed for other reasons [2009] HCA 35).

36 *Viasystems (Tyneside) Ltd v Thermal Transfer (Northern) Ltd* [2006] 2 QB 510; *Chen Qiangshi v Hong Fei CDY Construction Pte Ltd* [2014] SGHC 177, [197]-[203] per George Wei JC; *Shannon v Global Tunnelling Experts UK Ltd* [2015] EWHC 1267 (QB), [17] per Jay J.

37 *Biffa Waste Services Ltd v Maschinenfabrik Ernst Hese GmbH* [2009] QB 725, 744 [55] – 745 [56]; *Colour Quest Ltd v Total Downstream UK plc* [2009] EWHC 540 (Comm), [207]-[216] per David Steel J.

38 *Biffa Waste Services Ltd v Maschinenfabrik Ernst Hese GmbH* [2009] QB 725, 746 [59].

39 *TFW Printers Ltd v Interserve Project Services Ltd* [2006] BLR 299, 308 [42] per Dyson LJ.

40 *Appleby v Myers* (1867) LR 2 CP 615. Note, however, that in marine work where a marine spread is employed by the Contractor, for example, a pipeline barge, diving service vessel, and supporting vessels, payment by the Employer for named cyclone downtime at pre-agreed rates is not unusual. This is not to be confused with the allocation of risk for damage to the Works.

at its own cost, subject to any relevant insurance which provides coverage for the loss. Except to the extent that the Contractor can show that the loss or damage has been caused by any of the Employer's risks, the Contractor is liable to make good the loss or damage forthwith at its own cost, even if the loss or damage has occurred through no fault of the Contractor. The allocation of risk may even be such that the Contractor accepts the risk of damage to the Works caused by the negligence of the Employer. For example, a Contractor was held contractually responsible for damage caused to a jetty which it was constructing for the Admiralty, such damage having arisen in consequence of a negligently navigated Admiralty vessel colliding with the jetty.[41]

The Contractor's liability to make good the loss or damage is therefore not confined to those cases where there has been some breach of contract or statutory duty or some negligence on the part of the Contractor or any of its subcontractors or employees. The only other qualification on the Contractor's obligation to make good loss or damage would be an impossibility, which in the context of construction contracts is probably limited to some supervening event making Completion of the Works as a whole impossible and thereby frustrating the Contract (unless there is some contractual provision which provides relief to the Contractor). Frustration is discussed in ¶23.2.4.

The Contractor should be obliged not only to make good any defects in the Works which appear during the defects liability period, but also to make good any damage to the Works caused by such defects. Thus the Contractor would remain liable during the defects liability period for any loss or damage caused by its defective design, materials, or workmanship. This would also apply if loss or damage was caused by the Contractor during the defects liability period, for example, whilst carrying out Tests on Completion after a Taking-Over Certificate has been issued. Except in the case of loss or damage caused by materialisation of an Employer's risk, the Contractor is liable for loss or damage before Taking-Over irrespective of fault on the part of the Contractor. However, after the risk transfer date, the Contractor's liability for loss or damage to the work should be limited to those cases where the loss or damage is caused by the Contractor. Thus the Contractor's liability after Taking-Over must be founded upon some breach of contract or of statutory duty, or of negligence.

Construction contracts commonly require the Contractor to insure the Works themselves against various kinds of damage, especially damage by fire;[42] such provisions are designed to protect the Employer from claims, and to ensure that the Contractor has the financial resources to repair any damage to the Works. Contractual provisions relating to insurance are considered in Chapter 26.

24.3.4 Responsibility to rectify loss or damage

Where the Contractor has a responsibility to rectify loss or damage to the Works from 'any cause whatsoever,' these words may be wide enough to include any act or neglect of the Employer or its servants, so that the Contractor may be liable to reinstate the loss or

41 *AE Farr Ltd v Admiralty* [1953] 1 WLR 965.

42 *A E Farr Ltd v The Admirality* [1953] 2 All ER 512 (QB); *James Archdale and Co Ltd v Comservices Ltd* [1954] 1 All ER 210 (CA); *Gold v Patman and Fotheringham Ltd* [1958] 2 All ER 497 (CA).

damage free of charge notwithstanding that the Employer or its servants have negligently damaged the Works.[43] However, if there is an obligation on the Employer to ensure that the Site is in a particular state when it is first handed over to the Contractor, and the Employer in breach of that express obligation fails to do so, the Employer will have no remedy against the Contractor.[44]

A prudent Contractor undertaking such a contractual obligation will ensure that its insurance appropriately responds to such risks. The Contractor may, in addition to its obligation to take care of the Works, be required to indemnify the Employer for any loss and expense which the Employer may suffer as a consequence of the Contractor's negligence in carrying out the Works, if the Contractor's negligence causes damage to property on Site including property of the Employer and the Works.

The contractual requirement that the Contractor take out 'contractor's all risks' or 'contract works risk' insurance in 'joint names' may mean that there is no need to identify which insured party was responsible for the relevant damage,[45] but does not relieve the Contractor of its contractual responsibility for reinstating the Works if they are damaged.[46] It is through the requirement that the Contractor take out and maintain insurance against the possibility of the risk of physical damage eventuating that the Employer is protected by having a pool of funds available to carry out remediation should the Works or the Site be damaged.[47]

24.3.5 Passing of risk of loss or of damage to the Works

The risk transfer date in relation to the Works or a section thereof should be the earliest of either:

(a) The date of issue of the Taking-Over Certificate or
(b) The date when the Engineer is deemed to have issued the Taking-Over Certificate or when the Works are deemed to have been taken over[48] or
(c) The date of expiry of the notice of termination when the Contract is terminated by the Employer or the Contractor.

Once the risk of loss or damage to the Works has passed from the Contractor on the risk transfer date, its liability in respect of the Works is limited.[49] The responsibility for the care of the Works passes to the Employer, subject to the fulfilment of the Contractor's obligations in respect of Defects after Taking-Over and to making good loss or damage caused by the Contractor during the defects liability period.

---

43 *A E Farr v The Admiralty* [1953] 2 All ER 512 (QB).

44 *AMF International Ltd v Magnet Bowling Ltd* [1968] 1 WLR 1028.

45 *Cooperative Retail Services Ltd v Taylor Young Partnership Ltd* [2002] 1 WLR 1419, 1424 [14] per Lord Hope.

46 *Amec Civil Engineering Ltd v Cheshire County Council* [1999] BLR 303, 310 per HHJ Gilliland QC.

47 *Skanska Construction Ltd v Egger (Barony) Ltd* [2002] BLR 236, 241[17]-[19] per Latham LJ, [28] per Mance LJ (CA).

48 See JCT Standard Building Contract (2016 edn) clauses 2.33 and 2.34; 2017 FIDIC Red Book sub-clause 10.2; SIA Building Contract (1st edn 2016) clause 26; *P& M Kaye Ltd v Hosier and Dickinson Ltd* [1972] 1 WLR 146, 159 per Lord Pearson; *Skanska Construction (Regions) Ltd v Anglo-Amsterdam Corporation Limited* (2002) 84 Con LR 100; *Cenric Group Pty Ltd v Ziegler* [2019] NSWSC 1586, [37]-[39] per Leeming JA.

49 *TFW Printers Ltd v Interserve Project Services Ltd* [2006] BLR 299, 308 [39] per Dyson LJ.

24.3.6 Third parties – damage to property and injury to persons

The Contractor's liability in respect of loss or damage to the property of third parties and the property of the Employer other than the Works, and claims arising out of death or personal injury to the extent that such claims occur before the issue of the defects liability certificate, should be provided for in the Contract. The Contractor should be liable to the extent that the loss, damage, or injury is caused by its defective design, materials, or workmanship or by its negligence or breach of statutory duty or that of its subcontractor's employees and agents. This liability is based on fault.

The Contractor's liability arising from such a defaulting act is totally unaffected by the passing of the risk transfer date and of responsibility for the care of the Works from the Contractor to the Employer. It should be noted that not only is the Contractor made liable for such matters but it is usually required to indemnify the Employer against any such claims. The reason for this is that third parties whose property is lost or damaged, or whose person is injured, will, in the nature of things, be likely to take proceedings against the Employer rather than the Contractor. The risks of such liabilities being incurred by the Contractor can, however, easily be insured under an appropriate public third-party and products liability insurance policy.

Occasionally, the Employer or the Contractor carries out the work in such a way that it damages the property of third parties. Thus, Highway Authorities may recover the cost of special repairs from persons who have subjected a highway to damage. Any highway or bridge anywhere must be covered, since large special units for incorporation into engineering works may need to traverse the whole country by road from the point of manufacture to the Site. Specific authority would be required for persons to carry out temporary strengthening works to bridges or highways to enable their vehicles to use them without damage, though no doubt such authorities would have a general power to make such arrangements. These matters may also be prescribed in applicable legislation relating to the relevant authorities and utilities.

24.4 Employer's risks

In general terms the risks assigned to the Employer are usually either those over which the Contractor has no control (eg defects in the design of the works by the Employer or the Engineer), or risks of loss or damage which flow from the Employer's decision to construct the Works (eg damage which is the inevitable result of the construction of the Works in accordance with the Contract). Certain risks may not be capable of being transferred in some jurisdictions, such as the 'strict' liability arising from the duty to provide lateral support to adjoining properties. These are risks which it would not be fair or appropriate to allocate to the Contractor with the resulting legal liability which would flow from them. Some of these risks may not be insurable and, if they were allocated to the Contractor would result in the Contractor allowing in its price for potential liability which might never arise, resulting in an increased price to the Employer. For example, it may not be appropriate in the case of the risks of riot, commotion, or disorder to restrict these risks to those cases where the riot, and so on, occurs only in the Employer's country or the country where the Site is located. However, if the riot, and so on, is confined to the employees of the Contractor or of its subcontractors, this should be a Contractor's risk wherever the riot, and so on, occurs.

Any risk which an experienced Contractor could not have foreseen or, if it was foreseeable, against which reasonable measures to prevent loss, damage, or injury from occurring could not have been taken, should be allocated to the Employer. Again this reflects the Abrahamson Principles that risks allocated to the Contractor should be those against which it can reasonably control or protect itself. To the extent that loss or damage to property or death or personal injury occurs in consequence of any of the Employer's risks, the Employer should be made liable for them under the Contract and should be required to indemnify the Contractor against any such claims.

24.5 Consequences of Employer's risks

Legal liability to make good any loss or damage to the Works consequential on any Employer's risk materialising, would be at the Employer's expense. The Contractor would generally be required to carry out the necessary rectification work, provided that the Engineer gives the Contractor instructions to do so. The Contractor would then be entitled to be paid a reasonable price for making good the loss or damage agreed with the Employer. If the price cannot be agreed then the ultimate remedy for Contractor and Employer is to have the price determined by the applicable dispute resolution procedure.

24.6 Intellectual property rights

Where it is the Contractor's responsibility to design the Works, it must ensure that, in so doing or in manufacturing and operating the Works, the intellectual property rights of any third party are not infringed. Accordingly, the Contractor is usually required to indemnify the Employer against any such claims of infringement.

Similarly, it is appropriate if the Contract also provides that the Employer indemnifies the Contractor against any claims of infringement of intellectual property rights arising as an unavoidable result of the Contractor's compliance with the Contract, or as a result of the Works being used by the Employer in a manner inconsistent with the Contract.

24.7 Limitation of liability

Sometimes the legal liability of both parties is modified by limiting the damage recoverable to that reasonably foreseeable at the time the Contract was made, by restricting the parties' rights to make claims against each other for loss of profit, loss of use, loss of production, or loss of contract, or for indirect or consequential damage, except in specific circumstances. The Contractor's maximum liability may be stipulated and sometimes, except in the case of gross misconduct, any liability of the Contractor for loss or damage to the Employer's property after the defects liability period has expired is excluded. Of course this cannot affect any liability of the Contractor for any claims by third parties because they are not parties to the Contract.

The remedies provided by the Contract for the Employer and the Contractor are, except in the case of gross or deliberate misconduct or actions arising under fair trading legislation, usually intended to be the only remedies for claims which the parties may have against each other. The intention is that claims which do not fall within the provisions of the Contract are to be excluded altogether so that any claims that may be made against the other party must be based on some specific provision of the Contract and not upon some extraneous rule of law or practice. For example, if the claim has been excluded by the terms of the Contract, or has expired, it should not be possible to claim on an alternative basis that the cause of the claim is negligence rather than breach of contract. As with any other aspect of a specific Contract, the parties' intentions must be derived by construction of the terms of the Contract as a whole.

Indirect loss that flows from the direct losses caused by a breach of contract, for example, economic loss such as loss of profits or customers because a facility is defective or completed late, are referred to as **consequential losses**. These may be specific to a person's particular circumstances and may not be known by the other party to the Contract. It may be agreed that neither of the parties are liable to the other for claims for consequential losses, except the Contractor's liability for delay in Completion and the specific provisions of the Contract which entitle the Contractor to receive profit on extra costs that it has incurred in certain circumstances. It will have been noted that the latter would apply only in those cases where it can be said that the Contractor's claim to extra cost has arisen through some breach of contract by the Employer or those for which it is responsible. It may be argued that the Contractor who, by its breach of contract other than lateness, causes the Employer to lose the use of the Works, or to lose production or contracts, should be liable to the Employer. The availability of such a remedy will depend on the terms of the Contract.

Note that there is conflicting case law on the meaning of the term 'consequential loss' as used in exclusion clauses. There is English case law that the term refers to losses recoverable only under the second limb of *Hadley v Baxendale*[50] (damages 'such as may reasonably be supposed to have been in the contemplation of both parties, at the time they made the contract, as the probable result of the breach of it'). An alternative view expressed by Nettle JA of the Victorian Court of Appeal is that 'ordinary reasonable business persons would naturally conceive of 'consequential loss in contract as everything beyond the normal measure of damages, such as profits lost or expenses incurred through breach.'[51] To avoid any ambiguity and to ensure that those 'consequential losses' intended, and only those intended, are excluded, the term should be clearly defined in the Contract.

It is not possible for parties to contract out of certain aspects of fair trading legislation in an attempt to exclude liability for a contravention of such an *Act*.

24.8 Mitigation of loss or damage

When a contract has been breached, the innocent party is not entitled to sit back and allow damages to multiply. It has a duty to mitigate its loss and damage. To fulfill its obligation to mitigate, the claimant does not have to do everything that could conceivably be done to reduce or restrict the size of its claim. For example, if a Defect occurs in some part of the Works and causes damage which could be confined to that section of the Works, and if appropriate measures can be taken by the Employer, it must do its best to take those measures so as to prevent its loss from increasing. Mitigation of damages is considered in ¶27.11.1.

50 (1854) 9 Ex 341, 354–355.

51 *Environmental Systems Pty Ltd v Peerless Holdings Pty Ltd* [2008] VSCA 26 [93].

CHAPTER 25

Exceptional events

CONTENTS

25.1 Allocation of risks

There are certain legal presumptions that operate as to the allocation of risk, for example, where goods are being supplied, the risk of loss or damage to the goods is *prima facie* with the supplier until the point that title is transferred,[1] but the allocation of risk between the Employer and the Contractor depends upon what they have agreed.[2]

Even though a party has little or no ability to control a risk, a party may agree to accept that risk. A notable example of such acceptance of risk is *Independent Broadcasting Authority v EMI Electronics*,[3] in which the Contractor agreed to design and erect a structure and was found to be in breach of an express warranty that the structure would be fit for a particular purpose (even though the Contractor did not carry out any part of the design work, which it left to a specialist consultant). Also *Midland Expressway Ltd v Carillion Construction Ltd*[4] in which the Contract did not set out the work that the Contractor was to perform, but prescribed standards and performance levels that must be met, and in which the Contractor accepted the risk that the means it used would not necessarily accomplish the ends prescribed by the Contract. The parties may also agree that the risk of cost overruns are to be shared by means of a 'target cost' mechanism in

1 *Sale of Goods Act (1979)* (UK) s 20; *Consumer Rights Act 2015* (UK) s 29; *Sale of Goods Act 1923* (NSW) s 25; *Sale of Goods Ordinance (Cap 26) (HK)* s 22; *Sale of Goods Act (Cap 393, 1999 revised edition)* (Sing) s 20.

2 See *Persimmon Homes v Ove Arup and Partners Ltd* [2017] EWCA Civ 373, [57] per Jackson LJ; C B Chapman, S C Ward & B Curtis, 'Risk Theory for Contracting' in J Uff & P Capper (eds), *Construction Contract Policy* (Kings College London, 1989) Chapter 7; O'Reilly, 'Risk, Risk Allocation – an Overview' (1996) *International Construction Law Review* 502, 504; R Smith, 'Allocation of Risk – The Case for Manageability' (1996) *International Construction Law Review* 549; D S Jones, 'Philosophies of Risk Allocation – The Case for Foreseeability' (1996) *International Construction Law Review* 570; L Klee & R Teodoresescu, 'Romanian Experience with FIDIC Forms in Road and Bridge Construction' (2013) *International Construction Law Review* 432, 435.

3 (1980) 14 BLR 1.

4 [2005] EWCH 2810 (TCC), [571(4)] per Jackson J.

DOI: 10.4324/9781003206873-25

the Contract, such that the parties share in any 'pain' or 'gain' resulting from the project cost being greater or less than anticipated regardless of which party is responsible for the overruns or the savings.[5]

'Exclusion' clauses, also known as 'exemption' clauses, 'exception' clauses and 'protective' clauses, will usually operate so as to prevent the Employer from recovering damages from the Contractor for breach of a specified contractual obligation.[6] The definition and allocation of risk for and contractual consequences of the occurrence of *force majeure* or 'exceptional events'[7] is aimed at achieving the same result.

In general terms, the risks assigned to the Employer are either those over which neither party has control (eg war, rebellion, terrorism etc), those over which the Contractor has no control (such as defects in the design of the Works by the Employer or the Engineer), or risks of loss or damage which flow from the Employer's decision to construct the Works (eg damage which is the inevitable result of the construction of the Works in accordance with the Contract).[8] In practice, many of the risks apportioned to the Employer are risks for which insurance cannot be obtained or which can only be insured with difficulty or at a very high premium.

In equipment hire-contracts, exclusion clauses may be used so as to exempt the party who hired out the equipment from liability for losses occasioned by the use of the equipment, even if the loss was caused by an operator of the equipment who was supplied by the hirer.[9] Usually the party who hires out the equipment takes responsibility for any mishaps that occur when the equipment is being transported or erected,[10] but like all exclusion clauses used in contracts in the United Kingdom, Hong Kong, and Singapore such clauses must satisfy the requirement of reasonableness under the *Unfair Contract Terms Act 1977*.[11]

The time and money risk of adverse site conditions being encountered unexpectedly may be accepted by either party to a contract.[12]

5 See W Wilson, 'MTR Corporation Ltd – On Track for Mutual Benefit' (2001) *International Construction Law Review* 726–727.

6 See *Thomas National Transport (Melbourne) Pty Ltd v May and Baker (Australia) Pty Ltd* (1966) CLR 353, 376 per Windeyer J.

7 The 1999 FIDIC rainbow suite sub-clause 17.3 listed a number of 'Employer's Risks,' and a number of these were repeated in sub-clause 19.1 [Definition of *Force Majeure*]. The terminology of 'Employer's Risks' is a widely accepted and sensible nomenclature but was abandoned in FIDIC's ill-considered re-drafting in 2017. It is curious that the term '*Force Majeure*' was replaced by 'Exceptional Events.' If it was intended that 'Exceptional Events' were to be treated as being equivalent to incidents of *force majeure* as widely understood in the international arena, this could have been stated. An opportunity for a universal formulation of *force majeure* was missed.

8 See Julian Bailey, 'The Limits of Limitation Clauses' (2017) 33 *Construction Law Journal* 188; (2017) 33 *Building and Construction Law* 4.

9 See *Arthur White (Contractors) Ltd v Tarmac Civil Engineering Ltd* [1967] 1 WLR 1508 (HL(E)); *Phillips Products Ltd v Hyland* [1987] 2 All ER 620, 625–626; *Deutsche Bank AG v Chang Tse Weng* [2013] SGCA 49, [63]-[68] (noted by K Loi & K Low, 'Non-Reliance Clauses and the Unfair Contract Terms Act: Welcome Clarity from Singapore' (2014) *Journal of Business Law* 155).

10 See *Yarm Road v Hewden Tower Cranes Ltd* (2003) 90 Con LR 1, considering the model conditions in the Construction Plant Hire Association (1979 edn); *Baldwins Industrial Services Ltd v Segmentation Construction Ltd* (1992) 37 Con LR 20.

11 The *Unfair Contract Terms Act* imposes constraints on the extent to which contracting parties may attempt to limit or exclude their liability for breach of contract or negligence. The *Unfair Contract Terms Act* was enacted in Singapore in 1977 in terms virtually identical to those in the United Kingdom and replicated in Hong Kong in the *Control of Exemption Clauses Ordinance Cap 71*.

12 See *Downer Connect Pty Ltd v McConnell Dowell Constructors (Aust) Pty Ltd* [2008] VSC 443, [17] per Harper J; *Resource Piling Pte Ltd v Geospecs Pte Ltd* [2013] SGHC 231, [90] per Quentin Loh J. Unforeseeable physical conditions are an Employer's risk in the 2017 Red and Yellow Books (sub-clause 4.12), whereas Unforeseen difficulties are a Contractor's risk in the 2017 Silver Book (sub-clause 4.12).

The NEC4 ECC contract contains a mechanism for the early identification by the parties of risks that may materialise, aimed at avoiding them through the cooperation of the parties.[13]

The significance of *force majeure* to relieve a party from liability for the materialisation of risks in common law jurisdictions will depend on its use in an express contractual term, and its intended effect and operation must be found within the express or implied terms or the matrix of the particular contract.[14] It is essential to define *force majeure* events in the Contract, as there is no universally accepted definition of it.[15]

25.2 Definition of *force majeure*

As discussed in ¶2.3.2, the term *force majeure* does not have any precise meaning nor does it give rise to any special legal doctrine or consequences under the common law, although it is a well-known expression and a considerably more developed concept in French and other civil law systems. The term *vis major* means 'God-made' and comes from the Latin for 'act of God,' while *force majeure* covers both man-made and God-made events and comes from the French for 'superior force.' The words *force majeure* cover unforeseen circumstances of a serious nature which prevented one or both of the parties, partly or totally, from fulfilling their contractual obligations.[16] A *force majeure* clause is a contractual mechanism to excuse performance as a consequence of a risk event outside the control of either party.

As there is no common definition; each contract typically provides its own list. For example, the 2017 FIDIC rainbow suite defines 'Exceptional Event'[17] as an event or circumstance which:

(i) is beyond a Party's control;
(ii) the Party could not reasonably have provided against before entering into the Contract;
(iii) having arisen, such Party could not reasonably have avoided or overcome; and
(iv) is not substantially attributable to the other Party.[18]

The FIDIC definition includes, but does not limit an Exceptional Event to:

(a) war, hostilities (whether war be declared or not), invasion, act of foreign enemies;
(b) rebellion, terrorism, revolution, insurrection, military or usurped power, or civil war;
(c) riot, commotion or disorder by persons other than the Contractor's personnel and other employees of the Contractor and Subcontractors;
(d) strike or lockout not solely involving the Contractor's Personnel and other employees of the Contractor and Subcontractors;
(e) encountering munitions of war, explosive materials, ionizing radiation or contamination by radio-activity, except as may be attributable to the Contractor's use of such munitions, explosives, radiation, or radio-activity; and
(f) natural catastrophes such as earthquake, tsunami, volcanic activity, hurricane, or typhoon.[19]

13 See NEC4 clause 15. Express provision is made as to matters that are the 'employer's risk' and the 'contractor's risk' and an 'early warning register' is used as a project management tool.

14 I N Duncan Wallace, *Hudson's Building and Engineering Contracts* (Sweet and Maxwell London, 11th edn, 1995) 657.

15 The definition in FIDIC contracts being the most widely accepted.

16 *Force majeure* carries different meanings in different legal systems: see N Bunni, 'The Liability and Insurance Clauses of the FIDIC E&M Form' (1987) *International Construction Law Review* 172, 191–194.

17 The 1999 FIDIC rainbow suite used the term *Force Majeure*.

18 Sub-clause 18.1.

19 Ibid.

The following events could be added to the *force majeure* events listed above:

- Mobilization, requisition, or embargo
- Epidemic or pandemic.

Examples of *force majeure* events are given above, but *force majeure* events may also include circumstances that render a contract unprofitable, such as an increase in the cost of consumables or materials, (but will not usually do so)[20] and may also include workers' strikes which are not attributable to dealings of the Contractor with its workforce.[21]

COVID-19 had a substantial impact on the time and cost of the execution of construction projects, but rarely to the level of making performance impossible that would have frustrated the contract. Whether it came within the definition of a *force majeure* event depended on the specific wording in the relevant contract. Whilst COVID-19 satisfied (i) – (iv) in the FIDIC definition of Exceptional Event as noted previously, it does not obviously fit into any of the enumerated categories (a) – (f). It may nevertheless be a *force majeure* event because the list (a) – (f) is not an exclusive list. No doubt this ambiguity will be clarified by appropriate Particular Conditions in future contracts.

Force majeure clauses are interpreted by giving effect to the words used in the clause read in the context of the other contractual terms and the commercial background of the transaction.[22]

The scope of *force majeure* under *Civil Codes* varies widely as discussed in ¶2.3.2. *Force majeure* in the UAE is barely distinguishable from common law frustration, as it depends on impossibility of performance. In contrast, the provision in the Philippines *Civil Code* excuses performance for 'those events which could not be foreseen or which, though foreseen, were inevitable.'

The *UNIDROIT Principles* definition of hardship 'where the occurrence of events fundamentally alters the equilibrium of the contract' discussed in ¶2.3.2.4 are similar to many definitions of *force majeure*.

25.3 Consequences of *force majeure*

Where there is an appropriate *force majeure* clause in the Contract, the consequence of performance being so prevented is that the party affected is not considered to be in default or in breach of its obligations under the Contract. The usual practical consequence is that the Contractor is not considered to be in culpable delay under the Contract if the delay in question is caused by *force majeure*. In this situation, however, the Contractor should apply for an extension to the Date for Completion. The Contractor's entitlement to an EOT would, however, be subject to conditions precedent such as the obligation to mitigate the effect of the delay, where possible.

20 *Holcim (Singapore) Pte Ltd v Precise Development Pte Ltd* [2011] SGCA 1, [56]; *Thames Valley Power Ltd v Total Gas and Power Ltd* [2005] EWHC 2208 (Comm), [15] per Clarke J.

21 *Wing Hing Engineering Investment Ltd v Foric Ltd* [2008] HKCFI 1013.

22 *RDC Concrete Pte Ltd v Sato Kogyo (S) Pte Ltd* [2007] 4 SLR(R) 413, [54]; *Goldlion Properties Ltd v Regent Enterprises Ltd* (2009) 12 HKCFAR 512, [6] per Bokhary and Chan PJJ; *Holcim (Singapore) Pte Ltd v Precise Development Pte Ltd* [2011] SGCA 1, [49]; H Hunter, 'From Coronations to Sand Bans: Frustration and Force Majeure in the Twenty-first Century' (2011) 27 *Journal of Contract Law* 61, 69–75.

It is important to note that the parties are released from their obligations only to the extent that performance is prevented by *force majeure*. When any circumstances of *force majeure* occur, the Contractor is usually obliged to endeavour to continue to perform its obligations so far as is reasonably practicable. The Contractor may have to resort to alternative methods, for example, if an embargo prevents delivery of the software for the control system of a process plant, instead of purchasing the software under embargo, the Contractor may develop it itself, or purchase it elsewhere at a higher price. Some of the disruption of a *force majeure* hindrance to some part of the Works may be mitigated by accelerated work on another part. If the Contractor contemplates any such possibilities, it should notify the Engineer and inform it of the steps the Contractor proposes to take, including any reasonable alternative means for performance of work which is not prevented by *force majeure*. The Contractor should be precise in its description of the steps it proposes to take to secure a basis for claiming compensation and extension of time. The steps or alternative means proposed by the Contractor should not be acted upon unless the Engineer directs the Contractor to do so. It is in the interests of both the Engineer and the Contractor that such instructions are as precise as possible because of the relief claimed. If the Engineer's instructions in any way deviate from the Contractor's proposals, this should be explicitly stated by the Engineer in its instructions. If such instructions are not in writing, the Contractor should either confirm such instructions in writing or obtain written confirmation from the Engineer.

The right to compensation and extension of time arising from a *force majeure* event relates only to costs and delays incurred as a result of the *force majeure* event or complying with the Engineer's instructions, not costs incurred by doing more work than was instructed or work other than that which was instructed by the Engineer.

Prolonged *force majeure* may lead to the termination of the Contract. A wide variety of standard form construction contracts contain provisions for extension of time and delay costs, as well as suspension and termination clauses, in order to address the consequences of a *force majeure* event. For example, an Exceptional Event under the 2017 FIDIC Yellow Book provides for an EOT for events (a) – (f), Cost for event (a) and Cost for events (b) – (e) if the Exceptional Event occurs in the Country.[23] The 2017 FIDIC Yellow Book also provides for optional termination if the execution of substantially all the Works in progress is prevented or delayed for a continuous period of 84 days or multiple periods totalling more than 140 days.[24]

The consequences of a *force majeure* event may result in increased cost and substantial delay without reaching the high threshold of making performance impossible that would frustrate the contract. In these circumstances it may be in both parties' interests to be able to terminate the contract under the *force majeure* provisions.

25.4 Duty to minimise delay

The Contractor's general obligation is to continue the performance of its obligations so far as is reasonably practicable. The Contractor is obliged to minimise delay and mitigate

23 Sub-clause 18.4.
24 Sub-clause 18.5.

losses. If, for example, a civil war in a neighbouring country makes it impossible to procure pure gas for calibration purposes on the site for a refinery, the performance of building the refinery should go on unhindered. A war in the Employer's country may prevent delivery of the plant to the Site when it is finished in a year's time, but it does not prevent the Contractor from finishing the work on the plant that is being performed at its own premises in another country. Similarly, the outbreak of a pandemic (such as the COVID-19 pandemic) may affect the supply of goods both locally and internationally and the provision of services to and on the Site, but the Contractor should do what it can to continue with the Works.

The Contractor may also be required to submit regular notices if the *force majeure* event has continuing effect.

25.5 Release from performance under the law

Parties can be released from their performance obligations under a contract under the common law when the contract is frustrated:

> the law recognises that without default of either party a contractual obligation has become incapable of being performed because the circumstances in which performance is called for would render it a thing radically different from that which was undertaken by the contract.[25]

Thus, delay to Completion of the Works caused by an event outside the control of either party may be so great as to warrant termination because the Contract is frustrated under the common law. This is discussed in more detail in ¶9.1.6.

25 *Davis Contractors Limited v Fareham Urban District Council* [1956] AC 696, 729 per Lord Radcliffe.

CHAPTER 26

Insurance

CONTENTS

26.1 General requirements for insurances

An insurance contract is a contract of the utmost good faith.[1] A person taking out or renewing a policy of insurance must disclose to the insurer all material facts that may influence the mind of the insurer.[2] Circumstances giving rise to insurers' liability to indemnify are determined by the wording of the insurance policy itself, which is a contract;

1 *Manifest Shipping Co Ltd v Uni-Polaris Insurance code Ltd* [2003] 1 AC 469, 491 [42] per Lord Hobhouse; *CGU Insurance Ltd v Porthouse* (2008) 235 CLR 103, [49]. Under Australian statute law, the *Insurance Contracts Act 1984* (Cth) s13 places the obligation on both the insured, including any third-party beneficiary, under the policy and the insurer to act in the utmost good faith.

2 *Versloot Dredging BV v HDI Gerling Industrie Versicherung AG* [2016] UKSC 45, [87] per Lord Hughes JSC; *St Paul Fire & Marine Insurance Co (UK) Limited v McConnell Dowell Constructors Ltd* (1995) 74 BLR 112; *Insurance Act 2015 (UK)* s3; *Insurance Contracts Act 1984* (Cth) s21.

DOI: 10.4324/9781003206873-26

under the principle of freedom of contract the parties to a contract are usually free to agree on whatever terms they choose.

First party insurance is insurance against the risk that a party will suffer a loss which does not represent its liability to any other party, for example, where an owner insures itself against the risk of damage to its property due to fire, flood, or other events. **Liability insurance** is insurance that is expressed in terms that the insurer's liability to indemnify only arises where an event has occurred that renders the insured liable to a third party, or where there has been the notification of a claim in respect of such liability. Under first party insurance, the insurers' obligation to indemnify usually arises upon the happening of an event, whereas in the case of liability insurance, insurers' liability to indemnify arises from the 'occurrence' of an event that gives rise to a claim against the insured.[3] **Claims made liability** may arise from the making of a claim against the insured. The making of a claim plus the notification of that claim to the insurer may also give rise to the insurers' liability, known as **claims made and notified liability**. The burden of proving that the loss suffered falls within the terms of the insurance policy rests upon the party seeking to take the benefit of that insurance policy.[4]

Contractors are free to take out insurance of any kind against any risk, whatever the Contract may require. It may be reasonable to suppose therefore that contractual requirements for insurance would be limited solely to matters directly in the Employer's interest. However, this is not necessarily so, as the Employer may be severely prejudiced if the Contractor is unable to fulfil its contractual obligations due to the occurrence of a peril against which it could have insured but did not. The Contract should make provision for this eventuality to protect the Employer's position. It follows that the interest of the Employer, where the Contractor is liable, is to ensure that sufficient insurance funds are available to avoid delay to the project or increased costs of finding a substitute contractor due to the Contractor being financially crippled by a liability or a claim.

A contract of insurance may be described as a species of indemnity.[5] A contract of insurance has been described as a contract under which an insurer agrees to indemnify an identified or identifiable person against a loss suffered by that person, or to restore a loss that has been suffered, where the occurrence of that loss involved some element of uncertainty, and the assured had an insurable interest in the subject matter of the contract.[6] In other words, the insurer promises to hold a person harmless against a loss, or to make good the loss suffered by that person. Contractors and consultants may utilise general insurance policies that are applicable to all aspects of their business operations or may take out policies specific to particular projects.

In order to be entitled to an indemnity under the policy, a person must have an 'insurable interest' in the subject matter of the insurance, meaning that a person who seeks to be indemnified under an insurance policy must have the potential to suffer an insured loss.

---

3 See *McConnell Dowell Middle East LLC v Royal & Sun Alliance Insurance PLC* [2008] VSC 501; *Weir Services Australia Pty Ltd v AXA Corporate Solutions Assurance* [2018] NSWCA 100, [94]-[97] per Barrett AJA.

4 *British and Foreign Marine Insurance Co-Ltd v Gaunt* [1921] 2 AC 41, 47 per Lord Birkenhead LC; *Suncorp Metway Insurance Ltd v Owners Corporation SP 64487* [2009] NSWCA 223, [52] per Sackville AJA.

5 See *Bofinger v Kingsway Group Ltd* (2009) 239 CLR 269, [7]; *Alliance Ltd v Scandi Enterprises Ltd* [2017] UKPC 10, [7] per Lord Sumption (PC).

6 See Julian Bailey, *Construction Law Vol III* (London Publishing Partnership, 3rd edn 2020) [17.01].

Insurance plays a key role in risk allocation in virtually all engineering projects.[7] An earlier edition of *Hudson's Building and Engineering Contracts* made the following observations which are still generally applicable:

> It is in fact essential, in drafting a provision requiring insurance, for the contract to specify the exact risk to be insured against, the person or persons for whose benefit the policy is to be taken out, the amount of cover required and the effect of the obligation upon any indemnities which, under the contract, may be due from one party to the other in relation to the carrying out of the works. Otherwise the insurance of one party against a specific risk may only result in the insurance company being able to recover upon an indemnity from the other, which may defeat the whole purpose of the requirement to insure, or the protection conferred by the indemnity provisions may itself be affected.[8]

It is important that the information required for insurance of the Works is given by the Employer at the tender stage. Sensible limits for deductibles should be chosen on the advice of the Employer's insurance consultants. Any additional risks which are to be insured by the Contractor should be specified in the preamble to the tender documents.

Most risks can be covered by insurance, although the cost may be prohibitive. The insurers should be provided with a copy of the Contract documents, and the cover and exceptions should follow exactly the words of the Contract. Alternatively, the insurers should be asked to confirm in writing that they are covering the risks defined by the Contract. In doing so, it is important for the Contractor not to confuse insurance risks with commercial risks assumed by the Contractor under the Contract. It is common to see policies issued by leading insurers which do not comply with the requirements of the Contract. The interpretation of an insurance policy may be a difficult task for the Employer, and for that reason a practice is growing of specifying in the Contract that the Contractor must produce a certificate from its insurers stating that the requirements of the Contract have been complied with. If there are any special risks attached to the particular Works, or if anyone has doubts at any time as to whether a particular risk is covered, the parties should confirm the cover with the insurers in writing and argue later about who is liable for any extra premium.

In general, the insurance should be taken out by the Contractor for the benefit of itself and the Employer. The Contractor should be required in the Contract to insure the Works and Contractor's equipment in transit to the Site and whilst on Site, and to insure against third-party liability and its liability to its employees. There should be no difficulty in a Contractor obtaining such insurance under a standard Contractor's all-risks insurance policy. In some cases, it may be appropriate for the Employer to arrange the necessary insurance, or at least the insurance of the Works, during the construction stage and during the defects liability period. Because of the complexities of cover under such 'project insurance,' it is advisable to seek specialist insurance advice to ensure that adequate but not excessive insurance cover is available.

---

7 See the report of the FIDIC Task Committee on Insurance, 'Construction, Insurance and Law' (1986) *International Construction Law Review* 383, commented on by P Madge, 'Construction Insurance and Law' (1986) *International Construction Law Review* 458.

8 I N Duncan Wallace, *Hudson's Building and Engineering Contracts* (Sweet & Maxwell London, 8th edn 1959) 154.

Insurance policies usually place financial limits on the cover provided, which may be whatever the parties agree upon. Policies generally make provision for an excess or deductible as well as an upper limit to the cover provided. Whether the deductible is applicable to the total loss of the insured caused by a problem which manifests itself in many ways or whether the deductible is to be applied in respect of each individual issue caused by the underlying problem should be clarified.[9] A policy may also contain an aggregation provision which limits the total amount the insured is entitled to claim during the policy period.[10] Losses which are consequential upon the insured loss will also not usually be covered.[11]

26.1.1 Obligations of the Contractor

In order to provide adequate insurance to protect the Employer (and confirm that it has been provided at all relevant times), it is desirable that the Contract should require the Contractor to:

(a) Provide the policies or certificates of insurance for inspection, as well as receipts for the premiums at least on an annual basis
(b) Take out insurance policies with an insurer approved by the Employer
(c) Have the terms of the policies approved by the Employer, which approval should not be unreasonably withheld
(d) Be precluded from making any material alteration to the terms of any insurance without the Employer's approval
(e) Provide cover which will not be terminated for failure to pay premiums, and so on, without notice to the Employer
(f) Notify the Employer of any material change in the terms of the policy that may be introduced by the insurers themselves
(g) Comply with all of the conditions stipulated in the insurance policies which it is required to take out under the Contract. Failure to comply with a relevant condition could involve underwriters in withdrawing cover altogether under the relevant policy, for example, a failure by the Contractor to give notice of a claim at the earliest possible opportunity could cause both the Employer and the Contractor to lose their right to claim.

If the Contractor does not produce receipts for its premiums or other evidence of complying insurance cover, the Employer can normally insure at the Contractor's expense, and deduct the premiums from any moneys due or which become due.

In order to protect the Employer, the Engineer should always inspect the policies for conformance with the requirements of the Contract. Any doubtful points should be resolved by the Contractor's insurers in writing or brought to the Employer's notice. The Contractor has no remedy if the mere approval of the policy misleads it into believing that it has full

9 *Mitsubishi Electric UK Ltd v Royal London Insurance* (UK) Ltd (1994) 74 BLR 87.
10 See *AIG Europe Limited v Woodman* [2017] UKSC 18, [14] per Lord Toulson JSC.
11 See *Austria GmbH v Tokio Marine Europe Insurance Ltd* [2009] BLR 261, 279 [115] – [117] per Coulson J.

protection, but if the Engineer takes it on itself to advise the Contractor, it may be liable for negligence.[12]

Where the insurance is in the joint names of the Contractor and the Employer, the insurers will pay out money due under the policy jointly to the Employer and Contractor. The Employer should arrange for such insurance payments to be released to the Contractor on interim certificates. No retention should be deducted from these payments, since the Employer holds the retention deducted from payments for the damaged work which is being replaced.

The Contractor's insurance will generally be set out in more than one policy or in several sections in one policy, and there must be no gaps. Vehicles not being driven on a public road, for instance, may sometimes be excluded from the Contractor's ordinary motor insurance; however, they should not be excluded from its public liability cover for movable equipment. The fact that a policy is called 'Contractors' all risks' does not in fact mean that all risks are covered, and the policy conditions – particularly any special exceptions – must be considered carefully. The exclusion of liability undertaken by contract, which is included in ordinary public liability policies, must not appear in any insurance taken out by the Contractor or Employer.

In cases where the Contractor assumes liability under the Contract for defaults by the Employer or others, it is particularly important that the insurance policy provisions provide adequate cover. In *A E Farr v The Admiralty*,[13] due to negligent navigation the Employer's ship collided with the wharf which the Contractors were building. It was held that the words 'any cause whatsoever' which appeared in the liability clause in question, are 'about as wide as they can be,' so that the Contractors were liable to make good the damage caused by the Employer.[14] In the event that such liability is not covered by the Contractor's insurance, it would have to bear the costs of rectification from its own resources.

26.1.2 Exclusions

Insurers commonly exclude from cover under standard policies a number of risks which would be expected to be within the cover provided. They are apparently not prepared to insure against such risks without additional and perhaps unrealistic premiums, or under a different type of policy. In most Contractors' all-risks policies of insurance, unless there is a special item in the policy, defects due to bad workmanship or materials are excluded. Furthermore, an insurance policy may also exclude cover for indirect or consequential loss or damage, including any reductions in the contract price or liquidated damages for delay. The insurance policy may also exclude claims in relation to wear and tear, and shortages and theft, such provisions being standard exclusions in construction all-risks insurance policies. Finally, motor vehicle risks may be excluded from the insurance required to be affected by the Contractor under the Contract upon the basis that such risks will be covered by specific vehicle insurance.

---

12 *AMF International v Magnet Bowling Ltd* [1968] 2 All ER 789 (QB).

13 *AE Farr Ltd v The Admiralty* [1953] 2 All ER 512 (QB).

14 See also *AMF International v Magnet Bowling Ltd* [1968] 2 All ER 789 (QB).

In most Contractors' all-risks policies of insurance, only the excepted risks are excluded. Although defects due to bad workmanship or materials are typically excluded, damage to the Works by an accident caused by these defects are not excluded. The breadth of these common exclusions reinforces the importance of carefully scrutinising the insurance policy for conformity with the requirements of the Contract and obtaining the insurer's written confirmation.

Where there is an exclusion of damage due to a negligent act or negligent omission by the Employer or its agent 'during the currency of the contract' this might include a case where the Engineer failed to vary the work when a defect in the original design was discovered or so as to avoid threatened damage. The insurer bears the burden of proving that a policy exclusion applies.[15]

26.1.3 Responsibility to insure

The Contractor is normally required to insure against the various categories of damage for which it is contractually liable, including damage due to 'insurable' riot risks. The Contractor is also usually expressly liable to repair damage to the Works due to defective materials or workmanship during the progress of the Works, and during the defects liability period unless otherwise stated. There is no requirement to insure for these risks, and indeed it is unlikely to be commercially available at a reasonable price, at least in the common law world.

The insurance position in respect of major defects in design or construction is different in countries where decennial liability applies. **Decennial liability** is the joint liability of a Contractor and an architect or engineer for a period of ten years from the date of handover to compensate the Employer for any total or partial collapse of a building or installation, and for any defect which threatens the stability or safety of the building. In France, insurance against decennial liability is mandatory under Art L.242–1 of the *Insurance Code.*[16] Decennial liability also applies in other countries such as Egypt, the UAE, and some Francophone countries.

Insurance in the joint names of the Contractor and the Employer may be convenient in the special case of damage occurring during the defects liability period caused by the Contractor's operations, since by this time the Works will be occupied by the Employer, and it may be considered desirable for that reason to enable the Employer to sue on the policy itself. However, even in this case the liability as between Employer and Contractor is normally the Contractor's under the Contract, so that joint insurance is not strictly necessary to protect the Employer.

The Engineer should check that the Employer and its property are, in fact, covered by the Contractor's insurance, particularly where alterations are being made to an existing structure. This will have to be dealt with specifically, since if the policy is in joint names, property belonging to an insured is normally excluded from public liability cover. The cover should be at least for the amount in the tender. However, as the Contractor's ultimate

---

15 *Owners of Strata Plan 68372 v Allianz Australia Insurance Limited* [2014] NSWSC 1807, [86] per Ball J.

16 Insurance for decennial liability is discussed in David Brown & Michael Conrad, 'France' in Donald Charrett (ed), *The International Application of FIDIC Contracts* (Informa Law from Routledge, 2020) 153–155.

liability is not affected by insuring up to the specified amount, the Contractor may require a higher cover. This is particularly so where valuable machinery, and so on, which may be easily damaged, is being installed in the Works by the Employer.

The Employer is left to insure the Works, if it wishes, against the excepted risks which are not allocated to or insured by the Contractor.

Frequently the policy wording requires the insured to take all reasonable precautions to prevent a loss from arising, and to mitigate the size of any loss which is suffered. Generally, an insured is not entitled to be indemnified as a consequence of its own 'wilful misconduct.'[17]

26.2 Insurance for Works and Contractor's equipment

26.2.1 Contractor's equipment

The Employer is interested in ensuring that Contractor's equipment is adequately insured since the absence of certain Contractor's equipment from Site in consequence of loss or damage could cause considerable delay to Completion. The Contractor is, subject to the terms of the Contract, usually required to insure the Contractor's equipment effectively against all loss or damage caused by any of the Contractor's risks from the moment it is dispatched to Site until it is no longer required on Site.

26.2.2 The Works

The Contractor is usually required in construction contracts to insure the Works in the joint names of the Contractor and the Employer to their full replacement value, with stipulated deductible limits in **contract works insurance**. The risk insured is the risk associated with the physical loss of or damage to the Works under construction, including temporary works, and property associated with the performance of the Works. Such insurance does not cover Works being rendered practically useless but not damaged owing to a design error.[18] It may be necessary for the Contractor to discuss with insurers how the obligation to insure to full replacement value is to be satisfied.

It is customary for policies to be issued showing the original total contract price, inclusive of free issue materials, customs dues, freight, and insurance, if not already included, as the initial sum insured. This sum should be reviewed at appropriate intervals, and the Contractor should arrange with its insurers one of the various ways of adjusting its cover upwards for Variations, increases in quantities, and circumstances giving rise to changed risks to reflect the full replacement value at all times as required by the Contract.

The deductible limits or 'excesses' are the amounts which are to be borne by the Contractor itself on each and every claim. Considerable thought may need to be given by the Employer and Engineer, or the Employer's risk manager, to the sums to be specified as the deductible limits. Setting a high excess may mean a reduction in premium and theoretically lower tender prices, but it will also increase the extent to which claims for loss or damage to the Works have to be borne by the Contractor itself out of its

17 As to the meaning of 'wilful misconduct,' see *De Beers UK Ltd v Atos Origin IT Services UK Ltd* [2010] EWHC 3276 (TCC), [206] per Edwards-Stuart J.

18 *Transfield Constructions Pty Ltd v GIO Australia Holdings Pty Ltd* [1996] NSWCA 538.

own pocket (or by other insurers under a specific policy effected for the purpose) with a consequent increase in risk to the Employer. Fixing low deductible limits is likely to increase tender prices because of the increased cost of insurance and may not provide sufficient incentive for the Contractor to manage its work properly so as to minimise insured risks.

A construction contract should provide that the insurance of the Works is from the commencement date until the risk transfer date. It should also require that the Contractor is to maintain insurance against loss or damage during the defects liability period caused by the Contractor whilst completing any outstanding work or complying with its obligations to remedy defects. This should also apply to any of the Contractor's risks which occurred prior to the risk transfer date, where the damage or loss comes to light or occurs after the risk transfer date. Contractors should have no difficulty in insuring their liabilities for loss or damage to the Works after the risk transfer date by means of an appropriate extended maintenance insurance policy, but they are unlikely to be able to obtain insurance at a reasonable premium which covers the cost of repair of defective parts of the Works as opposed to damage caused by such defective parts.

Insurance provides compensation for loss of, or damage to, the Works caused by any of the Contractor's risks, and any other risks specified in the Contract. The risk of physical loss or damage covered will usually include the risk of damage proximately caused by fire, whether through accident, the negligence of an assured, or the negligence or deliberate act of a third party,[19] flood,[20] carelessness,[21] accident, or other adventitious events.[22] The width of the insuring provision must be analysed carefully, because it may afford cover for the cost of remedying physical damage to other parts of the Works caused by defects in design or construction, or the cost of taking steps to neutralise or mitigate the effects of delay or danger to the project caused by the physical damage in question. It is important to note that 'all risks' insurance does not usually provide cover for the cost of remedying defects in the Works themselves due to, for example, defective design and/or workmanship.[23]

The risks ordinarily borne by the Contractor such as the risk of damage to or destruction of materials brought by the Contractor to the Site before ownership of those materials has passed to the Employer are normally covered by such insurance.[24] The Contractor is usually obliged to take out 'all risks' insurance until the Works have been handed over

19 *Scottish & Newcastle plc v GD Construction (St Albans) Ltd* [2003] BLR 131, 138–139 [26] per Aikens J (CA).

20 See 'flood' defined in *Young v Sun Alliance & London Insurance Ltd* [1976] 3 All ER 561; *Board of Trustees of the Tate Gallery v Duffy Ledcor Construction Ltd* [2007] BLR 216.

21 *Construction Ltd v Northbridge Indemnity Insurance Co* (2016) SCC 37.

22 *CA Blackwell (Contractors) Ltd v Gerling* [2007] EWCA 94 (Comm) [40] per Judge Mackie QC; (affirmed [2007] EWCA Civ 1450).

23 *Simaan General Contracting Co- v Pilkington Glass Ltd (No 2)* [1988] 1 QB 758, 781–782 per Bingham LJ; *Kier Construction Ltd v Royal Insurance (UK) Ltd (No 1)* (1992) 30 Con LR 45, 72–76 per Judge Bowsher QC; *Canadian National Railway Co v Royal & Sun Alliance Insurance Co of Canada* [2008] 3 SCR 453; *Reilly v National Insurance & Guarantee Corporation Limited* [2018] EWCA Civ 1460; Patrick Mead, 'Policy Triggers and Exclusions in Construction Insurance' (2008) 24 *Building and Construction Law* 184.

24 When the materials are incorporated into the Works, they become fixtures and ownership is transferred to the Employer.

to the Employer.[25] This is because during construction the physical state of the Site is at risk of the Contractor. This is a useful means of enabling the Employer to include within the contract works insurance of as many of the Employer's risks as can reasonably be insured.

The contract works insurance may also insure for the cost of clearing the Site after damage and for loss from damage to plant. If the contract works insurance does not cover loss of or damage to plant in transit and Contractor's equipment to or from the Site by air, sea, or land, the Contractor should be required to affect the necessary transit insurance.

26.3 Insurance against injury to persons and damage to property

A construction contract should provide that the Contractor is required to insure against its liability to third parties for any death, or personal injury or loss of or damage to any physical property by taking out appropriate **public liability insurance**. Further, the Contract should require it to insure these liabilities until the issue of the last defects liability certificate. The Contractor should be on cover before it begins any work on Site and should insure for not less than the amount specified in the Contract. The amount specified in the Contract will not affect the Contractor's liability, and accordingly it may be prudent for the Employer to fix a reasonably high sum for the amount of insurance.

Subject to the terms of the Contract, public liability insurance is required to cover injury, loss or damage to any person or property including the Employer or its property (other than the Works), and surface rights and **servitudes** or easements (rights to enter the land of third parties), damage to land or crops with certain exceptions, and for at least the amount shown in the Contract.[26] Usually the Contractor is not required to insure for liability for interference with third-party rights which are the unavoidable result of the construction of the Works in accordance with the Contract.

Physical damage to the property of the insured is not ordinarily covered, nor economic loss suffered by third parties that arises out of physical injury or damage to property.[27]

A construction contract should require that the public liability insurance cover affected by the Contractor is issued in the joint names of the Employer and the Contractor for at least the amount stated in the Contract, with an extension of a cross liability cover so that the insurance shall apply to the Contractor and to the Employer as separate insureds.

As an injured third party may, in some cases, recover from the Contractor damages to be borne ultimately by the Employer under the indemnity provisions of the Contract, the Contractor may be wise to have full employer's and public liability insurance, without exception, unless it knows that the Employer has the resources or insurance to cover its liability to indemnify the Contractor.

25 *Jones v Crowley Colosso Ltd* [1997] EWCA Civ 2909.

26 See *C J Pearce & Co v Hereford Corporation* (1968) 66 LGR 647.

27 *Tesco Stores Ltd v Constable* [2008] EWCA Civ 362, [14] per Tuckey LJ; *AXA Insurance UK plc v Thermonex Ltd* [2012] EWHC B10 (Mercantile), [59]-[65] per Simon Brown QC; *Aspen Insurance v Sangster & Annand Ltd* (2018) 35 Const LJ 200, 208 [59] – 209 [65] per HHJ Waksman QC.

26.4 Insurance for Contractor's personnel

A construction contract should require the Contractor to take out appropriate employer's liability or workmen's compensation insurance. The party on whom the obligation to take out employer's liability insurance is imposed may be dictated by the Contract.[28] This type of insurance covers the risk associated with harm or injury suffered by employees arising out of or in the course of their employment. Private Contractors in the United Kingdom are required to take out employer's liability insurance to cover such risks under the *Employers' Liability (Compulsory Insurance) Act 1969* (UK), and there is a similar requirement under Singapore, Australian, and Hong Kong law. It is appropriate to check whether the contractual requirements exceed the required level of statutory insurance. Any such additional insurance requirement is of course likely to increase tender prices.

26.5 Professional indemnity

Professional indemnity insurance (known in the USA more descriptively as errors & omissions or malpractice insurance) provides a construction professional with cover against the risk of loss, arising as a result of liability to another party due to the professional's negligence.[29] The policy is typically designed to protect the insured against loss or liability resulting from any neglect, error, or omission in the design and/or construction of a structure,[30] and possibly legal expenses resulting from any action against the insured.[31] For example, in *George Wimpey & Co Ltd v Poole*,[32] it was alleged that a structure was designed without taking adequate consideration of pre-existing and available geotechnical information.

A professional indemnity policy usually only provides cover to the extent that it can be established that the professional failed to exercise due skill and care. It does not normally cover a construction professional against liability for failure to ensure that the design, workmanship, or both comply with a contractual obligation or a failure to satisfy a 'fitness for purpose obligation.' Importantly for consultants and specialist contractors, a professional indemnity policy may only cover the professional against positive acts of negligence in design but not breaches of contract flowing from the failure to supply materials or services in accordance with the relevant contract specification.[33] In Australia, professional indemnity insurance normally covers liability arising from misleading or deceptive conduct in breach of *Australian Consumer Law*.

In many situations, the only significant funds available to satisfy an award of damages arising from defective design are the proceeds of a professional indemnity insurance policy. The existence and cover provided by professional indemnity insurance are

28 See, for example, 2017 FIDIC Red Book sub-clause 19.2.5.

29 *Chubb Insurance Company of Australia v Robinson* [2016] FAFC 17, [131]-[152].

30 *Balderstone Hornibrook Engineering Pty Ltd v Gordian Runoff Ltd* [2008] NSWCA 243.

31 *Rust Consulting v PB Ltd* [2012] BLR 427, 431 [17] per Toulson LJ; *QBE Underwriting Ltd v Southern Colliery Maintenance Pty Ltd* [2018] NSWCA 53, [57]-[61] per Leeming JA.

32 (1984) 27 BLR 58.

33 *Vosten v Commonwealth* [1989] 1 Qd R 693; *Balderstone Hornibrook Pty Ltd v Paul Segaert Pty Ltd* [2008] NSWSC 972.

therefore of real interest to the Employer; it may not be financially viable to instigate litigation against a designer in the absence of insurance cover to satisfy any liability. As professional indemnity insurance is provided for claims made and notified, it is essential that a professional provides an 'alert' to its insurer as soon as it becomes aware of a potential liability in order to preserve its insured position. Failure to provide such an 'alert' could preclude obtaining professional indemnity insurance for that liability in a subsequent policy year.[34]

26.6 Product liability

The insurance covering the risk associated with the use of defective materials or other goods in the construction of particular works, and the associated risk that the defective materials or other goods may cause physical damage to persons or property is referred to as **product liability insurance**. Such policies do not usually cover the loss associated with damage to the defective product itself.[35]

26.7 Business interruption

The risk of impairment of revenue or profit, or of increased costs as a consequence of an adverse event during a project is referred to as 'business interruption' risk. **Business interruption insurance** cover may include 'delay in start-up,' 'advance loss of profits,' and 'industrial special risks'; the latter describes the risk of an increased cost of working or production flowing from physical damage to property, for example, building materials under the Contractor's control being damaged or destroyed by an accidental occurrence.

26.8 *Force majeure* and unforeseen site conditions

As discussed in ¶2.3.2 and ¶25.2, under the common law, *force majeure* is an exceptional event or circumstance which cannot be resisted or controlled and which satisfies the criteria stated in the contract, whereas in civil law systems, *force majeure* is defined in the relevant *Civil Code* and operates independently of party agreement. *Force majeure* is discussed in detail in Chapter 25. It is possible for project specific policies to insure some or all project participants against the risk of adverse economic effects flowing from *force majeure* events occurring or adverse site conditions[36] being encountered unexpectedly.[37]

---

34 For further details on professional indemnity insurance, see Dr Donald E Charrett, 'Is Conventional Insurance for Construction Projects Fit for Purpose?' (2018) 34 *Building and Construction Law* 253, or Donald Charrett, *Contracts for Construction and Engineering Projects* (Informa Law from Routledge, 2nd edn 2022) Chapter 23.

35 See *Pilkington United Kingdom Ltd v CGU Insurance PLC* [2004] BLR 97 (CA), in which the policy wording made it clear that the policy was not intended to apply where the damage was only to the defective product that was supplied.

36 Which may include contaminants on the Site.

37 G A Smith, T P Wilson & G E Bundschuh, 'Recent Developments in the Insurability of Force Majeure and (Not Completely) Unforeseen Condition Risks' (2001) *International Construction Law Review* 83.

26.9 Insurance in joint names

Joint names insurance refers to insurance taken out by one or more of the parties to the Contract in respect of identified risks (usually for contract works risk and sometimes other risks such as those associated with workplace injuries and similar matters), in the names of and for the benefit of one or more of the contracting parties, or third parties. In order to exempt a party from liability for damage caused by its own negligence, express words are usually required. A person must be sufficiently identified as an assured by the policy, otherwise cover will not be provided.[38]

26.10 Employer's insurance

Subject to the provisions of the Contract, the Engineer may advise the Employer to obtain insurance coverage as follows:

(1) Loss of profit from the Works through fire, and so on, causing delay in Completion, for which it has to give the Contractor an extension of time.
(2) The Works to Completion, except so far as the Contractor insures for damage by the Employer for maintenance operations, and so on. If the Employer occupies any part of the Works, it should insure the whole Works for any damage due to its occupation. It should be made clear that the Contractor continues the general insurance of the part occupied. Under the policies of some companies, when Completion of a part is certified, the Contractor's insurance of that part ends. The Engineer should check this so that the Employer may insure, if necessary, without prejudice to any argument about liability for the premium.
(3) Ordinary public liability to Completion.
(4) Personal injury or damage to the property of any person (including the Contractor) which it or its agents cause by a negligent act during the currency of the Contract.
(5) For liability to any employee of the Contractor or any subcontractor resulting from any act or default of the Employer or its agents or servants.
(6) Damage to materials supplied by the Employer or a contractor employed directly by it.
(7) For the Engineer's fees on rebuilding, which are not included in the Contractor's insurance.
(8) The original structure in the case of alterations, except as covered under item (2).

The Employer may also insure for damage to the Works due to the Engineer's design, which is also normally excluded from the Contractor's cover. Although the Engineer may have indemnity insurance which will cover damage due to its negligence, the level of that insurance may be significantly less than the possible damages resulting from a catastrophic loss or major rebuilding.

38 *Petrofina (UK) Ltd v Magnaload Ltd* [1984] QB 127 (in which it was held that a reference to 'subcontractor' in a 'joint names' all risks policy included a 'sub-subcontractor'; *Tokio Marine & Fire Insurance Co Ltd v Holgersson* [2019] WASCA 114; *National Oilwell (UK) Limited v Davy Offshore Ltd* [1993] 2 Lloyds Rep 582, 596–597 per Colman J.

The Engineer should warn the Employer to take out its own insurance as soon as Completion approaches, and not to wait until it issues its certificate, since the certificate is often delayed and the time of Completion backdated.

26.11 Claims between beneficiaries

Subrogation means that an insurer is entitled in equity to step in and exercise the insured's rights against any relevant third parties where it has fully indemnified the insured against a loss covered by a contract of insurance.[39] The effect of a 'waiver of subrogation' clause in an insurance policy is to prevent an insurer from exercising by way of subrogation one insured's rights against a co-insured party in respect of an insured event. A waiver of subrogation may be an express or an implied term of an insurance contract.[40] The purpose is that the insurance covers the party's loss, even if it was caused by the negligence or fault of the co-insured party.[41]

26.12 Remedy on Contractor's failure to insure

If a Contractor fails to take out insurance in the terms required by the Contract, then the Employer is usually entitled to take out such insurance in the Contractor's name and to pay the premiums as may be necessary to keep the insurance in force. The Employer is also then usually entitled from time to time to deduct the amount of the premiums paid by it from any monies due or which may become due to the Contractor; or it may recover the same as a debt due from the Contractor.

A contractual remedy of this kind is essential in the case of all obligations to insure, since until a risk has eventuated in respect of which there are neither Contractor's nor insurance funds available, the Employer is not in a position to show that any damage has resulted from the Contractor's failure to insure; and by then it is too late for it to have any effective remedy for the breach.

26.13 Notice

Compliance with provisions of a policy requiring the insured to notify the insurer of a claim and to cooperate with the insurer by supplying supporting information regarding the claim may be expressed to be a condition precedent to the insurer's liability under the policy. Prompt notification of a claim together with supporting information gives insurers an early opportunity to assess the claim, and to take such action as is appropriate under the circumstances. For this reason it is usually a requirement of an insurance contract that the insured must give notice to the insurer of a claim, or an occurrence that might or is expected to give rise to a claim 'immediately' or as soon as possible or when the insured

39 *Woodside Petroleum Development Pty Ltd v H&R-E &W Pty Ltd* (1999) 20 WAR 380; *Caledonia North Sea Ltd v British Telecommunications plc* [2002] BLR 139; *Dura (Australia) Constructions Pty Ltd v Victoria Managed Insurance Authority* [2012] VSC 114, [46] per Robson J.

40 *Bovis Lend Lease Ltd v Saillard Fuller & Partners* (2001) 77 Con LR 134, 189 [152] per HHJ Thornton QC.

41 *Talbot Underwriting Ltd v Nausch, Hogan & Murray Inc* [2006] EWCA Civ 889, [51] per Moore-Bick LJ.

becomes aware of the circumstances giving rise to the claim.[42] A requirement to give notice 'immediately' means 'with all reasonable speed considering the circumstances of the case.'[43] The interpretation of the words 'as soon as possible' was decided in *Kier Construction Ltd v Royal Insurance (UK) Ltd*[44] where it was held that: 'it is difficult to conceive of circumstances where a delay of four weeks between the acquisition of knowledge of an occurrence and the giving of notice in a commercial situation should be regarded as being within time even under the less stringent words 'as soon as possible.'

The insured must comply with the terms of the insurance policy, which may include a requirement that the insured must not admit liability or enter into a settlement agreement with the claimant without the insurer's written consent. The reason for this is that such conduct might cause prejudice to the insurer. The insurer may be entitled to refuse cover for the claim should the insured breach such a provision. Such provisions may create conflicts of interest for certifiers (under their professional indemnity insurance) who may themselves be responsible for issues which give rise to an entitlement to the Contractor but also obliged to administer the contract fairly and honestly. One such example might be the issue of late or incorrect drawings entitling the Contractor to an extension of time and the payment of time-related costs, which may amount to an admission of liability on their part.

26.14 The effect of insurance on liability

Insurance does not affect the contractual liability of the parties at all. If, for any reason, a claim against insurers is not met, then the loss will, subject to the terms of the Contract, be borne according to whether the cause or risk associated with the claim is an Employer's risk or a Contractor's risk. This also applies if the amounts for which the Employer has required insurance to be affected are inadequate to cover the claim, as the requirement for the Contractor to provide insurance of a certain level does not imply any cap on its liability. Any limitations of liability must be defined explicitly in the Contract.

It is for the person who seeks to be indemnified under the policy to establish that it has suffered a loss in respect of a risk covered by the policy, and that the policy responds in the particular circumstances.[45]

42 *Kier Construction Ltd v Royal Insurance (UK) Ltd* (No 1) (1992) 30 Con LR 45, 84–85 per Judge Bowsher QC.

43 *Aspen Insurance UK Ltd v Pectel Ltd* [2008] EWHC 2804 (Comm) [9] per Teare J.

44 (No 1) (1992) 30 Con LR 45, 84–85 per Judge Bowsher QC.

45 *Wallaby Grip Ltd v QBE Insurance (Australia) Ltd* [2010] HCA 9, [28].

CHAPTER 27

Employer's and Contractor's claims

CONTENTS

27.1 Claims are not disputes

It is important to clearly distinguish between a claim made by one party to a contract (either Contractor or Employer), and a dispute between the parties. A properly structured, articulated, and supported claim may persuade the other contracting party of the claimant's legal entitlement. Provided claims are submitted *bona fide* pursuant to a reasonably arguable legal basis, they are a legitimate assertion of a claimed entitlement, and deserve to be properly assessed by the other party on the basis of the facts, the contract, and the law. The following passage articulates this proposition in the context of the formal procedures built into the FIDIC contracts:

DOI: 10.4324/9781003206873-27

> Claims should not be regarded as either inevitable or unpalatable, and complying with claims procedures should not be regarded as being an aggressive act. Major projects give rise to major risks, which have to be dealt with if they occur. Whilst the Parties might prefer everything to remain unchanged, they should not instinctively seek to attribute blame if circumstances arise or events occur which give rise to an adjustment of the Contract Price. In these events, the claims procedures are specified so as to provide the degree of formality considered necessary for the proper administration of a building or engineering project. Complying with these procedures and maintaining a cooperative approach to the determination of all adjustments should enhance the likelihood of achieving a successful project.[1]

Claims and disputes were both covered in Clause 20 of the 1999 editions of the FIDIC rainbow suite, perhaps conflating these two separate issues. However, in the 2017 editions they are separated into Clause 20, Employer's and Contractor's Claims, and Clause 21, Disputes and Arbitration, to emphasise their distinct identities. In addition, both Claim and Dispute are new defined terms in the 2017 editions. Although many disputes arise out of claims that are rejected, a claim is not a dispute, and indeed many (perhaps most) claims are appropriately assessed and the results of that assessment accepted (even if the recipient does not agree with it).

A **dispute** or difference under a contract only arises when a determination on a claim is made that is not accepted by the claiming party. Thus, where the Engineer or the Employer determines a Contractor's claim adversely to the Contractor, a dispute only arises if the Contractor does not accept the Engineer's/Employer's determination.[2] The determination of the Contractor's claim in itself is not a decision on a dispute or difference, and it is necessary for the Contractor to formally disagree with the determination of its claim before a dispute comes into existence. This emphasises that, in contrast to the FIDIC Fourth Edition Red Book 1987,[3] the Engineer under a 2017 FIDIC contract has no role in the resolution of disputes. If the parties cannot agree on the resolution of a claim, the Engineer makes a *determination* on the *claim*; if a party does not accept the Engineer's determination and initiates a dispute, it is the DAB/DAAB that ultimately makes a *decision* on the *dispute*. It should be noted that the only references to the Engineer in Clause 21

1 *The FIDIC Contracts Guide* (FIDIC, 2000) 88, 89.

2 *Monmouth County Council v Costelloe & Kemple Ltd* (1964) 63 LGR 131 (1965) 63 LGR 429 (Court of Appeal) where Lord Denning MR stated: 'First point is this: Was there any dispute or difference arising between the contractors and employer? It is accepted that, in order that a dispute or difference can arise on this contract, there must in the first place be a claim by the contractor. Until that claim is rejected, you cannot say that there is a dispute or a difference. There must be both a claim and a rejection of it in order to constitute a dispute or difference.'

3 Clause 67.1 [Engineer's Decision] stated 'If a dispute of any kind whatsoever arises between the Employer and the Contractor in connection with, or arising out of, the Contract or the execution of the Works, whether during the execution of the Works or after their completion and whether before or after repudiation or other termination of the Contract, including any dispute as to any opinion, instruction, determination, certificate or valuation of the Engineer, the matter in dispute shall, in the first place, be referred in writing to the Engineer, with a copy to the other party. Such reference shall state that it is made pursuant to this Clause. No later than the eighty-fourth day after the date on which he received such reference the Engineer shall give notice of his decision to the Employer and the Contractor.'

[Disputes and Arbitration] of the 2017 Red and Yellow Books relate to her/his contract administration role.

The distinction between a claim and a dispute in the 2017 Yellow Book is made clear by the definitions of these terms:

> '**Claim**' means a request or assertion by one Party to the other Party for an entitlement or relief under any Clause of these Conditions or otherwise in connection with, or arising out of, the Contract or the execution of the Works.
>
> '**Dispute**' means any situation where:
>
> (a) one Party makes a claim against the other Party (which may be a Claim, as defined in these Conditions, or a matter to be determined by the Engineer under these Conditions, or otherwise);
> (b) the other Party (or the Engineer under Sub-Clause 3.7.2 [Engineer's Determination]) rejects the claim in whole or in part; and
> (c) the first Party does not acquiesce (by giving a NOD under Sub-Clause 3.7.5 [Dissatisfaction with Engineer's determination] or otherwise),
>
> provided however that a failure by the other Party (or the Engineer) to oppose or respond to the claim, in whole or in part, may constitute a rejection if, in the circumstances, the DAAB or the arbitrator(s), as the case may be, deem it reasonable for it to do so.

Disputes arising from claims thus involve three discrete steps:

(i) Claims for an EOT, an extension of the Defects Notification Period, or additional money from either Employer or Contractor.
(ii) Rejection or deemed rejection of the validity of the claim by the other contracting party or the Engineer administering the Contract.
(iii) The claimant's non-acceptance of the rejection or deemed rejection of the claim.

27.2 Claims

A **claim** is the submission of a formal request by one party to the other party under the provisions of the Contract or under the (common) law, for additional time or money arising out of circumstances or events concerning the execution of the project. Thus, a Contractor's claim is a request to the Engineer (or Employer) for an extension of time for Completion or for additional payment pursuant to the Contract or under the (common) law. An Employer's claim is an Employer's submission of a formal request or an assertion of an entitlement under the provisions of the Contract or the (common) law for payment of money or an extension of the defects liability period arising out of circumstances or events concerning the execution of the project.

To be a valid claim, such a request must be based on the terms of the Contract or on the Contractor's or Employer's common law or legal rights. It is important to remember that the onus of proof is on the claimant and all supporting evidence should be relevant and cogent. *Ex gratia* payments made for reasons of business policy are beyond the scope of this book but should not be totally disregarded in situations where there may not be any contractual or legal entitlement. Construction projects are subject to a range of risks and unforeseen events, and claims are therefore almost inevitable on construction contracts of any magnitude. Properly formulated claims should be viewed by the Employer as normal and routine, and not as evidence of aggressive or inappropriate conduct by the Contractor and should therefore be approached from a purely objective point of view.

There will always be unforeseen costs incurred by the Contractor during the performance of a construction contract. Some of these costs may be rightly seen as the Contractor's risks in wrongly evaluating the costs of performing the work. Some may be claimed under the Variations procedure. Some of the costs, however, may be of a kind that should rightly be borne by the Employer. Similarly, there are risks which, if they eventuate, result in delays to construction for which the Contractor may or may not be entitled to an EOT. For these reasons it is vital to have a claims procedure set out in the Contract.

In order to ensure that claims may be handled in an orderly way and late claims are avoided, Employers should establish in the Contract a reasonable and realistic procedure for dealing with claims. The main motivation behind any claims procedure in the Contract is to avoid surprise on the Employer's behalf, and therefore to have claims presented by the Contractor and determined as soon as possible after the occurrence of the circumstances which form the basis of each claim. It is equally important for the Contractor that submitted claims are processed within a reasonable time so that it is aware of its entitlements to time and money. If time and money claims are not handled during the contractual period in a timely and effective manner, the Contractor will not be able to plan its resources and cash flow and the potential for waste of time and cost in subsequent litigation or arbitration will be increased.

Once the Contract has been executed, it would be prudent for both the Contractor and the Employer to develop their own internal contract management manuals, setting out the timelines and procedures for the different claims to be made and administered under the Contract.

27.3 Claim procedures

27.3.1 Notification of Contractor's intention to claim

The first procedural step in submitting a Contractor's claim should be the Contractor's obligation to notify the Engineer or the Employer of its intention to make a claim for any additional payment or EOT. The Contract should provide that the notification must state the reasons for the claim. However, how much the Contractor must or can explain depends on the circumstances. It should be borne in mind that the notification only has the purpose of alerting the Engineer (and the Employer) to the intention of the Contractor to issue a claim against the Employer under or in connection with the Contract, and (in broad terms at least) the circumstance giving rise to the claim.

Some Contractors have no sensible routing for internal notification of claims. This frequently results in claims being submitted at a late stage, giving such Contractors a bad name by linking these 'late claimers' with those who deliberately wait until the end of the Contract and then surprise the Engineer with inflated claims. The time limit mandated in the Contract for submission of claims is therefore highly important to the Engineer and the Employer as well as the Contractor. Absolutely foolproof routines should be established internally by the Contractor to ensure that notifications are sent within the time limits set out in the Contract documents. As suggested, such risk management would be greatly enhanced by developing an internal contract management manual once the tender has been accepted and distributing this to all key personnel involved in claim management.

27.3.2 Detailed Contractor's claim

The second step in submitting a claim under a construction contract is usually an obligation for the Contractor to submit to the Engineer full and detailed particulars of the claim within a specified time limit. In other words, the Contractor must give details of its claim sometime after having notified its intention, in order to avoid losing its right to make the claim. The main rule established by the claim mechanism in the Contract should be that the Contractor must submit full and detailed particulars of its claim as soon as reasonably practical after the date of the notice of its intention to claim.

It is often acceptable to both the Contractor and the Engineer to postpone the submission of a fully detailed claim until very late in the Contract, or until Taking-Over, even though this scenario may not be provided for in the Contract. The reason is that the basis for the claim may be difficult to evaluate until more experience is gained. A fairly frequent example is claims for cost caused by disturbance because of many Variations, or delay in delivery of the Employer's 'free issue materials' (on the assumption that the Employer has accepted the risk for the delivery of such materials in the Contract). In such a scenario, the disturbance or delay has occurred, but the ultimate consequences are dependent upon subsequent events. These subsequent events may greatly influence the size of the claim, and both the Engineer and the Contractor may therefore be interested in a postponement of the submission of details of the claim until after those events have occurred. If the Engineer and the Contractor reach such an agreement, the agreement should be made or confirmed in writing for the purposes of evidence (ie to prevent the Employer subsequently claiming that the Contractor failed to deliver the required claim within the time specified in the Contract) and control.

27.3.3 Claim assessment

After the Contractor has submitted its claim, the Contract should then require the Engineer to determine, within a reasonable defined period of time, whether the Contractor is entitled to additional payment and/or extension of time. To enable the Contactor to plan its resources and cash flow as previously discussed, the Contract should not allow the Engineer to postpone its decision on a claim.

It should be emphasised that a delay in the assessment of a claim beyond the contractually specified time is only acceptable if both parties agree to it. In most cases the Contractor will need to know whether or not a claim, for example, for an EOT, has been accepted within the time provided for in the Contract. A rejection of an EOT claim may result in the projected time for Completion exceeding the contractual time for Completion, which could be averted by timely acceleration; however, there would be no need for acceleration if the EOT claim is accepted. In such circumstances the Contractor should expect determination of its entitlement (or not) to an EOT strictly within the time limit set in the Contract so that it can plan its resources accordingly.

If the Contractor is late in submitting the particulars of the claim as specified in the Contract, the Engineer should be entitled under the Contract to reject the claim. However, whether it is in fact entitled to do so will depend upon the terms of the Contract and the relevant law. The right of rejection gives the Engineer the means to discipline the Contractor so as to avoid the notorious late claims where appropriate, and to insist on precise and not tactical and imprecise claims. For more detail on the rights and obligations of the Engineer, refer to Chapter 8.

27.3.4 Time bars

Many contracts, including FIDIC, have strict time limits within which claims must be submitted as a condition precedent to any entitlement. The consequence of failure to comply with such a time limit is that the claim is subject to a **time bar** – there is no contractual right to the EOT and/or money claimed. Modern construction contracts almost invariably contain notice provisions that are set forth as conditions precedent to the recovery of additional compensation and/or time for claims for changes, changed conditions, suspensions in the work, and the like.

The general purpose behind time-barring clauses is to compel the parties to give notice of the possibility of claims for additional time or costs timeously in order to make it possible for the matters to be investigated at the time when they are still fresh in the minds of the people concerned, and the records and documentation are available for inspection and adjudication.

In regard to many of the time-barring provisions in the extension of time clauses it is to be noted that these clauses stipulate that a claim is to be submitted within a specified number of days after the occurrence or 'as soon thereafter as is reasonable.' In regard to weather, it is not difficult to understand that notice can be easily given within the specified period after occurrence. However, in regard to late information, extra work, or where latent defects exist in free-issue materials it is not always easy or possible to determine whether additional time is to be required or not. In this regard, the parties should adopt a reasonable attitude. As far as latent defects in free-issue materials is concerned, the doctrine of impossibility might be applied to time-barring clauses.

Whether or not a contractual time bar is enforceable will depend on the governing law of the contract. In a common law jurisdiction, where the terms of the contract are explicit, they cannot be ignored because they will generally be strictly enforced by the courts and the burden of proving its case rests upon the plaintiff.[4] However, whilst clearly worded time bars are generally enforceable in common law jurisdictions, they may not be in civil law jurisdictions. For example, in Italy a Contractor would be entitled to obtain additional compensation for a Variation where the Employer tacitly implicitly accepted the extra works, inferred from the Employer's behaviour in, for example, inspecting the Works or acting in a way showing its willingness to accept the Variation. Any contractual provisions relying on a time bar in such circumstances would always have to surmount the general principles of good faith and unjust enrichment. The Italian *Civil Code* also provides for circumstances where Variations were necessary[5] or unforeseeable[6] in the circumstances.

Time bars may not be enforceable in a number of other jurisdictions, for example, Brazil,[7] Peru,[8] and the UAE.[9]

27.3.5 Employer's claims

The previous discussion is based on a claim by the Contractor. However, the Employer may also have claims under the Contract for money to be paid by the Contractor, or for an extension of the Defects Notification period. Similar considerations to those previously discussed apply to Employer's claims. The Contract should provide for a formal procedure for the Employer to provide notification of a claim, and for its assessment in accordance with the Contract by the Engineer. The Contractor is entitled to timely notification of a claim so that it is not surprised, and it is entitled to timely determination of the Employer's

4 *Terson's Limited v Stevenage Development Corporation*, [1963] 3 All E.R. 863.

5 *Italian Civil Code* Art. 1660 Necessary Variations in Plans. If, in order to carry out the work according to standards of the trade, it is necessary to make variations in the plans, and the parties fail to agree in that respect, it is the duty of the court to establish what variations are to be made and the related variations in price. If the amount of the variations exceeds one-sixth of the total price agreed upon, the contractor can withdraw from the contract and can, according to the circumstances, receive a just indemnity. (Nicola Davide Romano, 'Italy' in Donald Charrett (ed), *The International Application of FIDIC Contracts A Practical Guide* (Informa Law from Routledge, 2019) 240, 253).

6 *Italian Civil Code* Art. 1664 Supervening hardship or difficulty in performance. If, as a result of unforeseeable circumstance, there have occurred such increases or reductions in the cost of the materials or of labor as to cause an increase or reduction by more than one- tenth of the total price agreed upon, the independent contractor or the customer can request that the price be revised. The revision can only be granted for that part that exceeds one-tenth.

If in course of work difficulties are revealed from geological conditions, water, or other similar causes not foreseen by the parties, which made the performance of the contractor considerably more onerous, he is entitled to just compensation therefor. (Nicola Davide Romano, 'Italy' in Donald Charrett (ed), *The International Application of FIDIC Contracts A Practical Guide* (Informa Law from Routledge, 2019) 240, 253).

7 Thiago Moreira & Caio Gabra, 'Brazil' in Donald Charrett (ed.), *The International Application of FIDIC Contracts A Practical Guide* (Informa Law from Routledge, 2020) 80.

8 Jaime Gray & Jonnathan Bravo, 'Peru' in Donald Charrett (ed.), *The International Application of FIDIC Contracts A Practical Guide* (Informa Law from Routledge, 2020) 301.

9 Erin Miller Rankin & Samantha Lord Hill, 'The United Arab Emirates' in Donald Charrett (ed.), *The International Application of FIDIC Contracts A Practical Guide* (Informa Law from Routledge, 2020) 395.

entitlement so that it can plan its work and cash flow accordingly. It is notable that clause 20 of the 2017 FIDIC rainbow suite articulates one procedure for both Employer's and Contractor's Claims.

27.4 Purpose and timing of notices

A **notice** may be defined as the formal written document required by the Contract to advise the Engineer or Employer of a state of affairs relevant to the Contract. A claim notice is the formal written document required by the Contract to advise the other party of the circumstances giving rise to a claim. The purpose of the notice is to enable the other party (or the Engineer) to appraise the situation and the problem concerned, to specify the form and nature of the records required to be kept, and to enable the evidence then available to be examined and thereafter at the time it becomes available.

A properly prepared Contractor's notice of claim to the Employer of a change in the Works will accomplish the following:

(a) Permit the Employer to make its own determination as to the character and scope of the issue.
(b) Permit the Employer to determine the course of action to be taken in coping with the issue(s) encountered.
(c) Permit the Employer to exercise control over cost and effort expended in resolving the issue(s).
(d) Ensure that both parties have an appropriate record of the dates and facts that initiated the claim situation.
(e) Permit resolution of the situation while the facts and circumstances are still fresh.

Failing to give the Employer notice prejudices the Employer's position because in not having been made aware of the issue(s), the Employer is unable to take steps to avoid the additional expenditures or time claimed by the Contractor. Claim notice requirements should be adhered to even if such compliance severely limits the amount of work the Contractor can proceed with prior to direction from the Employer or Engineer.

The timing of the notices required will be given in the Contract. Notice of intention to claim is in most cases required as soon as circumstances giving rise to the claim occur, so that the Engineer has the opportunity of investigating the claim reasonably close to the time when the material events occurred, and the facts can be established with reasonable certainty.

As previously noted, where the contract wording is clear that notification is a condition precedent to entitlement, failure to provide the contractually stipulated notification within the time provided for disqualifies the Contractor's claim for additional remuneration or extension of time that would otherwise have been allowable under the Contract in many jurisdictions.[10]

Notification of the possible time and cost consequences of changed circumstances at the earliest possible opportunity also enables the Employer to reconsider its position and, for

10 *Neodox v Borough of Swinton and Pendlebury* (1958) 5 BLR 34, 49 per Diplock J (QB).

example, to obtain necessary additional finance or make savings whilst it is still possible to do so.[11]

These principles have been well stated judicially:

> Obviously the provision is there [ie to provide notice of intent to claim] to enable the Engineer to keep a close check on extra and on additional expense, and the penalty for possible loss is introduced as a spur to the Contractor to provide these particulars regularly. It must be remembered that in large engineering undertakings construction work can get buried and difficult to trace. . . . As regards the condition precedent of monthly notices, it tends to confirm that this is a condition precedent to payment.[12]

27.5 Notice requirements

Once the formal notice of intention to claim has been submitted in accordance with the Contract, it is good practice to include the estimated amount due arising from the notified claim to be incorporated within, and included in, each and every interim valuation or application for payment. As events or circumstances demand, these estimates should be updated where and when necessary. The recognition of claims as they occur during the Contract, and their treatment as far as possible as measurement items, will avoid defences such as time barring, waiver, and estoppel.

Whilst notices are the formal channel of communication between the parties, much practical communication between the parties and between the Engineer and the Contractor takes place in meetings. However, even minutes of meetings signed by those present at the meeting should not be relied on as a formal notification unless specifically permitted under the Contract.

If not prohibited by the Contract, any such minutes or protocol should clearly state that its contents are to take effect as a notice or instruction under the Contract. It should also be required under the Contract that the minutes or protocol are signed by the authorised representatives of the giver and recipient of such notice or instruction. If these conditions are fulfilled, then the notice or instruction will usually be a valid notice or instruction for the purposes of the Contract.

It is of course always necessary to comply with the specific procedure for the provision of notices as specified in the Contract. For example, in the 2017 FIDIC rainbow suite, a Notice 'means a written communication identified as a Notice and issued in accordance with Sub-Clause 1.3.' Sub-clause 1.3 [Notices and Other Communications] is a detailed specification of the requirements for a Notice (which may be a paper original or in approved electronic form), including that it shall be identified as a Notice. Notwithstanding the Employer's knowledge of circumstances giving rise to a Contractor's claim by attendance at a site meeting evidenced by minutes, under the 2017 FIDIC contracts it is only the formal submission of a complying Notice in accordance with the contractual requirements that triggers the Contractor's entitlement to claim an EOT or payment of money.

11 *Crosby v Portland Urban District Council* (1967) 5 BLR 121, 122 (commentary by Humphrey Lloyd QC and Colin Reese) and 132 per Donaldson J.

12 *Alfred McAlpine & Son (Pty) Ltd v Transvaal Provincial Administration* (1974) 3 SALR 506 (SA).

27.6 Format of the claim

It is not possible to set down a standard format for claims submissions, as different circumstances require different treatments. Further, the format of the claim may be specified in the Contract. However, in general, a claim submission should be self-sufficient, self-explanatory, and self-supporting. A summary sheet setting out the salient facts and identifying the claim by number and description is useful as an introductory page to each claim.

The formal submission of a claim is, depending on the requirements of the Contract, essentially a detailed statement of the facts giving rise to the claim, supported by all relevant documentation (cross-referenced to the text), and concluding with an evaluation of the effects upon the time for Completion and/or costs of Completion of the Works. It usually makes for simplicity if the time and money effects are separately detailed and evaluated. It is essential to include all possible references to the clauses of the Contract or principles of law under which the claim is being submitted and upon which the claim is based. The correct formulation of the contractual basis of the claim from the outset is of paramount importance.

The submissions supporting the claim should be as complete as possible, covering all the facts and circumstances and all the consequences resulting which give rise to the claim. The expression 'full and detailed particulars' (often used in construction contracts to describe the information that the Contractor must provide in its claim to the Employer), means that the submission must contain a description of the circumstances which form the basis of the claim, with relevant evidence and documentation of the payment claimed and a reference to the legal basis of the claim. It must, in short, enable the Engineer to establish whether the Contractor is entitled to additional payment under the Contract, and to evaluate the claim. See, for example, *New South Wales v Austeel Pty Ltd* where the test for the requirements of a notice of dispute involved making an 'attempt to capture or describe the essence of the existing dispute or difference . . . but like any business document it is to be construed fairly in its context.'[13]

The Engineer is therefore usually not entitled to require further particulars beyond what is reasonably required for such an assessment. However, the Contract may specify that the Contractor is to provide further information on request, in which case the Engineer would be entitled to request such further information.

Notwithstanding the usual requirement for completeness, the Contract may provide for a series of submissions to be prepared and submitted as required from time to time, covering all the facts related to a single event or series of events and circumstances. It must be made clear to the Employer and/or its Engineer what the submission covers and where (and why) it is incomplete. Where a submission covers a consequence which increases due to the passage of time before settlement (eg a dispute related to recovery of increased costs on outstanding moneys claimed), the evaluation should be updated until such time as the circumstances giving rise to the claim cease to exist and/or the claim is settled. The Contract may require regular submission of updates for a claim with ongoing effect, and it will be necessary to ensure that those regular updates are submitted, unless the parties have agreed in writing otherwise.

13 *New South Wales v Austeel Pty Ltd* [2003] NSWCA 392, [19] per Mason P.

27.7 Delay claims

Where claims are time-based and comprise a formal request for an extension of time for Completion, delay statements prepared by the Contractor are extremely important documents. Contractors are sometimes reluctant to submit claims in the early stages of a project, anxious not to disturb the 'working relationship' on the site. The danger that this attitude presents is that it may mislead the Employer, and delays at the beginning of a project may have as much, if not more, impact as delays at the end.

Claims should be chronologically numbered, should state the cause of the delay, evaluate the delay, and record the effect on resources and the planned programme of Completion; they should also refer to records of correspondence, drawing receipts, or other pertinent records for cross-reference purposes and substantiation. Where there is more than a single cause of delay, each cause must be articulated in a separate delay statement. If there is any question of contention as to liability for delay, or where separate clauses of delay are concurrent, the delay statement should note this and deal with the issue of concurrency. Concurrent delay is discussed in ¶14.5.

The delay statements should describe, in as much detail as is necessary or required, what the Contractor had intended to do in the time and manner envisaged at the time of tender and therefore included in the tendered price; the reasons for which the intention had been prevented, hindered, or impeded, which were outside its control; and what it had to do or did as a consequence. The method of construction, rate of progress, and resources to be applied are those used in computing the tender or which are justified as reasonable in the circumstances, unless instructions have been given to accelerate, in which event the increased resources and accelerated rate of progress would be applied. The cost of such increased resources would be quantified and recovered by the Contractor separately. The conclusions should be clearly set out with suitable reference to the activity or operation shown on the Contract programme.

The evaluation of the effects of all causes of delay should be computed for each delay statement, and the periods thus computed inserted into a delay programme. A delay programme illustrates the anticipated impact of each delay on planned Completion of the Works (as set out on the Contract programme). Comparison of anticipated and delayed programme planning demonstrates the additional periods of time to which the Contractor is entitled (subject to the terms of the Contract). Further comparison with actual progress will demonstrate the effectiveness of steps in mitigation of the delay or measures to accelerate adopted by the Contractor. The delay programme thus demonstrates, in a graphic form, the final net delay (after concurrency and liability aspects) for which the Contractor is, subject to the terms of the Contract, entitled to be awarded extensions of time.

Where the additional time merits or attracts additional money, the evaluation of this additional money can be computed from the net delay shown on the delay programme. Where the completion of the work is achieved prior to the expiry of the illustrated net delay (as may be separately illustrated on the same delay programme) the Contractor must clearly demonstrate its entitlement to recover additional costs in respect of steps it has taken to mitigate the delays. Where the Contractor has taken accelerative measures on the instruction of, or as approved by the Employer, these should be described in detail.

Where a claim covers recovery of additional expenditure which is not a consequence of additional time but is, in itself, the cause of an entitlement to additional time, the additional time should be demonstrated and computed on a delay statement and shown on the delay programme; the additional expenditure recovery, subject to the terms of the Contract, can then include the effects of that additional time within the overall net delay evaluation.

Recovery of additional expenditure should be dealt with in a separate submission or a separate section of the submission, setting out the facts giving rise to the claim, the basis of the amount being claimed, the logic and reasons leading to the computation of the amount covered by the claim with fully detailed calculations, concluding in a summary which collects into a single amount all the individual elements being claimed.

If a claim as submitted is not accepted, it may be beneficial to conduct initial negotiations on a claim 'without prejudice', that is, cannot be used as evidence in any later arbitration or litigation to settle any dispute arising out of the claim. Agreement on the value of a legitimate claim from a reasonable compromise is generally preferable to a dispute arising from a rejection of a claim that is not accepted by the claimant. As discussed in ¶28.1.2, a standing Dispute Board can provide an appropriate 'without prejudice' forum that promotes dispute avoidance.

27.8 Supporting documentation for a Contractor's claim

27.8.1 Contractor's documentation

Documentation supporting the Contractor's claim often includes the tender make-up, method statement, resource schedule, construction programme, correspondence, records, diaries, minutes of site meetings, or other evidence which supports the existence of the grounds of the claim, proves its validity, and provides the facts upon which it can be evaluated.

All pertinent correspondence should be simple, unambiguous, and free of irrelevant adjectives, invective, or personality.

Minutes of meetings are usually prepared (depending on the terms of the Contract) by the Engineer and must be checked by the Contractor (and other attending parties) as being truly representative of the discussions. If they are not, the facts must be corrected at the next meeting or recorded in correspondence as being incorrect, and the corrected version must be given. With the assistance of voice-recognition technology, minutes can now be prepared and agreed on progressively in the same meeting after each item is dealt with.

The drawing register is usually (subject to the terms of the Contract) prepared and maintained by the Contractor's engineering staff. The register usually identifies and records the date of receipt of drawings, and, where a claim involves delay arising from issue of information, this may become a vital record.

In the normal day-to-day planning, organisation, and execution of a contract, discussions take place between the staff of the Engineer and the Contractor respectively. Where these discussions centre on the work being done or to be done, the effect may be an instruction which, in well-organised circumstances, is confirmed by a formal instruction, but is not necessarily dealt with as such at the time of the discussion. These discussions, whether by telephone or otherwise, should be recorded in a file note pending receipt of the formal instruction from the Engineer or formal confirmation of the instruction from the Contractor.

The site diary is usually prepared and maintained by the Contractor's site management and, on large, complex contracts, by heads of departments. It forms a daily record of events, such as resources employed, production achieved, weather conditions, and any and all other factors which have affected the day's operations and activities. The site diary is a very useful document which can also be utilised to record oral instructions, and so on, which should be subsequently confirmed. The more detailed and complete the site diary, the more useful it will be eventually for the purposes of submitting claims or in any subsequent disputes.

The ease and low cost of digital photographs provide the Contractor with a further tool for regularly recording progress on site. Comprehensive photographs of the site, taken from the same vantage points at regular intervals can provide powerful evidence of the actual sequence and timing of construction. It is imperative that each photograph be labelled with the date on which it was taken and by whom, and appropriately filed on computer hard drives or CDs/DVDs so that relevant photographs can be readily retrieved at a later date by persons who were not on the site. On large projects continuous time-lapse photographs taken from one or more fixed vantage points are a worthwhile investment to provide unequivocal evidence of the actual stage of construction at any point in time. For linear projects such as roads or railways that extend over many kilometres, a video of the site from start to finish can be taken by drone at regular intervals to provide a continuous record of construction progress.

As outlined in ¶14.3, the Contract programme is important in recording the Contractor's intended sequence of work items and recording progress as-built. It is in the Contractor's interest to prepare an appropriately detailed and credible programme of works at the outset of a project, and to update this on a regular basis to record the actual progress made against each work item. Such an up-to-date programme will be the best evidence to demonstrate the projected impact of a delaying event required to demonstrate the Contractor's entitlement to an EOT. Many contracts require the Contractor to submit an updated programme on a regular basis, or whenever events have occurred to impact planned progress. A programme prepared retrospectively to prove an entitlement to an EOT will rarely be as persuasive as one prepared and updated contemporaneously. It is usually difficult and expensive to reconstruct the sequence of events after the fact when the available evidence may be contentious. Ultimately the cogency of a programme will rely on the facts on which it is based; if the facts cannot be proven, the most sophisticated programme software and presentation will be to no avail.

Fullest possible use of other forms of documentation should be explored by the Contractor. These may comprise graphs, histograms, flow charts, as well as critical path diagrams which are all graphical methods aimed at illustrating the differences between the original planned intention and the actual methods, resources, and so on, utilised as a result of the events which created the claim.

27.8.2 Document management

Any construction project generates vast quantities of original documentation, with the inevitable number of copies. Access to this information is necessary for providing management information, in the compilation of claims, in the conduct of mediation, arbitration, or litigation, and in the preparation of discovery (disclosure) programs for litigation or arbitration. Perusal of the files to establish facts and formulate a claim or to arbitrate or litigate a dispute involves high costs.

Various proprietary document management systems are designed to satisfy multi-purpose user requirements and can be tailored to suit the individual needs of each project. These should be discussed in depth and agreed with the Employer prior to any work being undertaken. Briefly, such document management systems involve systematic processing of the documentation and recording of key data into an electronic database in an easily retrievable sequence, including daily digital images of key areas of the project.

The process results in an indexed database which enables the searching of documents relating to specific criteria, the listing of all such documents, a screen image of all documents, a printout of any document, and the creation of specific purpose files. The electronic database can be mounted on a network system so that all project personnel are able to have access to the data. Such a network can link two or more distant points such as the site office and the project head office. Access can be restricted to a variety of levels of use.

Quality assurance checks should take place throughout the process to ensure that all pages are readable on screen and that correct coding data is entered on the database. All types of documents from contracts, correspondence, and site diaries to digital images can be handled on the database. The end result is a cost effective, up to date, easily accessible and recoverable record of the project during and after the project life.

Not only does such an electronic database enable the efficient and timely documentation of claims, in the event of mediation, arbitration, or litigation, the necessary research, discovery, and formulation of evidence is greatly simplified, saving considerable time and expense.

27.9 Pre-completion and post-completion claims

Contractor's claims are usually made during a project but may also be submitted after project completion. However, it should be recognised that from a management and negotiation point of view, the respective bargaining positions of the parties are very different pre- and post-project completion.

During the pre-project completion stage, the Employer is focused on completion of the project on time and on budget. The question is: 'Has the tension between time, cost, and quality been resolved and communicated to the project managers? Which takes priority?'

Causation must be established in claims for extensions of time but there may be opportunities to avoid a delay to completion by re-sequencing the work, or by ordering acceleration of the work through engaging additional resources and working overtime; completion on time of individual work items can be of prime importance if they are on or close to the critical path. It may be possible to reduce time by omitting certain quality assurance steps considered to be excessive. The Employer's contract controls scheduler will be fully conversant with the Contract baseline schedule, and it should not be too difficult to establish whether the alleged delay has impacted the critical path. (Assuming that the Contract has been competently drawn, making provision for Employer's acts of prevention, how concurrency is to be dealt with, which methods of delay analysis are to be applied, and an up to date as-built programme is available.) Liquidated damages and incentives to meet milestones encourage the Contractor to meet the schedule but can never be a substitute for completion on time.

Claims for additional compensation are usually made and evaluated strictly in accordance with the requirements of the Contract. During project execution issues can be investigated at the time and before the work is covered over, and those with first-hand knowledge are able to establish the veracity of the claim. There is also the opportunity to maintain budget by legitimately relaxing the Employer's requirements if appropriate.

In jurisdictions with *Security of Payment* legislation the Contractor has the ability to file a payment dispute under the relevant *Act* and obtain an Adjudicator's determination of the Contractor's entitlement to provisional payment. In these circumstances the Contractor is legally entitled to suspend carrying out the work if the Employer does not pay the amount determined by the Adjudicator. Any such suspension of the work could have a ripple effect throughout the project and is therefore to be avoided at all costs. Some Contractors recognise the sensitivity of Employers to this outcome, and file spurious claims under the relevant *Act* with little sanction. Others, recognising the importance of completion on time, simply state that they are unable to complete the full scope of work for the contract price and appeal to the Employer to assist them to complete the Contract, holding the Contract and its administrators in contempt. Yet others blatantly threaten to withhold hand over of the work unless their claims are paid in full, knowing full well that the Employer is in a very weak position to resist such economic duress.[14]

The negotiating position of the parties may change radically in favour of the Employer after practical completion under the Contract or hand over of the project. From the award of the Contract, the Contractor is in a diminishing position of strength as the work progresses. There is a tipping-point after which the Employer has the capability to take over and complete the Works. After hand over:

- The Employer has possession of the Works and does not have to make any concessions to the Contractor to achieve Completion or hand over.
- The Employer can integrate any remaining work into the project so as to maintain the overall project schedule.
- The leverage which the Contractor had prior to hand over as to possession of the Works is lost, and the Employer will not have paid Contractor's claims which have been presented after Completion, and will be in no hurry to do so.
- Claims are frequently difficult to formulate and justify after the fact, when witnesses and records may no longer be readily available.
- Claims are more likely to be time barred if they are introduced for the first time at this stage.
- The Employer can usually self-perform or have other contractors perform any rectification of defects required if the Contractor fails to co-operate, as at this stage the Employer still usually retains 50% of the retention/performance securities.
- There should be no new claims as the work has been completed. Contractual remedies against late claims can be applied, and all unresolved clams should have been timeously notified as the work progressed and be in the dispute resolution process.
- The spectre of claims under *Security of Payment* Acts is diminished.
- The financial and schedule position of the Contract is known and can be compared against budget and project schedule.

14 Philip Loots & Dr Donald Charrett, 'Being Held to Ransom or "Wielding the Whip or the Rod"' (2014) 31(2) *International Construction Law Review* 211.

27.10 Common law and other legal rights

Unless expressly excluded by clear words in the Contract, the Contractor retains its common (or civil) law and other legal rights in addition to the remedies granted to it under the Contract. A claim may therefore be based upon a common law right, and the absence of a contractual clause upon which to base a claim does not necessarily invalidate the claim.

In a civil law jurisdiction, the *Civil Code* may contain provisions that would enable a party to make a claim not contemplated by the words of the Contract. For example, the German *Civil Code* provides in s313 Interference with the basis of the transaction:

(1) If circumstances which became the basis of a contract have significantly changed since the contract was entered into and if the parties would not have entered into the contract or would have entered into it with different contents if they had foreseen this change, adaptation of the contract may be demanded to the extent that, taking account of all the circumstances of the specific case, in particular the contractual or statutory distribution of risk, one of the parties cannot reasonably be expected to uphold the contract without alteration.

(2) It is equivalent to a change of circumstances if material conceptions that have become the basis of the contract are found to be incorrect.

(3) If adaptation of the contract is not possible or one party cannot reasonably be expected to accept it, the disadvantaged party may revoke the contract. In the case of continuing obligations, the right to terminate takes the place of the right to revoke.

27.11 Damages

The Contractor is entitled to claim damages which it has suffered in cases where a breach of contract by the Employer does not amount to repudiation of the Contract, or where, even though it does amount to repudiation, the Contractor does not elect to terminate the Contract. Claims for damages arising out of the Employer's breach of contract should be distinguished from contractual claims for extension of time and claims for additional payment.

There is no reason in principle why a claim for damages for breach of contract should not be submitted for assessment in the same manner as a claim under the Contract. For example, the 2017 FIDIC rainbow suite definition of Claim (¶27.1) includes a claim 'for any entitlement or relief under any Clause of these Conditions *or otherwise in connection with, or arising out of, the Contract or the execution of the Works*.' Notwithstanding his/her reluctance to adjudicate on such a claim, the Engineer is required to do so in accordance with sub-clause 3.7 of the 2017 FIDIC Red and Yellow Books. A rejection of such a claim, as with any other claim rejection, is grounds for initiating a dispute.

A claim for breach of contract frequently arises where the Contractor has been delayed in proceeding with the Works. It is then entitled to damages so as to place it in a position as if the delays had not occurred. Some of the categories of damages that it would be entitled to claim are as follows:

(a) Additional on-site expenses, for example, extra supervision and security expenses, extra expenses in connection with all equipment, and extra costs incurred in providing on-site accommodation, storage, and screening.

(b) Rises in costs of labour and materials: this may be claimed when there is no suitable price adjustment or escalation clause incorporated in the Contract.
(c) Standing time of labour and plant: this would depend upon whether the Contractor would be able to mitigate its loss by re-organising its labour force and equipment.
(d) Additional financing and insurance costs: this could also include interest on the late payment of retention monies and extra expenses for insurance and sureties over a longer period of time.
(e) Loss of profit and off-site overheads if the Contractor's resources could have earned profit elsewhere. Once again, this claim may be mitigated by re-organisation.
(f) Subcontractors: in certain cases where an Employer's delay has caused loss to a subcontractor for which the Contractor is liable, the Contractor may claim from the Employer the amount it has to pay to the subcontractor.
(g) Claims for disruption and acceleration: the proof and quantification of such claims is discussed in ¶14.6.2 and ¶14.6.3.

27.11.1 Mitigating damages

The duty on the part of the non-defaulting party to take all reasonable steps to reduce the ultimate amount of its damages in case of a breach of contract by the other party is a well-settled principle.

This duty is not always applied in construction disputes, perhaps due to lack of proper understanding of the construction process on the part of the courts. In reality, the opportunity exists and to mitigate almost always represents a cost-effective option, particularly in delay/acceleration situations.

Some likely settings where mitigation ought to be the order of the day are as follows:

- The Contractor, instead of working around the missing pump, or boiler, or transformer, stops and waits until the missing piece (to be supplied by the Employer) arrives.
- The Contractor, in the case of a major Employer-caused delay, orders the crew to report for work every day (and incurs show-up charges, presumably under the impression that ultimately the Employer will pay), instead of laying off the workmen and keeping a skeleton staff on hand only.
- During the construction of a module, the Contractor runs out of steel from the Employer designated supplier and, instead of looking for a new source, sits back and waits until the Employer finds a solution.

Mitigating the damages invariably involves the performance of changed, or perhaps even extra work. Most contracts warn the Contractor that no payment will be made for changed or extra work if performed without a prior written order. The question facing the Contractor is, therefore, which one of the two patently contradictory obligations are they to comply with? Are they to mitigate the damages the Employer could sustain, without waiting for a written order, or are they to play it safe and wait for a written order?

In such circumstances, adequate and timely communication from the Contractor to the Engineer should protect its position. If the Engineer is aware that the Contractor is suffering Employer caused delay, the Engineer can issue instructions appropriate to the circumstances, if necessary, including instructions to incur mitigation costs to avoid larger delay costs.

27.12 Example – Claim management under 2017 FIDIC rainbow suite

The 2017 FIDIC rainbow suite provides a detailed procedure for the submission of claims for payment and/or EOT in sub-clause 20.2. This procedure applies to both Contractor's claims for additional payment or an EOT and Employer's claims for payment or an extension of the Defects Notification Period, and is detailed (over four pages) under the following headings in the Yellow Book:

- Notice of Claim
- Engineer's initial response
- Contemporary records
- Fully detailed claim
- Agreement or determination of the Claim
- Claims of continuing effect
- General requirements

The Notice of Claim describing the event or circumstances giving rise to the Claim must be submitted as soon as practicable, and no later than 28 days after the claiming Party became aware or should have become aware of the event or circumstances. If this Notice of Claim is not submitted within 28 days it is time barred.

If the Engineer considers the Notice of Claim is time barred it must give a Notice to the claiming Party with reasons. In this case, the claiming Party may submit a fully detailed Claim including details of the reasons why it considers the Claim valid. If the Engineer does not give a Notice within 14 days, the Claim Notice is deemed valid. If the other Party disagrees with the deemed valid Claim Notice, it shall give the Engineer a Notice with reasons for its disagreement. The subsequent agreement or determination of the Claim shall include the Engineer's review of such disagreement.

The claiming Party is required to keep contemporary records as required to substantiate its claim. The Engineer may inspect these records without admitting any Employer's liability.

The fully detailed claim is to be submitted within 84 days of the claiming Party becoming aware or should have become aware of the event or circumstances giving rise to the Claim. This time period may be varied by agreement. A fully detailed claim is defined as one that includes:

(a) a detailed description of the event or circumstance giving rise to the Claim;
(b) a statement of the contractual and/or other legal basis of the Claim;
(c) all contemporary records on which the claiming Party relies; and
(d) detailed supporting particulars of the amount of additional payment claimed (or amount of reduction of the Contract Price in the case of the Employer as the claiming Party), and/or EOT claimed (in the case of the Contractor) or extension of the DNP claimed (in the case of the Employer).

If the fully detailed claim is not submitted within the required time, the Notice of Claim is deemed to have lapsed and the Engineer is to provide a Notice within 14 days to that effect. In the absence of such an Engineer's Notice, the Notice of Claim is deemed valid. If the other Party disputes such deemed valid Notice of Claim, it shall give the Engineer a Notice detailing its disagreement. The subsequent agreement or determination of the Claim shall include the Engineer's review of such disagreement.

After receiving the fully detailed Claim the Engineer shall proceed to agree or determine the claiming Party's entitlement under the Contract to additional payment, an EOT, or extension of the Defects Notification Period as appropriate. The agreement or determination shall include whether or not the Notice of Claim was a valid Notice or why late submission was justified. The Engineer may request further particulars of the Claim but shall nevertheless give its response on the contractual or other legal basis of the claim within the time limit specified in sub-clause 3.7.3.

Where the event or circumstance giving rise to the Claim is of continuing effect the fully detailed claim shall be considered as interim. The claiming Party shall submit further fully detailed Claims at monthly intervals, and a final fully detailed Claim within 28 days after the end of the effects resulting from the event or circumstances.

The Engineer shall include in each Payment Certificate such amounts in a Claim that have been reasonably substantiated, even before the fully detailed Claim has been agreed or determined.

Sub-clause 3.7 Agreement or Determination contains a very detailed procedure that the Engineer is required to follow after receiving a Notice of Claim. When carrying out its duties under sub-clause 3.7 'the Engineer shall act neutrally between the Parties and shall not be deemed to act for the Employer.' The Engineer is required to consult with both Parties and endeavour to reach agreement. If agreement cannot be reached the Engineer shall make a fair determination of the Claim in accordance with the Contract, taking into account all relevant circumstances. The Engineer shall give a Notice of agreement or determination within 42 days, or such other time as agreed by both Parties. If the Engineer does not give the Notice within the time limit, the Engineer is deemed to have given a Notice rejecting the Claim.

This detailed procedure for submission and assessment of Claims has the following notable features, not all of which are in common usage:

- The same binding procedure applies to Claims made by both the Contractor and the Employer. The Employer has no contractual entitlement to additional payment or an extension of the Defects Notification Period unless it complies with the specified procedure.
- There are strict time limits for submission of a Notice of the event or circumstances giving rise to a Claim, submission of a fully detailed Claim, the Engineer's initial response, and agreement or determination of a fully detailed Claim. The consequences of failure to comply with the time limits are defined, including time bars on the Claim.
- Notwithstanding the time limits, there is some 'wiggle room' for the Engineer to consider relevant circumstances if the time limits are not met.
- If the Engineer does not assess the Claim within 42 days it is deemed to be rejected, thus enabling the claiming Party to initiate a Dispute if it does not accept the deemed rejection.
- It is in a claiming Party's interests to submit its fully detailed Claim as soon as it has all of the required information, as the Engineer's assessment may not be available for 42 days. This period may give rise to difficulties near the end of a project where the Contractor may be facing significant liquidated damages for delay if it is not entitled to an EOT.
- Notwithstanding that the Engineer is appointed by the Employer, and acts for the Employer in many of its functions, in assessing a Claim the Engineer acts 'neutrally' and is not deemed to act for the Employer.
- It should be noted that this does not overcome the inherent conflict of interest that arises as a result of the Engineer being employed and paid by the Employer, in circumstances where the Claim stems from an act or omission or error of the Engineer. In such circumstances the Engineer may simply decline to assess a claim within 42 days because its Professional Indemnity Insurance Policy prohibits the making of any admission. As this is a deemed rejection of the Claim the Contractor must initiate a Dispute to have its Claim assessed.

27.13 Case study – Claims arising from COVID-19 under FIDIC Contracts

The worldwide advent of COVID-19 in 2020 had a substantial impact on economic life around the world, including the construction industry. Construction projects were significantly delayed, postponed, or terminated; those that continued were subject to increased costs as a result of the health measures required to keep workers safe – stringent cleaning and disinfection, physical distancing, and increased use of personal protective equipment (**PPE**), among other economic impacts. Contractors will inevitably seek costs and EOTs and a substantial number of claims can therefore be expected. At the time of writing (September 2021) the COVID-19 pandemic is far from over, and there is already anecdotal evidence of claims on many construction projects.

Early in the pandemic (April 2020) FIDIC issued the 'FIDIC COVID-19 Guidance Memorandum to Users of FIDIC Standard Forms of Works Contract.'[15] That Memorandum contains an outline of the provisions in FIDIC's standard forms of contract for works relevant to likely scenarios arising as a consequence of COVID-19:

> FIDIC's core purpose of drafting this Guidance Memorandum is to help Parties to a FIDIC contract to consider mutually satisfactory solutions and avoid disputes arising between them. COVID-19 pandemic is a unique broad scale and extraordinary event which should be recognised as such.

The Guidance Memorandum does not refer to any specific legal system or jurisdiction and cautions that the legal interpretation of the contract will depend upon matters such as the precise wording of the various documents in the Contract and the governing law. The Memorandum takes the approach of outlining a number of possible scenarios and suggests likely relevant responses by reference to relevant provisions of FIDIC contracts.

FIDIC's list of scenarios identifies the following circumstances that are expected to give rise to claims unique to the impact of COVID-19:[16]

1. The local authorities/government do not promulgate any new piece of legislation or regulation banning construction activity or works on Site. However, the Contractor is facing difficulties in mobilising personnel, who fear for their safety, and in obtaining Goods due to issues in the supply chain.
2. The Contractor is under the same circumstances as scenario No. 1 above. However, instead of facing difficulties in mobilising personnel or obtaining Goods, the Contractor is suffering delays caused by the authorities (for example, making repeated health and safety inspections on the Site).
3. The local authorities or government have promulgated changes to the Laws restricting construction activities and works on the Site. The Contractor is still able to proceed with the Works, however it is suffering delay and or incurring additional Cost as a result of those changes.

15 https://fidic.org/sites/default/files/COVID%2019%20Guidance%20Memorandum%20-%20PDF.pdf (accessed 15 March 2021).
16 Ibid.

4. The local authorities/government have issued an order(s)/decree(s) preventing construction activities (including lockdown, curfew, inaccessible quarantined areas, etc.), and execution of the Works on Site has now become impossible. Consequently, the Contractor and/or the Employer is prevented from performing obligations under the Contract.
5. Under scenario No. 4 above, can the Contractor subject this scenario to Clause 17 [*Risk and Responsibility/Care of the Works and Indemnities*]? Under Clause 17 the Contractor is entitled to a financial compensation in addition to an EOT, rather than only an EOT, when a natural *Force Majeure* or Exceptional Event occurs.
6. Under scenarios Nos. 1, 2, or 3, above, can the Employer or the Contractor resort to Clause 19 [*Force Majeure*], Clause 18 [*Exceptional Events*], or Clause 18 [*Exceptional Risks*] (in the relevant FIDIC contract as the case may be), to address such scenarios?
7. There has been no change in Laws of the Country nor real impact on the availability of personnel or on the supply chain so far. However, the personnel of the Employer (including the Engineer or the Employer's Representative, as the case may be) are, as a precaution, working remotely and hence are most of the time away from Site. As a consequence, the Contractor suffers delay and/or incurred additional Cost due to slow decision making.

27.14 Global claims

The claim procedures discussed in ¶27.3 are predicated on showing a causal connection between an event or circumstance, and an entitlement to additional time and/or money under the Contract. The normal procedure is to identify each individual event or circumstance impacting performance and prove how each event or circumstance results in a specific entitlement to time and/or money under the Contract. By contrast, in a global claim the Contractor seeks additional compensation or an extension of time where it has not shown the causal links between its asserted entitlement and events for which the Employer is liable under the Contract. Such a global claim may be in the form of a total cost claim or a total time claim.

Global claims do not come within the normal claims procedures in construction contracts, and are typically rejected by the Engineer or Employer, frequently triggering a dispute. As discussed in Appendix C, global claims may be upheld by a court or arbitral tribunal, provided specific requirements are fulfilled. However, as the cases make clear, such claims should only be made in circumstances where it is not possible to prove a contractual entitlement in the normal way.

CHAPTER 28

Dispute avoidance and resolution

CONTENTS

DOI: 10.4324/9781003206873-28

28.1 Dispute avoidance

The incidence and expense of disputes in construction contracts are notorious. The most time and cost effective 'dispute resolution' is undoubtedly dispute avoidance. There are various tools available to assist parties to avoid disputes.

28.1.1 Tools for dispute avoidance[1]

28.1.1.1 Tender and Contract documents

Dispute avoidance starts with the preparation of the contract documents and the tender documents. Selecting the most suitable form and terms of contract commensurate with the appropriate allocation of risks and rewards are the first requirements for a balanced contract. It is also necessary to clearly define the parties' rights and obligations as well as the scope and quality of work to ensure that the contract documents are unambiguous. In the authors' experience, unbalanced contract terms in which one party is liable for risks that it cannot manage or control is a frequent cause of disputes, notwithstanding the words of the Contract. Many writers suggest that adherence to the principle of balanced risk allocation enhances the prospect of successful contracts by encouraging contractual performance that minimises adverse outcomes and thereby reduces disputation.[2] The potential consequences of unbalanced risk allocation are discussed in ¶3.9.3.1.

In preparing its tender, the Contractor's understanding of the scope of work is fundamental in ensuring that the cost and time estimates incorporated in the tender are adequate. The time schedule needs to be commensurate with the resource and capacity availability, and to show a realistic time for execution of all the activities, as well as providing for some contingency for Contractor's risk events.[3]

---

1 For a more detailed treatment of this topic see: Donald Charrett, *Contracts for Construction and Engineering Projects* (Informa Law from Routledge, 2nd edn 2022) Chapter 24.

2 Donald Charrett, 'The FIDIC Golden Principles' in Donald Charrett (ed), *The International Application of FIDIC Contracts A Practical Guide* (Informa Law from Routledge, 2020) 23–30.

3 See Philip Loots & Dr Donald Charrett, 'Reconsidering Procurement Criteria and Procedures for Major Infrastructure Projects' (2017) *International Construction Law Review* 69, or Philip Loots & Donald Charrett, *The Application of Contracts in Developing Offshore Oil and Gas Projects* (Informa Law from Routledge, 2019) 97–110, where the authors suggest that the use of 'price' as the determining factor in construction procurement decisions is wrong, and that it should at least be replaced with a resourced schedule as the dominant parameter in bid evaluation.

Before the Contract is signed the Contractor should carefully assess its terms to ensure that they appropriately and clearly articulate the scope of work, the agreed risk allocation, and the parties' rights and obligations in respect of time, cost, and quality. Ambiguities in the scope of work or allocation of specific risks is a frequent source of claims that may lead to disputes. Specific contractual provisions on formal processes for risk identification and management such as in the NEC contracts are a useful dispute avoidance tool. So too is the requirement in sub-clause 8.4 of the 2017 FIDIC rainbow suite and sub-clause 16.1 of NEC3 for either party to give advance warning of any known or future probable events or circumstances that may cause delay, increase the contract price, or adversely affect the Contractor's work or the performance of the completed project. Similarly, sub-clause 68(2) of the 1999 ICE Conditions of Contract requires early warning of any matter which if unresolved might become a dispute.

28.1.1.2 Management of project execution

It is perhaps trite to observe that good management of project execution in accordance with the requirements of the Contract is a powerful tool for dispute avoidance, although no doubt unrealistic to expect that it will always be carried out. However, it is suggested that the following are important Contractor's project management procedures that will assist in dispute avoidance and should be properly implemented to the fullest extent possible:

- Ensure sufficient resources are applied to execute the contractual scope of work at all stages of the project.
- Prepare a credible programme reflecting the proposed methods and sequence of working achievable with the available resources, and regularly update it to reflect 'as-built' status.
- Complete the Works to the contractually required quality.
- Submit the design documents to the Employer in accordance with the requirements of the Contract.
- Maintain and manage comprehensive documentation from the start of the tender through the execution of the project to ensure that the best evidence is available to support/defend a claim.
- Familiarise with and apply the provisions of the Contract.

28.1.1.3 Communications

The importance of maintaining appropriate communication channels between the Contractor and Engineer/Employer during execution of the project should not be underestimated. A cooperative and professional working relationship based on good communication will enable many issues that arise to be resolved by mature discussion and perhaps some give and take.

Good communication is important in the submission and assessment of claims. In the first instance, as discussed in the previous chapter, this requires clear and comprehensive communication of a claimant's claim to the other party, both the factual basis of the claim, including supporting documents where appropriate, and the legal basis that supports the entitlement claimed. Secondly, if the claim is rejected by the recipient, the basis for rejection of the claim should be clearly communicated, including any additional or different facts (including documents), and the legal basis that supports the rejection. Inadequate or non-existent communications will inevitably result in misunderstanding or lack of understanding of the other party's position and may not satisfy the formal requirements of the Contract. Proper, professional management of claims strictly in accordance with the provisions of the contract can materially assist in averting disputes. The submission of poorly prepared and unsubstantiated claims that have no contractual legal basis will be counter-productive and may promote disputes.

It should be noted that the 'claim management' provisions of FIDIC contracts explicitly promote (and require) communication by all participants in the claim management provisions. Many provisions of FIDIC contracts make best practice project management a contractual obligation.

It is also suggested that claims and the inevitable unforeseen issues that arise during a project should be addressed and dealt with as they arise whilst contemporary information is available. Issues that are put in the 'too hard' basket inevitably become even harder to resolve with the effluxion of time.

28.1.2 Dispute Board role in dispute avoidance

A further powerful dispute avoidance tool is the appointment and operation of a full-term or standing **Dispute Board (DB)**. A Dispute Board comprised of an independent, impartial, and experienced panel that is familiar with the Contract, the project, and the contracting parties is in a position to assist them to recognise potential issues and find acceptable resolution of them before they fester and become real disputes. A standing Dispute Board is appointed at the start of the Contract and becomes and remains familiar with the project by reading project documents and meeting regularly with the parties on site. Further details of DBs and their role in resolving disputes is discussed in ¶28.10.

The DB generally has ultimate control of the agenda of the regular Site meetings, which should be 'without prejudice' and attended by senior off-site representatives of each party. The DB's success in dispute avoidance will ultimately depend on it taking a proactive role to promote communication between the parties and assist them to find their own resolution of issues. A DB's proactive role may include asking pertinent questions to encourage the parties to focus on the real issues or soliciting position papers on contentious issues. Its members are selected because of their experience, expertise, and skills: neither party will wish to be seen as unprepared or putting forward unsubstantiated claims. In fulfilling this dispute avoidance role, the DB functions in a similar way to a Mediator.

The most powerful tool the DB has is the perception that it is an independent arbiter that can provide a 'reality check' on a claim – if the DB, with its intimate knowledge of the project and the Contract has a particular view of an issue, why would an arbitral panel or a judge have a different view?[4]

4 See Philip Loots & Chief Engineer Robert Fraser, 'Alternative Dispute Resolution (ADR) in Practice in South Africa' (1999) 3 *Dispute Review Board Foundation Forum*, discussing the structuring and practical application of Dispute Boards using FIDIC documents for the construction of the Katse Dam and tunnels, Kingdom of Lesotho; and a retrospective assessment in: Philip Loots & Robert Fraser, 'Lean Dispute Avoidance for Lean Construction' (2016) 20(2) *DRBF Forum*.

The 2017 FIDIC rainbow suite specifically recognises the importance of the DB's role in dispute avoidance by renaming it the **Dispute Avoidance/Adjudication Board (DAAB)**. Specific guidance on dispute avoidance is given in sub-clause 21.3:

- The Parties may jointly request the DAAB to provide assistance and/or informally discuss any issue or disagreement.
- The DAAB may invite the Parties to make a joint request for assistance.
- The DAAB is not bound in any subsequent formal dispute adjudication by any informal assistance it has given.

28.1.3 Case Study: Australian experience with Dispute Boards

The Australian experience on major infrastructure projects worth many billions of dollars is that properly constituted standing DBs are very successful at dispute avoidance. Major government departments in NSW and Queensland responsible for large infrastructure projects now routinely require standing DBs – they are typically named Dispute Avoidance Boards, in recognition of their primary role. There have been relatively few DB adjudications on formal disputes, and many DBs have had no disputes to adjudicate. All disputes have been resolved within the DBs, and no disputes have had to be resolved by arbitration or litigation.

The contractual conditions for and operation of DBs in these contracts are essentially no different from the DAAB provisions in the 2017 FIDIC rainbow suite:

- The DB becomes familiar with the project by regular Site meetings with the parties.
- The parties can request the DB to provide an advisory opinion on a contentious issue.
- There are procedural rules for formal adjudication of disputes submitted in writing.
- The DB's determination is provisionally binding – the parties must comply with it unless and until it is overturned by agreement or arbitration/litigation.

28.2 Dispute resolution

28.2.1 The origins of disputes

The distinction between claims and disputes and the preconditions for a dispute to exist are discussed in ¶27.1. Many claims arise out of the Contractor being required, obliged, or compelled to do work which it had not tendered to do, or to do work under changed conditions or circumstances which it had not anticipated. Disputes arise when claims are rejected because the Engineer or Employer will not recommend or certify an extension of time and/or reimbursement within what the Contractor considers are the terms of the Contract or to the extent to which the Contractor considers it is entitled. The reasons for the Engineer's or Employer's refusal to recommend or certify reimbursement to the Contractor (which may or may not be justified under the Contract) are usually because of:

(a) Refusal to accept that the work is other than what the Contractor tendered to do,
(b) Refusal to accept that the circumstances in which the work was completed are other than the circumstances in which they were to be completed, or
(c) The Contractor's interpretation of the Contract is not accepted.

Disputes may also arise from the Engineer's/Employer's failure to recognise the Contractor's common (civil) law or statutory rights that are additional to its contractual rights.

28.2.2 The inception of a dispute

Absent an agreement or a relevant law to the contrary, a party in dispute over the provisions of a contract has the right, through litigation in court, for a judge to determine a binding and enforceable resolution. However, because of the perceived time and cost of litigation, most modern construction contracts provide for other methods of dispute resolution as precursors to or in substitution for litigation.

Modern construction contracts typically have sophisticated multistage provisions to provide for resolution of disputes between the contracting parties. The precondition for embarking on such 'contractual' dispute resolution procedures or referring a dispute to the courts is that there must be a difference or 'dispute' between the parties. Although it is usually obvious when the parties have a dispute, it is necessary that a dispute has formally come into existence before dispute resolution procedures can be commenced. The timing of when a dispute occurred may be particularly important where the Contract has provisions that make determinations by the Engineer binding and unreviewable unless they are disputed within a specified limited period of time.

An Engineer's certificate as to, for example, the Contractor's liability for liquidated damages, constitutes a determination which the Contractor may disagree with. However, should it fail to formally dispute the decision within the contractually stipulated time limit, the decision embodied in the certificate may become final. That is, the Contractor is precluded from implementing the dispute resolution procedures provided for in the Contract if it does not comply with the formal dispute notification requirements.

Conduct short of outright rejection of a claim may also constitute a dispute, for example, failing to reply to a request or demand,[5] or refusing to admit liability for payment.[6]

28.2.3 Engineer's decision

Contracts sometimes provide that the Engineer's determination about certain issues is binding, for example, in respect of claims less than a threshold amount, or for technical design and construction matters. Further, many construction contracts in the past (and even some contracts still used in Australia such as AS2124–1992 and NPWC3) invested the Engineer not only with the power to make a determination on a claim, but also to provide a 'decision' on a dispute about the Engineer's determinations. Some contracts even went as far as specifying that the Engineer was to act as Arbitrator in disputes between the Contractor and Employer, which in many instances were disputes about that same Engineer's determinations! The lack of independence and absence of procedural fairness in such an arrangement is obvious, and not consonant with current practice.

---

5 *Sandhurst Engineering Ltd v Citra Constructions Ltd* (1987) 3 BCL 198.
6 *Halki Shipping Corp v Sopex Oils Ltd* [1998] 2 All ER 23 (Court of Appeal).

Modern construction contracts typically provide that an Engineer's determination or decision can be disputed, and most contracts provide for the dispute to be resolved with the assistance of a third-party neutral and not the Engineer. The power of an arbitral tribunal to open up, review, and revise any decision, opinion, direction, certificate, or valuation of the Engineer appears to have been considered by the courts for the first time in the case of *Robins v Goddard*.[7] An arbitral tribunal is not, in general, bound by the approval, satisfaction, or certificate of the contractual certifier, unless there is some express term in the contract to the effect that a determination is final and binding.[8] The same principle applies where the courts are seized of a dispute instead of an arbitral tribunal.[9]

28.2.4 Alternative dispute resolution

The literature on dispute resolution frequently refers to ADR, which generally means 'alternative dispute resolution.' Whilst the term 'alternative' often means alternative to litigation in the courts, there is no universally accepted definition of which alternative methods come within the ambit of ADR. Some definitions refer to these being any alternative to court-based litigation (which would include arbitration), whilst other definitions confine ADR to those amicable dispute resolution methods in which the parties are encouraged to arrive at compromise solutions, usually with the assistance of a neutral person (which would exclude arbitration). For the purposes of this book, the term **alternative dispute resolution** or **ADR** will be taken to mean any method of dispute resolution that does not involve a judicial assessment in court litigation.

There are a number of different types of ADR in current use; however, there are numerous variants of each type, and no standard definitions. The Australian National Alternative Dispute Resolution Advisory Council (**NADRAC**) published a useful glossary of common ADR terms.[10] It should be noted that other authors may use different definitions, and there are many hybrid methods which combine features from several different methods described here.

28.2.5 Contractual dispute resolution

28.2.5.1 Ousting the jurisdiction of the court

The discussion on the doctrine of freedom of contract in ¶3.6.7 highlights that courts will uphold the terms of a contract properly entered into, providing it is not contrary to public policy or statute law. This important principle has far-reaching ramifications for the resolution of disputes between contracting parties. It means that, as with all other aspects of their commercial arrangement, parties are generally free to provide for any method(s) of dispute resolution they may choose.

7 [1905] 1 KB 294.

8 *Brodie v Cardiff Corporation* (1919) AC 337.

9 *Neale v Richardson* [1938] 1 All ER 753, 758 (CA) per Scott IJ.

10 NADRAC Glossary of ADR Terms www.asbfeo.gov.au/sites/default/files/Dispute%20Resolution%20Glossary.pdf (accessed 4 September 2021).

This principle is subject only to the qualification that it is against public policy to 'oust the jurisdiction of the court,' and a term that had that effect would not be enforceable.[11] This is a long-standing principle:

> As far as I have discovered, the first appearance of the phrase 'ousting the jurisdiction of the court' was in 1746 in *Kill v. Hollister* [1799] EngR 393; (1746) 1 Wils KB 129 (95 ER 532). It was there used in relation to a provision in an insurance policy that all disputes should be referred to arbitration. With the important limitation recognized in *Scott v. Avery* [1856] EngR 810; (1856) 5 HLC 811 (10 ER 1121), it is still true that the parties to a contract cannot remove disputes as to their contractual rights from the cognizance of the courts. That is because, as this Court has said:
>
> 'It is not possible for a contract to create rights and at the same time to deny to the other party in whom they vest the right to invoke the jurisdiction of the courts to enforce them': *Dobbs v. National Bank of A/asia Ltd.* [1935] HCA 49; (1935) 53 CLR 643, at p 652).[12]

In relation to contractually specified dispute resolution, in *Baulderstone Hornibrook Pty Ltd v Kayah Holdings Pty Ltd*[13] the judge did not uphold a contractual clause which provided for resolution of any dispute by the 'final and binding' decision of an independent third-party Expert. The Expert was empowered to make his decision in any manner that he saw fit, subject to observing the principles of procedural fairness and natural justice. However, the judge found that in the circumstances of a dispute involving matters of both fact and law, the dispute resolution clause was against public policy in that it '(a) purports to oust the jurisdiction of the court and (b) prescribes a procedure which is entirely unsuited to the resolution of disputes which may arise out of the contract.'

Dispute resolution clauses commonly include a requirement for a defined method of ADR to be undertaken before a dispute can be referred to court. For example, referral of a dispute to expert determination is a condition precedent to commencing litigation in clause 71 of the NSW Government GC21 contract. Similarly, clause W1.4 or W2.4 of the NEC3 contract requires all disputes to be referred to adjudication before submitting to the tribunal (litigation or arbitration). In *Fraserburgh Harbour Commissioners v McLaughlin & Harvey Ltd*,[14] Lady Wolffe held that the W2.4 clause of the NEC3 contract was mandatory, and a party could not avoid this by referring a dispute to court:

> In my view, it is clear from the language used, as well as its interrelationship with other parts of Clause W4.2, that these provisions were intended to be definitive as to the means for determining any disputes between the parties and the sequence in which they were to be taken.[15]

Such a contractual clause does not oust the jurisdiction of the court but is a contractual bar to resort to the court in the face of a contractual term prohibiting it from doing so.

---

11 See eg *ST v CT* (1224/16) [2018] ZASCA 73 [178] per Majiedt JA (Saldulker and Dambuza JJA and Plasket AJA concurring) [7].

12 *Brooks v Burns Philp Trustee Co Ltd* [1969] HCA 4; (1969) 121 CLR 432, [1969] ALR 321; (1969) 43 ALJR 131 per Kitto J.

13 (1998) 14 BCL 277.

14 [2021] ScotCS CSOH-8.

15 Ibid, [33].

28.2.5.2 Role of the courts

Irrespective of the dispute resolution mechanism in a contract, the courts have ultimate authority in respect of interpretation and enforcement of contract terms or deciding on the consequences of a breach of the contract. In many, if not most cases, the courts will keep the parties to the bargain they have made in respect of the method of dispute resolution they have chosen. The consequence is that a court will generally decline to determine a dispute between the parties, if the contract contains appropriate, valid, and certain provisions on a contractual method of dispute resolution. For example, if the contract contains an arbitration clause providing that all disputes arising under or in connection with the contract are to be decided by arbitration, a court will generally stay any litigation brought by one party in breach of the arbitration clause.

28.2.5.3 Features

Any method of ADR which the parties have provided for in their contract will be referred to as **contractual dispute resolution**. Contractual dispute resolution includes many but not all forms of ADR; for example, statutory adjudication applies as a result of statutory not contractual rights. What contractual dispute resolution methods all have in common is that they rely on agreement or contractual provisions to compel the parties to engage in the dispute resolution process, and, to the extent provided for in the contract, to implement the resolution of a dispute as determined by application of the process.

All methods of contractual dispute resolution can, and usually do, require that the proceedings and the outcome are confidential to the contracting parties. This is often one of the most important criteria in opting for contractual methods of dispute resolution in preference to litigation in the courts. For public policy reasons that justice must not only be done but must be seen to be done, hearings in court are open to the public, unless there are compelling reasons to the contrary (which would rarely apply to construction disputes). Large, high-profile companies are often reluctant, for understandable reasons, to be exposed to the relentless glare and public criticism arising from media reporting of litigation, and for that reason may choose contractual alternatives in which confidentiality can be enforced and maintained.

28.2.6 Third-party neutral

28.2.6.1 Role

With the exception of negotiation or Senior Executive appraisal, all of the methods of ADR discussed in the following sections involve the use of a **third-party neutral**. The role of such a neutral depends on the dispute resolution method: it may be facilitative (eg a Mediator), advisory (eg a Conciliator) or determinative (eg an Expert, Adjudicator, or Arbitrator), or it may involve a combination of these characteristics. The particular role may require a specific set of skills, for example, an Arbitrator may need an understanding of complex engineering issues, as well as considerable knowledge of contract law. Irrespective of the exact role and the necessary skills, any neutral must be independent of the disputing parties, without any perceived conflict of interest which could threaten the appearance of neutrality and must act fairly and impartially as between the parties. The role of any neutral can only be fully effective if both parties have full confidence in her/his independence and impartiality.

28.2.6.2 Selection

Perhaps the most fundamental distinction between litigation and all methods of contractual dispute resolution is the ability of the parties to select the most appropriate person(s) as the third-party neutral(s) for their selected method of contractual dispute resolution. Whilst in principle the parties may be free to agree on the identity of their third-party neutral, in practice such agreement may be difficult to achieve for any number of reasons in relation to the individual candidates, such as apprehension of bias, lack of track record, past performance, or for tactical reasons to delay the process. Accordingly, it is important that the contract has appropriate default provisions to enable the appointment of a third-party neutral within a reasonable timescale in the event that the parties cannot agree. This is frequently done by nominating an appropriate professional institution (such as the Chartered Institute of Arbitrators or the ICC) as the default appointer. Another alternative is to list a number of potential pre-agreed candidates in the contract from whom the third-party neutral will be appointed in accordance with a defined selection procedure.

28.2.6.3 Agreement with third-party neutral

By definition, a third-party neutral is not a party to the Contract but has obligations to both parties (which must be the same). The contract parties in turn have obligations to the third-party neutral. Accordingly, her/his services must be regulated by a separate contract, commonly referred to as a **Third-Party Agreement**. Such an agreement should define the scope of work for the third-party neutral, his/her responsibilities, the duration of services, compensation and reimbursement for services, and legal relations. The Third-Party Agreement almost invariably will require that the neutral maintains confidentiality about the dispute proceedings and outcome. As with best practice contracting, the Third-Party Agreement should be executed before the neutral commences his/her services. It is strongly recommended that the Third-Party Agreement should be a tripartite agreement between the neutral and the contract parties, to avoid any perception that the neutral owes any allegiance to either party. For the same reason, payment of the third-party neutral's invoices should ideally be separately paid in equal shares or authorised by both contract parties.

In the event of any inconsistency between the Contract and the Third-Party Agreement in respect of the dispute resolution, the Third-Party Agreement should prevail, as it is the only agreement which binds the third-party neutral. To avoid the possibility of any inconsistencies between these two contracts and to ensure that the parties agree on the dispute resolution method(s), it is desirable that the Contract specifically incorporates a draft of the Third-Party Agreement. This procedure is followed in the FIDIC contracts, which contain the General Conditions of Dispute Avoidance/Adjudication Agreement as an Appendix.

28.2.6.4 Indemnity

The role of the third-party neutral in any method of dispute resolution is to assist the parties to resolve their dispute in accordance with the agreement on the method of dispute resolution specified in the Contract, as well as any relevant legislative requirements, for example, the relevant *Arbitration Act* or *Security of Payment* legislation. Such legislation generally provides an indemnity for any actions of the neutral carried out in good faith.

The following are two examples of Arbitrator's indemnity.

Section 28(1) of the *International Arbitration Act 1974* (Cth) states:

> An arbitrator is not liable for anything done or omitted to be done by the arbitrator in good faith in his or her capacity as arbitrator.

Article 31.1 of the London Court of International Arbitration Rules similarly provides that an Arbitrator has wide immunity from suit:

> None of the LCIA. . ., any arbitrator, any Emergency Arbitrator and any expert to the Arbitral Tribunal shall be liable to any party howsoever for any act or omission in connection with any arbitration, save: (i) where the act or omission is shown by that party to constitute conscious and deliberate wrongdoing committed by the body or person alleged to be liable to that party; or (ii) to the extent that any part of this provision is shown to be prohibited by any applicable law.

Third-party neutrals appointed pursuant to various standard form contracts are not liable:

- NEC3 – for any actions undertaken in good faith.[16]
- FIDIC 1999 rainbow suite – for anything done or omitted to be done except if the act or omission is in bad faith.[17]
- FIDIC 2017 rainbow suite – for anything done or omitted to be done except in the case of fraud, gross negligence, deliberate default, or reckless misconduct.[18]

In the authors' view, this principle of quasi-judicial immunity for the third-party neutral for anything s/he does in good faith should be extended to all forms of contractual dispute resolution and included in the Third-Party Agreement, whether or not there is legislative backing for it. If the Third-Party Agreement does not provide immunity for the actions of the neutral, it would suggest that the parties are attempting to hold the third-party neutral personally or professionally liable for their efforts to resolve the parties' disputes. Such an indemnity from suit for an Expert was found by the Victorian Court of Appeal to be usual and reasonable and 'probably universally required by persons prepared to act as experts in the resolution of disputes of the nature with which this case is concerned.'[19]

28.2.7 Procedures for dispute resolution

With the exception of negotiation, all methods of dispute resolution are generally carried out in accordance with an agreed set of procedures (**Procedural Rules**). For example, litigation is conducted under the jurisdiction of the court in accordance with the relevant Rules of Court. Dispute resolution methods with statutory backing such as arbitration

16 Clause W1.2 (5).

17 General Conditions of Dispute Adjudication Agreement sub-clause 5.

18 General Conditions of Dispute Avoidance/Adjudication Agreement sub-clause 8.2.

19 *1144 Nepean Highway Pty Ltd v Abnote Australasia Pty Ltd (formerly known as Leigh Mardon Australasia Pty Ltd* [2009] VSCA 308, [28], [32].

or statutory adjudication must be conducted in accordance with the relevant legislation, although generally such legislation does not provide detailed procedures for the conduct of the dispute resolution process.

Methods of contractual dispute resolution generally provide that the third-party neutral can conduct the proceedings in any way s/he sees fit. Whilst this is a valuable power to be used when necessary, it is inappropriate to 'reinvent the wheel' for each new dispute; any method of contractual dispute resolution will be easier to implement and more readily accepted if a set of procedures have been agreed on by the parties before any dispute has arisen (which may be the only time they are prepared to agree on anything!). Whilst it may be necessary to create a 'bespoke' set of procedures for the requirements of a specific contract or a new method of dispute resolution, a variety of 'standard' Procedural Rules for most types of dispute resolution are readily available. The availability of such standard Procedural Rules is outlined in relation to the different methods of dispute resolution discussed in later sections. Even if such standard Procedural Rules are not appropriate in their entirety, they may be an appropriate starting point for contract-specific modifications. Such standard rules, like standard form contracts, have the great benefit of widespread usage, and a balanced and comprehensive form developed by a number of experienced and knowledgeable users.

It is desirable that the Contract details the procedures for the methods of contractual dispute resolution adopted by the parties. As those rules are to be implemented by the third-party neutral, it is also desirable for the Third-Party Agreement to incorporate or otherwise specifically refer to the Procedural Rules the parties have agreed to. For example, the 2017 FIDIC rainbow suite incorporate the Procedural Rules as an annex to the General Conditions of Dispute Avoidance/Adjudication Agreement.

28.2.8 Alternative methods of dispute resolution

The following methods of dispute resolution in current use are presented in order of increasing 'formality.' The term formality is used somewhat loosely to include issues such as the role of the third-party neutral and the rules/procedures within which s/he must operate, options available for possible outcomes, the extent to which the parties must be afforded natural justice, whether there is a 'hearing' and its procedures, the extent to which a resolution of the dispute is binding, and the availability of further dispute resolution processes if either party is unhappy with the outcome.

The spectrum of dispute resolution methods can be illustrated diagrammatically on a dispute resolution 'ladder' as in Figure 28.1.

As can be seen from the diagram in Figure 28.1, dispute resolution methods can be put into the following four broad classifications, each with distinctive characteristics. Whilst there are many different ADR methods, the methods within each classification share important common features:

1. **Negotiation**, in which the parties attempt to resolve their differences by discussions between their own representatives, without any assistance from a third party.
2. **Facilitation**, in which a third-party neutral facilitates discussions and negotiations between the parties, in order to assist the parties themselves to reach a resolution of a dispute acceptable to all parties.

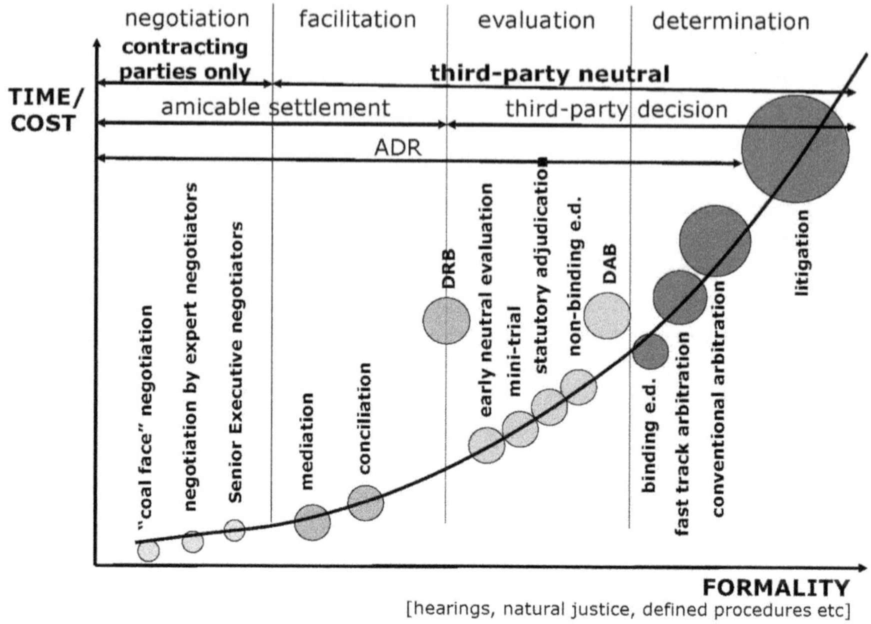

Figure 28.1 The dispute resolution 'ladder'

3. **Evaluation**, in which a third-party neutral evaluates the parties' evidence and submissions and provides an independent and impartial opinion of their legal rights.
4. **Determination**, in which a third-party neutral ensures the parties have natural justice to present their evidence and submissions and determines their legal rights in a binding decision.

An **amicable settlement** of a dispute achieved by negotiation or facilitation can materially assist in preserving the parties' business relationships because the outcome is not required to be 'winner takes all.' As will be clear from the following discussion on each different dispute resolution method, frequently there is no sharp demarcation between methods, and a particular method may combine aspects from more than one method, for example, facilitation and evaluation, such as in conciliation.

28.3 Dispute resolution methods in standard form contracts

The wide variety of dispute resolution methods included in current construction contracts is illustrated by the examples in Table 28.1, listing which rungs on the dispute resolution ladder are provided for in some standard form contracts. Also included for historical interest are the provisions in the contracts for design and construction of two famous bridges, the Quebec Bridge (1903) and the Sydney Harbour Bridge (1923).

Table 28.1 Dispute resolution methods in standard form construction contracts

Contract	Dispute Resolution Mechanism
FIDIC 1999 Red Book	1. 'Standing' Dispute Adjudication Board (not acting as arbitrators). 2. Amicable settlement [where notice of dissatisfaction has been served within 28 days after DAB decision]. 3. Arbitration under ICC rules [not less than 56 days after notice of dissatisfaction, even if no attempt at amicable settlement].
FIDIC 1999 Yellow Book FIDIC 1999 Silver Book	1. 'Ad hoc' Dispute Adjudication Board (not acting as arbitrators). 2. Amicable settlement [where notice of dissatisfaction has been served within 28 days after DAB decision]. 3. Arbitration under ICC rules [not less than 56 days after notice of dissatisfaction, even if no attempt at amicable settlement].
FIDIC 2017 Red Book FIDIC 2017 Yellow Book FIDIC 2017 Silver Book	1. 'Standing' DAAB (not acting as arbitrators). 2. Amicable settlement [where notice of dissatisfaction has been served within 28 days after DAAB decision]. 3. Arbitration under ICC rules [not less than 28 days after notice of dissatisfaction, even if no attempt at amicable settlement].
NEC3 Engineering and construction contract 2013 NEC3 Engineering and construction subcontract 2013	Option W1– used unless the *Housing Grants, Construction and Regeneration Act 1996* (UK) applies: 1. Adjudication by an Adjudicator appointed at the starting date [dispute must be referred within the time frame defined in the contract]. 2. Settlement by 'tribunal' [where notification of dissatisfaction is served within four weeks of the Adjudicator's decision]. The choice of 'tribunal' (Court, arbitration, or whatever) is specified by the parties in the contract, as is the arbitration procedure and identity of the Appointer (if arbitration is selected).
NEC4 Engineering and construction contract 2017	Option W1– used unless the *Housing Grants, Construction and Regeneration Act 1996* (UK) applies: 1. Negotiation by Senior Executives over a period of three weeks. 2. Adjudication by an Adjudicator appointed at the starting date [dispute must be referred within the time frame defined in the contract]. 3. Settlement by 'tribunal' [where notification of dissatisfaction is served within four weeks of the Adjudicator's decision]. The choice of 'tribunal' (Court, arbitration, or whatever) is specified by the parties in the contract, as is the arbitration procedure and identity of the Appointer (if arbitration is selected).
NEC4 Engineering and construction contract 2017	Option W3 – used unless the *Housing Grants, Construction and Regeneration Act 1996* (UK) applies: 1. Standing Dispute Avoidance Board makes 'a recommendation for resolving' a potential dispute. 2. Settlement by 'tribunal' [where notification of dissatisfaction is served within four weeks of the DAB's recommendation]. The choice of 'tribunal' (Court, arbitration, or whatever) is specified by the parties in the contract, as is the arbitration procedure and identity of the Appointer (if arbitration is selected).
ICC Model Turnkey Contract for Major Projects 2007	1. Combined Dispute Board in accordance with ICC Rules. 2. Arbitration under ICC rules after notice of dissatisfaction.

(*Continued*)

Table 28.1 (Continued)

Contract	Dispute Resolution Mechanism
ENAA Model Form of International Contract for Power Plant Construction 2012	1. Negotiation ('mutual consultation'). 2. Arbitration under ICC rules after notice that dispute exists. 3. Alternatively, if parties agree – expert determination under ICC Rules for Expertise. If a party issues a notice of dissatisfaction within 14 days with Expert findings, arbitration under ICC rules.
Contract for design and construction of Quebec Bridge 1903 (Canada)	1. Arbitration by three arbitrators, one appointed by the Owner, one appointed by the Contractor, and the third appointed by the first two arbitrators.
Contract for design and construction of Sydney Harbour Bridge 1923	1. Engineer's decision to be final and binding in respect of disputes for less than £1000, and technical issues in respect of design and construction. 2. Determination of the Board of Advice and Reference of the Department of Public Works, based on procedures determined by the Board. The Board's determination to be final and binding as to all matters of disputed fact. 3. Supreme Court decision on special case stated by the Board (without pleadings), if the Contractor disputes the Board's determination on a point of law within 14 days.

The following sections contain a brief description of the features of a number of different methods of ADR and contractual dispute resolution, in an endeavour to define their distinguishing features. Each method of contractual dispute resolution discussed in ¶28.4 and following sections has its own advantages and disadvantages, summarised in Table 28.3 in ¶28.14.

28.4 Negotiation

28.4.1 Contractual requirements

Freedom of contract means that the parties are always free to negotiate a settlement of any dispute between themselves, irrespective of whether or not the Contract formally provides for negotiations as a rung on the ladder of contractual dispute resolution methods. The same is of course true for any other method of contractual dispute resolution.

Because of the possible difficulty of getting a reluctant disputing party to agree to *ad hoc* negotiation, many modern construction contracts formally provide for negotiations as the first dispute resolution step, before any other methods can be implemented. For example, the ENAA Model Form of International Contract for Power Plant Construction 2012 provides that 'the parties shall seek to resolve any such dispute or difference by mutual consultation' before a party can serve a notice of dispute and trigger the arbitration clause.

Negotiation is sometimes required to be implemented as a staged process if initial negotiations at the 'coal face' do not resolve a dispute. Escalation of a dispute to senior executives who are not involved at the project level can bring a broader perspective beyond the immediate dispute, and bypass personnel who may have developed communication barriers.

For example, clause 37.1 of the CRINE/LOGIC General Conditions for Construction 2003 provides for a three-stage negotiation prior to ADR or litigation:

> Any dispute between the COMPANY and the CONTRACTOR in connection with or arising out of the CONTRACT or the WORK shall be resolved by the following procedure:
>
> (a) the dispute shall initially be referred to the COMPANY REPRESENTATIVE and the CONTRACTOR REPRESENTATIVE who shall discuss the matter in dispute and make all reasonable efforts to reach an agreement;
> (b) if no agreement is reached under Clause 37.1(a) the dispute shall be referred to the two persons named in Appendix 1 to Section I – Form of Agreement. Such persons are nominated one by the COMPANY and one by the CONTRACTOR. Such persons may be replaced by the party which nominated them by notice to the other party;
> (c) if no agreement is reached under clause 37.1(b) the dispute shall be referred to the Managing Directors of the COMPANY and the CONTRACTOR.

28.4.2 Settlement

The successful outcome of the negotiation of a dispute (or any other ADR method) between the parties must be formalised by a binding agreement. Settlement agreements are discussed in ¶28.12.

Clearly, a contractual obligation to negotiate a dispute cannot imply an obligation to actually reach a settlement by this route. An 'agreement to agree' is not sufficiently certain to constitute a legal agreement. However, a contractual obligation to negotiate in good faith as a condition precedent to commencing litigation may well be effective even in a common law jurisdiction, provided the process to be followed is sufficiently certain.[20] In those circumstances a court may stay any proceedings commenced in breach of the condition.

Negotiation is an inherently unstructured process, although there are many books and papers on effective techniques. As such, there are no Procedural Rules to be specified for dispute resolution by negotiation. The procedures to be adopted will depend on the parties' own preferences, negotiation skills, and experience, as well as their authorised 'room to move' in accordance with corporate policies and objectives.[21]

28.4.3 Advantages and disadvantages

The most significant advantages of negotiation are that it is an economical and speedy process which preserves relationships between the parties. The parties themselves 'own' the process and the outcome, and may be able to structure an innovative, positive sum outcome that provides a 'win-win' situation for both parties.

20 For example, a mediation agreement expressed to be a condition precedent to the commencement of arbitration was upheld in *Hooper Bailie Associated v Natcon Group* (1992) 28 NSWLR 194, whereas in the subsequent case of *Elizabeth Bay Developments Pty Ltd v Boral Building Services Pty Ltd* (unreported, NSW Supreme Court, Giles J, 28 March 1995) the agreement to mediate was not upheld because of lack of certainty in the process to be followed in the mediation.

21 See eg *Harvard Business School Executive Negotiation Program*; Roger Fisher, William Ury & Bruce Patton, *Getting to Yes* (Random House, 3rd edn 2012); Robert M. March, *The Japanese Negotiator: Subtlety and Strategy Beyond Western Logic* (Kodanasha International USA Ltd, 1991); Roy Lewicki, Bruce Barry & David Saunders, *Essentials of Negotiation* (McGraw-Hill International, 7th edn 2020).

Disadvantages include the fact that it does not allow for power imbalances between the parties, it does not necessarily make proper allowance for their legal rights, and the outcome may be dependent on the negotiating skills of the participants.

28.4.4 Application

Negotiation may be an effective method of dispute resolution in circumstances where:

- Both parties genuinely desire to reach a commercial settlement,
- There are good working relationships between the disputing parties,
- Both parties have approximately equal bargaining power, and
- The parties want to preserve their relationship.

28.5 Mediation/conciliation

28.5.1 The process

Mediation is a process of facilitated ADR in which a third-party neutral **Mediator** assists the parties to try and reach an amicable settlement on their own resolution of their dispute. The role of a Mediator is aptly defined in Rule 5.2 of the Resolution Institute (Australia) (**RI**) Mediation Rules 2016 as follows:

> The Mediator shall assist the parties to negotiate between themselves a mutually acceptable resolution of the Dispute, by:
>
> a. helping the parties to identify and define the issues in dispute;
> b. implementing a procedure which is aimed at achieving resolution of the Dispute quickly, fairly and cost-effectively;
> c. where appropriate, suggesting particular dispute resolution techniques for individual issues aimed at narrowing the issues in dispute quickly, fairly and cost-effectively;
> d. acting as the facilitator of direct negotiations between the parties.

Whilst every Mediator will bring their own skills and techniques to the mediations they conduct, there are several styles or processes of mediation. The following are distinct styles of mediation process:

- Facilitative mediation is a process in which a Mediator assists the disputing parties to identify the disputed issues, develop options, consider alternatives, and endeavour to reach an agreement about some issues or the whole dispute.[22]
- Settlement mediation focuses on positions from the parties' interests – what do the parties really want?
- Therapeutic or transformative mediation concentrates on the course of the dispute and the relationship between the parties.

22 NADRAC Glossary of ADR Terms www.asbfeo.gov.au/sites/default/files/Dispute%20Resolution%20Glossary.pdf (accessed 4 September 2021).

- Evaluative mediation is a term used to describe processes where a Mediator, as well as facilitating negotiations between the parties, also evaluates the merits of the dispute and provides suggestions as to its resolution.[23]

The International Mediation Institute (**IMI**) provides a referral service for certified Mediators whose mediation style is evaluative, facilitative, or transformative.[24]

In mediation, the Mediator takes an active role in providing an appropriate non-confrontational forum for the parties to discuss their issues of concern and explore ways of resolving their dispute in a way that is mutually acceptable. However, such a Mediator is 'hands off' in the sense that s/he does not apply any pressure to the parties to reach agreement and may not provide opinions on the merits or otherwise of proposed settlement initiatives.

By contrast, in a **conciliation**, the **Conciliator** takes a more proactive role in persuading the parties to adopt a settlement and may provide his/her own opinion on the merits of possible settlement options. Whilst the active participation of the third-party neutral is theoretically the distinguishing feature between mediation and conciliation, in reality the one may merge into the other, illustrated by the previous definition of evaluative mediation. Every mediation/conciliation is unique – in terms of the parties, their dispute, the facts, the third-party neutral, and the way in which the proceedings evolve. Some Mediators take a more proactive role than others and their mediations may be more like conciliations.

A comparison of the Mediation Rules and Conciliation Rules published by the RI illustrates the difference between mediation and conciliation previously referred to. Conciliation Rule 5.2 defines the role of the Conciliator in virtually identical terms to the Mediator's role previously defined, but in addition, Rule 5.5 empowers a Conciliator to:

- Make suggestions for settlement of the dispute.
- Express opinions as to what would constitute a reasonable resolution of the dispute.
- In the event of the conciliation being terminated without a settlement, the Conciliator may provide the parties with a written expression of opinion of what would constitute a reasonable resolution of the dispute or any part of it.[25]

28.5.2 Mediation rules

Whilst mediation is a more informal process than arbitration or litigation, it must nevertheless be conducted within a defined framework so that there is an agreed process that the parties understand and accept. Mediation is conducted in accordance with Procedural Rules that define the Mediator's role and the parties' rights and obligations.

23 NADRAC Glossary of ADR Terms www.asbfeo.gov.au/sites/default/files/Dispute%20Resolution%20Glossary.pdf (accessed 17 July 2020).

24 www.imimediation.org/find-a-mediator/?filter_mediation_style_49c98=174||172 (accessed 17 August 2020).

25 www.resolution.institute/documents/item/1965 (accessed 14 August 2020).

The worldwide acceptance of mediation as a cost-effective method of ADR is confirmed by the mediation rules published by every major international dispute resolution institution, such as:

- International Mediation Institute Model Mediation Rules[26]
- The American Arbitration Association (**AAA**) Construction Industry Arbitration Rules and Mediation Procedures 2015 (which includes procedures for large, complex construction disputes),[27] and also the 2013 Commercial Arbitration Rules and Mediation Procedures[28]
- ADR Institute of Canada (**ADRIC**) National Mediation Rules 2012[29]
- The Arbitrators' and Mediators' Institute of New Zealand Inc (**AMINZ**) Mediation Protocol[30]
- Chartered Institute of Arbitrators (**CIArb**) Mediation Rules 2018[31]
- International Institute for Conflict Prevention & Resolution (**CPR**) Mediation Procedure[32]
- Hong Kong International Arbitration Centre (**HKIAC**) Mediation Rules[33]
- International Chamber of Commerce (**ICC**) Mediation Rules 2014,[34] with accompanying guidance Notes (in three languages)[35]
- Resolution Institute (Australia) Mediation Rules 2016[36]
- Arbitration Institute of the Stockholm Chamber of Commerce (**SCC**) Mediation Rules 2014[37]
- Swiss Chambers' Arbitration Institution (**SCAI**) Rules of Mediation 2019[38]
- Singapore International Mediation Centre (**SIMC**) Mediation Rules[39]
- Singapore Mediation Centre (**SMC**) Mediation Procedure[40]
- Vienna International Arbitration Centre (**VIAC**) Rules of Arbitration and Mediation 2018.[41]

These institutional Procedural Rules generally cover many or all of the following aspects of the mediation process:

---

26 www.imimediation.org/resources/online/rules-and-clauses/ (accessed 17 August 2020).
27 www.adr.org/sites/default/files/ConstructionRules_Web.pdf (accessed 14 August 2020).
28 Ibid.
29 https://adric.ca/pdf/ADRMEDIATIONRULES2014.pdf (accessed 17 August 2020).
30 www.aminz.org.nz/Category?Action=View&Category_id=90 (accessed 17 August 2020).
31 www.ciarb.org/media/3291/mediation-rules.pdf (accessed 17 August 2020).
32 www.cpradr.org/resource-center/rules/mediation/cpr-mediation-procedure (accessed 17 August 2020).
33 www.hkiac.org/mediation/rules/hkiac-mediation-rules accessed 17 August 2020.
34 https://iccwbo.org/dispute-resolution-services/mediation/mediation-rules/ (accessed 14 August 2020).
35 https://cms.iccwbo.org/content/uploads/sites/3/2014/12/icc-mediation-guidance-notes-english.pdf (accessed 14 August 2020).
36 www.resolution.institute/documents/item/1897 (accessed 14 August 2020).
37 https://sccinstitute.com/media/49819/medlingsregler_eng_web.pdf (accessed 17 August 2020).
38 www.swissarbitration.org/files/838/Swiss%20Rules%202019/Web%20versions%202019/Mediation%20Web%202019/mediation_2019_webversion_englisch.pdf (accessed 17 August 2020).
39 http://simc.com.sg/v2/wp-content/uploads/2019/07/SIMC-Mediation-Rules-FINAL_A4.pdf accessed 17 August 2020.
40 www.mediation.com.sg/wp-content/uploads/2020/01/CMS-Mediation-Procedure-Rules-with-Annexes-31Jan2020-1.pdf (accessed 17 August 2020).
41 www.viac.eu/images/documents/vienna_rules/Wiener_Regeln_2018_Broschüre_en_Onlinefassung_Einzelseiten_2._Auflage_20200401.pdf (accessed 17 August 2020).

- Agreement of the parties to mediate their dispute
- Role of the Institution
- Appointment of the Mediator
- Commencement of mediation
- Mediator's role and obligations
- Responsibilities of the parties
- Representation and attendance
- Pre-mediation protocols
- Conduct of the mediation
- Privacy
- Confidentiality
- Termination of the mediation
- Extension of limitation period
- Other proceedings
- Settlement
- Costs, fees, and payments
- Limitation of the Mediator's liability
- Applicable law.

28.5.3 Settlement of a mediation/conciliation

Irrespective of the exact role that the third-party neutral fulfils, the successful outcome of a mediation/conciliation is an agreement to settle a dispute on terms acceptable to both parties. Such an outcome can be 'win-win,' in which both parties achieve something they desire, without necessarily conceding major important issues. Because it is a negotiated settlement, the outcome does not have to be confined to issues of strict legal rights under the Contract. It can include other outcomes that might be valuable in preserving an ongoing commercial relationship, for example, an agreement to consider a tender for a future contract.

As with a settlement achieved by negotiation between the parties themselves, it is essential that a settlement achieved by mediation/conciliation be documented in a legally binding form. Mediators/Conciliators are well aware of the importance of 'striking while the iron is hot,' and invariably insist on the parties drawing up a settlement agreement at the conclusion of the mediation/conciliation, and before the parties disperse. Whilst such a settlement agreement is intended to be binding, limitations of time at the mediation/conciliation often mean a more comprehensive agreement must be drawn up subsequently. In these circumstances, the first agreement should be the first type of 'Masters v Cameron' preliminary agreement, that is, the parties have reached finality in arranging all the terms of their settlement and intend to be immediately bound to the performance of those terms, but at the same time propose to have the terms restated in a form which will be fuller or more precise but not different in effect (see ¶5.3).

The legal process of drawing up the second formal agreement to settle the dispute, invariably drawn up by lawyers, sometimes requires significant further negotiation, as the parties may disagree on the scope of the settlement as documented in the preliminary agreement. It is thus very important that all of the important aspects of the settlement are precisely documented in the preliminary agreement executed at the conclusion of the mediation/conciliation.

28.5.4 Singapore Convention

The potential problems of enforcement of international arbitral awards were resolved by the implementation and widespread adoption of the *1958 New York Convention*, the efficacy of which made international arbitration the only practical avenue of dispute resolution for international commercial contracts until the recent advent of International Courts (see ¶28.13.2).

There is now an equivalent to the *New York Convention* for mediation: the *2019 United Nations Convention on International Settlement Agreements Resulting from Mediation* known as the *Singapore Convention on Mediation* (***Singapore Convention***). The *Singapore Convention* establishes a harmonized legal framework for the right to invoke settlement agreements as well as for their enforcement. It has been signed by 52 countries including the United States and China and has already entered into force in six countries (Belarus, Ecuador, Fiji, Qatar, Singapore, and Saudi Arabia). The United Nations Convention on International Trade Law (UNCITRAL) prepared the *Singapore Convention* and summarises its value and importance in the following words:

> The Convention is an instrument for the facilitation of international trade and the promotion of mediation as an alternative and effective method of resolving trade disputes. Being a binding international instrument, it is expected to bring certainty and stability to the international framework on mediation, thereby contributing to the Sustainable Development Goals (SDG), mainly the SDG 16 [*peace, justice and strong institutions*].[42]

The *Singapore Convention* applies to international written settlement agreements of commercial disputes resulting from mediation, which is defined as:

> A process, irrespective of the expression used or the basis upon which the process is carried out, whereby parties attempt to reach an amicable settlement of their dispute with the assistance of a third person or third persons ('the mediator') lacking the authority to impose a solution upon the parties to the dispute.[43]

The *Singapore Convention* has many similarities with the *New York Convention*, and also some modern additions. For example, a settlement agreement 'in writing' can be in electronic form and a regional economic organisation can participate on behalf of its constituent States. Article 5 states limited grounds on which a competent authority 'may' refuse to grant relief, including legal impediments, procedural irregularities in the settlement agreement, or the mediator's breach of relevant standards of conduct. In parallel with the *New York Convention*, enforcement can be refused where granting relief would be contrary to public policy.

The *Singapore Convention* has the potential to elevate mediation as a viable method to resolve international construction disputes in much less time and for much less cost than arbitration. At the time of writing that potential is limited by the *Convention* only being in force in six countries. It applies to settlement agreements concluded after the date when it enters into force.

42 https://uncitral.un.org/en/texts/mediation/conventions/international_settlement_agreements (accessed 27 January 2021).

43 *Singapore Convention* Art.2.3.

28.5.5 Advantages and disadvantages

Mediation has become a very important part of dispute resolution over the last 20 years in many countries. It is clearly regarded by governments and courts as an important alternative to litigation. Courts and tribunals may have the power to order litigants to mediate their dispute, frequently even over the objections of one party, for example, most parties to construction disputes in Australian courts or statutory tribunals are required to participate in some form of compulsory mediation before the court/tribunal hearing commences.

As a facilitated negotiation process, the advantages of mediation/conciliation include most of those listed previously under negotiation. In addition, the role fulfilled by an independent and experienced Mediator/Conciliator can 'level the playing field' and compensate for any power imbalance. A skilled Mediator/Conciliator can draw the parties out to reveal the real or underlying reasons behind the dispute and assist in formulating an appropriate resolution. The mediation/conciliation hearing may provide a forum in which a party can safely 'let off steam,' at the end of which the parties feel they have had their 'day in court' and that their case has been put and heard.

Possible disadvantages of mediation/conciliation include the fact that the outcome may not be synonymous with fairness and justice – the parties may have had their legal rights watered down. The lack of procedural protection that is available for, say, arbitration or litigation may reinforce inequality between the parties and may lead to ill-informed decision-making. The nature of the process in which the parties briefly articulate their position and negotiate in an endeavour to achieve consensus may be unsuitable for large complex disputes involving difficult questions of fact requiring substantial lay and expert evidence, cross examination, and so on. Although the process is 'without prejudice,' a party can obtain valuable information about the strengths and weaknesses of their opponent's case which can be useful in subsequent arbitration or litigation. As a consensual process, any resolution ultimately depends on both parties' commitment and cooperation, and there is no way of achieving resolution of the dispute if one party is totally uncooperative.

28.5.6 Application

Mediation/conciliation is particularly suitable for resolution of disputes in which:

- The issues at stake affect only a limited number of people,
- There is no requirement to establish a binding reason for future action,
- The issues are not purely legal,
- The parties are genuinely searching for a resolution to their dispute and not using the process for delay,
- A judicial remedy is not required such as an injunction to prevent assets from being removed from the jurisdiction,
- The issues of facts are straightforward,
- The dispute does not involve deep-seated values which cannot be resolved by negotiation, and
- All parties are able to participate effectively.

28.6 Early neutral evaluation

Early neutral evaluation is an evaluative ADR method in which a third-party neutral hears presentations by both sides at an early stage of the dispute and provides an evaluation of what the result might be if the dispute was arbitrated or litigated in court. The neutral's opinion of the likely outcome is not binding but is likely to be very persuasive if the parties selected the neutral because of her/his stature and experience. A reasoned opinion by the neutral can form the basis for substantive negotiations by the parties, based on a preliminary but expert view of the merits of each party's case.

The earlier such a process is carried out, the more cost-effective it will be if the parties use it to settle. However, against this must be balanced the requirement for the parties to carry out sufficient work on gathering evidence and formalising their case for presentation to the neutral for the evaluation to be relevant to the evidence and the real issues in dispute. The value of the neutral evaluation as a predictor of the likely outcome of litigation or arbitration will no doubt depend significantly on the level of preparation that has gone into the submissions.

As with any form of dispute resolution involving a third-party neutral, the efficacy of the process will depend largely on the skill and expertise of the neutral. Retired judges or Arbitrators who are experienced in construction disputes are likely to be the most effective neutrals to conduct early neutral evaluation. The advisory opinion of a Dispute Board (discussed in ¶28.10) is an example of an early neutral evaluation.

The advantages of early neutral evaluation include the modest time and costs involved, because of the relatively early stage in a dispute at which it can be conducted. The parties obtain a salutary reality check from an independent and experienced third-party neutral on the likely consequences of committing to time-consuming and expensive arbitration or litigation. The main disadvantage is that because of time and cost limitations, the case presented to the neutral has not been fully worked up, and therefore may not include the impact of compelling evidence that might ultimately be obtained via discovery in adversarial proceedings.

Early neutral evaluation may be worthwhile to help the parties determine the strength or weakness of their position in a dispute or help persuade or educate them in respect of the risks of escalating their dispute to arbitration or litigation. At the least it provides a reasoned basis for negotiations that can focus on the significant issues identified by the third-party neutral.

28.7 Mini trial

28.7.1 The process

A **mini trial** (sometimes called **Senior Executive appraisal**) is an evaluative method of ADR in which each party presents their best-case scenario to a panel comprising a senior executive from each of the parties, usually chaired by a neutral facilitator. The executives selected should not have been directly involved in the dispute, but normally have the authority to bind the parties they represent. Each party presents its position to the panel, usually with the aid of their lawyers. At the conclusion of the presentations, the Senior Executives may agree on the resolution of the dispute themselves, the panel as a whole may seek a solution acceptable to all the parties, or the neutral may express an opinion on the positions of each side in an endeavour to assist the parties to negotiate a settlement.

The mini trial process has some of the characteristics of early neutral evaluation, although it may require more preparation. The hearing is likely to be the first time that the Senior Executives have been exposed to a properly presented case by the opposing party, without the biases inevitable in internal presentations on a dispute prepared by someone 'at the coalface.' An appropriately qualified and experienced neutral chair of the panel can bring an independent and impartial perspective on the evidence and the law and provide a reality check on the consequences of not settling the dispute. The process, involving an abbreviated hearing, highlights for each party the strengths and weaknesses of their own and their opponent's case, and provides a more realistic perspective on the likely outcome if the dispute proceeds to arbitration or litigation.

28.7.2 Procedural Rules

There are no hard and fast rules for the conduct of a mini trial, as these will depend on the circumstances of the particular dispute, and the agreement of the parties on how they wish the proceedings to be conducted. The rules for a mini trial should, however, be agreed and documented beforehand. Fisher suggests that the Procedural Rules should cover the following issues, and gives an example of an agreement incorporating such rules:

(a) Production of documents,
(b) Discovery,
(c) Rulings by a third-party neutral,
(d) Exchange of briefs,
(e) Witnesses,
(f) Experts' reports, models, and other visual aids,
(g) What happens to existing litigation,
(h) Selection of Senior Executives for the panel,
(i) Confidentiality, and
(j) Time limits.[44]

28.7.3 Advantages and disadvantages

The advantages of a mini trial include:

- The modest time and costs involved, because of the relatively early stage in a dispute at which it can be conducted.
- Senior Executives are made aware of the strengths and weakness of their own and the other party's case without 'filtering' by personnel in their own organisations.
- The outcome is owned by the Senior Executives who negotiated it.
- Business relationships can be preserved.

The main disadvantage is that because of time and cost limitations, the case presented to the Senior Executives has not been fully worked up, and therefore may not include the impact of compelling evidence that might ultimately be obtained via discovery in adversarial proceedings.

44 S G Fisher, 'The Mini-Trial: A Guide to Success' in D Paul Edmond (ed), *Commercial Dispute Resolution* (Canada Law Book, 1989) 209–222.

28.7.4 Application

A number of authors have written on the features and advantages of mini trials.[45] It appears that the mini trial is a suitable method of ADR in circumstances where:

- Senior personnel who are prepared to make their own decisions are ready to listen, assess, take advice, and make deals.
- Disputes are part of the business environment for the parties and the senior management.
- The amount in dispute is large, and the parties' organisations are large.
- The dispute does not depend on the credibility of witnesses.
- There is sufficient trust between the parties to enable them to objectively look at the case being presented to them and work towards a compromise.
- It is important for the parties to maintain an ongoing business relationship.
- The dispute does not depend on the resolution of important legal principles.
- The dispute involves mixed questions of law and fact.
- The dispute involves complex technical issues.

28.8 Expert determination

28.8.1 The process

Expert determination is a method of ADR in which an independent impartial **Expert** is engaged by the disputing parties to determine those disputed questions of fact and/or law in the reference defined by the parties. The Expert makes a determination on an assessment of party submissions and relevant evidence provided to him/her. An expert determination may not require that the parties be afforded procedural fairness. Accordingly, a hearing at which witnesses give evidence and are available to be cross-examined is not essential.

An expert determination in which the reference is to determine the legal rights of the parties in respect of an entire, defined dispute may be indistinguishable from contractual adjudication (see ¶28.9.5). However, an expert determination may be more narrowly confined to factual/technical issues, the answers to which may assist the parties to negotiate the resolution of a broader dispute. The skills required of an Expert in such a narrowly defined determination may be mainly or entirely technical in a particular specialty field, whereas an Adjudicator of a dispute will generally need to also have significant legal skills in respect of the relevant contractual/statutory issues in dispute.

There are two distinct types of expert determination. In a non-binding expert determination (also called **expert appraisal**), the parties appoint an Expert to provide an advisory opinion on the merits of the factual/legal issues included in the reference. Ideally, the parties have agreed on the identity of the Expert, and therefore have confidence in her/

45 D Henderson, 'Mini-Trial of Construction Disputes' (1994) 4, *International Construction Law Review* 442; Sir Laurence Street, 'Senior Executive Appraisal' (1989) 6 *Australian Construction Law News* 9; Philip Naughton, 'Alternative Forms of Dispute Resolution – Their Strengths and Weaknesses' (1990) *Construction Law Journal* 195; P Hibberd & P Newman, *ADR and Adjudication in Construction Disputes* (Wiley, 1999) 115–122; H Astor & C Chinkin, *Dispute Resolution in Australia* (LexisNexis Butterworths, 2002) 94–99; S G Fisher, 'The Mini-Trial: A Guide to Success' in D Paul Edmond (ed), *Commercial Dispute Resolution* (Canada Law Book, 1989) 209–222.

his skills and expertise to provide a relevant and useful opinion. Dependent on the skill of the Expert, and the persuasiveness of his/her reasons, the determination may be sufficiently convincing that both parties accept it and settle their dispute accordingly. As a minimum, even if both parties do not accept it in its entirety, the determination is likely to assist the parties in their further negotiations, by virtue of the fact that it consists of an independent impartial view of the issues, and reasons for the conclusions reached. A non-binding expert determination may be indistinguishable from early neutral evaluation as discussed in ¶28.6.

The other type of expert determination is binding expert determination, in which the parties agree prior to the reference that they will accept the Expert's opinion as a binding, conclusive determination of the issues in the reference. Whilst in general the parties have freedom of contract to agree that the determination will be binding and conclusive, care must be taken to ensure that such an agreement cannot be construed to oust the jurisdiction of the courts. This is discussed further in ¶28.2.5.1.

As an example of the use of this method of ADR, the NSW Government General Conditions of Contract (Edition 2) provides for expert determination in the event that an issue is not resolved by Senior Executives within 28 days of its notification. Clause 71 covers appointment of the Expert, and provides that, subject to limited exceptions, the Expert's determination is final and binding if it requires payment by a party of an amount less than a contractually specified sum. Schedule 5 defines the expert determination procedure, including the role of the Expert as follows:

> 4.1 The Expert:
>
> 1 acts as an *Expert* and not as an arbitrator;
>
> 2 must make its determination on the basis of the submissions of the parties, including documents and witness statements, and the *Expert's* own expertise; and
>
> 3 must issue a certificate in a form the *Expert* considers appropriate, stating the *Expert's* determination and giving reasons, within 16 weeks, or as otherwise agreed by the parties, after the date of the letter of engagement of the *Expert* referred to in clause 71.3 of the GC21 General Conditions of Contract.
>
> 4.2 If a certificate issued by the *Expert* contains a clerical mistake, an error arising from an accidental slip or omission, a material miscalculation of figures, a mistake in the description of any person, matter or thing, or a defect of form, then the *Expert* must correct the certificate.

The Resolution Institute can appoint an Expert and has published Expert Determination Rules which can be used as appropriate Procedural Rules for the conduct of either binding or non-binding expert determination.[46] The ICC International Centre for ADR offers three distinct services: (1) proposal of Experts or neutrals; (2) appointment of experts and neutrals; and (3) administration of expert proceedings in accordance with the ICC Rules for the Administration of Expert Proceedings 2016.[47] These Rules are appropriate for non-binding and binding expert determinations.

46 www.resolution.institute/documents/item/1845 (accessed 17 August 2020).

47 https://iccwbo.org/content/uploads/sites/3/2015/01/2015-ICC-Expert-Rules-ENGLISH-version-1.pdf (accessed 3 August 2021).

28.8.2 Enforceability

Expert determination is a creature of contract only and has no statutory basis (unlike arbitration):

> Expert determination, on the other hand, is no more than a private contractual mechanism to which parties agree and which, as is dealt with above, does no more than create binding contractual obligations. It has no statutory backing as a process. It is not a process which resolves any dispute by the exercise of judicial, quasi-judicial, administrative, statutory or other power or jurisdiction.[48]

A binding expert determination will be legally enforceable as a matter of contract if the Expert did what was required of him/her by the agreement for expert determination:

> As the authorities on the subject make clear, the parties will be bound if the Expert did what the Contract, on its proper construction, required him to do, irrespective of the result. Conversely, the Determination will not be binding if the Expert went outside the ambit of what the Contract required him to do: see, for example: *Legal & General Life of Australia Ltd v A Hudson Pty Ltd* (1985) 1 NSWLR 314; *Holt v Cox* (1997) 23 ACSR 590; *AGL Victoria Pty Ltd v SPI Networks (Gas) Pty Ltd* [2006] VSCA 173; *Australian Vintage Ltd v Belvino Investments No 2 Pty Ltd* (2015) 90 NSWLR 367.[49]

In *Shoalhaven City Council v Firedam Civil Engineering Pty Limited*[50] the Contractor sought to set aside an expert determination on the basis that the Expert had not complied with the expert determination procedure as he had not provided reasons as required by the Contract. In rejecting that submission, the Australian High Court noted:

> The content of the requirement to give reasons must reflect the nature of the expert determination process, which is neither arbitral nor judicial. It must also be informed by the nature of the issues to be determined. Judicial observations in other cases about contractual requirements to give reasons in expert determinations or in arbitrations must be read according to their context. It may be accepted, as a general proposition, that a mistake in the reasons given for an expert determination does not necessarily deprive them of the character of reasons as required by the relevant contract nor deprive the determination of its binding force. There are mistakes which may have that effect and others that will not.[51]

28.8.3 Advantages and disadvantages

The advantages of expert determination stem from the independence and skills of the Expert. A non-binding determination provides the parties with a 'reality check' on their case and may dissuade them from proceeding to expensive litigation or arbitration, as well as providing a reasoned basis from which to negotiate a settlement. A binding determination resolves the defined issues in contention by means of an assessment of the relevant facts/law by an independent third-party neutral. The Expert can rely on her/his personal expertise on the issues in dispute (which can be an important factor in selection of the Expert) and is not confined to the evidence submitted by the parties. The time and cost of an expert determination are usually substantially less than for the more formal procedures of arbitration or litigation.

---

48 *Lainson Holdings Pty Ltd v Duffy Kennedy Pty Ltd* [2019] NSWSC 576, [59] per Hammerschlag J.

49 Ibid, [39].

50 [2011] HCA 38.

51 Ibid, [26] per French CJ, Crennan & Kiefel JJ.

The major disadvantage of non-binding expert determination is that it may not conclude the dispute between the parties if they are unable to subsequently negotiate a settlement. In that situation, substantial costs are likely to be thrown away, and the time taken to reach ultimate resolution increased. Binding expert determination suffers from the disadvantage that there may be no avenue to appeal a determination that is plainly wrong because it is based on errors of fact (a disadvantage it shares with arbitration) or law. As an Expert normally acts inquisitorially and may not hear evidence, the determination may not be based on all the available evidence.

28.8.4 Application

Expert determination is particularly suitable in disputes in which:

- There are complex technical issues,
- The questions of law are straightforward, and
- Both parties have confidence in the Expert's skill and ability to determine the issues fairly and justly.

28.9 Adjudication

28.9.1 The process

Adjudication of disputes is a recent addition to the range of available alternative dispute resolution methods, at least in its current form.[52] In essence, it is a method of dispute resolution in which an independent **Adjudicator** resolves a dispute by providing a reasoned, provisionally binding determination of the parties' contractual rights following an impartial assessment of the parties' submissions and other evidence. Key features of adjudication are that it is carried out within a strictly limited timeframe and is therefore (usually) relatively inexpensive, and (at least in the case of statutory adjudication) it does not alter or finally determine the parties' legal and contractual rights. The speed and economy of an adjudication make it an attractive dispute resolution mechanism for Contractors and subcontractors, for whom cash flow is vital, and the time involved in ultimate resolution of disputes is potentially financially crippling or fatal.

28.9.2 Statutory adjudication

28.9.2.1 Legislation

Statutory adjudication is the adjudication of a dispute in accordance with the requirements of a statute. Following the recommendations of the Latham Report *Constructing the Team*,[53] adjudication of construction disputes of all types and at any time was introduced

52 The famous English scientist Robert Hooke (1635–1703) 'carried out occasional views on properties in the city, providing professional adjudications in disputes between property owners or builders, usually for a fee of 10s': Stephen Inwood, *The Man Who Knew Too Much* (Pan Macmillan, 2002) 386.

53 Sir Michael Latham, 'Constructing the Team: Final Report of the Government/Industry Review of Procurement and Contractual Arrangements in the UK Construction Industry' *Report* (1994) 9(14).

as a statutory right in the UK in the *Housing Grants, Construction and Regeneration Act 1996* (***HGCRA***). Certain parts of the *HGCRA* relating to construction contracts were subsequently amended in the *Local Democracy, Economic Development and Construction Act 2009* (***LDEDCA***). As a result of the celerity and (relatively) low cost of statutory adjudications it is now well-established and accepted. Anecdotal evidence of the fall in the number of construction litigation cases in parallel with the rise in the number of statutory adjudications in the UK suggests that, notwithstanding the provisional nature of an adjudication determination, this legislation has had a substantial impact on reducing the number of disputes that require final resolution by mediation, arbitration, or the courts.

Since the implementation of the *HGCRA*, legislation providing for statutory adjudication of construction disputes has been passed in all Australian jurisdictions,[54] New Zealand,[55] Singapore,[56] the Isle of Man,[57] Malaysia,[58] Ireland,[59] and Ontario.[60]

28.9.2.2 Features of the legislation

These ***Statutory Adjudication Acts*** have been implemented to address one of the most enduring and intractable problems in the construction industry – to facilitate cashflow, the 'lifeblood' of the construction industry. The purpose of the *Construction Contracts Act 2002* (NZ) sums up these aims:

> The purpose of this Act is to reform the law relating to construction contracts and, in particular, –
>
> (a) to facilitate regular and timely payments between the parties to a construction contract; and
> (b) to provide for the speedy resolution of disputes arising under a construction contract; and
> (c) to provide remedies for the recovery of payments under a construction contract.[61]

These *Acts* (with the exception of Malaysia) provide for 'regular and timely payments' by providing an entitlement to progress payments. The 'speedy resolution' of disputes is provided by an entitlement to statutory adjudication. The *HGCRA* and the Isle of Man *Act* provide for adjudication of 'any difference,' and the NZ *Act* for adjudication of 'a dispute' if there is no agreement for international arbitration. Disputes in the other jurisdictions are confined to payment disputes. The *Statutory Adjudication Acts* do not finally determine the parties' contractual rights, but they do determine who 'holds the money,' at least provisionally.

54 *Building and Construction Industry Security of Payment Act 1999* (NSW); *Building and Construction Industry Security of Payment Act 2002* (Vic); *Construction Contracts (Security of Payments) Act 2004* (NT); *Building and Construction Industry (Security of Payment) Act 2021* (WA); *Building and Construction Industry (Security of Payment Act) 2009* (ACT); *Building and Construction Industry Security of Payment Act 2009* (SA); *Building and Construction Industry Security of Payment Act 2009* (Tas); *Building Industry Fairness (Security of Payment) Act 2017* (Qld).

55 *Construction Contracts Act 2002* (NZ).

56 *Building and Construction Industry Security of Payment Act 2004* (Sing).

57 *Construction Contracts Act 2004* (IoM).

58 *Construction Industry Payment and Adjudication Act 2012* (Malaysia).

59 *Construction Contracts Act 2013* (Ireland).

60 *Construction Act 1990* (Ont).

61 s 3.

The 'remedies for the recovery of payments under a construction contract' previously referred to are provided by expedited procedures to recover an adjudicated amount as a debt due by established court procedures. The legislation is based on the principle of 'pay now and argue later' in an endeavour to get payments to Contractors and subcontractors as expeditiously as possible.

This legislation cannot be contracted out of[62] and is arguably the largest constraint on freedom of contract for construction contract in the common law world as it

> to a large extent removes from the contracting parties the freedom they would otherwise have to agree upon their respective rights and obligations in relation to a construction project, and imposes upon them a regime of rights and obligations that they cannot bargain away.[63]

The *HGCRA* and the Isle of Man *Act* provide more freedom of contract than the other *Acts*, for example, in the UK the parties can define their own adjudication scheme, providing it satisfies the eight compliance points in the *HGCRA*; the parties can also nominate their own Adjudicator.

The *Acts* vary in length from a very brief 12 clauses in the Ireland *Act* to 245 in the Queensland *Act*. In addition to providing for prompt payment and statutory adjudication, the Queensland *Act* requires project bank accounts to be established for holding payments on trust for subcontractors. It also provides for continued use of subcontractor's charges as an alternative to adjudication. The Ontario *Act* (121 clauses) also provides for payments to be subject to trust obligations, as well as detailed provisions on the long-established mechanic's lien.[64]

28.9.2.3 Provisional determination of disputes

Statutory adjudication is a process which does not (in theory at least) provide a final resolution of any dispute. An Adjudicator's determination does not determine or affect the rights of the parties, and they can finally resolve their dispute through the courts, or the dispute resolution processes provided for in the Contract. On closer examination, however, some adjudication determinations involve decisions on claims of tens or hundreds of millions of dollars, and the lengthy period usually involved in arbitration or litigation to finally resolve such a dispute means that the determination of which party holds the money has profound cash flow significance for both Contractor and Employer, particularly in situations where there is a prospect of insolvency. In practice therefore, the 'provisional' outcome of a statutory adjudication may become the *de facto* final resolution of the dispute.

28.9.2.4 Enforceability

One of the greatest attractions of statutory adjudication is the ease and extent to which the Adjudicator's determination is enforceable. Broadly speaking, courts will only set aside a determination if there has been a breach of natural justice, lack of compliance with the

62 The *Construction Contracts (Security of Payments) Act 2004* (NT) permits parties to a 'high value' construction contract (> \$500m) to use a dispute resolution mechanism in accordance with the *Regulations* instead of adjudication.

63 Julian Bailey, *Construction Law Vol III* (Informa Law London, 2nd edn 2016) 1715.

64 Bruce Reynolds, Sharon Vogel & James Little, 'A Report on the Introduction of Prompt Payment and Adjudication Legislation in the Province of Ontario' (2019) 1 *International Construction Law Review* 73.

basic procedural requirements laid down in the relevant *Act*, or lack of jurisdiction. Courts recognise that determinations usually have to be completed on written submissions of the parties within a very limited time and on the balance of probabilities, and accordingly will not find a determination void merely because of error by the Adjudicator in respect of either the facts or the law. The following judicial statement made in respect of the *HGRCA* is equally applicable to other *Statutory Adjudication Acts*:

> the purpose of the scheme is to provide a speedy mechanism for settling disputes in construction contracts on a provisional interim basis, and requiring the decisions of adjudicators to be enforced pending final determination of disputes by arbitration, litigation or agreement, whether those decisions are wrong in points of law or fact. It is inherent in the scheme that injustices will occur. . . . The victims of mistakes will usually be able to recoup their losses by subsequent arbitration or litigation.[65]

Enforcement of statutory adjudication determinations is very straightforward in most jurisdictions, for example, in Australia a certified copy of the adjudication determination or an adjudication certificate issued by the Authorised Nominating Authority that appointed the Adjudicator is filed in court with a supporting affidavit and can then be enforced as a judgement of the court. If a respondent seeks to have such a judgement set aside, it cannot raise any cross-claim or defence in relation to matters arising under the Contract, or challenge the Adjudicator's determination.

28.9.2.5 Advantages and disadvantages

Statutory adjudication provides a speedy and relatively inexpensive method of at least provisionally resolving a payment dispute. As it does not affect the parties' legal rights, they are able to finally resolve their dispute and correct any wrong Adjudicator's determination by subsequent arbitration or litigation (providing the relevant party is still solvent).

The disadvantages of statutory adjudication stem from the prescriptive and confined nature of the *Security of Payment* legislation. The extent of these disadvantages varies between jurisdictions, because of the sometimes significant differences between the relevant legislation. Further, the legislation in a particular jurisdiction may be subject to review and modification following experience of its operation, and accordingly it is essential to refer to the relevant up-to-date legislation to determine the exact extent to which the following limitations apply.

28.9.2.6 Application

Statutory adjudication in most jurisdictions only applies to the class of payment disputes provided for in the legislation, which may exclude important cost issues such as Variations or latent ground conditions.[66] As an *Act* may be focused on ensuring cash flow to Contractors/subcontractors, it may not apply to many types of construction disputes such as extensions of time. There are very limited opportunities for extending the time for an adjudication, which may be inadequate for disputes over large and complex claims. In this context, it

65 *Bouygues (UK) Ltd v Dahl-Jensen (UK) Ltd* [200] BLR 49, [35].

66 *Building and Construction Industry Security of Payment Act 2002* (Vic).

is possible for a claimant to 'ambush' the respondent. A claimant can devote considerable resources over a number of months to prepare a comprehensive claim documented in dozens of lever arch files; the claimant will have a very limited time (perhaps no more than five business days) to prepare its response. Christmas Eve can be a very tactical date on which to serve such a claim; however, certain jurisdictions have now excluded Christmas and New Year from the counting of days!

Both parties can minimise the risks of being time barred by managing claims properly from the outset:

> A contractor who submits a properly justified claim for payment under the contract maximises the chances of being paid without dispute, but is also well placed to use the same claim in an adjudication, thus avoiding delays in writing up a detailed submission. A principal who rejects a claim with clear reasons is more likely to have the claim withdrawn, but also has a ready prepared response should the contractor seek adjudication. A contractor who puts in a poorly substantiated claim and has it rejected triggers a dispute and the time bar and if wishing to retain rights to adjudication must pull together the details of the claim under the pressure of the strict time frames of the Act.[67]

Statutory adjudication is an effective method of resolution of:

- Straightforward disputes over progress payments by Contractors, subcontractors, consultants, and suppliers of materials for construction which do not require significant input from experts or where factual issues are not complex.
- Disputes caused by the Employer using its 'power of the purse' for tactical or illegitimate reasons to withhold payments that should be made under the Contract.

28.9.3 Statutory adjudication process

As previously noted, at the time of writing, there are 14 jurisdictions that have *Statutory Adjudication Acts* which provide for an adjudication process in respect of disputes over progress payments claimed under a construction contract. Whilst all the *Acts* have broadly similar procedures in respect of claiming payments and adjudication of disputes, there are significant differences between them, including the times at which procedural steps must be undertaken. For example, the time from filing of an adjudication claim to the delivery of the Adjudicator's determination varies from a low of 15 business days in some Australian jurisdictions to up to 80 business days in Malaysia. The relevant legislation must be consulted to determine the specific requirements for a particular situation. More detailed information is available in the comprehensive texts which are available.[68] Guidelines for

67 Peter Gow, 'The Construction Contracts Act in Western Australia' (2008) 27(2) *The Arbitrator & Mediator* 33, 37.

68 For example, Julian Bailey, *Construction Law* (Informa Law, 2nd edn 2016); Andrew Burr, *International Contractual and Statutory Adjudication* (Informa Law from Routledge, 2017); Keith Pickavance, *A Practical Guide to Construction Adjudication* (Wiley Blackwell, 2016); Nick Henchie, *Adjudication for Architects A Practical Guide to Statutory Adjudication Introduced by the Housing Grants, Construction and Regeneration Act* (Stephen Cross, 2002); John Redmond, *Adjudication in Construction Disputes* (Blackwell Science, 2001); Sarah Lupton, *Architects Guide to Adjudication* (RIBA Publications, 1998); Marcus S Jacobs, *Security of Payment*

the procedures under the *Acts* in different Australian jurisdictions are available on the Internet.[69]

Not only are there significant differences in detail between the individual Australian *Acts*, there are also conceptual differences between the *Construction Contracts Act 2004* (WA)[70] and the NT *Act* (west coast model) and the *Acts* in the other jurisdictions (east coast model). The west coast model provides more freedom of contract than the east coast model and is more in harmony with the legislation passed in the UK and NZ:

> Whilst both models allow for a statutory adjudication scheme to determine, in the interim, disputed payment claims, they differ with respect to adjudicator appointment, submissions which may be considered by an adjudicator, and the approach which an adjudicator is to adopt in order to arrive at his or her determination. In all of these respects the East Coast Acts are more restrictive, disallowing mutual agreement of an adjudicator, consideration of reasons for withholding payment which have not been duly submitted in accordance with the statutory payment scheme, and discouraging an evaluative approach to adjudicators' determinations.[71]

The significant differences between the *Acts* means that there is no 'Australian adjudication' as such. The construction industry supports harmonisation of *Statutory Adjudication Acts* across Australia, and the Commonwealth Government implemented a comprehensive review to identify legislative best practice with a view to improving consistency in *Security of Payment* legislation. The report by John Murray AM made 86 recommendations for uniform legislation that addressed perceived shortcomings and inconsistencies in the existing legislation.[72] Whether this achieves the desired effect remains to be seen.

The features of the various *Statutory Adjudication Acts* are summarized in Table 28.1.

---

in the Australian Building and Construction Industry (Lawbook Co, 2014); Philip Davenport, *Adjudication in the Building Industry* (Federation Press, 3rd edn 2008); Anthony Hussey, *Construction Adjudication in Ireland* (Routledge, 2017).

69 NSW: www.fairtrading.nsw.gov.au/trades-and-businesses/construction-and-trade-essentials/security-of-payment (accessed 26 August 2020); Victoria: www.vba.vic.gov.au/building/security-of-payment (accessed 26 August 2020); Queensland: www.qbcc.qld.gov.au/sites/default/files/Protecting_your_payment_rights.pdf (accessed 26 August 2020); SA: www.sasbc.sa.gov.au/security_of_payment (accessed 26 August 2020); Tasmania; www.cbos.tas.gov.au/topics/products-services/problems/resolving-a-building-dispute/disputes-security-of-payment (accessed 26 August 2020); ACT: www.planning.act.gov.au/build-buy-renovate/for-industry/industry-resources/security-of-payments (accessed 26 August 2020); WA: www.commerce.wa.gov.au/building-and-energy/information-using-construction-contracts-act (accessed 26 August 2020); NT: https://nt.gov.au/__data/assets/pdf_file/0004/236803/resolving-construction-disputes-nt.pdf (accessed 26 August 2020);

70 At the time of writing (September 2021) the *Construction Contracts Act 2004* (WA) still applies to payment disputes which qualify under that *Act*; however, it will fall away with the effluxion of time because the *Building and Construction Industry (Security of Payment) Act 2021* (WA) (which is more aligned to the east coast model) is due to commence in August 2022. Certain parts of the *2021 Act*, including the statutory trust provisions, will not commence until six to twelve months thereafter. Contracts entered into after the commencement date will be subject to it, with earlier contracts instead continuing to be governed by the *Construction Contracts Act 2004* (WA). Reference in this work is generally made to the *Building and Construction Industry (Security of Payment) Act 2021* (WA) in anticipation of its coming into force.

71 Jeremy Coggins, Robert Fenwick Elliott & Matthew Bell, 'Towards Harmonisation of Construction Industry Payment Legislation: A Consideration of the Success Afforded by the East and West Coast Models in Australia' (2010) 10(3) *Australasian Journal of Construction Economics and Building* 14, 15 (citations omitted).

72 John Murray AM, 'Review of Security of Payment Laws' (2017) Australian Government www.ag.gov.au/sites/default/files/2020-03/review_of_security_of_payment_laws_-_final_report_published.pdf (accessed 27 August 2020).

28.9.4 Comparison of Security of Payment Acts in different countries

Table 28.2 Comparison of Statutory Adjudication legislation

	HGCRA[73]	**Australia**[74]	**New Zealand**[75]	**Singapore**[76]	**Isle of Man**[77]	**Malaysia**[78]	**Ireland**[79]	**Ontario**[80]
Legislation can't be contracted out of.	s104(5)	X[81]	s12	s36	s1(5)	s2	s2(5)	s5(1)
Residential property excluded.	YES s106	YES & NO	NO	YES s4(2)	YES s3	YES s3	YES s2(1)(b)	NO
Entitlement to progress payments.	s109	X	In default of agreement – s14	s5	s6		s3(1)(a)	s6.3
Parties can agree on mechanism for determining payments & timing.	s109(2)	X Time limits in some States	s14	ss6–8	s7	s36(1)	s3	s6.3
Default payment provisions.	s114	X	ss15–18	ss8(2),8(3)	s11	s36	s3(3) Subcontract – s3(4)	ss6.4–6.6

(*Continued*)

73 *Housing Grants, Construction and Regeneration Act 1996* (UK) as amended by *Local Democracy, Economic Development and Construction Act 2009* (UK).

74 *Building and Construction Industry Security of Payment Act 1999* (NSW); *Building and Construction Industry Security of Payment Act 2002* (Vic); *Construction Contracts (Security of Payments) Act 2004* (NT); *Building and Construction Industry (Security of Payment) Act 2021* (WA); *Building and Construction Industry (Security of Payment Act) 2009* (ACT); *Building and Construction Industry Security of Payment Act 2009* (SA); *Building and Construction Industry Security of Payment Act 2009* (Tas); *Building Industry Fairness (Security of Payment) Act 2017* (Qld).

75 *Construction Contracts Act 2002* (NZ).

76 *Building and Construction Industry Security of Payment Act 2004* (Sing).

77 *Construction Contracts Act 2004* (IoM).

78 *Construction Industry Payment and Adjudication Act 2012* (Malaysia).

79 *Construction Contracts Act 2013* (Ireland).

80 *Construction Act 1990* (Ont).

81 For example, *Building and Construction Industry (Security of Payment) Act 2021* (WA) s111. Because different *Security of Payment Acts* apply in each State and Territory of Australia, the relevant applicable *Act* must be referred to.

Table 28.2 (Continued)

	HGCRA[73]	**Australia**[74]	**New Zealand**[75]	**Singapore**[76]	**Isle of Man**[77]	**Malaysia**[78]	**Ireland**[79]	**Ontario**[80]
Date for payment after payment claim.		Specified maximum in 3 jurisdictions	20 working days in default of agreement s18	s8		s36(4)		Contractor 28 days – s6.4 Sub + 7 days s6.5
Interest on overdue payments.		X WA & NT – default only	On retention s18G	s8(5)				s6.9
Statutory procedures for claims and payments.	s114	X	ss19–24	ss10–11		ss5–7	s5	ss6.3–6.7
Non-paid party may stop work.	s112	X WA & NT – if adj amount unpaid	s24A	If adj amount unpaid s26	s9	If adj amount unpaid s29	ss5, 7	If adj amount unpaid s13.19(5)
Automatic entitlement to progress payment if formalities are not observed.	s111	X Not NT	s22					
"Pay when paid" and "pay if paid" clauses are void.	s113	X	s13	s9	s10	s35	s3(5)	ss6.5(4), 6.6(4)
Trust over monies payable.		Queensland; project bank account by Contractor						ss7–13
Provisions relating to retention.		Trust in 4 jurisdictions	ss18A-18I					ss22–30
Parties have the right to submit a defined type of dispute to adjudication.	Any difference s108	Payment dispute	A dispute if no international arbitration agreement s25	Payment claim dispute s12	Any difference s5(1)	Payment claim dispute s7	Payment dispute s6	Payment dispute s13.5(1)

	HGCRA[73]	Australia[74]	New Zealand[75]	Singapore[76]	Isle of Man[77]	Malaysia[78]	Ireland[79]	Ontario[80]
Defined adjudication procedures.	s108	X	ss25–71	ss13–17	s11	ss7–12	s6	ss13.6–13.16
Strict time limits for adjudication.	s108(2)	X	ss33,35,36–37,46	s17(1)		s12(2)	s6(6)	s13.13
Time for adjudication from notice of adjudication.	28 days	15–20 days	5 + 2 + 5 (+ 5 + 2) + 20 = 32 working days	7 + 7 + 7(14) = 21 days	7 + 28 = 35 days s5(2)	10 + 10 + 10 + 5 + 45 = 80 working days	7 + 28 days	7 + 5 + 30 = 42 days
Choice of Adjudicator.		ANA or Registrar (Q) NT – choice	Agreement or ANA s33			By agreement or AIAC appointment ss21–23	Agreement or panel chair s6(4)	Agreement or ANA s13.9(2)
Review of Adjudicator's determination.		Limited in 3 jurisdictions	By non-respondent Owner ss71A-71D	If adj amount > response by prescribed amount ss18–19				s13.18
Enforcement procedures for Adjudicator's determination.		File adjudication as judgement debt	ss73–76	Lien on unfixed goods and order of court ss23, 25, 27		Order of High Court s28	Order of High Court s6(11)	Filed determination enforceable as order of court s13.20
No contractual defences to court enforcement.		X	s74	ss27(6), 27(7)		s15		s13.18(5)
Representation		NO, exc WA & NT	s38B	s16(5)		s8(3)		
Natural justice	implicit		s41C	s16(3)		s24(c)		
Clauses in *Act*	17	36–245	107	45	16	41	12	121

28.9.5 Contractual adjudication

28.9.5.1 The process

Although statutory adjudication is typically confined to a certain class of payment disputes, the benefits of adjudication of other types of disputes arising out of or in connection with a construction contract can be achieved by contractual means. **Contractual adjudication** is a determinative method of ADR in which the parties agree in the Contract (or in a separate contract) for an independent Adjudicator to resolve a dispute by providing a provisionally binding determination of the parties' contractual rights, following an impartial assessment of the parties' submissions and other evidence. Care needs to be exercised in proper drafting of the adjudication provisions to avoid prohibited 'contracting out' of any applicable *Security of Payment* legislation.

This definition of contractual adjudication suggests that the process is essentially that of binding expert determination (discussed in ¶28.8), carried out within a strictly limited time period. The efficacy and acceptance of this process is based on the stature and competence of the Expert/Adjudicator; the parties will be more likely to accept the Expert's/Adjudicator's determination if they have been party to his/her selection on the basis of the skills and experience necessary for resolution of the particular issue or dispute.

There are various standard form Third Party Agreements for contractual adjudication, for example, NEC3 Adjudicator's Contract, for which guidance notes and flowcharts are also available. The ICE Adjudication Procedure 1997 published by the Institution of Civil Engineers contains Procedural Rules for adjudication under the *HRGCA*, as well as an Adjudicator's Agreement.

The FIDIC provisions for a DAB (1999 rainbow suite) or DAAB (2017 rainbow suite) decision on a dispute are provisions for contractual adjudication. Dispute Boards are discussed further in ¶28.10.[82]

Whilst contractual adjudication is intended to operate as a speedy 'rough and ready' form of ADR, in practice it can have many of the features of accelerated arbitration. Parties can provide written submissions and witness statements, and attend a hearing where witnesses are examined and cross-examined. The written decision of the independent, impartial Adjudicator may then be similar to an arbitral tribunal's award, but without the legislative backing of an arbitration award.

Contractual adjudication is the primary method of dispute resolution in the ICE Conditions of Contract – Measurement Version (7th edn 1999), available as of right to either party if agreement cannot be reached on other forms of ADR such as mediation or conciliation.[83] Such contractual adjudication, in accordance with the ICE Adjudication Procedure (1997), complies with the requirements for statutory adjudication under the UK *HGRCA*.

---

82 1999 rainbow suite: Sub-clause 20.4 [Obtaining Dispute Adjudication Board's Decision], Appendix General Conditions of Dispute Adjudication Agreement, and Annex Procedural Rules; 2017 rainbow suite: Sub-clause 21.4 [Obtaining Dispute Adjudication Board's Decision], Appendix General Conditions of Dispute Avoidance/Adjudication Agreement, and Annex DAAB Procedural Rules.

83 Clause 66B.

28.9.5.2 Advantages and disadvantages

The advantages of contractual adjudication include the short timeframe and limited costs involved in obtaining an independent third-party neutral's evaluation of the parties' contractual rights. As a process defined by the relevant contract, the parties have control over the process, including selection of the Adjudicator. Such a provisionally binding resolution of a dispute, even if ultimately disputed, enables the parties to deal with the issues in a timely fashion when the evidence and memories are fresh. The ultimate resolution of any disputed adjudication can usually be deferred to the end of the project, thereby enabling the parties to focus on Completion, rather than being distracted by preparation for dispute resolution.

Disadvantages of contractual adjudication mainly stem from the limited time and scope of the process. The short time period allowed for may be insufficient for complex legal and factual disputes which require careful consideration of large numbers of documents and other evidence.

28.9.5.3 Application

Contractual adjudication is an appropriate ADR method where:

- The parties are prepared to accept the Adjudicator's 'rough and ready' determination as provisionally binding and
- The disputed issues of fact and law are confined in scope.

28.10 Dispute Boards

28.10.1 The process

In the context of construction contracts, a DB comprises a board of one or three persons, independent of the contracting parties, engaged to perform an overview role of the execution of the project and the Contract. Its primary function is to assist the parties to avoid disputes if possible, or if avoidance is not possible, to assist them to a speedy, cost-effective, and acceptable resolution of disputes, and avoid the need for arbitration or litigation. The ICC defines a DB as follows:

> A Dispute Board ('DB') is a standing body composed of one or three DB Members. Typically set up upon the signature or commencement of performance of a mid- or long-term contract, they are used to help parties avoid or overcome any disagreements or disputes that arise during the implementation of the contract. Although commonly used in construction projects, DBs are also effective in other areas. These areas includes research and development; intellectual property; production sharing and shareholder agreements.[84]

The members of a Dispute Board need to be relevantly experienced in the type of project under construction and have a thorough understanding of contractual issues. They need to be respected for their experience and expertise, and they must be impartial. Both contracting parties must agree on membership of the DB.

84 https://iccwbo.org/dispute-resolution-services/dispute-boards/ (accessed 27 August 2020).

The usual selection process for a three-person DB is for the Employer to nominate one member, and the Contractor to nominate a second member. Notwithstanding their nomination by a party, each of those members must be independent of both contracting parties. Each party has the right of reasonable objection over the other party's selection. The Chairman is usually nominated by the party nominees, and then agreed to by the parties.

Standing DBs are organised at the start of the Contract, and before construction begins. The DB is provided with the contract documents, plans and specifications, and is provided with regular progress reports during the course of the project. Thus, the DB members become and remain familiar with the Contract, the project, and the participants from the beginning, and have an up-to-date knowledge of all the relevant issues which might impact on potential disputes.

The DB meets on regular site visits with representatives of the Employer and Contractor together and is briefed on progress and potential problems. The Board also carries out an inspection of the Works on each of its site visits, and thus obtains firsthand knowledge of the Site and the project. The aim of the Board's site meetings is to facilitate communication with the contracting parties, and encourage resolution of contentious issues at the job level, before they become actual disputes. With the acquiescence of both parties, it is able to provide an informal advisory opinion on a potential dispute.

Either party has the right to refer a dispute to the Dispute Board. Following such a referral, the Board will hold a hearing, question witnesses, consider submissions, and then provide a reasoned determination of the dispute, all within a defined limited time. The contractual effect of the Board's determination depends on whether the Dispute Board is a so-called Dispute Resolution (or Review) Board (**DRB**) or a Dispute Adjudication Board (**DAB**).

28.10.1.1 Types of DB

The determination of a DRB (the US model) is a recommendation to the parties of the DRB's considered opinion as to the appropriate resolution of the dispute. The DRB's recommendation has no contractual effect, unless the parties agree to implement it. However, notwithstanding the lack of a binding contractual effect of the DRB's recommendation, it is generally very persuasive because of the stature of the Board members, and the structured, fair, and independent process by which they came to their reasoned decision. The track record of success of this model in the USA supports its efficacy as an effective method of dispute resolution.

By contrast, the determination of a DAB (the European model) is a decision that is contractually binding on the parties unless and until it is overturned by agreement or in accordance with the contractual requirements for final determination of disputes (arbitration or litigation). There is a defined limited period of time after the DAB's decision within which either party may give notice of dissatisfaction with the DAB's decision. In the absence of such notice, the DAB's decision is finally binding on the parties. Even if one of the parties gives formal notice of dissatisfaction, the final resolution of the dispute by arbitration or litigation is usually deferred until the end of the project; in the meantime, the DAB's decision is binding on the parties.

Each contract on the Lesotho Highlands Water Project Phase 1 applied one of the different models so as to evaluate practical advantages and disadvantages of each model, and as a risk mitigation measure. The project included the Katse Dam, Africa's second-largest double curvature arch dam, 85 m high and 710 m long and a dual tunnel 5 metres in diameter and more than 200 km in length. A multitude of issues which arose during the course of the construction were successfully resolved, underground works being particularly suited to this form of dispute avoidance and resolution.[85]

28.10.1.2 DB procedures

A Dispute Board Manual is available on the Dispute Resolution Board Foundation (**DRBF**) website.[86] This manual succinctly addresses all of the important issues relating to Dispute Boards: their history, what they are, how they are established, the processes involved in their establishment and operation, and, importantly, their costs. The DRBF responded to the requirements for remote operation of DBs during the COVID-19 pandemic by publishing Best Practice Guidelines for Virtual Dispute Board Hearings and Checklist for Dispute Board Members in Preparation for Virtual Dispute Board Proceedings.[87]

28.10.1.3 International use of DBs

The DRBF website also provides a comprehensive database on projects around the world which have used DBs, identifying the Contractor and Employer, contract value, and the numbers of disputes heard, settled, or referred to other dispute resolution procedures.[88] As at August 2020, the database listed 2,815 projects in 57 countries, with a total contract value of US$278b. Two- thirds of the projects had no disputes referred to the DB. Eighty one percent of the disputes referred to the DB were settled, and only 15% of the disputes were referred to other dispute resolution tribunals. The countries that listed more than ten DBs and the number of DBs are as follows:

- USA 2,442
- Australia 71
- South Africa 31
- Canada 26
- India 25
- Tanzania 23
- Romania 23
- Ethiopia 18
- Lesotho 17
- Pakistan 15
- Mozambique 12

85 Drawing from their experience on the project, the practical advantages and disadvantages of each model of DB are discussed by legal counsel and chief engineer: see Philip Loots & Robert Fraser, 'Alternative Dispute Resolution (ADR) in Practice in South Africa' (July 1999) 3 *Dispute Review Board Foundation Forum*; and a retrospective on their article, Philip Loots & Robert Fraser, 'Lean Dispute Avoidance for Lean Construction' (November 2016) 20(2) *Dispute Review Board Foundation Forum*.

86 www.drb.org/concept/manual/ (accessed 28 August 2020).

87 www.drb.org/publications-data/library/coronavirus-covid-19/ (accessed 28 August 2020).

88 www.drb.org/publications-data/drb-database/ (accessed 27 August 2020).

The World Bank's 2019 Standard Procurement Document for Works adopts the 2017 FIDIC Red Book, including a standing DAAB, giving further international support for the use of DBs.[89]

28.10.2 *Contractual requirements for a DB*

The formal requirements for implementation of a DB comprise the following three contractual documents:

- **Dispute Board clauses** in the construction contract between Employer and Contractor;
- Procedural Rules defining the operations of the DB; and
- **Tripartite Agreement(s)** between Employer, Contractor, and DB Members, incorporating the Procedural Rules.

The Dispute Resolution Board Australasia Inc. (Region 3 of the DRBF) publishes a number of draft contract provisions on its website.[90] The AAA publishes DRB Operating Procedures,[91] DRB Hearing Rules and Procedures,[92] and DRB Guide Specifications.[93] Rules for a DAB are published by the Chartered Institute of Arbitrators,[94] ICE,[95] and the ICC.[96] The ICC also publishes a Model Dispute Board Member Agreement (Tripartite Agreement).[97] The 2017 FIDIC rainbow suite of contracts includes all of the required contractual requirements:

- General Condition sub-clauses 21.1 [Constitution of the DAAB], 21.2 [Failure to Appoint DAAB Member(s)], 21.3 [Avoidance of Disputes], 21.4 [Obtaining DAAB's Decision];
- DAAB Procedural Rules; and
- General Conditions of Dispute Avoidance/Adjudication Agreement.

28.10.3 *Advantages and disadvantages*

A standing DB, that is one that is set up at the beginning of a project and maintains an active involvement in the progress of the project by reading regular progress reports and making periodic site visits, is well placed to make an expeditious determination of any

89 http://pubdocs.worldbank.org/en/865231562944956956/SPD-Request-for-Bids-WORKS-after-prequalification.docx (accessed 28 August 2020).

90 www.drbf.org.au/document/example-db-provisions (accessed 27 August 2020).

91 www.adr.org/sites/default/files/document_repository/Construction_DRB_Operating_Procedures.pdf (accessed 27 August 2020).

92 www.adr.org/sites/default/files/document_repository/Construction_DRB_Hearing_Rules_Procedures.pdf (accessed 27 August 2020).

93 www.adr.org/sites/default/files/document_repository/The%20AAA%20Dispute%20Resolution%20Board%20Guide%20Specifications_0.pdf (accessed 27 August 2020).

94 www.ciarb.org/media/3934/ciarb-dispute-board-rules.pdf (accessed 28 August 2020).

95 Institution of Civil Engineers can, *ICE Dispute Resolution Procedures* (2012).

96 https://iccwbo.org/content/uploads/sites/3/2015/09/icc-dispute-board-rules-english-version.pdf (accessed 25 May 2021).

97 https://iccwbo.org/content/uploads/sites/3/2015/09/Model-Dispute-Board-member-Agreement-in-English-1.pdf (accessed 25 May 2021).

dispute, as its 'learning curve' will be minimal, and may be able to determine disputes as part of regular site visits.

The only real downside to such a DB is the not insignificant cost; board members will need to be paid a retainer to compensate them for reading site communications, maintaining appropriate files, and being available at short notice to participate in determinations of disputes, as well as daily remuneration and expenses for travel to site, site meetings, and dispute hearings.[98] A less effective but less expensive alternative is an '*ad hoc*' DB; a board that is only constituted when a dispute arises and is then required to read all the relevant background information, conduct site inspections and a hearing, and prepare a determination. The 1999 FIDIC Yellow and Silver Books provide for such an *ad hoc* DAB.

There are many similarities between the use of a DAB and contractual adjudication.[99] In particular, DAB and contractual adjudication provide for a provisionally binding determination to be made by a third-party neutral(s), chosen by the parties, who conducts the necessary investigations within a strictly limited and enforced period of time.

28.11 Arbitration

28.11.1 Overview

Arbitration is the private judgement of a dispute between parties by an independent, unbiased, and impartial **arbitral tribunal** which applies the principles of procedural fairness (natural justice) in a determinative process in which all parties have the opportunity and the right to present their case and rebut the case of their opponents. The arbitral tribunal typically consists of one or three **Arbitrators** who must consider all of the evidence presented by the parties and decide what are the relevant facts from the evidence which, when applied to the relevant principles of law (or, rarely, general justice and fairness[100]), determine the rights and obligations of the parties in relation to the dispute. The arbitral tribunal publishes its findings on the facts and the law and the rights and obligations of the parties applicable to the dispute in a written determination called an **award** which is binding on all parties to the arbitration. After the arbitral tribunal has handed down the award, the dispute between parties no longer exists, as the award irrevocably extinguishes the original cause of action that resulted in the arbitration.

Consistent with the doctrine of freedom of contract, where the parties have agreed to settle their dispute by private arbitration, the courts will usually stay court proceedings where the ambit of the dispute submitted to the court is within the parties' arbitration agreement. Such arbitration does not oust the courts' jurisdiction,[101] as the courts may be required to keep the parties to their agreement to arbitrate their dispute, and if necessary, to enforce the arbitral award.

98 See Dispute Resolution Board Foundation, *Dispute Board Manual A Guide to Best Practices and Procedures* (Dispute Resolution Board Foundation, 2019) Chapter 11 Costs and Fees 84–95.

99 Fenwick Elliott, '10 Days in Utopia' (May 2000) 27(1) *The Arbitrator and Mediator* 57, 58.

100 Also referred to as ***ex aequo et bono***, Latin for 'according to the right and good' or 'from equity and conscience.'

101 *Dobbs v National Bank of Australasia Ltd* (1935) 53 CLR 643, 656 per Starke J.

It is apparent from this description that an arbitral tribunal's role has many features in common with those of a judge, and it has been said that arbitration involves an inquiry in the nature of a judicial inquiry.[102] Further, legislation legitimising and regulating arbitration may provide an arbitral tribunal with certain powers and privileges that judges have, such as the ability to administer an oath/affirmation and not be liable for negligence in respect of anything done in the capacity of Arbitrator.[103]

28.11.2 Arbitration agreement

Litigation in a court of law is the default option for resolution of a commercial dispute because it is available as a matter of right to a party in dispute who has not made a consensual agreement with the other party(ies) to the dispute to adopt ADR to resolve the dispute. It is therefore readily apparent that parties who desire to use arbitration to resolve a commercial dispute must agree that they will submit their dispute to arbitration. Such an **arbitration agreement** may be made before there is any dispute between them, and parties entering into a construction contract may agree that any disputes or disputes of a particular type will be referred to arbitration. Even if there is no prior agreement to refer disputes to arbitration, it is usually (at least theoretically) possible for parties to agree to refer a dispute to arbitration after the dispute has arisen. However, because parties in dispute may find it difficult to agree on anything, such a post dispute agreement may be difficult to achieve in practice.

Thus, the fundamental characteristic of arbitration is that it is the product of a consensual arrangement to submit a dispute for determination by an arbitral tribunal in accordance with a contract known as the arbitration agreement. The arbitration agreement is the most important (contract) document in regulating the entire arbitration process. It is the primary source of the parties' rights in respect of any arbitration proceeding, and sets out what can be arbitrated, when the arbitration will take place, and the legal and procedural framework within which the dispute will be arbitrated.

The *lex arbitri* in some jurisdictions may require a valid arbitration agreement to be in writing. For example, the *International Arbitration Act 1974* (Cth) gives the *Model Law* the force of law in Australia and adopts Option 1 of Article 7 for the definition of an arbitration agreement (requiring the agreement to be in writing).

It is important to distinguish between the arbitration agreement (contract) to resolve a dispute by arbitration from the Contract between the parties, the (alleged) breach of which gave rise to the dispute. The Contract usually contains the agreement to settle disputes by arbitration within it (ie the arbitration agreement), but in law the Contract and the arbitration agreement are treated as separate contracts. Thus, for example, a Contract which is null and void because the necessary formalities were not complied with, or the conditions precedent were not fulfilled does not necessarily invalidate the arbitration agreement.[104]

---

102 *Hammond v Wolt* [1975] VR 108.

103 For example, *International Arbitration Act 1974* (Cth) s28.

104 *Heyman v Darwins* [1942] AC 436.

The universally accepted doctrine of **separability** means that an arbitral tribunal has jurisdiction to decide a dispute in accordance with the arbitration agreement, including the threshold issue of whether the Contract itself is valid.

Model Law Article 16(1) articulates the doctrine of separability as follows:

> The arbitral tribunal may rule on its own jurisdiction, including any objections with respect to the existence or validity of the arbitration agreement. For that purpose, an arbitration clause which forms part of a contract shall be treated as an agreement independent of the other terms of the contract. A decision by the arbitral tribunal that the contract is null and void shall not entail ipso jure the invalidity of the arbitration clause.

The arbitration agreement can provide for either *ad hoc* arbitration, or institutional arbitration. An **institutional arbitration** is one that is administered by a named institution, such as the ICC, SIAC, HKIAC, LCIA, and ICDR (a division of the AAA). An ***ad hoc*** **arbitration** is one that is conducted according to procedures agreed by the parties without any institutional supervision.

28.11.3 Arbitration agreement and the Contract

The primacy of the arbitration agreement over other sources of rules that regulate the conduct of arbitration proceedings reinforces the importance of the parties to a contract ensuring that their arbitration agreement has been properly thought through so that it adequately provides for the parties' preferred dispute resolution procedure. Particularly in an international arbitration, it pays dividends, prior to the onset of a dispute, for the parties to turn their minds to the many choices they can make which will have a substantial influence on the cost, efficiency, and effectiveness of the arbitration procedure, and formalise their choices in the arbitration agreement. Matters such as the location of the arbitration, *ad hoc* or institutional arbitration, the Procedural Rules governing the arbitration, choice of the *lex arbitri*, how many Arbitrators and how they are chosen, whether the arbitral tribunal must decide in accordance with the law and limitation of rights of appeal to a court are all significant issues over which the parties can exercise choices that may ultimately have a substantial influence on the arbitration process, and possibly the effectiveness of the outcome. The arbitral tribunal should be expressly empowered to review and revise any decision or instruction of the Engineer or any certificate of the Engineer.

Notwithstanding that arbitration proceedings have commenced, the Contractor should be obliged to continue the performance of the Contract in accordance with the Engineer's decision or instruction that is being challenged, unless the Employer orders work to be suspended in accordance with the terms of the Contract. If work is suspended, then the Contractor will, subject to the terms of the Contract, be entitled to recover the reasonable costs incurred and occasioned by the suspension. The clause should further provide that the fact that arbitration is taking place does not give the Employer grounds for withholding payments which have become due or are otherwise payable.

Any formal notice of arbitration must usually be given no later than a stipulated number of days after the issue of the final payment certificate. The final payment certificate should, except in certain circumstances, be conclusive evidence that both parties have performed all their obligations under the Contract. The final payment certificate would not be conclusive if arbitration or court proceedings under the Contract have been commenced before the expiry of the stipulated period after the issue of the final payment certificate. Under some arbitration rules the arbitration is not deemed to have been commenced until notice of the existence of the dispute has been given to the arbitration body itself, for example, Article 4.2 of the ICC Arbitration Rules and Article 5.2 of the ACICA Rules.

28.11.4 Applicable law

There are potentially three different systems of law that may be relevant to the arbitration of a dispute:

- The law governing the validity, scope, or interpretation of the arbitration agreement;
- The law governing the conduct of the arbitration (the procedural law, also known as the *lex arbitri* or the curial law); and
- The law governing the substance of the dispute (the substantive law).

In principle, the parties to an arbitration agreement may be able to make separate (and different) explicit choices for the systems of law that apply to each of these systems of law and record their choices in the arbitration agreement. Providing that these choices are not in conflict with statute or public policy, a court or arbitral tribunal would normally be expected to give effect to the parties' explicit choices of law. In many cases, however, the parties have not made explicit choices of law, and it falls to the arbitral tribunal or a court to determine the appropriate choice of law that applies to each aspect of the parties' relationship. In making such a determination, different considerations apply to each choice of law.

28.11.4.1 The law governing the arbitration agreement

The law governing the arbitration agreement is central to all questions arising from construction of the agreement itself, and indeed to the threshold question as to whether there is an arbitration agreement in existence that gives jurisdiction to the arbitral tribunal to conduct an arbitration. For example, the law governing the arbitration agreement determines whether the arbitral tribunal itself can determine if there is an arbitration agreement in existence, or whether that issue must be determined by an appropriate court within the jurisdiction of the law chosen.

Where the contract contains a choice of governing law:

> As a matter of principle and authority there are therefore strong reasons why an agreement on a choice of law to govern a contract should generally be construed as applying to an arbitration agreement set out or otherwise incorporated in the contract.[105]

The complexity of determining which system of law governs the validity and scope of the arbitration agreement where the parties have not made an explicit choice of the governing

105 *Enka Insaat Ve Sanayi AS v OOO Insurance Company Chubb* [2020] UKSC 38, [54] per Lord Hamblen and Lord Leggatt.

law of the contract is highlighted by the UK Supreme Court case *Enka Insaat Ve Sanayi AS v OOO Insurance Company Chubb*.[106] In that case the majority (Lords Hamblen, Leggatt, and Kerr) determined that, where the parties have not made a choice of the governing law of the contract, the arbitration agreement will be most closely connected with the law of the seat of arbitration.[107] The minority in dissent (Lord Burrows and Lord Sales) considered that the law with which the main contract is most closely connected governs the arbitration agreement, as this is the law with which in their view the arbitration agreement is also most closely connected.

28.11.4.2 The *lex arbitri*

The party autonomy derived from freedom of contract means that parties to an arbitration agreement can choose the place where the arbitration is to take place – known as the **seat of arbitration**. The procedural law applicable to an arbitration (also known as the curial law or the *lex arbitri*) is selected by the parties through their choice of the seat of arbitration. The choice of seat is usually based on the parties' selection of a neutral location where they consider the *lex arbitri* to support the arbitral process, as some international jurisdictions, such as Singapore and Hong Kong, are more 'arbitration friendly' than others.

The choice of a particular place as the 'seat' of the arbitration does not mean that hearings must be held or the award issued there:

> [T]he seat of an arbitration is a legal concept rather than a physical one. A choice of place as the seat does not dictate that hearings must be held, or that any award must actually be issued, in that place. As the Court of Appeal observed (at para 46), it is perfectly possible to conduct an arbitration with an English seat at any convenient location, anywhere in the world. . . . The point of agreeing a seat is to agree that the law and courts of a particular country will exercise control over an arbitration which has its seat in that country to the extent provided for by that country's law. A choice of seat can in these circumstances aptly be regarded as a choice of the curial law.[108]

The *lex arbitri* is usually articulated in fairly broad terms and does not purport to provide all the detailed procedures necessary for the conduct of an arbitration. The *lex arbitri* is usually supplemented by Procedural Rules, discussed in ¶28.11.7. Redfern and Hunter list a number of examples of issues which are likely to be covered by the *lex arbitri*.[109] The following Redfern and Hunter list is annotated with the relevant articles from the *Model Law* which is the basis of the *lex arbitri* in 116 jurisdictions:[110]

- The definition and form of an agreement to arbitrate (Article 7).
- Whether a dispute is capable of being referred to arbitration, that is, whether it is 'arbitrable' under the *lex arbitri* (Article 7).

106 [2020] UKSC 38.

107 Ibid, [170].

108 *Enka Insaat Ve Sanayi AS v OOO Insurance Company Chubb* [2020] UKSC 38, [38] per Lord Hamblen and Lord Leggatt.

109 Alan Redfern & Martin Hunter, *Law and Practice of International Commercial Arbitration* (Sweet & Maxwell, 4th edn 2004) 81.

110 https://uncitral.un.org/en/texts/arbitration/modellaw/commercial_arbitration/status (accessed 15 January 2021).

- The constitution of the arbitral tribunal and any grounds for challenge of that tribunal (Articles 10–15).
- The entitlement of the arbitral tribunal to rule on its own jurisdiction (Article 16).
- Equal treatment of the parties (Article 18).
- Freedom to agree upon detailed rules of procedure (Article 19).
- Interim measures of protection (Articles 17, 17A – 17G).
- Statements of claim and defence (Article 23).
- Hearings (Article 24).
- Default proceedings (Article 25).
- Court assistance if required (Articles 17H – 17J, 27, 34–36).
- The powers of the arbitrators, including any powers to decide as '*amiable compositeurs*'[111] (Articles 19, 20, 22–29, 32, 33).
- The form and validity of the arbitration award, and the finality of the award, including any right to challenge it in the courts of the place of arbitration (Articles 30, 31, 33, 34–36).

The applicable *lex arbitri* must be consulted to determine the exact position for each of these issues, particularly whether there are mandatory provisions. However, typically, many of the provisions of the *lex arbitri* are default options that define rights, obligations, or procedural issues in the event that the arbitration agreement between the parties has not made provision for these matters. However, with few exceptions, parties are generally free to choose their own rights, obligations, and procedures in place of the default options in the statutes.

It is apparent from the foregoing that the place of arbitration should be carefully considered and clearly defined in the Contract, as this defines the procedural law for the arbitration. The language of the arbitration should also be defined, as this will have practical implications for the costs of conducting the arbitration and may influence the choice of seat and arbitral tribunal.

28.11.4.3 The substantive law

The substantive law is the law applied by the arbitral tribunal to determine the parties' legal rights and obligations in dispute – the proper or governing law of the contract. This is discussed in more detail in ¶2.6. If the parties have not chosen the governing law in the Contract, it will be necessary for the arbitral tribunal to determine it.

Article 28(20) of the *Model Law* provides for the governing law to be determined under the *lex arbitri*: 'Failing any designation by the parties [of the rules of law applicable to the substance of the dispute], the arbitral tribunal shall apply the law determined by the conflict of laws rules which it considers applicable.'

Procedural Rules published by arbitral institutions usually give the arbitral tribunal the power to determine the governing law of the contract if the parties have not agreed.

111 An arbitral tribunal acting as ***amiable compositeur*** is not bound by strict rules of law but is entitled to decide according to their subjective sense of what is fair and just. An arbitral tribunal acting as *amiable compositeur* makes their award *ex aequo et bono*.

Example: Governing law determined by arbitral tribunal under Procedural Rules

The ICC Arbitration Rules in force from January 2021 provide for the governing law to be determined by the arbitral tribunal under the Procedural Rules in Article 21 Applicable Rules of Law:

1 The parties shall be free to agree upon the rules of law to be applied by the arbitral tribunal to the merits of the dispute. In the absence of any such agreement, the arbitral tribunal shall apply the rules of law which it determines to be appropriate.
2 The arbitral tribunal shall take account of the provisions of the contract, if any, between the parties and of any relevant trade usages.
3 The arbitral tribunal shall assume the powers of an *amiable compositeur* or decide *ex aequo et bono* only if the parties have agreed to give it such powers.

In addition to explicitly specifying the governing law in the Contract, it is also important to establish the ruling language of the Contract if versions of the Contract are prepared in different languages.

28.11.5 Interface with the law

As a private method of resolving disputes outside of the law courts, arbitration has a very long history.[112] It is now firmly supported by the legal systems in most jurisdictions as an alternative to litigation, backed up by legislation. That legislation provides for the enforceability of arbitral awards, and severely limits the circumstances in which parties who have made a valid arbitration agreement can seek the assistance of a court of law, including appealing the arbitral tribunal's decision. The legal privileges granted to the arbitral tribunal and to the arbitral process can be seen as a logical outcome of the fundamental principles of party autonomy and freedom of contract.

In a recent case in Poland,[113] the claimant argued that if a party does not have the funds to start arbitration and the given arbitration rules do not allow for exemption from the courts, this would infringe such party's right to a fair trial. The Warsaw Court of Appeals decided that a party's lack of funds to launch arbitration did not render the arbitration agreement ineffective. The court explained that by deciding on arbitration, the parties had accepted this means of dispute resolution with its pros and cons. One benefit of arbitration over litigation is the expeditiousness of the proceedings. However, at the same time, the parties to arbitration agree on the limitation of the procedural guarantees which exist in state court litigation.[114]

112 England's oldest surviving award is dated AD118. www.trans-lex.org/262120/_/england's-oldest-surviving-arbitral-award-with-an-introduction-by-derek-roebuck-/ (accessed 4 September 2021).
113 Warsaw Court of Appeals, 27 April 2020, VII AGz 35/20.
114 www.internationallawoffice.com/Newsletters/Arbitration-ADR/Poland/Kubas-Kos-Gakowski/Lack-of-funds-does-not-enable-parties-to-escape-arbitration?utm_source=ILO+Newsletter&utm_medium=email&utm_content=Newsletter+2021-01-21&utm_campaign=Arbitration+%26+ADR+Newsletter (accessed 29 January 2021).

However, the courts have an important role to play in support of arbitration, by providing judicial interpretation of the meaning of the legislative provisions, and the construction of arbitration agreements, as well as defining the legal principles on which the private rights inherent in freedom of contract are resolved in the light of relevant public policy principles. In appropriate circumstances the court will use its coercive powers in support of an arbitration, for example, by issuing a subpoena for a third party to give evidence at an arbitration hearing, or to implement interim measures such as the preservation of evidence or assets.

For over 400 years English law has supported the right of parties to a contract to choose arbitration as at least the first method of solving their disputes. However, there is a tension between freedom of contract and the principle that all persons are subject to the law, and that it is against public policy for the courts' jurisdiction in upholding the law to be ousted by any private arrangement.

In the past this has meant that judges have retained considerable power to intervene in arbitration proceedings, and to review and set aside or amend arbitral tribunal's awards. This possibility of judicial review was a significant constraint on the ability of arbitration to fulfil its fundamental objectives of providing a speedy, fair, economical and final method of resolving disputes in the forum chosen by the parties, and thereby avoid some of the perceived disadvantages of litigation in the courts. However, the modern trend is to severely circumscribe the circumstances in which parties to an arbitration can obtain the courts' assistance to circumvent the arbitration process or refuse implementation of the arbitral tribunal's award, and arbitration legislation has undergone considerable evolution to provide greater certainty to the outcome of the arbitral process.

This principle that, subject to important safeguards, parties who have freely entered into an arbitration agreement should be held to their bargain to settle their disputes by arbitration and not litigation is supported by the *lex arbitri* around the world, the *Model Law*, and the *New York Convention*. For example, the *Model Law* contains many important provisions that promote properly run arbitration as private, independent judgement of disputes with a final enforceable outcome, with very limited avenues to appeal to the courts.

28.11.6 Enforcement of an arbitral award

There is an essential interface between arbitration and the law as administered by the courts in enforcement of an arbitral tribunal's award. Modern *Arbitration Acts* provide for the courts to enforce an arbitral tribunal's award as if it were a judgement of the court and provide very limited ground for refusing recognition or enforcement. This is perhaps one of the most important aspects of an arbitration award as an alternative to a court judgement, since the full machinery of the law is available to a successful party to make the arbitral tribunal's award as effective as if it were a court judgement.

Typically, the only grounds on which a court may refuse enforcement are limited to issues that negate the basis of the agreement to arbitrate, the arbitral tribunal was not constituted or did not comply with the requirements of the arbitration agreement, or the award was inconsistent with relevant law or public policy.

Example: Recognition and enforcement of awards

Chapter VIII Recognition and Enforcement of Awards in the *Model Law* provides for court enforcement of an award, and limits the grounds on which it can decline to do so as follows:

Article 35. Recognition and enforcement

(1) An arbitral award, irrespective of the country in which it was made, shall be recognized as binding and, upon application in writing to the competent court, shall be enforced subject to the provisions of this article and of article 36.

(2) The party relying on an award or applying for its enforcement shall supply the original award or a copy thereof. If the award is not made in an official language of this State, the court may request the party to supply a translation thereof into such language.

Article 36. Grounds for refusing recognition or enforcement

(1) Recognition or enforcement of an arbitral award, irrespective of the country in which it was made, may be refused only:
   (a) at the request of the party against whom it is invoked, if that party furnishes to the competent court where recognition or enforcement is sought proof that:
      (i) a party to the arbitration agreement referred to in article 7 was under some incapacity; or the said agreement is not valid under the law to which the parties have subjected it or, failing any indication thereon, under the law of the country where the award was made; or
      (ii) the party against whom the award is invoked was not given proper notice of the appointment of an arbitrator or of the arbitral proceedings or was otherwise unable to present his case; or
      (iii) the award deals with a dispute not contemplated by or not falling within the terms of the submission to arbitration, or it contains decisions on matters beyond the scope of the submission to arbitration, provided that, if the decisions on matters submitted to arbitration can be separated from those not so submitted, that part of the award which contains decisions on matters submitted to arbitration may be recognized and enforced; or
      (iv) the composition of the arbitral tribunal or the arbitral procedure was not in accordance with the agreement of the parties or, failing such agreement, was not in accordance with the law of the country where the arbitration took place; or
      (v) the award has not yet become binding on the parties or has been set aside or suspended by a court of the country in which, or under the law of which, that award was made; or
   (b) if the court finds that:
      (i) the subject-matter of the dispute is not capable of settlement by arbitration under the law of this State; or
      (ii) the recognition or enforcement of the award would be contrary to the public policy of this State.

(2) If an application for setting aside or suspension of an award has been made to a court referred to in paragraph (1)(a)(v) of this article, the court where recognition or enforcement is sought may, if it considers it proper, adjourn its decision and may also, on the application of the party claiming recognition or enforcement of the award, order the other party to provide appropriate security.

The importance and significance of the *New York Convention* is discussed in ¶4.6. The adoption of this *Convention* in 160 countries provides a near universal acceptance of the principle of binding and enforceable arbitration awards that were procured in accordance with the arbitration agreement and the *lex arbitri*. The only grounds on which a court in a Convention country may refuse enforcement are limited to those articulated in the *Model Law*. The wording of Articles III – V of the *New York Convention* is in very similar terms to the *Model Law* Articles 35 and 36 in the previous example.

28.11.7 Procedural rules

As discussed in ¶28.11.4.2, an arbitration will be governed by the provisions of the *lex arbitri*, to the extent that these have not been negated by specific provisions made by the parties in their arbitration agreement. *Arbitration Acts* typically have default options that define certain procedural issues which apply if the arbitration agreement between the parties has not provided otherwise. However, there are many detailed matters relating to the conduct of an arbitration on which legislation is silent. It is therefore appropriate for the parties to have an agreed set of Procedural Rules to supplement the legislative provisions, and to ensure that the arbitration can be carried out efficiently and expeditiously.

The following examples of Procedural Rules are appropriate for *ad hoc* arbitrations:

- The UNCITRAL Arbitration Rules[115]
- The Resolute Institute Arbitration Rules 2020[116]

The following are examples of rules used for institutional arbitration administered by the named institution:

- The ICC Rules of Arbitration 2021[117]
- Australian Centre for International Commercial Arbitration (**ACICA**) Arbitration Rules and Expedited Arbitration Rules 2016[118]
- Arbitration Rules of the Singapore International Arbitration Centre 2016[119]

115 https://uncitral.un.org/en/texts/arbitration (accessed 26 January 2021).

116 www.resolution.institute/documents/item/1844 (accessed 26 January 2021).

117 https://iccwbo.org/dispute-resolution-services/arbitration/rules-of-arbitration/ (accessed 26 January 2021).

118 https://acica.org.au/wp-content/uploads/2016/02/ACICA_Rules_2016_Booklet.pdf (accessed 26 January 2021).

119 www.siac.org.sg/images/stories/articles/rules/2016/SIAC%20Rules%202016%20English_28%20Feb%202017.pdf (accessed 26 January 2021).

- Administered Arbitration Rules of the Hong Kong International Arbitration Centre 2018[120]
- The AAA Commercial Arbitration Rules and Mediation Procedures (including procedures for large complex commercial disputes) 2013[121]
- LCIA Arbitration Rules 2020[122]

The parties can of course devise their own bespoke rules, or make whatever modifications are appropriate for their individual circumstances by amending appropriate institutional Procedural Rules.

28.11.8 Third-Party Agreement

The Procedural Rules published by institutions that administer arbitrations generally provide adequate protections for the interests of appointed arbitrators in respect of payment of fees and indemnities. For example, in respect of liability, the ICC Arbitration Rules 2021 provide a very broad indemnity:

> The arbitrators, any person appointed by the arbitral tribunal, the emergency arbitrator, . . . shall not be liable to any person for any act or omission in connection with the arbitration, except to the extent such limitation of liability is prohibited by applicable law.[123]

Whilst certain legislative protection is typically provided to Arbitrators under the *lex arbitri*, it is highly recommended that the parties and the arbitral tribunal in an *ad hoc* arbitration execute an appropriate Third-Party Agreement. Such an agreement will ensure that issues such as payment of and security for the arbitral tribunal's fees, the arbitration procedures to be adopted, limitation of liability, and so on are documented and agreed. Such an agreement can be based generally along the lines of agreements commonly used for other forms of ADR.

28.11.9 Appeals

Arbitration is intended to be a final, binding, and enforceable resolution of a dispute. Accordingly, modern *Arbitration Acts* severely circumscribe the grounds on which a party can seek the court's aid in recourse against an award or in avoiding enforcement of an award. There are typically no avenues of appeal if the arbitral tribunal made an error in the facts and limited or no avenues of appeal if the arbitral tribunal made an error of law.

The only grounds for recourse against an award are typically confined to issues that negate the basis of the agreement to arbitrate, the arbitral tribunal was not constituted or did not comply with the requirements of the arbitration agreement, or the award was inconsistent with relevant law or public policy. In the event that any of these grounds are made out, a court may set the award aside, or refuse to enforce it.

120 www.hkiac.org/sites/default/files/ck_filebrowser/PDF/arbitration/2018_hkiac_rules.pdf (accessed 26 January 2021).

121 www.adr.org/sites/default/files/CommercialRules_Web.pdf (accessed 26 January 2021).

122 www.lcia.org/Dispute_Resolution_Services/lcia-arbitration-rules-2020.aspx (accessed 26 January 2021).

123 Article 41.

Article 34 of the *Model Law* provides that the only recourse against an award is for it to be set aside by a court. The grounds for setting aside do not include errors of fact or law by the arbitral tribunal and are confined to the grounds on which a court may refuse enforcement of an award in Article 36. Article 36 is reproduced in the example in ¶28.11.6.

28.11.10 Advantages and disadvantages

The advantages of arbitration include:

- The parties themselves have the ability to have an input into all stages of the process, starting with the arbitration agreement which defines the scope of disputes referred to arbitration and the method of selecting the arbitral tribunal.
- The parties' options include their choice of the arbitral tribunal, the location of the arbitration, and to a substantial extent, the *lex arbitri* which is to be applied to the arbitration, and the extent to which its legislative provisions apply.
- The arbitral tribunal can be expert in the technical and legal issues involved in the dispute.
- Arbitration results in a binding award, enforceable through normal court processes, that finally resolves the dispute.
- Privacy and confidentiality: unlike litigation in court which is open to the public, an arbitration is private, and the proceedings and award can generally be kept confidential.
- Most of the powers that a court can exercise in the conduct of civil litigation are available in an arbitration, either to the arbitral tribunal or by application to a court by a party or the arbitral tribunal.
- There are limited avenues of recourse against an arbitral tribunal's award, whilst preserving the parties' rights to seek the court's relief in the event that the arbitral tribunal breaches the rules of procedural fairness, or the arbitration award was improperly procured.

In principle, arbitration has the potential for many of the advantages of litigation (impartial judgement, known defined procedures, binding resolution of dispute) without some of the disadvantages (publicity, time, and excessive cost). Whether it achieves the holy grail of fairness, economy, and efficiency in any situation depends partly on the parties themselves, but also substantially on the arbitral tribunal, which ultimately decides how to regulate the proceedings to the extent that the parties have not themselves defined the procedure.

The usual disadvantages cited for arbitration are that it takes too long and costs too much because the procedures often may be almost indistinguishable from those of a court.

28.11.11 Fast track arbitration

A relatively recent innovation is the use of **chess clock arbitration**, in which a limited time for the hearing is set by the tribunal, with each party given equal time to present its case. The length of the hearing is set for a much shorter period than in a conventional arbitration where each party presents its entire case during the hearing. Each party must decide for itself how to allocate its limited hearing time between opening submissions, examination

in chief, cross-examination, re-examination and closing submissions. Timekeepers are employed to keep track of the time used by each party, using the equivalent of a chess clock. There is considerable emphasis on written submissions and delivery of evidence in chief via witness statements. This 'chess clock' process has been used successfully in large arbitrations in Australia and elsewhere, with the result that a final binding outcome has been achieved years earlier than it would have if a conventional litigation route been followed.

Chess clock hearings are but one example of a process of **fast track arbitration**, in which the aim is to achieve an arbitration award in the minimum time consistent with a fair process complying with the rules of natural justice (procedural fairness).

28.12 Settlement agreements

As noted, after an arbitral tribunal has handed down its award, the dispute between the parties no longer exists, as a valid award irrevocably extinguishes the original cause of action that resulted in the arbitration. Other methods of ADR will only formally resolve a dispute at the stage that the parties have entered into a binding and enforceable agreement which states the basis on which they have agreed to settle all issues in dispute between them. The key features of such an agreement are thus that it must be comprehensive so as to cover all issues in dispute and binding so as to preclude either party from reviving the dispute in another forum such as a court.

In the absence of such a binding agreement, any 'settlement' is illusory, as there is no sanction for a party which reneges on its agreement. Properly drawn up, a binding settlement agreement may be enforced through litigation: the courts will generally uphold the terms of a settlement agreement as a contract between the parties, providing it complies with the normal requirements for the validity of a contract such as certainty of terms and so on. It is usually appropriate to obtain legal advice in drawing up a settlement agreement for any significant dispute to ensure that it 'covers all bases.'

The nature of construction disputes is such that there are frequently a number of claims and cross claims between the parties, including claims for additional compensation and extension of time, Variations and defects in quality. Parties engaged in a dispute resolution process over a number of such issues may reach a 'global' settlement in which it is desired to resolve all known and possible future claims, so that the parties can finally conclude their commercial relationship. Whilst such a settlement may be desirable, the possible consequences need to be carefully thought through. It should be borne in mind that a characteristic of construction contracts is that the consequence of poor-quality construction may not be immediately apparent, and in some cases may not become manifest for a number of years. A global settlement which covers all possible future claims could preclude any further action being taken for defects which arose at a later date.

28.13 Litigation

28.13.1 Litigation in domestic courts

Litigation to resolve commercial disputes is available as of right in any jurisdiction subject to the rule of law. As previously discussed, if parties have entered into an arbitration agreement, courts will generally stay litigation commenced in respect of a dispute covered by the arbitration agreement, on the principle of the court upholding the parties' bargain to arbitrate.

In the absence of an arbitration agreement or resolution of a dispute by ADR, the parties to a dispute must resort to litigation in court to enforce their legal remedies. Further, litigation may be necessary as an adjunct to ADR or arbitration, in circumstances where a party wants to enforce its contractual rights in respect of the dispute resolution process itself, or the award, decision, agreement, or determination arising from such a process.

Litigation may be the preferred method of dispute resolution for some construction disputes, for example, where a binding decision made in public is desired to create a precedent to apply to similar future disputes. Some jurisdictions have specialist courts for construction disputes, such as the Technology and Construction Court (**TCC**) in England[124] and the Technology, Engineering and Construction List in the Supreme Court of Victoria (**TEC**).[125] Such courts have judges experienced in managing and hearing complex technical disputes, who actively case manage cases to minimise the time and cost of the litigation.

Proactive well-managed courts with appropriately experienced judges may in fact deliver a judgement on a construction dispute in less time and at less cost than arbitration. Singapore is a standout in court efficiency, in 2016 being placed first out of 140 countries by the World Economic Forum in terms of the efficiency of its legal framework in settling disputes.[126] Chief Justice Menon notes the following efficient performance by the Singapore courts that would be a challenge for many arbitral tribunals:

> On average, cases that do not involve heavy factual disputes are fixed for hearing within three to six weeks from the date they are filed. Trials that engage contested facts are generally heard eight weeks from the date of setting down, which is when the case is ready for hearing.[127]

Enforcement of a judgement within the jurisdiction is unproblematic, as the courts have the full coercive powers of the state at their disposal. However, attempting to enforce a judgement on a party outside the jurisdiction may be complex, costly, and ultimately ineffective. The use of domestic courts for resolution of international disputes is therefore usually inappropriate. However, there is a new breed of court intended for litigation of international commercial disputes.

28.13.2 International commercial courts

International commercial courts originated in the Special Economic Zones (**SEZ**) in the Gulf, before expanding to Asia and Europe. They are 'domestic courts rooted in the legal system of their home jurisdictions, but specially created and tailored in terms of structure

124 www.gov.uk/courts-tribunals/technology-and-construction-court (accessed 28 January 2021).

125 www.supremecourt.vic.gov.au/sites/default/files/assets/2017/09/c7/1ce0ae424/tec%2Blist%2Bbackground%2Bpaper.pdf (accessed 28 January 2021).

126 Singapore Supreme Court, *Shaping the Future of Justice, Annual Report 2016,* 44.

127 Chief Justice Sundaresh Menon, 'The Rule of Law and the SICC' (2018) *Singapore International Chamber of Commerce Distinguished Speaker Series* 6, www.sicc.gov.sg/docs/default-source/modules-document/news-and-article/b_58692c78-fc83-48e0-8da9-258928974ffc.pdf (accessed 27 January 2021).

and personnel to meet the needs of transnational commercial disputes.'[128] Institutionally and procedurally inspired by the Commercial Court of England and Wales, many of their judges are English or from other common law jurisdictions, and the law applied is predominantly common law. Notwithstanding their domestic bailiwick, their international profile comes from their case load, judges, bar, and rules. There are three broad types of international commercial court: SEZ, stand-alone courts, and international chambers within ordinary courts.[129]

28.13.2.1 SEZ courts

The SEZ courts are set up in the Special Economic Zones. The judges are mostly drawn from England and Wales, as well as other leading common law jurisdictions. The SEZ courts apply SEZ law as the default applicable law; however, the parties may agree on the law that shall apply to the dispute. The courts comprise:

- Dubai International Financial Centre (**DIFC**) Courts, established in 2004[130]
- Qatar International Court and Dispute Resolution Centre (**QIDRC**) established in 2009[131]
- Abu Dhabi Global Market (**ADGM**) Courts established in 2013[132]
- Astana International Financial Centre (**AIFC**) Court (Kazakhstan) established in 2015[133]

28.13.2.2 Stand-alone courts

The stand-alone courts establish a new jurisdiction for 'international commercial' cases. They have a domestic bench as well as international judges (SICC) or an international expert committee (CICC). These courts apply domestic law; however, the parties may agree on the law that shall apply to the dispute. The courts comprise:

- Singapore International Commercial Court (**SICC**) established in 2015 as a division of the High Court of Singapore[134]
- China International Commercial Court (**CICC**) established in 2018 by the Supreme People's Court of China[135]

28.13.2.3 International chambers within ordinary courts

The international chambers within ordinary courts have been set up to internationalise the domestic judiciary with a view to attracting cross-border cases. Their domestic judges have a good command of the English language. As with the stand-alone courts these courts apply

128 V K Rajah, 'W(h)ither Adversarial Commercial Dispute Resolution' (2017) 33 *Arbitration International* 17, 26.

129 Georgios Dimitropoulos, 'Litigation in the International Commercial Courts' *IBA Webinar* 18 November 2020.

130 www.difccourts.ae (accessed 27 January 2021).

131 www.qicdrc.gov.qa (accessed 27 January 2021).

132 www.adgm.com/adgm-courts (accessed 27 January 2021).

133 https://court.aifc.kz (accessed 27 January 2021).

134 www.sicc.gov.sg (accessed 27 January 2021).

135 http://cicc.court.gov.cn/html/1/219/index.html (accessed 27 January 2021).

domestic law, however the parties may agree on the law that shall apply to the dispute. They comprise:

- Chamber of International Commercial Disputes at the *Landgericht* Frankfurt am Main in the State of Hesse established in 2018[136]
- International Chambers at the Paris Commercial Court and the Paris Court of Appeal established in 2018[137]
- Netherlands Commercial Court (**NCC**) established in 2019[138]

28.13.2.4 Commercial Court of the High Court of England and Wales

The Commercial Court of the High Court of England and Wales was established in 1895 and has always had an international jurisdiction and focus. Since 2010 over 50% of its cases have involved only foreign parties, and more than 80% have involved at least one non-UK party.[139] However, it is not a truly international court as previously defined: it 'is meant to be and is an English court, with English judges, with English procedure, requiring English counsel, in London.'[140]

28.13.2.5 Singapore International Commercial Court

The SICC was the first stand-alone international commercial court and 'adds to and augments Singapore's position as a dispute resolution hub alongside the SIAC by providing a niche international commercial court whose services can be tapped on by businesses.'[141] The following features distinguish it from a domestic Singapore court:

- The cases SICC was envisaged to hear include cases where parties have agreed to have their disputes resolved either by *ad hoc* agreement or a choice of court clause in their contract.
- The judges are drawn from a pool comprising the judges of the Singapore Supreme Court and international judges from Australia, Canada, France, Hong Kong, Japan, the UK, and USA, that is both civil law and common law.
- Parties are able to be represented by lawyers of their choice who are not required to be permitted to represent parties before Singapore's domestic courts.
- The SICC uses simplified processes that enhance the efficiency of resolving transnational commercial disputes, based on best practices in other commercial courts and in international commercial arbitration.

---

136 https://ordentliche-gerichtsbarkeit.hessen.de/ordentliche-gerichte/lgb-frankfurt-am-main/lg-frankfurt-am-main/chamber-international (accessed 27 January 2021).

137 www.tribunal-de-commerce-de-paris.fr/en/home (accessed 27 January 2021).

138 www.rechtspraak.nl/English/NCC/Pages/default.aspx (accessed 3 August 2021).

139 https://acica.org.au/wp-content/uploads/2016/02/ACICA_Rules_2016_Booklet.pdf (accessed 26 January 2021) 26.

140 Lucy Reed, 'International Dispute Resolution Courts: Retreat or Advance – 10th John E.C. Brierley Memorial Lecture' (2017–2018) 4 *McGill Journal of Dispute Resolution* 129, 138, https://mjdr.openum.ca/files/sites/154/2018/09/Reed_PDF-1.pdf (accessed 28 January 2021).

141 Chief Justice Sundaresh Menon, 'The Rule of Law and the SICC' (2018) *Singapore International Chamber of Commerce Distinguished Speaker Series* 6 https://www.sicc.gov.sg/docs/default-source/modules-document/news-and-article/b_58692c78-fc83-48e0-8da9-258928974ffc.pdf (accessed 27 January 2021) 12.

- The SICC is a division of the Singapore High Court. Hence, SICC judgements enjoy the benefit of existing enforcement arrangements which Singapore has with other jurisdictions, including Australia, Hong Kong, India, the UK, and almost all member states of the European Union.
- The judge presiding over each case filed in the SICC will be appointed by the Chief Justice, and not by the parties to the dispute. Furthermore, none of the SICC judges currently practice as lawyers.[142]

28.13.2.6 Enforcement of international court judgements

Perhaps the greatest barrier to more widespread use of international commercial courts is the perception of the difficulties of enforcing a court judgement in another jurisdiction. There is, as yet no equivalent to the *New York Convention* for court judgements.

The Hague Conference on Private International Law was established to work for the progressive unification of the rules of private international law. In 2021 it has 86 member states plus the European Union.[143] It has produced the *Hague Convention of 30 June 2005 on Choice of Court Agreements* (***Hague Convention***),[144] aimed at ensuring the effectiveness of choice of court agreements (also known as 'forum selection clauses'). The *Hague Convention* entered into force on 1 October 2015. In January 2021 it had 32 contracting parties, including the 26 members of the European Union, the UK, Mexico, and Singapore. China and the USA have signed the *Convention* but are not yet contracting states.[145] The *Hague Convention* may potentially place court judgements on a much more even footing with arbitral awards even in relation to enforcement.[146]

Example: Enforcement under the Hague Convention

The *Hague Convention* defines an exclusive choice of court agreement in Article 3 a) as:

> an agreement concluded by two or more parties that meets the requirements of paragraph c) [writing or accessible information] and designates, for the purpose of deciding disputes which have arisen or may arise in connection with a particular legal relationship, the courts of one Contracting State or one or more specific courts of one Contracting State to the exclusion of the jurisdiction of any other courts;

The operative provisions are in Articles 5 and 6:

142 www.resolution.institute/documents/item/1844 (accessed 26 January 2021) 13–14.

143 www.hcch.net/en/states/hcch-members (accessed 28 January 2021).

144 www.hcch.net/en/instruments/conventions/full-text/?cid=98 (accessed 28 January 2021).

145 www.hcch.net/en/instruments/conventions/status-table/?cid=98 (accessed 28 January 2021).

146 Chief Justice Sundaresh Menon, 'The Rule of Law and the SICC' (2018) *Singapore International Chamber of Commerce Distinguished Speaker Series* 6 https://www.sicc.gov.sg/docs/default-source/modules-document/news-and-article/b_58692c78-fc83-48e0-8da9-258928974ffc.pdf (accessed 27 January 2021) 18.

Article 5 Jurisdiction of the chosen court

(1) The court or courts of a Contracting State designated in an exclusive choice of court agreement shall have jurisdiction to decide a dispute to which the agreement applies, unless the agreement is null and void under the law of that State.
(2) A court that has jurisdiction under paragraph 1 shall not decline to exercise jurisdiction on the ground that the dispute should be decided in a court of another State.
(3) The preceding paragraphs shall not affect rules -

a) on jurisdiction related to subject matter or to the value of the claim;
b) on the internal allocation of jurisdiction among the courts of a Contracting State. However, where the chosen court has discretion as to whether to transfer a case, due consideration should be given to the choice of the parties.

Article 6 Obligations of a court not chosen

A court of a Contracting State other than that of the chosen court shall suspend or dismiss proceedings to which an exclusive choice of court agreement applies unless -

a) the agreement is null and void under the law of the State of the chosen court;
b) a party lacked the capacity to conclude the agreement under the law of the State of the court seised;
c) giving effect to the agreement would lead to a manifest injustice or would be manifestly contrary to the public policy of the State of the court seised;
d) for exceptional reasons beyond the control of the parties, the agreement cannot reasonably be performed; or
e) the chosen court has decided not to hear the case.

28.13.2.7 Enforcement of SICC judgements

Chief Justice Menon suggests that cross border enforcement of SICC judgements may not cause intractable difficulties for the following reasons.

(a) Parties may comply voluntarily with the judgement of the SICC, as they generally do with other court judgements and arbitral awards.
(b) A court judgement creates a debt (also known as a money judgement), which may be sued upon in any other common law jurisdiction, and which can then be enforced in a straightforward summary manner. Also, in many civil law jurisdictions, including China and Japan.
(c) Singapore has a number of reciprocal enforcement agreements with other countries.
(d) The *Hague Convention on Choice of Court Agreements* may change the landscape for the cross-border enforcement of court judgements.
(e) The availability of enforcement options ultimately turns on their availability in key financial and commercial centres. A judgement of a Singapore court

is likely to be summarily enforceable in any common law jurisdiction, throughout the EU and Mexico, in Malaysia, Brunei, India, Pakistan, Sri Lanka, Hong Kong, the UK, Australia, New Zealand, PNG, and the Windward Islands pursuant to reciprocal agreements, in many ASEAN jurisdictions, China and Japan on the basis of reciprocity, and in a number of Middle East jurisdictions.[147]

28.13.3 Advantages and disadvantages of litigation

The advantages of litigation over ADR include:

- Judges are experts on the law.
- Plaintiffs can join a number of parties to ensure that all issues in dispute are heard at the one time, even if they relate to different contracts.
- A litigant dissatisfied with the judge's decision at first instance can generally appeal to a higher court.
- The costs of a judge and the court are generally significantly less than that of an arbitral tribunal.
- The judge may be a specialist with experience in hearing construction cases, for example, the TCC in England.
- Courts may apply modern technology and case management techniques to minimise the time and cost of litigation, for example, Victorian Supreme Court Practice Notes.[148]
- Judgements are public documents available to articulate and explain the law.
- Judgements (at least in the common law world) provide binding precedents that will be followed in subsequent court cases with similar facts.

The disadvantages of litigation include:

- The substantial time often required to complete the interlocutory processes, prepare for trial, and obtain a hearing date.
- The considerable time required for and substantial cost of discovery (disclosure) of all relevant documents (which in a large construction case can number in the hundreds of thousands).
- The parties have no choice in the judge assigned to hear the case.
- Even in specialist lists, the judge may not have sufficient familiarity with the technical aspects of design and construction work.
- High legal costs of court hearings because of the formality of the procedures, and the need for experts to assist the judge in understanding technical issues.
- The possibility of appeals from the decision of a judge at first instance, adding significant time and cost before a final resolution is achieved.

---

147 Chief Justice Sundaresh Menon, 'The Rule of Law and the SICC' (2018) *Singapore International Chamber of Commerce Distinguished Speaker Series* 6 https://www.sicc.gov.sg/docs/default-source/modules-document/news-and-article/b_58692c78-fc83-48e0-8da9-258928974ffc.pdf (accessed 27 January 2021) 17–18.

148 www.supremecourt.vic.gov.au/law-and-practice/specialist-lists-of-the-court/technology-engineering-and-construction-list (accessed 28 January 2021).

28.14 Comparison of alternative dispute resolution methods

Table 28.3 Comparison of different methods of dispute resolution

	Engineer's determination	Negotiation	Senior Executive negotiation	Mediation	Conciliation	DRB	Early neutral evaluation	Mini trial	Statutory adjudication	Non-binding expert determination (Expert appraisal)	Contractual adjudication	DAB	Binding expert determination	Arbitration	Litigation
Basis	Contract[149]	Agreement[150]	Agreement	Agreement	Agreement	Contract	Agreement	Agreement	Legislation (*SoP Act*)	Agreement	Agreement	Contract	Agreement	Agreement / legislation (*Arbitration Act*)	Legal rights (*Rules of Court*)
Resolver/ Assessor	Engineer	Parties	Senior Executives of the parties	Parties, facilitated by independent, impartial Mediator	Parties, with the assistance of independent, impartial Conciliator	Independent, impartial Board (3 or 1)	Independent, impartial neutral	Independent, impartial 'judge'	Independent, impartial Adjudicator	Independent, impartial Expert	Independent, impartial Adjudicator	Independent, impartial Board (3 or 1)	Independent, impartial Adjudicator/ Expert	Independent, impartial Arbitrator	Independent, impartial judge
Role of independent person	Give a ruling on the parties' rights under the Contract	-	-	Facilitate the parties' negotiations to settle their dispute on mutually acceptable terms	Encourage the parties to settle their dispute on mutually acceptable terms	Make an advisory determination of the parties' rights under the Contract	Make an advisory determination of the parties' rights under the Contract	Make an advisory determination of the parties' rights under the Contract	Make a provisionally binding determination of the parties' rights in accordance with the legislation	Make an advisory determination of the parties' rights under the Contract	Make a provisionally binding determination of the parties' rights under the Contract	Make a provisionally binding determination of the parties' rights under the Contract	Make a provisionally binding determination of the parties' rights under the Contract	Make a binding determination of the parties' rights under the Contract	Make a binding determination of the parties' rights under the Contract
Independent person's control over the DR process	Flexible	-	-	Flexible	Flexible	Flexible, as provided for in the Contract	Flexible, as provided for in the agreement	Flexible, as provided for in the agreement/ Contract	Flexible, but limited by the short timeframe available to complete the determination	Flexible, as provided for in the agreement	Flexible, but limited by the short timeframe available to complete the determination	Flexible, as provided for in the Contract	Adjudicator/ Expert is free to make enquiries/ conduct proceedings in any manner thought fit, subject to the Contract	Arbitrator is free to make enquiries/conduct proceedings in any manner thought fit, subject to the Arbitration Agreement and the *Act*	Judge is constrained by the parties' pleadings and *Rules of Court*
Party control over the DR process	Limited	Flexible	Flexible	Flexible	Flexible	Flexible, as provided for in the Contract	Flexible, as provided for in the agreement	Flexible	None	Flexible	Flexible, within the Procedural Rules in the agreement	Flexible, as provided for in the Contract	Flexible, as provided for in the agreement	Flexible, as provided for in the agreement	Limited

149 Contract refers to the construction contract.
150 Agreement refers to an agreement in the Contract or a separate agreement.

	Engineer's determination	Negotiation	Senior Executive negotiation	Mediation	Conciliation	DRB	Early neutral evaluation	Mini trial	Statutory adjudication	Non-binding expert determination (Expert appraisal)	Contractual adjudication	DAB	Binding expert determination	Arbitration	Litigation
Party selection of independent person	Selected by Employer	-	-	√	√	In a three-person board, each party nominates one member, and these two jointly appoint the third	√	√	Selected by authorised nominating body, or by party agreement, depending on the applicable legislation	√	√	In a three-person board, each party nominates one member, and these two jointly appoint the third	√	√	X
Private/ Confidential	√	√	√	√	√	√	√	√	Yes, unless the Adjudicator's determination is challenged in court	√	√	√	√	√	X
Finality of DR process (enforceability)	No, unless provided for in the Contract	No, however, binding settlement agreement can be drawn up and executed	No, however, binding settlement agreement can be drawn up and executed	No, however, binding settlement agreement can be drawn up and executed	No, however, binding settlement agreement can be drawn up and executed	DRB determination may be binding under the Contract, if the parties accept it	No, however, binding settlement agreement can be drawn up and executed	No, however, binding settlement agreement can be drawn up and executed	Determination is binding unless overturned for jurisdictional reasons or underlying dispute is finally determined by the DR process defined in the Contract	No, however, binding settlement agreement can be drawn up and executed	Adjudicator's determination is binding unless underlying dispute is finally determined by the DR process defined in the Contract	DAB determination is binding unless underlying dispute is finally determined by the DR process defined in the Contract	Expert's determination is binding unless it 'ousts the jurisdiction of the court'	Yes, subject to very limited grounds to overturn award or refuse enforcement.	Judgement is binding unless overturned by a Court of Appeal
Outcome	Determination of defined issue only – 'win/lose'	Flexible – parties are not confined to contractual rights: 'win/ win' possible, but there is no certainty of any outcome	Flexible – parties are not confined to contractual rights: 'win/ win' possible, but there is no certainty of any outcome	Flexible – parties are not confined to contractual rights: 'win/ win' possible, but there is no certainty of any outcome	Flexible – parties are not confined to contractual rights: 'win/ win' possible, but there is no certainty of any outcome	Expert opinion on contractual issues defined by the parties/ perceived by the Board	Expert opinion on legal outcome of the dispute – can be used in negotiations to achieve a noncontractual outcome	Expert opinion on likely legal outcome of dispute	Provisional determination of legal rights (England) or which party is to 'hold the money' – 'win/lose'	Expert opinion on issues defined by the parties – can be used in negotiations to achieve a noncontractual outcome, but there is no certainty of any outcome	Provisional determination of legal outcome of dispute – 'win/ lose'	Provisional determination of legal outcome of dispute – 'win/ lose'	Binding determination of legal outcome of dispute/issues defined by the parties – 'win/ lose'	Determination of legal outcome of dispute – 'win/ lose'	Determination of legal outcome of dispute – 'win/lose'
Time for DR process	As defined in the Contract	Short	Short	Short	Short	Short	Short	Short	Very short, but claim preparation time may be significant	Usually short, but depends on complexity of the issues	Usually short, but depends on complexity of the issues	Medium	Usually short, but depends on complexity of the issues	Long, but can be shortened by appropriate procedures, eg 'chess clock'	Long, but can be shortened by judicial case management

(Continued)

Table 28.3 (Continued)

	Engineer's determination	**Negotiation**	**Senior Executive negotiation**	**Mediation**	**Conciliation**	**DRB**	**Early neutral evaluation**	**Mini trial**	**Statutory adjudication**	**Non-binding expert determination (Expert appraisal)**	**Contractual adjudication**	**DAB**	**Binding expert determination**	**Arbitration**	**Litigation**
Cost	Low	Low	Low	Modest	Modest	Medium	Modest	Modest	Modest	Medium	Medium	Medium	Medium	High, but can be reduced by procedures	High, but can be shortened by judicial case management
Use/ acceptance	Extensively used in the past, less common now	Widely used/ accepted	Widely used/ accepted	Widely used/ accepted	Not as widely used as mediation	Extensively used in the USA for over 20 years, limited use to elsewhere	Limited use	Limited use	Widely used	Limited use	Limited use	Standard feature in FIDIC International contracts since 1999	Widely used	Widely used	Widely accepted, but often avoided because of concerns over time and cost
Hearing	Not normally	N/A	N/A	Informal	Informal	Yes, sufficient for all issues to be properly ventilated	Yes, of limited time and scope	Yes, of limited time and scope	Not normally	Not unless required by the Expert or agreed by the parties	If required by the Adjudicator or agreed by the parties	Yes, sufficient for all issues to be properly ventilated	Not unless required by the Expert or agreed by the parties	Yes, but may be limited in time in 'chess clock' arbitration	Yes
Natural Justice	No	N/A	N/A	N/A	N/A	Yes	Yes?	Yes?	Yes?	Yes	Yes	Yes	Yes	Yes	Yes
Procedures	In accordance with the Contract	N/A	N/A	At the discretion of the Mediator	At the discretion of the Conciliator	At the discretion of the DRB, subject to any Procedural Rules agreed by the parties	At the discretion of the neutral subject to any Procedural Rules agreed by the parties	At the discretion of the panel subject to any Procedural Rules agreed by the parties	At the discretion of the Adjudicator subject to any requirements of the relevant *Act*	At the discretion of the Expert, subject to any Procedural Rules agreed by the parties	At the discretion of the Adjudicator subject to any Procedural Rules agreed by the parties	At the discretion of the DAB, subject to any Procedural Rules agreed by the parties	At the discretion of the Expert, subject to any Procedural Rules agreed by the parties	At the discretion of the Arbitrator, subject to any requirements of the relevant *Act* and the Procedural Rules agreed by the parties	In accordance with the relevant *Rules of Court* and Practice Notes

CHAPTER 29

The impact of ICT on construction contracts

CONTENTS

DOI: 10.4324/9781003206873-29

29.1 Introduction

29.1.1 Low productivity in the construction industry

The construction industry in every country is essential to producing the infrastructure required for affordable, sustainable, healthy, peaceful, and happy lifestyles for as many people as possible in the modern world, and for achieving the United Nations' Sustainable Development Goals (**SDGs**).[1] There is an infrastructure deficit in many if not most developed and developing nations that will require increasing investment over the coming years. Notwithstanding the improvements in productivity in other industries such as manufacturing, there has been little change in productivity of construction sites in recent years. For example, data from the US Census Bureau shows that in the 45-year period from 1967 to 2012 the productivity of manufacturing industries more than doubled, whilst the productivity of on-site construction was essentially unchanged. The productivity of off-site construction in that same period improved by approximately 50%.[2] McKinsey notes that the worldwide construction sector productivity has only increased 1% over the last 20 years, although there are significant differences between countries.[3] The World Economic Forum noted a similarly abysmal productivity record and a reluctance to adopt new approaches:

> While most other industries have undergone tremendous changes over the past few decades, and have reaped the benefits of process, product and service innovations, the construction sector has been hesitant to fully embrace the latest innovation opportunities and its labour productivity has stagnated or even decreased over the past 50 years. This mediocre track record can be attributed to various internal and external challenges: the persistent fragmentation of the industry; inadequate collaboration between the players; the sector's difficulty in adopting and adapting to new technologies; the difficulties in recruiting a talented and future-ready workforce; and insufficient knowledge transfer from project to project, to name a few.[4]

1 The SDGs are the United Nations' framework for continuing development priorities such as poverty eradication, health, education and food security and nutrition, and a wide range of economic, social, and environmental objectives such as climate control and green energy for sustainable buildings. United Nations, 'Resolution adopted by the General Assembly on 25 September 2015' 6, https://documents-dds-ny.un.org/doc/UNDOC/GEN/N15/291/89/PDF/N1529189.pdf?OpenElement (accessed 25 March 2021).

2 R Sacks, C Eastman, G Lee & P Teicholz, *BIM Handbook: A Guide to Building Information Modeling for Owners, Designers, Engineers, Contractors, and Facility Managers* (John Wiley & Sons, 3rd edn 2018) 10.

3 McKinsey Global Institute, 'Reinventing Construction: A Route to Higher Productivity' (February 2017) 2, 3, www.mckinsey.com/~/media/McKinsey/Business%20Functions/Operations/Our%20Insights/Reinventing%20construction%20through%20a%20productivity%20revolution/MGI-Reinventing-construction-A-route-to-higher-productivity-Full-report.pdf (accessed 31 March 2021).

4 World Economic Forum & the Boston Consulting Group, 'Shaping the Future of Construction Inspiring innovators redefine the industry' (February 2017) 3, http://www3.weforum.org/docs/WEF_Shaping_the_Future_

Productivity improvement in the construction industry will require the embrace of modern technology:

> The industry has vast potential, however, for improving productivity and efficiency thanks to digitalization, innovative technologies and new construction techniques. Consider the rapid emergence of augmented reality, drones, 3D scanning and printing, Building Information Modelling (BIM), autonomous equipment and advanced building materials – all of them have now reached market maturity. By adopting and exploiting these innovations, companies will boost productivity, streamline their project management and procedures, and enhance quality and safety. To capture all this potential will require a committed and concerted effort by the industry across many aspects, from technology, operations and strategy to personnel and regulation.[5]

29.1.2 Requirements for increasing productivity

A 2017 McKinsey report noted that action in the following seven areas could boost construction productivity by 50–60%:

- Reshape regulation and raise transparency, for example, streamlining permitting and approvals processes, reducing corruption, and encouraging transparency on cost and performance.
- Rewire contracts by moving away from an adversarial environment to a more collaborative approach.
- Rethink design and engineering processes by greater use of value engineering, improved emphasis on constructability, and greater use of repeatable design elements.
- Improve procurement and supply chains, for example, by just in time processes that integrate procurement, logistics, delivery, and storage.
- Improve onsite execution, for example, the more rigorous use of planning, improvements in human safety, reduction of construction waste, and improvements in efficiency in building processes such as the use of prefabricated modular construction.
- Infuse technology and innovation, for example, by the use of 3D BIM, digital collaboration tools, drones and unmanned aerial vehicles for scanning, monitoring, and mapping.
- Reskill the workforce, for example, by the use of augmented reality/virtual reality in online learning systems.[6]

---

of_Construction_Inspiring_Innovators_redefine_the_industry_2017.pdf (accessed 25 March 2021).

5 World Economic Forum & the Boston Consulting Group, 'Shaping the Future of Construction A Breakthrough in Mindset and Technology' (2016), http://www3.weforum.org/docs/WEF_Shaping_the_Future_of_Construction_full_report__.pdf (accessed 21 March 2021).

6 McKinsey Global Institute, 'Reinventing Construction: A Route to Higher Productivity' (February 2017), www.mckinsey.com/~/media/McKinsey/Business%20Functions/Operations/Our%20Insights/Reinventing%20construction%20through%20a%20productivity%20revolution/MGI-Reinventing-construction-A-route-to-higher-productivity-Full-report.pdf (accessed 31 March 2021).

The use of appropriate information and computer technology (**ICT**) will be essential in each of these areas. The technologies are not disparate and may apply in different applications, like a complex orchestra of required instruments being used to create value for each of the situations.

29.1.3 Information and communication technology

The hardware and software that make up modern information and communication technology comprises both the underlying enabling technology, as well as the applications based on the use of the enabling technology. Without the applications that provide commercial solutions to real world problems, the technology itself is no more than a set of impressive and sophisticated technical achievements.

The application of information and computer technology is having an ever-greater influence on every aspect of our private and working lives (for good or ill). The infinite variety of music and other entertainment readily available at modest cost is on the plus side of the ledger, whilst screen addiction resulting in the loss of personal interactions is on the debit side. The unavoidable and rapid transition to remote working in many occupations due to the COVID-19 pandemic highlighted the extent to which appropriate ICT applications are already available and mature enough to provide for new ways of working.

ICT is typically applied in either enhancement applications, or disruptive applications. **Enhancement applications** enable new and more efficient ways of undertaking traditional tasks, for example, computer assisted discovery of documents required to be disclosed in litigation. **Disruptive applications** enable capabilities to do things that were not previously possible, for example, the use of building information modelling (**BIM**) to aggregate all of the information on design, construction, and operation requirements for a building in one electronic model. The impact of enhancement applications will be referred to as the **efficiency impact**, whilst the impact of disruptive applications is a paradigm shift. An efficiency impact will undoubtedly result in time and cost savings, often of significant magnitude. Implementation may require new tools and training but can generally be accommodated within existing organisational structures. However, its efficacy may be short lived as it may be superseded by a paradigm shift.

On the other hand, a paradigm shift will generally require completely new methods of working that may not be readily accommodated within traditional organisational structures. One striking well-known example of a paradigm shift is the way in which online 'free' applications such as Google and Facebook have decimated traditional media advertising. Diamandis and Kotler have observed that the ever-increasing rate of disruptive technology today is a consequence of formerly independent waves of exponentially accelerating technology beginning to converge with other independent waves of exponentially accelerating technology.[7] They expressed the pervasive impact of disruptive technology as follows:

7 Peter H Diamandis & Steven Kotler, *The Future is Faster Than You Think* (Simon & Shuster Inc New York, 2020) 8.

> When a new innovation creates a new market and washes away an existing one, we use the term 'disruptive innovation' to describe it. When silicon chips replaced vacuum tubes at the beginning of the digital age, this was a disruptive innovation. Yet, as exponential technologies converge, their potential for disruption increases in scale. Solitary exponentials disrupt products, services, and markets – like when Netflix ate Blockbuster for lunch – while convergent exponentials washed away products, services and markets, as well as the structures that support them.[8]

The following section briefly discusses some of the important enabling technologies that make the ICT applications possible and functional for the construction industry. This is followed by some current examples of known ICT applications relevant to construction projects that can achieve efficiency impacts or paradigm shifts in the operation of construction contracts, the execution of construction projects and the resolution of construction disputes.

The nature of future disruptive applications, by definition, is unpredictable and may well replace many of the current enhancement applications. As the scope of ICT applications is vast and evolving and expanding at an ever-increasing rate, the following can be no more than a small sample of ICT applications the authors are aware of that are relevant to construction contracts at one point in time.[9] In the construction industry disruptive technology may change not only cost and time, but also effort (man hours), safety, accountability, insight, and even aesthetics.

29.1.4 The security of ICT

All these technologies have an Achilles heel that needs to be addressed and managed – security of the data that is the lifeblood of ICT.

The ability of organisations to collect, store, process and retrieve data is now essential to their functioning and continued existence. However, IT failures occur in every country, to large and small companies, and in government, non-profit, and commercial organisations. Those failures may arise from internal issues, but the greatest threat is from external sources.

Data breaches are now common and widespread. Data may be stolen for malicious purposes or made publicly available because an organization inadvertently left data unprotected and exposed. Computers infected with ransomware can be made inaccessible to a company until it pays a large ransom (often in Bitcoin). In 2017 delivery company FedEx stated that a recent cyber attack cost its TNT division about US$300 million when its computer systems were severely disrupted by the NotPetya ransomware.[10] In a recent list of data breaches, 15 hacks were reported that exposed user details from 143 million to 3 billion accounts, including username and hashed password pairs, email addresses, dates of birth, and credit card details.[11]

---

8 Ibid, 9.

9 Reference to particular services or products in the following sections does not imply any endorsement by the authors of their efficacy or applicability. They are identified only to serve as concrete examples of currently available technology. Potential users would need to make their own assessment as to whether any service or product was appropriate for their circumstances.

10 www.bbc.com/news/technology-41336086 (accessed 29 July 2021).

11 www.csoonline.com/article/2130877/the-biggest-data-breaches-of-the-21st-century.html (accessed 30 March 2021).

Because data is essential to the running of any business, loss of data or the inability to access data due to inadequate cybersecurity is now an existential threat to organisations, large or small. The seriousness of this issue is highlighted by the following 2019 data:

> New research shows that data breaches are a huge factor in business failures. This is hardly surprising, because there were around 30 major data breaches in 2017 alone.
>
> The consequences of data breaches are severe for small businesses. One study found that 60% of all companies that suffer a data breach are forced into bankruptcy within six months. Despite the frightening lesson that they should learn from this, many small businesses are still reluctant to take their cybersecurity seriously. They believe that the probability that their company will be targeted by a cyberattack is too low to worry about.
>
> The sad reality is that around 20% of all companies will suffer a cybersecurity breach in the next year. This figure might actually start to increase as hackers become more brazen and invest more resources targeting small businesses.[12]

Construction companies maintain extensive data on contracts and subcontracts, payment transactions, intellectual property, construction records, personnel, clients, business development, and so on that has substantial monetary value, and this data needs to be airtight and secure. External and internal data and system perimeters need to be hardened and continually monitored to deal with constantly evolving threats.

The security of valuable commercial data used to be assured by keeping the physical records under lock and key in secure monitored premises. The security aspect of ICT is now critical to the entire ecosystem. There is no substitute for a well-resourced and expert IT department in medium and large enterprises. For smaller organisations that cannot support an IT department, cybersecurity should be an essential element in assessing the suitability of their external IT support.

29.2 Barriers to adoption of ICT in the construction industry

The characteristics of the construction industry are such that there are a number of significant barriers to the adoption of ICT that can significantly improve productivity and the bottom line for Contractors and Employers. These barriers include the following.[13]

Construction is a very competitive, high-risk industry worldwide, yet operates on very low margins: McKinsey states that the construction industry has bottom-quartile profit margins, with an average profit margin of only 4.4% over sales.[14] Given the commercial pressures to maintain profitable projects, the implementation of new technologies is a distraction to running the business. Companies have little capacity or appetite to invest in expensive technologies that may require years to show significant returns.

12 www.business2community.com/cybersecurity/1-in-8-businesses-are-destroyed-by-data-breaches-dont-be-a-statistic-02162471 (accessed 29 July 2021).

13 Rob Horne, 'Construction Risk Management – Technology to Manage Risk (ConTech)' in Charles O'Neill, *Global Construction Success* (Wiley Blackwell, 2019) 205, 209–210.

14 McKinsey Global Institute, 'Reinventing Construction: A Route to Higher Productivity' (February 2017) 10 www.mckinsey.com/~/media/McKinsey/Business%20Functions/Operations/Our%20Insights/Reinventing%20construction%20through%20a%20productivity%20revolution/MGI-Reinventing-construction-A-route-to-higher-productivity-Full-report.pdf (accessed 31 March 2021).

There is a view that ICT does not provide commercial solutions appropriate to construction which is heavily reliant on human interactions and the generation of trust. The technology may be perceived to be unproven and unreliable, and unsuitable to integrate with existing processes. New technology will inevitably require changes to traditional ways of working, and this is problematic in a conservative industry that has historically changed slowly and incrementally.

Some of the design and contract management technologies involve sharing of data with others in the contractual chain, and an automation of functions that are currently carried out by people. Contractors may be reluctant to lose some aspects of their traditional commercial control over the supply chain.

In a paper looking at potential economic opportunities from greater adoption of connectivity in four industries, McKinsey identified the following longstanding hurdles that echo the barriers to the adoption of ICT in the construction industry just outlined:

- Value chain coordination – players that rarely collaborate today may need to act in concert and resolve issues such as varying technical standards.
- Use case fragmentation – the value potential is fragmented across hundreds of use cases and different domains without a single source of significant demand. Applications have limited value unless they can be scaled over time and geography.
- Misaligned incentives – the players that assume the cost and risk of investment may not be the ones who capture the resulting value.
- Data complexities – cross-industry standards to ensure data privacy, security, ownership, and systems interoperability are still evolving.
- Deployment constraints – constraints such as physical roll out barriers, regulatory uncertainties, and long investment cycles may slow down adoption.[15]

Overcoming these barriers will require a willingness to rethink traditional methods of working, detailed investigation of the risks and benefits of suitable technology, and an acceptance of greater collaboration than the construction industry is used to.

29.3 Enabling technologies

29.3.1 Recent advances

The development and increasing use of the Internet has led to the creation of powerful new tools and increased ease-of-use to Internet users. Recent advances in ICT capabilities have been:

- Speed – dial-up connectivity to wired broadband to wireless.
- Portability and mobility – mainframe computers to desktop PCs to laptop PCs to network to smartphone/tablet.
- Storage – Megabytes to gigabytes to terabytes.

15 McKinsey Global Institute, 'Connected World: An Evolution in Connectivity Beyond the 5G Revolution' (February 2020) 8, www.mckinsey.com/~/media/McKinsey/Industries/Technology%20Media%20and%20Telecommunications/Telecommunications/Our%20Insights/Connected%20world%20An%20evolution%20in%20connectivity%20beyond%20the%205G%20revolution/MGI_Connected-World_Executive-summary_February-2020.pdf (accessed 31 March 2021).

- Communications – costly telephony to free (almost) telephony.
- Digitised currency – Reliance on paper money to reliance on money in electronic form.[16]
- Software availability from individual copies to software as a service provided by 'cloud' computing.
- Order of magnitude reductions in the costs of data communications.

29.3.2 Data

It has been observed that we are in the early stages of the fourth industrial revolution – the digital revolution characterized by a fusion of technologies that is blurring the lines between the physical, digital, and biological spheres. The first two industrial revolutions were founded on the application of energy to mechanise and create mass production, whilst the third industrial revolution used electronics and information technology to automate production.[17] The fourth industrial revolution is founded on data – the collection, storage, processing, and retrieval to extract information that can be applied to solve existing problems more efficiently and effectively, to solve problems that were previously intractable, and to solve problems that haven't even been formulated yet.

The possibilities of the scale and capacity of data storage are illustrated by Google, a company only founded in 1998, but now one of the largest technology companies in the world. In 2018, just one of its data centres in Oregon contained 225,000 computer servers jammed together to reduce speed of light delays, interlinked with fibre optic lines. The data centre is accessible to a fibre optic artery linking Asia to the United States with a bandwidth of 8.4 trillion bits per second. This combination of big data and vast computing power in the cloud is unprecedented in the history of computing: 'These machines gain control of their environment by excelling all others in the speed and density of their computations and transactions, and in the size of their data stores.'[18] Google's capacity to store and process data enables it to provide web services such as maps (Google Maps), videos (YouTube), scheduling (Google Calendar), documents (Google Docs), transactions (Google Checkout), translations (Google Translate), email (Gmail), and productivity software (Writely).[19]

Construction projects generate large quantities of data at all stages: in the contract documents that require detailed data to define the legal obligations and the technical requirements of the scope, time, cost, and quality of the work; in recording the progress and quality of the work, and in the extensive communications required to administer the contracts, make claims and payments and to articulate parties' submissions in the resolution of disputes. Such data can come from a wide variety of sources, including computers, tablets, phones, cameras, equipment, and sensors. Data needs to be reliable, accessible, usable, and secure. There are myriad applications now available to process this data to

16 Ethan Katsh, 'ODR: A Look at History' 30, www.mediate.com/pdf/katsh.pdf (accessed 25 February 2021).

17 World Economic Forum, 'The Fourth Industrial Revolution: What it Means, How to Respond' (January 2016), www.weforum.org/agenda/2016/01/the-fourth-industrial-revolution-what-it-means-and-how-to-respond/ (accessed 26 March 2021).

18 George Gilder, *Life After Google* (Regenery Gateway, 2018) 53.

19 Ibid, 58.

enable the necessary information to be extracted and presented in readily accessible ways that are suitable for the required functions.

The worldwide accessibility of the Internet, free applications and fast communication has made data storage in the cloud feasible and economical, through the use of vast data centres, such as the Google one previously described. However, the current model suffers from some serious deficiencies, chief among them being a lack of trust. Many writers believe blockchain technology will overcome these deficiencies, including George Gilder:

> As a global copying machine, the Internet founders in establishing origins, facts, truths, timestamps, and ground states. Beyond the slippery slopes of the Internet, the blockchain can provide an immutable database on which to build new structures of trust.[20]

Blockchain technology is discussed further in ¶29.3.5.

The **cloud** is one of the enabling technologies for data storage that makes universal access to data from anywhere in the world possible and affordable. In the words of one writer: 'The 'cloud,' then, is an artful name for the great new heavy industry of our times: gargantuan data centres composed of immense systems of data storage and processes, linked together by millions of miles of fibre-optic lines and consuming electrical power and radiating heat to an extent that excels most industrial enterprises in history.'[21] The cloud is available commercially from a number of very large corporations, such as Amazon, Google, and Microsoft. Data security laws applying in some countries, such as the European *General Data Protection Regulation*, may place constraints on which countries the cloud servers can be located in.

Cloud storage is now a USD46 billion dollar industry.[22] However, it is concentrated amongst a small number of providers – Amazon, Google, Microsoft, and Alibaba control about 70% of the cloud computing market, and Amazon alone controls 45%. 'If for some reason their services are interrupted, every government, company and user relying on them may fail to operate as intended. In some cases, mission-critical infrastructure would fail without access to these cloud services.' Such vulnerability is promoting different approaches to file storage based on blockchain, such as filecoin – a decentralised storage and distribution network that aims to compete with the cloud storage industry by providing an efficient and robust marketplace for data storage needs.[23]

29.3.3 Connectivity

The invention of writing (and money) enabled the connectivity and communication between large numbers of people essential for the first large scale societies over five thousand years ago. The connectivity today that is essential to modern life is enabled by worldwide high-quality audio and visual personal communications at very low cost. Connectivity is fundamental to the high-speed communications between users and devices and between devices and devices. In this context the term devices includes computers, tablets, mobile

20 Ibid, 210.
21 Ibid, 21.
22 www.alliedmarketresearch.com/cloud-storage-market (accessed 21 May 2021).
23 https://grayscale.com/wp-content/uploads/sites/3/2021/05/grayscale-building-blocks-filecoin-march-2021.pdf (accessed 21 May 2021).

phones, servers, sensors, and so on. The much-hyped Internet of Things envisages that any physical devices will be capable of connecting to the Internet.

Connectivity today is enabled by vast networks of fixed high bandwidth fibre-optic cables, and a range of technologies that use various parts of the electromagnetic spectrum such as 5G mobile telephony, wi-fi, low power wide area networks, and Bluetooth. Future technologies such as constellations of low earth orbit satellites and high band 5G hold the promise of global coverage, high speed, and highly secure cellular connectivity.[24]

The universal connectivity to the Internet brings with it some serious problems, including theft of information, malware that can cripple an organisation's ability to function, ransom demands to unblock hacked networks, identity theft, and fraud. As noted in ¶29.1.4, cybersecurity will be increasingly important in the years ahead, to ensure that connectivity of devices and things to any network is secure and reliable.

29.3.4 AI and machine learning

The term 'artificial intelligence' refers to enabling computers to perform tasks that resemble human thinking ability. It is widely used (and hyped) in connection with the current and future impacts of disruptive technology. Of the many possible definitions of this term, the following is used for the purposes of this book:

> **Artificial intelligence** (**AI**) is the capability of devices or mechanisms and machinery to perform functions usually associated with human intelligence, including scientific systems, reasoning, optimization through experience, and automated motor systems.[25]

Two other terms that are related to AI are machine learning and deep learning. Machine learning is generally regarded as a subset of AI. A useful definition is:

> The essential elements of **machine learning** are an automated approach to learning patterns from empirical data using training examples, usually large databases, with the development of a machine learning algorithm which when applied to new examples creates accurate predictions.[26]

Deep learning is a cutting-edge subset of machine learning involving more complex layers of data processing using algorithms that are inspired by the human brain that works in a hierarchical way.[27] The 'machines' used in machine learning and deep learning may include computers, smartphones, software, industrial equipment, robots, vehicles, and so on.[28]

---

24 McKinsey Global Institute, 'Connected World: An Evolution in Connectivity Beyond the 5G REVOLUTION' (February 2020) 2, www.mckinsey.com/~/media/McKinsey/Industries/Technology%20Media%20and%20Telecommunications/Telecommunications/Our%20Insights/Connected%20world%20An%20evolution%20in%20connectivity%20beyond%20the%205G%20revolution/MGI_Connected-World_Executive-summary_February-2020.pdf (accessed 31 March 2021).

25 H James Birx, *Encyclopedia of Anthology* (Sage Publications California, 2006) 281.

26 Joachim P Sturmberg & Carmel Martin, *Handbook of Systems and Complexity in Health* (Springer, 2013) 455.

27 Chirag Shah, *A Hands On Introduction to Data Science* (*Cambridge* University Press, 2020); Erik R Ranschaert, Sergey Morozov & Paul R Algra (eds), *Artificial Intelligence in Medical Imaging: Opportunities, Applications and Risks* (Springer, 2020) 353.

28 Bernard Marr, *Tech Trends in Practice: The 25 Technologies that are Driving the 4th Industrial Revolution* (Wiley, 2020) 4.

These concepts are important enablers of the fourth Industrial Revolution. They are the technologies behind the recent advances in the Internet of Things (**IoT**), virtual reality, chatbots, facial recognition, robots, automation, and self-driving cars.[29] However, at this stage, these applications are only as good as the data used to train them, and all sorts of bias can be introduced in the scope of the data and any algorithms involved. One should be wary of blindly accepting the outputs without understanding the underlying reasoning. The issues involved in designing appropriate AI are the subject of research by 'philosophers, computer scientists, political scientists, lawyers and sociologists, working together to develop democratically and culturally legitimate machine intelligence' at the Australian National University. Their four areas of research in designing democratic AI are: personalisation, automating governance, algorithmic ethics and human-AI interaction.[30]

The dark side of the relentless focus of applying mathematics to many fields of human endeavour was highlighted in a book written by Cathy O'Neil, a mathematician who had previously worked as a 'quant' at a Wall Street hedge fund and as a data scientist. She warned of the consequences of the reliance on mathematics and statistics in the Big Data economy in the following terms:

> The math-powered applications powering the data economy are based on choices made by fallible human beings. Some of these choices were no doubt made with the best intentions. Nevertheless, many of these models encoded human prejudice, misunderstanding, and bias in the software systems that increasingly managed our lives. Like gods, these mathematical models were opaque, their workings invisible to all but the highest priest in the domain: mathematicians and computer scientists. Their verdicts, even when wrong or harmful, were beyond dispute or appeal. And they tended to punish the poor and the oppressed in our society, while making the rich richer.[31]

The consequences of insufficient human input in autonomous ICT applications was recently brought into sharp focus in Australia by the AU$1.8 billion settlement of a class action against the Commonwealth of Australia over its use of an automated debt collection system over a four- year period. The system, colloquially known as the Robodebt system, attempted to identify overpayments of social security benefits at particular points of time through automatic data matching. This was conducted by using income information of social security recipients and comparing the notional or assumed fortnightly income with the actual fortnightly income provided to the government department. The Commonwealth then determined whether the person had been overpaid social security benefits and where that occurred it sought to recover the asserted debt. The evidence in the case revealed that the Commonwealth unlawfully asserted such debts, totalling at least AU$1.763 billion against approximately 433,000 Australians.[32]

The champions of AI postulate that within the foreseeable future the capabilities of AI will supersede human intelligence by extremely fast logic machines processing unlimited data, that will make redundant the jobs of many professionals, including some lawyers.

29 Ibid, 4.
30 https://hmi.anu.edu.au (accessed 29 July 2021).
31 Cathy O'Neil, *Weapons of Math Destruction* (Penguin Random House, 2016) 3.
32 *Prygodicz v Commonwealth of Australia (No 2)* [2021] FCA 364.

Author and futurist Ray Kurzweil has predicted that artificial intelligence will pass a valid Turing test[33] and therefore be considered to have achieved human levels of intelligence as soon as 2029.[34]

Some thought leaders such as Elon Musk and Stephen Hawking have warned of the existential dangers to humanity if AI ever supersedes human intelligence – which it would do very quickly if AI even reaches the level of general human intelligence. This danger is receiving serious attention. In a book written by Professor Nick Bostrom, Professor of Philosophy at Oxford University (and a physics and mathematics background) the threats from the possible achievement of AI greater than human intelligence are carefully articulated, and practical suggestions made as to how such threats can be mitigated.[35] Others are more sanguine, not accepting that the human mind functions by executing algorithms that can be emulated by faster and more powerful networked computers iteratively processing enormous amounts of data.[36]

Notwithstanding the advances in speech recognition and language translation based on AI, there are still significant limitations in current natural language processing. Systems struggle to understand language and speech above the sentence level, and with semantics and idiom.[37]

Whatever the future capabilities of AI, it is undoubtedly having an impact in today's society, and more specifically in the construction industry, enabling both enhancement technology and disruptive technology. There is ample scope to deploy current AI capabilities in many aspects of construction to improve the industry's poor record of productivity and low financial returns (without any existential threats to humanity). The examples of current ICT applications in the construction industry in ¶29.5 include those where AI is one of the enabling technologies.

29.3.5 Blockchain

Blockchain is arguably the most important advance in connectivity since the introduction of the Internet. Whilst blockchain is often conflated with cryptocurrencies, it is a distinct concept. Blockchain was the enabling technology for the first cryptocurrency, Bitcoin, and has since been applied not only to other cryptocurrencies but also to many other applications where trust is a necessary requirement in a transaction.

The foundational elements for blockchain were published in 2008 for a new 'trustless'[38] networked currency comprising:

---

33 The Turing test is a way to judge or otherwise an attempt to produce a thinking computer. It is based on the idea that if a person who interrogated a computer could not tell if it was a human or computer, then to all intents and purposes according to Turing, it is intelligent. Ben Coppin, *Artificial Intelligence Illuminated* (Jones & Bartlett Sudbury MA, 2004) 8.

34 Ray Kurzweil, *The Singularity is Near: When Humans Transcend Biology* (Penguin Books, 2006).

35 Nick Bostrom, *Superintelligence: Paths, Dangers, Strategies* (Oxford University Press, 2016).

36 For example, see George Gilder, *Life After Google* (Regenery Gateway, 2018) 72–73.

37 Toby Walsh, *Android Dreams: The Past, Present and Future of Artificial Intelligence* (Latrobe University Press Australia, 2017) 79.

38 Casey and Vigna object to 'some cryptocurrency fanatics' describing blockchain technology as 'trustless,' preferring to describe it as 'a tool upon which society can create the common stories it needs to sow even greater trust, to build social capital, and to forge a better world.' Michael J Casey & Paul Vigna, *The Truth Machine The Blockchain and the Future of Everything* (St Martin's Press, 2018) 34.

- A distributed ledger – a database with many copies that update themselves automatically
- A method of achieving consensus between the majority of networked computers to govern changes in the ledger
- A cryptographically secure currency
- 'Mining' incentives to encourage people to invest the computer time necessary to manage the currency
- 'Blocks' of transactions describing when people trade the currency, strung together in what's called a 'Merkle Tree' to form an immutable record, a 'blockchain.'[39]

One definition of a general **blockchain** is: a distributed ledger that uses a particular mechanism to ensure the integrity of the database, specifically block transactions with some form of mathematical proof of integrity of the transaction (such as proof of work).[40] A blockchain provides a distributed programming platform with good security: it creates trust in a trustless environment, the data is immutable, and large amounts of computing power are available.

The distributed ledger in a blockchain replaces trust in a single entity with trust in a peer-to-peer network where each of the copies talk to each other and automatically update themselves. A record of every transaction is available to everyone on the network, a record that can't be altered. A Merkle tree is the mathematical method of establishing an immutable history of transactions by linking a series of equations in a treelike structure in which the result of the first equation forms the input to the second equation and so on. The data in a group of transactions forming a block is input into a mathematical equation whose output is used as input to the next block, linking the blocks together in a Merkle tree, a blockchain. Thus, any change to the data in one block will change the input to the next block.

Horne has suggested three practical applications of blockchain for a construction project: a payment system based on shared data that releases funds very quickly; auditability of project decision making where everyone can see what has happened in close to real time; and using common data to reduce the need for separate commercial processes through the supply chain.[41]

29.3.5.1 Ethereum

The benefits of using blockchain in connection with construction projects are much broader than the use of cryptocurrencies. One widely used blockchain that has a range of potential applications in industry and commerce generally is called **Ethereum**, created in 2014. Whilst it has many of the same characteristics as the Bitcoin blockchain such as a cryptocurrency (called Ether, symbol **ETH**), mining and blocks, its value is in the ability to carry out computations in small computer programs in what are called smart contracts:

> Ethereum is software running on a network of computers that ensures that data and small computer programs called smart contracts are replicated and processed on all the computers on

39 David L Shirer, *Basic Blockchain* (Robinson Great Britain, 2020) 17.

40 Ibid, 136.

41 Rob Horne, 'Construction Risk Management – Technology to Manage Risk (ConTech)' in Charles O'Neill (ed), *Global Construction Success* (Wiley Blackwell, 2019) 234.

> the network, without a central coordinator. The vision is to create an unstoppable censorship-resistant self-sustaining decentralised world computer.[42]

For Ethereum to function as a decentralised world computer, it needs to calculate, store data, and communicate without relying on a central server:

- The calculations for smart contract code are run by the Ethereum Virtual Machine on all networked computers.
- The files of data are split into blocks, distributed and stored by participating nodes by a peer-to-peer protocol called Swarm. These nodes are compensated for storing and retrieving the data by ETH.
- An encrypted messaging protocol (Whisper) allows nodes to send messages directly to each other in a secure way that hides the identity of the sender and receiver from third parties.[43]

In the context of blockchains and cryptocurrencies, a **smart contract** comprises prewritten logic (computer code) stored and replicated on a blockchain, executed by a network of computers that can result in updates to the distributed ledger. The verification by many computers ensures distributed trustworthy calculations.[44] Once deployed, the coding in a smart contract is immutable. Notwithstanding the name, a smart contract is neither smart (as it encodes an algorithm that executes a strict set of rules), nor is it a legal contract.

Ethereum exists as a public permissionless version of the network accessible over the Internet. However, the publicly available Ethereum software can be slightly modified to create a private network that isn't connected to the main public network, ensuring that the tokens and smart contracts are private. In the authors' view, it is likely to be in the area of private blockchain networks that the majority of uses in the construction industry will be developed.

29.3.6 Virtual reality and augmented reality

Virtual reality forms the basis of modern computer games: powerful digital processing creates sophisticated animated images and sound that may be difficult to distinguish from the real world. **Virtual reality** can be defined as a digital animated representation of the physical world, displayed on specialised equipment in sufficient detail to be perceived as realistic. It typically involves the use of specialised equipment such as specialised headsets connected to a virtual reality program. **Augmented reality** is the use of virtual reality overlaid on top of an image of the real (physical) world.

29.4 Digital policies

Governments are responsible for the procurement of major infrastructure and for the management of extensive portfolios of operating facilities and assets. Recognising the efficiency dividends achievable with properly planned ICT policies, many governments

42 https://bitsonblocks.net/2016/10/02/gentle-introduction-ethereum/ (accessed 7 April 2021).
43 Ibid.
44 https://bitsonblocks.net/2016/02/01/gentle-introduction-smart-contracts/ (accessed 7 April 2021).

have implemented policies and strategies to reap the promised benefits of digitization. One such example is the Victorian digital asset strategy.

The Government of Victoria's digital asset strategy aims to create a 'Virtual Victoria' – a digital twin that supports integrated planning and the development of smart cities. Virtual Victoria will enable location, condition, and performance of infrastructure assets to be known digitally and in real time so that those assets can be used more productively. This strategy focuses on a whole of life philosophy and innovative approaches such as digital engineering which aims to create an efficient flow of information over the life-cycle of an asset by managing data in a systematic way. It is based on a common data environment (**CDE**) that aligns digital information systems, including drafting, geospatial information systems (**GIS**), building information modelling (BIM), electronic document management systems, project controls (time, costs, risks, etc), asset data, and other related systems.[45]

29.5 ICT applications for the operation of construction contracts

Construction contracts and projects involve a large volume of interconnected documents that can be overwhelming. The processes for a construction contract are complex and time consuming, and their management and communication currently require intense human capital. There are many contractual interfaces that need to be managed. There is frequently a disconnect between what a contract says and how it is administered. The contract is often 'put in the bottom drawer' and not consulted to determine the specific contractual requirements for the particular project, the contract administrator relying on past experience of administering contracts for similar projects.

There are already a number of ICT applications available to promote timely communications and assist contract administrators to administer a construction contract in accordance with its terms. The number and types of such applications will inevitably grow substantially over the coming decades. The following is a small sample of ICT applications currently used at the front end of construction projects.

29.5.1 BIM

Building information modelling (BIM) is a modelling technology and associated set of processes to produce, communicate, and analyse building models.[46] BIM processes emphasise information sharing and the breaking down of information silos between various professions and project stages.[47] BIM's significance has been summed up as follows:

> We believe that BIM represents a paradigm change that will have far-reaching impacts and benefits, not only for those in the construction industry but for society at large, as better buildings are built that consume fewer materials and require less labor and capital resources and that operate more efficiently.[48]

45 Government of Victoria, 'Victorian Digital Asset Strategy' www.opv.vic.gov.au/Victorian-Chief-Engineer/Victorian-Digital-Asset-Strategy (accessed 25 March 2021).

46 R Sacks, C Eastman, G Lee & P Teicholz, *BIM handbook: A Guide to Building Information Modeling for Owners, Designers, Engineers, Contractors, and Facility Managers* (John Wiley & Sons, 3rd edn 2018) 14.

47 'Australian BIM Strategic Framework' www.abab.net.au/wp-content/uploads/2020/01/ABAB_Australian_BIM_Strategic_Framework_Feb_2019.pdf (accessed 25 March 2021).

48 R Sacks, C Eastman, G Lee & P Teicholz, *BIM Handbook: A Guide to Building Information Modeling for Owners, Designers, Engineers, Contractors, and Facility Managers* (John Wiley & Sons, 3rd edn 2018) xxii.

Sacks et al identify the following three important characteristics of BIM:

- Building components that are represented with digital representations (objects) that carry computable graphic and data attributes that identify them to software applications, as well as parametric rules that allow them to be manipulated in an intelligent fashion.
- Components that include data that describe how they behave, as needed for analyses and work processes, such as quantity takeoff, specification, and energy analysis.
- Consistent and nonredundant data such that changes to component data are represented in all views of the component and the assemblies of which it is a part.[49]

There are various levels of sophistication and hence functionality of BIM. The UK Government BIM Task Group adopted the following concept of BIM Levels:

- Level 0 BIM – unmanaged computer aided drawing (CAD), typically two dimensional (2D) with information shared by traditional paper drawings.
- Level 1 BIM – a mixture of three-dimensional (3D) CAD for concept work, and 2D for construction documentation. Electronic sharing of data is carried out from a common data environment (CDE), and models are not shared between project team members.
- Level 2 BIM – collaborative working in which all parties use their own 3D models, but not working on a single shared model. Design information is shared through a common file format which enables any user to combine that data with their own to make a federated BIM model.
- Level 3 BIM – 'open BIM.' Full collaboration between all disciplines by using a single shared project model that is held in a centralized repository – normally an object database in cloud storage.[50]

Levels 0–2 BIM result in efficiency impacts in the traditional way of procuring construction projects, whilst Level 3 BIM represents a paradigm shift. Fully implemented Level 3 BIM can provide the following benefits.[51]

Preconstruction benefits to the Employer

- Concept, feasibility, and design benefits, for example, determining whether a building meets the required financial hurdles.
- Increased building performance and quality – evaluation of design alternatives using analysis/simulation tools on a schematic model prior to generating a detailed building model.
- Improved collaboration using integrated project delivery (IPD) for project procurement – BIM can be used by the project team from the beginning of design to improve understanding of project requirements and to extract cost estimates.

49 Ibid, 14.

50 TMD Studio, 'What is BIM and Why Do You Need It?' https://medium.com/studiotmd/what-is-bim-and-why-do-you-need-it-c4445eed7941 (accessed 24 March 2021).

51 R Sacks, C Eastman, G Lee & P Teicholz, *BIM Handbook: A Guide to Building Information Modeling for Owners, Designers, Engineers, Contractors, and Facility Managers* (John Wiley & Sons Hoboken, 3rd edn 2018) 21–25.

Benefits for design

- Earlier and more accurate visualisations of design – the 3D model generated by the BIM software will be dimensionally consistent in every view.
- Automatic low-level corrections when changes are made to the design – where desired objects are controlled by parametric rules, the 3D model will be free of geometry, alignment, and spatial coordination errors.
- Generation of accurate and consistent 2D drawings at any stage of the design.
- Earlier collaboration of multiple design disciplines – BIM technology facilitates simultaneous work by multiple design disciplines.
- Easy verification of consistency to the design intent, either quantitatively or qualitatively.
- Extraction of cost estimates during the design stage – an accurate bill of quantities and spaces can be extracted at any stage and used for cost estimation.
- Improvement of energy efficiency and sustainability, by linking the building model to energy analysis tools to allow evaluation of energy use during the early design phase.

Construction and fabrication benefits

- Use of design model as the basis for fabricated components, by transferring the design model to a BIM fabrication tool to program numerical control machinery.
- Quick reaction to design changes – a suggested design change can be entered into the building model to determine the consequences and evaluate the projected cost.
- Discovery of design errors and omissions before construction – conflicts and constructability problems can be identified before they are detected in the field.
- Synchronisation of design and construction planning – by linking a construction plan to the 3D objects in a design it is possible to simulate the construction process and show what the building and site would look like at any point in time.
- Better implementation of lean construction techniques – the accurate BIM model of the design and material resources required provides the basis for improved planning and scheduling of subcontractors.
- Synchronisation of procurement with design and construction – the quantities, specifications, and properties in the BIM model can be used to procure materials from product vendors and subcontractors.

Post construction benefits

- Improved commissioning and handover of facility information.
- Better management and operation of facilities.
- Integration with facility operation and management systems.

These benefits are theoretically available with today's technology, however, there are many legal and other hurdles to overcome before they can be fully achieved. The biggest hurdle arises from the fragmented nature of the construction industry – designers, contractors, subcontractors, and suppliers are separate organisations with their own legal rights to protect. Design involves a variety of different disciplines, such as architecture, foundation engineering, structural engineering, mechanical engineering, electrical engineering, and so on, and there are many challenges in these professionals collaborating in a team.

Many subcontractors are very small organisations with limited resources or incentive to invest in BIM technology. Profit margins for contractors are low, limiting their ability and willingness to invest in technology that will take years to recover their investment. There may be significant security concerns over the BIM model falling into the hands of a bad actor. There may also be legal challenges to documentation ownership and production, and who is responsible for their accuracy. Other obstacles to the rapid take up of BIM include lack of client understanding, engagement, and demand, cost of implementation, resistance to change, and disruption to the status quo, lack of digital planning and uneven skills and capability.[52]

These and other challenges indicate that the current adversarial forms of construction contract are not well-suited to open BIM. More collaborative forms of contract, such as an alliance contract, for example, as used for procurement of Heathrow Terminal 5, would be more appropriate to enable collaboration without the costly contractual silos inherent in traditional adversarial contracts.

29.5.2 Intelligent contracts

The term **intelligent contract** will be used to mean a contract in an electronic form that has processing capabilities built into it that can receive or output information relating to contractual functions and/or autonomously carry out contractual functions. This term is used in preference to the commonly used 'smart contract' to avoid confusion with the Ethereum concept previously discussed. Intelligent contracts have been envisaged as a way to harness the enabling technologies discussed to improve productivity in the construction industry: processing of large data, connectivity, blockchain, AI, and machine learning.

One such application is based on what is referred to as intelligent document format (**IDF**). IDF is used for understanding and management of complex documents such as contracts, regulations, standards, and manuals that typically involve a large number of interrelated documents that can change over time. The users of this technology have Internet access to a single up-to-date version of the documents that can be searched and navigated via interlinked clauses and pop-up definitions. Documents can be annotated and interrogated to extract all contractual obligations and entitlements and export them to a spreadsheet. It is designed for collaborative working, and for providing a traceable history of amendments.[53]

The use of IDF is an established enhancement application that applies modern ICT to achieve new efficiencies and promote collaboration using existing documentation for established forms of contract. Other proposals for intelligent contracts are disruptive applications that will require new ways of working and new paradigms.

A number of writers have proposed the use of blockchain to address the problem of delayed payments and insolvencies in the construction industry. One such proposal is for a payment system based on intelligent contracts and administered by an independent third party. This proposal is for the head contractor to maintain control of the bulk of the project funds as they are earned but paid to subcontractors automatically by an intelligent

52 'Australian BIM Strategic Framework' www.abab.net.au/wp-content/uploads/2020/01/ABAB_Australian_BIM_Strategic_Framework_Feb_2019.pdf (accessed 25 March 2021).

53 https://assets.digitalmarketplace.service.gov.uk/g-cloud-12/documents/92196/592944090436974-service-definition-document-2020-10-06-1244.pdf (accessed 8 April 2021).

contract once certain predefined conditions are met. Payment claims would be adjusted based on an objective measure of the believability of the claimant and the respondent; the believability to be determined from the history of previous projects and associated with an individual identifier stored in the blockchain. The author of this proposal postulates that it would result in increased trust and collaboration, improved efficiency, and auditability of the payment process.[54] There are a number of legal and practical issues that would need to be resolved to implement this proposal, not the least of which would be the willingness of contractors to surrender their power of the purse to an intelligent contract.

Other writers have more ambitious aims for intelligent contracts, one suggesting that an intelligent contract could create an all-encompassing contract process that ensures all parties adhere to the terms agreed, provides protection of payment, insurance, and data as well as the potential to increase efficiency and reduce risk.[55] In a Master's thesis, McNamara posits that the adversarial relationships and lack of trust inherent in the construction industry could be addressed by making contracts trustless, using blockchain and BIM as the source of the data to be used by an intelligent contract. He acknowledges that the adoption of intelligent contracts will have many significant challenges, including their unalterable nature, confidentiality, software reliability and compatibility issues, and a perceived lack of control and/or surrender to an automated third-party. Perhaps the biggest challenge at this point would be the limitations of natural word processing to extract sophisticated enough algorithms to handle unexpected issues such as *force majeure* and other circumstances where a human certifier is normally required.[56]

29.5.3 Document management

There are a number of software applications currently used to manage documents for a construction project, for example, Aconex, Procore, Teambinder, and Open Windows. These cloud-based applications are designed to manage the types of issues that occur on every project: business workflow, document storage, document production, contract access, email management, reporting, and payment processing.

Document management applications typically enable all participants in a project to have controlled access to a single information database from any device with Internet access. Coordination is promoted by use of a single source of truth from a centralized database. Distribution of documents such as design information for review or requests for information is simplified and transparent, with automatic production of transmittals. The time to prepare Variation requests with appropriate supporting documentation is reduced. Relevant up-to-date information is available on site, and can be instantly updated with, for example, photographs taken in the field. The results of site inspections or punchlists can be updated in real time and available immediately in the head office. Progress information

54 Angus Faulkner, 'Security of Payment – Can the Blockchain Help us Avoid Another Carillion?' Paper delivered at the Society of Construction Law Conference, Hunter Valley August 2018.

55 Alan McNamara, 'Automating the Chaos: Intelligent Construction Contracts' in Infotech Open (ed), *Smart Cities and Construction Technologies* (2020), www.intechopen.com/books/smart-cities-and-construction-technologies/automating-the-chaos-intelligent-construction-contracts (accessed 24 March 2021).

56 Alan McNamara, 'Is the First Step to Implementing Intelligent Contracts in the Construction Industry through BIM Integration?' (23 November 2017) *Thesis for MSc in International Construction Law at the University of the West of England, Bristol* 32.

is available to support invoicing and payments. The production of up-to-date operation and maintenance manuals based on as- built information is simplified. An audit trail of all communications is maintained, simplifying disclosure of documents if required in resolving disputes.

Other specialised types of software such as Revu enable rapid design reviews by allowing all members of a design and construction team to mark up and collaborate on the same documents in real time or at any time, integrating with many document management systems.[57]

29.5.4 Data management

The amount of data generated or used by any business is increasing at an exponential rate. It comes from many sources and systems, and it is a major challenge to extract information from such disparate sources of data in a readily understood form. There are many applications written to provide a user-friendly interface so that timely data is processed into relevant information and made available to those who need it. For example, the Teradata Corporation provides the Vantage platform, built for a hybrid multi-cloud reality to solve complex data challenges at scale.[58]

Another widely used application is provided by Tableau. The Tableau platform is designed to connect to virtually any data source and provide interactive visual analytics of the data. It can be used in-house, on-line in a public cloud, or accessible via mobile devices.[59] Such an application can be very valuable in providing senior executives with a tailored interface that provides up-to-the-minute access to key information in a readily digestible form. It can also have applications in a dispute resolution process by presenting information derived from large data sets in a readily understood visual format.

29.5.5 Contract administration

A construction contract for a large project involves a number of documents with detailed 'legal' and 'technical' requirements that must be construed as a whole. There are usually prescriptive processes for the submission of requests for payment, variations, claims, and disputes, often time barred for late submission. Administering such a contract is complex and requires access to large volumes of contractual and factual information, an ideal candidate for the application of ICT. The Onetrack software to be released in 2022 is an enhancement application for contract administration with the following functionality, as outlined by the developer, Phillip Greenham, a construction lawyer with many years of experience.

OneTrack is a workflow management tool designed to assist in the management of construction contracts and similar contracts with complex and varied administrative processes. In contrast to tools which manage business workflows, Onetrack guides the user through the contractual processes in the underlying contract. It collects all of the

57 www.bluebeam.com (accessed 24 March 2021).
58 www.teradata.com/Solutions (accessed 27 April 2021).
59 www.tableau.com/products (accessed 27 April 2021).

data necessary for the contractual provisions to produce an outcome. It then applies the contractual rules and makes a recommendation to the contract administrator as to the contractually appropriate outcome. The software does not impose the contractual outcome on the parties. The judgement, flexibility, and decision making which is a critical part of effective contract management is reserved to the contract administrator. However, the use of OneTrack will ensure that this judgement, flexibility, and decision making is made with full knowledge of the formal contractual outcome, is visible, recorded, auditable, and the reasons for it known. The output produced by OneTrack, in circumstances where this judgement, flexibility, and decision making have been deployed will preserve the integrity of the contract for future application and prevent confusion arising between the parties as to the status and relevance of the contractual rules in the future.

In addition to guiding the contract administrator through the contractual workflows, OneTrack will make available to the contract administrator those provisions of the contract relevant to the circumstances under consideration and provide explanation and narrative to assist the contract administrator in understanding the relevant provisions and making the decisions necessary to support the successful completion of the project.

The knowledge of, and management of critical time frames is a key aspect of the support which OneTrack offers. Through the use of a configurable traffic light system, the contract administrator will always be aware of the administrative tasks which are outstanding and the time remaining for the completion of those tasks. This information will assist senior managers from identifying any bottlenecks in the administration of contracts for which they are responsible. The visibility of these bottlenecks will assist in making decisions as to resource allocation, training, and recruitment.

It is anticipated that the timely, consistent and contractually compliant decisions which result from the use of OneTrack will reduce the number of formal disputes which arise in relation to a project. The ability of OneTrack to efficiently provide all the data relevant to any dispute that does occur will assist in the more efficient and timely resolution of any formal disputes which do arise. The uncertainty surrounding the outcome of such disputes will also be reduced.

It is expected that the combination of the ability to better manage administrative resources and the beneficial impact on formal disputes from the use of Onetrack will result in a reduction in costs associated with contract administration and dispute resolution.

29.6 ICT applications for the execution of construction projects

The challenge of on-site construction is encapsulated in the following:

> Inconsistency, inaccuracy, and uncertainty in design make it difficult to fabricate materials off-site. As a result, most fabrication and construction must take place on-site and only after exact conditions are established. On-site construction work is costlier, more time-consuming, and prone to produce errors that would not occur if the work were performed in a factory environment where productivity is higher, work is safer, and quality control is better.[60]

60 Sacks, R., Eastman, C., M., Lee, G., & Teicholz, P., M, *BIM Handbook: A Guide to Building Information Modeling for Owners, Designers, Engineers, Contractors, and Facility Managers* (John Wiley & Sons Hoboken, 3rd ed.2018) 5.

As noted in ¶29.1.1, significant improvements in on-site productivity will need to draw on ICT applications. The opportunities and challenges of implementation have been summed up by the World Economic Forum:

> The industry has vast potential, however, for improving productivity and efficiency thanks to digitalization, innovative technologies and new construction techniques. Consider the rapid emergence of augmented reality, drones, 3D scanning and printing, Building Information Modelling (BIM), autonomous equipment and advanced building materials – all of them have now reached market maturity. By adopting and exploiting these innovations, companies will boost productivity, streamline their project management and procedures, and enhance quality and safety. To capture all this potential will require a committed and concerted effort by the industry across many aspects, from technology, operations and strategy to personnel and regulation.[61]

The World Economic Forum outlined an industry transformation framework to achieve this potential. This framework is articulated for company level, sector level and government actors. Significantly, under best practices, both front-loaded and cost-conscious design and project planning and innovative contracting models with balanced risk-sharing are identified as driving enhanced productivity.[62]

McKinsey has suggested the following five ways to transform productivity and project delivery through new technologies and improved practices:

- Higher-definition surveying and geolocation,
- Next-generation 5-D building information modelling,
- Digital collaboration and mobility,
- The Internet of Things and advanced analytics, and
- Future-proof design and construction.[63]

Higher definition surveying and geolocation can be achieved by the integration of high-definition photography, 3-D laser scanning, and geospatial information systems (GIS). A robotic total station enables surveying to be carried out by one person.[64] Light detection and ranging (**lidar**) provides high-quality 3-D images that can be used in conjunction with drones, ground penetrating radar, and magnetometers to generate above ground and below ground images of a project site. The use of high-quality survey with GIS allows maps, images, distance measurements, and GPS positions to be overlaid.[65] Better quality site data can assist in minimising the later discovery of latent conditions and provide more accurate design information.

61 World Economic Forum, 'Shaping the Future of Construction A Breakthrough in Mindset and Technology' (May 2016) 3, http://www3.weforum.org/docs/WEF_Shaping_the_Future_of_Construction_full_report__.pdf (accessed 27 April 2021).

62 Ibid, 9.

63 McKinsey Productivity Sciences Center Singapore, 'Imagining Construction's Digital Future' (June 2016), www.mckinsey.com/~/media/McKinsey/Business%20Functions/Operations/Our%20Insights/Imagining%20constructions%20digital%20future/Imagining-constructions-digital-future.pdf?shouldIndex=false (accessed 31 March 2021).

64 https://bim360resources.autodesk.com/connect-construct/what-is-a-robotic-total-station-heres-everything-you-need-to-know (accessed 29 July 2021).

65 Ibid 4, 5.

The **Internet of Things** (IoT) is the combination of sensor and wireless technologies that connects physical objects to the Internet so that data can be accessed from anywhere. Objects such as construction machinery, equipment, materials, structures, or clothing have sensors attached that transmit critical performance parameters to a central database. One type of sensor is a radio frequency identification (**RFID**) device that uses radio frequency transmission to automatically identify and track objects in a real-time location system (**RTLS**).[66] RTLS is a technology system that provides the current location of a given object or individual, first used commercially in the 1990s by healthcare facilities in the United States. This has applications in construction, for example, control of materials and inventory, tracking tool usage, automatic collision protection of workers and machinery, and automating time sheets. The Leadenhall building in London is an example of the use of the IoT to coordinate the delivery or prefabricated components to a very constricted site by using RFID sensors on the prefabricated components.[67]

Virtual and augmented reality are already being used in the construction industry, particularly at the concept and design stages. There are also many opportunities for the use of this technology during construction, provided the design model is available. For example, the ability to be 'in' a virtual model of the partly constructed facility can assist in training workers for specific tasks or carrying out safety assessments of proposed procedures. As with many of the available (and future) technologies, the greatest benefits will ultimately come from a conjunction of applications, such as the use of a BIM model, advanced surveying techniques and augmented reality.

This brief discussion of the ICT applications in construction is only a small sample of those currently available and in use. Given the rapid pace of technology change in the 21st century, many of the existing applications will evolve and change, and there will no doubt be new applications that are not yet even at the concept stage. The challenge for the construction industry will be to make the required commitment and investment in training, hardware, and software necessary to reap the benefits that ICT promises.

29.7 ICT applications for the resolution of construction disputes

ICT is helping lawyers utilise information in areas of case management,[68] and legal research, in which legal software harnesses the power of artificial intelligence and machine learning to generate query results and assess the research and drafted pleadings to ensure lawyers cite cases correctly and use the most significant relevant cases.[69] Data analytics analyses large amounts of information to glean insights and trends. Legal data analytics

---

66 See eg https://constructionexec.com/article/is-real-time-location-sensing-the-future-of-construction (accessed 29 July 2021); www.highstreetcentre.com.sg/2021/07/17/rfid-enabled-rtls-what-are-the-benefits-of-using-them/#:~:text=The%20basics%20of%20RFID%20RTLS%20RFID%20is%20a,advanced%20RFID%20asset%20tracking%20systems%20or%20security%20protocols (accessed 29 July 2021).

67 Trevor Thomas, 'OK Google, turn on the D9 Dozer: The Use and Potential of the Internet of Things in the Building and Construction Industry' (2018) Paper delivered at the SoCLA conference in the Hunter Valley, August 2018, 18.

68 See eg *Embracing Technology Changes in Your Law Practice*, L. FUEL (July, 13 2018), www.lawfuel.com/blog/embracing-technology-changes-in-your-law-practice/.

69 See eg Lohr, 'A.I. is Doing Legal Work, It Won't Replace Lawyers, Yet' (29 Mar 2017) *NY Times*; Karen Turner, 'Meet "Ross", the Newly Hired Legal Robot' (16 May 2016) *Washington Post*, www.washingtonpost.com/news/innovations/ep/2016/05/16/meet-ross-the-newly-hired-legal-robot/.

software can analyse thousands of court filings and their results to predict case outcomes, allowing improved legal decision-making.[70]

Construction disputes are renowned for their complexity and the time and cost incurred in their resolution. There is considerable scope for the application of ICT to assist in dispute resolution processes to reduce their time and cost. The following examples are a sample of some of the ways in which ICT is being applied to the resolution of disputes.

29.7.1 Discovery

Discovery (also referred to as disclosure) and inspection of relevant documents is a long-established right in common law litigation, and not one that lawyers willingly forgo. Because of the substantial documentation required for the execution of any significant construction project (in the hundreds of thousands or millions for a large project), construction disputes typically involve large numbers of documents. The costs of discovery and inspection may be in the millions of dollars, and the greatest component of the legal costs.

Courts are cognisant of the cost of discovery and the consequent costs of inspection and may tailor orders for discovery to suit the requirements of the particular dispute. For example, the *Civil Procedure Rules 1998* (Eng) provide the court with a choice of six options for disclosure, ranging from no disclosure to full disclosure at the *Peruvian Guano*[71] level: all 'documents which it is reasonable to suppose may contain information which enables that party to advance its own case or to damage that of any other party, or which leads to an enquiry which has either of those consequences.'[72] Similarly, the *Civil Procedure Act 2010* (Vic) provides the court with broad powers to 'make any order or give any directions in relation to discovery that it considers necessary or appropriate,' and lists 11 optional types of orders.[73]

29.7.1.1 Electronic discovery

ICT is a two-edged sword in respect of discovery. Whilst it offers the capability to carry out discovery more effectively, there may be terabytes of documents that are potentially discoverable and may be expensive to locate. The ubiquitous use of mobile phones, emails, and other electronic documents has resulted in an exponential increase in material that needs to be reviewed for potential discovery. A document for the purposes of discovery is typically defined along the lines of 'anything in which information of any description is recorded.'[74] Accordingly, an electronic document is still a document for the purposes of discovery, including emails, text messages, photos, videos, and so on. The search for electronically stored documents and information and organisation of that material for litigation is referred to as **e-discovery** or **e-disclosure**, electronic discovery/disclosure or computer-aided discovery/disclosure.

70 Laura Olsen, 'Data-Driven Decisions: Using Legal Analysis to Up Your Game' (4 Apr 2018) *State Bar of Wisconsin*, www.wisbar.org/newspublications/insidetrack/pages/article.aspx?Volume=10&Issue=6&ArticleID=26261 (accessed 25 February 2021).

71 *Compagnie Financiere et Commerciale du Pacifique v Peruvian Guano Co* (1882) 11 Q.B.D. 55.

72 Rule 31.7.

73 s55.

74 *Civil Procedure Rules 1998* (UK) Rule 31.4.

The majority of discoverable documents in any significant construction dispute are typically now in electronic form, and accordingly e-discovery is not optional. Any (potentially) relevant hard copy documents are therefore normally scanned, (possibly) converted to text format, and added to the database of native electronic documents, all subject to e-discovery. Rules for e-discovery emphasise the need for the parties to confer and attempt to agree to the parameters, before any part of the process is undertaken.[75] The TeCSA/SCL/TECBAR eDisclosure Protocol[76] is useful to record the results of discussion on e-disclosure and is endorsed by UK courts.[77]

In his Preliminary Report on Review of Civil Litigation Costs in the UK, Jackson LJ described the steps in e-disclosure in the context of the *Civil Procedure Rules* (Eng) under the following headings:

(1) Information management – the organization by potential litigants of their electronic information so that relevant categories can be found.
(2) Identification of the documents/information that will have to be searched, and the places that will have to be searched.
(3) Preservation – determination of whether data has to be preserved in the state it was in originally. Metadata changes with every access to data and additional time and expense are required to preserve the original metadata if this is required.
(4) Collection – the process of taking data off the original location and storing it on another computer for processing and retrieval.
(5) Processing the data into a form that is suitable for review.
(6) Review and analysis to cull the documents to only those that are relevant to the issues in dispute.
(7) Disclosure of the information, either electronically or in hard copy.
(8) Presentation of material in court, selected from the disclosed documents, either electronically or in hard copy.[78]

Steps (1) and (2) will generally have to be carried out by the litigant or a person in the litigant's organisation. Step (3) will be determined by the litigant's legal team. Steps (4) and (5) require technical skills and are often carried out by specialist service providers who provide the appropriate software and carry out the basic organisation and coding of documents based on the legal team's requirements. The software may carry out basic tasks such as identifying and removing duplicate documents. Step (6) is the most expensive and time-consuming part of the process. It requires substantial input from the legal team to determine what issues are relevant to the litigation, and a time-consuming review of the documents to cull those that are not relevant and identify those documents that are subject to privilege and will not be disclosed to the other side. Steps (7) and (8) are essentially technical, using the technology set up in steps (4) and (5).

75 Practice Direction 31B – Disclosure of Electronic Documents (UK); Supreme Court of Victoria, 'Practice Note SC Gen 5 Technology in Civil Litigation'; Federal Court of Australia, 'Technology and the Court Practice Note (GPN-TECH)' Part 3; Federal Court of Australia, 'Litigation using Electronic Discovery' www.fedcourt.gov.au/law-and-practice/practice-documents/practice-notes/gpn-tech/electronic-discovery (accessed 26 April 2021).

76 https://tecbar.org/wp-content/uploads/2016/05/2013-eDisclosure-Protocol.pdf (accessed 30 April 2021).

77 *Triumph Controls UK Limited & Ors v Primus International Holding Co & Ors* [2018] EWHC 176 (TCC) [16].

78 The Honourable Rupert Jackson, *Review of Civil Litigation Costs: Preliminary Report* (The Stationary Office UK, 2009) 378.

The scale and some of the challenges and potential pitfalls of e-disclosure are revealed in *Digicel (St Lucia) Ltd v Cable & Wireless.*[79] This case arose from an application for specific disclosure after the defendant had already reviewed 1.1m documents and spend £2m in legal fees and disbursements of £175,000. There had been no prior discussions between the parties on appropriate protocols. The judge ordered the parties to confer and discuss the process for retrieving information from back up tapes. He ordered additional keyword searches but emphasised that the extent of the required reasonable search was subject to considerations of proportionality.

It is therefore apparent that the large number of documents generated by modern ICT has inevitably added a substantial financial burden to 'standard' discovery of relevant documents. Under modern *Civil Procedure Rules* judges tailor their orders for discovery to the exigencies of the specific case, and endeavour to minimise the financial burden to the minimum necessary for the justice of the case. Nevertheless, in a complex construction case 'standard' discovery may still be ordered – discovery of all relevant documents on which the litigant relies, the documents which adversely affect his/her own case, and the documents which adversely affect or support another party's case.[80]

29.7.1.2 Technology assisted review

A recent application of ICT to reduce the time and costs of e-discovery is computer assisted review or **technology assisted review (TAR)** – the application of predictive coding technology to identify relevant documents in a collection of electronic documents. This technique has been endorsed by courts in suitable cases in a number of jurisdictions: USA,[81] Ireland,[82] UK,[83] and Victoria.[84] The technique is far more sophisticated than a keyword search, as it involves the use of AI to 'train' the software to recognise relevant documents from a representative sample. The software analyses the documents in the representative sample for common concepts and language used. Based on that training the software reviews and categorises each document in the complete set as relevant or not. The results of the categorisation are validated by human review based on statistical sampling. The sampling is repeated as much as necessary to achieve the agreed level of accuracy. This process is described in more detail in *Pyrrho Investments Limited.*[85] Many papers are available on technology assisted review.[86]

---

79 [2008] EWHC 2522 (Ch).

80 eg *The Civil Procedure Rules 1998* (UK) s35.6.

81 *Da Silva Moore v Publicis Group* (US District Court – Southern District New York) F.R.D. 182; *Moore v Publicis Groupe*, SA, 2013 WL 4483531, 11 Civ 1279 (ALC)(AJP.

82 *Irish Bank Resolution Corporation Limited v Quinn* [2015] IEHC 175; [2015] 3 JIC 0306.

83 *David Brown v BCA Trading Ltd & Ors* [2016] EWHC 1464 (Ch); *Triumph Controls UK Limited & Ors v Primus International Holding Co & Ors* [2018] EWHC 176 (TCC).

84 *McConnell Dowell Constructors (Aust) Pty Ltd v Santam Ltd & Ors* [2016] VSC 734.

85 *Pyrrho Investments Limited v MWB Property Limited* [2016] EWHC 256 (Ch) [19] – [24].

86 e.g., Elle Byram, 'The Collision of the Courts and Predictive Coding: Defining Best Practices and Guidelines in Predictive Coding for Electronic Discovery' (2013) 29 *Santa Clara Computer & High Tech L.J.* 675; Brandon L. Garrett, 'Big Data and Due Process' (2014) 99 *Cornell L Review Rev. Online* 207; Clive Freedman, 'Technology Assisted Review Approved for use in English High Court Litigation' (2016) 13 *Digital Evidence and Electronic Signature Law Review* 139; Edward Sohn, 'Top Ten Concepts to Understand About Predictive Coding' (2013) *Association of Corporate Counsel*, www.acc.com/resource-library/top-ten-concepts-understand-about-predictive-coding (accessed 4 May 2021).

The reported uses of TAR in litigation indicate that, properly conducted, it is reliable and not only saves considerable time and expense, but also may be more accurate than human review of all documents.[87] Courts have ordered TAR in circumstances where, after de-duplication, in one case 681,000 documents remained to be reviewed,[88] and in another, 1.4m.[89] In one case TAR was projected to cost £132,000 whereas a keyword search was likely to cost £250,000 – £338,000.[90]

The technology is now sufficiently accepted that courts have issued guidelines on the use of TAR in discovery.[91] Indeed, in the US by 2015 in *Rio Tinto PLC v Vale S.A.*[92] Judge Peck of the United States District Court for the Southern District of New York stated:

> In the three years since *Da Silva Moore*, the case law has developed to the point that it is now black letter law that where the producing party wants to utilize TAR for document review, courts will permit it.

29.7.2 Court proceedings

In recent years, courts have been implementing ICT at various stages of proceedings – filing documents in court, electronic court file, e-trials, videoconferencing, and virtual hearings. Some of these ICT applications were implemented before the advent of COVID-19 in 2020, but the pandemic greatly accelerated their take-up. The Federal Court of Australia 'expects parties and their legal representatives to consider and discuss, as early as practicable in the preparation or conduct of the proceeding, how the use of technology, may lead to increased efficiency and cost effectiveness.'[93]

29.7.2.1 Redcrest[94]

The Redcrest system of electronic filing of court documents has been used by the Supreme Court of Victoria since 2014. Proceedings in the Commercial Court are initiated by filing an Originating Process in Redcrest. Each party to a proceeding is required to appoint a Case Manager who must register on the system and manage the party's engagement with Redcrest. The Case Manager has the responsibility of informing the Court of the current status of authorized users, and for receiving all notifications of the filing of documents and bringing those notifications to the attention of any other relevant users with access to the case page. There are 11 categories of documents filed in Redcrest, including outlines of submissions and arguments, expert and lay evidence and chronologies, that are designated confidential and only made available to the Court and registered users for that case. Whilst such confidential documents form part of the court record, they will not

---

87 *Irish Bank Resolution Corporation Limited v Quinn* [2015] 175 IEHC [66] – [69].

88 *Irish Bank Resolution Corporation Limited v Quinn* [2015] 175 IEHC.

89 *McConnell Dowell Constructors (Aust) Pty Ltd v Santam Ltd & Ors* [2016] VSC 734.

90 *David Brown v BCA Trading Ltd & Ors* [2016] EWHC 1464 (Ch) [3].

91 eg Supreme Court of Victoria Practice Note SC Gen 5 Technology in Civil Litigation.

92 14 Civ. 3042 (RMB)(AJP).

93 Federal Court of Australia, 'Technology and the Court Practice Note (GPN-TECH)' www.fedcourt.gov.au/law-and-practice/practice-documents/practice-notes/gpn-tech (accessed 3 May 2021).

94 www.supremecourt.vic.gov.au/sites/default/files/assets/2017/12/02/0966bc081/CC5RedCrestPNandSummary_Secondrevision21122017.pdf (accessed 3 May 2021).

be available to anyone without authorized access to the case page. The Court may make further orders for privacy and confidentiality of any other documents filed in Redcrest. All documents filed in Redcrest must be in PDF format, preferably in text searchable format and following the Redcrest Document Naming Protocol. Documents requiring signatures must be electronically signed in the specified format. Supreme Court Practice Note SC CC5 provides guidance on the use of Redcrest by practitioners.[95] Detailed instructions on the use of Redcrest are available in the Redcrest e-Filing User Guide.[96]

The Federal Court of Australia provides a similar eLodgement facility to file court documents.[97]

29.7.2.2 Hearings

As an example of a modern court familiar with the benefits of ICT, the Federal Court of Australia has a range of technology and equipment in courtrooms to support the efficient hearing of proceedings. This technology includes videoconference facilities; document cameras; wi-fi; computer/power access points for court users; and for approved cases, the ability to webcast television footage or stream part of the proceeding.

The Federal Court's eCourtroom is a virtual courtroom that allows for evidence to be considered and orders made online without the need for in person court appearances. The transcript facility records all messages posted by the registrar, judge, or any parties; this is viewable by the public as well as the parties. Documents posted are only viewable by the parties.[98] In addition to *ex parte* applications, the eCourtroom was used extensively during the COVID-19 pandemic to proceed with full trials where appropriate.

Electronic documents may be used in 'face-to-face' trials by the use of an electronic court book used by the judge, counsel, and witnesses in the courtroom. Such an e-trial may require the use of an external service provider to ensure that documents are made available to all participants expeditiously; delays in access to electronic documents may result in a longer trial than the use of traditional hard copy court books.

Lawyers preparing complex evidence for a hearing now have a range of technologies available; in addition to the commonly used videos and PowerPoint presentations, other technologies such as virtual reality may provide evidence with powerful visual impact.

29.7.3 Online dispute resolution

The Internet's rapid communication and information processing capabilities have opened up opportunities for creative approaches and responses to problem-solving for disputes that do not go to court. There are a greater number of disputes stemming from online activities than anyone predicted. Online dispute resolution (**ODR**) is also applied to traditional kinds of disputes occurring off-line, and the boundary line between the online and off-line worlds is much less clear than it used to be: 'the digital world merges with the physical

95 www.supremecourt.vic.gov.au/sites/default/files/assets/2017/12/02/0966bc081/CC5RedCrestPNandSummary_Secondrevision21122017.pdf (accessed 3 May 2021).

96 www.redcrest.com.au/redcrestdocs/docs/RedCrest_e-Filing_User_Guide_November_2020.pdf (accessed 3 May 2021).

97 Federal Court of Australia, 'Technology and the Court Practice Note (GPN-TECH)' www.fedcourt.gov.au/law-and-practice/practice-documents/practice-notes/gpn-tech (accessed 3 May 2021).

98 Ibid.

world.'[99] The new challenge for ADR is finding tools that can deliver trust, convenience, and expertise for many different kinds of conflicts.[100]

Information and communication technology and its use in ADR, known as online dispute resolution, is an evolutionary development which promises to provide revolutionary changes to the way disputes are avoided and resolved in the near future. If ODR is to be resorted to, users will look to price, convenience, trust, and a perception of low risk. The marketplace for ODR is now in off-line disputes as well as those originating online, and public sector disputes as well as those originating in the private sector.[101]

Three of the features of ICT relevant to ODR are that it provides more communication channels, it deals with information in ways that were not possible previously, and it helps redefine groups and group dynamics.[102] The metaphor employed to explain the use of ODR is the 'Fourth Party'[103] in which the Fourth Party primarily assists the third-party neutral (eg Mediator, Arbitrator, or Adjudicator) by providing convenience and efficiencies. Appropriate software manages the flow of information and interactions between disputants online in a manner that facilitates a resolution of their dispute.

According to Daniel Rainey 'ODR, in the broader sense, is simply the intelligent application of information and communication technology to any conflict engagement process. I say "intelligent" application, but in many cases it's probably the "unwitting" application of ICT – we have integrated technology into what we do professionally because we have integrated the same technology into our everyday lives.'[104] The normal functions that third-party neutrals employ in the steps of standard ADR models now use online technology to help fulfil those functions in ODR. For example, it is common to use survey and scheduling platforms to help handle intake, get agreements to mediate in place, and gather all of the information needed to convene meetings of the parties.

In 1997, the Hewlett Foundation provided a grant to the University of Massachusetts to establish the Center for Information Technology and Dispute Resolution (later the National Centre for Technology and Dispute Resolution).[105] The goal of the Center was to support the development of the field of ODR. ODR has gained traction around the world through the Center's Cyberweek, an all online conference, and physical conferences held around the world in Geneva (2002 and 2003), Melbourne (2004), Cairo (2006), Liverpool and Victoria (Canada) (2008), Haifa (Israel) (2009), Buenos Aires (2010), Chennai (India) (2011), Prague (2012), and so on.

---

99 N Gershenfeld, *When Things Start to Think* (Coronet Books, 1999) 10.

100 E Katsch & J Rivkin, *Online Dispute Resolution: Resolving Disputes in Cyberspace* (Wiley, 2001) 73: 'No ODR system will be successful unless it is convenient to use, provides a sense of trust and confidence in its use, and also delivers expertise. Described a little differently, such systems need to facilitate access and participation, have legitimacy, and provide value.'

101 Ethan Katsch, 'ODR: A Look at History' 30, www.mediate.com/pdf/katsh.pdf (accessed 25 February 2021).

102 Daniel Rainey, 'Conflict Engagement and ICT: Evolution and Revolution' (2016) 3 *International Journal of Online Dispute Resolution* 2.

103 Ethan Katsch & Janet Rifkin, *Online Dispute Resolution: Resolving Conflicts in Cyberspace* (Jossey-Bass, 2001).

104 Daniel Rainey, 'Conflict Engagement and ICT: Evolution and Revolution' (2016) (3)2 *International Journal on Online Dispute Resolution* 77, 81, www.tncourts.gov/sites/default/files/docs/rainey_daniel_2019oct_mediation_workshop.pdf (accessed 17 August 2021).

105 www.odr.info.

Systems such as eBay's private Resolution Centre or public systems such as court ODR systems have focused on a number of areas such as the application of artificial intelligence to dispute resolution using information gathered from parties to automate steps in the process, provide guidance or even determine optimal outcomes for disputes. ADR processes have been replicated by convening and conducting them wholly online, focusing on using technology as a communication intermediary for party-party and party-Mediator interaction.[106] The use of video conferences, virtual hearings, and other ODR technologies increased dramatically as a consequence of the COVID-19 constraints on movement and assemblies. The considerable experience gained in the conduct of virtual arbitration hearings in 2020 has been well documented,[107] as has the conduct of virtual mediations using ubiquitous general platforms such as Zoom or Teams.[108]

29.7.3.1 ODR applications

In 1999 eBay engaged the University of Massachusetts Amherst Centre for Information Technology and Dispute Resolution to conduct a pilot project to mediate disputes online between buyers and sellers.[109] eBay subsequently included ODR as an option for buyers and sellers in the event a transaction was unsuccessful. By 2010, the number of disputes handled by eBay reached the phenomenal figure of 60 million.[110]

Ninety percent of e-commerce disputes are 'resolved' by 'Fourth Party' algorithms created to provide information and other paths to resolution without the 'interference' of a human third party. Online apps encourage parties to engage in direct negotiation by leading them through rational decision-making steps without a third party.

China says that millions of legal cases are being decided by 'internets courts' that do not require citizens to appear in court. The 'smart court' includes non-human judges powered by artificial intelligence and people seeking legal action can register their case on the Internet. They can then take part in a digital court hearing. China's first Internet court was established in Hangzhou in 2017. From March to October 2019, China's official Xinhua news agency reported that users completed more than 3.1 million legal activities through the court system. The Internet court system operates 24 hours a day 7 days a week and even though virtual judges are used, human judges observe the process and can make major rulings. Ni Defeng, VP of the Hangzhou Internet Court has said that the use of blockchain is particularly useful in helping to reduce paperwork and create clearer records of the legal

106 Ayelet Sela, 'Can Computers be fair? How Automated and Human-Powered Online Dispute Resolution Affect Procedural Justice in Mediation and Arbitration' (2016) 33 *Ohio State Journal on Dispute Resolution* 91, 100.

107 eg Chartered Institute of Arbitrators, 'Guidance Note on Remote Dispute Resolution Proceedings' www.ciarb.org/media/9013/remote-hearings-guidance-note_final_140420.pdf (accessed 3 May 2021); International Chamber of Commerce, 'ICC Guidance Note on Possible Measures Aimed at Mitigating the Effects of the COVID-19 Pandemic' https://iccwbo.org/publication/icc-guidance-note-on-possible-measures-aimed-at-mitigating-the-effects-of-the-covid-19-pandemic/ (accessed 3 May 2021).

108 eg Supreme Court of Victoria, 'Virtual Mediations Zoom User Guide' www.supremecourt.vic.gov.au/sites/default/files/assets/inline-files/Virtual%20Mediations%20-%20Zoom%20User%20Guide_0.pdf (accessed 3 May 2021); Federal Court of Australia, 'National Practitioners/Litigants Guide to Online Hearings and Microsoft Teams' www.fedcourt.gov.au/online-services/online-hearings (accessed 3 May 2021).

109 E Katsch, J Rifkin & A Gaitenby, 'E-commerce, E-Disputes and E-Dispute Resolution: In the Shadow of eBay Law' (2000) 15 *Ohio State Journal on Dispute Resolution* 705, 708–709.

110 Katsch & Rabinovitch-Einy, *Digital Justice Technology and the Internet of Disputes* (Oxford University Press, 1st edn 2017) 35.

process. Courts nationwide are using some form of online tools to help deal with cases. Ni Defeng believes that the system's ability to provide quick results helps give citizens more quality justice.[111]

In the USA, Government agencies, such as the National Mediation Board[112] and the Office of Government Information Services (OGIS)[113] are adopting and promoting ODR as a means of resolving problems with citizens. Cybersettle has moved beyond its original focus on insurance disputes and is helping to resolve claims brought against New York City.

29.7.3.2 Software

An increasing number of choices of appropriate software for ODR are available. General purpose videoconferencing platforms such as Zoom, Teams, and Webex have been widely used for ADR meetings and hearings during the COVID-19 pandemic. The need for virtual platforms has also encouraged and expanded the use of purpose written ADR platforms, such as the Community Court of Modria.com, FairOutcomes.com and Immediation.com.

The Immediation platform, designed and implemented by a Victorian barrister experienced in courtroom practice, is accessible by computer or mobile phone and provides all the online facilities required for ADR and court processes: videoconferencing, breakout rooms, document display, and tools for drafting and signing settlement agreements and other documents.[114] It has been used for mediations, including mediations with unrepresented parties, arbitrations, and providing services to Commonwealth and Victorian courts. It was used for the International Willem C Vis Commercial Arbitration Moot in 2020, involving 560 hearings in 30 countries. Security has been built into the platform with firewalling, global load balancing, and encryption of all data, and tested using military level methodology.

ADR practitioners can undertake online training in ODR, for example, the ODR Practitioner Certification Program by ODR Foundations Training (USA),[115] and the ODR Practitioner's Certificate by the Resolution Institute (Australia).[116] These courses cover technologies such as web video applications, text applications, e-mail services, e-signature services, and online voting platforms.

29.7.3.3 The challenges of ODR

It is said that fast, inexpensive, informal, and extrajudicial processes that currently motivate courts to implement ODR systems which include online and automated case management, automated and assisted negotiation processes, and the diversion to online mediation as currently contemplated by court administrators, marginalise or eliminate traditional roles and activities of lawyers. This is a development that is expected to have deep and destructive ramifications for the legal profession.[117]

---

111 Bryan Lynn, 'Robot Justice, The Rise of China's 'Internet Courts' (11 December 2019), https://learningenglish.voanews.com/amp/robot-justice-the-rise-of-china-s-internet-courts-/5201677.html (accessed 11 February 2021).

112 www.nmb.gov (accessed 25 February 2021).

113 www.nara.gov/ogis (accessed 25 February 2021).

114 www.immediation.com (accessed 3 May 2021).

115 https://odrfoundationstraining.com (accessed 4 May 2021).

116 www.resolution.institute/events/event/odr-prac-cert (accessed 4 May 2021).

117 Noam Ebner & Elayne Greenberg, 'What Dinosaurs Can Teach Lawyers About How to Avoid Extinction in the ODR Evolution' (2019) 19–0004 *St. John's School of Legal Studies Research Paper Series*, www.onlinemediators.com/evolution.pdf (accessed 25 February 2021).

While it can be expected that future increases in power and reductions in cost will occur, increasingly powerful ICT provides capabilities for manipulating and, to a considerable extent, removing constraints of time and space that are present in the physical environment. The success of virtual processes in court and ADR during the COVID-19 pandemic will inevitably accelerate the uptake of ODR to achieve time and cost savings.

Dispute resolution practitioners and parties who find themselves working in different contexts, cultural locations, legal jurisdictions, and organisational frameworks might require different technological toolboxes. Practitioners will have to develop perspectives best suited to their own workflow, subjective experience of the dispute resolution cycle, dispute resolution practices, evolution with technology, contextual needs, or way of addressing problems.[118]

The integration of technology in our daily lives gives increased confidence in the ability to avoid and resolve disputes using ODR. But individual behavioural, psychological, cognitive, physical, and interactional changes may not have received adequate attention and may require us to also consider a 'Fifth Party' in the dispute resolution process, that is, the power of ICT to facilitate external influence via social media and the Internet. There appears to be an increasing tendency for 'confidential information' and 'fake news' to be leaked by disgruntled losers, woke interventionists, influencers, hackers, and activists with minority or hidden agendas masquerading under the banner of 'public opinion.' Reality and perceptions become intentionally blurred. The aim is to apply pressure on legitimate and truly beneficial solutions arrived at by parties directly affected. To ignore the 'Fifth Party' (the 'outside' influences and forces of public opinion, whether truly interested parties, representative or not), in the daily conduct of 'business as usual,' and in particular in dispute avoidance and dispute resolution may result in failed outcomes and catastrophic reputational damage. The result is that ICT has brought us great advantages, but also significant dangers, which we must adjust to.

29.7.3.4 The future of ODR

Rainey[119] anticipates that in the not-too-distant future artificial intelligence (AI) will enable true driverless mediation – not just leading the parties through a series of steps but actually operating as a virtual Third/Fourth Party. This will no doubt depend on the achievement of significant advances in natural language processing.

Existing ODR platforms have enabled tasks to be performed more quickly over distance, but in future ODR is likely to involve greater advances in information processing and more use of AI. If a negotiation problem is appropriately modelled, a computer may be able to act as an intelligent agent using optimisation algorithms that seek the best solution. Optimisation algorithms can utilise detailed and highly accurate information from all

118 A Carrel & N Ebner, 'Mind the Gap: Bringing Technology to the Mediation Table' (2019) 2 *Journal of Dispute Resolution* 1, 27; see also Noam Ebner, 'The Technology of Negotiation' in C Honeyman & A K Schneider (eds), *The Negotiator's Desk Reference (Vol 2)* (St Paul DRI Press, 2017) 174, which identifies three phases of a cycle: 'negotiators . . . go through a cyclic process which includes learning about negotiation in general, preparing for a specific negotiation, and conducting that negotiation . . . reflection on this negotiation experience adds to the negotiators general stockpile of knowledge, and the negotiators cycle continues.'

119 Daniel Rainey, 'Conflict Engagement and ICT: Evolution and Revolution' (2016) 3(2) *International Journal on Online Dispute Resolution*, 82.

parties, information that they would never provide each other and which in some cases would not be of interest to a human mediator. For any dispute other than one involving the very simplest of issues, such optimisation is beyond the capabilities of any unassisted human. One trajectory of ODR may be in the direction of the role that information can play not only in how disputes are resolved but how they can be prevented.

GLOSSARY OF TERMS

Terms are capitalised where they have a specific meaning in the context of a construction contract (the **Contract**), where they are capitalised in common usage, or where they refer to a person. The Contract should be consulted for the specific meaning of these terms, and any others listed here which are defined terms in a specific contract.

Terms are italicised where they are non-English words, and where they are legislation, regulations, or conventions.

FIDIC refers to definitions in standard form contracts published by the International Federation of Consulting Engineers.[1]
NEC refers to definitions in the NEC ECC contract.[2]
NADRAC refers to definitions in the NADRAC Glossary of ADR Terms.[3]
SCL refers to definitions in the Society of Construction Law Delay and Disruption Protocol (2nd edn 2017).[4]

Term	Meaning	Defined in Section
AAA	American Arbitration Association	**¶28.5.2**
AACE	Association for the Advancement of Cost Engineering	**¶14.6.2**
Abrahamson Principles	Principles of fair and balanced risk allocation, articulated in Max W Abrahamson, 'Risk Management' (1983) *International Construction Law Review*, 241, 244.	**¶3.9.2**
ACC	*Australian Contract Code.*	**¶2.9.2.3**
acceleration	Speeding up the execution of the **Works** under a contract by the application of more resources than were originally planned, for example, additional manpower, existing manpower working longer or additional shifts, or additional equipment.	**¶14.6.3**
acceleration	Definition in SCL Delay and Disruption Protocol 2nd Edition.	**SCL**

1 www.fidicterms.org/wiki/index.php/Category:Contracts_and_Agreements (accessed 23 July 2021).
2 www.neccontract.com/About-NEC/NEC-Dictionary (accessed 23 July 2021).
3 www.asbfeo.gov.au/sites/default/files/Dispute%20Resolution%20Glossary.pdf (accessed 4 September) 2021).
4 www.scl.org.uk/sites/default/files/documents/SCL_Delay_Protocol_2nd_Edition_Final.pdf (accessed 23 July 2021).

Term	Meaning	Defined in Section
Accepted Contract Amount	FIDIC definition (Red, Pink, Yellow, Blue-Green and Emerald Books)	**FIDIC**
Accepted Programme	NEC definition.	**NEC**
Accepted Programme	Definition in SCL Delay and Disruption Protocol 2nd Edition.	**SCL**
access dates	NEC term identified in the Contract Data.	**NEC**
ACICA	Australian Centre for International Commercial Arbitration.	**¶28.11.7**
ACL	*Australian Consumer Law.*	**¶2.11**
act of prevention	An act by one contracting **party** (usually the **Employer**) which prevents or delays the other party from performing its obligations under a contract.	**¶14.7.6**
Activity	Definition in SCL Delay and Disruption Protocol 2nd Edition.	**SCL**
activity float	Definition in SCL Delay and Disruption Protocol 2nd Edition.	**SCL**
activity schedule	NEC term identified in the Contract Data provided by the Contractor.	**NEC**
activity-on-the-node network	Definition in SCL Delay and Disruption Protocol 2nd Edition.	**SCL**
***ad hoc* arbitration**	An **arbitration** that is conducted according to procedures agreed by the parties without any institutional supervision.	**¶28.11.2**
additional conditions of contract	NEC term identified in the Contract Data.	**NEC**
ADGM	Abu Dhabi Global Market. A financial free zone in Abu Dhabi, established pursuant to Federal Law No. 8 of 2004. (UAE)	**¶28.13.2.1**
adhesion contract	See **contract of adhesion**.	
adjudication	A method of dispute resolution in which an independent **Adjudicator** resolves a **dispute** by providing a reasoned provisionally binding determination of the **parties'** contractual rights following an impartial assessment of the parties' submissions and other evidence. Adjudication is commonly carried out pursuant to the provisions of ***Security of Payment* legislation (statutory adjudication)**, or in accordance with contractual provisions on dispute resolution (**contractual adjudication**).	**¶28.9.1**
Adjudication	NADRAC glossary of common ADR terms.	**NADRAC**
Adjudicator	The independent person (**third-party neutral**) who carries out an **adjudication**.	**¶28.9.1**
Adjudicator	NEC term identified in the Contract Data.	**NEC**

Term	Meaning	Defined in Section
Adjudicator nominating body	NEC term identified in the Contract Data.	**NEC**
ADR	Any method of **dispute** resolution that does not involve a judicial assessment in court litigation.	**¶28.2.4**
ADR	NADRAC glossary of common ADR terms.	**NADRAC**
ADR clause	An agreement by the contracting **parties** to adopt a specific form of **ADR** in the event of, or on the occurrence of, a **dispute**, and the contractual consequences of the decision of the third-party neutral.	
ADRIC	ADR Institute of Canada.	**¶28.5.2**
Advance Payment Certificate	FIDIC definition (Red, Yellow, and Emerald Books)	**FIDIC**
Advance Payment Guarantee	FIDIC definition (Red, Yellow, Silver, and Emerald Books)	**FIDIC**
advisory dispute resolution process	NADRAC glossary of common ADR terms.	**NADRAC**
affermage contract	A public-private sector arrangement under which the private operator is responsible for operating and maintaining the utility but not for financing the investment.	**¶3.5.5**
AFC	Approved for construction (drawings).	
AI	**Artificial intelligence**.	**¶29.3.4**
AIFC	Astana International Financial Centre (Kazakhstan).	**¶28.13.2.1**
alliance contract	A **construction contract** in which the risks and rewards are intended to be shared in a non-adversarial relationship between the parties.	**¶3.5.4**
alternative dispute resolution	Any method of dispute resolution that does not involve a judicial assessment in court litigation. Alternative dispute resolution includes **negotiation**, **mediation**, **conciliation**, **expert determination, adjudication**, and **arbitration** and is alternative to litigation.	**¶28.2.4**
amiable compositeur	An **arbitral tribunal** acting as *amiable compositeur* is not bound by strict rules of law but is entitled to decide according to their subjective sense of what is fair and just. An arbitral tribunal acting as *amiable compositeur* makes their **award *ex aequo et bono.***	**¶28.11.4.2**
amicable settlement	A settlement of a **dispute** achieved by nonconfrontational methods (such as **negotiation** or **mediation/conciliation**), thereby preserving business relationships.	**¶28.2.8**

Term	Meaning	Defined in Section
AMINZ	The Arbitrators' and Mediators' Institute of New Zealand Inc.	**¶28.5.2**
AMPLA	An Australian organisation of lawyers founded in the 1970s to promote technical excellence, education, innovation, and collaboration in the law on energy, resources, renewables, and commodities. It publishes a number of example agreements. www.ampla.org/News-Resources/Publications/Example-Documents (accessed 21 January 2021).	
animus contrahendi	Mind to contract. (Latin)	**¶10.9**
arbitral tribunal	A panel of **Arbitrators**, usually one or three.	**¶28.11.1**
arbitration	The private judgement of a **dispute** between contracting **parties** by an independent, unbiased and impartial **arbitral tribunal** which applies the principles of **procedural fairness** (natural justice) in a process in which all parties have the opportunity and the right to present their case and rebut the case of their opponents.	**¶28.11.1**
Arbitration	NADRAC glossary of common ADR terms.	**NADRAC**
arbitration agreement	An agreement by **parties** to resolve a **dispute** between them by **arbitration**. An arbitration agreement can be entered into prior to the existence of a dispute, or after a dispute has occurred.	**¶28.11.1**
arbitration procedure	NEC term identified in the Contract Data.	**NEC**
Arbitrator	The person who conducts an **arbitration**. S/he considers all of the evidence presented by the **parties** and decides what are the relevant facts from the evidence which, when applied to the relevant principles of law (or, rarely general justice and fairness), determine the rights and obligations of the parties in relation to the dispute. The Arbitrator publishes his/her findings on the facts and the law and the rights and obligations of the parties applicable to the dispute in a written determination called an **award** which is binding on all parties to the arbitration.	**¶28.11.2**
Architect	See **Engineer**.	
artificial intelligence	The capability of devices or mechanisms and machinery to perform functions usually associated with human intelligence, including scientific systems, reasoning, optimization through experience, and automated motor systems.[5]	**¶29.3.4**
as-built programme	Definition in SCL Delay and Disruption Protocol 2nd Edition.	**SCL**
as-planned versus as built windows	Definition in SCL Delay and Disruption Protocol 2nd Edition.	**SCL**
assessment interval	NEC term identified in the Contract Data.	**NEC**

5 James Birx, Encyclopedia of Anthology (Sage Publications California, 2006) 281.

Term	Meaning	Defined in Section
assignment	The means by which a **party** legally transfers to another the whole or part of its rights or obligations under a contract.	**¶9.12.1**
augmented reality	The use of **virtual reality** overlaid on top of an image of the real (physical) world.	**¶29.3.6**
Australian Consumer Law	This legislation comprises a schedule to the *Competition and Consumer Act 2010* (Cth), which is the harmonised re-enactment of the *Trade Practices Act 1974* (Cth).	
Automated dispute resolution processes	NADRAC glossary of common ADR terms.	**NADRAC**
Automated negotiation (or blind-bidding)	NADRAC glossary of common ADR terms.	**NADRAC**
award	An **Arbitrator's** written findings on the facts and the law applicable to a **dispute**, and his/her determination of the rights and obligations of each **party** in relation to the dispute. An award is binding on all parties to the **arbitration**, and a final award irrevocably extinguishes the cause of action between the parties.	**¶28.11**
B2B	Business to business.	
B2C	Business to consumer.	
Bank	FIDIC definition (Pink Book)	**FIDIC**
Base Date	FIDIC definition (Red, Pink, Yellow, Silver and Emerald Books)	**FIDIC**
base date	NEC term identified in the Contract Data.	**NEC**
bespoke contract	A **contract** in which the terms are specifically prepared for the particular project, contracting **parties**, the **Site** and scope of work.	**¶1.4**
bid	A tender, ie an offer to enter into a **contract**.	
bidder	A **Tenderer**, ie a person, firm or company which submits a **tender** for a contract.	
bill of quantities (BoQ)	A schedule briefly describing each different type of constructional element and listing the quantity of each required for a complete construction project. A bill of quantities is prepared by a **quantity surveyor**, usually engaged by the **Employer**. A **Tenderer** can prepare a **tender** from a BoQ by multiplying the unit rate for each different type of constructional element by its quantity and summing all the items.	**¶19.1**
Bill of Quantities	FIDIC definition (Red and Emerald Books).	**FIDIC**
bill of quantities	NEC term identified in the Contract Data provided by the Contractor.	**NEC**
bill of quantities contract	A **measurement contract** which uses a **bill of quantities** to evaluate changes in the **Works** during the course of the **Contract**. The bill of quantities forms part of the Contract.	**¶19.1**

Term	Meaning	Defined in Section
BIM	Building Information Modelling. The process of generating and managing a set of electronic information generated and maintained throughout the life cycle of a building. Also used for Building Information Model - a set of electronic information generated and maintained throughout the life cycle of a building	**¶29.1.3**
blockchain	A distributed ledger that uses a particular mechanism to ensure the integrity of the database, specifically block transactions with some form of mathematical proof of integrity of the transaction (such as proof of work).[6]	**¶29.3.5**
Blue-Green Book	FIDIC Form of Contract for Dredging and Reclamation Works – First Edition 2006, Second Edition 2016.	
BOO	Build, own, operate. A form of **construction contract** which requires the **Contractor** to build a facility, own and operate it.	**¶3.2**
BOOT	Build, own, operate transfer. A form of **construction contract** which requires the **Contractor** to build a facility, own and operate it for a period, and ultimately (perhaps after a period of many years) transfer ownership and operating responsibility to the **Employer**.	**¶3.2**
BoQ	**Bill of quantities**.	
Borrower	FIDIC definition (Pink Book)	**FIDIC**
BOT	Build, operate, transfer. A form of **construction contract** which requires the **Contractor** to build a facility, operate it for a period and then transfer operating responsibility to the **Employer**.	**¶3.2**
BOTT	Build, operate, train, transfer. A form of **construction contract** which requires the **Contractor** to build a facility, operate it for a period, train the **Employer's** personnel and transfer operating responsibility to the Employer.	**¶3.2**
boundaries of the site	NEC term identified in the Contract Data.	**NEC**
breach of contract	Failure or refusal to comply with the terms of the contract agreement, entitling the other **party**(s) to the contract to damages and possibly other remedies.	**¶2.11**
buildability	The ability of a **design** to be implemented physically in a manner that is safe, sound and otherwise in accordance with the terms of the relevant construction contract; it may embrace both the physical possibility of implementing a design, and the practical ability to do so.	**¶13.1**
building contract	A species of **construction contract**, the primary object of which is construction of one or more buildings, and in which the non-building work is a minor component of the total work, and is ancillary to the building, eg civil engineering of roadworks.	**¶3.1.2**

6 David L Shirer, Basic Blockchain (Robinson Great Britain, 2020) 136.

Term	Meaning	Defined in Section
business interruption insurance	Insurance for the risk of impairment of revenue or profit, or of increased costs as a consequence of an adverse event during a project.	¶26.7
CAD	Computer Aided Design or Computer Aided Drawing.	¶6.9
case law	The judgements of judges on specific disputes, published in **Law Reports** that is, collectively, the written statement of the **common law**.	¶1.4
Case presentation (or Mini-trial)	NADRAC glossary of common ADR terms.	NADRAC
casus fortuitus	A happening so exceptional or extraordinary as not to be foreseeable. (Latin)	¶14.7.4
CDE	Common data environment.	¶29.4
CESMM	Civil Engineering Standard Method of Measurement issued by the **ICE**.	¶21.4.1
change/ variation	Definition in SCL Delay and Disruption Protocol 2nd Edition.	SCL
chess clock arbitration	An **arbitration** in which a limited time for the hearing is set by the **arbitral tribunal**, with each party given equal time to present its case.	¶28.11.11
choice of law	The law of the **legal jurisdiction** that the parties have chosen to regulate their legal rights and obligations – **the proper law of the contract**.	¶2.6
CIArb	Chartered Institute of Arbitrators.	¶4.6
CICC	China International Commercial Court.	¶28.13.2.2
CISG	*United Nations Convention of Contracts for the International Sale of Goods* of 11 April 1980. Also known as the *Vienna Convention.*	¶9.1.8
civil engineering contract	A species of **construction contract**, the primary object of which is the construction of civil engineering works such as roadworks or tunnelling, and which involves the movement of significant quantities of soil and rock.	
civil law	In a civil law system, the governing legislature enacts detailed legislation that endeavours to codify the law in a given area.	¶1.4
claim	The submission of a formal request by one **party** to the other party under the provisions of the **Contract** or under the (common) law for additional time or money arising out of circumstances or events concerning the execution of the project.	¶27.2
Claim	FIDIC definition (Red, Yellow, Silver, and Emerald Books)	FIDIC
claims made and notified liability	Insurer's liability under **liability insurance** arising from the making of a claim plus the notification of that claim to the insurer.	¶26.1
claims made liability	Insurer's liability under **liability insurance** arising from the making of a claim against the insured.	¶26.1
Client	See **Employer**.	

Term	Meaning	Defined in Section
Client	NEC term identified in the Contract Data.	**NEC**
Client's objective	NEC term identified in the Contract Data.	**NEC**
cloud	'An artful name for the great new heavy industry of our times: gargantuan data centres composed of immense systems of data storage and processes, linked together by millions of miles of fibre-optic lines and consuming electrical power and radiating heat to an extent that excels most industrial enterprises in history.'[7]	**¶29.3.2**
Co-mediation	NADRAC glossary of common ADR terms.	**NADRAC**
codification	Codification of the law is a comprehensive statement of all the principles that determine the legal outcome resulting from a given set of factual circumstances.	**¶1.4**
cold commissioning	The **plant** has been tested, checked, and run to demonstrate that it is ready to be placed into operation, and consists of **dry commissioning** and **wet commissioning**.	**¶11.7**
collapsed as-built	Definition in SCL Delay and Disruption Protocol 2nd Edition.	**SCL**
collateral contract	A contract which is entered into by persons A and B as consideration for B's entry into a separate contract with person C (or alternatively with A).	**¶9.1.3.3**
Combined or hybrid dispute resolution processes	NADRAC glossary of common ADR terms.	**NADRAC**
Commencement Date	FIDIC definition (Red, Pink, Yellow, Silver, and Emerald Books)	**FIDIC**
commissioning	Bringing something newly produced into working condition.	**¶11.7**
common law	The law as stated by judges in their reasoning in giving judgement in the disputes brought before them. The principle is that earlier judicial decisions, usually of the higher courts, made in a similar case, should be followed in the subsequent cases. See ***stare decisis***.	**¶1.4**
compensable delay	A **delay** for which a party is entitled to additional payment.	**¶14.4**
compensable event	Definition in SCL Delay and Disruption Protocol 2nd Edition.	**SCL**
compensation	Definition in SCL Delay and Disruption Protocol 2nd Edition.	**SCL**
Compensation Event	NEC definition.	**NEC**
Completion	The **stage** where the **Works** have been completed except for minor defects that do not prevent the **Employer** from **Taking-Over** the Works.	**¶16.1**
Completion	NEC definition.	**NEC**

7 George Gilder, *Life After Google* (Regenery Gateway, 2018) 21.

Term	Meaning	Defined in Section
Completion Date	NEC definition.	**NEC**
completion date	NEC term identified in the Contract Data.	**NEC**
completion date	Definition in SCL Delay and Disruption Protocol 2nd Edition.	**SCL**
Completion Schedule	FIDIC definition (Emerald Book).	**FIDIC**
Compliance Verification System	FIDIC definition (Red, Yellow, Silver, and Emerald Books)	**FIDIC**
conciliation	A process of facilitated **negotiation** in which a **Conciliator** assists the **parties** to try and reach agreement on their own resolution of their **dispute**, taking a proactive role in persuading the parties to adopt a settlement, and may provide his/her own opinion on the merits of possible settlement options.	**¶28.5.1**
Conciliation	NADRAC glossary of common ADR terms.	**NADRAC**
Conciliator	The **third-party neutral** who conducts a **conciliation**.	**¶28.5.1**
concurrency	Definition in SCL Delay and Disruption Protocol 2nd Edition.	**SCL**
concurrent delay	Delay caused by more than one event when the causes are within the control or risk shared by both parties.	**¶14.5.1**
concurrent delay	Definition in SCL Delay and Disruption Protocol 2nd Edition.	**SCL**
condition	NEC term identified in the Contract Data.	**NEC**
condition [of a contract]	A fundamental contractual term, breach of which by one party gives the other party a right to terminate the contract.	
conditions of contract	The contract document(s) which specifies the **parties'** overall obligations under the **Contract** and the allocation and consequences of risks. In a **standard form contract** the conditions of contract typically consist of **General Conditions** and **Special Conditions** or **Particular Conditions**.	**¶3.3**
Conditions of Contract	FIDIC definition (Red, Yellow, Silver, and Emerald Books)	**FIDIC**
conditions of contract	NEC term identified in the Contract Data.	**NEC**
Conference/ Conferencing	NADRAC glossary of common ADR terms.	**NADRAC**
conflict of laws	Where there is more than one **legal jurisdiction** whose laws may govern the private rights under a contract.	**¶2.6**
conflict of laws rules	The rules of law applied to determine preliminary issues where more than one **legal jurisdiction** is involved in a **dispute**.	**¶2.6**
Consensus building	NADRAC glossary of common ADR terms.	**NADRAC**

Term	Meaning	Defined in Section
consequential loss	Indirect loss that flows from the direct losses caused by a civil wrong such as **breach of contract**, for example, economic loss such as loss of profits or customers because a facility is defective or completed late. Consequential losses may be specific to a person's particular circumstances.	**¶24.7**
consideration	Something of value given by one **party** to another in return for the other party's promise to perform an agreed service or action. (common law)	**¶2.10.1**
construct only contract	The 'traditional' form of **construction contract** between an **Employer** and **Contractor** in which the Contractor constructs the **design** prepared for the Employer by the Employer's engineer/architect (who has a separate **design contract** with the Employer).	**¶3.4**
construction contract	Any contract where one person [including a corporation] agrees for valuable consideration to carry out construction of a physical structure (including building or engineering works) for another.	**¶3.1.1**
construction management contract	A form of **construction contract** in which the **Employer** engages a **Construction Manager** to act as the Employer's agent to program, coordinate, and manage the **design** and construction activities which are divided into packages which are separately undertaken by trade contractors contracted directly to the Employer. Also called an **EPCM** contract.	**¶3.4**
Construction Manager	The **Contractor** in a **construction management contract** who has contractual responsibility for programming and coordinating the **design** and construction activities.	**¶3.4**
construction of contract terms	The process of construing the terms of a contract to determine what the **parties'** objective intentions were at the time they entered into the contract.	**¶1.6**
constructive acceleration	Definition in SCL Delay and Disruption Protocol 2nd Edition.	**SCL**
consulting engineer	An independent engineer engaged by the **Employer** or the **Contractor** to provide engineering services such as **design** and supervision. A consulting engineer may be engaged by the Employer as the **Engineer**.	
contra proferentem	A rule of construction devised by the courts where there is doubt about the meaning of a contract, the words will be construed against the person who put them forward.	**¶2.13.3**
contract	A legally binding agreement voluntarily entered into between two or more **parties** that is enforceable in a court of law according to its terms. Each party accepts obligations in exchange for rights granted by the other party in order to achieve the contract objective.	**¶1.8** **¶2.2**
Contract	The **construction contract** being referred to.	**¶3.1.1**
Contract	FIDIC definition (Red, Pink, Yellow, Silver, and Emerald Books)	**FIDIC**
Contract	NEC definition.	**NEC**

Term	Meaning	Defined in Section
Contract Administrator (CA)	Definition in SCL Delay and Disruption Protocol 2nd Edition.	**SCL**
Contract Agreement	FIDIC definition (Red, Pink, Yellow, Silver, and Emerald Books)	**FIDIC**
contract code	A comprehensive statement of all the principles of contract law that determine the legal outcome resulting from a given set of factual circumstances.	**¶1.4**
contract completion date	Definition in SCL Delay and Disruption Protocol 2nd Edition.	**SCL**
Contract Data	FIDIC definition (Red, Pink, Yellow, Silver, and Emerald Books)	**FIDIC**
Contract Data	NEC definition.	**NEC**
contract documents	The documents which make up the legally enforceable agreement between the parties in a contract. The contract documents are usually listed in a **construction contract**, and in addition to the **conditions of contract** may include the **tender** and **letter of acceptance**, **specifications**, drawings, and **bills of quantities**.	**¶3.3**
contract of adhesion	A standard form contract written by the contracting party with overwhelming bargaining power and presented to the weaker contracting party on a take-it-or-leave-it basis, without any opportunity to negotiate terms.	
contract price	The total amount payable to the **Contractor** for providing the **Works**.	**¶21.1.1**
Contract Price	FIDIC definition (Red, Pink, Yellow, Silver, and Emerald Books)	**FIDIC**
Contract Risk Management Plan	FIDIC definition (Emerald book).	**FIDIC**
Contract Risk Register	FIDIC definition (Emerald book).	**FIDIC**
contract works insurance	Insurance of the **Works** in the joint names of the **Contractor** and the **Employer** to their full replacement value, with stipulated deductible limits. Usually required from the commencement date of the **Contract** until the risk is transferred to the Employer. It may also require providing cover against loss or damage during the **defects liability period** caused by the Contractor whilst completing any outstanding work or complying with its obligations to remedy **Defects**.	**¶26.2.2**
Contractor	The party to a construction contract (the **Contract**) who carries out the work.	**¶3.1.1**
Contractor	FIDIC definition (Red, Pink, Yellow, Silver, and Emerald Books)	**FIDIC**
Contractor	NEC term identified in the Contract Data.	**NEC**
Contractor	Definition in SCL Delay and Disruption Protocol 2nd Edition.	**SCL**

Term	Meaning	Defined in Section
Contractor Delay	Definition in SCL Delay and Disruption Protocol 2nd Edition.	**SCL**
Contractor Delay to Completion	Definition in SCL Delay and Disruption Protocol 2nd Edition.	**SCL**
Contractor Delay to Progress	Definition in SCL Delay and Disruption Protocol 2nd Edition.	**SCL**
Contractor Risk Event	Definition in SCL Delay and Disruption Protocol 2nd Edition.	**SCL**
Contractor's contingency	The time remaining from the planned completion of all the Contractor's activities required for Completion until the **Date for Completion** under the Contract.	**¶14.3.2**
Contractor's Documents	FIDIC definition (Red, Pink, Yellow, Silver, and Emerald Books)	**FIDIC**
Contractor's Equipment	FIDIC definition (Red, Pink, Yellow, Silver, and Emerald Books)	**FIDIC**
Contractor's Key Equipment	FIDIC definition (Emerald Book)	**FIDIC**
Contractor's Key Personnel	FIDIC definition (Emerald Book)	**FIDIC**
Contractor's Personnel	FIDIC definition (Red, Pink, Yellow, Silver, and Emerald Books)	**FIDIC**
Contractor's planned completion date	Definition in SCL Delay and Disruption Protocol 2nd Edition.	**SCL**
Contractor's Proposal	FIDIC definition (Yellow and Emerald Books)	**FIDIC**
Contractor's Representative	FIDIC definition (Red, Pink, Yellow, Silver, and Emerald Books)	**FIDIC**
Contractor's risks	Those risks for which the **Contract** assigns the legal responsibilities and liability for the risks materialising to the **Contractor**.	**¶24.1**
contractual adjudication	A determinative method of **ADR** in which the parties agree in the **Contract** (or in a separate contract) for an independent **Adjudicator** to resolve a **dispute** by providing a provisionally binding determination of the parties' contractual rights, following an impartial assessment of the parties' submissions and other evidence.	**¶28.9.5.1**
contractual dispute resolution	Any method of dispute resolution alternative to litigation in the courts which the **parties** have provided for in their contract. Contractual dispute resolution includes all forms of **ADR**.	**¶28.2.5.3**
Core Clauses	NEC definition.	**NEC**

Term	Meaning	Defined in Section
cost	Actual costs properly incurred plus allowable overhead charges. Does not include profit unless the relevant definition in the **Contract** specifically includes it.	**¶21.1.13**
Cost	FIDIC definition (Red, Pink, Yellow, Silver, and Emerald Books)	**FIDIC**
cost plus	See **cost reimbursable**.	
Cost Plus Profit	FIDIC definition (Red, Yellow, Silver, and Emerald Books)	**FIDIC**
cost reimbursable	A term used in a **measurement contract**, or part of a **lump sum contract**, such as a **Variation**, in which the **Contractor** is paid its costs for labour and materials used in the **Works** plus a margin for overheads. Profit is generally only included in the margin if the relevant **Contract** definition provides for it. The margin is generally fixed in the Contract.	**¶21.1.6**
Country	FIDIC definition (Red, Pink, Yellow, Silver, and Emerald Books)	**FIDIC**
CPM	**Critical path method**.	**¶14.3.2**
CPR	International Institute for Conflict Prevention and Resolution.	**¶28.5.2**
critical delay	'[A] delay to progress of any activity on the critical path [which] will, without acceleration or re-sequencing, cause the overall project duration to be extended.' Definition in SCL Delay and Disruption Protocol 2nd Edition.	**SCL**
critical path	A term used in **CPM** to denote the sequence of activities which must all be started at their scheduled start times and completed in the time scheduled for their duration to avoid extending the time for **Completion**.	**¶14.3.2**
critical path	Definition in SCL Delay and Disruption Protocol 2nd Edition.	**SCL**
critical path analysis (CPA)	Definition in SCL Delay and Disruption Protocol 2nd Edition.	**SCL**
critical path method	A mathematical method of scheduling a set of project activities to determine the shortest overall time for **Completion**. Also referred to as critical path analysis or network analysis.	**¶14.3.2**
critical path method (CPM)	Definition in SCL Delay and Disruption Protocol 2nd Edition.	**SCL**
culpa in contrahendo	The law applicable to a non-contractual obligation arising out of dealings prior to the conclusion of a contract. (Germany)	**¶1.5**
culpable delay	Definition in SCL Delay and Disruption Protocol 2nd Edition.	**SCL**
currency of this contract	NEC term identified in the Contract Data.	**NEC**
DAAB	See **Dispute Avoidance/Adjudication Board**.	
DAAB Agreement	FIDIC definition (Red, Yellow, Silver, and Emerald Books)	**FIDIC**

Term	Meaning	Defined in Section
DAAB or **Dispute Avoidance / Adjudication Board**	FIDIC definition (Red, Yellow, Silver, and Emerald Books)	**FIDIC**
DAB	**Dispute Adjudication Board**.	
damages	An award by a court or **Arbitrator** of a sum of money to compensate a party for the loss suffered as a result of another contracting party's breach of contract.	
Date for Completion	The date by which the **Contractor** must achieve **Completion** of the **Works** in order to comply with the requirements of the **Contract**.	**¶14.1.1**
date for completion	Definition in SCL Delay and Disruption Protocol 2nd Edition.	**SCL**
Date of Completion	The date on which the **Contractor** actually achieved **Completion** of the **Works**.	**¶14.2.1**
Date of Completion	FIDIC definition (Red, Yellow, Silver, and Emerald Books)	**FIDIC**
day	FIDIC definition (Red, Pink, Yellow, Silver, and Emerald Books)	**FIDIC**
daywork	Work performed on a piecemeal basis and which is not properly capable of being measured according to any method of measurement prescribed by the **Contract**. It is usually of a minor or incidental nature.	**¶20.5**
Daywork Schedule	FIDIC definition (Red, Yellow, Silver, and Emerald Books)	**FIDIC**
DB	**Dispute Board**.	**¶28.1.2**
DB	FIDIC definition (Pink Book)	**FIDIC**
DBB	Design-bid-build: a **construct only contract** (USA).	**¶3.4**
DBFO (design, build, finance, operate)	Essentially the same as a **BOO** contract.	
DBOT	Design, build, operate, transfer.	
DCMF	Design, construct, manage, finance.	
de minimis non curat lex	The law takes no notice of trifling matters. (Latin)	
decennial liability	The joint liability of a **Contractor** and an architect or engineer for a period of ten years from the date of handover to compensate the **Employer** for any total or partial collapse of a building or installation, and for any defect which threatens the stability or safety of the building.	**¶26.1.3**
deed	A legal document signed, sealed, and delivered that passes an interest, right, or property to another person, or creates a binding obligation. A deed is a special form of contract which complies with specified formalities and has a longer limitation period than applies to a simple contract. Also known as a specialty.	

Term	Meaning	Defined in Section
deep learning	A cutting-edge subset of **machine learning** involving more complex layers of data processing using algorithms that are inspired by the human brain that works in a hierarchical way.	**¶29.3.4**
default rules	The applicable law which supplements the **Contract** with issues the parties did not regulate. Also referred to as *jus dispositivum* or suppletive rules.	**¶1.8**
defect	Any defective work in the general sense.	**¶18.1.1**
Defect	A **defect** in which material supplied or work carried out by the **Contractor** does not satisfy the quality requirements of the **Contract**.	**¶18.1.1**
Defect	NEC definition.	**NEC**
Defects Certificate	NEC definition.	**NEC**
defects correction period	NEC term identified in the Contract Data.	**NEC**
defects date	NEC term identified in the Contract Data.	**NEC**
defects liability certificate	A certificate issued by the **Engineer** at the end of the **defects liability period** detailing that, in the opinion of the Engineer, there are no outstanding **Defects**, or alternatively listing the remaining known Defects.	**¶21.7.1**
defects liability period	The period after **Completion** or **Taking-Over** during which the **Contractor** has a contractual obligation to rectify **Defects**. Sometimes referred to as the maintenance period.	**¶18.1.2**
Defects Notification Period	FIDIC definition (Red, Pink, Yellow, Silver, and Emerald Books)	**FIDIC**
defendant	The person/company defending an action brought against him/her/it in a court by the plaintiff (or, in a criminal case, the prosecution).	
Defined Cost	NEC definition.	**NEC**
delay	Any event which extends the duration of one aspect (or multiple aspects) of a project.	**¶14.4**
Delay Damages	FIDIC definition (Red, Yellow, Silver, and Emerald Books)	**FIDIC**
Delay Damages	NEC definition.	**NEC**
delay event	Definition in SCL Delay and Disruption Protocol 2nd Edition.	**SCL**
Delay to Completion	Definition in SCL Delay and Disruption Protocol 2nd Edition.	**SCL**
Delay to Progress	Definition in SCL Delay and Disruption Protocol 2nd Edition.	**SCL**
delict	A remedy similar to the tort of negligence in English law. (South Africa)	
dependencies	Which activities are dependent on other activities in a **network**.	**¶15.1**

Term	Meaning	Defined in Section
design	All plans, drawings, sketches, instructions, and descriptions that determine the way the **Works** (or parts of it) are to be constructed. Design includes the writing or selection of **specifications** as well as the production of plans and drawings and any element of choice on the part of the designer, such as requirements as to materials or working methods.	**¶11.1.1**
design and construct contract	A construction **contract** in which the **Contractor** prepares the **design** to satisfy the **Employer's** requirements, and then constructs that design.	**¶3.4**
design contract	A contract for the preparation of a **design** to be constructed under a **construction contract**.	
design life	The time for which a constructed facility is designed, implicitly or explicitly, to perform for its intended purpose with expected maintenance but without major repair being necessary.	**¶11.3.3**
design parameters	The required functions, service life, and assumptions made for the design of a facility.	**¶11.3.1**
determination	A decision of an entity (such as the **Engineer** or a **Dispute Board**) in the exercise of its decision-making function.	**¶8.5.1**
determination	A style of **ADR** in which a **third-party neutral** ensures the **parties** have natural justice to present their evidence and submissions and determines their legal rights in a binding decision.	**¶28.2.8**
Determinative case appraisal	NADRAC glossary of common ADR terms.	**NADRAC**
Determinative dispute resolution processes	NADRAC glossary of common ADR terms.	**NADRAC**
DIFC	Dubai International Financial Centre.	**¶28.13.2.1**
direct fee percentage	NEC term identified in the Contract Data provided by the Contractor.	**NEC**
Disallowed Cost	NEC definition.	**NEC**
discharge	The release of obligations under a contract. (common law)	
dispute	A dispute or difference under a contract exists when a determination on a claim is made that is not accepted by the claiming party.	**¶27.1**
Dispute	FIDIC definition (Red, Yellow, Silver, and Emerald Books)	**FIDIC**
Dispute Adjudication Board	A **Dispute Board** that provides a provisionally binding decision on a **dispute** referred to it. In the absence of a notice of dissatisfaction, the DAB's decision is finally binding on the parties.	**¶28.10.1**
Dispute Avoidance/ Adjudication Board	A standing **Dispute Board** appointed under a FIDIC Contract to assist the **parties** in avoiding disputes, and to provide a provisionally binding decision on a **dispute** referred to it; if neither party issues a notice of dissatisfaction within a defined time, the decision becomes final and binding.	**¶28.1.2**

Term	Meaning	Defined in Section
Dispute Board	A panel of one or three suitably qualified and experienced independent persons appointed under a contract to be available to confer with the **parties** to assist in the avoidance of **disputes**, or if necessary to provide a determination on a dispute referred to it. A Dispute Board may be a **Dispute Avoidance/Adjudication Board (DAAB)**, a **Dispute Adjudication Board (DAB)**, a **Dispute Review Board (DRB)** or a **Dispute Resolution Board (DRB)**.	**¶28.1.2**
Dispute Board clause	The clause in a contract between **Employer** and **Contractor** in which they agree to use a **Dispute Board** to recommend a resolution of or resolve a **dispute** between them.	**¶28.10.2**
Dispute counselling	NADRAC glossary of common ADR terms.	**NADRAC**
Dispute resolution	NADRAC glossary of common ADR terms.	**NADRAC**
Dispute Resolution Board (DRB)	A **Dispute Review Board**.	
Dispute resolution practitioner	NADRAC glossary of common ADR terms.	**NADRAC**
Dispute Review Board (DRB)	A **Dispute Board** in which the Board's determination of a **dispute** is not binding unless accepted as such by both parties within a contractually defined period of time.	**¶28.10.1**
disruption	'Disturbance, hindrance, or interruption to a Contractor's normal working methods, resulting in lower productivity or efficiency in the execution of particular work activities.' Definition in SCL Delay and Disruption Protocol 2nd Edition.	**¶14.6.2** **SCL**
disruption event	Definition in SCL Delay and Disruption Protocol 2nd Edition.	**SCL**
disruptive applications	**ICT** applications that enable capabilities to do things that were not previously possible.	**¶29.1.3**
divisible contract	A contract in which the total financial compensation payable by the Employer is divisible.	**¶21.1.17**
DNP	**Defects Notification Period.** FIDIC definition (Red, Yellow, and Silver Books)	**FIDIC**
doctrine of prevention	See **prevention principle**.	
domestic building contract	A building contract in relation to **domestic building work** as defined in the relevant statute.	**¶3.1.3**
domestic building work	Work in connection with the construction of a home as defined in the relevant statute.	**¶3.1.3**
domestic mandatory rules of law	Rules of law of a given **legal jurisdiction** which apply to all contracts for which the **proper law of the contract** is the law of the **legal jurisdiction**.	**¶1.8**
DR	Dispute resolution.	

Term	Meaning	Defined in Section
Drawings	FIDIC definition (Red, Pink Books).	**FIDIC**
DRB	**Dispute Review Board** or **Dispute Resolution Board**.	
DRBF	Dispute Resolution Board Foundation.	**¶28.10.1.2**
dry commissioning	**Plant** has been manufactured, trial-fit, passed quality control testing, disassembled, and packed ready for transport without solvents or process fluids yet introduced.	**¶11.7**
duration	The time it takes to complete an activity.	**¶15.1**
duration	Definition in SCL Delay and Disruption Protocol 2nd Edition.	**SCL**
e-disclosure	The search for electronically stored documents and information and organisation of that material for inspection electronically. Also referred to as **e-discovery**.	**¶29.7.1.1**
e-discovery	The search for electronically stored documents and information and organisation of that material for inspection electronically. Also referred to as **e-disclosure**.	**¶29.7.1.1**
early neutral evaluation	An evaluative **ADR** process in which a **third-party neutral** hears presentations by both sides at an early stage of a **dispute** and provides an evaluation of what the result might be if the dispute was arbitrated or litigated in court.	**¶28.6**
Early neutral evaluation	NADRAC glossary of common ADR terms.	**NADRAC**
Early Warning	NEC definition.	**NEC**
ECC	NEC Engineering and Construction Contract.	**¶3.10.2**
ECI contract	Early contractor involvement contract.	**¶3.5.2**
economic duress	The use of illegitimate economic pressure to overcome free will and induce a contracting party to provide extra-contractual benefits that it does not freely consent to.	**¶21.13**
economic loss	In the context of damages intended as compensation for loss suffered as a consequence of a wrongful act by another, economic loss is confined to financial loss, and does not include personal injury or damage to property.	
efficiency impact	The increased efficiency resulting from the implementation of an **enhancement application**.	**¶29.1.3**
EIC	European International Contractors.	**¶3.10.2**
ejusdem generis	A rule of **construction of contract terms** in which general words may be restricted to the same genus as the specific words immediately preceding them. (Latin)	**¶2.13.3**
election	Choosing from a number of different rights or remedies.	
Employer	The **party** to a **construction contract** for whom the work is done. Also referred to as the Principal or the Owner or Client.	**¶3.1.1**
Employer	FIDIC definition (Red, Pink, Yellow, Silver, and Emerald Books)	**FIDIC**
Employer	NEC term identified in the Contract Data.	**NEC**
Employer	Definition in SCL Delay and Disruption Protocol 2nd Edition.	**SCL**
Employer Delay	Definition in SCL Delay and Disruption Protocol 2nd Edition.	**SCL**

Term	Meaning	Defined in Section
Employer Delay to Completion	Definition in SCL Delay and Disruption Protocol 2nd Edition.	**SCL**
Employer Delay to Progress	Definition in SCL Delay and Disruption Protocol 2nd Edition.	**SCL**
Employer risk event	An event which is the risk or responsibility of the **Employer** under the **Contract**.	**¶14.7.1**
Employer Risk Event	Definition in SCL Delay and Disruption Protocol 2nd Edition.	**SCL**
Employer's Equipment	FIDIC definition (Red, Pink, Yellow, Silver, and Emerald Books)	**FIDIC**
Employer's Personnel	FIDIC definition (Red, Pink, Yellow, Silver, and Emerald Books)	**FIDIC**
Employer's Representative	FIDIC definition (Silver Book)	**FIDIC**
Employer's requirements	The **Employer's** requirements for the facility to be provided under a **construction contract**, including performance requirements, data, and information provided by the Employer, a statement of intended purpose of the facility, and criteria for testing and performance of the completed **Works**.	**¶11.4.1**
Employer's Requirements	FIDIC definition (Yellow, Silver, and Emerald Books)	**FIDIC**
Employer's risks	Those risks for which the **Contract** assigns the legal responsibilities and liability for the risks materialising to the **Employer**.	**¶24.1**
Employer-Supplied Materials	FIDIC definition (Red, Yellow, Silver, and Emerald Books)	**FIDIC**
end of liability date	NEC term identified in the Contract Data.	**NEC**
Engineer	The person, firm, or company which fulfills the contract administration role of the Engineer for the purposes of and as defined in the **Contract**. The term is synonymous with Architect or Superintendent as used in certain contracts.	**¶8.1.2**
Engineer	FIDIC definition (Red, Pink, Yellow, and Emerald Books).	**FIDIC**
engineer	The person/entity providing one or more 'engineering' (including project management) services in relation to one or more aspects of a construction project, such obligations being defined under the engineer's contract with the **Employer**.	**¶8.1.2**
Engineer's contract	The agreement between the **Employer** and the **Engineer** containing the terms of the Engineer's engagement.	**¶8.1.1**
Engineer's Representative	A person delegated by the **Engineer** (usually in writing) to exercise certain powers as provided for in the **Contract**.	**¶8.2.1**
Engineer's Representative	FIDIC definition (Red, Yellow, and Emerald Books).	**FIDIC**

Term	Meaning	Defined in Section
engineering contract	A species of **construction contract**, the primary object of which is the construction of an industrial facility designed by **engineers**, such as an offshore oil and gas platform or a mineral processing facility. Although construction of buildings may be part of an engineering contract, these are ancillary to the main functional purpose of the facility.	
enhancement applications	**ICT** applications that enable new and more efficient ways of undertaking traditional tasks.	**¶29.1.3**
entire agreement	A clause in a **contract** to the effect that the written terms constitute the entire agreement and understanding between the **parties**, and that any representations made during negotiations prior to entry into the contract have no contractual effect.	**¶2.16**
entire contract	A contract in which the **Contractor** is not entitled to payment of the **contract price** or any part thereof until the work has been fully completed where the **Contract** does not make express provision for progress payments.	**¶21.1.17**
EOT	**Extension of time**.	
EPC contract	Engineer, procure, and construct contract. A **construction contract** (also referred to as a turnkey contract) in which the **Contractor** takes total responsibility for the engineering (**design**), procurement, and construction, and provides a fully equipped facility ready for operation (at the 'turn of the key').	**¶3.4**
EPCM contract	Engineer, procure, and construction management contract. A **construction contract** in which the **Employer** engages a **Construction Manager** to act as the Employer's agent to program, coordinate, and manage the **design** and construction activities which are divided into packages which are separately undertaken by trade contractors contracted directly to the Employer. Also called a **construction management contract**.	**¶3.4**
EPIC contract	Engineer, procure, install, and construct contract. Essentially the same as an **EPC contract**.	
equipment	The appliances and machinery brought by the **Contractor** onto the **Site** to carry out the **Works**, and afterwards removed.	**¶9.1.11.3**
Equipment	NEC definition.	**NEC**
equity	The separate body of law, developed in the English Court of Chancery, which supplements, corrects, and controls the strict rules of the **common law**.	**¶1.6**
estoppel	A party in legal proceedings is precluded ('estopped') from asserting a position contrary to that which it has already established by its promise, representation, or conduct. Thus, whenever a party has by its promise, representation, or conduct induced another to make an assumption that something is or will be the case, that party may be estopped from going back on the representation that led to the assumption.	**¶14.11**
ETH	The cryptocurrency used by **Ethereum**.	**¶29.3.5.1**

Term	Meaning	Defined in Section
Ethereum	**Blockchain** software running on a network of computers that ensures that data and small computer programs called **smart contracts** are replicated and processed on all the computers on the network, without a central coordinator.[8]	**¶29.3.5.1**
evaluation	A style of **ADR** in which a **third-party neutral** evaluates the **parties'** evidence and submissions and provides an independent and impartial opinion of their legal rights.	**¶28.2.8**
Evaluative mediation	NADRAC glossary of common ADR terms.	**NADRAC**
ex aequo et bono	Latin for 'according to the right and good' or 'from equity and conscience.' An **Arbitrator** authorised to act *ex aequo et bono* has the power to dispense with strict consideration of the law and consider solely what they consider to be fair and equitable in the circumstances.	**¶28.11.1**
Excavation	FIDIC definition (Emerald Book)	**FIDIC**
exceptio generalibus derogant	An exception departing from the general. (Latin)	
Exceptional Event	FIDIC definition (Red, Yellow, Silver, and Emerald Books)	**FIDIC**
exchange rates	NEC term identified in the Contract Data.	**NEC**
excusable delay	A **delay** caused by the **Employer** or the Employer's agents or due to a neutral event beyond the control of the **Contractor**.	**¶14.4**
excusable delay	Definition in SCL Delay and Disruption Protocol 2nd Edition.	**SCL**
Expert	The independent **third-party neutral** who conducts an **expert determination.**	**¶28.8.1**
expert appraisal	Non-binding **expert determination**.	**¶28.8.1**
Expert appraisal	NADRAC glossary of common ADR terms.	**NADRAC**
expert determination	A method of **ADR** in which an independent impartial **Expert** is engaged by the disputing **parties** to determine those disputed questions of fact and/or law in the reference defined by the parties.	**¶28.8.1**
Expert determination	NADRAC glossary of common ADR terms.	**NADRAC**
Expert mediation	NADRAC glossary of common ADR terms.	**NADRAC**
express term	A term of a contract which is explicitly stated or defined by the parties to be part of the contract.	
expressio unius est exclusio alterius	A rule of construction in which the express mention of one thing excludes the other. (Latin)	**¶2.13.3**

8 https://bitsonblocks.net/2016/10/02/gentle-introduction-ethereum/ (accessed 7 April 2021).

Term	Meaning	Defined in Section
extension of time	A formal extension of the contractually specified **Date for Completion** approved by the person nominated in the **Contract**.	**¶14.7.1**
Extension of Time or EOT	FIDIC definition (Red, Yellow, Silver, and Emerald Books)	**FIDIC**
extension of time (EOT)	Definition in SCL Delay and Disruption Protocol 2nd Edition.	**SCL**
Facilitated negotiation	NADRAC glossary of common ADR terms.	**NADRAC**
facilitation	A style of **ADR** in which a **third-party neutral** facilitates discussions and negotiations between the **parties**, in order to assist the parties themselves to reach a resolution of a **dispute** acceptable to all parties.	**¶28.2.8**
Facilitation	NADRAC glossary of common ADR terms.	**NADRAC**
facilitative ADR	An **ADR** process where a dispute resolution practitioner assists the parties to a **dispute** to identify the disputed issues, develop options, consider alternatives, and try to reach an agreement about some issues or the whole dispute. (NADRAC) Examples of facilitative processes include **mediation**, facilitation, and facilitated negotiation.	**¶28.2.1**
Facilitative dispute resolution processes	NADRAC glossary of common ADR terms.	**NADRAC**
Fact finding	NADRAC glossary of common ADR terms.	**NADRAC**
fast track	A method of project execution in which construction is started before the **design** has been completed.	**¶3.9.2.1**
fast track arbitration	An expedited **arbitration** process in which the aim is to achieve an arbitration **award** in the minimum time consistent with a fair process complying with the rules of **natural justice** (procedural fairness).	**¶28.11.11**
Fast-track arbitration	NADRAC glossary of common ADR terms.	**NADRAC**
Fee	NEC definition.	**NEC**
FEED	Front end engineering design. The engineering **design** carried out at the start of a project to confirm its technical and economic feasibility and determine the basic parameters to be used for subsequent detailed design. The term is commonly used in procurement of facilities for extracting and processing minerals and oil and gas.	**¶8.1.8**
FIDIC	International Federation of Consulting Engineers (Fédération Internationale des Ingénieurs-Conseils).	**¶1.9**
FIDIC	FIDIC definition (Red, Pink, Yellow, Silver, and Emerald Books)	**FIDIC**
FIDIC Golden Principles	The essential features of a FIDIC Contract that make the risk/reward allocation fair and balanced.	

Term	Meaning	Defined in Section
final certificate	A statement by the Engineer or the Employer that the Contractor has completed all the Works in accordance with the Contract.	**¶17.4**
final payment	The payment to be made by the **Employer** following receipt of the **final payment certificate**.	
final payment certificate	A certificate issued by the **Engineer** at the conclusion of the **defects liability period** (or maintenance period) certifying that all known **Defects** have been rectified and the Engineer is satisfied that the **Contractor** has fulfilled its contractual obligations.	**¶18.8**
Final Payment Certificate or FPC	FIDIC definition (Red, Pink, Yellow, and Emerald Books)	**FIDIC**
Final Statement	FIDIC definition (Red, Pink, Yellow, Silver, and Emerald Books)	**FIDIC**
First-party insurance	Insurance against the risk that a party will suffer a loss which does not represent its liability to any other party.	**¶26.1**
fit for purpose	The requirement that a **design** or a constructed facility is suitable to fulfill the known purpose.	
float	A term used in **CPM** for the amount of free time available before an activity must start so that it does not extend the overall time for **Completion**. Activities on the **critical path** have zero float.	**¶14.3.2**
float	Definition in SCL Delay and Disruption Protocol 2nd Edition.	**SCL**
force majeure	Under the common law, *force majeure* is an exceptional event or circumstance which cannot be resisted or controlled and which satisfies the criteria stated in the **Contract**. In **civil law** systems, *force majeure* is defined in the relevant *Civil Code* and operates independently of party agreement, which means that it will protect an obligee even if the contract does not contain a *force majeure* clause.	**¶2.3.2**
Force Majeure	FIDIC definition (Pink Book)	**FIDIC**
Foreign Currency	FIDIC definition (Red, Pink, Yellow, Silver, and Emerald Books)	**FIDIC**
forfeiture	See **termination**.	
forum	The place where the issue is being decided.	**¶1.8**
free float	Definition in SCL Delay and Disruption Protocol 2nd Edition.	**SCL**
freedom of contract	The ability of legal persons (eg natural persons over 18 years of age and properly constituted companies) to enter into a binding agreement to do anything, provided it is not contrary to the law or **public policy** (and in some **legal jurisdictions**, morals).	**¶4.3.1**
frustration	The termination of a contract by operation of law on the emergence of a fundamentally different situation that was not in the contemplation of either party.	**¶2.3.1**

Term	Meaning	Defined in Section
functus officio	Has exhausted its mandate, for example, an **Arbitrator** is *functus officio* at the time s/he has handed down his/her final **award**.	**¶21.8.1**
fundamental change in circumstances	A **civil law** principle similar to the principle of **frustration** of contract in **common law** countries. If the circumstances change fundamentally after the execution of a contract so that the performance of the contract would be onerous for one **party**, that party has the right to terminate the contract or to modify some articles of the contract.	
Gantt chart	A horizontal bar chart with activities represented by bars on a timescale, with the names of the activities in a column on the left.	**¶15.4.2**
Gantt chart	Definition in SCL Delay and Disruption Protocol 2nd Edition.	**SCL**
garantie décennale	Decennial liability. (France) The statutory liability for a **Contractor** (10 years), in so far as stability and security of the building are affected by **latent defects.**	**¶1.8**
General Conditions	The **conditions of contract** in a **standard form contract** which are of a general nature and are not specific to the project, the **parties**, the **Site**, or the specific scope of work.	**¶3.3**
General Conditions	FIDIC definition (Red, Yellow, Silver, and Emerald Books)	**FIDIC**
generalia specialibus non derogant	Things general do not restrict things special. (Latin)	
Geotechnical Baseline Report or GBR	FIDIC definition (Emerald Book)	**FIDIC**
Geotechnical Data Report or GDR	FIDIC definition (Emerald Book)	**FIDIC**
GIS	Geospatial information systems.	**¶29.4**
global claim	A claim by the **Contractor** for additional compensation or an extension of time where it has not shown the causal links between its asserted entitlement and events for which the **Employer** is liable under the **Contract**.	**¶C.1**
global claim	Definition in SCL Delay and Disruption Protocol 2nd Edition.	**SCL**
Goods	FIDIC definition (Red, Pink, Yellow, Silver, and Emerald Books)	**FIDIC**
governing law of the contract	The law that governs the **parties'** contractual relations. The governing law of a contract provides the legal rules for determining issues in connection with its formation, validity, interpretation, and the rights and obligations of the contracting parties. Also known as the proper law of the contract.	**¶2.6**
Green Book	FIDIC Short Form of Contract (1999).	

Term	Meaning	Defined in Section
Hague Convention on Choice of Court Agreements	*Hague Convention of 30 June 2005 on Choice of Court Agreements*. The **Convention** applies in international cases to exclusive choice of court agreements concluded in civil or commercial matters.	**¶28.13.2.6**
Hague Principles	*Principles on Choice of Law in International Commercial Contracts (2015)* published by the Hague Conference on Private International Law.	
hammock	Definition in SCL Delay and Disruption Protocol 2nd Edition.	**SCL**
hanging activity	Definition in SCL Delay and Disruption Protocol 2nd Edition.	**SCL**
hash	Mathematical operator transforms one number into another number, often used in cryptography as a way of concealing the original number.[9]	
head contract	A **contract** for construction of a facility between the owner or user of the facility (**Employer**) and a contractor (**Contractor**) who takes responsibility for construction of the complete **Works** in accordance with the requirements of the **Contract**. The Contractor generally employs one or more **subcontractors** to execute some (but not all) of the Works.	**¶3.1.1**
Head Contractor	The **Contractor** for a **head contract**.	**¶3.1.1**
head office overheads	Definition in SCL Delay and Disruption Protocol 2nd Edition.	**SCL**
head office overheads and profit formulae	Definition in SCL Delay and Disruption Protocol 2nd Edition.	**SCL**
HGCRA	*Housing Grants, Construction and Regeneration Act 1996* (UK)	**¶28.9.2.1**
HKIAC	Hong Kong International Arbitration Centre.	**¶4.6**
hot commissioning	A phase of **commissioning** when the **plant** and systems are energised, and when the actual performance of the individual plant components is demonstrated and confirmed against their specified performance, involving the introduction of feedstock and process fluids.	**¶11.7**
Hybrid dispute resolution processes	NADRAC glossary of common ADR terms.	**NADRAC**
IBA	International Bar Association.	**¶4.6**
ICC	International Chamber of Commerce.	**¶3.10**
ICE	Institution of Civil Engineers (UK).	**¶3.10.1**

9 David L Shirer, *Basic Blockchain* (Robinson Great Britain, 2020) 157.

Term	Meaning	Defined in Section
ICSID Convention	*Convention on the Settlement of Investment Disputes between States and Nationals of Other States*. The ***ICSID Convention*** is a treaty ratified by 154 Contracting States. It entered into force on October 14, 1966. Also known as the *Washington Convention*.	
ICT	Information and communication technology.	**¶29.1.2**
IDF	Intelligent document format.	**¶29.5.2**
IFC	Issued for construction (drawings).	
IMI	International Mediation Institute.	**¶28.5.1**
impact	Definition in SCL Delay and Disruption Protocol 2nd Edition.	**SCL**
impacted as-planned analysis	Definition in SCL Delay and Disruption Protocol 2nd Edition.	**SCL**
implied term	A term of a contract which the **parties** have not expressly stated.	
implied term of cooperation	Each *party* agrees to do all that is necessary to be done on his/her part to enable the contract to be performed.	**¶2.14.3**
imprévision	The unexpected (it presumes the fulfilment of certain conditions specifically imposed by the law) (France).	**¶2.3.3**
in rem claim	A claim *in rem* literally means 'against the thing.' It is taken directly against property and it can be brought even though the owner has no personal liability.	**¶2.5**
incentive schedule	NEC term identified in the Contract Data.	**NEC**
incentivised target cost contract	A **construction contract** in which the **Contractor** is rewarded or penalised based on its performance measured against a target cost.	**¶3.5.3**
indemnity	An undertaking given by A to B that A accepts some liability or responsibility which would otherwise fall on B.	
Indirect negotiation	NADRAC glossary of common ADR terms.	**NADRAC**
injunction	A court order that compels or prevents a course of action. Usually an injunction is granted to stop a party from doing or continuing to do an illegal act.	
innominate contract	A **contract** that does not come within the defined class of **nominate contracts**. (civil law)	**¶1.4**
innominate term	An innominate term of a **contract** is between a condition and a warranty. If the consequences of breach are such as to deny the innocent party the benefit of the contract, it will be entitled to terminate the contract, otherwise the innocent party will only be entitled to damages.	**¶22.3.2**
institutional arbitration	An **arbitration** that is administered by a named institution.	**¶28.11.2**
intelligent contract	A contract in an electronic form that has processing capabilities built into it that can receive or output information relating to contractual functions and/or autonomously carry out contractual functions.	**¶29.5.2**

Term	Meaning	Defined in Section
intellectual property	Statutory and **common law** rights which protect the owners of creative and intellectual effort, for example, copyright, patents, trademarks.	
interest rate	NEC term identified in the Contract Data.	**NEC**
interim payment certificate	A payment certificate, usually issued by the **Engineer** as agent for the **Employer**, certifying the amount of a **progress payment** due to the **Contractor**.	**¶21.3**
Interim Payment Certificate or IPC	FIDIC definition (Red, Pink, Yellow, and Emerald Books).	**FIDIC**
international arbitration	**Arbitration** in which (a) the parties to an arbitration agreement have, at the time of the conclusion of that agreement, their places of business in different States; or (b) one of the following places is situated outside the State in which the parties have their places of business: (i) the place of arbitration if determined in, or pursuant to, the arbitration agreement; (ii) any place where a substantial part of the obligations of the commercial relationship is to be performed or the place with which the subject-matter of the dispute is most closely connected; or (c) the parties have expressly agreed that the subject matter of the arbitration agreement relates to more than one country. (UNCITRAL Model Law on International Commercial Arbitration[10])	
international construction contract	A **construction contract** for the provision of goods and services in which: (a) the parties to the Contract have, at the time of the conclusion of their agreement, their places of business in different **legal jurisdictions**; or (b) one of the following places is situated outside the **legal jurisdiction** in which the parties have their places of business: (i) the **Site**; or (ii) any place where a substantial part of the obligations for the **Works** is to be performed.	**¶2.5**
international mandatory rules of law	Rules of law which must be applied within the **jurisdiction**, even if the **proper law of the contract** is that of another **jurisdiction**.	**¶1.8**
Internet of Things	The combination of sensor and wireless technologies that connects physical objects to the Internet so that data can be accessed from anywhere.	**¶29.6**
interpretation of contract terms	Synonymous with **construction of contract terms**. 'Interpretation of a promise or agreement or a term thereof is the ascertainment of its meaning.' s200 American Restatement of Contracts (2nd)	
Investigation	NADRAC glossary of common ADR terms.	**NADRAC**

10 https://uncitral.un.org/sites/uncitral.un.org/files/media-documents/uncitral/en/19-09955_e_ebook.pdf (accessed 23 July 2021).

Term	Meaning	Defined in Section
IoT	**Internet of Things.**	**¶29.3.4**
IP	**Intellectual property**.	
IPD	Integrated project delivery.	**¶3.5.4**
ITC	**Incentivised target cost contract**.	
JCT	Joint Contracts Tribunal, publisher of standard forms of contract.	
JICA	Japan International Cooperation Agency.	**¶3.9.3.1**
joint and several liability	Under common law, where two or more persons are liable for wrongdoing to a plaintiff, each wrongdoer is separately liable to the plaintiff for the entire liability, as well as all the wrongdoers collectively being liable. Under joint and several liability a plaintiff may enforce the entire liability against all or any one or any combination of wrongdoers.	
joint names insurance	Insurance taken out by one or more of the parties to the Contract in respect of identified risks (usually for contract works risk and sometimes other risks such as those associated with workplace injuries and similar matters), in the names of and for the benefit of one or more of the contracting parties, or third parties.	**¶26.9**
Joint Venture or JV	FIDIC definition (Red, Yellow, Silver, and Emerald Books)	**FIDIC**
Judicial dispute resolution (or judicial ADR)	NADRAC glossary of common ADR terms.	**NADRAC**
jurisdiction	The authority, capacity, and decision-making power of a court or tribunal to decide a matter in **dispute** between contracting parties, for example, an **Adjudicator** has jurisdiction to determine a payment **dispute** subject to the relevant **Security of Payment legislation**. Also used in the sense of a **legal jurisdiction**.	
JV Undertaking	FIDIC definition (Red, Yellow, Silver, and Emerald Books)	**FIDIC**
key date	Definition in SCL Delay and Disruption Protocol 2nd Edition.	**SCL**
Key Date	NEC definition.	**NEC**
key dates	NEC term identified in the Contract Data.	**NEC**
lag	Definition in SCL Delay and Disruption Protocol 2nd Edition.	**SCL**
language of this contract	NEC term identified in the Contract Data.	**NEC**
latent condition	A **Site** condition not known to the **parties** at the time they entered into the **Contract**, but which subsequently becomes manifest, for example, rock which had not been detected by pre-contract geotechnical investigations but which was revealed by the **Contractor's** excavations.	**¶9.7.1**
latent defect	A defect which a reasonable inspection at the time of **Taking-Over** would not have been discovered.	**¶18.11**
law of the contract	NEC term identified in the Contract Data.	**NEC**

Term	Meaning	Defined in Section
law of the forum	The procedural law that applies to any court proceedings, including the coercive power of the court in support of arbitration proceedings.	**¶1.8**
Law Reports	Published and widely available books containing the judgements of judges in determining the outcome of specific disputes between the parties to litigation. Such judgements usually contain the detailed reasoning that the judge went through in determining the outcome of a **dispute**. In common law systems, the judgements in the Law Reports, collectively, constitute the statement of the **common law** in the judges' reasoning behind the individual judgements.	**¶1.4**
Laws	FIDIC definition (Red, Pink, Yellow, Silver, and Emerald Books)	**FIDIC**
LCIA	London Court of International Arbitration.	**¶4.6**
LDEDCA	*Local Democracy, Economic Development and Construction Act 2009* (UK), an *Act* amending the ***HGCRA***.	**¶28.9.2.1**
lead	Definition in SCL Delay and Disruption Protocol 2nd Edition.	**SCL**
legal definitions	Words or phrases having a precise definition which is often specified by case law.	
legal jurisdiction	The geographic area that is subject to a unique set of laws. For example, in Australia, each of the eight States and two Territories is a separate legal jurisdiction, because the Parliament in each of those States and Territories has passed laws that apply within the geographical limits of the State or Territory.	**¶1.4**
legal person	A legal person is an entity on which the legal system confers rights and obligations and includes natural persons and artificial bodies such as corporations or companies.	**¶1.8**
legal privilege	A communication (including an oral communication or a document) has legal privilege if the communication cannot be used as evidence of any admission in subsequent legal proceedings or arbitration.	
Letter of Acceptance	FIDIC definition (Red, Pink, Yellow, and Emerald Books).	**FIDIC**
letter of acceptance	The formal acceptance by the **Employer** of the **Contractor's tender** for the execution of the **Works**.	**¶5.4**
letter of intent	A document issued prior to entry into a contract, which signifies the **Employer's** intent to enter into a contract with a preferred **Tenderer** at a future time.	**¶5.2**
Letter of Tender	FIDIC definition (Red, Pink, Yellow, and Emerald Books).	**FIDIC**
level of effort	Definition in SCL Delay and Disruption Protocol 2nd Edition.	**SCL**
lex arbitri	The law governing the **arbitration**. The substantive law that gives an **Arbitrator jurisdiction** to determine a **dispute** instead of the courts. (Latin)	**¶2.5**
lex causae	The law or laws applicable to the cause of action. (Latin)	

Term	Meaning	Defined in Section
lex constructionis	The law relating to construction projects which is widely accepted internationally in **legal jurisdictions** subject to the rule of law and which recognises the parties' **freedom of contract**, irrespective of the specific impact of **statute law**. (Latin)	**¶1.2**
lex contractus	The law that governs the legal consequences of the rights and obligations the **parties** have assumed under their contract, that is, the **proper law of the contract.** (Latin)	**¶2.5**
lex domicilii	The law of the habitual residence of a person. (Latin)	**¶2.5**
lex fori	The **law of the forum**. (Latin)	**¶1.8**
lex loci arbitri	The law of the **seat of arbitration**. (Latin)	**¶2.5**
lex loci contractus	The law of the place where a contract is made. (Latin)	**¶2.5**
lex loci delicti	See ***lex loci delicti commissi.***	
lex loci delicti commissi	The law of the place where a wrong is committed. (Latin)	**¶2.5**
lex loci rei sitae	The laws applicable to the execution of the **Works** at the **Site**. (Latin)	**¶2.5**
lex mercatoria	The Law Merchant: an a-national system of best practice in international commercial law, which has evolved by international custom and usage, and which is free from legal technicalities. (Latin)	**¶4.7**
lex rei situs	The law of the location of the thing. (Latin)	**¶2.5**
liability	An obligation or responsibility enforceable at law.	
liability insurance	Insurance that is expressed in terms that the insurer's liability to indemnify only arises where an event has occurred that renders the insured liable to a third party, or where there has been the notification of a claim in respect of such liability.	**¶26.1**
lidar	Light detection and ranging.	**¶29.6**
limitation period	The period during which proceedings in court or in an **arbitration** on a cause of action may be commenced, or an interlocutory step taken in proceedings. The relevant periods are defined in legislation. Different periods apply to causes of action based on a simple contract or on a contract executed under **deed**, or on a 'building action' (as defined in the relevant legislation).	**¶3.6.2**
line of balance	A project/production analysis method designed to create a project in which each team or pool of resources works with minimal interruption.	**¶15.4.3**
Lining	FIDIC definition (Emerald Book)	**FIDIC**
liquidated and ascertained damages, liquidated damages, LADs, LDs	Definition in SCL Delay and Disruption Protocol 2nd Edition.	**SCL**

Term	Meaning	Defined in Section
liquidated damages	An agreed pre-estimate of loss and damages specified in the **Contract** for a specified breach of contract. In its most common form, it is applied in respect of delay damages for each day that the **Date of Completion** exceeds the **Date for Completion**. (common law)	¶14.2.1
liquidation	Termination of a company's existence by realising its assets, discharging its liabilities, and distributing any surplus to the creditors who are entitled.	
Local Currency	FIDIC definition (Red, Pink, Yellow, Silver, and Emerald Books)	FIDIC
logic links	Definition in SCL Delay and Disruption Protocol 2nd Edition.	SCL
lump sum contract	A contract in which a stipulated amount is paid for work (usually described by reference to an end result) to be performed. Fixed price contracts are the most common form of lump sum contracts and provide for the payment of an agreed amount with provision for adjustment for **Variations** to the scope of work or scope of performance or any extra costs incurred as a result of delays.	¶21.1.5
machine learning	An automated approach to learning patterns from empirical data using training examples, usually large databases, with the development of a machine learning algorithm which when applied to new examples creates accurate predictions.[11]	¶29.3.4
Main Options	NEC definition.	NEC
maintenance period	The specified period after the **Date for Completion** during which the **Contractor** has the contractual obligation to rectify **Defects** and also to repair or maintain the **Works**. The term may be synonymous with **defects liability period**.	¶18.1.3
mandatory [rules of] law	Provisions of a statute which the parties to a **contract** may not derogate from.	¶1.8
Materials	FIDIC definition (Red, Pink, Yellow, Silver, and Emerald Books)	FIDIC
MDB	Multilateral development bank.	¶3.10.1
measurement contract	A contract in which the **Contractor** is paid for the work it performs, based on measurement of the actual quantities of each different element of construction, applied to pre-agreed rates in the **Contract**. A measurement contract may use a (re-measured) **bill of quantities** with a schedule of rates, or cost plus reimbursement of materials and labour used by the **Contractor** on the **Works**.	¶21.1.6
Mechanical Completion	Physical completion of a facility, ready to be commissioned.	¶16.1
Med-arb	NADRAC glossary of common ADR terms.	NADRAC

11 Joachim P Sturmberg & Carmel Martin, *Handbook of Systems and Complexity in Health* (Springer, 2013) 455.

Term	Meaning	Defined in Section
mediation	A process of facilitated **negotiation** in which a **third-party neutral** assists the **parties** to try and reach an **amicable settlement** on their own resolution of their **dispute**.	**¶28.5.1**
Mediation	NADRAC glossary of common ADR terms.	**NADRAC**
Mediator	A person independent of the **parties** to a contract who conducts a **mediation** with the aim of assisting the parties to achieve an **amicable settlement** of a **dispute**.	**¶28.5.1**
Merkle tree	A mathematical construct for a stream of data that builds on itself to ensure the integrity of the data; if one historical part of the tree is changed, the entire edifice becomes corrupted providing a warning that there was an effort to make a change.[12]	**¶29.3.5**
method of measurement	NEC term identified in the Contract Data.	**NEC**
method statement	Definition in SCL Delay and Disruption Protocol 2nd Edition.	**SCL**
milestone	A discrete point in the progress of the **Works** at which certain identified activities have been completed.	**¶14.3.1**
milestone	Definition in SCL Delay and Disruption Protocol 2nd Edition.	**SCL**
Milestone	FIDIC definition (Emerald Book)	**FIDIC**
Milestone Certificate	FIDIC definition (Emerald Book)	**FIDIC**
milestone payment	A payment that is due on the achievement of a specified **milestone**.	**¶21.1.11**
mini-trial	A method of **ADR** in which each **party** presents their best-case scenario to a panel comprising a senior executive from each of the **parties**, usually chaired by a neutral facilitator. Also called Senior Executive appraisal.	**¶28.7.1**
Mini-trial	NADRAC glossary of common ADR terms.	**NADRAC**
mitigation	Definition in SCL Delay and Disruption Protocol 2nd Edition.	**SCL**
Model Law	***UNCITRAL*** *Model Law on International Commercial Arbitration*. Adopted by UN Resolution 40/72 in 1985 with amendments adopted by UN Resolution 61/33 in 2006.	**¶4.6**
month	FIDIC definition (Red, Yellow, Silver, and Emerald Books)	**FIDIC**
moral rights	The rights of an individual author of an artistic work conferred by the relevant *Copyright Act* which provides for the following three rights of authorship: (a) the right of attribution, (b) the right against false attribution, and (c) the right of integrity.	
Multi-party mediation	NADRAC glossary of common ADR terms.	**NADRAC**

12 David L Shirer, *Basic Blockchain* (Robinson Great Britain, 2020) 159.

Term	Meaning	Defined in Section
must start/ must finish	Definition in SCL Delay and Disruption Protocol 2nd Edition.	**SCL**
mutatis mutandis	Notwithstanding differences between two things being compared because of their different situations, the basic point remains the same. (Latin)	
NADRAC	National Alternative Dispute Resolution Advisory Council. (Australia)	**¶28.2.4**
named suppliers	NEC term identified in the Contract Data provided by the Contractor.	**NEC**
natural justice	A well-defined concept which includes two fundamental rules of fair procedure: • A person may not be a judge in their own cause (the rule against bias) • A person's defence must always be fairly heard (the right to procedural fairness).[13]	
NCC	Netherlands Commercial Court.	**¶28.13.2.3**
NEC	New Engineering Contract published by the Institution of Civil Engineers.	**¶3.10.2**
negative lag	Definition in SCL Delay and Disruption Protocol 2nd Edition.	**SCL**
negative total float	Definition in SCL Delay and Disruption Protocol 2nd Edition.	**SCL**
negotiation	In the context of dispute resolution, negotiation is a style of **ADR** in which representatives of the contracting parties meet and discuss their differences, generally without the presence of third parties, with a view to **amicable settlement**.	**¶28.2.8**
negotiorum gestio	Enables one who intervenes without authority in another's affairs for the latter's benefit to claim reimbursement and indemnity. (civil law) See *Rome II* Article 11.	**¶1.5**
network	A representation of the logical sequence of activities and the relationship or the links between them.	**¶15.1**
network analysis	See **critical path method**.	
network logic	The logical relationships between activities in a **network**.	**¶15.1**
New York Convention	*United Nations 1958 New York Convention on the Recognition and Enforcement of Foreign Arbitral Awards*.[14]	**¶4.3.5**
No-objection	FIDIC definition (Red, Yellow, Silver, and Emerald Books)	**FIDIC**
NOD	Notice of Delay.	**¶14.7.2**
NOD	Notice of Dissatisfaction. FIDIC definition (Red, Yellow, and Silver Books).	**FIDIC**
nominate contract	Contracts of a 'standard' type which are governed by particular statutory rules. (civil law)	**¶1.4**

13 Sir William Wade & C Forsyth, *Administrative Law* (Oxford University Press, 9th ed, 2004) 440.
14 www.newyorkconvention.org/english (accessed 24 July 2021).

Term	Meaning	Defined in Section
nominated subcontractor	A subcontractor of the **Contractor** nominated by the **Employer**, under rights provided for in the **Contract**.	**¶9.3.1**
non-compensable delay	A **delay** that does not entitle a party to additional payment.	**¶14.4**
non-compensable event	Definition in SCL Delay and Disruption Protocol 2nd Edition.	**SCL**
non-critical delay	A delay to an activity that is not on the **critical path** of the construction **programme** and therefore does not affect the project **Completion** date.	**¶14.4**
non-excusable delay	A delay that is **attributable** to the **Contractor** or the Contractor's agents and therefore does not entitle the Contractor to an **EOT** or compensation.	**¶14.4**
non-excusable delay	Definition in SCL Delay and Disruption Protocol 2nd Edition.	**SCL**
non-mandatory [rules of] law	Provisions of a statute which the **parties** can opt out of by appropriate agreement otherwise in their **contract**.	**¶1.8**
NOP	Non-Owner participant in an **alliance contract**.	**¶3.5.4**
noscitur a sociis	A rule of construction in which a word of ambiguous meaning may take its character from the surrounding words if they have a common characteristic. (Latin)	**¶2.13.3**
notice	A formal written document required by the **Contract** to advise the other **party** of a state of affairs relevant to the **Contract**.	**¶27.4**
Notice	FIDIC definition (Red, Yellow, and Silver Books).	**FIDIC**
Notice of Dissatisfaction or NOD	FIDIC definition (Red, Pink, Yellow, Silver, and Emerald Books)	**FIDIC**
novation	A form of **assignment**, whereby the assignee third party takes over the full contractual rights of the assignor, as though named as an original party to the transaction.	**¶9.12.5**
O&M manuals	Operations and maintenance manuals.	**¶16.1**
ODR	Online dispute resolution.	**¶29.7.3**
On-line dispute resolution, ODR, eADR, cyber-ADR	NADRAC glossary of common ADR terms.	**NADRAC**
ordre public	**Public policy**. (France)	**¶4.3.5**
Others	NEC definition.	**NEC**
Owner	See **Employer**.	
pacta sunt servanda	A Latin phrase that means that agreements are to be kept.	**¶1.2**
pari passu	Equally, without preference on one side or the other. (Latin)	**¶10.10.2**
parol evidence rule	Oral (parol) evidence is not admissible to add to, vary, or contradict the written terms of a contract. (common law)	**¶2.12**

Term	Meaning	Defined in Section
Part	FIDIC definition (Red, Yellow, and Emerald Books).	**FIDIC**
Particular Conditions	See **Special Conditions**.	**¶3.9.1**
Particular Conditions	FIDIC definition (Red, Yellow, Silver, and Emerald Books)	**FIDIC**
Parties	NADRAC glossary of common ADR terms.	**NADRAC**
Parties	NEC definition.	**NEC**
Partnering	NADRAC glossary of common ADR terms.	**NADRAC**
party	One of the entities or persons who enter into a contract.	
Party	FIDIC definition (Red, Pink, Yellow, Silver, and Emerald Books)	**FIDIC**
Path	Definition in SCL Delay and Disruption Protocol 2nd Edition.	**SCL**
payment certificate	A certificate issued by the **Engineer** to the **Employer**, showing the amount of payment due in response to the **Contractor's payment claim**. A payment certificate can be either an interim payment certificate for a progress payment, or a final payment certificate for the final payment.	**¶21.5**
Payment Certificate	FIDIC definition (Red, Pink, Yellow, and Emerald Books).	**FIDIC**
payment claim	A **Contractor's** claim for payment to the **Employer**. **Security of Payment legislation:** a payment claim complying with the statutory provisions of the relevant *Security of Payment* legislation.	**¶21.5**
payment schedule	**Security of Payment legislation:** A schedule provided by an **Employer** in response to a payment claim by the **Contractor**, complying with the relevant *Security of Payment* legislation.	
PC item.	**Prime cost item**.	
PC sum	**Prime cost sum**.	
PCs	**Particular Conditions**.	
PDR (Primary Dispute Resolution)	NADRAC glossary of common ADR terms.	**NADRAC**
penalty	Under the **common law**, a clause stipulating a consequence for breach of a term of the contract will be an unenforceable penalty if the consequence is out of all proportion to the legitimate interests of the innocent party in performance of the primary obligation.[15] By contrast, some **civil law jurisdictions** allow penalty clauses where the pre-agreed amount of damages for breach of contract or non-performance can be higher than the actual damages that could reasonably be expected.	**¶1.4.1**

15 The rule against penalties is a rule of contract law based on public policy. It is a question of construction of the parties' contract judged by reference to the circumstances at the time of contracting; the public policy is that the courts will not enforce a stipulation for punishment for breach of contract. *Cavendish Square Holdings v Makdessi* [2015] 3 WLR 1373, [243] per Lord Hodge.

Term	Meaning	Defined in Section
Performance Certificate	FIDIC definition (Red, Pink, Yellow, Silver, and Emerald Books)	**FIDIC**
performance damages	**Liquidated damages** for failure to meet the specified performance criteria of the **Contract**.	**¶16.4**
Performance Damages	FIDIC definition (Yellow and Silver Books).	**FIDIC**
performance security	Security provided by the **Contractor** for the due fulfilment of its obligations under the **Contract**.	**¶9.2.1**
Performance Security	FIDIC definition (Red, Pink, Yellow, Silver, and Emerald Books)	**FIDIC**
Performance Tests	Tests carried out on the finished **Works**, or any part of them, and made to determine the ability of the finished Works to fulfil their intended function (as opposed to tests of their materials or workmanship to determine their compliance with the **Contract**).	**¶13.3**
period for reply	NEC term identified in the Contract Data.	**NEC**
permanent works	The works, as specified in the **Contract**, which the **Contractor** is required to provide and hand over to the **Employer**.	**¶9.1.11.3**
Permanent Works	FIDIC definition (Red, Pink, Yellow, Silver, and Emerald Books)	**FIDIC**
PERT	Programme Evaluation and Review Technique. A **critical path** network analysis scheduling method which allows for randomness in estimated start times and activity durations.	**¶15.1**
PERT	Definition in SCL Delay and Disruption Protocol 2nd Edition.	**SCL**
PFI	Private Finance Initiative.	
Pink Book	FIDIC Conditions of Contract for Construction MDB Harmonised Edition for Building and Engineering Works Designed by the Employer (MDB Harmonised Edition 2010).	**FIDIC**
plaintiff	The person who commences an action in court by making a claim against a defendant.	
planned completion date	Definition in SCL Delay and Disruption Protocol 2nd Edition.	**SCL**
planning	The structured identification and visualisation of activities, events, and resources required to deliver a project as well as the relationships between them.	**¶15.1**
plant	The machinery and apparatus which the **Contractor** is required to provide and hand over to the **Employer** as part of the **permanent works** and as specified in the **Contract**.	**¶9.1.11.3**
Plant	FIDIC definition (Red, Pink, Yellow, Silver, and Emerald Books)	**FIDIC**
Plant and Materials	NEC definition.	**NEC**
PPE	Personal protective equipment.	**¶27.13**

Term	Meaning	Defined in Section
PPP	Public Private Partnership. A form of contract between a private operating company and a government in which the private company contracts to design, build, and operate a public facility on behalf of the government.	**¶3.5.5**
practical completion	**Completion** of the **Works** save for minor deficiencies that can be readily remedied and which do not impair the Works as a whole. (common law)	**¶16.1.1**
Practical Completion	Definition in SCL Delay and Disruption Protocol 2nd Edition.	**SCL**
precedence diagram	Definition in SCL Delay and Disruption Protocol 2nd Edition.	**SCL**
precedence network	A network based on the systematic listing of each of the activities' predecessors – the activities that must logically precede each activity.	**¶15.1**
precedent	A previous judgement of a court cited as an authority for deciding a case with a similar set of facts.	
Preliminaries	Generally, the first item in a **bill of quantities** in which the **Contractor** prices the provision of items applying to commencement of the **Works**, or the Works as a whole, for example, temporary offices, insurances, temporary lighting, hoardings, fencing, and so on. The item description will define whether it includes all of the Contractor's overheads or not.	**¶19.6**
prevention principle	Neither **party** shall do anything to prevent or delay the other from performing the **contract**.	**¶2.15**
prime cost item	A specified item of known work, **plant**, or materials in a **bill of quantities** or the **Contract** which is assigned a dollar value by the **Employer** for tender pricing purposes. That value may or may not cover the actual cost of the item; however, the final **contract price** includes the actual cost, plus applicable markup.	**¶20.4**
prime cost sum	The amount of money assigned to a **prime cost item** for tendering purposes.	**¶20.4**
Principal	See **Employer**.	
private international law	The principles for dealing with conflicts between the domestic laws of two or more states, arising from private matters in an international context. Also called **conflict of laws**.	**¶2.6**
Private judging	NADRAC glossary of common ADR terms.	**NADRAC**
privity of contract	The relationship between the **parties** to a **contract** (and not third parties) which binds each of them to their contractual obligations and entitles them to enforce the contractual promises made by other parties (subject to limited statutory and common law exceptions).	**¶2.10.1**
procedural fairness	See **natural justice**.	
procedural law	Procedural law regulates the formal requirements of the way a **dispute** about **substantive law** issues is to be conducted in court or another judicial tribunal.	**¶2.6**

Term	Meaning	Defined in Section
Procedural Rules	The rules governing the procedure for the conduct of a dispute resolution method.	**¶28.2.7**
procurement law	Statute laws regulating the procurement of goods and services by a government or government agency.	
product liability insurance	Insurance covering the risk associated with the use of defective materials or other goods in the construction of particular works, and the associated risk that the defective materials or other goods may cause physical damage to persons or property.	**¶26.6**
professional indemnity insurance	Insurance covering a construction professional against the risk of loss, arising as a result of liability to another party due to the professional's negligence.	**¶26.5**
programme	A schedule of the activities, their start times and durations required for **Completion** of the **Works**.	**¶14.3.1**
Programme	FIDIC definition (Red, Yellow, Silver, and Emerald Books)	**FIDIC**
Programme	FIDIC definition (Red, Yellow, Silver, and Emerald Books)	**FIDIC**
programme narrative	Definition in SCL Delay and Disruption Protocol 2nd Edition.	**SCL**
programming	A skillset of time management divided into **planning** and **scheduling**.	**¶15.1**
progress payment	Advance payments made 'on account' of the eventual contract price, usually following the issue of an **interim payment certificate**.	**¶21.3**
project bank	NEC term identified in the Contract Data.	**NEC**
project management contract	A **construction contract** in which the **Employer** engages a **Project Manager** to act as its agent with control over the whole project, which may or may not be divided into discrete parts.	**¶3.4**
Project Manager	The **Contractor** in a **project management contract** who has contractual responsibility to act as the **Employer's** agent with control over the whole project.	**¶3.4**
Project Manager	NEC term identified in the Contract Data.	**NEC**
prolongation	The extent to which a **delay** impacts **Completion**.	**¶14.6.1**
prolongation	Definition in SCL Delay and Disruption Protocol 2nd Edition.	**SCL**
proper law of the contract	The law that governs the **parties'** contractual relations. The proper law of a contract provides the legal rules for determining issues in connection with its formation, validity, interpretation, and the rights and obligations of the contracting parties. Also known as the **governing law of the contract**.	**¶2.6**
proportionate liability	Each **defendant** is liable for its proportionate share of the **plaintiff's** damages that are assessed by the court. Proportionate liability only exists to the extent it is defined by a relevant statute.	**¶6.19**
Provide the Works	NEC definition.	**NEC**

Term	Meaning	Defined in Section
provisional quantity	An item in a **bill of quantities** for work which is not reasonably predictable in quantity before the work is carried out.	**¶19.2**
provisional sum	A sum included in the **contract price** to cover items of work, goods, or services that the **Employer** may or may not require, or for contingencies. The **Contractor** will only be paid for provisional sums expended following the **Engineer's** instructions. Payment for provisional sums normally comprises the actual amount expended, plus a predetermined mark-up to cover overhead and profit.	**¶20.4**
Provisional Sum	FIDIC definition (Red, Pink, Yellow, Silver, and Emerald Books)	**FIDIC**
public liability insurance	Insurance against liability to third parties for any death or personal injury or loss of or damage to any physical property.	**¶26.3**
public policy	Public policy is largely concerned with the potential for manifest unfairness or injustice within a given situation. Courts may disregard or refuse to give effect to contractual obligations which, whilst not directly contrary to any express or implied statutory prohibition, nevertheless contravene 'the policy of the law' as discerned from a consideration of the scope and purpose of the particular statute.	**¶4.3.5**
punch-list item	An item of defective work that requires rectification.	**¶17.2**
QA	**Quality assurance.**	
QC	Quality control.	
QIDRC	Qatar International Court and Dispute Resolution Centre.	**¶28.13.2.1**
QM System	FIDIC definition (Red, Yellow, and Silver Books).	**FIDIC**
quality	The attributes the client is prepared to pay for.	
quality assurance	A formalised process of recording conformance with a documented set of procedures which specify the steps to be followed to achieve a **quality** product.	
Quality Management or QM System	FIDIC definition (Emerald Book).	**FIDIC**
quantity surveyor	A professional trained to measure the quantities of different elements of construction and prepare **bills of quantities** and estimates of the costs of construction.	
quantum meruit	Reasonable remuneration or 'what one has earned' (Latin). A *quantum meruit* is the award of just and fair compensation for a benefit which has been accepted, based on the principle of restitution for unjust enrichment in circumstances where there is no subsisting contract.	**¶21.12**
rainbow suite	The major construction contracts published by **FIDIC**.	**¶3.10.1**
re-measurement contract	See **measurement contract**.	
rebus sic stantibus	Doctrines or rules relating to changed conditions.	**¶4.8.1.1**

Term	Meaning	Defined in Section
rectification	Correction by a court of the written terms of a **contract** where it does not express the agreement made by the **parties**.	**¶6.5**
Red Book	FIDIC Conditions of Contract for Construction for Building and Engineering Works Designed by the Employer (First Edition 1999)/(Second Edition 2017).	**¶4.5**
Referrers (or referring agencies)	NADRAC glossary of common ADR terms.	**NADRAC**
renunciation	See **termination**.	
renvoi	Sending back. The situation where a **forum** court is directed by its choice of laws rules to the law of another country whose rules in turn direct the matter back to the forum court.	**¶2.6**
repudiation	Repudiation of a contract occurs where one **party** is in breach of a fundamental term of a **contract**, or has shown by her/his conduct an intention not to be bound by the contract terms, and the other (innocent) party elects to accept the repudiation, thereby bringing the contract to an end.	**¶22.3.2**
required service life	The **service life** specified by the **Employer**.	**¶11.3.2**
rescind	The **common law** right to terminate a contract for breach is referred to as the right to rescind it, leaving intact rights and obligations already accrued. It is also sometimes used to describe the annulment of a contract from the outset (*ab initio*), for example for misrepresentation.	
rescission	**Common law** termination of a contract, leaving intact rights and obligations already accrued.	**¶22.3.2**
resource	Definition in SCL Delay and Disruption Protocol 2nd Edition.	**SCL**
resource levelling	Definition in SCL Delay and Disruption Protocol 2nd Edition.	**SCL**
restitution	A remedy which restores a party, as far as is possible, to the position it was in before it suffered the loss or injury.	
retention free amount	NEC term identified in the Contract Data.	**NEC**
retention fund	See **retention money**.	
retention money	A portion of the amount certified in an **interim payment certificate** set aside or retained by the **Employer** until a later date when the **Contract** has been completed. Retention monies withheld are set aside as security for the due **Completion** of the **Works** and to provide funds for the rectification of **Defects** should the **Contractor** fail to do so.	**¶21.6.1**
Retention Money	FIDIC definition (Red, Pink, Yellow, Silver, and Emerald Books)	**FIDIC**
retention percentage	NEC term identified in the Contract Data.	**NEC**
retrospective longest path analysis	Definition in SCL Delay and Disruption Protocol 2nd Edition.	**SCL**

Term	Meaning	Defined in Section
Review	FIDIC definition (Red, Yellow, Silver, and Emerald Books)	**FIDIC**
revised programme	Definition in SCL Delay and Disruption Protocol 2nd Edition.	**SCL**
RFID	Radio frequency identification.	**¶29.6**
RI	Resolution Institute (Australia), formerly known as the Institute of Arbitrators and Mediators (IAMA).	**¶28.5.1**
RIBA	Royal Institute of British Architects.	**¶10.5.5**
risk	The chance of something happening that will have an impact on objectives.	
risk event	An event that, if it occurs, has an impact on fulfilment of the contractual objectives.	
Risk Event	Definition in SCL Delay and Disruption Protocol 2nd Edition.	**SCL**
Risk Register	NEC definition.	**NEC**
risk transfer date	The date on which the **risk** of loss or damage to the **Works** passes from the **Contractor** to the **Employer**.	**¶24.3.2**
rolling wave programming	Definition in SCL Delay and Disruption Protocol 2nd Edition.	**SCL**
Rome Convention	See ***Rome I***.	
Rome I	*Convention on the Law Applicable to Contractual Obligations. Regulation (EC) No 593/2008 of the European Parliament and of the Council of 17 June 2008 on the law applicable to contractual obligations.* Corrigenda dated 4 July 2008 and 14 August 2009.	**¶4.3.5**
Rome II	*Regulation (EC) No 864/2007 of the European Parliament and Of the Council of 11 July 2007 on the law applicable to non-contractual obligations.*	
RTLS	Real-time location system.	**¶29.6**
SCAI	Swiss Chambers' Arbitration Institution.	**¶28.5.2**
SCC	Stockholm Chamber of Commerce.	**¶28.5.2**
schedule	Definition in SCL Delay and Disruption Protocol 2nd Edition.	**SCL**
Schedule of Baselines	FIDIC definition (Emerald Book)	**FIDIC**
Schedule of Contractor's Key Equipment	FIDIC definition (Emerald Book)	**FIDIC**
Schedule of Payments	FIDIC definition (Red, Yellow, Silver, and Emerald Books)	**FIDIC**
Schedule of Performance Guarantees	FIDIC definition (Yellow, Silver and Emerald, Books)	**FIDIC**
schedule of prices	See **schedule of rates**.	
schedule of quantities	See **bill of quantities**.	

Term	Meaning	Defined in Section
schedule of rates	A schedule in the **Contract** of the rates to be charged by the **Contractor** for specified labour, equipment, or material in the event that its use is directed by the **Engineer**.	**¶21.1.5**
schedule of rates contract	A **measurement contract** in which the **Contractor** is paid in accordance with a **schedule of rates** for the work it actually performs.	**¶19.1**
Schedule of Rates and Prices	FIDIC definition (Yellow, Silver, and Emerald Books).	**FIDIC**
Schedules	FIDIC definition (Red, Pink, Yellow, Silver, and Emerald Books).	**FIDIC**
scheduling	The analytical sequencing of activities based on their relationships. Scheduling is the mathematical calculation of activity timing and **float** thereby determining a project's duration and the **critical path** to its completion.	**¶15.1**
SCL Protocol	The Society of Construction Law Delay and Disruption Protocol (2nd edn, Feb 2017).	**¶14.4**
Scope	NEC definition.	**NEC**
Scott Schedule	A Scott Schedule is used in dispute resolution proceedings and tabulates with particularity: the claimant's claim, the respondent's response, and the tribunal's (judge, **Arbitrator**, or **Adjudicator**) comments and evaluation of the claimant's entitlement.	
SDG	United Nations' Sustainable Development Goals.	**¶4.4.2** **¶29.1.1**
seat of arbitration	The place where the proceedings in an **arbitration** are conducted.	**¶28.11.4.2**
section	A discrete part of the **Works** which can be completed by the **Contractor** and subject to **Taking-Over** by the **Employer** independently of other sections.	**¶16.1.1**
Section	FIDIC definition (1987 Red, Red, Pink, Yellow, Silver, Gold, and Emerald Books).	**FIDIC**
section	NEC term identified in the Contract Data.	**NEC**
***Security of Payment* legislation**	Legislation relating to the statutory entitlement to progress payments and the process of **adjudication** for their rapid recovery during the execution of a **construction contract**.	**¶1.2**
Senior Executive appraisal	See **mini-trial**.	
Senior executive appraisal	NADRAC glossary of common ADR terms.	**NADRAC**
separability	The doctrine of separability is that an **arbitration agreement** is legally considered to be a separate agreement (or a **collateral contract**) to the contract that contains it.	**¶28.11.2**
separable contract	See **divisible contract**.	

Term	Meaning	Defined in Section
service life	The time that a constructed facility is in functional operation.	**¶11.3.2**
servitude	A non-owner's intangible interest in land, giving rights over the land short of actual possession. An easement is one form of servitude.	**¶26.3**
set-off	An amount due to one **party** which reduces (set off against) a greater amount due to the other party.	**¶10.11**
SEZ	Special Economic Zone.	**¶28.13.2**
share range	NEC term identified in the Contract Data.	**NEC**
shop drawings	Drawings of all the dimensional, material, and fabrication details required for manufacture of components such as structural steel or joinery in a workshop.	**¶7.10**
Shuttle mediation	NADRAC glossary of common ADR terms.	**NADRAC**
SIAC	Singapore International Arbitration Centre	**¶4.6**
SICC	Singapore International Commercial Court.	**¶28.13.2.2**
Silver Book	FIDIC Conditions of Contract for EPC/Turnkey Projects (First Edition 1999)/(Second Edition 2017).	**¶4.5**
SIMC	Singapore International Mediation Centre.	**¶28.5.2**
Singapore Convention	The 2019 *United Nations Convention on International Settlement Agreements Resulting from Mediation*.[16]	**¶28.5.4**
Site	The place(s) made available by the **Employer** for execution of the **Works**.	**¶6.17**
Site	FIDIC definition (Red, Pink, Yellow, Silver, and Emerald Books)	**FIDIC**
Site	NEC definition.	**NEC**
Site Information	NEC definition.	**NEC**
slack	Definition in SCL Delay and Disruption Protocol 2nd Edition.	**SCL**
smart contract	Prewritten logic (computer code) stored and replicated on a **blockchain**, executed by a network of computers that can result in updates to the distributed ledger.	**¶29.3.5.1**
SMC	Singapore Mediation Centre.	**¶28.5.2**
Special Conditions	The **conditions of contract** in a **standard form contract** which are specific to the project, the **parties**, the **Site**, or the specific scope of work, and supplement or replace provisions in the **General Conditions**.	**¶3.3**
Special Provisions	FIDIC definition (Red, Yellow, Silver, and Emerald Books)	**FIDIC**
specialia generalibus derogant	Specific words derogate from general words. (Latin)	

16 https://uncitral.un.org/en/texts/mediation/conventions/international_settlement_agreements (accessed 23 May 2020).

Term	Meaning	Defined in Section
specialty	A contract executed under seal. (common law)	**¶2.10.1**
specific performance	A court order compelling a **party** to fulfil its obligations to another party under a **contract**. (common law)	
specification	A document which describes technical requirements for the **Works** to be constructed.	
Specification	FIDIC definition (Red, Pink, Yellow, and Silver Books).	**FIDIC**
SPV	Special purpose vehicle. A company that enters into a concession contract with a government in a **PPP**.	**¶3.5.5**
stage	A discrete part of the **Works** which must generally be completed before the next stage can be commenced, for example, **design** may constitute the first stage of a **design and construct contract** which must be completed and 'signed off' by the **Employer** before the **Contractor** is entitled to proceed with the construction stage. **Completion** of a stage may constitute the achievement of a **milestone**.	**¶16.2**
standard form contract	**General Conditions** of contract prepared by an organisation independent of the contracting parties, in a standard form intended to be used by many **parties** for a number and range of **construction contracts** of a particular type.	**¶3.9.1**
standard method of measurement	A predetermined method of measuring work, the most common in use being the **CESMM**, applied by engineers and quantity surveyors for estimating, tendering and payment of work.	**¶19.3**
Star Rate	A reasonable rate for valuing a **Variation** derived from sources outside the **Contract** based on industry custom and practice.	**¶20.1.9**
stare decisis	'The decision stands' (Latin). The doctrine under which a **common law** court is required to follow previous decisions in the same legal **jurisdiction**, unless they are inconsistent with a higher court's decision or determined to be wrong in law.	**¶1.4**
starting date	NEC term identified in the Contract Data.	**NEC**
state of the art	The art and science that would be applied by competent and experienced practitioners involved in the relevant practice of engineering, not necessarily the science of engineering as known to academics researching at the cutting edge of known technology.	**¶11.3.1**
Statement	FIDIC definition (Red, Pink, Yellow, Silver, and Emerald Books)	**FIDIC**
statute law	The law enacted by the Government in legislation or regulations.	**¶1.6**
statutory adjudication	The adjudication of a **dispute** in accordance with the requirements of a statute.	**¶28.9.2.1**
Statutory Adjudication Acts	Statutes providing for **statutory adjudication** of construction disputes.	**¶28.9.2.2**
Statutory conciliation	NADRAC glossary of common ADR terms.	**NADRAC**

Term	Meaning	Defined in Section
stop clock arbitration	**Chess clock arbitration**.	
sub-network	Definition in SCL Delay and Disruption Protocol 2nd Edition.	**SCL**
subcontract	An agreement between the **Contractor** and a third party for the performance by the third party of some or all of the contractual obligations of the **Contractor** under a **head contract**. The **Employer** is not a party to a subcontract.	**¶3.1.1**
subcontracted fee percentage	NEC term identified in the Contract Data provided by the Contractor.	**NEC**
subcontractor	A party in contract with the **Contractor** under a **subcontract**.	**¶3.1.1**
Subcontractor	FIDIC definition (Red, Pink, Yellow, Silver, and Emerald Books)	**FIDIC**
Subcontractor	NEC definition.	**NEC**
subrogation	An insurer is entitled in equity to step in and exercise the insured's rights against any relevant third parties where it has fully indemnified the insured against a loss covered by a contract of insurance.	**¶26.11**
substantial completion	**Completion** of the **Works** save for minor deficiencies that can be readily remedied and which do not impair the Works as a whole. (common law)	**¶16.1.1**
Substantial Completion	Definition in SCL Delay and Disruption Protocol 2nd Edition.	**SCL**
substantive law	The law applying to the substance of a legal relationship, for example, a contract, in contrast to the **procedural law**.	**¶2.6**
sui generis	Belonging to a species all of its own; unique.	
sujétions imprévues	Technical difficulties of an unforeseeable nature and of sufficient magnitude to affect fundamentally the Contractor's performance. (France)	**¶2.3.2.2**
Superintendent	See **Engineer**.	
Supervisor	NEC term identified in the Contract Data.	**NEC**
suppletive rules	Relevant default rules for a nominated type of contract. Also referred to as default rules or *jus dispositivum*.	**¶1.8**
surety	An accessory obligation in terms of which a person makes itself responsible for the performance of the **Contractor's** obligations.	**¶9.2.1**
suspension	Performance of all or part of the **Works** is put on hold.	**¶14.7.3**
Taking-Over	Taking-Over, sometimes referred to as 'provisional acceptance,' occurs at the end of the construction **stage** of the **Works** or a section of the Works when, after passing the **Tests on Completion**, the Works can be used for their intended purpose and are taken over by the **Employer** and the **Contractor's** obligations to remedy **Defects** commence.	**¶16.2**
Taking-Over Certificate	A certificate issued under the **Contract**, when the **Engineer** (or **Employer**) considers that the whole (or part) of the **Works** has reached **Completion** and is ready for **Taking-Over**.	**¶16.2**

Term	Meaning	Defined in Section
Taking-Over Certificate	FIDIC definition (Red, Pink, Yellow, Silver, and Emerald Books)	**FIDIC**
TAR	**Technology assisted review**.	**¶29.7.1.2**
TCC	Technology and Construction Court (England).	**¶28.13.1**
TEC	Technology, Engineering, and Construction List in the Supreme Court of Victoria.	**¶28.13.1**
technology assisted review	The application of predictive coding technology to identify relevant documents in a collection of electronic documents.	**¶29.7.1.2**
temporary works	All **works** (other than **equipment**) required by the **Contractor** for the execution and **Completion** of the **Works** and the remedying of any **Defects** which are not part of the **permanent works**.	**¶9.1.11.3**
Temporary Works	FIDIC definition (Red, Pink, Yellow, Silver, and Emerald Books)	**FIDIC**
tender	An offer to enter into a **contract**.	
Tender	FIDIC definition (Red, Pink, Yellow, Silver, and Emerald Books)	**FIDIC**
tender documents	A set of documents issued by the **Employer** in its invitation to **tender**, or a set of documents submitted by a **Tenderer** in its tender.	
tender period	The period from issue of the **Employer's** invitation to **tender** until the date for submission of **tenders**.	
Tenderer	A person, firm, or company which submits a **tender** for a **contract**.	
termination	The process in which a **party** brings a contract to an end by its own action before the contract has been fully performed by one or other or both parties.	**¶22.3.1**
Tests after Completion	Tests carried out after the **Taking-Over Certificate** has been issued.	**¶16.5**
Tests after Completion	FIDIC definition (Red, Pink, Yellow, Silver, and Emerald Books)	**FIDIC**
Tests on Completion	Tests to be carried out on **Completion**, the passing of which leads to acceptance and **Taking-Over** of the **Works** by the **Employer** who thereby regains possession of the **Site**.	**¶16.2**
Tests on Completion	FIDIC definition (Red, Pink, Yellow, Silver, and Emerald Books)	**FIDIC**
Third-Party Agreement	An agreement between the contracting **parties** and a **third-party neutral** engaged to assist them in dispute resolution.	**¶28.2.6.3**
third-party neutral	A person independent of the contracting **parties** who has a defined role in a dispute resolution procedure to assist the parties to reach a resolution, or to provide a judgement on the merits of the **dispute**. Third-party neutrals include **Arbitrators, Adjudicators, Conciliators, Mediators, Experts,** and **Dispute Boards**.	**¶28.2.6.1**

Term	Meaning	Defined in Section
time at large	The stipulated time for **Completion** in the **Contract** no longer applies because of delay to the **Works** caused by the **Employer**. (common law)	**¶14.7.6**
time bar	A provision in a contract which precludes the exercise of a contractual right, if specified obligations are not carried out within the defined time period.	**¶27.3.4**
time chainage diagram	A diagram showing the duration of activities through time as well as distance, portraying a geographical representation of project progress.	**¶15.4.3**
Time for Completion	FIDIC definition (Red, Pink, Yellow, Silver, and Emerald Books)	**FIDIC**
time impact analysis	Definition in SCL Delay and Disruption Protocol 2nd Edition.	**SCL**
time is of the essence	A **condition** in a contract that the contractual obligations must be completed by a stipulated time. (common law)	
Time Risk Allowance	NEC definition.	**NEC**
Time Risk Allowance	Definition in SCL Delay and Disruption Protocol 2nd Edition.	**SCL**
time slice analysis	Definition in SCL Delay and Disruption Protocol 2nd Edition.	**SCL**
tort	An act by a person/company, which is a breach of the general duty of care that the law imposes on all members of the community generally, and which causes loss or harm to another.	
total cost claim	A claim where the composite sum sought by the **Contractor** is computed by reference to the amount of money required to ensure that the total money received is not less than the total money expended or expected to be expended on the project.	**¶C.1**
total float	Definition in SCL Delay and Disruption Protocol 2nd Edition.	**SCL**
total time claim	A claim in which a number of legal bases for a time extension are alleged and the **Contractor** seeks as a time extension the difference between the number of days which the project took to complete less the **time for Completion** including extensions allowed provided in the **Contract**.	**¶C.1**
tribunal	NEC term identified in the Contract Data.	**NEC**
Tripartite Agreement	An agreement between **Employer**, **Contractor**, and **Dispute Board Members**, incorporating the **Procedural Rules**.	**¶28.10.2**
true concurrent delay	The occurrence of two or more delay events at the same time, one an **Employer risk event**, the other a **Contractor risk event**, the effects of which are felt at the same time. For concurrent delay to exist, each of the Employer risk event and the Contractor risk event must be an effective cause of delay to **Completion** (ie the delays must both affect the critical path). Definition in SCL Delay and Disruption Protocol 2nd Edition.	**¶14.5.1**
Turnkey contract	**EPC contract**.	

Term	Meaning	Defined in Section
UCC	***Uniform Commercial Code*** (USA).	**¶2.9.2.2**
UNCITRAL	United Nations Commission on International Trade Law.	**¶4.6**
Underground Works	FIDIC definition (Emerald Book).	**FIDIC**
Unforeseeable	FIDIC definition (Red, Pink, Yellow, Silver, and Emerald Books)	**FIDIC**
UNIDROIT	International Institute for the Unification of Private Law, an independent intergovernmental Organisation with its seat in Rome.	**¶4.7.1.1**
Uniform Commercial Code	A comprehensive modernisation of various statutes relating to commercial transactions including sales, leases, negotiable instruments, bank deposits and collections, funds transfers, letters of credit, bulk sales, documents of title, investment securities, and secured transactions.[17] It has been enacted (sometimes with modifications to suit local conditions or presentation style) in all of the 50 US states, as well as in the District of Columbia, the Commonwealth of Puerto Rico, Guam, and the U.S. Virgin Islands. (USA)	**¶2.9.2.2**
unjust enrichment	A benefit received for which the recipient is obliged to make **restitution** to the party at whose expense it was unjustly obtained. See ***quantum meruit***.	
unliquidated damages	Damages which have not been predetermined in monetary terms by the parties in a **dispute**. They must be proved as the actual loss suffered as a result of the other contracting party's **breach of contract**.	
UP	*UNIDROIT Principles of International Commercial Contracts.*[18]	**¶2.7**
Updated Programme	Definition in SCL Delay and Disruption Protocol 2nd Edition.	**SCL**
value engineering	'[A] systematic approach to delivering the required function at lowest cost without loss of quality, performance or reliability.'[19]	**¶20.2**
Variation	An increase, decrease, or change to the originally agreed scope of work, as directed by the **Employer**, which the **Contractor** has a contractual obligation to perform.	**¶4.2.1**
Variation	FIDIC definition (Red, Pink, Yellow, Silver, and Emerald Books)	**FIDIC**
Variation Order	A written instruction, in the form required by the Contract, to the **Contractor** from the **Engineer** (or **Employer**) to carry out a **Variation**.	**¶20.1.6**

17 www.ali.org/index.cfm?fuseaction=publications.ppage&node_id=86 (accessed 6 March 2020).

18 www.unidroit.org/english/principles/contracts/principles2016/principles2016-e.pdf (accessed 24 July 2021).

19 David Blockley, *New Dictionary of Civil Engineering* (Penguin Books, 2005).

Term	Meaning	Defined in Section
Variation Price Request	A written request by the **Engineer** (or **Employer**) for a cost estimate and the effect on the **programme** of carrying out the work required for a proposed **Variation**.	**¶20.3**
VIAC	Vienna International Arbitration Centre.	**¶28.5.2**
virtual reality	A digital animated representation of the physical world, displayed on specialised equipment in sufficient detail to be perceived as realistic.	**¶29.3.6**
waiver	An election by a **party** not to enforce a right it is entitled to under a contract.	**¶14.11**
warranty	A contractual term, breach of which gives rise to a right to claim damages, but not to a right to reject the subject matter of the contract or to treat the contract as repudiated.[20]	
Washington Convention	The *ICSID Convention on the Settlement of Investment Disputes between States and Nationals of Other States*, a treaty ratified by 154 Contracting States.[21]	
wayleave easement	Permission to make or use a way across private land and includes permission to erect overhead wires and the like.	**¶7.5**
WBS	Work breakdown structure.	**¶15.5.3**
weather data	NEC term identified in the Contract Data.	**NEC**
weather measurements	NEC term identified in the Contract Data.	**NEC**
wet commissioning	Operation of **plant** for the first time for the purposes of trialing or testing its performance and the discharge of waste as in pipelines, transformers, pumps, and the like.	**¶11.7**
White Book	FIDIC Clients/Consultants Model Services Agreement (Fifth Edition 2017)	**¶8.1.2**
without prejudice	A label used for any communication (including an oral communication as well as a document) for which it is intended to claim **legal privilege**, so that the communication cannot be used as evidence of any admission in subsequent legal proceedings or **arbitration**. The term is used when making settlement offers without wanting to admit or imply liability.	
Working Areas	NEC definition.	**NEC**
working areas	NEC term identified in the Contract Data provided by the Contractor.	**NEC**
Works	The work, materials, and **plant** which the **Contractor** is or may be required to carry out and complete or provide under the **Contract**, and includes **Variations**, rectification of **Defects**, **temporary works**, and **equipment**.	**¶9.1**
Works	FIDIC definition (Red, Pink, Yellow, Silver, and Emerald Books)	**FIDIC**
Works	NEC definition.	**NEC**

20 Butterworth Concise Australian Legal Dictionary.

21 https://icsid.worldbank.org/sites/default/files/ICSID%20Convention%20English.pdf (accessed 24 July 2021).

Term	Meaning	Defined in Section
works	Definition in SCL Delay and Disruption Protocol 2nd Edition.	**SCL**
Works Information	NEC definition.	**NEC**
year	FIDIC definition (Red, Yellow, Silver, and Emerald Books)	**FIDIC**
Yellow Book	FIDIC Conditions of Contract for Plant and Design-Build for Electrical and Mechanical Plant and for Building and Engineering Works, designed by the Contractor (First Edition 1999)/(Second Edition 2017).	**¶4.5**

APPENDIX A

Matters for consideration when drafting a construction contract

CONTENTS

The following notes have been drawn up as a general guide for Engineers and Project Managers when construction contracts are to be awarded and where the persons involved may not have experience in contractual matters. The notes are deliberately drafted to put forward the best position for the Employer; it is acknowledged that some of the points would not be acceptable to a contractor in the negotiations prior to award. However, by identifying these issues, management will be aware of the risks involved and in a position to take measures to minimise such risks.

Most, if not all, of these issues will be covered in standard form General Conditions or Contract Data to be completed for the particular project. Special Conditions may be necessary to modify the General Conditions in a standard form if they do not represent the Employer's preferences or desired risk allocation.

A.1 Definitions

It is most important to define what is meant by the terms Employer, management, Engineer, commission, the Works, and so on. The Engineer may be a consulting engineer acting as agent on behalf of the Employer or an employee of the Employer. Employer refers to the Employer who contracts with the Contractor and who may or may not be the owner of the facility. Management may also refer to the Employer. Where delegation of powers is provided for it is necessary to ensure that the nature and extent of the power delegated are clearly spelled out.

A.2 The financial status of the Contractor

It is obviously important to ascertain that the Contractor is financially stable and not likely to be placed in liquidation prior to completion of the Contract. Preliminary enquiries on this should include:

(a) Banker's references,
(b) Discreet enquiries in the construction industry,
(c) Inspection of latest accounts,
(d) Company searches,
(e) The ability to provide a performance bond in the form of a demand guarantee, and
(f) Whether the Contractor is by repute regarded as a professional constructor.

A.3 The time element and liquidated damages (LDs)

Time has always been important but has now become of critical importance due to inflation in construction costs. The Contract should therefore include the following provisions:

(a) A Contract Completion date given in terms of a specified number of weeks after notice to proceed.
(b) Contractually binding and LD-related key dates during the course of construction.
(c) The power for the Engineer to accelerate the works (at the cost of the Contractor if it is behind schedule, but otherwise at the cost of the Employer).
(d) Clearly defined conditions under which the Contractor is entitled to an extension of time and under which circumstances such extensions of time entitle the Contractor to payment of time-related charges or costs.

Some incentive to make a Contractor complete on time or earlier should also be considered if the Employer stands to benefit from early Completion. Although some people consider that LDs work well, it has often been found in practice that they are an inadequate incentive in the overall context of the Contract. LDs coupled with a bonus clause may therefore be preferred, giving the Contractor additional payment for early Completion; the amount of the bonus should obviously only be calculated with reference to the advantage to the Employer, if any, of early completion.

A.4 Drawings, specifications, schedule of quantities, and quality assurance

The drawings, specifications, and schedule of quantities (if any) are of crucial importance and should contain as full a description as possible of the Works to be constructed. They should include all criteria which are important to the Employer. In particular, the Contract should provide:

(a) A definite description of the nature and the extent of the work to be done.
(b) For the work to be done to the specified description, but where there is no such description, to whichever is the better of the relevant (specified) standard or the current best construction practice.
(c) For performance requirements to be defined, particularly as to durability, capacity, conversion efficiency, use of utilities, pollution, manning, ambient conditions (heat, humidity, corrosion, atmospheric conditions), continuance of operation, mechanical quality including ease and frequency of maintenance, compatibility with other equipment and spares, product purity and energy consumption.
(d) For guarantees of the performance requirements listed in the specifications for the full duration of the defects liability period. The Contract should spell out what the consequences of failure to meet a performance requirement will be – for example, whether the Contractor is to remedy the defects or merely to have a monetary liability, and whether the Contractor is liable for consequential damages or not.
(e) That quality assurance be imposed in accordance with clearly predetermined procedures and standards.
(f) The order of precedence of the various documents forming part of the Contract in the event of a conflict or ambiguity.

A.5 The Engineer's powers

The best way to ensure a satisfactory project is by close day-to-day supervision by the Engineer and the Employer's qualified personnel. The powers required include:

(a) The power to require the Contractor to comply promptly with all directions notwithstanding that it considers them to be outside the Contract, and if it does consider them to be outside the Contract, to notify the Engineer in writing within a specified number of days failing which it should be deemed to accept that the direction is within the Contract.
(b) The power to test materials off site.

(c) The power to expedite directly with the supplier.
(d) The power to inspect and reject all materials and workmanship both before and after installation.
(e) The power to require samples and prototypes to be fabricated and submitted for approval.
(f) The power to remedy any defect if the Contractor does not do so itself, where any part of the Works is rejected, and to charge the Contractor with the cost thereof.
(g) The power to require work to be opened up.
(h) The power to require details of non-contractual programmes, including soft copies of the data to enable the Engineer to run the software.
(i) The power to remove personnel or subcontractors from the Site.
(j) The power to 'time bar' any claim if details of the claim are not delivered by the Contractor within the time limits set out in the Contract.

A.6 Role of the Engineer, Architect, or Project Manager

Consideration should be given to employing the Engineer, Architect, or Project Manager on a fixed fee basis or to giving them some bonus payment for completion within time and cost. Alternatively, engaging a construction manager who takes design and management responsibility on a target price or a fixed price basis.

A.7 Safety, pollution, and hygeine

An increasingly heavy burden is imposed by law in these matters and the Contract should provide:

(a) The Contractor shall comply with all laws and regulations governing safety during construction.
(b) The plant is to be designed and installed so that when it is in operation it will comply with safety laws and regulations.
(c) The Contractor is required to comply with site safety regulations in force from time to time.
(d) Any hazard specific to the Site is provided for.
(e) The Contractor is required to keep the Site free of rubbish and to clear the Site after Completion.
(f) The Contractor is required to take all reasonable steps to minimize electrical and magnetic emissions, dust, mud, fumes, smell, vibration, noise, excess lighting, or polluting effluent.
(g) The Works comply with prevention of pollution legislation concerning effluent discharge and discharge into the atmosphere.
(h) The Contractor is required to make available fire-fighting, first aid, and medical facilities on the Site.
(i) The Contractor's employees are restricted to certain areas.
(j) The Contractor is responsible for fencing and lighting.
(k) The Contractor is prohibited from carrying out blasting, welding, or other hazardous activities without prior notice.
(l) The Contractor's employees shall wear protective clothing where necessary.
(m) The Contractor shall ensure that its equipment and tools are well maintained.
(n) The Contractor shall notify the Engineer before delivering materials and equipment to Site and before excavating.
(o) The Contractor is required to take care not to damage cables, pipes, and so on, and is required to provide lateral support and to shore up and cover excavations adequately.
(p) The Contractor shall report any accident promptly to the Engineer and follow all protocols and procedures.

Statutory requirements impose a duty on the responsible person to take reasonable steps to ensure that the Site and any plant or substances on site are safe and without risk to health. This duty extends to persons who are not the Contractor's employees. It is therefore important to ensure that this duty is transferred to the Contractor in the Contract.

A.8 Industrial relations and Site discipline

This is a controversial and difficult subject, most of which cannot be adequately covered in contractual terms. But the following points should be considered for inclusion in the Contract:

(a) Appropriate priorities are included regarding membership or otherwise of unions.
(b) The Contractor shall avoid pay differentials between employees of the same grade.
(c) The Employer has the right to search persons and vehicles, enforce security measures, and to institute a personnel identification system.
(d) The Contractor shall not poach labour from the Employer or the Engineer.
(e) The Contractor has the power to eject troublemakers from the Site or to refuse admission to them.

A.9 Planning permission and industrial development approvals

Planning permission is a matter of prime importance which should be resolved before the Contact is let. Planning permits can take an indeterminate time to be awarded, particularly if there is significant opposition to the proposed project. Local authorities are capable of either refusing permission or imposing such onerous conditions as to make the project no longer worthwhile. The Contract must make provision for compliance by the Contractor with stated planning conditions and clearly designate responsibility for the procurement of planning approval.

A.10 Financing

In cases where the Contractor is unable to obtain credit as inexpensively as the Employer, it will be worthwhile, in order to keep the price of the quotation down, to provide as much financing as is prudent. This can be effected by:

(a) Progress payments according to costs incurred, and prompt payment within 30 days.
(b) Paying for materials when they come on site and ownership has passed to the Employer.
(c) A reasonable level of retention.
(d) Neutral funding or payments in advance subject to satisfactory security furnished by the Contractor.

A.11 Escalation

Contracts extending over more than a year are typically subject to escalation either by reference to certain indices or by reference to actual material and labour costs. Here the following points should be borne in mind:

(a) Provided the indices are a correct reflection of inflation, the index method is to be preferred as it minimizes disagreements and reduces the administrative workload.
(b) Where the escalation clause is linked to actual materials costs it is worthwhile ordering as much material in advance as possible – provided that rates of interest are lower than rates of inflation. However, one should ensure that the ownership vests in the Employer and that payment is not made until that time unless alternative security is given. The amount

pre-ordered will also have to be limited by considerations such as storage area on Site or at approved places off site, deterioration, and pilferage.

(c) Any escalation clause must have a cut-off date at the contractual time for Completion – this gives the Contractor a powerful incentive to complete on time.

(d) For a contract of six months or less in duration it is probably preferable to ask for a fixed price not subject to escalation. There is some risk in this, but it does avoid the administrative cost of checking work done against indices. Even for contracts of one-year duration it could be worthwhile asking the Contractor to submit a fixed price as an alternative to its price in escalation. The Contractor should be asked what rate of escalation it has assumed in arriving at its fixed price.

(f) When considering an escalation clause and the percentage split between plant, labour, materials, and so on, one should consider the variation of the Contractor's costs over a period of time. The first six months may be low in labour, the final six months may be high, and if the percentage split between the various indices does not reflect this change, one or other of the parties will be out of pocket.

(g) In certain 'measure and value' contracts with monthly certificates, escalation is paid from the base date to the end of the relevant month in which the work is measured (not the month in which the work was done). Where the claim of the Contractor is ultimately successful, the amount of that claim may be included in the monthly certificate after the award is made in respect of that claim, and therefore measured in the month to which that certificate relates. It might then be argued that it should be escalated to the end of that month, rather than only up to the time when the work to which the claim is related was carried out.

(h) A Contractor will realize that inflation may exceed interest rates and it may 'rear end load' its tender by putting in low rates for early works and high rates for later works. (The Contractor will not mind being out of pocket and having to finance work early in the Contract, at say X % per annum, if it knows that it can recover escalation later on, at the rate of, say, 2X % per annum).

(i) Many Contractors consider that an escalation formula based upon a fixed portion of 15% not subject to escalation does not adequately protect the Contractor against escalation. These Contractors will make provision for such shortfall elsewhere in the Contract. Those who do not, may not complete the Contract. A more realistic fixed portion might be considered if the escalation formula is to fulfil its true function, depending upon the circumstances.

A.12 Subcontracting and nominated subcontractors

The Employer will require control over the subcontractors who will be employed on the Site and must be able to prevent the Head Contractor from subcontracting an unreasonable amount of the work. The Contract should therefore include an absolute bar against subcontracting without the Employer's consent (except with regard to nominated subcontractors). This consent must not be unreasonably withheld. A list of selected subcontractors with approximate values of the subcontracts may be agreed with the Head Contractor.

The number of nominated subcontractors provided for in the Contract must be carefully considered. In general, it is desirable to have as few nominated subcontractors as possible because there is no privity of contract between the Employer and the nominated subcontractor and contractual difficulties in enforcing the subcontract may therefore arise. Many forms of nominated subcontract provide opportunities of relieving the Head Contractor of responsibility where nominated subcontractors default. Where nominated subcontractors are placed in liquidation or where, despite the efforts of the Head Contractor, they fail to perform, practical difficulties may also arise for the Employer. However, against this must be balanced the advantage of not having too many direct contractors on site as in these circumstances it is easy for one contractor to blame damage to work, disruption, and delay on other contractors. The use of non-nominated or selected subcontractors is generally to be preferred.

A.13 Design responsibility

It is important to make it clear who is responsible for the design of both the permanent works and the temporary works and to make the designer warrant that designs provided by it are suitable for the purpose intended. Wherever design is carried out, the designer must carry adequate design insurance, and in the event of any mishap an independent designer should be commissioned to investigate the cause.

A.14 Ground conditions

'Unforeseen ground conditions' may be a fertile field of claims. Ways to minimize the Employer's exposure are:

(a) A thorough investigation by professional engineers to determine geotechnical conditions by an adequate number of bore holes and/or test pits should be completed before sending out invitations to tender. If the investigation forms part of the tender documents, the Contractor should be entitled to rely upon it. In addition to determining the foundation material for its suitability to support the structures to be placed on or in it, ground conditions should also be checked for, for example, hardness of rock, obstructions, marshiness, corrosive elements. The tenderers should be provided with all geotechnical information available.
(b) Provisional sums for likely hazards should be allowed for.
(c) Insist that the tenderers inspect the site and core-boxes before the Contract is let.
(d) Strictly limit the occasions where the Contractor can claim extra time and/or money to circumstances which would be unforeseeable to an experienced Contractor.
(e) Prohibit the use of disclaimer clauses where the Engineer has been commissioned and paid to carry professional responsibility for geotechnical investigations and for the parameters determined from its engineering analyses of such information.

A.15 Liaison with other contractors

Disruption by other contractors is a frequent source of delay and claims and, although the solution is mostly practical, the Contract should contain:

(a) A duty to liaise with other contractors.
(b) A back-charging clause whereby the Employer can reclaim from the Contractor any amount the Employer has paid to another contractor as a result of the Contractor's breach of contract or delay – although this may be difficult to negotiate.

A.16 The services supplied by the Employer

The Contract should spell out what the Employer will supply and at what costs, if any. For example:

(a) Water supply,
(b) Electricity or gas supplies,
(c) Canteen facilities,
(d) Sanitary and changing facilities,
(e) Car parking,
(f) Office and staffing facilities,

(g) First-aid facilities,
(h) Security services,
(i) Telecommunications,
(j) Unloading facilities,
(k) Accommodation for personnel, and
(l) Hoisting and craneage.

A.17 Insurance

It is important that adequate contractor's all risks cover, including contractors' plant and equipment and temporary works and third-party liability cover is taken out. These should be taken out in the joint names of the Contractor and the Employer for the duration of the construction period. It is emphasised that the designer should be required to carry adequate design liability (professional indemnity) insurance. The limit of indemnity and deductible amount under each policy should be realistic, and the exclusions to each policy should be studied carefully. The Contractor will be obliged to effect mandatory workmen's compensation insurance and third-party motor vehicle insurance while making use of public roads. The Contractor should also be required to carry public liability insurance against claims by third parties.

A.18 Patents and registered designs

If the Contractor is providing the design, it should provide an indemnity against all expenses and financial losses resulting from infringement of intellectual property rights caused by the construction of the Works or use of any process used in it.

If the Employer is providing the design, it is not reasonable to ask the Contractor to give this indemnity. Indeed, the Employer may then reasonably be required by the Contractor to give such an indemnity.

A.19 Copyright and patterns

The Contract should specify who owns copyright, and patterns used in the design. In respect of copyright, if the ownership remains with the Contractor, the Employer should insist on an irrevocable, royalty free licence to use the copyright for the purposes of operations, maintenance, repairs, and – if possible – plant renewal.

A.20 *Force majeure*, additional time and compensation to the Contractor

In many standard forms of contract these clauses are vaguely drafted, giving the Contractor an opportunity for instituting spurious claims. It is therefore important to define precisely those circumstances in which additional time and/or money can be claimed. In particular the following causes should be resisted, as they involve risks that should be assumed by the Contractor:

(a) Inclement weather;
(b) Shortage of materials and plant or equipment, otherwise than as a result of genuine *force majeure* circumstances (eg fire at supplier's works or pandemic); and
(c) Shortage of labour.

It is also vitally important to insist upon a strict time limit within which claims must be made (eg notice of event within 28 days, full details within 42 days) so that contemporaneous records can be kept. Otherwise the Contractor may lodge several claims at the end of the Contract when the evidence has been lost, employees have been transferred to other projects, and the employees remaining cannot clearly recollect what actually happened.

A decision will need to be made as to whether the Contractor is entitled to an extension of time only, in respect of *force majeure* circumstances, or to additional expenses as well. The amount of compensation should only be the Contractor's out-of-pocket expenses and reasonable overhead costs unavoidably arising as a result of the delay and which are not otherwise payable under the provisions of the Contract.

A.21 Time barring of claims

To ensure that claims are dealt with as they arise, it is suggested that the following provisions be inserted:

(a) The Contractor shall notify the Engineer or Employer of any unusual event or *force majeure* circumstances, within 14 days of when it became aware or should have become aware of such event or circumstances arising.
(b) Within 28 days of the Contractor becoming aware or should have become aware of an event or circumstances that it considers entitles it to additional time or payment, it must submit details of the circumstances or event to the Engineer, failing which the claim will be treated as waived.
(c) Unless any Engineer's instruction is objected to within 14 days, the instruction is to be treated as being in accordance with the Contract.
(d) In respect of Variation orders, the Contractor accepts the Engineer's determination of value unless the Contractor objects thereto and notifies such objection within 28 days.
(e) Adjudication, expert determination, conciliation, or mediation is to be used as a means of breaking any deadlock between the parties with minimum delay, and a precondition to arbitration or litigation.
(f) There should be no bar to interim litigation or arbitration before the project is completed.

A.22 Takeover and performance tests

Cold commissioning, hot commissioning, dry commissioning, and wet commissioning are examples of terms which must be clearly defined. Whether the work is considered as complete for the purposes of the imposition of LDs on completion of erection, or after successful commissioning, must be set out in the Contract.

In contracts involving mechanical and electrical instrumentation, the Contract should set out in detail what standards of performance are to be met by equipment to be installed and what tests should be undertaken to determine whether such standards of performance have been achieved.

A.22.1 Mechanical quality and standards of performance

Even without any express warranty on the part of the seller, the law presumes every contract of sale to be subject to the implied warranty that the equipment sold is free from latent defects or deficiencies which render it unfit for the purpose for which it is bought. Latent, or hidden defects, are defects which are not apparent to an ordinary inspection. The test whether the defect renders the thing unfit for the purpose for which it was bought is an objective test – that is, whether the average reasonable person, had s/he known of the defect, would have bought the thing in question. This test is of great importance for it determines whether or not the purchaser is entitled to have the sale cancelled or whether it is confined to a reduction in the price. The degree of deficiency in the performance of the equipment necessary to render the equipment unfit may vary, depending upon its intended application, and proof of the dividing line between fitness and unfitness may in practice be difficult and costly to determine. Equipment purchased for application A may, for example, be required to produce an entirely different standard of performance from the same equipment when used in application B. For these reasons, it may be desirable, from the point of view of buyer and seller alike, to specify at the time of purchase, and to include in the Contract, figures of merit, against which the performance of the equipment may be measured and evaluated.

Mechanical performance or, more correctly, mechanical quality is a combination of a number of factors. It is, however, generally agreed that a machine must be:

- Available for work when called upon to do so.
- So constructed as to require a minimum number of hours under repair per working hour.
- Reliable in so far as it does not fail frequently.
- Rapidly repairable when it does fail.

The true measure of product effectiveness is its ability to maintain reasonable figures of merit at a reasonable cost for an extended period in a given operating environment. The following sections provide formulae to determine five different figures of merit to assess the mechanical performance of mechanical equipment.[1]

A.22.2 Availability

This is a commonly used and widely misunderstood ratio.

A simple formula for availbility is:

$$\%A = \frac{0 \times 100}{S}$$

Where O = total operating hours
S = total scheduled hours

Availability expressed in this way is no more than a measure for manipulating a previously assumed relationship between fixed and variable costs. This ratio is not a measure of mechanical performance in that there is nothing to indicate whether mechanical or management failures are responsible for the fact that operating hours are less than scheduled hours.

The following formula is a measure of mechanical performance during scheduled hours:

$$\%A = \frac{S - D}{S} \times 100$$

Where S = scheduled hours
D = downtime hours during scheduled hours

This formula does not account for repair effort expended outside scheduled hours and the relationship is thus very sensitive to variations in S. For example, if the machine is scheduled for 12 hours per day and had broken down to the extent that it required an eight-hour repair. Availability can vary from 33% if the repair must be undertaken during scheduled hours, to 100% if the repair can be completed outside scheduled hours. If the machine is scheduled for 24 hours per day, then availability is 66% as there is no opportunity to do work outside scheduled hours.

Formulae that break down scheduled time into its components provide a more meaningful figurer of merit:

1 Philip Loots, *Construction Law and Related Issues* (Juta & Co, 1999) 526.

$$\%A = \frac{W + Sd + Sf}{T} \times 100$$

or

$$\%A = \frac{T - (Md + Mf)}{T} \times 100$$

Where T = scheduled hours or total shift hours
Md = service time
Mf = break-down time
Sd = standing time
Sf = inclement weather time
W = working time

Only scheduled hours are recorded and $T = Md + Mf + W + Sd + Sf$

The only definition of availability which the authors are aware has been tested in law is that contained in *The South African Railways Standard Conditions of Contract* E 160.[2]

The definition used is:

$$\%A = \frac{To - Tb}{T} \times 100$$

Where To = scheduled hours
Tb = all periods during which the plant is unable to produce work due to a defect in the machine.

A.22.3 Repair ratio

The shortcomings inherent in the definition and calculation of availability suggest the use of a more simple and direct measure of mechanical performance. The repair ratio measures the number of hours the machine has spent under repair per working hour and the following definition may be used:

$$RR = \frac{Td}{W}$$

Where RR = repair ratio
Td = breakdown time
W = working time

A.22.4 Frequency of failure

The frequency of failure (or reciprocal of the mean time between failures) is a measure of the reliability and mechanical quality in that it is sensitive to the number of events which have contributed to the total breakdown time, Td:

$$V = \frac{N \times 100}{W}$$

Where V = number of mechanical failures per 100 working hours
N = number of mechanical failures
W = working time

2 See Philip Loots, *Construction Law and Related Issues* (Juta & Co, 1995) 327.

A.22.5 Mean time to repair

The time taken to effect each repair is also of value when assessing mechanical quality. The following formula is proposed:

$$RT = \frac{Td}{N}$$

Where RT = average time broken down
Td = breakdown time as assessed by parties involved or consulted
N = number of mechanical failures

A.22.6 Utilization

A measure of equipment utilization is often calculated to give an indication of the extent to which the machine has been used for the available hours. The following can be used:

$$UT = \frac{W}{T - Td} \times 100$$

Where UT = utilization
T = scheduled hours
Td = breakdown time
W = working time

A.22.7 Summary

Five different figures of merit as previously defined may be used to assess the mechanical performance of mechanical equipment. These, using common symbols, are:

(a) Availability

$$\%A = \frac{T - Td}{T} \times 100$$

(b) Repair ratio:

$$RR = \frac{Td}{W}$$

(c) Frequency of failure:

$$V = \frac{N \times 100}{W}$$

(d) Mean time to repair:

$$RT = \frac{Td}{N}$$

(e) Utilization:

$$\%UT = \frac{W}{T - Td} \times 100$$

Where T = scheduled hours
Td = breakdown time

W = working time
N = number of failures

Provisional acceptance should not take place until after the tests to evaluate the figures of merit have been satisfactorily completed. There should be a sufficiently large amount of money payable to the Contractor on provisional acceptance to give it every incentive to ensure that the plant does pass the tests as soon as possible.

A.23 Defects liability period

Once the project is provisionally accepted and taken over, it is normal to have a period (usually 12 months) during which the Contractor is liable to rectify defects. Here the following points should be considered:

(a) Whether there should be a further defects liability period in respect of any defects which manifest themselves during the first period and which are then rectified.
(b) A sufficient amount of retention money should be retained until final acceptance to ensure the Contractor fulfils its obligations to rectify defects.
(c) The Employer should have the power to rectify defects at the Contractor's expense if the Contractor does not respond or complete rectification promptly.
(d) Whether performance guarantees should also apply during the defects liability period and for how long thereafter (subject to exclusions where due to operator negligence).
(e) The Contract should make clear the extent of the Contractor's liability in respect of latent defects once the defects liability period had expired.
(f) If a defect does arise during the defects liability period, the Contract should also make it clear whether the Employer's rights are limited to requiring the Contractor to remedy the defect under the defects clause, or whether the Employer also has the right to recover a penalty or damages.

A.24 Retention money

The amount of retention should be such as to give the Employer reasonable protection from bad workmanship and design where applicable, and it should provide an incentive to the Contractor to complete its outstanding obligations in order that the retention be released but should not be excessive as this would increase the Contractor's tender price. It is recommended that some retention monies should always be withheld until the end of the defects liability period.

A retention of between 5% and 10% of the contract price is normal, a half payable upon Completion or provisional acceptance and the remaining half upon expiry of the maintenance/defects liability period or final acceptance.

A.25 Contractor's liability for defects

Although not desirable from the Employer's point of view, it is now common in engineering contracts for the Contractor's liability to be limited along the following lines:

(a) No liability for consequential loss or no liability at all beyond, say, 10–15% of the contract price.
(b) No liability for defects during the defects liability period other than the obligation to rectify defects.

(c) No liability whatsoever for defects arising after the defects liability period.

Notwithstanding the above, the interests of the Employer and the circumstances of each case must be carefully considered. In the light of these, the following points become much more important:

(a) Close supervision by the Engineer over the Contractor during construction and the express definition and inclusion of this task in the agreement between the Employer and the Engineer.
(b) Detailed inspection and documentation of defects requiring attention prior to provisional and final acceptance.
(c) Consideration of consequential loss insurance.

It is desirable that limitation of liability should not apply to design defects; however, this may be difficult to achieve in practice because of the limits of professional indemnity insurance.

A.26 Suspension and termination for convenience

The Employer should have the right to suspend the operation of the Works for up to, say, three months at a time and also to terminate the Contract altogether on notice of, say, three months at its discretion. For suspension, the Contractor will obviously need to be compensated for additional out-of-pocket expenses and overheads, and in the case of termination for convenience, it should be entitled to a settlement giving a reasonable profit for the work done and a contribution towards prospective loss of profits.

A.27 Termination for default

It is most important to have an effective termination for default clause. Most clauses are rather narrowly drafted. It should be possible to terminate in the following circumstances:

(a) The insolvency or liquidation of the Contractor (although this may be prohibited under *ipso facto* provisions in legislation).
(b) Where the Contractor fails to provide a compliant programme, update a programme, or is significantly behind programme without justifiable cause.
(c) Where the Contractor is materially in breach of contract.
(d) Where the Contractor fails to remedy any material breach of contract within seven days of being given notice requiring it to remedy the breach.

If termination for default has occurred, the Employer should have the right to:

(a) Use all plant and materials on Site.
(b) Complete the project by making use of another contractor.
(c) Hire the Contractor's employees.
(d) Take assignments of subcontracts and suppliers.
(e) Recover damages from the Contractor.
(f) Withhold retentions and monies due and payable to the Contractor, pending final assessment of the Contractor's liability.
(g) Call in demand guarantees or sureties.

A.28 Training, spares, operating manuals, as-built drawings

The following provisions should be considered for insertion into the Contract:

(a) The duty of the Contractor to train operating and maintenance personnel.

(b) The provision of spares lists and recommendations as to levels of spares to be held in stock, in time for ordering and delivery prior to provisional acceptance.
(c) The delivery of operation, maintenance, and repair manuals.
(d) The delivery of as-built drawings.

As-built drawings and operation and repair manuals are particularly important and final payment should be conditional upon receiving them.

A.29 The effect of certificates of provisional and final acceptance

It is important to avoid any clause whereby the effect of the giving of the certificate is to waive any of the Employer's rights as to undiscovered faulty work (or design) or latent defects. Moreover, if possible, it is desirable to include a clause to the effect that certificates are for payment purposes only and do not constitute an acceptance by the Employer that the Contractor has complied with its contractual obligations.

A.30 Arbitration and litigation

As an intermediate step the parties should agree to an appropriate ADR procedure, to provide a provisionally binding determination of a dispute, pending final determination by arbitration or litigation if necessary.

Arbitration is often the most suitable means of final dispute resolution for construction disputes, particularly in the case of international contracts. An arbitration clause should be in the Contract, as it may not be possible to get the agreement of the parties for arbitration once a dispute has crystallised.

Litigation should only be selected as the final method of dispute resolution if courts suitable for construction disputes are available in the jurisdiction, if neither party will have an inherent advantage, and enforcement of a judgement in a relevant jurisdiction can be readily achieved.

A.31 Governing law

The Contract should state the language to be used, the law by which it is governed, and that the parties submit to the jurisdiction of the relevant tribunal for the purposes of service, trial, and the enforcement of any judgement or award.

APPENDIX B

Risk factors in the construction of infrastructure projects

CONTENTS

The Employer and the Tenderers involved in infrastructure projects must be fully aware of the risks inherent in the construction and testing of the Works, and the risks of working in the area of the Site so as to best allocate and deal with them. The lawyer tasked with the insurance and preparation of contracts for the construction of infrastructure must also have a good understanding of the main risk factors involved in each category of work.

The following highlights the main risks relevant to construction of different types of infrastructure projects.

B.1 Airport works

With perhaps the exception of the construction of entirely new airports, this work is normally divided into two categories – land side and air side.

Land side works include the construction, alteration, and repair of buildings, the installation and servicing of plant, and any other work where there is no possibility of contact with aircraft operations. This work can be assessed in the same way as general building work at any other location.

Air side contracts are concerned with such work as the construction or extension of runways and aprons, the installation of airport lighting, and the provision of refuelling facilities. In the case of work on existing airports, special measures need to be taken at both design and construction stages to avoid interference with air traffic and the normal functioning of the airport. Damage to buried services or flooding of the Works caused by interference with existing drainage could be hazards with a consequential risk of closing down the airport partly or totally; this would normally attract very significant damages.

In each case the potential third-party exposure requires special consideration. Due to the increasing weight, value, and passenger carrying capacity of modern jet aircraft it is quite common for the Contractor to be asked to provide a third-party policy with a very high indemnity. The premium for such cover may well be completely disproportionate to the size of the Contract involved. The site plan showing the areas of operations and their proximity to the main runways, when considered in conjunction with the funnel diagram showing the maximum permitted angles and heights for aircraft approach, will enable a realistic assessment of the risks to be made.

By their very nature airports are, whenever possible, built on flat, open ground, and are consequently exposed to such natural perils as storm, tempest, and water damage. The risks of loss or damage to the work during such processes as drainage, grading, laying of aggregate, and casting of concrete for the runways are reasonably obvious for an inland airport, although special attention should be given to the possibility of damage to expensive items of Contractor's equipment such as large paving machines and concrete batching plants. Many airports, however, are built in coastal areas and, frequently, an extension of the runway to cope with larger and heavier aircraft necessitates work in the sea. Such work is exposed to entirely different perils and needs to be considered under the heading of seaworks in ¶B.14.

B.2 Bridges

Almost any structure designed to cross a gap comes within this category. Bridges may cross over and under roads, including flyovers and underpasses, over and under railways, over rivers, gorges, and chasms, and across harbours and low-lying ground. The main types of structure are as follows:

(a) Single span on piers or abutments,
(b) Multi-span on piers,
(c) Arch,
(d) Cantilever, and
(e) Suspension and cable stayed.

It should be noted that (a) and (b) may be either of constant section or variable section, and (a), (b), and (c) may be static or opening either by the swing principle or lifting as in the case of the bascule or counter-poise or balanced bridge design.

The materials used may be steel, reinforced concrete, prestressed concrete, or a combination of all three with decking generally of reinforced concrete, welded steel, or light alloy. Small bridge structures may be constructed of stone or brick.

The risks involved may be considered under the four headings:

(a) Abutments
(b) Foundations
(c) Piers
(d) Superstructure

B.2.1 Abutments

These are often concrete retaining walls, possibly having piled foundations, depending on the topography of the chosen site. The embankment may also be retained by reinforced earth construction or, where sloped, may simply be protected against scouring by precast units or by grassing.

The abutments will usually retain the backfill supporting the approaches to the bridge as well as drainage media to relieve excessive pressure from saturated soil. The risks to be considered relate to the slip or collapse of embankment material adjacent to an abutment, and failure is in many cases due to flood damage where scour occurs due to excessive flow velocities brought about by reduced flow areas under the bridge. Erosion of abutment foundations is not uncommon in flat river valleys with a meandering watercourse in which changes to the riverbank at the structure causes washout of the material behind and under the abutment.

B.2.2 Foundations

The foundations which are to support the piers either on land or in water will consist of a bed plus the foundation structure itself. The bed may either be rock or concrete piles of sufficient strength to support the weight of the finished structure. In the case of piers in water, the bed must also be of sufficient depth to be free from any danger of disturbance by scouring caused by the tide or other currents, including abnormal floods.

The foundation structure may be any of the following:

(a) Reinforced concrete footing or piles with pile cap,
(b) Caisson, or
(c) Monolith.

B.2.2.1 Reinforced concrete footing or piles

A reinforced concrete footing will be cast in situ. On land this will be in open excavation which may require shuttering to prevent the collapse of the sides and dewatering to lower the water table. Where the pier is to be in water, sheet piling will be driven into the water bed to form a coffer dam. Any damage to, or overtopping of, the coffer dam could result in the inundation of the foundation works causing damage to the concrete and possibly the loss of any equipment working within the coffer dam. On completion the sheet piling is either withdrawn by means of a crane or the upper portion is cut off by torch below the level of the riverbed after any space between the foundation and the sheeting has been filled with concrete.

Piles of concrete or steel may be driven by a pile driver or cast in situ concrete within a driven steel liner. In view of the unknown founding depth of piles or liners until they have been driven, adequate lengths of pile or liner need to be available for possible founding depths inferred from the geotechnical investigations. Suitable equipment may be required to splice pile lengths.

B.2.2.2 Caissons

Caissons are large shafts of steel or concrete erected on cutting curbs and sunk down either on land or on the riverbed or seabed by excavation from within. The sides of the shaft may be built up as the sinking proceeds. During such sinking, bentonite is frequently used to reduce side friction and, in such cases, the excavation from within must be more strictly controlled to prevent tilting due to differential ground conditions. Where required, after sinking, side friction may be restored by cement grouting from holes drilled from within. When final depth is reached, the bottom of the well is plugged with concrete and the inside filled, usually with sand. A concrete cap is then formed upon which the pier structure may be erected.

B.2.2.3 Monolith

Monoliths are used where very heavy loads have to be carried and a foundation structure of large superficial area is required. They consist of a number of caissons or a large cellular structure which is sunk in the same way as caissons. When used for foundation works in water it should be noted that both caissons and monoliths may be precast and floated into position for sinking on the river or seabed. Much will depend upon the experience of the contractor in towing, sinking, and correctly positioning such structures.

B.2.3 Piers

The materials used may be brick, stone, steel, timber, or concrete depending on the type of bridge, its design, and possibly on the local availability of materials. It is, however, normally of reinforced concrete cast in situ, but precast units may also be used. For in situ casting, the risks to be considered are the possibility of collapse of the false-work or shuttering, the possibility of damage by impact and, for 'wet' conditions, the overtopping or failure of the coffer dam. Consideration should be given to the difficulties of the site with regard to access, possible obstruction to the movement of cranes, and the required 'reach' of cranes relative to the size and mass of the loads being lifted.

B.2.4 Superstructure

The various methods of bridge-building differ considerably in this respect.

B.2.4.1 Single or multispan on piers and abutments

Such bridges may comprise prestressed concrete beams precast in a factory, or fabricated steel girders that can span between piers. The size and weight of such beams require special transport arrangements, and may require checking the adequacy of existing bridges to carry the load.

Longer spans are typically made of individual precast concrete units which are erected and secured together by longitudinal post-tensioning to form each span or cantilever. They fall into various categories:

(a) Span-by-span construction, where all the segments of one span are erected on a supporting truss or gantry and longitudinally post-tensioned together.
(b) Balanced cantilever, where segments are erected sequentially in cantilevers on each side of an initial segment placed on top of the pier, with temporary towers providing stability.
(c) Progressive cantilever, where segments are erected in cantilever in one direction, progressing over all the piers. Additional temporary piers or towers with cable stays are needed.

Other concrete bridge construction systems include incremental launching, partial precast, cast-in-place, and post-tensioned segmental girders. Success in segmental construction depends on the accuracy of the concrete casting operations. Problems in launching bridge sections can arise due to lack of such accuracy and due to bridge bearings not being placed at the same level. Collapse of prestressed structures has been caused by corrosion of the post-tensioned tendons at joints due to the ingress of chlorides through ineffective waterproofing and inadequate protection of the tendons at joints, exacerbated by opening of the segments due to superimposed loads and a damp environment. The cracking of box girder bridges has also been experienced due to poor detailing or bad workmanship and cracking due to temperature differences with subsequent failure by fatigue of the tendon couplers has occurred.

Falsework failures may be caused by impact loads, for example, during concreting, or inadequate strength or stability to carry the construction loads. Any deficiencies may be overlooked by inadequate review of the design and construction – sometimes caused by lack of clarity with respect to responsibility and poor communication – and lack of regular inspection.

B.2.4.2 Arch

An arch bridge may be supported by an abutment at each end that transmits the entire thrust in the arch into adequate bearing material in the ground. In a bowstring arch bridge, the horizontal component of thrust in the arch is resisted by the structure at the deck level, and the vertical component of the thrust by the abutment.

It is possible for such a bridge to carry heavier loads and to provide a longer span than is the case with a simple beam bridge. An arch bridge may be made of steel or concrete, and the arch may be above or below the decking. Steel railway bridges are an example of the arch above the decking, whereas concrete road bridges are the commonest example of the arch below the decking. It is normal to have more falsework for the construction of arch bridges than is the case with beam bridges.

B.2.4.3 Cantilever

This is usually a symmetrical three-span bridge, of which each of the outer sections is anchored at the shore or abutment and overhangs into the central span about one-third of its length. The suspended central section resting on the cantilever arms occupies the remaining one-third of the span. The method of working varies considerably with each design and requires careful evaluation. This type of bridge is normally used to provide a large span over water and the third-party risk of damage to shipping can be considerable.

B.2.4.4 Suspension and cable-stayed

These bridges rely on cables above the deck for structural support rather than from piers below and can provide long uninterrupted spans over water or difficult terrain, or where access must not be disrupted. Areas subject to earthquakes and typhoons may have limitations on span length and opinions vary as to the maximum span length possible with present-day materials. Major suspension bridges in various parts of the world are well known to engineers and laymen alike and bridges in this category are normally major engineering feats.

The towers carrying the main cables may be constructed in steel or concrete or a combination of the two. For long periods during construction the towers will be in a temporary state because they are designed to withstand both wind and loading forces when they are themselves braced by the supporting cables anchored on each side. The normal risks of placing large prefabricated sections or in situ concrete at considerable heights must be considered.

Cable anchorages for suspension bridges are normally constructed of mass concrete embedded in sound rock. Depending upon the geology of the site these could reach a considerable depth before bedrock is found and the risks are those of normal large-scale foundation work. For a suspension bridge the cables are strung from anchorage to anchorage across the top of the towers, and the hangers to support the bridge sections are attached to the cables. Methods of installing the deck sections vary from hoisting into position from below to working outwards from existing fitted sections. Problems arising in the construction of suspended crossings include difficulty in stabilising the unfinished deck during construction until the bridge is fully braced and stiffened. The major risk lies in the effect of high winds on the partially completed structure.

Hazards to bridges may arise from motor vehicle collisions, impact by high vehicles, and failure of erection equipment resulting in heavy loads being dropped during erection. In river or harbour locations, the dangers of carrying out construction activity in busy shipping lanes with fast tidal currents and damage to or by shipping are considerable.

B.3 Electricity transmission lines

Transmission and distribution cables are usually designed with two basic factors in mind. The first is the ability of the cable to transmit the required load with a sufficient safety factor; the second is the provision of a dielectric which will satisfactorily help to dissipate any excess heat generated. The almost universal use of oil-impregnated paper insulated cables is due to the fact that the component materials of the installation are so stable chemically and electrically that they can be operated at relatively high temperatures (70–85 degrees C). The use of these materials is more economical than alternative types of dielectric although cross-linked polyurethane may be favoured for voltages of less than 33kV. Solid type oil-impregnated cables are unsuitable for high voltages because ionisation appears in the cavities in the dielectric, leading to destruction of the insulating paper and the impregnant. In the higher voltage ranges, therefore, cables are designed to contain an oil or gas cooling medium which is often supported by ducted water. The ducted water may be within the outer covering of the cable or the cable may be laid in water troughs where very high voltages are envisaged. In the external gas pressure cable, the cable may be placed in a gas pressure container consisting of a steel pipeline into which the cable is drawn after the pipe has been tested for gas tightness.

The installation of transmission and distribution cables in the ground is usually a relatively simple matter from a technical point of view. Depending upon the working pressure and radius of cable it will usually be installed in a trench with approximately 1 m cover on a bedding of sand or soil pounded down to form a stone-free base. Sumps will be introduced at regular intervals, cut below the level of the trench so that water will drain off and can then be pumped out. Sand or soil will usually top the cable to a depth of about 100 mm, and then it is covered with tiles or reinforced concrete slabs aligned with the cable to act as a warning to anybody excavating in the area in the future. The ducted or piped system is an alternative usually employed in crowded areas where frequent trench excavation would be inconvenient and expensive. Ducts or pipes are buried in the ground with manholes at regular intervals from which the cables may subsequently be drawn. The ducts are usually of PVC, glazed earthenware, or cement with spigot and socket ends set in a concrete base. Steel and cast iron may also be used. Cables may be laid under water by means of cable-laying barges or ships, or in the case of short distances, by winching. The possibility of damage by storm, abnormal currents, impact with shipping, and corrosion must be considered. Marine liabilities arising from the use of vessels will normally be separately insured.

With the impregnated paper insulated type of cable, jointing is possible so that small areas of damage can be fairly easily repaired. With oil-filled cables, however, it is not possible to make joints other than at the maker's works or where provision has been made during the manufacture of the cable. For this reason, substantial losses can be experienced following fairly minor damage to an oil-filled cable. There is also the hazard of the loss of oil following such damage, which may result in third-party claims for pollution.

When crossing difficult territory, transmission lines are frequently strung on masts or towers. Strict security is normally impossible, and the cable often presents a high theft risk. Wind, heavy rain, and ice are hazards which should be taken into account at the design stage of the towers and cable.

B.4 Dams

Dams may take several different forms depending upon the use to which they are to be put, the geographical and geological features of the site, and the prevailing climatic conditions. They are, however, primarily concerned with the containment or regulation of water and, as such, bunds, coffer dams, barrages, and weirs are included in this category.

B.4.1 Embankment dams

The earliest known and simplest method of making a dam is to build an embankment of earth and/or rock with a watertight membrane to prevent leakage. This type of dam is eminently suitable for sites where there is a considerable depth of loose material lying on top of solid rock. This loose material would not be a suitable foundation for a concrete dam but with treatment it is frequently strong enough to support an embankment dam.

There are four principal types:

(a) Earth embankment dam with a central core of impervious clay or concrete;
(b) Rock-filled dam built only of large rocks which is then rendered watertight by means of a concrete skin on the upstream surface;
(c) Zoned fill embankment containing both soil and rock in different zones which is made watertight by the use of an impervious rolled earth core; and
(d) Roller-compacted concrete dams.

Seepage takes place through and under all dams, both earth and concrete, the engineering problem being to control it so that it has no harmful effects. Seepage through an embankment is considered to be potentially more dangerous than seepage through a concrete dam as erosion may then occur with the possibility of the dam being carried away. For this reason, particular care is necessary in the design and implementation of methods to prevent unacceptable seepage, such as carrying a watertight membrane or core down to an impervious foundation or injection grouting the foundation itself.

Overtopping of earth dams due to lack of sufficient spillway capacity is, however, considered to be the most frequent cause of failure. Piping has also been a frequent cause of dam and bund failures where seepage water emerges from an embankment or adjacent ground surface under sufficient pressure and with sufficient velocity to wash away the material. Certain 'dispersive' soils are unsuitable for use without prior treatment, requiring the careful selection and treatment of materials from borrow pits.

B.4.2 Gravity dams

The gravity dam relies entirely on its own deadweight for stability against toppling and lateral movement and may be solid, cellular, or of buttressed construction. It is normally entirely of concrete.

B.4.2.1 Solid gravity dams

The main features of these dams are their simplicity of concept and their robustness of construction, leading to permanence and low maintenance. The height of the gravity dam is limited by the strength of the foundations and, where rock is at a considerable depth below the surface, an earth dam may be more economical. Bad grouting and poor design of the foundation may cause cracking in the downstream base.

B.4.2.2 Buttressed and cellular gravity dams

These dams differ from solid gravity dams in the following respects:

- (a) The area subject to uplift is much reduced with a resultant saving in deadweight concrete, making them cheaper to construct.
- (b) The weight of water on the sloping upstream face can be harnessed as a stabilising feature.
- (c) The material of the structure is used more efficiently at higher stresses.
- (d) A degree of flexibility and provision for settlement can normally be allowed for.

The main types of buttressed dams are:

- (a) Slab and buttress dams;
- (b) Multi-arch buttress dams;
- (c) Solid head buttress dams;
- (d) Massive buttress dams (these have straight, nearly vertical upstream walls, the downstream face being arched into the buttress); and
- (e) Cellular and hollow gravity dams (which are, to all effects, hollowed out gravity dams and have largely been developed in Europe).

The use of buttressed dams may prove more economical particularly in locations where procurement of transport and basic materials is costly or where materials are scarce, but these dams may also be more open to damage or destruction by sabotage than gravity dams. Their structural thinness may render them susceptible to deterioration – particularly in certain conditions of exposure.

B.4.3 Arch dams

The prime requirements for the site of an arch dam are that:

- (a) Foundation rock which includes the sides of the valley should be watertight and strong enough to be able to withstand the thrusts from the arch.

(b) The shape of the valley is suitable for the use of a stable arch form (the valley sides should be steep and the slope on the two sides roughly equal).

B.4.4 Spillways

A most important feature of any form or type of dam is the spillway to discharge and control water during periods of abnormal flow or rainfall. This is especially vital in the case of embankment dams. The following types of spillways exist:

(a) A specially designed section of a gravity dam or section in an embankment.
(b) A chute spillway – isolated but usually adjacent and with its crest normal to the dam.
(c) A side-channel spillway, where the flow passes over the spillway crest into a channel whose centre-line is parallel to the crest of the dam.
(d) A shaft spillway – which has a vertical flaring intake connected to an outlet conduit carrying the water through or around the dam.

Problems with spillways are often associated with the very high velocities attained by the water flowing in them and include scouring of the foundation downstream and cavitation damage to the spillway apron.

B.4.5 Coffer dams

A coffer dam is a temporary dam constructed so as to exclude water and soil from a construction site and allow work to be undertaken inside the coffer dam in relatively dry and safe conditions. The structure is generally subjected to large pressures. Coffer dams may be considered under two headings – those built of soil, concrete, or timber, and those of steel sheet piling. The choice of type depends upon the requirement of the work, the estimated pressures, the type of soil, and cost and time considerations.

In its simplest form a coffer dam consists of an earth embankment, but where a high pressure is expected it is more usual to use either a concrete wall or a diaphragm of interlocking steel sheet piles. Sheet pile diaphragms are usually far from watertight, and if constructed as a single skin, necessitate heavy bracing which forms an obstruction in the working area. Sheet piled coffer dams are, therefore, typically made of two skins filled with excavated material between them and are tied together with tie bolts. The structure then becomes stable without the use of external shoring. Alternatively, cellular coffer dams formed of special curved piles are often used.

Most dams are constructed across existing river valleys and provision must therefore be made for the normal flow of the river during the construction of the dam. To enable the foundations of the dam to be constructed in the dry as far as is possible, it is necessary to divert the natural flow of the river. The diversion may involve either restricting the flow to a small part of the riverbed, and thus completing the dam foundations in sections, or of providing a diversion channel or tunnel past the site of the proposed dam and sealing off the complete riverbed with a coffer dam.

Whichever type of coffer dam is used, the most important consideration is the height of the coffer dam compared to the highest recorded water level of the river at that point during the past 10 or 20 years. In considering this point, allowance must also be made for the discharge capacity of the diversion channel or tunnel and any additional ponding which may be caused by a limitation in this capacity to cope with the river in flood. The capacity of the coffer dam to withstand the forces of the river at all times of the year will, to a large extent, govern the possibility of damage to the main dam structure. If, however, it is considered impossible to construct a coffer dam and diversion arrangements sufficient to withstand the river at all times of the year, so that overtopping of the coffer dam becomes inevitable, then due allowance must be made by means of providing for the damage which will result both to the coffer dam and the main dam.

It will be seen, therefore, that the critical times in dam construction are first, the diversion of the river by means of a coffer dam and, second, the final closure of the main dam and the diversion channels allowing ponding to commence in the reservoir area. The timing of these activities is critical and the contractor's proposed working schedule, together with rainfall and river flow figures for the previous 10 to 20 years or more are absolutely vital.

The third-party risk arising out of dam construction is normally light because the location is generally in a remote area. In the case of a steep-sided valley, however, a failure of the dam after commencement of ponding could cause a tidal wave which may engulf habitation some distance downstream. Other risks may arise from the operation of a quarry, the transportation of materials, and claims under the cross liabilities clause where several contractors or subcontractors are insured jointly.

The failure of a coffer dam is seldom due to the failure of its component parts. It is almost always due to failure of the ground at the base inside the coffer dam, where the soil may change its mechanical properties due to the forces exerted upon it, or where it may prove incapable of resisting these forces.

B.5 Reservoirs

The construction of reservoirs for the conservation of water may be carried out by the closing of a natural valley with a dam, the formation of an artificial lake by excavation and sealing as in pumped storage schemes, or the construction of concrete containers above or below ground. The risks arising from the construction of dams have already been discussed in the previous section.

Pumped storage schemes require a lake or reservoir above and below the powerhouse and it is unlikely that both will exist naturally. One or the other will need to be created by excavation and by lining of the excavated area with waterproof concrete or bitumen to prevent water loss.

The construction of concrete reservoirs above or below ground will involve the usual hazards associated with mass excavation and concrete construction.

The main problem with all reservoirs, however, is that of adequate sealing to prevent water losses. The only possible method of testing is to fill the reservoir with water and any leakage then discovered may prove expensive to repair. Finding the precise location of the cause of leakage may be time-consuming and expensive. Failure of the reservoir during testing may result in flood damage to third-party property and possibly loss of life.

B.6 General buildings

B.6.1 Foundations

Foundations are intended to carry the weight from a building to the ground on which the building rests in such a way as to avoid uneven settlement in relation to the structure. In the case of high-rise buildings, they also resist wind loads or earthquake loads in regions susceptible to earthquakes.

The soil, foundations, and superstructure are interrelated. In all foundation work investigation of the ground is an essential prerequisite of sound design. Preliminary information regarding the subsoil is mostly obtained by trial boreholes; the sciences of soil mechanics and geology enable the nature of the soil's strata to be known and an assessment of the most satisfactory method of construction to be made.

In the event of the load on the foundations being high, there is a tendency for the soil beneath to be forced down and outwards giving rise to heaving on the surface and allowing the foundation to sink. The depth and type of the foundation should therefore be such that the weight of the soil coupled with the shear resistance of the soil will prevent this from occurring. The foundations for very tall modern buildings can be extremely elaborate and can often be considered as a civil engineering project within a building project.

Failures have been known to occur and the cost of rectifying differential settlement to high-rise building can be considerable. Difficulties also arise where the new structure is to be much higher than the surrounding buildings because new foundations will be founded considerably below those of adjoining properties; the consequent risk of subsidence and cracking to third-party properties must be alleviated by adequate support of the excavation. Buildings with rigid monolithic frames or flexible frames with precast facings are sensitive to differential movement. Settlement of foundations may be caused by any of the following:

(a) Moisture changes,
(b) Subsidence, and
(c) General movement.

B.6.1.1 Moisture changes

These may be the result of:

- Climatic changes so that, for example, clay dries out and shrinks;
- A variable water table (the level of standing water in the subsoil) particularly applicable to sites on reclaimed land adjacent to rivers or the coastline; or
- The effects of tree roots.

It is important to note the proximity of the building site to fast-growing and water-seeking trees. Within a few years of planting, the roots of these trees can extend 20 metres and more. Conversely, the removal of such trees may cause an increase in groundwater and affect the water-table.

B.6.1.2 Subsidence

Mass movement of ground may occur in areas where mining has taken place or on filled or made-up ground or as a result of extensive dewatering activities.

B.6.1.3 General movement

The tendency is for the upper strata of clay soils to move downhill on sloping sites, and landslips on slopes previously considered stable may be the result of work carried out on adjoining land.

The majority of building foundations are constructed from mass or reinforced concrete. They may be either shallow foundations, which transfer the load to the soil at a level close to the lowest floor of the building (eg strip footings, slabs, and rafts) or deep foundations such as piles and piers.

B.6.2 Mass concrete foundations

The hazards associated with the laying of mass concrete are frost or the sudden incursion of water. In locations where there is a high water table it is usually desirable to lower the water level by pumping to avoid upward pressure of the water. This is particularly the case in the construction of basements where the weight of the partially-complete building is insufficient to prevent the basement from floating. Other methods of preventing the ingress of water are the well-point system of dewatering, the forming of a temporary coffer dam by driving steel sheet piling, or the construction of permanent diaphragm concrete walls in a bentonite slurry trench. In suitable circumstances, groundwater can be frozen by refrigeration or work may be carried out within a caisson which is later incorporated into the foundation construction. Dewatering by pumping out water lowers the water table under adjacent structures, which may result in settlement and cracking of adjacent buildings with consequent third-party claims.

B.6.3 Piled foundations

A piled foundation would normally be used where no firm bearing strata exist at a reasonable depth. The dimensions, materials used, and method of inserting the pile are many and varied. It is a common misconception that piles must be either driven or bored, preformed, or cast in situ. Piles may now be installed by top driving, bottom driving, boring, coring, vibrating, drilling, jetting, jacking, ramming, pulling down, washing out, blowing out, and mudding or by a combination of these methods. The equipment used may be single-acting or double-acting hammers, operated by air, diesel, or steam, low-frequency and high-frequency vibrators, and augers and hammer grabs. The piles themselves may obtain a firm set on rock or other load bearing strata or may be of the friction type. The type of power required can only be decided after a close study of the ground conditions revealed by the geotechnical investigations on each site.

Another popular misconception is that it is possible to avoid noise and vibration by utilising bored piles rather than driven piles. The installation process involved in both types lead to vibration in the surrounding soils and nearby surfaces and structures to extents varying according to many factors. What is of more importance than attempting the distinction is to determine the level of vibration which is acceptable on a given site. Only screwed, drilled, or jacked pilings are totally vibration free. Driving with an internal drop hammer on an internal piling at the base of the piling tube is much quieter than top driving a driven pile or temporary lining of a bored pile.

Apart from the possibility of breakage or damage to precast or preformed piles during handling or driving, there is always the risk of the effect on uncured concrete in the ground of running water, acids, and other deleterious substances. There is a practice in some places amongst some specialist piling contractors to offer to the employer a guarantee for up to five years against any damage to the superstructure resulting from a failure of the piles.

B.6.4 System building

The use of system or modular building is increasing because of the saving in construction time and labour that it facilitates. There are many different systems in use but, basically, they all involve the erection of standard factory-prepared component parts. These are principally cast concrete panels and beams but many also include complete plumbing systems. In view of the great variety of systems, and the continually evolving designs, it is important that a detailed assessment of each system submitted, including the manufacturers brochures, are studied. General points to consider when dealing with system buildings are as follows:

(a) Size and value of largest component,
(b) Actual method of erection,
(c) Method of storing major component parts,
(d) Height factor – high rise buildings,
(e) Location of factory, and
(f) The transit risk.

B.6.4.1 Size and value of largest component

A wall may be fitted as one complete unit. This could have a considerable value and a mishap whilst placing the wall could prove to be costly not only in respect of the replacement value of the wall unit but also in terms of damage to work already completed.

B.6.4.2 Actual method of erection

At a certain stage the building may be vulnerable to collapse. In one particular system the gable ends of the building are erected and temporarily supported until the sidewalls are placed into position and the four tied together. A windstorm at this stage of the work may cause collapse of the gable ends.

Collapse has also occurred in cases where there has been a lack of adequate temporary props to stabilise the units prior to release of crane slings and until other units ensure stability. Inadequate grouting space at joints has also caused major problems.

B.6.4.3 Method of storing major component parts

Storage and vehicular traffic should be carefully planned so as to avoid impact of vehicles with the stockpile which can cause considerable damage. Lifting large and heavy components into position may require the segment to be swung over the stockpile and this risk must also be taken into consideration.

B.6.4.4 Height factor – high-rise buildings

Where the building is to be multi-storied an additional hazard is involved in the lifting of component parts. The method of keying-in of the panels must also be considered because falling parts may cause considerable damage to stockpiles, contractor's equipment, third-party property, and even injury or death.

B.6.4.5 Location of factory

There are occasions where, for large developments in remote areas, it is more economical to set up a temporary factory on site. An allowance must therefore be made for the manufacturing processes involved.

B.6.5 Steel-framed buildings

There have been several instances of the collapse of steel frames in buildings nearing completion. Subsequent investigations have revealed that the cause was an abnormal stress imposed on the structure due to incorrect or inadequate bolting of a fairly small but critical section. Lightweight cladding is often used in connection with steel-framed buildings and this is more susceptible to damage during storage and erection than brick or concrete panels. In the light of recent catastrophic fires, the fire resistance and combustibility of cladding requires special attention.

B.6.6 Tall buildings

Foundations will generally be of considerable depth and complexity. All the materials and structural sections to be incorporated in the higher floors have to be lifted or transported by hoist or crane to their final position. Any errors in hoisting or placing into position could result in damage not only to the unit concerned but also the complete structure and surrounding third-party property.

The equipment used by the Contractor will include several large items, such as tower cranes, which are of much greater value than the equipment used on smaller buildings. On completion of the structure, the dismantling and removal of the tower cranes can be an extremely hazardous operation and a number of third-party claims have resulted from accidents arising at this time.

If scaffolding is erected to a great height the collapse of such scaffolding can cause injury and death, and considerable damage to the structure which would lead to costs in addition to the cost of replacing the scaffolding.

A fire in the upper stories of a partially completed tower block could prove extremely difficult to fight.

Many tall buildings are erected in town or city centres on congested sites so that the only possible location for huts, temporary offices, and material storage is within the partially completed framework. Even materials which normally would be stored well away from the building under construction have to be placed close to or even within the structure. Materials which are susceptible to damage from the elements may also be stored within the lower floors. Materials comprising timber and other inflammable substances, in addition to huts and temporary buildings constitute a considerably increased risk to the partially completed structure. It is not always obvious which materials will create an increased fire hazard because even non-combustible items will be seriously damaged or destroyed by fire originating in the packing materials.

B.7 Groundworks

The works to be considered under this heading differ from all other construction works in that very little is constructed. Most of this work can form part of a construction contract but it is also possible for it to be left as a separate contract or as a subcontract where the subcontractor is required to arrange its own insurance. The work involved may be subdivided as follows:

(a) Earth moving,
(b) Mass excavation,
(c) Trenching,
(d) Shaft sinking, and
(e) Piling.

B.7.1 Earthmoving

This will normally form part of a major project such as road building, or may be the preliminary work to the construction of a large industrial complex or power plant. Earthmoving will also form a large part of the work involved in the construction of an earth embankment dam.

Apart from the possibility of damage to embankments caused by heavy rainfall or flooding, subsidence, or collapse, the major risk in this type of work concerns the Contractor's equipment. The cost of salvaging large and expensive items of equipment which have been inundated with floodwater, which have tipped over on a steep slope, or which have become bogged down in marshy ground can be considerable. The equipment used on large earthmoving projects is extremely expensive. Damage to tyres arising out of normal usage must also be taken into account.

B.7.2 Mass excavation

This is normally associated with foundation works or the construction of basements utilising the methods already described. In all cases except shallow excavations, where the soil conditions allow the use of a reasonable unsupported batter (slope), some support to the sides of the excavation will be necessary. Concrete diaphragm walls constructed in a bentonite slurry or walls of close concrete piling constructed before excavation begins should be self-supporting. In the case of steel sheet pile coffer dams, within which excavation is to take place, there is always the risk of some instability. This may be caused by not driving the piling to a sufficient depth so that the toe is uncovered during excavation, by the flow of groundwater scouring beneath the toe, or by ground or ground water pressure where no waling beams and cross strutting have been employed in a single skin coffer dam. Whatever the method of supporting the sides of the excavation, there is always the risk of inundation due to heavy rain or floodwater, or the complete breakdown of the dewatering pumps. A careful assessment should be made of the total value of contractor's equipment which may be in use within the excavation at any one time. Other methods of supporting vertical sides of excavations such as geo-nails and ground anchors are used, and the prescribed excavation procedures must be carefully followed.

B.7.3 Trenching

Trenching is often a major civil engineering undertaking, and as with mass excavation, the main hazards are collapse of the trench sides and inundation of the trench. The objectives of trench support systems should be to hold up the ground so that work in the trench can proceed safely, and to avoid ground movements which could damage adjacent structures or buried services. Most fatalities are due to lack of, or inadequate, trench support, sometimes because of apparently stable soil becoming unstable and collapsing in abnormal weather conditions. Trenches may also become filled with salt, sand, mud, snow, and other detritus requiring careful re-excavation. The seriousness of the hazard in such work calls for regular inspection and primarily depends on the length of trench which is to be left open. This is often curtailed by work specifications as well as the climatic conditions which may be expected during the period of the work.

B.7.4 Shaft sinking

Shaft sinking works are associated with the construction of tunnels and mining projects; the hazards present in shaft sinking, and the construction of horizontal shafts or tunnels is dealt with under ¶B.17.

B.7.5 Piling

Piling work has already been mentioned under ¶B.6.3, but it is included in the category of groundworks because some present-day piles are of such large diameter that they virtually become shaft excavations. Piles in this category would be of cast in situ concrete. Piling in a built-up area may involve hazards peculiar to such situations.

B.8 Heavy industries

This category embraces steel mills, rolling mills, and other metalworking industries such as aluminium and copper smelting and refining. A feature of the contract for such plant, much of which has a high weight load factor, is the substantial foundation work necessary to carry heavy plant. Close investigation into site conditions is therefore desirable. It is reasonable to expect that the Employer or Contractor will seek expert technical advice on the load-bearing properties of the soil and satisfactory evidence of this should be obtained. In areas where mining has been carried out the risk of subsidence is of particular importance.

Large blast furnaces will be used in the smelting and refining processes and whilst they present no special problems during construction, the refractory brickwork linings constitute a serious hazard during the testing and commissioning period when heat is first introduced into the furnace for drying out purposes. This creates a risk of damage by cracking. The remedy may involve taking out and completely rebuilding the brickwork at a very high cost. In normal operating conditions such brickwork has a limited life and periodical replacement is regarded as an operating risk. The normal practice of contractor's all risk insurers is to exclude damage to refractory brickwork lining arising from drying out or subsequent operations, although cover will be granted in respect of other insured risks such as impact or an explosion, even if this arises during the testing period. Where gas or oil-fired furnaces are used, the risk of an ignition type of explosion is present at all times after initial start-up. With electric arc furnaces the heavy-duty transformers constitute a heavier than normal breakdown and/or disruption risk during testing. Leakage in a furnace transformer induction coil could result in overloading with possibility of widespread damage from explosion. A flue gas explosion risk could also exist, depending on the source of waste heat and whether there is any supplementary firing of the boilers.

The value of rolling mill machinery is very high and although much of the plant will be extremely robust, and small losses are unlikely, high repair costs can be anticipated if damage does occur.

Breakdown risks during testing are mainly associated with large gearboxes and synchronous DC motors driving the rollers. The smaller and less robust rollers employed in the final stages of rolling will probably be highly polished and more susceptible to accidental damage than those used in the initial stages of the process.

Fire risks do not normally present problems, although there have been instances in aluminium rolling plants where the rollers are sprayed with paraffin as a cooling lubricator. This could of course seriously increase the risks of fire during testing and commissioning.

In aluminium plants the alumina powder is prepared from the basic ingredient of bauxite after treatment with a caustic solution, followed by filtering and drying processes. The powder is then heated and combined with other ingredients in what are known as pot line furnaces. These pot lines consist of large numbers of small cells or furnaces in which electrolytic action takes place to form molten aluminium. A problem encountered with this process is the large supply of electric current required. A failure in the electricity supply would cause the aluminium to harden, resulting in considerable, perhaps irreparable, damage to cells or furnaces. It is therefore essential to ascertain whether a secondary supply of current is available during commissioning. Similarly, any failure of the main transformers can result in serious damage. The problem of liquids solidifying in metal furnaces is not restricted to aluminium plants and may also affect other metal refining processes. Expensive replacement and repair costs can be expected including the digging out of solidified contents of furnaces or plotlines.

Contractor's equipment will need to include several heavy duty cranes capable of lifting the large items of plant involved. The tendency towards lifting increasingly large prefabricated units has resulted in frequent use of one or more mobile cranes together with static lifting equipment for the same lift. This type of multiple-lift operation has become necessary due to considerations of bulk as well as weight load. It is considerably more hazardous than if carried out by a permanently installed crane in controlled factory conditions. There is always the danger that the moving load will suddenly impose a disproportionate stress on one of the cranes causing the eventual collapse of both. A mobile crane with lifting capacity of 150 tonnes or more will be very costly to replace. To this must be added damage to the equipment being lifted and surrounding works plus any damage to third-party property and the resultant consequential losses. A careful technical appraisal of the lifting methods should be made before cover is sought and it may be necessary to employ a specialist engineer for this purpose, with specific insurance for each lift.

A special third-party risk arises during the testing and commissioning because of the danger of the release into the atmosphere of caustic solutions in untreated chemical smoke.

B.9 Miscellaneous industries

In addition to the specific industries dealt with elsewhere in this Appendix, there is a wide range of industries which account for the remainder of manufacturing activities. General consideration of the hazards applying to these miscellaneous industries has been divided into three sections as follows:

(a) Environmental hazards,
(b) Erection hazards, and
(c) Testing hazards.

B.9.1 Environmental hazards

B.9.1.1 High structures

High-capacity goliath cranes are now produced with a significant overall height. Aerials and masts are also erected to considerable height and present a real collapse risk if hit by a storm when partly erected and before the guy ropes can be properly fixed. Ice load conditions should also be investigated in connection with exposed tall structures, particularly when constructed on high ground. The factor of safety levels considered by designers in relation to weather conditions foreseeable at the contract site, whether wind or ice loading, are naturally geared to the resistance of the completed structure and may offer no protection during the erection period.

B.9.1.2 Water hazards

Apart from the obvious risks where machinery is being installed beside or over water, consideration should be given at other locations to problems of water ingress and evacuation in partially completed structures. This is particularly relevant where electronic equipment is to be installed. The fact that high value sensitive equipment is involved is no guarantee that adequate safeguards have been considered.

B.9.1.3 Theft

Recurring theft losses can be expected where valuable materials such as copper cabling or smaller electrical equipment are spread over a large area which cannot be adequately fenced. Items such as railway signalling, and line-side equipment are particularly vulnerable. Arrangements for handing over completed works with concomitant cessation of responsibility are therefore particularly important.

B.9.1.4 Subsidence

For all works of a massive or movement sensitive nature, the steps taken by contractors to ensure the stability of foundations and ground support must be clarified. Structures such as rotary kilns are of considerable length and weight so that, in any areas with a history of ground movement, whether on or below the surface, special consideration of the foundations is required.

B.9.2 Erection hazards

B.9.2.1 Lifting operations

Mobile cranes with extended jibs can be seriously affected by wind forces during high lifting operations.

B.9.2.2 Computer and instrumentation equipment

High values in the form of delicate machinery will be concentrated in comparatively small bulk, and faulty handling can lead to serious losses. There is also a need to provide specially equipped storage if installation cannot be carried out immediately on delivery. Once installed, a dust-free atmosphere must be carefully preserved during completion of surrounding works.

B.9.2.3 Paper-making machines

The highly polished cylinders found on such machines are susceptible to scoring during installation operations, the susceptibility varying according to the nature of cylinder finish. The distance of the manufacturer's premises from the contract site would have a considerable bearing upon the repair costs, as it is unlikely that facilities will be available on-site.

B.9.2.4 Pharmaceutical works

It is possible that there will be a preponderance of glass lined tanks in such works and the degree to which any repair is practicable must be clearly established. The value of the more susceptible items must be related to the overall contract price.

B.9.2.5 Testing hazards

Assessment of testing hazards will normally be based on experience of normal machinery breakdown, plus an allowance for the extra hazards which initial operational running presents and the initial uncertainty involved in updated processes or equipment which has been enlarged in scale. When considering testing hazards it is necessary to separate the susceptibility of certain machinery to breakdown from the risks inherent in the process – for example, the fire or explosion risk arising out of the materials fed into the machinery. Machinery involving a comparatively high breakdown risk may be employed on a non-hazardous process, whereas machinery offering a much lower breakdown risk may be required in the processing of highly volatile substances.

B.10 Oil and chemical industries

Considerable progress has been made in the development of the processing of by-products or waste gases from oil refineries. This has resulted in the growth of the petrochemical industry. A range of materials has emerged from such development, varying from fertilisers to plastics, detergents, industrial and domestic heating media in the form of rich gas, and materials for building, clothing, and furnishing – the latter being perhaps better known collectively as man-made fibres. All are developments of the processing of the basic hydrocarbons found in crude oil. The type of plant with which we are concerned here includes oil refineries, petrochemical complexes, chemical plants, fertiliser plants, gas treatment plants, oil gasification plants, the liquefaction of natural gas, and natural gas plants.

Such progress frequently brings its own problems, particularly when the ultimate aim is increasing output coupled with minimum capital expenditure and running costs and keen competition within the industry itself. The problems associated with new developments and experimentation, new techniques involving higher or lower temperatures and pressures, faster throughput and vast complexes, have resulted in many disastrous loss experiences. Contract values are rising continuously, reflecting the increased size of plant and emphasis on economies of scale. Similarly, the values of the major individual items are also increasing.

B.10.1 Natural hazards

In addition to the normal assessment of exposure to windstorm, earthquake, and so on, it should be remembered that for reasons of effluent discharge and access to feedstock the works will often be located adjacent to the sea or a river. There is, therefore, always the risk of damage by flood. Contracts may also include the construction of piers, jetties, and submarine pipelines for loading and unloading purposes.

B.10.2 Erection hazards

The size and weight of major units, particularly high distillation and fractionating columns, reactors, drums, and so on, will frequently necessitate the use of two cranes for lifting and lowering operations.

Accidents resulting in the toppling over of, and the damage to, both cranes and the load are common. Partly erected columns, towers, chimneys, and flare-stacks are all prone to storm damage unless suitably guyed and braced. The method of erecting tall columns should be closely investigated. They may be erected in ring sections and welded in situ or prefabricated into larger sections and hoisted into position for welding, or completely prefabricated on the ground where space permits, and hoisted into position as a complete unit.

The erection of storage tanks is also subject to storm damage or collapse risks. The dismantling of disused tanks frequently constitutes a considerable fire and explosion hazard, especially where cutting torches are employed.

B.10.3 Testing hazards

In addition to the normal machinery breakdown risks there is a considerably increased risk of fire and explosion due to the fact that hydrocarbons are being processed. Once feedstock has been introduced into the system for the start-up trials and commissioning operations, complete processes are involved.

New design features may be incorporated into machinery and process plant with the result that the incidence of breakdown during commissioning is far higher than in plants of tried and proven design. Extensions to existing plants are mostly intended to improve efficiency and output while new plant invariably incorporates updated designs and new processes; higher and lower operating temperatures and pressures, fluctuating loads, and inadequate safety margins, controls, and safety devices have all led to metallurgical and other failures.

Most processes require a catalyst to assist the basic chemical reaction. The value of the catalyst will vary considerably according to the type of plant involved. The catalyst can easily be spoiled, poisoned, or lost due to faulty operation of the plant and, as a result, it is normal to exclude loss or damage to the catalyst from any operational cause after introduction of feedstock.

B.10.4 Third-party hazards

It should be remembered that, for contracts involving alterations and/or extensions to existing facilities, considerable values can be at risk in the event of a fire or explosion caused by the Contractor during testing operations. There is also the danger of the release into the atmosphere of caustic solutions in untreated chemical smoke or pollution of water from effluent discharge.

B.11 Pipelines

In recent years the construction of pipelines has increased enormously throughout the world. Water, oil, gas, and chemical products are now conveyed enormous distances by pipelines varying in diameter from a few centimetres to several metres. The discovery of natural gas and oil under the sea has resulted in special problems, and the laying of sub-sea pipelines is considered under the heading of seaworks in ¶B.14. The comments in this section apply primarily to the laying of pipelines on land.

A large number of losses of considerable magnitude have been experienced on pipeline contracts, often from the most unexpected causes.

Assuming that fabrication and supply of the pipe does not form part of the construction contract, the work may be subdivided into the following sections:

(a) Clearing and grading,
(b) Stringing,
(c) Excavation,
(d) Lining-up,

(e) Welding,
(f) Coating and wrapping,
(g) Placing, and
(h) Testing.

A pipeline contractor will schedule these operations sequentially along the length of the pipeline. If any part of the site is not available immediately after the preceding section has been cleared, the Contractor will either be delayed or will have to remobilise equipment in another area; in either event this may result in substantial claims for extra time and money.

B.11.1 Clearing and grading

The equivalent to site preparation works comprises straightforward clearance of vegetation and the forming of gradients where required by contract conditions. In rocky areas, however, a certain amount of blasting may be necessary to establish the required levels. It is important that the right-of-way should allow the Contractor a reasonable area on both sides of the proposed trench line for use of mobile plant and equipment. Work in congested areas does, of course, require special consideration from the third-party point of view.

B.11.2 Stringing

Pipes are stacked along the proposed route so that sections may be drawn from these stacks as required, and are laid end-to-end (stringing), either on the ground or raised on timbers as near as possible to the lining of the proposed trench.

B.11.3 Excavation

Whenever possible the trench will be dug by a mobile excavator although blasting may be necessary in rocky areas. Buried pipelines normally have a minimum cover of 1 m so that the depth of the trench will vary according to the diameter of pipe. To maintain levels, however, it may be necessary to establish quite deep cuttings in undulating land and the major risk arises from the flooding and collapse of the trench. Frequently the trench is not shored or protected in any way, so it may be filled by heavy rain fall or flood waters, sand, or dust or the sides of the trench may collapse. The method of excavation and the length of trench which will be left open at any one time are therefore of particular importance. From this point of view, it is preferable for the welding, placing, and back-filling operations to proceed as quickly as possible after excavation.

Particular attention should be paid to road, rail, or river crossings. Road crossings may be by means of pipe jacking, thrust boring, or in open trench. In the latter case there is the risk of injury to road users and damage to vehicles. Third-party claims may also arise out of damage to other underground services during the excavation process. Frequently, plans provided by public utility authorities, purporting to show the location of their services, prove to be inaccurate.

Rail crossings may use a pipe bridge where the rail track is in a cutting, or pipe jacking, thrust boring, or trenching beneath the lines where appropriate. In either case there may be a risk of interference with rail traffic and heavy liabilities if passenger trains are involved.

River crossings may also be by pipe bridge, or by laying on the riverbed or in a prepared trench in the river bed. Much will depend upon the depth, rate of flow, and navigability of the river. It must be noted that in some situations pipelines are laid above ground on concrete haunches so that little or no excavation is required.

B.11.4 Lining-up

This is normally a manual operation by which the pipe ends are brought together in exact alignment preparatory to a welding operation. There are, however, some automatic welding sets in use which incorporate an internal hydraulic clamp to ensure perfect alignment.

B.11.5 Welding

This is normally undertaken manually using electrodes and therefore relies heavily upon the skill of the operator. Automatic welding facilities are now being used more frequently. It should be noted that most locations require the provision of firefighting facilities to prevent fires caused by sparks from the welding process. Welds should be checked for faults before the final coating and wrapping. The advantage of the x-ray method of testing is that a permanent record is available for inspection in the event of a fault developing during testing but, due to the cost factor, it is not normal for land lines to be tested in this way at each weld. Other methods of non-destructive testing may be employed. The percentage of welds tested must be adequate and in conformity with the requirements of the specification. For sections under water this should be 100%.

It will be appreciated that the comments made so far relate solely to the use of steel pipes. Pipes made of glazed earthenware, PVC, and cast iron may also be used. The methods of jointing will vary from the use of bitumen compounds, cement, and resin to bolting, and in the case of PVC pipes, the fusion of flanges by passing an electric current through previously incorporated electrodes. While glazed earthenware and cast iron pipes are susceptible to cracking and fracturing, they are normally manufactured in short lengths, and a reasonable level of access is usually sufficient to cater for most breakages. The use of asbestos cement is prohibited in most countries because of the health dangers posed by asbestos.

B.11.6 Coating and wrapping

Most steel pipes are coated and wrapped before final laying. Where this is carried out at the manufacturer's premises there is an increased risk of damage during transit, storage, and welding. If carried out on-site, however, there is an increased fire risk arising from the use of bitumen and coal tar enamel. In either case the welded joints of the pipe must be coated and wrapped on the site.

B.11.7 Placing

It is normal for considerable lengths of pipe to be welded, coated, and wrapped before laying in the trench, and the actual laying operation can involve the use of several side-boom tractors or pipe-laying machines. A large proportion of the value of the contractor's equipment is to be found in such machinery.

B.11.8 Back-filling

It is important that the backfilling should be completed as quickly as possible after the pipe has been laid to prevent collapse and/or flooding of the trench. If this is not done the pipe may be floated out of the trench by a flood, causing considerable expense in the excavation and relaying. Unfortunately, the disadvantage of backfilling the trench before testing is the difficulty of locating a leak. This can add considerably to the cost of the repair, although joints may be left open.

B.11.9 Testing

The testing of pipelines is usually confined to air and hydrostatic tests, the latter being favoured for high-pressure testing. The contract specification will generally state the nature of the tests to be carried out and depression limits to be achieved.

A steel pipeline may be subjected to a series of tests as follows:

(a) Sectional area tests,
(b) High level hydraulic testing, and
(c) Final air test.

B.11.9.1 Sectional area tests

After completion of laying and backfilling of sections of the pipe, they will be cleaned, sealed, and subjected to a specified air pressure. This pressure is sustained for a specified period. Any significant drop in pressure signifies leakage.

B.11.9.2 High level hydraulic testing

This method is otherwise known as high yield testing. One important purpose of hydrostatic pipeline testing is the discovery of defects in the pipeline and one of the most positive ways to accomplish this is to test at high pressure. This method of testing provides an extremely efficient means of revealing faults in material and workmanship during both manufacture and installation on site. Loss of the testing medium through damage to the pipe by over-pressurisation may result in considerable transport costs where water is scarce. A burst in the pipeline during such a high-pressure test would result in the discharge of water at a high velocity with the consequent risk of damage to third-party property or injury to persons.

B.11.9.3 Final air test

Sometimes a final air test is required after the high-level hydraulic test. This would, however, be at a fairly low pressure.

B.11.10 Other pipeline issues

Pipe jacking is particularly useful for passing pipes through obstructions such as railway embankments where open trench methods are not feasible. A hydraulic jack is used to push pipe sections, protected by a shield on the leading pipe, through the soil. For larger pipes, miners or tunnelling machines excavate the soil, working inside or beyond the end of the pipe. One of the problems associated with pipe jacking is friction, but this may be overcome by the use of bentonite, or by other means, to produce the desired working condition. Thrust boring is a method of forcing a hole through ground before insertion of the pipe. Specialist subcontractors may be used for these processes.

Cathodic protection may be needed in a pipe-laying contract. This is an electrical system designed to counteract high soil corrosion potential. Neither the installation nor the existence of such a system presents any serious hazard.

A combination of a high water table and an empty buried pipeline may cause the pipeline to 'float,' resulting in catastrophic damage over a considerable distance. Empty canals can suffer the same fate.

B.12 Power stations

Power stations, also referred to as power plants, generating stations, or generating plants, are industrial facilities for the generation of electric power and are usually connected to an electrical grid. They fall into eight categories:

(a) Coal-fired,
(b) Gas-fired,
(c) Geothermal,

(d) Hydroelectric,
(e) Pumped storage,
(f) Solar power,
(g) Wind turbine, and
(h) Nuclear.

The eighth category is not being considered here in view of the highly complex and specialised techniques involved, although they offer a sensible and environmentally acceptable means of generating power, provided adequate safeguards are put in place during their design, construction, and operation, and provision is made for the safe storage and disposal of spent fuel.

B.12.1 Coal-fired

In addition to general preparatory site work, the work will usually consist of the construction of foundations and power station buildings. Chimneys and cooling towers call for special consideration. With the drive for anti-pollution methods, chimneys are constructed at great heights using slip-forming methods and must be designed to withstand considerable wind forces.

Thermal stations are normally located adjacent to rivers or the sea, or over coalfields and the risk of flooding or subsidence must always be considered. The construction of cooling water intakes may involve the use of coffer dams, the hazards of which have been referred to in ¶B.4.5.

A feature of the construction of major power stations over recent years has been the installation of very large turbines. Risks associated with such machinery should not be underestimated. All turbines should be carefully investigated for design and prototype features. New techniques of design, construction, and materials are constantly evolving, and large turbines are invariably custom-built. Manufacturers will probably wish to consider employing the latest advances in design. It is these new designs and techniques which, in spite of the most careful calculations, supervision, and planning, can upset the finely balanced controlled conditions at the time of testing, resulting in the all too frequent breakdowns during the commissioning of power station plant. Troubles in this context usually mean very costly claims for contractor's all risk insurance and litigation.

The machinery component of the contract is largely bound up with the expensive and highly specialised work of installing generating equipment and water tube boilers. The boiler installation will take up much of the time for the overall construction as it will be built in situ.

Turbine equipment, generators, electrical distribution gear, and transformers, however, do not normally reach the site until much later in the construction programme. The build-up of values does not therefore proceed at a uniform rate. With a single large turbine, the value at risk will rise very substantially when the stator and rotor arrive on site.

The period of hot-testing – that is, after steam is introduced into the turbine following the final steaming tests and floating of the boiler valves – is often longer than with certain other types of machinery, possibly as long as six months. Fires can occur in boilers during testing. Since failures of steam turbines can be of catastrophic proportions, the need for adequate insurance cover for testing cannot be overemphasised.

The large size and weight of power station plant requires careful planning of transportation to the Site. Strengthening of existing bridges may be required to avoid damage.

B.12.2 Gas-fired[1]

Gas-fired power stations or natural gas power plants are thermal power stations which burn natural

1 https://en.wikipedia.org/wiki/Gas-fired_power_plant (accessed 5 September 2021).

gas to generate electricity. They are fossil fuel power stations in which chemical energy stored in natural gas, mainly methane, is converted successively into thermal energy, mechanical energy, and finally, electrical energy. Plant types include a simple cycle gas-turbine in which hot gas drives a gas turbine to generate electricity; combined cycle gas turbine in which simple cycle gas turbines are combined and followed by a heat recovery steam generator and a steam turbine. The most common configuration is two gas turbines supporting one steam turbine. They are more efficient than simple cycle plants.

Reciprocating engine plants use reciprocating internal combustion engines and are much smaller than other types of natural gas-fired electricity generators. They are typically used for emergency power or to balance variable renewable energy such as wind and solar.

Natural gas power stations generate almost a quarter of the world's electricity and create a significant component of greenhouse gas emissions, but about half that of coal-fired power stations and in general more than ten times that of nuclear power and renewable energy. However, they can be useful in providing seasonal dispatchable generation to balance variable renewable energy where hydropower or interconnectors not available.

Power stations deriving motive power to the generators from gas turbines present design problems and the turbine manufacturer's past experience must be investigated. Generally, a shorter installation period applies because gas turbines will be constructed at the maker's works and delivered complete to the Site.

Widespread destruction can result from testing because of disruption of steam in gas turbines and steam pressure or flue gas explosion of water tube boilers. It is important to remember that, where separate contracts are let, the civil works will probably be third-party property to the plant installation contractor.

Gas-fired power plants can be modified to run on hydrogen, thus eventually reducing carbon emissions.

B.12.3 Geothermal

Geothermal power is electrical power generated from geothermal energy. Technologies in use include dry steam power stations, flash steam power stations, and binary cycle power stations. In ground that is hot but dry, or where water pressure is inadequate, injected fluid can stimulate production. Developers drill two holes into a candidate site and fracture the rock between them with explosives or high-pressure water. Then they pump water or liquefied carbon dioxide down one borehole, and it comes up the other borehole as a gas. This approach is called hot dry rock geothermal energy in Europe or enhanced geothermal systems in North America. Much greater potential may be available from this approach than from conventional tapping of natural aquifers. Geothermal electricity generation is currently used in 26 countries, while geothermal heating is in use in 70 countries.

Geothermal power is considered to be a sustainable, renewable source of energy because the heat extraction is small compared with the Earth's heat content and greenhouse gas emissions of geothermal electric stations are on average less than 5% of that of conventional coal-fired plants. The development of binary cycle power plants and improvements in drilling and extraction technology may enable enhanced geothermal systems over a much greater geographical range. A demonstration project in Switzerland was shut down after it triggered earthquakes. Demonstration projects are under construction in Australia, the United Kingdom, and the United States of America. The potential of enhanced geothermal systems was estimated in a report by the Massachusetts Institute of Technology which concluded that investing US $1 billion in research and development over 15 years would allow the creation of 100 GW of electrical generating capacity by 2050 in the United States alone.

At present, geothermal wells are rarely more than 3 km deep. Upper estimates of geothermal resources assume wells as deep as 10 km. Drilling near this depth is now possible in the petroleum industry, such as Exxon's Z-12 well in the Chayvo field, Sakhalin. The deepest research well in the world, the Kola Superdeep Borehole is 12.3 km deep (7.6 miles). The technological challenges are to drill wide bores at low cost and to break large volumes of rock.

B.12.4 Hydroelectric

Most hydroelectric power stations will be constructed in remote and inaccessible locations where the water supply is available. The machinery employed does not present the same degree of breakdown risk as for thermal stations. The most serious risks arise less out of testing or operational failures than out of design, general handling, and environmental risks.

Restricted access and working space complicate the handling of large and heavy components. The plant is normally installed in a powerhouse situated well below the dam or in an underground cavern. Both locations present a serious risk of flooding and/or rock fall.

B.12.5 Pumped storage

Where the supply of water is limited and there is a fluctuating demand for electricity produced, a pumped storage scheme may be employed. This involves the provision of an upper and a lower reservoir between which the water will pass. A reversible water turbine will be installed. During peak demand hours, the machine acts as a water turbine providing motive power to an electric generator. At off-peak hours the process is reversed and the turbine acts as a pump to return the water from the reservoir at the base of the hill to the reservoir at the top. The generator acts as a motor with power supplied from the grid to drive the pump.

A considerable part of such projects is made up of civil engineering work, details of which will be found under the sections dealing with dams, reservoirs, and tunnels.

B.12.6 Solar power

Solar power is the conversion of energy from sunlight into electricity, either directly using photovoltaics (PV), or indirectly using concentrated solar power (CSP), or a combination. Photovoltaic cells convert light into an electric current using the photovoltaic effect. The array of a photovoltaic power system produces direct current (DC) power which fluctuates with the sunlight's intensity. For practical use this usually requires conversion to certain desired voltages or alternating current (AC) through the use of inverters. Multiple solar cells are connected inside modules. Modules are wired together to form arrays, then tied to an inverter, which produces power at the desired voltage, and for AC, the desired frequency/phase. The current largest photovoltaic power station in the world is the Bhadla Solar Park in Rajasthan, India, with a generation capacity of 2,245 MW and occupying an area of 5,700 hectares.[2]

Solar power plants use one of two technologies: photovoltaic systems use solar panels, either on rooftops or in ground mounted solar farms, converting sunlight directly into electric power, while concentrated solar power, also known as concentrated solar thermal plants, use solar thermal energy to make steam which is thereafter converted into electricity by a turbine.

Concentrated solar power systems use lenses or mirrors and solar tracking systems to focus a large area of sunlight into a small beam. Among the best-known technologies are the parabolic trough, the compact linear Fresnel reflector, the dish, and the solar Power Tower. Various techniques are used to track the sun and focus light. In all these systems a working fluid is heated by the concentrated sunlight, and is then used for power generation, for example, to make steam, which is thereafter

2 https://en.wikipedia.org/wiki/Bhadla_Solar_Park (accessed 5 September 2021).

converted into electricity by a turbine, or energy storage. Hybrid systems combine PV and CSP with one another or with other forms of generation such as diesel, wind, and biogas, enabling the system to modulate power output as a function of demand or at least reduce the fluctuations in solar power and the consumption of non-renewable fuel.

Long-distance transmission allows remote renewable resources to displace or supplement fossil fuel consumption.

The main risks relate to damage by extreme weather events.

B.12.7 Wind turbine

Wind turbines provide a clean energy source and use little water, emitting no greenhouse gases and no waste products. They convert the wind's kinetic energy into electrical energy. However, energy harnessed by wind turbines is intermittent and is not a dispatchable source of power. Turbines are manufactured in a wide range of sizes with either horizontal or vertical axes. Hundreds of thousands of large turbines, in installations known as wind farms, now generate over 650 GW of power, of which 60 GW is added each year. They are an increasingly important source of intermittent renewable energy and are used to lower energy costs and reduce reliance on fossil fuels. Large three-bladed horizontal axis wind turbines (HWAT) with blades in front of the tower produce the overwhelming majority of wind power in the world today. These turbines have the main rotor shaft and electrical generator at the top of the tower and must be pointed into the wind. Small turbines are pointed by a simple wind vane, while large turbines generally use a wind sensor coupled with a yaw system. Most have a gearbox, which turns the slow rotation of the blades into a quicker rotation that is more suitable to drive an electrical generator. The blades are usually coloured white for daytime visibility by aircraft and range in length from 20 to 80 m. Offshore wind turbines are built up to 8 MW currently and have a blade length of up to 80 m.

Typically a 1.5 MW wind turbine as frequently seen in the United States has a tower 80 m high; the rotor assembly (blades and hub) weigh 22,000 kg, and nacelle which contains the generator, weighs 52,000 kg. The concrete base for the tower is constructed using 26,000 kg of reinforcing steel and contains 190 m^3 of concrete. The base is 15 m in diameter and 2.4 m thick near the centre. As of 2018, global production of wind turbines used 450,000 tons of copper per year.

Wind turbines produce electricity as one of the lowest priced renewable energy sources.

Risks include environmental degradation such as visual impact, noise, bird strikes, ice accretion on turbine blades due to in-cloud icing and freezing rain events, and navigation hazards.

B.13 Roads

Most major road building projects will involve the construction of a number of bridges crossing roads, railways, and rivers. Consideration of the construction of such bridges may be found in ¶B.2. Apart from these major bridge structures there will also probably be certain minor underpasses and culverts to allow pedestrian access and to traverse minor streams crossing the proposed route. These do not, however, present particular hazards. The type of road construction used will depend largely on the territory, but whatever the method of surfacing, the following points should be noted:

B.13.1 Earth moving

A considerable amount of earthmoving is normally involved in all road construction contracts and the major hazard is the possibility of damage to the heavy, expensive equipment in use. This point has already been made under the heading of groundworks in ¶B.7. The site of a road contract frequently stretches over many kilometres and, as a result, access is often over roads and bridges which were not designed for the heavy loads imposed by modern machinery. Third-party claims may therefore be expected for damage caused in this manner, and when considering the extent of the cover, particular attention should be paid to the contract conditions relating to the use of extraordinary traffic.

B.13.2 Embankments

The construction of embankments to carry the road over low-lying or marshy areas may result in claims for damage by flood water, heavy rainfall, subsidence, and collapse. The time allowed for settling and consolidating of the embankment before proceeding with the laying of the subbase and paving of the road should be seen to be adequate. The difficulty of salvaging heavy equipment from marshy ground should not be overlooked.

B.13.3 Cuttings

Cuttings may be necessary to maintain the line of the road and to reduce gradients. This will be either a large earth moving activity, in which case particular attention should be paid to the slope of the sides of the cutting, or it will involve a considerable amount of rock blasting with the consequent risk of damage to construction equipment and possibly third-party property.

B.13.4 Benching

If the road is required to traverse a steeply sloping hillside, the construction of this section will be part cutting and part embankment. On the embankment side there is an even higher risk of subsidence and collapse and in some cases, piling is necessary to support the benching. In addition to subsidence and collapse, particular hazards are rock-fall and washing away by heavy rains or thawing snow.

B.13.5 Retaining walls

Where soil stability is suspect, retaining walls may be constructed in either cuttings and/or benchings to prevent the soils from falling onto or away from under the road. An alternative method used in some instances is to use rock bolts to stabilise loose material, and then spray a concrete mixture on to the face of the soil to prevent deterioration caused by weather. Reinforced earth construction is also used for high retaining walls.

B.13.6 Quarrying

A plentiful supply of crushed stone aggregate is required for most roadworks, both for road bed materials, and for concrete aggregate. Quarries will therefore be established at convenient locations as necessary. The quarries will probably contain heavy stone-crushing machinery and mobile loaders which will be exposed to the risk of blasting and perhaps falling rock in the quarry. There may also be the risk of flooding and of a considerable third-party hazard if the quarry is located in a built-up area.

B.13.7 Paving

Large, complicated, and expensive automatic stripping and paving machines may be included under the Contractor's equipment items. The risks related to the bitumen or concrete laying operation are those of water damage and frost. The design of the layers and the choice of materials for use in the pavement are critical to durable road pavements.

B.13.8 Traffic

Most roadworks are associated with the improvement of existing facilities and there will therefore be numerous connections with, and/or alterations to roads carrying traffic. Although not a catastrophe risk, this is always a potential source of high incidence third-party claims, particularly where operations involve working over traffic. Traffic management will usually be a significant activity that will require prior planning.

B.14 Seaworks

Here one is concerned with the principal classes of work known to insurers as 'wet risks.' The primary perils to be considered in each case are storm, tempest, water damage, subsidence, collapse, and impact by shipping.

B.14.1 Sea walls

These may be constructed for the protection of low-lying coastal areas to prevent coastline erosion or to facilitate land reclamation schemes. The walls are normally of massive concrete construction, founded on piles or on rock. If the rock is relatively near the surface, excavation will probably be necessary within the protection of a steel sheet pile coffer dam. Permanent steel piles are often driven on the seaward side of the wall to form a deep toe and prevent undermining by the action of the sea. The completed wall may itself be protected by a formation of concrete tetrapods, dolos, or large rocks to break the force of the waves. The fact that such a wall is necessary will point to the danger of damage to the works by the sea during construction. The time of carrying out such work is obviously critical. In some cases, it is necessary to remove an existing seawall before completion of the new. The consequent risk of flooding at this time may result in third-party claims.

Contractor's equipment should be withdrawn to the landward side of the Works in the event of a storm or on the completion of work each day.

B.14.2 Jetties and dolphins

These structures are a development of the original landing stage and mooring buoy, where it is necessary to provide deep water unloading, loading, or bunkering facilities for modern vessels whose draft will not permit them to be brought closer to the shore.

The dolphin is a fairly simple structure normally comprising three or more raking piles (driven at an angle) with a concrete cap. They may be provided for an independent mooring or may be connected by walkways to a jetty.

The jetty will consist of a head, usually parallel to the shore, providing berthing space and plant for loading and unloading vessels. This plant may comprise large fixed or rail mounted cranes, counterbalanced cantilever arms, or just pipelines and pumping facilities. The head will be connected to the shore by an arm which normally provides vehicular as well as passenger access. The normal method of construction of the jetty is to drive piles, sometimes of timber but mostly of steel or concrete, working outwards from the shore. Jack-up barges may be used as fixed platforms for the driving of piles. Otherwise as the work progresses, the piling frame may be moved forward on the piles already driven. A temporary jetty may also be constructed to facilitate access to the working area. The piles are then connected by means of a heavy steel framework or concrete beams and topped with a deck, usually of concrete.

The hazards will depend to a large extent on the depth of water, the length of the piles, the size of the tide, the wave heights, and storm intensity and frequency. Once again contractor's equipment should be withdrawn in the event of a storm although it may not be practicable or necessary to do so at the end of each work day. However, where construction is exposed to the sea, provision must be made for the unexpected occurrence of king-waves and the platform should be jacked-up beyond reach at the end of each day's work. There is an additional risk with such work of impact from passing shipping or from the Contractor's own floating equipment. One of the better features of this work, however, is that in order to provide a safe anchorage for vessels, the jetty will, wherever possible, be built in a relatively sheltered position.

B.14.3 Moles and breakwaters

Construction methods vary between tipping the fill material from trucks working out from the shore to depositing the material from hopper barges. Loss of the fill due to the action of the tide or local currents should be allowed for by the Contractor in its price, but an unexpected storm can result in the washing away of large quantities of fill material. The fill is normally armoured by the placing of graded rock, the largest sizes normally being positioned by the use of a crane which can work either from the partially completed mole or from a barge. Additional armouring is provided by the use of concrete tetrapods or blocks. In the latter case, however, careful preparation of the seabed is required to prevent subsidence. Occasionally moles will be constructed by the use of steel sheet piles filled with mass concrete.

By virtue of the fact that these structures are designed to provide protection from heavy seas, they are themselves vulnerable to severe damage during construction.

B.14.4 Harbours

A natural harbour will normally be found in a comparatively sheltered bay or inlet or at varying distances upstream in navigable rivers. Because the basic protection already exists, development can proceed at a slower pace. The artificial harbour, however, is almost invariably designed to serve a specific commercial enterprise so that the site location is dictated largely by the need to provide access. This may well mean working in an exposed location. It follows that the first protective breakwater will have little or no protection from the sea during its construction and is, therefore, probably the worst of all 'wet risks' to be encountered. In the later stages of harbour construction risks tend to decrease as the outermost structures take shape and break the direct impact of the waves.

The total work involved will consist of the construction of breakwaters, jetties, piers, quay walls, unloading facilities, warehouses, roads, and the like.

B.14.5 Docks

Whilst much of the work involved is described previously under 'harbours,' mention should be made of the particular hazards involved in the construction of dry dock facilities. Deep excavation is necessary over a large area in close proximity to the sea or tidal waters. It is likely that a considerable amount of dewatering will be necessary to reduce the water table, and the danger of flooding is ever-present. It may also be necessary to use large quantities of explosives for rock excavation. As such work could well be in a congested area, the third-party exposure requires special attention. The installation of the dock gates will involve the handling of bulky and heavy equipment in difficult working conditions.

The value of contractor's equipment used in the excavation is always of importance because of the inherent dangers in working behind a coffer-dam. As in the case of reservoirs, testing can only be carried out by filling the dock with water and any faults then discovered in the operation of the dock gates can prove costly and difficult to rectify.

B.14.6 Pipelines

Pipelines laid in water may take many forms. For river crossings, pipes may be of steel or PVC and may either be welded or bolted together. For major pipeline projects in the sea, however, it is normal to use only steel.

The three main methods of laying pipelines are:

(a) Winching,
(b) Laying from a barge or pipe lay vessel, and
(c) Reel lay.

B.14.6.1 Winching

The process of winching the pipe means that it will be prefabricated onshore in long lengths and then pulled from the shore by means of a cable attached to a winch on a craft anchored at sea. The pipe may be either:

(a) Dragged as a deadweight in a previously dredged trench;
(b) Pulled in a condition of negative buoyancy with the aid of buoyancy tanks so that it floats just above the seabed; or
(c) Floated on the surface with the aid of flotation tanks.

Winching is suspended at regular intervals to allow the joining together of the long sections onshore. Obviously, the larger the area onshore which is available for preparation of pipe strings the less interruption there will be in the winching program. Details should be sought of any stand-by equipment available in the event of a winch breakdown and of the precautions taken while negotiating the surf zone.

Horizontal directional drilling may be used to avoid the surf zone by tunnelling beneath it, commencing onshore some distance from the beach, tunnelling beneath it, and exiting a safe distance away from the shore on the seafloor.

B.14.6.2 Laying from a barge

By this method, sections of pipe are welded together, coated, and laid over the stern of the barge as it moves forward along the line of the proposed route. This method has the advantage that there is no pulling of the pipe in the trench, but it has the disadvantage that all of the work must take place at sea over a correspondingly longer period. The risk of storm damage is therefore greater. A further complication of this method is the continual supply of pipes to the laying barge which constitutes a marine transit risk, if the pipe is not manufactured on-board.

Because of the expense of locating and repairing the leaks in a pipeline once it has been laid, it is imperative that all welds are x-rayed before launching. Further hazards are underwater currents causing a whipping action and resulting in bending or twisting, the breakage of the pipeline during towing, and the loss of complete sections during a storm. The season in which the laying operation will take place is therefore critical. Damage may also be caused to the pipeline by impact from shipping or vessels dragging anchors.

Third-party hazards from damage to shipping, the close proximity of other pipelines in the area of laying, connections to land-based installations, and the risk of pollution arising from failure during the testing and maintenance periods are all possible.

B.14.6.3 Reel lay

The reel lay method is suitable for pipelines of small diameter. In the reel lay method, pipe is welded onshore into long lengths, which are coated and spooled onto a large storage reel on a vessel. The pipe is plastically deformed around the hub of the reel. Pipe diameters of up to 450mm can be spooled onto a horizontal reel.

When the pipe is laid offshore, it is pulled off the reel over an aligner at the top of the lay ramp, passed through a straightening system, and the process of lowering the pipe to the seabed is controlled by linear tensioners which grip hold of the pipe as it passes. The main benefit of this approach is that much of the welding, coating, and testing is undertaken onshore. It not only significantly reduces the offshore installation time, but the offshore spread is also less than for a pipelay barge, as no anchor handling is required.

The unreeling process requires careful control to ensure that the pipe is not subject to excessive plastic strain.

B.15 Sewage disposal works

Sewage works are essential throughout the world to improve human health and to prevent the pollution of rivers and streams which can become seriously affected if trade and domestic effluent is not purified before discharge. Such purification involves not only the removal of matter in suspension but also the stabilisation of organic impurities to prevent secondary decomposition after the effluent has passed into the water. In this manner the oxygen content of the river water will be maintained at a suitable level.

Crude sewage (ie before treatment) contains enormous quantities of anaerobic bacteria and relatively few aerobic bacteria, but by prolonged aeration it is possible to destroy large quantities of the former and encourage the latter to multiply. The anaerobic bacteria cause the sewage to decompose and the aerobic bacteria to combine with oxygen to enable the organic matters to form stable and harmless compounds such as nitrates.

The chief methods of sewage treatment consist of land treatment or some combination of sedimentation tanks with or without use of chemical precipitants, septic or hydrolytic tanks, activated sludge tanks, and contact beds or percolating filters. Construction will mostly be in low-lying areas and will consequently be subject to the risk of flood or other water damage.

B.15.1 Land filtration

This normally involves flat or levelled land surrounded by earth walls or banks presenting few problems and may be regarded as a normal earthmoving project. There may be some concreting work for drainage channels.

B.15.2 Sedimentation tanks

These are normally straightforward concrete tanks with a depth of between 2 m to 3 m through which effluent is passed slowly to allow the organic solids to settle. Sludge is drawn off to a smaller sludge-removal chamber also constructed of concrete.

B.15.3 Septic tanks

The construction is similar to that of sedimentation tanks. The concept is that the sludge is allowed to remain for a longer period resulting in greater decomposition and smaller quantities of solid.

B.15.4 Contact beds

Watertight concrete tanks, frequently circular in construction, are filled with clinker onto which the sewage is sprayed by revolving sprinklers. The maximum depth of excavation does not normally exceed 3 m and no special problems are presented.

It is normal for a pump-house to be connected to the treatment works and, although this will include the deepest point of excavation, the hazards will depend upon the subsoil of the particular location. The methods of construction and machinery involved are traditional.

The greatest hazards arising out of sewage disposal works are as follows:

(a) Laying of sewage pipes and
(b) Construction of the sewage outfall.

B.15.4.1 Laying of sewage pipes

This involves a pipeline contract such as has been described in ¶B.11. Damage to the pipes, collapse of trenches, interference with traffic, and possible subsidence of adjoining third-party property are the main perils.

B.15.4.2 Construction of the sewage outfall

If the discharge is into a river, a simple coffer dam may be sufficient for the construction of the outfall. If the river is tidal, a valve chamber will be included to prevent backup. An outfall into the sea would be subject to the hazards described under the heading of 'pipelines' in ¶B14.6 and would be used by coastal communities, industries, and utilities in disposing of waste water and effluents.

Problems may arise with the dynamics of the seafloor – erosion, deposition, and the liquefaction of bottom sediments, removal of protective rock by wave action, currents, waves, and a phenomenon known as vortex-shedding. Other problems from marine traffic such as bottom-trawling, hooking by anchors, dredging, and cable-sawing by anchor cables and trawler warps may be experienced. Possible material failure due to lack of or inadequate corrosion protection, corrosive effluent, and thermal effects should be taken into account. An outfall can wear when the pipe moves on the seabed or where abrasive materials pass the pipe. Plastic outfalls are particularly subject to this type of failure and to puncturing by rock back-fill and the like.

Construction problems such as diver error or damage from construction debris or moving boulders also occur.

B.16 Stone and ceramic industries

The establishment of quarries or open cast mining sites may be the subject of contractor's all risk insurance. The plant to be supplied can be divided into that which will be employed in excavation of the raw material and that which will be used for the crushing process.

The excavation plant will include heavy duty digging items such as excavators, draglines, and hydraulic shovels together with the more portable items such as rock drills and bores. It is most important to establish that this equipment is not used by the Contractor as construction equipment to assist with the site clearance. The testing risk is high because of damage that may be caused by falling rock, toppling over, or fatigue fractures. The possibility of damage by blasting operations should be taken into account.

Rock crushers are of massive construction, driven by powerful electric motors. Even short commissioning periods can bring losses as a result of foreign bodies entering a crusher. The repair or replacement of the large casings in jaw or gyratory cone crushers can prove very expensive. Secondary and tertiary crushers and rock mills (as distinct from ball or rod mills) will handle smaller sizes of rock but still represent a heavy risk during commissioning. In remote areas, repair or replacement costs will be considerably increased due to the difficulties of transportation. Third-party risk is normally restricted to that arising from the use of explosives.

B.17 Shaft sinking and tunnels

B.17.1 Shaft sinking

Although shaft sinking works are normally associated with mining projects, they are also commonly used to provide access to additional workfaces for tunnel boring machines, other equipment, and construction materials. Contractors tendering for shaft sinking contracts frequently seek to limit their risk by qualifying their tenders.

A test borehole on the site of the proposed shaft should disclose full information about all strata through which the shaft will pass. Although there are always inherent risks in the use of explosives and working at great depth, the results of any serious difficulties are likely to be more expensive to the Contractor in terms of delay and remedial works than to the insurance underwriter in terms of an insurance claim.

The presence of ground water, or water bearing strata, may be dealt with either by the method of freezing the surrounding areas using refrigeration pipes or by curtain grouting in advance of sinking the shaft. Curtain grouting, if effectively carried out, has the advantage of being a permanent protection, whereas any breakdown in the refrigeration process could result in the flooding of the shaft. It is normal for the shaft lining to be constructed as the sinking proceeds, and there is always the possibility of damage to this lining if too large an explosive charge is inadvertently used.

Raise boring methods, where vertical shafts are drilled upwards from underground workings or tunnels, involve the use of expensive machines which may be subjected to the hazard of rock-falls.

B.17.2 Tunnelling

Details of the type and conditions of the strata to be met when driving a tunnel can be obtained from the study of bore-hole cores: the greater the number of boreholes over the proposed route, the more accurate the assessment. It is, however, an unfortunate fact that faults and fissures can and do occur within a few metres of a borehole and yet remain undetected until the tunnel reaches that point. Methane gas, rock bursts, rock falls, and underground watercourses of high pressure and high temperature are frequently experienced during rock drilling.[3,4]

Tunnels may be major civil engineering projects or a comparatively small part of larger projects, for example, diversion tunnels for dams. Tunnelling methods may be employed for road and rail tunnels through mountains, under rivers and harbours, turbine halls, surge chambers, access tunnels, tail races, and temporary diversion tunnels, underground railway networks, sewers, water supply schemes, and many others. Whatever their purpose, there are basically only four methods by which the tunnel will be constructed:

(a) Blasting,
(b) Boring,
(c) Prefabrication, or
(d) Cut-and-cover.

B.17.2.1 Blasting

For tunnelling through hard rock, blasting is probably the only method which may be employed. Apart from the foreseeable risk of damage to the Contractor's equipment by blast, there are the ever-present risks of roof collapse, flooding, and the ignition of underground gas pockets. In the case of

3 This example was used by the South African Association of Mining Contracting Companies.
4 Philip Loots, *Construction Law and Related Issues* (Juta &Co, 1st edn 1995) 233.

blasting, multi-boom drilling machines are very expensive items and if there is a roof collapse, major damage can be expected. Provided the rock is sound, the tunnel will only be lined if it is necessary to maintain an accurate profile or prevent loss of water – for example, in the case of pressure tunnels for hydro schemes. In addition to the drilling machines, a considerable amount of equipment will be at risk in the tunnel for mucking out and transportation purposes.

B.17.2.2 Boring

In soft rock and clay, and sand and gravel soils, it is possible to use boring machines and tunnelling shields. When tunnelling through known water-bearing strata it is likely that a small diameter pilot tunnel will be driven, possibly using compressed air to counteract the water pressure. The pilot tunnel will be lined with cast-iron segments through which grout tubes can be inserted into the surrounding soil. The area of the proposed tunnel can then be grouted with either cement or chemical grants to check the permeation of water. The excavation of the main tunnel can then proceed with relative safety.

When tunnelling under water, fissured or broken ground may be grouted from boreholes sunk into the river or seabed. This may involve the construction of temporary jetties.

In many cases it will be necessary for the tunnel to be lined and in areas of high instability it is essential that the lining follows as closely behind the shield or boring machine as is practicable. There is no risk of damage by blasting, so lining segments are used to provide a base for the hydraulic rams which propel the shield or boring machine. The tunnel segments may be cast iron, steel, or concrete.

Boring machines and tunnelling shields are complicated machines, of highly sophisticated design and often purpose made. A collapse or squeezing of the tunnel or flooding could result in serious damage or entrapment to these items.

B.17.2.3 Prefabrication

The immersed tube tunnel may be used as a method of crossing rivers and waterways. This method entails the prefabrication of sections of the tunnel, usually in concrete but also in steel. These are then sunk into position, aligned, and joined together. The jointing of the sections involves the use of divers and complicated systems of air-locks. Individual sections of concrete tunnel, which will probably be constructed in a dry dock and towed into position, may weigh as much as 25,000 tons. The loss of one of these sections by breaking loose from the tow, impact from shipping, or by sinking in the wrong position poses a serious risk. Risk exposure is also linked to the towing and sinking procedures and will depend upon the length of time spent on sinking the units and on the equipment used for locating and bedding them in the trench. The risks in this type of tunnel are more related to pipeline laying and caisson work than normal tunnelling procedures.

B.17.2.4 Cut-and-Cover

For the construction of shallow tunnels, such as for underground railway systems and some urban freeways, this method is often preferred. The normal procedure is to excavate a pit in the open after having protected the Site by means of close piling or steel sheet piling or a diaphragm wall. The base, sides, and roof of the tunnel are then formed in the open pit which is finally backfilled, and the surface is reinstated. An alternative method, which has been employed where it is important for the roadway or ground level to be reinstated as quickly as possible, is achieved by close piling both sides of the route of the proposed tunnel and then casting in a shallow excavation, the concrete roof of the tunnel bearing upon the piles. The ground surface can then be reinstated and the tunnel excavated beneath the already formed roof.

In both cut-and-cover methods the principal risks are collapse of the excavation, inundation by heavy rain or floodwater, or failure of the dewatering system and the consequent damage to the

Contractor's equipment. The third-party hazard is frequently considerable because of the vibration and possible weakening of support for buildings which adjoin the route. In the case of underground railway systems, many of these buildings may be of considerable age and any damage may therefore be very costly.

B.18 Third-party risks – General

The following issues may be relevant to many different types of contract and are of particular importance to the realistic assessment of risks.

B.18.1 Fire and explosion

These perils are among those likely to have the most serious consequences as enormous damage can be caused to vulnerable property adjacent to the Works. Great care is necessary to assess the possibility of any consequential losses which may result from even minor damage to process plant.

In many plant construction contracts there will be extensive welding work with the consequent danger of sparks igniting inflammable gases or liquids. During testing and commissioning, feedstock may be introduced into the system involving process hazards. These activities can result in serious damage by fire and/or explosion to any existing plant surrounding the site and to any sections of the Works already completed and handed over to the Employer.

B.18.2 Use of explosives and demolition

Full details should always be obtained as to the amount and type of explosive, the size of charges, precautions taken to prevent flying fragments, the age, condition, and proximity of any nearby property, and arrangements to keep any third parties at a safe distance.

If there is property immediately adjoining the Site, it may be advisable to take seismic recordings before establishing the size of the charges to be used. Only qualified and experienced blasters should undertake this work. It is important that the storage, transportation, and use of the explosives is arranged in such a manner that it complies exactly with the regulations applicable to the location of the Site.

Implosion is a well-known and spectacular technique used to demolish major structures. As with all demolition, careful planning is essential for the success of the operation and the safety of personnel, adjacent structures, and services. Surveys of properties in the vicinity of blasting operations are usually called for in order to avoid claims for damage.

B.18.3 Vibration, weakening, or removal of support

In certain instances, resultant damage will either be the inevitable consequence of the work or, if controllable, will result from the exercise of less care and attention than is necessary on the part of the Contractor or the Engineer. If excavation or tunnelling work is undertaken near to, or below, the level of the foundation of existing property there will be a serious risk of damage if the sides of the excavation are not adequately supported or if there is a collapse of overburden into a heading. It is emphasised that this risk is not in any way confined to work involving interference with, or underpinning of, foundations. The majority of claims arising from these perils occur where the excavation or tunnel is close to, rather than adjoining, a building or its foundations.

Assessment involves consideration of the age, condition, proximity, and use to which neighbouring property is put, but the experience of the Contractor and any subcontractors is of paramount importance. The Contractor's experience is also a vital consideration if underpinning work carried out. Any proposal to expose individual lengths of foundation greater than 2 m at any one time requires further investigation of the working method.

A serious risk of removal of support can arise if extensive dewatering work is involved. It may be necessary to lower the level of groundwater to construct foundations, and large-scale pumping, particularly in peaty or sandy soils, can cause subsidence and collapse of buildings some considerable distance from the Site.

The use of one of the many different forms of piling can cause widely varying degrees of vibration which may result in damage to surrounding property. It is vital to know the use to which such property is put because many items of machinery and electronic apparatus are particularly sensitive to vibration and consequential losses may be high.

B.18.4 Underground services

A contractor engaged in roadworks, sewer, cable, or pipe-laying operations will almost inevitably cause some damage to other underground installations when working in a built-up area. With the increase in the use of mechanical plant, the likelihood of digging up or damaging other pipes and/or cables is ever-present. To any repair costs may be added consequential losses suffered by users of the pipe or cable. For example, damage to an electricity cable within the grounds of a factory may halt production completely and result in sizeable losses.

In view of this it should be ascertained whether appropriate steps have been taken to locate underground services on the Site, bearing in mind that municipal drawings are not always accurate.

B.18.5 Use of cranes

There have been a great many third-party claims resulting from toppling over, or collapse of, tower cranes either when working or during erection or dismantling. The jib may traverse a wide radius carrying heavy loads over traffic, pedestrians, or buildings, and there is always the risk of something being dropped. The use of mobile cranes increases the risk of impact damage. Equipment must be maintained and checked on a daily basis.

B.18.6 Mechanically propelled equipment

The Contractor should require insurance cover for all liability arising from the use of mechanically propelled equipment except that which is compulsorily insurable under local legislation governing the use of vehicles on the highway.

The important factors are, therefore, the amount and type of equipment in use and the extent of the Site definition. It should be remembered that, normally, the Contractor will be responsible for liability arising from use of hired equipment, even when operated by an employee of the owner of that equipment.

B.18.7 Subcontractors

Much will depend on how much and what type of work has been subcontracted and whether the subcontractors are responsible for their own actions under the terms of the subcontract. The work may be particularly hazardous, as for example demolition, piling, scaffolding, or specialist engineering work in a petrochemical complex. It is vital to know whether the subcontractor is sufficiently experienced in the type of work and whether it is adequately insured for both third-party and employer's liability risks to protect its indemnity to the Head Contractor. In the case of labour-only subcontractors, or labour gangs, where the legal relationships may be difficult to establish, they may be treated as employees of the Head Contractor for insurance purposes, rather than having to rely upon any subcontract indemnities.

B.18.8 Consequential loss

Due allowance must be made for the possibility of consequential losses far exceeding the cost of repair following damage to property. Because of the complicated nature of production processes in some factories, or the type of plant in which electrical or mechanical works may be undertaken, even minor damage can result in a substantial claim. In addition to halting the process by cutting off an essential supply, and the consequent spoiling of a batch of product, there may also be a large claim for loss of production.

APPENDIX C

Global claims

CONTENTS

C.1 Global claim/total cost claim/total time claim

The term global claim is typically applied to a claim for compensation by the Contractor in circumstances where it has not shown the connection between the compensable events and the additional costs claimed. For example, the Society of Construction Law Delay and Disruption Protocol defines a global claim as:

> one in which the Contractor seeks compensation for a group of Employer Risk Events but does not or cannot demonstrate a direct link between the loss incurred and the individual Employer Risk Events.[1]

However, a global claim can take the form of a total cost claim or a total time claim. A **total cost claim** is one where the composite sum sought by the Contractor is computed by reference to the amount of money required to ensure that the total money received is not less than the total money expended or expected to be expended on the project. A total cost claim is asserted where the Contractor alleges a number of legal bases for financial compensation and claims as the measure of this compensation the difference between its total cost of performing the contract and payments received under the Contract. A **total time claim** is a claim in which a number of legal bases for a time extension are alleged and the Contractor seeks as a time extension the difference between the number

1 www.scl.org.uk/sites/default/files/documents/SCL_Delay_Protocol_2nd_Edition_Final.pdf (accessed 23 July 2021).

of days which the project took to complete less the time for Completion including extensions allowed provided in the Contract.

A more general definition of **global claim** that encompasses total cost claims and total time claims is therefore: a claim by the Contractor for additional compensation or an extension of time where it has not shown the causal links between its asserted entitlement and events for which the Employer is liable under the Contract.

The admissibility of a global claim has been tested in a number of cases, for example, *John Holland Construction and Engineering Pty Ltd v Kvaerner R J Brown Pty Ltd*,[2] in which a global claim was permitted where it was impractical to disentangle that part of the loss which was attributable to each head of claim, and where this difficulty had not been brought about by delay on the part of the Contractor (see also *Wharf Properties Ltd v Eric Cumine Associates (No 2)*[3]). The assertion that the Contractor has not shown any causal connection by way of pleading or particulars of the individual delay events and the overall delay claimed is often made.[4]

C.2 Damages for breach of contract

In accordance with ordinary principles of contract law, a party which suffers a loss because of breach of contract by another party is entitled to recover the loss and damage suffered as a consequence of the breach. Provided that breach is established, and it is proved that loss has flowed from that breach, courts have been reluctant to refuse to award substantial damages even though the claimant has been unable to estimate precisely the relevant loss.

Where a Contractor has been required to perform a contract in circumstances which are more onerous as a result of events for which the Employer has contractual liability, any loss must be proved on the balance of probabilities. Where the consequence of the events has been loss of productivity or where, for some other reason, it has led to extra costs to the Contractor in the performance of the work and where these consequences are intermingled with those for which the Employer bears no responsibility, the tribunal of fact is entitled to make an estimate after taking into account all the contingencies, probabilities, and chances involved.[5]

In such a case a rational starting point might be to compare the cost of performance in fact with the expected cost had no event occurred. In a construction project where a multiplicity of factors combine to produce the actual cost of performance to the Contractor, it is inevitable that some informed estimate must be undertaken in assessing the claim. 'Informed' because the assessment must be made by the application of rational principles to the facts as proved by evidence properly before the tribunal and the reasons must demonstrate this.[6] Where this assessment is made by the tribunal on the evidence put forward by the parties and that tribunal adopts a method which is fair to both parties, it will not easily be susceptible to attack for error of law.[7]

2 (1996) 8 VR 681.

3 (1991) 52 BLR 1.

4 See *Nauru Phosphate Royalties Trust v Matthew Hall Mechanical and Electrical Engineers Pty Ltd* (1992) 10 BCL 179; D Byrne, 'Total Costs and Global Claims' (1995) 11 *Building and Construction Law Journal* 397, and *McAlpine Humberoak Ltd v McDermott International Inc* (1992) 58 BLR 1.

5 *In re an arbitration between Taylor Woodrow International Ltd v The Minster of Health* (1978) 19 SASR 1, 13, per Bray CJ.

6 An arbitral tribunal might, in the appropriate case, act on evidence which is not admissible in court and which may, again in the appropriate case and subject to the requirements of natural justice, bring to bear its own expertise.

7 *Graham Evans & Co Pty Ltd v SPF Formwork Pty Ltd* (unreported, NSW Sup Ct, Brownie J, 9 April 1991) 31.

C.3 Adjustment of contract sum or time

The Contractor's entitlement to extra time or money under the Contract will necessarily depend upon the terms of the contract itself. The two English cases on global claims which have received the most attention are as follows.

In *J Crosby & Sons Ltd v Portland Urban District Council*[8] the Arbitrator in a preliminary award submitted no less than 29 specific questions of law to the Court.[9] The Contractor took 46 weeks more than the stipulated 52 weeks to carry out the work. The Arbitrator found that the Contractor had been delayed in the execution of the work, but that part of the delay was due to matters for which it was contractually responsible. The balance of the overrun, namely 31 weeks, was due to nine matters for which the Employer was solely responsible. These matters were various directions given by the Engineer which were, for the most part, Variations as to differing matters, but one was an order to suspend work for a time. In his award the Arbitrator contented himself with a simple finding that delays totalling 31 weeks were caused by the nine matters.[10] He made no attempt to dissect any particular delay which was attributable to any one of these matters. He awarded £8,835 as compensation for the delay. The court case concerned the propriety of this assessment. The Arbitrator did, however, make the following finding:

> The result, in terms of delay and disorganisation, of each of the matters referred to above was a continuing one. As each matter occurred its consequences were added to the cumulative consequences of the matters which had preceded it. The delay and disorganisation which ultimately resulted was cumulative and attributable to the combined effect of all these matters. It is therefore impracticable, if not impossible, to assess the additional expense caused by delay and disorganisation due to any one of these matters in isolation from the other matters.[11]

Donaldson J rejected an argument that the Arbitrator should have assessed the delay and financial consequences flowing from each event, saying that where the events produce an extremely complex interaction of effects on the work it would be entirely artificial to require a tribunal of fact to make an apportionment which has no basis in reality.[12]

The *Crosby* case was primarily concerned with the amount of compensation awarded to the Contractor for the Employer's delays. This is the sum of £8,835 whose make-up is also obscure, except that it is said to have been arrived at after making allowance for certain delays for which specific compensation was awarded. Again, the award was supported by the court which said of the Arbitrator:

> I can see no reason why he should not recognise the realities of the situation and make individual awards in respect of those parts of individual items of the claim which can be dealt with in isolation and a supplementary award in respect of the remainder of these claims as a composite whole.[13]

---

8 (1967) 5 BLR 121.

9 A practice deplored by Donaldson J who described the list as an 'examination paper' set by the Arbitrator for the Court: (1967) 5 BLR 121, 127.

10 (1967) 5 BLR 121, 133.

11 (1967) 5 BLR 121, 133–134.

12 (1967) 5 BLR 121, 136. In their commentary in this case the editors of BLR described this as a 'judicial approval of a widespread and common sense method of measuring claims' but are careful to limit its applicability to those cases in which it is difficult, if not impossible, to make an apportionment. See also (1967) 5 BLR 121, 123.

13 (1967) 5 BLR 121, 136.

In the second English case,[14] question nine asked whether the Contractor could recover claims for direct loss and or expense under clauses 11(6) or 24(1) of the JCT contract in respect of an alleged event when it was not possible for the Contractor to state in respect of that event the amount of loss or expense attributable to it.[15] The question raised an issue which differed from that in the *Crosby* case in that it involved, not a number of events, but only the one which might give rise to an entitlement under different clauses of the contract. In the *Crosby* case there were a number of events which might have given rise to an entitlement under differing provisions of the contract.

Vinelott J confirmed that where it was impractical to disentangle the consequences of a multiplicity of events which might give rise to an entitlement under different contractual provisions, the Arbitrator might make a global award reflecting the loss attributed to all of them, provided that the conditions as to liability had been satisfied under each of the provisions and provided further that the difficulty of dissection had not been the result of the Contractor's delay in making the claim.[16]

These two English cases stand as authority for the proposition that it is legitimate for a tribunal to make a global award of a sum of money payable under a contract, notwithstanding that:

- The events which give rise to the entitlement are numerous and differ,
- The contractual provisions under which the entitlement arises are various, provided that the contractual requirements for each have been satisfied, and
- No specific amount has been proved to flow from any one of these events.

But, in them, the court emphasises[17] the right of the tribunal to make such an award arises where and only where:

- The loss and expense attributable to each head of claim cannot in reality be disentangled.
- There is a complex interaction between the consequences of the events.
- The inability to disentangle the consequence of these events is not the result of delay on the part of the Contractor in making the claim.

It is self-evident but essential to avoid double counting, particularly where the delays for which compensation is payable under the Contract are the result of Variations for which extra payment is allowable under the Variation provision in the Contract.

These cases were concerned with the question whether a global award can stand as a matter of law. They do not, in terms, deal with the form of pleading the claim. Second, the two English cases concern claims which were made for extra payment under the Contract. They were not claims for damages for breach of contract.[18] Third, neither of the two cases, in terms, addresses the question of the total cost claim or an award made on such a claim.

The Privy Council has endorsed the authority of these decisions within the limits of the facts on which they were decided and on the issue which they dealt with.[19]

> Those cases establish no more than this, that in cases where the full extent of extra costs incurred through delay depend upon a complex interaction between the consequences of various events, so that it may be difficult to make an accurate apportionment of the total extra costs, it may be proper for an arbitrator to make individual financial awards in respect of claims which can

14 *London Borough of Merton v Stanley Hugh Leach Ltd* (1985) 32 BLR 51 (Ch D).

15 (1985) 32 BLR 51, 52.

16 (1985) 32 BLR 51, 102.

17 *J Crosby & Sons Ltd v Portland Urban District Council* (1967) 5 BLR 121, 136, per Donaldson J; *London Borough of Merton v Stanley Hugh Leach Ltd* (1985) 32 BLR 51, 102, per Vinelott J.

18 *Wharf Properties Ltd v Eric Cumine Associates* (1991) 52 BLR 1.

19 The quantification of the financial consequences of breaches, not their factual consequences: *Wharf Properties Ltd v Eric Cumine & Associates* (1991) 52 BLR 1, 21.

conveniently be dealt with in isolation and a supplementary award in respect to the financial consequences of the remainder as a composite whole.[20]

The question, then, is how may a claimant present and a tribunal determine a claim where it is not possible to prove the loss which flows from a number of events which, individually, constitute a breach of contract or which give rise to a contractual entitlement (a 'compensable event')? Very often it is possible to compare the performance of part of the work which is affected by a compensable event or events with a comparable part which is not so affected or, if this be not available, with a specially constructed comparable activity. This method, called in the US 'the measured mile method,'[21] is particularly useful in loss of productivity claims. The advantage of this method, provided the standard is truly comparable in all other respects, is that it is not necessary to make an adjustment for the Contractor's own inefficiencies. These are presumed to be included in the standard against which the affected work is measured.

C.4 Total cost/time assessment

C.4.1 Principles

Total cost claims are considered more benevolently where they are brought, not for damages for breach of contract, but for a contractual adjustment of the agreed price. The courts have, however, laid out a series of strict principles for their disposition.[22]

- The total cost method is a less reliable manner of assessing extra cost flowing from an event than proof of direct costs so incurred. It will be adopted only if a more reliable method is impossible or highly impracticable, or where the plaintiff's inability to prove its claim was not the result of its failure to maintain proper records.
- The contract price is realistic.
- The actual costs are reasonable.
- The claimant is not responsible for any of the added costs.

Where a claimant is or ought to be able to prove the amount of its loss by the production of records of actual loss or extra cost incurred because of the compensable events or where the claimant ought to be able to demonstrate this loss by some other method such as the measured mile approach, there is no place for the total cost/time methodology. The claimant seeking to invoke this methodology must therefore demonstrate that the interrelated nature of the claims prevents the presentation of the claim on a case-by-case basis,[23] or that the problem was so pervasive or occurred with such frequency that it was impossible to distinguish the claimed particular additional cost or expense from that which would have been incurred without the compensable events.[24] Associated with this is the insistence of the court that the claimant not be able to rely upon the total time/cost methodology where its inability to prove the claim by more orthodox methods is due to its own failure to maintain adequate and proper site records which might have been sufficient to prove the amount of the actual loss. The mere fact that the claimant's records do not in fact show in segregated form the claimed increased

20 *Wharf Properties Ltd v Eric Cumine & Associates* (1991) 52 BLR 1, 20.

21 Or a 'should cost' claim: G D Ruttinger & C S Hamrick, 'Proving Federal Equitable Adjustment Claims' (May 1993) *Construction Briefings (2d series)* 4.

22 *JD Hedin Construction Co Inc v US* 347 F 2d 235 (Ct Cl, 1965); *W R B Corporation v US* 183 Ct Cl 409 (1968), 426; *Boyajian v US* 423 F 2d 1231 (Ct Cl, 1970), 1243; *Servidone Construction Corporation v US* 931 F 2d 860 (CA Fed Cir, 1991), 861; *Youngdale and Sons Corporation Co Inc v US* 27 Fed Cl 516 (Ct Fed Cl, 1993), 541.

23 *Transpower Constructors v Grand River Dam Authority* 905 F 2d 1413 (10th Cir, 1990), 1417.

24 *Concrete Placing Co v US* 985 F 2d 585 (Cl Ct, 1992).

costs does not confer a licence to present a total costs claim,[25] but where it appears that the records kept were normal for the industry and reasonable, and that the maintenance of further records which might have shown this extra cost would be especially burdensome or grossly unfair, this requirement will not prove to be an insuperable bar.[26]

C.4.2 Methodology

It is necessary to acknowledge at the outset that the presentation of a total cost/time claim is a theoretical exercise. No particular part of the claimed overrun is attributed to any particular compensable event. To a practitioner in the field of construction law this is not, of itself, a surprising or insuperable obstacle,[27] but it is appropriate to consider exactly what is involved in the theory under consideration. The total cost/time method of assessing a claim is merely a particular demonstration of the readiness of a court to draw a factual inference where direct evidence is lacking in circumstances where otherwise a claimant will suffer injustice. The claimant must have proved the first two ingredients of the cause of action, namely, the compensable event and the fact that some extra cost or some delay has been caused by that event. In such a case there is a natural resistance to denying the claimant relief on the ground only that the measure of its entitlement has not been established.

In the simplest situation, where an extra item of compensable work is carried out in the course of a contract, the cost of performing that item is equal to the cost of performing the whole project less the cost of carrying out the contract work. If we assume that the agreed contract price is equal to the cost of carrying out the contract work, the extra cost incurred in performing the extra item of work might be expressed as the difference between the total cost of performing the whole project less the contract price.[28] Underlying the validity of such a conclusion there are three assumptions or elements which must be identified:

(a) The contract price is realistic, that is, it is equivalent to the reasonable price of performing the contract work.
(b) The actual cost figure represents the reasonable cost of carrying out the project including the extra work.
(c) No factor other than the compensable event is responsible for the difference between the actual cost and the contract price.

A similar logic underpins a total time claim. In a typical project where a total cost/time claim is made, each of these assumptions or elements may be subject to serious doubt and there may be difficulties of proof for each. Characteristically, the project will be a complex one; there will be a

---

25 *Boyajian v US* 423 F 2d 1231 (Ct Cl, 1970), 1242; *Huber, Hunt and Nicholas Inc v Moore* 136 Cal Rptr 603 (CA (Cal), 1977), 622. Mere assertion of the difficulties of separating the extra costs will not suffice: B B Bramble & M T Callahan, *Construction Delay Claims* (Wiley, 2nd edn 1992) [12.7].

26 *Skip Kirchdorfer Inc v US* 14 Cl Ct 594 (1988), 607; *Neal & Co Inc v US* 945 F 2d 385 (CA Fed Cir, 1991), 389. The position may be otherwise where the contract requires that the records be kept.

27 The quantification of loss of contribution to offsite overheads or profit due to prolongation is commonly made by an application of the Hudson formula which is equally theoretical and based on assumptions which are often unproved and are, in many cases perhaps, unprovable.

28 A more familiar example of this methodology in the context of sale of goods is to be found in the case where a profit-making machine is sold with defects. In such a case the court has no difficulty in dealing with a claim which alleges that the expected capacity of the machine was so much, the actual performance was somewhat less, and that the difference in profit should be recovered from the defendant. See, for example, *Burns v MAN Automotive (Aust) Pty Ltd* (1986) 161 CLR 653.

large number of compensable events whose impact on the job will be difficult to disentangle.[29] It will be a rare case where the evidence will show that all three of the assumptions have been justified, so as to entitle the claimant to maintain a pure total cost/time assessment. More usual will be the case where this must be modified.

C.4.3 The contract price or time is realistic

The assumption is that the contract price/time for the whole project is realistic in the sense that the work might, without any compensable event, have been carried out for the price or within that period. It assumes that the Contractor would have 'broken even' in the absence of the compensable events.[30] The total cost claim facing the Court of Claims in the leading case of *Boyajian v US*[31] was put in terms of difference between the actual cost and contract receipts. The claimant's adoption of contract receipts rather than contract price was presumably intended to pick up, in addition to the contract price, any adjustments to it. To ignore these adjustments would be to allow double recovery. It has the further advantage that the total cost assessment is limited to those claims which have not been dealt with in a more conventional way. The assumption which the court was asked to make in that case was, not only that the contract price was realistic, but that the adjustments to it were realistic also.

If the claimant has underpriced the work, this will, of course, have the effect of inflating the amount of the claim and the court will be astute to reject such a price as a basis for the claim. There may be good commercial reasons for bidding below cost, although this may not be a common practice in normal economic conditions. On the other hand, having regard to the fact that a contract for an agreed price to be performed within an agreed time underlies the relationship between the parties[32] a claimant will not be heard to argue that the agreed price[33] or time[34] was greater than reasonable.

The proper proof of how this element is made out in each case is a matter of evidence. Usually, the tender is produced, and the estimator swears to its validity. In support of this, or perhaps in substitution,[35] an independent expert may express an opinion on the matter.[36] This evidence may be corroborated by evidence of competitive tenders at a similar amount.[37] In the case where the Employer has, itself, analysed and approved the tender as reasonable, evidence of this may be very persuasive.[38]

Where the claim concerns time, the position is similar. However, time programmes pose particular difficulties and, in the hands of a skilled programmer, may be used to demonstrate whatever is required. In the usual tender it is the Employer, not the Contractor, which specifies the contract time. Where a Tenderer submits a bid to carry out the whole of the Works within that time, it is likely that

---

29 These are the requirements of the first principle laid down in the US cases and, it will be recalled, in *Crosby's* case and *Merton's* case in England.

30 *Laburnum Construction Corp v US* 325 F 2d 451 (Ct Cl, 1963), 458.

31 423 F 2d 1231.

32 *Fattore Coy Inc v Metropolitan Sewerage Commission of the County of Milwaukee* 505 F 2d 1 (CA 7th Cir, 1974), 5.

33 *Oliver-Finnie Co v US* 279 F 2d 498 (Ct Cl 1960), 506.

34 *Glenlion Construction Ltd v The Guiness Trust* (1987) 30 BLR 89, 104–5 (Official Referee).

35 *W R B Corporation v US* 183 Ct Cl 409 (1968), 427 (failure to produce a reliable breakdown of estimates).

36 *Sternberger v US* 401 F 2d 1012 (Ct Cl, 1968), 1015 (uncontradicted evidence of expert unsatisfactory).

37 *Great lakes Dredge and Dock Co v US* 96 F Supp 923 (Ct CI, 1951); *Nauru Phosphate Royalties Trust v Matthew Hall Mechanical and Electrical Employers Pty Ltd* (1992) 10 BCL 179; 12 Aust Const LR 99 (SC Vic); *EC Ernst Inc v Koppers Coy Inc* 626 F 2d 324 (CA 3rd Cir, 1980) (time-claim); *Youngdale & Sons Construction Co Inc v US* 27 Fed Cl 516 (Ct Fed Cl, 1993), 543.

38 B A Aaen, 'The Total Cost Method of Calculating Damages in Construction Cases' (1991) 22 *Pacific Law Journal* 1185, 1200.

its ability to achieve the Date for Completion depends upon its planning, including the resources it will bring to bear on the project. Very often a reconstruction of the construction programme with resources, made subsequently, may be viewed with suspicion. This suspicion may be dissipated somewhat by evidence that the Employer has, at an early stage, examined and approved (or not objected to) the Contractor's construction programme including its sequence of work and resources.

In some cases where the contract price is not found to be realistic, the court has applied a modified total cost approach by using as a starting point the sum which it finds to be a realistic price for the performance of the contract work. This sum may be proved by expert evidence or by averaging those unsuccessful tenders which are considered realistic.[39]

Another variation of this method, but one which has been found less satisfactory, is to dissect from the contract price that component which is referable to the part of the work affected by the compensatory events and to compare this component with the actual cost of the performance of that part of the work.[40] This approach has to be viewed with some suspicion, for it is not uncommon to find in such a dissection an unjustified loading of certain components to favour those which are likely to be affected by Variations and disruptions.

There are many reasons for a Contractor to compress components of its initial programme, particularly if it is to be used to encourage subcontractors. Consequently, there is great scope for argument as to the location and validity of the critical path.

C.4.4 The actual cost/time is reasonable

In the case of cost, some component for profit, on-site and off-site overheads should be included, for these are built into the contract price with which comparison is to be made. This assumption or element involves two components. The first is that the work done under the contract specification must have been carried out within the contract price and time. Put another way, so far as the original contract work is concerned, 'reasonable' means the realistic price/time in terms of the first element. The second element is that the extra or affected work was performed at a reasonable cost[41] and within a reasonable time.

The importance of recognising these two components, especially the first, is demonstrated by the following simplified example. Suppose a project comprises ten activities. The compensable event is one which would normally increase the time or cost for performing activity number five. If at the time of the event, the efficiencies of the contract are such that it is running under budget and ahead of time, the effect of the compensable event on the project as a whole may be nil. The same consequence may flow where the Contractor, which is previously on programme, is able to absorb the consequence of the compensable event by rescheduling activities or redeploying resources.[42] If, on the other hand, an inefficient Contractor is running behind budget and programme, the impact of the compensable event on the project as a whole will be exaggerated, unless the consequences of the Contractor's own inefficiencies are isolated and brought to account.

Given that the overall contract price has been shown to be realistic, the tribunal may be ready to accept without much proof that the contract work, other than that affected by the compensable event, was carried out within budget and time. This may be particularly the case if it accepts, too, that the Contractor is not responsible for the overrun which is charged to the Employer. The difficulty is

39 As in *Great Lakes Dredge and Dock Co v US* 96 F Supp 923 (Ct Cl, 1951).

40 *Phillips Construction Co v US* 394 F 2d 834; *WRB Corporation v US* 183 Ct Cl 409 (1968), 426 (Claims 22 and 26). For example, labour: *Oliver-Finnie v US* 279 F 2d 498 (1960).

41 B A Aaen, 'The Total Costs Method of Calculating Damages in Construction Cases' (1991) 22 *Pacific Law Journal* 1185, 1201.

42 As it may be contractually obliged to do.

that, in the typical case where these claims are made, this can never be proved since by definition it is not possible to disentangle the impact on the work as a whole from the compensable event.[43] In general, the validity of the total cost/time claim depends very much on proof of the reasonableness of the actual costs incurred. This assumes that the Contractor has been efficient in the deployment of its resources and, of course, that it has not been billing other work to the project.

The requirement of reasonableness does not require that the Contractor show that it was not reasonable to adopt a different and cheaper construction method.[44] Moreover, it may be supposed that the court will view with some benevolence the efforts of a Contractor seeking to perform the contract work in circumstances of difficulty where that difficulty has been the result of a compensable event.[45] Nevertheless, the claimant must allege what the total cost of performing the work is, and, in due course, prove it by the production of proper accounts or otherwise support it by expert opinion of its reasonableness.

C.4.5 The claimant bears no responsibility for the overrun

This assumption or element is perhaps the most precarious of all. It will be the rare case indeed where no overrun cost beyond the contract price and no time overrun beyond the contract period is due to an act or omission for which the Contractor is responsible. In the typical total cost/time claim the Contractor offers a great number of events which are said to have required extra cost and time. Almost inevitably, it will not persuade the tribunal that all of them are contractually the responsibility of the Employer. A failure with respect to these extra costs and items will destroy the third assumption or element, which is that no part of the overrun is due to the Contractor.

The claimant must show that the whole of the claimed overrun is the consequence of the compensable events for which the Employer is contractually responsible.

It is this assumption or element which provides the most material for those who would reject the legitimacy of the total cost/time method. The philosophy behind a fixed price or fixed term contract is that the Contractor must carry out the work for that price and within that time unless it is able to establish an entitlement under the contract for extra payment or extra time. The effect of a total cost/time claim, it is said, is to transform such a contract into one to be performed for a reasonable price[46] and within a reasonable time.[47]

Leaving to one side the facts of any given case, such a conclusion overlooks the first assumption (the contract price is realistic) and the first component of the second assumption (the work done under the contract specification must have been carried out within the contract price and time). If one accepts that, so far as the specified work unaffected by the compensable events is concerned, the price and the actual cost are the same, this criticism disappears.

The third assumption underlying the total cost/time method of assessment and the third element to be shown by the claimant is that the extra cost or time is not caused by events within the area of risk

43 If it were possible, then the total cost/time approach would not be warranted.

44 *Great Lakes Dredge and Dock Co v US* 96 F Supp 923 (Ct Cl 1951), 925.

45 B A Aaen, 'The Total Cost Method of Calculating Damages in Construction Cases' (1991) 22 *Pacific Law Journal* 1185, 1201–2. See also *US on behalf of Taylor & Polk Construction Inc v Mill Valley Construction Inc* 29 F 3d 154 (CA 4th Cir, 1994), 162.

46 See, for example, the comment of the Arbitrator which was accepted as a non-appealable conclusion of fact in *Wormald Engineering Pty Ltd v Resources Conservation Co International* (1988) 8 Aust Const L R 28, 32, per Rogers CJ Comm D; (1988) 8 BCL 158.

47 In *McAlpine Humberoak Limited v McDermott International Inc (No 1)* (1992) 58 BLR, 21, the Court of Appeal rejected as a 'novel doctrine of quasi frustration' an argument to the effect that a delay by the Employer causes time generally to be at large. See also *Trollope & Colls Ltd v North West Metropolitan Regional Hospital Board* [1973] 2 All ER 260, 266, per Lord Pearson.

apportioned to the Contractor under the Contract. The assumption may be unwarranted as, indeed, it may be in many cases, but once made, the conclusion follows.

It is easy to make such an assumption but difficult to prove or disprove it. In making such an assertion the Contractor usually pays insufficient attention to the matters for which under its contract it is legally responsible. There may be risks which might occur in the most carefully conducted business such as bad weather, industrial disputes, or unavailability of materials. Second, the Contractor is, naturally enough, inclined to attribute great effect to the impact of the compensatory events. Who can say whether the Contractor is or is not responsible for industrial unrest (assuming this to be the Contractor's risk under the contract), when the workforce has become disenchanted with the administration due to an unreasonable number of late Variations (assuming this to be a compensable event)? The consequence is that the burden of proof effectively passes to the defendant to produce evidence of non-compensatory events which caused or contributed to the overrun. This may be a very onerous burden in a project where the Contractor is in possession of the detail of the day-to-day running of the project and the Employer is dependent upon the Engineer for this information.

Ultimately, it is the claimant who bears the burden of proving the amount of its loss or its time extension.

The position is complicated where the Contractor accepts responsibility for part of the overrun and seeks to claim the balance only. This is the modified total cost/claim which is, for practical purposes, the most likely to be encountered since it is a very unusual case where the Contractor will seriously seek to establish the third element in its purity. What the Contractor here is contending for is that it is not responsible for a given percentage only of the overrun except the part caused by certain non-compensatory events.

It is in this sense that the US cases speak of the total cost/time method of assessment as a starting point. The Contractor in such a case calculates the difference between the actual cost and the contract price and then reduces this sum in various ways. In total time claims, this is commonly done even if it is not the apparent methodology.[48] Again, it is necessary to bear in mind that it is the Contractor who bears the burden of adducing evidence sufficient to satisfy the tribunal that the proposed allocation of responsibility is proper. If it is unable to do so, the consequence must be that the claim fails unless there is some alternative basis for assessing it.[49] But where there is evidence that permits an allocation of responsibility to the Employer for the consequences of its compensable acts, there is no reason why the tribunal should not be ready to apply a modified total cost/time approach to the task of assessment.[50]

C.4.6 Causation

The cause of action in contract requires that the Claimant prove that the loss has been caused by the breach. The claimant must prove extra cost was incurred or delay suffered because of the compensable event. When the interaction of the event with other compensable events is complex, the court may deal with them globally as was the situation in the *Crosby* case.

The requirement that the claimant prove that loss was caused by the compensable event is associated with the third assumption underlying the total cost/time claim that the Contractor is not responsible for the overrun.

In a conventionally presented claim, the claimant will prove the compensable event and then demonstrate its adverse impact in terms of time or cost on the project. Generally, this exercise must

---

48 For example, *J Crosby & Sons Ltd v Portland Urban District Council* (1967) 5 BLR 121.
49 *Phillips Construction Co v US* 394 F 2d 834 (Ct Cl, 1968), 838.
50 *Boyajian v US* 423 F 2d 1231 (Ct Cl, 1970), 1244.

be undertaken in respect of each event relied on. The total cost/time claim turns this presentation on its head: first, certain compensable events are established; second, it is proved that the project cost more or took longer than it ought; third, it is accepted that events which caused this overrun may be compensable or not; fourth, it is proved that no non-compensable event caused or contributed to the overrun; and finally, the conclusion is drawn that the overrun must have been caused by the compensable events.

So understood, it is clear that in a total cost/time claim, causation is sought to be inferred rather than proved.

If evidence shows that the Contractor is responsible for some of the overrun then the claim fails as a total cost/time claim[51] unless there is some rational method for separating this part of overrun from the total overrun and of quantifying it.[52]

This requirement of causation requires that the claimant demonstrates some 'discernible nexus' between the compensable events and the consequent delay[53] or 'a proper nexus which relates each event relied upon to the money claimed.'[54] Where, however, the complexity of the consequences of the compensable event makes it impossible or impracticable for the Contractor to identify the specific relationship between the events and the cost/time consequence, it is permissible to maintain a claim for a single composite amount.[55]

C.4.7 Pleading and global claims

The rules of pleading vary in detail from jurisdiction to jurisdiction and in arbitration there are none at all.[56] Nevertheless, underlying the delivery of the statement of claim and defence and points of claim and points of defence, by whatever name they are called, there is the need to permit the orderly trial of a dispute by disclosing, with as much particularity as is reasonably necessary, the factual and legal basis of the claimant's case and of the respondent's defence.

Their objective is to put the other party on notice of the case to be met and to inform the tribunal of the issues so that they may be addressed and so that rulings on relevance may be made. In a complex construction case this may require delicate judgement, for the amount and extent of detail required will depend upon the relationship between the parties and the expertise of the tribunal.

Mid Glamorgan County Council v J Devonald Williams & Partner[57] was a decision of the Official Referee Mr J A Tackaberry QC in which he undertook a useful analysis of the *Crosby* case and the *Merton* case, noting that in each of them the court saw no difficulty with a global claim where it was impractical or impossible to distinguish individual effects of particular events that contributed to the overall delay.

Imperial Chemical Industries PLC v Bovis Construction Ltd was a pleading summons brought before Official Referee Judge Fox-Andrews. It concerned the form of a Scott Schedule in a claim in which the Employer sought, against each defendant, the whole of the extra cost of the project, some

51 *Lichter v Mellon-Stuart Company* 305 F 2d 216 (CA 3rd Cir, 1962) (Contractor conceded that if a substantial part of the added cost was non-compensable the whole claim must fail as there was no basis for separation). See *Wunderlich Contracting Co v US* 351 F2d 956 (Ct Cl, 1965), 969.

52 In which case the assessment becomes a modified total cost/time assessment.

53 *Wharf Properties Ltd v Eric Cumine Associates* (1991) 52 BLR 1, 21 (PC).

54 *Mid Glamorgan County Council v J Devonald Williams & Partner* (unreported, Official Referee, 17 September 1991), [56.3].

55 See *Mid Glamorgan County Council v J Devonald Williams & Partner* (unreported, Official Referee, 17 September 1991), [56.4], [69] (a modified total cost claim).

56 *Pace South Australian Superannuation Fund Investment Trust v Leighton Contractors Pty Ltd* (1990) 55 SASR 327.

57 Unreported, Official Referee, 17 September 1991.

£19m. His Honour expressed the view that, on the authorities, a claim for a global sum, representing the extra costs incurred by reason of a number of breaches of contract without relating any part of the costs to any particular breach, was not in principle, unsustainable, where the factual consequences were intermingled. He did, however, observe that because of the degree of artificiality of the claim 'it is the more imperative that it should be properly particularized.'[58] His Honour then analysed the sufficiency of the particulars and directed that in many respects they would need to be improved and enlarged.

Nauru Phosphate Royalties Trust v Matthew Hall Mechanical and Electrical Employers Pty Ltd[59] was an application in the Supreme Court of Victoria arising out of an arbitration. The claim for disruption and loss of productivity caused the difficulty. In its final form, this was in very general terms and no attempt was made to relate the matters complained of to their impact on the claimant's work, nor on the loss of productivity complained of, nor any part of the global sum claimed. The Arbitrator made a number of pertinent observations and ordered that particulars be given.[60] Having received certain of these particulars he fixed the commencing date for the hearing. The Employer was dissatisfied with the claim as it stood and applied to remove the Arbitrator for misconduct[61] on the ground that he had denied it natural justice, alternatively for an order striking out the claim for an abuse of process.[62] The Employer's application was unsuccessful. Nevertheless, Smith J subjected some of the cases referred to previously including some of the United States decisions, to a very illuminating analysis. It was submitted on behalf of the Employer that 'the points of claim must be specific in providing a discernible connection or nexus between any events relied upon and the consequent disruption alleged.'[63] His Honour rejected this submission, concluding that the English cases:

> do not, in my view, purport to permit only the quantum to be dealt with in a global way. They permit a party to proceed with a global claim where it is not possible to spell out the interaction of events and their relationship to the quantum claimed – in other words the 'nexus.'[64]

This passage highlights the difficulty with respect to causation in the discussion of total cost/time claims. It is necessary for a claimant to demonstrate that some loss has flowed from the disrupting event relied upon and, if it is necessary to do so, this causation should be alleged as a material fact in the pleading. In many cases this may not be necessary because it is evident to the parties and to the tribunal that, for example, a late instruction meant that workers were idle for some time or had to move to another workface or lost the efficiencies which are to be derived from the repetition of standard work. In other cases, the tribunal will require that the nexus be spelt out so that the respondent will understand the case to be met.

This is well illustrated by a decision of the Supreme Court of Queensland, *Ralph M Lee Pty Ltd v Gardner & Naylor Industries Pty Ltd*[65] which is an extreme case. The subcontractor's statement of claim alleged as an implied term of the building subcontract that the Contractor would take all steps as were reasonably required to enable the subcontractor to comply with the Contractor's construction

---

58 (1992) 32 Con LR 90, 101.
59 (1992) 10 BCL 179; 12 Aust Const LR 99 (Vic Sup Ct).
60 (1992) 10 BCL 179, 185–186.
61 Pursuant to the uniform *Commercial Arbitration Act* s 44.
62 Ibid, 47.
63 (1993) 10 BCL 179, 194.
64 As was ordered in *Imperial Chemical Industries PLC v Bovis Construction Ltd* (1992) 32 Con LR 90, and would doubtless have been ordered in *Mid Glamorgan County Council v J Devonald Williams & Partner* (unreported, Official Referee, 17 September 1991).
65 (1992) 10 BCL 179, 195.

program. The pleading then alleged in general terms late access and late instructions in breach of that term. Finally, the subcontractor said that, as a consequence, it was delayed, the particulars provided being an annexed as-built program. Not surprisingly, the Court acceded to an application that the statement of claim identify the facts relied on to found a causal connection between the breach and the delay and the consequent damage. Moynihan J observed that a plaintiff might seek to make out a disruption claim by showing that 'the works required many more man hours than ought to reasonably have been required and seek to establish the necessary nexus between breach and disruption by arguing that the breaches were capable of causing disruption and that there was no other explanation.' There are, of course, other ways in which the plaintiff might seek to demonstrate that the breaches caused loss of productivity. Either way, in this, the likely area of real contest at trial, the defendant was entitled to have the plaintiff indicate how the case as to causation was put.

In *Bernhard's Rugby Landscapes Ltd v. Stockely Park Consortium Ltd*[66] the position in relation to composite claims was restated.

A claimant is entitled to plead or prove its claim, whether on liability or quantum, in the way it chooses.[67] However, the defendant is entitled to know the case it must meet. A plaintiff may, within the very generous limits affecting claims which are said to disclose no cause of action, choose to take the risk of presenting its case as it sees fit. There is no power in the court to stay or dismiss a claim on the ground that it is likely to be unsuccessful.[68] Such a principle is entirely consistent with the often expressed view that global claims should be made only when, and to the extent that, it is impossible or impractical to prove the claim by evidence of direct loss, a view which is applicable *a fortiori* to total cost/time claims. But even such claims cannot be summarily dismissed as not disclosing a cause of action.

In order to ensure fairness, the court must require a party to set out its case with sufficient particularity. Where a global or a total cost/time claim is made, the tribunal may, where appropriate, direct particularisation including particularisation of the matters relied on as showing the impracticality of the more conventional method of assessment. Where the case depends upon the causal effect of an interaction of events, the nexus must be stated in an intelligible form. Sufficient particularity is a matter of fact and degree in each case. A balance must be struck between excessive particularity and basic information. The approach must also be cost effective.

C.5 Case study: Global claims

The Extra Division, Inner House of the Court of Session, in the case of *John Doyle Construction Limited v Laing Management (Scotland) Limited*[69] considered whether a global claim could succeed where the defendant was not liable for all the delay and disruption but only part of it.

John Doyle Construction Limited (JDC) was engaged as the subcontractor and Laing Management (Scotland) Limited (LMS) was the management contractor, on two separate work packages for the construction of office headquarters of the Scottish Widows Fund (namely WP2010 and WP2011).

WP2011 was delayed by 22 weeks and consequently JDC brought an application in the Commercial Court for an extension of time and made a 'global claim' for the 22 weeks delay,

66 (1998) 14 Const.L.J.329;(1997) 82 BLR 39. See also *John Holland Construction and Engineering Pty Ltd v Kvaerner R.J. Brown Pty Ltd* (1996) 82 BLR 81.

67 *Mid Glamorgan County Council v J Devonald Williams & Partner* (unreported, Official Referee, 17 September 1991).

68 See, for example, *Wharf Properties Ltd v Eric Cumine Associates* (1991) 52 BLR 1, 19–20; *British Airways Pension Trustees Ltd v Sir Robert McAlpine & Sons Ltd* (1994) 72 BLR 26, 33–34 per Saville LJ, Beldam and Neill LJJ concurring.

69 [2004] ScotCS 141.

the related delay, and disruption costs in the amount of £4,807,144.16. It was alleged that some of the delay was due to the late completion of WP2010 which ultimately resulted in the late start of WP2011 and further delay which was not caused by LMS. The statement of claim identified that the claim was made as a 'global claim' because it was impossible to 'identify the causative links between each such cause of delay and disruption, and the cost consequence thereof.' LMS sought to have the global claim struck out on the basis that it included some delays for which LMS was not responsible.

The claim made by LMS to have the global claim struck out was unsuccessful at first instance. The Commercial Court held that while the global claim may fail in respect of events which were not the fault of LMS, it should not fail in its entirety.

LMS appealed the decision to the Court of Session where Lord MacFayden again dismissed the application. The case was then appealed to the Inner House Court of Session where on 11 June 2004 it was again held that LMS was unsuccessful and the matter was referred to trial.

In its decision, the Court of Session suggested a three-pronged approach when considering whether a global claim is successful:

- Where particular events can be directly linked to individual loss, then they should be extracted from the global claim and argued separately. This is unlikely to be very common as the nature of a global claim is that the loss cannot be directly linked to an individual event.
- If there are concurrent delays, the claimant must prove that the defendant is the 'dominant' cause of each event leading to the delay. If it can be proven that the defendant is the 'dominant' cause of the delay then the concurrent events which are not the responsibility of the defendant can be ignored when assessing the loss or damage payable to the claimant.
- Where the claimant cannot or fails to prove that the defendant is the 'dominant' cause of the loss, the loss shall be apportioned between each cause, dependent on responsibility. While this method is similar to that adopted in assessing contributory negligence, it is a very rough and ready approach.

The court also held that causation must be treated with common sense. That is, it should be reasonably obvious that a particular event caused the loss, notwithstanding that other events played a part in its occurrence.

INDEX

Page numbers in *italics* indicate figures; page numbers in **bold** indicate tables.

www.ingramcontent.com/pod-product-compliance
Ingram Content Group UK Ltd.
Pitfield, Milton Keynes, MK11 3LW, UK
UKHW051703240926
475702UK00037B/2806
* 9 7 8 1 0 3 2 0 7 4 2 6 9 *